Encyclopedia of British Humorists

GARLAND REFERENCE LIBRARY OF THE HUMANITIES (VOL. 906)

Encyclopedia of British Humorists

Geoffrey Chaucer to John Cleese

Volume 1 A–K

Edited by
Steven H. Gale

GARLAND PUBLISHING, INC.
New York & London
1996

Library of Congress Cataloging-in-Publication Data

Encyclopedia of British humorists : Geoffrey Chaucer to John Cleese / edited by
    Steven H. Gale.
        p.   cm. — (Garland reference library of the humanities ;
    vol. 906)
    Includes bibliographical references and index.
    ISBN 0-8240-5990-5
    1. English wit and humor—Bio-bibliography.   2. Humorists, English—Biog-
raphy—Dictionaries.   3. English wit and humor—Dictionaries.   I. Gale,
Steven H.   II. Series.
PR931.E54   1996
827.009—dc20
[B]   95-2282
                                                                             CIP

Cover photograph: Gertrude Lawrence and Noel Coward. Courtesy of the Bettmann
Archive. Photo researcher Marjorie Trenk.

Cover design by Larry Wolfson Design, NY

Printed on acid-free, 250-year-life paper
Manufactured in the United States of America

To Kathy, Shannon, Ashley, Kristin,
my father, Norman A. Gale, and Linda,
the Goodwins, the Johnsons, the Corums,
and in memory of my mother, Mary Wilder
Haase, and my brother, Bill, as always,
with all my love and thanks

Contents

Acknowledgments

I appreciate the work done by Elaine Wesley in checking sources, helping with the correspondence, typing, and all of the other details that go into producing a manuscript, by Kim Bales, who helped with the typing, and by Lisa Gayle Brown and Laurel Chipman, who aided with the finishing touches. Reference librarians Susan Martin, Amanda Sexton, and Linda Um Bayemake Joachim at Kentucky State University's Blazer Library and the reference librarians (including Beverly Kunkle, Mildred Polsgrove, Rita Douthitt, Glen Lewis, Nancy Rice, and Mary Greathouse) at the Paul Sawyier Library in Frankfort, Kentucky, also helped me track down factual and bibliographic information. As he always does, Don Nilsen of Arizona State University freely shared his knowledge of the field of humor studies as he suggested scholars who might contribute to the volume, and I especially appreciate the willingness of John S. Batts of the University of Ottawa to take the time to carefully review my introduction and to offer extremely valuable advice and information, particularly regarding twentieth-century humor. Similarly, I cannot overemphasize the value of Shannon Gale's work in compiling the index. Ashley Gale and Kristin Gale helped in manuscript preparation. Editors Gary Kuris, who has done so much to extend the field of humor studies, and Phyllis Korper, along with Chuck Bartelt, Pamela Chergotis, Rita Quintas, Managing Editor Helga McCue, Copy Editor Donna Pintek, Desktop Production Associate Dora Kubek, Production Editor Alexander Metro, and many others at Garland also deserve to be recognized.

I thank, too, the many scholars who worked diligently to produce thoughtful, insightful, and comprehensive interpretations and historically accurate essays. It was a long and difficult process and the scholars accepted editorial advice with equanimity and patience, and they did their best to produce the kind of coverage required for their individual entries. While British writer Edward De Bono stated that "humour is by far the most significant activity of the human brain," humor criticism has not been so readily appreciated; American cartoonist Saul Steinberg declared that "trying to define humor is one of the definitions of humor," and American humorist E.B. White claimed that "analyzing humor is like dissecting a frog. Few people are interested and the frog dies of it." I think that the entries in this encyclopedia prove that both Steinberg and White were wrong—that the exercise can be interesting and fun as well.

As always, I want to thank my wife, Kathy, and my three daughters, Shannon, Ashley, and Kristin, for their motivation, inspiration, and help, and especially for their patience.

Preface

For the purpose of definition, the British in *Encyclopedia of British Humorists* refers to those nations located in the British Isles—England, Ireland, Scotland, and Wales—and entries on all of the principal British literary humorists are included in this volume. This, of course, involves a tremendously wide range of time, authorial talent, literary approaches, and subject matter. The subjects range from *Beowulf* and the works of Geoffrey Chaucer to the writing of P.G. Wodehouse and John Cleese. Also included are those writers in between, such as Henry Bunbury, who is credited with creating the forerunner to the modern comic strip, and the contemporary humorists who developed in the twentieth-century Oxbridge milieu. Indeed, some authors, like Philip Sidney, who have generally been considered mainstream writers and not humorists, are seen in a new light. Sometimes, as in the case of E.M. Forster, who called humor "that estimable adjunct of the educated man," humor has been a recognized yet somewhat neglected element of an author's style; sometimes, as with Winston Churchill, the writer's primary occupation has not been literary and therefore the author has not been considered a humorist. Others, such as Andrew Marvell, who were considered humorists in their own times but today tend to be known for other qualities in their writing, are reexamined as humorists. There is even an entry on one subject-author for whom an entry is included in the *Encyclopedia of American Humorists*—Thomas Chandler Haliburton. As is the case with T.S. Eliot and W.H. Auden, both North America and Britain claim Haliburton in their literary histories.

A few readers might quibble about the exclusion of a couple of minor writers (such as Robert Herrick and Thomas Coryate, who among other things dabbled in humor, be it satire, parody, or epigram), but as with the *Encyclopedia of American Humorists,* I relied upon scholars who were experts on and/or who specifically wanted to write about particular authors. Thus, I did not seek to cover *every* English writer of humor, being content instead to include those about whom interest, knowledge, and enthusiasm were demonstrated rather than looking to fill the pages of this volume through assignments in order merely to fill the pages. This in turn permitted me to include major (read "serious") literary figures who are not considered to be humorists primarily but who consistently utilize humor in their works. The expansion of focus is thus based on the concept of literary humor, and the word *humorist* in the title of this encyclopedia indicates someone who works primarily within a literary medium, as opposed to comic or comedian, which implies performance (such as Benny Hill, the Two Ronnies [Barker and Corbett], and others—who write jokes, but who are basically performers, either as stand-up comics or actors).

In concept, I wanted to include in this encyclopedia articles on all major (that is, the best and most important) and representative humorists from the beginnings of British literature to the present. As with the *Encyclopedia of American Humorists,* identifying those writers was not as easy as it might at first seem to be. The two most important questions that arose were: What is British, and what is the definition of a humorist? For the purpose of the *Encyclopedia of British*

Humorists, British includes authors who were born in and/or wrote most of their humorous materials in the British Isles.

As for what is a humorist, I had to make some arbitrary decisions (which included some of the determining factors discussed above)—otherwise the volume would have been endless. One of my first decisions was to focus on those writers who are known primarily as humorists. On the one hand, of course, even preeminent humorists such as Wodehouse did not write exclusively humorous material, but their reputations are based on their humorous writings. On the other hand, many major British authors utilize humor in their work but are not recognized for this aspect of their canon above all other elements—Forster, A.E. Housman, and Harold Pinter come to mind. There are also authors (such as H.G. Wells and Churchill) whose main body of work was not humorous but who wrote humorous books. In these cases only the humorous works have been examined closely.

Once the definition of my subject was set, I contacted approximately 200 literary scholars, primarily in America and Great Britain, and supplied them with a list of about 150 names to be considered for inclusion in the encyclopedia. I asked them to let me know which names they thought would be appropriate (or inappropriate) for inclusion; I welcomed their suggestions of additional names to be considered, and I asked if they were interested in writing an entry or if they could recommend anyone else who would be especially well-suited to write an entry on a particular author. I ended up with well over 230 possible entries; a good number of those included in the encyclopedia were chosen from the additional suggestions that I received.

Over a period of five years, the list of subject authors was refined and writing assignments were made. Scholars were instructed in the format—which was to include biographical and bibliographical information (primary sources and annotated secondary sources) for easy, quick reference and a detailed literary analysis for in-depth study that would be useful to either laypeople or established scholars. Occasionally an entry does not fit this format exactly. A few scholars felt that their subject author's life or work could be better understood if minor variations from the strict categorization were allowed, and in some instances certain information simply was not available. The themes and techniques of the subject's best and most representative works were to be examined, and there was to be a brief summary that included an assessment of the importance and influence of the subject in the area of British humor. By and large, the length of the entry reflects the importance of the subject author, though this is not always a completely accurate yardstick, especially if the scholar who wrote the entry felt that the subject had not received an appropriate amount of critical attention previously.

The final choice of subject authors also included another important element. I was looking for scholars to write on each subject who had some expertise on the subject and who were recognized as good writers. This means that not every subject author whom I would have liked to include in the *Encyclopedia of British Humorists* is included; in a few instances I chose not to include an entry if I could not count on its being as well written as possible (or if an entry was submitted that I did not feel met that standard), and I did not want to seek out someone to write on a humorist who did not already have an interest in the writer purely to be able to include another entry. Conversely, some lesser writers were included because of the enthusiasm of an expert on that particular author and because of my desire to expose a wider audience to a figure who has heretofore been neglected (several are examined for the first time in this volume).

Ironically, one of the things about the contributions that I, as an editor, found interesting was the difficulty that some major literary scholars had in approaching the subject of humor in a scholarly fashion, for humor is a subject too often given short shrift in literary analysis. This is ironic because "humor" has become a seriously big business in the last two decades of the twentieth century. In the United States there are numerous annual meetings devoted to the application of humor to the workplace, in the field of medicine (à la Norman Cousins), and in our everyday lives. Steve Allen, Sid Caesar, and other comedians have become featured speakers at these gatherings. In Britain this movement is exemplified in videotapes created by Cleese, whose thirty-five-minute-long *Humour Is Not a Luxury* is advertised as being filled with the wisdom of a man who believes that "when humor is present we lose not seriousness, but only solemnity" and who describes how humor can "facilitate learning; help change people's behavior, promote an increase in creativity; make it easier to respond to stress; [and] make individuals more effective and organizations more productive."

There has been an effort to make the essays in this volume consistent in format, though for the reasons indicated above that has not always been possible. Some of the subject authors' lives and works simply did not lend themselves to the general format (as in the case of the *Beowulf* and *Gawain* poets, for example). Occasionally there is information missing—certain dates of births, marriages, and deaths, for instance, could not be definitely ascertained for a number of the subjects, and there were even problems with the dating of some of the texts. Wherever there is no date, or where the date has not been established with any degree of certainty, that is apparent in the text, though this does not mean that efforts were not made to determine the factual material; some material just is not available to scholars now (and it may never be). The essays also incorporate a variety of styles and critical approaches (for example, some include footnotes, most do not). Individual scholars were permitted to write as individuals within the context of the standard format.

I had to make a series of arbitrary decisions regarding pseudonyms too. Instead of listing all authors by their birth names, in some cases I listed them by their pseudonyms. In making these decisions, I used the criterion of which name a lay audience would most likely recognize. Thus, Noel Coward appears as Noel Coward rather than as Yorick, a name that he used in his writing; Charles Lutwidge Dodgson, on the other hand, appears as Lewis Carroll because the pseudonym is certainly more familiar to readers than the birth name.

Part of the joy of working on this six-year-long project came from the passion and careful work shown by many of the scholars whose essays appear in the volume. Most tried religiously to meet their deadlines (several went so far as to use overnight express mail deliveries or fax machines to ensure that they did so) and to create entries that go beyond facile, shallow summations of other people's research. Their willingness to contribute original scholarship was admirable. I was pleased by the consistently high quality of the submissions and the cooperative attitude shown when I made editorial suggestions. (Note: I did standardize spellings to the American form, except in quotations and titles.)

The result of all of this is the *Encyclopedia of British Humorists,* which is intended to be the most comprehensive and up-to-date reference text on British humorists ever published, with scholarly articles on authors from the earliest-extant British literature through today, including all of the chief humorists as well as a wide range of the finest and most representative of the rest.

There are 203 entries in this encyclopedia covering 206 humorists (there are three pairs). These entries involve the work of 118 scholars from seven countries (the United States, Canada, England, Scotland, Ireland, France, and Australia), and the essays represent the efforts of experts from an extremely diverse field of disciplines: literature and English departments (including specialists in both English and American literature), naturally, but there are also members of departments as disparate as business, drama, and sociology, along with librarians and several independent scholars as well. The range in backgrounds of the scholars adds to the richness of points of view and theoretical approaches to the concept of humor and to specific subject matter. This diversity suggests, too, that the subject of humor, and British humor in particular, is one that appeals to a wide range of people and that this volume not only will fill a reference need but also will be of interest to those who enjoy humor for its own sake.

Frankfort, Kentucky

Humor has justly been regarded as the
finest perfection of poetic genius—
Thomas Carlyle

Chronological Index

This chronology contains the known birth and death dates of the authors and the dates of their major humorous literary works.

Eighth century	*Beowulf*
Fourteenth century (?)	John Scoggin
ca. 1300	Howleglas born
ca. 1340	Geoffrey Chaucer born
1350	Howleglas died
ca. 1350	The Gawain/Pearl Poet born
ca. 1385	*Second Shepherds' Play* (Wakefield Master) performed
ca. 1365–1390	*Sir Gawain and the Green Knight* written
ca. 1369–1394	*The Canterbury Tales* (Geoffrey Chaucer) written
ca. 1400	The Gawain/Pearl Poet died
October 25, 1400	Geoffrey Chaucer died
ca. 1460	William Dunbar born
ca. 1460	John Skelton born
ca. 1500	Wakefield Master born
1503	*The Tretis of the Tua Mariit Wemen and the Wedo* (William Dunbar) published
1509	*Howleglas* (Howleglas) published
1504–1511	*The Tunning of Elinor Rumming* (John Skelton) written
ca. 1522	William Dunbar died
1529	John Skelton died
1550(?)	Wakefield Master died
ca. 1552	Walter Ralegh born
1554	Philip Sidney born
ca. 1556	George Peele born
July 11, 1558	Robert Greene born
1559	George Chapman born
ca. 1560	Thomas Deloney born
February 1564	Christopher Marlowe born
April 1564	William Shakespeare born
ca. 1565	William Kempe born
1567	Thomas Nashe born
ca. 1569	Robert Armin born
ca. 1572	Ben Jonson born
1572	John Donne born
July 1, 1574	Joseph Hall born

March 8, 1859	Kenneth Grahame born
March 26, 1859	A.E. Housman born
May 2, 1859	Jerome Klapka Jerome born
May 9, 1860	James Matthew Barrie born
September 18, 1861	Owen Seaman born
June 11, 1862	Violet Florence Martin born
September 8, 1863	W.W. Jacobs born
September 28, 1864	Barry Eric Odell Pain born
1865	*Alice's Adventures in Wonderland* (Lewis Carroll) published
August 27, 1865	Thomas Chandler Haliburton died
December 30, 1865	Rudyard Kipling born
January 23, 1866	Thomas Love Peacock died
September 21, 1866	H.G. Wells born
1867	"The Owl and the Pussycat" (Edward Lear) published
July 27, 1867	E.F. Benson born
1868	*The Ring and the Book* (Robert Browning) published
December 8, 1868	Norman Douglas born
September 25, 1869	St. John Hankin born
May 23, 1870	Mark Lemon died
June 9, 1870	Charles Dickens died
July 27, 1870	Joseph Peter René Hilaire Belloc born
December 18, 1870	Hector Hugh Munro born
May 18, 1872	Bertrand Arthur Russell born
August 24, 1872	Max Beerbohm born
December 17, 1873	Ford Madox Ford born
January 25, 1874	W. Somerset Maugham born
May 29, 1874	G.K. Chesterton born
November 30, 1874	Winston S. Churchill born
July 10, 1875	E.C. Bentley born
1879	*The Egoist* (George Meredith) published
January 1, 1879	E.M. Forster born
January 1880	Henry Howarth Bashford born
March 1, 1880	Lytton Strachey born
March 30, 1880	Sean O'Casey born
May 30, 1880	James Robinson Planche died
February 5, 1881	Thomas Carlyle died
	Frederick Lonsdale born
October 15, 1881	P.G. Wodehouse born
1882	*Vice Versa* (F. Anstey) published
January 18, 1882	A.A. Milne born
February 2, 1882	James Joyce born
November 18, 1882	Wyndham Lewis born
December 6, 1882	Anthony Trollope died
February 17, 1884	Charles Stuart Calverley died
1885	*The Mikado* (W.S. Gilbert) performed
January 17, 1886	Ronald Firbank born
December 12, 1886	Ben Travers born
July 25, 1887	Henry Mayhew died
September 7, 1887	Edith Sitwell born
January 29, 1888	Edward Lear died
December 7, 1888	Joyce Cary born
1889	*Three Men in a Boat* (Jerome Klapka Jerome) published
October 27, 1889	Enid Algerine Bagnold born

December 12, 1889	Robert Browning died
September 24, 1890	A.P. Herbert born
1892	*The Diary of a Nobody* (George and Walter Weedon Grossmith) published
January 3, 1892	J.R.R. Tolkien born
1894	*Trilby* (George Du Maurier) published
July 26, 1894	Aldous Leonard Huxley born
1895	*The Importance of Being Earnest* (Oscar Wilde) performed
November 3, 1895	Archibald Gordon Macdonell born
1896	*A Shropshire Lad* (A.E. Housman) published
	The Wheels of Chance (H.G. Wells) published
	Many Cargoes (W.W. Jacobs) published
October 7, 1896	George Du Maurier died
November 4, 1896	J.R. Ackerley born
January 14, 1898	Lewis Carroll died
November 29, 1898	C.S. Lewis born
1899	*Some Adventures of an Irish R.M.* (Somerville and Ross) published
December 16, 1899	Noel Pierce Coward born
1900	*Kim* (Rudyard Kipling) published
	Eliza (Barry Eric Odell Pain) published
February 1, 1900	Stephen Potter born
November 30, 1900	Oscar Wilde died
December 16, 1900	V.S. Pritchett born
1901	*Man and Superman* (George Bernard Shaw) performed
May 3, 1901	John Henry Noyes Collier born
1902	*Far from the Madding Crowd* (Thomas Hardy) published
1902	*Erewhon Revisited Twenty Years Later* (Samuel Butler) published
1902	*The Path to Rome* (Joseph Peter René Hilaire Belloc) published
January 5, 1902	Stella Dorothea Gibbons born
June 18, 1902	Samuel Butler died
June 25, 1903	George Orwell born
October 28, 1903	Evelyn Arthur St. John Waugh born
1904	*Reginald* (Saki) published
August 26, 1904	Christopher Isherwood born
October 2, 1904	Graham Greene born
November 28, 1904	Nancy Mitford born
1906	*Peter Pan* (James Matthew Barrie) performed
April 13, 1906	Samuel Beckett born
August 28, 1906	John Betjeman born
February 21, 1907	W.H. Auden born
December 18, 1907	Christopher Fry born
1908	*The Man Who Was Thursday: A Nightmare* (G.K. Chesterton) published
	The Wind in the Willows (Kenneth Grahame) published
December 25, 1908	Quentin Crisp born
May 9, 1909	George Meredith died
June 15, 1909	St. John Hankin died
1911	*Zuleika Dobson* (Max Beerbohm) published
February 4, 1911	Geoffrey Willans born
May 29, 1911	W.S. Gilbert died
June 10, 1911	Terence Mervyn Rattigan born
October 5, 1911	Brian O'Nolan born

February 15, 1912	George Mikes born
March 1, 1912	George Grossmith died
1913	*Trent's Last Case* (E.C. Bentley) published
April 19, 1913	Michael Wharton born
June 2, 1913	Barbara Pym born
October 27, 1914	Dylan Thomas born
1915	*The Good Soldier* (Ford Madox Ford) published
December 21, 1915	Violet Florence Martin died
February 4, 1916	Gavin Ewart born
September 13, 1916	Roald Dahl born
November 14, 1916	Hector Hugh Munro died
1917	*South Wind* (Norman Douglas) published
April 21, 1917	Francis Cowley Burnand died
September 9, 1917	Albert Vajda born
1918	*Eminent Victorians* (Lytton Strachey) published
February 1, 1918	Muriel Sarah Spark born
January 29, 1919	N.F. Simpson born
June 14, 1919	Walter Weedon Grossmith died
May 19, 1920	Sandy Wilson died
April 16, 1921	Peter Ustinov born
1922	*The Flower Beneath the Foot* (Ronald Firbank) published
	Ulysses (James Joyce) published
	Facade (Edith Sitwell) published
April 16, 1922	Kingsley Amis born
1923	*St. Joan* (George Bernard Shaw) performed
	Jeeves (P.G. Wodehouse) published
February 9, 1923	Brendan Behan born
April 17, 1923	Lindsay Gordon Anderson born
1924	*Augustus Carp, Esq.* (Henry Howarth Bashford) published
	A Passage to India (E.M Forster) published
	Juno and the Paycock (Sean O'Casey) performed
1927	*Misleading Cases* (A.P. Herbert) published
1924–1928	*Parade's End* (Ford Madox Ford) published
April 23, 1924	Colin Welch born
November 7, 1924	Wolf Mankowitz born
1925	*The Last of Mrs. Cheyney* (Frederick Lonsdale) published
March 22, 1925	Gerard Hoffnung born
1926	*Winnie-the-Pooh* (A.A. Milne) published
May 15, 1926	Peter Levin Shaffer born
May 21, 1926	Ronald Firbank died
1927	*Lucia in London* (E.F. Benson) published
	The Constant Wife (W. Somerset Maugham) published
	Misleading Cases (A.P. Herbert) published
	The Childermass, vol. 1 of *The Human Age* (Wyndham Lewis), published
June 14, 1927	Jerome Klapka Jerome died
July 15, 1927	Ann Jellicoe born
1928	*Decline and Fall* (Evelyn Arthur St. John Waugh) published
January 11, 1928	Thomas Hardy died
March 4, 1928	Alan Sillitoe born
March 30, 1928	Tom Sharpe born
May 5, 1928	Barry Eric Odell Pain died
January 9, 1929	Brian Friel born

February 6, 1929	Keith Spencer Waterhouse born
September 20, 1929	Henry Livings born
1930	*Private Lives* (Noel Pierce Coward) performed
	Cakes and Ale (W. Somerset Maugham) published
October 10, 1930	Harold Pinter born
January 10, 1931	Peter Barnes born
1932	*Hindoo Holiday* (J.R. Ackerley) published
	Cold Comfort Farm (Stella Dorothea Gibbons) published
	Brave New World (Aldous Leonard Huxley) published
January 21, 1932	Lytton Strachey died
July 6, 1932	Kenneth Grahame died
September 7, 1932	Malcolm Stanley Bradbury born
1933	*England, Their England* (Archibald Gordon Macdonell) published
January 1, 1933	Joe Orton born
September 8, 1933	Michael Frayn born
March 10, 1934	F. Anstey died
1935	*Mr. Norris Changes Trains* (Christopher Isherwood) published
January 28, 1935	David Lodge born
1936	Peter Tinniswood born
January 18, 1936	Rudyard Kipling died
February 2, 1936	Owen Seaman died
April 30, 1936	A.E. Housman died
June 14, 1936	G.K. Chesterton died
October 20, 1936	Simon Gray born
June 19, 1937	James Matthew Barrie died
July 3, 1937	Tom Stoppard born
September 5, 1937	Ella D'Arcy died
June 27, 1938	Alan Coren born
1939	*At Swim-Two-Birds* (Brian O'Nolan) published
April 12, 1939	Alan Ayckbourn born
June 26, 1939	Ford Madox Ford died
October 27, 1939	John Cleese born
November 17, 1939	Auberon Alexander Waugh born
February 29, 1940	E.F. Benson died
January 13, 1941	James Joyce died
January 16, 1941	Archibald Gordon Macdonell died
September 1, 1943	W.W. Jacobs died
1944	*The Horse's Mouth* (Joyce Cary) published
1945	*Animal Farm* (George Orwell) published
	Blithe Spirit (Noel Pierce Coward) performed
1946	*How to Be an Alien* (George Mikes) published
April 2, 1946	Sue Townsend born
August 13, 1946	H.G. Wells died
1947	*The Age of Anxiety* (W.H. Auden) published
	Gamesmanship (Stephen Meredith Potter) published
August 23, 1947	Willy Russell born
1948	*The Loved One* (Evelyn Arthur St. John Waugh) published
	The Browning Version (Terence Mervyn Rattigan) performed
March 1948	*The Lady's Not for Burning* (Christopher Fry) performed
1949	*Love in a Cold Climate* (Nancy Mitford) published
August 25, 1949	Martin Louis Amis born
October 8, 1949	Edith Anna Oenone Somerville died
1950–1956	*Chronicles of Narnia* (C.S. Lewis) published

Pseudonyms

Encyclopedia of British Humorists

A

Ackerley, J[oe] R[andolph]

Born: London, November 4, 1896
Education: Rossall School, Lancashire,
*   1908–1914; Magdalene College, Cam-*
*   bridge, 1919–1921*
Died: Herne Hill, Kent, England June 4, 1967

Biography

J.R. Ackerley begins his autobiography, *My Father and Myself*, with the arresting sentence, "I was born in 1896 and my parents were married in 1919." As this indicates, Ackerley's life was in some ways an unconventional one; in others, however, it was typically bourgeois, even repressed. His well-to-do father, Roger Ackerley, was a self-made man, a fruit importer who had earned the sobriquet of "the Banana King." He and Ackerley's mother, Janetta Aylward, brought up their three children in a series of large houses in Richmond.

Roger and Janetta's strange menage had precedents in Janetta's family, and Ackerley's biographer points out that, "although the Aylwards were middle-class, cultured and outwardly respectable, the family tree is a network of illegitimacy and sexual irregularity."[1] When Roger died in 1929 a final secret came out: he had been keeping a second family, comprised of three teenage daughters and their mother, Muriel Perry.

Ackerley and his brother Peter were educated at Rossall School in Lancashire. In 1914 Ackerley entered the East Surrey Regiment, serving in the Battle of the Somme, among other campaigns. He was taken prisoner in 1917 and spent the remainder of the war in hospitals and POW camps in Germany and, later, in Switzerland; there, on the advice of Arnold Lunn, he wrote a play, *The Prisoners of War*.

In 1919, Ackerley went up to Magdalene College, Cambridge, where he studied English literature. He left in 1921 and spent several years drifting unhappily in his attempts to become a writer. He wrote a good deal of poetry, some of which was published in *Poems by Four Authors* (1923). This period saw the beginning of many lifelong friendships, notably that with E.M. Forster. Ackerley and his new friends were openly homosexual.

In 1923, on Forster's recommendation, Ackerley obtained the post of secretary/companion to the Maharajah of Chhatarpur; he stayed in India for six months, keeping copious journals.

The Prisoners of War was produced in London in 1925 and was a success both *d'estime* and *de scandale*, dealing, as it did, with homosexual love. Ackerley became a rising literary star. However, he was not a highly productive writer, and in 1928 he joined the British Broadcasting Corporation (BBC), starting in the Talks Department. He was to stay with the BBC until retirement, spending twenty-four years as literary editor of its weekly magazine, *The Listener*. In this capacity he became an extremely influential figure, attracting contributors such as Forster, John Maynard Keynes, Virginia Woolf, and Kenneth Clark, and promoting the early work of such writers as W.H. Auden, Christopher Isherwood, Cecil Day Lewis, and Stephen Spender. The standard of reviewing was said to be the highest in England. With his left-wing bent and his pleasure in calling a spade a spade, he did much to change the BBC's traditional prudery and political conservatism.

Ackerley's account of his Indian journey, *Hindoo Holiday*, was published in 1932. The book was tremendously successful, Ackerley's only great commercial success.

In 1945, Ackerley acquired a friend's Alsatian dog, Queenie. Queenie became the great love that Ackerley had sought all his life, and he devoted his next two books, *My Dog Tulip* (1956) and *We Think the World of You* (1960) to her. The latter book—Ackerley's only novel—won the W.H. Smith Annual Literary Award.

Ackerley spent the better part of his last years caring for his aunt and sister, speaking out in the cause of animal rights, and rewriting his family memoir. He died in Kent, England, in 1967; *My Father and Myself* was published posthumously in 1968.

Literary Analysis

With the exception of *Hindoo Holiday*, none of Ackerley's books are straightforwardly comedic works. All, however, are infused with black comedy of the most deeply sardonic vein. Ackerley bitterly regretted his estrangement from his father; though the two were friendly and affectionate with one another, their respective secrets prevented their ever enjoying a more than superficial relationship. Ackerley's belief that this secretiveness had been emotionally destructive caused him to be obsessed with personal and family roots and with the truth in whatever form it might be found; and when the truth contained an element of the grotesque, he confronted it with great relish. Gleeful enumeration of the most humiliating personal facts—always in elegant, limpid prose—is Ackerley's literary stock-in-trade.

Perhaps as a result of these preoccupations, his work is almost obsessively autobiographical—most of it is statedly so (*Hindoo Holiday, My Dog Tulip, My Father and Myself*). His two "fictional" works, *The Prisoners of War* and *We Think the World of You*, are lifted straight from life, so much so that the publishers of *We Think the World of You*, fearing libel suits, urged Ackerley to make as many circumstantial changes as possible.

Ackerley's life, certainly, was rich in material for black humor. He began with every advantage—money, brains, spectacular good looks—and ended up a rather solitary eccentric, his life wrapped up in that of his dog. He was fully aware of the inherent absurdity: "once upon a time," he wrote, "I was a handsome young man, regarded as one of the most promising writers of the day, much sought after by everyone, involved in countless exciting love affairs—and now look at me, grey-haired and going deaf, a dog lover and grovelling about . . . in a public park."[2]

The Prisoners of War (1925) now appears rather melodramatic, something of a period piece; its interest largely lies in its treatment of homosexuality, unusual for a commercial play of the time. It seemed fresh and interesting for the new generation who had come of age after the war; the young Stephen Spender and Christopher Isherwood, among others, were intrigued by the piece's audacity.

Hindoo Holiday has become a classic of its kind. The 1920s and 1930s were a heyday for travel/adventure books written by amateur explorers or professional writers traveling for pleasure. Sometimes, as with Norman Douglas's *South Wind*, they formed the nucleus of a novel, though usually they were simply travel narratives. Forster's *The Hill of Devi*, the travel books of Peter Fleming, Evelyn Waugh, Robert Byron, and others, are all still popular; so is *Hindoo Holiday*, which stands with the best of them. In his review of the book Waugh said that it "leaves the reviewer in some difficulty as to the terms in which he must praise it . . . the difficulty is to control one's enthusiasm and to praise it temperately."[3] The book contains a series of portraits, but it is constructed around that of the Maharajah himself, a very funny, but simultaneously moving portrayal. In his "Introduction," Ackerley writes of how he came to be employed by the Maharajah: "He wanted someone to love him—His Highness, I mean . . . He wanted a friend. He wanted understanding, and sympathy, and philosophic comfort; and he sent to England for them."[4] While the first merit of the book is its humor, many Indian readers were impressed by its truth: the Aga Khan wrote an introduction to the French edition, and the eminent Indian scholar Saros Cowasjee said that it was "the only book about India by an Englishman in which I have not been conscious of the author's nationality while reading it."[5]

In 1956, Ackerley published *My Dog Tulip*, a short book (comprised of several essays) detailing life with his bitch, Queenie. There would seem to have been no precedent in Ackerley's life for the great love he bore Queenie. An irritable middle-aged man, deeply misogynistic, he had devoted much of his life to the pursuit of the Ideal (male, youthful, working-class) Friend. The irony was not wasted on him when his affections were finally returned by a dog—a spoiled, capricious, feminine beauty, resembling only too closely the possessive women whom Ackerley had for so many years excoriated.

The book is partly a lyrical impression of love and the passage of time. It is also partly a tease. In it Ackerley challenges conventional notions (prevalent not only among the bourgeoisie but also in his own liberal and humanistic circle) of the primacy of human doings and relationships. Ackerley portrays Tulip as, in many ways, a typical romantic heroine, and while lovingly extolling her beauty and goodness, he also, mischievously, details her every bodily function, including the sexual and the scatological. Though more than half-serious, it is also deliberately written to provoke, and in this it succeeds. Many of Ackerley's friends and admirers could not bring themselves to like or approve of the book, but they had to admit that nothing quite like it had ever been written.

The same could be said for Ackerley's only novel, *We Think the World of You*. General consensus, after more than thirty years, has proclaimed this eccentric book a minor masterpiece. In it, Ackerley tells the story of his acquisition of Queenie (or Evie, in the novel). It is narrated by Frank, a middle-aged civil servant. Evie had been owned by Frank's feckless lover Johnnie, who, jailed for housebreaking, leaves the dog to the not-so-tender mercies of his family. Though fond of Evie in their way, they take no notice of her needs, always subordinating hers to their own. Frank enters into battle with his lover's stubborn parents, unattractive and unpleasant wife Megan, and horrible baby to finally rescue this beautiful princess from her dreary dungeon.

The book's deceptively simple structure as what Ackerley called a "fairy story for adults" encompasses a complex interweaving of themes. It is a penetrating examination of the class system and of the rigid, hopelessly conflicting values of the classes, specifically the intellectual/professional, represented by Frank, and the working classes, represented by Johnnie and his family (Ackerley's offbeat vision of this might have sprung from his own ambiguous place in that system). It is an ironic indictment of conventional Christian mores, and a vindication of individual freedom—however eccentric—over the conventions of society and the family, very much in the mode of Samuel Butler. The novel is also, surreptitiously, a sly study in subjectivity. The reader is inclined to take the first-person narrator's descriptions of his unattractive foes at face value; eventually, however, it becomes evident that Frank's judgments are colored by his own neuroses. His misogyny and, in spite of his obsession with male youth and beauty, his real misanthropy, make him a comically unreliable narrator. The book's "villains" seldom actually say anything objectionable, though Frank's perpetual ire makes it seem as though they do:

"It's Megan, Frank."

Why did she always have to begin like that, I wondered irritably, as though anyone could possibly mistake that sickening Welsh voice. (*We Think the World of You*, 21)

As Ackerley himself put it: "Frank is an unstable, maladjusted man, obsessed and frustrated, and the story is subtly contrived to turn completely over so that his 'persecutors' can be viewed in a sympathetic light."[6]

Ackerley was seldom satisfied with his work and tended to spend years writing and rewriting. *My Father and Myself* was begun in 1933, four years after the death of Roger Ackerley; it was not finished until 1967, the year of his own death. It was probably his best piece of work, and still has a wide circle of admirers, though its graphic sexual disquisitions make less startling reading now than they did upon its publication in 1969. Like *We Think the World of You*, it conforms to no real literary "type," and Truman Capote, speaking for many, called it the most original autobiography that he had ever read.

Ackerley himself described the book as a quest for the truth. As its title suggests, it is a parallel exploration of himself and of his father, and of the secrets at the core of their lives. The events of Roger Ackerley's youth were well-kept secrets, and Ackerley suspected that his father's "guardsman-to-grandee" success story might have found its origins in a financially advantageous homosexual liaison. Ackerley links this, as well as his father's reluctance to marry his mother and the existence of his second family, to his own emotional life, discussing in detail the self-destructiveness of his sex life and his experiences during World War I, where he brutally examines his own behavior for any signs of cowardice. The book is deeply moving; at the same time it is ludicrously funny.

A

These are the works on which Ackerley's reputation rests. He was also a prolific poet, but his poetry, being primarily serious, does not enter into the domain of this study.

Summary

As an editor, J.R. Ackerley was instrumental in forming the character and quality of post-war literary journalism. As a writer, his most notable characteristics, exemplified in *Hindoo Holiday* and *We Think the World of You*, are black—sometimes farcical—humor, and brutal honesty. All of his work is in one way or another autobiographical; his nearest literary allies are Samuel Butler, E.M. Forster, and Christopher Isherwood.

Notes

1. Peter Parker, *Ackerley* (New York: Farrar, Straus, Giroux, 1989): 10–11.
2. Diaries, March 12, 1950; quoted in Parker, 268.
3. *The Spectator*, April 16, 1932.
4. *Hindoo Holiday* (London: Chatto and Windus, 1932; Penguin Books, 1983): Preface.
5. Indian edition of *Hindoo Holiday* (India: Arnold/Heinemann, 1979): "Introduction."
6. Quoted in Parker, 349.

Selected Bibliography
Primary Sources

Books
Poems by Four Authors. London: Bowes and Bowes, 1923.
The Prisoners of War: A Play. London: Chatto and Windus, 1925.
Hindoo Holiday: An Indian Journal. London: Chatto and Windus, 1932; rev. ed. 1952.
Escapers All (ed.). London: The Bodley Head, 1932.
My Dog Tulip: Life with an Alsatian. New York: Secker and Warburg, 1956; rev. ed. London: The Bodley Head, 1966.
We Think the World of You. London: The Bodley Head, 1960.
My Father and Myself. London: The Bodley Head, 1969.
E.M. Forster: A Portrait. London: Ian McKelvie, 1970.
Micheldever & Other Poems. London: Ian McKelvie, 1972.
The Letters of J.R. Ackerley. Ed. Neville Braybrooke. London: Duckworth, 1975.
My Sister and Myself: The Diaries of J.R. Ackerley. Ed. Francis King. London: Hutchinson, 1982.

Anthologies Containing Poems by J.R. Ackerley
Church, Richard, and M.M. Bozman. *Poems of Our Time: 1900–1942*. London: J.M. Dent, 1945.
Coote, Stephen. *The Penguin Book of Homosexual Poetry*. Penguin, 1983.
Davison, Edward. *Cambridge Poets, 1914–1920*. W. Heffer and Son, 1920.
Moult, Thomas. *The Best Poems of 1922*. London: Jonathan Cape, 1923.
Newbolt, Sir Henry. *The Mercury Book of Verse*. London: Macmillan, 1931.
Squire, J.C. *Second Selections from Modern Poets*. London: Martin Secker, 1924.

Secondary Sources

Biographies
Furbank, P.N. *E.M. Forster: A Life*. Vol. I: *1879–1920*, London: Collins, 1983. Vol. II: *1921–1970*, London: Collins, 1985. There is a good bit of material about Ackerley here, and indeed about his entire circle of friends.
Parker, Peter. *Ackerley: A Life of J.R. Ackerley*. London: Constable and Co., 1989. New York: Farrar, Straus, Giroux, 1989. A first-rate biography, with considerable literary merit of its own; as amusing and pleasurable to read as Ackerley's own work.
Petrie, Diana. *The Secret Orchard of Roger Ackerley*. A family memoir by one of the half-sisters of whose existence Ackerley was for so many years unaware. A fascinating companion piece to *My Father and Myself*.

Brooke Allen

Adams, Douglas (Noel)

Born: Cambridge, March 11, 1952
Education: Brentwood School, Essex; St. John's College, Cambridge

Biography

Born on March 11, 1952 in the great university city of Cambridge and educated at an excellent private school (Brentwood School in Essex),

Douglas Adams has a bohemian familiarity with and affectionate contempt for intellectuality. The son of a Cambridge graduate student in theology who divorced his mother a few months after his birth, he grew up in the university community. After receiving his B.A. degree in English, he spent several years writing for radio and television, performing in and sometimes directing stage reviews in London, Cambridge, and on the Edinburgh Fringe. He worked as a hospital porter, a barn builder, a chicken-shed cleaner, bodyguard, radio producer, and script editor of the *Dr. Who* series on television. He was not, as some sources assert, involved with the *Monty Python* group.

In 1978, he wrote a series of comic science-fiction radio dramas called *The Hitchhiker's Guide to the Galaxy*. Expanded and revised, scripts for this series were the basis for the books *Hitchhikers Guide* (1979) and *The Restaurant at the End of the Universe* (1980). The books, in turn, were transformed into record albums, a computer game, and the six-episode BBC television series *Hitchhiker's Guide to the Galaxy* (1981). Adams continued his hitchhiker narrative in *Life, The Universe, and Everything* (1982) and *So Long, and Thanks for All the Fish* (1984). In 1985, he published the original hitchhiker radio scripts, and in 1986, he collaborated on *The Utterly, Utterly Merry Comic Relief Christmas Book*. In 1983, he went to Hollywood where he wrote a screenplay based on the series. A few years of frustration followed during which he tried unsuccessfully to negotiate the production of his script. Then, in 1987, he discovered that his bookkeeper had defrauded him and that he owed a considerable tax debt. Returning to writing, he concluded that he had "written one Hitchhiker book too many." He attempted to change genres with *Dirk Gently's Holistic Detective Agency* (1987) followed by *The Long Dark Tea-Time of the Soul* (1989) which continued Dirk Gently's adventures.

Perhaps the six-foot-five Adams was describing himself in this sketch of the character Richard MacDuff in *Dirk Gently*: "Tall. Tall and absurdly thin. And good-natured. A bit like a preying mantis that doesn't prey. A non-preying mantis if you like. A sort of pleasant genial mantis that's given up preying and taken up tennis instead."

In 1988, he began work on a BBC radio series concerning nearly extinct animals somewhat ironically titled "Last Chance to See," a project that took him to China, New Zealand, Thailand, Brazil, Madagascar, Chile, and Zaire. Once again, the radio scripts were expanded into a book, *Last Chance to See* (1991).

Though he had resolved not to, in 1992 he wrote a fifth hitchhiker novel, *Mostly Harmless*, with the subtitle *The Fifth Book of the Increasingly Inaccurately Named Hitchhiker's Trilogy*.

He lives, according to his agent's biography, in Islington "with a lady barrister and an Apple Macintosh." Adams identifies the English romantic poets as his major inspiration, but he is also fascinated with computer technology and Stephen Hawkings's speculations on the origins of the universe. His first six novels sold ten million copies but, reflecting on their success, he suggested that he had hidden behind jokes, and he has expressed the desire to be remembered for something more substantial than the Hitchhiker series.

Having achieved that goal in *Last Chance to See*, he indulged himself with *Mostly Harmless*.

Literary Analysis

Adams's tremendous popular success transcends the small realm of science-fiction parody (though often he does directly mimic science-fiction writers), or even the wider world of science fiction as social satire, although that element also frequently informs his work. Like a magic-realist painter, Adams is philosophically intrigued with vivid juxtaposition, and his work, in addition to devouring the juicier morsels of science-fiction imagination and satirizing the trivialities of modern life, often reflects a surrealistic audacity and a sophisticated taste for the ironies involved in the search for epistemological verities—as one critic put it: "Posh-school Science Fiction" (Brown, 1032).

Adams says that he enjoys "taking what's essentially a dream and making it as real as possible," yet his work abounds in preposterous names, bizarre characters, and instantaneous and totally improbable plot twists. The aspect of reality with which he challenges himself in his novels is his perception that "every particle of the universe affects every other particle, however faintly or obliquely" (*The Long Dark Tea-Time of the Soul*, 110).

Adams's method is to introduce five or six seemingly unconnected plots and then to bring them crashing together in an unexpected denouement. While this strategy may sometimes be confusing to his readers, the brilliance of his style and the range of his intellect seem to function best in this chaotic ferment. Earth is destroyed in the first chapter of *Hitchhiker's Guide* by subhuman Vogons making way for a hyperspace bypass. The two-headed president of the galaxy steals a spaceship on a whim and goes to the world of planet designers accompanied by three survivors of Earth's holocaust and a paranoid robot. There we find out that Earth is not Earth but actually is a supercomputer run by mice trying to find out the meaning of Life, the Universe, and Everything—which has turned out to be "42," an answer that raises more questions than it answers. Thus ends the first book of the five-book "trilogy." Almost every chapter—and many of the chapters are very short—ends with an imminent cataclysm which is averted by the improbable intervention of a new plot element at the last moment.

Knitting all of these improbable plot lines together requires more and more inventive fabrication on Adams's part—a feat that he achieves with seemingly giddy, almost frantic, improvisation. Nevertheless, the most unlikely fancy usually turns out to be integral to a carefully worked out scenario.

The texture of his writing, the one-sentence paragraphs, the short chapters ending with imminent catastrophes or inexplicable revelations, the intercutting of shifting points of view, resembles the style of Kurt Vonnegut. But, Adams is less terse, frequently focusing closely on the stream of consciousness of a lone character, ornamenting his narrative with asides and digressions that are clearly his own. In *Long Dark Tea-Time*, Kate Schechter, airport bound on a trip to Norway, ruminates about the inconveniences of travel:

> She was not a superstitious person, or even a religious person, she was simply someone who was not at all sure she should be flying to Norway. But she did find it increasingly easy to believe that God, if there was a God, and if it was even remotely possible that any godlike being who could order the disposition of particles at the Creation of the universe would also be interested in directing traffic on the M4, did not want her to fly to Norway either. All the trouble with the tickets, finding a next door neighbor to look after the cat, then finding the cat so it could be looked after by the next door neighbor, the sudden leak in the roof, the

missing wallet, the weather, the unexpected death of the next door neighbor, the pregnancy of the cat—it all had the semblance of an orchestrated campaign of obstruction which had begun to assume godlike proportions. (*Tea-Time*, 2)

The juxtaposition of the cosmic and the trivial, the catalogue of annoyances, the unexpected events, the focus on a character's consciousness, and the digressive and leisurely pace are all typical of Adams's literary style. And, though Kate is a relatively minor character and this elaboration on her ruminations might seem disproportionately detailed, as though once he started Adams could not control his playful essay on the discontents of modern travel, the speculation on the doings of God or gods and the extent to which they might meddle in mortal affairs turns out to be integral to the theme of the novel. One of the delights of Adams's style is the way in which the seemingly irrelevant proves integral, and in this Adams's style mirrors the theme of interconnectedness that informs all of his work.

Though the Dirk Gently books still retain elements of science-fiction parody and improbable juxtaposition, they are less frenetic than the *Hitchhiker* series, and occasionally Adams slows the pace and broadens his range to include such matters as a description of the faculty eccentrics dining in a college resembling his college at Cambridge, an essay on the relationship between quantum physics and aesthetics, or a demonstration of the process by which subjects of post-hypnotic suggestion rationalize their actions.

In Sherlock Holmes's mechanistic world, after all other hypotheses have been disproved, whatever remains, no matter how improbable, must be the correct solution. Adams's detective, Dirk Gently, operates in a chaotic quantum universe abuzz with the uncertainty principle, clouded with fuzzy logic, awash in low probability events. His theory, which just might be the rationalization of a totally undisciplined mind, is that, since everything is contingent upon everything else, everything is a clue and that wherever he happens to go and whatever he might be inclined to do all amount to working on the case.

In the second Dirk Gently book, *The Long Dark Tea-Time of the Soul*, his bemused detective is supplanted in significance by the cosmic scope of the case on which he is working. The trail of improbable clues and shifts in point of view leads to a struggle between Zeus and Odin over the disposition of the remnants of their powers in the modern world. The book concludes with a titanic confrontation in Valhalla which is probably Adams's comic masterpiece. Here he has left behind the science-fiction parody for which he is best known and revives and apotheosizes the genteel comic Pan-in-Sussex genre of the Edwardian fantasy satirists, setting it far from the country house weekend and the vicar's croquet party. In *Dirk Gently's Holistic Detective Agency* we have a rendition of a *Topper* situation, a spectral consciousness set in a London in which one's personal computer can be programmed to figure out how to get a large designer sofa up the twisted stairway to one's flat and in which one puzzles over fragmentary spirit messages on the answering machine.

Summary

Despite his considerable success as a writer, Douglas Adams's distinctive and sophisticated achievements as a humorist have attracted very little critical attention. Though he works in popular genres such as the mystery, science fiction, and fantasy novel, his work is so original, skidding hectically along the margin between nonsense and quantum physics, that he is discounted even by those who praise him: "an eccentric master in a field of giggly schoolboys" (Brown, 1032). It is likely that he is doomed to be remembered mainly as the author of the *Hitchhiker's Guide to the Galaxy* series—works that he felt declined in quality as the series progressed until he moved to the detective genre with the Dirk Gently books and proved himself with *Last Chance to See*—a work on ecology that retained his witty, individualistic style. Adams has expressed an ambition to write more seriously and personally and may find a new audience for a more mature style.

Selected Bibliography
Primary Sources

Novels
The Hitchhiker's Guide to the Galaxy. London: Pan, 1979; New York: Crown, 1980.
The Restaurant at the End of the Universe. London: Pan, 1980; New York: Crown, 1982.
Life, the Universe, and Everything. London: Pan, and New York: Crown, 1982.
So Long, and Thanks for All the Fish. London: Pan, 1984; New York: Crown, 1985.
Dirk Gently's Holistic Detective Agency. New York: Simon and Schuster, 1987.
The Long Dark Tea-Time of the Soul. New York: Simon and Schuster, 1988.
The More Than Complete Hitchhiker's Guide. New York: Crown, 1986. Includes an introduction by Adams.
Last Chance to See. New York: Harmony Books, 1991. Co-authored with Mark Carwardine, though all actual writing is by Adams.
Mostly Harmless. New York: Harmony Books, 1992.

Plays
The Hitchhiker's Guide to the Galaxy. Radio play, 1978; TV series, 1979.

Television Plays
The *Doctor Who* series.

Secondary Sources
"Adams Anew." *Oregonian*, March 26, 1989. Interview with Adams in which he discusses his theories of literature.
Brown, Richard. "'Posh-school' Science Fiction." *Times Literary Supplement* (September 24, 1982): 1032. Intellectual background of Adams's world view.
Colker, David. "'Hitchhiker' Creator Returns to Earth." *Los Angeles Herald Examiner* (July 6, 1987). Review of Dirk Gently and interview in which Adams discusses his decision to abandon the Hitchhiker series.
Easton, Tom. "The Long Dark Tea-Time of the Soul." *Analog Science Fiction—Science Fact* (February 1988): 187–88. A review of the book from the science-fiction perspective.
Gaiman, Neil. *Don't Panic: The Official Hitchhiker's Guide to the Galaxy Companion.* New York: Pocket Books, 1988. A jokey compendium of interviews with Adams, biographical material, and hitchhiker marginalia and trivia.
Jonas, Gerald. "Hitchhiker's Guide." *New York Times Book Review* (January 25, 1981): 24. An appreciation of Adams's sense of humor in *Hitchhiker's Guide*.
Sipchen, Bob. "A Cosmic Detour With

'Hitchiker' Author." *Los Angeles Times*, March 17, 1989. Interview and review of Adams's career.

William Donnelly

Addison, Joseph

Born: Milston, Wiltshire, England, May 1, 1672

Education: Charterhouse School, 1686–1687; Magdalen College, Oxford University, M.A., 1693

Marriage: Charlotte, Countess Dowager of Warwick, August 9, 1716; one child

Died: June 17, 1719, London

Biography

Joseph Addison—essayist, dramatist, and Whig politician—was a classical scholar who, along with his friend Richard Steele, was the chief contributor to the periodicals the *Tatler* and the *Spectator*. His prose style modeled the "middle way" for essay writing, an enormous stylistic influence from his own century down to modern times.

The eldest son of Reverend Lancelot Addison and his wife Jane, Joseph was born on May 1, 1672, in Milston, Wiltshire. Addison attended various schools relative to his father's parishes. At Charterhouse in London, at age fourteen, he began a lifelong friendship with his future collaborator, Richard Steele, who was two months older than he. Both attended Oxford, where Addison became a Latin scholar. He received an M.A. from Magdalen College in 1693 and remained as a fellow for thirteen years (1698–1711). He published poems in Latin and English, but only with "The Campaign" (1704), celebrating Marlborough's triumph at Blenheim, did he achieve fame.

Courted by influential Whig statesmen, Addison toured Europe as a diplomat (1699–1704) and met notable philosophers such as Pierre Bayle and G.W. Leibniz. Back home in London he was a member of the Kit-Cat Club, an association of prominent Whigs that also included literary figures Steele, William Congreve, John Vanbrugh, and, for a while, Jonathan Swift. Addison held a number of political offices, including a sinecure vacated at the death of John Locke, but more importantly, a seat as a Member of Parliament (1708–1719), Secretary of State for Irish Affairs, and shortly before his death, Secretary of State.

During Addison's term as Irish Secretary, Steele began the *Tatler* (April 12, 1709), a periodical to which Addison contributed approximately forty-nine essays plus twenty-two shared essays (about one-fourth of the total of those printed in the 271 issues of the journal). Published three days a week, the *Tatler* continued until January 2, 1711; it was succeeded by the *Spectator* (March 1, 1711, to December 6, 1712, 555 issues), which was published daily. Just as Steele had set the tone for the *Tatler*, Addison did so for the *Spectator*, creating the most memorable characters and discoursing on philosophy and the arts in his 251 essays (about one-half of the total). Popular and profitable, both journals were collected and published in volume form at that time, the former as *The Lucubrations of Sir Isaac Bickerstaff Esq.* and the latter under its own name (over fifty editions of the *Spectator* were published before 1800).

During these years, Addison reigned supreme among the literati of London, who met at Button's coffeehouse, prompting Swift to write of Addison that "if he had a mind to be chosen king, he would hardly be refused." However, Addison's relations with Swift and Alexander Pope became more and more strained, and Pope parodied Addison in *The Dunciad* and more pointedly in "Epistle to Dr. Arbuthnot."

Addison's other literary activities included his successful play *Cato* (1713), the most respected tragedy of the century but a rulebound museum piece by modern standards, and a comedy, *The Drummer* (1716). For half a year he ran his own periodical, *The Free-Holder* (1715–1716), and at this time he married Charlotte, Countess Dowager of Warwick; the couple had one child, a daughter born in 1716. Appointed Secretary of State under the new king George I, he resigned due to ill health and died soon afterward in London on June 17, 1719.

In his last years, Addison was estranged from Steele and betrayed him in print as well as politics. They were always an odd couple: Addison was eminently successful and prosperous, aloof and correct, manic about debts, reticent to the point of being unable to speak in Parliament; Steele was gregarious and rambunctious, a free spirit. Addison was probably a secret alcoholic. As he lived a measured life of propriety, so he married and so he died. He lies interred in Westminster Abbey.

Literary Analysis

Addison is important in the tradition of British humor in several ways. First, along with Steele, he instituted such high standards for periodical essays that his style and topics were often emulated but usually considered nonpareil. Second, he created an innovative cast of humorous characters who mildly satirized social situations. Third, his philosophy of wit and propriety defined early eighteenth-century culture and literature. These characters and discourses, which mirrored as well as influenced his times, have remained the hallmarks to evaluate the spirit and prose of the Age of Enlightenment.

To understand Addison's style is to understand both the movement toward a simple but elegant prose and the prototypical status of the *Tatler* and the *Spectator*. His plain, sensible prose mirrored the urbanity of a well-bred society, a departure from the intrusions of metaphysical wit and the excesses of Restoration frivolity. It was a prose mandated by the Royal Society (Thomas Sprat's *History of the Royal Society*, 1667) and practiced by John Dryden, for whom Addison wrote the "Preface" to his great translation of Virgil's *Georgics* (1697). This famed "middle style" used by Addison promoted the prevailing view of wit by aligning inventiveness with sense and decorum, a social prose for a social age. As Samuel Johnson testified in his *Lives of the Poets* (1781), "Whoever wishes to attain an English style, familiar but not coarse, and elegant but not ostentatious, must give his days and nights to the volumes of Addison."

The influence of the periodical essay, begun in 1704 with Daniel Defoe's newspaper, the *Review,* was heightened and its literary scope considerably broadened with the *Tatler* and *Spectator* papers. These single-paged, double-sided broadsides (folio half sheets) were extremely popular (3000 or more copies per issue), especially considering that copies were read aloud in coffeehouses and shared among friends (in *Spectator* 10 it was claimed that twenty people read or heard each copy). Topics ranged from duelling, gaming, ladies' fashions, and stage immorality to John Milton, the sublime, and the imagination. As early as the fourth issue Mr. Spectator declared, "I shall take it for the greatest glory of my work, if among reasonable women this paper may furnish tea-table talk." Letters from readers often occupied an entire issue, and thus was born participatory journalism. The direct impact is most obvious in the plethora of contemporary imitators (e.g., *Female Tatler, Tit for Tat, Tatling Harlot*), but continued down through the ages in Johnson's the *Rambler* in the mid-eighteenth century, in William Hazlitt's contributions to the *Morning Chronicle* and *Examiner* and Charles Lamb's essays under the name of Elia in the *London Magazine* early in the next century, in Charles Dickens's *Household Words* in the 1850s, and finally in today's syndicated columns. Even more significant, though, is the readership that the *Tatler* and the *Spectator* spawned, just preceding the emergence of novel-writing (with Samuel Richardson and Henry Fielding in the 1740s). Journalism's nurturing of widespread reading and discussion laid the groundwork for the popularity of novels and for the sympathetic and eccentric types that showed up as characters in them.

Humor in the *Spectator* consisted of character sketches and social satire. Of these, Addison is known primarily—perhaps only—for his characters, which is justified because they supplied continuity and served as prototypes for the early English novels by Fielding, Oliver Goldsmith, and Tobias Smollett. His social sketches, though fewer in number, are funnier to the modern reader but seldom anthologized.

The first character is Mr. Spectator, well-known in the various coffeehouses, who provides the frame, as well as the narration, for the whole journal: "I have acted in all the parts of my life as a looker-on, which is the character I intend to preserve in this paper" (*Spectator* 1).

Other characters began as literary types used for social commentary, especially in light of Addison's Whig agenda for plain dealing and bustling trade: Captain Sentry, the military advocate; the Clergyman, who discourses loudly but neglects his office; and The Templar, who cares very little about legal studies. But, in Sir Roger de Coverley, the Tory landowner who resists all of the Whig progress that was currently making England prosperous, and Will Honeycomb, a throwback to the gallants of the Restoration, Addison developed characters beyond type. Sir Roger, introduced in No. 2, became the subject of a series of *Spectator*s portraying his endearing but annoying combination of good nature and folly.

The satire on Sir Roger, whose refrain was "much might be said on both sides," showed that old Tories were too obsolete to be trusted to run the country. Yet, Sir Roger received great deference from all and told genial stories, such as the one about his own youth during the Commonwealth years when factions divided the country. When he asked directions to a religious site, he was beset by challengers at each turn, first one party, then the other. "Upon this, says Sir Roger, I did not think fit to repeat the former question, but going into every lane of the neighbourhood, asked what they called the name of that lane. By which ingenious artifice he found out the place he enquired after, without giving offence to any party" (*Spectator* 125).

Although Addison's influence was considerably less in the earlier periodical, he is credited with shifting the focus of the *Tatler* from news and politics to society and humor. He created characters that added charm and diversity, although they remained types and were good for only one issue. In the character Tom Folio, book connoisseur, Addison attacked pedants who ignore the textual sense in order to focus on textual details. Of Virgil, Folio exclaims that he "could find but two faults in him: One of them in the *Aeneids*, where there are two comma's instead of a parenthesis; and another in the Third *Georgick*, where you may find a semicolon turned upside down" (*Tatler* 158).

English tastes were represented in Ned Softly, a poet who is a "true English reader, incapable of relishing the great and masterly strokes of this art; but wonderfully pleased with the little Gothick ornaments of epigrammatical conceits, turns, points and quibbles, which are so frequent in the most admired of our English poets" (*Tatler* 163). When Ned forces his sonnet on Mr. Bickerstaff, he defends every conceit, even his allusion to Cupid: "'But Ah! it wounds me like his dart.' My friend Dick Easy assured me, he would rather have written that *Ah!* than to have been the author of the *Aeneid*."

Literary critics continued to be satirized in the personage of Sir Timothy Tuttle, who is so devoted to former critics, ancient authors, and the unities that genuine merriment or sympathy play no role in his judgments. His lady friend "laughed very heartily at the last new comedy which you found so much fault with. But Madam, says he, you ought not to have laughed; and I defy any one to show me a single rule that you could laugh by" (*Tatler* 165). Addison's modern editor, Donald Bond, calls these character sketches "the finest achievement in fiction before Richardson." *Spectator* papers 106–131 were published as cheap reprints in

England and America as "The DeCoverley Papers."

Social topics in the *Spectator* were greatly varied. In a high-spirited ridicule of Italian operas, Addison devoted one issue to the role of the lion in Francesco Mancini's *Hydaspes*. In response to complaints that the combat on stage between lion and warrior was merely sham, Addison concluded: "Besides, this is what is practised every day in Westminster Hall, where nothing is more usual than to see a couple of lawyers, who have been tearing each other to pieces in the court, embracing one another as soon as they are out of it" (*Spectator* 13). Addison scoffed at the whole notion of Italian operas performed in London: "For there is no question but our great grandchildren will be very curious to know the reason why their forefathers used to sit together like an audience of foreigners in their own country, and to hear whole plays acted before them in a tongue which they did not understand" (*Spectator* 18).

In another issue Addison provided a fictitious history of the cat-call, a small instrument used for whistling inside the theater but which he compares to "the voice of some of our British songsters" and its effects to "the roasting of a cat" (*Spectator* 361). The instrument is best at a British theater because "it very much improves the sound of nonsense." Addison determined that the critic used the cat-call "to express by it the whole art of criticism. He has his base and his treble cat-call; the former for tragedy, the latter for comedy; only in tragi-comedies they may both play together in consort. He has a particular squeak to denote the violation of each of the unities, and has different sounds to show whether he aims at the poet or the player. In short, he teaches the smut-note, the fustian-note, the stupid-note, and has composed a kind of air that may serve as an act-tune to an incorrigible play, and which takes in the whole compass of the cat-call."

Finally, in the extension of the *Spectator* (1714), Addison contributed several commentaries, including his description of the Widow-Club, consisting of nine oft-widowed women whose attitudes resembled those of Geoffrey Chaucer's Wife of Bath: "Their conversation often turns upon their former husbands, and it is very diverting to hear them relate their several arts and stratagems, with which they amused the jealous, pacified the cholerick, or wheedled the good-natured man, 'till at last, to use the club-phrase, *They sent him out of the house with his heels foremost*" (*Spectator* 561).

In these ways, Addison's humor consistently satirized London life and people. His social commentary was reflective rather than polemical, such as when he told his readers that they preferred operas in the Italian language "to ease themselves intirely of the fatigue of thinking" (*Spectator* 18). His characters were "humours" portraits modeled after character sketches by Ben Jonson, Thomas Overbury, and John Earle of the previous century. Although modern critics object that he treated only the surface of life, this matched his intention to "enliven morality with wit, and to temper wit with morality" (*Spectator* 10). His humor was pre-described by Overbury one hundred years earlier: "It is a picture (reall or personal) quaintlie drawne in various collours, all of them heightned by one shadowing" (1616).

Addison addressed humor, wit, and the imagination in a number of *Spectator*s, in order to rehabilitate wit to the social and moral prerogatives of the times. Thus, the author described the constitution and pleasures of humor rather than the creative process itself. Later, more rigorous philosophers such as Emmanuel Kant or the poet Samuel Taylor Coleridge brought new insights into the operations of the mind and imagination, but Addison more simply cultivated the gentlemanly accomplishment of participating in humor.

Humor was the topic for *Spectator*s 35, 47, and 249 and was distinguished from wit in the famous sequence of *Spectator*s 58–63. In a lively analogy, Addison defined humor by allegorizing its genealogy based on wit, mirth, good sense, and truth, concluding that "as true humour generally looks serious whilst everybody laughs that is about him, false humour is always laughing whilst everybody about him looks serious" (*Spectator* 35). False humor avoids reason, ridicules the individual rather than the vice, and is indifferent to its targets, he contended.

These judgments on the functions of the mind repeated the neoclassical assumption of conformity, that people are at all places and at all times alike. This view, based on Locke's theory of the association of ideas and indirectly corroborated by Newton's optics, shifted the discussion to behavior rather than fundamental propositions. Applying this psychology to literary criticism marked a significant step away from the strictly moral values of the Renaissance humanists and signaled the beginning of subjectivism in criticism. Aesthetic truths for Addison meant behavior that is proper. The uniformity of his reading public in the coffeehouses and theaters of eighteenth-century London verified his theory that we need no new truths about humor or the imagination: we simply must learn to apply wit in a civilized way to our behavior.

Addison offered style and elegance to his readers, and his inclusion of women as both audience and subject has had a lasting effect. However, his prominence, as well as his politics, made him a natural target for lampoons. In "Epistle to Dr. Arbuthnot," Pope showed his disdain for Addison's rule at Button's, where "by flatterers besieged" Addison sat in order to "Like Cato, give his little senate laws, / And sit attentive to his own applause" because Addison could "Damn with faint praise, assent with civil leer, / And without sneering, teach the rest to sneer." Pope concluded: "Who would not weep, if Atticus were he?"

In "The Enthusiast" (1744) Joseph Warton concurred:

What are the lays of artful Addison
Coldly correct, to Shakespeare's
     warbling wild?

Nevertheless, critics as far ranging as Johnson in the eighteenth century, Thomas Babington Macaulay in the nineteenth century, and Peter Gay in the twentieth century have all concluded that to know the early eighteenth century is to know the writing of Addison, that the period was truly the Age of Addison.

The question arises, why is Addison now relegated to minor literary status? The initial answer is that his works were always taken in small doses and his topics do not match the interests or moods of our own times. Robert Otten's volume on Addison concludes that hardly any scholarly work is being done on Addison's writing today, nor is any significant upsurge expected in Addison studies in the foreseeable future. In a similar diagnosis, Brian McCrea's *Addison and Steele Are Dead* (1990) posits that Addison and Steele were too successful in their clarity and commitment to popularity. While Pope and Swift followed in the footsteps of Milton in defining and educating an elite readership, Addison strove for common sense and anti-pedantry: "It was said of Socrates, that he brought philosophy down from heaven, to inhabit among men; and I shall be ambitious to have it said of me, that I have brought philosophy out of closets and libraries, schools and colleges, to dwell in clubs and assemblies, at tea-tables, and in coffee-houses" (*Spectator* 10).

In this way, Addison's prose becomes almost too simple to study. His subjects were conversational and public, not scholarly and private. He favored analogy over symbol because he believed common knowledge was true knowledge. He domesticated satire rather than armed it to disgrace individuals (see *Spectator*s 16 and 34) or degrade the species, "the fault which Juvenal and Monsieur Boileau are guilty of" (*Spectator* 209; see also *Spectator* 35) and which is evident in Swift's *Gulliver's Travels*. In his time, Addison was preferred to Pope and Swift, but that has not provided enough study material nearly three centuries later, especially given the mood of critical theory in English departments in the late twentieth century. McCrea supplies a much-needed argument that follows up on Louis Milic's "The Reputation of Richard Steele: What Happened?" (1975), that today we reject not their sentiment but their clarity and simplicity, the very goal of their publications.

Summary

Joseph Addison's collaboration with Richard Steele established high standards for periodical essays, attested to by the enormous popularity of the *Tatler* and the *Spectator* and by the myriad of contemporary imitators and successors in the following centuries. Their essays both shaped and mirrored the times in their general approach that wit should be reunited with moral and social values. A great portion of the charm of the *Tatler* and the *Spectator* essays lay in the geniality of their fictive characters who were eccentric and marked for gentle satire. Addison discussed humor and wit in a number of *Spectator* essays. His essay style established the famous "middle way" of prose, in line with the good sense and accessibility of his characters and philosophy.

Selected Bibliography
Primary Sources

With Richard Steele
The *Spectator*. Ed. Donald F. Bond. 5 vols. London: Samuel Buckey and Jacob Tonson, 1712–1713; Oxford: Clarendon, 1965.
The *Tatler*. Ed. Donald F. Bond. 3 vols. London: J. Morphew, 1711; Oxford: Clarendon, 1987.

Secondary Sources
Berry, Reginald. "Modifying a Whole Landscape: False Humour, Good Nature, and Satire in the *Spectator*." *Thalia*, 3, 1 (Spring 1980): 3–10.
Courthope, William John. *Addison*. New York and London: Harper, 1901. English Men of Letters Series.
Dwyer, John. "Addison and Steele's *Spectator*: Towards a Reappraisal." *Journal of Newspaper and Periodical History*, 4, 1 (Winter 1987–1988): 2–11.
Gay, Peter. "The *Spectator* as Actor: Addison in Perspective." *Encounter*, 29 (December 1967): 27–32.
Macaulay, Thomas Babington. *Essays on Milton and Addison*. Ed. Thomas Marc Parrott. New York and London: Globe School Book Company, 1901.
McCrea, Brian. *Addison and Steele Are Dead*. Newark: University of Delaware Press, 1990. An ingenious analysis of Addison and Steele's reputation and the professionalization of literary criticism in modern times.
Milic, Louis. "The Reputation of Richard Steele: What Happened?" *Eighteenth-Century Life*, 1 (1975): 81–87.
Otten, Robert. *Joseph Addison*. Boston: Twayne, 1982. A thorough treatment of Addison's works and influences.
Smithers, Peter. *The Life of Joseph Addison*. Oxford University Press, 1954; 2nd ed. 1968. The standard, but old-fashioned, biography that focuses on Addison's politics.
Thackeray, William Makepeace. The English Humorists of the Eighteenth Century: A Series of Lectures. New York: Harper and Brothers, 1853.

Joel Athey

Amis, Kingsley

Born: London, April 16, 1922
Education: City of London School, 1934–41; St. John's College, Oxford, B.A., 1947; stayed on to research B.Litt. thesis, but left without the degree in 1949
Marriage: Hilary Ann Bardwell, 1948; three

children; marriage dissolved, 1965; married Elizabeth Jane Howard, 1965; separated, 1980
Died: London, October 22, 1995

Biography

Kingsley Amis was born in South London on April 16, 1922, the son of Rosa and William Robert Amis. He was brought up in Norbury, a suburb ten miles south of London. His father was a senior clerk in the export department of Colman's Mustard and commuted to London daily.

Amis grew up in a typically lower-middle-class suburban milieu, which he later re-created in his book *The Riverside Villas Murder*. Though his parents were themselves without intellectual interests, they encouraged their son's academic precocity, and in 1934 he won a scholarship to the City of London School, where he remained for the next seven years. In 1941, Amis went on to win an exhibition to read English at St. John's College, Oxford.

In 1942, he was called up for military service and commissioned in the Royal Corps of Signals. He rose to the rank of lieutenant, serving in France, Belgium, and Germany. At the end of the war he returned to Oxford, where he received a degree with First Class Honors in 1947. He stayed on for two more years, working on a B.Litt. thesis on Victorian poetry and its reading public. He married Hilary Ann Bardwell in 1948. Amis left the University in 1949 without receiving the degree, but his choice of thesis subject testified to a lifelong interest in Victorian poetry (he was later to write on Lord Tennyson, G.K. Chesterton, and Rudyard Kipling). Among the important friendships that he formed at Oxford were those with Philip Larkin and John Wain.

In 1949, Amis went to the University College of Swansea in Wales as a lecturer in the English department; he remained there for twelve years. (Wales and the Welsh provide background material for much of Amis's work, from *That Uncertain Feeling* [1955] to *The Old Devils* [1986].) While at Swansea, he published several collections of poetry as well as four novels, including *Lucky Jim* (1954), his first novel and still his most popular.

Unlike *Lucky Jim*'s hero, Amis found academic life congenial. In 1961, he moved back to England from Swansea to become director of studies in English at Peterhouse, Cambridge, and it was not until 1963 that he left academia to devote his time to writing. That same year his seventeen-year marriage to Hilary Bardwell was dissolved, and he went to live with fellow-author Elizabeth Jane Howard, whom he married in 1965. The couple lived in Hertfordshire and later in Hampstead, with frequent trips abroad (including Amis's stints as visiting professor in the United States); they separated in 1980, however. Amis shared a house in London with his first wife and her present husband, a situation which he wryly likened to that of an Iris Murdoch novel. He died in London on October 22, 1995, a month after suffering injuries in a fall.

Amis was the father of three children by his first wife—one of these, Martin, is a highly successful novelist in his own right.

Literary Analysis

Amis can lay legitimate claim to being one of the outstanding serious novelists of the post-war era, as well as to being one of the period's more versatile poets. Still, many readers think of Amis primarily as a comic writer, and he is certainly best known as the author of *Lucky Jim*, which enchanted and enraged the literary world on its appearance in 1954. With its relish for the ribald, its broad farce, its perceived anti-intellectualism, its frequent vulgarity, and its anti-Romantic emphasis on the here and now, the good things in life ("nice things are nicer than nasty ones"), *Lucky Jim* was the most vibrant of the works by the new generation of writers challenging the upper-middle-class literary Mandarins of the 1930s and 1940s.

In the novel Jim Dixon, a young lecturer at a provincial university, is forced to toady to his absurd superiors (personified by the pretentious, arty Professor Welch) and is emotionally blackmailed by his neurotic colleague, Margaret Peel. Dixon eventually escapes his bondage and moves on to a better job and a better girl. When *Lucky Jim* appeared, the protagonist was seen as the prototype for a new generation of state-educated intellectuals. Walter Allen's now famous review of the novel begins, dramatically, with the statement, "A new hero has risen among us . . . In contact with phoneyness he turns just as red as litmus paper does in contact with acid."[1]

Allen linked the novel with Wain's *Hurry On Down*, which had appeared the previous year and which also deals with a lower-middle-class youth trying to move up in the world. In 1956, with John Osborne's play *Look Back in Anger*, Amis and several other young writers—and their literary alter-egos—were forced by the media into an uneasy grouping under the sobriquet "Angry Young Men." Insofar as they can be seen to form a school or a movement, Amis, Osborne, Wain, John Braine (*Room at the Top*), Colin Wilson (*The Outsider*), Alan Sillitoe (*Saturday Night and Sunday Morning*), and William Cooper (*Scenes from Provincial Life*) do share certain preoccupations. Their heroes, like themselves, tend to be lower-middle-class, provincial, well-educated through grammar schools and scholarships, and generally overqualified and dissatisfied in the rigidly stratified class system that the Welfare State has failed to destroy. They aim at upward mobility, often through marriage to upper-middle-class girls—the process that Geoffrey Gorer describes as hypergamy.[2]

Fresh and revolutionary though these writers seemed at the time, it is possible in retrospect to see the new style (as John Holloway did in 1957) as constituting an anti-Modernist reversion to the nineteenth-century traditions of English fiction: preoccupation with the class system, money, power, social mobility, and marriage. Jim Dixon, Holloway pointed out, has more in common with Arthur Kipps and Mr. Polly than with any more threatening figures.[3] Politically, the supposed left-wing bias of the Angry Young Men amounted to very little; the only genuine radical in the group was Sillitoe, and Amis was so repelled by the political excesses of the 1960s that he "turned right," as he put it, while still comparatively young. In any case, only by a vigorous stretch of the imagination can Amis's early novels be considered at all political.

Somehow the sunny-natured Jim Dixon and the bitter, indiscriminately enraged Jimmy Porter of *Look Back in Anger* melted into one character in the minds of the literary establishment (e.g., Stephen Spender, Evelyn Waugh), who believed the barbarians to be at the door. Somerset Maugham, in a famous excoriation, called the new heroes "scum." But, Jim and Jimmy have little in common, and Amis chafed at being yoked with the so-called angries. "I don't like these glum chums," he complained,[4] remarking that "some of these presumptive colleagues one wouldn't like to be seen drinking with."[5] Characteristically, he refused to contribute to *Declaration*, an "angry" anthology published in 1957. In his review of Wilson's *The Outsider*, Amis castigated the Nietzschean emoting of the author as mere adolescent self-dramatization and posited that the real question

in life is "how am I to live?" rather than the *Outsider's* "who am I?" Like that of other traditional comic writers, his notion of morality grows from conventional tolerance, demanding that the misfit ultimately adjust to his society rather than indulging in permanent rebellion. Amis's heroes tend to adapt to the world they so clearly cannot change.

Despite the hysteria that it caused among the conservative, *Lucky Jim* is no more than superficially political or sociological; it is principally a comic work, in the tradition of Henry Fielding, P.G. Wodehouse, and Waugh. In fact, it is a very traditional, play-by-the-rules example of New Comedy, with Jim in the role of *eiron* or self-deprecator, the smarmy Bertrand Welch as *alazon* or impostor, Welch Senior as the intractable *senex* (combining that role with the traditionally comic one of pedant), and the rich, powerful Gore-Urquhart as the final redeeming agent who makes the hero's fortune and unites him with the object of his love. Some critics have pointed out that the novel conforms with all of the elements of myth: Jim survives the labyrinth of the minotaur Welch, defeats a rival in combat, and is united with the captive heroine. The fact that Jim is both underdog and Everyman makes these archetypal elements all the more forceful.

As satire, *Lucky Jim* marks the memorable beginning of Amis's long and distinguished attack on hypocrisy and cant in all of their forms. He believed with Fielding (an acknowledged idol) that "the only source of true Ridiculous . . . is affectation."[6] Much of *Lucky Jim* and *I Like It Here* are devoted to mocking those who pretentiously revere "culture." This attitude has given Amis a reputation for philistinism among those who confuse his characters' personae and opinions with his own. Thus, Jim Dixon's complaint about "filthy Mozart" has, absurdly, been taken for Amis's own evaluation. In youth he wrote that "nobody wants any more poems about philosophers or paintings or novelists or foreign cities or other poems. At least I hope they don't."[7] The target here is not culture itself, but people who are pretentious about culture, and these people are ruthlessly caricatured. A typical example is Professor Welch in *Lucky Jim*, who waffles on ad infinitum: "Now a recorder, you know, isn't like a flute, though it's the flute's immediate ancestor, of course. To begin with, it's played, that's the recorder, what they call a bec, that's to say you blow into a shaped mouthpiece like that of an oboe or a clarionet, you see . . . " (*Lucky Jim* chapter 1).

This attitude is characteristic of another school with whose name Amis has been linked, the "Movement." Though this, too, is a rather artificial classification, invented by literary journalists of the 1950s, its very looseness gives it a certain validity. Movement writers include Amis's friend Larkin, Donald Davie, D.J. Enright, Thom Gunn, John Holloway, Wain, and Elizabeth Jennings, who as a group challenged, a little more coherently than the angries, the British upper classes' cultural monopoly.

The Movement writers share certain attitudes, such as a strongly anti-Romantic stance, and stylistic concerns, foremost among which is clarity of expression, a rejection of Modernist obscurity. "What I think I am doing," Amis says, "is writing novels within the main English-language tradition; that is, trying to tell interesting, believable stories about understandable characters in a reasonably straightforward style: no tricks, no experimental tomfoolery."[8] Amis eschews what he considers the excesses of Modernist stylistics: "Style, a personal style, usually turns out in practice to mean a high idiosyncratic noise level in the writing, with plenty of rumble and wow from imagery, syntax, and diction."[9] His brilliant parody of Henry James in *I Like It Here* acts as an illustration of this belief. In his poetry and prose Amis, like other Movement writers, debunks the common notion of "poetic" language, with its elaborate and arcane diction, that is evident in the works of Dylan Thomas and John Keats. Like Larkin, he joined a literary tradition of linguistic reticence. In poetry John Betjeman is an important model; in prose, his models were Anthony Powell and Waugh, who shared with Amis a mastery of the most limpid and classical prose combined with a sharp ear for the colloquial and the contemporary.

Lucky Jim was followed by *That Uncertain Feeling* (1955), a novel which, while still comic in situation and character, is altogether a more somber piece of work, and perhaps more in keeping with the "Angry Young Man" formula. John Lewis is an assistant librarian in the Welsh town of Aberdarcy; he lives with his wife Jean and their baby in a cramped flat. He takes up with Elizabeth Gryffudd-Williams, a scion of local society, and, as a result of his infidelity, temporarily joins the fast set—a vivid portrait of what passes for aristocracy in a provincial backwater:

While Elizabeth got going at a cocktail cabinet mainly constructed of glass and chromium, I thought of all the money that must have been spent on the things in here . . . There was a television set with a gigantic magnifying lens at hand; there was a phonograph obviously capable of dispensing recorded music for several days without attention; there was a curious mirror with cherub-like creatures crawling out of the frame . . . (*That Uncertain Feeling,* chapter 9)

At the end John gives up both Elizabeth and the promise of more interesting work and retreats with Jean to their native village—a sad ending, finally, in spite of the couple's reconciliation.

I Like It Here (1958) is the story of a writer, Garnet Bowen, who makes a reluctant working visit to Portugal. Through the character of the xenophobic Bowen, Amis satirizes not, as some critics seemed to think, the continent of Europe itself, but both the insular xenophobes like Bowen and their opposites, the cultural snobs who so often appear as the butt of Amis's humor. *I Like It Here* was considered by many critics to be a thin novel, but it is interesting in many ways, not the least of which is its status as Amis's most "literary" book, the book that carries the greatest number of references to writers and writing, from Bowen's search for Jamesian "Great Tradition" writer Wulfstan Strether to his pilgrimage to Fielding's tomb.

Take A Girl Like You (1960) is the longest of Amis's books, and took him the longest time to write, having been begun in 1955. It gives meticulous attention to the social and sexual mores of its period (which is that immediately preceding the sexual revolution), and the seduction of Jenny Bunn (working-class, Northern, provincial, virginal) by the dashing Patrick Standish (a Londoner, well-off, unscrupulous, and flash) deliberately follows Richardson's *Clarissa.* Like *That Uncertain Feeling*, this is an amusing but fundamentally sad book; Patrick is the first of the Amis "heroes" to be unsympathetic, though certainly not the last. *One Fat Englishman* (1963) has a thoroughly nasty central character, the odious Roger Micheldene: "of the seven deadly sins, Roger considered himself qualified in gluttony, sloth, and lust but distinguished in anger" (*One Fat Englishman* chapter 1). This is another "Englishman abroad" novel, this time with America as the

A

location, but it is never lightheartedly funny like *I Like It Here*. Its blackness, its combination of distaste, rage, and despair, look forward to the bleakness and *accidie* of the later novels.

With the exception of *I Want It Now* (1968), none of Amis's novels after the first four can truly be considered comic. In spite of its darker implications, *I Want It Now* is, like *Lucky Jim*, essentially a fairy tale: Ronnie Appleyard, a sleazy TV "personality," pursues the troubled heiress Simona Quick, a seeming nymphomaniac whose sexual excesses, it turns out, cover up a fearful frigidity. Ronnie is the ultimate media hypocrite, still a fairly new phenomenon in the 1960s. Mouthing fatuities about social problems he cares nothing about, he speaks straight into the camera doing a "sincerity routine, . . . with raised eyebrows and a lot of nodding" (*I Want It Now* chapter 1). But, as he comes genuinely to love Simona, Ronnie's sins and vices melt away until he really becomes a Prince Charming, wakening his princess with a kiss and rescuing her from her witch-mother with the help of her benevolent but ineffective father.

I Want It Now marks the end of Amis's work in the traditional genre of comedy. His later novels, like *One Fat Englishman*, are basically studies in unhappiness, unsatisfied lusts, wasted love, depression, and despair. The fact that they continue to display Amis's trademarks of farce, linguistic pyrotechnics, and, above all, black humor, has made readers continue to regard Amis as a comic writer, and many perceive a lessening in his comedic power rather than, as is really the case, a heightened seriousness in his work.

In *The Anti-Death League* (1966), with its eschewal of farce, its limited verbal wit, and its focus on death, fate, and God, Amis began this serious trend. *Girl, 20* (1971), though a hilarious book—one of Amis's funniest—is also a bitter one, examining within the fashions of the Swinging Sixties the denial of age and the ruin of youth. *Ending Up* (1973) is also extremely funny, while also being in many ways the blackest of Amis's books. Recalling Arnold Bennett's *The Old Wives' Tale* and Muriel Spark's *Memento Mori*, it is the story of five old people living together in straitened circumstances in a cottage and grew out of Amis's reflections on what his own eclectic household might come to in twenty years. The old people's pettiness,

their malice, their pitiful pleasures are brilliantly recorded; it is finally their own malevolence that brings about their dramatic, almost simultaneous deaths (a scene almost Jacobean in its extravagance).

Jake's Thing (1978) is a study of impotence in an aging university professor; it is another example of Amis's proficiency in the genre of black humor and much ridicule is heaped on the therapists and psychoanalysts who try to restore Jake's libido. As with *Lucky Jim*, the protagonist's personality and opinions became confused in the public mind with Amis's own, and the author was widely criticized for his supposed misogyny. This is strange in light of the fact that women have very clearly functioned as the moral center of many of Amis's novels: Jean Lewis, Jenny Bunn, Barbara Bowen, Margaret Anvil in *The Alteration* (1976), Helene Bang in *One Fat Englishman*—all provide the strength, love, and moral fiber that their men so significantly lack. Jake Richardson's discovery that his sexual impotence stems from a fundamental dislike of women is a sad one, pointing ultimately to misanthropy, a disgust with the entire human race, rather than to misogyny as such; Jake is another of Amis's sufferers from *accidie*.

Stanley and the Women (1984) is concerned with madness—both of the clinical variety (as seen in the title character's son) and in its more common guises, neurosis and narcissism. *The Old Devils* (1987) deals with the return to a small Welsh community of a successful television personality and his wife, and the events that this return sets in motion among their group of friends, now all approaching old age. This novel won Amis a long-overdue Booker Prize. Amis produced two more novels, *Difficulties With Girls* (1989) and *The Folks Who Live on the Hill* (1990), since *The Old Devils*.

Amis was also an accomplished poet, having published verse steadily since the 1940s. The dominant influences on his poetic voice were W.H. Auden (in the 1940s) and Robert Graves (in the 1950s); one can also see an affinity with Betjeman, in the simplicity and jokiness, the nostalgia, and in the precision of detail. Amis was an expert practitioner of what he classifies as *vers de societe*: "a kind of realistic verse that is close to some of the interests of the novel: men and women among their fellows, seen as members of a group or class in a way that emphasizes manners, social forms, amusements, fashion (from millinery to philosophy), topicality, even gossip."[10]

Like Graham Greene, Amis made frequent attempts to break the boundaries of genre. He wrote several "Experiments" (similar to Greene's "Entertainments") which explore the possibilities of genre fiction; and, like Greene, he did not consider a piece of work less worthy of serious attention because it is written in a "popular" form. As a matter of fact, he disapproved of the distinction between "popular" and "high" culture and exercised his interest in popular literature by editing several anthologies (see, for example, his *Faber Popular Reciter, The Golden Age of Science Fiction, The New Oxford Book of Light Verse*). He expressed the opinion that all literature—not just the popular kind—is escapist in its assumption that sense and coherence can be found in human experience. When asked whether his ghost story *The Green Man* (1969) was to be taken seriously, Amis answered that it should be taken very seriously indeed. Upon examination it does, indeed, prove to be among the most ambitious and comprehensive of Amis's works, with its examination of the nature of human and divine responsibility. Other "Experiments" include two murder mysteries (*The Riverside Villas Murder*, 1973, and *The Crime of the Century*, 1987), a James Bond-type novel, which Amis authored under the pseudonym Robert Markham (*Colonel Sun*, 1968), and a Sherlock Holmes–type story (*The Darkwater Hall Mystery*, 1978).

Along with *The Green Man*, the most interesting of these experiments is *The Alteration*. This is what is known, in science fiction, as an "Alternate World" story; that is, it takes place in the present, but with a significant fact of history changed so as to create a new version of the twentieth century. In this case, Henry VIII's older brother Arthur lived to have children and the Reformation never occurred. It is 1976, but the world is very different, dominated by a Catholic Church which has turned into something approaching an international police state. The book describes the adventures of a ten-year-old boy, Hubert Anvil, the most perfect soprano in the world, whom the Church is determined to claim as a castrato.

The Alteration has precedents in the Utopian fiction of Lucian and Thomas More and, of all Amis's work, it is the most obviously Swiftian. It achieves the ruthless force and outrageous plausibility of *A Modest Proposal*. The comparison with Swift, in fact, characterizes the kind of change that gradually came over the tenor of Amis's work. The Fieldingian faith in *Lucky Jim*—that true love allied with common sense can conquer all—gave way, as the 1960s wore on, to a Swiftian disgust, an inextricable combination of the comic with the grotesque. Amis was a good hater, but the high spirits with which his hatred was tempered in youth changed to a darker mood so that he can be seen, in approaching old age, to be more truly angry than he ever was as a young man.

In any case, Amis's humor has always been more decorative than structural, dependent, above all, on his idiosyncratic and spectacular use of language. As with Wodehouse, much of the comedy of Amis's novels depends for its effect on the literal interpretation of cliches and figures of speech:

> " . . . The young fellow playing the viola had the misfortune to turn over two pages at once, and the resulting confusion . . . my word . . . "

> Quickly deciding on his own word, Dixon said it to himself and then tried to flail his features into some sort of response to humor. (*Lucky Jim,* chapter 1)

Amis also achieves superb comic effects through scrupulously exact recreations of the linguistic pretensions of recognizable social groups, as with Welch's answer to the perfectly straightforward question of whether he planned to stay in the country for long:

> He went on chewing for a moment, pondering. "I doubt it," he said at last. "Upon consideration I feel it incumbent upon me to doubt it. I have miscellaneous concerns in London that need my guiding hand. . . . But it's very pleasant to come down here and to know that the torch of culture is still in a state of combustion in the provinces." (*Lucky Jim,* chapter 4)

Professional jargon, from the academic to the medical, is another target. In *Jake's Thing*, Amis ridicules psychoanalysts and therapists:

A

In a non-genital sensate focusing session the couple lie down together in the nude and stroke and massage the non-genital areas of each other's bodies in turns of two or three minutes at a time for a period of up to half an hour . . . Now we come to the use of the nocturnal mensurator. If you'd just step over here, Mr. Richardson. (*Jake's Thing,* chapter 4)

Amis also exploits the comic possibilities of circumlocution, as when Patrick Standish speaks to God:

I'm not trying to get credit with you by saying I know I'm a bastard. Nor by saying I'm not trying to get credit. Nor by saying I'm not trying to by saying . . . trying . . . you know what I mean. Nor by saying that. Nor by saying that. (*Take a Girl Like You,* chapter 20)

Another unfailing source of humor is Amis's schoolboy pleasure in the scatological; for instance, the telegram in *I Like It Here*:

ALL MY LOVE GOE SWITH YOU MY FARLINGS SEND ALL NEWS AND KEEP PHOTOGRAPHAL BUM TO SHOW ON RETURN BON VOYAGE + MOTHER

There is a God, Bowen thought. (*I Like It Here,* chapter 3)

As we have seen, Amis has been the victim of numerous misperceptions: that he is Jim Dixon, that he is Jake Richardson, that he is a misogynist, that he was first a left-wing radical and is now a right-wing fascist. Actually, Amis's deeply skeptical brand of humor makes nonsense of any real political stance. He put forward his own view of his politics when he said "I have not changed—I stand exactly where I was 20 or 30 years ago, opposed to totalitarianism in all its forms."[11] However, it must be admitted that he fueled all of these misperceptions through his own wish to provoke: "Annoying people," he says, "is part of one's life work."[12] Like his predecessor Waugh, Amis enjoyed being noisily on the "untrendy" side of any issue. It is partly due to this jocular belligerence that he has not, so far, been taken as seriously as his gifts warrant.

Summary

Kinglsey Amis is widely perceived as a comic writer, though his work (with the notable exception of *Lucky Jim*) tends to be fundamentally serious. However, even his darkest novels are notable for their use of farce, complex Wodehousian linguistic jokes, black humor and parody.

Notes

1. Walter Allen, review of *Lucky Jim*. From *The Beat Generation and the Angry Young Men*. Ed. Gene Feldman and Max Gartenberg (Secaucus: Citadel Press, 1984), pp. 339–40.
2. Geoffrey Gorer, "The Perils of Hypergamy." In *The Beat Generation and the Angry Young Men*.
3. John Holloway, "Tank in the Stalls: Notes on the 'School of Anger.'" In *The Beat Generation and the Angry Young Men*, pp. 364–372.
4. Quoted in Kenneth Allsop, *The Angry Decade* (Wendover: John Goodchild, 1985), p. 8.
5. Quoted in John McDermott, *Kingsley Amis: An English Moralist* (London: Macmillan, 1989), p. 21.
6. Preface to Henry Fielding, *The Adventures of Joseph Andrews* (London: Millar, 1742).
7. Quoted in McDermott, p. 28.
8. *Contemporary Novelists*. Ed. James Vinson, 3rd ed. London: St. James Press, 1982.
9. Quoted in McDermott, p. 238.
10. Introduction to *New Oxford Book of English Light Verse* (London and New York: Oxford University Press, 1978).
11. Quoted in McDermott, p. 36.
12. J. Silverlight, "Kingsley Amis—the Writer and the Symbol" (*Observer,* January 14, 1968): 13.

Selected Bibliography

Primary Sources

Novels
Lucky Jim. London: Victor Gollancz, and New York: Doubleday, 1954.
That Uncertain Feeling. London: Victor Gollancz, 1955; New York: Harcourt Brace Jovanovich, 1956.
I Like It Here. London: Victor Gollancz, and

New York: Harcourt Brace Jovanovich,
1958.

Take a Girl Like You. London: Victor
Gollancz, 1960; New York: Harcourt
Brace Jovanovich, 1961.

One Fat Englishman. London: Victor
Gollancz, 1963; New York: Harcourt
Brace Jovanovich, 1964.

The Egyptologists (with Robert Conquest).
London: Jonathan Cape, 1965; New
York: Random House, 1966.

The Anti-Death League. London: Jonathan
Cape, and New York: Harcourt Brace
Jovanovich, 1966.

(as Robert Markham) *Colonel Sun*. London:
Jonathan Cape, and New York: Harper
and Row, 1968.

I Want It Now. London: Jonathan Cape,
1968; New York: Harcourt Brace
Jovanovich, 1969.

The Green Man. London: Jonathan Cape,
1969; New York: Harcourt Brace
Jovanovich, 1970.

Girl, 20. London: Jonathan Cape, 1971; New
York: Harcourt Brace Jovanovich, 1972.

The Riverside Villas Murder. London:
Jonathan Cape, and New York:
Harcourt Brace Jovanovich, 1973.

Ending Up. London: Jonathan Cape, 1973;
New York: Harcourt Brace Jovanovich,
1974.

The Alteration. London: Jonathan Cape,
1976; New York: Viking Press, 1977.

Jake's Thing. London: Hutchinson, and New
York: Viking Press, 1978.

Russian Hide-and-Seek. London:
Hutchinson, 1980.

Stanley and the Women. London: Hutchinson,
1984; New York: Summit, 1985.

The Old Devils. London: Hutchinson, 1986;
New York: Summit, 1987.

The Crime of the Century. London: J.M.
Dent, 1987.

Difficulties With Girls. London: Hutchinson,
1988; New York: Summit, 1989.

The Folks Who Live on the Hill. London:
Hutchinson, 1990; New York: Summit,
1990.

Collections of Short Stories
My Enemy's Enemy. London: Victor
Gollancz, 1962; New York: Harcourt
Brace Jovanovich, 1963.

Dear Illusion. London: Covent Garden Press,
1972.

Collected Short Stories. London: Hutchinson,
1980.

Verse
Bright November. London: Fortune Press,
1947.

A Case of Samples: Poems 1946–1956.
London: Victor Gollancz, 1956; New
York: Harcourt Brace Jovanovich,
1957.

The Evans Country. Oxford: Fantasy Press,
1962.

*A Look Round the Estate: Poems 1957–
1967*. London: Jonathan Cape, 1967;
New York: Harcourt Brace Jovanovich,
1968.

Collected Poems 1944–1979. London:
Hutchinson, 1980; New York: Viking
Press, 1981.

Criticism
*New Maps of Hell: A Survey of Science Fic-
tion*. New York: Harcourt Brace
Jovanovich, 1960; London: Victor
Gollancz, 1961.

The James Bond Dossier. London: Jonathan
Cape, and New York: New American
Library, 1965.

*What Became of Jane Austen? and Other
Questions*. London: Jonathan Cape,
1970; New York: Charles Scribner's
Sons, 1971.

Kipling and His World. London: Thames and
Hudson, 1975; New York: Charles
Scribner's Sons, 1976.

Secondary Sources

Bibliographies
Gohn, J.B. *Kingsley Amis: A Checklist*. Kent,
Ohio: Kent State University Press, 1976.
Published, unpublished, and secondary
sources through 1975.

Salwak, D.F. *Kingsley Amis: A Reference
Guide*. Boston: Hall, 1978. The best
guide to his critical reputation. Includes
a list of dissertations on Amis.

Books About Amis
Bradford, Richard. *Kingsley Amis*. London:
Hodder & Stoughton, 1989. A fairly
good study, though from a highly academic point of view, discussing Amis
within the context of F.R. Leavis's
"Great Tradition."

Gardner, Philip. *Kingsley Amis*. Boston: Twayne, 1981. An extensive study of the novels and poetry through *Jake's Thing*; a sound introduction.

McDermott, John. *Kingsley Amis: An English Moralist*. London: Macmillan, 1989. An excellent overview of Amis's career; McDermott is especially interesting when dealing with the vagaries of Amis's critical reputation.

Salwak, D.S., ed. *Kingsley Amis in Life and Letters*. London: Macmillan, 1990. A *Festschrift* containing everything from personal reminiscences to critical essays to appreciations from fellow-writers. Informative and entertaining.

Books Significantly Mentioning Amis

Allsop, Kenneth. *The Angry Decade*. London: Peter Own, 1958. A good contemporary account of the Fifties writers.

Bergonzi, Bernard. *The Situation of the Novel*. London: Macmillan, 1970. Discusses the early "Experiments."

Feldman, Gene, and Max Gartenberg, eds. *The Beat Generation and the Angry Young Men*. Secaucus, NJ: Citadel Press, 1984. An anthology containing, among other things, Allen's review of *Lucky Jim*, Amis's "Socialism and the Intellectuals," and an excellent article on Amis and the other "angries" by John Holloway.

Lodge, David. *The Language of Fiction*. London: Routledge & Kegan Paul, 1966. Chapter 7 deals with Amis.

Morrison, Blake. *The Movement*. Oxford: Oxford University Press, 1980. A first rate account.

Rabinowitz, Rubin. *The Reaction Against Experiment in the English Novel, 1950–1960*. New York: Columbia University Press, 1967. A good view of the aesthetic context in which Amis's early books were written.

Brooke Allen

Amis, Martin Louis

Born: Oxford, August 25, 1949
Education: Numerous schools in Britain, Spain, and the United States; Exeter College, Oxford, B.A., 1971
Marriage: Antonia Phillips, 1984; two children

Biography

Martin Amis was born in Oxford on August 25, 1949, one of the first children of the age of nuclear proliferation: "four days later, the Russians successfully tested their first atom bomb, and deterrence was in place. So I had those four carefree days, which is more than my juniors ever had" (Amis, *Einstein's Monsters*). Despite the shadow of the bomb, Amis's childhood seems to have been happy, though rather scattered as he attended over a dozen schools. The son of one of the most successful novelists of post-war Britain, Kingsley Amis (and his wife Hilary Ann Bardwell), Martin learned, and was free to enjoy, clearly, independent intellectual habits. This independence may well have been influenced and encouraged by keenly satirical intelligence, the most recognizably similar temperamental trait between the father and his son.

Martin appeared to be close to his father despite forming a markedly different political outlook from him. Kingsley has a reputation for being both a great ludic wit and a political reactionary. Martin indulgently describes the reaction of his father on the subject of his son's *bête noire*, nuclear arms:

> When I told him I was writing about nuclear weapons, he said, with a lilt, "Ah I suppose you're . . . 'against them,' are you?" Epater les bien-pensants is his rule . . . "Think of it. Just by closing down the Arts Council we could significantly augment our arsenal. The grants to poets could service a nuclear submarine for a year . . . " (Amis, *Einstein's Monsters*)

Martin took a First in English at Exeter College, Oxford, in 1971 and entered journalism, becoming an editorial assistant on the *Times Literary Supplement* in 1972. In 1973, he published his first novel, *The Rachel Papers*, in which it is tempting to read an autobiographical element as the adolescent Charles Highway displays an intense attention to literature and provides brutally iconoclastic, and at the same time penetrating, appraisals of classic English literature (one can also perhaps hear Amis mimicking his father in this). The novel won the 1974 Somerset Maugham Award.

In 1975, Amis was made assistant literary editor of the *Times Literary Supplement*, a position that he held until taking up the literary editorship of the *New Statesman* in 1977. Two years later, having published three commercially successful novels, Amis became a full-time writer, though he has continued in journalism, contributing to the *Observer* and most recently to the *Independent on Sunday*. In his journalism he has frequently displayed an interest in what might be called subjects of a "trash aesthetic" nature; recently, for example, he has been interested in Madonna.

Martin lives in London with his wife, Antonia Phillips, a professor of aesthetics whom he married in 1984 and with whom he has had two sons. He keeps a separate flat in the city where he works in a highly disciplined fashion. One of the characters in his novel *Money* observes about the author's working lifestyle:

> I tell you, this Martin Amis, he lives like a student. I had inspected his flat with an adman's eye, mindful of outlay and lifestyle, of vocational expenditure. And there was nothing, no tape recorders or filing cabinets or electric typewriters or word processors. Just his pastel portable, like an ancient till. Just biros, pads, pencils. Just two dust-furred rooms off a sooty square, with no hall or passage. And he earns enough. Why isn't he living right up to the hilt of his dough? He must have a bad book-habit, this character. How much are books? It seems he has the reading thing real bad.

Perhaps Martin's choices of personae and subject-matter (both of these aspects of his writing being emersions in the vernacular material culture of the late twentieth century) disguise his working and intellectual rigor for some readers. Even when his frequently observed stylistic flamboyance is allowed, the often crass lifestyle that he writes about is off-putting for many. However, it is his ability to make people extremely uncomfortable which, as well as drawing extreme admiration from the literary establishment and a large audience, makes Martin Amis the "hottest property" in the British novel industry in the early 1990s.

Literary Analysis

Amis is one of the most vicious satirists of the modern urban world. His close rendering of the voices of twentieth-century self-detachment, the linguistic energy of the self-contained registers of hedonistic and materialistic living, make him one of the greatest modern exponents of dramatic irony. He captures the "style" of modern living and shows this life collapsing under the weight of a confidence that it is not entitled to. In this free appropriation of the most dominant registers of the day without any explicit reference to a more "cultured" discourse, Amis's great debt to American rather than British fiction is apparent.

Amis's first novel, *The Rachel Papers*, features the appropriation of received culture by and within the liberated sexual culture of the late 1960s, as the adolescent Charles Highway turns his pursuit of a place reading literature at Oxford into a fashion accessory. That genre of British fiction, a carry-over from the 1950s, featuring a working class hero or "lad of parts" rising through the educational system, is reworked into the picaresque mode as Highway's sexual appetites prime all of his activities. The question of Highway's self-awareness with his literateness in Freudian thinking is comically raised as he imagines himself addressing the necessary older woman who becomes his conquest in the novel:

> Me? Me, I'm devious, calculating, self-obsessed—very nearly mad, in fact: I'm at the other extreme: I will not be placed at the mercy of my spontaneous self. You trust to the twitches and shrugs of the ego; I seek to arrange these. Doubtless we have much to learn from one another. We're in love; we're good-natured types, you and I, not moody or spiteful. We'll get by.

Ambivalence over the extent of modern self-awareness is continued in Amis's second novel, *Dead Babies* (1975), as it declares itself a Menippean satire. The naming of this mode indicates the way in which the twentieth-century mind "narrates" its own modernity according to principles of sexual fragmentarianism. This conscious hedonism of a group of individuals undertaking a weekend orgy at an English country-house is undermined as a vile, manipulating hidden hand utilizes the self-absorption of the other characters for his own ends. The predatory "Johnny" demonstrates how ripe for exploitation modern "self-awareness" can be if excessively indulged. In the novel old-fashioned madness or "split personality" trounces a laissez-faire personal morality expressed in the "hippy" vernacular of sex and drugs.

A

In *Success* (1978), Amis again treats shallow excess in providing the almost fabulistic pairing of Gregory Riding, seemingly sexually irresistible and extremely successful in every sphere of his life, and his foster-brother, Terry, unattractive and extremely unsuccessful in life. The novel reads almost as a parody of much modern sensationalistic fiction. As the roles are suddenly reversed, however, we realize that we are dealing with a situation that has to be qualified with reference to a psychological complexity that undercuts the material surfaces of life. The spectacular success and failure, recorded in the alternating reflections of the two brothers, highlight both the psychological vacuity and the psychological malaise of power-driven (both sexual and material) modern society. As in *Dead Babies*, the comedic effect derives from a grim explosion of the hedonistic facade of human life. Of all of Amis's novels, *Success* is perhaps the one which highlights its writer as something of a traditional moralist, a fact sometimes obscured by Amis's Swiftian dwelling on the bodily functions.

The fictive playfulness apparent in his earlier work takes up a more central position in Amis's *Other People* (1981). Characters are provided with clearly functional names: Mary Swan is suffering from amnesia and the policeman Prince helps her pursue her lost past. It turns out that her forgotten identity is the malevolent Amy Hide who has perhaps been murdered by Mr. Wrong (who may actually be Prince and also the narrator). *Other People* shows Amis's utilization of novel form and literary conventions to create a dystopian vision for the reader. Thus begins a trend in Amis's writing (though the element is by no means absent from his earlier work) toward a kind of Post-Modern comedy where the artifice of the novel is used to comment ironically on the artifice of the "real" world.

With *Money* (1984) Amis most explicitly satirizes the control or narration of "personal" lives by large financial interests. The novel stands as a refutation of the Reaganite and Thatcherite 1980s. The supposed crassness and alienation of the decade are searingly expressed by the central character, John Self:

Watching television is one of my main interests, one of my chief skills. Video films are another accomplishment of mine: diabolism, carnage, soft core. I realize, when I can bear to think about

it, that all my hobbies are pornographic in tendency. The element of lone gratification is bluntly stressed. Fast food, sex shows, space games, slot machines, video nasties, nude mags, drink, pubs, fighting, television, handjobs. I've got a hunch about handjobs, or their exhausting frequency. I need that human touch. There's no human here so I do it myself. At least handjobs are free, complimentary, with no cash attaching.

Self, a would-be film producer, attempting to put together a huge film deal as he moves in the power-charged financial and media worlds of London and New York, is shown, finally, not to be in control of his wheelings and dealings but instead to be the victim of the plotting of another individual who has been psychologically damaged by Self. A serious jolt is delivered then to the reader, who has been enjoying the spectacle of cheap appetites pursued and indulged with childish excess and who is suddenly confronted with the comeuppance of Self. This is a familiar pattern in Amis's fiction. Those who can live with the crass selfishness of modern society are often destroyed by those that it has touched more deeply.

London Fields (1989) is Amis's most accomplished work. It manifests an unusual coherence between the literary object itself and its themes. On one level the complexity of the plot points to the complexity of the world; on another, the transparently suitable names (for example, Nicola Six who stands for sex) point to how threadbare modern life has become. This ambivalence allows alternative possibilities: is the twentieth-century world complicated or is it narrow and squalid? Nicola Six, disgusted by the neuroses of the modern world, seeks her own destruction and becomes involved with low-life Keith Talent, a veritable riot of sexist and criminal crassness pursuing his dream of becoming a famous darts player. In a passage that signals Nicola's claustrophobia in a neuroses-ridden world, the reptilian nature of human life (a favorite metaphor of Amis's) is enunciated, while at the same time a new focusing of the destructive capabilities of mankind occurs:

As the first crocodile tear began to smear her vision, Nicola gazed into the fingerprint contours and saw—and saw crocodiles. She saw the reptile house in Keith Talent's brain. What iguanas and ana-

condas, what snoozing geckos anguished there, presided over, perhaps,
by a heraldic basilisk, a rampant cockatrice! . . . It wouldn't be her who
romped and basked with Keith and
rolled with him in the mud. It would be
Enola, Enola Gay.

Along with a typically comical piece of stylistic excess and reference to a nuclear world (the
bomber used to drop the atomic bomb on Japan was named *Enola Gay*), we find here a
newer note of concern for the world in larger,
"greener" terms. This new note was apparent
beginning in Amis's collection of short stories
Einstein's Monsters (1987).

In *Time's Arrow* (1991), which follows
Einstein's Monsters and *London Fields*, Amis
also deals with the concrete historical threat of
the twentieth century. The novel provides a new
twist to the author's often ironical distortion of
perspective in being the biography of a Nazi
doctor written backwards. This methodology
brilliantly focuses the twisted mentality of Nazi
"medicine":

> One morning of diagonal sleet and fro-
> zen puddles we were unloading some
> Jewish families at a rude hamlet on the
> River Bug. It was the usual sequence:
> we'd picked up this batch from the mass
> grave, in the woods, and stood waiting
> by the van on the approach road while
> the carbon monoxide went about its
> work . . . Among them was a mother and
> a baby, both naked, naturally, for now.
> The baby was weeping . . . probably
> from earache. Its mother already looked
> exasperated by these cries. Indeed she
> looked stunned—stopped dead in the
> face. . . . I was concerned.

The technique of *Time's Arrow* creates a
damning statement on the twentieth century. It
provides us with the ultimate in unhappy "endings" in implying by its technique that there is
no returning from the animalistic excesses of the
century to a more innocent time. At the same
time, however, *Time's Arrow* (along with
Einstein's Monsters and *London Fields*) suggests that Amis is embarking on a more positively polemical direction in his fiction whereas
in earlier work his diagnoses were much more
oblique. The reader's laughter, always a morally
dubious response to Amis's "comedy," has

much less license as Amis reaches his most
mature achievement.

Summary
Martin Amis is an acidic satirist of contemporary
western society. His fiction features explosive tales
of neurotic excess, more often than not delivered
with an ironical stylistic excess. In this he is very
much a moralist, albeit an often oblique one.

Selected Bibliography
Primary Sources
The Rachel Papers. London: Jonathan Cape,
  1973; New York: Knopf, 1974.
Dead Babies. London: Jonathan Cape, 1975;
  New York: Knopf, 1976.
Success. London: Jonathan Cape, 1978; New
  York: Harmony, 1987.
Other People: A Mystery Story. London:
  Jonathan Cape, and New York: Viking
  Press, 1981.
Money: A Suicide Note. London: Jonathan
  Cape, 1984; New York: Viking Press,
  1985.
*The Moronic Inferno and Other Visits to
  America*. London: Jonathan Cape, 1986;
  New York: Viking Press, 1987. A collec-
  tion of Martin Amis's journalism espe-
  cially interesting for his views on con-
  temporary American fiction.
Einstein's Monsters: Five Short Stories. Lon-
  don: Jonathan Cape, and New York:
  Harmony, 1987.
London Fields. London: Jonathan Cape,
  1989; New York: Harmony, 1990.
Time's Arrow. London: Jonathan Cape, 1991;
  New York: Harmony, 1992.

Secondary Sources
Hamilton, Ian. "The Company He Keeps."
  Sunday Times (London, March 8, 1981):
  43. Interview.
Miller, Karl. "Twins." In *Doubles: Studies in
  Literary History*. Oxford: Oxford University Press, 1985, pp. 402–15. Examines *Success*, *Other People*, and *Money*.
Morrison, Susan. "The Wit and Fury of Martin Amis." *Rolling Stone*, no. 578 (May
  17, 1990): 95–102. An interview that
  deals with some popular conceptions and
  misconceptions about Martin Amis.
Stout, Mira. "Down London's Mean Streets."
  New York Times Magazine, February 4,
  1990. Interesting as an incisive summa-
  tion of Amis's career to 1990.

A

Rawson, Claude. "The Behaviour of Reviewers and their Response to Martin Amis's Novel *Other People*." *London Review of Books* (May 7–20, 1981): 19–22. Fascinating article on the molding of critical opinion in relation to Amis.

Gerard Carruthers

Anderson, Lindsay Gordon

Born: Bangalore, India, April 17, 1923

Education: Educated in England at South Coast preparatory school and a public school, Cheltenham College. Read classics for a year at Wadham College, Oxford, while doing pre-officer training for military service, for which he had volunteered. Served in the 60th Rifles and the Intelligence Corps during World War II, the last year of which was spent in India doing cryptography. After the war, he returned to Wadham College, Oxford to read English.

Died: Dordogne region of France, August 30, 1994

Biography

Born in Bangalore, India on April 17, 1923, the son of Alexander Vass, an officer in the British army and Estelle Bell (Gasson) Anderson, Lindsay Anderson grew up in England, where his family returned when he was two years old. His parents were of Scottish extraction—"a fact to which he attributes his moral intransigence as well as a sense of not belonging to the English theatre or English cinema as such."[1] He remained in many ways an always-outspoken outsider: a director of films who scorned and refused to compromise with the commercial film-making "establishment," a public-school and Oxford-educated man whose second feature-length film, *If . . .* (1969), is among the century's most scathingly satirical indictments of the British public school system. While at Wadham College, Oxford, he studied Classics and English—a fact that is reflected in the fact that the erudition (both cinematic and literary) and unobtrusive allusiveness of his films are unrivaled in popular cinema.

While at Oxford and later in London, he founded (with Karel Reisz) and edited the magazine *Sequence* (1947–1952). Throughout the 1950s, he wrote about films and the theater for *The Times*, the *Observer, Encore*, and *Sight and Sound*; his criticism was notable not only

for its acumen but also for its often exhortative intensity, reflected in such titles as "Stand Up! Stand Up!" "Vital Theatre?" and "Get Out and Push!"

Anderson's first films were documentaries made for Sutcliffe Ltd. of Wakefield. In 1952, he wrote *Making a Film*, a study of the making of Thorold Dickinson's *Secret People*, and directed the documentary *Wakefield Express*. He produced and played in James Broughton's *Pleasure Garden* (1952) and, with Guy Brenton, made the documentary *Thursday's Children*, which won an Academy Award for the Best Documentary of 1953. Together with Reisz and Tony Richardson, he launched the Free Cinema Movement, a series of six programs screened at the National Film Theatre between 1956 and 1959. The films were deliberately designed to challenge orthodoxy both in cinema and in society, emphasizing the social responsibility of the film-making artist whom they sought to free from the constraints of commercial production; furthermore, they sought to stimulate liveliness and personal expression, taking as their subject "the significance of the everyday." Anderson's foremost contributions, the independently made *O Dreamland* (1953) and *Every Day Except Christmas* (1957), are depictions of actual people and places—a provincial amusement park and the Covent Garden market, respectively.

In 1957, Anderson began his association with the English Stage Company, which had been founded the year before by George Devine at the Royal Court Theatre; he first directed Kathleen Sully's *The Waiting of Lester Abbs* (1957), followed by Willis Hall's *The Long and the Short and the Tall* (1959). His association with the Royal Court continued throughout its heyday in the 1960s and 1970s; in 1964–1965 he was joint artistic director of the English Stage Company. During the late 1960s and early 1970s, he was most noted for directing a number of plays by David Storey, including *In Celebration* (1969), *The Contractor* (1969), *Home* (1970), *The Changing Room* (1971), and *Life Class* (1974). Their friendship began when Anderson directed his first feature film, *This Sporting Life* (1963), based on Storey's screenplay adapting his own first novel (1960); it was, in fact, Anderson who encouraged Storey to become a playwright.

In 1969, Anderson's second feature film, *If . . .*, brought him into international prominence as a film-maker. The story of a student rebellion in an English public school, the movie was both a critical and commercial success on both sides of the Atlantic—in part because its subject matter seemed to embody the *Zeitgeist* of the late 1960s. Based on a story by David Sherwin, with whom Anderson co-authored the script, the film is a dark and acerbic social satire that intermingles fantasy and reality. Its climax is a machine-gun shoot-out on the school quadrangle following the school's commencement ceremony, which has been disrupted by the student rebels who set the chapel afire. The film's intermittent, often abrupt, seemingly random transitions from color to black-and-white, which initially disconcerted many moviegoers and critics alike, was attributed to budgetary constraints—although the technique also provided a uniquely cinematic means of achieving the counterpart of the Brechtian "alienation effect." Malcolm McDowell made his film debut in the role of Mick Travis, the leader of the student rebels.

Anderson's next major film, *O Lucky Man!* (1973), was based on an original idea by McDowell and developed into a script by Sherwin and Anderson. It is a pointedly satiric picaresque allegory whose protagonist—a Candide-like innocent cum young-man-on-the-make in contemporary Britain—undergoes a series of more-or-less horrific experiences until, down-and-out and wandering the streets of London, he wanders into an open audition, gets cast by Anderson for *If . . .* , and attains (perhaps) a Zen-like enlightenment at the film's end.

Britannia Hospital (1982), which concludes the "Mick Travis trilogy," was again a collaboration of Anderson, Sherwin, and McDowell; the latter's character is not only killed but dismembered in a particularly macabre way, as if to make sure that no more "sequels" will be made. Other films that Anderson directed include the screen adaptation of two plays, Storey's *In Celebration* (1975) and David Berry's *The Whales of August* (1987). *Glory! Glory!* (1989) is a satire on American televangelism, from a script by Stan Daniels.

Throughout Anderson's career as a film-maker, he continued to direct in the theater, working not only at the Royal Court but also in London's West End (where he directed the first unexpurgated production of Joe Orton's *What the Butler Saw* in 1975), and more recently at the National Theatre. He had also directed a number of plays in New York, includ-

ing the American debuts of many of Storey's plays. Anderson died on August 30, 1994, while on vacation in the Dordogne region of France.

Literary Analysis

Although his cinematic oeuvre is comparatively small considering the three decades that his career as a film director spanned, his films are a unique and innovative contribution to contemporary cinema, remarkable alike for their innovative technique, their fiercely satiric animus, and their witty intertextual allusiveness (including references and homages to other films as well as literary works). His reputation as a satirist derives primarily from the four films that he directed: the three "Mick Travis" films (*If . . .* , *O Lucky Man!*, and *Brittania Hospital*) plus *Glory! Glory!* Among these, the first two are not only the most renowned but also the only ones on which Anderson's name appears as a co-author of the screenplay.

Widely known as the "story of a student rebellion in an English public school," *If . . .* seemed particularly topical in the late 1960s—and especially in the United States. Opening within just months of the "siege of Chicago" at the Democratic National Convention, the campus strike at Harvard, and the student-led tumult at Columbia, when anger-laden confrontations between students and administrators filled the daily news, Anderson's film seemed immediately "relevant," that favorite catch phrase of the day. The film's advertising logo—a student carrying a parcel of schoolbooks alongside the parcel of schoolbooks over his arm—is surely among the most revealing images of the era, epitomizing a younger generation's hopes and the elder generation's fears. Defiant and irrevocably committed, violently resisting the injustices and persecutions of an oppressive and tradition-laden institution that he longs to overthrow, McDowell's character is arguably *the* anti-hero of his times, much as Jimmy Porter was in John Osborne's play *Look Back in Anger* in the more staid, less politicized mid-1950s.

Yet, as Anderson insisted (much to the disappointment of the ideologues of the day), his film is far from being a comradely call to arms. As he remarked in the preface to the published script, the fact that the film's making and release occurred at the time of "the world-wide phenomenon of student revolt" was merely a "coincidence"—"fortuitous" though it was for purposes of the film's publicity and box-office

A

appeal. The film's "basic tensions, between hierarchy and anarchy, independence and tradition, liberty and law, are always with us," he maintained.[2] In contrast to such now-dated films as Michelangelo Antonioni's *Zabriskie Point* (1970) and Stuart Hagmann's *The Strawberry Statement* (1970), *If . . .* contains very few topical references to the 1960s; quite apart from the incendiary passions and social upheavals of its day, Anderson's film is primarily an attack on the long-held moral *values* which uphold the oppressive system that the school embodies and which sanction the institutionalized brutality that its traditions sustain—issues that certainly transcend the topical interests of the late 1960s, when the film was released. Precedents for even the most harsh, violent, and radical incidents in Anderson's film can be found in the history of the English public schools (recounted, for example, in Jonathan Gathorne-Hardy's *The Old School Tie: The Phenomenon of the English Public Schools* [New York: Viking, 1977]) and in such fictional accounts of public school life as Thomas Hughes's *Tom Brown's Schooldays* (1858) and Rudyard Kipling's *Stalky and Co.* (1899). However much the revolt led by the students in *If . . .* may have stirred controversy among moviegoers of its day, in fact it is merely the modern counterpart of a number of such rebellions that actually took place in English public schools in earlier times (including one at Harrow in 1805, led by seventeen-year-old Lord Byron himself, who laid a trail of gunpowder below one of the school's corridors and intended to blow up the entire school; he and his cohorts desisted only because they realized that the explosion would destroy all of the signatures carved on the school walls).

Because it is a scathingly satirical account of a rebellion in a boys' school, intensely conveying the students' point of view in a series of autonomous chapters that include scenes of stark violence as well as evident fantasy, *If . . .* has often been compared to Jean Vigo's classic film *Zero de Conduite*. Filmed in France in 1932 but banned there until 1945 because of its allegedly incendiary political content as a metaphoric incitement to revolution, Vigo's film ends with its four rebels on the roof of their school as the havoc that they have created continues to rage below. Anderson has acknowledged seeing Vigo's film "again, before writing started, to give us courage" ("Preface," 11), but comparisons which suggest or imply that the later film is merely a remake or imitation overlook crucial differences between the two. Among the foremost of these is Anderson's naturalistic style which, even when dealing with fantasy, is quite unlike the surreal exaggeration of Vigo; Anderson admitted that in directing *If . . .* the films made by "John Ford ('old father, old artificer') and Humphrey Jennings (romantic-ironic conservative) were in [his] bloodstream" ("Preface," 9). Vigo's schoolboys' revolt is carried out with a bombardment of books, rocks, and old shoes rather than the fully adult weapons that Anderson's rebels use, though Anderson's film also ends with the boys atop the school roof. Mick Travis and his cohorts fire at fellow students and adults alike, whereas the latter were the target in Vigo's film. Anderson's only distinctively surreal sequence in *If . . .* (in which the school chaplain is resurrected) is a direct homage to Vigo, in whose film an instructor is shown tied to his bed with a coverlet and turned up vertically in what Vigo referred to as a "crucifixion." Even the two actors (Robert LeFlon in Vigo's film, Geoffrey Chater in Anderson's) look remarkably alike.

Presented in a series of eight individually titled segments ("chapters"), the plot of *If . . .* is comprised of events occurring within a single academic year. In the first segment, "College House . . . Return," the corridors are crowded as new boys move into their residence halls; amid much clamor and confusion, new boys (addressed as "scum") soon learn their place in the hierarchy of the school as they are dispatched to carry trunks or to warm lavatory seats for upperclassmen. In the senior dormitory, Mick arrives wearing a dark hat and scarf that conceals a mustache which, as an emblem of individuality and emerging manhood, must be shaved off as the school year begins. The second and third chapters ("College: 'Once again assembled . . .'" and "Term Time") characterize the routine of school life, from the opening chapel service through the various masters' small cruelties and sarcastic ironies in the classroom—though the latter pale in comparison to those practiced among the boys themselves in the roughhousing of the dormitories and, more systematically, in the enforcement of discipline. The juxtaposition of such scenes of wanton but (implicitly) officially sanctioned cruelty and the chapel services makes it unmistakably but tacitly clear that any semblances of *genuinely* Christian attributes—forgiveness, compassion, forbearance, or mercy toward those who lack strength, power, or influence—are very rare indeed.

In contrast to the preceding segments, the fourth chapter ("Ritual and Romance") provides lyrical relief—and release—as Mick and his cohort Johnny Knightly (played by David Wood) venture into the nearby town in violation of school rules. Temporarily, at least, they leave behind the insular school world of chapel, classes, and required games. In the town, they linger before shop windows displaying dresses and lingerie—alluring symbols of all the desires that school confinement is supposed to suppress. Driving out of a motorbike showroom (without authorization), the renegades cross long stretches of green countryside, relishing their illegal and daring freedom on a literal "joyride" that defies both the school's and society's rules. At a roadside cafe, Mick's flirtation with a young waitress turns suddenly (and probably only in his imagination) into an intense bout of lovemaking on the floor, accompanied by animalistic snarls and the "Sanctus" chorale from the *Missa Luba* on the jukebox. In the final scene, the waitress joins the rebels on their motorcycle tour across the countryside.

The fifth segment, "Discipline," contains the film's most protracted scenes of violence as Mick and his roommates are mercilessly flogged for their "general attitude" as "unruly elements." While his compatriots' flogging is heard rather than seen, Mick's punishment—eight brutally powerful strokes with a cane, administered with a running start as Travis is stretched out in cruciform position against a piece of gym equipment—is shown (in part) on screen. Despite its savagery, a ritualistic formality is maintained: stoical silence is *de rigeur*, and the victim must thank his persecutor at the end of the ordeal. Notably, however, Mick's expression remains defiant. The consequences of such persecution become clear in the sixth segment, "Resistance," as Mick and his roommates form a blood-bond, avowing that "one man can change the world—with a bullet in the right place" (113).

The seventh segment, "Forth to War," includes scenes of the school's requisite military training. The Chaplain, in full military uniform, leads the College Cadet Corps into mock-battle, encouraging them to issue the "yell of Hate." Suddenly, though again presumably in fantasy, the battle becomes more earnest; Mick fires on the Chaplain, who later is resurrected from a drawer in the Headmaster's cupboard—the film's most decidedly surreal moment, its clearest indication that at least some of the

film's incidents are not *objectively* "true." The Headmaster assigns the trio extra work, cleaning out the under-stage area of the school's auditorium. There, mysteriously joined by the waitress from the cafe, they discover stocks of ammunition, guns, and mortar shells that they will put to use in the film's final segment, "Crusaders." On the school's commencement day, with church officials, the military, the alumni, the parents, the faculty, and their classmates assembled in their finest regalia, the rebels set fire to the under-stage area. As the assembled masses flee the smoke-filled room, the rebels (and the waitress identified only as The Girl) fire on them with machine-guns from their vantage-point on the roof. The headmaster is shot through the forehead by The Girl, but those on the ground begin to mount a counterattack of their own. The film ends with a close-up of Mick, still defiantly firing away; the word "if . . . " in scarlet is superimposed on the screen.

Like the film's famous intermittent switching between color and black-and-white (a technique also used in Anderson's segment of *The White Bus* in 1966), the intermingling of fantasy and reality in *If . . .* has the effect of keeping the viewer constantly uncertain and *en garde*. It demands the viewer's constant, active attention and prevents mere passive absorption of the film as entertainment. More than just a consequence of budgetary constraints, the use of the black-and-white sequences in *If . . .* constitutes a uniquely cinematic counterpart of the Brechtian "alienation effect," distancing the audience from the action and providing "an incitement to thought," as Anderson acknowledged in the preface to the published script—adding that "there is no symbolism involved in the choice of sequences filmed in black-and-white, nothing expressionistic or schematic. Only such factors as intuition, pattern, and convenience" (10). In adapting the now-familiar stage technique to the medium of film in such an innovative way, Anderson in effect redefines the role of the moviegoing audience—in exactly the way that he had sought to do in the theater a decade earlier when, writing in *Encore* magazine, he had sought audiences that would "come to the theatre to work—not just to sit, and be 'absorbed,' made to laugh or cry by an expert machine, being 'entertained' . . . [Instead, they would] come, not with the passive expectation of 'entertainment,' nor just with mouths wide open for another slab of minority culture, but themselves prepared to give something, to work, with minds open and alert, themselves creative."[3] Recognizing alike the satiric animus that prevails throughout *If . . .* and its intermingling of interior and exterior "realities" (akin to that in Keith Waterhouse's novel *Billy Liar* [1959], the stage version of which Anderson directed in 1960), such an audience might then recognize the full significance of the "last word" imposed on the screen as the film ends. Mick is the ultimate inversion of the ethic embodied in Kipling's famous poem, which in many ways he nevertheless fulfills. Fighting fiercely from the battlements, outnumbered while manning his isolated barricade, he *is* in fact keeping his head while all about him are (literally) losing theirs and blaming it (with good reason) on him. He must trust himself when all may doubt him, and must think, without letting thought distract his aim. He has dreamed of freedom—undeterred by prefects, parents, masters—and now treats their impostures just the same. Whether his revolt ends with triumph or disaster, he risks all that is more serious than the ruggers' pitch and toss. He must force his will and nerve and sinew to serve his turn long after school-induced attempts at subduing it would seem to have made such willful endurance gone. "Essentially," Anderson concludes in his preface, "the heroes of *If . . .* are old-fashioned boys. They are not anti-heroes, or drop-outs, or Marxist-Leninists or Maoists or readers of Marcuse. Their revolt is inevitable not because of what they *think*, but because of what they *are*" (12). The issues that their revolt raises thus remove the film from the narrow passions and politics of its day, even as its innovative techniques transcend the conventions of cinematic narrative in uniquely Brechtian ways.

O Lucky Man! is clearly the most "epic" of Anderson's films in the Brechtian sense of the term. It is more ambitious than *If . . .* in the array of social targets that it satirically assails (the modern business ethos, the judicial system, medical research, the military-industrial complex, social "reformers," among many others). McDowell's character, though again named Mick Travis, is not *necessarily* the same as his namesake in the earlier film, which is supposedly being cast at the end of *O Lucky Man!*, its ostensible "sequel."

Again, Anderson's film technique is innovative in markedly Brechtian ways: most of the actors appear in multiple roles, and many of them also had roles in *If . . .* (including Chris-

tine Noonan, "The Girl" in *If . . .* , who turns up in *O Lucky Man!* accompanying a patron of a sleazy provincial strip club). Although the film has the episodic structure that is typical of picaresque fiction, its plot segments are separated by musical interludes in which songwriter Alan Price and his band appear. Their songs—performed from a "Limbo" space defined in the script as "black curtains encircling a central space"—provide jaunty yet cynical commentary on the action (while providing an emotional "distancing" effect), and the satiric animus and iconoclastic wit of their lyrics are comparable to those of Brecht and Kurt Weill. The musicians also become involved in the film's plot, rescuing Mick in their van after one of his mishaps. Numerous self-reflexively cinematic devices (akin to the use of the black-and-white sequences in *If . . .*) are used in *O Lucky Man!* including segment titles ("Once upon a time," "coffee for the breakfast table," etc.), singalong words to some song lyrics (in eight languages), blackouts, and occasional directional indicators ("North," etc.)—although the latter are, predictably, quite random as well. There are also a number of brief films within the film, beginning with a prologue in which the hands of a Mexican field-worker (McDowell) are chopped off after he is caught slipping a few coffee beans into his shirt, continuing through a 1950s-style stag movie involving Santa Claus, and culminating in a commercial sales film showing the effects of commercial development in third world countries and eventually of the devastation wrought by a napalm-like chemical weapon euphemistically referred to as "honey."

O Lucky Man! based on McDowell's original idea, is partially autobiographical. The film has also been concisely described as François Voltaire's *Candide* crossed with John Bunyan's *Pilgrim's Progress* and brought up to the twentieth century. Like McDowell before the beginning of his acting career, Mick begins as a coffee salesman in northern England—and is a much more conventional, earnest, ambitious, and naive young man than the protagonist of *If. . . .* The film is also far more allusive than its predecessor: there are quotations from William Blake and from William Shakespeare's *Merchant of Venice* ("All that glitters is not gold," Travis is warned by the daughter of a London tycoon whose executive assistant and fall-guy he has become); parodies of scenes from earlier films are included (e.g., *The Bird Man of Alcatraz*), as are allusions to McDowell's own previous movies (particularly Stanley Kubrick's *A Clockwork Orange*). Even a favorite Marxist slogan is mocked: "Revolution is the Opium of the Intellectuals" is spray-painted on an outdoor wall.

Like *If . . .*, *O Lucky Man!* has a provocative, memorable, yet ambiguous ending, though it is much more joyous than that of the previous film. After Mick has been cast by Anderson at the open audition for *If . . .*, he and the director (or director-to-be) exchange words when Anderson insists that he smile. After several refusals (his terrible experiences having caused him to lose the ability, perhaps), Mick is swatted across the face with the rolled-up script—a secular counterpart of a Zen satori, a prefigurement of spiritual enlightenment. "A faint smile begins to break at the corner of his mouth," the script specifies, though the question is posed as to whether it is "the smile of Understanding? or of Obedience?" (188). The film's final sequence takes place at the cast party on completion of the film, with all of the actors/characters reunited in a joyous, swirling dance amid falling balloons and Price's reprise of the film's theme song. "The getting of wisdom is still the principal thing," Anderson remarks in his preface to the script (8), alluding to the verse from *Proverbs* that provided the epigraph of *If . . .* ("Wisdom is the principal thing; therefore get wisdom: and with all thy getting get understanding" [*Proverbs* 4:7]). Anderson adds that Mick "seems to me to arrive, after journeying through the world of illusion, at some kind of acceptance of reality. But acceptance is not conformism" (8–9).

In *Britannia Hospital*, as in *If . . .*, a familiar British institution is a symbol for the society at large; the National Health [Service] becomes a metaphor for the "national health" of contemporary Britain. Chaotic, beset by union grievances as well as class distinctions (as wealthy "private" patients, including corrupt government officials from third world countries, are privileged far beyond their counterparts in the "public" wards), the hospital is managed by the beleaguered administrator Vincent Potter (played by Leonard Rossiter), who is preparing for a visit from a "royal personnage" who will commemorate the five hundredth anniversary of the hospital's founding. Mick, who has become a television news reporter, goes "undercover" to investigate experiments that are being conducted by one Professor Millar (Graham Crowden), whose gro-

tesque experiments were first seen in *O Lucky Man!* as he grafted a human head onto the body of a pig; Mick, who was scheduled for surgery and experimentation in the previous film, escaped the hospital by bolting through the window, much as the reconditioned Alex does in *A Clockwork Orange* after receiving the Ludovico Technique. In *Britannia Hospital,* Professor Millar is at work on two experiments. The first, a literally Frankenstein-like creation of a living human being from assembled corpse-parts, eventually involves Mick, whose severed head is stitched onto a multi-racial composite body before literally coming apart at the seams in a violent final confrontation with the Professor. His second project, known as Genesis, is the creation of an autonomous, disembodied, hyperintelligent, oversized, living, superhuman brain that is one hundred thousand times more powerful than our own.

The Brechtian techniques that characterize the previous "Mick Travis" films are absent from *Britannia Hospital*, which is more conventionally naturalistic in its narrative style. It features a considerable amount of black, grotesque, and gruesome comedy that might (charitably) be described as in the "Monty Python" tradition or (less charitably) as gratuitous, pre-adolescent "gross-out" humor (e.g., Millar slices apart a human brain and then purees it in a blender; he serves it to a television technician, who drinks it as Millar crunches on one of the leftover parts himself). The dichotomy between applied scientific technology and strife-ridden human relations pervades the film, much as it did in Mary Shelley's *Frankenstein* and the early science fiction of H.G. Wells, which are the film's primary literary progenitors.

These tensions culminate in the film's climax as, in a too-close recapitulation of the final scenes of *If . . .*, a band of sixties-style protesters storms the hospital grounds; a riot ensues as the band plays "God Save the Queen." In the film's final sequence, however, Millar addresses the entire populace—royalty and rioters alike—in an auditorium where he unveils the Genesis project with an eloquent and impassioned speech that heralds "only a new intelligence [which] can save mankind" by leading the world into a new era. When the autonomous brain begins to speak its piece, however, the words of superhuman wisdom turn out to be Shakespeare's: the "What a piece of work is a man" speech from *Hamlet*, a line of which ("how like a god") it repeats over and over as the film ends. Bizarre as it undoubtedly is, the image may well also be among the most indelibly memorable in contemporary cinema.

Glory! Glory! is a similarly audacious institutional satire, although—for the first time in Anderson's canon—the film's target is a distinctly American phenomenon: televangelism. Yet, in part because of the widely publicized trials and travails of a number of televangelism's *actual* practitioners (Jimmy Swaggart, Jim and Tammy Faye Bakker, et al.), the film's depiction of graft, greed, hypocrisy, and sexual indulgence among the pseudo-pious lacks the shock value that it might otherwise have. Richard Thomas portrays the "straight-arrow" son of a charismatic televangelist, although his probity nearly destroys the enterprise that his father has built. A dynamic but foul-mouthed rock-and-roll singer (played by Ellen Greene) in the guise of a devout miracle worker is brought in to rescue the financially ailing enterprise. *Glory! Glory!* is, like all of Anderson's films, deftly crafted, with much wit, visual humor, and sharp intelligence; the relationship between religion and show business is often acerbically shown, for example. Still, because the film's subject provides a too-ready target, it is on the whole a less significant work than any of the films in the trilogy.

In a profile published in *Drama: The Quarterly Theatre Review* in 1987, C. Paul Ryan characterized Anderson as "a realistic man who has never confused collaboration with compromise, coolness with coldness, or intimacy with mere familiarity. . . . He is a displaced Celt who has consistently described himself as an anarchist . . . in that he believes that ultimate responsibility rests with the individual and that everyone—the artist above all—has a social responsibility to fulfill."[4] In the same interview, Anderson summarized his work as a writer, satirist, and director: the films "are shot through with suspicion and dislike of institutions and institutional thinking. They appeal to the intelligence—not the intellect—and that's about it. I'm accused of being pessimistic, which is true, but I think the optimistic thing about a work of art is not any hopeful formulation that it may end up with, but essentially the vitality of the work itself." From the outset of his career, such vitality, intelligence, artistry, and wit were the hallmarks of his unique films; those films remain consistently among the most provocative satires of their times.

Summary

As a critic, stage director, and film-maker, Lindsay Anderson was consistently outspoken, iconoclastic, and provocative, with a passionate commitment to social and moral reform as well as conspicuous intelligence that pervades his works. His satire—in the exact tradition of Ben Jonson's—is erudite, allusive, witty, unsparing, wide-ranging, and austere; it is best exemplified in his two best-known films, *If . . .* and *O Lucky Man!*, which are remarkable for their innovative cinematic techniques as well as their ability to stimulate discussion and stir controversy years after their initial release.

Notes

1. Elizabeth Sussex, *Lindsay Anderson* (New York: Praeger, 1969), p. 7.
2. Anderson, "Notes for a Preface," *If . . .* (New York: Simon and Schuster, 1969), p. 7. All subsequent references are from this edition.
3. Anderson, "Vital Theatre?" *Encore*, 4, 2 (November–December 1957): 12–13.
4. C. Paul Ryan, "Still Out There Pushing: Lindsay Anderson in Interview," *Drama: The Quarterly Theatre Review*, no. 166 (4th quarter, 1987): 7.

Selected Bibliography
Primary Sources

Feature Films Directed
This Sporting Life. 1963.
The White Bus. 1966. Anderson's contribution is a forty-six-minute short story filmed mostly in black-and-white with occasional color segments; it was one of three episodes planned for the film.
If . . . . 1969.
O Lucky Man! 1973.
In Celebration. 1975.
Britannia Hospital. 1982.
The Whales of August. 1987.
Glory! Glory! 1989.

Film Scripts (co-authored with David Sherwin)
If . . . . Modern Film Scripts. New York: Simon and Schuster, 1969.
O Lucky Man! London: Plexus Publishing Ltd., 1973.

Books of Film Criticism
About John Ford. New York: McGraw-Hill, 1981.

Making a Film: The Story of "Secret People." London: Allen & Unwin, 1952; New York: Garland, 1977.

Articles and Essays
"The Court Style." In *At the Royal Court: 25 Years of the English Stage Company.* Ed. Richard Findlater. New York: Grove Press, 1981, pp. 143–48. Reminiscences of the early years of the English Stage Company at the Royal Court, emphasizing that its "tone was far more humanist than intellectual [and] liberal, if you like, in its strong rather than its soppy sense"—a characterization equally applicable to Anderson's own work as well.
"Get Out and Push!" In *Declaration.* Ed. Tom Maschler. London: MacGibbon & Kee, 1957, pp. 153–78. A witty and excoriating attack on British complacency and a plea for contemporary culture to tackle the social and cultural realities of the mid-twentieth century; other contributors to the volume include Doris Lessing, Kenneth Tynan, and John Wain.
"Glory Days." *Plays and Players* (May 1986): 6–9. Reflections on the early days of the Royal Court Theatre.
"Sport, Life and Art." *Films and Filming,* 9, 9 (February 1963): 15–18. Discussion of the making of *This Sporting Life,* his particular approach to the novel, and his views of film as art; includes his now-famous remark that the artist's "duty is to be a monster."
"Stand Up! Stand Up!" *Sight and Sound,* 26 (Autumn 1956): 63–69. Renowned example of Anderson's provocative, exhortatively expressed, intensely idealistic views of what cinema can and should be.
"Vital Theatre?" *Encore,* 4, 2 (November–December 1957): 10–14. See also his letter to the editor, *Encore,* 4, 4 (March–April 1958): 43–45, further defining and defending his views, in response to an editorial "A View from the Gods" by "Groundling" (*Encore,* 4, 3 [January–February 1958]: 4–7) and a letter to the editor by T.C. Worsley in the same issue. Anderson's initial essay, Worsley's letter, and Anderson's reply have been reprinted in *New Theatre Voices of the Fifties and Sixties: Selec-*
tions from Encore Magazine, 1956–1963, ed. Charles Marowitz, Tom Milne, and Owen Hale (1965; London: Eyre Methuen, 1981), pp. 41–51. Controversial, idealistic, lucid, and impassioned exposition of Anderson's views of the role and nature of the theater in modern society—engaging and *engagé* at the same time.

Interviews
Coveney, Michael. "To Court a Philistine Nation." *Plays and Players,* 23, 3 (December 1975): 14–17. Wide-ranging discussion of the Royal Court, his directorial style, the inadequacy of journalistic reviewing, the philistinism of much contemporary culture, and the general "national breakdown."
Cowie, Peter. "An Interview with Lindsay Anderson." *Film Quarterly,* 17, 4 (Summer 1964): 12–14. Excellent though brief early assessment of Anderson's views of the theater and film scene, shortly after he completed *This Sporting Life.*
Flatley, Guy. "Anderson: We Have to Make Our Own Acts of Courage." *New York Times* (July 1, 1973): sec. 2, 9, 17. Focuses on *O Lucky Man!,* American politics, and general attitudes about movies.
———. "I Never Saw a Pinter Play." *New York Times* (November 29, 1970): sec. 2, 1, 5. Flatley's conversation with Anderson and David Storey is primarily related to the New York production of *Home,* but it offers insight into their working relationship and a bantering humor not often evident in Anderson's other interviews.
Gelmis, Joseph. "Lindsay Anderson." In *The Film Director as Superstar.* Garden City, NY: Doubleday, 1970, pp. 93–110. Detailed discussion of politics, film-making, and specific aspects of his documentaries, *This Sporting Life,* and *If . . . .*
Gray, Paul. "Class Theatre, Class Film: An Interview with Lindsay Anderson." *Tulane Drama Review* 11 (Fall 1966): 122–29. Anderson assesses the impact of class on British cinema, in contrast to the work of various European directors; he also contends that "For me the cinema is a poetic medium, while the theatre is less exclusively poetic."

Levin, G. Roy. "Interview with Lindsay Anderson." *Documentary Explorations: 15 Interviews with Film-makers*. Garden City, NY: Doubleday, 1971, pp. 57–73. Focuses primarily on politics and film, politics and the artist, and documentaries in general.

Robinson, David. "Stripping the Veils Away." *The Times* (April 21, 1973): 7. Thoughtful discussion of many aspects of *O Lucky Man!* and Anderson's aspirations as a director.

Ryan, C. Paul. "Still Out There Pushing: Lindsay Anderson in Interview." *Drama: The Quarterly Theatre Review*, 166 (4th quarter 1987): 5–7. Retrospective assessment of art and society thirty years after his essay in *Declaration*. Anderson concedes that the "rather cold tradition of English art . . . has persisted, and has won," though he characteristically refuses to make any concessions to the *Zeitgeist*, including the philistine rejection of "truthful art" and of "this terrible middle-class thing of clinging desperately to some—even if fictitious—idea of hope."

Sussex, Elizabeth. "Lindsay Anderson's New Film." *The Times* (London: November 29, 1968): 14. Discussion of the "relevance" of *If . . .* , then-current politics, and Anderson's views on anarchy.

Secondary Sources

Bibliographies
Silet, Charles P. *Lindsay Anderson: A Guide to References and Resources*. Boston: G.K. Hall, 1979.

Books and Articles
"The Artist as Monster." *Time* (July 23, 1973): 87–88. Brief biographical profile.

Cunningham, Frank R. "Lindsay Anderson's *O Lucky Man!* and the Romantic Tradition." *Literature/Film Quarterly*, 2, 3 (1974): 256–61. Cunningham assesses major literary backgrounds of the film within the romantic period.

Graham, Allison. *Lindsay Anderson*. Boston: Twayne, 1981. Thorough overview of Anderson's film career through *O Lucky Man!,* prepared with Anderson's cooperation. Focuses on "his progressive involvement in artistic responses to social and political issues and increasing concern with the difficulty of creating 'new identities' and 'new images' in a class-bound society."

Hutchings, William. "*If . . .* Then—*And* Now: Lindsay Anderson's *If . . .* and the Schoolboy Rebels of Fact, Fiction, and Film." *Papers on Language and Literature*, 23, 2 (Spring 1987): 192–217. Establishes *If . . .* within the context of similar schoolboy revolts in English fiction (Hughes's *Tom Brown's School Days*, Kipling's *Stalky and Co.*), memoirs by George Orwell and Cyril Connolly, and history. Also assesses the film in terms of stage plays that Anderson directed earlier in the decade—particularly John Arden's *Serjeant Musgrave's Dance* and Keith Waterhouse and Willis Hall's stage adaptation of Waterhouse's novel *Billy Liar*.

Lavery, David. "*O Lucky Man!* and the Movie as Koan." *Literature/Film Quarterly*, 3, 1 (1980): 35–40. Discusses the Zen aspects of the film.

Lovell, Alan. "Brecht in Britain—Lindsay Anderson (on *If . . .* and *O Lucky Man!*)." *Screen*, 16, 4 (Winter 1975/1976): 62–80. Overview of Brecht's impact on British theater in general and Anderson's films in particular; a transcribed panel discussion after the essay focuses primarily on differences between Brecht's political ideology and Anderson's views, as opposed to "certain stylistic features."

———, and Jim Hillier. "Free Cinema." In *Studies in Documentary*. New York: Viking, 1972, pp. 133–67. Useful survey of the "Free Cinema" movement and Anderson's contribution to it.

Robinson, David. "Anderson Shooting *If . . .* ." *Sight and Sound*, 37, 3 (Summer 1968): 130–31. Insightful and anecdotal "insider's" account of Anderson's working style, focusing on the climactic scene of *If . . .* as it was being filmed at the school that Anderson himself attended.

Storey, David. "Working with Lindsay." In *At the Royal Court: 25 Years of the English Stage Company*. Ed. Richard Findlater. New York: Grove Press, 1981, pp. 110–15. Anecdotal reminiscence of the production process for Storey's plays *The Contractor, Home, The Changing Room*, and others.

Sussex, Elizabeth. *Lindsay Anderson.* New York: Frederick A. Praeger, 1969. Meticulously detailed, valuable study of Anderson's film works through *If . . .*, prepared with his full cooperation. Especially strong on the early short films and biographical details based on interviews.

Taylor, John Russell. "Lindsay Anderson." In *Directors and Directing: Cinema for the Seventies.* New York: Hill and Wang, 1975, pp. 69–99, 278–88 [filmography]. Contends that "among the directors at present working in the British cinema, Lindsay Anderson is the only one, of any generation, who is truly an international figure, who can without apology or special pleading be considered in the same frame of reference as [Pier Paolo] Pasolini or [Miklos] Jancso or [Satyajit] Ray—who is, in short, undoubtedly and unarguably an *auteur.*"

William Hutchings

Anstey, F.

Born: St. George's Terrace, London, August 8, 1856

Education: private school Surbiton; King's College School, 1872–1874; Trinity Hall, Cambridge, 1875–1876

Died: Holland Park, London, March 10, 1934

Biography

Thomas Anstey Guthrie, the son of a military tailor, also named Thomas Anstey Guthrie, and a professional pianist and organist, Augusta Amherst Austen, was born in London on August 8, 1856, the eldest of four children. His childhood was filled with toys, books, pictures, and visits to the seaside, circuses, and magic shows. His experience at the private school that he first attended was a lonely one; the school reappears in *Vice Versa* (1882) as Crichton House. He much preferred being a day-boarder at King's College School (1872–1874), where he edited the school magazine. Having studied law at Trinity Hall, Cambridge, he entered Middle Temple, London in 1876 and passed his bar exam in 1881 but never became a practicing attorney.

Guthrie had published poems, burlesques, and articles in university periodicals and comic journals, but his first important work was the novel *Vice Versa*, which, after two laudatory

reviews by Andrew Lang, became a best-seller. He decided to give up the law and devote his life to writing, using the pseudonym F. Anstey. His speedy celebrity brought him a secure income and contact with many literary figures, and in 1885 he was invited to become a contributor to *Punch*, joining its Table in 1886. Throughout the rest of his career he alternated parodies and imaginary conversations written for *Punch* with novels and children's stories. He also dramatized a number of his works, starting with *Vice Versa* in 1883.

Anstey led the static and unruffled life of a literary bachelor. His nature was shy and retiring, and, as was the case with Lewis Carroll, his closest friendships were with children. For the invalid son of solicitor Horace Pym he wrote and illustrated a number of stories, many of which remain unpublished. He was keenly sensitive to bad reviews and charges of plagiarism, and was more disappointed than he admitted publicly when his attempts at serious fiction, such as *The Pariah* (1889), were dismissed by the critics. None of his later works achieved the popularity of his first volumes, and the high-water mark of his earnings came around 1900. Thereafter, despite favorable notices, his books failed to win readers, although his plays continued to be well received. In large part this is because Anstey had little interest in the artistic and social fads of the Edwardian era and failed to direct his satiric shafts at them. His last years were devoted to cycling tours of France, translations of Moliere, and copying and coloring Renaissance engravings. He died of pneumonia on March 10, 1934 at his home on Holland Park Road, London.

Literary Analysis

Anstey's most durable works are his humorous ones, and they fall naturally into four categories: parodies, "overheard" dialogues, fantastic romances, and social satires.

The parodies, light in touch and so close to their originals that they might be mistaken for the real thing, were composed exclusively for *Punch*. The first were a series of "Model Music Hall Songs," lampoons of standard music-hall fare stripped of the innuendo that might offend the London County Council. Anstey, who had written a well-researched essay on London music halls for *Harper's Weekly*, knew whereof he spoke, and his samples of the lyrics of serio-comics and coster comedians bear all of the earmarks of the genuine articles. In his *Mr.*

A

Punch's Young Reciter: Burglar Bill and Other Pieces (1892) he carried out the same exercise on the kind of parlor recitations that plagued middle-class households; in particular his "Burglar Bill," about a housebreaker reformed by a golden-haired tot, was a devastating send-up of rhetorical sentimentality. *Mr. Punch's Pocket Ibsen* (1893) was one of the many comic attacks launched on the Henrik Ibsen productions mounted by the Independent Stage Society. Without overdoing things, Anstey managed to catch the ponderous absurdities of the Norwegian playwright as he appeared in William Archer's stilted translations. Edmund Gosse, who had discovered Ibsen for England, was one of the book's biggest fans.

Anstey's acute ear for colloquial speech certified the accuracy of *Voces Populi* (1890, 1892). He would visit a public event such as an exhibition of paintings or a Lord Mayor's Show and capture it in dialogue, reproducing with vivid accuracy the temperaments and tastes of the speakers who convened there. These were never mere transcriptions of overheard discourse, for Anstey occasionally worked from an anecdote, but he had an almost Dickensian ability to distill character into a memorable phrase or speech. What may mar these works for a modern audience is Anstey's snobbishness. His contemporaries marveled at the clinical mercilessness of his observations, which often lack joviality in his eagerness to skewer cads and prigs. To a reader nowadays, he seems too anxious to establish his superiority to 'Arry and 'Arriet. This reflects Anstey's own social anxieties; in his youth, schoolmates teased him for being the son of a tailor, and he shared the Victorian sensitivity to matters of caste. Like George Bernard Shaw's Professor Higgins, he used speech patterns to pigeonhole and classify his fellow Englishmen, certifying his own gentlemanliness in the process.

Vice Versa, Anstey's first success and his most enduring, set the style for most of his later fantastic novels. A magical "Garuda stone" transforms Mr. Bultitude, a humorless businessman, into the physical semblance of his son, and he must undergo the humiliations of a schoolboy while retaining his own sensibility. The son, on the other hand, now inhabiting his father's body, romps through the mysteries of high finance. This topsy-turvydom is a counterblast to the didacticism of most school stories. It also serves as a moving novel of education: Mr. Bultitude comes to learn of the joys and sorrows of childhood, and, as one critic puts it, "the return to normality [is] not a disappointment but a triumph" (David Grylls, *Guardians and Angels*). The book makes a perennial appeal to the English nostalgia for schooldays and enjoyed success as a play and later as a film with Peter Ustinov as the headmaster. Without crediting Anstey, Hollywood has lifted the plot for a modernized and Americanized version starring Judge Reinhold and Fred Savage in *Vice Versa*.

Having discovered a formula—an ordinary middle-class life turned inside-out by the interference of a supernatural agency—Anstey proceeded to repeat it with variations throughout the rest of his career. In *The Tinted Venus* (1885), a lowly barber causes a statue of Venus to come to life and the vivified goddess proceeds to get him into one embarrassing imbroglio after another. *A Fallen Idol* (1886) features a malevolent Asian effigy which curses the hero's existence, and the magic flask of *The Brass Bottle* (1900) emits a genie who disturbs the career and love life of an aspiring architect. In *The Talking Horse* (1892) the title creature wrecks the romance of his hapless owner. A somewhat more complicated structure appears in *Tourmalin's Time Cheques* (1891), which is about a mechanism that allows the hero to return to a past experience for limited periods. This promising premise is vitiated by Anstey's conventionality, and, after putting his protagonist in an almost inextricably fatal situation, he gets him out of it by showing the whole previous action to be a dream.

Anstey admitted that he devised his plots first and only then the characters with which to people them. The mechanical nature of these plots would be less obtrusive if Anstey had the capacity for drawing well-rounded and memorable characters or even for liking them, but, for the most part, his heroes are dreary, unimaginative plodders whom he enjoys putting in dangerous and distressing predicaments. The psychological sensitivity shown in *Vice Versa* is a rare commodity in the later books. His female characters, when they are not pretty lay figures, tend to be ghastly harridans, heartless flirts, or arid man-eaters. Still, the ingeniousness of his basic conceits is entertaining, and has been much exploited by the popular arts. *A Tinted Venus* served as a source for *One Touch of Venus*, a play and later a film co-written by American humorists S.J. Perelman and Ogden Nash. *The Brass Bottle* was made, with remarkably few alterations, into a film with Tony Randall as the architect and Burl Ives as the genie.

Anstey's one attempt at creating a comic character who would be more prominent than the intrigue in which he is featured was Baboo Jabberjee, an over-educated and conceited Bengali, whose ignorant attempts to break into English society are the motive force in *Baboo Jabberjee, B.A.* (1897) and *A Bayard from Bengal* (1902). Although Anstey's original concept had been sparked by his delight in the ornate and solecism-filled language of Babus (English-writing Hindus), the comedy now seems steeped in racism and overdone in its buffoonery.

The social satires in dialogue are, in contrast, carried out with a deft touch that led Anstey's contemporaries to evoke the names of Eugene Labiche, Jean Baptiste Moliere, and Oliver Goldsmith in describing them (it is no coincidence that Anstey wrote an essay on Labiche for *The London Mercury* and spent much of his later life translating Moliere). One novel in this category, *The Travelling Companions* (1892), in which two disagreeable gentlemen are compelled to share one another's distasteful company on a European tour, might be regarded as a jokey precursor of E.M. Forster's *A Room with a View* (1908). *The Man from Blankley's* (1893) is a delightful tour de force, the tale of a dinner party with hired waiters which keeps to the classic unities; it was successfully staged in 1901, 1906, and 1917, though a revival in 1930 showed how tied it was to obsolete character types and forms of etiquette. *Lyre and Lancet* (1895) takes a rather hackneyed tale of mistaken identities at a country-house weekend and, by casting it entirely in dialogue, keeps it crisp and sparkling. Anstey's almost Jamesian attention to the niceties of genteel intercourse led Sir John Squire to declare that the collection of sketches *Salted Almonds* (1906) was revolutionary in bridging "the gulf between Mark Lemon and Burnand on the one hand and A.A. Milne and A.P. Herbert on the other."

Summary
Like the man himself, F. Anstey's accomplishments are controlled and modest, and he never appealed to a broad public, especially outside of late-Victorian England. This seems to be because, doggedly Tory and upwardly mobile, he shared the beliefs and prejudices of his time, and his comedy drew chiefly from ideas of class and decorum which have dated badly. Never-theless, the ingenuity of his best plots and his superlative ear for dialogue continue to appeal to new readers.

Selected Bibliography
Primary Sources
Vice Versa; or A Lesson for Fathers. London: Smith, Elder, 1882; rev. 1883, 1894 (with additions).
The Giant's Robe. London: Smith, Elder, 1884.
The Black Poodle and Other Tales. London: Longmans, Green, 1884.
The Tinted Venus, a Farcical Romance. Bristol: J.W. Arrowsmith, 1885.
A Fallen Idol. London: Smith, Elder, 1886.
The Pariah. London: Smith, Elder, 1889.
Voces Populi, 2 series. London: Longmans, Green, 1890, 1892.
Tourmalin's Time Cheques. Bristol: J.W. Arrowsmith, 1891, 1905.
The Talking Horse and Other Tales. London: Smith, Elder, 1892.
Mr. Punch's Young Reciter: Burglar Bill and Other Pieces. London: Bradbury, Agnew, 1892.
Mr. Punch's Model Music-Hall Songs and Dramas. London: Bradbury, Agnew, 1892.
The Travelling Companions: A Story in Scenes. London: Longmans, Green, 1892; rev. 1908.
Mr. Punch's Pocket Ibsen. London: Heinemann, 1893, 1895 (enlarged).
The Man from Blankley's and Other Sketches. London: Longmans, Green, 1893.
Under the Rose: A Story in Scenes. London: Bradbury, Agnew, 1894.
Lyre and Lancet: A Story in Scenes. London: Smith, Elder, 1895.
The Statement of Stella Maberly, Written by Herself. London: T. Fisher Unwin, 1896.
Baboo Jabberjee, B.A. London: J.M. Dent, 1897.
Puppets at Large: Scenes and Subjects from Mr. Punch's Show. London: Bradbury, Agnew, 1897.
Paleface and Redskin, and Other Stories for Boys and Girls. London: Grant Richards, 1898.
Love among the Lions, A Matrimonial Experiment. London: J.M. Dent, 1898.
The Brass Bottle. London: Smith, Elder, 1900.

A

A Bayard from Bengal. London: Methuen, 1902.

Only Toys! London: Grant Richards, 1903.

Salted Almonds and Other Tales. London: Smith, Elder, 1906.

Vice Versa, a Farcical Fantastic Play in Three Acts. London: Smith, Elder, 1910.

The Brass Bottle, A Farcical Fantastic Play in Four Acts. London: Heinemann, 1911.

Percy and Others: Sketches, Mainly Reproduced from Punch. London: Methuen, 1915.

In Brief Authority. London: Smith, Elder, 1915.

The Last Load: Stories and Essays. London: Methuen, 1925.

The Man from Blankley's, A Comedy of the Early Nineties. London: Hodder and Stoughton, 1927.

Four Moliere Comedies, Freely Adapted. London: Oxford University Press, 1931.

Humour & Fantasy: Vice Versa, The Tinted Venus, A Fallen Idol, The Talking Horse, Salted Almonds, The Brass Bottle. New York: E.P. Dutton, 1931.

Three Moliere Plays, Freely Adapted. London: Oxford University Press, 1933.

A Long Retrospect. London and New York: Oxford University Press, 1936.

Secondary Sources

Bibliographies

Turner, Martin John. *A Bibliography of the Works of F. Anstey.* London: Privately printed, 1931.

Articles and Chapters in Books

Beerbohm, Max. *More Theatres 1898–1903.* New York: Taplinger, 1968, pp. 370–4, 507–10. Reviews of Anstey's plays as they were produced on the London stage.

Grylls, David. *Guardians and Angels: Parents and Children in Nineteenth-Century Literature.* London: Faber & Faber, 1978, pp. 103–07. A literary analysis of *Vice Versa* within the tradition of English school stories.

Spielmann, M.H. *The History of "Punch."* London: Cassell, 1895, pp. 396–401. Recollections of Anstey as a collaborator on the humor journal.

Squire, Sir John. "'F. Anstey,'" *London Mercury*, 29, 174 (April 1934): 517–21.

Obituary survey of his works and personality.

Laurence Senelick

Armin, Robert

Born: King's Lynn, Norfolk, 1569 (?)
Education: Probably grammar school; apprenticed to a goldsmith and later to professional actors
Died: 1616 [?]

Biography

No funny man in history ever originated as many classic comic roles as did the Elizabethan clown Robert Armin. When in 1599 Will Kempe left the Lord Chamberlain's Men, William Shakespeare's acting company, Armin joined the group as a specialist in fool and clown roles. Armin—his nicknames included "Snuffe" and "Pincke"—thus may have originated the roles of Touchstone in *As You Like It*, Thersites in *Troilus and Cressida*, Lavatch in *All's Well That Ends Well*, Feste in *Twelfth Night*, and King Lear's Fool, as well as continuing to act older roles (notably Dogberry in *Much Ado about Nothing*) and those of other playwrights (Abel Drugger in Ben Jonson's *The Alchemist*). No comic ever had such a palette of brilliant parts.

Armin was born in Norfolk, but he had reached London by 1581, when he was apprenticed to a goldsmith there; apprenticeships usually began at about twelve years of age, which suggests that his birth year was around 1569. He may have attended grammar school until his apprenticeship began; he had some knowledge of Latin and Italian. By 1590, he had begun to write and act. His first extant written work is a preface to Gilbert Dugdale's *A Brief Resolution of the Right Religion* in 1590. Armin is mentioned as a writer in Thomas Nashe's *Four Letters Confuted* (1592), in which he is treated as a well-known pamphleteer and comic. None of these early pamphlets remain, but around 1600 he wrote *Foole upon Foole* and *Quips upon Questions*, two popular jest books. Indeed, the former helped stoke a vogue for "fool" books in the first decade of the seventeenth century.

Armin may also have compiled *Tarlton's Jests* (1600; 1616), which contains the famous story in which the great clown Dick Tarlton "made Armin his adopted sonne, to succeed him." Tarlton, by far the most famous clown of his day, prophesies that Armin will "enjoy my clownes sute after me." The profession of clown in Elizabethan England was a hard shop to get into, and Armin would definitely have had to serve an apprenticeship with a "master merryman." If his master was Tarlton, Armin had the very best teacher in the business. But, the *Jests* is the only authority for this story, and Armin may have written it as a self-advertisement. (At one point Tarlton, twelve years dead, reminds the reader that "men may see" Armin "at the Globe.") It is also interesting to note that Will Kempe, Shakespeare's first clown, is referred to by many as Tarlton's heir-apparent.

Armin had a busy career as a comic actor. In the 1590s, he belonged to a traveling troupe called the Lord Chandos' Men (where he often played the role of the clown Grumball); his all-time career move to the Lord Chamberlain's Men came in 1599. For about the next decade he belonged to Shakespeare's company (though not as a shareholder), and his fortunes followed theirs. In 1600, he signs his name as "*Clonnico de Curtanio Snuffe*" ("Snuffe, clown at the Curtain [Theater]"); by 1605, this had changed to "*Clonnico del mondo Snuffe*" ("Snuffe, clown of the world" [i.e., the Globe Theater]). Shakespeare's company had indeed left the Curtain in 1599 and had been at the Globe for more than five years in 1605. Along with the rest of Shakespeare's company Armin became a servant to King James in 1603.

Armin was also a playwright. *The History of the Two Maids of More-clacke* was published in 1609 but was written while Queen Elizabeth was still alive. *The Italian Tailor's Boy* is a translation, and *The Valiant Welshman* was printed around the time of his death. By 1609, he complains that he cannot act as he would like (perhaps because of infirmity). He appears in the list of players for Ben Jonson's *The Alchemist* (1610) and in the list of "Principall actors" in the First Folio of Shakespeare's plays (1623). Nothing is known about his family background or whether he married. He is mentioned as dead in 1616. The time and place of his death are not known.

Literary Analysis

Armin has become the center of a long-standing debate about the development of Shakespeare's comic art. Shakespeare, so goes the argument, wrote with the individual members of his troupe in mind. Around 1599, Shakespeare's comic writing shifts from the knock-about farce of Gobbo in *The Merchant of Venice* and Bottom in *A Midsummer Night's Dream* to the more "verbal" clowning of the Touchstone-Thersites-Feste-Lavatch-Fool line. It just so happens that Shakespeare's company changed fools in 1599. Kempe, who presumably acted the older, rougher clown roles, was replaced by Armin. Perhaps Shakespeare's new angle on clowning, his new sadness, linguistic density, and philosophical depth, derive at least in part from Armin's clowning style.

This argument is interesting because it raises the possibility that someone other than Shakespeare helped write his comic parts. Collaboration was the name of the game in performance art, then as now, and scholars have imagined a wide range of contributions for Shakespeare's clowns. Some believe that the clowns more or less wrote their parts; others have concluded that Shakespeare "gagged" his clowns, allowing little or no ad-libbing on his sacred script.

But if one actually reads Armin's extant written humor, one quickly realizes that the connection between individual clown actors and the nature of their stage characters was a coincidence. Armin's comic forte, at least as a writer, lay in situation and character rather than in words. As H.F. Lippincott points out, *Foole upon Foole* shows that Armin is far more interested in the "natural" fool—the numbskull, dement, village idiot—than in the "artificial" fool who couches great wisdom in his verbal clowning. *Foole upon Foole* purports to be a discussion of "six sorts of sottes" or professional fools. The stories included appear to be quite original for their genre, and some may have a basis in fact. Since Armin claims to have known these fools personally, *Foole upon Foole* has been treated as a historical document by some scholars. Many of his tales have to do with the hard life of the jester in court and abroad. What Armin is most interested in is not truth or language or even characterization, but rather the things done and said in his stories. In the following tale, for instance, the famous jester Will Sommers tries to cheer up Henry VIII with a joke:

> Now tel me saies Wil (if you can,) what it is that being borne without life, head, nose, lip, or eye, and yet runs terribly throgh the world till it dyes?
> This is a wonder quoth the King, and no question, and I know it not: Why quoth

Will it is a fart. At this the King laught hartily, and was exceedingly merry, and bids Will ask any reasonable thing and he would grant it.

Armin's interest lies in the jest and the audience's reaction here. We learn a great deal about the tricks of the jester's trade, including the rough use of the bad jester, the competition and territoriality of professional clowns, and the use of the jester's stick with a carved head (which may have been used like a ventriloquist's dummy). Armin also shows his hand at improvised verse (the jester's stock in trade), as in this thumbnail description of John of the Hospital:

> Some thing tall dribling ever,
> Bodie small merrie never:
> Splay footed visage black,
> Little beard it was his lack.

John, an innocent "natural" fool, also appears in *The History of the Two Maids of More-clacke*. (A woodcut of Armin as John appears on the cover of the printed play.)

Quips upon Questions is meant to be a series of forty-five extempore comebacks on innocent-seeming questions. These show that the humorist had some talent for spontaneous jesting, but even this demonstration is diminished by some very tortured verse. Here is part of one such question-and-answer session. As in much of Armin's humor, it is in dialogue form:

> What is shee?
> What is that Woman: Sir she was a
>   Mayde.
> O, but she is not now. How happens
>   this?
> Yes, sir, she is, but therewith ill apayde:
> Mayde is she, no Mayde by one deede
>   amisse.
> In deede, one deede, which lately for she
>   did,
> From Maydes estate I must her needes
>   forbid.

Obviously, the answer to the question is "She's a whore," although it takes a long time and not too much wit to get there. Armin's three extant plays involve convoluted plots, undistinguished writing, and extremely corrupt texts; it is difficult to find a master writer at work in them.

Armin is a poor versifier, and it is very hard to imagine that he could have had much influence on the wonderful verse spoken by the later Shakespearean fools. Armin's great contribution to his roles, then, must have been in the way that he played them. It is unlikely that he was any less "physical" or any more exclusively "verbal" than other great clowns of the day. That is because, by modern standards, the Elizabethan clown was expected to be astoundingly versatile. Armin would not have gotten far without the ability to sing, dance, tumble, and improvise jokes. As Feste in *Twelfth Night*, for example, Armin would have been expected to dance, impersonate, cross-dress, and sing one- and two-part songs.

Further, like any Elizabethan actor, Armin would have been expected to master a very large number of parts. (Some actors mastered twenty or more parts for ready delivery, a simply astonishing number by our standards.) The "wise fools" of Shakespeare are only the parts that we read most often today; they certainly were not what Armin usually acted, or acted most often. As mentioned, he would have needed to know the older clown roles as well. For instance, he may well have acted the role of the Sommers, Henry VIII's clown, in Samuel Rowley's *When You See Me, You Know Me* (1604; 1616). Sommers is an aggressive, bawdy fool, making telling observations on the serious action, but also showing a talent for physical humor and extemporizing. Sommers is neither wholly physical nor wholly verbal, and neither was Armin's style.

Summary

There is less contemporary testimony to Robert Armin's skills or reputation than there is for Tarlton or Kempe. But, no one could have survived on the Elizabethan and Jacobean stage for twenty years, as it appears that Armin did, without being versatile and very good.

The question remains as to how much of a role to assign to Armin in generating the "wise fools" of Shakespeare. No doubt in actual performance Armin would try to get as much mileage out of his lines as possible, and he probably discussed his parts with Shakespeare as the company prepared plays. Nonetheless, we should probably forgo the idea that Armin could actually have written the "wise fool" roles. This is not to take away from Armin the clown. Rather, it makes clear that the revolution in Shakespeare's clowns had more to do with a revolution in Shakespeare's writing (1599–1600 was, after all, a turning point for him personally and artistically) than it did with a personnel change in his troupe. What this leaves us is the memory of a great clown. Armin achieved fame for two decades as a pamphleteer and actor, and when one scans the parts that he helped to memorialize, one wonders whether any clown will ever have the like opportunity again.

Selected Bibliography

Primary Sources

Preface to *A Brief Resolution of the Right Religion.* London: 1590.

Foole upon Foole, or, Sixe Sorts of Sottes. London: W. Ferbrand, 1600, 1605.

Quips upon Questions. London: W. White, 1600, 1601, 1602.

Tarlton's Jests. London. Registered 1600; printed 1616.

Preface to Gilbert Dugdale, *A True Discourse of the Practises of Elizabeth Caldwell and Others to Poison Her Husband.* London: 1604.

A Nest of Ninnies. London: J. Deane, 1608. An expanded edition of *Foole upon Foole.*

The History of the Two Maids of More-clacke. London: T. Archer, 1609.

Phantasma, The Italian Taylor and His Boy. London: 1609.

The Valiant Welshman. London: R. Lownes, 1615.

Collected Works. Ed. John P. Feather. New York: Johnson Reprint Corporation, 1972. A collection of all the known, and some of the doubtful, productions of Armin's pen.

Secondary Sources

Books

Baldwin, T.W. *Organization and Personnel of the Shakespearian Company.* Princeton: Princeton University Press, 1927. An influential study of how Shakespeare's work was shaped by his fellow players, including the clowns.

Baskervill, C.J. *The Elizabethan Jig.* Chicago: University of Chicago Press, 1929. Discusses the "jig," a popular entertainment form in Elizabethan England, and connects it with the careers of Armin, Kempe, and Tarlton.

Lippincott, H.F., ed. *A Shakespeare Jestbook. Robert Armin's 'Foole upon Foole'* *(1600).* Salzburg: University of Salzburg Press, 1973. A very good study of *Foole upon Foole*, along with a good discussion of Armin's life, literary talent, and place in Shakespeare's works.

Welsford, Enid. *The Fool: His Social and Literary History.* New York: Farrar & Rinehart, 1936. This is the best introduction to the profession of fool in Elizabethan times.

Biographies

Chambers, E.K. "Robert Armin." In *The Elizabethan Stage.* Oxford: Clarendon, 1927. Vol. 2, pp. 229–301.

Cook, Edward D. "Robert Armin." In *Dictionary of National Biography.* Ed. Leslie Stephen and Sidney Lee. Oxford: Oxford University Press, 1960. vol. 1. pp. 558–59.

Articles

Feather, John P. "A Check-List of the Works of Robert Armin." *Library*, 5, 26 (June 1971): 165–72. Feather argues, convincingly, that Armin wrote some of the pamphlets bearing Richard Tarlton's name.

Ingram, William. "Minstrels in Elizabethan London: Who Were They, What Did They Do?" *English Literary Renaissance*, 14 (1): 29–54. This article discusses how the occupation of "minstrel" overlapped with those of the fool and musician.

Somerset, J.A.B. "Shakespeare's Great State of Fools, 1599–1607." In Gray, J.C., *Mirror up to Shakespeare.* Toronto: University of Toronto Press, 1984, pp. 68–81. Somerset argues that Armin's written works make it clear that his interests were hardly in the "wise fool" line.

John Timpane

Armstrong, John

Born: Castleton Manse, Liddesdale, Roxburghshire, ca. 1709
Education: University of Edinburgh, M.D., February 4, 1732
Died: London, September 7, 1779

Biography

Tragicomic and comically tragic, the life of John Armstrong resolved out of a blurring of genres. Armstrong had the discomfiting habit of writing humorously on serious topics, seriously on absurd topics, and confusingly on all topics. His audience seldom knew how to interpret him, either in text or in life; consequently, his formidable capacities often went unused and unrewarded. James Beattie, the Scots poet, reports that Armstrong was temperamentally "inert" as well as abrasive in manner. He was his own worst enemy.

About Armstrong's early life very little is known. Born ca. 1709 in Castleton Manse, Liddesdale, Roxburghshire, he was descended from a Scots family of moderate fortune and less moderate social standing. During his adolescence, he maintained verse correspondences with several leading poets, including James Thomson and David Mallett. Ambitious as the young Armstrong might have been, it was clear from the start that he would need to supplement his literary income with the increments afforded by a trade. Medicine was his choice, a natural enough selection considering the vigorous tradition of medical research in the universities of eighteenth-century Scotland. Armstrong's Edinburgh degree, however, conferred no guarantee of success. The intense rivalry between Scots and English physicians pushed Armstrong to the perimeters of professional society, a serious predicament in a period during which social connections were equal with competence in securing generous patients.

After taking his medical degree at Edinburgh in 1732, Armstrong migrated to London, where he opened a practice in 1735. The "physician and poet," as the catalogue of the British Library describes him, had already drawn attention to himself by publishing a selection of best-selling medical pamphlets—many on the topic of his doctoral dissertation, venereal disease. Ten years of meager income but ample publication was consummated by Armstrong's appointment as Physician to the Hospital for Lame, Maimed, and Sick Soldiers, in London (1746). Through this post Armstrong was able to befriend the middle management of the military, finally securing for himself, in 1751, the lucrative position of Physician to the King's Army in Germany (this segment of the army was composed of those divisions of the King's Army that were engaged in European wars). Armstrong's Teutonic encampment lasted several years. Upon his return, he qualified for a lifelong half-pay pension, certainly not enough to support a high-profile lifestyle but sufficient to ease his chronic fiscal

urgencies. Armstrong eventually accumulated enough money to make a miniature, late-life grand tour in 1770 at the age of sixty-one. He toured France with Henri Fuseli, the visionary painter. One of his continental calls was on Tobias Smollett, the picaresque novelist, who was taking the cure at Leghorn. By the end of his life Armstrong had published enough poetry to earn the right to regular ridicule, the most notable of his verse critics being the satirist Charles Churchill.

Armstrong died on September 7, 1779 in his apartment in London. To everyone's surprise, he left behind a mattress stuffed with a large sum of money, amalgamated either through thrift or through sources of income that have vanished from the historical record.

Literary Analysis

If Armstrong had accomplished nothing else, the attribution to him by the editor of the *Dictionary of National Biography* of the most "nauseous" poem ever written would be reason enough to celebrate him. Armstrong's unsympathetic biographer alludes to *The Oeconomy of Love* (1736), a misguided piece through which Armstrong had intended to discourage masturbation. This literary non-masterwork may not be by any strict definition a comic work, but it symptomatizes the confusion that surrounds the classification of and reaction to Armstrong's works. It thus helps to explain this bumbling bard's perpetual career problems.

The *Oeconomy* tries to mediate the contemporary quarrel over autoeroticism. Rather than affect the punitive, retributive, and clinical discourse of his medical confreres, Armstrong turns to verse. He affects a hieratic, Miltonic style, deploying ringing blank-verse iambs to warn against excessive self-induced pleasures. Unfortunately for Armstrong, by the middle of the eighteenth century the Miltonic style had been linked with mock-heroic poetry, especially the mock-Miltonic spoofs of John Philips. The knee-jerk reaction to Armstrong's medical-Miltonic exercise was one of nervous laughter, not edification. For bridegrooms of the eighteenth century, for example, the discovery that a bride was less than a virgin was no small or laughing matter. Armstrong, never reluctant to take on the toughest topics, portrays such an encounter in a serio-comic scene that joins the sanctimoniousness of Milton with the beer-barrel comedy of John Gay and John Philips:

But hapless he,
In nuptial Night, on whom a horrid Chasm
Yawns dreadful, waste and wild; like that thro' which
The wand'ring *Greek*, and *Cytherea's Son*,
Diving, explor'd Hell's adamantine Gates:
An unessential Void; where neither Love
Nor Pleasure dwells, where warm Creation dies
Starv'd in th' abortive Gulph; the dire Effects
Of Use too frequent, or for Love or Gold.

Armstrong's absurd juxtaposition of domestic disappointment against the strains of religious epic tempts us to smile while his gravely didactic refrains keep our lips tense, even pursed. Is this a comedy or a sermon—or both? Armstrong compounds the problem of generic compartmentalization both by his extraordinary periphrases (the penis becomes the "tumid Wonder") and by his good-natured, lighthearted, coffee-house style. He educates with candy rather than sticks, holding out the prospect of becoming a happy parent of many healthy children to those whom he fears might be tempted inadvertently to diminish their reproductive capacities through autoerotic overkill. Armstrong's Augustan audience, alas, thought the versifying physician was treating a subject of high seriousness with untoward waggery. He picked up the reputation of a pornographer and panderer. Armstrong never quite erased the stigma of his early work, his publication of an expurgated edition of the *Oeconomy* in 1768 only making matters worse rather than better.

Had Armstrong not inadvertently sullied his reputation, he doubtless would have joined the Earl of Chesterfield, Horace Walpole, and Tobias Smollett among the masters of soft comedy, mirthful didacticism, and cheerful diaries. Armstrong is the unsung master of that mock-Miltonic strain that had vaulted Philips and his followers into fame. With elegance, poise, and wit, he invokes his muse to sing not of the creation of the world but of the dire penalties for self-stimulation: "Thy bounties, *Love*, in thy soft raptures when / Timeliest the melting Pairs indulge, and how / Best to improve the genial joy, how shun / The snakes that under rosy plea-sures lurk, / I sing: If thou fair *Cytherea* deign / Gracious to smile on my attempt" (*Oeconomy of Love*). One reason that Armstrong's readers could not overcome their initial assumption that Armstrong was writing humorously was that a good deal of Augustan humor turned on this very ability to treat shocking topics in dainty ways or to treat dainty topics in shocking ways.

The same comic sensibility suffuses Armstrong's most serious pieces. In his *An Essay for the Abridging of the Study of Physick* (1735), a deadly serious attack on medical education and the health profession, he unexpectedly inserts a comical dialogue between four mythological characters, Mercury, Hygeia, Charon, and Pluto, who were traditionally associated with healing (or its failure). "To secure my self from having a *Pill* or *Powder* cramm'd down my Throat too, not a Rag of a Quack comes into the Boat as long as I'm Master," declares Charon. In Armstrong's sharp, bumpkinish, scatological humor we hear the cadences of great future novelistic buffoons like Smollett's Lieutenant Bowling or Frances "Fanny" Burney's Captain Mirvan.

Like so many moderately well-to-do gentlemen of his period, Armstrong was an avid diarist. He might not have kept a personal diary punctiliously, but he often published his work in the form of personal sketches set down in private journals by pseudonymous characters, chiefly "Lancelot Temple, Esq." and "Noureddin Ali, formerly of Damascus." The "Lancelot Temple" materials, published as *Sketches or Essays on Various Subjects* (1758), describe a program for the production of humorous personal histories.

> The sententious Manner of Writing is apt to be too dry, and to give Disgust by its oracular Air and a dogmatical overbearing Pretension to Wisdom. Perhaps it would be better if its Severity was alleviated with a comfortable Mixture of human Nonsense. For to be Perpetually *wise*, is forbidding, unsocial, and something that does not become human Nature.

Influenced by Lord Shaftesbury and the Abbe Morvan de Bellagarde, Armstrong counsels the shuffling and disordering of dry, intellectural pieces. Broken up into witty remarks, he hopes that prose potsherds might congregate again into pleasing, amusing artifacts. In his *Sketches* he presents an array of light parodies of a variety of wisdom literatures, from almanacs to medical handbooks. He counsels, "abstain from hemlock, henbane, deadly mandrake, arsenic, sublimate, & c., for most physicians agree, that all these plants are more or less unwholesome." Darting from point to point, Armstrong makes the point that the making of points is occasionally funny.

Writing in the persona of Noureddin Ali in *The Muncher's and Guzzler's Diary* (1748), Armstrong demonstrates his fragmenting technique. He builds a delightful parody of farmer's almanacs out of a scaffold of tautologies: "If the wind does not blow from the south this month, we shall have it from the east or the north, except it comes from the west. For my own part, I have never yet known a south wind blow from the north-east; tho' I have oftener than once felt an easterly blast from the south-west"—and so forth. Armstrong's title for this work is itself something of an amusing orgy of onomastic emissions: *The Muncher's and Guzzler's Diary: The Wits', the Critics', the Conundrumist's, the Farmer's, the Petit-Maitre's Pocket Companion: The Jacobite's, the Whig's, the Freethinker's, the Methodist's Breviary: The London, the Rome, the Constantinople, the Pekin, the Cairo, the Mexican, the Brentford Calendar: the Gentleman's, the Lady's, the Old Woman's, the Child's Manual: The Male, the Female, the Hermaphrodite Prognosticator: The Mole's, the Salamander's, the Butterfly's, the Whale's, the Allegator's [sic], the Phoenix's, in a Word, The Universal Almanac.*

Armstrong wrote a great many didactic poems, most of which have been rendered technologically obsolete. Yet even in his relatively dry disquisitions on good taste, courteous behavior, benevolence, and assorted abstract virtues, Armstrong finds a way to turn a witty phrase. He proves his point about the importance of the superior senses by conjecturing about Horace's skill as a *cuisineur*: "The grosser Senses too, the Taste, the Smell, / Are likely truest where the Fine prevail: / Who doubts that *Horace* must have cater'd well?" (*Taste*, 1753). Both Milton and antiquity get roasted as Armstrong serves up satire on a lazy Susan—er, lazy *Paradise Lost*. Lest he ignore Catholic while relishing Protestant intellectuals, Armstrong looks for the same combination of etiquette, instruction, and wit in famous Roman clerics. In his *Sketches* he notices that "Though there may be something awkward and imperti-nent in what, as a superficial spectator, I am going to say, Clement the fourteenth has an appearance and manner very agreeable. If one may presume to judge from a few transient views, there is a pleasant good-natured Archness in his Look." Armstrong's remark carries a special pungency when we remember that he was one of the foremost advocates, during the Enlightenment, of the doctrine of physiognomy, the theory that people's looks reflected their characters. In the person of Clement, Armstrong discovers the most salient of all examples of the convergence of didacticism and good humor. Clement personifies Armstrong's theory of comedy.

Armstrong is one of those lost men of the literary tradition. The talk of the town but someone who, owing to his choice of salacious subject matter, could not be talked about, he managed to bury himself in his own fame. His prose and poetry sail smoothly, slickly, and speedily over the sea of comedy in a way that would daunt the bravest admirals of the buffooning armada, but his elusiveness and his resistance to easy classification make him ineligible for study by all but the most persistent. Sir Walter Ralegh once said of Lord Halifax that only the English literary tradition was rich enough to overlook so great a genius; so with Armstrong, no one label, discipline, or approach has been able to build a plinth adequate to display his enormously admirable works and witticisms.

Summary

John Armstrong blew away his audience with a bellows-full of breezy puffs. Socially handicapped by an unadvised pseudo-mock-heroic on masturbation, he tried to make up for the deficit by penning poems, chapbooks, and textbooks on such grave topics as "benevolence." Yet even in his heaviest works, his didacticism is relieved by grace notes of good wit. Armstrong's style is aphoristic, his sentences or lines beginning on serious chords but ending in mirthful flourishes. In his sketches and pseudonymous diaries he anticipates the gruff but lovable comic characterizations of Smollett, Burney, and all of the great English novelists.

Selected Bibliography

Primary Sources
An Essay for the Abridging of the Study of Physick. London: 1735.
The Oeconomy of Love: A Poetical Essay. London: 1736.

The Muncher's and Guzzler's Diary (written
  under the pseudonym "Noureddin Ali,
  formerly of Damascus"). London: 1748.
Taste: An Epistle to a Young Critic. London:
  1753.
Sketches or Essays on Various Subjects (written under the pseudonym "Lancelot
  Temple, Esq."). London: 1758.

Secondary Source
Gilfillan, G. *Memoirs of Armstrong*. In John
  Armstrong, *Poetical Works*. Ed. G.
  Gilfillan. London: 1858.

Kevin Cope

Auden, W[ystan] H[ugh]

Born: York, February 21, 1907
Education: St. Edmund's School, Hindhead,
  Surrey, 1915–1920; Gresham's, Holt,
  Norfolk, 1920–1925; Christ Church,
  Oxford, B.A. in English, 1925–1928
Marriage: Erika Mann, 1935; no children;
  Auden maintained a relationship with
  Chester Kallman, 1939–1973
Died: Vienna, September 29, 1973

Biography
W.H. Auden was born February 21, 1907 in
York, in northern England, the third and youngest son of George and Constance Bicknell
Auden, members of the professional middle
class. George Auden was a doctor, and
Constance Bicknell, daughter of the Vicar of
Wroxham, was educated at London University,
where she became a nurse. George was widely
read in Saxon and Norse antiquities and passed
that interest on to his youngest son. But, Wystan
remained closest to his mother, reflecting often
that the closeness that he shared with her had
affected him as an adult; he believed that his
homosexuality grew out of his close identification with his mother.

In 1908, Auden's family moved from York to
Birmingham and settled in Solihull, a mining village situated at the southeastern edge of the city
and the place where Auden discovered his fascination for things mechanical and for the bleak
landscapes of industrial cities, their smoking chimneys and sooty factories, and their imposing gas-
works. Auden never lost his fascination for such
desolate places which inspired what came to be
known as the "Pylon School" of poetry.

Wystan was a boarder at St. Edmund's, a
boys' prep school at Hindhead in Surrey, which

he attended from 1915 to 1920. With fellow
pupil Harold Llewellen Smith, Auden formed
the St. Edmund's School Literary Society in
1920. In the same year, Auden left St. Edmund's
for a public school, Gresham's, in Holt.

In 1925, having won a scholarship in natural science, Auden settled into Christ Church
in Oxford with classmates Cecil Day Lewis,
Louis MacNeice, Richard Crossman, Stephen
Spender, and (Sir) John Betjeman. In 1926 and
1927, his work was published in the annual
series of volumes by Oxford undergraduates,
Oxford Poetry. In 1928, he went down from
Oxford, having taken a Third on his examinations for the B.A. degree and spent the next year
in Berlin with a former classmate from St.
Edmund's, Christopher Isherwood.

By 1930, Auden was hired as a schoolmaster at Larchfield Academy, a private boys'
school. At this time T.S. Eliot commissioned
him to write book reviews for the *Criterion*. By
1932, Auden was preparing the first edition of
The Orators for publication; it was completed
in February and published in May. Auden left
Larchfield Academy that summer and accepted
an invitation to stay in London with his friend,
Robert Medley, who encouraged Auden's involvement with the Group Theater, officially
constituted in the winter of 1932. Auden again
found work as a schoolmaster, this time teaching at the Downs School in Colwell. Until 1935,
Auden supported himself by teaching at the
Downs School and tutoring in London. In
1933, he wrote *The Dance of Death* for the
Group Theater and sent off a copy to Faber &
Faber. The one-act play was published even
before it was performed onstage. In 1934,
Auden saw the publication of his first American
volume, *Poems*, by Random House. The
Isherwood-Auden political satire, *The Dog
Beneath the Skin*, was published in May 1935
after much revision, and his next Group Theater Project, *The Ascent of F6*, was published
in 1936. In 1935, Auden married Erika Mann,
the daughter of Thomas Mann, so that she
could escape from the dangerous political situation in Germany on a British passport. Although the marriage was never consummated,
Mr. and Mrs. Auden never divorced and remained lifelong friends.

After three more years of teaching, Auden
left the Downs School, finding employment as
a writer and assistant director with a film unit
attached to the British General Post Office
(GPO) under documentary filmmaker John

Grierson. During his six months with the GPO, Auden met the young composer Benjamin Britten, also a member of the GPO. Britten's music and Auden's verse combined in *Night Mail*, a documentary about the "Postal Special" train that ran nightly from London to Glasgow. Other films for which Auden shared responsibility were *Coal Face*, *Calendar of the Year*, and *God's Chillun* (which was never released).

From 1936 until 1939, Auden traveled extensively, first to Iceland, then to Spain to drive an ambulance for the Spanish Loyalists (his services were declined). In Iceland he met MacNeice, and together they produced a travel book, *Letters from Iceland*, published by Faber & Faber, who also subsidized the Iceland trip. In 1937, Auden won King George's Gold Medal for his volume of poems, *Look, Stranger!* (1936), also published by Faber & Faber (as *On This Island* in America).

By 1939, following a sojourn in war-torn China with Isherwood when the two writers were commissioned by Faber & Faber and Random House to co-write a travel book (*Journey to a War*, 1939), Auden emigrated to the United States, where, on May 6, 1946, he became an American citizen. During World War II, Auden was made an honorary major in the U.S. Army, serving with the Strategic Bombing Survey for the U.S. Army in Germany.

For the next thirty years, Auden continued to travel and to write as well as to teach in a number of American schools and universities, starting in 1940 and again in 1946 at the New School for Social Research, New York. Auden lectured at Oxford University as Professor of Poetry.

The 1940s and 1950s were prolific periods for Auden in terms of his writing, and he earned numerous awards and recognition for his poetry and drama, but he would never be named Poet Laureate. He and Chester Kallman also collaborated on a number of opera librettos for Britten and Igor Stravinsky. Throughout 1940, the poet was a member of the editorial board of a little magazine, *Decision*, edited by his brother-in-law Klaus Mann. At this time, Auden also published a new book of poetry, *The Double Man* (reprinted as *New Year Letter* in England). Earlier in the year he had published *Another Time*, the volume of verse that contained the greatest number of his finest, most familiar poems, "Musee des Beaux Arts," "Spain, 1937," "In Memory of W.B. Yeats," and "September 1, 1939" among them.

In 1941, Auden accepted a teaching position at the University of Michigan, and he participated in his first Writer's Conferences at Olivet College. In August of the same year, his mother died, and his distress at her death provided the inspiration for him to write a Christmas Oratorio in her memory. He called it "For the Time Being."

In 1942, Auden was awarded a Guggenheim Fellowship and took an appointment as Lecturer in English at Swarthmore College, as well as a second teaching job at Bryn Mawr. In March 1945, Auden was the recipient of a $1,000 poetry prize awarded by the American Academy of Arts and Letters.

Auden continued to elicit teaching engagements following the war, first at Bennington College in Vermont in 1946, and then in 1947, he taught religion at Barnard College. The next year, Auden was awarded the Pulitzer Prize for *The Age of Anxiety* (1947). In 1949, Auden delivered the Page-Barbour lectures at the University of Virginia. These lectures became the subject of his next book, *The Enchafed Flood* (1950). Another new volume of poetry, *Nones*, was published in 1951. He returned to teaching at Smith College in Massachusetts in 1953. In January 1954, Auden was the recipient of the Bollingen Poetry Prize and was also appointed to the poetry advisory committee of the National Arts Foundation, the precursor of the National Endowment for the Arts. *The Shield of Achilles* (1955) earned Auden a National Book Award.

In 1956, Auden was nominated for the Oxford University Professorship of Poetry. The Professor was required to give one lecture during each term for a period of five years. Auden was declared the winner of the election in February, and he arranged to give his inaugural address in June. The following year, he began his Professorship at Oxford, and the lectures that he gave there were later collected and revised for publication in a volume entitled *The Dyer's Hand* (1962).

On May 3, 1957, Auden's father died. In June the writer learned that he had won the Feltrinelli Award in Italy, which provided a cash award as well. With the cash, Auden and Kallman purchased a farmhouse in the village of Kirchstetten, Austria, where they would return each April to spend the summer.

Auden's next award was the Poetry Society of America's gold medal "for distinguished service to poetry" on January 23, 1959. Early in 1962, Christ Church elected Auden to an Honorary Studentship, or fellowship.

While in New York, Auden was a frequent guest on radio and television programs and supported himself by reviewing books and giving poetry readings. In June 1964, he received an honorary degree from Swarthmore College and in October he attended the international PEN conference in Budapest. In the autumn, Auden was a participant of the artists-in-residence project sponsored by the Ford Foundation and for six months he lived in West Berlin. At the same time, Auden also took part in the Congress of African and European Writers and learned that he had won the Austrian State Prize for European Literature. In the spring of 1967, Auden won yet another literary award, the 1967 National Medal for Literature, presented by the National Book Committee.

By 1970, although his health was visibly declining, Auden continued to give poetry readings and to speak at all manner of symposia; in December, he was part of a visiting scholar program at the Downstate Medical Center in Brooklyn, New York. Auden spent his last winter, 1972, in New York, preparing a return to Christ Church in April, where he was given permanent tenancy of a cottage there.

Auden continued to attend international poetry conferences, reviewing books and continuing to write and edit his poetry. In September 1973, Auden and Kallman went to Vienna where, on September 28, Auden gave a poetry reading at Palais Palffy for members of the Austrian Society for Literature. The next morning, September 29, 1973, he was found dead in his bed. Although he was offered a place of honor in Poet's Corner in Westminster Abbey and received a plaque there in 1974, Auden's wish was to be buried in Kirchstetten, Austria, where he had spent many happy summers. On Thursday, October 4, 1973, he was buried after a simple graveside service in the village churchyard.

Literary Analysis

For over forty years, Auden took his calling as poet and a dramatist quite seriously yet never altogether solemnly. Throughout his lengthy career, Auden showed himself to be virtually indefatigable in stylistic versatility and in the sheer volume of his artistic and critical works. Although he thought of himself first and foremost as a poet, he created with equal skill and intelligence plays and opera libretti; in addition, he was an editor of little magazines and books, a skillful translator, a regular contributor to periodicals in the United States and abroad, and a consistently witty and incisive book reviewer. Auden wrote for film and radio, and collections of his literary criticism and reviews, *The Dyer's Hand and Other Essays* (1962), as well as his prefaces, introductions, and "afterwords" (*Forewords and Afterwords*, 1973) reveal him to be a literary critic of major stature. As a Shakespearean critic, his analyses are both evaluative and appreciative. His is not the formal, systematic criticism associated with Eliot or I.A. Richards but tends more toward what is sometimes called theoretical criticism. However, it is his poetry for which Auden is most often read and studied today, and his poetry survives in the same way that he declares that Yeats's poetry will survive: it may make nothing whatever happen, but it will remain as a standing judgment of the world which it cannot change. For Auden, in the end, poetry becomes celebration, an instrument of healing and forgiveness; it is a poetry inspired by his intellectual and spiritual quest to understand the paradox of man as fallen yet free, and to come to terms with the spiritual dangers of his artistic calling.

No one can discount the tremendous influence of Eliot's *The Waste Land* on poets of the 1930s, especially Auden, for it was Eliot's groundbreaking dictum that the subject matter of poetry need not be beautiful or extraordinary that excited the imaginations of poets known as the Auden Group, for their world had become increasingly ugly. Eliot's use of quotation, his creation of stark yet highly visual imagery, and even his forays into obscurity offered a vision of what the world had come to as a result of the errors of past generations. Auden and those of his literary set were determined to show the way to preventing the same kinds of errors through their creation of literary works that were modes of action that could make something happen and that assigned the poet/artist a very active role in the creation of such works.

Auden's artistic career is generally divided into three periods or "stages," each period marked by particular themes or preoccupations. "Early Auden" identifies the period 1930–1938, wherein the poet assumes the positions of smirking schoolboy and monitor, social critic and detached clinician, the diagnostician of the ills of a society in which he finds more to deplore than to admire. Alienation, isolation, and history as an immutable force are recurring themes. By the end of 1938, Auden's poetry reflects a shift in perspective from the private realm of dense, sometimes obscure schoolboy humor and inside jokes, revolutionary politics, and psychological theory to the public realm, where the poet exhorts, warns, even prophesies: "To-morrow, perhaps the future . . . But to-day, the struggle."[1]

The years 1939–1949 mark what is often called Auden's American period. Having emigrated to the United States in January 1939, Auden's self-imposed exile from England suggests that he was responding both to the crisis facing Western Europe, another World War, and to an artistic, ideological crisis that was deeply personal, for Auden realized that poetry would make nothing happen. The answer to crisis and to public chaos was not liberal ideology or politics. The end of the epoch, another recurrent theme, and the failure of art to influence the outcome of history meant that the convictions and the cliches of what came to be known as the "Auden Generation" had been sham, though well-intentioned. In America, Auden moves gradually from diagnostician to healer. Love becomes possible through human sympathy and empathy. The author's preoccupation with quests during the 1930s moves from a quest for physical love toward a quest for a more Christian kind of love. In America, he responds to a society at odds with Christianity, a society in opposition to the directives of *agape*.

From 1948 to 1973, Auden assumes the role of grand old man of his genre; critics have remarked that during this period he seems more settled, less strident. There is less smartness for its own sake in his poetry. Auden's shifts in artistic and philosophical perspective reveal an artist becoming more certain that the cure for social ill, for the foibles of men, is still love, but that love is now celebrated because it can be achieved through Auden's vision of *agape*—his knowledge that the cure for man's guilt and sinfulness is Christian grace—forgiveness rather than blame, celebration rather than proclamation.

While never considered an essentially humorous poet, during this final period Auden writes poetry that is more relaxed, more conversational, lighter in tone and technique, and, finally, more comic. Politics and public matters figure much less frequently in the works of his final years. Critics, in general, have found Auden's works following *The Age of Anxiety*

(*The Shield of Achilles* [1955], *Homage to Clio* [1960], *About the House* [1966], *City Without Walls* [1969], *Epistle to a Godson* [1972], and *Thank You, Fog* [1974]) less memorable than his 1930s poetry, which is unsteady in tone, questionable in taste, and still too-too clever. But, by the end of his career, Auden had shifted to subjects that were more personal and that paid homage to earthly happiness and the natural world, to a more settled domesticity and a celebration of ordinary human activities. Critics saw these changes as evidence that Auden had gone soft, that he had undergone a religious re-conversion, personally *and* artistically. Still, the writer's final period signifies no more than the maturity of a restless mind and the opportunity once more to exercise his tremendous range and virtuosity. The intellectual quest has given way to acceptance and celebration. Life has become for him a secular pleasure rather than a religious necessity. If there is one line of Auden's that forms a continuous thread throughout his career, it would be "Bless what there is for being" ("Precious Five").

As he matured, Auden insisted that art was "a game of knowledge," a "conjuring trick"[2]; however, his emphasis was increasingly on gamesmanship. By 1973, Auden had come as close as he would be able to in resolving the tensions apparent in his poetry throughout his career: the relation between art and moral purpose, the possibility of art imposing an order on life beyond man's puny power, and the relation of art to truth. Auden insisted to the end that art could not be separate from the ethical activity of producing it: if art and life can effect consequences for each other, art alone cannot express man's fullest vision of life, nor can it lead man to the entire truth about himself and his place on the grand stage of life. What art can do, and in a way least painful, is to lead man to a greater awareness of what he is like. Nevertheless, it is man's choice as to what he is to do about his discovery. Through comedy, art could reveal man's deficiencies and excesses in all their farcical glory. When the later Auden advanced to a poetry of acceptance, his advancement revealed an acceptance of the disparities and incongruities in human existence, an acceptance of the way man is, and of the difficulty of his choices in the face of ethical necessity. Auden's comic vision, unlike the satire of his verse before 1950, treats its subjects with compassion and sympathy instead of judgment. Although men are sinful and imperfect, they are fundamentally good. Their behavior is often absurdly funny, but Auden's laughter is always empathetic.

Ever conscious of his reading public but often uncertain as to how to reach it, the early Auden sought to speak as though readers were part of the in-group, appealing to their outlook and their opinions, taking their side in what he believed to be the need for a more progressive art that would help bring about change, change not only in poetic form and style, but actual social and political change. Poetry, for the early Auden, could be a means of influencing world events; we have only to read *Spain* or *In Time of War* (1938) to see that "The dangers and the punishments grew greater; / And the way back by angels was defended / Against the poet and the legislator" (2, *In Time of War*).[3] The decade of the 1930s was a period of grimness and uncertainty, and at nearly every turn observers tended to agree that crisis loomed for Great Britain. Early in the decade, the manifestations of this crisis were seen in largely economic terms. In Auden's poem "Get There if You Can," written in April 1930, the depression landscapes, the debris of machines long stilled, and the images of decay and disuse all illustrate the continuing preoccupations of the literary prophets comprising the Auden Generation.

It was also during this period that Auden began to devise his particular philosophy of the comic; he had remarked to his friend John Pudney as early as 1931 that, in spite of the desolation of the times, or perhaps because of it, "On the whole, I believe that in our time it is only possible to write comic poetry; not the *Punch* variety, but real slapstick."[4] Thus, we have *The Orators* (1932). In the midst of the economic, social, and political chaos of England in the 1930s, it is Auden's voice that cries out: "O teach me to outgrow my madness!"

Stylistically, Auden's manner during the 1930s became a collective idiom; young English poets became unabashed imitators and disciples of the precocious young poet from Oxford. His poetry is packed with the everyday details of social life, rife with psychological observations about human behavior; his public themes—the rise of fascism in Europe, unemployment in England, decaying factories, and rusting locomotives—bespeak a politically conscious artist. What characterizes Auden's poetry most during his early career and to the end is his ability to create a mood rather than a particular voice or persona without abandoning what have since

come to be defined as "Audenesque" qualities: landscapes and maps, catalogs and lists, isolated heroes, quests and journeys. Sometimes the early Auden is luxuriantly clever, flip, mocking; at other times, he is the austere, detached clinician, reporting the observations that his scientist's eye records. Looking for order where there is none, he strives to create it:

> About suffering they were never wrong
> The Old Masters, how well they understood
> its human position; how it takes place
> While someone else is eating or opening
> a window or
> Just walking dully along . . . ("Musee des
> Beaux Arts," *Another Time*)

Moreover, in most Auden poems there is a heavy use of definite articles, the effect of which is to allow readers to participate in his sometimes obscure private experiences. This classifying, specifying impulse allows the poet to chart reality as something known and intelligible, yet the effect is of distance between the speaker and his subjects: "To lie flat on the back with the knees flexed / And sunshine on the soft receptive belly, / " (18, 9, *Poems, 1931–1936*).

Disturbing syntax, the use of strange adjectives, and the use of the vocative—"O where are you going? said reader to rider"—and sometimes bizarre or overreaching similes are all distinctive of the Audenesque. Joining an abstract idea to a concrete fact creates the unforgettable:

> Lay your sleeping head my love,
> Human on my faithless arm. ("Lullaby,"
> 1–2)

In addition, there is that peculiarly Audenesque sense of humor revealed through tone, diction, and even usage. Auden's tone can be at once ironic, witty, mocking, and sometimes campy: "All of us believe / We were born of a virgin / (for who can imagine / his parents copulating?), / And cases are known / of pregnant Virgins. / But the Question remains: / from where did Christ get / that extra chromosome?" ("The Question"). In the case of this poem, the speaker achieves humor through irreverence, and yet the "truth" of the poem is likewise underscored. In matters of word choice, Auden is an intellectual bowerbird, raiding the *OED* for bright, shiny archaisms, cadging a scrap here and there, jazzing in the modern idiom:

. . . You don't need me to tell you what's
going on: the ochlocratic media,
joint with under-the-dryer gossip
process and vent without intermission
all today's ugly secrets. Imageable
no longer, a featureless, anonymous
threat from behind, to-morrow has us
gallowed shitless: if what is to happen
occurs according to what Thucydides
defined as "human," we've had it,
    are in for
a disaster that no four-letter
words will tardy . . . ("Epistle to a
    Godson," *Epistle to a Godson
    and Other Poems*, 25–36)

Auden's sense of humor, especially early in his career, at times baffled those readers new to the idiosyncrasies of the Auden Group; parody, satire, punning, and name-dropping occurred regularly in his 1930s works. In *The Orators*, among other cronies, Isherwood's name appears, as does Spender's. In the same work, book 2 "Journal of an Airman," Auden skewers sacred cows; Lords Beaverbrook and Rothermere appear as a composite figure, clearly The Enemy: "Beethameer, Beethameer, bully of Britain."

As he matured and tried to understand the nature of his audience, Auden left behind the foolery and self-mockery of British schoolboy humor and satire; he realized that it is one thing to satirize the foibles of one's rather exclusive circle and the circle's objects of satire, for everyone in the circle will understand the joke. Beyond that, though, the problem that so often confronted Auden was the absence of any body of attitudes or beliefs that poet and audience held in common. As a response to the problem of audience, his poetry deepened and sharpened in its wit, its irony replaced with a more compassionate, understanding, or "knowing" sense of the satiric that becomes increasingly more comic than satiric, although many critics believe that Auden was dominantly a satirist. However, Auden himself believed that satire was but a type of comedy. In his essay "Notes on the Comic," in *The Dyer's Hand and Other Essays*, he makes a distinction between the two on the basis of the difference in their effects. Falstaff is comic because in his speech on honor (*Henry IV*, part 1, act 5, scene 2) the disparity between the way he sees himself—"a daredevil who plays highwayman"—and the way he really is, a coward afraid to die on the battlefield—is em-

barrassingly clear. The speech itself, "irrespective of the speaker," is "a comic criticism of the feudal ethic as typified by Hotspur." The comic disparity arises from two conditions: "the circumstances under which the speech is uttered, and the character of the speaker." Satire, however, derives its effect from the writer's judgment of his characters. A political figure can be an object of satire because "though in possession of his moral faculties, [he] transgresses the moral law beyond the call of temptation," often at the expense of others, which is not funny. Satire serves to point up the guilt of both the object of satire and his victims, who share in their own victimization as a result of their vices. Both are guilty. Auden concludes his essay by arguing that formal literary satire is no longer possible in the modern world because satirist and audience diverge in their ideas of how "normal people can be expected to behave . . . satire cannot deal with evil and suffering."[5]

What Auden suggests in the final paragraph of "Notes on the Comic" is that it is no longer possible in the contemporary world for an artist and his audience to share certain moral assumptions. Satire merely trivializes evil and suffering; it seeks to change what is into what ought to be. Nonetheless, Auden understands the art of comedy as a means of helping us accept the contradictions between what is and what ought to be. Comic art persuades us to recognize those contradictions as facts of life against which it is useless to rebel. That is why Auden's satire before 1945 fails to amuse. In the end, he recognized that satire was an inappropriate form of communication for his own age since artist and audience diverged in matters of attitudes and common standards or norms. As Lunatic Clergyman, Auden found that the comic was a better, gentler vehicle for truth; though the matter might be comic, the message could still be serious. Drawing upon Kierkegaard, Auden selected this aphorism, which clearly illustrates his idea of the comic, for the *Viking Book of Aphorisms*: "If a man wants to set up as an innkeeper, and he does not succeed, it is not comic. If, on the contrary, a girl asks to be allowed to set up as a prostitute and she fails, it is comic."

Encouraged by his "discovery" of Kierkegaard, after 1950 Auden seems to have found a philosophy of the comic art that bridges the gaps between comedy and tragedy and helps the artist resolve his own inner conflicts so that they become acceptable unities. The logic of this philosophy is simple: all that a man knows and is comes about as a result of his interaction with the environment. In the vastness of cosmic uncertainty, nothing of this knowledge is ever certain. Man makes up his own world based on what he observes because he can do nothing else. No matter what world man creates as a result, it is always wrong. God alone knows the make-up of the world, and man knows nothing empirically about God; all he can do is blunder about, trying to act certain in the midst of his uncertain universe. Divine necessity impels man to seek out and know God, who, by definition, is unknowable through limited human means. Since man cannot evade life, he may occasionally seek to escape it, and he does so by choosing different ways of living. Man can choose to accept the absurdity of his predicament, becoming resigned and despairing, or he can choose to embrace his lot with joy for its divine beneficence and with humor for the comic spectacle of fallen man attempting to deny what he really is. Kierkegaard rejected neither of these responses. The first he saw as tragic, the second, comic. What he believed was that both responses should be embraced at once because life is both tragic *and* comic.[6] Such a neat resolution of life's comic/tragic paradox suited Auden's own temperamental contradictions. While his comic tendencies are apparent as early as 1930, it is only after his discovery of Kierkegaard that they emerge most fully formed.

Auden's comic sense arises from his innate awareness of and his ability to see the ludicrous side of every situation. Life with its parade of human follies becomes more amusing than painful; it is, at times, gloriously farcical, happily absurd. If satire cannot convey the depth of human suffering without trivializing it, comedy can present suffering as part of a larger comic view of man's attempts at self-knowledge. While never strictly didactic, Auden understood the value of entertaining while obliquely instructing. He also understood that self-knowledge could be a painful quest; why shouldn't the image men saw reflected in art's mirror be the same kind of image men saw reflected in a circus mirror?

Auden fancied that he was more entertainer than instructor, and he seems to have striven for audience surprise as well as amusement. Role-playing became part of the craftsmanship that characterizes Auden's virtuosity. He was reporter and journalist, yes, but as the range of his canon attests, he could just as easily transform himself into any number of personae: a nice old sort, Prospero of *The Sea and the Mirror*, the Horatian or Byronic verse epistolarian of *Letter to Lord Byron*, the domesticated, homey old queen of *About the House*, sanctifying the common and the everyday. Thus, given Auden's boyhood penchant for wearing peculiar hats, it is no coincidence that among his favorite artistic hats was that of a clergyman—a lunatic clergyman, to be sure—and in that role, the over-solemnity with which so many of his readers regarded his poetry could be modified somewhat, although only if readers approached it in the spirit in which it was written: ironic, playful, and parodying, but informed with a restless, probing intelligence. Such poetry virtually demands the quality of lightness, and lightness, or light verse, according to Auden, could be produced only when poet and audience shared the same interests and perceptions. Because light verse "tends to be conventional, to accept the attitudes of the society in which it is written,"[7] Auden believed that it made a much better vehicle for reaching its audience than satire. However, the artistic problem that Auden faced in writing "light" verse was the responsibility of the artist to be both entertaining and truthful. The artist who is close to the everyday life of his audience has a more difficult time being honest and truthful; on the other hand, the artist who stands apart from his audience may find it easier to be honest and truthful, albeit more difficult to communicate with them as one of them.

Auden knew that light verse was truly popular verse, and he believed that its popularity served a social function. Light verse was a poetry of the people, and as Eliot decreed, "modern" poetry did not necessarily have to deal with elevated subjects or Grand Ideas, things which often repulsed modern readers. Light verse appealed to Auden, first, because he was good at it (and through his efforts light verse achieved a certain respectability). Second, light verse was the perfect vehicle for the poet's experiments with popular forms such as ballads, jazz lyrics, and blues. The schoolboy smirking of the prose sections of *The Orators*, the sustained pastiche of "Letter to Lord Byron," and Auden's forays into parody in *The Age of Anxiety* all attest to the poet's facility in different kinds of comic expression. His later works in *About the House* (1966) and his *Goodbye to the Mezzogiorno* (1958) demonstrate his continuing ability to create verse that is "light" yet in no way silly or frivolous.

Finally, it is Auden's approach to subjects not commonly associated with comedy or lightness that gives his light verse its charming eccentricity and audience appeal. Very traditional forms, like ballads, come dancing to life thanks to Auden's gift for creating contrast and balance; the humor is very often ironic and depends upon the poet's facility with compression, brevity, and apposition of what the poem says and the associations that it brings to mind. Ironic ballads like "Victor," about a man who has murdered his unfaithful wife, and "Miss Gee," about an old maid whose virginity implodes into cancer which kills her, are comic because they fulfill an essential of the comic: they demonstrate the conflict between what is and what should be.

Unfortunately, what Auden intended and what often did not come through in his light and comic verse after 1940 was his sharpening sense of the comic state of all human beings. In a world beset by social, economic, and political chaos, the poet's voice, he believed, should be the one stabilizing force that attempts to draw order and sanity from chaos. In order to do this, the poet must try to understand: if sinful, fallen man can manage to smile ironically at what he recognizes to be his foibles, then perhaps his bumbling attempts to transcend them or deny them or ignore them might be forgiven. Man's complacency, unawareness, and self-deception become Auden's satiric and then comic targets. But, the poet remains sensitive to the dilemma that artists face: they cannot easily represent both Truth and the human condition, which suffers an aversion to the Truth and to Truth-tellers: "Can poets (can men in television) / Be saved? . . . / And all poor s-o-b's who never / Do anything properly, spare / Us in the youngest day when all are / Shaken awake, facts are facts" ("Compline").

What lends itself well to the humor that seems so often just beneath the surface of an Auden poem is, finally, his technical virtuosity, for Auden is unmatched in the ease and variety of his use of numerous traditional poetic forms. He is a recognized master of the sonnet; his facility with ballads, ironic odes, lyrical verse, the villanelle, and even clerihews and what he called "Shorts"—witty, pungent epigrams—is one reason that he was so often dismissed as a writer of pastiche and light colloquial verse. Still, his use of the mock-heroic

epic form for his longer works succeeded during a time when the longer poem was all but dead. *The Age of Anxiety* (1947), which Auden subtitles a "baroque eclogue," is a pastoral form unsuited to the poem's setting, a bar in New York, and its subject matter, four modern-day denizens of that bar during World War II. *The Age of Anxiety* is full of Auden's imitation of Old English metric patterns counterpointed by the characters' catalog of modern-day pettinesses, revealed in what they say. In conjoining the remoteness of Anglo-Saxon tone and vocabulary with the modern idiom, Auden creates irony between an epic measure and the banality of modern men's apparent concerns and the elusiveness of their real concerns. The "baroque" element uses wit as a means of vision. The reader is affected as a result of the shock and extravagance of the comic (yet sympathetic) undercurrent while, at the same time, the seriousness of the work and its central theme, the conditional reasons for men's anxiety, are in no way diminished. Such is Auden's uniqueness of poetic expression, his response to the conditions of modern life. Yet Auden's penchant for the unusual also accounts for the sometimes difficult nature of his poems, particularly, his longer works. But, it must be remembered that an Auden poem in general tends to exploit contrast and the unusual or the peculiar precisely for the comic effect.

Auden himself was "unusual" in that he was one of very few twentieth-century poets who was able to combine talents for writing witty, sometimes brilliantly humorous verse concurrently with the serious. In fact, to find an equally talented artist with a similar capacity for combining the comic with the serious, it is necessary to go back to Byron, a poet whom Auden much admired.

While Auden, early on, attempted to attend to the task of "serious" artists, putting the wasteland in order, to enter into the spirit of modern times, the poet had to devise a philosophy of the comic. And, he understood that sense of the comic to be the perception of individuality in conflict with unchanging forces. Thus, Auden himself observes in "Notes on the Comic" that "a sense of wit and humor develops in a society to the degree that its members are simultaneously conscious of being each a unique individual and of being all in common subjection to unalterable laws." Again, for Auden, the most important element of the comic is contradiction. In the ordinary events of life, this contradiction occurs in "the clash between the laws of the inorganic which has no *telos*, and the behavior of living creatures who do have one." Auden's uniqueness of expression, in conjunction with subjects both common and familiar, results in that contrast between the individual and his inevitable clash with the immovable laws of society; this result, while often comic, even unwittingly so, is never cruel or frivolous. It is Auden's approach to subjects not commonly associated with comedy that gives his light verse its charming but sometimes eccentric comic bite.

Through tone, meter, and a variety of traditional forms, Auden could move from the shameless to the sly confidence, from the leader's exhorting trumpet to the skylarking of a privileged clown. He could speak with the most uncluttered simplicity of tone and image while sometimes reverting to the densest, most symbol-laden obscurity. Whenever Auden has been charged with being "difficult," it is most often because he is an artistic, stylistic chameleon, difficult to pin down. Auden's cheek, however, is easier to trace: it most often arises from his deliberate attempts to flout conventional ideas of poetry as well as artistic decorum, as in this dedication to Isherwood that begins *The Orators*: "Private faces in public places / are much wiser and nicer / than public faces in private places."

Auden's technical expertise very often gives rise to a sense of formality in his verse. His traditional forms, like odes and ballads, spring to life as a result of his gift for creating contrast while at the same time achieving balance between the form and the subject matter of his verse. In his final period, Auden's occasional poems, his greetings, and his verse epistles, far from suggesting any "modernist" preoccupations, very often mimic poets of the eighteenth century—John Dryden and Alexander Pope as well as William Shenstone and Matthew Prior. The witty, urbane civility blends well with the highly personal Audenesque voice. Those many masks, the many voices, the wealth and range of his knowledge make Auden a virtual community of individual talents all in collaboration.

Thus, Auden's artistic career demonstrates a man capable of putting on many faces, and throughout his career it is obvious that he enjoyed experimenting with a wide variety of styles and voices, wearing and discarding those

personae like so many hats. He was the undergraduate Marxist; he was the clinical Freudian; he was the re-converted High Anglican as well as the lunatic clergyman. He aspired to drive an ambulance in Spain during the Fascist uprising, but perhaps because the Spanish had heard of his execrable driving habits, he ended his Spanish sojourn doing what he did best: talking about the war in his poem "Spain." At the end, ill and lonely, dreading death, yet hoping that when it came, it would come quickly and painlessly, he continued to find humor: "In a coughing fit / he felt he was throwing up / hard Capital F's" ("Addenda to 'Profile'").

Politics, religion, psychology, and social awareness characterize much of Auden's poetry and demonstrate his place in the tradition of great English poets. He has the ethical keenness of a John Milton or a William Langland, the wit of a Pope or a Dryden, and the technical facility of a Wilfred Owen or a Gerard Manley Hopkins. His poetry can be, on its face, serious, intellectual, probing, even philosophic; in tone, it can be mocking, ironic, comic, and self-parodying. But above all, Auden knew himself well enough never to take himself too seriously.

Auden was unquestionably a "modern" poet. Though the form might be traditional, "modern" poetry, as demonstrated by Auden, used diction and imagery in startling and unconventional ways. The subject matter, as his limerick, "The Aesthetic Point of View" shows, does not have to be lofty or serious. Such light or occasional verse achieves its comic yet instructive purpose through less-than-serious means:

> As the Poets have mournfully sung,
> Death takes the innocent young.
> The rolling-in-money
> The screamingly funny,
> And those who are very well-hung.

The simple and innocent first lines expressing an obvious cliche in conventional diction give way to colloquial feminine rhymes in lines three and four. The last line is what shocks and amuses in the speaker's use of suggestive slang. The curious turn of an apparently simple idea is what jolts; the shock of the unexpected is what finally pleases. The effect today is the same; the poem shocks less than it amuses. The limerick at first appears frivolous. Indeed, its frivolity is its point since the poem condemns the frivolity and amorality of an aesthetic point of view which appreciates only how interesting or striking a situation is rather than what it means.

Auden's poetry both early and late tends always to illustrate his intellectual and artistic preoccupations, and it is possible to see a shift in these preoccupations shortly after he emigrated to the United States. In the 1930s, his themes are remembered for their sociopolitical significance, and his "message" often involves duality or contradiction, tension and complexity. It is the treatment of recurring preoccupations such as social responsibility, love, quests, the psychological causes of physical illness, the dichotomies between art and life, and man's relation to God that make up Auden's themes in the 1930s. Men and society are seen as sick, and it is a profound soul sickness, taking the form of physical and neurotic sickness. The individual represses his natural urges and, according to Auden's understanding of psychology, that itself is sick. After the 1930s, the poet's themes shift to *agape* love, social engineering, the good life, technology for better or worse, the nature of art, and the dichotomy between history and nature. Freud, Groddeck, and Marx are traded for Kierkegaard; Auden no longer accedes to the impulse to analyze, manipulate, modify, or assess. Subjects, people, and experience become things to delight in. The intellectual quest gives way to acceptance and celebration. With the help of Kierkegaard, Auden recognizes that although men are sinful and imperfect, they are fundamentally good. Their behavior is sometimes absurdly funny, especially when men speak in ostentatious and self-important voices, but Auden's laughter is empathetic, not cruel. He knows that human nature is probably not amenable to change, but he does believe that it can be improved. After 1941, life gradually becomes for him a secular pleasure, not a religious necessity. By 1948, in his essay "Squares and Oblongs" Auden had taken the position that:

> . . . the only popular art will be comic art, like Groucho Marx or Li'l Abner, and this will be unpopular with the Management. Whatever their differences, highbrows and lowbrows have a common enemy, The Law (the Divine as well as the secular), and it is the Law which it cannot alter which is the subject of all comic art. What is not comic will either be highbrow art, or popular or official magic.[8]

Summary

W.H. Auden achieved his literary fame in the 1930s, and he is commonly associated with other prominent British literary figures who also earned recognition for their work at the same time. Cecil Day Lewis, Louis MacNeice, Stephen Spender, and Auden were the principles in what has been called "the Auden Group." Yet, of all the members of the "Auden Group," it was Wystan Hugh who moved far ahead of his peers in both talent and technique. Today he is regarded as a master of light verse, and his comic vision embraces man's tragedies and triumphs. In any examination of modern British literature after Eliot, it is Auden whose name remains a touchstone of the era. In terms of his humor as he demonstrates it in his light and occasional verse, Auden remains a consummate artist who can be satirical, chatty, serious, deliberately corny, slapstick, witty, self-deprecating, and pompously slick without ever taking his tongue out of his cheek.

Notes

1. *Spain* (London: Faber & Faber, 1937).
2. *New Year Letter* (London: Faber & Faber, 1941), p. 90.
3. Unless otherwise noted, all quotations of Auden's poems come from W.H. Auden, *Collected Poems*, ed. Edward Mendelson (New York: Random House, 1976).
4. Quoted in Humphrey Carpenter, *W.H. Auden: A Biography* (Boston: Houghton Mifflin, 1981), p. 129. Carpenter quotes from a letter by Auden to Pudney currently held in the Henry W. and Albert A. Berg Collection, the New York Public Library, Astor, Lennox, and Tilden Foundations.
5. "Notes on the Comic," *The Dyer's Hand and Other Essays* (1962; New York: Vintage, 1968), pp. 371–85.
6. For a more thorough discussion of Auden and Kierkegaard, see Justin Replogle, *Auden's Poetry* (Seattle and London: University of Washington Press, 1969).
7. W.H. Auden, "Introduction," *Oxford Book of Light Verse* (1938; London: Oxford University Press, 1979), pp. vii–xx.
8. "Squares and Oblongs," *Poets at Work*, ed. Charles D. Abbott (New York: Harcourt Brace Jovanovich, 1948), pp. 165–81.

Selected Bibliography

Primary Sources

Verse

Poems. S.H.S. (Privately printed by Stephen Spender), 1928.

Poems. London: Faber & Faber, 1930; rev. ed. 1933; New York: Random House, 1934.

The Orators: An English Study. London: Faber & Faber, 1932; rev. ed. 1966.

Look, Stranger! London: Faber & Faber, 1936; as *On This Island.* New York: Random House, 1937.

Spain. London: Faber & Faber, 1937.

Selected Poems. London: Faber & Faber, 1938.

Some Poems. London: Faber & Faber, 1940.

Another Time. New York: Random House, and London: Faber & Faber, 1940.

The Double Man. New York: Random House, 1941; as *New Year Letter.* London: Faber & Faber, 1941.

For the Time Being: A Christmas Oratorio. New York: Random House, 1944; London: Faber & Faber, 1945.

Collected Poetry. New York: Random House, 1945.

The Age of Anxiety: A Baroque Eclogue. New York: Random House, 1947; London: Faber & Faber, 1948.

Collected Shorter Poems, 1930–1944. London: Faber & Faber, 1950.

Nones. New York: Random House, and London: Faber & Faber, 1951.

The Shield of Achilles. New York: Random House, and London: Faber & Faber, 1955.

The Old Man's Road. New York: Voyages Press, 1956.

Goodbye to the Mezzogiorno. Milan, Italy: All 'Insegna del Pesce D'Oro, 1958.

Selected Poetry. New York: Modern Library, 1959.

Homage to Clio. New York: Random House, and London: Faber & Faber, 1960.

About the House. New York: Random House, 1965; London: Faber & Faber, 1966.

Collected Shorter Poems, 1927–1957. London: Faber & Faber, 1966; New York: Random House, 1967.

Collected Longer Poems. London: Faber & Faber, 1968.

Selected Poems. London: Faber & Faber, 1968.

City Without Walls and Other Poems. London: Faber & Faber, 1969.

Academic Graffiti. London: Faber & Faber, 1971.

Epistle to a Godson and Other Poems. London: Faber & Faber, and New York: Random House, 1972.

Thank You, Fog, Last Poems. New York: Random House, 1974.

Collected Poems. Ed. Edward Mendelson. New York: Random House, 1976.

The English Auden: Poems, Essays and Dramatic Writings 1927–1939. Ed. Edward Mendelson. New York: Random House, 1977.

Plays

The Dance of Death. London: Faber & Faber, 1933.

The Dog Beneath the Skin; or, Where is Francis? Co-authored with Christopher Isherwood. London: Faber & Faber, and New York: Random House, 1935.

The Ascent of F6. Co-authored with Christopher Isherwood. London: Faber & Faber, 1936; New York: Random House, 1937.

On the Frontier. Co-authored with Christopher Isherwood. London: Faber & Faber, 1938; New York: Random House, 1939.

The Rake's Progress. Co-authored with Chester Kallman, opera libretto for Igor Stravinsky. London and New York: Boosey and Hawkes, 1951.

The Magic Flute. Co-authored with Chester Kallman, after the libretto of Schikaneder and Gieske. New York: Random House, and London: Faber & Faber, 1956.

Elegy for Young Lovers. Co-authored with Chester Kallman, opera libretto for Hans Werner Henze. Mainz, Germany: B. Schott's Sohne, 1961.

Die Bassaricen (The Bassarids). Co-authored with Chester Kallman, opera libretto for Hans Werner Henze. Mainz, Germany: B. Schott's Sohne, 1966.

Travel

Journey to a War. Co-authored with Christopher Isherwood. London: Faber & Faber, and New York: Random House, 1939; rev. ed. 1973.

Translations

No More Peace! by Ernst Toller. Trans., with Edward Crankshaw. London: John Lane, and New York: Farrar and Rinehart, 1937.

Caucasian Chalk Circle, by Bertolt Brecht. Trans., with James and Tania Stern. London: Methuen, 1960.

Literary Criticism (a selection)

The Enchafed Flood: or The Romantic Iconography of the Sea. New York: Random House, 1950; London: Faber & Faber, 1951.

Making, Knowing, Judging. Oxford: Clarendon, 1956.

The Dyer's Hand and Other Essays. New York: Random House, 1962; London: Faber & Faber, 1963; New York: Vintage, 1968.

Selected Essays. London: Faber & Faber, 1964.

Secondary Worlds. London: Faber & Faber, and New York: Random House, 1969.

Forewords and Afterwords. New York: Random House, 1973.

Other Works

Letters from Iceland. With Louis MacNeice. London: Faber & Faber, and New York: Random House, 1937.

Journey to a War. With Christopher Isherwood. London: Faber & Faber, and New York: Random House, 1939; rev. ed. 1973.

The English Auden: Poems, Essays and Dramatic Writings, 1927–1939. Ed. Edward Mendelson. New York: Random House, 1977.

Secondary Sources

Bibliographies

Bloomfield, B.C., and Edward Mendelson. *W.H. Auden: A Bibliography 1924–1969*. Charlottesville: University Press of Virginia, 1972. 2nd ed. The fullest bibliography to date.

Biographies

Carpenter, Humphrey. *W.H. Auden: A Biography*. Boston: Houghton Mifflin, 1981. Explores and analyzes Auden's poetry in great detail, in the context of his life; biographical errors (apocryphal stories)

are also corrected here.

Isherwood, Christopher. *Lions and Shadows*. London: Hogarth Press, 1938. London: Methuen, 1985. A pseudo-biography (many of the stories are exaggerated). "Hugh Weston" in the book is really Auden.

Norse, Harold. *Memoirs of a Bastard Angel: A Fifty-Year Literary and Erotic Odyssey*. New York: William Morrow, 1989. Contains a great deal of biographical-anecdotal detail about Auden. Norse, a friend and secretary of Auden's, claims that he was Chester Kallman's lover until Kallman met Auden. Norse depicts the literary and homosexual subculture of the 1930s, 1940s, and 1950s candidly and vividly, especially in his revelations of Auden's sex life.

Osborne, Charles. *W.H. Auden: The Life of a Poet*. New York: Harcourt Brace Jovanovich, 1979. A personal and chatty biography, since Charles Osborne was a personal friend of Auden's. Stephen Spender and John Lehman supplied additional details, making this biography intimate as well as thorough.

Books

Bahlke, George W. *The Later Auden: From "New Year Letter" to About the House*. New Brunswick, NJ: Rutgers University Press, 1970. Bahlke's purpose is to refute the contention that Auden's later work (meaning his poetry after 1944) was silly, shallow, and had lost the force and novelty of his 1930s poetry. The author's focus is on four longer works of Auden's: *New Year Letter,* "The Sea and the Mirror," *For the Time Being,* and *The Age of Anxiety.*

Beach, Joseph Warren. *The Making of the Auden Canon*. Minneapolis: University of Minnesota Press, 1957. The intention of Beach's book, as he himself describes it, is "to present a record of the facts in regards to Mr. Auden's procedure in making up the texts" of his 1945 and 1950 collected editions of poems. Beach attacks Auden's practice of revising previously published poems and his inattention to the chronological order of the poems selected for those collections. Beach argues that Auden's refusal to respect the proper chronology and the original texts of so many of his poems reveals his lack of development as a poet; any individual poem that manifests "success" has achieved that success purely by accident.

Callan, Edward. *Auden: A Carnival of Intellect.* New York: Oxford University Press, 1983. The author elucidates the intellectual and philosophical foundations upon which Auden's art was built. He explores the life of the poet, his world and his work, tracing his poetic development through the political upheaval in Great Britain during the 1930s. Callan says that Auden became aware of the dangers of political Romanticism as he saw the ascension of Adolf Hitler and other self-absorbed romantics during the 1930s. Callan also examines the influence of Christian philosophers and theologians on Auden's later work. Throughout the book, Callan elucidates Auden's intellectual interests, his imagery and mythology, historical events, and influential persons in the context of their contributions to the range and versatility of Auden as a consummate artist.

Everett, Barbara. *Auden.* Writers and Critics Series, No. 042. Edinburgh and London: Oliver and Boyd, 1964. Everett treats the unity of Auden's work in the face of critics who claim that there is no unity in Auden's work. Using Auden's own critical responses to the attacks on his work, Everett shows, in chronological fashion, the thematic elements that can be found in Auden's work from first to last.

Fuller, John. *A Reader's Guide to W.H. Auden.* New York: Farrar, Straus, and Giroux, 1970. This book is mostly a guide to the sources and allusions within Auden's poetry and drama that are considered more "difficult" and in need of commentary. Fuller explores these elements in chronological order and organizes Auden's work into four periods (1927–1932, 1933–1938, 1939–1947, and 1948–1957) and includes a chapter on Auden's work after 1957.

Hoggart, Richard. *Auden: An Introductory Essay.* London: Chatto and Windus, 1951. A survey of Auden's work, tracing his development from the 1930s to 1950. Hoggart includes chapters on Auden's landscapes and their symbolic impor-

tance, his use of various forms and meters, and his change in theme after 1939; also treats Auden's post-war themes.

Hynes, Samuel. *The Auden Generation: Literature and Politics in England in the 1930s.* New York: Viking Press, 1976. A literary study that examines the historical, political, and social milieus existing in Great Britain at the time that Auden and others "came of age" and began writing. The literature of the 1930s and the growth of particular literary forms comprise most of the book.

Mendelson, Edward. *Early Auden.* Cambridge, MA: Harvard University Press, 1983. A critical, interpretive study which delves into Auden's infamous obscurities and more difficult themes from his works up to 1939 and elucidates them clearly. Captures the influence of Auden's childhood and later intellectual development upon the moral foundation of his art. Mendelson notes that Auden "came to write poetry that, more than any other, contributed to the understanding of his time."

Nelson, Gerald. *Changes of Heart: A Study of the Poetry of W.H. Auden.* Perspectives in Criticism 21. Berkeley and Los Angeles: University of California Press, 1969. Nelson studies Auden's attempt during the 1940s to change the temper of his work to a more metaphysical and even "religious" point of view. The poems themselves are examined in the light of this new poetic persona; the ideas and attitudes of characters in Auden's longer works are also examined.

Replogle, Justin. *Auden's Poetry.* Seattle and London: University of Washington Press, 1969. Replogle examines Auden's poetic development, finding in it particular "stages" or periods from the 1930s to the 1960s that move the style and ideas toward his greatest achievement, the comic poetry of the later Auden.

Spears, Monroe K. *The Poetry of W.H. Auden: The Disenchanted Island.* New York: Oxford University Press, 1968. Rev. ed. A chronological investigation of Auden's poetry up to the 1960s, which emphasizes the poetry itself instead of the ideas that underlie the poetry. Spears declares that his aim is to set the facts straight and to provide an unobstructed background and context to understanding Auden's poetry. Includes a bibliography of Auden's major works and provides indexes to both titles and first lines of poems.

Articles

Allen, Walter. "W.H. Auden: The Most Exciting Living Poet." *Listener*, 47 (1952): 640–41. Allen examines the impact of Auden's first publication, *Poems* (1930), in the way that it changed an entire generation's understanding of what poetry was capable of. What is important in this article is Allen's discussion of the manner in which Auden achieved his new poetic landscapes.

Bayley, John. "Our Northern Manichee." *Encounter*, 21 (1963): 74–81. Bayley discusses Auden as literary critic, using *The Dyer's Hand and Other Essays* to reveal the poet as a model of critical firmness and clarity who brings to his criticism the "forthrightness of moral judgment." Auden's particular form of Manichaeanism underscores the dualism between words as objects of play and words as objects of craft.

Cook, F.W. "The Wise Fool: W.H. Auden and the Management." *Twentieth Century*, 168 (1960): 219–27. Auden's comments on the Master/Servant, King/Fool relationship in his article, "Balaam and the Ass: On the Literary Use of the Master-Servant Relationship" (*Encounter*, 3 [July 1954]: 35–53) seem to Cook to assert more than meets the eye: in the article, Cook believes that Auden reveals his own role and methods as Poet, which mirror the function and methods of the Fool as a literary device. Cook uses Auden's own perception of the Fool in *King Lear* to analyze the later poetry.

Jarrell, Randall. "From Freud to Paul: The Stages of Auden's Ideology." *Partisan Review*, 12 (Fall 1945): 437–57. Jarrell claims that after 1939 Auden turned his back on his early belief that poetry could initiate social and political change when he became a Christian. Auden's views, Jarrell says, are psychologically determined: "A complex of ideas, emotions, and unconscious attitudes about anxiety, guilt, and isolation" makes up the heart of Auden's poetics.

Mendelson, Edward. "The Fading Coal vs. The Gothic Cathedral or What to Do about an Author both Forgetful and Deceased." *Text: Transactions of the Society for Textual Scholarship*. Ed. D.C. Greetham and W. Speed Hill. New York: AMS Press, 1985, pp. 409–16. The subject of the article is Auden's infamous habit of revising previously published works and in some cases removing established poems from the body of work he wished to preserve. Mendelson essays two models of the process by which authors compose. In the "fading coal" model the most revealing moment of literary composition is the earliest; whatever follows is pure dross. In the gothic cathedral model "any lengthy work of literature will exhibit thousands of details" that come about after the initial composition; thus, the "finished" work will reflect something entirely different from what its author first intended. There is no clear way of distinguishing composition from revision. Mendelson addresses the nature of the problems faced by textual editors who have no recourse to the authors whose works they edit.

Ostroff, Anthony, ed. "A Symposium on W.H. Auden's 'A Change of Air.'" *Kenyon Review*, 26 (1964): 190–208. George P. Elliott, Karl Shapiro, and Stephen Spender each offer a brief analysis of the poem to which Auden replies in conclusion.

"Sixteen Comments on Auden." *New Verse*, 26–27 (1937): 1–30. Auden's friends and fellow-poets devote short essays to Auden the Man and Auden the Poet: Isherwood writes of the early verse; Spender discusses the development of Auden's "politics"; Geoffrey Grigson provides "Auden as a Monster"; Kenneth Alcott remarks on Auden's connection with the theater; Edgell Rickard provides "Auden and Politics"; Edwin Muir, George Barker, Frederick Prokosch, Allen Tate, Cecil Day Lewis, Graham Greene, Dylan Thomas, and others offer brief comments as well.

Spears, Monroe K. "Late Auden: The Satirist as Lunatic Clergyman." *Sewanee Review*, 59 (Winter 1951): 50–74. Spears argues that modern criticism, in general, is not equipped to elucidate and evaluate the kind of poetry characteristic of Auden. Spears says that "[Auden] is not primarily a lyric poet; his work belongs to a genre with a different purpose and tradition, and it can be properly understood only when it is approached in terms of this convention. For Auden is dominantly a satirist."

Melinda Adams

Austen, Jane

Born: Steventon, Hampshire, December 16, 1775
Education: Brief periods at two schools, one run by Mrs. Cawley, one by Mrs. Latournelle; from age nine, at home under the guidance of her father and brothers
Died: Winchester, July 18, 1817

Biography

Jane Austen was born December 16, 1775, the seventh of eight children born to George and Cassandra (Leigh) Austen, in Steventon, Hampshire. George Austen, a surgeon's son, was left a penniless orphan at an early age but was educated by an uncle, Francis Austen, a successful Tonbridge attorney. He served as a Fellow at his college, St. John's, Oxford, then was ordained in 1760. The next year another relative, Thomas Knight of Godmersham in Kent, presented him with the living (a church benefice) at Steventon, to which his Uncle Francis added that of Deane, a mile and a half away. The income was sufficient for his marriage, on April 26, 1764, though as the family grew, careful planning and economies were required.

Cassandra Leigh was the great-granddaughter of the eighth Lord Chandos and a grandniece of George Frederick Handel's patron, the first Duke of Chandos. Another ancestor, Sir Thomas White, was the founder of St. John's College, Oxford, and the Merchant-Taylor School, while another, Sir Thomas Leigh, was the Lord Mayor of London who escorted Elizabeth I to her coronation. Other family connections included the Duke of Lancaster, the Duke of Marlborough, and William Pitt, prime minister during much of Jane's lifetime. Several of the women who married her brothers could also claim aristocratic descent. The Austen line was not so distinguished, tracing its roots to medieval clothiers who had prospered in both numbers and distinction. However, George was known for his good looks, affectionate and even-tempered personality, and his scholarly abilities, which enabled him to educate his children and other youths. Cassandra was described by her great-nephew as having strong common-sense, a lively imagination, and wit in both conversation and writing.

Their first child, James, was born in 1765, followed by George in 1766, Edward in 1768, Henry in 1771, Cassandra in 1773, Francis in 1774, Jane in 1775, and Charles in 1779. James became a clergyman, serving first at Deane, part of his father's "living," then succeeding his father at Steventon. George was an "invalid" about whom little is known except that he had "seizures" and that he lived apart from the family but was apparently well cared for since he lived to be seventy-two. Edward was adopted by childless relatives, taking their name, Knight, and inheriting their estate. Henry originally planned to become a clergyman but switched to the military service to win the hand of his vivacious, widowed cousin Eliza de Feuillide, who was ten years his senior. Francis and Charles both had successful naval careers.

Jane and her sister Cassandra never married, though both experienced a wide range of family relationships. Jane seems to have had several "almost romances," one of which is thought to have ended in the premature death of the young man. In 1802, Jane was very briefly—overnight—engaged to Harris Bigg-Wither. The sisters were always very close to each other, were popular with their nieces and nephews, and were often called upon to manage their own or their brothers' households in times of childbirth or illness.

Jane's formal education was limited. In 1783, she and Cassandra were sent to school with Mrs. Cawley, widow of the Principal of Brasenose, first in Oxford, then in Southampton, but were brought home to be nursed through severe cases of "putrid fever." In 1784, they tried the Abbey School, at Reading, under Mrs. Latournelle, but soon returned home. Henceforth they read and studied under the guidance of their father and brothers, becoming moderately proficient in French, Italian, English literature, drawing, and piano. That this was an unusually rich, nonformal education is attested to by evidence in Austen's juvenilia of her acquaintance with more than fifty works, including those by William Shakespeare, Joseph

A

Addison, Alexander Pope, Samuel Johnson, Samuel Richardson, Henry Fielding, Horace Walpole, Oliver Goldsmith, Richard Brinsley Sheridan, James Boswell, Johann Wolfgang von Goethe, Frances "Fanny" Burney, Maria Edgeworth, Charlotte Smith, William Cowper, Thomas Grey, and Sir Walter Scott. Furthermore, her brother James was editor of the *Loiterer*, an Oxford journal published in 1789–90. Jane's juvenilia is full of allusions to and ideas from these sources, for the family enriched its somewhat isolated situation by sharing reading, writing, and amateur theatrical performances.

Despite some eye problems—possibly nearsightedness and the strain of working in the inadequate lighting characteristic of the time—at twelve Jane began to spend hours writing humorous sketches and letters. In 1790, she produced the fairly long work entitled *Love and Freindship* (her spelling), and in 1791, "A History of England from the Reign of Henry IV to the Death of Charles the First, by a Partial, Prejudiced, and Ignorant Historian," in which the family's strong Stuart sympathies gave her a vehicle for some adolescent rebellion. There are three volumes of her juvenilia and letters. Unfortunately for scholars, at her death her sister destroyed a large number of her letters, apparently for fear that some of the wit and comments on personal events might be inappropriate for her reputation.

Between 1793 and 1795 she wrote her first novel, the epistolary *Lady Susan*, and began the epistolary *Elinor and Marianne*, which would be revised and published as *Sense and Sensibility* in 1811. During the next two years, she completed *First Impressions*, an early version of *Pride and Prejudice* (1813). By 1798 she had completed *Northanger Abbey*.

In 1800, without consulting Cassandra or Jane, their father decided to retire and move to Bath. Jane disliked Bath, and the loss of the Steventon income was a serious blow to the family's comfort. The sisters' unhappiness was exacerbated by the personality of Mary Lloyd, James's second wife, who now became mistress of Steventon. They were, however, very fond of Mary's unmarried sister, Martha Lloyd, who later became a member of their household after Mr. Austen's death in 1805 and then in 1828 became the second wife of Francis Austen. Mary Austen and the three young women lived in several different lodgings until, in 1809, Edward offered them the Chawton Cottage on his estate in Hampshire. His first wife, Elizabeth,

had just died giving birth to their tenth child. Edward was Cassandra's favorite brother, and she was of considerable assistance to his eldest child, Fanny, who was now in charge of the household. Although the cottage was small, Jane found the courage to renew her writing.

In 1811, she published *Sense and Sensibility*, anonymously, at her own expense. It came out in November, in three volumes. In 1813, *First Impressions* was revised and published as *Pride and Prejudice: A Novel. In Three Volumes. By the Author of Sense and Sensibility*. In 1814, *Mansfield Park* was published, again anonymously and in three volumes. It was sold out by November. In 1815, *Emma*, the revised version of an earlier novel titled *The Watsons*, was finished and published, and *Persuasion* was begun. In 1816, a second edition of *Mansfield Park* appeared and Austen's authorship was generally known, but signs of her final illness were apparent. Modern scholars diagnose the symptoms as those of Addison's Disease, which begins slowly but accelerates, especially under stress. Henry's bankruptcy and a period of serious illness, during which she nursed him, may have hastened Jane's decline. She lost some of her meager funds in his bank failure. Her total earnings during her lifetime were less than 700 pounds.

In 1817, a third edition of *Pride and Prejudice* was published, and Austen completed the first eleven chapters of *Sanditon*. In May she was moved to Winchester, sixteen miles from Chawton, to take advantage of better medical help. She continued to write to the very end, which came on July 18, 1817. She was buried at Winchester Cathedral. *Persuasion* and *Northanger Abbey* were published after her death, their authorship still officially anonymous.

Literary Analysis

Nearly two centuries of popular and critical interest in Austen's novels attest to her artistic achievement. Although her popularity was assured with the publication in 1813 of *Pride and Prejudice* (still the public's favorite), her work attracted only slight critical attention, such as comments in letters and reviews that spoke of the "liveliness of her characterization," the "high comedy," the "ethical standards," and the "cleverness" of the volumes. The novels were praised for the accuracy of their pictures of life, though some critics found them "earthbound" and "uninspiring."[1] The earliest notable comment came from Sir Walter Scott who at the request of John Murray reviewed *Emma* for the *Quarterly Review*.[2] Scott drew attention to the neatness of the prose style, the precision of the character-drawing, the creation of a fictional world faithful to the events and situations of ordinary life. He even saw her achievement as the beginning of a new novel form, a break with those works of fiction in which "the action and characters obey laws remote from the necessities of human existence."[3] In 1821, Bishop Richard Whately took up Scott's term "the modern novel," emphasizing Austen's unobtrusive morality as an advance over the didacticism of other writers, and praising her "economy" in handling plot, action, and characterization.[4]

Unfortunately, much of the public and many professional writers and critics were not ready for this newness. Still, in an unsigned but readily acknowledged article entitled "The Novels of Jane Austen," published in *Blackwood's Edinburgh Magazine* in July 1859, the respected critic George Lewes claimed that Austen was a greater artist than Scott or Emily Brontë or Fielding because she was able to portray authentic human life with "the greatest economy of art." He compared her "mimetic powers" of characterization to Shakespeare's, considered her second to none in truthfulness, and praised her "authorial unobtrusiveness."[5]

As critical interest grew, the commonest complaint was that Austen seemed to ignore the large events of her times, such as the French Revolution and the Napoleonic Wars, and that her ironic humor lacked intensity or passion, or the "high seriousness" that Matthew Arnold and his contemporaries required.[6] However, some modern critics see Austen as the bridge between the Augustan and Romantic periods, emphasizing her portrayal of individuality within a static social structure. Others are interested in her attacks on materialism or her feminism. As critical insights into her themes increased, her techniques came to be considered controversial. She is accused by some of failure to use such standard criteria as vivid detail, fresh metaphors, and symbols. Some suggest that she omitted specific detail because she was nearsighted; others insist that she found description unnecessary because she developed her characters as a dramatist, through dialogue and action (*Pride and Prejudice* was easily made into a popular play and a movie). Her metaphors are said to be trite and her stance as the ironic observer too "detached" for symbolism.

But, R.F. Brissender finds all of these techniques in *Mansfield Park*, citing for an example the scene in which Fanny Price watches the sunlight reveal the dirt of her parents' slovenly home as her father reads from his paper the "dirty" news of Maria Rushworth's desertion of her husband to run off with Henry Crawford.[7]

The present quantity of Austen criticism is proof of the appeal of her work. A recent bibliography covering just eleven years, from 1973 to 1983, contains 1,045 entries, some of which are multiple author collections.[8] And, while numerous critical analyses inevitably produce inconsistencies, reflecting varied viewpoints and foci, Austen was remarkably consistent in scope, themes, and techniques. She limited her material to people, places, and customs that she knew well, keeping the larger world in the background. Much of the material in her published novels was revised from earlier creations, and her life and letters reveal her literary philosophy, that of a careful observer who could laugh at the Human Comedy without bitterness or a betrayal of basic morality.

One of her major themes was exposing as silly the sentimental and gothic novels popular in her day. *Sense and Sensibility*, her first published novel, is a revision of an earlier novel entitled *Elinor and Marianne*. It features contrasting heroines, Elinor and Marianne Dashwood. Upon their father's death, the sisters experience social and financial hardships, intensified by frustrated romances. Marianne reacts to events and her surroundings in the manner of the popular novelistic heroine, effusively and melodramatically. Elinor exercises common sense and hides her suffering. Marianne must be disillusioned about her romantic attachment to an unworthy young man and marry a good man whom she had originally spurned as too old for romance. Elinor is finally united with the man she loves, Edward Ferrars, when his tenacious and insincere fiancée, Lucy Steele, marries his selfish and insincere brother, Robert.

None of Austen's other heroines in the published novels so obviously indulge in "sensibility," but the heroine of *Northanger Abbey*, one of her last works, must learn that even a quite untypical heroine must be disabused of her novelistic notions of friendship and gothic abbeys. Catherine Morland is introduced as the rather tomboyish daughter of a country parson. She visits Bath with an irresponsible older couple, is courted by the insincere Thorpes, then becomes a guest of the aristocratic Tilneys at

A

their abbey home. There she indulges the fancy that General Tilney murdered his wife. She is taught the truth by the General's son Henry, a witty, sophisticated clergyman. Actually, the General is unromantically modernizing the abbey and proves his "villainous" nature by turning Catherine out when he learns that she does not have prospects of a rich dowry. Henry, who had been ordered to court her, then drop her, is now in love with her and defies his father's materialistic criteria for marriage, but submits to Catherine's parents' dictum that the young couple first secure the General's consent. This they receive when Henry's sister, Eleanor, is allowed to marry her true love because he has unexpectedly inherited a title and wealth.

This materialistic interpretation of marriage is castigated in all Austen's novels. She does not deny the importance of financial security for establishing a family, and her favorite heroine, Elizabeth Bennet, wins the wealthiest of all her heroes in *Pride and Prejudice*. However, nearly all the antagonists of her heroines disclose their Midas mentality, as in the following exchange in *Sense and Sensibility* between Elinor and her half-brother, John, as they discuss a proposed marriage between Edward Ferrars and a Miss Morton, who is very wealthy. When Edward reveals that he has been secretly engaged to Lucy Steele, his ambitious mother disowns him and seeks to secure Miss Morton for her second son, Robert. Elinor comments:

> "The lady, I suppose, has no choice in the affair."
> "Choice—how do you mean?" responds her brother.
> "I only mean, that I suppose from your manner of speaking, it must be the same to Miss Morton whether she marry Edward or Robert."
> "Certainly, there can be no difference; for Robert will now to all intents and purposes be considered as the eldest son; and as to anything else, they are both very agreeable young men." (chapter 4)[9]

Nearly all of Austen's heroines are frustrated or misled by the financial interests of those about them. In *Pride and Prejudice*, the Bennet girls are threatened with the law of entail, which means that Longbourn, their home, will belong to a distant male relative, William Collins, upon the death of Mr. Bennet. This leads the sycophantic Mr. Collins to assume that any one of the Bennet girls would be happy to accept his impersonal proposal to ensure her future position as mistress of Longbourn. Mrs. Bennet agrees and is furious with Elizabeth when she refuses, especially so when Charlotte Lucas, formerly Elizabeth's friend, marries Mr. Collins, although she neither likes nor respects him. With superb ironic humor Austen portrays Collins's long-winded pomposity and Mrs. Bennet's hysterical protests, contrasted with Mr. Bennet's laconic cynicism, when the issue is brought to him:

> "Come here, child," cried her father as she appeared. "I have sent for you on an affair of importance. I understand that Mr. Collins has made you an offer of marriage. Is it true?"
> Elizabeth replied that it was. "Very well—and this offer of marriage you have refused?"
> "I have, sir."
> "Very well. We now come to the point. Your mother insists upon your accepting it. Is it not so, Mrs. Bennet?"
> "Yes, or I will never see her again."
> "An unhappy alternative is before you, Elizabeth. From this day you must be a stranger to one of your parents. Your mother will never see you again if you do *not* marry Mr. Collins, and I will never see you again if you *do*." (chapter 20)

Austen's most obvious theme is marriage as it should be and all too often is not. Few of her established marriages are admirable; most of her parents fall far short of the ideal, and the general concepts of courtship are the stuff of comedy—and tragedy. She does have a few wholesome exceptions, such as the Hargraves and the Crofts of *Persuasion* and the Gardiners in *Pride and Prejudice*. The best known of her "failures," the Bennets, afford much of the humor in *Pride and Prejudice*, he with his wit and she with her "mean understanding" and her obsession with marriage for her five daughters. Having chosen his spouse unwisely, Mr. Bennet now ridicules her and takes no responsibility for the development of his daughters, until the youngest, Lydia, must be rescued from the tragic consequences of her flirtation with

Wickham. Mr. Bennet even fails to help Elizabeth, his favorite daughter, properly evaluate Wickham and Darcy. Mrs. Bennet's lack of intelligence and true refinement embarrasses her oldest daughters, Jane and Elizabeth, encourages the folly of the youngest, Kitty and Lydia, and permits Mary, the middle daughter, to become a pedantic fool. In *Mansfield Park*, Fanny Price's mother is incapable of managing her family or household; her father thinks only of his unrefined interests. Mrs. Price's sisters, Lady Bertram and Mrs. Norris, also betray marriage and motherhood. Lady Bertram is little more than a vegetable, totally uninterested in either her husband or her children. Mrs. Norris married for security, was relieved when her clergyman husband died, and considers herself "charitable" in misguiding her Bertram nieces into snobbery and abusing Fanny to teach her humility. Sir Thomas Bertram discovers belatedly the price of his neglect of true parenting when his daughter Maria marries, for wealth, the rather stupid Mr. Rushworth while her emotions are excited by the sophisticated Henry Crawford.

All of Austen's novels are comedies in that in the end true love triumphs and none of her villains and fools are more miserable than they deserve to be. Her insistence that courtship and marriage require more than role playing is dramatized by the self-exposure of the "fools" who use social custom to mask their selfishness and shallowness. Her interest in the individuality of those cast as hero and heroine was a forerunner of much modern fiction, with its highly developed concern with the individual's sense of his- or herself. This was a challenge not only to the literature that preceded her but also to the society which she so successfully portrayed that its values and assumptions are viable today. While the granting of clerical "livings" was a well-established practice of the English Church, Austen clearly reveals its shortcomings, even announcing her concern with its problems as the theme of *Mansfield Park*. The struggle that Edmund Bertram faces in choosing between "taking orders" or finding some other profession to satisfy Mary Crawford may well reflect the author's reaction to her brother Henry's choices before and after marrying Eliza de Feuillide. And, Mr. Eliot in *Emma* and Mr. Collins of *Pride and Prejudice* are clergymen unworthy to provide spiritual leadership.

Another "flaw" in the English social system of Austen's day was the snobbery characteristic of its undemocratic structure. The novelist clearly mocks its false pride in the character of Lady Catherine de Bourgh in *Pride and Prejudice*, and she draws in harsh lines Sir Walter Elliot, of *Persuasion*, whose only reading was the *Baronetage*, wherein he might contemplate his lineage. Austen also indicts the related problem of education, not only for girls but also for young men who, lacking qualifications for useful occupations, are easily induced to spend their time flirting or gambling, or must suffer a denial of their personal convictions to please the relatives who control their income.

Austen's special achievement is her development of all of her themes with humor. Julia Prewitt Brown, in her critical analysis *Jane Austen's Novels: Social Change and Literary Form*, points out that:

> The picture of ordinary, middle-class domestic life that nineteenth-century readers found so convincing is not merely a convenient background for a comedy of manners and values, meant to teach us the limitations of our lives. It constitutes, rather, a foreground of social and moral change, conceived with an irony that accurately reflects its tensions.[10]

She goes on to label three of the novels, *Northanger Abbey*, *Pride and Prejudice*, and *Emma*, ironic comedy; the other three, *Sense and Sensibility*, *Mansfield Park*, and *Persuasion*, she classifies as satiric realism. The difference, she claims, is that in satiric realism the misery is real. Nevertheless, Austen touches even the realism with incongruities and other comic relief that softens its sting. In *Sense and Sensibility* when it becomes apparent that Marianne will marry Colonel Brandon, the voluble Mrs. Jennings asserts that "They had in fact nothing to wish for, but the marriage of Colonel Brandon and Marianne, and rather better pasturage for their cows" (chapter 42).

From the broad parody of her juvenilia and the biting wit of her letters to the subtle irony of her published novels, Austen skillfully uses reversal, literalization, protraction, condensation, and exaggeration to mock conventions that have become artificial. In one of her early sketches, "Jack & Alice," she begins:

> Mr. Johnson was once upon a time about 53; in a twelvemonth afterwards he was

54, which so much delighted him that he was determined to celebrate his next birthday by giving a Masquerade to his children & Freinds [sic].

Thus, Austen achieves hyperconvention and anticonvention in one sentence.[11] Extracts from her letters illustrate other techniques, such as exaggeration and reversal. Writing to Cassandra, from Steventon, on October 27, 1798, she reported: "Mrs. Hall, of Sherborne, was brought to bed yesterday of a dead child, some weeks before she expected, owing to a fright. I suppose she happened unaware to look at her husband."[12] And, from Castle Square, on December 9, 1808: "I am very much obliged to Mrs. Knight for such a proof of the interest she takes in me, and she may depend upon it that I *will* marry Mr. Papillon, whatever may be his reluctance or my own. I owe her much more than such a trifling sacrifice."[13] An example of literalization in *Pride and Prejudice* correctly puts the finishing touch on the character of Miss Bingley. When the marriage of Jane Bennet and Mr. Bingley is certain, "Miss Bingley's congratulations to her brother, on his approaching marriage, were all that was affectionate and insincere" (chapter 18). Perhaps Austen's best-known irony is the opening sentence of *Pride and Prejudice*: "It is a truth universally acknowledged, that a single man in possession of a good fortune, must be in want of a wife." And, so skillfully does Austen blend the author's voice with the voices of her characters that countless readers are sure that the novelist's portrait can be found in Elizabeth Bennet, her favorite heroine.

Summary

Jane Austen began writing at an early age, and although she died while comparatively young, forty-one, and published only six novels, there is wide agreement that she is one of the great humorists in the English language. Despite her lack of formal education and personal contact with the other professional writers of her day, she had a true sense of artistic values and used to advantage the cultural resources of her family. The family encouraged her talent but after her death sought to protect her image as a refined member of genteel society. None of the modern critical analyses has uncovered any serious breaches in this image, but they have revealed the accuracy of her portrait of her world and the artistry with which she created credible characters at the same time that she was challenging harmful social customs and satirizing human folly. Her work is so consistent that her unfinished novel, *Sanditon*, could be credibly finished by an anonymous scholar-writer, and critically analyzed to reveal not only Austen's careful use of detail but her interest in current philosophical and social change.[14] She was strongly influenced by Johnsonian principles, but she was also in agreement with the growing emphasis on the values of individuality. Her early novels followed the popular epistolary form, but her revisions produced stories that are inherently dramas, with the reader discovering both characters and plots through dialogue and action; consequently, she is often compared to Shakespeare, despite the difference in their material. And while she intends her readers to smile, even laugh, at the pomposity or other foibles of her characters, she employs humor to call attention to the ways in which her audience falls short of reasonableness and honesty.

Notes

1. B.C. Southam, ed., *Jane Austen: The Critical Heritage* (New York: Barnes & Noble, 1968), p. 9.
2. Unsigned review of *Emma, Quarterly Review* (March 1816), XIV, 188–201; see also Southam, pp. 58–69.
3. Southam, p. 13.
4. Bishop Richard Whately, unsigned review of *Northanger Abbey* and *Persuasion, Quarterly Review*, 24 (January 1821): 353–76; see also Southam, pp. 87–105; comment, p. 19.
5. "The Novels of Jane Austen," *Blackwood's Edinburgh Magazine* (July 1859), LXXXVI, 99–113; see also Southam, pp. 148–66.
6. Southam, p. 25.
7. "*Mansfield Park*: Freedom and the Family," in *Jane Austen: Bicentenary Essays*, ed. John Halprin (New York: Cambridge University Press, 1975), pp. 156–71.
8. Barry Roth, *An Annotated Bibliography of Jane Austen Studies, 1973–83* (Charlottesville: The University Press of Virginia, 1985).
9. Since there are many acceptable editions of the Austen novels, quotation references are to chapters rather than pages.
10. Julia Prewitt Brown, *Jane Austen's Novels: Social Change and Literary Form* (Cambridge, MA: Harvard University

Press, 1979), pp. 4–5.
11. Claudia L. Johnson, "'The Kingdom at Sixes and Sevens': Politics and the Juvenilia," in *Jane Austen's Beginnings: The Juvenilia and Lady Susan*, ed. J. David Grey (Ann Arbor: University of Michigan Research Press, 1989), p. 46.
12. Penelope Hughes-Hallett, ed., *My Dear Cassandra: The Letters of Jane Austen* (New York: Clarkson N. Potter, 1990), p. 22.
13. Hughes-Hallett, p. 71.
14. Jane Austen and Another Lady, *Sanditon* (Boston: Houghton Mifflin, 1975).

Selected Bibliography

Primary Sources

Sense and Sensibility. London: Thomas Egerton, 1811.

Pride and Prejudice. London: Thomas Egerton, 1813.

Mansfield Park. London: Thomas Egerton, 1814.

Emma. London: John Murray, 1815.

Northanger Abbey and *Persuasion*. London: John Murray, 1818.

MSS: *The Watsons*; *Lady Susan*; *Sanditon* (incomplete); *Jane Austen's Letters to Her Sister Cassandra and Others*, edited by R.W. Chapman. Oxford University Press, 1952.

Secondary Sources

Bibliographies

Roth, Barry. *An Annotated Bibliography of Jane Austen Studies, 1973–83*. Charlottesville: The University Press of Virginia, 1985. A useful bibliography of Austen criticism, organized by year.

———, and Joel Weinsheimer. *An Annotated Bibliography of Jane Austen Studies, 1962–72*. Charlottesville: The University Press of Virginia, 1973. Valuable resource.

Biographies

Chapman, R.W. *Jane Austen—Facts and Problems*. Oxford: Clarendon, 1948. A brief reference work, especially useful in relating biography to works.

Halprin, John. *The Life of Jane Austen*. Sussex, England: Harvester Press, 1984. A modern, sympathetic biography.

Hodges, Jane Aiken. *The Double Life of Jane Austen*. London: Hodder and Stoughton, 1972. A perceptive account of Austen's life based chiefly on extant letters.

Lascelles, Mary. *Jane Austen and Her Art*. Oxford: Oxford University Press, 1939. Often quoted biography, revealing modern insights into Austen's art.

Tucker, George Holbert. *A Goodly Heritage: A History of Jane Austen's Family*. Manchester: Carcanet New Press in association with Mid Northumberland Arts Group, 1983. This family biography, including Austen and Leigh ancestors and descendants, is essential genealogical research.

Books

Austen, Jane, and Another Lady. *Sanditon*. Boston: Houghton Mifflin, 1975. This attractive completion of Austen's unfinished novel, by Austen scholar Marie Dobbs, includes a helpful analysis of themes and techniques.

Bloom, Harold, ed. *Jane Austen: Modern Critical Views*. New York: Chelsea House Publishers, 1986. This collection of modern critical analyses varies from friendly to unsympathetic; there are also seven pages of bibliography.

———. *Jane Austen's Mansfield Park: Modern Critical Interpretations*. New York: Chelsea House Publishers, 1987. Complex insights.

Brown, Julia Prewitt. *Jane Austen's Novels: Social Change and Literary Form*. Cambridge, MA: Harvard University Press, 1979. This analysis focuses on the changing social and economic forces of Austen's day, as seen from a modern point of view.

Fergus, Jan. *Jane Austen and the Didactic Novel: Northanger Abbey, Sense and Sensibility and Pride and Prejudice*. New York: Barnes & Noble, 1983. An analysis of Austen's first three novels in which her improvement on the didactic conventions of the eighteenth century is demonstrated.

Folsom, Marcia McClintock, ed. *Austen's Pride and Prejudice*. New York: Modern Language Association, 1993. Approaches to Teaching World Literature series.

Gillis, Christopher. *A Preface to Jane Austen*. Preface Series: Critical Studies of Major

A

Writers. London: Longman Group, Ltd., 1974, 1985. This is a concise introduction to Austen study, useful enough for a second edition.

Grey, J. David, ed. *Jane Austen's Beginnings: The Juvenilia and Lady Susan*. Ann Arbor: University of Michigan Research Press, 1989. Significant insights through study of the juvenilia, and an annotated bibliography.

Halprin, John, ed. *Jane Austen: Bicentenary Essays*. New York: Cambridge University Press, 1975. Helpful critical analyses from a historical viewpoint.

Hughes-Hallett, Penelope, ed. *My Dear Cassandra: The Letters of Jane Austen*. New York: Clarkson N. Potter, 1990. This attractive selection of illustrations and letters illuminates the Austen work.

Kirkham, Margaret. *Jane Austen, Feminism and Fiction*. Totowa, NJ: Barnes & Noble, 1983. This offers plausible support for Austen's inherent feminism.

Leavis, Q.D. *A Critical Theory of Jane Austen's Writings*. New York: Cambridge University Press, 1963. Essays that relate Austen's mature novels to her earlier work, including her letters.

McMaster, Juliet. *Jane Austen's Achievement*. Papers delivered at the Jane Austen Bicentennial Conference at the University of Alberta. New York: Barnes & Noble, 1976. The emphasis in these papers is on Austen's artistry and influence.

Monaghan, David. *Jane Austen: Structure and Social Vision*. London: Macmillan & Co., 1980. Balanced, modern criticism of each novel.

Nardin, Jane. *Those Elegant Decorums: The Concept of Propriety in Jane Austen's Novels*. Albany, NY: State University of New York Press, 1973. These analyses of Austen's literary use of cultural mores give depth to her "comedy of manners."

Norman, Sherry. *Jane Austen*. New York: ARCO Publishing, 1966, 1969. Good "layman's" analysis of Austen and her works.

Southam, B.C., ed. *Jane Austen: The Critical Heritage*. New York: Barnes & Noble, 1968. This review of Austen's critical reception from her time to the present is essential to an understanding of Austen's genius.

Weinsheimer, Joel, ed. *Jane Austen Today.*

Athens: University of Georgia Press, 1975. Eight American and Canadian critics appraise Austen's novels from the viewpoint of current literary theory.

Articles

Cheng, Yung-Hsiao T. "Clergymen in Jane Austen's Novels." *Fu Jen Studies: Literature & Linguistics*, No. 11 (1978): 25–40. Cheng finds that Austen's clergymen are depicted as typical middle-class gentry, either honest and conscientious or mercenary and selfish.

Hall, Judith. "*Sanditon's* 'Other Lady.'" *Woman's Journal* (London: August 1975): 71. Marie Dobbs discusses her completion of *Sanditon*.

Newman, Karen. "Can This Marriage Be Saved: Jane Austen Makes Sense of an Ending." *Journal of English Literary History*, 50 (1983): 693–710. Austen's contrast between novelistic conventions and realities in a patriarchal society is discussed.

Oliphant, Mrs. Unsigned article: "Miss Austen and Miss Mitford." *Blackwood's Edinburgh Magazine* (March 1870), CVII, 294–305. Mrs. Oliphant compares these two nineteenth-century women authors with keen and sympathetic insight.

Scott, Sir Walter. Unsigned review of *Emma*. *Quarterly Review*, 14 (March 1816): 188–201. This first noteworthy review of Austen's talent is perceptive, though brief.

Tatham, Michael. "Mary Crawford and the Comic Heroine." *New Blackfriars: A Monthly Review*, 60 (1979): 11–26. Examines the reversal of the virtues of Mary Crawford and Fanny Price in *Mansfield Park*.

Whately, Richard, Bishop. Unsigned review of *Northanger Abbey* and *Persuasion*. *Quarterly Review*, 24 (January 1821): 353–76. Bishop Whately's comments were significant both ethically and artistically for Austen's contemporaries.

Esther M.G. Smith

Ayckbourn, Alan

Born: Hampstead, London, April 12, 1939
Education: Haileybury School, Herefordshire, 1951–1956

Marriage: Christine Roland, July 30, 1959;
    two children

Biography

Although his family background included stage performers and a professional writer as well as a violinist and bank manager, Alan Ayckbourn arrived almost haphazardly at his combined vocation of playwright, theater manager, and director. He was born in Hampstead, London, on April 12, 1939. Throughout his school years he intended to pursue a career in journalism, largely influenced by the example of his mother, Irene Worley, who churned out novels and magazine stories on a typewriter in the kitchen and gave the boy his own small typewriter.

Worley was the daughter of a Shakespearean actor and a music-hall male impersonator. After her divorce—when their son was four—from Horace Ayckbourn, first violinist with the London Symphony Orchestra, she became a very successful romance writer whose works were syndicated under the name Mary James. At seven, Ayckbourn was sent to a local boarding school but spent weekends at home. His mother's remarriage in 1946 to banker Cecil Pye took the family to live in a succession of Sussex towns much like the suburban settings that Ayckbourn would later use in his comedies. Indeed, his sardonic treatment of marriage in those plays undoubtedly owes much to the gradual deterioration of what he saw as a "tempestuous relationship" between his mother and stepfather. It was Ayckbourn who finally took his mother away from her unhappy situation in 1956 and found her a job that enabled her to return to writing.

Ayckbourn's interest in theater was awakened by his French teacher, Edgar Matthews, at Haileybury School in Herefordshire, "a very tough school," which he attended on a Barclay's Bank Scholarship from 1951 to 1956. There he played cricket and rugby, edited the house magazine, created end-of-term revue sketches, and joined the Senior Literary and Debating Society. But, for him, the highlights of those years were the school Shakespeare productions that toured abroad in the summer. In 1955, he toured the Netherlands as Peter in *Romeo and Juliet*, and in 1956 he traveled in the eastern United States and Canada, playing Macduff in *Macbeth*. Upon completing his studies at Haileybury, Ayckbourn sought Matthews's advice on how to break into theater and was given a letter of introduction to the intimidating Sir Donald Wolfit, the last of the great actor-managers. Ayckbourn was hired on a Friday to begin work on Monday on a revival of Fritz Hochwalder's *The Strong Are Lonely* for the 1956 Edinburgh Festival. He got the job of assistant stage manager and the walk-on role of a sentry, he recalls, because he was willing to work for low pay and, having served in the cadet force, could be relied upon to stand at attention for forty-five minutes without fainting, as a previous sentry had done, during Wolfit's big scene.

That three-week stint at the Edinburgh Festival motivated Ayckbourn to seek more theatrical experience. He took an unpaid position as a student assistant stage manager at the Connaught Theatre Repertory Company in Worthing. During his six months there, he worked his way around virtually every department from the loading dock to operating a limelight. In 1957, he became assistant stage manager with Hazel Vincent Wallace's company in Leatherhead, which also gave him the opportunity to act a number of small roles in weekly repertory. That summer brought his first association with Stephen Joseph, founding director of a theater-in-the-round company in Scarborough, Yorkshire. Joseph, son of publisher Michael Joseph and actress Hermione Gingold, pioneered arena staging in England and nurtured a generation of playwrights. After a winter season with Frank Hauser's Oxford Theatre, Ayckbourn rejoined the Scarborough company, continuing to combine stage management with acting. Over the years until Joseph's death of cancer in 1967, Ayckbourn came to regard that "half genius, half madman" as his mentor (Watson, 18).

Ayckbourn claims that he was challenged to write his first play because he did not like the one being staged at the time: he was playing Nicky in *Bell, Book and Candle*. His first four plays, *The Square Cat* (1959), *Love after All* (1959), *Dad's Tale* (1960), and *Standing Room Only* (1961)—all produced at Joseph's Library Theatre in Scarborough, but never published—were written under the pen name Roland Allen. The name was a blend of his own and that of Christine Roland, whom he married on July 30, 1959. Ayckbourn's assumption of responsibility for night feedings of the two sons born to the young couple established his longstanding habit of writing at night. He and his wife are amicably separated.

In 1962, Ayckbourn became a founding director of the Victoria Theatre, Joseph's theater-in-the-round in Stoke-on-Trent. There he acted such major roles as Vladimir in *Waiting for Godot*, Sir Thomas More in *A Man for All Seasons*, and Starbuck in *The Rainmaker*, making his last appearance as an actor in *Two for the Seesaw* in 1964. His Christmas play for children, *Xmas vs. Mastermind* (1962), directed by Peter Cheeseman, is recalled by Ayckbourn as "the most disastrous play I've ever done." The local success of his next effort, *Mr. Whatnot* (1963) warranted its transfer, with embellishments, to London's West End. Opening at the Arts Theatre in August 1964, *Mr. Whatnot* was trounced by the critics, which nearly drove Ayckbourn from the theater forever. He took a position as a producer of radio drama for the BBC in Leeds, where he remained for six years. His work on developing scripts with other writers gave him valuable insights about the craft of playwriting, and he continued to write an annual play for the summer season at Scarborough. The best of these were *Meet My Father* (1965), which he later retitled *Relatively Speaking*, and *How the Other Half Loves* (1969).

In 1970, Ayckbourn returned full-time to Scarborough as artistic director of the Library Theatre, nurturing it along well enough that the company was able to construct its own facility for year-round productions. Opened in 1976, it was named the Stephen Joseph Theatre. Ayckbourn now lives in Joseph's former house, which had once been a vicarage. During his more than twenty years at the helm of the theater that his mentor founded, he has settled into a regular pattern, once a year taking a week or so to write a new play. He works quickly, writing an outline in longhand, from which he dictates improvised lines to his secretary and companion Heather Storey. The rest of the year is devoted to running the company, which includes directing four or five plays each season by other dramatists, and he occasionally directs productions at the National Theatre in London. About half of his forty plays have received London productions, usually about a year after their Scarborough premieres.

Literary Analysis

The English middle-class milieux of Ayckbourn's plays are peopled with variations on the insensitive husband and the wife who finds her emotional outlet in an obsession with her children, in organizing things (a household, a village pageant, a career), or in madness. There is virtually no such thing as a happy or well-adjusted marriage in the entire canon. Ayckbourn has commented that in his early plays he drew upon the anger that he felt "about not being able to carry on with my marriage. For anybody who marries under twenty, it is a miracle if it survives till they are thirty" (Raymond, 26). Only one couple, Richard and Anthea in *Joking Apart*, lives happily together after twelve years—and they are not married. "In some psychological way," says Ayckbourn, "when we are outside marriage, we work a bit harder to keep a relationship together" (Raymond, 26). Noting that "bad relationships make good theatre" (Raymond, 26), he has tended to keep the married couple in the forefront of his comedies. His plays of the late 1980s hint at a mellowing view of marriage in that they end on a note of optimism for the future. At the same time, however, there is a darker, almost vicious, undercurrent in plays such as *A Small Family Business*, *Man of the Moment*, and *Revengers' Comedies*, all of which incorporate a character's death. *Just Between Ourselves* "continued my small progress," says Ayckbourn, "first started in *Absent Friends*, towards my unattainable goal: to write a totally effortless, totally truthful, unforced comedy shaped like a flawless diamond in which one can see a million reflections, both one's own and other peoples'" (Page, *File on Ayckbourne*, p. 44).

Experimentation with theatrical form has become a hallmark of Ayckbourn's work. Many of his devices arose from the limitations of the space in which he worked in Scarborough; this led him, for example, to call for a composite setting in which an upper-class drawing room overlaps with a squalid, lower-middle-class living room (*How the Other Half Loves*), or to require his actors to mime running up and down the stairs of a three-story house, all played on a level stage floor (*Taking Steps*, 1979). *The Norman Conquests* (1973) is a trilogy with the action of each play occurring simultaneously with the other two in a different part of the house or garden. *Sisterly Feelings* (1978) is a play in four scenes, but there are two different versions of the second and third scenes; the sequence that is performed depends upon a coin toss at the end of Scene One. *Intimate Exchanges* carries the same conceit to an extreme, as there are sixteen different variants for this two-character play. *Woman in Mind* alternates reality and hallucination.

Relatively Speaking (1965), the play that launched Ayckbourn into the front rank of British dramatists, began as a conscious exercise in writing a well-made play. "I think this is important for a playwright to do at least once in his life," Ayckbourn commented, "since as in any science, he cannot begin to shatter theatrical convention or break golden rules until he is reasonably sure in himself what they are and how they were arrived at" (Billington, 21). The play is remarkable in the way that it sustains mistaken identities beyond credibility yet makes the device seem credible. On a Sunday morning, Ginny—telling her current lover, Greg, that she is off to visit her parents—goes to the country house of her older lover, Philip, to break off their relationship. Greg finds the address, travels there himself, and takes Philip and his wife Sheila to be Ginny's parents. Philip, however, assumes that Greg is Sheila's young lover who hopes to seduce her away. Ginny is forced to play Philip's daughter in front of Greg while behaving like Philip's secretary in front of Sheila. Amazingly, the dramatic soufflé does not fall, and a comic spirit prevails despite the problems in the marriage of Philip and Sheila. The superior insight of both women allows them a kind of triumph over the easily duped men.

The two superimposed living rooms of *How the Other Half Loves* allow the action to proceed simultaneously in the homes of Frank Foster and his employee Bob Phillips. Attempts to cover up Fiona Foster's affair with young Phillips involve an innocent third couple, the hapless Featherstones (they are called the Detwilers in the American adaptation). The farcical highlight occurs in act 2 (the end of act 1 in the American version), when the Featherstones are the dinner guests of the Fosters and the Phillipses on two successive nights, but the two dinners are presented simultaneously with the Featherstones/Detwilers seated on swivel chairs that allow them to be present at one or the other dinner table as demanded in the dialogue. The satiric treatment of class differences, mingled with the theme of marital discord, becomes even more pointed in *Absurd Person Singular* (1972). The action occurs in the kitchen while a Christmas Eve party is progressing in the offstage living room, but each of the three acts is set in a different kitchen on three successive Christmases. In act 1, Jane and Sidney are timorously entertaining their social superiors. Jane's neurotic obsession with cleanliness carries over with hilarious effect to Eva's slovenly kitchen in act 2. Eva, feeling rejected by her boorish husband, Geoffrey, and oblivious to the party guests who spill into her kitchen, is bent on committing suicide. Act 3, set in the banker's kitchen, wrings humor and bite out of the reversal of fortune that has occurred: the banker and Geoffrey are economically in thrall to Sidney, who has become a ruthless developer. We see how financial considerations dictate the social hierarchy.

The Norman Conquests is composed of three self-contained plays: *Table Manners,* set in the dining room; *Living Together,* set in the living room; and *Round and Round the Garden,* located in the garden of the same house. Each two-act play is composed of action that occurs offstage during the other two plays, all performed by the same six characters, and yet each work stands as an independent entity. The house is occupied by an unseen invalid mother and her spinster daughter, Annie. Annie's older brother, Reg, and his wife, Sarah, arrive for the weekend so that Annie can go off on a small break from her drudgery. However, Sarah learns that Annie is planning to spend the weekend with Norman, the husband of Annie's sister Ruth. Sarah puts a stop to their plan and calls Ruth to insist that she join them all for the weekend. The cast is completed by Annie's oafish suitor Tom, a veterinarian. The mainspring of the action is the character of the irrepressible Norman, who works his charms on all three women. At the end of *Round and Round the Garden,* all three reject him, but there is no doubting his sincerity when he shouts after them: "I only wanted to make you happy" (*The Norman Conquests,* 184). One of Ayckbourn's most popular works, *The Norman Conquests* won best play awards from the *London Evening Standard* and *Plays and Players.*

Ayckbourn indulged in a deliberate change of pace with *Absent Friends* (1974). He recalls that "it was a terrifying risk when it was first produced. I'd never pitched anything in quite such a low key before" (*Three Plays,* 8). The dramatic situation derives from the recent death of a young man's fiancee. A teatime gathering intended to console him brings together three wives, two of their husbands, and their bereaved acquaintance, whose attitude upon arrival at the end of act 1 upsets all expectations. Much of the hilarity stems from his utterly misguided "pop psychology" interpretation of the three troubled marriages. The relative somberness of that play contrasts with one of

Ayckbourn's funniest and most popular plays, *Bedroom Farce* (1975), for which the setting is three side-by-side bedrooms. The action involves constant cross-cutting among them by four married couples. No adultery is contemplated, merely the hope of getting some sleep. As usual in Ayckbourn's comedies, the women—apart from the hopeless Susannah—prove far more resourceful and insightful than their self-absorbed husbands.

Ayckbourn refers to his next three efforts as his "winter plays." After twenty years as a summer repertory theater, the Scarborough Theatre-in-the-Round Company shifted to a year-round schedule. Thus, Ayckbourn wrote *Just Between Ourselves* (1976), *Ten Times Table* (1977), and *Joking Apart* (1978) in December for January production. The first play truly reflects Ayckbourn's concern with "the everyday damage people inflict on one another" (Nightingale, 1991, 6). In *Ten Times Table*, perhaps the last of the plays in which hilarity predominates over bitterness, the playwright spoofs committee meetings, in this case a committee charged with planning the village pageant. The action culminates on Festival Day in a behind-the-scenes Armageddon. In *Joking Apart* Richard and Anthea are set up as a charmed couple possessing every talent and virtue. However, the action, spanning twelve years, suggests that they exemplify "the blithe destructiveness of the good" (Billington, 124).

The deadly violence that intrudes into Ayckbourn's plays of the late 1980s is prefigured in *Season's Greetings* (1980), which builds to a possibly-fatal shooting. Four couples (three of them married) have come together in one household for the Christmas holidays. Clive, the guest of the unmarried sister, unintentionally invites sexual aggression by the other women and ends up the victim. A full measure of comedy is wrung from devices such as the children's toys under the Christmas tree where a seduction occurs and the bumbling husband who insists on foisting his boring puppet shows upon the household. The potent mix of merriment and pain has earned the play a number of critical comparisons to Anton Chekhov's work.

The allegorical *Way Upstream* (1981), called "a state-of-the-nation play" by Michael Billington (160), places two couples on a boat (England) for a seven-day vacation trip up the River Orb (earth) to Armageddon Bridge. The arrogant capitalist, Keith, and his libidinous wife, June, dominate the reasonable but passive Alistair and Emma. En route, the boat is commandeered by the vicious Vince, who brings aboard his girlfriend, Fleur, a child of the decadent aristocracy. The mitigatedly hopeful ending has Alistair and Emma finding within themselves the unsuspected resources to begin afresh, perhaps like the couple whose initials they share, Adam and Eve. In production, the technical extravagance of the moving boat in real water may have skewed critical assessment of the work's genuine merit. *A Chorus of Disapproval* (1984) again picks up the theme of the "innocent" whose passivity only promotes discord. The narrative line is tied to preparations for a small-town production of John Gay's *The Beggar's Opera*, but this is merely a pretext for exploring rampant greed and adultery in this cross-section of English life.

Woman in Mind (1985) proceeds harrowingly from a situation that is pure farce: Susan has stepped on the end of a garden rake and knocked herself out. The resulting head injury leads her to hallucinate an ideal family in counterpoint to the insensitive characters with whom she lives in reality. Reality and fantasy at first collide, but gradually overlap, becoming equally unpleasant traps as Susan slips into madness. Ayckbourn's supporting characters exhibit even greater self-seeking callousness in *A Small Family Business* (1987). When Jack becomes head of the family firm, he vows to run it on principles of trust and honesty, but he is soon caught up in a spiral of events progressing from his complicity in covering up his daughter's shoplifting to massive fraud, drug money-laundering, and the illicit disposal of the corpse of a blackmailer killed by his daughter. "What the play's really about," Ayckbourn has said, "is the virtual nonexistence of set moral codes any more, and the fallacy of trying to live by one. I think now the only thing we can do—and in a way cannot help doing—is to make up our own moral codes as we go along" (Page, *File on Ayckbourn*, p. 78). Because Ayckbourn wrote *A Small Family Business* to premiere at the National Theatre, he was scenically less restricted than usual; the setting is a cross-section of a two-story house which at various times serves for scenes set in the separate homes of different branches of the family. Billington points out the theatricality of a sequence near the end of the drama, in which Jack races at ground-floor level to his relatives' houses to raise money for the blackmailer while on the floor above we see the blackmailer's threat to Jack's wife inside his own home.

Henceforward (1987) and *Man of the Moment* (1988) both demonstrate how technology threatens to destroy human feeling. *Henceforward* offers a horrific vision of the future in which gangs of marauding feminists control the streets while most human endeavors—including artistic creativity—have become dependent upon technology. Indeed, the apartment setting requires elaborate video effects. Jerome is a composer whose medium is recorded sound; however, he has suffered an artist's block ever since his wife and daughter left him. The play's cleverest touch is Jerome's robot, Nan. Although subject to Jerome's programming of her, she serves as a metaphor for the changing roles of women. She was designed as a child-care robot, but Jerome uses her for household management, in which capacity she exhibits considerable independence of spirit: she persists in presenting mugs of coffee or glasses of orange juice upside down. Television is the force that subverts traditional values in *Man of the Moment*. Vic Parks, a criminal turned media celebrity, is a brutish egotist whose life is shown in contrast to that of the unassuming and decent Douglas Beechey. When the facts of their encounter—and Vic's drowning in the swimming pool—are transformed into a television program, a new reality is callously created for the viewing public.

To date, Ayckbourn's brand of comedy has fared less well with American audiences, particularly New York audiences, than with the English. "Perhaps it's because my work tends to fall between the cultural and the boulevard," he suggests. "People may think me either too lightweight or not lightweight enough." Benedict Nightingale (*New York Times*, February 10, 1991) offers one-liners whereas Ayckbourn prefers verbal understatement; Americans are squeamish about laughing at subjects that they do not deem fit for comic treatment, while Ayckbourn's increasingly dark comic vision focuses upon "the everyday damage people inflict on one another;" Americans like upbeat comedies that reaffirm moral certainties, but Ayckbourn explores moral gray areas, concluding only that "everything and everyone conspires against us." Ayckbourn comments: "Humor is a very difficult trans-Atlantic traveler, and I suspect the New York ear is more finely attuned to the verbal side. But in my plays a line only becomes funny when it's seen in the context of all the other lines. The humor comes from character and situation. If you try to structure fragile lines into laugh lines, the result is resolutely unfunny." Responding to Nightingale's article in a letter to the editor, Thomas Monsell faulted "the intricate structurings of [Ayckbourn's] plays," and asserted that Americans "seem to prefer straight lines, not Chinese boxes . . . His plays seem like games that the audience has to put up with rather than experiences they can share."

Ayckbourn continues to experiment with form and content in his recent plays such as *The Revengers' Comedies* (1989), *Body Language* (1990), and *Wildest Dreams* (1991), and *Communicating Doors* (1994). In recent years, he has written several children's plays, including *Mr. A's Amazing Maze Plays* (1990) and *Callisto 5* (1990). *A Word from Our Sponsor* (1993) was scheduled to have its American premiere at the 1994 International Theatre Festival of Chicago.

Summary

While American audiences are gradually discovering Alan Ayckbourn's humor, the British public holds firm to the opinion that it is the best thing to hit the comic stage since Moliere. Ayckbourn's plays are perhaps best summed up in his own words: "A comedy is just a tragedy interrupted."

Selected Bibliography

Primary Sources
Joking Apart and Other Plays. London: Penguin, 1982.
Three Plays. New York: Grove, 1979.
The Norman Conquests. New York: Grove, 1979.
Recent titles are available in single-play paperback editions from Faber & Faber.

Secondary Sources
Billington, Michael. *Alan Ayckbourn*, 2nd ed. New York: St. Martin's Press (Modern Dramatists), 1990. Lively and reliable survey of the plays through *The Revengers' Comedies*.
Blistein, Elmer M. "Alan Ayckbourn: Few Jokes, Much Comedy." *Modern Drama*, 26 (March 1983): 26–35. Analyzes Ayckbourn's comic technique with emphasis on *The Norman Conquests*.
Dukore, Bernard F., ed. *Alan Ayckbourn: A Casebook*. New York: Garland, 1991. A collection of commissioned essays on various aspects of Ayckbourn's

workincluding a study of Ayckbourn's women characters.

———. "Craft, Character, Comedy: Ayckbourn's *Woman in Mind*." *Twentieth Century Literature*, 32 (Spring 1986): 23–39. Dukore looks at the action of that play in terms of phases in Susan's progression into madness.

———. "Alan Ayckbourn's Liza Doolittle." *Modern Drama*, 32 (September 1989): 425–39. Analyzes Sylvie's narrative through-line and its implications in *Intimate Exchanges*.

Kalson, Albert E. "Alan Ayckbourn" in *British Dramatists since World War II. Dictionary of Literary Biography 13, Part I: A-L.* Ed. Stanley Weintraub. Detroit: Gale Research, 1982, pp. 15–32. Kalson's pithy analyses zero in on the essence of Ayckbourn's work.

———. "Old Friends Reminisce." *The Pinter Review* (1989): 53–57. Explores "Pinter's shadow in Ayckbourn's background," especially as *Old Times* may have influenced *Absent Friends*.

———. "On stage, off stage, and backstage with Alan Ayckbourn." *Themes in Drama 10: Farce.* New York: Cambridge University Press, 1988, pp. 251–58. Considers Ayckbourn's use of theatrical space for farcical purposes.

Kerensky, Oleg. *The New British Drama: Fourteen Playwrights since Osborne and Pinter.* New York: Taplinger Publishing Co., 1977, pp. 114–31. An overview of characteristic comic techniques and thematic patterns in the plays through *Confusions*.

Nightingale, Benedict. "Can the Ayckbourn Curse Be Broken?" *New York Times* (February 10, 1991): sec. 2, pp. 5, 6. Examines the difficulty of cultural transferral of Ayckbourn's British comedy to American audiences. Follow-up letter from Thomas Monsell (March 10, 1991): Sec. 2, p. 4.

———. "It's Not Cricket, but the Score Is: Ayckbourn, 37; Shakespeare, 36." *New York Times* (August 3, 1989): C17, C24. Ayckbourn at fifty reflects upon his accomplishments and the increasing seriousness of his plays.

Page, Malcolm, compiler. *File on Ayckbourn.* London: Methuen, 1989. Contains chronology, a brief description, and production data for each of the plays, along with quotations from reviews and critical studies, and a bibliography.

———. "The Serious Side of Alan Ayckbourn." *Modern Drama*, 26 (March 1983): 36–46. Shows the seriousness with which Ayckbourn depicts marriage.

Raymond, Gerard. "Alan Ayckbourn Takes Manhattan." *TheaterWeek* (February 25, 1991): 22–27. *Absent Friends* and *Taking Steps* placed within the context of Ayckbourn's life and work.

Watson, Ian. *Conversations with Ayckbourn.* London: Faber & Faber, 1988. Lively interviews with Ayckbourn cover his life and work; this is the essential volume on Ayckbourn.

White, Sidney Howard. *Alan Ayckbourn.* Boston: Twayne Publishers, 1984. An appreciation of Ayckbourn's plays through *Way Upstream*.

Felicia Hardison Londre

B

Bagnold, Enid Algerine
Born: Rochester, Kent, England, October 27,
1889
Education: Prior's Field, Godalming, Surrey,
1902; Villa Thioleyre, Lausanne, 1906;
Madame Yeatman's Protestant Institute
for Young Ladies, Paris, 1907;
Blackheath Art School, London, 1907;
Walter Sickert Art School, London, 1911
Marriage: Sir Roderick Jones, July 8, 1920;
four children
Died: London, March 31, 1981

Biography
The elder daughter of Arthur Henry and Emily
Bagnold, Enid Bagnold was born in Rochester,
Kent, on October 27, 1889. Her father was a
major in the Royal Engineers, distinguished for
his engineering and practical skills. From him
she learned the personal discipline that was to
be an important element of her life and writing.
Her father's army career ensured that she had
an itinerant childhood, including three years in
Jamaica from 1899 to 1902. On her family's
return to England, she attended Prior's Field,
the unconventional boarding school for children of the intellectually distinguished run by
Aldous Huxley's mother. In 1906, she went to
finishing schools in Lausanne and Paris.

After four years of unsuccessful submissions, her first poem was published in the *English Illustrated* magazine in 1907, quickly followed by another in the progressive *New Age*.
By 1917 she was appearing regularly in the
periodicals *New Statesman* and *Nation*. She
continued to write poetry throughout her life.

Bagnold attended London's Blackheath Art
School in 1908 and then moved on to the
Walter Sickert Art School in Camden Town,

London, in 1911. The visuality of painting was
of particular assistance in developing her use of
imagery. She became associated with the area's
artistic society, which included Lovat Fraser,
Ralph Hodgson, and Henri Gaudier-Brzeska
(who created a sculpture of her head), and became personally involved with author Frank
Harris, for whom she slaved for five months on
the ladies' magazine *Hearth and Home*. When
this journal collapsed, they edited *Modern Society*, another short-lived publication for which
she wrote most of the material.

Returning to the family home at Shooter's
Hill, West London in 1914, Bagnold joined the
sparkling society that surrounded the Baron
and Baroness d'Erlanger and included the Austrian aristocrats, the Bibesco brothers.

With the outbreak of war, she joined the
Red Cross and worked in the Royal Herbert
Hospital, Woolwich. She condensed her experiences there into *Diary Without Dates* (1918),
a book that made national headlines and resulted in her dismissal from the nursing service
for her revelations of the uncaring hospital routine. Beginning in November 1918, she spent
six months as a Volunteer Ambulance Driver
(VAD) in France.

Marriage on July 8, 1920, to Sir Roderick
Jones, chairman of Reuters International News
Agency and eleven years her senior, involved her
in a busy life as hostess to his many diplomatic
associates. In addition, the couple had two children. In 1924, North End House, Rottingdean,
Sussex became the main family home and was
to remain so until 1980.

Bagnold maintained a strict and lifelong
routine of spending three hours every morning
shut away in a room dedicated to writing. She
was not, however, a prolific author partly be-

cause she was unwilling to neglect her husband and children for the sake of her work. Nor did she find writing easy and, unable to rest on the laurels of past successes, was subject to spells of great anxiety and depression when faced with difficulty in beginning a new work.

Involvement in a pantomime in 1939 awakened in her an interest in the theater that was to challenge and frustrate her for the rest of her life. Overall, her plays had less popular success than her novels but her greatest success, *The Chalk Garden* (1955), gained her the American Academy of Art and Letters Silver Medal for Distinguished Achievement in Drama.

Bagnold's last original work was her autobiography, published in 1969. An unsuccessful and consequently very painful hip replacement in that same year resulted in a dependency on morphine which, combined with a series of strokes, rendered her virtually unable to write. She died at home in Hamilton Terrace, St. John's Wood, London, in 1981.

Literary Analysis
Bagnold drew almost completely from herself for her subjects and themes. The characters of her plays and novels were rooted firmly in real people; thus, the Countess Flor di Folio in *Serena Blandish* was based so much on Baroness Catherine d'Erlanger that it almost resulted in a libel action; Lady Diana Cooper provided the model for Lady Maclean in *The Loved and Envied* and the brothers Bibesco were the leading characters of *The Last Joke*.

Bagnold's first two books were also virtually autobiographical. *The Happy Foreigner* (1920), relating the experiences of a VAD in France, although written as a novel was in reality much nearer reportage than fiction and both this volume and *Diary Without Dates* use a fragmentary style suited to a documentary flavor. These works also reveal a facility with language which is a mark of her work. Her imagery has a strong pictorial quality which developed as a result of her interest in painting, and in *The Happy Foreigner* she draws a vivid scene of the desolation of the war-ravaged areas.

Overall, *Diary Without Dates* is a thought-provoking book full of pathos, but it also exhibits flashes of humor that are very English in their understatement. They demand, as do many of her plays, a certain interpretation by the reader of the tone of the author's voice. For instance, she bemoans the effect of the life and uniform on her appearance: "My ruined charms cry aloud for help . . . I was advised last night on the telephone to marry immediately before it was too late. A desperate remedy. I will try cold cream and hair tonics first." Her perception of character and ability to express it in a few well-chosen words was already formed. She describes the different types of hospital visitors in a few short sentences—the woman who acts as though it were a school treat, another who asks the soldiers about their acquaintances "exactly as though she was talking about Cairo in the season," and finally, the Limit who embarrasses the author with compliments in front of the men: "She went away and said she hoped to come again." Bagnold adds darkly with another flash of wry humor, "And she will."

The unlikelihood of a number of Bagnold's plots is not immediately noticeable. For example, *Serena Blandish or the Difficulties of Getting Married* progresses at an accelerated pace. At the time of writing, the author was much influenced by the classic French writers introduced to her by Antoine Bibesco, and Voltaire's method, in evidence in *Candide*, of sweeping the reader along with no time for consideration is well suited to her parody of modern society.

In later plots, it is Bagnold's "sharply substantiated sense of things"[1] which lends the air of reality to the tales. The down-to-earth characters, for instance, together with an understanding of their relationships and a strong sense of place set *National Velvet* (1935) so firmly in the actual world that it is easy for readers to accept the wish fulfillment of the plot in which a young girl rides her horse in the Grand National (the 1994 film version of the novel starred Elizabeth Taylor). She had also used this technique in *Alice and Thomas and Jane*, an earlier story especially for children.

It is this reality which is at the core of the humor running throughout the book. The observations of family life, the rituals and trials, especially of small children, are captured so exactly that it results in a gentle amusement of recognition. The daughters, rising from the meal table, mutter at speed and without thought, "For whatayave received, thank God!" Donald, the little boy who collects his spit in a bottle, is perhaps the greatest source of humor. Velvet wakes him and tells him that he has slept too long.

"I've slept too long," moaned
    Donald. . .
"Slept *too long*," he wailed self-pityingly.
Mrs. Brown washes him and he returns.
"I've slept too long," he said in quite a
    different voice, engagingly, socially.
"Yes, we heard," said Mr. Brown.

Her later works tend more to be vehicles for Bagnold's contemplations. The theme of *The Loved and Envied* takes over the story to the extent that the characters submerge under the ideas. Lewis Gannet of the *New York Herald Tribune* wrote, "most of her network of characters were vehicles for her ideas about love and age, rather than flesh and blood individuals,"[2] while William Collins described it as "almost dauntingly literate."[3] Her first play, *Lottie Dundass*, displays the faults of an inexperienced playwright in the imbalance of words and action and the lack of characterization and, as she progressed, Bagnold was to concentrate more and more on the language of her plays to the detriment of characterization and the lucidity of the themes. In *The Last Joke* she explores death and aging, but these themes are lost behind a richness of idiom which drew criticism at the time as "an intellectual vacuum behind the teeming undergrowth of lush metaphors and exotic imagery."[4]

The Chalk Garden was her most successful play, described as "the finest artificial comedy to have flowed from an English . . . pen since the death of Congreve."[5] However, as with the humor previously, much relied on the reading of the words and Bagnold herself placed considerable emphasis on their delivery. Thus, the lines in which the young girl discusses the fate of a murderess are not, on examination, such a witty exchange, but they can appear very witty indeed when delivered with the assurance and hauteur intrinsic in the character:

Laurel: "Was she hung?"
Mrs. St. Maugham: "Hanged, my darling, when speaking of a lady."

The Chalk Garden is written in an artificial language reminiscent of Ivy Compton-Burnett and is a triumph of shrewd character observation and language, tightly written without a single careless line. However, the final version was the result of several years cooperative writing with her producer, Irene Selznick. Bagnold liked to fill her plays with epigrams which she called her "plums" and Selznick worked on rounding out the stereotypical characters and making the "plums" a little more digestible. A film version, directed by Ronald Neame, was released in 1964. The movie starred Deborah Kerr, Haley Mills, John Mills, Dame Edith Evans and Felix Aylmer; it was well received.

Similarly, it was necessary for director Noel Willman to make the characters in *Call Me Jacky* (in which Mrs. Basil voices Bagnold's ideas on senility and death) more three-dimensional in order to turn it into the more successful *A Matter of Gravity*.

A character who recurs often in Bagnold's writing is the masculine woman, a matriarchal figure who is immensely strong emotionally. Mrs. Brown in *National Velvet* is the wise, calm cornerstone of the family who speaks little but understands much, fighting quietly but inexorably for her children and their dreams. Facing her husband's opposition to entering the horse in the race, she "rose like a sea monster from its home. After her years of silence she grunted with astonishing anger, and William, powerless and exasperated, stung like a gnat upon a knotted hide." Lady Maclean in *The Loved and Envied*, though beautiful, is not feminine and "was nearing the large period of the wise woman, when having been a woman to men, she now remained a woman only for herself."

Such emphasis on the strong female figure has resulted in Bagnold's being described as a feminist writer. *The Squire* (1938), which broke new and courageous ground in its descriptions of childbirth, explores without sentiment the binding of a mother with her newborn babe. Men and sex have no part in the immediate scene and the book was acclaimed by *Time and Tide* as a "really important book, a mark in feminist history as well as a fine literary feat. Here at last is a portrait of a woman in her essentially feminine phase of life and yet neither siren nor appendage."[6] Bagnold's remarks on the matriarch ("We ought to be called 'wumen' some different word. 'Wumen' are hard-working, faulty, honest, female males") and characters such as that of the leading role in *The Chinese Prime Minister*—a woman who decides to leave her husband to launch herself into a new and independent life—lend substance to the label of feminist. However, the emphasis on women resulted less from a desire to assert women's equality or importance than from the fact that the author drew so much of her material from herself.

B

Fears of death and losing her looks haunted the writer increasingly as she got older. Her awareness of the inevitable end provided an impetus to her writing career and became more and more apparent in her work. The subject of death appears fleetingly in earlier books: Mrs. Brown in *National Velvet* "thought of death occasionally with a kind of sardonic shrug" and tells Velvet, "Childbirth an' being in love. An' death. You can't know 'em until you come to 'em. No use guessing and dreading." The Squire expresses Bagnold's own awareness: "After 40, the sense of beauty grows less acute; one is troubled instead by a vast organ note, a hum of death."

Bagnold's importance lies in her observations of British life and character. In her most successful works, her sharp characterization and ear for dialogue create a humor born out of the accuracy of her observation. Bagnold was an acute observer of the human condition, using the life she knew to illustrate fears and problems common to all; "The root is personal experience, the flower is universal."[7] Her characters are usually affluent and urbane because she drew them from the society in which she mixed. *Serena Blandish* captures a hard, postwar gaiety in a bitter parody described in the *Times Literary Supplement* as "a brilliant tract for the times."[8] *The Squire* provides an excellent and humorous insight into life in an English country house; *National Velvet*, is a realistic depiction of British working-class family life of the period. Bagnold's generally affluent settings drew criticism in the socially-aware decades of the 1950s and 1960s, and the emphasis on society and aristocratic lifestyle at a time when low-life dramas were fashionable reduced her influence on future writers.

Summary

Enid Bagnold's skill lay in her acute observation of English character and life which she portrayed in economic and exact prose. Her most successful and well-remembered work was *National Velvet*. Her plays, while witty, are written in an artificial language and concentrate on expressing her ideas, which had less general appeal than did her novels because she paid less attention to the lives of her characters.

Notes

1. Christopher Morley, "Book of Genesis," *Saturday Review of Literature* (October 1, 1938): 7.
2. Lewis Gannet, *New York Herald Tribune* (January 1951).
3. William B. Collins, *Philadelphia Enquirer* (October 28, 1975).
4. Milton Shulman, *Evening Standard* (September 29, 1960).
5. Kenneth Tynan, *The Observer* (April 15, 1956).
6. *Time and Tide* (October 22, 1938).
7. *The Girl's Journey* (contains *The Happy Foreigner* and *The Squire*) New York: Doubleday, 1954. Foreword by Arthur Calder-Marshall.
8. *Times Literary Supplement* (December 1924).

Selected Bibliography

Primary Sources
A Diary Without Dates. London: Heinemann, 1918.
The Happy Foreigner. London: Heinemann, 1920.
Serena Blandish or the Difficulties of Getting Married. London: Heinemann, 1924.
National Velvet. London: Heinemann, 1935.
The Squire. London: Heinemann, 1938.
Four Plays. London: Heinemann, 1970. Includes *The Chalk Garden*, *The Last Joke*, *The Chinese Prime Minister*, and *Call Me Jacky*.

Secondary Sources
Biographies
Sebba, Anne. *Enid Bagnold*. London: Weidenfeld and Nicolson, 1986. A well researched biography containing much information from interviews and letters.

Books and Articles
Anonymous. *The Times* (April 1, 1981). Obituary.
Cockburn, Claud. *Bestseller: The Books that Everyone Read 1900–39*. London: Sidgwick and Jackson, 1972. Includes an examination of the appeal of *National Velvet* to the nation.
Stine, Jean, ed. *Contemporary Literary Criticism*. Vol. 25. Detroit, MI: Gale Research, 1983, pp. 71–79. Collection of reviews of works as published.

Helen Gazeley

Barnes, Peter

Born: London, January 10, 1931
Education: Stroud Grammar School
Marriage: Charlotte Beck, October 14, 1961

Biography

Peter Barnes was born in London on January 10, 1931. Although his father, Freddie, converted from the Church of England to Judaism to marry Barnes's mother, Martha Miller, the family was not strict in its observance of Judaism. Before the War, the Barneses moved to Clacton-on-Sea where they ran amusement stalls. During World War II, Peter was sent to the Stroud Grammar School in Gloucestershire. His family joined him soon afterward, and his father found work in a munitions factory.

Despite the war, Barnes dreamed of going to the movies in London, and he left school at seventeen for a position on the Greater London Council. He then served in the Royal Air Force in 1949 and 1950, returning to a position on the Greater London Council as the film critic for their in-house magazine. He left to become a freelance film critic and in 1956 became a story editor for Warwick Films. Also in 1956, he wrote his first screenplay, *Violent Moment*, adapted from a short story, and he has continued to write assigned screen plays. His first stage play, *The Time of the Barracudas*, starring Laurence Harvey and Elaine Stritch, was produced in 1963 in San Francisco and Los Angeles. But, it was with *The Ruling Class* (1968) that Barnes became a celebrity.

He married Charlotte Beck on October 14, 1961. The couple are still married and they have no children.

Literary Analysis

Pretense, one of Barnes's major themes, is present in virtually every one of his works. His characters must pretend to be someone noteworthy or they cannot exist. Additionally, if the noteworthy characters who have any authority, or position of authority, do exist, they are usually corrupt and deserving of contempt.

Most often in Barnes's plays the virtuous individual is in direct confrontation with an evil, corrupt world. In addition, the element of hypocrisy is present in all of his religious leaders who are perforce authoritative, political, and evil. Faith or a sense that God exists is found only in the most simple characters.

Barnes presents these characters in an inherently theatrical manner rather than in a realistic slice-of-life mode. Many of his characters play act and don the most ornate costumes in order to better deceive themselves. In what some critics consider his best play, *The Ruling Class*,[1] the protagonist (the 14th Earl of Gurney, played by Peter O'Toole in the film), convinces himself that he is the son of God. Of course, this type of reasoning must be mad, yet Barnes succeeds in chiding the British for assuming such lordly attitudes.

The Ruling Class can serve as a model for the themes and representative humor that follow in Barnes's later work in that the playwright luckily found his unique voice in working out his first major drama.

Barnes, a historic revisionist, researches his historical plays, which have anarchy at their core, daily at the British Museum. A "New Wave" dramatist (along with Arnold Wesker, John Arden, Harold Pinter, John Osborne, Edward Bond, and Joe Orton—the screenplay *Violent Moment* was written the same year that *Look Back in Anger* changed the theatrical landscape), Barnes's acknowledged influences range from the Jacobeans, with their film-like scene changes and bloody on-stage violence, to the Germanic heritage, especially Bertolt Brecht with his cynical, satirical sense, his theatrical alienation effects and great love of costume, and his socialistic antipathy for the upper classes, and to George Bernard Shaw for his plays-of-ideas and socialist bent. In addition, there is a combination of Jean Genet's and Antonin Artaud's outrageous theatricalities simultaneously being infused with the "schtick" of vaudevillian comedians and the high wit of an Oscar Wilde.

Barnes's writing shares similarities with the work of Peter Weiss, especially *Marat Sade*, and the contemporaneity of fellow British writers, such as Howard Brenton, Bond, and David Hare, in that he, too, is attracted to such curious subjects as molestation, prostitution, and murder. However, for the most part Barnes utilizes songs and corny jokes in place of excremental imagery. He feels that his contribution in the chain of dramaturgical influences extends to the work of Howard Barker.[2]

Perhaps the author's most skillful and unique dramatic device is his use of one-liners at the most inopportune moment. The "bad joke" creates a macabre, Kafkaesque black humor while still remaining hysterically funny.

Although Barnes has stated that "It is usually more interesting to ignore the medium than to accommodate it, better if you make it conform to you, than you to it" (*The Spirit of Man & More Barnes' People*, viii), in actuality, he never ignores the medium but is superb at crafting it anew. Like a cubist painter, the dramatist does not meld form and content together; he holds the elements ajar at angles so that his composition has a unique edge. For example, a frequent element found in his radio plays is blindness where the unseeing audience "visualizes" characters who are blind.

Moreover, in all his venues, Barnes is not only aware of his audience but also frequently assigns it a place in the play. He claims that he is not an autobiographical writer. Nevertheless, he is, at the very least, a self-conscious one. For instance, in *The Three Visions* (1986), a three-character play, a middle-aged writer named Barnes is listening to sound effects in a radio broadcasting studio when his younger namesake challenges him. They agree that they are in a dream and the younger Barnes recalls a dream in which he is chased by a tiger over a precipice. He clings to a vine at which a mouse starts to nibble. Even so, with one bare hand he grabs for a strawberry.

The middle-aged Barnes does not recall this dream and claims that it sounds very literary, which is why he never uses dreams in his writings.[3] Both the older and younger characters have plastic knees which, they claim, came from falling off the stage while directing *Bartholomew Fair* at the Roundhouse Theatre in 1978. In comes an OLD MAN to warn that the same thing had happened to him. Old age is not too good to him since the younger Barnes did not take good care of himself. He has a similar dream, though the strawberry is now a raspberry and the tiger, a lion.

The old man, like Barnes himself, writes light verses for music no longer written. The latest piece is crudely called "Yank My Doodle, It's a Dandy." Upon hearing this, the young Barnes requests, "Yank My Doodle," to which the old man answers in true Barnesian self-conscious humor, "I'm sorry I'm too old for that sort of thing now!" At the end of *The Three Visions*, the three Barneses sing a song about the knee—the only thing about them which will endure.

Barnes's major theatrical works, *The Ruling Class*, *The Bewitched* (1974), *Laughter!* (1978), and *Red Noses* (1985), call for large casts suitable for a repertory company like the Royal Shakespeare Company, which has performed many of his plays. He wants his plays to be "universal and vast," but the exigencies of producing theater today also require that they be subsidized.

An authentic Cockney, Barnes is also perverse about writing plays with subject matter that could not be considered entertainment. *Laughter!*, produced at the Royal Court Theatre, includes an exclamation point in its title because the first act depicts the unpredictably despotic viciousness of Ivan the Terrible, and the second act is set in Auschwitz. In *Laughter!* Barnes is dealing with man's inhumanity to man. He seeks to show that cruelty, having been a personal affair based on whim in feudal times, has progressed into something more systematic: "It is now more widespread because it is organised" and "Sir Peter Hall said it would have closed the National if he would have done it."[4]

Literary Analysis

Barnes' People II (1984) consists of seven short two-people dialogues, which the playwright calls "duologue." They are actually problem plays that contain the themes with which Barnes is perennially concerned.

Acting Exercise was, along with *Worms*, originally written for the review *Somersaults*. In *Acting Exercise*, Willet interrupts Rowan, an actor having trouble making his lines seem sincere, by accusing him of stealing his wife, who is his agent Murray's new secretary. Rowan, with self-conscious humor, retorts, "I've only just gone to Murray—changing agents is as useful as changing deck chairs on the Titanic" (2). However, when Rowan succeeds in convincing Willet that his wife was just trying to make him jealous, Willet joyously exits, acting with sincerity the lines that he will cry out to his wife. Rowan, convinced that he had done such a marvelous job deluding Willet, throws new conviction into his acting rehearsal.

In *Acting Exercise*, Barnes is conscious of his audience. Rowan berates the audience's behavior by recalling that he found himself "in front of audiences who resembled delegates from the local mortuary in winding sheets" (4).

In *Worms*, Barnes addresses the hypocrisy of religious leaders. A shabbily dressed old woman comes to confession because of her sins: pride, envy, covetousness. Not only had she wanted two bowls of soup instead of her usual one, she was also bothered by her dream to sleep in a real bed. Her major sin, though, was loving people who did not believe in God. The priest, who finds a connection between this simple woman's trust and a heretic's vision, gives her penance for her sins, and finds new faith through her simple devotion.

In *Silver Bridges* two robber barons, Cornelius Vanderbilt and Jay Gould, get their kicks as they count the money that they can steal from each other while the rest of the world goes without.

The Right Time and Place is about the confrontation of a psychiatrist, who mans a suicide hot line, and a would-be suicide who is so depressed that she could "buy artificial flowers and have them die on her" (34). The psychiatrist agrees and climbs out on the window sill leaving the depressed would-be suicide no real choice but to attempt to change the psychiatrist's mind. In typical Barnesian humor, the would-be suicide cries out, "I came here for help and what do I get? Competition!" (37). In joining her psychiatrist on the window sill, she remembers that she has "a terrible head for heights. I'll be sick." "Not over me please," answers the good doctor. As they realize that their deaths will not be taken seriously, they try to return inside, acknowledging that "it's not so easy going back" (40), but that for suicide you need "the right time and place."

In *Moondog Rogan and the Mighty Hamster*, two female wrestlers practice for a match that their promoters have decided will be a draw. The grunts emanating from their rehearsal, consisting of hammerlocks, headlocks, legdives, and head scissors, provide a background for "female bonding." Their professional gripes include one wrestler who was so heavy that "when she had a facelift her surgeon got a hernia" (14). The self-effacing Barnes includes their opinion that they "should have applied for an Arts Council Grant long ago" (12), and he injects them with self-respect, drowning out their conversation with the roar of the crowd.

The Spirit of Man & More Barnes' People (1990) contains three one-act plays, *A Hand Witch of the Second Stage, From Sleep and Shadow*, and *The Night of the Simhat Torah* under the umbrella title, *The Spirit of Man*. Seven monologues entitled "Madame Zenobia," "Slaughterman," "The Road to Strome," "Billy and Me," "Losing Myself," "Houdini's Heir," and "A True-Born Englishman" are included under the coverall *More Barnes' People*.

In "Madame Zenobia," an Irish fortune teller tells her unhappy story, which is filled with irony. Her drinking husband, in response to her wish to live a sedentary life in one small home, had wished that they "had a half million," realizing that there is no good to "dreaming when yer not asleep." But, in getting her wish to stop traveling and live in one place, she is there only long enough to have her son die. "Walls weaken us," she concludes (57).

To keep the attention of his students a professor tells them a metaphorical story in "Slaughterman," because "There is always a marked discrepancy between the milk in the coconut and the hair on the shell" (60). Although ancient ritual professed that a cow or bull's soul was liberated during its slaughter, he, as the animals' butcher, only experienced their terror. Once he was shattered by slaughtering a mother cow who had a calf within her. He left one form of butchering by retiring to academia where he could cater to calves.

In "A True-Born Englishman," Bray puts down the English by saying that they were born for service: "I don't want to talk politics but it's why it's right for us to change from a manufacturing economy to a service one. Everyone agrees we English make the best valets and maids; we know how to take orders" (98). Bray uses old vaudeville jokes as he tells how he got the job as footman at Buckingham Palace. In answering the questionnaire, he filled in age, height, and color of eyes correctly "but under 'Sex' I wrote 'Yes please'" (99), and Bray details how he rose through the ranks to become Keeper of the First Door. He chides the British class structure, speaking about his mother's politics: "She was so conservative . . . she thought of having her heart transplanted to her right to counteract the mistake made by the Creator" (98) and "ideas only come . . . from the top. When they came from the opposite direction it would be a signal for the end of our way of life" (101). And in Barnes's self-conscious fashion, Bray continues, "I found out early on, people with ideas end up living under a hedge without a penny piece" (101). As "A True-Born Englishman" was considered antiroyalty,[5] it was never produced by the BBC.

There are four characters in "A Hand Witch of the Second Stage,"[6] a one-act play which is set in 1437: 1) a misogynistic, credulous priest called Father Nerval; 2) Marie Blin, the woman accused of witchcraft; 3) Claude Delmas, the sodden drunk who bears witness against Marie Blin; and 4) Henri Mondor, the executioner.

The play includes most of Barnes's major themes. If Marie is proven guilty of witchcraft, then all of her lands and possessions go to the accuser. The executioner tells her that "To be the truth, it can only be hard earned, nicked from bone, torn from mouth and metres of gut. Truth's never given free" (10). In order to circumvent the executioner's truth, which he euphemistically calls his "Art of Persuasion" (12), Marie affirms that she is a witch and that the testimony of the drunken Delmas was the truth. She names the names of the most powerful of France as also having made a pact with the devil.

Barnes, the humorist, has Marie agree to be a witch, but only a hand witch of the second stage, there being various levels of witchery proficiency. A hand witch of the second stage is able to perform magic with hand gestures, flexed fingers, and subtle wrist, and is even able to squeeze a heart to death. Delmas finds himself gasping for breath.

The naming of the rich and powerful creates a problem for Father Nerval in that he is sure that such people have the authority to refuse to be named.

Barnes's sense of the theatrical as being a form of virtual reality is evidenced when Marie's hand fills with blood. To "defeat Authority" one has to use "Authority's weapons" (19). Marie thanks God for giving her the wit to help herself. The play ends with the lines "Wit, cunning and endurance are more important than heroism, / Though heroism in small doses, helps too" (20).

In *The Bewitched*, which Barnes considers his most representative and best play because "I have included every one of my themes in it,"[7] the author concentrates on the horrors and diseases of power. The result is that "Black comedy, macabre satire, and the song, 'That's Entertainment' unite the ruling forces of the nation in hideously bizarre jollity," according to one critic (Marriott). Also included are such songs as "Lucky in Love" and "Clap Yo Hands," which provide an absurdist background for the Spanish court of Carlos II.

In the prologue, Philip IV is shown to be so powerful that obeisance in the court includes a dwarf who must somersault backwards in exiting rather than turn his back on Philip IV. This weakened Philip IV feels forced to copulate with his wife Mariana to beget an heir for the Spanish throne, and the result is the insipid Carlos II.

There was much discussion surrounding the production, especially its dramatization of an auto-da-fé. Richard Watts found the use of the song, "Oh what a day for an auto-da-fé" referential to Candide.[8] Robert Cushman found that scene "where the king and the queen are done up in vast effigies of themselves and united by a huge golden phallus, spectacular but confusing."[9] Finally, Michael T. Leech found that the auto-da-fé was like a "therapeutic treatment designed to give the king an erection."[10]

The Bewitched, which lists forty-one characters on its "dramatis personae" page,[11] concerns the realm of Carlos II in fifteenth-century Spain. Barnes examines Carlos II and his court from their point of view and sense of position in the world. How do they justify their existence as rulers or, for instance, such an event as an auto-da-fé?

Ronald Bryden, in the introduction to *The Bewitched*, writes that "it is a neo-Jacobean play which crystallizes, clarifies and pins down what it is that links the Jacobeans and his [Barnes's] contemporaries . . . Only a writer saturated as Barnes is in the language of Jonson, Marston and Middleton could have produced the brilliant, thorny, fantastic speech of Carlos' courtiers, the two great verse tirades the stammering king speaks in the lucid aftermath of epilepsy" (ix).

Along with *The Bewitched*, Barnes is especially fond of *Lament for Armenians and Grey Viruses*, which is included in the paperback *Barnes' People II* (1984). According to the dramatist, "It's about two tramps who are sitting down and just talking. I tried to write a short play which is about nothing at all, just style where two creative characters are doing nothing—just talking. How they say things—not what they say—but how they say things is what I worked on. I didn't quite succeed, the trouble being that the audience constructs a meaning in the succession of sentences and that when it hears the 'lament' or sees it, the audience reads a little story into it and gives it meaning, but there was no story there."[12]

An analysis of *Lament* reveals a cry of very humorous but unconnected logic: "Asthma and wet dreams 're brought on by cockroaches with leaky feet." The characters, although drunk, are creative with their language ("I'm rubbishing here") as well as poetic ("I used to work, till the last sunbeam faded"). The lamenting tramps are also smart, "But honour doesn't go to the wise or success to the good—only to those who swim with the tide." One complains that he is "the Wandering Jew" who has "never been anywhere," and the other agrees that "the earth is a prison and we rush about but the sky surrounds us on all sides and I can't get out." In this dark piece, "hope is a terrible torture" and the world does not end with a "whimper," but with "Plop, plop . . . plop, plop . . . " (50–58).

The Real Long John Silver and Other Plays (1986) is an anthology of eight short, three-character, one-act plays produced on the radio. In his introduction to the volume Barnes tells the story of an opera singer who jumps to his death when he misinterprets the crowd who comes to cheer him as having come to jeer him. Barnes says of himself that "he has not yet felt the urge to jump," even though the proper praise and recognition due him as a writer may still not be forthcoming. Like his characters, the writer aims to be and, of course, is someone noteworthy.

In *The Real Long John Silver* a husband, a wife, and a friend all dress up as Long John Silver (complete with the parrot and peg leg) in order to enter a costume party, but they spend so much time fighting about which one should enter as Silver that they miss the party. The resolution is that one shoots the other with either a mock or real gun. Which one has lied or told the truth is unclear. Seemingly, the moral message is that the truth is whatever the perception of that truth is.

In *After the Funeral*, one of the "Other Plays" in the anthology, Anna has died and Harry is bemoaning that fact to his friends who, being similarly upset, are following a most correct behavior for mourning. The shock of finding out, however, that the three men are pimps and the deceased Anna nothing more than Harry's favorite whore is quickly overshadowed by the three men's joining together to inappropriately sing "Unforgettable" as a tribute to a most unforgettable whore. It is expected that Harry will carry on with the business of living by calling in another whore, the moral message being that "life force" is the "business" of living.

Elements within *After the Funeral* that bear the Barnes signature (or are referential to the author) include the fact that when Harry wanted to take Anna away from a brothel in Casablanca, he shot her left knee cap (the incident recalls the biographical *The Three Vi-*sions). *After the Funeral* is also referential to Genet's *The Balcony*. One of Anna's clients liked to set up a table in his bedroom to resemble "The Last Supper" and Anna would arrive as Mary Magdalene wearing a veil and sandals.

Aside from *The Ruling Class, Red Noses* is probably Barnes's best known work in the United States. There were two major productions, at The Goodman Theatre of Chicago and The Trinity Rep in Providence, Rhode Island. Although the subject matter—the bubonic plague—was about as appealing a subject as Auschwitz was in *Laughter!*, producers and critics found that the play's deathly fourteenth-century plague had great relevance to the current AIDS crisis. By way of explanation, a note was included in the program of the 1987 Goodman Theatre production:

In 1347, under siege by a Tartar army in the Crimean port of Kaffa, Genoese trade merchants see their only hope for survival in a strange and terrible sickness cutting through the ranks of their enemy. But when the Tartars turn to the strategy of sharing their malady with the Genoese, by catapulting corpses infected with the disease into Kaffa, the sickness takes virulent hold in the besieged city, and the only course left for the Genoese is flight. They take to their ships and sail for the Mediterranean, bearing with them the passenger that would in three years' time kill a third of Europe—the Black Death.

The critics were not unanimous in their praise. Hedy Weiss's headline blared, "Stinker of a script plagues Goodman's 'Red Noses,'" and Roy Porter's title read "Gags for God—it's not funny." Nevertheless, K. Kelly in writing of Artistic Director Adrian Hall's farewell at the Trinity Rep theater, thought *Red Noses* "majestic."

Sheridan Morley concludes: "By viewing a time and place of unspeakable horror through the eyes of people who in later lives would doubtless have been staging the camp concerts at Dachau, Mr. Barnes has achieved his usual theses about a stand-up comic being a lot more useful than a pope in a real crisis. He also has a nicely cynical turn of phrase ('the continued existence of Christianity proves that almost anything can be made to work in the end') and a deep love for old jokes ('I've had to suffer for my art, now it's your turn,' says the blind juggler to his moribund audience)" (50).

Barnes's most recently written *and* produced play is the two-act *Sunsets and Glories* (1990). With only twenty-four characters, small by Barnes's standards, the play retains all of the flavor and themes of his previous plays. In act 1, the Council of Cardinals surprisingly chooses a deeply religious hermit, Peter Morrone, not necessarily a play on words, to become the Pope in Rome. The name does, however, point out that the Pope has to be worldly in order to see and deal in politics. Morrone, being a celestial figure, was unsuited for the position and like a moron, he selects a former lawyer for the papacy. Nevertheless, the unscrupulous lawyer, who reigns in act 2 as Pope, is definitely more suited for the position and abler to meet its exigencies than is Morrone.

Revolutionary Witness & Nobody Here But Us Chickens (1989) is another combination volume. *Revolutionary Witness* consists of four monologues which independently constitute a behind-the-scenes fictional history of the French Revolution from the point of view of the involved citizen, and *Nobody Here But Us Chickens* is an umbrella title for three one-act plays (*Nobody Here But Us Chickens, More Than a Touch of Zen*, and *Not as Bad as They Seem*) about ordinary people who are handicapped in some way.

Not As Bad As They Seem features a wife whose husband arrives home while her lover is still in her bed. The problem—and humor—stems from the fact that all three are blind.

Bye Bye Columbus, which was commissioned by the British Broadcasting System to commemorate the 500th Anniversary of Columbus's discovery of America (and published in 1993), does so in typical Peter Barnes fashion. There are no heroes, only the usual cynical aphorisms: "Marriage is a funeral where you smell your own flowers"; "He's a man who brightens a room just by leaving it"; "Lies carry their own truth"; "I'll do anything for everything"; and "Learn to love yourself, it's the only affection you can count on." In Barnes's screenplay, Columbus (portrayed by Daniel Massey in the broadcast) is a monster. Not only power hungry but also power crazed, he tells the story of his discovery to a parrot that irreverently parrots the voice of God giving Columbus his God-given command. Columbus decides to take natives back to Ferdinand and Isabella as slaves. Upon being reprimanded and reminded that Isabella wants her subjects converted, not consigned, and that there was no money or manner for provisions for the extra people, Columbus replies, "We ship cannibal slaves—they can eat each other on the journey."[13]

Summary

Peter Barnes, originally a film and theater critic, is a theatrical chameleon, adept at writing, adapting, and directing. As a translator/adaptor of classics such as Frank Wedekind's *Lulu*, his facility with language is such that he is able to positively transform the words of the original to suit the present voice and ear.

On the one hand, Barnes is a great painter of huge historical canvases, filling the theatrical stage both visually and orally with larger than life sets and huge casts of disparate voices who tumble out of history, revisioned through Barnes as a "truthful liar." On the other hand, he is a skillful monologist who is able to tightly confine a unique voice and vision to one ten-minute narrative radio voice.

Barnes's signature permeates his canon. He holds authority figures up for examination and finds them, through very colorful and anti-realistic means, absurd and deserving of pity.

Much has been written about Barnes's facility with language, his injections of old, corny jokes at inopportune moments as if life itself were an inappropriate regurgitation, and his anti-authority/pro-socialist stance for a requisite life-force. Nevertheless, his greatest gift is his singular skill at establishing some sense of empathy for a totally unlikable lot. He brings a high canonical figure down to earth, shows the character's fears, dreams, and shabby reality—as well as his insane, evil justification for his behavior—and has the character remain, although totally despicable, understandable.

Because of the unparalleled success of his adaptation of Elizabeth von Arnim's *Enchanted April* (1991), audiences are likely to enjoy much more of Barnes's prodigious talent. He has been commissioned by the BBC to adapt and direct Charles Dickens's *Hard Times*[14] for the television screen, and his own screenplay *The Trial of Socrates* was aired by the BBC in 1993. Additionally, it can be hoped that there will be future productions of three of the author's unpublished and unproduced works: 1) *Heaven's Blessing*, a biblical comedy; 2) *Clap Hands, Here Comes Charlie*, which Barnes has been working on for the past twenty-five years; and

3) *Eggs 'n Gravy*, an adventure story set in Italy, where the olfactory senses are seduced by some cooking on the stage.

Notes

1. For an excellent discussion on *The Ruling Class* and other major works by Barnes, consult the definitive critical edition of his work: Bernard F. Dukore, *The Theatre of Peter Barnes* (Portsmouth, NH: Heinemann, 1981).
2. Interview with Peter Barnes, London, August 18, 1993. Hereinafter "Interview."
3. This is also the case in Barnes's works.
4. Sheridan Morley in *Punch* (July 10, 1985): 50.
5. Barnes readily admits to being anti-royalty or anti-authority. Interview. (London, August 18, 1993).
6. First broadcast by BBC-TV as the first part of the trio *The Spirit of Man* on August 23, 1989. It was produced by Richard Langridge and directed by the author.
7. Interview. (London, August 18, 1993).
8. *New York Post* (September 14, 1974): 16.
9. *The London Observer* (May 12, 1974).
10. *After Dark* (July 1974).
11. In The Royal Shakespeare Company production which opened May 7, 1974, director Terry Hands doubled nine actors.
12. Interview. (London, August 18, 1993). Barnes comments in much the same manner in his "Introduction" to *Barnes' People II: Seven Duologues*, p. v.
13. Quotes taken from the videotape.
14. *Hard Times* was aired by PBS on March 8, 1993; October 25, 1993; and March 10, 1994.

Selected Bibliography

Primary Sources
The Frontiers of Farce. London: Heinemann, 1977.
Barnes' People II: Seven Duologues. London: Heinemann, 1984.
The Real Long John Silver and Other Plays. London: Faber & Faber, 1986.
Plays: One. London: Methuen, 1989.
Sunsets and Glories. London: Methuen, 1990.
Revolutionary Witness & Nobody Here But Us Chickens. London: Methuen, 1989.
The Spirit of Man & More Barnes' People. London: Methuen, 1990.
Barnes Plays: Two. London: Methuen, 1993. Contains *Bye Bye Columbus*.

Plays
The Time of the Barracudas, 1963.
Sclerosis, 1965.
The Ruling Class, 1968.
Leonardo's Last Supper, Noonday Demons, 1970.
Lulu (adaptor), 1972, Bristol Old Vic.
The Bewitched, 1974.
The Devil Is an Ass, 1976.
For All Those Who Get Despondent, 1976.
The Frontiers of Farce, 1976.
Laughter!, 1978.
Bartholomew Fair, 1978.
Antonio (adaptor), 1979.
The Devil Himself (adaptor), 1980.
Somersaults, 1981.
Collected Plays, 1981.

Screenplays
The White Trap, Anglo Amalgamated, 1959.
Breakout, Anglo Amalgamated, 1959.
The Professionals, Anglo Amalgamated, 1961.
Off Beat, British Lion, 1965.
Ring of Spies, with Frank Launder, BL, 1965.
Not with My Wife You Don't!, with Norman Panama and Larry Gelbart, Warner Brothers, 1966.
Violent Moment, Artists/Schoenfeld, 1966.
The Ruling Class, United Artists, 1972.
Enchanted April, 1991.

Teleplays
The Man with the Feather in His Hat, ABC (Britain), 1960.
Bye Bye Columbus, PBS, 1992.
The Trial of Socrates, 1993.
Hard Times, 1993.

Radio Plays
Eastward Ho! (adaptor), BBC, 1973.
My Ben Jonson, BBC, 1973.
Lulu (adaptor), 1975.
Antonio (adaptor), BBC, 1977.
The Two Hangmen: Brecht and Wedekind, 1978.
A Cheap Maid in Cheapside, Middleton (adaptor), BBC, 1979.
Eulogy of Baldness from Sysius of Cyrene (adaptor), BBC, 1980.

B

The Soldier's Fortune (adaptor), BBC, 1981.

The Atheist, Thomas Otway (adaptor), BBC, 1981.

Barnes People, BBC, 1981.

For the Conveyance of Oysters, from a work by Gorky, 1981.

The Soldier's Fortune, from the play by Thomas Otway, 1981.

The Dutch Courtesan (adaptor), BBC, 1982.

The Singer, Wedekind (adaptor), 1982.

The Magician, Gorki (adaptor), 1982.

The Dutch Courtesan, Marston (adaptor), 1982.

A Mad World My Masters, Middleton, 1983.

Barnes People II, 1984.

The Primrose Path, Feydeau, 1984.

A Trick to Catch the Old One, Middleton, 1985.

The Old Law, Middleton and Rowley, 1986.

Woman of Paris, Henri Becque, 1986.

Barnes People III, 1986.

No End to Dreaming, 1987.

The Magnetic Lady, Jonson, 1987.

Short Stories

"Madame Zenobia." 1989.

"Slaughterman." 1989.

"The Road to Strome." 1989.

"Billy and Me." 1990.

"Losing Myself." 1990.

"Houdini's Heir." 1990.

"A True-Born Englishman."

Articles

With T. Hands, I. Wardle, C. Blakely, J. Hammond. "Ben Jonson and the Modern Stage." *Gambit* 6 (1972): 5–30.

"Still Standing Upright: Ben Jonson, 350 Years Alive, anniversary celebration by a disciple and fellow dramatist." *New Theatre Quarterly*, 3, 11 (August 1987): 202.

Secondary Sources

Articles and Chapters in Books

Barker, Clive. "On Class, Christianity, and Questions of Comedy." *New Theatre Quarterly*, 6, 21 (February 1990): 5–24.

Bly, Mark, and Doug Wager. "Theater of the Extreme: An Interview with Peter Barnes." *Theatre*, 12, 2 (Spring 1981): 43–48.

Bryden, Ronald. "Introduction" to *The Bewitched*. London: Heinemann, 1974.

Carlson, Susan. "Cosmic Collisions: Conventions, Rage and Order." *New Theatre Quarterly*, 3, 12 (November 1987): 303–16.

Cornish, Roger, and Violet Ketels, eds. *Landmarks of Modern British Drama: The Plays of the Sixties*. London: Methuen, 1985.

Dukore, Bernard F. "Newer Peter Barnes, With Links to the Past." *Essays in Theatre*, 5, 1 (November 1986): 47.

———. "Red Noses" and "Saint Joan." *Modern Drama*, Vol. 30.

———. "People like you and Me: The Auschwitz plays of Peter Barnes." *Essays in Theatre*, Vol. 3.

Esslin, Martin, *Plays and Players* (January 1969).

———. "Green Room." *Plays and Players*, 21 (August 1974): 12–13.

Ferris, Paul. *London Observer* (March 11, 1984): 22.

Fields, Steffi. *Women's Wear Daily* (August 2, 1972): 18.

Hiley, Jim. "Liberating Laughter: Peter Barnes and Peter Nichols in Interview." *Plays and Players*, 6, 293 (March 1978): 14–17.

Hobson, Harold. "Introduction" to *The Ruling Class*. In *Barnes. Plays: One*. London: Methuen, 1989.

Kelly, Kevin. *The Boston Globe* (May 11, 1989). Review of Adrian Hall's majestic farewell at the Trinity Rep theater on May 11, 1989 thought *Red Noses* "majestic."

Marriott, R.B. "The Stage and Television Today." *Plays in Performance* (May 16, 1974).

Morley, Sheridan. *Punch* (July 10, 1985): 50.

Nightingale, Benedict. "Green Room." *Plays and Players* (July 1974).

Porter, Roy. "Gags for God . . . it's not funny." *London Times Literary Supplement*, July 26, 1985.

Shafer, Yvonne. "Peter Barnes and the Theatre of Disturbance." *Theatre News* (December 1982): 7–9. Interview with Barnes.

Shorter, Eric. "The Daily Telegraph" (November 9, 1968).

Weiss, Hedy. "Stinker of a Script Plagues Goodman's 'Red Noses.'" *Chicago Sun Times* (October 7, 1987): 45 Review.

Wilkes, Angela. "Desperate Acts on a Large

Scale." *Sunday Times* (June 30, 1985): 43. Interview with Barnes.

Books

Cave, Richard Allen. *New British Drama in Performance on the London Stage, 1970–1985.* New York: St. Martin's Press, 1988.

Dukore, Bernard F. *The Theatre of Peter Barnes.* London: Heinemann, 1981.

Taylor, John Russell. *The Second Wave.* London: Methuen, and New York: Hill and Wang, 1971.

Worth, Katharine J. *Revolutions in Modern English Drama.* London: G. Bell & Sons, 1972.

Marjorie J. Oberlander

Barrie, James Matthew

Born: Kirriemuir, Forfarshire, Scotland, May 9, 1860
Education: Edinburgh University, M.A., 1882
Marriage: Mary Ansell, July 9, 1894; divorced, 1910
Died: London, June 19, 1937

Biography

James Barrie, the creator of Peter Pan, was a journalist and novelist before becoming one of London's most popular playwrights. The son of David Barrie, an industrious Scottish weaver and his pious wife Margaret, both of whom favored education for all of their children, Barrie was the ninth of ten children, the third boy. Two influences on young Barrie were the Auld Licht ("Old Light") strict Calvinist religion of his parents and the accidental death of David, the middle brother, who was his mother's favorite. The grievous effect of David's death on his mother tempered all of Barrie's later activities.

At Edinburgh University, Barrie studied literature. His college career was followed by two years, apprenticeship on the Nottingham *Journal.* His best pieces were sentimental sketches from provincial Scottish life, which resulted in *Auld Licht Idylls* (1888) and *A Window in Thrums* (1889). *The Little Minister* (1891), his novel written in the same style, was a best-seller.

In London, Barrie's play, *Walker, London* (1892), ran for 511 performances, and he married its leading lady, Mary Ansell on June 19, 1894. This was typical of Barrie's hold on

people; the diminutive five-foot-one charmer surrounding himself with attractive people. Yet, he was impotent and, in October 1910 after fifteen years of marriage, he divorced Mary when she ran off with Gilbert Cannan, an author and friend of D.H. Lawrence. Lawrence later portrayed Barrie as Bertie in his short story "The Blind Man."

Barrie was regarded as an eccentric genius by his contemporaries. He collaborated with Arthur Conan Doyle and received admiring letters from fellow-Scotsman Robert Louis Stevenson. But meeting the five boys of the neighboring Davies family was the most important event in Barrie's adult life: the yarns that he told them eventually became the Peter Pan stories. He wrote daily to Sylvia Davies, their mother. Their father, Arthur Davies, never reconciled himself to these intrusions, but when he died of cancer his final wish was for Barrie to care for his family. Sylvia died three years later, and Barrie became Uncle Jim, supporting the boys through Eton, joining them on summer travels, writing letters, worrying. Three of the boys served in France during World War I, where George, the oldest, was killed.

Meanwhile, Barrie became famous, especially with *The Admirable Crichton* (1902), *Peter Pan* (1904), and *What Every Woman Knows* (1908). He was a favorite of the American impresario of theater, Charles Frohman, who later went down on the *Lusitania,* as well as a friend of explorer Captain Robert Scott. Scott's final letter from his ill-fated race to the South Pole in 1913 was to Barrie, asking the writer to take care of Mrs. Scott and their son.

Barrie's final relationship was with Lady Cynthia Asquith, the daughter-in-law of the Prime Minister. Again, the husband did not appreciate Barrie's letters and attentions paid to his wife, but for twenty years Cynthia and Barrie depended on each other. By this time Barrie was rich enough to support the Asquiths—even though he deeded perpetual rights to *Peter Pan* to Great Ormond Street Hospital for Sick Children—and she handled all his affairs, for he never knew how much or even where his money was.

After the war, Barrie produced successful fantasy plays—*Dear Brutus* (1917) and *Mary Rose* (1920)—and a one-act mystery, *Shall We Join the Ladies?* (1921), that ran for 407 performances. Honors came to Barrie, including a Baronetcy (1913), and the positions of

Rector of St. Andrews (1919), and Chancellor of Edinburgh University (1930). He died in London on June 19, 1937, and was buried in Kirriemuir.

Literary Analysis

Barrie gained early success as a journalist and novelist composing vignettes of provincial Scottish life. Although his own model was Stevenson, Barrie became master of the Kailyard (cabbage-patch) school of young writers creating a sentimental view of Scotland through dialects, provincialisms, and gentle irony. His most successful novels were *Sentimental Tommy* (1896) and *Tommy and Grizel* (1900).

More important to understanding Barrie's writing is *Margaret Ogilvy* (1896), a panegyric to his mother. Barrie's entire opus is open to Freudian interpretations based on the Oedipal nature of this work. He never forgave himself for being unable to replace his brother David (dead at age fourteen) and console his mother, and the motif of every Barrie work removes guilt by resurrecting the mother who was laid low by David, the boy who literally never grew up. By using her maiden name, the story transposes his mother back to her virginal state (later, in *Peter Pan*, the father must reside in the dog house). Barrie's own sexual impotence, fascination with young boys, and incessant use of family names can be diagnosed *ad infinitum*.

As a dramatist, Barrie achieved early success with *Walker, London*, and ten years later *The Admirable Crichton* ran for 328 performances. These plays established the Barrie genre of romance and sentiment. *Peter Pan*, *What Every Woman Knows*, and *Dear Brutus* also rely on fantasy lands where people get second chances to improve their lives.

As Barrie's comic masterpiece and chief social commentary, *The Admirable Crichton* satirizes the status of master and servant. Its premise stemmed from Conan Doyle's question ten years prior to the play: If a king and a seaman were stranded on an island, who would rule? In Barrie's play, Lord Loam, his son Ernest, and daughter Lady Mary are shipwrecked with their servants Crichton and Tweeny. "Nature will decide for us" becomes the play's theme, so it is no surprise when two years later the capable Crichton is "Gov," with Lady Mary aspiring to marry him and Ernest pursuing Tweeny. However, after they are rescued and returned to England (act 4 is titled "The Other Island"), all revert to their original roles, and Ernest's published account of their "heroic" exploits relegates Crichton to a footnote.

The humor in *Crichton* correlates to this social dichotomy. In England, when Crichton justifies his dutiful laugh at Ernest's lame epigrams with, "My lady, he is the second son of a peer," Lady Mary replies, "Very proper sentiments" (1). Later, stranded on the island, Lord Loam and Lady Mary are offended when Crichton takes charge: Loam loftily orders, "Take a month's notice," and Mary chimes in, "And don't come to me, Crichton, for a character" (2). The entertainment continues into the final act with Lady Brocklehurst's imperious interrogations of the castaways, where she resembles Lady Bracknell in Oscar Wilde's *The Importance of Being Earnest*. With Wildean echoes, she observes, "I thought cricket educated Englishmen for everything," and of Ernest's book, "It is as engrossing as if it were a work of fiction." Barrie, however, sustains romance, as Lady Mary opines about the island, "Father, I have lived Arabian nights. I have sat out a dance with the evening star."

Crichton's stance as a determinist who never questions social roles sustains the parody of aristocratic norms. It is Barrie's conception on the Darwinian struggle, his rendering of Rousseau's argument for innate goodness, Carlyle's hero-worship, and ultimately Nietzsche's Will to Power, but with a twist. Comedy prevails over their linear prescriptions as Barrie exhibits a fractured world rather than a comforting one of order or benevolence: regal England remains juxtaposed with the natural island, master with man. Crichton, named after a sixteenth-century Scottish warrior, contrasts with Loam, whose name suggests his earthbound lack of vision and resolve, witnessed in his cry: "I shall assert myself. Call Crichton." Barrie promotes his ironic stance with rhetorical puns and literary allusions.

George Bernard Shaw, who was writing *Man and Superman* at the time, missed this understated satire when he compared Crichton to his New Man, Enry Straker, for Straker and his emerging talents open up new social boundaries, whereas Crichton merely characterizes these boundaries.

Peter Pan, the fantasy tale of a boy who never grows up, has become the most popular children's play ever, as well as a great work of children's literature. It evolved over a period of years: a six-chapter digression in *The Little White Bird* (1902) was converted into the three-act play *Peter Pan, or The Boy Who Would Not Grow Up,* two years later. In 1906, the novel *Peter Pan in Kensington Gardens* was issued, later to be modified to *Peter and Wendy* (1911) and then simply *Peter Pan.* The final version is the 1928 five-act play.

The play delightfully demonstrates Barrie's grasp of a child's sense of humor and fair play. Children, then as now, accepted the macabre results of adult actions, such as when Mr. Darling does penance in Nana's dog house, or when Hook explains, "Pan flung my arm to a crocodile that happened to be passing by" (2). A homey humor related Neverland kids to their mothers, when Nibs tells us, "All I remember about my mother is that she often said to father, 'Oh how I wish I had a cheque book of my own,'" and when Slightly was named because his mother wrote "Slightly Soiled" on his shirt collar. Hook is so courtly that even his victims "note that he always says 'Sorry' when prodding them along the plank" (2). For older kids, Hook is "not wholly evil: he has a Thesaurus in his cabin, and is no mean performer on the flute" (4). Later, nearing success in murder and mayhem, Hook exults, "Split my infinitives, but 'tis my hour of triumph!" (5,1). The triumph will not, of course, be Hook's, who is no match for Peter Pan's speed and cunning, and his final muttering before jumping to the crocodile is "Floreat Etona" ["May Eton flourish"], an echo of the Duke of Wellington's praise of the playing fields of Eton as the embryo of England's victory at Waterloo.

Barrie's own account of the genesis of the play ("I have no recollection of having written it") can hardly be believed, but no doubt the story is the result of his fantasy tales told to the Davies boys. On one level the story is basic escapism, with adventures, pirates, and a flight from reality as Peter directs, "second [star] to the right and then straight on till morning."

However, the reader or playgoer learns to discount the Walt Disney version, for in Barrie's story Peter Pan has no memory, subsists on internecine rivalries, has no need for parents, and forgets even Wendy, Tinkerbell, and Captain Hook. The enemy is Time, signified by the ticking clock in the crocodile's stomach. When the clock stops, Hook is outfought and devoured, after which Peter assumes Hook's role, cigar, hat, and hook.

An Oedipal situation is indicated in several ways. Wendy is alternately the mother/sister of the Lost Boys and wife/mother of Peter. Her impregnation is signified when she is shot in the breast by one of the boys, and then according to Peter's instructions they build a house around her, "busy as tailors the night before a wedding." Replete with symbolic chimney made from father's stovepipe hat, the house is perfected when Wendy emerges and the boys sing out, "We've made the roses peeping out, / The babies are at the door, / We cannot make ourselves, you know, / 'Cos we've been made before."

Children in the audience are glad when Peter slays Hook, in part because the same actor who plays Mr. Darling also plays Hook. Hence, a psychodrama of the unconscious, with its glance into vague sexuality, gratifies the Oedipal conflict. Barrie's claim in 1922, and later in the preface to the 1928 version, to have no recollections of the composition of *Peter Pan,* thereby deferred to his own preconscious or repressed concepts.

Adults respond to a creation myth in *Peter Pan.* Barrie acknowledged fairy tales, nursery stories, adventure narratives, and penny dreadfuls as his inspirations, and in the 1909 revival used a drop-curtain patterned as a sampler with "Thank You" to Lewis Carroll, Charles Lamb, Robert Louis Stevenson, and Hans Christian Andersen embroidered on it. Hook, of course, resembles *Treasure Island's* Long John Silver, while the fantasy theme parallels Lamb's "Dream Children" and "The Child's Angel," reissued in 1902. The harlequin tradition—Peter is clearly a harlequin, with wooden sword, tights, and mask—and its clowns were later elevated by Barrie in his ballet *The Origin of Harlequin* (1905).

Influences on Barrie were as widespread as English empiricist Francis Bacon and Romantic poet William Wordsworth. In Bacon, whose works were republished in the 1880s, Barrie discovered the fantastic island *New Atlantis* (1624); in *The Wisdom of the Ancients* (1609), he saw linguistic potential for humor, as well as the Pan and Cupid myths treated from a darker, more ambivalent perspective. In Wordsworth, who declared, "The child is father of the man," Barrie perceived the divinity of the child, which certified that Peter Pan will defeat Hook, who is, after all, Peter's creation.

How does *Peter Pan* fit into contemporary adolescent fiction, which is usually so topical? The work by Barrie—not the Disney film—emphasizes the price of adhering to childhood, and its most frequent epithet for the paradise of childhood is "heartless." The cost is a removal from nurturing love, which for Peter is "the one joy from which he must be forever barred." Hence, childhood is a paradise well lost, reminiscent of John Milton's promise to Adam. As good adolescent literature, *Peter Pan* shows the rewards of maturity in spite of the splendidness of childhood's anarchy.

The joy and sentiment of *Peter Pan* established the play as a theatrical institution, especially at Christmas. In 1978 and again in 1991, it was performed on Broadway, and in 1982 by the Royal Shakespeare Company at the Barbican. Three film versions of *Peter Pan* are the 1924 silent film, the 1953 Disney cartoon, and the 1955 NBC musical with Mary Martin. Spielberg's 1991 film *Hook* is a $50-million twist with Robin Williams (as Peter), Dustin Hoffman (Hook), and Julia Roberts (Tinkerbell) playing grown-up Neverland people.

A parallel romantic fantasy occurs in Steven Spielberg's movie *E.T.*, where the bedtime story that inspires the children to save E.T. is the episode from *Peter Pan* in which the boys must believe in Tinkerbell in order to save her life.

The legacy of *Peter Pan* is not only its creation of a new myth, but its impact on the theater. It was a theatrical spectacle involving a huge cast, clever mechanical devices, complex lighting, and even audience participation, when Peter asks the children in the audience to clap in order to save Tinkerbell. The domestic scene is nearly as fantastic as the Neverland; after all, the play opens with Nana the dog preparing the bath. Barrie, ever the theorist, wrote *Notes on the Acting of a Fairy Play* (1903) to complement his creative efforts.

The play offered some of the most coveted roles in English theater for the first half of the twentieth century, from Noel Coward as one of the children in 1913 to the great actresses who played the title role over the decades. Shaw responded to the play's popularity by writing *Androcles and the Lion* (1913) for children.

Peter Pan has entered the world's vocabulary, as documented in Roger Green's *Fifty Years of Peter Pan* (1954) and applied in an unrigorous psychology text, *The Peter Pan Syndrome* (1983) by Dan Kiley.

Other dramas followed. *What Every Woman Knows* presents many Barrie characteristics. Here, wise but unglamorous Maggie manipulates her husband through his infidelity crisis until the humorless Scotsman finally recognizes his wife's merits and devotion. She promises throughout "not to behave as other wives do," but the play's theme contradicts this, for it suggests that behind every successful man there is a shrewd woman who manages him while keeping his ego intact.

Again, Barrie gives everyone a second chance to grow up. Typically, there is a startling lack of love, or even need for passion, but an abundance of Scotch practicality. When the seductress Sybil mutters "Practical?" the stage direction reads, "She has heard the word so frequently today that it is beginning to have a Scotch sound." Other asides emphasize this quality: "He envies the English way of dressing for trees and lawns, but is too Scotch to be able to imitate it" and "Kilts were only invented, like golf, to draw the English north."

Bursting from every scene is Maggie's worthiness—who is patterned after Barrie's mother, Margaret Ogilvy. Those who intuitively see Maggie's excellence are her father Alick and her brothers David and James, easily identified as the three boys in the Barrie family. Barrie, his whole life spent atoning for his brother's death, identifies David as "the ablest person in the room" and James as married and stupid. The play, coinciding with Barrie's own divorce, skipped over his current moods and harked back to his years in Kirriemuir.

Still another fantasy land is created in *Dear Brutus*, where an assortment of married couples are lured into Lob's magic wood, which appears every Midsummer Eve. The sulky, the happy, the egocentric, the alcoholic, the selfish—all are given a second chance to alter their pasts. The enchantment matches the spirit of William Shakespeare's *A Midsummer Night's Dream*. Few improvements result, however, which reinforces the theme borrowed from *Julius Caesar*: "The fault, dear Brutus, is not in our stars, but in ourselves." The dream child Margaret—again, Margaret Ogilvy—is killed off by marriage and reality.

The modernism in *Dear Brutus* is the therapeutic value that is assigned to dream analysis of repressed desires acted out. Even if things are not made better, the dreamers absorb the experience as clearly as a re-found reality and are presumably wiser for it.

For many, Barrie's sentiment and romance represent one portion of early modern British theater, a counter to the portion by Shaw's social commentary and literariness. The two playwrights were neighbors at 10 Adelphi Terrace in London.

Summary
The reputation of James Barrie rests primarily on *The Admirable Crichton* and *Peter Pan*. Barrie said, "I should feel as if I had left off my clothing, if I were to write without an island." His plays and novels reflect his own prototypic situation with his mother and brothers. Today he is regarded as a skillful but limited comic dramatist, although R.D.S. Jack argues convincingly for Barrie as an important visionary in the theater. Most important, though, *Peter Pan* has found its way into the world's literature alongside *Alice in Wonderland* and *The Wizard of Oz*.

Selected Bibliography
Primary Sources
The Plays of J.M. Barrie. Ed. A.E. Wilson. London: Hodder and Stoughton, 1947.

Secondary Sources

Biographies
Dunbar, Janet. *J.M. Barrie: The Man Behind the Image*. Boston: Houghton Mifflin, 1970. A psychological biography.
Geduld, Harry. *Sir James Barrie*. New York: Twayne, 1971. A reliable overview of Barrie's life and art.

Books and Articles
Blackburn, William. "*Peter Pan* and the Contemporary Adolescent Novel." *Proceedings 9th Annual Conference Children's Literature Association*, 1982.
Delany, Paul. "Who Was 'The Blind Man'?" *English Studies in Canada*, 9, 1 (March 1983): 92–99.
Egan, Michael. "The Neverland of Id: Barrie, Peter Pan and Freud." *Children's Literature*, 10 (1982): 37–55.
Gilead, Sarah. "Magic Abjured: Closure in Children's Fantasy Fiction." *PMLA*, 106, 2 (March 1991): 277–93.
Green, Martin. "The Charm of Peter Pan." *Children's Literature*, 9 (1981): 19–27.
Jack, R.D.S. *The Road to the Never Land: A Reassessment of J.M. Barrie's Dramatic Art*. Aberdeen, Scotland: Aberdeen University Press, 1991. The most important study of Barrie's drama, emphasizing the author's metaphysical vision and satire.
Russell, Patricia. "Parallel Romantic Fantasies: Barrie's *Peter Pan* and Spielberg's *E.T.*" *Children's Literature Association Quarterly*, 8, 4 (Winter 1983): 28–30.

Joel Athey

Bashford, Sir Henry Howarth
Born: Bedford, England, January, 1880
Education: Bedford Modern School; the London Hospital, University of London, M.D., 1908; B.S. (London), M.R.C.S. (England), 1904; L.R.C.P. (London), 1939
Marriage: Margaret Eveline Sutton, 1908; four children
Died: Pewsey, Wiltshire, August 15, 1961

Biography
A son of Frederick and Eleanor (Howarth) Bashford, Henry Howarth Bashford was born into a middle-class English family in Bedford in January 1880 and brought up in the home counties. His grandfather, the rector of a fashionable West-end church, had been Chaplain-in-ordinary to Queen Victoria. Henry was sent to a fee-paying public school, Bedford Modern, where he received his secondary education. Thereafter he studied medicine in London, qualifying with the M.R.C.S. (Member of the Royal College of Surgeons) and L.R.C.P. (Licentiate of the Royal College of Physicians) in 1904, and obtaining his M.D. in 1908. Bashford held residence appointments at the hospital prior to joining the medical staff of the General Post Office, where he devoted himself to special industrial health problems. There he rose to chief medical officer (1933–1943). In 1938, he was knighted and appointed a member of the Industrial Health Research Board. Bashford was elected L.R.C.P. in 1939. In 1943, he became the Medical Advisor to the Treasury, retiring in 1945. From 1941 to 1944 he was Honorary Physician to King George VI.

After his marriage in 1908 to Margaret Eveline Sutton of Basildon, Berkshire (she bore him one son and three daughters), Bashford regularly published volumes of fiction, some non-fiction, essays, and even poems for children. His most successful books were about famous medical men or about being a doctor;

he also wrote numerous slighter works, the titles of which hint at their content: *Vagabonds in Perigord*, *Fisherman's Progress*, and so forth. Bashford wrote under a literary pseudonym, "Peter Harding," as well. He contributed essays to magazines and published occasional articles in that distinguished organ of British medical opinion, *The Lancet*.

A success in his chosen profession, Bashford wrote and edited almost two dozen books, an achievement that may easily be overlooked in a career which brought him many accolades in English society; he was made a Fellow of the Hunterian Society and a Knight of Grace Order of St. John of Jerusalem, and was knighted by King George VI.

Oddly enough, *Augustus Carp, Esq. By Himself, Being the Autobiography of a Really Good Man*, his only work of humor and one that may well prove to be his enduring literary monument, was published anonymously in 1924. Bashford was never linked to this book in his own lifetime. After *Augustus Carp, Esq.'s* appearance and a mixed reception which the author may have anticipated, this work suffered neglect. At Sir Henry's death in Pewsey, Wiltshire on August 15, 1961, the authorship of *Augustus Carp, Esq.* was still a literary puzzle; only a 1965 appeal for information by novelist Anthony Burgess brought about a correct attribution.

Literary Analysis

When *Augustus Carp, Esq. By Himself, Being the Autobiography of a Really Good Man* (hereafter *Augustus Carp, Esq.*) was published in May 1924, contemporary reviews were less than kind. Perhaps the anonymity of its writer did nothing to help bring the novel an appreciative readership. Illustrations in the book probably enhanced the mystery because these were simply labeled as being by "Robin," recently identified by Robert Robinson as Marjorie Blood, a woman who subsequently entered the Order of the Sacred Heart and taught at Roehampton convent in south-west London as "Mother Catherine." Burgess has outlined the difficulties of an anonymous work receiving a favorable review and he worried about possible misreading; could it really have been viewed as "a solemnly intended essay in self-regard"? At any rate, his assessment of "a small mean nature enlivened by elephantine attempts at humor" appeared in his review in *The Bookman* (vol. 60: 1924, 214).

Bashford's theme in the book is hypocrisy, especially religious hypocrisy, in the Carp household at Mon Repos (complete with stubborn English pronunciation), Angela Gardens, Camberwell, a location south of the River Thames and in reality removed from Bashford's own residence in Hampstead, a fashionable northern suburb of London. The autobiographer's father, on whom much humor falls, is determined to conduct himself as an independently-minded member of the lower-middle class and successfully brings up his son in his own obnoxious image.

Bashford was a member of the Church of England, but his depiction of the extreme degree of low-church-cum-Puritan earnest Anglicans represented by father and son Carp surely owes more to a fertile imagination than any real-life pariah of St. James-the-Least-of-All. Pompous in speech, dress, and manner, Pa Carp cuts a preposterous figure with his "lower middle height," "large and well modelled nose," "massive ears," and powerful voice; moreover, he seems oblivious to his own harsh un-Christian way of treating his wife, his sisters-in-law, or even his temporary charlady. The father, ridiculously high-minded and high-handed, is both quick to see offense and prone to threaten legal action, even against members of his own "sershle soakle," though he meets his match in Mrs. O'Flaherty, the char', and in a like-minded rival sidesman, Alexander Carkeek. The "spiritual crisis" induced by the latter's donation of a brass lectern to the church, felicitously sustained via droll narration, mock-heroic diction, and exaggeration, introduces one of the best sustained pieces of humorous writing in the book.

The autobiographer son of "the Collector of Outstanding Debts for The Consolidated Water Board" reviews with deadpan seriousness his own life from an infancy plagued by ill-health and through school days marked by zeal for studying the Bible (even his pet rabbit is named "Isaiah"), and by a recreational talent for "Nuts in May" and ducks and drakes, his only athletic exercises. Thoroughly priggish and often a Twain-like innocent, glib Augustus is absolutely against swearing, drinking, dancing, and smoking, and he battles obtusely with his schoolmasters and fellow students over their blasphemies, cheating, and worldliness. He is given to inflated diction and extravagant hates:

Hitherto, like my father, when travelling by tram or omnibus, I had always insisted upon complete immobility prior both to entrance into and departure from one of these public conveyances; and many a conductor had been reported by us both for failing to secure the requisite lack of motion. (44)

This humbug leads to several humorous episodes, backed by a blend of hyperbole, parodies, comic analogies, and inversions, even bathos, perhaps the best example of which involves the besting of Augustus by an avenging actress, Mary Moonbeam, who introduces him to "Portugalade," a cordial health drink which Augustus finds "peculiarly attractive to the nostril" and "no less grateful to the tongue." Days later, before giving a public lecture, Augustus is treated to a dinner by Mary, during which that beverage was "again served to my annoyance in wine-glasses." Swaying under its spell in the presence of his tee-total employer, Augustus, sometimes as gullible as Swift's Gulliver, falls from the stage and thus fails to complete a public address, anticipating Kingsley Amis's Jim Dixon. Argue though he will that he has suffered from "port-poisoning," he loses his job.

As befits comedy, the autobiography closes after Augustus's marriage and the birth of a son. The insufferable Augustus praises Providence for seeing "fit to reward my efforts & the crowning satisfaction of becoming a father."

Appreciation of the literary humor of *Augustus Carp, Esq.* is recent and belated. Perhaps there is substance to Stephen Leacock's remark in *My Discovery of England* that in the first several decades of the twentieth century, humor was not something longed for or even highly regarded by the English.

Augustus Carp, Esq. certainly meets Leacock's requirement for English humor in terms of form: the book is a series of anecdotes. Moreover, it conforms to Leacock's observation that for the English the point lies in the humorous telling rather than in some culminating fireworks. Bashford frequently draws humor from surprising juxtapositions of ideas and language, as in Augustus's recapitulation of Simeon Whey's first sermon with its clusters of quasi-Biblical phrasing.

Among Bashford's shortcomings is an English reliance on pun and hidden quotation which ranges from silliness to pedantry. An anti-dancing tract by Augustus's friend, Ezekiel Stool, is titled "The Chorus Girl's Catastrophe." At better moments, with nods to Dr. Spooner and Mrs. Malaprop, a vacillating vicar is described as "a weed before the rind." Pa Carp's high-falutin language is reminiscent of E.F. Benson's amusing characters and their determined anglicizing (and mangling) of French expressions. Bashford also likes Latin tags and convoluted sentences which parody Victorian autobiography. The writer's characteristic humor shows its English pedigree too by avoiding both slang (for the most part) and Twain-y misspellings.

Some of the niceties of Bashford's humor are restricted to those readers aware of the minutiae of Anglicanism and class barriers. There is a turn-of-the-century feel to the book, transcended by an occasional quip about Anglican parsons which might come straight from the "Beyond the Fringe" or "Monty Python" crowd; a friend's sons are described as "Xtian lads of about my own age, and each with an impediment in his speech, both [of whom] were destined on this account for eventual ordination in the Church of England."

Summary

Henry Bashford's "neglected masterpiece," *Augustus Carp, Esq.*, contains great moments of humor. Some of its pages have inevitably lost their early sparkle because our awareness of late Victorian/Edwardian London society is less sure and our grasp of some English allusions and of contemporary language is more tenuous. Since its reissue in 1966, however, *Carp* has been lauded. Now, a generation later, Burgess's praise may be viewed as over-enthusiastic, but the book is likely to retain much of the acclaim of this generation and to take its place among the classics of English humor such as Jerome K. Jerome's *Three Men in a Boat* and George and Weedon Grossmith's *Diary of a Nobody*.

Selected Bibliography

Primary Sources
Augustus Carp, Esq. By Himself, Being the Autobiography of a Really Good Man. Il. "Robin." London: Heinemann, 1924; Boston: Houghton Mifflin, 1924; London: Heinemann, 1966; Harmondsworth, Middx.: Penguin Books, 1987; New York: Viking Press, 1987. London: Folio Book Soc., 1988.

Tommy Wideawake. London and New York: John Lane, 1903.

The Manitoban: A Romance. London and New York: John Lane, 1904.

The Trail Together: an Episode. London: Heinemann, 1906.

The Corner of Harley Street. London: Constable, 1911.

Pity the Poor Blind. London: Constable, and New York: Holt, 1913.

Vagabonds in Perigord. London: Constable, and Boston: Houghton Mifflin, 1914.

Songs Out of School. London: Constable, 1917.

Sons of Admiralty: a short history of the naval war, 1914–18. London: Constable, and New York: Doubleday, 1919; co-authored with Archibald Hurd.

The Plain Girl's Tale. London: Collins, 1919.

Half-Past Bedtime. London: Harrap, 1922; Boston: Houghton Mifflin, 1921.

The Happy Ghost. London: Heinemann, and New York: Harpers, 1925.

Behind the Fog; a Tale of Adventure. London: Heinemann, 1926.

The Harley Street Calendar. London: Constable, and Boston: Houghton Mifflin, 1929.

Lodgings for Twelve. London: Constable, 1935.

Doctors in Shirt Sleeves. Musings on hobbies, meals, patients, sport, and philosophy, ed. London: Kegan Paul, 1939.

Fisherman's Progress. London: Constable, 1946.

Wiltshire Harvest. London: Constable, 1953.

Secondary Sources

Anon. *Antioch Review,* 46 (Spring 1988): 276. A favorable review of "this treasure."

Anon. *The Bookman,* 60 (1924): 214. Overall rather critical of the "elephantine humor."

Anon. *The New Yorker,* 64 (April 4, 1988): 102. "A sublime ferocious farce." "Some of the best lines, delivered deadpan, are given to drinkers, smokers, dancers and adulterers."

Burgess, Anthony. "Introduction" to *Augustus Carp, Esq. By Himself, Being the Autobiography of a Really Good Man.* London: Heinemann, 1966, pp. xi–xiv. A totally neglected writer of a solitary masterpiece.

———. "Postscript" to *Augustus Carp, Esq. By Himself, Being the Autobiography of a Really Good Man.* Harmondsworth: Penguin Books, 1987, pp. 187–91. Burgess recalls a long-standing, personal enthusiasm for "one of the great comic novels of the twentieth century." Praises the professional craft of the humorist.

———. *Bookseller* (September 24, 1966): 1768–69. *Augustus Carp, Esq.* This review addresses a new generation of readers.

———. Letter in *Times Literary Supplement,* 3307 (July 15, 1965): 602. The original appeal for information about authorship of *Augustus Carp, Esq.*

Khan, Naseem. *New Statesman,* 114 (December 4, 1987): 31. A brief review in which Khan finds the book "incomparable," "a wonderful slapstick satire on hypocrisy."

Robinson, Robert. "Introduction" in *Augustus Carp, Esq. By Himself, Being the Autobiography of a Really Good Man.* Harmondsworth: Penguin Books, 1987, pp. xi–xvi. Robinson reflects on a lifetime's admiration for this coterie work whose lingo insinuated itself into his family's affections. He sketches his favorite characters/caricatures, those well-remembered incidents, and favorably compares this work with the Grossmiths' humorous portrayal of lower-middle-class London life.

John S. Batts

Beaumont, Francis

Born: At the family estate Grace Dieu, Leicestershire, 1584 or 1585

Education: Matriculated at Broadgates Hall, Oxford, in 1597; entered Inner Temple, London in 1600.

Marriage: Ursula Isley, ca. 1613; two children

Died: Kent, March 6, 1616

Biography

Third son of Francis Beaumont, Justice of the Common Pleas, Francis the dramatist belonged to the younger branch of a distinguished Leicestershire family. He was born in 1584 or 1585 at the family estate, Grace Dieu. He matriculated at Broadgates Hall in Oxford with his two brothers in 1597; there is no record of a degree being conferrred. When his father died in 1598, the eldest son, Henry, left Oxford to take up his inheritance; he may have been accompanied by his brothers.

Although apparently slated to follow the paternal path by studying law at the Inner Temple, which he entered in 1560, once in London both Francis and John showed more interest in literary than in legal pursuits. Long associated with the literary and theatrical life of Elizabethan England, the Inns of Court proved congenial; their overlapping intellectual and poetic circles included John Donne, Sir John Davies, William Browne, and John Marston, and their members provided an educated, articulate, sophisticated audience for innovative drama as well as poetry. Beaumont's earliest known work, a playful *Grammar Lecture* that wittily mocks the manners of his fellow Templars, was delivered at one of their Christmas revels and survives in manuscript. His first verses were probably those signed "F.B." which were prefixed to his brother John's 1602 mock panegyric, *The Metamorphosis of Tobacco*, and Francis is generally accepted as the author who in the same year wrote the anonymous *Salmacis and Hermaphroditus* as a contribution to the late-Elizabethan fad for wittily erotic, mini-epic poems based on Ovidian mythology.

Beaumont's interests soon turned theatrical, and he began writing for the fashionable, avant-garde children's companies whose private theaters had been revived in 1599–1600. There he became friends—and, according to legend, roommates—with John Fletcher, with whom he soon formed one of the most famous collaborative teams in literary history. Although the text of *Love's Cure* exists only in a later version revised by Philip Massinger, Beaumont and Fletcher may have collaborated on the original script for the boys of Paul's as early as 1605. Before that company's demise in 1606, Beaumont wrote *The Woman Hater*, printed in 1607 as having been acted by them. Writing next for the Children of the Queen's Revels at the Blackfriars theater, Beaumont found congenial colleagues that included, besides Fletcher, the poet-playwrights Ben Jonson, George Chapman, and Marston, along with the troupe's talented leading actor Nathan Field. One of Beaumont's closest literary friendships was with Jonson, and he wrote commendatory verses for the first quartos of Jonson's *Volpone*, *Epicoene*, and *Catiline*, as well as for Fletcher's unsuccessful pastoral play *The Faithful Shepherdess*. For the Blackfriars children Beaumont composed

The Knight of the Burning Pestle (ca. 1607; printed 1613), today his most admired play although a commercial failure at the time, and around 1608, in their first certain collaboration, he and Fletcher borrowed plots from Philip Sidney's *Arcadia* for the apparently popular tragedy *Cupid's Revenge* (printed 1615).

When the Blackfriars troupe was suppressed by King James for one too many politically inflammatory plays, its theater was taken over by the King's Men, the adult company that held the building's lease and whose principal playwright was William Shakespeare. Beaumont and Fletcher continued to collaborate for the reorganized Revels Children, composing two comedies for them (*The Coxcomb*, ca. 1609, and *The Scornful Lady*, ca. 1610), but their most famous collaborations were written for the King's Men and performed at both the private Blackfriars and public Globe theaters. While Shakespeare was producing his last plays, Beaumont and Fletcher turned out three very successful and influential dramatic romances of their own: *Philaster* (ca. 1609), *The Maid's Tragedy* (ca. 1610), and *A King and No King* (1611). According to modern scholars, Beaumont also contributed a scene or two to some of Fletcher's plays of this period, just as Fletcher apparently helped touch up *The Woman Hater* before publication; there is disagreement over whether *The Noble Gentleman* is an early Beaumont script heavily revised by Fletcher, or wholly a late-Fletcher composition. Finally, in 1660 the folio's publisher Humphrey Moseley entered in the Stationers' Register under Beaumont's name the title of a play about which nothing more is known, *The History of Madon, King of Britain*.

Beaumont seems to have maintained his contacts with the Inns of Court, and on February 20, 1613 his *Masque of the Inner Temple and Gray's Inn* was performed as part of the elaborate court celebrations for the marriage of Princess Elizabeth to the Elector Palatine. Although his financial circumstances remain a mystery, and hence whether he turned playwright for economic reasons is unknown, Beaumont was a gentleman by birth, and he moved easily in country as well as London literary circles. His poetic brother John, a close friend of Michael Drayton, succeeded Henry in 1605, and visits to Grace Dieu became literary as well as familial occasions. Beaumont wrote verse epistles and elegies for various prominent noblewomen and seems to have shared with Jonson the favor of Sidney's daughter Elizabeth, countess of Rutland. His poems, some of them fashionably Donnean and wittily libertine, were not collected and printed until 1640, well after his death. Reticence about publication would not have been unusual in this period for one of Beaumont's social standing. It is probably no coincidence that, with the exception of the masque, none of his dramatic works printed in his lifetime—his own or those written with Fletcher—appears with his name on the title-page; the first quarto to claim even his partial authorship, *The Scornful Lady*, was entered in the Stationers' Register thirteen days after Beaumont's death.

Around 1613, Beaumont married a Kentish heiress, Ursula Isley, and presumably lived a gentleman's life on her estates until his death. (Fletcher took over from Shakespeare as principal dramatist for the King's Men and continued to write, prolifically, until his death in 1625.) Whether marriage and comparative affluence led Beaumont to turn his back on his former life and reclaim his social position, or whether the stroke that he suffered around 1613 (the "apoplexe" described by Thomas Pestell in his elegy on Beaumont) incapacitated him for London theatrical pursuits, is not known. He lived on for three years, fathering two daughters. The author died in Kent on March 6, 1616, and was buried in what became known as Poets' Corner in Westminster Abbey. His reputation persisted, and when Moseley brought out the first folio in 1647 (thirty-four previously unpublished plays, plus Beaumont's masque), the collection of preponderately Fletcher and Fletcher-Massinger works appeared under the title *Comedies and Tragedies* "written by Francis Beaumont and John Fletcher, Gentlemen"; when the plays already in print were added in 1679 for the second folio (fifty-two plays), the authorial ascription did not change.

Literary Analysis

Although Beaumont wrote with Fletcher in all genres and developed with him the kind of romantic tragicomedy that became the seventeenth century's most popular dramatic form, he began his literary career with comedy—the wittily erotic epyllion *Salmacis and Hermaphroditus* and his first two plays. The tragicomedies use stock comic characters and situations to leaven the action's apparently fatal trajectory and to create the "middle mood"

appropriate to the new form's hybrid tone and final happy ending, and he continued to collaborate with Fletcher on comedies for the boys' troupes. Commendatory verses to the first folio repeatedly extol both men for their "wit," a term that already included, along with its older reference to good judgment and discretion, the more modern sense of sparkling expression and liveliness of fancy. John Earle compares Beaumont favorably with Menander, Plautus, and Aristophanes. William Cartwright and John Berkenhead also credit him with great judgment as well as the firm sense of structure responsible for one of the collaborations' most admired features, their teasingly convoluted, carefully modulated, dramatic plotting. Later, explaining the dominance of their plays on the Restoration stage, Dryden cited the gaiety of their comedies, the easy, gentlemanly fluency of their language (at a time when Shakespeare was beginning to sound antiquated), and a wittiness surpassing Jonson.

These two other legs of the seventeenth-century "Triumvirate of Wit," whom Beaumont and Fletcher briefly excelled in popularity, also suggest the two locales with the strongest influence on Beaumont's developing dramaturgy. He began writing for the private theaters, known for modish social and political satire and for comedies of contemporary London life, and Jonson and Marston provided immediate models. The impress of Marston's works, especially *The Dutch Courtesan* (acted 1603–1604; printed 1605), is clear as early as *The Woman Hater*, which borrows from *The Dutch Courtesan*'s subplot for one of its own and whose plucky, independent-minded heroine Oriana at times echoes Marston's Crispinella (who in turn quotes Montaigne on the evils of Custom). As his commendatory poems and two verse epistles to Jonson indicate, Jonson was an admired artist and became a close friend; the epistles also compliment Jonson by adopting, uncharacteristically for Beaumont, the heroic couplet favored by his neo-classicist colleague. Still, in neither form nor tone are Beaumont's plays—alone or with Fletcher—truly Jonsonian.

Whether or not he knew Shakespeare personally before writing for the King's Men, Beaumont certainly knew his works. Members of the first generation to begin writing under the influence of a substantial Shakespearean *oeuvre*, both Beaumont and Fletcher turned to this proven, public-theater dramatist as well as to their own early associates. Under the influence of Shakespeare's plays, as well as Sidney's *Arcadia*, they came to specialize in romantic tragicomedy and tragedy as well as comedies based on love rather than financial intrigue. When they sought an ordering principle for comedy's loose multiplicity of incident, they turned not to Jonson or Plautus but to the traditional Elizabethan—and Shakespearean—double plot.

Specific borrowings and allusions appear in Beaumont's first dramas: parodies of speeches from *Hamlet*, *Othello*, and *Antony and Cleopatra* in *The Woman Hater*; a comic use of Hotspur's paean on honor in *The Knight of the Burning Pestle*. Later, in the joint plays and continuing in Fletcher's work after 1613, Shakespearean speeches, characters, situations—even whole plays—get recycled in the works of the "Beaumont and Fletcher" canon. To such bifold dramatic authority Beaumont brought intelligence and a talent for independent creation, and the private theaters, always receptive to novelty, proved a locale conducive to dramatic experiment. It was there that, despite individual early failures, he and his new partner began forging the much-admired "Beaumont and Fletcher" comic as well as tragicomic style.

In fusing their private and public theater heritages, Beaumont and Fletcher developed the clever, out-spoken heroine favored by Marston but also associated with Shakespeare's high-Elizabethan comedy (preeminently *Much Ado About Nothing*'s Beatrice and Benedick, but also the resourceful women who disguise themselves as men of other works). To her courtship they adapted two features of satiric city comedy: the portrait of contemporary life and manners, and the intrigue plotting that controlled its dramatic structure. Elements of this mixture are evident in *The Woman Hater*, although there the witty exchanges take place between Oriana and Gondarino, the title's misogynist, not Oriana and the Duke whom she will marry. The transvestite heroine is not a feature of Beaumont's first comedy (although she would soon appear in *Cupid's Revenge* and *Philaster*), but her potential for comically inverting traditional sex roles—as well as her implicit challenge to their status as socially normative and definitive—proved attractive from the start. In *The Woman Hater*, Gondarino's anti-feminist obsession finds its match in the virtuous but also intelligent and self-confident Oriana. Oriana takes the initiative to punish his foul-mouthed slander of her whole sex by turning on him his own stereotype of women as talkative, lustful, and aggressive. She reverses the convention of masculine wooing and chases Gondarino all over his own house, peppering him with courtly compliments and threatening her eternal devotion.

A Shakespearean fondness for multiple plots, ranging from royalty to gentry courtiers to city craftsmen, also marks Beaumont's dramatic debut and extends *The Woman Hater*'s range of comic types. In the most developed subplot Lazarello, the "hungry courtier" who gave the 1649 quarto its subtitle, becomes obsessed with obtaining the head of an umbrana fish for his dinner; this humorous character's repeatedly frustrated pursuit of his gustatory goal is raised to the mock-heroic level, then further embellished with comically inappropriate verbal allusions to contemporary tragedies and extended flights of Petrarchan hyperbole that convert the lowly fishhead into an object of erotic desire. In a more truncated and conventional subplot, a mercer who admires learning is gulled into marrying a prostitute by a pandar posing as a scholar-magician. These subsidiary actions contribute to the romantic main plot familiar satiric portraits of social types (borrowed largely from city comedy), but they are maintained at the level of farce and thus help keep the play's tone light.

In this early play the innovative woman is not wholly successful. Oriana's self-conscious violations of decorum provide several very funny scenes for the audience, but they do not shock Gondarino out of his unmanly hatred of women and unnatural isolation from society; the Petrarchanly inclined Duke proves in his way as conventional as the misogynist and, unable to accept as innocent her bold behavior or frank speech, agrees that she should be put to the ultimate test of female virtue: the choice of death or dishonor. Yet although the refreshing world of comic possibility and individual freedom suddenly narrows in the denouement, much of the main plot's sheer fun has depended on Oriana's playful role-reversal and verbal agility. At the very end, allowed to choose Gondarino's punishment, she rescues this comedy from its brush with mortality: bound to a chair, the woman hater must endure being publicly "wooed" and fondled by a bevy of ladies.

Oriana proved a precedent. Beaumont and Fletcher are usually credited with bringing a new feminism to English comedy with well-born, independent-minded ladies who challenge their gentlemen-gallants on an equal footing. In *The Coxcomb* and, especially, *The Scornful Lady*, the dramatists reassigned some of the private theaters' urbane, often scurrilous, wit from sarcastic asides or set speeches on standard satiric topics to the prickly interchanges of the romantic couple whose courtship is now the play's primary focus. Such "wit duels" proved a model for Restoration comedy. In the joint comedies Beaumont and Fletcher also adopted an upper-class social milieu more appealing to the restricted audience of Restoration drama, and they set a precedent for the later comedy's preoccupation with the social effects of a double standard of sexual morality. The most popular play in the whole "Beaumont and Fletcher" canon, *The Scornful Lady* was steadily performed well into the eighteenth century.

In other ways, too, Beaumont—alone and in his collaborations with Fletcher—provided some of the materials, if not the final emphasis, of Restoration comedy. The polished restraint, cool distance from daily life, and ironic self-consciousness of the Restoration hero already mark the wittily cynical observations of Count Valore in *The Woman Hater*, himself developed from the children's companies' "satiric commentator" figure. Although they lack the later *de rigueur* libertine philosophy, Mercury (*The Coxcomb*) and Lovelace (*The Scornful Lady*) could—and did, in revivals—comfortably share the stage with William Congreve's and William Wycherley's sophisticated male protagonists. *The Scornful Lady* deftly updates the witty exuberance of Elizabethan romantic comedy with topical satire, stylish double entendre, and a new style of wooing to complement the "new" woman. Old-fashioned courtship has become a battleground on which each side struggles for dominance and private satisfaction, and this harder edge is underlined in the subplots, where economics and opportunism weigh more heavily than romance.

Both innovative and eclectic in his use of conventional theatrical materials, from the beginning Beaumont demonstrated a chameleon-like talent—and taste—for literary parody and burlesque. *The Woman Hater* abounds in recognizable character types and dramatic devices as well as direct borrowings and parodied speeches. Through the hilariously vapid Lazarello, Beaumont zestfully also mocks most of the outmoded literary languages of his day—not only Petrarchanism, but also Euphuism and the rhetoric of chivalric romance. This aspect of his dramaturgy was especially aimed at his private-theater audience's assumed sophistication in literary taste as well as playgoing, and it gives Beaumont's early comedy a metadramatic dimension that found full flower in *The Knight of the Burning Pestle*'s high-spirited burlesque of both literary conventions and contemporary plays.

Expanding the conventional Induction's apparently spontaneous pre-play discussion among players and audience members, Beaumont fashions an unusual vehicle for exploring the nature of dramatic creation and performance. As though erupting from the Blackfriars audience itself, a grocer and his wife climb on stage to sit with the gallants. They object to the theater's intended offering, a city comedy called *The London Merchant*, and demand that the actors perform—if not instead of, at least in alternating scenes—a citizen-adventure story to be dictated by them and to star their own apprentice, Rafe. Initially, the play's focus seems wholly satiric, aimed at the boorish, egoistic citizens—their demand that the theater conform to their wishes and flatter their class; their outmoded taste in literature; their failure as audience and as playwrights—and against public theaters like the Red Bull and Curtain, where exactly the named plays they prefer could be found.

Yet, the citizens' lack of literary sophistication or theatrical experience is fundamental to Beaumont's larger, non-satiric concerns, and what looks to become a struggle between art and life turns into an interrogation of their interrelations as well as, in its unique way, a genuinely festive comedy. The very qualities that make the obstreperous citizen-audience an actor's nightmare also increase their usefulness in Beaumont's scheme: they become child-like commentators on, and interrupters of, two plays, one of which they create out of a mishmash of the stock characters, situations, and old-fashioned rhetorical style of chivalric romance. Miguel Cervantes' non-dramatic burlesque of many of the same romances, *Don Quixote*, may lie behind Beaumont's initial conception, but Beaumont has turned its central epistemological confusions to boldly original theatrical uses.

The citizens generate most of *The Knight*'s hilarity, both in their own hopelessly disjointed knightly romance and in their naive responses to this new experience—playgoing. They swing rapidly between under- and over-distancing and have trouble telling fiction from fact, even in the events of the play that they make up themselves. When dissatisfied with the plot of *The London Merchant*, they order Rafe to intervene and, in his character as the Knight of the Burning Pestle, to right its wrongs. They also provide two of the most vital, fully realized London tradesmen in Renaissance drama, and their enthusiasm for the imaginative satisfactions that only art can provide is contagious. Their untutored reactions also expose the arbitrariness and dependence on shared convention of the theater's own professional offering. Like an early seventeenth-century Luigi Pirandello, Beaumont holds the mirror of life up to art in order to probe the pleasures, and limits, of his new medium.

Real life proved as intractable as *The Knight*'s fractious citizens. The comedy's first audience may indeed have missed what the quarto's publisher calls in his dedicatory epistle the play's "privy marke of *Ironie*." Beaumont may also simply have asked too much. He created a fresh, uncommon play by disconcertingly juxtaposing, and subverting, two established forms; for good measure, bits of well-known plays (*Mucedorus*, *The Spanish Tragedy*, *Macbeth*) crop up unexpectedly. The play's success depends on the audience's willingness to follow the constant shifts between levels of illusion; it must maintain an alert, imaginatively engaged yet also critical perspective as apparently familiar material is put to unexpected uses. Beaumont succeeds in giving the impression that he has brought real people on stage, but the ensuing confusion explodes narrative expectations and continuity; it may have led his first audience to feel as resentful as the play's boy-actors, taken captive against their will.

Summary

Critically disparaged in the nineteenth and twentieth centuries, the "Beaumont and Fletcher" phenomenon was enormously influential in its time; late in the seventeenth century it helped determine the shape both of Restoration comedy and the emergent comedy of manners, and of the serious heroic drama that evolved, with substantial French borrowing, from their brand of romantic tragicomedy. Ironically, since he apparently tried to avoid public association with his stage compositions, Beaumont's early fame (and death) made him a commercially negotiable property. Despite a brief career and a handful of plays, he was made joint author of all fifty-two works in the "Beaumont and Fletcher" second folio. As a result, Beaumont's literary reputation has largely suffered the critical fate of that canon. However, Beaumont has begun to receive his due in recent studies in attribution, which sift out Beaumont from other contributors subsumed under his name and express appreciation of his strikingly modern exploration of metadramatic issues in *The Knight of the Burning Pestle*. *The Knight* is now regarded as a minor comic masterpiece, as well as the first great English dramatic burlesque, and it was in the collaborations with Beaumont that the influential "Beaumont and Fletcher" style was first forged.

Selected Bibliography
Primary Sources

Original quartos, folios, manuscripts
The Woman Hater. London, 1607.
The Knight of the Burning Pestle. London, 1613.
The Scornful Lady. London, 1616.
Poems. London, 1640. Rpt. with additions, 1653. Not all by Beaumont.
Comedies and Tragedies. London, 1647. First folio; includes *The Coxcomb*.
Fifty Comedies and Tragedies. London, 1679. Second folio.
Grammar Lecture. British Library, Sloane MS. 1709, fols. 12–22.

Modern Editions
The Works of Beaumont and Fletcher. Ed. Alexander Dyce. 11 vols. London: Edward Moxon, 1843–1846. Best edition of its time; reprints documents from Beaumont's life as well as the poetry.
The Works of Francis Beaumont and John Fletcher. Variorum Edition. Ed. A.H. Bullen, et al. 4 vols. London: G. Bell & Sons, 1904–1912. Twenty plays; series never completed.
The Works of Francis Beaumont and John Fletcher. Ed. Arnold Glover and A.R. Waller. Cambridge English Classics. 10 vols. Cambridge: Cambridge University Press, 1905–1912. Folio of 1679 with appendix of variants in first folio and quartos; useful for those plays not yet edited for Bowers edition and for 1647 commendatory verses.

The Dramatic Works in the Beaumont and Fletcher Canon. Ed. Fredson Bowers, et al. 7 vols. to date. Cambridge: Cambridge University Press, 1966–. Standard modern edition; old spelling.

The Knight of the Burning Pestle. Ed. John Doebler. Regents Renaissance Drama Series. Lincoln: University of Nebraska Press, 1967.

———. Ed. Michael Hattaway. The New Mermaids. London: Ernest Benn, 1969.

———. Ed. Sheldon P. Zitner. The Revels Plays. Manchester: Manchester University Press, 1984.

Secondary Sources

Bibliographies

Smith, Denzell S. "Francis Beaumont and John Fletcher." In *The Later Jacobean and Caroline Dramatists: A Survey and Bibliography of Recent Studies in English Renaissance Drama.* Ed. by Terence P. Logan and Denzell S. Smith. Lincoln: University of Nebraska Press, 1978. Items largely restricted to 1923–76; some helpful annotations.

Tannenbaum, S.A. *Beaumont and Fletcher (A Concise Bibliography).* Elizabethan Bibliographies, no. 3. New York: Samuel A. Tannenbaum, 1938. Especially useful for nineteenth-century commentary and location of excerpted selections, scenes, and songs.

Biographies

Gayley, Charles Mills. *Beaumont, the Dramatist.* London: Duckworth, 1914; New York: Russell & Russell, 1969. Standard biography; enthusiastic but sometimes inaccurate.

Books

Bliss, Lee. *Francis Beaumont.* Twayne's English Authors Series. Boston: Twayne, 1987. Life and theatrical background; literary analyses of plays written alone or with Fletcher.

Finkelpearl, Philip J. *Court and Country Politics in the Plays of Beaumont and Fletcher.* Princeton: Princeton University Press, 1990. Finds in the comedies, too, a political critique of the Jacobean court and its ideology.

Macaulay, George Campbell. *Francis Beaumont: A Critical Study.* London: Kegan Paul, Trench & Co., 1883; New York: Lemma, 1972. Early defense of Beaumont and attempt to differentiate him from Fletcher; has been superseded on questions of authorship and dating.

Maxwell, Baldwin. *Studies in Beaumont, Fletcher, and Massinger.* Chapel Hill: University of North Carolina Press, 1939. Relevant essays treat a source for *The Knight*, dating of *The Scornful Lady*, and the "hungry knave" character.

Sprague, Arthur Colby. *Beaumont and Fletcher on the Restoration Stage.* Cambridge: Harvard University Press, 1926; New York: Benjamin Blom, 1965. Best survey of frequency of revival and nature of later adaptations.

Waith, Eugene M. *The Pattern of Tragicomedy in Beaumont and Fletcher.* New Haven: Yale University Press, 1952. Brief discussion of the early comedies.

Wallis, Lawrence B. *Fletcher, Beaumont & Company: Entertainers to the Jacobean Gentry.* New York: King's Crown Press, 1947. Most complete study of dramatists' reputation; some attention to the early comedies.

Articles

Bliss, Lee. "*Don Quixote* in England: The Case for *The Knight of the Burning Pestle.*" *Viator,* 18 (1987): 361–80. Examines ways *Don Quixote* might have been known in England by 1607.

———. "'Plot mee no plots': The Life of Drama and the Drama of Life in *The Knight of the Burning Pestle.*" *Modern Language Quarterly,* 45 (1984): 3–21. Critical study of the play, especially as metadrama.

Doebler, John. "Beaumont's *The Knight of the Burning Pestle* and the Prodigal Son Plays." *Studies in English Literature,* 5 (1965): 333–44. Doebler discusses this "genre," including *Eastward Ho,* and Beaumont's inversion of the pattern.

Eccles, Mark. "Francis Beaumont's *Grammar Lecture.*" *Review of English Studies,* 16 (1940): 402–14. Discusses and reprints this early work, from the original British Library copy (Sloane MS. 1709, fols. 12–22).

Finkelpearl, Philip J. "'Wit' in Francis Beaumont's Poems." *Modern Language*

Quarterly, 28 (1967): 33–44. Suggests that Beaumont learned from Jonson to reject false wit and ostentatious rhetoric.

Gale, Steven H. "The Relationship between Beaumont's *Knight of the Burning Pestle* and Cervantes' *Don Quixote*." *Anales Cervantinos*, 12 (1972): 87–96. Discussion of the evidence that Beaumont was familiar with Cervantes' novel and the influences and borrowings that appear in the play.

Hoy, Cyrus. "The Shares of Fletcher and his Collaborators in the Beaumont and Fletcher Canon." *Studies in Bibliography*, 8–9, 11–14 (1956–1961). Most sophisticated attempt to ascribe shares, though least helpful in distinguishing Fletcher from Beaumont.

Miller, Ronald F. "Dramatic Form and Dramatic Imagination in Beaumont's *The Knight of the Burning Pestle*." *English Literary Renaissance*, 8 (1978): 67–84. Excellent study of how satire dissolves into metadramatic exploration.

Samuelson, David A. "The Order in Beaumont's *Knight of the Burning Pestle*." *English Literary Renaissance*, 9 (1979): 302–18. Interesting on relations among competing plots.

Upton, Albert W. "Allusions to James I and His Court in Marston's *Fawn* and Beaumont's *Woman Hater*." *PMLA*, 44 (1929): 1048–65. Argues for extreme political topicality.

Lee Bliss

Beckett, Samuel

Born: Foxrock, near Dublin, Ireland, April 13, 1906

Education: Portora Royal School; Trinity College, Dublin, B.A., 1927; Fellowship, l'Ecole Normale Superieure, Paris, 1928–1930; Trinity College, Dublin, 1930–1931, M.A., 1931

Marriage: Suzanne Deschevaux-Dumesnil, March 25, 1961

Died: Paris, December 22, 1989

Biography

Samuel Beckett was born in Foxrock, near Dublin, Ireland, on Good Friday, April 13, 1906, the second of two sons to William and May (Mary) Beckett. His father was a quantity surveyor who made a good living for his family. A bon vivant, William loved his two sons, sports, good food, and drinking with his business associates and friends. An active swimmer and hiker, he encouraged the boys to be fearless, competitive athletes, teaching them to swim, for example, by throwing them into the water from a ten-foot drop before they were five years old.

Beckett's mother was very different—a complex and difficult woman. According to biographer Deirdre Bair, Mary had been a nurse before her marriage but afterward devoted herself to her family, her animals (she kept donkeys and many dogs), and right living. Throughout Beckett's childhood, she had sudden mood swings ("severe tension headaches, dark depressions and thundering rages"[1]), but she also told funny stories, served jam cakes to the boys' friends, and took the neighborhood children for rides in her donkey cart. A harsh disciplinarian who tried to defeat Samuel's seeming willfulness, she often beat him "severely." She disapproved of her husband's easy-going ways, made the boys feel guilty for preferring their father to her, and saw to it that the family observed proper religious practices. Many traces of her personality and conflicts appear in Beckett's characters. For example, she paced the house ceaselessly at night when her insomnia raged, as does May in *Footfalls*.

Samuel and his brother Frank received a good education at the Portora Royal School, a boarding school at Enniskillen, County Fermanagh, where Oscar Wilde had also been a pupil. Sam was on the cricket team, boxed, studied piano and French, and did well enough academically. In 1923, he went on to Trinity College, Dublin, where he blossomed, majoring in modern languages, studying modern French poetry and Dante with especial intensity. He was groomed for an academic career by his mentor, Dr. Rudnose-Brown, and was encouraged to study in France. While still an undergraduate, he made several trips to France and Germany. There he visited his father's sister, Cissie Beckett, who had married a penniless but charming, intelligent Jew who later became an art and antiques dealer in Germany. Samuel saw a lifestyle immersed in art and culture with looser behavioral codes. He apparently fell in love with his beautiful cousin, Peggy Sinclair, but she did not want to get seriously involved with him, and the romantic element in their relationship ended well before her death in 1933.

Along with his graduation from Trinity in 1927, he won a two-year graduate fellowship to l'Ecole Normale Supérieure in Paris (1928–1930). It was there that he met James Joyce and the group of writers and artists in his circle. In this period Beckett produced some translations of avant-garde French and Italian poetry, an important book on Proust, early short stories ("Assumption") and the essay "Dante . . . Bruno . . . Vico . . . Joyce" written for *Our Exagmination Round His Factification for Incamination of Work in Progress*, a volume intended to introduce Joyce's *Finnegans Wake*, then called *Work in Progress*, to a wider audience.

Beckett and Joyce were brilliant linguists and scholars, intellectually cosmopolitan Irishmen living abroad, deeply committed to literature, and Joyce's influence on Beckett was very strong at this time. Beckett's writing shows this influence: an elegance of diction, a plethora of literary allusions, quotations, parodies, and puns, a highly intellectual, objective style based on deep, philosophical reflection. During this period, Beckett read the works of René Descartes and his follower, Arnold Geulincx. He agreed that a man "must realize that he can only achieve true independence in his own mind . . . not act against passion but [be] indifferent to it" (Bair, 91–92). The desire to live in and valorize the mind, searching there for the essence of the self while devaluing the body, may have encouraged the introversion, agony, and ontological despair of his later fiction.

In 1930, Beckett's poem, *Whoroscope*, won a literary prize and was published. It exhibits some of his basic characteristics and comic themes: the punning title, the obsession with Descartes' philosophy (the separation of self into body and mind), the erudition, the focus on the odd angle (in this case, Descartes' appetite for eggs developed to a stage that most people would find distasteful).

Joyce did more than stimulate Beckett's intellectual development. Joyce relied personally on the younger man who was happy to run his errands, read to him, and write the essay detailing Joyce's debt to Dante. With his good friend Alfred Peron, Beckett made the first translation of the Anna Livia Plurabelle section of *Finnegans Wake* into French. Unfortunately, Joyce's daughter, Lucia, who became mentally ill, also became infatuated with Beckett. Since Beckett could not respond to Lucia's romantic interest in him, he was banished from Joyce's social circle.

Still, Beckett continued to be influenced by Joyce's work, almost as a negative and a positive resemble each other. Joyce loved all of the small pleasures of life with passion; his work is full of delight in food, lace underwear, the geography of Dublin, Irish song, the puns languages inevitably create. If Joyce tried to include everything in his writings, Beckett did the opposite. Israel Shenker quotes Beckett as saying "I'm working with impotence, ignorance. My little exploration is that whole zone of being that has always been set aside by artists as something unusable—as something by definition incompatible with art. I think anyone nowadays, who pays the slightest attention to his own experience finds it the experience of a non-knower, a non-can-er."[2] Beckett's characters are pared down to the most concentrated form possible with almost no possessions, appetites, or even specific environments. If Joyce's work can be epitomized by Molly Bloom's great affirmative "Yes," Beckett's writings begin with an equally great "No!" Perhaps the only thing that saves his characters from complete despair is their willingness to hang on despite their difficulties. "I can't go on this way," "That's what you think," and "I can't go on; I'll go on" are typical of his characters' statements.

In 1930, Beckett returned to Trinity College to take his master's degree, which he received in 1931, and to begin teaching. Unfortunately, he hated teaching and quit the profession by 1932. He then tried to develop a career as a published writer of criticism, poetry, translations, and fiction. In 1933, he moved to London. An unpublished novel, *Dream of Fair to Middling Women*, was reworked into a series of short stories called *More Pricks Than Kicks*, which was published in 1934. Unable to support himself independently by his writing in London, Beckett traveled back home periodically for long visits with his parents. Even in Dublin, he had to rely on his parents to give him an allowance (mentioned, but not spelled out in his father's will). His mother's continuing insistence that he change his unconventional lifestyle, stop his heavy drinking and his writing, and settle down to a bourgeois life, "becoming a man," threw him into self-destructive rages marked by severe psychosomatic illnesses (including attacks of influenza, boils on the neck and anus, and long periods of severe headaches).

During 1933, Beckett began work on *Murphy*. He spent much of his time visiting the hospital where his friend Dr. A.G. Thompson worked. There (and again later in London) he got much of the background material that went into the description of the "Magdalen Mental Mercy Seat" in the novel. A deeply philosophical work based on Geulincx but also influenced by psychoanalysis, *Murphy* was rejected by forty-two publishers before it was finally published by Routledge in 1938.

In 1933, Beckett's father died. Samuel spent some time helping his mother cope with her bereavement, but finally he persuaded her that he would improve his health by going into analysis in London and with her support he moved there again in 1934. A slim volume of his poems, *Echo's Bones*, was privately published in 1935.

Although he was in analysis for two years during which his doctor tried to get him to break away from his mother, Beckett could not achieve separation from her. On one occasion his doctor invited him to hear a lecture by Carl Jung in which the latter discussed the relationship between creativity and the unconscious and also spoke of a young child whose dreams revealed that she was dying, although there seemed no specific physical cause. "She had never been born entirely," Jung said (Bair, 209). Beckett felt that this description fitted his own condition, helping to explain his need for his many return visits to his mother despite the anguish that they caused him.

For some time during 1935, Beckett thought that he would like to learn film technique. Although he abandoned the notion, his interest in the black-and-white silent films persisted. Some of his later theatrical tricks came from the cinematic comic tradition, and his film (called *Film*, part of a trilogy—the other segments being written by Eugene Ionesco and Harold Pinter) starred the motion picture comic Buster Keaton. At this time Beckett also became interested in art. During 1936, he traveled to Germany, mainly to visit museums. He was upset that the Nazis had removed so much modern art (created by Jews) from the museums, but seemed otherwise uninterested in the rise of Fascism. After another disastrous return to his mother's home he left again, now for Paris, where he had been his happiest. From October 1937 on he made France his home, although he returned to Ireland to be with his mother for one month each year (except during World War II) until her death in 1950.

In January 1938, a pivotal accident occurred. Out for an evening with friends, Beckett was knifed in a mugging. Ultimately, the wound turned out not to be serious. However, it looked very dangerous. A passing pedestrian who stopped to help also visited him in the hospital where their relationship developed.

This woman, Suzanne Deschevaux-Dumesnil, was his companion for the rest of his life. Believing in Beckett's genius and sharing his need for intense privacy, Suzanne undertook the task of caring for him. She supported him financially through her sewing when that was necessary, acted as his agent occasionally, lived and traveled with him, yet encouraged him to establish separate friendships with others as he wished. The two finally married in 1961.

In Paris, he had reestablished his relationships with Joyce's circle, but with the difficult political situation there were few publishing opportunities among his old friends. Again, he wrote some short poems and worked on a translation of *Murphy* into French.

Beckett was back in Ireland when World War II broke out, but he insisted on returning to Paris to share the dangers of the war with his friends. Although he and Suzanne walked south in 1940, they returned to the occupied capitol and joined a resistance group engaged in dangerous underground work. By 1942, the Gestapo had infiltrated his group (fewer than half survived the war). When Alfred Peron was seized and killed by the Nazis, Mme. Peron warned them, and Beckett and Suzanne fled from Paris, making their way to the unoccupied southern part of France mainly by walking at night and hiding during the day. Living quietly in Roussillon for two and a half years, waiting for the war's end, Beckett passed the time partly by writing *Watt*, his last novel to be written first in English.[3] In 1945, he was awarded the Croix de Guerre with a gold star for his work in the resistance.

After the war, Beckett again returned to Ireland to visit his family. To get back to France, he joined an Irish Red Cross unit going to St. Lo. There he acted as interpreter and administrator for the Irish voluntary field hospital. That work concluded, he returned to Paris and began the most fertile years of his writing career.

During this period, he wrote four novellas: *La Fin*, 1946 (*The End*, 1954), *Premier Amour*, 1946 (*First Love*, 1972), *Le Calmant*, 1946 (*The Calmative*, 1967), and *L'Expulsé*, 1946 (*The Expelled*, 1962), as well as his trilogy of novels, *Molloy*, 1947 (in English, 1951), *Malone Meurt*, 1948 (*Malone Dies*, 1956), and *L'Innommable* (*The Unnamable*, 1958). Despite some critical recognition, Beckett had great difficulty finding publishers; his books did not sell well and he found both the writing and marketing of his manuscripts a torment.

Seeking some relief, he turned to the theater. He wrote the unpublished and unproduced *Eleutheria* in 1947 and *En Attendant Godot* in 1948, though the latter was not produced until 1953 (*Waiting for Godot* was first produced in London in 1955). Owing much to his wartime experiences with Suzanne, this play had universal reverberations. Many playgoers, expecting a conventional comedy, walked out of the early productions; others understood that here was a remarkable, incredibly original contribution to contemporary theater. Guided by intelligent critical response, audiences began to appreciate this avant-garde playwright. *Fin de Partie* (*Endgame*), set in a dying universe, followed in 1957. From this time forward, Beckett's dramatic works (about thirty, all told) became moderately to highly commercially successful, not on Broadway, but with more thoughtful audiences. To make sure that his plays were staged exactly as he envisioned them, Beckett traveled occasionally to oversee productions in the United States and Germany. Otherwise, he and Suzanne continued to live quietly in their simple country farm house and in their apartment in Paris.

He won Obie (New York City Off-Broadway) awards in 1958, 1960, 1962, and 1964 along with a London *Evening Standard* award in 1955. With Jorge Luis Borges, he shared the International Publishers Prize in 1961. In 1969, he was awarded the Nobel Prize for literature, which he reluctantly accepted, although he refused to write an acceptance speech or attend the awards dinner.

As his fame as a playwright grew, he was besieged by publishers for new works. During the 1970s, he published various short works and revised materials written earlier. *Mercier et Camier*, for example, was written in French in 1946, revised and published in French in 1970 (English, 1974). In the early 1980s, he continued to write and publish increasingly shorter pieces—some for radio, film, and television (*Breath*, a playlet, takes thirty seconds to perform), and other short prose (*A Piece of Monologue*) dealing with the same existential issues that had always preoccupied him. Short prose

pieces after 1980 include *Ill Seen Ill Said* (1981), *Worstward Ho* (1983), and *Disjecta* (1983). Short plays include *Ohio Impromptu* (1981, not so short), *Quad* (1982), *Catastrophe* (1982), and *What Were* (1983). Beckett died in Paris on December 22, 1989.

Literary Analysis

In March 1975, the experimental theater group, Mabou Mines, under the direction of Lee Breuer, produced Beckett's *The Lost Ones*.[4] David Warrilow, looking very gaunt, recited the text, "peopling" it, so to speak, with inch-high white paper figures removed from a case that he carried. He set these paper actors in a miniature cylinder, suggestive of the "Abode where lost bodies roam each searching for its lost one. Vast enough for the search to be in vain." The audience, in the round, sat on bleachers covered, as was the entire small auditorium (floor, seats, ceiling) by dark gray felt. As they entered the theater, ticket holders were given pocket binoculars. They could view the mannikin actors through either end of the binoculars. At two points in his recital, Warrilow stripped and "became" one of the characters, while two other actors who had been sitting quietly near him joined in the action. At another moment, he placed a figure in his left ear, as he described the climbers moving through tunnels in the cylinder wall, and "removed" the figure from his right ear, which meant, of course, that the figure had crawled through the "tunnel" of his head while he spoke. While describing the crawling, Warrilow maintained his dignity and equanimity—merely lifting one eyebrow and then the other, only hinting at his subliminal discomfort as the figure "crawled" within.

Given the deliberate and effective changes in the audience's perception of the materiality and size of the characters, given the invitation to the long view offered by the binoculars and the dispassionate text, spectators were nudged toward a God-like stance. Certainly, I felt myself an observer viewing at long distance the fruitless behavior of a pitiable lot of insects.

As Warrilow recited the text, the audience learned that the very small percentage of inmates who no longer desire to climb are called the "vanquished." Most of the inmates of the cylinder are "seekers" and "climbers" who strive ceaselessly to reach the top of one of the ladders scattered throughout the space. After a while, they climb back down. Sometimes they change their minds as they arrive at the front of their line. They pass up their turn, choosing instead to start over at the end of another line. Auditors heard of the seekers' frantic, useless compulsion to move: "[T]he need to climb is too widespread. To feel it no longer is a rare deliverance" (*The Lost Ones,* 10). Yet, viewers see the figures standing perfectly still. Impasse.

Described as circling perpetually in the arena, the mannikins are reminiscent not only of Dante's circles in Hell, but also of Wall Street tycoons and social climbers or scholars and students. Beckett's description is so stripped of clutter that it becomes universal and horrifyingly amusing. At the same time, we could classify Warrilow's trick, the passage through the "hollow" head, as the kind of low comedy that belongs to family dinners where quarters are pulled from children's ears by jolly uncles.

These extremes of humor (bleak, black, even cruel on the one hand, music hall or vaudeville on the other) illustrate the broad range of comedy found in Beckett's work. In these texts whose theme is the suffering and destitution of all humanity, how can we explain the presence of such comedy? Instead, let us simply recall the terrible events of the twentieth century, so grotesque that they can be confronted only by the bleakest kind of farce. Equally important to understanding Beckett's work is his life history, since the intersection of the large and small worlds helped to form Beckett's unique vision.

The roots of Beckett's writing are many and complex. Undoubtedly, his pessimistic philosophy grew partly out of his personal life history, with a very difficult, demanding mother who never hesitated to evoke his feelings of guilt toward her. Although he downplayed the importance of his Protestant upbringing by calling Christianity a "mythology" with which he happened to be familiar, a spiritual or religious quest certainly underlies his work, full as it is of references to the Bible, to humanity's sins and need for God's pity. But God failed to appear, either to the Irish expatriates and other intellectuals of his generation or to the philosophers, writers, and poets read by Beckett. In his texts, as in theirs, there is a spiritual void, a *cri de coeur* to whatever God there might (or might not) be to care for suffering humanity. The absence or death of God was certainly brought home to Beckett's generation by its experiences of both world wars, the Holocaust, and the Cold War with its threat of nuclear annihilation. In this atmosphere, Beckett's nightmares express for many readers their own sense of the human condition. To mention this background is not to explain away Beckett's power to claw. However, when a writer has put his endless searching and agony into words and then makes us laugh at his creatures' dilemmas, his writing, his articulation of existential anguish in itself offers us comfort. Readers of Beckett may feel like the child whom he describes in *That Time,* whispering to himself to make himself not alone.

Beckett's works demonstrate a consistent line of development in some ways: his prose becomes more concise; his vocabulary simpler; he is less interested in displaying his erudition; the jejune bathroom jokes and jokes revolving about slightly profane language diminish in number; the novels and plays lose a conventional plot line and conventional "characters" who resemble people we might conceivably meet. The trilogy reaches the deepest possible focus on an individual consciousness in *The Unnamable.* Then the plays (foreshadowed by *Mercier and Camier*) pick up from there by introducing the notion of the couple. There is then a slowly expanding exploration of the mostly sado-masochistic but occasionally satisfying relationships which can occur between any two, ranging from the master-slave relationship of Pozzo and Lucky to the nostalgic memory of "the dear face" in *Ohio Impromptu.*

However, in other important respects, Beckett's philosophy, his themes, and approach to literature were already completely formed when he was twenty-five and wrote his monograph on *Proust.* Speaking of Proust, Beckett says, "Suffering opens a window on the real and is the main condition of the artistic experience." "Art," he adds, is the "one ideal and inviolable element in a corruptible world" (*Proust,* 28). If this seems a bit too solemn, he also remarks that "The attempt to communicate where no communication is possible is . . . horribly comic like the madness which holds a conversation with the furniture" (*Proust,* 63).

Already present is his concentration on suffering along with the stance that can view suffering as "horribly comic." In the early collection of short stories, *More Pricks Than Kicks,* the main character, Belacqua (named after a character from Dante) is guilty of the sin of sloth. Belacqua's adventures in Dublin exhibit Beckett's penchant for irony. For example, in "Love & Lethe" Belacqua proposes a suicide pact to Ruby, which she accepts, although she would prefer an affair because she is dying anyway. However, the pistol misfires and they end up having sex instead.

In "Yellow," Belacqua is awaiting an operation when he thinks about how to behave: "Was it to be tears or laughter? *It came to the same thing in the end* [emphasis mine] but which was it to be now? It was too late to arrange for the luxury of both" (*More Pricks Than Kicks*, 163). Wanting to make "a certain impression on other people," Belacqua chooses laughter. He thinks about the funny story of the priest who, not wanting to take the Lord's name in vain, agrees to be shot in an amateur production only if they will let him change the line from "By God! I'm shot!" to "Upon my word!" or something of that kind, but the production was so amateur that the revolver went off indeed and the man of God was transfixed: "Oh!" he cried, "Oh . . . ! . . . By CHRIST! I *am* SHOT!" (*More Pricks Than Kicks*, 172). Ironically, though Belacqua "bounced up on to the [operating] table like a bridegroom . . . the anesthetic mixture was too rich, and, like the priest in the joke, 'By Christ! he did die!'" (*More Pricks Than Kicks*, 174).

The book was somewhat favorably reviewed. References were made to Beckett's cleverness and his humor, "the last weapon against despair" (as the book jacket had it), but the extremely arcane references and elaborate style worked against the book's popular acceptance.

Murphy, Beckett's first published novel, is transitional in the sense that it has a fairly conventional plot line, characters, and denouement, but with the deeply philosophical underpinnings from Descartes and Geulincx and focus on Murphy's mind (as opposed to his body) which will become increasingly important in the trilogy. Again love is used mainly for comedy. Almost everyone is in love with a person who loves someone else, except for Murphy and Celia. Theirs (possibly the most harmonious heterosexual relationship in all of Beckett's work) is "a striking case of love requited" (*Proust*, 16). Celia, a prostitute, forces Murphy to get a job so that she can quit hers. However, the job forces Murphy to live as an attendant in a mental institution; thus, instead of bringing them together, the job parts them. Murphy comes to admire the inmates of the institution, especially Mr. Endon, whose chess playing is designed to ignore the opposition and stay, insofar as possible, in his initial positions on the board. Murphy dies (either accidentally or in a kind of passive suicide) when his gas jet explodes, triggered by some person using the toilet downstairs (he had been siphoning the gas for his otherwise unheated garret through a jerry-built gadget). This accident occurs just as he is about to return to Celia. In another ironic note, his bones are scattered on the floor of a pub whereas he wanted them flushed down in "the necessary house" in the Abbey Theatre.

Some of the grotesque humor is derived from disgusting descriptions of women's infirmities, such as Miss Carridge's body odor or Miss Rosie Dew's duck disease. There are many puns: "Celia, s'y la." We find names like Ticklepenny, Dr. Killiecrankie, and Miss Counihan who is a love interest. A minor character, Cooper, never sits (prefiguring Watt and Clov). Much of the incidental humor is derived from parodies of Shakespearean references, from inappropriate diction, and from subtle references to esoteric subjects. A scene in the mortuary depends upon confusion and cross-purposes in the dialogue.

Pertinent to Beckett's humor is his reply, when asked to cut *Murphy*, that "The wild and unreal dialogues . . . cannot be removed without dulling and darkening the whole thing. They are the comic exaggeration of what elsewhere is expressed in elegy, namely, if you like, the Hermeticism of the spirit. . . . There is no time and no space in such a book for *mere* relief. The relief has also to do work and reinforce that from which it relieves" (Bair, 243). Note that, for Beckett, comic relief is serious business. It is, therefore, difficult to do justice to his comedy out of context, since it depends so much on just what it is "reinforcing."

Watt, Beckett's next novel, was written while he was in hiding during World War II. In the novel Watt goes to work for Mr. Knott (who has God-like attributes) for a while, then leaves and ends up in an asylum, telling his story, more or less, to the narrator, Sam, who tells it, but not in the same order, to us.

As with many of Beckett's texts, it must be said that not everyone finds *Watt* funny. Some of the humor is really cruel. For example, Sam and Watt feed frogs to rats, then the rats to their relatives: "Watching with *glee* [italics mine] as the lucky relatives tear the rat apart, Sam reflects, 'It was on these occasions, we agreed, after an exchange of views, that we came nearest to God'" (*Watt*, 156). Another illustration of Beckett's cruel sense of humor is his treatment of humanity's physiological weaknesses: disfigurement, disease, aging, death, the cloacal both in the gastrointestinal and sexual systems are all emphasized. Watt, like many of Beckett's protagonists, is physically grotesque. Ironic treatment of sex is shown in Watt's relationship to his aging "paramour," Mrs. Gorman, the fishwife, and the advertising for "Bando," an aphrodisiac (in French, the verb "bander" means to have an erection). This novel (again, typically) abounds in ironic biblical and religious references. For example, "[Watt] would turn the other cheek . . . if he had the energy," and "'Poor woman, God forgive her,' said Tetty. 'Faith I wouldn't put it past him,' said Mr. Hackett" (*Watt,* 16). There are also the inevitable puns as Watt (What?) goes to work for Mr. Knott, who is *not* God, just as Godot is not God. Beckett finds it funny that Mr. Graves, the gardener, says "turd" for "third" and "fart" for "fourth." The "hardy laurel" bush laughs (a pun on the clowns of American film, Stan Laurel and Oliver Hardy).

Characteristic here as well as in the trilogy of novels to follow is the obsessive quality of the writing. In another kind of punning/wordplay, at times when Watt talks to Sam he changes the order of words in a sentence, the order of sounds in a word, the order of sentences in a paragraph, the order of letters in a word and words in a sentence, the order of the words in a sentence and the sentences in the paragraph, and all the possible combinations of these changes (*Watt,* 168). There are two pages detailing the sound patterns made by three croaking frogs: krik, krak, krek (*Watt,* 137–38).

An extension of this obsessiveness leads to a unique kind of humor found in the fiction from *Watt* on, as Beckett's protagonists try to explain, while their fanatically obsessive and logical ruminations multiply geometrically—what?—anything at all—with precision and fidelity to experience. As Fred Miller Robinson phrases it, "We are obligated, for reasons unknown, or because we are human, to wrench meaning out of chaos. This painful undertaking is the 'ancient labor' at which Watt labors" (F.M. Robinson, 134). The contrast between the earnestness of the attempt and the absurdity of the task becomes irresistibly comic. As Robinson reminds us, experience cannot be caught in language, "because language, with its syntax and sentences, is designed to elucidate the elusive, not to confront the fact of elusiveness itself. The more language attempts to fix . . . what cannot be fixed, the more it parodies

its own mechanism. This is how much of [Beckett's comedy] works . . . The result is a vaudeville of language, an explosion of hectic and futile reasoning" (F.M. Robinson, 130).

Beckett wrote his trilogy of novels in French after World War II in fairly rapid succession, saying that it was easier to write in French without style. Materially, his conditions were very poor. The pre-war world of Beckett's associates in Paris had fallen apart, and most people were in a state of post-war shock. Nevertheless, these three novels, increasingly terrifying in their bleak view of existence, would quite possibly have been exactly as they are no matter what the external conditions of Beckett's life were. Discussing the role of modern painters whom he admired, Beckett stated his view of the nature of the artist succinctly: "there is nothing to express, nothing with which to express, nothing from which to express, no power to express, no desire to express, together with the obligation to express."[5]

It was in this post-war mood that Beckett began the trilogy, which he considered his best work aside from *Endgame.* The three novels document the paradoxical task of the writer as he tries using language to "express" (i.e., to capture) his essence, pared of contact with the ordinary world of the realistic novel. The cast of characters diminishes. In *Molloy,* Molloy begins by seeking his mother, but ends in a ditch. *Malone Dies* begins "I shall soon be quite dead at last in spite of all," and although Malone creates characters and plot within the novel, dying is the central subject. In *The Unnamable,* although as usual characters from earlier works reappear, the unnamable himself exists in a post-death limbo, finally reduced to Worm, a "tiny blur, in the depths of the pit . . . come into the world unborn, abiding there unliving, with no hope of death."[6]

Despite this inevitably doomed attempt to describe the essence of an abortive, timeless, wordless self in a work written (and read) in time, there are grotesque bits of humor in these increasingly desperate monologues. For instance, in *Molloy* there are seven wonderfully absurd, perfectly logical, dead-pan pages devoted to explaining how Molloy distributes his sixteen sucking stones in four pockets so as to suck each in turn without repeating any before going the whole round. He finally throws away all but one, and then loses (or swallows?) the last (*Molloy,* 93–100). Another amusing passage explains how "three hundred and fifteen farts a day" are "nothing" when "mathematics" are called upon to "help you know yourself" (*Molloy,* 39).

In *Samuel Beckett: The Comic Gamut,* Ruby Cohn obligingly lists a number of comic devices present in the trilogy and gives examples of each. In Beckett's creation of the Saposcat family in *Malone Dies,* Cohn details "the comic brilliance of language" (Cohn, 1962, 125). Beckett's treatment of the Saposcats offers a parody of the *Bildungsroman,* using such typical comic devices as parody of the Bible or Shakespeare, incongruity, jargon, litotes (understatement), non sequiturs, and so forth. Cohn gives examples of the ironic tone: "Humbly to ask a favour of people who are on the point of knocking your brains out sometimes produces good results" (*Malone Dies,* 238). Discussing Lemuel's violent blows to his own head with a hammer, Macmann finds this "understandable, for it too is . . . sensitive, and difficult to miss, and the seat of all the shit and misery, so you rain blows upon it, with more pleasure than on the leg for example, which never did you any harm, it's only human" (*Malone Dies,* 97). Cohn feels that the "grotesque extravagance of these violently cruel actions tumbles them into the comic mode" (Cohn, 1962, 154). Apparently, Beckett thought the same. He has Malone comment on the stories that he has been told: "all funny, not one not funny" (*Malone Dies,* 98).

Another critic who appreciates Beckett's cruel humor is Valerie Topsfield, who finds Macmann's love affair with Moll in *Malone Dies* a source of "bawdy humour" (Topsfield, 84). After describing Moll's degeneration (she was "beginning to smell," "subject to fits of vomiting," "her hair began to fall out in abundance," and "her complexion, now rapidly turning from yellow to saffron"), the narrator continues, "The sight of her so diminished did not damp Macmann's desire to take her, all stinking, yellow, bald and vomiting, in his arms. And he would certainly have done so had she not been opposed to it. One can understand him (her too). For when one has within reach the one and only love requited of a life so monstrously prolonged, it is natural one should wish to profit by it, before it is too late, and refuse to be deterred by feelings of squeamishness excusable in the faint-hearted, but which true love disdains" (*Malone Dies,* 94). The sweet reasonableness of the argument combined with the disgusting description and ending with the in-

vocation of what "true love disdains" is an absolutely brilliant manipulation of tone. Is it funny? That may be a matter of taste.

The subtle humor to be found in Beckett's mixture of objective description and more lyrical language appears more clearly in context. F.M. Robinson cites, for example, a passage near the end of *Molloy* in which Moran, ruminating about the orderly dance of the bees, says, "And all during the long journey home, when I racked my mind for a little joy in store, the thought of my bees and their dance was the nearest thing to comfort. For I was eager for my little joy, from time to time!" (*Trilogy,* 169). Robinson explains that "For I . . . joy" is at once "sardonic and lyrical, a typically Beckettian comic utterance" (F.M. Robinson, 140).

In the last novel of the trilogy, *The Unnamable,* Beckett again invokes previous fictional characters, as the narrator who exists first as a head with weeping eye sockets and a rump, ends in a jar spewing forth the contents of his consciousness in the only remaining way—through words. Malone, Molloy, Murphy, Basil (a new one) renamed Mahood all appear, followed by the new Worm. In Cohn's words, Beckett "reduces the comic to the hysterical, but also to the pathetic: 'I'll laugh, that's how it will end, in a chuckle'" (Cohn, 1962, 123).

In *The Unnamable* Beckett plays on his own fascination with the womb as a place of darkness, silence, and security as the narrator describes his expulsion into outer world as "an atonement for an unknown sin." Resisting the limitations of language and the unsatisfying social constructs available to us, Beckett forces us to confront our unhoused position in the universe. By stripping his characters of all of their ordinary activities and trappings, he faces them with the void of being in an inexplicable world—and this situation, so impossible, flips into absurdity.

Given the state of entropy at the end of *The Unnamable,* it is not surprising that Beckett felt finished as a writer. But, his agony during the writing of the trilogy had forced him to take a respite, so to speak, by moving to another kind of writing that he felt would be less bleak. *Waiting for Godot* was the result. Classed as an "absurdist" drama, it was recognized, fortunately, as a theatrical masterpiece. Beckett now turned from fiction to drama, thus enriching, bemusing, and amusing a needy world.

Before looking at the plays, a brief glance at *Mercier and Camier*, written in 1946, would be useful because it contains for the first time the male couple who will reappear in various guises in many of the dramas. These two, like many literary doubles, seem to be two halves of one personality: mind versus body—optimist versus pessimist—one who needs and one who needs to be needed. *Mercier and Camier* is the story of a journey which peters out inconclusively after (though not because) a bicycle, an umbrella, and a raincoat (all objects that Beckett treasured at various times) are lost or discarded. As in *Waiting for Godot*, the notion of continuing to try is as important as the balance between laughter and tears. As Topsfield reminds us, Mercier recommends that Camier acquire a sense of proportion: "When you fear for your cyst think of your fistula. And when you tremble for your fistula consider your chancre. This method holds equally for what is called happiness" (*Mercier and Camier*, 58). "In distancing themselves from the assaults of providence," Topsfield claims, "they are on the way to the *risus purus* which laughs at fate" (*Mercier and Camier*, 69).

In *Waiting for Godot*, there are two sets of couples: Pozzo and Lucky (master and slave) and Vladimir and Estragon (friends and equals who call each other Didi and Gogo respectively). The relationship between master and slave portrayed here is paradigmatic, as Lucky desperately holds on to the heavy bag filled with sand that he carries for Pozzo in order to "impress" him so that Pozzo will keep him. When Gogo pities Lucky and tries to comfort him, he is rewarded with a kick in the shins. When Pozzo is reproached for his beastly cruelty toward Lucky, he begins to snivel and complains about how awful it is for him to have a slave like Lucky hanging about. When they return in act 2, Pozzo has gone blind and Lucky gone dumb, but they are still literally tied to each other.

While Vladimir and Estragon are not tied literally, either to each other or to Godot, they struggle with their ambivalent attachments to each other and to their difficult task, which is to pass the time somehow while waiting for the appearance of the mysterious Mr. Godot who, it is implied, will somehow take care of them. The inability of people to stop relying on their fantasies of rescue by other, powerful personages who will take care of them and the inability of longtime companions to separate are themes that reappear in Beckett's works. "I'm going" is followed several times by the stage direction "He does not move," just as the last line of the play, "Yes, Let's go," is followed by the stage direction "They do not move." Impasse.

Given, of course, is the basic theatrical situation, the "two hours traffic" upon the stage. The audience comes, expecting to be amused or at least taken out of its existential boredom for that two hours by the make-believe actions of the actors. In *Waiting for Godot*, though, the actors themselves are stuck on stage and have trouble finding ways to pass the time. Among other things, they fight, make up, comfort each other for their bodily dysfunctions, get excited about hanging themselves (it will give them an erection), and try it with a rope belt that breaks, leaving Gogo's trousers down. Again, in a context in which not much is happening, these activities are very amusing and offer a commentary on the very state of existential discomfort which the audience had tried to avoid by coming to the theater.

No matter how different the audience may initially feel itself to be from Didi and Gogo, by becoming the audience watching such seemingly trivial events unfold on stage viewers share Vladimir and Estragon's state of anxious frustration as Godot, the object of their desire, fails to appear. Since the unattainable object of desire exists for almost every human being, the audience sees itself more clearly. By stripping his characters of the ordinary plot progression with climax and resolution, Beckett faces them and the audience with the futility of their games, of their ways of coping with an inexplicable and unsatisfying world—allowing the audience to see that their own ways are, rather than merely frustrating, laughable indeed.

Among other comic devices in *Waiting for Godot* are the stock characters, the exaggeration of their qualities (Lucky "thinking," for example, or their all falling and being unable to rise in act 2), the repetition and circularity of the plot (inherently comic devices according to Henri Bergson), the assertion of claims of the body in the midst of philosophical cogitation (such as Gogo's difficulties with his feet and boots, Didi's trouble with urination, the chewing of and discussion about the carrot and radish, Pozzo's throat atomizer). The exchange of hats (patterned after a Marx Brothers film comedy routine), the lice in Didi's hat, the difficulties with zippers and trousers, characters' imi-

B

tation of the tree, and Gogo's attempt to hide behind it are childish. Their breaking of theatrical convention by commenting on the audience, seeing it as a "bog," is funny, as is their voicing of the audience's thoughts in the complaint, "Nothing happens, nobody comes, nobody goes, it's awful!" Lucky's dance and monologue and their attempt to stop it are grotesque. And so on.

Critics complained that *Waiting for Godot* was the play in which nothing happened, twice—but that is certainly far from true. However, *Endgame*, which followed in 1956, is a one-act play in which "nothing" happens once. It takes place in a room with two small, high windows (some interpret this setting as being the human skull) in which Hamm, the crippled, blind master confined to his armchair on castors, dominates Clov, the servant, while Nagg and Nell, Hamm's legless parents, converse from the two ash cans in which they are set.

The drama's title is taken from a term in chess. Usually, in the endgame the board is almost empty, just as here the four characters seem to be the lone survivors in a post-apocalyptic world (unless Clov has correctly spotted a small boy outside the shelter). In chess the king, who can at best move only one square at a time, often cannot move at all without putting himself in jeopardy during the endgame. As capturing the king would violate his divine rights, the game ends before he would be taken in the next move. Similarly, the play ends as Hamm (with his kingly attributes of pride and arrogance) remains immobilized in the middle of the room, while Clov stands on the threshold poised to leave, but not moving. Impasse.

Again the play is ghastly in tone, but leavened with humor that reinforces the grim material. The play begins with Clov trying to look out of the two windows using a small stepladder. He has to go back for the ladder each time, as he keeps forgetting it (later, he exaggerates the same joke by deliberately dropping a telescope, having to get off the ladder to retrieve it, etc.). As he looks out of the windows, as he removes the covers from Nagg's and Nell's ashbins, as he removes a bloody handkerchief from Hamm's face (hints of Veronica's veil), he laughs. What kind of laughter is this? Perhaps we should look at Beckett's definition of laughter, given earlier in *Watt*. As Arsene describes it there, "The bitter laugh laughs at that which is not good, it is the ethical laugh. The hollow laugh laughs at that which is not true, it is the

intellectual laugh . . . But the mirthless laugh is the dianoetic laugh [i.e., the laugh of pure reason], down the snout—Haw!—so. It is the laugh of laughs, *the risus purus*, the laugh laughing at the laugh, the beholding, the saluting of the highest joke, in a word the laugh that laughs—silence please—at that which is unhappy" (*Watt*, 48). To enjoy laughing at that which is unhappy is also mentioned by Nell who says, "Nothing is funnier than unhappiness." "Oh!" replies Nagg, and the stage direction is "*Shocked*" (*Endgame*, 18). If the audience members are unable to share Nell's view, they will miss much of Beckett's humor.

Yet even here, slapstick and more conventional kinds of humor are used. Many of the conversations between Hamm and Clov become witty as they exaggerate the sadomasochistic elements found in most normal relationships. Often a question such as "Do you want—" will be answered "No" before the subject is named. Other such refusals of humane interaction abound. When Hamm asks to be readied for bed, for example, Clov refuses: "I can't be getting you up and putting you to bed every five minutes. I have things to do." After a pause, Hamm's reply is, "Did you ever see my eyes?" This seems to be a non sequitur, but of course Hamm is saying that his martyrdom is greater than Clov's, so Clov should not refuse him a favor. They exchange many lines in which adherence to logic demonstrates logic's absurdity. Hamm threatens not to feed Clov, and Clov replies that then he will die (and, by implication, be freed from Hamm's domination). So Hamm threatens to feed him just enough to keep Clov from dying. "Then we won't die," says the sassy Clov. Shifts in tone are also funny in context: "Any phone calls?" asks Hamm. When Clov finds a flea in his pants, he sprinkles insecticide in his dropped pants. Asked if he got the flea, Clov replies, "Looks like it. (He drops the tin and adjusts his trousers). Unless he's laying doggo." His grammar corrected by Hamm, he replies "Ah? One says lying? One doesn't say laying?" The humor of an exquisite concern for correct diction in the midst of all of this horror is enhanced by its being a mildly sexy joke, as Hamm replies, "Use your head, can't you. If he was laying we'd be bitched" (*Endgame*, 34; Hamm means that evolution might produce more human beings again from this flea—a dreaded prospect).

As Nagg and Nell strain to kiss from their respective ashcans, they look like Punch and

Judy figures. But, they cannot achieve physical contact. Nor can they connect in their conversation, for when Nagg tells a long, shaggy dog story about a tailor who takes longer to make a pair of trousers than it took God to make the world, Nell refuses to laugh. Nagg wants to believe that it was this tailor story that made Nell laugh while they were canoeing on Lake Como, but she rejects his appeal and says that it was simply because she was happy to be on the lake that day.

Hamm, like Beckett and many of the protagonists in the novels, is a creator of stories, which he recites to his captive audience, Clov and his parents. But, his story, too, is about domination and subjugation. All of these ways of demonstrating how flat, stereotypical characters try to dominate and control each other throw light on real life's ironies.

Pratfalls and slapstick dominate *Act Without Words: A Mime for One Player* (1957), in which the lone actor is teased by having a carafe of water hung just out of reach. No matter how he is encouraged to try to reach it (boxes to stand on magically appear), the carafe remains tantalizingly just out of reach. Like Didi and Gogo, he cannot even hang himself. The tree branch will not let him.

In the radio play *All That Fall* (1957) part of the humor comes from our visualization of Mrs. Rooney's great bulk. As her polite neighbor tries to hoist her into his car without touching her body in a sexually suggestive way, the text bumbles into one double entendre after another. In this play, more specifically grounded in Irish village life than any of Beckett's other dramas, there is also the humor to be gained from the village gossip and from the sounds of rural Ireland. Undercutting the humor are the Rooneys' physical problems and several deaths, the last being the accidental death of a child.

Beckett returned to prose in *How It Is*, written in 1956. Here he again "admit[s] the chaos and does not try to say that chaos is really something else."[7] Although the text poetically describes an infinitely self-replicating universe of torturers and the tortured, Topsfield believes that here the writer finally achieves a resolution of his conflicting feelings about tragedy and humor; as she reads it, the conflict between tears and laughter disappears; they are truly now the same (Topsfield, 130).

Beckett's unique mixture of humor and pathos ranging from vaudevillian to existential reappears in the next play, *Krapp's Last Tape*

(1958). Some of his humor comes from the protagonist's inability to give up his bad habits such as his reliance on alcohol or his passion for bananas (though they cause his constipation). The bananas offer other opportunities for humor. They are locked in his desk drawer, reached only after much fumbling. They look funny as he eats them (the vaudeville term "top banana" is relevant to the actor's manner here). Krapp slips on the skins, tosses the skins offstage, and so forth. A more ironic level of humor is reached as the sixty-nine-year-old Krapp, obviously a failure, listens to the earlier more optimistic birthday tapes that he made glorifying his life's ambitions.

Happy Days (1961) takes the term "black humor" to new heights as Winnie, first buried up to her waist (act 1) and then up to her neck (act 2), keeps up a happy prattle of the sort we expected from an air-headed breakfast television talk show hostess who has been instructed to be upbeat at all costs as she chats on about the increasing deaths from AIDS. Winnie keeps up her spirits during her "happy day" as she brushes her teeth, puts on her lipstick, etc. Her speech is filled with stale cliches ("can't be cured, genuine pure, nothing like it, that is always what I say, another happy day"), archaic diction ("tis, beseech, enow, God grant, damask cheek, dire need"), and misquotations from Shakespeare.

In addition, there is some of the humor of the couple to be found in the way in which Winnie tortures Willie by demanding his attention and hitting him on the head with her umbrella and in his resistance to her relentless cheeriness. One of Beckett's favorite themes, the decrepitude of old age, gets a workout at the play's end as Willie crawls toward Winnie in his morning coat, apparently unable to do more than croak out the ambiguous syllable, "Win," while he approaches the gun lying between them.

What slowly alters the nature of the late plays and prose works is the recognition by Beckett of the significant role of the other as listener, mirror, helpmate, even beloved. Krapp remembers a lyrical moment with a woman in a rowboat. Mrs. Rooney has gone to meet her husband's train as a birthday present to him, and they share a laugh together over the silence of God. Despite their mainly ironic tone, there are important memories of remembered closeness with a mother or a girl which are not undercut in *Footfalls*, *Rockabye*, and *That Time*.

B

And in the late *Ohio Impromptu*, not only does the relationship between Listener and Reader seem totally symbiotic, but the reader seems to be there, as Virgil was for Dante, at the behest of a beloved "shade" to "comfort" the listener.

Summary

Even allowing for occasional moments of tenderness, Samuel Beckett's humor is slight sweetening for bitter fruit. As Maurice Charney points out, Beckett is "our greatest practitioner of tragic farce" (Charney, 111) that is "the terribly serious, even savage comic humor" which Charney associates with Ionesco, Friedrich Durrenmatt, Joe Orton, and Tom Stoppard. This mode has become so widespread that it is hard to point to a few specific individuals who imitate Beckett, although his influence on Pinter, American playwright David Mamet, and Eastern European writers such as Vaclav Havel is apparent.

In his useful study, Charney lists many components of comedy, almost all of which are exemplified in Beckett's works. Beckett's humor grows out of his innovative treatment of character, of plot structure, of literary style, of his obsessive desire to tell some hard truths about humanity. Trapped in an existential void, Beckett's characters are funny, in part, because they seem mechanical, as invulnerable as clowns or cartoon figures. They never seem to die (unless they are already dead and in limbo), although they are incredibly abused by their author to the point of being grotesques. Deprived of all of the ordinary means and necessities of life, they nevertheless possess a wild energy that expresses itself in their indomitable will to go on living, or, at the very least, talking, trying to explain "it all" (see, for example, the play *Not I*, which consists only of a spotlight, a dim, shadowy listener, and a mouth that can't seem to stop talking). At the least eccentric, they possess a fine education and an intelligence that augments the ordinary cunning of classic comic figures. Their mania for the exact expression of the truth allied with their intense and narrow persistence renders them inhuman and mocks our notions of intelligence or free will.

Beckett's plots, if they exist at all, are illogical, discontinuous, or circular and lead to insane asylums, accidents, random violence, brutal murders, and all of the weaknesses of ill health, extreme old age, or decrepitude. One must laugh in order to avoid crying at the characters' ontological predicaments.

The breadth of Beckett's humor is amazing. Some of it is based on bathroom jokes, on mild obscenities, on comic disgust with body smells, on pratfalls, trouser-dropping, flea scratching, Ireland, humanity's inability to control or do without material objects which resist human will, or the expression of childish hostility. Some is based on our awareness of the futility of our insatiable desire for meaning; some of his humor arises as, from a great distance, he assumes a lofty view of humanity's absurdity in the face of an inscrutable universe that has no discernible purpose.

Beckett's brilliant ability to manipulate language and tone is most difficult to illustrate out of context. However, he puns, parodies, and plays on the preposterousness of language and human logic. The subtlety, irony, and beauty of his writing are admirable.

It is surprising that, in spite of the gloom and depression of Beckett's world view, there is so much humor underlying the bleakness of the rest. The fact that this writer who claims that "Nothing is funnier than unhappiness" can amuse in the midst of his charnel house is the most amazing and unaccountable joke, perhaps, of them all.

Notes

1. Deirdre Bair, *Samuel Beckett: A Biography* (New York: Harcourt Brace Jovanovich, 1978), p. 13. Though some critics dispute the absolute accuracy of this account, it has been relied on herein.

2. Israel Shenker, "A Portrait of Samuel Beckett, the Author of the Puzzling *Waiting for Godot*," *New York Times* (May 6, 1956): sec. 2, p. 1. Though there is some question whether Shenker actually met Beckett, the quote is a fair representation of his approach.

3. Beckett did all the translations from English to French and vice versa (in a few cases with a collaborator).

4. A videotape of Brever's 1976 New York Shakespeare Festival production is available for viewing at TOFT, Lincoln Center Library, New York.

5. "Three Dialogues with George Duthuit," *Transition*, 49, 5 (December 1949).

6. Quoted in Michael Robinson, *The Long Sonata of the Dead: A Study of Samuel Beckett* (New York: Grove Press, 1969), p. 198.

7. Tom F. Driver, "Beckett by the Madeleine," *Columbia University Forum* IV (Summer 1961): 21–25.

Selected Bibliography
Primary Sources

Short Stories and Miscellaneous Texts
(translations by Beckett unless otherwise noted)
More Pricks Than Kicks. London: Chatto and Windus, 1934; New York: Grove Press, 1970.
Nouvelles et Textes pour Rien. Paris: Editions de Minuit, 1955; trans. with Richard Seaver as *Stories and Texts for Nothing,* New York: Grove Press, 1967.
From an Abandoned Work. London: Faber, 1958.
Imagination morte imaginez. Paris: Editions de Minuit, 1965; trans. as *Imagination Dead Imagine,* London: Calder and Boyars, 1965.
Assez. Paris: Editions de Minuit, 1966; trans. as *Enough,* in *No's Knife,* 1967.
Bing. Paris: Editions de Minuit, 1966; trans. as *Ping,* in *No's Knife,* 1967.
Tetes-Mortes. Paris: Editions de Minuit, 1967; trans. in *No's Knife,* 1967. Includes *D'Un Ouvrage Abandonne, Assez, Bing, Imagination morte imaginez.*
No's Knife: Selected Shorter Prose, 1945–1966. London: Calder and Boyars, 1967. Includes *Stories and Texts for Nothing, From an Abandoned Work, Imagination Dead Imagine, Enough, Ping.*
L'Issue. Paris: Georges Visat, 1968.
Sans. Paris: Editions de Minuit, 1969; trans. as *Lessness,* London: Calder and Boyars, 1971.
Sejour. Paris: Georges Richar, 1970.
Premier Amour. Paris: Editions de Minuit, 1970; trans. as *First Love,* London: Calder and Boyars, 1973.
Le Depeupleur. Paris: Editions de Minuit, 1971; trans. as *The Lost Ones,* London: Calder and Boyars, 1972.
The North. London: Enitharmon Press, 1972.
First Love and Other Shorts. New York: Grove Press, 1974.
Fizzles. New York: Grove Press, 1976.
For to End Yet Again and Other Fizzles. London: Calder and Boyars, 1976.
All Strange Away. New York: Gotham Book Mart, 1976; London: Calder and Boyars, 1979.
Four Novellas (The Expelled, The Calmative, The End, First Love). London: Calder and Boyars, 1977; rpt. as *The Expelled and Other Novellas,* London: Penguin, 1980.
Six Residua. London: Calder and Boyars, 1978.
Mal vu mal dit. Paris: Editions de Minuit, 1981; trans. as *Ill Seen Ill Said,* London: Calder and Boyars, and New York: Grove Press, 1981.
Disjecta: Miscellaneous Writings and a Dramatic Fragment. Ed. with a foreword by Ruby Cohn. New York: Grove Press, 1984.

Verse
Whoroscope. Paris: Hours Press, 1930.
Gedichte. Wiesbaden, Limes Verlag, 1959. Collected poems in English and French, with German translations.
Poems in English. London: Calder and Boyars, 1961; New York: Grove Press, 1963.
Collected Poems in English and French. London: Calder and Boyars, and New York: Grove Press, 1977.

Novels
Murphy. London: Routledge, 1938; New York: Grove Press, 1957.
Molloy. Paris: Editions de Minuit, 1951; trans. with Patrick Bowles, Paris: Olympia Press, and New York: Grove Press, 1955; London: Calder and Boyars, 1959.
Malone meurt. Paris: Editions de Minuit, 1951; trans. as *Malone Dies,* New York: Grove Press, 1956; London: Calder and Boyars, 1958.
L'Innommable. Paris: Editions de Minuit, 1953; trans. as *The Unnamable,* New York: Grove Press, 1958; London: Calder and Boyars, 1959.
Watt. Paris: Olympia Press, 1953; New York: Grove Press, 1959; London: Calder and Boyars, 1963.
Comment C'Est. Paris: Editions de Minuit, 1961; trans. as *How It Is,* New York: Grove Press, and London: Calder and Boyars, 1964.
Mercier et Camier. Paris: Editions de Minuit, 1970; trans. as *Mercier and Camier,* London: Calder and Boyars, 1974; New York: Grove Press, 1975.

B

Company. London: Calder and Boyars, and New York: Grove Press, 1980.

Plays (Stage, film, radio, and television)

En Attendant Godot. Paris: Editions de Minuit, 1952; trans. as *Waiting for Godot: A Tragicomedy*. New York: Grove Press, 1954; London: Faber, 1956.

Fin de Partie: Suivi de Acte sans Paroles. Paris: Editions de Minuit, 1957; trans. as *Endgame: A Play in One Act; Followed by Act Without Words: A Mime for One Player*. New York: Grove Press, and London: Faber, 1958.

All That Fall. New York: Grove Press, 1957; as *All That Fall: A Play for Radio*, London: Faber, 1957.

Krapp's Last Tape. Included in *Krapp's Last Tape and Embers*, 1959; rpt. in *Krapp's Last Tape and Other Dramatic Pieces*, New York: Grove Press, 1960.

Embers. Included in *Krapp's Last Tape and Embers*, 1959; in *Krapp's Last Tape and Other Dramatic Pieces*, 1960.

Act Without Words II. Included in *Krapp's Last Tape and Other Dramatic Pieces*, 1960; rpt. in *Eh Joe and Other Writings*, 1967.

Happy Days. New York: Grove Press, 1961; London: Faber, 1962, bilingual edition, ed. James Knowlson, London: Faber, 1978.

Cascando. Paris: Editions de Minuit, 1963; trans. as *Cascando: A Radio Piece for Music and Voice*, included in *Play and Two Short Pieces for Radio*, 1964; in *Cascando and Other Short Dramatic Pieces*, 1968.

Play. Included in *Play and Two Short Pieces for Radio*, 1964; in *Cascando and Other Short Dramatic Pieces*, 1969.

Play and Two Short Pieces for Radio. London: Faber, 1964. Includes *Words and Music* and *Cascando*.

Eh Joe. Included in *Eh Joe and Other Writings*, 1967; in *Cascando and Other Short Dramatic Pieces*, 1968.

Come and Go: Dramaticule. London: Calder and Boyars, 1967; rpt. in *Cascando and Other Short Dramatic Pieces*, 1968.

Eh Joe and Other Writings. London: Faber, 1967. Includes *Act Without Words II* and *Film*).

Cascando and Other Short Dramatic Pieces. New York: Grove Press, 1968. Includes *Words and Music, Eh Joe, Play, Come and Go, Film*.

Breath and Other Shorts. London: Faber, 1971. Includes *Come and Go, Act Without Words I* and *II*, and the prose piece *From an Abandoned Work*.

Ends and Odds: Dramatic Pieces. New York: Grove Press, 1976. Includes *That Time, Footfalls, Tryst, Not I*; as *Ends and Odds: Plays and Sketches*. London: Faber, 1977. Includes *Not I, That Time, Footfalls, Ghost Trio, . . . but the clouds . . . , Theatre I and II, Radio I and II, Rough for Radio, Shades*.

Rockaby and Other Works. New York: Grove Press, 1981.

Rockaby and Other Short Pieces. New York: Grove Press, 1981. Includes *Ohio Impromptu, All Strange Away, A Piece of Monologue*.

Three Plays. New York: Grove Press, 1984. Includes *Ohio Impromptu, Catastrophe, What Where*.

Screenplay

Film, 1965. Published as *Film*. New York: Grove Press, 1969; London: Faber, 1971.

Secondary Sources

Bibliography

Andonian, Cathleen. *Samuel Beckett—A Reference Guide*. Boston: G.K. Hall, 1989. A very useful annotated bibliography of books and articles through 1984 from which most of this list is drawn. Contains, at a guess, well over 2,000 entries.

Federman, Raymond and John Fletcher. *Samuel Beckett: His Work and His Critics, An Essay in Bibliography*. Berkeley: University of California Press, 1970. A thorough, detailed, annotated bibliography through 1966.

Biography

Bair, Deirdre. *Samuel Beckett: A Biography*. New York: Harcourt Brace Jovanovich, 1978. The only biography to date. A study of the life and works.

Books

Alvarez, A. *Beckett*. London: Fontana-Collins, and New York: Viking, 1973. General overview of life and works for the "ordinary reader," placing Beckett in the absurdist tradition.

As No Other Dare Fail: For Samuel Beckett on His 80th Birthday by His Friends and Admirers. London: Calder and Boyars, 1986. New York: Riverrun, 1986. Articles by such well-known Beckett scholars as Knowlson, Esslin, Gontarski, and Bishop on a variety of issues: narrative technique, role of the reader, etc.

Beja, Morris, ed. *Humanistic Perspectives.* Columbus: Ohio State University Press, 1982. Essays first offered at the Beckett symposium at Ohio State University in May 1981.

Ben-Zvi, Linda. *Women in Beckett: Performance and Critical Perspectives.* Chicago: University of Illinois Press, 1990. The treatment of women characters and accounts by actresses of their work with Beckett.

Bishop, Tom, and Raymond Federman, eds. *Samuel Beckett.* Paris: Editions de l'Herne, 1976. Reminiscences, tributes, and influence studies. Includes chronology and bibliography.

Burkman, Katherine H. *Myth and Ritual in the Plays of Samuel Beckett.* Cranbury, NJ: Associated University Presses, 1987. Relates Beckett's practices to various theories of myth and discusses his characters' uses of rituals.

Charney, Maurice. *Comedy High and Low: An Introduction to the Experience of Comedy.* New York: Oxford University Press, 1978. A clear discussion of comic theory which draws a wide range of examples from farce to film to Beckett.

Cohn, Ruby. *Samuel Beckett: The Comic Gamut.* New Brunswick, NJ: Rutgers University Press, 1962. Very useful study of comic devices in his works using Bergson's categories. Cohn examines works through *How It Is.*

———. *Back to Beckett.* Princeton: Princeton University Press, 1973. An analysis of Beckett's poetry and prose in which Cohn demonstrates Beckett's obsession with mortality.

———, ed. *Samuel Beckett: A Collection of Criticism.* New York: McGraw-Hill, 1975. Includes a chronology of the life and works, and articles on subjects such as Beckett's themes and his involvement with art.

Duckworth, Colin. *Angels of Darkness: Dramatic Effect in Samuel Beckett with Special Reference to Eugene Ionesco.* London: George Allen and Unwin, 1972. Studies dramatic structure and impact on audiences.

Esslin, Martin, ed. *Samuel Beckett: A Collection of Critical Essays.* Englewood Cliffs, NJ: Prentice-Hall, 1965. Useful translations from French and German criticism. Links Beckett to the cultural and philosophical traditions of which he is part.

———. *The Theatre of the Absurd.* Garden City, NY: Doubleday, 1969; rev. 1969. Includes a chapter on Beckett's life and works.

Federman, Raymond. *Journey to Chaos: Samuel Beckett's Early Fictions.* Berkeley: University of California Press, 1965. Study of the short stories and novels through *How It Is.*

Finney, Brian. *Since "How It Is": A Study of Samuel Beckett's Later Fiction.* London: Covent Garden Press, 1972. Studies opposites, like order and chaos, and form and content.

Fletcher, John, and John Spurling. *B: A Study of the Plays.* London: Methuen, 1972. Discusses the evolution of Beckett's fiction before turning to an analysis of the plays.

Gontarski, Stanley E., ed. *On Beckett: Essays and Criticism.* New York: Grove Press, 1986. Essays comparing the earlier and later works of Beckett.

Graver, Lawrence, and Raymond Federman, eds. *Samuel Beckett: The Critical Heritage.* London: Henley, 1979. Eighty-three articles, interviews, and reviews which deal with each of Beckett's works.

Harvey, Lawrence E. *Samuel Beckett, Poet and Critic.* Princeton: Princeton University Press, 1970. Intensive study of Beckett's early poetry, criticism, and prose through *Watt.*

Helsa, David H. *The Shape of Chaos: An Interpretation of the Art of Samuel Beckett.* Minneapolis: University of Minneapolis Press, 1971. Considers the existential, philosophical basis of the works before 1960.

Jacobsen, Josephine, and William Mueller. *The Testament of Samuel Beckett.* New York: Hill and Wang, 1964. An examination of fictional techniques, including a chapter on comedy.

B

Kenner, Hugh. *Samuel Beckett: A Critical Study*. New York: Grove Press, 1961, rev. 1968. An analysis of formal, philosophical and mathematical domains with emphasis on the Cartesian.

Kott, Jan. *Shakespeare Our Contemporary*. New York: Doubleday, 1964. A comparison of the tragic in Shakespeare with the grotesque in Beckett, esp. *King Lear* and *Endgame*.

Knowlson, James, and John Pilling. *Frescoes of the Skull: The Later Prose and Drama of Samuel Beckett*. London: Calder and Boyars, 1970. Studies Beckett's early and late writing as well as his critical writing.

Murray, Patrick. *The Tragic Comedian: A Study of Samuel Beckett*. Cork: Mercier Press, 1970. General introduction.

Reid, Alec. *All I Can Manage, More than I Could: An Approach to the Plays of Samuel Beckett*. Dublin: Dolman Press, 1968. Study of the plays through *Come and Go* showing how Beckett enlarges the scope of the theater through his unique plays.

Robinson, Fred Miller. *The Comedy of Language*. Amherst, University of Massachusetts, 1980. A very useful chapter on Beckett, esp. *Watt*.

Robinson, Michael. *The Long Sonata of the Dead: A Study of Samuel Beckett*. New York: Grove Press, 1969. Introduces the works and ideas. Especially good on the trilogy.

Schlueter, June, and Enoch Brater, eds. *Beckett's Waiting for Godot*. New York: Modern Language Association, 1991. Approaches to Teaching World Literature series.

Smith, Joseph H., ed. *The World of Samuel Beckett*. Baltimore: Johns Hopkins University Press, 1991. A study from a dozen scholars placing Beckett's subjectivity in formal, existential, and psychological contexts.

Topsfield, Valerie. *The Humour of Samuel Beckett*. New York: St. Martin's Press, 1988.

Winkler, Elizabeth. "The Clown and the Absurd: Samuel Beckett." In *The Clown in Modern Anglo-Irish Drama*. Bern: Herbert Lang, 1977. Compares Beckett's use of the clown to others such as Shaw and Synge.

Worth, Katherine, ed. *Beckett the Shape Changer*. London: Routledge & Kegan Paul, 1975. Essays first offered at a Beckett symposium, University of London.

Vera Jiji

Beerbohm, Max

Born: London, August 24, 1872
Education: Charterhouse, 1885–1890;
Merton College, Oxford, 1890–1894
Marriage: Florence Kahn, May 4, 1910;
Elizabeth Jungmann on April 20, 1956
Died: Rapallo, Italy, May 20, 1956

Biography

Henry Maximilian Beerbohm, best known simply as "Max," was both a skilled caricaturist and essayist whose work from the 1890s to the 1920s delighted and entertained many. From his pen came essays and sketches which captured the spirit of his era and the essence of its major personalities. Born the ninth child of Julius Ewald Beerbohm, a prosperous grain merchant, and his scond wife Eliza Draper, on August 24, 1872, he was educated at Charterhouse (1885–1890) and Merton College, Oxford (1890–1894). He received no formal art training but delighted in designing cartoons and caricatures of his teachers and classmates. He never completed his degree at Oxford, but at Merton he enjoyed an active social life. He became friends with writers and artists such as Reginald Turner, William Rothenstein, and Oscar Wilde and joined the social club, The Myrmidons.

On weekends during his college years Beerbohm enjoyed life in London, where he had connections with the theater world. His half brother, Herbert Beerbohm Tree, was a preeminent actor and theater manager of the day, and the contacts and experiences that Tree provided gave Max subjects and themes for his pen. In 1895, he traveled with his brother on an American tour, initially in the capacity of secretary.

In 1894, Aubrey Beardsley introduced Beerbohm to Henry Harland, then in the process of founding *The Yellow Book*. Harland included Max's essay "A Defense of Cosmetics" in the first issue. Although Beerbohm had published articles in the Chicago *Chap-Book*, the *Daily Chronicle*, *Daily-Mail*, and *Parade*, this piece established his reputation as a dandy and as a part of the Decadent Movement. He contributed several caricatures and essays to both *The Yellow Book* and the *Savoy* and enjoyed an active social life with such 1890s luminaries as Beardsley, Harland, Richard LeGallienne, Edmund Gosse, and Will Rothenstein. John Lane published *The Works of Max Beerbohm* (1896), *The Happy Hypocrite* (1897), and *More* (1899) at the famous Bodley Head publishing house. Around the turn of the century *Caricatures of Twenty-Five Gentlemen* (1896), three exhibitions at Carfax Gallery (1901, 1904, 1907), *A Book of Caricatures* (1907), and *Yet Again* (a collection of essays, 1909) helped to ensure Max's position and popularity. His witty caricatures, parodies, and essays won him a devoted following. It was quite "the thing" for a famous actor, writer, artist, or politician to be caricatured or parodied by Max.

In 1898, Beerbohm became a drama critic for the *Saturday Review*, a position that he held for twelve years. George Bernard Shaw, in recommending Beerbohm as his replacement in this position, provided the epithet "the incomparable Max" which stayed with him throughout his life. Beerbohm left his position on the *Saturday Review* in 1910 and on May 4 of that year he married Florence Kahn, an actress from Memphis, Tennessee. They settled in a lovely villa called Villino Chiaro in Rapallo, Italy. This was to be home for Beerbohm until his death in 1956. Although residing in Italy, he continued to be a literary and artistic figure of importance in England. In 1911, he published both *Cartoons* and his satiric novel of Oxford life, *Zuleika Dobson*, and held the first of several exhibitions of drawings at Leicester Galleries. Noteworthy publications of his middle years were: *A Christmas Garland* (1912), which contained sixteen parodies of famous writers; *Fifty Caricatures* (1913); *And Even Now* (1920), a collection of essays; and *Rossetti and His Circle* (1922), often considered among his best works in caricature. He was knighted in 1939.

Beerbohm and his wife returned to England during both world wars. During World War II, he did a series of radio broadcasts which had a great deal to do with creating his image as the traditional Edwardian who looked nostalgically to a golden, pre-war past. These broadcasts, frequently based on earlier essays, were published in *Mainly on the Air* (1946). After the war, the Beerbohms returned to their reclusive existence in Rapallo. They occasionally entertained eminent visitors such as Americans Thornton Wilder, Ezra Pound, Edmund Wilson, and S.N. Behrman (who wrote *Portrait of Max* based on these visits). When Florence died in 1951, Elizabeth Jungmann became the author's housekeeper and constant companion. He married her on April 20, 1956, exactly one month before he died at age eighty-four.

Literary Analysis

Beerbohm was a master on a small scale, but a master nonetheless. His accomplishments are in those sub-categories of art and literature characterized by brevity—the caricature and the essay. His appeal was never to a broad, popular audience; his audience was and remains a relatively small, sophisticated one. Max's world is the educated world of Oxford and of the prominent literary, theatrical, and artistic circles of London at the turn of the century. Although he lived to see the second half of the twentieth century and lived abroad for over forty years, in essence his work remains bounded by London and by the years 1890–1920.

In the 1890s, Beerbohm adopted a lifestyle, a system of values, a manner and mode of dress, and he rarely diverged from these early patterns. He had no training in art; he had no formal academic degree. He was simply Max, doing what Max liked to do and doing it well. As W.H. Auden says of him: "At an astonishingly young age, he knew exactly the sort of person he was, and he never showed the slightest desire to be anyone else."[1] In this statement Auden captures the essence of Max, just as Max so often captured the essence of his subjects in his parodies and caricatures. He knew the limitations of his own talents, and in a 1921 letter to his fellow caricaturist Bohun Lynch he summarizes his achievement: "My gifts are small. I've used them very well and discreetly, never straining them; and the result is that I've made a charming little reputation."[2] Whether these self-imposed limitations spring from laziness, as the critic Roger Lewis asserts,[3] or whether, more likely, they derive from an honest sense of self, he managed to make a significant mark in literary and artistic history and to earn Shaw's apt description as "incomparable."

Beerbohm's *Yellow Book* essay "In Defense of Cosmetics" elicited spirited criticism and established his reputation as a Decadent writer and dandy. Wilde influenced his writing style, and his caricatures of Wilde are among his best known. A keen observer, he captured his friends and acquaintances in his drawings. His caricatures of the great literary and political figures of the 1890s are valuable resources for students of the period, for they provide a humorous insight into personalities which no other source can provide.

Beerbohm defined caricature as "that which, on a small surface, with the simplest means, most accurately exaggerates, to the highest point, the peculiarities of a human being, at his most characteristic moment, in the most beautiful manner."[4] Max's special talent lay in capturing "the highest point" and the "most characteristic moment" in his unique style. Caricature requires exaggeration of negative features and, thus, often offends the subject of the drawing. The surprising fact about Max's caricatures is that they so rarely did. Rudyard Kipling, a favorite subject, was reportedly not amused by Max's studies of him, but most often his targets were flattered and felt privileged to be drawn by Max. In his work there is little malice and much delight.

Of course, some of his subjects are unknown today and, therefore, of little interest. How many now would realize the aptness of his drawings of Henry Labouchere, Sir Hedworth Williamson, or the Earl of Rosebery? But, Beerbohm's renditions of famous political, literary, and artistic figures continue to entertain. With his pen he captured such political luminaries as King George IV, Arthur Balfour, and Winston Churchill (although he never felt that he did Churchill justice).

Beerbohm's main appeal in the twentieth century derives from his caricatures and parodies of famous literary figures. One popular series of drawings, "The Young and the Old Self," shows his vision of such figures as H.G. Wells, Shaw, Joseph Conrad, and Arnold Bennett as old men. Some are particularly prophetic. Among the caricatures that will always delight readers and literary scholars are his "Walt Whitman, inciting the bird of freedom to soar" (1904), "Mr. Thomas Hardy composing a lyric" (1913), "Mr. W.B. Yeats, presenting Mr. George Moore to the Queen of the Fairies" (1904), "Some Persons of 'the Nineties'" (1925), "Mr. Henry James revisiting America" (1905), and the humorous "Henry James" (ca. 1904), which shows James kneeling before a closed apartment door surreptitiously inspecting two pairs of shoes, one male and one female. And, Beerbohm did not limit himself to contemporary writers and artists. Among his subjects are Homer, Dante Alighieri, William Shakespeare, and Lord Byron. The Pre-Raphaelite Circle held a particular fascination for him, too, and he published a series of sketches entitled

Rosetti and His Circle in 1922. Beerbohm's self-caricatures demonstrate his ability to perceive his own idiosyncrasies as clearly and honestly as he saw others'.

As with his drawings, Beerbohm's parodies of and essays about well-known literary figures are probably the most frequently enjoyed today. The parody of James in "The Mote in the Middle Distance" is undoubtedly his best known, but in *A Christmas Garland* (1912) he also skillfully captures the rhythms and eccentricities of Kipling, Wells, Conrad, George Meredith, and twelve others. Among his essays about writers and artists is "No. 2: The Pines," which recounts Max's meeting Algernon Charles Swinburne at Walter Watts-Dunton's. In "A Clergyman" he delightfully analyzes a particular exchange between Dr. Samuel Johnson and an obscure churchman, and in "Quia Imperfectum" he deals with the charm and appeal of various artistic and literary fragments such as Tischbein's portrait of Johann Wolfgang Goethe or Samuel Taylor Coleridge's "Kubla Khan."

The topical nature of much of Beerbohm's work creates problems for modern readers. Both his subjects and his style are often dated. The leisurely, quietly speculative essays that convey the observations of a cultured London gentleman possess an antiquated quality. Beerbohm's world is the pre-war London of the privileged class. Essays like "A Club in Ruins," "Going Back to School," and "Fashion and Her Bicycle" interest the historian of the era more than the general reader, as do character studies such as "King George the Fourth" or an analysis of "Whistler's Writing." But, such essays as "Ichabod," in which Beerbohm analyzes what drives people to collect things, contain timeless observations. He is a master of the personal essay on the seemingly commonplace; he writes of household fires, of seeing friends off on trips, and of names given to streets. He entertains his readers with his humorous and unusual perspective. Often he takes the unexpected angle, as in "Going Out for a Walk" when he begins, "It is a fact that not once in all my life have I gone out for a walk. I have been taken out for walks; but that is another matter." In "An Infamous Brigade" he bids a fireman who is pouring water on the flames to "desist from his vandalism. I told him that I had driven miles to see this fire, that great crowds of Londoners, poor people with few joys, were there to see it also, and I asked him who was he that he should dare to disappoint us."

The words most often used to describe the author's inimitable prose style in these essays are "delicate," "delightful," and "elegant." The topics are treated lightly and humorously. Mock seriousness is his favorite humor technique; he deals with such matters as hatboxes ("Ichabod"), books mentioned in other books ("Books within Books"), and the fragment of a fan ("The Relic") as if they were matters of high seriousness.

Beerbohm's fiction has certain affinities with his caricatures and essays, for he continues to satirize and parody. *The Happy Hypocrite*, a small book published by Lane in 1897, parodies Wilde's *The Picture of Dorian Gray*: Beerbohm's roguish hero assumes a saintly mask to win his lover and surprisingly takes on good qualities while wearing it. *Seven Men* (1919) contains five short stories, but the fiction merges with the personal essay, for Beerbohm himself is involved in all five and he incorporates personal acquaintances and experiences in the narration. "Enoch Soames" is particularly interesting to modern critics because of the circularity of its plot line. Soames, the erstwhile poet, goes into the future to discover that the only fame that he achieves is as an imaginary character in a satire by Max Beerbohm. *Zuleika Dobson*, Beerbohm's sole novel, stands as a model of sustained satiric fantasy. Zuleika is a *femme fatale* who conquers Oxford and leads all of the undergraduates to commit suicide. Oxfordians delight in the satire of university customs, types, and rituals of a by-gone day, but most readers, while they can admire Beerbohm's lucid and flexible style, find the novel strained. After this short foray into the genre, Beerbohm never attempted another novel. Obviously the well-wrought miniature appealed to his taste, not the more ambitious canvas.

Beerbohm had no interest in being popular and disdained crowds and wide fame. He was willing to do BBC broadcasts during the war because to him the voice was part of the literature, but he drew the line at television. When Behrman suggested that he do a television series for NBC, Beerbohm adamantly refused, saying, "No, television is not literature, it is actuality."[5] He felt that the viewers would concentrate on him rather than on what he was saying. His work was a serious matter to him, and even though it meant passing up chances to make much-needed money, he would not violate his principles. Beerbohm was a remarkably consistent man. His quiet, ordered life seems an anomaly in the twentieth century. The topics and themes of his fiction, caricatures, and essays should date him, but he continues to charm and entertain.[6]

Summary

Sir Max Beerbohm was a master of satiric and parodic humor. His caricatures, parodies, and essays have irrevocably conditioned how we see the 1890s and its most prominent figures. His wit is urbane and sophisticated; his subjects are most often literary and artistic. He portrays a limited world, but he does it in an inimitable, delightful way. His caricatures, considered works of art with their watercolor washes and masterful single strokes, capture the essence of his subjects' personalities succinctly and humorously. As an essayist he is held up as a model of a polished, mellifluous style. No one more clearly represents the Edwardian manner and perspective than "the incomparable Max."

Notes

1. W.H. Auden, "One of the Family." *The New Yorker* (October 23, 1965): 228.
2. Lynch quotes this letter in full in his preface to *Max in Perspective* (London: Heinemann, 1922), pp. viii–ix.
3. Roger Lewis, "The Child and the Man in Max Beerbohm," *English Literature in Transition*, 27, 4 (1984): 296–303. Lewis characterizes Max as an "inert imp" who did not deserve the attention that he received. His is definitely the minority view. This essay appears with four others in a 1984 issue of *ELT* dedicated completely to Beerbohm.
4. Quoted in J.G. Riewald, ed., *Beerbohm's Literary Caricatures* (Hamden, CT: Archon Books, 1977), p. 18.
5. S.N. Behrman, *Portrait of Max* (New York: Random House, 1960), p. 265.
6. Between 1980 and 1991 at least twelve articles and two full-length studies of Beerbohm were published. Martin Maner in "Beerbohm's *Seven Men* and the Power of the Press," *English Literature in Transition*, 34, 2 (1991): 133–51, goes so far as to claim that "he anticipated postmodernism" in his insights into the problems of twentieth-century mass culture and that *Seven Men* is "an anomaly, a postmodernist fiction written before its time."

Selected Bibliography
Primary Sources

Drawings
Caricatures of Twenty-Five Gentlemen.
London: Leonard Smithers, 1896.
A Book of Caricatures. London: Methuen,
1907.
Fifty Caricatures. London: Heinemann, 1913.
Rosetti and His Circle. London: Heinemann,
1922.
Things New and Old. London: Heinemann,
1923.

Writings
*The Works of Max Beerbohm with a Bibliog-
raphy by John Lane.* London: John Lane,
1896.
The Happy Hypocrite. London: John Lane,
1897.
More. London: John Lane, 1899.
Yet Again. London: Chapman & Hall, 1909.
Zuleika Dobson. London: Heinemann, 1911.
Seven Men. London: Heinemann, 1919.
And Even Now. London: Heinemann, 1920.
The Works of Max Beerbohm. 10 vols.
London: Heinemann, 1921–1928.
Mainly on the Air. London: Heinemann,
1946.

Secondary Sources

Bibliographies
Gallatin, A.E., and L.M. Oliver, comps. *A
Bibliography of the Works of Max
Beerbohm.* The Soho Bibliographies III.
London: Rupert Hart-Davis, 1952. The
standard bibliographic reference to
Beerbohm's caricatures and writings.
Hart-Davis, Rupert, comp. *A Catalogue of
the Caricatures of Max Beerbohm.*
London: Macmillan, and Cambridge,
MA: Harvard University Press, 1972.
Illustrated catalogue of drawings from
1885 to 1956 which lists data on origi-
nal publication and present owners.

Biographies
Behrman, S.N. *Portrait of Max.* New York:
Random House, 1960. An excellent
combination of biography and memoir,
based on personal interviews with
Beerbohm in his last years.
Cecil, David. *Max, A Biography.* London:
Constable, 1964. The authorized biogra-

phy, focuses more on the life than the
works.

Critical Studies
Danson, Lawrence. *Max Beerbohm and the
Act of Writing.* Oxford: Clarendon,
1989. An important critical study which
examines Beerbohm's forward-looking
tendencies.
Felstiner, John. *The Lies of Art: Max
Beerbohm's Parody and Caricature.* New
York: Knopf, 1972. A significant work
exploring the motives behind Beerbohm's
parodic works.
Jackson, Holbrook. *The Eighteen-Nineties: A
Review of Art and Ideas at the Close of
the Nineteenth Century.* London: Grant
Richards, 1913. Puts Beerbohm in con-
text of the 1890s. Beerbohm read and
praised this work.
Lynch, Bohun. *Max in Perspective.* London:
Heinemann, 1922. A fellow caricaturist
and friend writes rather effusively of
Beerbohm's achievements.
McElderry, Bruce R., Jr. *Max Beerbohm.*
New York: Twayne, 1972. A succinct
overview of Beerbohm's life and works,
good for the general reader.
Mix, Katherine Lyon. *Max in America.*
Brattleboro, VT: Stephen Greene Press,
1974. A detailed study of Max's trip to
America with Herbert Beerbohm Tree
and of his relations with Americans, particularly his wife and American
expatriots.
Riewald, J.G., ed., *Beerbohm's Literary Caricatures.* Hamden, CT: Archon Books,
1977. A reproduction of 104 Beerbohm
caricatures featuring famous writers,
with background and exposition for
each.
———, ed. *The Surprise of Excellence: Modern Essays on Max Beerbohm.* Hamden,
CT: Archon Books, 1974. A selection of
essays published between 1943–1970 by
such writers as Harold Nicolson,
Edmund Wilson, Evelyn Waugh, W.H.
Auden, John Felstiner, and David Cecil.
Jill Tedford Owens

Behan, Brendan
Born: Dublin, February 9, 1923
*Education: French Sisters of Charity School,
Dublin, 1928–1934; Christian Brothers*

School, Dublin, 1934–1937; Day Apprentice School, 1937; Hollesley Bay, Borstal, 1939–1941.
Marriage: Beatrice ffrench-Salkeld, February 19, 1955; one child
Died: Dublin, March 20, 1964

Biography

Born in Dublin on February 9, 1923, Brendan Behan was the first son of Stephen and Kathleen Kearney Behan. He attended the French Sisters of Charity School (1928–1934) and the Christian Brothers School (1934–1937), and then in 1937 the Day Apprentice School, where he was to learn the trade of house painting. He had no further formal education, but during and after his incarceration he read extensively in English and Irish literature as well as Irish history; he also taught himself Gaelic, in which he wrote poetry and *An Giall*, the original version of his play *The Hostage.*

The Behans' was an intensely nationalistic household; Brendan became a member of Fianna Eireann in 1931 and joined the Irish Republican Army (I.R.A.) in 1937, when he was fourteen. Two years later he was arrested in Liverpool, convicted of helping an I.R.A. bomb-planting campaign, and sentenced to three years' incarceration in a Borstal (reform school) at Hollesley Bay. In 1941, at the end of his term of confinement in England, he was deported to Ireland under an Expulsion Order. The next year, he was arrested following a row at Glasnevin Cemetery on Easter Sunday; he was then sentenced to fourteen years in prison for shooting a policeman. Behan's sentence was commuted in the general amnesty of 1946; after his release from prison, he became a house painter and apprentice writer. During the next ten years, he led a rather nomadic existence, traveling through England, Ireland, and France. His experience during this time included pimping in Paris and doping racing greyhounds as well as becoming a free-lance writer for various newspapers and a broadcaster for Radio Eireann. *The Scarperer*, a novel, was published serially in the *Irish Times* (under the pseudonym Emmet Street) in 1953, and his weekly column was published in that newspaper from 1954 through 1956. In February 1955, Behan married Beatrice ffrench-Salkeld; the couple had one child, daughter Blanaid, who was born in 1964.

Behan's experiences in the borstal and the prison provided the central subject for much of his writing. *The Quare Fellow*, about the events in a prison on the eve of an execution, was first produced in 1954 (directed by Alan Simpson) at the fifty-five-seat Pike Theatre in Dublin. However, his fame was established by the London production, directed by Joan Littlewood, which opened at the Theatre Royal, Stratford, East London in 1956. Further acclaim came in 1958 with the publication of the autobiographical narrative *Borstal Boy*, and he began translation of his Gaelic play *An Giall*, which had opened that year at Damer Hall, Dublin. As *The Quare Fellow* had been, the English version, *The Hostage*, was directed by Joan Littlewood at the Theatre Royal in London the following year. *The Quare Fellow* was also produced off-Broadway in 1958, under the direction of Jose Quintero.

As Behan's literary reputation rapidly grew, so did his public notoriety—fueled by public drunkenness, rowdiness, and dissipation that increased in his later years, even as his witty extemporizations, colorful anecdotes, and bursts of song won him a wide popular audience that had little interest in or knowledge of his writings. This part of his public persona (which seemed to confirm stereotypical views of the comically drunken Irishman) was firmly established in 1956 when Behan appeared—quite incoherently drunk—on the BBC television program *Panorama*, hosted by Malcolm Muggeridge. After 1958, his behavior became increasingly erratic, as he drunkenly enjoyed both his fame and new-found wealth but required hospitalization more and more frequently. Despite occasional attempts to remain sober and muster the discipline required to resume his writing, such efforts failed. While press coverage continued to celebrate his often-witty public pronouncements and appearances (including tours of the United States and Canada), his drinking binges and brawling, which sometimes resulted in his arrest, continued until he died.

Late in 1963, Behan returned to New York, of which he had become fond, associating it with wealth, fame, and his creative power. His final books, *Brendan Behan's Island* (1962), *Brendan Behan's New York* (1964), and the posthumously-published *Confessions of an Irish Rebel* (1965), were compiled and edited by Rae Jeffs from tape-recorded conversations. As a result of this procedure, they are quite unlike the carefully crafted prose of *Borstal Boy*. Behan returned to Dublin in July 1963, quite ill. Us-

B

ing the death of John F. Kennedy as an excuse to start a final binge, he remained drunk or in a diabetic coma until he died in Meath Hospital, Dublin, on March 20, 1964.

An acclaimed stage adaptation of *Borstal Boy* by Frank McMahon was produced in Dublin (1967) and on Broadway (1970). A play titled *Richard's Cork Leg*, "edited with additional material by Alan Simpson," was posthumously produced at the Peacock Theatre in Dublin in 1972, performed by the Abbey Theatre Company.

Literary Analysis

In 1939, at the age of sixteen, two days after having crossed the border from Ireland into England, Behan was arrested in Liverpool for possession of explosives which he intended to use in helping to implement the Irish Republican Army's plant-bombing campaign. He had been a Volunteer in the 2nd Battalion, Dublin Brigade of the I.R.A. for the previous three years. *Borstal Boy* is Behan's forthright account of his life as a teenaged inmate or young prisoner (Y.P.) in the English penal system. Each of the book's three parts depicts his life in a different place of incarceration: first in the adult prison to which he was remanded during the two months that he awaited trial; then in the boys' prison to which he was temporarily transferred; and finally in the borstal (reform school) in which he served two years of his three-year sentence.

Borstal Boy opens with the sudden arrival of the police at the boarding house where Behan was staying in Liverpool, their confiscation of the bomb-making materials in his possession, and his immediate arrest. After his initial interrogation at the Criminal Investigation Department (C.I.D.) offices where he refused to answer questions but agreed to make a statement that was both determinedly partisan and wholly unrepentant, he was briefly confined in the Dale Street lock-up before being transferred to Walton Prison to await trial. With remarkable candor and surprising objectivity, Behan recounts the details of prison life: the extreme regimentation, the constant indignities, the routine (extending to the point of regulating when prisoners' bowel movements were and were not to be allowed), the prison-issue clothing (including Boy Scout-like shorts to be worn even in mid-winter), the meager food, the monotonous labor of sewing mail-sacks, the "screws" (guards), the threat of "chokey" (solitary con-

finement for infractions of the rules), and—in his particular case—the anti-Irish jeers and anti-I.R.A. resentments of the English authorities and other prisoners alike. Yet against all such means of dehumanization, the young captive retains a certain heroic indomitability: he steadfastly refuses to recant his nationalist beliefs; he defiantly disagrees with the prison-provided priest who condones the Catholic Church's excommunication of the I.R.A. and mistakenly terms him merely an ignorant boy; and he proves his willingness to fight even the fully adult prisoners when goaded too far. He finds, too, sources of pleasure and satisfaction—in books from the prison library, in cigarettes and newspapers that he is permitted to buy, and particularly in his friendship with two English Y.P.s, Charlie and Ginger, who are also seventeen years old. Because they were under the age of eighteen at the time of their offenses, they could not be given an adult prison term (Behan's could have been up to fourteen years). The judge's harsh reprimand of Behan, sentencing him to three years in the borstal, concludes the first part of the book.

The book's second, and shortest, part takes place in London's Feltham Boys' Prison, where Behan and his "chinas" ("mates") await the bureaucratic decision on the specific Borstal Institution in which they will serve their terms. From the moment of their arrival at Feltham, where they are designated as Allocations (temporary inmates to be transferred elsewhere), conditions are markedly less severe than in Walton Prison: fewer restrictions are placed on speech and movement, the food is better and more abundant, and the beds are located in a shared dormitory area rather than individual cells. After initially and deliberately demonstrating a willingness to fight and a potentially volatile temper in order to establish his status as a "terror" among the others and thus forestall trouble later, Behan readily adjusts to the new prison's easier routines. Though excommunicated from the Roman Catholic Church, he is required by English law to attend its services in the prison chapel and, though he cannot receive the sacraments, he is even allowed to serve the Mass. The religious services are depicted with considerable humor and occasional irreverence, being valued by the boys less for their spiritual content than for the opportunity to socialize with one another and to escape the workaday monotony of prison life. The second section ends as Behan shares with his English friends a cache of I.R.A.-provided tobacco and chocolates, secretly passed to him by a fellow I.R.A.-member who is also serving as an altar-boy.

The final section of the book is set in Hollesley Bay, a Borstal near the coast of Suffolk, where conditions are far less restrictive than in the other institutions where he has been confined. However, because his heroically indomitable spirit is best displayed in adversity, the portrayal of his experience in the Borstal itself lacks the narrative force and suspense of the preceding sections in which his circumstances were far less benign. After an initial period during which he is engaged in field labor, Behan is reassigned to work as a painter—the trade in which he had been a fourth-year apprentice before his criminal conviction. Among his new acquaintances is Ken, whose middle-class background, attitudes, and experiences separate and isolate him from the other boys far more than Behan's Irishness and political views have ever done. Ken plans and attempts an ultimately unsuccessful escape, after which he is confined in "chokey." For the others, life settles into a relatively comfortable routine of work and camaraderie, harvesting fruit from the borstal orchards and swimming in the ocean. Without the narrative tension that was present in the first two parts, the final hundred pages seem more a random collection of anecdotes often interspersed with the words of favorite songs. Shortly before his release after serving two years of his sentence, Behan learns that Charlie (who had been released from the borstal somewhat earlier and returned to naval service) has been killed in the war. The book ends with Behan's return to Dublin on a train and his welcome (in Gaelic) by the Irish immigration control officer.

Because they belong to an outlawed political organization, and because their activities, if they are to be successful, must be accomplished anonymously and become known only by their (often literally explosive) effects, members of the I.R.A. remain covert subversives, necessarily attempting to stay out of the public eye. *Borstal Boy*, however, is a surprising and extraordinarily intimate self-portrait of an I.R.A. member as a young man: its first-person narrative is not only unexpectedly unpolemical but also compassionate, always frank, and often witty, disarmingly human, and remarkably humane.

Inspired in part by the Irish revolutionist John Mitchel's *Jail Journal, or Five Years in British Prisons* (1854), *Borstal Boy* would seem to fit within the literary subgenre of such autobiographical accounts of prison life as Jean Genet's *Thief's Journal* (1948, trans. 1964), Alexander Solzhenitsyn's *One Day in the Life of Ivan Denisovich* (1963), Eldridge Cleaver's *Soul on Ice* (1968), and Jack Abbot's *In the Belly of the Beast* (1981). The unique tone of Behan's writing—its often hilarious comedy, its almost complete lack of bitterness, its literary allusiveness, its emphasis on resilience and irrepressibility, its inclusion of frequently bawdy songs and mirth-filled banter—sets it apart from the aforementioned works. The nature of Behan's crime also differentiates *Borstal Boy* from other books of this kind: his intended bombing attempt is now known to have been unauthorized by the I.R.A. leadership, independently undertaken and poorly planned, having little if any chance of success at the heavily guarded military installation that he had targeted. It seems primarily a rash act of adolescent bravado and derring-do rather than the work of a humorless zealot like those depicted, for example, in Feodor Dostoyevsky's *The Possessed* (1867), Graham Greene's *The Quiet American* (1955), or Joseph Conrad's *The Secret Agent* (1907).

Fundamentally, *Borstal Boy* is more nearly comparable to the novels of England's so-called "Angry Young Men" of the mid-to-late-1950s (Kingsley Amis, Alan Sillitoe, John Braine, Keith Waterhouse, et al.) in its emphasis on working-class experience, its anti-authoritarianism, its inclusion of sometimes "coarse" language and formerly "unmentionable" subject matter, its comic "vulgarity," and its uninhibited frankness about the body and all of its functions. It particularly resembles Sillitoe's non-autobiographical novella, *The Loneliness of the Long-Distance Runner* (1959), whose first-person narrator is also a teenaged borstal boy, a self-styled "outlaw," and a resilient anti-hero with wit, "cunning," and anti-authoritarian defiance. The vitality of both protagonists is effectively communicated through the vigor of their authors' occasionally-profane prose. Behan's, particularly, is laced with prison argot as well as Cockney rhyming slang.[1] Though shocking to staid readers of the 1950s, the frequent obscenities not only contribute to its humor and its consistently frank tone but also are essential to an accurate portrayal of its characters. Behan's many painstaking revisions refined the book's style into a type of "vulgar" lyricism having its origins in the language really used by men in a state of confinement.[2]

Although there can be no doubt that when challenged by the authorities or teased by the English boys about Ireland or the I.R.A.'s bombing campaign, Behan was always ready with a retort both historically accurate and profanity-laden, few such polemics are to be found within the book itself. Apart from his initial defiant statement after being apprehended (intended largely for propaganda purposes in England and for notice at home in Ireland) and his genuinely angry outburst against the condescension and smugness of the priest in Walton Prison, Behan's commitment to the I.R.A. remains a subordinate theme of *Borstal Boy*. Instead of emphasizing the ideology that sets him fundamentally apart from his captors, his church, and his fellow inmates (almost all of whom are English), Behan repeatedly shows his humane solidarity with and genuine compassion for his fellow prisoners, whatever their crimes may have been. Though he is ready to fight whenever necessary, and acts of sometimes brutal violence recur throughout the first two parts of the book, "Paddy" Behan's repeated acts of kindness—consoling, encouraging, and defending others as needed, always ready to share with them a joke, a song, or an allocation of tobacco or chocolate—earn him the esteem and affection of his compatriots.

Behan's attitude toward the church undergoes a radical transformation during the course of *Borstal Boy* as his prison experience soon causes him to lose his initially secure faith: "Walton scalded my heart with regard to my religion . . . [and] cured me of any idea that religion of any description had anything to do with mercy or pity or love."[3] The priest there, Behan contends, is "an active enemy" (321) who condones his expulsion from the Church, offers no consolation of any kind, and belittles his political views. In Feltham Prison Behan enjoys but does not join in the other boys' bawdy irreverence during the services; in the borstal, he finds that he has lost interest in religion entirely. He remarks without bitterness that his expulsion from the church was "like being pushed outside a prison and told not to come back" (322). He willingly serves the Mass, but he does so solely "in memory of my ancestors" (322). Ironically, the book's one authentic religious experience is felt by a boy known as Chewlips during his first visit to a Catholic Mass, but his potentially life-transforming conversion is thwarted by prison authorities who prevent him from attending further Catholic services because his identification card states that he is a member of the Church of England. For Chewlips, as for Behan, it is social institutions and the bureaucratic agents of church and state, whether priests or prison guards, that constantly frustrate rather than encourage the development or expression of humane values and the autonomy of the individual—both of which such institutions continually and insidiously try to suppress.

At times, Behan reveals that, notwithstanding his adolescent bravado and his sincere support of the Irish cause, his devotion to political goals is less fervid than it appears. In Walton Prison he contrasts himself with the more ardently defiant Callan, an older I.R.A. member whose shouted political slogans and sly subversions of prison routines earn him a severe beating from the guards, and later he expresses a frank preference for the company of his English friends in the boys' prison and the borstal rather than the ideologues of the bombing campaign. For all of his support of the I.R.A. and his pride in his Irish heritage, Behan ultimately celebrates individual autonomy rather than any institutional authority—whether that of the Catholic church, the British Empire, the penal system, or even the I.R.A. The book's epigraph, from Virginia Woolf's *Orlando*, describes a "crew of young watermen or postboys . . . [who] roared and shouted the lewdest tavern songs, as if in bravado, and . . . were sunk with blasphemies on their lips" (ix). Later in the epigraph they are said to have been Irish rebels and are, clearly, as irrepressibly high-spirited as Behan himself.

The fact that Behan's humane values, wit, and personal integrity are so utterly irrepressible accounts in large part for the vitality and warmth that typify his writings for the stage as well. In *The Quare Fellow*, as in *Borstal Boy*, these values are juxtaposed against all of the dehumanizing aspects of prison experience which, notwithstanding all of its incipient violence and cruelty, is depicted with the author's characteristic blend of naturalistic detail, raucous comedy, and song. The play depicts events occurring before, during, and after the execution of a condemned man (referred to in prison argot as a "quare fellow"). Although the title character is never seen on stage, his plight remains the focus of the play as the events that occur during his final hours are compellingly described by the on-stage characters: the other inmates (two of whom must dig the grave in which he will be buried), the governor of the prison, and the priest whose duty it is to administer the last rites.

Like Leonid Andreyev's novel *The Seven Who Were Hanged* (1908), *The Quare Fellow* is a forthright and eloquent albeit understated condemnation of capital punishment, in which Behan confronts the audience with the grim details of the execution process. Nevertheless, the writers' strategies are quite different. Whereas Andreyev has the reader accompany the condemned men and women on literally every step to the gallows in a work whose unremitting moral earnestness is unrelieved by humor, Behan—like Anton Chekhov and, later, David Storey—places the play's central event as well as the title character off-stage, exploring and exploiting the dramatic effectiveness of "interior" rather than "exterior" action and allowing intermittent moments of both comedy and song.

The play's tone is no less unorthodox than its form. Humor and song are essential, authority-defying assertions of vitality in the face of the imposed constrictions and repressions of the anti-life. Thus, as the play opens, an unseen prisoner's song defies the injunctions of the *"large block Victorian lettering [of] the word 'SILENCE'"*[4] that dominates the stage set's prison wall. Similarly, the on-stage prisoners' frequently off-color badinage constantly confirms their life-affirming, irrepressible interest in now-forbidden pleasures: drink, tobacco, and the women prisoners ("mots") whom they can see hanging out wash. Authority is ultimately unsuccessful in its demands for conformity: song subverts silence, swigs of methylated liniment are better than no drink at all, and the Bible is cherished because its pages can be torn out and used to roll mattress stuffing into makeshift cigarettes. Furthermore, authority is inherently capricious: the quare fellow is to be hanged for murder while another (who beat his wife to death with a "silver-topped cane") is reprieved. The same fundamental concern about the unfathomable arbitrariness of the grace granted by those in unaccountable but unchallengeable authority perplexes Didi and Gogo in Samuel Beckett's *Waiting for Godot* as they ponder the vastly different plights of the crucified thieves. A grimly ironic, absurdist paradox occurs late in act 1, when Silver-Top attempts to hang himself. The man who has been condemned to death, receiving no re-

prieve, clings to life in his final hours; meanwhile, the man whose sentence has been commuted, who is now "committed" to and for "life" in prison, attempts his own execution.

Throughout the second act, the half-dug grave for the quare fellow is visible on stage and is made the object of jokes by the prisoners in the exercise yard—only the newest inmate finds their jibes disconcerting. Despite the on-going rough humor, tension mounts among the prisoners. As the time nears, the play becomes more didactic, as Warder Regan suggests just after the arrival of the hangman that a corrupt society is to blame for capital punishment. The act ends with Regan quoting Home Office instructions on how to treat the condemned: officials are to maintain *"an air of cheerful decorum,"* ready to play games such as draughts and Snakes and Ladders or to chat about sports events with the victim-to-be.

In the two scenes of the third act, Behan's satire becomes increasingly bitter, juxtaposing the petty concerns of the presiding authorities against the enormity of the execution that is about to take place. The warders are mere civil servants, uncaring functionaries seeking "pay, promotion, and pension" (106); the hangman is a drunken itinerant executioner who once left his paraphernalia in a pub and who insists that precautions be taken so that no prisoner swipes any of his breakfast. All of the officials fail to react in any moral or humane way to the inherent horror of the prisoner's impending death; they distract themselves with perfunctory formalities, rituals, and proprieties of order, as do members of the society outside the prison walls in whose name the deed is done—a group that includes, of course, the audience in the theater. The evangelist who accompanies the hangman is a teetotaling hymn-writer whose song about God, mercy, and forgiveness provides a bitterly satiric counterpoint to the executioner's heedless calculations of the gallows "drop" needed to accommodate a given prisoner's weight. Warder Regan's ensuing lengthy and didactic reflections against capital punishment are far less theatrically effective than Prisoner C's lonely Gaelic song for the condemned man which is much more heart-felt and consoling than the pious platitudes of the evangelist's hymn.

The play's brief final scene concerns the moment of execution itself, the completion of the grave, and the prisoner's sole memorial—his prison number carved into the wall (or, more accurately, *miscarved*, since a 7 is easier to cut than a 9. The prisoner is thus finally denied the autonomy and identity of his own number, much less his own name. The comedy of the earlier scenes is notably diminished, though the prisoners do laconically describe the approach to the gallows as if it were a horse race. The warders cross themselves at the moment of death, but from the prisoners there "comes a ferocious howling" (121). Later, however, they argue over how to dispose of the dead man's last letters; those who want to smuggle the letters out and sell them to the Sunday papers are no less mercenary than the Roman soldiers who gambled over Christ's robe.

Like *The Quare Fellow*, *The Hostage* depicts events that surround the execution of a character whom the audience never sees—an eighteen-year-old I.R.A. member sentenced to die in a Belfast jail for having killed an Ulster policeman. As in the previous play, the crucial event takes place offstage, but this time none of the characters is a public official or directly involved in the death of the condemned man. The setting is a run-down brothel that is used by I.R.A. members as the hideout, in effect a makeshift prison, where a young British soldier, Leslie Williams, is held hostage in retaliation and eventually killed, albeit by accident. Yet, despite this grim subject, the play is full of raucous, life-affirming humor as well as Behan's most bitterly acerbic satire. Its structure is more indebted to the innovations of Bertolt Brecht's Berliner Ensemble and to the music-hall stage than to the conventions and formulae of the "well-made play." Originally written in Gaelic under the title *An Giall*, it attracted relatively little attention until the translated and much-revised version was produced by Joan Littlewood's Theatre Workshop. The extent to which the final form of the play is attributable to Littlewood's improvisational, collaborative "workshop" methods remains a matter of critical debate.

The play opens with "*a wild Irish jig*" that is danced by the "*pimps, prostitutes* [including "a homosexual navvy, Rio Rita"], *decayed gentlemen, and their visiting 'friends'*" in the "*old house in Dublin that has seen better days*" (129–30). Like the bar in Eugene O'Neill's *The Iceman Cometh* or the brothel in Genet's *The Balcony*, the brothel is, in fact, a microcosm of its society. "This is nineteen-sixty," its middle-aged manager remarks, "and the days of heroes are over this forty years past" (131). As are their counterparts in Brecht's *The*

Threepenny Opera (the first London production of which occurred in 1955), Behan's characters are unheroic, disreputable outcasts who, nevertheless, fundamentally and exuberantly affirm life through their raucous banter and their ostensibly "immoral" activities, offenses against traditional moralists' life-stifling proprieties. The house's "real owner isn't right in the head and thinks he's still fighting in the Troubles or one of the anti-English campaigns before that" (129). When the dance ends, an ineptly-played blast from an offstage bagpipe introduces the play's more somber theme; the "Dead March" is to be played "for the boy in the Belfast jail when they hang him tomorrow" (130). The piper, known as Monsewer, is an ardent I.R.A. supporter who "lives in a world of his own, peopled by heroes and enemies . . . [and] spends much of his time making plans for battles fought long ago against enemies long since dead" (134). Most of his hearers are unable to understand him because of his sentimental allegiance to the Gaelic language, and his anachronistic patriotism and ersatz-heroic quests are fundamentally quixotic. Even his compatriot, the brothel-keeper, recognizes that "the I.R.A. and the War for Independence are as dead as the Charleston" (131). Catholicism is also a target of Behan's satire: Miss Gilchrist, a social worker from the St. Vincent de Paul Society, embodies a shallow and irrelevant piety, ready with hymns and tracts for any occasion but making ultimately no difference in the issue of the prisoner's impending death. The first act ends as the captive soldier is dragged in while the residents dance a swirling reel. Implausibly, the captive leads them in song, "There's no place on earth like the world" (169–70).

The second act develops a love story between the prisoner, Leslie, and Teresa, a nineteen-year-old maid who has come from a convent school to work at the prison. Despite differences in their religion and nationality (he is an English Protestant), despite the inherent peril in the situation and intermittent interruptions, the young couple becomes well acquainted. Eventually they consummate the relationship in an upstairs bedroom. Behan's characterization of the English "enemy" is, as in *Borstal Boy*, surprisingly humane. Leslie is remarkably undoctrinaire about both religion and politics. In Ireland solely because he was sent there, he is uninterested in news of the royal family and the larger "Irish question" alike. Although the fact that he and Teresa have sex shocked many staid theatergoers of the late 1950s, theirs is in fact the only non-exploitative, non-commercial, even "innocent and genuine" act of love occurring among any of the inhabitants of the house. Subsequently, however, Leslie learns that he is to be shot, since the I.R.A. prisoner has been executed. Nevertheless, he closes the second act with another rollicking song, following which a bugle sounds and he sharply salutes.

As the third act opens, "the atmosphere is one of death and dying" (207). Still, even while the house's inhabitants mourn the death of the Belfast prisoner, they become increasingly attached to and protective of Leslie, whose song is now the solemn hymn "Abide With Me" (213). The fanaticism of the I.R.A. officers and Monsewer, like the absurdity of Leslie's plight, becomes increasingly apparent. The possibility that the threat is a bluff, that he is to be questioned by Intelligence Officers rather than shot, is maintained, and the love interest established in the second act continues in the third. Suddenly, an explosion shakes the stage, filling it with smoke as the police attack the house. Mulleady, one of the residents, has turned informant and brings the police to the rescue (one of the house patrons, ostensibly a Russian sailor, has been "a police spy all along" [232]). A full-scale battle ensues on stage, as "*whistles and sirens blow, drums beat, bombs explode, bugles sound the attack, bullets ricochet and . . . bodies hurtle from one side of the stage to the other*" (233). Through it all, absurdly, Monsewer slowly marches upright, ceremoniously blowing the bagpipe. During the fracas, Leslie makes a break for freedom but is killed in a "*deafening blast of gunfire*" (235), presumably from the attackers, not the defenders, of the house. After the battle, Teresa laments his death, promising never to forget him "till the end of time" (236).

Such an ending, appropriately anti-war, bitterly ironic, arguably even tragic (with Leslie and Teresa a modern-day Romeo and Juliet of sorts), would be relatively conventional. But, as in the preceding acts, a merry song provides the play's finale, an extremely controversial scene that has astonished and perplexed audiences since the original production. As "*a ghostly green light glows on the body[,] . . . Leslie slowly gets up and sings*:

The bells of hell
Go ting-a-ling-a-ling
But not for you or me.

Oh death, where is thy sting-a-ling-a-ling
Or grave thy victory?" (236)

The entire cast then joins in with him for a final chorus of the song which, as always in Behan's work, reaffirms the vitality of the life-force—and here particularly mocks the sentimentality of the conventionally theatrical ending. It is an anti-illusionist *coup de theatre*, effectively undercutting the audience's emotional response in essentially the manner of a Brechtian "alienation effect," as do the characters' occasional direct address to the audience which deliberately violates the theater's "fourth-wall effect," as was not done in *The Quare Fellow*. The intermingling of serious action and raucous song is also a staple of Brechtian theater, the influence of which peaked in Britain during the late 1950s and extended particularly into the ensemble work and collaborative methods of Littlewood's Theatre Workshop.

In the years following the success of *The Hostage*, a number of books were published under Behan's name, though in the strictest sense they were not actually written by him, since they were compiled and edited from tape-recorded conversations. Among them, *Brendan Behan's Island: An Irish Sketchbook* and *Brendan Behan's New York* are essentially compilations of anecdotes and observations. Although Behan was a duly famous raconteur and the stories thus recorded are often entertaining, the transcription remains a ramshackle, shapeless work, despite the best efforts of his editor, Jeffs. Throughout the years that these later volumes were being compiled, drink, illness, and dissipation were taking their soon-to-be-fatal toll on the inimitably exuberant, innovative, ardently Irish, working-class writer. Though he was not the first writer to find in the solaces of drink a release from the pressures of popular acclaim, Behan was among the first whose compulsively self-destructive behavior was chronicled and exploited in the glaring lights of television and the celebrity-sustaining popular press.

The novelist Flann O'Brien provided an especially eloquent and insightful obituary of Behan, describing him as "delightful rowdy, a wit, a man of action in many dangerous undertakings where he thought his duty lay, a reckless drinker, a fearless denouncer of humbug and pretence, and so a proprietor of the biggest heart that has beaten in Ireland for the past forty years."[5]

Summary

Uniquely among the young working-class writers who came to prominence in the 1950s, Brendan Behan subsumes "anger" into life-affirming vitality in works that are filled with raucous humor and song. In his writings for the stage and his prose narrative *Borstal Boy*, Behan drew on his experience in English borstals and prisons in which he served time for participation in activities of the outlawed Irish Republican Army. Yet, surprisingly, even the grimmest aspects of his experiences there are subsumed into irreverent comedy, replete with accounts of secret subversions and indomitable high-spiritedness.

The recurrent juxtaposition of brutal violence and raucous humor, of dehumanizing repression and life-affirming song is a key feature of Behan's style, a fact that has led detractors to contend that his works are diffuse and not unified. Nevertheless, these works are remarkable for their compassion, their transcendence (and, later, satiric denunciation) of ideological extremism, their affirmation of common humanity and the vitality of the life-force. In his later years, Behan was also a notoriously-often-drunken celebrity, a renowned raconteur, an unfailingly irreverent and inimitably Irish wit whose demise was as untimely as it was unfortunate.

Notes

1. A glossary of the book's frequently-used slang terms is provided, though its definitions are sometimes euphemistic. Not all terms are included, but most of those omitted are sufficiently clear in context.
2. Although the original manuscript of *Borstal Boy* is no longer extant, the published text appears to have been extensively and inconsistently edited. Sometimes dashes are substituted for the more offensive words, with or without the first or last letter being indicated; at other times, the same words are spelled as if in dialect (e.g., "fugh," "facquing").
3. Brendan Behan, *Borstal Boy* (New York: Knopf, 1959), pp. 321–22. Subsequent quotations are from this edition and have been inserted parenthetically into the text.
4. Brendan Behan, *The Quare Fellow*, in *Brendan Behan: The Complete Plays* (New York: Grove Press, and London: Methuen, 1978), p. 39. All subsequent references to Behan's plays are from this collection and have been inserted parenthetically into the text.
5. Quoted in Ulick O'Connor, *Brendan* (1970; New York: Grove Press, 1973), pp. 318–19.

Selected Bibliography
Primary Sources

Prose Works
Borstal Boy. London: Hutchinson, 1958; New York: Knopf, 1959.
Brendan Behan's Island: An Irish Sketchbook. London: Hutchinson, 1962. A compilation of tape-recorded conversations and previously published short pieces. Illustrated with drawings by Paul Hogarth.
Brendan Behan's New York. New York: Bernard Geis Associates, 1964. Another compilation of tape-recorded conversations, also illustrated by Hogarth.
Confessions of an Irish Rebel. London: Hutchinson, and New York: Bernard Geis Associates, 1965.
Hold Your Hour and Have Another. London: Hutchinson, 1963; Boston: Little, Brown, 1964. A collection of columns written for the *The Irish Times*, 1954–1956. Illustrated with drawings by Beatrice Behan.
The Scarperer. Garden City, NY: Doubleday, 1964; London: Hutchinson, 1966. Book form of a serial written for *The Irish Times* in 1953.

Plays
The Big House. In *Evergreen Review*, 5 (September-October 1961): 40–63.
Brendan Behan: The Complete Plays. London: Methuen, and New York: Grove Press, 1978.
The Hostage. London: Methuen, 1958; New York: Grove Press, 1959.
Moving Out and A Garden Party: Two Plays. Ed. Robert Hogan. Dixon, CA: Proscenium Plays, 1967.
The Quare Fellow. London: Methuen, 1956; New York: Grove Press, 1957.
The Quare Fellow and The Hostage. New York: Grove Press, 1964.
Richard's Cork Leg. Ed. and completed by Alan Simpson. London: Methuen, 1973; New York: Grove Press, 1974.

Poetry

Life Styles: *Poems, with Nine Translations from the Irish of Brendan Behan*. Trans. Ulick O'Connor. Dublin: Dolmen Press, 1973.

Poems and Stories. Dublin: Liffey Press, 1978.

Secondary Sources

Bibliographies

Mikhail, E.H., ed. *Brendan Behan: An Annotated Bibliography of Criticism*. Totowa, NJ: Barnes & Noble, 1980.

Books and Articles

Ahrens, Ruediger. "National Myths and Stereotypes in Modern Irish Drama: Sean O'Casey, Brendan Behan, Brian Friel." *Fu Jen Studies*, 21 (1988): 89–110. Argues that Behan's "vitality, originality, and popularity" are underappreciated since most criticism focuses on the man rather than the works which are made to seem "nostalgic and sentimental reminiscences."

Behan, Beatrice (with Des Hickey and Wes Smith). *My Life with Brendan*. London: Leslie Frewin, and Los Angeles: Nash, 1973. Memoirs by Behan's wife.

Behan, Brian. *With Breast Expanded*. London: MacGibbon & Kee, 1964. A brother's reminiscences.

Behan, Dominic. *My Brother Brendan*. London: Leslie Frewin, 1965; New York: Simon and Schuster, 1966. More brotherly reminiscences.

Bordinat, Philip. "Tragedy Through Comedy in Plays by Brendan Behan and Brian Friel." *West Virginia University Philological Papers*, 29 (1983): 84–91. Contends that both writers used comedy to "intensify tragic impact by humanizing their characters through comedy," though Behan's approach is comic while Friel's (in *The Freedom of the City*) is epic.

Boyle, Ted. E. *Brendan Behan*. New York: Twayne, 1969. Useful, concise overview of Behan's life and works, including a chapter on "Some Relevant Theories of Comedy." Focus is on "this peculiar juxtaposition of laughter and death . . . [that] could be said to be his most characteristic theme."

Brown, Richard. "*Borstal Boy*: Structure and Meaning." *Colby Library Quarterly*, 21, 4 (December 1985): 188–97. Insightful assessment of Behan's "ingratiating but conceptually limited narrator" who is "fueled by his emotions over immediate experience." Brown argues that the book's "nearly utopian third part and its melancholy, anti-climactic ending are actually well-shaped to conclude a surprisingly mature political argument, which is reflected in the process of the narrator's growing up."

Burgess, Anthony. "The Writer as Drunk." *Urgent Copy: Literary Studies*. London: Jonathan Cape, 1968; Harmondsworth: Penguin, 1973, pp. 98–102. Contrasts Behan and Dylan Thomas, preferring the latter; Behan "was a man with a lot of talk in him but very limited creative gifts" who "sometimes reads like a man eager to get his five hundred words done before the pub opens." *Borstal Boy* is "a fine autobiographical book"; the plays are "of little shape but immense vigour."

Cardullo, Bert. "*The Hostage* Reconsidered." *Eire-Ireland: A Journal of Irish Studies*, 20, 2 (Summer 1985): 139–43. Contends that Behan's play is interesting "not for its literary merit or originality but for the production given it by Joan Littlewood's Theatre Workshop, which was a landmark in the elevation of the director to superstar status in our century."

Gray, Nigel. "Every Tinker Has His Own Way of Dancing." *The Silent Majority: A Study of the Working Class in Post-War British Fiction*. New York: Barnes & Noble, 1973, pp. 73–99. Gray discusses the characters in *Borstal Boy* as an example of the "solidarity that exists between brothers in a family that ignores national boundaries."

Jeffs, Rae. *Brendan Behan, Man and Showman*. London: Hutchinson, 1966. Reminiscences by the editor of Behan's tape-recorded works; covers the period from 1957 through his death.

Kearney, Colbert. *The Writings of Brendan Behan*. New York: St. Martin's Press, 1977. Overview of Behan's life and works, focusing on narrative technique and comparing *Borstal Boy* to James Joyce's *A Portrait of the Artist as a Young Man*. Behan is seen as an iconoclast, "pushing broadmindedness to its limits" both in the theater and in his personal activities.

Marcus, Steven. "Tom Brown in Quod." *Partisan Review*, 26, 2 (Spring 1959): 335–44. Discusses Behan's development as "the unmaking of a fanatic" and notes the similarity of his experience in the Borstal to that of boys in an English public school; part three of *Borstal Boy* "intimates a failure of inwardness" and manifests "virtually no impulse to construe his experience as symbolic of modern life."

McCann, Sean, ed. *The World of Brendan Behan*. London: New English Library, 1965; New York: Twayne, 1966. Useful collection of essays and reminiscences.

Mikhail, E.H., ed. *The Art of Brendan Behan*. Totowa, NJ: Barnes & Noble, 1979. Compilation of forty-nine articles and reviews, emphasizing Behan the writer rather than Behan the man. Arranged chronologically.

———. *Brendan Behan: Interviews and Recollections*. 2 vols. Totowa, NJ: Barnes & Noble, 1982. Collection of extracts from published memoirs and interviews given by those who knew Behan; there are fifty-one items in volume 1 and fifty-five in volume 2. Mikhail's introduction insightfully compares Behan and Oscar Wilde.

O'Connor, Ulick. *Brendan*. London: Hamish Hamilton, 1970; Englewood Cliffs, NJ: Prentice-Hall, 1971; New York: Grove Press, 1973. Excellent, judicious biographical and critical study.

Paul, Ronald. "A Broth-of-a-Boy: Brendan Behan's *Borstal Boy*." *"Fire in Our Hearts": A Study of the Portrayal of Youth in a Selection of Post-War British Working-Class Fiction*. Gothenburg Studies in English 51. Goteborg, Sweden: Acta Universitatis Gothoburgensis, 1982. Detailed analysis of the "class matrix," "class ideology," and "class nexus" of Behan's book.

Porter, Raymond J. *Brendan Behan*. New York: Columbia University Press, 1973. Columbia Essays on Modern Writers 66. Brief and general introduction to Behan's writings.

Simpson, Alan. *Beckett and Behan and a Small Theatre in Dublin*. London: Routledge & Kegan Paul, 1962. Memoir of Behan and his family by the proprietor of the Pike Theatre, Dublin.

Taylor, John Russell. "Brendan Behan." *Anger and After: A Guide to the New British Drama*. London: Methuen, 1963; rev. ed. 1969, pp. 123–30. Overview of Behan's major plays, emphasizing "his roughness, his irreverence, his distaste for any establishment, even the establishment of rebellion" but seeing him as a product of "the new questioning spirit in Britain."

Witoszek, Walentyna. "The Funeral Comedy of Brendan Behan." *Etudes Irelandaises*, 11 (December 1988): 83–91. Witoszek discusses the puzzling presence of laughter in Behan's writings in which execution is imminent. Though Death is the "central character" of all of Behan's plays, "there is this orgiastic, swinging atmosphere of carnival madness," which is analyzed in terms of ritual, "the Irish *topos* of the *laughing death*," and Mikhail Bakhtin's theories of the carnivalesque.

William Hutchings

Belloc, Joseph Peter René Hilaire

Born: La Celle St. Cloud, Paris, France, July 27, 1870

Education: The Oratory School, Birmingham, 1880–1887; Balliol College, Oxford, 1893–1895

Marriage: Elodie Hogan, June 16, 1896; five children

Died: Guildford, Surrey, July 16, 1953

Biography

The son of a French father, Louis Belloc, and an English mother, Bessie Rayner (Parkes) Belloc, Hilaire Belloc was born at the family home on the edge of Paris on July 27, 1870, nine days after Pope Pius IX had promulgated the doctrine of Papal Infallibility at the close of the First Vatican Council in Rome and two days before Prussia declared war on France. The family fled to London on the last train to leave Paris before the start of the siege, and when they returned a year later, they found that the house and surrounding area had been devastated by the occupying German troops. Soon afterward, Louis Belloc died of sunstroke, whereupon his widow returned to live permanently in England, first in London, then in Sussex.

At the age of ten, Hilaire was sent by his mother to the Oratory School in Birmingham, over which the aged Cardinal Newman presided. He stayed until he was seventeen, when he spent an abortive term at the College Stanislas in Paris. Three years later, in 1890, he met a young Californian girl, Elodie Hogan, in London, and immediately fell in love with her. When she returned home the next year believing that she had a vocation to be a nun, he pursued her, earning his fare across the United States by selling sketches that he made as he went, but, for the time being, she resisted his courtship. Belloc then completed his eighteen months as a conscript in the French Army (thus safeguarding his French nationality for the time being), stationed in Toul, on the borders of the lost provinces of Alsace and Lorraine, which had been annexed by the new German Empire following the Franco-Prussian war. In 1893, he went up to Balliol College, Oxford, to read history. He became President of the Oxford Union and had high hopes of gaining a Fellowship at All Souls College on completing his degree two years later. But, All Souls rejected him, not least because of his belligerent Catholicism, and this became an abiding bitterness which grew throughout his life, partly because it condemned him to write for profit, a profit won with difficulty from an audience that he felt to be basically hostile to him.

In 1896, by which time Elodie had tried her vocation and failed, he traveled to California a second time, in the face of fierce opposition from his mother, to find Elodie recovering from a nervous breakdown. They were married in Napa, Elodie's birthplace, on June 16, and returned to England to live, first in Oxford and three years later, as his hopes of an academic career finally died, in the publishing center of London. In order to maintain his growing family (the couple had five children), he wrote steadily in several genres: political journalism, children's verse, essays, fiction. In June 1901, he set out to walk from Toul, the place of his military service, to Rome, and published his account of the journey as *The Path to Rome* (1902). Meanwhile, his opposition to the Boer War drew him towards the Liberal Party, and in 1906 he was elected to the House of Commons as part of that party's landslide victory. The party, however, with its roots in religious nonconformity, was essentially alien to him,

and at the second election of 1910 he declined to stand again. The breach with the party was completed in 1913 when a political weekly, the *New Witness* (that Belloc, along with G.K. Chesterton's younger brother, Cecil, had founded) accused government ministers of corruption in awarding a contract for the establishment of wireless telegraphy stations in Great Britain to the Marconi Company, in which they had bought shares—although, as the ministers were eventually to prove, they had done so in the American and not the British Company. Though Cecil Chesterton was fined £100 for criminal libel against a director of the company, Belloc saw this as the final confirmation of the corruption inherent in a parliamentary political system.

After a short illness, Elodie died on February 3, 1914, at the house, King's Land, which he had bought in his beloved Sussex as a family seat. (Belloc described the house and its family rituals in "A Remaining Christmas" [*A Conversation with an Angel*].) His biographer, Robert Speaight, states that "Her room was closed and never again used during Belloc's lifetime; but as he passed it on his way to bed, he would always pause outside the door and trace upon it the sign of the Cross" (Speaight, 342).

When the First World War broke out the following August, Belloc saw it as the second great attempt by Prussian militarism to overcome Catholic Europe. His articles on the progress of the fighting, written for a weekly journal, *Land and Water*—which had been founded to deal exclusively with the war—reached a readership of 100,000. His family bereavements continued, however, when his eldest son, Louis, was killed on a flying mission in August 1918.

Financial necessity compelled Belloc to continue writing at high pressure: historical studies, satirical novels, Catholic apologetics, and more nonsense verse. But, the world he knew had changed beyond recognition, and the fact that the cradle of National Socialism was Catholic Austria and Bavaria made nonsense of his thesis that German militarism had been the result of the imposition of Prussian atheism upon the gentle Catholic southern German states. It was the loss of his second son, Peter, in April 1941, while on active service in the latest resulting war, the third to have marked his life, that finally broke his health and spirit, though he himself was to live on for another twelve years. On July 12, 1953, his daughter discovered him lying near the fire in his study, and he was taken at once to the Franciscan Missionaries' nursing home at Guildford, Surrey, where he died four days later from shock and burns.

Literary Analysis

In 1911, Belloc wrote that he was compelled to write books "just like a man searching the hillside to draw fire. If they won't buy one kind of book, I write another" (quoted in Speaight, 330). His friend, Edmund Clerihew Bentley, wrote of him, in the facetious and compressed verse-form named "clerihew" after its inventor:

> Mr. Hilaire Belloc
> Is a case for legislation ad hoc;
> He seems to think nobody minds
> His books being all of different kinds.

Unquestionably, the works that he saw himself as being called to write were the historical studies, studies which he would have wished to produce in an academic rather than a commercial context, and which all contributed to a single picture of the Catholic Church operating through history as the agent of Providence, in light of his final assertion that "The Faith is Europe, and Europe is the Faith" (concluding words of *Europe and the Faith*). Since, however, he wrote for a society with a strong anti-Catholic tradition of long standing, such works were not likely to have large sales.

All of his humorous works were thus incidental to his main enterprise, and indeed are humorous in the old sense of the word defined by the *Oxford English Dictionary* as "full of humours or fancies," rather than being designed to arouse laughter. Though Belloc wrote and wrote and was obliged to go on writing for money, he never sought to ingratiate himself with his readers, while his own laughter was scornful as he fixed his gaze upon the Protestant, imperialist, mercantile society in which he lived and from which he felt himself fundamentally estranged. His humorous writings are thus a reminder that humor is essentially dependent upon an awareness of disparities and incongruities such as he saw all around him.

The fact that these incongruities can be just as easily tragic as comic means that there is no clear dividing-line between his humorous and serious works. What gives them consistency is the tone of voice: forceful, sometimes didactic, sometimes hectoring, but always expressing itself in masterly lucidity. The recurrent movement in and out of seriousness is constantly to be seen in the ten collections of essays gathered from his regular journalism (plus one posthumous collection), all given inconsequential titles which may be exemplified by five of the series: *On Nothing* (1908), *On Everything* (1909), *On Anything* (1910), *On Something* (1910), and finally, in desperation, simply *On* (1923). It appears again in *The Cruise of the "Nona"* (1925), in which, in the course of recounting the cruise in his sailing-boat from Holyhead in northwest Wales, 'round Land's End to its home-mooring in Shoreham, Sussex, he meditates on politics, on history, on literature.

The least enduring of his humorous works are the fourteen satirical novels ("he generally dictated a novel during Holy Week," according to Speaight [330]), most of them illustrated by his friend, G.K. Chesterton, starting with *Emmanuel Burden* in 1904 and ending with *The Hedge and the Horse* in 1936.

Essentially, the novels fail in their humor because of the narrow range of his targets and the sour dislike with which Belloc regards them. His *bêtes noires* all appear again and again: the effete political establishment, adroit at retaining political power while manipulating the gullible middle-class electorate; the wealthy Jews who marry into that establishment, hiding their origins and supra-national loyalties by buying peerages to which they apply bogus, ancient-sounding titles; dim-witted offspring of the establishment who have to be found wives and jobs to provide them with capital and income; and stupid middle-class academics, exploited and mocked by the wealthy and powerful.

If anywhere, Belloc's own sympathies lay with old-fashioned English Tories. During his unhappy years as a Liberal Member of Parliament, he was disconcerted to find that the most congenial fellow-Member was George Wyndham, who had been the Secretary of State for Ireland in the previous Conservative Government, and his inability to square his gut-sympathy with his political and religious convictions led to the lack of any positive value-center in his fiction.

Far more substantial and enduring are the rumbustious account of his walk from Toul to Rome, *The Path to Rome*, illustrated with his own pencil sketches, and—ten years later—a eulogy of Sussex (which is also a farewell to his youth), *The Four Men: A Farrago* (1912). His greatest linguistic debt in the first of these is acknowledged by the invocation of François Rabelais in the prefatory "Praise of this Book," in whose name Belloc produces a variety of styles, all characterized by their vigor and freedom. The book culminates in a picture of God surveying His creation and showing a forgetfulness about the remote and inconspicuous planet Earth and an ignorance of the reason why various of its inhabitants keep placing themselves in strange postures that irritate the Archangel Michael, who had fought there with the Devil on mankind's behalf:

> "Sire!" cried St. Michael, in a voice that shook the architraves of heaven, "they are worshipping You!"

> "Oh! they are worshipping me! Well, that is the most sensible thing I have heard of them yet, and I altogether commend them. *Continuez*," said the Padre Eterno, "*continuez!*"

> And since then all has been well with the world; at least where *ils continuent*. (*The Path to Rome*, 443–44)

But there is a purpose in Belloc's tomfoolery. Writing in the tradition of Jonathan Swift's *A Tale of a Tub* (1704), a work that he describes as immortal in an essay on Swift in *A Conversation with a Cat*, he is mocking the Protestant who believes that Christ died specifically in order to save him.

If *The Path to Rome* abounds in high spirits, *The Four Men* is an altogether graver book, which, exceptionally, took Belloc five years to complete. The four men of the title (of whom three are partly supernatural figures and partly projections of aspects of Belloc, who appears as "Myself") wander through the deserted countryside of the County of Sussex, arguing, reminiscing, and telling each other stories, over the five days from October 29 to November 2, culminating in All Saints' Day and All Souls' Day, the Day of the Dead. The gravity shot through by sardonic humor that characterizes Belloc's writing is well illustrated by Grizzlebeard's tale of his first love: "'But what a vision is that! . . . I mean the unrestricted converse with such a friend at the very launching of life! . . . to find a shrine which shall so sanctify our outset: to know, to accompany, and to adore!'" (217). On returning after an absence of several months, however, he is dis-

illusioned to find that his love has married a man who manufactured "'rectified lard, and so well, let me tell you, that no-one could compete with him'" (218). Yet although "I saw reality all bare, original, evil and instinct with death" (219), the original vision remains with him: "But that first woman still sits upon her throne. Not even in death, I think, shall I lose her" (222). Finally, Grizzlebeard solemnly pours away his beer upon the ground "for a symbol of what befalls the chief experience in the life of every man" (223–24). The co-existence of disillusionment with the original vision in all its strength is what creates the peculiar Bellocian melancholy.

Most enduring of all, however, are the children's verses, which he started writing while still at Oxford. Though the same *bêtes noires* appear as in the novels, it is only the academic analyst who is aware of them. What comes through to the intended reader is the kind of manic violence to which children eagerly respond, as, for instance, in the stories of "Jim, Who ran away from his Nurse, and was eaten by a Lion," or "Henry King, Who chewed bits of String, and was early cut off in Dreadful Agonies." The first of these collections, *The Bad Child's Book of Beasts* (1896), illustrated by his Oxford friend and contemporary, Lord Basil Blackwood, with a naivete reminiscent of Edward Lear, sold out its first edition of 4,000 within four days and was immediately reprinted. There followed *More Beasts for Worse Children* (1897), *A Moral Alphabet* (1899), *Cautionary Tales for Children* (1907), and *More Peers* (1911). Much later, but no less successfully, followed *New Cautionary Tales* (1930) and *Ladies and Gentlemen* (1932), illustrated in a professional and sophisticated style by E.C. Bentley's son, Nicolas.

Basically, the verses parody Victorian moral certitudes as preached to children:

> The vulture eats between his meals,
> And that's the reason why
> He very, very rarely feels
> As well as you and I.
> His eye is dull, his head is bald,
> His neck is growing thinner.
> Oh! what a lesson to us all
> To only eat at dinner!

But, the straight-faced declaration deconstructs itself, and elsewhere the Victorian code is overtly satirized, as in the verse on the letter "X" in *A Moral Alphabet*:

No reasonable little Child expects
A Grown-up Man to make a rhyme
   on X.
MORAL
These verses teach a clever child to find
Excuse for doing all that he's inclined.

Summary

Hilaire Belloc's humor is a strange mixture of aggressiveness and melancholy, which are themselves the expression of his fierce religious convictions tempered by a deep skepticism. The stressfulness of the mixture is heightened by his sense of being at odds with English society, both in his Catholic optimism and in his classical melancholy, as he himself was painfully aware. His essay, "On Irony" (in *On Anything*), concludes, in his characteristic lapidary style, with what amounts to a self-estimate: "No man possessed of irony and using it has lived happily; nor has any man possessing it and using it died without having done great good to his fellows and secured a singular advantage to his own soul."

Selected Bibliography

Primary Sources
The Path to Rome. London: George Allen, 1902.
Caliban's Guide to Letters. London: Duckworth, 1903.
Emmanuel Burden. London: Methuen, 1904.
On Nothing. London: Methuen, 1908.
On Everything. London: Methuen, 1909.
On Anything. London, Methuen, Constable, 1910.
On Something. London: Methuen, 1910.
First and Last. London: Methuen, 1911.
The Four Men: A Farrago. London: Thomas Nelson, 1912.
This and That. London: Methuen, 1912.
Europe and the Faith. London: Constable, 1920.
On. London: Methuen, 1923.
The Cruise of the "Nona." London: Constable, 1925.
Short Talks with the Dead. London: Cayme Press, 1926.
A Conversation with an Angel. London: Jonathan Cape, 1928.
A Conversation with a Cat. London: Cassell, 1931.
Cautionary Verses. London: Duckworth, 1942. Collected Edition.

Cahill, Patrick, ed. *One Thing and Another*. London: Hollis and Carter, 1955.

Secondary Sources

Biographies
Speaight, Robert. *The Life of Hilaire Belloc*. London: Hollis and Carter, 1957. The first, official biography, published shortly after Belloc's death.
Wilson, A.N. *Hilaire Belloc*. London: Hamish Hamilton, 1984. A franker and more speculative work than Speaight, though written with the full support of the surviving members of Belloc's family.

Books and Articles
Boyd, Ian, ed. *Chesterton Review* (Saskatoon, Saskatchewan), 12 (May 1986). Hilaire Belloc Special Issue (includes articles by Ralph J. Coffman and Michael H. Markel on the Belloc archives at Boston College).
Clerihew, E. (pseud. for E.C. Bentley). *Biography for Beginners*. London: T. Werner Laurie, 1905.
Donaldson, Frances. *The Marconi Scandal*. London: Hart-Davis, 1962.
Jago, David. "The Stoicism of Hilaire Belloc." *Renascence* (Milwaukee, WI), Vol. 27, no. 2 (Winter 1975).
McCarthy, John P. *Hilaire Belloc: Edwardian Radical*. Indianapolis: Liberty Press, 1978. A lucid account of the years of Belloc's greatest political effectiveness.

David Jago

Benson, E[dward] F[rederic]

Born: Wellington College, Berkshire, July 27, 1867

Education: Marlborough and at King's College, Cambridge, where he was exhibitioner (1888) and scholar (1890); he took a first class degree in both parts of the classical tripos (1890, 1891)

Died: London, February 29, 1940

Biography

E.F. Benson was the third son of six children born on July 27, 1867, to Mary (Sidgwick) and Edward White Benson while his father, later to become Archbishop of Canterbury, was headmaster of Wellington College, Berkshire. The entire family was literary and also plagued, in varying degrees, with what was known then as "neurasthenia." Benson, known to his wide circle of acquaintances as "Fred," seems to have been the least affected of the children by bouts of severe depression and melancholia. His eldest brother, Martin, died from meningitis while at Cambridge; he was eighteen. Arthur Christopher Benson, the eldest of the remaining Benson children, became widely known and appreciated for his writings on the attainment of spiritual serenity, with such titles as *The House of Quiet* and *The Thread of Gold* to his credit. Nellie, the elder of the two Benson daughters, died suddenly of diphtheria when she was only twenty-seven. Maggie, the second daughter, edited her father's work after his death and produced a book on personal moral philosophy, *The Venture of a Rational Faith*. The youngest child, and the Archbishop's favorite, was Hugh, who, while fulfilling his father's aspirations for him by entering the clergy, left the Church of England for the Roman Catholic Church in which he was ordained as the Very Reverend Monsigneur Hugh Benson.

From Wellington College, the family moved in 1873 to Lambeths, where Edward Benson took up his new duties as Archbishop. Benson's mother, nicknamed "Minnie," was twelve years the junior of the Archbishop, having been attached to him since she was twelve and marrying when she was eighteen. Lambeths afforded the Benson family an introduction into select society, and young Fred, gregarious and witty, soon came to be the familiar acquaintance of upper-class nobility and royalty. Minnie maintained a deep and cheerful faith in the face of the severe emotional difficulties of both Arthur and Maggie, recording in her diary after she was widowed the resolve to weave her life "into a garment of praise, not into a cowl of heaviness."[1] The Bensons often traveled together, including a visit to Switzerland where Fred, an active and moderately accomplished amateur athlete, climbed the Matterhorn. He also engaged in a passionate pursuit of cricket, rugby, and golf.

Educated at Marlborough and at King's College, Cambridge, where he was exhibitioner (1888) and scholar (1890), Benson nonetheless was an indifferent, if able, student, until he was introduced to classical studies. As a result of this introduction, he joined the number of late Victorians who were ardent Hellenists, and after taking his degree with first classes in both parts of the classical tripos (1890, 1891) he worked in Athens for the British School of Archaeology (1892–1895) and in Egypt for the Society for the Promotion of Hellenic Studies (1895).

His own temperament, in contrast to that of his father and brothers, was highly social and urbane. He claimed Henry James, among other literati, as a friend, and visited him at Lamb House in Rye, Sussex, where James lived for eighteen years, and where Benson was to spend the last twenty years of his own life. James made useful, if severe, comments on Benson's first (and highly successful) novel, *Dodo*, prior to its publication in 1893. The character of "Dodo" was allegedly based on Margot Tennant, later Countess of Oxford and Asquith.

Benson divided his time between England, Scotland, Switzerland, and finally Capri, where he shared a summer villa with John Ellingham Brooks, an openly practicing homosexual (despite the dangerously illegal nature of such a practice at the time). Benson's most intense romantic friendships were with those of his own sex, and this was apparently true for the rest of his family as well. While Benson never openly admitted, or to certain knowledge practiced, homosexuality, he was close friends with those who did, including Lord Alfred Douglas, Brooks, Oscar Wilde, and others. The notorious trial of Wilde (discussed at some length by Benson in *As We Were*) caused many with homosexual sympathies to leave England, and the island of Capri became an idyllic place where individuality was encouraged for numbers of expatriates. Benson's reminiscences of Capri are enlivened with descriptions of colorful individuals, parties, and nightly gatherings at Morgano's Cafe which included Maxim Gorki, the Russian writer then in exile, and Compton MacKenzie, among others.

While he felt immediate delight for the village of Rye, Benson did not make it his home until 1919; at this time he also lived part of the year at his house in Brompton Square. He was Mayor of Rye from 1934 to 1937, and while there lived in Lamb House until his death in 1940. The West Window in Rye Church was given by Benson in memory of his parents, and the figure of his servant Charles Tomlin appears as a shepherd, with Benson's Welsh collie, Taffy, and Benson himself dressed in his red mayoral robes in the bottom righthand corner. Rye commemorates Benson's memory with the "Tilling Society," which is based on Benson's re-creation of Rye as the village of Tilling in his popular Mapp and Lucia stories.

Like many others of his class and age, Benson was an immensely private man whose closest friends were unaware of the final bouts he suffered of depression, physical pain, and self-pity. He died of cancer of the throat in London on February 29, 1940.

Literary Analysis

Benson's interest in archaeology led him to work in such diverse genres as biography, the historical novel, and the occultic tale. He published numerous critically maligned though commercially successful light novels as well, many of which were marred by unbelievable plots, cutout characters, and maudlin sentimentality, though critical opinion has varied. Michael Sadleir has written that "A few of his books are so nearly first rate that the reader becomes regretfully aware that none quite reaches that level . . . He would re-use one of his series of groupings, embellishing it with new and amusing dialogue, with new and crushing incidental detail, yet in fact writing the same story two, three, or even four times over."[2] Benson's serious efforts at biography, including *Charlotte Bronte* (1932), *King Edward VII* (1933), and *Daughters of Queen Victoria* (1939), for the latter of which he was granted access to previously unpublished correspondence, were more successful.

It is, however, the invention of Mrs. Emmeline Lucas (known familiarly as "Lucia," wife of Lucas, pronounced in the Italian mode) and that of Miss Elizabeth Mapp (who "might have been forty, and had taken advantage of this opportunity by being just a year or two older"[3]) for which Benson is most appreciated today. These two formidable females preside over their respective original villages of Riseholme and Tilling, surrounded by lesser but vividly drawn characters who provide material for the exercise of power strategies by Lucia and Mapp. Because Benson views the gossipy intrigues of his characters with acuity and a sense of deep enjoyment, the reader finishes these volumes with something of the same pleasure and tolerance for human foibles that Geoffrey Chaucer and Charles Dickens can evoke. Albeit satiric, these stories do not partake of satire's subtextual narrative of high moral outrage. Quite the opposite is true: the reader has no wish to see any of these characters develop morally, only strategically; the vices and follies of society are made ridiculous but with warmth and sympathy, and the "Luciaphiles" in Lon-

don discover one another through their enraptured trackings of Lucia's social career. "Nobody wants to spite Lucia," says Lord Tony in *Lucia in London*. "We all want her to have the most glorious time . . . " "'She's ridiculous!' said Marcia, relapsing a little. 'No, you mustn't feel that,' said Adele. 'You mustn't laugh at her ever. You must just richly enjoy her.'" What will Mrs. Quantock take up as her next "fad" (Guruism, spiritualism, vegetarianism, golf?) and more important, how will Lucia annex and exploit it? Can Elizabeth Mapp become Tilling's first mother among her social set and thus vanquish Lucia forever? It is the large questions of life that are marginalized; Lucia's colonization of London slices through divorce cases, art movements, developments in psychology—all are mere rungs on the dizzying climb of her social advancement.

The nineteenth century enjoyed a revival of the "comedy of manners" (devised by Ben Jonson and George Chapman in the sixteenth century and first revived a hundred years later by Goldsmith and Congreve). Benson carries the genre further, however, in his brilliant choice to place his hermetic high society in the tiny villages of Riseholme and later Tilling. His natural gift for close and judicial observation led him to satiric portraiture, and his own class experience made the self-absorption of an enclosed and privileged society a perfect stage for his own "comedy of manner." Like Oscar Wilde, Benson deflates the pretensions of "serious art" while he nonetheless hopes to be taken seriously. But, unlike Wilde, whose view that style is all caused him to celebrate appearance as reality, Benson uses the fundamental comic effect of incongruity between what the character pretends and what the viewer knows to be "true" as the driving force of his art. In this sense, Benson remains conservative, believing there to be a difference between appearance and reality which can be exploited. He mocks the avant-garde of his day, particularly in *Lucia in London* (1927). When Lucia's husband, Peppino, inherits a legacy from his mad aunt, the couple moves to London, once derided as a "fiddling little ant-hill by the Thames"[4] but now a Mecca of the Modern where Lucia's social ambitions can grow exponentially.

Through characters like Sophy Alingsby, who is "tall and weird and intense, dressed rather like a bird-of-paradise that had been out in a high gale, but very well connected," Benson filters his contempt for those who preferred "stories without a story, and poems without meter or meaning."[5] Lucia's pretensions are equally transparent, but her village of origin, Riseholme, writhes under the knowledge that however exasperating and hypocritical this "poseuse" may be, "there was something about her that stirred you into violent though protesting activity."[6] And in *Miss Mapp,* Benson evokes the illicit "love duel" characteristic of the "comedy of manners," further degrading those witty and often amoral lovers into the sham heroes of Captain Puffin and Major Flint, whose quarrel derives from the most trivial offense and is whipped into a scandalous duel by the excited Tillingites, led by Miss Mapp. The actual duel, however, never takes place.

Benson's very prose style might be the best evidence of his fundamental attack against the high culture that he admired and from which he felt excluded, as critics continued to deride his more serious efforts. Interlarded allusion and satiric reference to popular movements like spiritualism, as in the episode of the nonexistent duel, exemplify Benson's parody of the sublime. Tilling's vicar, known as "the Padre," has gone to find and prevent the duel among the sand dunes. As the duelists, arriving on the tram from the golf course, are eagerly awaited, Miss Mapp considers the possible denouements, and after ticking the possibilities off on her fingers, she arrives at "IV. The Padre might arrive with a stretcher. Query—Whose? V. The Padre might arrive with two stretchers. VI. Three stretchers might arrive from the shining sands, at the town where the women were weeping and wringing their hands." But, when all three figures disembark, clearly unharmed, "[i]t is no use denying that the Cosmic Consciousness of the ladies of Tilling was aware of a disagreeable anticlimax to so many hopes and fears."[7]

Avoiding the temptation to be merely witty, Benson discovered and made intrinsic to his comic vision the sympathetic feeling for character which enriches his natural tendencies to satire, an essentially judgmental genre. In this, too, he remains primarily conservative, using a clever handling of situation and intrigue to critique social behavior and character type, while allowing his main characters individual consciousness of self. Daisy Quantock (the Queen Pretender while Lucia is away in London), for example, has ideas but "doesn't carry her ideas out in a vivid manner that excites interest and keeps people on the boil." In contrast, Benson gives us Lucia, who is perfectly aware of the discrepancy between what the larger world sees as important and what she sees. "On the boil! That's what we all ought to be, with a thousand things to do that seem immensely important and which are important because they seem so . . . What does it matter to me whether it's [Duchess] Marcia's ball, . . . or playing duets with poor dear Georgie . . . so long as I find it thrilling?"[8] Olga Bracely, the great opera singer who lands in Riseholme thinking that it is a quiet retreat, becomes embroiled in the political intrigues of village life, asking Georgie Pillson (Lucia's chaste devotee), "Is it all of you who take such tremendous interest in [events] that makes them so absorbing, or is it that they are absorbing in themselves, and ordinary dull people, not Riseholmites, don't see how exciting they are?"[9] In this question, posed by Benson's possibly most sympathetic character, we hear his riposte to a world which decided that his art, like the lives of his villagers, was hopelessly "trivial."

Benson's style in these stories derives from a nicely balanced disparity and, indeed, inversion, of "high" and "low." In other words, the conventional moral order is reversed; petty struggles for social supremacy in two tiny, insular English villages receive the treatment of military campaigns, and serious ethical questions are made to seem, if not positively pretentious, at the least irrelevant. Considering Benson's experiences with a puritanical (and often tyrannical) father and several very earnest siblings, it is not surprising that a genial and gregarious temperament such as his would find the farcical intricacies of power dynamics far more interesting than a graver treatment of the same themes.

This very mastery of the trivial is both Benson's triumph and his failing. Many of the novels with larger, non-episodic plot structures lose themselves at some point either to muddiness of concept or carelessness with regard to language and accuracy. It is as if either more serious subjects failed to grip his imagination for long or his habits as an author prevented him from fully exploring a complicated theme. The fluency with which he wrote is demonstrated by his rate of publication: from 1893 to 1936, excepting the years 1899 and 1909, Benson published at least one book every year. In some years there were as many as three, with a total of ninety-seven books; perhaps his skill of revision atrophied as a result. The problem of sentimentality also ruins many otherwise good moments in Benson, much as it troubled Dickens (whom Benson admired); as a result, Benson is at his most finely tuned when he has no great moral point to make.

When he is engaged in a more analytical task, such as in the commentary of *As We Are* (1932), his writing approaches that of the best socio-cultural essayists. Using the fictional "parable house" of the Edwardian country house called Hakluyt, seat of Lord and Lady Buryan, Benson explores the three generations in transition from the Great War: the older, traditional landowners; the generation that fought in the war; and the new generation of "bright young things." Benson describes that which he knows—the upper class—with insight and compassion, while at the same time critiquing the less affable qualities of conservative dowagers hardened into selfishness and unsentimental, extravagant pleasure-seekers. He sketches such "Emminent Men" as Arthur Balfour and Randall Davidson, Archbishop of Canterbury. Various writers—D.H. Lawrence and James Joyce among them—are dissected with relish, though modern critics would disagree with some of Benson's literary assessments.

Although some critics have missed the sense of raw emotion, Benson's literary temperament is finally very like that of Georgie Pillson, the male spinster of the Lucia stories, who was "gentle in all his ways."[10] However, both in the "Victorian peep-show," *As We Were* (1930), and *As We Are*, Benson's restraint is used to advantage in narrating events that easily could have been submerged in bathos, producing instead a moving elegaic tone. Such reminiscences, which are enhanced by talents of closely observed detail in human affairs, are rich as sources for the social historian and as examples of elegant, fluid prose, the latter of which has been largely overlooked.

In one of those serendipitous moments in history, Benson delivered *Final Edition* (1940) to his publisher only ten days before he died. In many ways, it is exemplary of his best work, avoiding the twin dragons of sentimentality and frivolity that undermine many memoirs; his difficulty with extended and sustained narrative plot was also mitigated by the genre of autobiography, which both furnished him with a ready-made plot and allowed him to exploit his gift for episode. The volume must, however, still answer to criticism such as that recorded by Virginia Woolf in her diary: "My Times [Book Club] book this week is E.F.

Benson's latest autobiography—in which he tried to rasp himself free of his barnacles. I learn there the perils of glibness."[11] Desmond Shawe-Taylor more kindly observed that "Benson had the discrimination and self-criticism to see what was petty in his busy intellectual life and what was trivial in his productions. In the middle of a prosperous and admired career he deliberately set himself to make a clean sweep and do better."[12]

Summary

E.F. Benson continues to delight readers with his satires of English village life in the 1920s and 1930s, the Mapp and Lucia stories (*Queen Lucia, Lucia in London, Miss Mapp, The Male Impersonator, Mapp and Lucia, Trouble for Lucia*). An archaeologist for several years, Benson wrote numerous historical novels and several collections of ghost stories which were less successful than his early phenomenal debut at the age of twenty-five with *Dodo*, a light social satire allegedly based on the life of Margot Tennant, later Countess of Oxford and Asquith. Historical interests also led to his many biographies, which include *Charlotte Bronte, King Edward VII*, and *Daughters of Queen Victoria*, for which latter work he was granted access to previously unpublished correspondence. His reminiscences and analytical commentaries about late Victorian and post–World War I Britain (*As We Were: A Victorian Peep-show, As We Are*, and what some see as his best serious work, *Final Edition*) offer the useful perspective of a well-traveled and well-known socialite whose experience embraced both Victorian and modern times.

Notes

1. An excerpt of Mary Benson's diary, cited by E.F. Benson in *Final Edition*, p. 18.
2. Michael Sadleir, in *The Dictionary of National Biography, 1931–1949*, ed. L.G. Wickham Legg (London: Oxford University Press, 1949), p. 70.
3. The opening lines of *Miss Mapp*, in *Make Way for Lucia* (New York: Thomas Y. Crowell, 1977), p. 293.
4. From *Lucia in London* (Crowell, 1977), p. 176.
5. *Ibid.*, p. 202.
6. *Ibid.*, p. 185.
7. *Ibid.*, p. 360 (*Miss Mapp*).
8. *Ibid.*, p. 270 (*Lucia in London*).
9. *Ibid.*, p. 140 (*Queen Lucia*).

10. *Ibid.*, p. 108.
11. Entry for November 1, 1940. *The Diary of Virginia Woolf*, ed. Anne Olivier Bell (New York: Harcourt Brace Jovanovich, 1977–1984).
12. Desmond Shawe-Taylor, in *A Library of Literary Criticism: Modern British Literature*, p. 78.

Selected Bibliography

Primary Sources

Autobiographies
As We Were: A Victorian Peep-show. Longmans, Green, 1930; London: Hogarth Press, 1985.
As We Are: A Modern Review. Longmans, Green, 1932; London: Hogarth Press, 1985.
Final Edition. New York: D. Appleton-Century, 1940.

Biographies
Charlotte Bronte. London: Longmans, Green, 1932.
King Edward VII. London: Longmans, Green, 1933.
Daughters of Queen Victoria. London: Cassell, 1939.

Social Satire
Dodo. London: Methuen, 1893.
Queen Lucia. London: Hutchinson, 1920.
Miss Mapp. London: Hutchinson, 1922.
The Male Impersonator. London: Elkin Mathews and Marot, 1929.
Lucia in London. London: Hutchinson, 1927.
Mapp and Lucia. London: Hodder and Stoughton, and Garden City, NY: Doubleday, Doran, 1931.
Lucia's Progress. London: Hodder and Stoughton, 1935. American title: *The Worshipful Lucia.* New York: Doubleday, 1935.
Trouble for Lucia. London: Hodder and Stoughton, 1935.
Make Way for Lucia. New York: Thomas Y. Crowell, 1977. Includes all of the Mapp and Lucia novels, originally published between 1920 and 1939.

Historical Fiction
The Vintage. London: Methuen, 1898.
The Capsina. London: Methuen, 1899.

Horror and Occultic Fiction
The Luck of the Vails. London: Heinemann, 1901.
Spook Stories. London: Hutchinson, 1928.

School Stories
The Babe, B.A. London: G.P. Putnam's Sons, 1897.
David Blaize. London: Hodder & Stoughton, 1916.

Secondary Sources

Books
Newsome, David, ed. *Edwardian Excursions: From the Diaries of A.C. Benson, 1898–1904.* Selected and introduced by Newsome. London: John Murray, 1981. Presents vignettes of Edwardian life, including Benson family anecdotes, through Arthur Benson's eyes, whose diary at his death numbered some four million words.
Palmer, Geoffrey, and Noel Lloyd. *E.F. Benson: As He Was.* Luton, Beds.: Lennard Publishing, 1988. The first full-length biography to appear on Benson. Makes extensive use of the voluminous Benson family journals, books, diaries, and letters. Particularly valuable is an annotated bibliography, combining biography and literary analysis, though unfortunately presented in essay form, rendering quick reference difficult.
Reavell, Cynthia, and Tony Reavell. *E.F. Benson: Mr. Benson remembered in Rye, and the world of Tilling.* Rye: Martello Bookshop, 1984. Contains a history of Lamb House, correspondences between Rye and the fictional village of Tilling, anecdotes of Benson's domestic life, and the memoirs of Charlie Tomlin, Benson's manservant from 1918 to 1941.

General Reference
Block, Maxine, ed. *Current Biography 1940.* New York: H.W. Wilson, 1940.
Kunitz, Stanley J., ed. *Living Authors.* New York: H.W. Wilson, 1937.
———, and Howard Haycraft. *Twentieth Century Authors.* New York: H.W. Wilson, 1942.
Sadleir, Michael. "E.F. Benson." In *Dictionary of National Biography 1931–1949.* L.G. Wickham Legg, ed. London: Oxford University Press, 1949.

Shawe-Taylor, Desmond. "E.F. Benson." In *A Library of Literary Criticism*: *Vol. I, Modern British Literature*. Ruth Temple, ed. New York: Frederick Ungar, 1966.

Obituaries
Manchester Guardian, March 1, 1940, p. 12.
New York Herald Tribune, March 1, 1940 p. 16.
New York Times, March 1, 1940, p. 21.
Publishers Weekly, March 9, 1940, vol. 137, p. 1089.
Wilson Library Bulletin, April, 1940, vol. 14, p. 546.

Deanne Lundin

Bentley, Edmund Clerihew (E.C.)

Born: London, July 10, 1875
Education: St. Paul's School, London, 1887–1894; Merton College, Oxford University, 1894–1898
Marriage: Violet Alice Mary Boileau, 1902; three children
Died: London, March 30, 1956

Biography

Edmund Clerihew Bentley was born in London on July 10, 1875. Through his father, John Edmund Bentley, a civil servant, Edmund was related to preacher and writer John Bunyan and to Richard Bentley, the publisher of the nineteenth-century popular magazine *Bentley's Miscellany*, which had been edited by Charles Dickens. Edmund's mother was Margaret Richardson Clerihew, and it was her surname—of obscure Scotch origin—that became her son's middle name, then, briefly, his *nom de plume*, and finally the name of the light verse form he invented.

He attended St. Paul's School in London from 1887 to 1894, where he was much influenced by his masters, including R.F. Cholmeley and the then Head Master, Frederick Walker. His friendship with G.K. Chesterton, begun at preparatory school and continued through St. Paul's, Oxford University, and beyond, was perhaps the most important of his life. It was at St. Paul's that Bentley began to write the four-line nonsense verses that were later called "clerihews" (a "baseless biography"): he and five friends, including Chesterton, kept a notebook of their efforts, which was comically illustrated. At Oxford he read history, debated at the Union Society (and served as its president), wrote hu-

mor and light verse for undergraduate magazines, and rowed for his college, Merton. His dedication to rowing may have cost him the First in history that he coveted, but he later reflected that he "would not have missed the river for all the academic distinctions there ever were."[1]

While studying history he took an interest in law, and upon going down from Oxford in 1898 he read for the bar, passed the examinations, became a pupil in Sir William Hansell's chambers in London, and had the opportunity to observe the workings of the law. Although this taught him to admire the British system of justice, he was already writing for the *Speaker*, a Liberal weekly, and drifting toward a career in journalism. He worked on the Liberal *Daily News* as a reporter and eventually became deputy editor.

He married Violet Alice Mary Boileau in 1902; they had three children, a girl and two boys. The younger son, Nicolas, illustrated the *New Cautionary Tales* of Hilaire Belloc, Bentley's friend from Oxford, as well as some of the published clerihews. These poems appeared in four successive books, beginning in 1905 with *Biography for Beginners*, illustrated by Chesterton, and published under the name E. Clerihew. Successive volumes were called *More Biography* (1929) and *Baseless Biography* (1939), but finally the publisher succumbed to the popular practice of calling the little verses after their creator, and the grand collection was titled *The Complete Clerihews of E.C. Bentley*.

In 1912, Bentley left the *Daily News* for the *Daily Telegraph*, where he worked until 1934 (he returned briefly to the journal in 1939, at the onset of World War II). In 1913, he published his first novel, the detective story *Trent's Last Case*, which was dedicated to his friend Chesterton, whose first book of Father Brown mysteries had come out two years earlier. Unlike *Biography for Beginners*, which enjoyed a steady but unremarkable popularity, *Trent's Last Case* became, and continues to be, a very popular novel. It still appears on lists of the best mystery novels in English, in large part because of the character of Philip Trent, an amateur but gentlemanly sleuth who is more human—and therefore more sympathetic—than the coolly omniscient detective type then prevailing in the genre. The story relies both on suspense and on wry humor; it is possible to see elements of Trent in Dorothy Sayers' Lord Peter Wimsey, whose humor and a touching sense of his own fallibility temper the customary cool omniscience. (Bentley parodied Sayers and Lord Peter to great effect in a short story called "Greedy Night.")

World War I precluded further attempts at writing fiction in favor of Bentley's newspaper work and volunteer relief efforts. But, the novel's popularity continued to grow, and despite the finality implied by its title, Bentley belatedly produced two sequels, the novel *Trent's Own Case* (1936) and the short-story collection *Trent Intervenes* (1938). These are considered to be inferior to *Trent's Last Case*, perhaps, as his son Nicolas suggests, because its author had not kept up with the developments that he had helped to initiate in the genre. He also wrote a book of autobiographical reminiscences, *Those Days* (1940), and "an enigma," *Elephant's Work* (1950). He died in London on March 30, 1956.

Nicolas Bentley's memoirs, *A Version of the Truth*, portray the elder Bentley as a reserved but loving father and husband who derived "more pleasure than anything else he achieved in life" from seeing the term "clerihew" included in the *Oxford English Dictionary* during his own lifetime.[2] Nicolas provides an entertaining account of the literary circle in which his parents traveled and in which he grew up, including his impressions of Chesterton, Belloc, and Max Beerbohm. However, he does not describe Bentley's last years as happy ones. He and his wife (who died in 1949) were bombed out of their flat during the Blitz and lived thereafter in reduced circumstances. Bentley, who was an athlete as a young man, became a hypochondriac and a drinker. Nicolas portrays his father as plagued by a sense of never having fulfilled his youthful potential, though Bentley's own *Those Days*, published when he was sixty-five, suggests a thoughtful man who took a discreet pride in the modest achievements of his career. This is probably appropriate for someone who is best remembered for a literary form that he nearly perfected when he was eighteen.

Literary Analysis

Sir Humphrey Davy
Was not fond of gravy
He lived in the odium
Of having discovered Sodium.[3]

Bentley was sixteen years old and a schoolboy at St. Paul's when he wrote those lines. By his own account, they sprang into his mind while he was sitting in a science class. He wrote more verses and circulated them among his friends, who responded in kind. The form was quite loose; although all clerihews contain two rhyming couplets, the meter can vary widely. Most lines are roughly dipodic, with two chief stresses, although, as in Anglo-Saxon accentual and Middle English alliterative verse, there may be a number of other stressed syllables in the line. The third line of the clerihew tends to be particularly cluttered in this way.

The first line almost always contains the name of the subject, sometimes by itself ("Dante Alighiere"), sometimes not ("The digestion of Milton"). In any case, the first rhyme is almost always made with the subject name. Whatever unlikely association this produces is usually taken up and elaborated by the second couplet. Hence:

Daniel Defoe
Could tie himself in a bow.
He thought it was rot
Tying one's self in a knot.[4]

This novelty verse form became popular with Bentley's set. "Nothing quite so preposterous had occupied our attention before," he confesses in his autobiography (*Those Days*, 150). The friends compiled a notebook of their efforts, which they called a "Dictionary of Biography." Bentley's opening verses noted, in imitation of adolescent naivete, that:

Biography
Is different from Geography.
Geography is about maps,
While Biography deals with chaps.

The notebook was inscribed by Bentley to Maurice Solomon, who donated it to the archives of St. Paul's School, and it became available in 1982 in an Oxford University Press facsimile edition, *The First Clerihews*. The illustrations, by Chesterton, crowd the margins and the spaces between the verses and have worked into them little symbols representing the poems' authors. By far the greatest number of them are labeled with a sketch of a dodo bird representing Bentley himself. Chesterton's emblem is a gavel; L.R.F. Oldershaw's, a stag's head; W.P.H. d'Avigdor's, a double pi (looking like the Greek letter with an extra vertical leg); a triple 6 stands for Maurice Solomon; and a pipe is the token of Chesterton's father, Edward.

The friends may have adopted these symbols partly out of caution, for the clerihews occasionally invoke the names of persons associated with St. Paul's School, but their use also reflects a schoolboy taste for secret codes and inside jokes. Although only twenty-one of the 132 clerihews in the notebook appeared (most in revised form) in the books that Bentley published as an adult, the clerihew as a form still succeeds or fails on whether it delivers the *frisson* of sophomoric pleasures derived from being silly about important elders. The earliest clerihews, like the original Humphry Davy one, almost all play upon the names of figures, both historical and contemporary, who pass before the schoolchild's eyes. Thus, after verses on William Thackeray, Christopher Columbus, and St. Paul's Form Master Cholmeley ("Mr. R.F. Cholmeley / Behaved rather rumly"), Bentley and Solomon remedied an important omission:

> What fools we've been!
> We've forgotten the Queen!
> She removes her crown, it is said,
> When she goes to bed.

In 1930, at an editor's request, Bentley produced a facetious account of the birth of the clerihew, which he reproduces in his autobiographical book, *Those Days*. In this humorous essay he discusses the essential features of the form. Mere historical accuracy, he declares, is not biography. He cites as an example of a failed clerihew the following:

> Frederick the Great
> Became King at twenty-eight.
> In a fit of amnesia
> He invaded Silesia.

"In this," he explains, "there is nothing with which the dry-as-dust historiographer could possibly quarrel . . . Truthful and reliable—yes; even slavishly so. But where is the human appeal? Where is the probing psychological touch?" (157). For the purposes of the clerihew "biography" is a twist on the known facts of a life, usually sparked by a fortuitous rhyme with the name of the hapless subject. A near-perfect example is found in the clerihew on Philip Snowden:

> Mr. Philip Snowden
> Was rarely mistaken for Woden.

> People as a rule were much more
> Apt to mistake him for Thor.[5]

The only slightly fractured feminine rhyme of Snowden / Woden; the enormous improbability of the pairing; the second couplet, which takes the outrageous statement of the first with polite credulity—these are absolutely typical of the clerihew. And though the effect is gently mocking (as is the illustration by Chesterton, in which Snowden holds up Thor's hammer with no more expression than if he were raising a croquet mallet while Bentley looks on appraisingly), it is, like almost all clerihews, apolitical and not particularly pointed. As Gavin Ewart points out, "the classical clerihew is free from malice . . . It's mainly a question of tone, and the tone of the clerihew is both civilized and dotty."[6]

Ultimately, biography itself is the butt of every joke, with the peculiarity of human nature in general coming a close second; hence the "Index of Psychology, Mentality and Other Things Frequently Noted in Connection with Genius" appearing at the end of *Complete Clerihews* which allows the reader to seek clerihews under headings from "Absurdity" (which directs the reader to George III) to "Zulus, table manners of, resort to" (indicating The Duke of Fife, whose clerihew tells us that he left off using a knife and fork, but makes no comparison of his table manners to those of Zulus). This index is of little use in finding a clerihew on Miguel de Cervantes or Savonarola, but it aims a number of very funny barbs at the practice of indexing, with entries such as the following:

> Day, rainy, preparedness for (FORD)
> Dejection, stanzas written in, nowhere
>   near Naples (MILTON)
> Delicacy (BRIGHAM YOUNG)
> Diet, indiscretion in (MILTON, HENRY
>   I); morbid delicacy in matter of
>   (DAVY, BESANT, MARCONI, but
>   *cf.* BUNYAN)

The clerihew's gentle nonpartisan bemusement has kept it young and vigorous, and most of Bentley's verses are still fresh. Although the form is not attempted as often as the limerick, Ewart notes that occasional magazine contests still challenge entrants to compose clerihews, and collections of light verse always contain some, by Bentley and others. Finally, the clerihew is surely the closest ancestor of a light-verse form invented in the twentieth century, the "double dactyl" of Anthony Hecht and John Hollander.

Summary

E.C. Bentley is known principally for his invention of the brief nonsense verses called "clerihews" in which he satirized historical, political, and literary figures. They may be about either historical or contemporary figures, but rarely contain any direct political commentary or satire. Bentley's friend G.K. Chesterton collaborated on satiric verses with him at St. Paul's and later illustrated some of the published clerihews. Besides his unique contribution to British literary humor, Bentley was a journalist, and he also published four novels, including the landmark mystery novel *Trent's Last Case*, as well as a volume of memoirs which includes some sober reflections on war and politics.

Notes

1. Edmund Clerihew Bentley, *Those Days* (London: Constable, 1940), p. 118.
2. Nicolas Bentley, *A Version of the Truth* (London: Andre Deutsch, 1960), p. 32.
3. Edmund Clerihew Bentley, *The First Clerihews* (Oxford: Oxford University Press, 1982), p. 7. In *Biography for Beginners*, the second line reads "Abominated gravy"; in *The Complete Clerihews*, "Detested gravy."
4. *The First Clerihews*, p. 18.
5. Edmund Clerihew Bentley, *The Complete Clerihews of E.C. Bentley* (Oxford: Oxford University Press, 1981), p. xiii.
6. Gavin Ewart, Introduction to *The Complete Clerihews* (Oxford: Oxford University Press, 1981), p. xiii.

Selected Bibliography

Primary Sources
Clerihews Complete. London: T.W. Laurie, 1951.
The Complete Clerihews of E.C. Bentley. Illustrated by Nicolas Bentley, G.K. Chesterton, Victor Reingarrim, and the author; with an introduction by Gavin Ewart. Oxford: Oxford University Press, 1981. First published in Great Britain as *Biography for Beginners* (London: T.W. Laurie, 1905), *More Biography* (London: Methuen, 1929), and *Baseless Biography* (London: Andre Deutsch Ltd., 1939).
Those Days. London: Constable, 1940. Autobiographical reminiscences.
Elephant's Work, an enigma. New York: Knopf, 1950.
Trent's Case Book. New York: Knopf, 1969. Includes *Trent's Last Case*, *Trent's Own Case*, and *Trent Intervenes*.
"Greedy Night." In Dorothy L. Sayers's *Lord Peter: A Collection of All the Lord Peter Wimsey Stories*. Compiled by James Sandoe. New York: Harper and Row, 1972.
The First Clerihews. E. Clerihew Bentley with G.K. Chesterton, L.R.F. Oldershaw, Edward Chesterton, W.P.H. d'Avigdor, and Maurice Solomon; illustrated by G.K. Chesterton. Oxford: Oxford University Press, 1982.

Secondary Sources
Bentley, Nicolas. *A Version of the Truth*. London: Andre Deutsch, 1960. A memoir by Bentley's son Nicolas, an artist who illustrated his father's *Baseless Biography*. Much of the book focuses on Nicolas Bentley's schooling and adult experiences (which include stints as a clown, an actor, and a fireman in London during the Blitz), but the first part includes reminiscences about his extended family (including G.K. Chesterton). He portrays Bentley as a reserved but loving father, something of an enigma even to those closest to him, and plagued by a sense of never having fulfilled his early promise.
Ewart, Gavin. Introduction to *The Complete Clerihews of E.C. Bentley*. Oxford: Oxford University Press, 1981, pp. ix–xix. Ewart's introduction condenses the most pertinent facts from Nicholas Bentley's book and draws also upon E.C. Bentley's memoir *Those Days*. He reviews the general subject matter and approach of the clerihew and reproduces, for purposes of comparison and amusement, eighteen clerihews by other dabblers in the form.
Gilmour, John, and Nicholas Wall. "The Clerihew: Its History and Bibliography." *The Book Collector*, 29, 1 (Spring 1980): 23–35. Includes the origins of the clerihew, analysis of the form, illustrations, sample clerihews by Bentley and others, and bibliographical references to clerihews published in books.

B

Mead, Hugh. "Bentley and St. Paul's." In *The First Clerihews*. Oxford: Oxford University Press, 1982, pp. ix–xiv. The Librarian of St. Paul's School provides some historical context for Bentley's public school years, discussing the requirements and atmosphere of St. Paul's. The characters of Head Master Frederick Walker and Form Master R.F. Cholmeley are covered, as is the unofficial institution of the Junior Debating Club, to which Bentley and the other creators of the first clerihews belonged. Mead also includes one of a series of fables that Bentley wrote for the club magazine.

Redman, Ben Ray. "Introduction" to *Trent's Case Book*. New York: Knopf, 1964, pp. v–xii. In the introduction to an omnibus collection of the two novels and the short story collection featuring Bentley's detective Philip Trent, Redman gives an account of how the Trent books came to be written and a brief analysis of Bentley's influence on the detective story genre, particularly on the characterization of the detective himself.

Nancy Cohen

The *Beowulf* Poet

Anonymous: eighth century

Biography

We know nothing of the author of *Beowulf* save what can be derived from the text itself. We know of no other works by him. In all likelihood the poet was a man of the first half of the eighth century, a native of Britain. Whether he was from the north, midlands, or the south is a matter of dispute. This poet was admirably skilled not only in his use of much legendary material of Scandinavia, the fifth- or sixth-century setting of *Beowulf*, but also and especially in his development of the 3,182-line poem's highly sophisticated form. He was a master of traditional Old English style and poetic rhetoric, his talents surpassing those of other fine authors of the period.

Literary Analysis

Beowulf, composed in the Old English oral tradition in the early eighth century, is a serious and edifying epic concerned with heroism, sacrifice, and the inevitability of death, dragons, and doom. At the same time, throughout this grim poem there is a stolid Germanic humor which at once relieves and underlines the poem's heaviness. It has been said that a German joke is no laughing matter: this is true of the majority of *Beowulf's* Anglo-Saxon humor, which is wry and dry, as is most of the sparse comedy in earliest English literature. The *Beowulf* author nudges his audience's funnybone with ironies and wit and with quick switches in mood and situation, thus sharing with them his clear and omnipresent awareness of life's inevitable surprises here in this *middangeard* (the "middle-yard") of earth. Their mutual understanding of the wide-ranging incongruities that permeate the nature of transitory things is the basis of the humor found in the poem.

A typically humorous moment in the poem occurs when Beowulf, "a man happy in victory," having slept most contentedly following his defeat of the dreadful monster Grendel and the subsequent heavy feasting, greets old King Hrothgar in the morning by asking "if the night had been agreeable according to his desires." Hrothgar replies, "Do not ask about pleasure"—for Grendel's mother has attacked during the night, slaughtering one of the king's best retainers. The best of times meets the worst of times in this brief scene. The incongruity between Beowulf's polite and lighthearted query and Hrothgar's mournful response certainly is funny—but not laughable—and in this way great men clash, reminding the poem's audience yet once more of how inescapably and unpredictably oxymoronic life is: the feasts can't last; but then neither can the fights. "That now is gone; this too will go" is the way the consolation is phrased in another Old English poem, *Deor's Lament*. With this understanding, our Anglo-Saxon ancestors could smile wryly at life's twists and re-enter the temporary fray.

In order to more easily find and appreciate the humor in *Beowulf*, it helps to locate the poem in the corpus of Old English literature. All that remains of this material is contained in four manuscripts, but what exists gives us a rather wide spectrum of literary types. *Beowulf* is the only imaginative work of any substantial length, but there are also assorted saints' lives and other biographies, homilies, battle-accounts, and other bits of history, poems of longing and lament, legends of bravery, and assorted charms, riddles, and gnomic (proverbial) verses.

In all of these we can observe the Old English mindset at work, and again and again we see, as they did, some humor in the inevitable and unpredictable conjunction of opposites in life. Their brooding outlook, fostered by the primitive conditions in cold, damp, and dark northern Europe, was relieved by their occasional hard scrambles for joy and triumph in their meadhalls and on the battlefields. Additionally, the thick and quick penetration of Christianity into Britain during the seventh century served to reinforce the native Old English sense that life was an either/or proposition: while one lived, life alternated between happiness and sorrow, both unstable and incomplete conditions; only after death, in heaven or hell, would one experience pure and eternal joy or suffering.

This pattern of sudden alterations can be found throughout Old English literature. For example, it is apparent in the famous poem "The Battle of Malden" when in that battle the enemy Viking leader demands tribute and the Old English hero Byrhtnoth replies, "Hear, you seafarer, what this people say. They will give spears to you as tribute"—thus providing a bit of comic relief in the midst of great danger. Similar quick changes, this time between the straightforwardly descriptive and the subtly humorous, are found most clearly in Old English riddles. In these often overtly amusing pieces, humor exists in the recognition of congruence between apparent incongruities, between the literal statement and the implicit, concealed meaning. Penis-riddles (which have remained popular in English tradition) illustrate this beautifully. For example, Riddle 44 (of the ninety-five metrical riddles preserved in the Exeter Book) plays on the familiar *double-entendre* of "key" and "penis":

A strange item hangs by the thigh of a man, under its master's garment. It is pierced in the front; it is stiff and hard and it has a good fixed place. When the man pulls his own robe up over his knee, he intends to poke with the head of this hanging thing that familiar hole of equal length which it has often filled before.

Another penis-riddle, actually about an onion, works on the same principle:

I am a marvellous creature, bringing joy to women, and of good use to those who stay near me. I harm no person except just my destroyer. My place is lofty. I

stand up in a bed. Underneath, in a place, I am hairy. Sometimes a very pretty peasant girl of great courage attempts to lay hold on me, razes my redness, despoils my head, clamps me in fastness. This curlyhaired woman who in this way holds me soon feels my meeting: her eye gets wet. (Riddle 25, Exeter Manuscript)

Although *Beowulf* has no lewd humor and no riddles, the response to its kennings is similar to the response to Old English riddles. These two-word metaphors for common objects, so familiar in Old English literature, are in a sense mini-riddles—bits of wit which tickle listeners or readers when their apparent incongruity resolves into clarification. The sun, for example, is in *Beowulf* a "world-candle," the body, a "bone-house," wounds are "hate-bites," a sword, "battle-lightning," and blood is "sword-sweat."

There are similarly thought-provoking and subtly humorous incongruities in non-metaphorical descriptions as well in *Beowulf* and throughout the Old English corpus. In the poem "Seafarer," for example, the speaker expresses both his delight in the seafaring life along with his clear realization of its awful hardships. That both observations are, paradoxically, true is amusing: the poem presents this inherent contradiction as a simple fact of life here on this middle-earth. Beowulf's behavior toward Unferth, King Hrothgar's counselor, amuses us with the same sort of paradox. When Unferth accuses the newly arrived warrior of idle boasting and ribs him about losing a youthful swimming contest, Beowulf responds quite harshly, it seems, by pointing out that not only is Unferth wrong, but he also is a hell-bound kin-killer, a warrior unable to handle his beer, and too wimpy to help his own king by ridding their meadhall of a monster. However, their argument does not dampen the fun in the hall, where good cheer and laughter immediately take over once again. Later in the poem, in fact, Beowulf and Unferth get along fabulously, Unferth lending Beowulf the ancient battle-treasure, the sword Hrunting, for which—even after it turns out to be useless in battle—Beowulf most politely thanks him.

The two warriors' sharp exchange in the meadhall more likely amused than disturbed Hrothgar and his subjects. Such *flytings*, or sharply barbed attacks exaggerating a bit of

B

truth in order to provoke laughter, were common in British courtly entertainment and literature throughout the Middle Ages. Typical of the humor in *Beowulf*, Unferth's particular *flyting* suggests an incongruity (a weak and deceitful hero) as a truth, to the amusement of those assembled. Beowulf's response, though harsher, is *flyting* in kind, hardly the stuff to shock or dismay the boisterous beer drinkers who probably made up much of the poem's audience.

Flyting is an example of humorous overstatement in *Beowulf*. Much more prevalent in the poem, and in all Old English literature, is ironic understatement, or *litotes*, humorous also because of incongruity. In *Beowulf* many examples of *litotes* are patterned on the contrast between the constant hope for joy and the strong likelihood of sorrow. For instance, sea-monsters that Beowulf slaughters "had not any joy of the feast." Grendel, readers are told, has left his "grasp" (hand, arm, and shoulder) as a calling-card in the meadhall. "Nor by that has the wretched being bought any comfort," the author remarks, adding that the mere to which Grendel returns to die "was no pleasant place." And, when Beowulf, now old, sets out to fight the dragon which will do him in, the *scop*, or poet, remarks, "That was no pleasant journey."

Other pointed and witty ironic statements are similarly patterned, underlining the fact that Old English society depended upon strength and occasional joy but was fully aware of the tenuous hold which humans have upon security and happiness. An excellent example occurs when old Beowulf, snapping off his sword in the dragon's head-bone, finds himself defeated by the strength of his own ever-mighty grip: "Too strong was the hand," we are told; "he was not any the happier for it." Grendel's strength, too, comes to nothing in the end: "the arm and the shoulder: there all together was Grendel's grasp," hanging in the meadhall. The central Old English notion that halls are places of gift-giving and happiness is nicely played upon in a funny description of Grendel's mother's reception of Beowulf in her home. The hero has just thrown her to the floor by her hair, and "she in turn paid him his gift with her grim claws . . . and sat on the hall-guest."

This wry acceptance of the oxymoronic state of life determines a common mode of presentation in Old English homilies wherein we can find, for example, amusing descriptions of the double-edged pleasure of earthly existence. One highly effective sermon graphically describes a recently damned soul bemoaning the time when it dwelt in the gluttonous body which had taken pride in its surfeit of earthly delicacies but which now has become "food of worms," a "gluttonous sack" of "corruption and foulness and carrion." (One problem with gluttony, it seems, is that it is an attempt to "have it all" here on earth; the appalling impossibility of that thus would have contributed to the perceived deadliness of this sin.)

Beowulf contains one of these two-sided Christian sermons advising against the foolishness of heathen pleas "to the Devil" for assistance against Grendel:

> Sometimes they honored idols at heathen temples, with their words urged that the soul's slayer [the Devil] would give aid for the distress of the people . . . in their hearts they were mindful of hell, they knew not the Ruler. . . . Woe to him who in grievous affliction shall thrust his soul into the fire's bosom, expect no comfort, nor any change. Well is the man who may, after his death-day, seek the Lord and seek peace in the Father's bosom!

It was clear to the folk who composed and enjoyed *Beowulf* that only in heaven or in hell would, or should, humans experience pure joy or sorrow—"weeping without consolation" or "continual summer without any change," as one homily states. Theirs were difficult lives, often presenting sudden and uncontrollable changes. Kings, courtly retainers, or clodbusters, their cultural background and general expectations were those of the peasant. And like today's medical personnel in a war zone or in a large inner-city hospital, they inevitably found humor in the sometimes appalling incongruities of life. For the Old English, these incongruities were found in the contrasts between rough joys, as of the meadhall, and the devastations that inevitably followed the feasting. These first English people found humor in its opposite; they would have agreed with Mark Twain that "the secret source of humor itself is not joy, but sorrow."

Beowulf reminds us that humor is not merely for laughs. For the Old English man or woman, humor, especially irony, served to further strengthen social bonds because humor works only if you are in on the joke. The laughter that they shared in the meadhall, albeit quickly passing, reinforced their kinship-bonds.

Grendel and his mother (like all monsters, the *scop* reminds us, condemned by God as kind of Cain) never are in on *any* jokes, for their kind is damned on earth, irrevocably alienated, and thus completely "deprived of joy." They are, in fact, angered to deeds of slaughter by sounds of human laughter.

Little has been published on the humor in *Beowulf*. Still one scholar, Thomas Gardner, suggests that by playing with the wording and placement of traditional Old English oral formulas, the *Beowulf*-poet intentionally creates humor. Gardner points out that:

> When the slain Æschere is first mentioned, he is especially praised for being one of those who *hafelan weredon* ("protected heads"). The next time he is mentioned, his bodiless head is sighted on the cliff overlooking Grendel's mere. It seems unfair to the poet to think of this amusing piece of irony as accidentally achieved. Æschere's demise comes up one more time in the poem with a word for "head" and another decapitation in the near context. As far as this last example is concerned, the "audience" must have experienced it as something less than serious that the word *heafomaga* ("head-kinsmen" = "near relatives") should have been chosen immediately after Beowulf mentions cutting off the head of Grendel's mother (and particularly in the light of what the "audience" already knows about the heads that have been rolling).[1]

Inspired by Gardner's observations I find it funny that Grendel's last victim, the warrior Hondscioh (whose name means "glove") is unable to contain Grendel's grip, which Beowulf then immediately *is* able to contain— and in fact rip off. The "hand-grip" jokes continue in the poem, emphasizing the humor in the horror. For example, just after describing Grendel's "grip" hanging in the hall, the author tells us: "Then was it commanded that Heorot [the hall] be within quickly adorned by hands."

The Old English were in many ways rough, but they were neither unperceptive nor unintelligent. As John Leyerle and other critics have pointed out, *Beowulf* is intricately structured with amazingly complex interlacings of character, plot, theme, time, and place. The ability of its audience (however wide or narrow it might have been) to sort out all of these threads into an entertaining and edifying whole raises our estimation of these early medieval folk. These ancestors of today's British were pattern-seekers and puzzle-solvers, people who relished finding unexpected congruities among life's multiplicities. The witty humor found in *Beowulf* exactly fits their temperament in its subtlety, its irony, and its ability to touch upon not only the pleasures but also the pains inevitable in the human condition.

Summary

The humor in *Beowulf* is at once subtle and outrageous, befitting the canny peasant-stock society that relished it. It works mostly on the audience's perception of ironies and incongruities, especially those which would be apparent in a life of many hardships and occasional quick joys. The jokes in this epic poem serve not only to amuse, but also to provoke reflection and to reinforce social bonds.

Notes
1. Thomas Gardner. "How Free Was the *Beowulf* Poet?" *Modern Philology*, 71 (1973): 111–27.

Selected Bibliography
Primary Sources

Editions
Klaeber, Fr. *Beowulf and the Fight at Finnsburg*. Boston: Heath, 1950. 3rd ed. with Supplement.
Wrenn, C.L. *Beowulf, with the Finnesburg Fragment*. New York: St. Martin's Press, 1973. 3rd ed. rev. W.F. Bolton.

Translations
Kennedy, Charles W. *Beowulf, the Oldest English Epic*. London: Oxford University Press, 1940. An excellent verse translation, though somewhat hard to follow.
Donaldson, E. Talbot. *Beowulf*. New York: Norton, 1966. Smooth and accurate prose.
Raffel, Burton. *Beowulf*. Amherst: University of Massachusetts Press, 1971; paperback rpt., New York: Mentor, 1963. Artful and somewhat free verse translation.

Bibliography

Short, Douglas D. *Beowulf Scholarship: An Annotated Bibliography*. New York: Garland, 1980.

Historical Background

Stenton, Sir Frank. *Anglo-Saxon England*. Oxford: Clarendon, 1971. 3rd ed. Provides thorough, readable, and accurate background.

Whitelock, Dorothy. *The Beginnings of English Society*. Baltimore: Penguin Books, 1952. A standard text for understanding the milieu of *Beowulf*.

Books

Chambers, R.W. *Beowulf: An Introduction*. Cambridge: The University Press, 1963. 3rd ed. with Supplement by C.L. Wrenn. Contains a full range of most valuable information.

Articles

Kaske, R.E. "*Beowulf*." In *Critical Approaches to Six Major English Works*. Ed. R.M. Lumiansky and Herschel Baker. Philadelphia: University of Pennsylvania Press, 1971, pp. 3–40. An allegorical approach to the poem, showing Beowulf as the ideal Christian hero.

Leyerle, John. "The Interlace Structure of *Beowulf*." *University of Toronto Quarterly*, 37 (October 1967): 1–17. A landmark essay on the complexities of the poem's structure.

Tolkien, J.R.R. "*Beowulf*: The Monsters and the Critics." *Proceedings of the British Academy*, 22 (1936): 245–95; published by Oxford University Press, 1936. An interesting and influential essay on several aspects, including the poem's structure and the role of monsters.

Margaret Downes

Betjeman, Sir John

Born: Highgate, London, August 28, 1906
Education: Byron House, Highgate 1915; Highgate Junior School, 1916; Dragon School ("Lynam's"), Oxford 1917–1920; Marlborough College, Wiltshire, September 1920–1924; Magdalen College, Oxford University 1925–1928
(no degree)
Marriage: Penelope Valentine Hester Chetwode, 1933; two children
Died: Trebetherick, Cornwall, May 19, 1984

Biography

In the late eighteenth century Sir John Betjeman's family emigrated from Holland (or Germany) to London. In 1820, his great grandfather founded a family firm which designed furniture, glassware, and silver. John, an only child, was born on August 28, 1906 to Ernest Edward Betjeman, a prosperous but stone-deaf business man, and Mabel Bessie Dawson, who later ran a millinery and dress shop on Buckingham Street. The family advanced financially and moved from 52 Parliament Hill Mansions, Highgate, London, where John was born, to 31 West Hill, Highgate, a semi-detached house.

At Byron House, a Montessori school in Highgate, in 1915 John met his first love, Peggy, daughter of Admiral Sir Herbert Purey-Cust. At Highgate Junior School, his favorite master in 1916 was T.S. Eliot. Estranged from his father because he knew that he must be a poet, the ten-year-old boy submitted a manuscript, "The Best of Betjeman," to "the American master, Mr. Eliot / That dear good man, with Prufrock in his head." Subsequently, while at the Dragon School ("Lynam's") in Oxford from 1917 to 1920, John submitted poetry, sketches, and prose to *The Draconian* and enjoyed leading roles in dramatic presentations. Although the move to Marlborough public school, Wiltshire, in 1920 filled him with the sense of "Doom! Shivering doom!" whenever he considered the great bullies to be faced, the faculty included Christopher Hughes, who took the boys on sketching and watercolor expeditions in the Wiltshire countryside. At Marlborough, the youth met Sir Arthur Elton, Louis MacNeice, Bernard Spencer, and Anthony Blunt (later Keeper of the Queen's pictures and unmasked spy), and established a high-brow satirical magazine, the *Heretick*.

After the Spartan discipline and accommodations of Marlborough, John luxuriated in the freedom and privacy of Oxford when he matriculated at Magdalen College in 1925. Quickly deciding that he had no talents to offer the athletic crowd ("The Hearties"), he went completely aesthetic and aristocratic. At Oxford he met W.H. Auden, Martyn Skinner, Lionel Perry, John Dugdale, Lord "Billy" Clonmore,

Evelyn Waugh, Harold Acton, and Edward James (the private publisher of Betjeman's first book of poetry, *Mount Zion*). John co-edited the *Cherwell* with Christopher Sykes. His great champion was the Dean of Wadham College, C. Maurice Bowra; contrarily, his tutor, C.S. Lewis, dismissed him as "a pretentious playboy." In all justice it should be said that the unconverted Lewis could scarcely admire the undergraduate who was an antiquarian without being a scholar and who attended Anglo-Catholic Mass at Pusey House. Having failed the Divinity Moderations, Betjeman left Oxford without a degree in 1928 and began to teach at Heddon Court School, Barnet, Hertfordshire, where his pose as a cricket expert was quickly exposed. Through the recommendation of Professor Bowra, however, he was rescued to become assistant editor of the *Architectural Review* in 1931, the same year that his Oxford friend James privately published his first volume of poetry. His articles on the castles and halls of obscure Irish peers in the *Review* caught the attention of Lord Beaverbrook of the *Evening Standard*, who took him on as film critic. The *Standard*'s policy of gentleness to movies advertised in its pages led the young critic to perfect the technique of a favorable review which yet conveys the impression that his subject was really a "terrible film."

In 1933, he became editor of the Shell Oil Company series of topographical guidebooks to Britain and married Penelope, daughter of Sir Philip (later Lord) Chetwode, Commander-in-Chief of the India forces. Lady Chetwode lamented that "we ask people like that to our houses, but we don't marry them." The Betjemans would have two children.

Also in 1933, Chapman & Hall published *Ghastly Good Taste: A Depressing Story of the Rise and Fall of English Architecture*, and four years later John Murray brought out *Continual Dew: A Little Book of Bourgeois Verse*. The year 1938 saw the publication of *An Oxford University Chest*, 1939, *Antiquarian Prejudice*, and in 1940, *Old Lights for New Chancels* was published.

During World War II, Betjeman served the Ministry of Information for one year in Dublin, was transferred to the media division of the Admiralty, became a popular BBC broadcaster, and then settled in the books department of the British Council (1944–1946). *New Bats in Old Belfries* came out in 1945, in the middle of the British Council period. After two architectural studies, *Vintage London* (1942) and *English Cities and Small Towns* (1943), he produced the Penguin book on his illustrator, John Piper, in 1944. *A Few Late Chrysanthemums* and *Poems in the Porch*, both published in 1954, preceded the 1957 Spring Term Poet-in-Residency at the University of Cincinnati and were followed by *Collected Poems* (1958), which sold over 100,000 copies and made him one of the most popular poets since Lord Byron. *Summoned by Bells* (1960) was an epic-length, mostly blank verse poem with a disturbing self-consciousness not present in his earlier work and an introspective vein which became characteristic of his later work.

Plump, rumpled, and wispy-haired, the unlikely-looking architecture historian and poet insisted that his two passions did not compete for his attention. Architecture, for Betjeman, is the human setting in which poetic events occur, the "outward and visible manifestation of society's spiritual condition." He was a chief factor in the restoration of Victorian Gothic to critical favor; his travel guides were personalistic but inviting; his television lectures enormously popular; and he was constant in his use of poetry to preserve an unspoiled countryside. His worship of tradition often appeared as a snobbery inconsistent with his careless dress and simple accommodations.

Betjeman's honors and awards were many: the Heinemann (1949), Foyle (1959), Loines (1956), Duff Cooper (1958), and Queen's (1960) awards, appointment as Commander of the British Empire (1960), knighthood in 1969, Poet Laureate (1972), and Honorary Fellow of the Royal Institute of British Architecture (1971), of Keble College (1972) and of Magdalen College (1975).

A weekly columnist for the *Spectator*, book critic for the *Daily Telegraph*, and frequent guest on the BBC, during the week, Betjeman maintained a small apartment on Cloth Fair near Smithfield Market in London (until he was driven out by the early morning noise of lorries), and on weekends joined his wife at "The Mead," Wantage, Berkshire. His urban life and her devotion to horses and gardening turned their marriage into occasional visits, but also an enduring friendship.

In the mid-1970s, Betjeman suffered a number of strokes and the ravages of Parkinson's Disease. Having already left Cloth Fair for Radnor Walk, Chelsea, in 1972 he took up terminal residence at the site of his boyhood holidays, Trebetherick, Cornwall. Although Penelope had become a Roman Catholic in 1948, John remained an enthusiastic though somewhat doubtful Anglo-Catholic to the end. He died on May 19, 1984, of complications brought on by strokes and the increasing debility of Parkinson's Disease.

Literary Analysis

The knighting of John Betjeman by Queen Elizabeth II came as no surprise to the public. Was he not a favorite of Princess Margaret, a former Oxonian (without degree), an ardent defender of the Victorian Gothic Revival, a pillar of the Anglo-Catholic establishment, and a bon vivant with aristocrats who lived in historic country houses? His wife's passion for horses and gardening provided added credentials for both princesses and country lords. Even his carefully cultivated image of a bumbling, untidy, absent-minded, friendly old duffer boosted his popularity among commoners.

Still, Betjeman's appointment as Poet Laureate raised quite different issues. Eliot had pontificated: "Poets in our civilization, as it exists at present, must be *difficult*." Ezra Pound, Eliot himself, and Auden heeded the admonition and were difficult, indeed, feeding a light academic industry of thousands of graduate students devoting theses, dissertations, scholarly papers, and articles to an unrestrained feeding-frenzy of explication. Should England, then, have an "official poet" who had simply sidestepped all of the technical experiments and artistic esoterica that produced the literary milieu of Modernism?

It is important to note that in bypassing the bibliophiles, Betjeman fell right into the current of William Wordsworth, Alfred, Lord Tennyson, Thomas Hardy, Matthew Arnold, Rudyard Kipling, A.E. Housman, and even his own predecessor, Cecil Day Lewis. Much of Eliot's instruction to younger poets was based on the despairing recognition that there no longer existed a body of commonly-shared culture to support the modern poet. But, Sir John, with all of his poetry selling more than 5,000 copies on publication and the first edition of his *Collected Poems* rapidly reaching 100,000 in sales, proved that the popularity of Tennyson, Kipling, and Housman could be achieved in the modern era if the poet wrote memorably about the old things that had shaped and moved him and aroused matching echoes in the memories of his readers.

Consider, for example, the much-anthologized "Subaltern's Love-Song," the two Myfanwy poems ("Myfanwy" and "Myfanwy at Oxford") and the less well known "Olympic Girl." Read for pleasure, they are slightly absurd trifles about an unathletic aesthete's crush on crashing big girls. However, Tennyson's *The Princess* and the novels of Charles Reade immediately come to mind with their great, strong Junoesque heroines who perform their strenuous rescues of limp aesthetic males clearly not worthy of their attention and a frightful nuisance in the bargain. Is no important social judgment being made here? Remember that Myfanwy, Miss J. Hunter Dunn, and the Olympic Girl are not figures of fun; boyish in strength, goddess-like in beauty, they speak eloquently about the males with whom they consort, the society that they inhabit, and the gender tensions of the modern world. Strength and beauty can be intimidating and masochism can become a default-substitute for equal love.

Besides writing essays on architecture, Betjeman's poetry is characteristically, like Hardy's, the celebration of place. The list is staggering: Leamington health spa, Oxford, Cambridge, Croydon, the Cadogan Hotel, the Downs, Holy Trinity, Trebetherick, Westminster Abbey, St. Barnabas, Bath, St. Enodoc—the list can be multiplied many times. The poet seems always to respond first to sight and sound—a woman's glove, the vox humana on the organ, the tombs of leading statesmen, the Anglican Service "In Westminster Abbey" (*Old Lights for New Chancels*). The lady of the glove is entirely human and as such, identifiable with the reader. Yet, consider the sting of savage satire: this woman just wants to feel better about herself; she has squeezed in a brief prayer in the Abbey before her really important luncheon engagement; she prays to a Gracious Lord to bomb the Germans and spare the British—particularly her residence at 189 Cadogan Square. She bargains with God for His favors: she will attend Evening Service whenever she can find the time; she will send white feathers to men who have not enlisted; she will even go so far as to interrupt her social calendar by joining, albeit not so far as serving in, the Women's Army Corps. In a particularly wicked admission, she acknowledges that the British forces have an unnaturally large group of black soldiers from Jamaica, Honduras, and Togoland, but she adds, above all "protect the whites."

In 1960, Betjeman emulated Wordsworth's *Prelude* with a ninety-seven-page epic of childhood and youth, *Summoned by Bells*, generally in rapid-moving blank verse, but shifting to rhyme when the poet's emotions are particularly stirred. It is possible to read this as a charming *Tom Brown's School Days* of privileged childhood, fine public schools, and the Jazz Decade of the 1920s at Oxford. To do so misses the most incisive and poignant meanings of the poem. What are the "Bells"? Of course, they summon a boy to school, a family to church, and the living to a funeral. chapter 1, "Before MCMXIV," confesses that the family name had originally one "n." In the nineteenth-century enthusiasm for all things Germanic, the "n" became "nn." Then, during World War I, when all things German were an anathema, the double "nn" became single "n" again!

Maid Sarah was so "bad-tempered that she scarcely spoke." Hateful nursemaid Maud forced him to eat chewy bits of fish, threatened to return the boy to baby diapers and bottles, rubbed his face in the food that he left, removed his teddybear Archibald, and inflicted him with such searing visions of Hell that he never escaped them. The early days with his father were warm; but chapter 2, "The Dawn of Guilt," portrays a youth expected to take over the factory on Pentonville Road. His determination to be a poet spells disappointment to his mother, estrangement from his father, and betrayal of the factory hands whose livelihood depends on him. In later years his father presses him again to take on the firm; the books of architecture and poetry are no substitute. His father's "kind grey eyes look woundedly" at the middle-aged poet, the workmen will have to seek work elsewhere, and the red stone family obelisk "Points an accusing finger to the sky."

Chapters 3, 4, and 5 trace the boy from Byron House, amid rivals for the favor of Peggy Purey-Cust who attack him violently and on the basis of his name call him a German spy, to Cornwall summers as a welcome refuge from school bullies. At Dragon School he evades a fight with "the perfect boy" (whom he admired) by confessing the fraudulent illness of his Mater. But, Ronnie Wright becomes his best friend and Gerald Haynes the ideal schoolmaster.

The family move to Chelsea (chapter 6) further cements his friendship with Ronnie. Marlborough School is full of "impending doom" (chapter 7) with fagging and flogging, but "architecture and literature—ecstasy."

Chapter 8 details a characteristic father–mother row, but chapter 9 opens the door to the freedom, luxury, and privacy of Oxford. A "Betjeman set" develops—songs, dinners, High Mass, sherry with dons—but someone seems to have neglected to warn the youth of coming examinations and so he leaves Paradise degreeless. He is rescued from a miserable situation as private schoolmaster by that deus ex machina, the wealthy and discriminating James, who privately publishes his first slender book of verse.

Nostalgia, yes, privilege aplenty, but sadistic nursemaids, a disappointed father, beatings by schoolmates, and Oxford brilliance unrewarded by an Oxford degree all reveal the astringent side of Betjeman's sentimentality about people, buildings, and England.

The Earl of Birkenhead, who compiled the *Collected Poems of John Betjeman* (1971), called his friend "one of modern England's few upper-class licensed jesters." And, Sir Maurice Bowra, an Oxford undergraduate with both Birkenhead and Betjeman, described him as "a mind of extraordinary originality, there is no one else remotely like him." In the Introduction to the same collection, it was the even more controversial poet Philip Larkin who penned the epigram: "If the spirit of our century is onwards, outwards, and upwards, the spirit of Betjeman's work is backwards, inwards, and downwards"—incidentally rather aptly describing himself.

Beside the occasional poem, the subjects of his verse are the lay of the land, religion which he loves but cannot entirely accept, people in the past whom he loved even if they did not love him, Victorian architecture on a modest, human scale of coziness, and the shadows of childhood and death, neither of which he can avoid. So he is able to move from the entirely banal and middle-class comfort of Miss J. Hunter Dunn, athletic girl tennis-star, the six-o'clock news and a lime juice and gin ("A Subaltern's Love-song," *New Bats in Old Belfries*) to the suburban ferocity of an Edwardian couple in London for work and shopping: "Cancer has killed him. Heart is killing her" ("The Metropolitan Railway," *A Few Late Chrysanthemums*). "Early Electric" transformed their early lives and moved them with ease across a lovely landscape. Now he's dead and she is dying; the trees they loved are cut down; the site of the villa they bought with such passionate planning is now occupied by the Odeon cinema.

If Betjeman describes a place, like the rowing sheds on the Oxford Isis, it is shown from the view of elderly dons attending the funeral of a former student ("I.M. Walter Ramsden," *A Few Late Chrysanthemums*). It was John Sparrow who noted (*Selected Poems*, Preface, John Sparrow, John Murray, 1948): "he cannot see a place without seeing also the life that is lived in it, without becoming conscious of its human associations."

In "The Dear Old Village" (*Late Chrysanthemums*) he speaks of children being bused eleven miles to "a fine school." All is descriptive, reflective, yet it is perfectly clear that the poet prefers windows that squint beneath thatch to the "vita-glass" windows of the new school. He deplores and laments the girls who clerk in Woolworth's and the boys who lost the warm plough horse for a smelly, noisy tractor. The general comic tone is satiric concerning the modern "improvements" he hates, and wryly nostalgic about the old things that he loves. The language is simple, the rhythms familiar—the only surprises come from the sudden insertions of "Woolworth" girls or "Heinz Ketchup."

On behalf of the town of Slough, he issues a savage invitation: "Come, friendly bombs, and fall on Slough" because everything in it is "tinned": fruit, meat, milk, beans, minds, and breath ("Slough," *Continual Dew*, 1937). "Trebetherick" (*Old Lights for New Chancels*) has some of the same incongruous mix of ferocity and the banal. The town of Trebetherick reminds him of a brutal past when shoresmen waited hopefully to plunder the ships that foundered on their rocky beach. Then the inhumane landsmen were somehow picturesque and romantic. Now "Ralph, Vasey, Alastair, Biddy, John and I" merely get sand in their sandwiches and wasps in their picnic tea. Even the Lake District so dear to Wordsworth is now simply a place to drink "non-alcoholic wine," to shake the "H.P. Sauce and spill Heinz's Ketchup" on the tablecloth ("Lake District," *Old Lights*).

In "Huxley Hall" (*A Few Late Chrysanthemums*), he meditates on the grim doctrine of the Fall of Man. But, the setting continually trivializes the theology: a "vegetarian dinner," a "lime-juice minus gin." When he writes a poetic preface to *High and Low* (1966), he pays brief tribute to John Milton, William Cowper, Wordsworth, Tennyson, and even muted recognition to Ernest Dowson, Byron, George Crabbe, Thomas Moore, and Thomas Campbell. As for himself: "How can I, / A buzz-ing insubstantial fly, / Compare with them?" The best he can do is to recall with wry amusement that at least he has the same publisher (John Murray) that they had and then go on to express his somewhat surprised gratitude to the people who buy his verses.

Without radical poetic experiment, with slight pretense to pompous inspiration, his method is chiefly the *argumentum ad absurdum*. The old world warmed humanity; the new world "tins" and plasticates it.

Summary

John Betjeman was a best-selling poet, popular television commentator, architectural scholar and preservationist, and intimate friend of country characters as well as aristocrats and royalty. Criticism is deeply divided concerning his literary significance. Many consider him a competent writer of light, humorous occasional verse, entirely unaffected by the ferment of Pound and Eliot. Larkin and Auden pointed out his lucidity, delicate lyricism, and fine ear for dialogue, his command of language, and his metrical skill. Auden particularly defended his use of light, humorous verse as the vehicle for serious truth about himself and contemporary society.

Selected Bibliography
Primary Sources
(Because so many of John Betjeman's publications were combinations of prose, poetry, and architecture, they are listed as mixed-genre, chronologically.)

Mount Zion. London: Edward James, 1931.

Ghastly Good Taste: A Depressing Story of the Rise and Fall of English Architecture. London: Chapman & Hall, 1933.

Continual Dew: A Little Book of Bourgeois Verse. London: Murray, 1937.

An Oxford University Chest. London: Miles, 1938.

Antiquarian Prejudice. London: Hogarth Press, 1939.

Old Lights for New Chancels. London: Murray, 1940.

Vintage London. London: Collins, 1942.

English Cities and Small Towns. London: Collins, 1943.

John Piper. Harmondsworth: Penguin Books, 1944.

New Bats in Old Belfries. London: Murray, 1945.

Slick But Not Streamlined: Poems and Short

Pieces. Sel. and intro. by W.H. Auden. Garden City, NY: Doubleday, 1947.

Selected Poems. London: Murray, 1948.

The English Scene. London: Cambridge University Press, 1951.

First and Last Loves. London: Murray, 1952.

A Few Late Chrysanthemums. London: Murray, 1954.

Poems in the Porch. London: S.P.C.K., 1954.

The English Town in the Last 100 Years. Cambridge: Cambridge University Press, 1956.

Collected Poems. London: Murray, 1958.

Summoned by Bells. London: Murray, 1960.

Ground Plan to Skyline, with Richard M. Farren. London: Newman Neame Take Home Books, 1960.

A Ring of Bells. London: Murray, 1962.

The City of London Churches. London: Pitkin Pictorials, 1965.

High and Low. London: Murray, 1966.

A Pictorial History of English Architecture. London: Murray, 1972.

London's Historic Railway Stations. London: Murray, 1972.

A Nip in the Air. London: Murray, 1975.

The Best of Betjeman. Sel. by John Guest. London: Murray, 1978.

Secondary Sources

Brooke, Jocelyn. *Ronald Firbank and John Betjeman*. London: Longman, Green, 1962. Writers and Their Work Series. From Oxford into his mature years Betjeman is seen as an "original mind" who made his influence felt in poetry and conversation rather than learned articles. Above all else, the poet of nostalgia.

Harvey, Geoffrey. *The Romantic Tradition in Modern English Poetry*. New York: St. Martin's Press, 1986. Exceptionally high estimate of his poetic significance presented with good examples in brief compass.

Press, John. *John Betjeman*. London: Longman Group, 1974. Writers and Their Work Series. Press considers his immense popularity in poetry and on television; pays much attention to his architectural prose and argues that his best poems intermingle setting, the past, the present, and the specter of death.

Stanford, Derek. *John Betjeman: A Study*. London: Spearman, 1961. Contains some valuable information and photo-

graphs not to be found elsewhere.

Taylor-Martin, Patrick. *John Betjeman: His Life and Work*. London: Allen Lane, 1983. Biography with some poetical criticism and a bibliography. Taylor-Martin fails to convince that deep meanings underlie the charming surface of Betjeman's verse.

Thwaite, Anthony. *Poetry Today: A Critical Guide to British Poetry, 1960–1984*. London: Longman, 1985, pp. 7–10. Meagre but incisive treatment.

Elton E. Smith

Bradbury, Malcolm Stanley

Born: Sheffield, Yorkshire, September 7, 1932

Education: West Bridgford Grammar School, Nottingham; University College, University of Leicester, B.A. with honors, 1953; University of London, M.A., 1955; Indiana University, 1955–1956; Yale University, 1958–1959; University of Manchester, Ph.D., 1964

Marriage: Elizabeth Salt, October 1959; two children

Biography

Malcolm Stanley Bradbury was born on September 7, 1932, in Sheffield, in the North of England, to Arthur and Doris Ethel Marshall Bradbury. One of the first beneficiaries of the Education Act of 1944 which guaranteed free education to all, he attended West Bridgford Grammar School in Nottingham. Bradbury then went on to the redbrick University of Leicester. He was the first in his family to attend university and graduated with a B.A. with honors in 1953.

After taking an M.A. at the University of London in 1955, Bradbury spent a year at Indiana University (1955–1956), where he studied American literature, taught freshman composition, and wrote brief pieces for *Punch* on such subjects as the impossibility of getting socks darned in America. After another stint in America, at Yale (1958–1959), he returned to England, published his first novel (*Eating People Is Wrong*), married Elizabeth Salt, and took up his first university position, "all," as he later recollected, "in the space of a few days" in 1959.[1] He and his wife have two sons.

Bradbury's two sojourns in America, and hence his fresh perspective on English mores, inspired two humorous books, *Phogey! Or,*

How to Have Class in a Classless Society (1960) and *All Dressed Up and Nowhere to Go: The Poor Man's Guide to the Affluent Society* (1962), which anatomize the virtues and vices of the English national character such as "Stiff Upper Lippery," "Superiority to Foreigners," and "Muddling Through." The penetrating observation of sociologically revealing habits and behavior that marks his novels is already on display: food, drink, vocabulary, and domestic artifacts are all scrutinized for potential humor, pretension, or absurdity. In 1964, Bradbury received his Ph.D. from the University of Manchester with a thesis on the *American Literary Expatriates in Europe: 1815 to 1950*; much of his later critical work has centered on modernism and the contemporary novel. He rose rapidly through the ranks of lecturer, senior lecturer, and reader at the Universities of Birmingham and East Anglia, becoming Professor of American Studies in 1970 at the age of thirty-eight, very young by British standards.

Bradbury's academic career has flourished. He has held many prestigious academic appointments and fellowships in America, England, and elsewhere in Europe, while continuing to be based at the University of East Anglia. In addition to his many academic publications, Bradbury has also written an impressive number of novels, short stories, humorous books, and radio and television plays. A television adaptation of *The History Man* (1975), which had previously won the Heinemann/Royal Society of Literature Award, appeared in 1981.

Literary Analysis
Bradbury has noted with pleasure that his first stories were published in a local newspaper, the *Nottinghamshire Guardian*, which had also published D.H. Lawrence's first story. But, the literary tradition in which Bradbury has placed himself does not include the humorless Lawrence. As a novelist, he has declared his indebtedness to Evelyn Waugh and E.M. Forster, both of whom have also been subjects of his critical scrutiny. Bradbury stands in a long line of British social satirists which includes Jane Austen, Tobias Smollett, Henry Fielding, Thomas Love Peacock, Charles Dickens, and, in this century, Forster, Waugh, Kingsley Amis, and Simon Gray. Bradbury's bailiwick is academic society. He focuses his mordant but not entirely unsympathetic gaze on the intellectual types and social fads that define it; the academic world is an enclosed one, and some characters, such

as the perceptive social psychologist Flora Beniform, reappear in various works.

To his chagrin, Bradbury's novels have usually been identified solely as examples of the campus novel, a genre that rose to fame with the publication of Kingsley Amis's brilliantly comic *Lucky Jim* in 1954. There is much circumstantial evidence to support this judgment. With one exception, Bradbury's novels take place on either a fictional campus or the global campus. With the partial but notable exception of *The History Man*, his novels conform to the expectations of the campus novel genre: a naive hero, set-pieces such as the faculty meeting or (usually drunken) lecture, a supporting cast of recognizable academic types, and periodic dips from comedy into farce. Furthermore, Bradbury's own academic itinerary has provided much of the background material for his novels. His first novel, *Eating People Is Wrong* (1959), partly depicts the new outsiders' entrance into academic life; Indiana University in the American Midwest is comically resurrected as Benedict Arnold University in his novel *Stepping Westward* (1965); *The History Man* chillingly chronicles life on the faculty of an increasingly embattled university; Bradbury's many travels for the British Council inform *Rates of Exchange* (1983); his experiences as a radio and television scriptwriter are served up in *Cuts* (1987); the slippery mortality of current literary criticism pervades *Doctor Criminale* (1992).

The label of campus novelist has continued to stick to Bradbury, especially with the success of novels like *Changing Places* and *Small World* by his contemporary, fellow academic, and sometime collaborator David Lodge. Both writers tend to be placed in the house of fiction half humorously dubbed by Howard Jacobson—himself an academic and author of a campus novel—"Bradbury's Lodge."[2] Bradbury himself has self-parodically created a composite English comic novelist, Brodge, the author of *Changing Westward*, about whom one inhabitant of his fictional Slaka opines, "I think he is very funny but sometimes his ideological position is not clear."[3] In recent years both Lodge and Bradbury have made this conflation one of their favorite jokes, as in Bradbury's "The Wissenschaft File" from *Unsent Letters: Irreverent Notes from a Literary Life* (1988) and Lodge's ventriloquized afterword to Bradbury's *My Strange Quest for Mensonge*.

Understanding Bradbury solely as a humorous "campus novelist," however, does not do justice to the serious social commentary and stylistic innovation in his work. Even in *Eating People Is Wrong*, Bradbury attempts to enlarge the conventions of the campus novel. Through the microcosm of the quad, common room, and lecture hall, he deals with issues of intellectual honesty and fashion, the public implications of private values (notably liberal humanism), and the problems of the well-meaning but hesitant heart. What might seem at first to be a genre limited in style, substance, and audience has at times proved in Bradbury's hands to be a remarkably sensitive instrument not only for exercising social satire of an increasingly keen sort but also for registering changes in the political and ideological climate. Indeed, his novels can fruitfully be considered as "Decade Novels." The popularity of his novels has increased as their scope has widened; *Rates of Exchange*, for example, was nominated for Britain's prestigious Booker Prize; his work is now as favorably reviewed in such publications as *Harper's* and *Newsweek*, as well as in the more academic *Times Literary Supplement* and *Critical Quarterly*.

The world of his fiction, while consistently humorous, cannot with justice be considered wholly comic, and the characters with whom the reader most sympathizes seldom meet with happiness or success. Although Bradbury's authorial stance generally supports liberal ideals challenged by doctrinaire ideologies, those ideals (and the characters who most embody them) prove ineffectual and are consistently defeated.

With the publication of *Eating People Is Wrong*, Bradbury was taken by many readers to be an Angry Young Man, along similar lines to Kingsley Amis, whose *Lucky Jim* five years earlier had also been set on a campus, depicted the collision between the old Oxbridge-educated academic and the new redbrick product, and was funny. Like Amis, Bradbury was quick to dissociate himself from the Angries, although for different reasons: "I was not an angry young man, perhaps, since to me the angry young men were all old, ten years older than I was. But I was a niggling one."[4] The older Bradbury nonetheless now believes that the novel is "very much *of* its time, and very much *about* its time."[5]

More than his other novels, *Eating People Is Wrong* deals with the issue of class. In the novel (which Bradbury wrote throughout the 1950s and concluded while in hospital for a serious heart operation) nobody is lucky, especially not the unnerving and unwashed Louis Bates whose class background most resembles Amis's Jim Dixon. The novel centers on Stuart Treece, liberal head of the English Department at a provincial redbrick university, who means well despite the difficulties of life. "It is well I am a liberal, and can love all men," he thinks, "for if I were not, I doubt I could" (chapter 1). Treece's failures of imagination and nerve follow him through the novel, even when the comic pitch is at its highest as when he plays unwilling host to Carey Willoughby, a bona fide Angry Young Man. Their unhappy association ends on a train platform with Willoughby characteristically stealing the complete Scott-Moncrieff translation of Marcel Proust for himself ("Culture should be freely accessible to all," he says) and Lawrence's *Etruscan Places* for Treece. Just as characteristically, Treece anonymously posts back the Lawrence and cash for the Proust to the bookseller. By the novel's end Bates is in a mental hospital after botching both his course and his suicide attempt while Treece has botched his romance with the significantly named post-graduate student Emma Fielding (working on the fish imagery in William Shakespeare's tragedies). Treece is left with only the cold comfort of his liberal guilt: "I suppose all you can say for us is, at least we can feel guilty" (chapter 9).

Stepping Westward, *Rates of Exchange*, and *Doctor Criminale* travel through an exotic abroad with a chastened return home. As picaresque novels, they display many characteristics of the genre: stylistic flamboyance and deft set-pieces as well as haphazard plotting and flat characterization. More unusually, they assume great knowledgeability of the very ideas of subjects such as genre. Their "heroes" are not only typically unheroic, but unheroic in a sophisticated way: "not . . . character[s] in the world historical sense" at all. *Stepping Westward* is full of clever near-parodies and playful borrowings from Bradbury's literary ancestors, including the Waugh-like shipboard scenes, the Amis-like lecture on "The Writer's Dilemma," and the *Lolita*-like romp through the Southwest. (Vladimir Nabokov, author also of the campus novel *Pnin*, appears intermittently as the aptly named Dr. Jochum.) The novel's protagonist, James Walker, was hired through a series of comic mistakes and machinations to teach writing—or at least writing as understood by American service universities: "How to under-

B

line. Use of the comma . . . [A] service course to enable [freshmen] to communicate with one another without sex."[6] Despite his misadventures with writing and romance, Walker remains a cipher; his return to the enclosed normalcy of England, where walking can appropriately cover the space, comes as no surprise. In *Rates of Exchange*, Petworth's travels through Slaka, an imaginary eastern European country, are part of a bleaker vision of international and interpersonal relations where literature—such as the works of "William Woolworth"[7]—is only one commodity competing among many. Bradbury appropriately draws attention to words—those shifting and shifty signifiers—since his protagonist Petworth is a linguist ("an expert on real, imaginary and symbolic exchanges among skin-bound organisms working on the linguistic interface") whose training in deep structure does him little good in calculating the changing values or rates of exchange of the people around him. In a more light-hearted spirit, the spin-off mock travel book *Why Come To Slaka?* (1986) reproduces Bradbury's comic linguistic skill without the grim political implications of the novel. The more recent *Doctor Criminale* takes on similar comic targets but is the most stylish and accomplished of the three. The narrator, a youngish English "journo" named Francis, working unfamiliarly on the interface of literature and television, tries to track down the brilliant but mysterious Doctor Bazlo Criminale, "the intellectual as frequent flyer."[8] Here we visit the parallel worlds of conventions of intellectuals and intellectual conventions, "the most conventional form of convention there is" (241). Francis is a child of the Age of Deconstruction: "We demythologized, we demystified. We dehegemonized, decanonized. We dephallicized, we depatriarchalized; we decoded, we de-canted, we de-famed, we demanned" (9). As such, he finds himself well able to follow philosophizing and manners, but illprepared to decipher Criminale's history, both private and public. Bradbury ambitiously confuses and confounds our expectations of the comic—even the grimly comic—novel. But, the increasingly dark exchanges and the portrayals of real emotional failures are only variously successful; too often Bradbury's stylistic grace is marred by narrative clutter and sloppy pacing.

The History Man, Bradbury's best book, avoids these problems; its tight circle of characters and tense narrative distinguish it from his more episodic works. Howard Kirk, the novel's protagonist, embodies the radical con man. While at first he appears as a canny and amusing manipulator of people and events, an agent in the plot of history, he emerges as a monster who—after many other successful machinations—corrupts the novel's only sympathetic character, Annie Callender, and causes his wife's despair. Howard would, of course, deny both charges, claiming instead that historical inevitability was working through him. Despite the true horror of Howard's character, his selftransformations are strangely compelling. Bradbury himself, like Annie, is both repelled and seduced by Kirk: "Howard is the only person who acts in the book, the only real actor; all the other characters are in a sense self-satisfied."[9] The ambivalence in the novel's presentation of Howard has troubled some critics (including Bradbury himself) who consequently view the novel as either conservative propaganda or a covert plea for liberalism. Stylistically accomplished, this darkly comic novel is a truly disturbing and deeply ambiguous book that bears attentive reading.

Bradbury's comic strengths are solidly grounded in his complementary public interests as professor, literary critic, and novelist. All of his books, like the tour-de-force *Mensonge*, are typically filled with verbal play and professional in-jokes that, although possibly intimidating or obscure to the uninitiated, amuse and provoke knowledgeable participants and onlookers. As he promises, "I'll be your implied author, if you'll be my implied reader."[10] Bradbury is ever self-conscious about the literariness of literature; his favorite comic gambits—word play, allusion, and parody—repeatedly draw attention to the fragility and artifice of fictions. His parody of a brittle Muriel Spark dialogue reveals much of his own postmodern awareness of literary conventions: "You must understand, Mercy, I have been in a novel before. I know what it's like. It is extremely uncomfortable, unless one manages to stay entirely peripheral to the main line of the action, and not to draw attention to oneself in any way. I have always thought . . . that the best way is to be a member of the servant classes, or to be asleep in another room most of the time."[11] Many other contemporary novelists on whom he has published well-received "straight" studies have also provided him with subjects for the devastating parodies in *Who Do You Think You Are?* (1976). From the fertile pen of Iris Murdoch, he provides a selection from "a new work called *The Sublime and the Ridiculous*" which has "many characters, some of them hardly used at all, who can—under fresh titles like *The Necessary and the Contingent* or *The Many and the Few*—be put through fresh sexual permutations." Murdoch, for example, is skewered in the opening sentence from *The Sublime and the Ridiculous*: "Flavia says that Hugo tells her that Augustina is in love with Fred."[12] Occasionally, he even borrows literary characters such as Miss Adela Quested, now rather elderly, "who had had that bit of trouble with the Indian boy all those years back and now had virtually to live in retirement away from the hordes of research students who were always pursuing her."[13] Bradbury's rewritings can also be more subtle. Henry Babbacombe and Lord Mellow in *Cuts* owe much to William Boot and Lord Copper of Waugh's *Scoop*.

Bradbury is particularly skilled at taking words to unsuspected places via metaphor and idiom. *Cuts*, for example, begins with a bravura chapter that, while ostensibly setting the stage for a critique of Thatcherism, is really exploring and explicating the word "cut":

> Ministers were cutting the ribbon to open small new stretches of motorway; in the Treasury they were cutting their coats according to their cloths. They were chopping at the schools, hewing at the universities, scissoring at the health service, sculpting the hospitals, shutting down operating theatres—so that, in one sense at least, there were actually far *fewer* cuts than before.[14]

Verbal translations, whether between languages, dialects, classes, or occupations interest him. *Rates of Exchange*, with translations of all kinds as its explicit subject, provides many comic examples. In Slaka, where the official language can change overnight, the "hero" Petworth's own name is unstable, rendered variously as Petwurt, Petwit (a blow at his learning?), Pervert, and Pumwum. Bradbury's description of this complicated linguistic economy is just as funny as the language he creates. As Marisja Lubijova, Petworth's guide, informs him:

> [Slakan] is not so complicated . . . All you must know is the nouns end in "i," or sometimes two or three, but with many exceptions. We have one spoken language and one book language. Really there are only three cases, but sometimes seven. Mostly it is inflected, but also sometimes not. It is different from country to town, also from region to region, because of our confused history. Vocabulary is a little bit Latin, a little bit German, a little bit Finn. So really it is quite simple, I think you will speak it very well, soon.[15]

Bradbury's facility with creating comic languages such as Slakan can sometimes play him false, as in *Doctor Criminale* where large amounts of bad stage Italian are evidently meant to be funny.

Not surprisingly, given the subject matter of his novels and the frequently self-obsessed proclivities of academics, Bradbury has already been the subject for a fair amount of academic speculation. In "The Wissenschaft File" he mimics the earnest student whose gifts for humor are somewhat limited: "If your books are funny, please tell me where, and send me your ontology of the comedic and your theoretiks of the humoristic, and how you like to compare yourself with Aristotle, Nietzsche, Bergson and Freud."[16] While Bradbury himself is perhaps the foremost critic and commentator on his work, his self-interpretations can be misleading; as Blake Morrison perceptively notes, "Bradbury the novelist gets the better of Bradbury the critic."[17] Nonetheless, Bradbury's novels largely continue to amuse and provoke, frustrate and fascinate.

Summary

Malcolm Bradbury's talents for literary parody and pastiche are considerable, and much of the humor in his books derives from them. His novels, although frequently categorized as "campus novels," expand and, in the case of *The History Man*, transcend the genre.

Notes

1. Afterword to *Eating People Is Wrong* (London: Arena, 1976), p. 291.
2. Howard Jacobson, *Coming from Behind* (New York: St. Martin's Press, 1983), p. 29.
3. *Rates of Exchange* (London: Secker & Warburg, 1983), p. 269.
4. Preface to *All Dressed Up and Nowhere to Go* (rev. ed.) (London: Pavilion, 1982), p. 8.

5. Afterword to *Eating People Is Wrong* (London: Arena, 1976), pp. 293–94.
6. *Stepping Westward* (London: Secker & Warburg, 1965), p. 232.
7. *Rates of Exchange*, p. 189.
8. *Doctor Criminale* (New York: Penguin Books, 1992), p. 26.
9. Quoted in Heide Zeigler and Christopher Bigsby, *The Radical Imagination and the Liberal Tradition* (London: Junction, 1982), p. 75.
10. *Rates of Exchange*, author's note.
11. *Who Do You Think You Are?* (London: Secker & Warburg, 1976), p. 173.
12. *Ibid.*, pp. 153, 155.
13. *Ibid.*, p. 152.
14. *Cuts: A Very Short Novel* (London: Hutchinson, 1987), p. 2.
15. *Rates of Exchange*, p. 93.
16. *Unsent Letters* (New York: Viking Penguin, 1988), p. 3.
17. Blake Morrison, "Stepping Eastward," *Times Literary Supplement* (April 8, 1983): 345.

Selected Bibliography
Primary Sources

Novels
Eating People Is Wrong. London: Secker & Warburg, 1959; New York: Knopf, 1960.
Stepping Westward. London: Secker & Warburg, 1965; Boston: Houghton Mifflin, 1966.
The History Man. London: Secker & Warburg, 1975; Boston: Houghton Mifflin, 1976.
Rates of Exchange. London: Secker & Warburg, 1983.
Cuts: A Very Short Novel. London: Hutchinson, and New York: Harper and Row, 1987.
Doctor Criminale. New York: Penguin Books, 1992.

Plays
Co-authored with David Lodge and James Duckett. *Between These Four Walls*. First produced in Birmingham, 1963.
Co-authored with David Lodge, James Duckett, and David Turner. *Slap in the Middle*. First produced in Birmingham, 1965.
Co-authored with Elizabeth Salt. *This Sport-*

ing Life. Radio play, 1974–1975.
Co-authored with Christopher Bigsby. *The After Dinner Game*. 1975.
The After Dinner Game: Three Plays for Television. London: Arrow Books, 1983. Includes *Love on a Gunboat* and *Standing in for Henry*.

Humor
Phogey! Or, How to Have Class in a Classless Society. London: Max Parrish, 1960.
All Dressed Up and Nowhere to Go: The Poor Man's Guide to the Affluent Society. London: Max Parrish, 1962.
Who Do You Think You Are? Stories and Parodies. London: Secker & Warburg, 1976.
All Dressed Up and Nowhere to Go. (rev. ed. with *Phogey!*) London: Pavilion, 1982.
Why Come to Slaka? London: Secker & Warburg, 1986.
My Strange Quest for Mensonge: Structuralism's Hidden Hero. With a foreword/afterword by Michel Tardieu translated by David Lodge. London: Andre Deutsch, 1987; New York: Viking Penguin, 1988.
Unsent Letters: Irreverent Notes from a Literary Life. London: Andre Deutsch, and New York: Viking Penguin, 1988.

Poems
Co-authored with Allan Rodway. *Two Poets*. Nottingham: Byron Press, 1966.

Literary Criticism
Evelyn Waugh. Edinburgh: Oliver & Boyd, 1964.
Possibilities: Essays on the State of the Novel. London and New York: Oxford University Press, 1973.
Co-authored with James McFarlane. *Modernism: 1890–1930*. Harmondsworth and New York: Penguin Books, 1976.
No, Not Bloomsbury. New York: Columbia University Press, 1988.

Secondary Sources

Book
Morace, Robert A. *The Dialogic Novels of Malcolm Bradbury and David Lodge*. Carbondale and Edwardsville, IL: Southern Illinois University Press, 1989. The most extensive study of Bradbury's

work so far, Morace reads Bradbury's work—both literary criticism and fiction—through Bakhtinian and post-Bakhtinian glasses in his concern for Bradbury's role as a realist. Strong on engaging with other Bradbury critics, weak on Bradbury as a humorist.

Articles and Interviews

Burton, Robert S. "A Plurality of Voices: Malcolm Bradbury's *Rates of Exchange*." *Critique: Studies in Modern Fiction*, 28 (Winter 1987): 101–106. Burton analyzes the comic effects of Bradbury's stylistic play.

Schellenberger, John. "University Fiction and the University Crisis." *Critical Quarterly*, 24, 3 (1982): 45–48. A Briskly useful comparison of British campus novels and plays with current trends in British academic and political life.

Todd, Richard. "Malcolm Bradbury's *The History Man*: The Novelist as Reluctant Impresario." *Dutch Quarterly Review of Anglo-American Letters*, 11, 3 (1981): 162–82. Todd relates theories of history and fiction in Bradbury's plotting; followed by an interview.

Widdowson, Peter. "The Anti-History Men: Malcolm Bradbury and David Lodge." *Critical Quarterly*, 26, 4 (1984): 5–32. By far the most incisive questioning of Bradbury's liberal humanist position in both literary criticism and novels.

Zeigler, Heide, and Christopher Bigsby, eds. "Malcolm Bradbury." In *The Radical Imagination and the Liberal Tradition: Interviews with English and American Novelists*. London: Junction, 1982. The most revealing interview with Bradbury.

Dissertations

Bostock, Paddy. *Poststructuralism, Postmodernism and British Academic Attitudes, with Special Reference to David Lodge, Malcolm Bradbury and Gabriel Josipovici*. Ph.D. dissertation, Council for National Academic Awards, United Kingdom, 1989. Of limited academic appeal, Chapters 3 and 4 consider the ideological interplay between Bradbury's literary criticism and novels.

Elphick, Linda Lois. *"A World Without Real Deliverances"*: Liberal Humanism in the Novels of Malcolm Bradbury. Ph.D. dissertation. Ball State University, 1988. The most extensive study of Bradbury's novels through *Rates of Exchange*, treating the novels as political satires.

Weigenstein, Steven Christopher. *The Contemporary Academic Novel: A Study in Genre*. Ph.D. dissertation. University of Missouri—Columbia, 1987. Places *The History Man* within the conventions and development of the academic novel.

Alexandra Mullen

Browning, Robert

Born: Camberwell, May 7, 1812
Education: At home, in private schools, a few months at University College, London, 1828–1829
Marriage: Elizabeth Barrett, September 12, 1846; one child
Died: Venice, December 12, 1889

Biography

Except for his famous elopement to Italy with Elizabeth Barrett, Robert Browning had more drama in his poetic career and his poems than in his life. The son of Dissenter parents, he was born in Camberwell near London on May 7, 1812. His father, also named Robert Browning, was a well-to-do clerk in the Bank of England who amused himself by writing jocular children's verses and illustrating them with grotesque caricature drawings, an art at which his son also tried his hand during his boyhood. Except for a few months (1828–1829) at University College, London, Browning was educated at home or at private schools. In 1833, he published his highly Shelleyan *Pauline*, which was harshly attacked by several critics. This he followed with two long semi-philosophical "soul dramas," *Paracelsus* (1835) and *Sordello* (1843), although before the appearance of the latter he had become interested in writing for the theater, and two plays, *Strafford* (1837) and the melodramatic *A Blot in the 'Scutcheon* (1843), both written for the eminent actor-manager Charles Macready, were staged to lack-luster receptions. However, in *Pippa Passes* (1841) and the following six "Bells and Pomegranates" booklets (1842–1846)[1] Browning found his true lyric voice and perfected his most effective form, the dramatic monologue. This is the form in which most of his humor appears.

Browning's romance and elopement to Italy with Elizabeth, then a better known poet than he, came in 1845–1846. The couple was married on September 12, 1846 and their son, "Pen," was born in 1849. In 1850, *Christmas-Eve and Easter Day* was published; it was a Victorian statement of religious faith comparable in importance to Alfred Tennyson's *In Memoriam*, which appeared the same year, Matthew Arnold's *Empedocles on Etna* (1852), and John Henry Newman's *Apologia pro Vita Sua* (1864). Five years later, in 1855, Browning published the two volumes of *Men and Women*, which contained fifty of his finest monologues plus "One Word More," a touching personal dedicatory poem to his wife. *Men and Women*, together with *Dramatis Personae* (1864) and especially *The Ring and the Book* (1868–1869), his superb elaboration of a sordid Roman murder story into ten long dramatic monologues, at long last brought him the fame and popularity that swelled in his later years to near-idolatry. Unfortunately, in 1861, before the publication of the latter two books, Mrs. Browning had died, but in "Oh Lyric Love," a passionate elegiac conclusion to book 1, Browning dedicated *The Ring and the Book*, often judged his masterpiece, to her memory.

Browning's later volumes[2] never reached the heights of *Men and Women* and *The Ring and the Book*, but he continued energetically to the end of his life, pouring out excellent philosophic and lyric poems. His last volume, *Asolando*, was published on December 12, 1889, the day of his death in Venice. He was buried with high acclaim in Westminster Abbey.

Literary Analysis

Browning is best known not as a humorist but as a creator of characters, an innovator in poetic style, an optimistic philosopher, and the perfecter of the dramatic monologue. But, under and supporting the artistic success, serious teaching, and keen psychological analysis of most of his best poems lies a sometimes light but often wry, dark, grotesque, and ironic humor that in part looks forward to the madhouse world of Franz Kafka, the theater of the absurd, and the black humor of the twentieth century. It is a humor at which one does not laugh out loud but chuckles inwardly. It is serious humor—a sense of incongruity that causes the mind to laugh while the heart feels sympathy as the mind confronts serious, even tragic problems.

In several works Browning enunciates his theory of comedy. In *Aristophanes' Apology* (1875), for instance, Balustion argues that truth may lurk in jest's surprise, and Aristophanes, clearly speaking for Browning, defends laughter as a cleansing agent and contends that the best writing incorporates both the comic and the serious. As an epigraph for *Ferishtah's Fancies* (1884), Browning quotes Jeremy Collier's remark that William Shakespeare's "genius was jocular, but, when disposed, he could be very serious"; Browning, who saw himself partly in Shakespearean terms, clearly thought of himself as in part a comic writer. He titled one of his volumes *Jocoseria* (1883), another *Asolando* (1889), a pun on the name of the town Asolo and the Italian verb *asolare*, "to amuse oneself at random."

A good argument can be made as to why Browning turned to humor. He had, of course, his father's example as a caricaturist and teller of amusing tales. More importantly, having at the outset of his career been sharply criticized by John Stuart Mill and others for his Shelleyan, self-revelatory *Pauline*, he dared not put himself forward unarmored again. He needed a defense. He found that defense primarily in dramatic method, particularly through the development of the dramatic monologue form in which he could speak vigorously through his characters, but, if attacked, could assert that it was not he but his character who was speaking. In part his humor served the same purpose: he could always back away and argue that what he had proposed was only said in fun. The ambiguities between personal and dramatic and between seriousness and fun could act as a protective shield and leave him free to voice even his most personal and unorthodox opinions.

Of the several varieties of humor and comedy in Browning's poems, the simplest is merry-hearted fooling, the light whimsy that gives zest to "Waring" (1842), parts of "Development" (1889), "Nationality in Drinks" (1845), and "Garden Fancies" (1845).[3] All of these are serious poems, but the speculations about the whereabouts of Waring, the story of Browning's learning Greek from his father (the cat represented Helen of Troy), and the amusing fate of the pedantic volume by Sibrandus Schafnaburgensis are all told in a gay mood, the darker undertones subdued. Despite its moralizing end in "dust and ashes," "A Toccata of Galuppi's" (1855) has much the same lilt, though the epigrammatic final twist in "What of soul was left, I wonder, when the kissing had to stop?" does make the reader, like the narrator, feel "chilly and grown old."

Another kind of humor found abundantly in Browning's poetry is playful humor of style. How can one help being amused with a poem that, like "The Soliloquy of the Spanish Cloister" (1842), begins with the word "Gr-r-r"? Indeed, Browning was a pioneer in bringing outré stylistic effects to serious poetry. Another such stylistic technique that he utilized is the comic double rhyming of "The Glove" (1845), a poem stylistically humorous though deeply serious in intent:

> "Sire," I replied, "joys prove cloudlets:
> Men are the merest Ixions"—
> Here the king whistled aloud. "Let's
> . . . Heigho . . . go look at our lions!"
> Such are the sorrowful chances
> If you talk fine to King Francis.

Related closely to such comic movement of expression is the intentionally vulgar, amusingly doggerel rhythm of "Shop" (1876).

The stories that Browning tells in his poems are frequently humorous. Muckle-mouth Meg, of the poem of the same name (1889), is actually, despite her nickname, a very pretty girl. Her mouth is not too large, but at the end of the poem her eager lover vows to kiss her and kiss her until her mouth really does widen into a "muckle-mouth." "Doctor —" (1880) is also a comic story, telling, as do so many fabliaux, how a bad wife can cheat even the Devil.

Comic characters fill the poems. On the lighter side we find Mr. Sludge the Medium, a delightfully clever and engagingly witty rascal. On the darker side is Johannes Agricola, the extreme egotist, the utter believer in predestination, whose motto is "Sin all you wish, for tomorrow you will be saved." His grim and fantastic spiritual pride, albeit reminiscent of Tennyson's more sober St. Simon Stylites, has a spark of comic madness that Tennyson's lacks. Another partially comic character is Fra Lippo Lippi, the friar caught by the local vice squad at night in the red-light district of Florence, the vital lover of life who at the age of eight forswore all commerce with women for a mouthful of bread and who drew legs and arms on the musical notes in the holy antiphonary, the painter who watches the Prior's niece with the small breasts. All through the poem there are details of Fra Lippo Lippi's comic twists and personality quirks, serious and dedicated artist and "theologian" though he is. Despite his bitterness and malice, the speaker of "Soliloquy of the Spanish Cloister"—as he slyly snaps off Brother Lawrence's prize lilies, piously drinks his orange juice in three gulps to frustrate the Arians, lusts after black-haired Dolores, and thinks up ways to damn Brother Lawrence while cheating the Devil out of his own soul— is also fundamentally comic. Bishop Blougram, playing with unsuspecting Mr. Gigadibs, pretending that his faith is based on worldly concerns while really it is founded far more deeply, jokingly converts Gigadibs to serious belief without even revealing his own real faith and is charming in his subtle yet good-natured humor. Viewed more satirically are the comic lawyers of *The Ring and the Book*, each concentrated on his own concerns, neither caring a hoot about the plight of Guido or the murder of Pompilia; each prepares a cogent argument today on one side as he would, if paid, prepare an equally strong one on the other tomorrow.

There is also humor of situation. Consider the plight of the speaker of "A Light Woman" (1855). In order to save his friend from a designing female, the narrator seduces her himself (she falls into his hands as easily as a ripe pear from the branch). Now, though he does not want her, he has her; he cannot in good conscience just drop her—and his friend is furious with him: "Robert Browning, you writer of plays, / Here's a subject made to your hand!" Browning's own plays were tragedies, but here a potentially tragic plot is treated as comedy. Another comic situation develops in "Pan and Luna" (1880). To shield her nakedness, Luna modestly plunges into a cloud to escape Pan. But, what happens? Pan takes advantage of the cloud to enjoy her, and instead of being indignant Luna chases him into the woods to continue the sport.

These situations are basically light in mood, although the humor is often black humor, bordering on the horrible or macabre. Actually, at the bottom much of Browning's famous grotesqueness is comic. Johannes Agricola, confident that however much he sins he will attain heaven, has already been mentioned. In "The Heretic's Tragedy" (1855), John the Templar pleads that he should not be burnt for heresy. How can he be a heretic, he argues, when he himself has roasted three Turks? In the macabre, yet on one level witty, story of "Gold Hair" (1864), the girl, thought by the villagers

B

"inviolate / Of body and soul," is piously buried "in the very space / By the altar." Ironically, when her corpse is dug up years later, her beautiful gold hair proves to be not a halo of pure saintliness but the depository for the golden coins that she had earned through sin. "The Laboratory" (1845) is, in part, a Browningesque jibe at France—one of several poems in which the poet attempts to catch the mood of certain places and eras. Still, it too has its element of grim comedy. Once in possession of the deadly poison bought to kill her successful rival, the fine lady of the ancient regime will go to "dance at the King's." In her perverted vanity she even offers to let the old apothecary kiss her full on her mouth.

Even more effective is the black humor of what Browning calls a "madhouse cell," "Porphyria's Lover" (1842). Happy and pleased that Porphyria has left the "gay feast" and come through the rain and storm to lie in his arms, in order to eternalize the one fleeting moment when she is wholly and passionately his, her lover winds her hair "In one long yellow string . . . / Three times her little throat around, / And strangled her." He then sits all night with her head propped on his shoulder, certain that he has done right. If he had done wrong, God certainly would have protested, would he not? "And yet God has not said a word!" The psychology is grim and mad and grotesque, but the exaggerated situation is also comic.

Irony is another large element in Browning's humor. The dying Bishop "orders" his tomb at Saint Praxed's Church, although even he knows that his illegitimate sons, whom he has always for propriety's sake called his "nephews" but now at last acknowledges, will give him nothing, or almost nothing, of what he wants. The bishop is apparently a pious man and sincerely mouths platitudes from *Ecclesiastes* on the vanity of the world and the brevity of man's life. When his church burns down, though, he steals for himself the "lump" of lapis lazuli, which with amusing irreverence he describes as "Blue as a vein o'er the Madonna's breast." His one great triumph, which cancels out Old Gandolf's successful appropriation of the best corner of the church for his tomb, is in his winning and keeping— this holy bishop of the Church—as his mistress the boys' beautiful mother. There is also something humorous as well as irreligious about the bishop's promise to use his influence with Saint Praxed in Heaven to gain for his sons horses, Greek manuscripts, and especially "mistresses with great smooth marbly limbs." What the bishop wants carved on his tomb is unmistakably comic in its ironic juxtaposition of pagan and Christian elements:

> Did I say basalt for my slab, sons?
>   Black—
> 'Twas ever antique-black I meant! How
>   else
> Shall ye contrast my frieze to come
>   beneath?
> The bas-relief in bronze ye promised me,
> Those Pans and Nymphs ye wot of, and
>   perchance
> Some tripod, thyrsus, with a vase or so,
> The Saviour at his sermon on the mount,
> Saint Praxed in a glory, and one Pan
> Ready to twitch the Nymph's last garment off,
> And Moses with the tables . . .

And, who cannot but smile at the lines:

> Peace, peace seems all.
> St. Praxed's ever was the church for
>   peace;
> And so, about that tomb of mine, I
>   fought
> With tooth and nail to save my niche, ye
>   know?

But, if the irony in "The Bishop Orders His Tomb" (1845) is gentle, that in "My Last Duchess" (1842) is harsh. The proud Duke heartlessly has his charming, friendly young Duchess done away with solely because of her outgoing nature and what appeared to him to be her lack of reverence for his 900-year-old name and position. Nevertheless, however grim, the poem has elements of dark, ironic humor. The most vivid, of course, is that hinted by the title itself: the Duke is talking about his "last" duchess to the envoy who has come to arrange for his marriage to his "next" duchess. His whole purpose in telling about the past is to warn of what may happen in the future: the new duchess must be careful not to be like the past one! And, there are further ironies. In talking to the ambassador about his duchess, the Duke really reveals more about himself than about her. By attempting to blacken his former wife's character, he blackens his own. There is a further bitter humor in the fact that he can appreciate the beauty of her portrait but could not enjoy the beauty of his living wife. There is also dark humor in his admiration for Claus of Innsbruck's bronze casting of Neptune taming a sea-horse: the Duke, too, knows how to "tame" or "break" unruly natures!

An even more subtle kind of humor in Browning's poems lies in the ambiguity with which the writer presents many of his ideas and characters. This amusing, consciously planned ambiguity is particularly effective when Browning seems to be questioning or at least acting as *advocatus diaboli* against some of the ideas which, elsewhere, he champions most strongly. Thus, though in several of his serious poems such as "In a Gondola" (1842), Browning appears to preach that the best fate is to die at the ecstatic height of one's existence (especially at the ecstatic height of love), this is the very doctrine which leads Porphyria's lover to strangle her with her long yellow hair. Which poem should we believe? In "Porphyria" Browning is exaggerating Browning to such an extent that the result is almost a joke—on Browning. In "Andrea del Sarto" (1855) and other poems, Browning seems to preach that "a man's reach should exceed his grasp, / Or what's a heaven for?" Yet in "A Grammarian's Funeral" (1855), the grammarian, though born with the face and throat of lyric Apollo, has pushed aside all of the joys of living to ruin his health and squander his life on the driest details of Greek grammar. Is one to believe here, as Browning tells us elsewhere, that God will "make the heavenly period / Perfect the earthen," or is this satire? The doubt injects humor.

Again, Browning believes, as he shows clearly in *The Ring and the Book*, that in dire circumstances God often sends a Perseus to save an Andromeda from the monster, a Saint George to battle the dragon, a knight to strike "God's stroke." On the surface this is what seems to be happening in "Count Gismond" (1842). But, is it really happening? Is the woman who is speaking really pure or has Count Gauthier, who only recants his accusation when faced with death, really embraced her body "a night long"? Why does she refuse to speak of the matter in front of Gismond? Why does one of her sons look so different from the other? One wonders, and the wondering, the possible self-satire, introduces a touch of humor (see also "Incident of the French Camp," 1842, which may or may not be serious: "Smiling the boy fell dead"!).

There is the same kind of humorous ambiguity in "Pictor Ignotus" (1845). In this poem a painter, who has spent his life monotonously painting "endless cloisters and eternal aisles / With the same series, Virgin, Babe and Saint," says he could have been popular, made a tremendous splash in the art world, drawn all eyes to himself—but he did not want to become commercial, to have his pictures bought and sold. But could he have done so? Is he speaking the truth or merely rationalizing? The question is especially piquant because at the time that he wrote the poem Browning was himself receiving few plaudits for his work. Presumably one must take seriously the concept of elective affinities in "Cristina" (1842), though there is possibly a glint of irony in the rejected lover's rationalizing statement, "She has lost me, I have gained her." However, when in a patently didactic way in a brief poem amusingly entitled "Transcendentalism: A Poem in Twelve Books" (1855) Browning vigorously attacks didacticism in poetry, one may suspect that, playing both sides of the field, he is having fun with the reader. And, when in "The Flight of the Duchess" (1845) the Duchess escapes from the absurd pseudo-medievalism of her husband's castle to what seems an equally unreal fairyland Gipsy life, one again wonders (despite the autobiographical overtones) just how serious Browning really is. Is the Duchess merely going from one kind of romantic impossibility to another? Is the author again playing with the reader?

Browning also employs a highly effective humor of sophistry (what Willaim B. Raymond calls casuistry), of playing around with ideas so skillfully that the reader smiles. In "Mr. Sludge, 'the Medium'" (1864) Sludge's turnings and twistings of self-justification, which always only get him deeper into guilt, are highly comic. Sludge is a despicable charlatan, but an amusing one who is almost likable. Bishop Blougram's discussions with Gigadibs, already mentioned, include arguments so successful that Gigadibs (for the wrong reasons!) packs up and goes to Australia. There is humor as well in "How It Strikes a Contemporary" (1855). The poet is "God's spy" writing "letters" back to his master, "the town's true master if the town but knew." Yet, the town, unconscious of the shabby poet's real power, insists on imagining him in a secret bower of bliss eating "his supper in a room / Blazing with lights, four Titians on the wall, / And twenty naked girls to change his plate!" The absurdity is double; it involves the townspeople's lack of perception of the truth on the one hand and their foolish fancyings on the other. There is even humor, or at least wit, in the very serious and sincere poem "One Word More" (1855), Browning's dedication of his volume *Men and Women* to his wife. To show his truest love the artist Raphael, whom one would expect to paint a picture, writes a poem; the poet Dante, on the other hand, paints a picture. But if there is wit here, how much more is there in "A Forgiveness" (1876), a poem that could easily have been cast into one of the most amusing and subtle stories of Henry James, for the title, like that of James's "The Pupil," is ironic. While he thought his wife loved her lover, the husband of the poem scorned her. It is only when she convinces him that she really loved him (her husband) and sinned only because he ignored her that his contempt turns to hatred. This hatred he satisfies by his vengeance on her lover. When he has thus through vengeance purged his hatred, he forgives her (hence the title), but only after he has killed her! The reasoning is grim, but its very subtlety makes it in one sense at least, like the turn-around subtlety of James's "The Beast in the Jungle," humorous.

A last element of humor in Browning is satire. Much of this, such as in his satire on Napoleon III in *Prince Hohenstiel-Schwangau* (1871) or that on Alfred Austin in "Pacchiarotto" (1876), is related to ideas and personages of his own time. At the same time, Browning is most successful when he satirizes the issues and movements of his own day by using people from the past to comment on them. The shift in time perspective is itself partially humorous; one does not expect a Renaissance Pope to be entering into the great Victorian controversy between the idolators of Euripides and the defenders of Aeschylus and Sophocles, for instance. The device is used with great skill in "The Epistle of Karshish the Arabian Physician" (1855), in which (though the ostensible date is within the lifetime of Lazarus, who was raised from the dead by Jesus) Browning subtly attacks nineteenth-century higher criticism and the Huxleyan faith in scientific evidence. The poem has, of course, an even larger theme—the justification of God's refusal to give man foreknowledge of heaven. Karshish's medical jargon, his view of Jesus as merely a skilled Nazarene physician who was accused of wizardry and died in a tumult some years before, his wholly scientific explanation of the "miraculous" raising of Lazarus, and even his explanation of the earthquake at the Crucifixion as prefiguring the death of his and his correspondent's old teacher are amusing in their refusal to admit the possibility of divine intervention—and as indirect commentary on Lévi Strauss and T.H. Huxley. The last few lines, in which the doubting Karshish doubts his doubt and catches a vision of the beauty of divine faith, turns the humor and satire into pathos and emotion.

Much the same method is used in "Cleon" (1855), in which Browning satirizes Victorian Hellenism, that Matthew Arnoldian faith in Greek culture as a guide to life. Cleon is the perfect Hellenist—writer, poet, philosopher, scientist, musician, sculptor, architect—but, ironically, he is still unhappy, for he sees that all of his accomplishments are useless if all end with death. And, with an odd echo of "Porphyria's Lover," if immortality were indeed a fact, surely Zeus would have sent some messenger to tell men so, but he has not. As for the Jew Paulus (St. Paul), to whom Cleon's patron Protos has written a letter, Cleon has only scorn for him and says that his "doctrine could be held by no sane man." One side of the joke is that Protos, because of his intellectual, cultural, and racial pride, will not see that the solution to his basic problem is right before his face. The other side is that this portrait of an ancient Greek cleverly satirizes the Arnoldians of Browning's own day. Similarly, in the amusing picture of the half-man Caliban in "Caliban on Setebos" (1864), Browning launches a double-pronged satiric attack on the proponents of Deistic "natural philosophy" and on the Calvinists. Caliban, the Darwinian "missing link," in entertainingly distorted third-person barbaric speech constructs by reasoning from nature a subtle though simple theology that reflects his own experiences, doubts, and fears. In its emphasis on fear of the jealous God Setebos, it also sounds very much like harsh Victorian Calvinism. It is funny to hear this grotesque brute-man in his rough jargon mouthing sophisticated religious ideas.

Perhaps the most stimulating of all of Browning's humor is his satirizing of his own doctrines and ideas by exaggerating them or putting them into the mouths of villains. "Porphyria's Lover" is one example. Bishop Blougram echoes many of Browning's basic ideas, but he does not mean them. Even the rascal Sludge is, like James Russell Lowell's Poe, three-fifths of him Browning and two-fifths sheer Sludge. Again, in *Fifine at the Fair* (1872), the villain Don Juan expresses many of Browning's own ideas in spite of being unmistakably a deep-dyed villain. The same technique is used in *The Inn Album* (1875). This highly amusing, quizzical self-satire, which one must watch carefully to catch, is certainly one of the most effective elements of Browning's art. Browning is often compared to Percy Bysshe Shelley, but he actually shares with another great Romantic poet, Lord Byron, a cardinal merit as a person and as an artist—the ability to laugh understandingly at himself.

Summary

Robert Browning is a great poet—a very powerful one, a very idealistic one, a very serious one. At times he is a quite didactic one, as in "Rabbi Ben Ezra" (1864) and "Abt Vogler" (1864). He is not a Henry Wadsworth Longfellow or Lord Tennyson or John Milton, for in the subjects, style, characterization, action, situations, ambiguity, construction, or thought of most of his best poems there is some element of humor, whether playfulness, wit, comedy, caricature, irony, self-satire, ambiguity, amusingly exaggerated melodrama, or the comic grotesque. In many other poems, where few or none of these qualities appear, the fundamental force of his art often arises from an artistry which, though not in itself humorous, is closely allied to humor. Thus, Browning is not only a great Victorian poet but also a great Victorian humorist.

Notes

1. In addition to *Pippa Passes* and *A Blot*, these were: *King Victor and King Charles* (1842), *Dramatic Lyrics* (1842), *The Return of the Druses* (1843), *Colombe's Birthday* (1844), *Dramatic Romances and Lyrics* (1845), and *Luria and A Soul's Tragedy* (1846).
2. *Balustion's Adventure* (1871), *Prince Hohenstiel-Schwangar* (1871), *Fifine at the Fair* (1872), *Red Cotton Night-Cap Country* (1873), *Aristophanes' Apology* (1875), *The Inn Album* (1875), *Pacchiarotto* (1875), *La Saisiaz* (1878), *Dramatic Idyls* (1879–1880), *Jocoseria* (1883), *Ferishtah's Fancies* (1884), and *Parleyings with Certain People of Importance* (1887).

3. In each instance throughout this article the poems mentioned to illustrate a particular kind of humor in Browning are only a few from many that could be cited. The date following each poem is that of the volume in which it was first published in full.

Selected Bibliography
Primary Sources

Collected Works and Letters
The Complete Works of Robert Browning. Ed. Charlotte Porter and Helen A. Clarke. 12 vols. New York: The Kelmscott Society, 1898. Florentine Edition.
The Works of Robert Browning. Ed. F.G. Kenyon. 10 vols. London: Smith, Elder, 1912. Centenary Edition.
The Complete Works of Robert Browning. Ed. Roma King et al. 6 vols. to date. Athens, OH and Waco, TX: Ohio University Press, 1969–.
The Poetical Works of Robert Browning. Ed. Ian Jack and Margaret Smith. 4 vols. to date. Oxford: Oxford University Press, 1982–.
The Brownings' Correspondence. Ed. Philip Kelley, et al. 10 vols. to date. Winfield, KS: Wedgestone Press, 1984–. This edition, in addition to hitherto unpublished letters, will eventually include almost all of the letters of Robert and Elizabeth Barrett Browning now scattered among many previously published collections.

Secondary Sources

Bibliographies and Handbooks
Broughton, L.N., C.S. Northrup, and Robert Pearsall. *Robert Browning: A Bibliography, 1830–1950*. Ithaca, NY: Cornell University Press, 1953; New York: B. Franklin, 1970. Standard bibliography of Browning's works.
Honan, Park. Chapter on Robert Browning in *The Victorian Poets: A Guide to Research*. Ed. Frederic E. Faverty. 2nd ed. Cambridge, MA: Harvard University Press, 1968.
Peterson, William. *Robert and Elizabeth Barrett Browning: An Annotated Bibliography 1951–1970*. New York: Browning Institute, 1974. Thorough and useful.

Drew, Philip. *An Annotated Critical Bibliography of Robert Browning*. London: Harvester, 1989.

DeVane, William Clyde. *A Browning Handbook*. 2nd ed. New York: Appleton, 1955. Still invaluable.

Biographies

Griffin, William Hall, and Harry Christopher Minchin. *The Life of Robert Browning*. London: Macmillan, 1910; rev. ed. 1938; Hamden, CT: Archon Books, 1966. Seminal biography.

Ward, Maisie. *Browning and His World*. 2 vols. New York: Holt, Rinehart, Winston, 1967–1969. Use with some caution.

Irvine, William, and Park Honan. *The Book, the Ring, and the Poet: A Biography of Robert Browning*. New York: McGraw Hill, 1974. The best modern biography.

Critical Studies (with special relevance to Browning's humor)

Altick, Richard D., and James F. Loucks II. *Browning's Roman Murder Story: A Reading of The Ring and the Book*. Chicago: University of Chicago Press, 1968.

Chesterton, G.K. *Robert Browning*. New York: Macmillan, 1916. Graceful and stimulating.

Cohen, J.M. *Robert Browning*. London: Longman, Green, 1952.

Fotheringham, James. *Studies in the Mind and Art of Robert Browning*. London: H. Marshall and Son, 1900. 4th ed., rev. See esp. Chap. XX: "Browning's Humor."

Jack, Ian. *Browning's Major Poetry*. Oxford: Clarendon, 1973.

King, Roma A., Jr. *The Bow and the Lyre: The Art of Robert Browning*. Ann Arbor: University of Michigan Press, 1964.

Langbaum, Robert B. *The Poetry of Experience: The Dramatic Monologue in Modern Literary Tradition*. New York: Random House, 1957.

Melchiori, Barbara. *Browning's Poetry of Reticence*. New York: Barnes & Noble, 1968.

Nichols, Ashton. "'Will Sprawl' in the 'Ugly Actual': The Positive Grotesque in Browning." *Victorian Poetry*, 21 (1983): 157–70.

Priestly, F.E.L. "Some Aspects of Browning's Irony." In *Browning's Mind and Art*. Ed.

Clarence Rupert Tracy. Edinburgh and London: Oliver and Boyd, 1968, pp. 123–42.

Raymond, William O. *The Infinite Moment, and Other Essays in Browning*. Toronto: University of Toronto Press, 1965.

Russell, Frances Theresa. *One Word More on Browning*. Stanford, CA: Stanford University Press, 1927. See esp. Chap. IV: "His Pungency and Wit."

Shaw, W. David. *The Dialectical Temper: The Rhetorical Art of Robert Browning*. Ithaca, NY: Cornell University Press, 1968.

Sullivan, Mary Rose. *Browning's Voices in The Ring and the Book*. Toronto: University of Toronto Press, 1969.

Symons, Arthur. *An Introduction to the Study of Browning*. London: J.M. Dent and Co., 1916.

Wolfe, Thomas P. "Browning's Comic Magician: Caliban's Psychology and the Reader's." *Studies in Browning and His Circle*, 6, 2 (1979): 7–24.

Curtis Dahl

Bunbury, Henry William

Born: Suffolk, 1750
Education: Westminster School and St. Catharine's Hall, Cambridge (no degree)
Marriage: Catherine Horneck, August, 1771; two children
Died: Keswick, May 7, 1811

Biography

Born in 1750 in Suffolk, Henry William Bunbury was the second son of the Reverend Sir William Bunbury, heir to properties in Barton and Mildenhall, Suffolk, which had formerly belonged to his powerful relations, the Hanmers. Henry William's brother, Sir Charles Bunbury, an avid sportsman and sometime politician, married the former paramour of King George III, Lady Sarah Lennox, in 1762 and became a member of Samuel Johnson's Literary Club in 1773 but is best known as the triumphal owner in both the 1801 Derby and Oaks— a double victory never before achieved and an indication of equine interests shared by Charles's more creative younger brother.

First attending school at Bury St. Edmunds near Mildenhall, Henry William continued his education at Westminster School and then at St. Catharine's Hall, Cambridge, but he never earned a university degree. His artistic skill and an attraction to the ludicrous (which was to imbue both his drawings and his literary efforts) had manifested themselves as early as his Westminster days, one adolescent product of which is an etching entitled "A Boy Riding upon a Pig." A portrait of Bunbury during his teens by his eventual friend and artistic admirer Sir Joshua Reynolds shows him already carrying his beloved sketchbook, and, by 1770 (a year spent, in part, studying drawing in Rome), he was exhibiting his work at the Royal Academy. With the support first of Reynolds and then of Benjamin West, he continued as an exhibitor during the next several decades. Although he aspired to no higher artistic rank than aristocratic dabbler, etchings of his works by Thomas Rowlandson and others achieved widespread popularity. Both David Garrick and Horace Walpole, who assembled the definitive collection of his graphic works, compared him—with the characteristic exaggeration of friendly encomium—to William Hogarth.

Bunbury's relatively less powerful and more good-humored satiric art is the product of a varied and fulfilling life spent among extraordinary people. In August 1771, Bunbury married the beautiful Catherine Horneck, with whom he had two sons. Catherine's close friend Oliver Goldsmith was a frequent guest at card parties held in the Bunburys' Great Barton home. Reynolds served as godfather to Bunbury's second son, Henry, the eventual heir to the Bunbury title, while the family Bible was given to Catherine by Johnson. Bunbury corresponded with Garrick and shared an amateur's passion for theatrical productions with Sir W. W. Wynne, at whose home Bunbury was often a guest. He was chosen equerry to the Duke and Duchess of York in 1787—a court appointment which gained him the acquaintance of, among others, Frances "Fanny" Burney—and he was also elected a militia officer by his West Suffolk neighbors.

Bunbury's life was not perpetually happy and prosperous, however. As second son, Henry William was not nearly as well off as his brother Charles, whose divorce from his wife Sarah, occurring as Henry William was beginning his own marriage, took seven years to settle and cost the Bunbury family several thousand pounds. His and Catherine's finances appear to have been adequate for a time despite this catastrophic drain on the Bunbury resources but by 1791 Henry William was in serious enough straits to be seeking Walpole's help in finding inexpensive living quarters. The deaths in 1798 of his elder son, Charles John, and in 1799 of his beloved Catherine deepened his troubles, and he sought a change of scene by moving to Keswick, where he continued his creative efforts despite an affection for brandy. There, on May 7, 1811, he died.

Literary Analysis

Bunbury's accomplishments as a humorist involve such an entanglement of literary and visual art that it becomes impossible to discuss one without including the other. Purely as a caricaturist, his primary interests were the foibles, posturings, and petty vanities of Continental and English social life, particularly but not exclusively within the fashionable circles of his direct experience. The Continental travel, which culminated in his short period of study in Rome, provided material for several of his graphic works, including "La Cuisine de la Poste" and "View on the Pont Neuf at Paris," engravings of which were produced from his designs by John Harris and placed on sale in 1771. In both works, Bunbury uses costume and accoutrement to overwhelm individual identity and suggest social station, with angular and sometimes shrunken faces functioning as pedestals for wigs and oversized hats, and thin shanks serving to display ostentatious hose, gargantuan boots, and other preposterous footwear. "Richmond Hill," engraved by William Dickinson and sold in 1782, pokes fun at the dandyism of the English, not only of dress but of horse and equipage.

Bridging the gap between the graphic and the literary productions are two extraordinary visual works of 1787, "A Long Minuet as Danced at Bath" and "The Propagation of a Lie." Sometimes cited as precursors of comic strip art, the two works are only a few inches high, but the former is seven feet long and the latter six feet. "A Long Minuet" portrays a series of elegantly dressed couples of comically diverse physique and physiognomy attempting, with varying degrees of success, to strike the graceful poses demanded by the dance. "The Propagation of a Lie" again presents a series of fashionably costumed and bewigged figures, but to the humor of facial expression and awkward pose Bunbury adds captions which, though they fail to achieve the continuity of modern comic strip dialogue, add narrative reality to this portrait of vacuous gossip.

Another work of 1787, *An Academy for Grown Horsemen*, which was followed by a 1791 sequel, *Annals of Horsemanship*, fully integrates words with illustrations and constitutes, along with its successor, a significant contribution to the humor of sport. The twelve plates of the former work and the sixteen plates of the latter, with titles such as "How to Be Run Away With," "How to Lose Your Way," and "How to Travel Upon Two Legs in a Frost," portray, with Bunbury's usual gift for the ludicrously awkward, the potential misadventures of the fashionable rider, while the commentary of the pseudonymous "Geoffrey Gambado, Esquire," adds an appropriate tone of pomposity to these instructions in the equine social graces. One vexing bibliographic problem is the extent to which Gambado is the creation of Bunbury and the extent to which Captain Francis Grose, named as collaborator by more than one source, assisted in Gambado's creation.

Of more direct literary interest than any of the above examples of Bunbury's satiric activities is his participation at the turn of the century in the production of the Gothic ballad parodies, individual poems and entire anthologies dedicated to belittling the horror ballads of Matthew Gregory ("Monk") Lewis, Robert Southey, Walter Scott, Samuel Taylor Coleridge, and others. Publication of the Gothic ballads themselves began in 1796 with the appearance of a half dozen translations and adaptations of Gottfried August Burger's "Lenore," the tale of a blasphemous bride carried off to the grave by the risen corpse of her paramour. The enthusiastic reception of the many versions of the poem, particularly of the masterful translation by William Taylor of Norwich, inspired emulation at the dawn of the British Romantic period by many of Britain's most promising young poets. Their efforts, in turn, drew a mocking reaction from a slew of parodists, prominently including Bunbury.

Bunbury enjoyed lampooning fashionable bad taste, particularly when the social elite were involved, and since two Members of Parliament (Lewis and John Thomas Stanley), another prominent socialite (William Robert Spencer), and the Poet-Laureate, Henry J. Pye, had translated or adapted Burger's poem, and since, further, a rival aristocratic amateur (Lady Diana Beauclerk) had illustrated one of the translations, Bunbury found the opportunity for satiric response irresistible. In addition, Bunbury's residence in the Lake District, in proximity to horror balladists Southey and Coleridge, may have helped to draw him into the satiric fray.

Never one to alienate the targets of his humor, Bunbury published one of his poems, "The Little Grey Man," in Lewis's *Tales of Wonder* (1801), the most prominent of the period's collections of horror poetry. The good-natured Lewis included a number of parodies in his collection, including some from his own pen. Bunbury's contribution is unique, however, in that it teeters so delicately between true horror and humorous excess that it becomes impossible to classify. The story is that of a young woman, distraught over the fate of her warrior lover and ambiguously threatened by an evil imp. This is very much in keeping with the ballads written in emulation of "Lenore," but the testy complaints of the imp while munching on a human heart and the blood-spattered deaths of the lovers amidst shrieking victims of execution suggest that Bunbury's intention was to reduce the Gothic ballad to absurdity by pushing it to its grotesque limits. Similarly indicating that Bunbury was playing with the conventions of the form for comic purposes is the poem's fifth stanza, a veritable compendium of Gothic cliches concluding with the bathetic entrance of what is ostensibly the poem's embodiment of ultimate evil:

> One evening so gloomy, when only the
>   owl
> (A tempest impending) would venture to
>   prowl;
> Mary-Ann, whose delight was in sadness
>   and gloom,
> By a newly made grave sat her down on
>   a tomb;
> But ere she to number her sorrows
>   began,
> Lo! out of the grave jump'd a Little Grey
>   Man!

The cumulative effect of this oddly mixed poem is to give the reader the impression that the Gothic ballad, with little assistance from the parodist, parodies itself.

Also mingled in content but more blatantly parodistic in purpose is *Tales of Terror* (1801), a volume that Bunbury is known to have illustrated and whose poetry, in whole or in part, he is likely, although not certain, to have written. The color illustrations, suggesting the macabre excesses of later pulp horror art, are the volume's most memorable feature. The frontispiece, set in a graveyard, shows several skeletal figures digging up and feasting on rotting corpses. A fold-out panel accompanying "The Wolf-King; or Little Red-Riding-Hood" depicts Grandmummy, her breasts exposed, being disemboweled by the wolf in bloody anatomical detail. A strategically displayed gin bottle, a spilling chamberpot, a teetering toilet chair, and a defecating bird add to the illustration's grotesque absurdity. A bit less extreme is the picture appended to "Grim, King of the Ghosts," which portrays Nancy eloping with the worm-eaten Grim while a nearby dog chews at a heart. Furthermore, lest the reader begin the volume unaware of its humorous intent, a skull in cap-and-bells grins from the title page, with a copy of Mother Goose propped before him.

The poetry quickly underlines the purpose of the humor. The book opens in heroic couplets with an "Introductory Dialogue" between the author and a friend. This friend urges the author to abandon the writing of tales for which "A nursery's praise shall be your best renown." The author replies that "Satire gives weapons for a nobler use" than killing "a *ghostly muse*":

> That task is *ours*: if I can augur well,
> Each day grows weaker her unheeded
>   spell,
> Her eager votaries shall fix her doom,
> And lay her spirit in Oblivion's tomb.

The friend agrees that the sort of monstrous poetic production then in fashion is not likely to last, or at least his hopes are that it will not. The author then claims that he himself is not a prey to fashion and attempts to defend his Gothic creations by saying that "the soul" requires a variety of pleasures and that it needs sometimes to turn "From classic brightness to Gothic gloom." After this, he concludes with a catalogue of Gothic delights.

The author's intention in *Tales of Terror*, to ridicule Gothic balladry, is then accomplished by allowing both the satiric spirit of "the friend" and the Gothic enthusiasm of "the author" free reign in the other poems of the book. The two urges, after all, are destructive of the "ghostly muse." Of the nineteen narratives in *Tales of Terror*, most, if taken out of context, could be assumed to be attempts at serious ballad-writing (serious enough, in fact, that Percy

and Elizabeth Shelley's *Original Poetry of Victor and Cazire* is partially plagiarized from the book's contents). Parts of the volume are very clearly parody, however, and the last poem, "The Mud-king, or Smedley's Ghost," in which "one of those hapless bards whose fates and fortunes are celebrated in the Dunciad" lures a moon-struck balladist to leap into the slime of Fleet Ditch, drives home the point that this is an attack in the tradition of Alexander Pope on poetic bad taste.

Tales of the Devil (1801), a work known definitely both to have been illustrated and written by Bunbury, continues the attack on the fashion for horror poetry. Declaring itself to be "From the Original Gibberish OF Professor LUMPWITZ, S.U.S. and C.A.C. IN THE UNIVERSITY OF SNORINGBERG," the volume begins with various allusions to "The Rime of the Ancient Mariner." The "Advertisement" states the hope that "the rage for phantoms" has "not entirely subsided in this Country" since Professor Lumpwitz has been put to "heavy expence . . . in purchasing the original of these Tales, from the Rider of a Bohemian Cheesemonger." The "Preludio" further echoes Coleridge's poem by narrating a framing encounter between a wandering "Stranger" and a poor "Fishmonger" who agrees, to the delight of the Stranger, to hear his "longest tale for a shilling." To this offer, the Stranger replies:

> Good luck to thee, brave Fish-monger,
> In sale of thine oysters and ling;
> "None ever would hear a tale of mine
>   out,
> "But I gave him five shil-ling;"

The Stranger then tells four tales rather than the Ancient Mariner's one, but they are tales which, like the work of Thomas Love Peacock, William Ainsworth, and Thomas Hood, explore the possibilities of grotesque humor beyond simple Gothic parody. "Earl Widgeon," "The Phantom of Funkingberg," "Simon Sniggle," and "The Hospodar," as well as their accompanying illustrations, create humorous effect largely by juxtaposing everyday experience, particularly as an aristocrat or a sportsman would know it, and the diabolical. The result, although marred by doggerel awkwardness, is grotesque comedy which can be enjoyed for its own sake as well as for its momentary satiric purpose.

B

Summary

Henry William Bunbury was an artist and writer of the late eighteenth and early nineteenth century notable for several comic achievements. His graphic art belittled the fashionable vanities of both England and the Continent, particularly sartorial dandyism, and earned him flattering comparisons to Hogarth. Two of his drawings, "A Long Minuet" and "The Propagation of a Lie," anticipated later comic strip art, while his books *An Academy for Grown Horsemen* and *Annals of Horsemanship* contributed to the humor of sport. Finally, through his work as Gothic ballad illustrator and parodist, particularly in *Tales of Terror* and *Tales of the Devil*, he prepared the way for later practitioners of grotesque humor.

Selected Bibliography
Primary Sources

Prose
An Academy for Grown Horsemen. London: W. Dickinson, 1787.
Annals of Horsemanship. London: W. Dickinson, 1791.

Poetry
Tales of Terror. London: W. Bulmer, 1801.
Tales of the Devil. Bury St. Edmunds: G. Ingram, 1801.

Secondary Sources

Articles and Books
Buss, Robert William. *English Graphic Satire and Its Relation to Different Styles of Painting, Sculpture, and Engraving: A Contribution to the History of the English School of Art.* London: Virtue & Company, 1874. Buss dedicates several pages to discussing Bunbury's style as a visual artist and to describing the techniques used by collaborators to transfer his designs to engraving plates.
Dobson, Austin. "Henry William Bunbury." In *The Dictionary of National Biography*, ed. Leslie Stephen and Sidney Lee. Vol. 3, pp. 267–68. 1917; London: Oxford University Press, 1950. Among the more complete biographical sketches.
Grego, Joseph. *Rowlandson the Caricaturist: A Selection from His Works, with Anecdotal Descriptions of His Famous Caricatures and a Sketch of His Life, Times,* *and Contemporaries.* 2 vols. London: Chatto and Windus, 1880. Includes important details about Bunbury's personal and professional life and quotes from his obituary in the *Gentleman's Magazine*.
Kunzle, David. *The Early Comic Strip: Narrative Strips and Picture Stories in the European Broadsheet from C. 1450 to 1825.* Berkeley: University of California Press, 1973. Kunzle reproduces "A Long Minuet" and "The Propagation of a Lie" and analyzes their importance to later comic strip art.
O'Connor, Robert H. "'The Rime of the Ancient Mariner' and *Tales of the Devil*: A Note." *The Wordsworth Circle*, 14, 2 (1984): 81–82. Describes the satiric attack on Coleridge in *Tales of the Devil* and presents evidence that Bunbury may have written all or part of *Tales of Terror*.
Paston, George. *Social Caricature in the Eighteenth Century.* 1905; New York: Benjamin Blom, 1968. A discussion of Bunbury's comic treatment of horsemanship and includes information about his other artistic endeavors, his professional and social standing, his aesthetic tastes, and his personality.
Riely, John C. "Horace Walpole and the Second Hogarth." *Eighteenth Century Studies*, 9, 1 (1975): 28–44. The best available study of Bunbury's career prior to the Gothic ballad parodies.

Dissertation
O'Connor, Robert H. "The Gothic Ballad in British Romantic Literature." Ph.D. dissertation, Bowling Green State University, 1979. An anthology and critical study of both the serious and the comic Gothic poetry of the late eighteenth and early nineteenth centuries, including certain of the works of Bunbury.

Robert H. O'Connor

Burnand, Francis Cowley

Born: London, November 29, 1836
Education: Eton, 1851–1854; Trinity College, Cambridge, 1854–1857
Marriage: Cecelia Victoria Ranoe, 1860; seven children; Rosina Paysan Jones, 1874; six children
Died: Ramsgate, April 21, 1917

Biography

Francis Cowley Burnand was born in London on November 29, 1836, the son of Emma Cowley and Francis Burnand, a stockbroker of Savoy-Swiss ancestry. Burnand began writing stage pieces while at Eton, which he attended from 1851 to 1854. After arriving at Trinity College, Cambridge in 1854, he was a founder of the Cambridge Amateur Dramatic Club (A.D.C.). He remained at Cambridge for three years. When his conversion to Roman Catholicism in 1858 ended his plans for a career in the Church of England, he entered the seminary of the Oblates of St. Charles. Despite Cardinal Manning's urging, Burnand soon decided that his true vocation was not the priesthood. So began his career as a writer for the stage. Although called to the Bar in 1862, he never seriously practiced. By then, he had made his mark as an inexhaustible source of comic writing.

Burnand authored over one hundred farces, burlesques, pantomimes, light musical pieces, and melodramas, including collaborations with both W.S. Gilbert and Arthur Sullivan. He also wrote for the comic periodical *Fun* until Mark Lemon, the founding editor of *Punch*, recruited him as a regular contributor in 1863. Welcomed to his first *Punch* dinner by William Makepeace Thackeray, who called him "the New Boy," Burnand served *Punch* for forty-three years—seventeen as a staff writer, then twenty-six more as editor.[1] He injected new life into *Punch*, making the 1880s one of the high points in the comic weekly's long history. His interest in the journal began fading in the 1890s, though, as he spent more and more time at home in Ramsgate, adding to his string of stage and literary pieces and working on his memoirs (which appeared as *Records and Reminiscences* in 1903). *Punch*'s foundations, however, were sturdy enough to uphold Burnand's own reputation as "the Commandant of the Household Brigade of British Mirth," and in 1902 he was knighted—the first time that a *Punch* writer had been so honored.[2]

Edged out of the editorship in 1906—the first time in *Punch* history that its publishers had successfully forced a change on the artistic side of the enterprise—Burnand loudly protested his forced retirement. He toured England with a lecture entitled "Nearly Fifty Years of *Punch*" to give his side of the story.

Burnand married twice—to Cecelia Victoria Ranoe during the winter quarter of 1860 in Chelsea, and to Rosina Paysan Jones in 1874—and was the father of thirteen children, seven by Cecelia (who died in 1870) and six with Rosina. Later in life, he edited the *Catholic Who's Who and Year Book*. He died in Ramsgate on April 21, 1917.

Literary Analysis

Burnand was a talented and prolific writer in genres which seldom rise above the momentarily amusing. His sentimental and melodramatic efforts for the stage are numbingly conventional. *The Deal Boatman* (1863), for instance, reproduces the Steerforth plot from *David Copperfield*—a wealthy and urbane youth runs off with the adopted daughter of a simple but noble boatman on the eve of her marriage to a decent but rugged sailor. In Burnand's hands, however, this story becomes a weepy trifle: the rake immediately marries the girl and when his uncle threatens to disinherit the happy couple, some timely discoveries reveal that the bride is the uncle's own long-lost daughter.

His comic theatrical works tend to be cheerfully tedious. Burnand is at his best when laughing at the stage conventions of his day. A work that he describes as "A Tragical, Comical, Demoniacal, and whatever-you-like-to-call-it Burlesque," *Alonzo the Brave; or, Faust and the Fair Imogene* is for the most part a mechanical parody of *Faust*, but it occasionally springs to life in passages like this chorus from a banqueting scene:

> Wine, oh! divine, oh! that is the thing
> An Operatic Chorus should sing,
> Wave o'er our heads the cups full of air,
> Action impossible if wine were there.
> Now then to laugh as our orders are,
> Ha, ha, ha, ha, ha, ha, ha, ha![3]

Burnand was most famous, however, for his ability to rattle off literally hundreds of pages of joking and wordplay. M.H. Spielmann called him "probably the most prolific punster" in an age addicted to the practice. Less kindly, another contemporary noted that, "When it comes to be a question of a volume of four hundred pages, with an average of ten puns to a page, the reader is likely to suffer from an indigestion."[4] The following passage from *The Frightful Hair; or Who Shot the Dog?* (1868), a travesty of Edward Bulwer-Lytton's *The Rightful Heir*, is typical Burnand:

Look down unblushing sun upon the
    fate
Of my departed poor canine companion,
Night draw they *cur-tain* o'er the *cur
    ta'en* from me,
Lest shrieking *cur-lews* week the poor
    cur lost.
He was my Tray for breakfast, lunch,
    and dinner,
The good dog Tray—*tray bon*—to cheer
    my life.
Together we made up the day's repast,
I bringing viands, he his little whine.
Upon his hinder legs he'd ask for bits,
For want taught him, like me to be a
    beggar.
He'd give his paw to me to signify
That he could feel for me, a *paw*
    relation.[5]

As such fooling suggests, Burnand's predictable comicalities and his fatal weakness for
puns make his longer works all but unreadable
today. Books like *The Incompleat Angler*
(1887) or *The Real Adventures of Robinson
Crusoe* (1893) deliver exactly what their titles
suggest and no more. In the latter parody, the
main character's real name is actually Jack
Robinson. He changes it on board ship for practical reasons—he is a blackmailer and a thief—
by adding a verse to a sea shanty:

No matter what weather,
We're jolly together
And jolly we've been, though it blew so,
This Cruise—you may bet it;
We'll never forget it—
We called it our Robinson Cruise, O![6]

The puns follow Crusoe onto his solitary
island. At one point, he concludes that "If there
were man-eating animals about, then I would
far rather have my clothes on than be found by
one of these beasts without them":

At all events there would be some chance
for escape with clothes on, as the most
determined and voracious man-eating
animal likes his food raw and rather objects to man dressed; whether well
dressed or badly dressed doesn't matter.[7]

The narrative jokes are just as broad and
labored. After rescuing supplies from his foundered ship, for instance, Crusoe spends his time
turning "a large sort of cupboard on wheels"
into "a first-rate bathing machine," and "a
screen covered with fancy pictures" into a "nice
compact bachelor's dining-room."[8] Burnand is
relentless at churning out such fun, but the
reader's delight fades and dies well before completing *Crusoe*'s 214 pages.

This same fondness for burlesque and
wordplay, however, made Burnand an inspired
choice for *Punch*. When extended only through
a paragraph or two, such joking can be lively
and clever, and in R.G.G. Price's opinion,
Burnand's youthful high spirits supplied a
needed shot of energy at a time when *Punch*
was losing its edge.[9] His first major contribution, *Mokeanna, or the White Witness* (1863),
was an inspired parody of the sensational fiction then appearing in the *London Journal*.
Lemon not only accepted Burnand's piece but
printed it in a mock-up of the *London Journal*
layout and even persuaded such notable artists
as Sir John Millais, "Phiz" (Hablot Knight
Browne), John Gilbert, and *Punch*'s own
Charles Keene and George du Maurier to lampoon their own original illustrations. Most of
Burnand's notable *Punch* writings were takeoffs
and parodies. The "Out of Town" series followed in *Punch*'s long tradition, started by Gilbert à Beckett, of legal burlesques. Burnand's
popular sendups of such writers as Ouida
and Victor Hugo also looked back to the
1840s—most notably to William Makepeace
Thackeray's "Novels by Eminent Hands."

Burnand's greatest *Punch* triumph, however, was somewhat atypical. Price has described the "Happy Thoughts" series as that
rare phenomenon, "a humorous classic in the
pages of *Punch* that lives on outside them."[10]
Begun in 1866, these short essays soon gained
a popularity which only Douglas Jerrold's
"Mrs. Caudle's Curtain Lectures" of the 1840s
had previously enjoyed. Arthur Prager aptly
describes the typical "Happy Thought" piece as
a "short chronicle of personal misadventure, the
little domestic disaster in which the first-person
narrator is the wretched victim of some embarrassment beyond his ability to control," and
though Prager's claim that "the narrator had
never before been the butt in humorous stories"
is overstated—Thackeray's early "Fat Contributor" series for *Punch* comes to mind—
Burnand's "absurd young man" was undeni-
ably an ancestor of the poor souls created by
Robert Benchley, S.J. Perelman, Stephen
Leacock, P.G. Wodehouse, generations of

Punch writers, and even Jack Benny and Woody Allen.[11] Due to popular demand, "More Happy Thoughts" followed. Single volume editions appeared, and Burnand gave "Happy Thoughts" public readings as well.

Though a far more prolific literary contributor than Lemon, Burnand also left his greatest mark on *Punch* by serving as its editor. Taking charge after the death of Tom Taylor in 1880, Burnand revitalized *Punch*. He was lucky enough to have inherited Keene, John Tenniel, and du Maurier, but he supplemented this outstanding artistic staff by first adding Harry Furniss and then over the years Phil May, E.T. Reed, and Bernard Partridge. On the writing side, Burnand enlisted Henry Lucy, whose "Essence of Parliament: The Diary of Toby, M.P." became one of *Punch*'s most popular features. E.J. Milliken, who created the popular cad 'Arry, and Owen Seaman, who eventually became *Punch*'s editor, were also Burnand recruits.

This new blood did not, however, impede Burnand's efforts to transform *Punch* into a national institution. The rough edges and feistiness which had marked the early years had by now all but disappeared. Burnand's self-proclaimed lack of political sympathies or antipathies allowed for a moderate amount of tolerance and debate, and on ethnic and religious issues *Punch* became far more polite. A Catholic himself, Burnand put an end to the anti-Catholic jokes. The Welsh and French jokes disappeared as well, and *Punch*'s anti-semitic strain and its fondness for ridiculing drunks survived only because some of the artists insisted on retaining these features.

Under Burnand, *Punch* became more comfortable and predictable. The du Maurier and Tenniel cuts appeared in the same places each week. A book review section was added, and so was a new gathering of comic bits called "Charivaria." During the 1880s, *Punch* sustained a tone which Prager has described as "scholarly, avuncular, mild and middle-aged," and which Price has called a dedication to leisure and fun.[12] The crowning event in this climb to total respectability was *Punch*'s fiftieth anniversary in 1891. The reprinting of complete library sets marked the occasion, and so in its way did the 1895 publication of Spielmann's massive hagiography, *The History of "Punch."*

Unfortunately, this same sense of achievement also led to complacency and stagnation. During the last sixteen years of his editorship, Burnand spent less and less time in the office, and by the turn of the century, *Punch* was essentially running itself. The regular contributors churned out their weekly assignments and occasionally left or died. New submissions were not encouraged. Burnand's own outside writing remained steady, but at *Punch* he served primarily as a gray eminence and master of ceremonies. Faced with this decline, Bradbury and Agnew (formerly Bradbury and Evans), *Punch*'s owners, repeatedly tried to nudge him out. As early as 1891, Lucy was offered the editorship but declined, and in 1903, F.H. Townshend became *Punch*'s first art director.

In 1906, Burnand unwillingly announced his retirement to his *Punch* readers. He wrote, lectured, and edited for another decade, but he severed all connections with the publication he had served for more than forty years.

Summary

Though a tireless writer for the stage, F.C. Burnand owes his literary reputation to his many years as a contributor and editor for *Punch*. His talent for punning, parody, and light comic essays was perfectly suited to the needs of England's premier comic weekly, and as its editor he gave it the second wind necessary to carry it into the twentieth century.

Notes

1. M.H. Spielmann, *The History of "Punch"* (New York: Cassell, 1895), p. 365.
2. *Ibid.*, p. 367.
3. *Alonzo the Brave*, p. 30.
4. M.H. Spielmann, *The History of "Punch"* (New York: Cassell, 1895) pp. 151, 366–67.
5. *The Frightful Hair*, p. 8.
6. *Crusoe*, p. 79.
7. *Ibid.*, p. 120.
8. *Ibid.*, p. 138.
9. R.G.G. Price, *A History of Punch* (London: Collins, 1957), p. 90.
10. *Ibid.*, p. 91.
11. Arthur Prager, *The Mahogany Tree: An Informal History of Punch* (New York: Hawthorn Books, 1979), p. 144.
12. Prager, 141; Price, 124.

Selected Bibliography

Primary Sources

Periodicals
Punch, or The London Charivari. February, 1863 to 1906.

Literary Works and Collections

Burnand was so prolific, and he gathered material so quickly into collections, that in 1893 Bradbury, Agnew, & Co., *Punch*'s owner and publisher, was advertising a "Selected Uniform Illustrated" edition of his writings. The following texts represent a sampling of his most popular works.

Happy Thoughts. London: Bradbury, Evans & Co., 1868.

The New History of Sandford and Merton. London: Bradbury, Evans & Co., 1872.

Strapmore: A Romance by Weeder. London: Bradbury, Agnew & Co., 1878.

The Incompleat Angler. London: Bradbury, Agnew & Co., 1887.

The Real Adventures of Robinson Crusoe. London: Bradbury, Agnew & Co., 1893.

Burnand also wrote over one hundred farces, burlesques, light musical pieces, pantomimes, and melodramas. Among the most notable are:

Alonzo the Brave; or, Faust and the Fair Imogene. London: Thomas Hailes Lacy, 18–. First performed at Cambridge in 1857.

Black-Eyed Susan. London: Strand, 1867. A parody of Douglas Jerrold's play.

Cox and Box, or the Long-Lost Brothers (1867). A lyric adaptation written with Arthur Sullivan of J. Maddison Morton's farce *Box and Cox*.

The Deal Boatman: A Serio-comic drama in Two Acts. London: T.H. Lacy, 18–. First performed September 21, 1863.

The Frightful Hair; or Who Shot the Dog? London: Phillips, 18–. First performed December 28, 1867.

Memoir

Records and Reminiscences, Personal and General. London: Methuen, 1903.

Secondary Sources

Books, Chapters in Books, and Articles

Howes, Craig. "*Punch*." In *The 1890s: An Encyclopedia of British Literature, Art, and Culture*, ed. G.A. Cevasco. New York: Garland, 1993, pp. 486–87.

Milne, A.A. "Francis Cowley Burnand." In *Dictionary of National Biography 1912–1921*, ed. H.W.C. Davis and J.R.H. Weaver. Oxford: Oxford University Press, 1927, pp. 77–78.

Prager, Arthur. *The Mahogany Tree: An Informal History of PUNCH*. New York: Hawthorn Books, 1979. Heavily anecdotal history from the beginnings to 1979. Illustrations, bibliography.

Price, R.G.G. *A History of PUNCH*. London: Collins, 1957. The best history and by a *Punch* contributor. Unlike Spielmann, Price is sharply evaluative, and even dismissive, of certain periods and contributors. Bibliography, some illustrations, very useful appendices on the origins of *Punch*, and on "Drawing and Reproduction," by Kenneth Bird.

Savory, Jerold J. "Punch." In *British Literary Magazines: The Victorian and Edwardian Age, 1837–1913*, ed. Alvin Sullivan. Westport, CT: Greenwood, 1984, pp. 325–29. Historical overview.

Speedie, Julie. "Burnand, Francis Cowley." In *The 1890s: An Encyclopedia of British Literature, Art, and Culture*, ed. G.A. Cevasco. New York: Garland, 1993, p. 88.

Spielmann, M.H. *The History of "Punch."* New York: Cassell, 1895. The most detailed source of information about *Punch*'s first fifty years. Heavily illustrated, with information about virtually every contributor. Its major weakness is Spielmann's genial and uncritical approval of almost everyone and everything connected with *Punch*.

Craig Howes

Burney, Frances "Fanny"

Born: King's Lynn, Norfolk, England, June 13, 1752
Education: no formal education
Marriage: Alexandre d'Arblay, July 1793; one son
Died: London, January 6, 1840

Biography

Frances Burney was the fourth of the six children of Charles Burney, the noted music historian, and his first wife, Esther Sleepe. Frances was born on June 13, 1752 at King's Lynn in Norfolk; her mother died when Frances was only ten years old. Subsequently her father married Mrs. Allen, a widow with three children, and Frances grew up in a very large household of talented and intelligent children. The eldest son, James, reached the rank of Rear Admiral in the navy after having served with Captain Cook; her second brother, Charles, became chaplain to George III. Both of Frances's sisters, Susan and Esther, were very accomplished in music and art; her half-sister Sarah joined Frances as a novelist, publishing four novels. The Burneys had moved to London in 1760, where Charles Burney's connections and his talents led to a circle of friends which included David Garrick, who probably introduced Frances to the delight of mimicry and role playing.

Frances was very shy and quiet as a child, especially around strangers. Her father thought of her as an unremarkable child who was "wholly unnoticed in the nursery for any talents or quickness of study." By the time she was eleven, she had been nicknamed "the old lady." She did not receive any formal education, but taught herself with the aid of her father's large and well-chosen library.

Her first novel, *Evelina, or, A Young Lady's Entrance into the World*, published anonymously in 1778, received great praise from the literary establishment including Samuel Johnson, who remarked that "there were passages in it that might do honor to Richardson"—a high compliment indeed from Dr. Johnson. After writing a satiric drama, *The Witlings* (1779), which her father persuaded her not to publish, Frances wrote a second, more serious, romantic novel, *Cecilia, or, Memoirs of an Heiress* (1782).

In 1786, Frances was offered the post of Second Keeper to the Robes of Queen Charlotte, a post that she accepted for economic and family reasons, despite her aversion to the position. She was not flattered by the prestige and resented the complete lack of privacy and independence which such a position required. Her father persuaded her to remain in the position for five years, during which time her only writings were some historical tragedies which were definitely inferior to the satire and humor of her earlier work.

Burney married the French emigre and former adjutant general of the Marquis de Lafayette, Alexandre d'Arblay, in July, 1793, against the wishes of her father. The action signaled a new kind of independence for Burney and her maturation beyond the diminutive "Fanny" of her father and Daddy Crisp, another mentor and father figure for her. During

her early married life, she wrote *Camilla, or, A Picture of Youth* (1796) to earn funds to support her husband and young son Alex. She also wrote comedies, but these were not performed.

In 1802, Frances followed her husband to France, where she remained for ten years and wrote little. In 1812, she returned to England and completed and published *The Wanderer, or, Female Difficulties* (1814), her fourth novel, to earn money to support her son's education at Cambridge University. After her father's death in 1814 and her husband's death in 1818, Burney wrote primarily memoirs and journals. She wrote no more fiction. The writing of the last twenty-five years of her life has a more somber, memorializing tone rather than the romantic and satiric tone of her earlier writing. Burney died in London on January 6, 1840.

Literary Analysis

There is some disagreement among critics about just how to describe Burney's modes of satire and humor, but there is general agreement that in those modes lie her greatest strengths as a writer. Earlier critics, such as Patricia M. Spacks, emphasize the insecurity of Fanny Burney and her fear of censure. Burney wrote in her journal, "The fear of doing wrong has been always the leading principle of my internal guidance."[1] In this regard it is important to note that Burney burned the manuscript of her first novel, the story of Caroline Evelyn, the mother of Evelina, because she felt that it was evidence of her irresistible drive to write, an activity unbecoming to a proper young woman. She felt guilt at any kind of self-display, and thus when she did publish *Evelina*, she published it anonymously. In one section of her journal Burney writes, "I would a thousand times rather forfeit my character as a writer than risk ridicule or censure as a female."[2]

Burney's first three novels are about young women who, with no mother to help them, must find their way in the world, a world both fascinating and frightening, one in which embarrassment is a constant threat. These novels follow a rather set plot line but their interest lies in the social comedy, the mimicry of absurd middle-class characters, and the farcical episodes. In the author's first and most popular novel, *Evelina, or, A Young Lady's Entrance into the World*, the heroine is the unacknowledged daughter of an English baronet; her mother died in childbirth, so she has been raised in the country by a guardian, the kind and other-worldly Mr. Villars. Evelina is taken to London by friends, where she meets her rude and egotistical grandmother Mme. Duval and her extremely vulgar British relatives. She is attracted to Lord Orville and courted by the unscrupulous Sir Clement Willoughby while trying to learn the intricate patterns of London society and frequently embarrassing herself or being embarrassed by her vulgar, middle-class relatives, the Branghtons.

Most of the positive women in the novel are quiet and unassuming; the aggressive behavior of Mme. Duval makes her an object of ridicule, especially in one scene in which she ends up in a ditch without her wig after the carriage has been overturned by Sir Clement and his friends pretending to be robbers. One minor character, however, Mrs. Selwyn, is an exception to these patterns. She is an outspoken woman who frequently puts the men in their places. Late in the novel three men are commenting on the proper qualities in women; Mrs. Selwyn answers them all. Lady Louisa, a shallow and silly woman, has been commenting on her weakness:

"But I'm a sad weak creature—don't you think I am, my Lord?"

"Oh, by no means," answered he, "your Ladyship is merely delicate—and devil take me if ever I had the least passion for an Amazon."

"I have the honor to be quite of your Lordship's opinion," said Mr. Lovel, looking maliciously at Mrs. Selwyn, "for I have an insuperable aversion to strength, either of body or mind, in a female."

"Faith, and so have I," said Mr. Coverley, "for egad I'd as soon see a woman chop wood, as hear her chop logic."

"So would every man in his senses," said Lord Merton; "for a woman wants nothing to recommend her but beauty and good nature; in every thing else she is either impertinent or unnatural. For my part, deuce take me if ever I wish to hear a word of sense from a woman as long as I live!"

"It has always been agreed," said Mrs. Selwyn, looking around her with the utmost contempt, "that no man ought to be connected with a woman whose understanding is superior to his own. Now I very much fear, that to accommodate all this good company, according to such a rule, would be utterly impractical, unless she should choose subjects from Swift's hospital of idiots." (*Evelina*, 361–62)

Many of the characters in the novel regard Mrs. Selwyn as a negative character, but readers love her and cheer as she "chops logic" with the men. There are many other humorous episodes in *Evelina*, as when a monkey is introduced as a relation, and the race between two old ladies. There is also the extravagant satire on middle-class values and speech.

The delighted and delightful response to the satire and comedy of *Evelina* encouraged Burney to write her comic play, *The Witlings*, which, unfortunately, is accessible only in manuscript. Margaret Doody, one of Burney's recent scholars, regards the play as a "real achievement" and highly unusual for any woman to write, especially the reticent Burney. Doody notes that "Comedy in particular was thought to require an unabashed knowledge of life and manners which it would ill become a lady to assume—it is a *bold* form" (Doody, 76–77). The play begins with milliners at work in a shop, an unusual setting, since women working was not a normal part of traditional drama. Burney satirizes the blue-stockings in a series of characters including Lady Smatter. Doody places these characters in a tradition which includes Jean Baptiste Molière's *Les femmes savantes*, William Congreve's Lady Froth in *The Double Dealer*, and John Gay's and Alexander Pope's Phoebe Clinket in *Three Hours After Marriage*. This satire includes Lady Smatter's comments: "I declare, if my pursuits were not made public, I should not have any at all, for where can be the pleasure of reading Books . . . if one is not to have the credit of talking of them?" (Doody, 80). Still, this adventuresome comic writer was not permitted to try her hand. Her father and Daddy Crisp disapproved; she must write literature more appropriate to a lady.

Charles Burney encouraged Frances to write another novel and she published *Cecilia, or, Memoirs of an Heiress*. This work is not as comic and satiric as *The Witlings* but returns to the more mixed mode of *Evelina*. In it she continues the satire on the anti-feminism of the eighteenth-century world; she also ridicules the shallow life and values of the party-goers. The authorial irony in this novel, especially in regard to a mother doting on an only son, is often seen as an influence on the authorial voice of Jane Austen. The reader of *Cecilia* is reminded of Austen's Mrs. Musgrove and her "large fat sighings" over the loss of her son in *Persuasion*. Frances's father still called her the "little Burney" and "Fannikin," but her voice was strong and her satiric comments on her world and its injustice rang true.

During her years as Second Keeper of the Robes for Queen Charlotte, when Burney did not write any fiction, she did write several dramatic tragedies, only one of which, *Edwy and Elgiva* (1790) was performed, and it was very unsuccessful. After her marriage to d'Arblay, she returned to fiction and published *Camilla, or, A Picture of Youth*. This novel was highly successful and provided her with the money that she needed for her family, but it does not have the social satire of the earlier works. Until recently most critics have viewed the plot as melodramatic. Several episodes in the novel support this reading: a seven-year-old child, Eugenia, Camilla's sister, is crippled for life; her father is sent to debtor's prison for his daughter's debts; ill and in despair, the heroine Camilla is finally rescued by Edgar; they are reconciled and married. But, more recent critics read the novel as a "festive" work, one full of irony and satire, especially regarding the idea that "women are mainly objects of moral and physical scrutiny" (Doody, 227). Doody also argues that the novel contains a pervasive "game-and-play motif." Judy Simons refers to the work as illustrating the "tension between conformist text and mutinous subtext" which Austen was to use so very well (95–96).

After *Camilla*, Burney returned to the writing of comedy. In a brief time she wrote three plays: *Love and Fashion* (1798–1799), which was to be performed at Covent Garden until Burney's authorship was revealed in the advertisements and her father again persuaded her to withdraw her work; *A Busy Day* (1800–1801); and *The Woman Hater* (1800–1801). *Love and Fashion*, as the title indicates, is a satire on the materialistic society and its emphasis on fashions, manners, and show.

A Busy Day is the most comic of the three dramas; it has the funniest and most light-hearted scenes of any of the three. Eliza Watts, the heroine of *A Busy Day*, is an heiress who has just returned from Italy. As in *Evelina*, Burney uses the contrast between the behavior and language of the well-bred young lady and that of the vulgar relations to provide much of the comedy. Eliza's modesty is completely misunderstood by her boorish relative, Miss Watts. For example, in one scene Miss Watts asks about Eliza's "lover" and entreats Eliza to bring him to see her:

> I want monstrously to see him. I intend, when you are married, you should *Shaproon* me everywhere, for I hate monstrously to go out with Ma! Don't you think Ma's monstrous mean? And Pa's so vulgar, you can't think how I'm ashamed of him. Do you know I was one day walking in the Park, with some young ladies I'd just made acquaintance with, quite the pelite sort, when all of a sudden I felt somebody twitch me by the elbow: so I screatched and called out, La, how impertinent! and when I turned round saying, do pray, Sir, be less free of you hands, who should I see but Pa.[3]

This statement reminds readers of *Evelina*'s absurd Branghtons and their insensitive and boorish language.

The Woman Hater uses the traditional comic plot stratagems of confused identities and problems with inheritance. Doody views the plot line as a variant of that in William Shakespeare's *The Tempest*. Mistaken identities, a confusion of fathers and daughters, provide the comic plot line. On a deeper level the play reveals the misogyny of the society and its tyranny. At one point Sir Roderick, the titular "woman-hater," says, "Why, what does a woman spend her life in? D'ye know? Doing nothing but mischief; talking nothing but nonsense, & listening to nothing but flattery! Sitting, with her two hands before her, all day long, to be waited on; & sighing & moping, because her noodle pate can't hit upon things to give trouble fast enough!" (*The Woman Hater*, 4, 16, 40). It is unfortunate that none of these plays was performed, but Frances could not deny her father's demands that her comedies remain unexposed to public scrutiny.

Burney's comic talents are not used very often in her final novel, *The Wanderer, or, Female Difficulties*. In this work Juliet is the most lonely but the most self-sufficient of Burney's heroines. The novel is the work of a mature woman, not a young girl. Ironically, *The Wanderer* was criticized for just that mature quality: "The Wanderer has the identical features of Evelina—but of Evelina grown old; the vivacity, the bloom, the elegance, 'the purple light of love' are vanished; the eyes are there, but they are dim; the cheek, but it is furrowed, the lips, but they are withered."[4] *The Wanderer* is a serious novel in which the writer examines the difficulties of being a woman in a world dominated by weak men. The critical response by male reviewers supports Burney's portrayal of those difficulties. Burney herself describes her heroine as "a being who had been cast upon herself; a female Robinson Crusoe, as unaided and unprotected, though in the midst of the world, as that imaginary hero in his uninhabited island."[5]

In addition to the works listed above, Burney was a prolific writer in several modes; she wrote twenty volumes of journals and letters and one biography, *Memoirs of Dr. Burney* (1832). *Evelina* and *Camilla* are currently her most widely known works, but recent feminist criticism has begun to focus attention on her journals, her comic plays, and *The Wanderer*.

Summary
As one critic suggests, modern readers should no longer address Burney by the diminutive "Fanny"; we should use the name that she chose to write under, "Frances." Frances Burney is much more than just a "cheerful little Augustan chatterbox."[6] She is a comic writer who, like Henry Fielding before her, mocks the superficiality, hypocrisy, and affectation of her society. She also, like Austen after her, underlines the difficulties of women struggling to please, to marry, and to survive with integrity in a society that permitted them few options. Furthermore, the ideas and episodes which she develops are conveyed through an intelligent, often humorous, and frequently ironic authorial voice.

Notes
1. Quoted in Patricia M. Spacks, *Imagining a Self: Autobiography and Novel in Eighteenth-Century England* (Cambridge, MA: Harvard University Press, 1976), p. 160.
2. Quoted in Judy Simons, *Fanny Burney* (Totowa, NJ: Barnes & Noble, 1987), p. 23.
3. Quoted in Simons, p. 132.
4. John Wilson Croker, *Quarterly Review*, 2 (April 1814), pp. 125–26.
5. Quoted in Margaret Doody, *Frances Burney: The Life in the Works* (New Brunswick, NJ: Rutgers University Press), p. 350.
6. Doody, p. 387.

Selected Bibliography
Primary Sources

Novels
Evelina, or, A Young Lady's Entrance into the World, 1778; New York: Norton, 1962; ed. Edward A. and Lillian D. Bloom, Oxford: Oxford University Press, 1982.
Cecilia, or, Memoirs of an Heiress, 1782.
Camilla, or, A Picture of Youth, 1796, ed. Edward A. Bloom and Lillian D. Bloom, Oxford: Oxford University Press, 1983.
The Wanderer, or, Female Difficulties, 1814.

Plays
The Witlings, 1779 (comedy)
Edwy and Elgiva, 1790 (tragedy performed unsuccessfully)
Hubert DeVere, 1790–1791 (tragedy)
The Siege of Pevensey, 1790–1791 (tragedy)
Love and Fashion, 1798–1799 (comedy)
A Busy Day, 1800–1701 (comedy)
The Woman Hater, 1800–1801 (comedy)

Memoirs, Journals, and Letters
Brief Reflections Relative to the Emigrant French Clergy, 1793.
"Narrative of the Illness and Death of General d'Arblay." 1823.
Memoirs of Dr. Burney, 1832.
The Journals and Letters of Fanny Burney. Ed. J. Hemlow et al. Oxford: Oxford University Press, 1972–1984.

Secondary Sources

Bibliographies
Gran, Joseph A. *Fanny Burney: An Annotated Bibliography.* New York: Garland, 1981.

Books
Adelstein, Michael. *Fanny Burney.* New York: Twayne, 1968. Adelstein charges Evelina and her author with snobbism; a rather conventional reading of Burney's works.

Doody, Margaret. *Frances Burney: The Life in the Works*. New Brunswick, NJ: Rutgers University Press, 1988. A serious and perceptive treatment of Burney's life, all of her works, and the connections between them.

Hemlow, Joyce. *The History of Fanny Burney*. Oxford, England: Oxford University Press, 1958. Important and thorough research on Burney's life and writings.

Simons, Judy. *Fanny Burney*. Totowa, NJ: Barnes & Noble, 1987. A brief but helpful analysis of Burney's works; especially good section on the heroines of the novels.

Straub, Kristina. *Divided Fictions: Fanny Burney and the Feminine Strategy*. Lexington, KY: University of Kentucky Press, 1987. Straub examines the tension that results from the novelist's sense of "female ephemerality."

Articles and Chapters of Books

Bloom, Lillian D. and Edward A. Bloom. "Fanny Burney's Novels: The Retreat from Wonder." *Novel: A Forum on Fiction*, 12 (1979): 215–35.

Croker, John Wilson. "The Wanderer; or Female Difficulties. By the author of Evelina, Cecilia and Camilla." *Quarterly Review*, 2 (April 1814): 123–30. Croker reviews *The Wanderer*.

Cutting, Rose Marie. "Defiant Women: The Growth of Feminism in Fanny Burney's Novels." *Studies in English Literature*, 17 (1977): 519–30.

Newton, Judith. *Women, Power and Subversion*. Athens, GA: University of Georgia Press, 1967, pp. 23–54. Good reading of *Evelina*.

Poovey, Mary. "Fathers and Daughters: The Traumas of Growing Up Female." *Women and Literature*, 2 (1982): 39–58. Analysis of Evelina's confrontation with her father—she views it as a revenge for the treatment that she has received.

Rogers, Katherine. "Fanny Burney: The Private Self and the Published Self." *International Journal of Women's Studies*, 7 (March-April 1984): 110–17. Rogers examines the reticence and passivity of Burney in her life and novels.

Skilton, David. "Sterne, Sentiment and Its Opponents." In *The English Novel:*

Defoe to the Victorians. Newton Abbot, England: David & Charles, 1977, pp. 45–59. "Fanny Burney was foremost among novelists of this period who refused to grant sentiment pre-eminence over reason."

Spacks, Patricia M. "Dynamics of Fear: Fanny Burney." In *Imagining a Self: Autobiography and Novel in Eighteenth-Century England*. Cambridge, MA: Harvard University Press, 1976, pp. 158–92. Spacks analyzes Burney's fear of censure and determination to please.

Martha Rainbolt

Burns, Robert

Born: Alloway, Scotland, January 25, 1759
Education: Sporadic until 1775
Marriage: Jean Armour, August 5, 1788; nine
*   children by Armour, four by other women*
Died: Dumfries, July 21, 1796

Biography

Robert Burns, the eldest child of William Burness (as the poet spelled his own name until he was twenty-eight) and Agnes Brown, was born in poverty on January 25, 1759, at Alloway in rural Ayrshire, and was never far from poverty during his entire life. His schooling was always spotty because he was often needed to help his father in the field. William Burness was a tenant farmer and Burns learned with his father and later on his own account that the annual rent must be paid, whether the soil was productive or not, and whether the crop was good or bad. He discovered early that in order to survive he must develop a shield against the buffetings of fate; part of that shield was humor. He learned to play hard, just as he learned to work hard. He was an outgoing person and a welcome guest after a day's work. According to contemporary reports, he was a brilliant conversationalist (one acquaintance said that as brilliant as was his poetry, his conversation was even better), at home with the highest or the lowest.

Burness held leases on farms, first at Mount Oliphant (1766–1777) and then at Lochlea (1777–1784); after their father's death Robert and his brother Gilbert rented Mossgield, where Gilbert remained until 1798.

Robert had an affair with Elizabeth Patton, a servant at the farm, which resulted in the birth of his first illegitimate child in 1785. By 1786,

Burns felt that there was no future for him in Scotland—Jean Armour, the girl whom he loved, was pregnant with twins, but her father would not allow the couple to marry—so Burns decided to emigrate to Jamaica. It is thought that he planned to take with him Mary (or Margaret) Campbell, but she died of a fever, leaving the poet with lifelong grief for the loss of his "Highland Mary."

For some years Burns's poems and songs had circulated in manuscript, and before his planned departure he was persuaded to publish them. On July 31, 1786, his *Poems, Chiefly in the Scottish Dialect* were issued from the press in Kilmarnock, and he became a celebrity almost overnight. Thus encouraged, he determined to go to Edinburgh to bring out an enlarged edition. The second edition (and a third one in London) appeared in 1787, but instead of the few weeks that he had expected to spend in Edinburgh, he spent over eighteen months there. Here he was entertained by the Edinburgh lierati and met Mrs. Agnes M'Lehose, with whom he had a short-lived but passionate love affair; he later immortalized her in these lines from "Ae Fond Kiss":

> Had we never lov'd sae kindly,
> Had we never lov'd sae blindly!
> Never met—or never parted,
> We had ne'er been broken-hearted.

By the time Burns left Edinburgh to take up the lease of a farm at Ellisland, not far from the port of Dumfries, he had finally married his beloved Jean when in February 1788 they contracted an irregular marriage (they lived together but had no marriage certificate), which was recognized by the church on August 5. He had nine children with Jean (he fathered four additional children by other women). As a precaution against the possible failure of his farm, Burns had taken instruction in the Excise, and before long he had himself appointed as an officer, riding an arduous 200 miles a week, as well as tending his farm. This turned out to be too much for him, and the farm, he found, was a bad bargain, so he transferred to port duty with the Excise in Dumfries. He was to spend the rest of his life there.

While in Edinburgh, Burns met James Johnson, a music engraver who was engaged in publishing Scottish songs. The poet agreed to help Johnson and he contributed three songs (of one hundred) to the first volume of *The Scots Mu-* *sical Museum,* which appeared in 1787. Johnson's intention was to publish all of the Scottish airs that he could find, adding words where needed. During Burns's lifetime, Johnson published volumes one through five; the sixth and last volume appeared in 1803. From Volume 2 on, Burns was the unnamed editor of the series, contributing songs for tunes for which there were no words, emending old words to make the songs more poetic, and writing new (but frequently quite similar) words for indecent songs. The project was to remain a constant interest to the poet, and in his last letter to Johnson, Burns prophesied, "your Publication will be the text book & standard of Scottish Song & Music." Burns was absolutely right.

A second song-writing project took up a good deal of the poet's time beginning in 1792 when he started supplying new and refurbished songs to George Thomson for his *Select Collection of Original Scotish* [sic] *Airs* which appeared between 1793 and 1818 in eight parts. Because most of Burns's letters to Thomson have survived, whereas many to Johnson do not appear to have survived, we know more about how Burns approached the task of gathering material from old collections of songs, chapbooks, and the oral tradition to supply texts for Thomson than we do about his relation with Johnson. The measure of the poet's enthusiasm for the project can be gauged by his reply to Thomson when asked how much he would charge: "As to any remuneration, you may think my Songs either *above*, or *below* price." Burns never took a penny for his contributions to the *Select Collection* or Johnson's *Museum.* Unlike Johnson, Thomson engaged well-known musicians to supply him with settings. Where Johnson published airs as they already existed, Thomson had composers arrange the airs anew; among those engaged were Joseph Haydn and Ludwig von Beethoven. Thomson must have been pleased to get Burns's work free, because we later see him haggling with Beethoven over the composer's fee per tune.

Though worn out by overwork and the legacy of doing a man's work as a boy, Burns remained active until the end, sending a last song to Thomson on July 12, 1796, just nine days before his death in Dumfries on July 21. Almost immediately elements of the Burns legend began to appear: he was called a drunkard, a fornicator, and in 1800 it was suggested by his official biographer, the medical doctor James Currie, that the poet had venereal disease, an accusation for which there is not a shred of evidence. Dozens of inferior poems were published as his, and tales of where he slept (and with whom) proliferated. There was a good side to this myth-making though. Almost no home in Scotland was without its copy of Burns's poems: in the thirty years that followed the lapse of copyright in 1802 there were 281 *editions* of the poet's complete works, not counting selections or books containing poems or songs of his. It is probable that at no time since then has some edition of the poet's work not been available.

Literary Analysis

Burns's humor derives from a double strain— that of the eighteenth-century Augustans, and a much older tradition going back to the Scottish Chaucerian poets, particularly William Dunbar and Robert Henryson. In this latter vein there were two eighteenth-century Scottish poets, Allan Ramsay and Robert Fergusson, both of whom played an important role in Burns's development as poet and humorist. With these masters as guides, he evolved into one of the greatest humorists of the English language. (I use the word "English" to denote both the language of England and that of Scotland; Scots is a dialect of the English language, although it differs greatly from the standard accepted in South-East England—Chaucer's English.)

Even in the first edition of his poems we see Burns the satirist fully formed. In the 1786 volume we find two of the poet's best-known poems, "To a Mouse" and "To a Mountain Daisy," written in the popular and typically Scottish verse form called "standard habbie." A companion piece demonstrates Burns's genius at unmasking hypocrisy—"To a Louse, On Seeing one on a Lady's Bonnet at Church":

> Ha! whare ye gaun, ye crowlan
> ferlie! [crawling wonder]
> Your impudence protects you sairly
> [indeed]. . .

Burns goes on to suggest that the louse will "dine but sparely, / On sic [such] a place." The louse should go elsewhere:

> Swith [off!], in some beggar's haffet
> squattle [temple squat];
> There ye may creep, and sprawl, and
> sprattle, [scramble]
> Wi' ither kindred, jumping cattle, [beasts]
> In shoals and nations; [families]

> Whare *horn* nor *bane* ne'er daur un-
> settle, [horn or bone comb]
> Your thick plantations.

The poet follows the louse's progress until it reaches the top of the lady's bonnet, with young Jenny still unaware of its presence, and he ends the poem with this admonition:

> O wad some Pow'r the giftie gie us
> *To see oursels as others see us*!
> It wad frae monie a blunder free us
> An' foolish notion:
> What airs in dress an' gait wad lea'e us,
> And ev'n Devotion!

The ability of the satirist to paint the particular in such a way that it serves to illuminate the general, as Burns has done in this pen-portrait, was to find its greatest achievement in the author's "Holy Willie's Prayer." The story behind the poem is that a friend of the poet's, Gavin Hamilton, was brought before the Kirk Session and eventually the Presbytery of Ayr for "unnecessary absences from church" (five times in two months), for "setting out on a journey . . . on the Sabbath," and for "habitual . . . neglect of family worship." To the consternation of the Kirk, and especially of William Fisher, one of the most fundamentalist of its elders, Hamilton was absolved. For some time there had been a struggle between the ultra-conservative faction, which believed implicitly in the doctrine of predestination and rigid adherence to the dictates of the Church of Scotland, and a more enlightened faction of the Church, with Fisher a staunch believer in the narrow interpretation of doctrine. Burns imagines him at prayer after the Hamilton case:

> O thou that in the heavens does dwell!
> Wha, as it pleases best thysel,
> Sends ane to heaven and ten to hell,
> A' for thy glory!
> And no for ony gude or ill
> They've done before thee.
> What was I, or my generation,
> That I should get such exaltation?
> When from my mother's womb I fell,
> Thou might hae plunged me deep in hell,
> To gnash my gooms [gums], and weep,
> and wail,
> In burning lakes,
> Yet I am here, a chosen sample,
> To shew thy grace is great and ample. . .

Holy Willie then catalogues his own sins, particularly those of drunkenness and fornication. But, in his self-revealed knowledge that he is one of God's elect, hence bound for Heaven, he turns the blame on God for his misdoings:

> Maybe thou lets this fleshly thorn
> Buffet they servant e'en and morn,
> Lest he o'er proud and high should turn,
> That he's sae gifted;
> If sae, thy hand maun [must] e'en be
> borne
> Until thou lift it.

But, for Robert Aiken (Hamilton's lawyer), who has brought God's elders to disgrace, making them the butt of laughter, Willie prays to God not to hear his supplication: "in thy day o' vengeance try him!" The poem ends with Willie's request to God that he be rewarded:

> But Lord, remember me and mine
> Wi' mercies temporal and divine!
> That I for grace and gear [wealth] may
> shine
> Excell'd by nane!
> And a' the glory shall be thine!
> Amen! Amen!

Thus, in what has been called the greatest short satire in the English language, Burns not only destroyed his target, but delivered what may have been the death-blow to the whole rigid idea of predestination as espoused by the fundamentalist wing of the Presbyterian Church in Scotland.

Burns took on the follies of his church in other satires too. The "Auld Lichts" (old lights) condemned the Revd. William McGill of Ayr for his book *The Death of Jesus Christ* (1786), which he was obliged to recant. In a splendid satire, "The Kirk's Alarm," Burns named most of the principals in the undignified debate which ensued, opening with the lines:

> Orthodox, Orthodox, who believe in
> John Knox,
> Let me sound an alarm to your
> conscience;
> A heretic blast has been blawn i' the
> West—
> That what is not Sense must be
> Nonsense, Orthodox,
> That what is not Sense must be
> Nonsense.

Among those taunted by Burns we find "Holy Will" again; this time he is accused of having "pilfer'd the alms o' the poor," and Burns says he should "swing in a rape [rope] for an hour." In the last stanza Burns turns his satire on himself:

> Poet Burns, Poet Burns, wi' your priest-
> skelping [bashing] turns,
> Why desert ye your auld native shire?
> Tho' your Muse is a gipsey, yet were she
> even tipsey,
> She could ca' us nae waur [worse] than
> we are, Poet Burns,
> She could ca' us nae waur than we are.

Burns never authorized the publication of "The Kirk's Alarm" because, although they were fighting a rearguard action, the Auld Lichts were not without influence.

Another quarrel which came under the writer's scrutiny was the disagreement between two ministers over their parish boundary, which gave rise to Burns's "The Twa Herds: or The Holy Tulzie" [quarrel]. The two ministers concerned were both Auld Lichts, and Burns begins the poem:

> O a' ye pious, godly Flocks
> Weel fed in pastures orthodox,
> Wha now will keep you frae the fox,
> Or worrying tykes? [dogs]. . .

As usual, Burns named names in this satire, including that of John Russell, one of the "herds," finishing up with his suggestion for a solution:

> Then Orthodoxy yet may prance,
> And Learning in a woody dance;
> [hangman's noose]
> And that curst cur ca'd Common Sense
> Wha bites sae sair,
> Be banish'd o'er the seas to France,
> Let him bark there.

In a lighter vein Burns satirized the Communion service, an annual affair held at Mauchline. "The Holy Fair" is a poem which owes a good deal to Robert Fergusson's "Hallow-Fair." Much of the work is given over to good-natured comic descriptions of the antics of the various invited preachers, including Russell:

> But now the Lord's ain trumpet touts,
> [sounds]

Till a' the hills are rairan, [roaring]
An' echos back return the shouts,
Black Russell is na spairan:
His piercin words, like highlan swords,
Divide the joints an' marrow;
His talk o' Hell, whare devils dwell,
Our vera 'sauls does harrow'
Wi' fright that day.

By no means, however, are all of those drawn to the Holy Fair penitents; Burns ends the poem with reference to those others:

There's some are fou o' *love divine*;
There's some are fou o' *brandy*;
An' monie jobs that day begin,
May end in *Houghmagandie* [fornica-
    tion]
Some ither day.

The author's political satires are only slightly less telling, although they are now somewhat dated. Among the best of them we count his election ballads.

As mentioned earlier, the last eight years of Burns's life were spent in writing songs rather than poems. One of the best-known of his songs is "The De'il's awa wi' th' Exciseman," written while he was a member of that service:

The deil cam fiddlin thro' the town,
And danc'd awa wi' th' Exciseman;
And ilka wife cries, auld Mahoun,
    [every; the Devil (Mahomet)]
I wish you luck o' the prize, man.

As a writer of songs, Burns is known for his tender and melancholy depiction of love, but he also wrote funny songs about the other side of that emotion. An example is "What can a Young Lassie do wi' an auld man?" when she has been forced to wed him. Her husband is always complaining, and Jenny herself complains, "O, dreary's the night wi' a crazy auld man!" Following the advice of her aunt she decides:

I'll cross him, and wrack him until I
    heartbreak him,
And then his auld brass will buy me a
    new pan.

Love is not always disinterested, as we see in the irony of "Hey for a Lass wi' a Tocher" [dowry]:

Your beauty's a flower, in the morning
    that blows,
And withers the faster the faster it
    grows;
But the rapturous charm o' the bonie
    green knowes, [knolls]
Ilk Spring they're new deckit wi' bonie
    white yowes. [each; ewes]

Although Burns had very friendly relationships with several physicians, he also included the medical profession in his satires. The subject of "Death and Doctor Hornbook" is John Wilson, schoolmaster at Tarbolton, who also thought of himself as something of an authority on medical matters. (The name satirizes the use of the hornbook as a teaching aid in Burns's day.) Following an old tradition, Burns has the persona of the poem meet Death on the road, in this case as he is weaving his way homeward after an evening of strong ale. Death quickly sets his mind at ease: he has not come for him, but to complain of Dr. Hornbook, who is taking away most of his trade. Death has a plan, though, as we see in the penultimate stanza:

But hark! I'll tell you of a plot,
Tho' dinna ye be speakin o't;
I'll nail the self-conceited Sot,
    As dead's a herrin:
Niest time we meet, I'll wad a groat,
    [next; wager; penny]
He gets his fairin'! [his deserts]

Just then the church bell sounds "Some wee, short hour ayont the *twall*" [beyond the twelve], and the narrator and Death part: "I took the way that pleas'd mysel, / And sae did *Death*."

Nothing else that Burns wrote can compare for sheer Rabelaisian abandon with "Love and Liberty—A Cantata," usually called "The Jolly Beggars." The work, consisting of 316 lines, was probably written in 1785, but Burns did not publish it during his lifetime. In fact, when asked about it by George Thomson (who published the work in 1818), Burns answered, "I have forgot the Cantata you allude to, as I kept no copy, & indeed did not know that it was in existence," a statement that may not be quite accurate. The scene of this bacchanalian revelry is Poosie Nansie's tavern in Mauchline where a group of vagabonds are met for a night of boisterous abandon. Each member comes forward to sing his or her song and then there

is a recitativo. A discharged soldier leaves the
company:

> I am a Son of Mars who have been in
>   many wars,
> And show my cuts and scars wherever I
>   come;
> This here was for a wench, and that
>   other in a trench,
> When welcoming the French at the
>   sound of the drum.

He is followed by his paramour, who characterizes herself thusly:

> I once was a Maid, tho' I cannot tell
>   when,
> And still my delight is in proper young
>   men:
> Some one of a troop of Dragoons was
>   my dadie,
> No wonder I'm fond of a Sodger Laddie.

The cantata ends with all singing a chorus about
how little they care for the niceties of life:

> A fig for those by law protected!
> Liberty's a glorious feast!
> Courts for Cowards were erected,
> Churches built to please the Priest.

There are precedents for "The Jolly Beggars," but none which can come close to Burns's
achievement. Matthew Arnold wrote that it had
"breadth, truth, and power which makes the
famous scene in Auerbach's cellar, of Goethe's
Faust, seem artificial and tame beside it, and
which are only matched by Shakespeare and
Aristophanes."

There is no comic tale of diablerie in the
English language to match Burns's "Tam o'
Shanter," the story of Tam getting drunk after
a market day at Ayr, while his wife Kate, who
knows how market days end up, stays at
home, "Gathering her brows like gathering
storm, / Nursing her wrath to keep it warm."
As the evening wears on, "The landlady and
Tam grew gracious, / Wi' favours, secret,
sweet, and precious." At the height of the
evening, we are told, "Kings may be blest, but
Tam was glorious, / O'er all the ills o' life victorious!"

Burns uses more than one voice in the
piece, such as his switch to pure English immediately after the lines quoted above:

> But pleasures are like poppies spread,
> You seize the flower, the bloom is shed;
> Or like the snow falls in the river,
> A moment white—then melts for ever;
> Or like the rainbow's lovely form
> Evanishing amid the storm.
> Nae man can tether time or tide;
> The hour approaches *Tam* maun ride. . .

Note how deftly Burns changes his poem from
standard English to broad Scots as he shifts
from commentary to the narrative. Having arrived at the ruins of Alloway Kirk, the insouciant Tam beholds a dance of supernatural beings
taking place:

> Warlocks and witches in a dance;
> There sat auld Nick, in shape o' beast;
>   [the Devil]
> A towzie tyke, black, grim, and large,
>   [shaggy dog]
> To gie them music was his charge:
> He screw'd the pipes and gart them
>   skirl. . . [made; scream]

The graves are open and their inhabitants have
come out: "As *Tammie* glowr'd [stared],
amaz'd, and curious, / The myrth and fun grew
fast and furious." Tam is particularly taken
with an attractive young dancer, and shouts out,
"Weel done, Cutty-sark!" [short skirt], whereupon the whole hellish legion takes off after
him. But, they had not counted on the mettle of
Tam's mare, Maggie, who was able to get completely across the keystone of a bridge (which
the supernatural pursuers could not cross) with
the exception of her tail which Cutty-sark
snatched, leaving the mare with nothing but a
stump for the rest of her life. Burns ends his
splendid performance warning his readers:

> Whene'er to drink you are inclin'd,
> Or cutty-sarks run in your mind,
> Think, ye may buy the joys o'er dear,
> Remember Tam o' Shanter's mare.

Even the warning is, of course, ironic; a mare's
tail would be a small price to pay for such an
evening of fun and adventure. Thus Burns
laughs at the entire concept of the story with a
moral, so dear to Scottish reformers.

I cannot conclude an essay on humor in
Burns without addressing the question of his
bawdy poems and songs. During his lifetime,
Burns made a collection of these and not long

after his death there appeared *The Merry Muses of Caledonia; A Collection of Favourite Scots Songs, Ancient and Modern* (1799). The words "ancient and modern" are accurate; several of the poems to be found in this first edition of *The Merry Muses* are indeed old; several were gleaned from oral sources.

The best of the bawdry written by or collected by Burns is humorous, some of it outrageously so. One of the political songs which Burns wrote (to the tune "The Campbells are Coming") was "When Princes and Prelates," composed shortly after Dumouriez had defeated Austria at Jemappes on November 6, 1792. The poem opens:

> When Princes and Prelates and het-
> headed zealots
> All Europe have set in a lowe, [flame]
> The poor man lies down, nor envies a
> crown,
> And comforts himself with a mowe.
> [fornication]
> When Brunswick's great Prince cam a
> cruising to France
> Republican billies to cowe, [fellows]
> Bauld Brunswick's great Prince wad hae
> shawn better sense,
> At hame with his Princess to mowe.

Burns closes the song with the suggestion that everyone have a bumper and toasts authority:

> Here's George our gude king and
> Charlotte his queen,
> And lang may they tak a gude mowe!

Burns also included religion in his bawdy songs, but without ever being offensive. In a highly amusing letter to Thomson, the poet wrote:

> Do you know a drole Scots song, more famous for its humour than delicacy, called, The grey goose & the gled? . . . the tune is positively an old Chant of the ROMISH CHURCH; which corrobrates (sic) the old tradition, that at the Reformation, the Reformers burlesqued much of the old Church Music with setting them to bawdy verses. As a farther proof; the common name for this song is, Cumnock Psalms. As there can be no harm in transcribing a stanza of a Psalm, I shall give you two or three . . .

> As I looked o'er yon castle wa',
> I spied a grey goose & a gled; [buzzard]
> They had a fecht between them twa,
> [struggle]
> And O, as their twa hurdies gade.
> [buttocks went]

After four more stanzas, Burns finished with the remark, "So much for the Psalmody of Cumnock," and Thomson annotated the letter, "Delicate psalmody indeed."

But if Burns has been censured by some for writing bawdy songs, he also "cleansed the mouth of Scotland" by rescuing many more songs from the oral tradition and writing decent words to them. Notable among these are the non-comic songs "Green Grow the Rashes, O" and particularly "John Anderson."

Burns's humor runs the gamut from erotic (both specific and suggestive), through political satire, religious satire (but never vicious satire), the bacchanalian, and on to songs which gently chide his fellow beings. There are few greater humorous poets in the English language than this humble Scottish author, of whom Ralph Waldo Emerson said: "He grew up in a rural district, speaking a patois unintelligible to all but natives, and he has made that Lowland Scotch a Doric dialect of fame. It is the only example in history of a language made classic by the genius of a single man." That genius is nowhere better displayed than in Burns's satires and humorous verse.

Summary

Robert Burns brings together two different literary strains of humor. The first of these draws upon early Scottish poets such as Dunbar, Henryson, and Douglas (from whose *Eneados* Burns took the epigraph for "Tam o' Shanter"). These poets were well versed in the classics, and there is a strain of Juvenalian satire in their poetry which we find echoed in that of Burns. He also drew upon the earthy humor of ballads and songs from the oral tradition. These, and the work of Laurence Sterne (he greatly admired *Tristram Shandy*) gave Burns the basis for his ribald humor, explicit and satisfying. Allan Ramsay and Robert Fergusson, who had themselves learned from the early Scottish "Makars," reinforced these influences but also showed Burns how earlier methods could be applied to contemporary situations.

The other strain in the satire of Burns is subtle and well-honed, deriving much from the poetry of Pope, who was one of the major influences on the poetry of the Scottish writer. From Pope he learned to portray the absurd as though it was sweet reason.

Burns learned his lessons well from these several masters, but it was his own genius which fashioned some of the greatest comic poems and songs in the language.

Selected Bibliography

Primary Sources

The Poems and Songs of Robert Burns. Ed. James Kinsley. 3 vols. Oxford: Clarendon Press, 1968. The standard reference edition, the first such to include the material from *The Merry Muses.* Contains the music for the songs, variant readings and commentary. A one-volume edition without the critical apparatus is available.

Secondary Sources

Carlyle, Thomas. "Robert Burns." Edinburgh: Ptd. for Constable & Co.: 1828. A review of John Gibson Lockhart's *Life of Robert Burns.* With unerring discernment Carlyle recognized the genius of Burns, although he accepted the tales of his failings somewhat uncritically. The essay remains one of the greatest ever written on the poet.

Crawford, Thomas. *Burns: A Study of the Poems and Songs.* Edinburgh and London: Oliver & Boyd, 1960. Concentrating on the poems and songs as literature, Crawford has produced the best critical study in the field. The work is based on exhaustive analysis of the works themselves, with significant attention to the background, both social and literary, that produced them.

Currie, James. *The Works of Robert Burns; with an Account of his Life, and a Criticism of his Writings. To which are Prefixed, some Observations on the Character and Condition of the Scottish Peasantry.* Liverpool: Printed by J. M'Creery; for T. Cadell, Jr., London; W. Creech, Edinburgh, 1800. 4 vols. Dr. James Currie, a Dumfries physician who had settled in Liverpool, edited the first collection of the poet's works. He obtained information from Burns's friends, and many of the poet's correspondents sent letters from Burns for Currie to pub-

lish. The Life which companied Burns's work was, by the editor's admission, written in such a way as not to offend anyone, and avoids controversy. Nevertheless, the biography remains a standard work; by 1820 it had gone through nine editions. Currie donated his profits to the poet's widow, enabling her to bring up her family and live out her life comfortably.

Daiches, David. *Robert Burns.* New York: Rinehart, n.d. [1950]. This study of Burns strikes a balance between readability and scholarship. The best all-around work on the poet.

Emerson, Ralph Waldo. *Celebration of the Hundredth Anniversary of the Birth of Robert Burns,* at the Boston Burns Club. January 25, 1859. Boston: Printed by H.W. Dutton and Son, 1859. One of the most sensitive assessments of Burns. Reprinted in Emerson's *Works.*

Fitzhugh, Robert T. *Robert Burns: The Man and the Poet.* Boston: Houghton Mifflin, 1970. In this work we find a tender and racy human being, a great poet who could stoop to writing petty epigrams, a man in whom all the contradictions are inconsequential when we wish finally to assess him as an artist.

Henley, William Ernest. *Burns: Life, Genius, Achievement.* Edinburgh: T.C. & E.C. Jack, and London: Whittaker 1898. This long essay was originally part of an edition of Burns's works, edited by Henley with Thomas F. Henderson. In his essay Henley debunked some ideas dear to Burns idolators and brought upon himself the wrath of many Scots. On the whole, it is a very good assessment of Burns and his work.

Lindsay, Maurice. *Robert Burns.* London: MacGibbon & Kee, 1954; 2nd ed. revised and enlarged, 1968. This is a popular, but by no means condescending, biography of Burns by a Scottish poet and prose writer who has a real feeling for the country and its writers.

McGuirk, Carol. *Robert Burns and the Sentimental Era.* Athens, GA: University of Georgia Press, 1985. A detailed examination of the poet's debt to eighteenth-century authors.

Roy, G. Ross. "The 'Sighan, Cantan, Grace-Proud Faces.'" *Scotia: American-Cana-*

dian Journal of Scottish Studies, 6 (1982): 26–40. The title comes from Burns's rhyming epistle "To the Rev. John M'Math, inclosing a copy of *Holy Willie's Prayer*, which he had requested" of 1785. The article is a study of Burns's Kirk satires.

Snyder, Franklyn Bliss. *The Life of Robert Burns*. New York: Macmillan, 1932. The first really scholarly and accurate life of the poet.

G. Ross Roy

Butler, Samuel

Born: Langar Rectory, Nottinghamshire, December 4, 1835
Education: Shrewsbury School, 1848–1854; St. John's College, Cambridge University, 1854–1858, First Class degree in Classical Tripos
Died: London, June 18, 1902

Biography

Born December 4, 1835, at Langar Rectory, Nottinghamshire, Samuel Butler was one of four children of the Reverend Thomas and Fanny Butler (a fifth child died in infancy). Samuel's childhood was spent austerely; in the atmosphere of the rectory affection was less important than piety, as Butler recorded in his posthumously published novel, *Ernest Pontifex, or The Way of All Flesh* (1903). Unhappy at home, he was no happier at Shrewsbury School (1848–1854). Only at St. John's College, Cambridge (1854–1858), where for the first time he had a room of his own and control over his own actions, did he express a sense of happiness. His isolation and demands for autonomy and privacy, as well as his uncompromising integrity and his contempt for authority and much of society, were to mark his difficult relationships with others throughout his life and were to cause the best of his writing to take the form of social satire.

Butler's family assumed that, following graduation from Cambridge with a First Class degree in the Classical Tripos, Samuel would be ordained into the Anglican clergy, but a period of social work in London shook Samuel's faith in the sacraments of the church, and he refused ordination. There followed a lengthy quarrel with his father over his future. Samuel wanted to study art; his father insisted upon a more practical course of action. Even-

tually, his father subsidized his emigration to New Zealand.

Butler arrived at Christchurch, New Zealand, when the settlement was no more than a decade old, and he became one of the pioneers who opened up the frontier to English settlement. His early explorations of the mountains led to his claiming land that he named Mesopotamia. Stocking his claim with sheep, he was to amass a fortune before his return to England, although much of his money was subsequently lost through the speculations of a banker and through his support of young Charles Paine Pauli, a dandy whom Butler met in 1863 and who exploited Butler's generosity until his death in 1897.

Butler and Pauli returned to England in 1864. Even though he supported Pauli, the novelist was rarely to see the other man in the years to come. Without him, Butler established a routine that would last until his death. He took quarters in Clifford's Inn where he would live (except for one business trip to Montreal and vacations on the Continent) until his last illness. He studied art at the South Kensington Museum and at Cary's and Heatherley's art schools, and though his art had been exhibited at the Royal Academy, he eventually gave up this study for his writing. Butler read at the British Museum, where he established three lasting friendships and two important relationships with employees. Miss Eliza Mary Ann Savage, whom he met at Heatherley's, edited and encouraged his writing until her death in 1885; Henry Festing Jones was a friend and companion until near the end of Butler's life and, after his death, was to be his most important early biographer. In the last months of Butler's life, R.A. Streatfeild, whom he had also met at the British Museum, became his primary adviser and was named his literary executor. For twenty years, Butler paid a pound a week to Lucie Dumas; their sexual arrangement lasted until her death in 1892. Fifteen years after meeting her, he told her his correct name and address. Left wealthy once more after his father's death, in 1887 Butler hired Alfred Cathie as valet, clerk, and general attendant. Apart from Pauli, these were the only significant personal relationships in his life.

Butler maintained this narrowly restricted life which he had chosen until 1901, when his health failed. Physicians disagreed, diagnosing either cancer or pernicious anemia. The author died in London on June 18, 1902. Following his funeral on June 21, his ashes were buried, the place unmarked, in the grounds of the crematorium at Woking.

Literary Analysis

Although there are flashes of wit even in Butler's most combative tracts, his reputation as a writer and humorist rests on four works: *Erewhon*, *Erewhon Revisited*, *Ernest Pontifex, or The Way of All Flesh*, and the notebooks that he kept from 1874 until his death (in 1912, Jones published the first selection as *The Note-Books of Samuel Butler*, and other editions followed). These four works have in common the writer's enjoyment of looking at authorities and conventions from an eccentric angle and thus seeing them as absurd, but *Erewhon* and *Erewhon Revisited* fit within the tradition of Utopian fiction, *Ernest Pontifex* is autobiographical, and the notebooks are made up of brief essays, aphorisms, and paragraphs containing witty insights.

However, these works are only part of an impressive body of writing. Butler had published articles while still a student at Cambridge, and he was to continue publication in the Christchurch *Press*. His writing increasingly reflected his interest in Charles Darwin's theory of evolution (as proposed in the *Origin of Species*, 1859), and in the relationship of man and technology. Butler's first major publication was edited by his father—*A First Year in Canterbury Settlement* (1863); he was to repudiate this travel essay, but it provided the early chapters of his important *Erewhon* some years later and it remains of interest to students of New Zealand history. In 1865, he published *The Evidence for the Resurrection of Jesus Christ* and, in 1873, *The Fair Haven*, the first a straightforward and the second a satiric attack on the evidences of the crucifixion and resurrection. (His father claimed that *The Fair Haven* caused the death of Samuel's mother, which may have caused the novelist to hold back *Ernest Pontifex* for posthumous publication.) These tracts are part of an extensive religious literature of the period.

Butler's first successful publication was *Erewhon*. It appeared anonymously in 1872 and was so much in demand that a second edition, slightly revised, was published later in the year. Edward Bulwer Lytton had published *The Coming Race* in the previous year, thus, apparently, leading to a rumor that this new Utopian tract was in the same vein and by the same author. Certainly, sales fell after *Erewhon* was identified as the work of an unknown.

Erewhon owes something to Butler's experiences in New Zealand and something, in its sardonic view of human affairs, to Jonathan Swift's *Gulliver's Travels* (1726). Like Swift's narrator, Butler's (unnamed in *Erewhon* but identified as Thomas Higgs in *Erewhon Revisited*) is sometimes a lucid observer of human follies and sometimes himself a fool, observed critically by beings who make more sense than he does. (His insistence upon keeping an English sabbath is perceived, for example, as a "fit of sulkiness."[1]) Of Butler's novels, *Erewhon* is the least structurally coherent. The first chapters, taken from his own pioneer experiences, with one exception lack humor until Higgs passes over the mountain range, daring to pass by some grotesque fallen statues that are generally interpreted as the Ten Commandments. The exception, in these early chapters, is Higgs's condescending treatment of his Maori companion Chowbok, whom Higgs is determined to convert, lecturing him by the fireside on "original sin, with which I was myself familiar, having been the grandson of an archdeacon by my mother's side."[2] His motive in converting Chowbok is to gain credit in heaven; for the Erewhonians, later, he has broader plans, since their conversion will entail selling them into slavery. Throughout the novel, Butler's treatment of Christianity is both satiric and bitter.

Much that follows Higgs's passage over the mountain range into Erewhon is conventional Utopian fiction—a young man finds a new world, is guided by an attractive young woman, discovers that world's follies and some of his own, and ultimately escapes. Here, however, the narration is frequently interrupted by tracts attributed to Erewhonian philosophers, either on the evolution of machinery or on the rights of animals and vegetables. Apart from the religious satire, the satire is directed at theories of evolution, of penality, of education, and of zealous reformers concerned with issues such as the rights of animals.

Once in Erewhon, Butler's attack upon the church is lighter and wittier. The Erewhonians' real religion is a kind of paganism, a worship of beauty, that offends the pietistic Higgs. The Erewhonians also revere Mrs. Ydgrund (the conventional figure of Mrs. Grundy, the voice of common sense). While these are the religious tenets that the Erewhonians follow, they preach the false religion of the Musical Banks, much as, in Butler's view, the English pay lip service on the sabbath to values they scorn the remainder of the week. The Erewhonians insist on regularly visiting these banks, where they make great show of depositing certain coins in hopes that there will be a return on their investment in some distant future. Like the English in the nineteenth century, the Erewhonians have attempted to renew these institutions by fixing their image while still ignoring their substance: "they had put fresh stained glass windows into all the banks . . . and repaired the buildings, and enlarged the organs; the presidents, moreover, had taken to riding in omnibuses and talking nicely to people in the streets."[3] Yet, even a church worker is offended when Higgs tries to pay him with the coin of the church instead of the currency used in everyday life. The satire on the English church is extensive and obvious.

In Erewhon criminals are hospitalized while victims of illness are imprisoned and harshly reprimanded by judges who severely punish them. A wry and bitter humor is gained by hearing a judge berate a patient for tuberculosis, but the comedy does not obscure Butler's serious point, that it is absurd to blame a man for being the product of his environment and heredity, whatever the result may be. It is not absurd to confine him away from society, Butler writes, or even to kill him if he is dangerous to those he lives among, but it is ridiculous to accompany this by lengthy lectures implying that all he has become is well within his control.

There is also a witty twist to the Erewhonian argument about the rights of animals. The Erewhonians abolished the slaughtering of animals for food; the immediate result was a wave of suicidal mania, which, "hitherto . . . confined exclusively to donkies, became alarmingly prevalent" among sheep and cattle which would "scent out a butcher's knife if there was one within a mile of them, and run right up against it if the butcher did not get it out of their way in time."[4] Eventually, an Erewhonian philosopher proves that vegetables, too, have their rights, leaving the Erewhonians free only to eat vegetation that has died a natural death. In the face of indigestion and near starvation, the Erewhonians had returned to a normal diet by the time of Higgs's appearance, having proven, primarily, the futility of legislating against the animal needs of man.

The lengthy "Book of the Machines" chapters, purportedly written by Erewhonian philosophers, are not intended for comedy but are the simplest working out of Butler's evolutionary theory, and there are witty twists to his conclusions that machines are simply part of human evolution so that a man with a shovel or a train is more highly evolved than a man who must work his garden with his hands or travel on his feet.

The amount of space given over to evolutionary theory in *Erewhon* points to what was virtually an obsession for almost two decades—Butler's quarrel with Darwin and with Darwinian theory. At first an admirer of Darwin, Butler later came to condemn Darwin's theory as arrogantly eliminating will, purpose, and intelligence from the world. Working along the same lines as his later contemporaries, George Bernard Shaw and Henri Bergson, Butler evolved his own theory. In his readings, Butler discovered how much Darwin had derived, without appropriate credit, from French thinker J.B. Lamarck, from his own grandfather Erasmus Darwin, and from others, and Butler attacked not just Darwin's theory but the man himself in an abrasive assault reminiscent of his attack upon his father and the church in its indictment of an authority that misuses its power. Butler developed both attack and theory in a series of lengthy volumes: *Evolution, Old and New* (1879), in which he compares Darwin's theories with those of earlier thinkers; *Unconscious Memory* (1880), in which he develops a theory of unconscious memory inherited from ancestors as the basis of evolution; *Luck or Cunning?* (1887), in which he opposes his theory to that of Darwin; and in the series of 1879 *Examiner* articles "God the Known and God the Unknown," in which he explores the theological implications of his theory. While these volumes remain important to those interested in the history of ideas in the late Victorian period, they are virtually unreadable by others today, and the abrasive tone of Butler's attack did little to win admirers in his own time.

After about 1880, Butler's thought took new directions. *Alps and Sanctuaries* (1881) and *Ex Voto* (1888) were appreciations of the native religious art of Italy. In the 1890s, he published an oratorio, a cantata, and other musical works, and he began work on English translations of the *Iliad* and the *Odyssey*, attempting to reduce the poetic translations of his period to the everyday English of ordinary men and women. His translation of the *Iliad* appeared in 1898 and of the *Odyssey* in 1900, and this work was said to have influenced the writing of James Joyce.[5] Butler's study led him to conclude that the *Odyssey* had been written by a woman, and his work *The Authoress of the Odyssey* appeared in 1897; it influenced poet Robert Graves. Butler's last scholarly preoccupation was with William Shakespeare's sonnets; he identified the object of the sonnets as a Mr. W.H. in *Shakespeare's Sonnets Reconsidered* (1899). He wrote a sympathetic biography of his own grandfather in *The Life and Letters of Dr. Samuel Butler* (1896); the older Butler had once been headmaster of Shrewsbury School but had died when Samuel was still an infant.

At the end of his life, Butler returned to the novel form, for which he will remain best known. *Erewhon Revisited Twenty Years Later* appeared in 1901; *Ernest Pontifex, or The Way of All Flesh* in 1903, seriously edited by literary executor R.A. Streatfeild; in 1964, editor Daniel F. Howard produced Butler's own version.

Erewhon Revisited is both a more coherent narrative and more wickedly humorous than *Erewhon*. The primary satire remains organized religion. In *Erewhon*, Higgs finally escapes the country in a balloon, taking with him Arowhena, whom he marries in England, and intending to return to enslave the Erewhonians in the name of Christianity. When he does return, however, he is a mellower man and is horrified to learn what the Erewhonians have created in his name. The balloon has vanished from Erewhonian mythology; instead, priests describe Higgs and "his earthly bride on their heavenward journey, in a chariot drawn by four black and white horses—which, however, Professor Hanky had positively affirmed to have been only storks,"[6] for Erewhon is now oppressed by priests and scholars, represented by such figures as Professors Hanky and Panky. Higgs is expected to return to judge the wicked. The calendar has been changed; a new era begins with Higgs's ascension, and Higgs is worshipped as the Sunchild. Alleged droppings from the horses are preserved in reliquaries, and on holidays children buy sweets shaped as horses' droppings. Then there is Yram, daughter of Higgs's jailor in Erewhon. When Higgs took the young society girl Arowhena to England, he left Yram pregnant. She later bore a son who was taught that he had two fathers, one on earth (the man whom Yram married) and one in heaven. Despite

Butler's denials, the ridicule of Christianity is again unmistakable.

Satire mingles with evolutionary theory and bitterness in *Ernest Pontifex*. In a working out of his evolutionary theory in the early chapters, Butler shows how young Ernest recapitulates the characteristics of his ancestors. Once past these chapters, Butler shows how the child's promising character is deformed by parents, religion, and education. Characters are portrayed in broad satiric brushstrokes; Theobald and Christina, young Ernest's parents, are caricatures of religious priggishness and self interest disguised as pious zeal. Contemplating martyrdom, Christina exclaims that "We, dearest Theobald . . . will ever be faithful. We will stand firm and support one another even in the hour of death itself." Turning her eyes to heaven, she prays, "Oh Lord . . . spare my Theobald, or grant that he may be beheaded."[7] Ernest is not merely crippled by his education, he is left so ignorant as to be unfit for earning a living and for understanding such practical matters as sex. He commits a witless assault on a good woman because he cannot distinguish her from a "bad" one, and he is sentenced to prison. In this novel, which was among the first to overtly debunk the Victorian verities of hearth and education, there are the seeds of much modern social criticism; the novel influenced such writers as Joyce, Virginia Woolf, E.M. Forster, and Aldous Huxley.

Butler's notebooks are the jottings of a quarter of a century. The writer's wit sparkles more spontaneously here than anywhere else. Parts have been published; the complete six volumes are in the Butler Collection of the Chapin Library, Williamstown, Massachusetts, with copies in the British Library and the library of St. John's College, Cambridge. These notebooks include autobiographical materials and short essays, but their best features are the pure aphorisms. For example, Butler writes: "Life is the art of drawing sufficient conclusions from insufficient premises"[8]; "All progress is based upon a universal innate desire on the part of every organism to live beyond its income"[9]; "Our ideas are for the most part like bad sixpences, and we spend our lives trying to pass them on one another"[10]; "Death is only a larger kind of going abroad."[11]

Summary

Samuel Butler is among the most influential writers of the late Victorian period. His attitudes reflect not the age in which he lived but the age that would follow him. He was among the first to celebrate rather than to decry the loss of faith in church, home, and family. He made respectable the debunking of all three. In all of his writings he extols the values and language of everyday—even in his translations of the *Iliad* and *Odyssey*—at the expense of the pretentious and the pedantic. In *Erewhon* and *Erewhon Revisited*, in *Ernest Pontifex, or The Way of All Flesh* and the notebooks, he celebrates the end of Victorian verities and the advent of modernism, with its disjunctures, materialism, and change. Even in his most difficult writings—his works on evolution—he is an important source for an understanding of changing religious thought and the battle to reconcile evolution and faith.

Notes

1. Samuel Butler, *Erewhon, or Over the Range* and *Erewhon Revisited Twenty Years Later* (New York: Random House, 1955), p. 69.
2. *Ibid.*, p. 35.
3. *Ibid.*, p. 145.
4. *Ibid.*, p. 266.
5. Peter Raby, *Samuel Butler: A Biography* (London: Hogarth, 1991), p. 264.
6. Butler, p. 368.
7. Butler, *Ernest Pontifex, or The Way of All Flesh*, ed. Daniel F. Howard (Boston: Houghton Mifflin, 1964), p. 48.
8. Butler, *Samuel Butler's Note Books*, ed. Geoffrey Keynes and Brian Hill (New York: Dutton, 1951), p. 222.
9. *Ibid.*, p. 191.
10. *Ibid.*, p. 60.
11. *Ibid.*, p. 144.

Selected Bibliography
Primary Sources

Collected Edition
The Collected Works of Samuel Butler. Ed. Henry Festing Jones and A.T. Bartholomew. London: Jonathan Cape, 1923–1926. 20 vols. "Shrewsbury Edition."

Novels
Erewhon, or Over the Range. London: Trübner, 1872. Rev. ed. London: Grant Richards, 1901. Ed. Hans-Peter Vreur and Daniel F. Howard. Newark: University of Delaware Press, 1981. Well annotated edition, but based on the 1872 text, with Butler's substantial 1901 changes in an appendix.

Erewhon and Erewhon Revisited. Ed. Lewis Mumford. New York: Random House, 1925. Modern Library edition with 1901 text of *Erewhon*.

Ernest Pontifex, or The Way of All Flesh. London: Grant Richards, 1903. Ed. Daniel F. Howard. Boston: Houghton, 1964. Restores text to Butler's original without Streatfeild emendations.

Correspondence
The Correspondence of Samuel Butler with His Sister May. Ed. Daniel F. Howard. Berkeley: University of California Press, 1962.

The Family Letters of Samuel Butler. Ed. Arnold Silver. Stanford: Stanford University Press, 1962.

Letters Between Samuel Butler and Miss E.M.A. Savage, 1871–1885. Ed. Geoffrey Keynes and Brian Hill. London: Jonathan Cape, 1935.

Notebooks
Further Extracts from the Note-Books of Samuel Butler. Ed. A.T. Bartholomew. London: Jonathan Cape, 1934.

The Note-Books of Samuel Butler. Ed. Henry Festing Jones. London: Fifield, 1912.

The Note-Books of Samuel Butler, Volume I (1874–1883). Ed. Hans-Peter Breur. Lanham, MD: University Press of America, 1984.

Samuel Butler's Note Books. Ed. Geoffrey Keynes and Brian Hill. London: Jonathan Cape, and New York: Dutton, 1951.

Secondary Sources

Bibliographies
Bethke, Frederick John. *Three Victorian Travel Writers: An Annotated Bibliography of Criticism on Mrs. Frances Milton Trollope, Samuel Butler, and Robert Louis Stevenson*. Boston: G.K. Hall, 1971. Contains some material on Butler's place in travel and New Zealand literature not included in Breur (below).

Breur, Hans-Peter, and Roger Parsell. *Samuel Butler: An Annotated Bibliography of Writings About Him*. New York: Garland, 1990. Most complete compilation of secondary sources.

Harkness, Stanley. *The Career of Samuel Butler (1835–1901): A Bibliography*. London: Bodley Head, 1955. Complete chronology of works by Butler up to Shrewsbury edition.

Biographies

Holt, Lee F. *Samuel Butler*. Boston: Twayne, 1989. Rev. ed. Excellent introductory study and bibliography.

Jones, Henry Festing. *Samuel Butler Author of Erewhon (1835–1901): A Memoir*. 2 vols. London: Macmillan, 1919; New York: Octagon Books, 1968. Detailed, sometimes undigested mass of information but still essential for serious Butler study.

Raby, Peter. *Samuel Butler: A Biography*. London: Hogarth, 1991. Excellent and readable study.

Stillman, Clara G. *Samuel Butler, a Mid-Victorian Modern*. New York: Viking Press, 1932. Good general discussion.

Criticism

Bissell, Clyde T. "A Study of *The Way of All Flesh*." In *Nineteenth Century Studies*. Ed. Herbert Davis. Ithaca: Cornell University Press, 1940. Bissell shows the relationship of the novel and Butler's evolutionary theories.

Buckley, Jerome Hamilton. *Season of Youth: The Bildungsroman from Dickens to Golding*. Cambridge, MA: Harvard University Press, 1974. The place of *Ernest Pontifex, or The Way of All Flesh* in the tradition of novels about growing up is discussed.

Dawson, Carl. *Prophets of Past Time: Seven British Autobiographers, 1880–1914*. Baltimore: Johns Hopkins University Press, 1988. Difficult but valuable study of Butler's theories and *Ernest Pontifex, or The Way of All Flesh*.

Fleishman, Avrom. *Figures of Autobiography*. Berkeley: University of California Press, 1983. *Ernest Pontifex, or The Way of All Flesh* as autobiography.

Garnett, R.S. *Samuel Butler and His Family Relations*. London: Dent, 1926. A study of Butler's depiction of his family and compares it with information from other sources.

Jeffers, Thomas L. *Samuel Butler Revalued*. University Park: University of Pennsylvania Press, 1981. Relates Butler's thought to that of such figures as Locke and Hume.

Knoepflmacher, U.C. *Religious Humanism and the Victorian Novel: George Eliot, Walter Pater, and Samuel Butler*. Princeton: Princeton University Press, 1965. Butler compared Butler with other Victorian doubters.

Maison, Margaret M. *The Victorian Vision: Studies in the Religious Novel*. New York: Sheed, 1961. Butler's *Fair Haven* and *Ernest Pontifex* placed within tradition of religious fiction of the time.

Willey, Basil. *Darwin and Butler: Two Versions of Evolution*. New York: Harcourt Brace Jovanovich, 1960. Lucid introduction to a complex controversy.

Betty Richardson

Byron, Lord George Gordon

Born: London, January 22, 1788
Education: Harrow, 1801–1804; Trinity College, Cambridge, 1805–1808, M.A.
Married: Annabella Milbanke, January 2, 1815; one child
Died: Missolonghi, Greece, April 19, 1824

Biography

Byron's mother, Catherine Gordon Byron, named him George Gordon at his christening; he ought to have been "George Byron," but his father, Captain John Byron, was nowhere to be found when the child was born in London on January 22, 1788, and George's mother doubted that the father would return. The Gordons were a Scottish family, and Catherine took the child back to Edinburgh, Scotland, and later to Aberdeen. Both families were of noble lineage, but Captain Byron had spent the little money that he inherited and, after marrying Catherine, spent hers too. As a result, Catherine had to borrow heavily to support herself and her son for the next ten years. Then in 1798, deaths in the Byron family put the boy in line to become the sixth English baron of that name. From that time on, no one called him George; friends, lovers, strangers, even his mother called him simply "Byron" (or, more formally, "Lord Byron").

With the title, he inherited Newstead (the family estate in England), other heavily mortgaged properties, and the accumulated debt of two generations of profligate and unproductive Byrons. Still borrowing against potential future income, Byron and his mother moved to England, living sometimes in the decaying abbey on their property, more often in the town nearby. Byron attended the elite public school Harrow from the ages of thirteen to sixteen (1801–1804). There he studied Greek with some small success and read widely on his own. Equally important, he learned to be at ease among the boys from aristocratic families and he began to come to terms with a disability that he was born with, a painful clubbed foot that caused him to limp. He also began to write poetry.

He attended Trinity College at Cambridge University (1805–1808), where, though he continued reading on his own, he learned almost nothing systematic from his classes; he was too much involved in living the life of a young nobleman—socializing, drinking, gambling, and indulging in sexual affairs (including at least one liaison with a male friend). Among his early published writings, two efforts attracted notice: a book of lyrics, *Hours of Idleness* (1807), and a satire, "English Bards and Scotch Reviewers" (1808). After leaving Cambridge with an M.A. in 1808, Byron embarked on a two-year tour of Europe and found that he felt much at home there, particularly in the eastern Mediterranean countries of Turkey, Greece, and Albania.

On his return to England in 1811, he polished and published the manuscript that he had begun on his travels, *Childe Harold's Pilgrimage*—a kind of moody travelogue: scenes of Europe described by a melancholy narrator. It was a great and immediate success, and for the next four years Byron continued to publish astonishingly popular poetry, becoming one of the most famous men in England. He spoke on political issues before the House of Lords (as was his right as a nobleman); he was on the management committee of the new Drury Lane theater. He attended all of the most important events, and was seen with the best, and worst, people. He carved out for himself a reputation as a social and literary lion and a seeker of pleasure, toying with scandal, and actually creating considerable scandal with Lady Caroline Lamb, a married woman whose indiscretions in their affair made it the talk of London high society.

In the midst of all of this, Byron established closer contact with his half-sister Augusta, now married and the mother of several children.

Augusta had been raised by the family of her mother (the first wife of John Byron) and had corresponded with Byron occasionally over the years; they had seen each other at least a few times. But when they met in London in 1813 for the first time in three years, they were charmed by each other's company. They fell in love; sometime during the summer of 1813, they entered into a sexual relationship.

His friends had often counseled him to marry and settle himself; such public scandals as seemed to follow Byron were bad for his reputation, his literary celebrity notwithstanding. An established literary career, any career, could easily be destroyed if one went too far. Now, mortified at his behavior with Augusta and fearful that if the truth were known he would be ruined, Byron fixed upon one Annabella Milbanke, a woman on the fringe of his social circle. He joked with friends about needing a wife who would reform him. In truth, he probably did hope that Annabella would keep him from at least some of his more dangerous vices. They were married on January 2, 1815. Tormented by guilt and now feeling trapped, Byron treated Annabella dreadfully for nearly a year, verbally abusing and demeaning her, hinting at his affair with Augusta, deliberately frightening her, and coercing her into sexual practices which she found repellent. A daughter, Augusta Ada, was born in December of that year.

In January of 1816, Annabella left on the pretext of visiting her parents, taking the infant girl with her. Byron never saw either of them again; he was notified that his wife was filing for a legal separation. Because they had ostensibly parted on friendly terms with no indication that Annabella was not returning, Byron was able to convince himself in later years that he had been the wronged party in this marriage.

He left England, never to return, in May 1816—escaping from the remorse that he felt about the marriage, his sexual indulgences, and the resultant scandals brought down around the guilty and innocent alike; escaping from the realization of how he had so far bungled his first tries at public life; escaping from creditors; and escaping from the press, which had been viciously attacking him for a year both for his "immoral" poetry and his liberal political affiliations.

For the next two years, living first in Geneva, and then in Rome and Venice, he threw himself into a life of unrestrained sensuality, but he also wrote prodigiously: two more cantos of *Childe Harold* (1816–1818), *The Prisoner of Chillon* (1816), *Manfred* (1817), and several other lengthy works. In 1818, he began the comic poem *Don Juan*, which became the most widely read of his later works. In 1819, he fell in love with the Countess Teresa Guiccioli; in 1820, Teresa separated from her husband, and she and Byron lived comfortably and happily together for three years. In addition to the sixteen cantos of *Don Juan*, he also wrote several verse dramas during this period.

Byron was always interested in the history and politics of Greece and saddened by the 400-year Turkish domination of the birthplace of democracy. In 1821, the war for Greek independence from the Ottoman Empire began, and the poet watched its progress carefully. In 1823, he accepted the invitation of a group of like-minded Englishmen to travel to Greece on their behalf to support the revolution. In Greece for nearly a year, Byron worked to bring unity to the various Greek factions and used much of his own money organizing and training troops. He died in Missolonghi from complications of a fever on April 19, 1824.

Byron's life has been the subject of nearly as much investigation and analysis as has his poetry. Indeed, since he often took himself as a subject, his life and his poetry are not easily separated, and readers have been tempted with Byron, more than with most other poets, to read his works as veiled accounts of his life. Sometimes this is justified, sometimes not, but both the life and the poetry are involved in the paradoxical mark that Byron left on literary history. Most writers are content to have a single persona associated with their life work. Byron defined two personas for the nineteenth century. He represents that most romantic of figures, the isolated, alienated hero, the very voice in European literature of that day of remorse, exile, existential anguish, and struggle for freedom. And yet, from this voice and this life comes, in a huge outpouring for six years, *Don Juan*, the longest and one of the two or three greatest comic poems of the English language.

Literary Analysis

Byron's literary output falls into three periods. His early poems, written before his European tour, were influenced directly by the models that he had taken to himself at school: Horace among the ancients, but more importantly John Dryden and Alexander Pope and the sentimental lyricists of the eighteenth century. Rather than sentimentality, though, Byron's early lyrics often leave the impression of mere exaggeration. The emotional extremism of "To Caroline" (1807) is typical:

> Think'st thou, I saw thy beauteous eyes,
> Suffus'd in tears, implore to stay;
> And heard unmov'd thy plenteous sighs,
> Which said far more than words can
>   say?

Byron wrote dozens of such lyrics in his youth, as did many young men of his day. Satires in the eighteenth-century mode were popular, too, and Byron tried his hand at this form, most successfully in "English Bards and Scotch Reviewers," a work spurred by negative reviews of his own *Hours of Idleness*. In this work he paints upon a broader canvas, assessing the literary merit of English poets and critics in a manner based largely on Pope's *Dunciad*:

> Shall gentle Coleridge pass unnoticed
>   here,
> To turgid ode, and tumid stanza dear?
> Though themes of innocence amuse him
>   best,
> Yet still obscurity's a welcome guest.
>   (255–58)

"English Bards" was Byron's most successful work through 1809, but there was still little to suggest at this point that he would ever make a mark as a comic poet. Only his letters, which throughout his life sparkled with wit, enthusiasm, and a deep interest and involvement in the public literary life, foreshadowed the comic genius to come. Away from England for some months in 1809, he wrote back to a friend, "Hodgson! send me the news, and the deaths and defeats and capital crimes and the misfortunes of one's friends; and let us hear of literary matters, and the controversies and the criticisms."

The middle period of Byron's life and poetry begins with the publication of cantos 1 and 2 of *Childe Harold's Pilgrimage* (1812), which propelled him into the literary spotlight, and closes with his final departure from England in 1816. *Childe Harold* resembles the early poems in several respects: the heightened sensitivity to impressions is still there (verging on melodrama, by modern standards), though now attached to scenes of the desolation wrought by war and tyranny—a subject perhaps more appropriate to emotional extremes. There is much nostalgia for the heroic past (often expressed in an archaic vocabulary) and a thorough and profound sense of weariness. But, the major advance shown in *Childe Harold* over his earlier works, and an aspect that its readers found attractive, is its ambitious scale. In "English Bards" Byron had looked about England to take stock of the contemporary literary scene; in this work he assesses the whole spiritual condition of Europe during the Napoleonic wars. Furthermore, it was a novelty: a poem of considerable skill (its Spenserian stanzas are a most demanding form) written by an aristocrat.

There is nothing that one would call "humor" in *Childe Harold*—indeed, most readers have found it rather too gloomy—but there is a striking, sustained tone of bitterness that would turn easily to humor in Byron's later works. It is as if the quasi-serious accusations of "English Bards" were broadened into indictments of nations, histories, even of time itself. The sweeping perspective of the poem, interrupted by prolonged, cynical meditations on particular scenes and characters, is very similar to that of the later *Don Juan*.

Byron welcomed the acclaim that followed the publication of *Childe Harold*. To the social status of a baron, he now could add the popular acknowledgement of literary genius, substantial progress for a young man who could remember a life of uncertain prospects in Edinburgh and who was never so secure in himself that he could do without praise. He wanted the praise; he courted it. It was at least in part to repeat the success of *Childe Harold* that Byron published, in rapid succession, a series of six verse tales (the "Oriental tales," so called because they are set in eastern Europe and the Middle East) in which he worked out the character of what has come to be known as the "Byronic hero," like Harold in mood, but a man of action:

> There was in him a vital scorn of all:
> As if the worst had fall'n which could
>   befall
> He stood a stranger in this breathing
>   world,
> An erring spirit from another hurled;
> A thing of dark imaginings . . . (*Lara*, 1,
>   313–17)

Allusions to the character of Satan in John Milton's *Paradise Lost* appear in all of the Byronic heroes through *Manfred* (1817), sometimes left vaguely mysterious, sometimes filled out by suggestions of criminality and incestuous desires. That by 1815 seven such heroes had sprung from Byron's pen, and that *Childe Harold* was known to be at least in part an autobiographical account of Byron's visit to Europe, inclined many readers to identify Byron with these characters.

For too long Byron felt immune, believing, correctly at first, that such identifications would be countered by what people actually knew of him. The poet was highly visible during these years, taking advantage of every pleasure that high society could offer, both the accepted and the illicit. Writing from such a position, he could afford, he thought, to play the role of the alienated criminal in his verse, trusting that any impression that he was actually morose or anti-social was sure to be corrected in tomorrow's newspaper account of his latest social appearance (or escapade).

When, however, he began to realize the gravity of his conduct with Augusta, and when he compounded his guilt by mistreating his wife, and when he began to see himself excoriated in the press every day—then the roles must have seemed much less like play. It must have appeared supremely ironic to Byron that he now seemed doomed to live out in tormented earnest the sufferings that he had created in his literary works.

Tangible changes in Byron's poetry appear after his departure from England in 1816. What he had casually called in a letter of 1813 "my natural love of contradiction and paradox" became now a near obsession with the duality of life, reality and fabrication, plain actions and hidden motivations, and the intricacies of time and of language, which the author began to work out in the plots, characters, and literary style of his poems. His experiences had modified his hatred of hypocrisy. Patent hypocrisy and hidden motive ("cant" is the term that he used for it) he never ceased to hate, but his writing was now infused with a broad recognition that human life is inherently deceptive. Appearance never quite discloses reality; motives are never altogether simple; human existence is always split by an awareness that what happens now will be compromised by what happens in the future. In one of his "Stanzas for Music" (probably 1814), he wrote of hope, happiness, love, and memory:

Alas! it is delusion all—
The future cheats us from afar:
Nor can we be what we recall,
Nor dare we think on what we are.

It seemed increasingly to him that life was more than immediate experiences and memories; the immediate moment was always complicated by subsequent events, and by other people. Such complications now pervaded his own life. While at college, Byron used to visit Newstead with his friends for a few days of riding, shooting, and drinking. There were no sexual orgies there. Still, suggestions of such scenes in the life of Childe Harold were taken from the poem and used by critics as evidence of Byron's immorality. All of his works were ransacked for evidence of sin, debauchery, and degeneration, and there was just enough symbolic truth in these new interpretations of old works to trouble Byron deeply.

In two poems of this period the old Byronic hero reaches a thematic and artistic climax. The paradoxes are vivid in the poetic drama *Manfred*, in which the title character, a magician, seeks to escape from the inevitable contradictions of human life, held up against the unity and simplicity of nature. Similar references to the "mixed essence" of human nature run through the two new cantos of *Childe Harold's Pilgrimage* (1816–1818), along with an oddly passive and resigned heroism, aimed as much at survival as at positive accomplishment.

It has often been thought yet another paradox of Byron's life and work that the great comic poem *Don Juan* emerges from this period of profound introspection, but one can guess at how it might have happened. There is a kind of heroism in Byron's acceptance of paradox and in his attempt, not to resolve divisions, but to multiply them, sometimes to revel in them. What might be an element of resignation brought at least a degree of peace within which Byron's sense of humor could operate. Even at a time of genuine pain (early in 1817), he could write to his friend, the poet Thomas Moore, of the third canto of *Childe Harold*: "I was half mad during the time of its composition, between metaphysics, mountains, lakes, love unextinguishable, thoughts unutterable, and the nightmare of my own delinquencies. I should, many a good day, have blown my brains out, but for the recollection that it would have given pleasure to my mother-in-law."

By any conventional standard, Byron's life during these years was far from peaceful; he involved himself in both local and national Italian political controversies (including joining a revolutionary organization) and, until he met Teresa Guiccioli, continued to indulge in dangerous romantic attachments. However, he was not subject to the daily assaults on his self-esteem and reputation which he had suffered in England, nor to immediate criticism of his writings. He had recently read John Hookham Frere's *Whistlecraft* and had been led from that to some works by Frere's model, the Italian poet Luigi Pulci. He wrote a light satire of his own in the same manner, *Beppo, A Venetian Story* (1818), mocking the inconsistent Venetian moral code and human inconsistency in general.

Byron enjoyed writing *Beppo*, and this was an enjoyment different in character from the relief afforded by work on the darker poems of 1816 to 1818. Several times in *Beppo* he pauses to comment directly upon his poems and his manner of composing in a way that he had not attempted before in work meant for publication:

> Oh that I had the art of easy writing
> What should be easy reading! Could I
>   scale
> Parnassus, where the Muses sit inditing
> Those pretty poems never known to fail,
> How quickly I would print (the world
>   delighting)
> A Grecian, Syrian, or Assyrian tale;
> And sell you, mix'd with western senti-
>   mentalism,
> Some samples of the finest Orientalism.
> (*Beppo*, stanza 51)

Other references to his supposed stylistic shortcomings (here accompanied by a sarcastic dig at his own earlier Oriental tales) appear in *Beppo*, along with casual comments regarding the mechanical elements of the poem:

> It was the Carnival, as I have said
> Some six and thirty stanzas back . . .
> (*Beppo*, stanza 56)

This sometimes led to broader remarks on the nature of writing:

> My pen is at the bottom of a page,
> Which being finished, here the story
>   ends;

'Tis to be wished it had been sooner
    done,
But stories somehow lengthen when
    begun. (*Beppo,* stanza 99)

These interruptions of and comments upon the processes of composing are usually taken to indicate Byron's discovery of a new sort of enthusiasm for writing. In any case, he was especially pleased by reports of *Beppo*'s success in England, and by the summer of 1818 he was projecting a much longer work in the same style.

Byron's remarks in his letters and in the text of the poem itself indicate that he was unsure just what sort of thing *Don Juan* would be, but "epic" is the term that he uses most frequently. As the term is applied to the ancient works of Homer and Virgil or the later Christian epics such as Dante's *Divine Comedy* and Milton's *Paradise Lost,* the epic is a narrative poem about the creation of a civilization or about the fall of one world order and the rise of a new. The epic hero is a central agent in this struggle, embodying his cultures' values and beliefs; the narrator of the epic is a comprehensive voice of the civilization, understanding it and expressing its belief systems as fully and as widely as possible.

None of this would appear to be true of *Don Juan* (pronounced "Jew-on") at first glance. On the contrary, it looks as though Byron is deliberately standing the tradition on its head. European civilization is presented as already fallen, thoroughly decadent and irredeemable; the hero is more acted upon than active; and the narrator, when not hopelessly self-contradictory, is scornful to the point of loathing all systems of belief. But, "epic satire" is a term that Byron uses for the work, and it is quite possible that he wished his readers to make an effort to see the poem in the epic tradition. He planted reminders such as "My poem's epic" in the most decidedly farcical passages to suggest that a slapstick epic was the only sort possible for his own degraded era.

Byron says many things about the poem. One kind of comment is frequent:

I don't know that there may be much
    ability
Shown in this sort of desultory rhyme;
But there's a conversational facility,
Which may round off an hour upon a
    time.

Of this I'm sure at least, there's no
    servility
In mine irregularity of chime,
Which rings what's uppermost of new or
    hoary,
Just as I feel the "Improvisatore." (*Don
    Juan,* 15, 20)

The poem has always been read more for its improvisational style than its contributions to the epic tradition. From this point of view, *Don Juan* is a series of apparently spontaneous performances at the level of the stanza or sequence of stanzas in which the main subject is nearly always the poet's current attitude and, frequently, his experiences of writing. In 1827, William Hazlitt called *Don Juan* "a poem written about itself." It is that, but it is also a poem about writing in general and about other writers, living and dead, and their subjects.

Thus, the poem begins with a lively seventeen-stanza "Dedication" to the current Poet Laureate of England, Robert Southey, and his fellow "Lake poets," William Wordsworth and Samuel Taylor Coleridge. These are lines much in the spirit of "English Bards and Scotch Reviewers," but in control and confidence they are far advanced beyond the earlier satire:

Bob Southey! You're a poet, Poet
    Laureate,
And representative of all the race;
Although 'tis true that you turn'd out a
    Tory at
Last,—yours has lately been a common
    case:—
And now, my epic renegade! what are ye
    at,
With all the Lakers in and out of place?
A nest of tuneful persons, to my eye
Like "four and twenty blackbirds in a
    pie,"

"Which pie being open'd, they began to
    sing"—
(This old song and new simile holds
    good)
"A dainty dish to set before the King,"
Or Regent, who admires such kind of
    food.
And Coleridge, too, has lately taken
    wing,
But, like a hawk encumber'd with his
    hood,
Explaining metaphysics to the nation—

I wish he would explain his Explanation
. . .
And Wordsworth in a rather long
    "Excursion,"
(I think the quarto holds five hundred
    pages)
Has given a sample from the vasty
    version
Of his new system to perplex the sages.
'Tis poetry—at least by his assertion,
And may appear so when the dogstar
    rages;
And he who understands it would be
    able
To add a story to the Tower of Babel.
    (Dedication, 1–2, 4)

Assaults of this kind are common in *Don Juan*, and not just against poets: scientists, philosophers, politicians, critics—any public author is liable to come in for a share of abuse or praise. There is little in the poem that does not in some way participate in the ongoing discourse on the public and private life of writing. Byron's own practice as a writer is constantly examined, as in the stanza cited earlier: "I don't know that there may be much ability / Shown in this sort of desultory rhyme"; and above, "This old song and new simile holds good." From the first moment of the poem proper, stanza 1 of canto 1, we encounter not just a story, but all of the thoughts, motives, and self-scrutiny of an author at work on a story. The beginning of the poem is the author's settling down to think:

I want a hero: an uncommon want,
When every month and year sends forth
    a new one,
Till, after cloying the gazettes with cant,
The age discovers he is not the true one;
Of such as these I should not care to
    vaunt,
I'll therefore take our ancient friend Don
    Juan,
We have all seen him in the pantomime
Sent to the devil, somewhat ere his time.

The stanza of *Don Juan* (as in the works of Frere and Pulci) is the *ottava rima*, an internally complex, clearly closed stanza. It is especially adaptable to brief stylistic flourishes—little self-contained masterpieces of the poetic craft. The ABABAB rhyme scheme of the first six lines (the sestet) encourages—even forces—word play. The alternating ten-

and eleven-syllable lines give the verse something of the rhythm of a ballad (often a vehicle for humor in English poetry). The final couplet, introducing a third rhyme, inevitably sounds like a summary remark. The stanza requires resourcefulness; it lends itself to wit rather than to sustained philosophical commentary.

The form is not particularly suited to narration: the stanzas are too internally involved and end too positively for the poetry to pick up much forward momentum. However, forward momentum is not the effect that Byron is after. He writes in canto 14, stanza 7:

This narrative is not meant for narration,
But a mere airy and fantastic basis,
To build up common things with
    common places.

Certainly most readers have agreed: the story line of *Don Juan* is mainly a pretext to keep writing and to keep people reading while the important things are "built up." "Common things" here means things that human beings have in common, ordinary things, and also base, unpleasant things; "common places" means stock responses (such as clichés), the "common places" of rhetoric (standard arguments), and remarks of the sort to be found in a "commonplace book"—a kind of reading journal kept by many people of the day.

The plot, such as it is, follows Don Juan through his youth and early adulthood. Despite what Byron says (and one has to get accustomed to his changing his mind), this is not the Don Juan of the pantomime (a moral play, often for children), not the dueller and libertine of legend. From the time that he appears as a youth in Seville, Byron's Juan that has no well-defined character at all but seems rather to take on the colors of his environment and the expectations of others. As a boy, he studies the classics and the lives of the saints and acts the "young philosopher" (1, 50). When he falls in love with Donna Julia, an older married woman, he becomes the very type of the tormented young lover, affording Byron an opportunity to bring in Wordsworth and Coleridge again:

Young Juan wander'd by the glassy
    brooks
Thinking unutterable things; he threw
Himself at length within the leafy nooks

Where the wild branch of the cork forest
  grew;
There poets find materials for their
  books,
And every now and then we read them
  through,
So that their plan and prosody are eli-
  gible,
Unless, like Wordsworth, they prove un-
  intelligible.
He, Juan (and not Wordsworth), so pur-
  sued
His self-communion with his own high
  soul,
Until his mighty heart, in its great mood,
Had mitigated part, though not the
  whole
Of its disease; he did the best he could
With things not very subject to control,
And turn'd, without perceiving his con-
  dition,
Like Coleridge, into a metaphysician . . .
In thoughts like these true wisdom may
  discern
Longings sublime, and aspirations high,
Which some are born with, but the most
  part learn
To plague themselves withal, they know
  not why:
'Twas strange that one so young should
  thus concern
His brain about the action of the sky;
If you think 'twas philosophy that this
  did,
I can't help thinking puberty assisted. (1,
  90–91, 93)

This is a fair sample of the versification of
Don Juan: abrupt changes in tone (including
here a parody of Wordsworth's style), alterna-
tion of simple and complex grammar, simple
rhymes (so called "masculine," i.e., end-stressed
rhymes) giving way to double and triple "feminine" rhymes (i.e., in which the final syllable is
unstressed). The passage is also typical of *Don
Juan's* peculiar sort of narration: a bit of plot is
the occasion for poetical flourish and word
play, much speculation on "common things"
(the longings of adolescence here), commentary
on the nature of writing, and potshots at contemporary writers.

Juan and Julia are discovered by Julia's
husband; in canto 2 Juan escapes by ship. The
ship founders in a storm; the surviving sailors,
adrift in a longboat, resort to cannibalism (a

scene presented humorously—and quite shocking to Byron's English readers), in which Juan,
though present, does not participate. He swims
to an island where he is found by a woman
named Haidee who tends to him and becomes
his second great love. The rest of canto 2 and
all of canto 3 are given to a lengthy description
of this affair. Again Juan is discovered (this time
by Haidee's father); Haidee dies of grief; Juan
is sold into slavery. Through various intrigues
he finds himself attired as a woman of a Turkish harem; new sexual adventures and misadventures follow (in scenes even more scandalous to the English readers—who, of course,
kept reading).

He is again discovered and escapes. In
canto 7 he falls in with a Russian regiment
marching to the siege of a Turkish fort. In another character shift seemingly evoked by the
moment, Juan distinguishes himself in battle.
He is sent to the court of Catherine the Great
where he becomes the empress's sexual favorite. In canto 10 he is selected for a diplomatic
mission to England. A brief journey across Europe gives Byron a chance to revisit poetically
several of the locales that were important in
Childe Harold.

The rest of the poem is set in England.
There is little in the way of action: Juan is forced
to kill a highwayman; he becomes the sexual
target of two aristocratic women; he becomes
attracted to a third. Rather than to action, these
six cantos are devoted to a detailed and leisurely
treatment of the vanities and hypocrisies of
British high society, deploying many of Byron's
memories and most of his resentments in a description of the English as a repressed, passionless, and generally trivial people.

Don Juan is unfinished. Byron had completed sixteen cantos and begun a seventeenth
when he was interrupted by his involvement in
the Greek revolution. Had he been able to continue the poem, though, it is unlikely that he
would have altered the rambling, spontaneous
character of the plot. He was clearly not trying
to create a tightly controlled narrative. In fact,
he probably conceived of *Don Juan* less as a
single, unified work than as a series of passages
and episodes. That is how the poem was published during his life—in smaller groups of two
or three cantos at a time.

In any case, the structure of the poem as it
exists is not epic, but is rather in the tradition
of the *picaresque*, a satirical form going back
several centuries in European literature, a con-

B

venient genre for a writer who wishes to touch on a great many issues. The picaresque narrative is built around a series of adventures encountered by a wandering (typically young, innocent, male) hero, with episodes clearly designed to reveal the hypocrisy and vanity of human behavior. The hero of the picaresque is usually unimpaired by his experiences; he remains idealistic in the face of all human venality, and he is often rewarded in the end by being placed in ideal circumstances. The narrator of the tale is usually just off stage, sometimes representing himself as an observer or as a historian, often speaking directly to the reader. Miguel Cervantes' *Don Quixote* is the masterpiece of the genre and was very much on Byron's mind during his composition of *Don Juan* (though in *Don Quixote* the hero is aged and idealism is the peculiar form of his insanity). *Don Juan* is closely related to several of the great British novels of the eighteenth century, which are also picaresque satires: Henry Fielding's *Tom Jones* and Tobias Smollett's *Roderick Random*, and especially Laurence Sterne's *Tristram Shandy*. Byron was quite familiar with these novels, claiming to have read them while a boy. François Voltaire's *Candide* seems to have been a model as well.

But, there is one prominent difference in Byron's tale. In these other picaresques the hero is idealistic, clinging to an optimistic view of life and humanity, regarding all villains and villainous motives as exceptions to the general rule of human decency; the hero's moral consistency is his strength. In Juan we sense almost nothing of a core of ideals that he carries with him from one situation to another. He learns little, remembers little; he is almost completely re-created by each new situation. Some readers have, therefore, considered Juan psychologically unrealistic. Still, there is much to suggest that Byron was trying to represent a certain perspective on human psychology: not that human beings are selfless or selfish, as such, not that they are necessarily hypocritical (though they may be), but rather that, paradoxically, true honesty looks like, is in fact like, hypocrisy. Of one character's apparent dishonesty, Byron writes:

> 'tis merely what is called mobility,
> A thing of temperament and not of art,
> Though seeming so from its supposed
> facility;

And false—though true; for surely
they're sincerest,
Who are strongly acted on by what is
nearest. (16, 97)

Describing himself in an 1823 conversation with his friend Lady Blessington, Byron is recorded as having said, "if I know myself, I should say, that I have no character at all . . . I am so changeable, being everything by turns and nothing long." These and similar statements apply easily to both the main character and the narrator of *Don Juan*, making the poem seem a mirror of Byron's mind, an elaborate record of spontaneous trains of thought extended over a period of years. Byron encourages this interpretation in such remarks as "I write what's uppermost, without delay" (14, 7).

It is difficult to know where to stop applying the thorough irony of the poem. He also writes:

> The regularity of my design
> Forbids all wandering as the worst of
> sinning . . . (1, 7)

This is clearly not true; the poem wanders extravagantly. The "regularity" of the design is not found in consistent development, but rather in the unusual, imaginative rules by which the world of *Don Juan* operates. Byron had been made painfully aware of the difficulties and dangers of fame, in particular of the unexpected ways that one's own writing can be interpreted and misinterpreted. These perceptions are expanded into something approaching a metaphysics in *Don Juan*.

The situation of the writer is the starting point: the writer is an ordinary human being, subject to the usual petty, material human problems and distractions. But, as he writes, aware that *what* he writes is aimed at some future reader and may in fact outlast his own earthly existence, it is as if he is poised on the brink of the unknown. The potential immortality of writing creates a spiritual world analogous to the world of ghosts and spirits that is-lluded to in *Manfred* and *Childe Harold 3* and *4*. Byron keeps the crucial moment of writing in the foreground of the poem, often referring to himself at that moment—seated at his desk, pen in hand:

> What is the end of fame? 'tis but to fill
> A certain portion of uncertain paper:
> (1, 218)

. . .

But let me change this theme, which
    grows too sad,
And lay this sheet of sorrows on the
    shelf;
I don't much like describing people mad,
For fear of seeming rather touched
    myself—
(4, 74)
Why, just now,
In taking up this paltry sheet of paper,
My bosom underwent a glorious glow,
And my internal Spirit cut a caper . . .
(10, 3)

References to the immediate experiences of
writing are often a prelude to philosophical
monologues on all of the themes together: the
passage of time and the uncertainty of the
future, the divided existence of humankind,
and the life of the writer. Here, for instance,
after noting his publisher's complaint that cantos 1 and 2 were likely to offend readers:

'Tis all the same to me; I'm fond of yield-
    ing,
And therefore leave them to the purer
    page
Of Smollett, Prior, Ariosto, Fielding,
Who say strange things for so correct an
    age;
I once had great alacrity in wielding
My pen, and liked poetic war to wage,
And recollect the time when all this cant
Would have provoked remarks which
    now it shan't . . .
Of poets who come down to us through
    distance
Of time and tongues, the foster-babes of
    Fame,
Life seems the smallest portion of exist-
    ence;
Where twenty ages gathers o'er a name,
'Tis as a snowball which derives assis-
    tance
From every flake, and yet rolls on the
    same,
Even till an iceberg it may chance to
    grow;
But after all is nothing but cold snow. (4,
    98, 100)

The "poetic war" mentioned here is, of
course, carried on in writing: in literary interpretation and plain slander, in parody and imitation

(as in the stanzas cited earlier describing Juan's
Wordsworthian longings), and occasionally in
praise for another writer. At stake in the war, in
these lines and throughout the poem, is the future of Byron's own name and reputation, and
not only in his own generation but far beyond.
"The future cheats us from afar," Byron had
written. *Don Juan* is an attempt to reach into
that future, to counter the cheat. All of this gives
writing an odd, unworldly importance, which
Byron seems to enjoy spelling out in detail.

The direct address to the reader, common
to many eighteenth-century literary works, is
motivated in *Don Juan* by a concern to take
charge of the interpretation of the poem. Byron
avoids directly attacking the readers of the
poem. He tries usually to enlist the reader's sympathy, striking out at those critics who willfully
misinterpret him:

They accuse me—*ME*—the present
    writer of
The present poem—of—I know not
    what,—
A tendency to under-rate and scoff
At human power and virtue, and all that;
And this they say in language rather
    rough.
Good God! I wonder what they would
    be at!
I say no more than has been said in
    Dante's
Verse, and by Solomon and by
    Cervantes,
By Swift, by Machiavel, by
    Rochefoucault,
By Fenelon, by Luther, and by Plato;
By Tillotson, and Wesley, and Rousseau,
Who knew this life was not worth a
    potato. (7, 3–4)

His condemnation is as strong as it can be when
he writes of such readers and when he writes
directly to them, as in a few lines further on:

Dogs, or Men! (for I flatter you in saying
That ye are dogs—your betters far) ye
    may
Read, or read not, what I am now
    essaying
To show ye what ye are in every way.
    (7, 7)

Always close at hand to the flippancies and
petty literary squabbling and dispute is the se-

rious discourse on the human condition in which distinctions are constantly on the verge of disappearing into some mystical, unknown but longed-for unity:

> Between two worlds life hovers like a
>   star,
> 'Twixt night and morn upon the
>   horizon's verge:
> How little do we know that which we
>   are!
> How less what we may be! (15, 99)

Ultimately, it has not been in Byron's rancorous "poetic war" that the readers of *Don Juan* have found their chief delight. It is, rather, in such grand sentiments as these, framed in this distinctive meditative style which moves with grace and confidence from microscopic examinations of human motive and the intricacies of language outward to regard all of Europe, and further out, embracing all human history and possibility.

There were other delights of a different sort during the years 1817–1823. The episodic progress of *Don Juan* enabled Byron to complete several additional complex and no less provocative works: a series of tragedies on historical figures, more verse narratives, dramatic monologues, and briefer satires on English manners and events. Two works in 1821 caused a public furor in England at least equal to any caused so far by *Don Juan*. In *Cain*, a tragedy based on the *Genesis* story, the old Byronic hero appears in two new, contrasting manifestations: the tormented Cain, struggling for spiritual freedom in what seems to him a cosmic prison; and Lucifer, who appears to have gained a degree of personal autonomy by rebellion and defiance, though at the cost of embracing evil and duplicity. Lucifer appears again in *The Vision of Judgement* (an *ottava rima* satire of 106 stanzas), arguing with Michael the Archangel outside the gates of Heaven over the soul of George III, the recently deceased king of England.

As the public eagerly read (and as often eagerly condemned) his poetry, there was no decline in their fascination with Byron himself during these years as he moved at or near the center of European political, moral, and literary controversies. Though Byron continued to discourage biographical interpretations of his works, his protests grew less frequent and less vehement; he may simply have given up. In truth, the side of himself that he showed his friends in person and in letters, and the subjects and manner of the relatively few "personal" lyrics that he wrote during these years reveal a man and a set of ideas much in tune with the more carefully wrought narrative persona of *Don Juan*. He was a man occasionally more weary of the struggle than he was quite willing to admit to in public:

> On My Thirty-Third Birthday
> 22 January 1821
> Through life's road, so dim and dirty,
> I have dragged to three and thirty.
> What have these years left to me?
> Nothing—except thirty-three.

Furthermore, he was still struggling, though at times feeling the futility of his struggle, for emotional and political freedom. The following frequently reprinted "Stanzas," like the birthday poem above, first appeared in a letter to his friend Moore:

> When a man hath no freedom to fight
>   for at home,
> Let him combat for that of his neighbors;
> Let him think of the glories of Greece
>   and of Rome,
> And get knocked on the head for his
>   labours.
> To do good to mankind is the chivalrous
>   plan,
> And is always as nobly requited;
> Then battle for freedom wherever you
>   can,
> And, if not shot or hang'd, you'll get
>   knighted.

Of the "first" Byronic hero—the Harold, the Lara—much can be seen in subsequent literature; he enters British and American fiction especially, becoming Heathcliff, Rochester, Captain Ahab, and a thousand other mysterious, tormented heroes. The influence of the Byron of *Don Juan* (and of the letters, published soon after his death and always widely read) is at once more subtle and more direct, and less purely literary. In another conversation with Lady Blessington, Byron summed up himself: "There are but two sentiments to which I am constant—a strong love of liberty, and a detestation of cant." These sentiments unify *Don Juan*, if loosely and inconsistently, and they are one way of organizing the several disparate attitudes associated with Byron in the intellectual history of Europe and America: cynicism, worldliness, skepticism, scorn, a capacity for depressions and exaltations verging on madness, an irreligious spirituality, an aristocratic friendliness, and always a questing after freedom in all of its forms, no matter how difficult or dangerous.

Summary

Lord Byron's poetry is a diverse, paradoxical body of work, representing two distinct contributions to intellectual history: a voice of outright rebellion against tyranny and conventional morality, found in the Byronic hero, and a voice of thorough skepticism, embodied in the narrator of *Don Juan*, which doubts the effectiveness of any human effort.

Don Juan is unique in British literature: a satire in the tradition of the epic. The poem's greatest achievement is its narrator, who is intended, like the narrators of past epics, to represent the spirit of his age and of his culture, and to stand apart from that culture. The epic struggle of *Don Juan* is a "poetic war"—a competition of writers and reputations fought on the battleground of the reader's mind. However, in the poem the epic traditions are brought to bear not on heroic accomplishments but on the sad predicament of human life, with all of its uncertainties, duplicities, and contradictions.

Selected Bibliography

Primary Sources

Hours of Idleness. Newark: S. and J. Ridge, 1807.

"English Bards and Scotch Reviewers. A Satire." London: James Cawthorn, 1809.

Childe Harold's Pilgrimage. A Romaunt. London: John Murray, 1812.

Lara, A Tale. London: John Murray, 1814.

Childe Harold's Pilgrimage. Canto the Third. London: John Murray, 1816.

The Prisoner of Chillon, and Other Poems. London: John Murray, 1816.

Manfred, A Dramatic Poem. London: John Murray, 1817.

Beppo, A Venetian Story. London: John Murray, 1818.

Childe Harold's Pilgrimage. Canto the Fourth. London: John Murray, 1818.

Don Juan. London: Thomas Davidson, 1819.

Don Juan. Cantos III, IV, and V. London: Thomas Davidson, 1821.

Cain, A Mystery. London: John Murray, 1821.

The Vision of Judgment. Suggested by the Composition so Entitled by the Author of Wat Tyler. Liberal, I, 1822.

Don Juan. Cantos VI, VII, and VIII. London: John Hunt, 1823.

Don Juan. Cantos IX, X, and XI. London: John Hunt, 1823.

Don Juan. Cantos XII, XIII, and XIV. London: John Hunt, 1823.

Don Juan. Cantos XV, XVI. London: John and H.L. Hunt, 1823.

Letters and Journals of Lord Byron, with Notices of His Life. Ed. Thomas Moore. 2 vols. London: John Murray, 1830.

Byron's Letters and Journals. Ed. Leslie A. Marchand. 12 vols. Cambridge: Harvard University Press, 1973–1982.

Lord Byron: The Complete Poetical Works. Ed. Jerome McGann. 7 vols. New York: Oxford University Press, 1980–1986.

Secondary Sources

Blessington, Lady Margaret. *Journal of Correspondence and Conversations between Lord Byron and the Countess of Blessington*. London: Henry Colburn, 1834. Blessington knew Byron only for a few months, but she is considered an acute observer of his personality; her records of their conversations are generally regarded as accurate in substance and tone.

Cooke, Michael G. *The Blind Man Traces the Circle*. Princeton: Princeton University Press, 1969. Cooke treats the skepticism in Byron's poetry as an indirectly affirmative philosophy.

Garber, Frederick. *Self, Text, and Romantic Irony: The Example of Byron*. Princeton: Princeton University Press, 1988. Garber examines the appearances of "doubling" (of characters, ideas, and poetic elements) in Byron's work, finding in it a way of accounting for his thorough irony and his distinctive notions of divided human identity.

Gleckner, Robert F. *Byron and the Ruins of Paradise*. Baltimore: Johns Hopkins University Press, 1967. In Byron's work Gleckner finds a continuity of theme based on a perception of a world fallen from unity and truth into sin and chaos; *Don Juan* is a comprehensive record of this world.

Marchand, Leslie A. *Byron: A Biography*.

New York: Knopf, 1957. The most comprehensive and trusted biography of Byron; source of material here on Byron's social life and reputation.

Ridenour, George M. *The Style of "Don Juan."* New Haven, CT: Yale University Press, 1960. An analysis of the rhetoric (i.e., the low, middle, and high styles defined by classical rhetoricians) of *Don Juan*; demonstrates Byron's erudition and skill in coordinating style and subject.

Terrance Riley

C

Calverley, Charles Stuart (Blayds)

Born: Martley, Worcestershire, December 22, 1831

Education: Private tutors; Marlborough; Harrow, 1846–1850; Balliol College, Oxford University (Prize Scholarship), 1850–1852 (removed for having committed offenses against college discipline); Christ's College, Cambridge University, 1852–1856; elected Fellow of Christ's College, 1858

Marriage: Ellen Calverley, 1865; three children

Died: February 17, 1884

Biography

The son of the Reverend Henry Blayds, Charles Stuart Calverley was born at Martley in Worcestershire on December 22, 1831. His mother was the daughter of Thomas Meade of Chatley, Somersetshire. Blayds was the name taken by the Calverley family, of ancient Yorkshire lineage, at the beginning of the nineteenth century. The use of the original name was resumed in 1852.

Educated by private tutors, he spent three months at Marlborough school and was admitted to Harrow preparatory school September 9, 1846. Athletic and social, he was renowned for his jumping ability, popular for his wit and sweetness of spirit, and respected for his extraordinary gift for verbal memory and Latin versification. Although not an omnivorous reader, his translation of Latin verses, which he admitted was so spontaneous as almost to be an improvisation, won him a scholarship to Balliol College, Oxford University, where he was admitted November 25, 1850 at the age of nineteen. Although he won the Chancellor's Prize

for Latin poetry, he was indolent by nature, a social personality with a good ear for music and a sweet singing voice. Very clever at caricature and parody, he gave himself especially to light, humorous verse. His great popularity led him into boyish recklessness and in 1852 he was dropped from the college roster for having committed offenses against college discipline.

In October of that year he matriculated at Christ's College, Cambridge University. Widely popular, he managed to stay on good terms with the college authorities. Although he never appeared to work hard, his apparent careless ease nevertheless won him the Camden medal in 1853 and 1855, as well as the Browne medal for a Greek ode the latter year, the Latin essay prize in 1856, and a second in the Classical Tripos that same year. Two years later he was elected Fellow of Christ's College, in which capacity he both tutored and lectured.

In 1862, Calverley's first volume, *Verses and Translations*, was published by Deighton, Bell, and Company. Then the lackadaisical but much-honored undergraduate turned to the study of law with great zest and was called to the bar of the Inner Temple, having vacated his university fellowship because of marriage to his first cousin, Ellen Calverley of Oulton Hall, Yorkshire, in 1865. All seemed directed steadily ahead; he liked the law and made a strong impression on senior barristers by his conduct of the Northern legal circuit. Then, during the hard winter of 1866–1867, vacationing at the estate of his wife's family, he fell very forcibly on his head while skating and suffered a concussion. At first the injury was neglected, but the accumulation of symptoms made the family take the accident more seriously. As he gradually became incapable of serious or sustained effort, he was forced to abandon the practice of law. Nevertheless, he published *Translations into English and Latin* (1866), *Theocritus Translated into English Verse* (1869), and *Fly Leaves* (a collection of parodies, 1872).

Walter J. Sendall, editor of the *Literary Remains*, described Calverley physically as short, with a powerful Greek head and crisp curling dark hair, a man built for speed and endurance. Psychologically Professor Sendall thought him to be kind, considerate, charming, and independent, with "a certain infirmity of will," and Seeley used the telling phrase "a hero asleep" (*The Literary Remains, A Memoir*).

The onslaught of Bright's Disease lowered the highspirited humorist into a profound depression and on February 17, 1884 he died and was buried in Folkestone Cemetery.

Literary Analysis

In some ways the task of the translator and the parodist represent opposite ends of the same continuum, and both are at the same time profoundly conservative.

Moses Hadas has observed that the translator has the least room for independence of thought or uniqueness of expression. It is not originality but high technical proficiency in language and meter that are required. Thus, in his translation of Theocritus, Calverley managed to surrender mind and pen to the technique and tradition of the Greek pastoral so that his translations are highly regarded even to the present time. When the Heritage Press decided to publish an English version of Virgil's *Eclogues* in 1960, it chose the translation that Calverley had made almost a century earlier.

The parody, on the other hand, represents a refusal to surrender to the tone and style of another writer. This is the point at which the parodist exposes to scorn the particular idiosyncrasies of personal style. It is unusual that the parody should be published as a volume; its fate was more usually the transient forms of periodicals, street ballads, minstrel shows, music halls, burlesques, pantomimes, and the Savoy Operettas of W.S. Gilbert and Arthur Sullivan. Often called "the most celebrated parodist in the language," with unique power of imitation and an unsparing eye for the ridiculous, Calverley was much more like Alexander Pope than William Wordsworth, and it comes as no surprise that his favorite novelist was William Makepeace Thackeray. Always impatient with

mysticism, and the champion of decorum and common sense, he took good-natured aim at the stilted phrase, the pretentious claim, deliberate authorial obscurity, and sickly sentimentality. His chief targets tended to be Alfred, Lord Tennyson (whom he very much admired), Robert Browning (whom he deplored), and a host of women poets: Anna Matilda, Jean Ingelow, Mrs. Felicia Dorthea Hemans, and Elizabeth Barrett Browning.

In this regard, *The Athenaeum*, No. 2817, editorialized thus: "We wish that some of these prolific small poets . . . would write as good poetry in earnest as Mr. Calverley does in play. His burlesque is far more poetical than their loftiest or prettiest attempts." Even in these parodies, however, Professor Seeley refers in Calverley's "Memoir" to "his elfish mockery, the exuberant playfulness of a powerful mind and tender, manly nature."

Walter Jerrold and R.M. Leonard anthologized ten of Calverley's parodies (not necessarily his best) in *A Century of Parody and Imitation* published in 1913 by Oxford University Press and republished in 1968 by Gale Research Company: "Ode to Tobacco" (Longfellow), "Beer" (Byron), "Wanderers" (Tennyson), "Proverbial Philosophy" (Tupper), "The Cock and the Bull" (Browning), "Lovers, and a Reflection" and "Ballad" (Jean Ingelow). Although the parodist attempts to imitate the style of the original, the results tend not to be word-for-word parodies of specific poems. Thus, in the manner of Longfellow, he praises tobacco "Sweet when the morn is grey; / Sweet, when they've cleared away / Lunch; and at close of day / Possibly sweetest." In parody of Byron's exotic style he celebrates "that mild, luxurious, / And artful beverage, Beer." His parody of Tennyson sounds more like Wordsworth out roaming over the hills with his dog and meeting a tinker. Perhaps the Calverley touch is supplied by the offer of "a whiff / Of 'bacco . . . (A pipe was all he needed)."

A delightful example of his tendency to cut down the high Romantic effusion can be found in the 1862 *Verses and Translations*: "Voices of the Night: The dew is on the roses, / The owl hath spread her wing; / And vocal are the noses / Of peasant and of king: / Nature (in short) reposes; / But I do no such thing."

The "Memoir" from *The Literary Remains* expresses Calverley's resentment that "genius should seem to take so much pains to be unintelligible"—a shaft shot at Browning and others of what Calverley called the "mystical school." Probably his most celebrated parody was "The Cock and the Bull," an attack on Browning's 80,000-line *The Ring and the Book*. He particularly satirized Browning's attempt to express masculine bravado, the large chunks of technical language, the absence of the lyrical impulse, and the intermingling of Latin and English. The title "The Cock and the Bull" is a fairly inept parody of *The Ring and the Book*. The poem is a dramatic monologue with the many self-interruptions and short-hand concisions of Browning's fractured style: "You see this pebble-stone? It's a thing I bought / Of a bit of a chit of a boy i' the mid o' the day— / I like to dock the smaller parts-o'-speech, / As we curtail the already cur-tail'd cur." Calverley's last line from "Reading" indicates his downright factuality in the face of Romantic fantasies: "And if thou canst not realize the Ideal, / Thou shalt at least idealize the Real." In his parody of Tennyson's "Locksley Hall," he pricks the false bubble of hysterical Romantic rhetoric and replaces the whole monologue in a domestic setting of calculated banality. Thinking of himself as a modern Horace, admiring Virgil above other poets, he nevertheless was very expert in parodying the Mantuan's style.

In his own day, Calverley's contemporaries considered him to be in the company of Henry Fielding, Jonathan Swift, Laurence Sterne, Lewis Carroll, Thomas Hood, and J.K. Stephens. Although he never achieved the solid literary success of these contemporary satirists, he nevertheless remains a fine translator, a sharp-eyed parodist whose career ended on the hard surface of an icy pond.

Summary

Charles Stuart Calverley is a clear case of a minor talent whose reputation was enormously inflated by his association with Harrow, Oxford, and Cambridge, and by the glowing recollections of former classmates as they nostalgically recalled a witty, charming athlete who had an exceptional gift for language. In his slight literary remains Calverley stakes out an exceptional achievement in three areas. His translations of standard Greek and Latin texts have stood the test of the years and are still in use today. His parodies of Browning, Tennyson, Virgil, and William Morris provide amusing sidelights on major writers and the extravagances of their style. His light, occasional verse is lean, disciplined, and exact. His comedic point of view is always the good-natured exposure of personal eccentricities, the Romantic "agony," and the sentimental fervor.

Selected Bibliography
Primary Sources
Verses and Translations. Cambridge: Deighton, Bell, 1862.
Theocritus Translated into English Verse. Cambridge: Deighton, Bell, 1869.
Fly Leaves. Cambridge: Deighton, Bell, 1872.
The Literary Remains, A Memoir. Ed. Walter J. Sendall. London: George Bell and Sons, 1885.
The Complete Works of Charles Stuart Calverley. Biographical Notice by Sir Walter J. Sendall. London: George Bell and Sons, 1901.
Verses and Translations. London: Blackie and Son, 1905. Introduction by Owen Seaman.
Virgil, *The Eclogues*. Trans. C.S. Calverley. New York: Heritage Press, 1960. Introduction by Moses Hadas.

Secondary Sources

Books
Babington, Percy L. *Browning and Calverley; or Poem and Parody*. London: John Castle, n.d. Line-by-line analysis of "The Cock and the Bull" related to lines in *The Ring and the Book*.
Jerrold, Walker, and R.M. Leonard. *A Century of Parody and Imitation*. London: Oxford University Press, 1913.
Kitchin, George. *A Survey of Burlesque and Parody in English*. Rpt. New York: Russell & Russell, 1967 (first published 1931). A six-page commentary beginning: "But now we come to one of the great masters of parody, beside whom the brightest humorist we have mentioned appears almost coarse." Selections from Calverley parodies of Browning, Matthew Arnold, Tennyson, Ingelow.
Macdonald, Dwight, ed. *Parodies: An Anthology from Chaucer to Beerbohm— and After*. New York: Random House, 1960. A six-page general essay on the art of parody by the editor; includes "The Cock and the Bull" and Calverley's parody of William Morris, entitled "Ballad."
Miles, Alfred H., ed. *The Poets and the Po-*

etry of the Nineteenth Century. Vol. 10 (Humour). London: George Routledge & Sons, 1967. A useful four-page introduction by Walter Whyte and two selections from *Fly Leaves*: "Wanderers" and "The Cock and the Bull."

Articles
Ince, R.V. "Calverley and Some Cambridge Wits of the Nineteenth Century." *Athenaeum*, 2 (October 24, 1885): 533. Helpful in relating Calverley to other humorists of the age.
The Living Age:
From *The Spectator*. Some examples of Latin and English verse. Rpt. in *The Living Age*, April–May–June 1884, Vol. 161, pp. 124–26.
From *The Saturday Review*. "He could write every kind of verse with almost unmatched excellence, but having nothing to say, like some other poets, he said nothing but mirthful follies." Rpt. in *The Living Age*, January–February–March 1886, Vol. 168, pp. 126–28.
From *Temple Bar*. Some recollections of Charles Stuart Calverley, "king of the college" (Christ's College, Cambridge). Contains some quotations from *Payn's Literary Recollections*. Rpt. in *The Living Age*, January–February–March, 1887, Vol. 172, pp. 421–26.

Elton E. Smith

Carey, Henry

Born: ca. 1687
Marriage: Unknown; possibly at least one child
Died: London, October 4, 1743

Biography
Little is known about the early life of Henry Carey, including the exact date of his birth, which probably took place in 1687. It is generally accepted that he was the illegitimate son of George Savile, the Marquis of Halifax, but a recent biographer, Henry J. Dane, disputes that claim in a doctoral dissertation. He argues that Carey was the son of Mary and Henry Carey, Sr., but his evidence for this assertion is only circumstantial. It seems probable that tradition is correct, especially since Carey gave the name Savile to three of his sons and dedicated several works to members of the Savile family.[1] In

1713, he wrote a preface to his first volume of poems in which he states that he had devoted his early years to a study of music. There is also internal evidence from these early poems that his mother was a schoolmistress.

In the early part of his life Carey taught music at boarding schools while writing songs, farces, and poetry. In 1715, with the performance of his farce *The Contrivances: or More Ways than One*, he became part of the London literary circle, especially since he was praised by Joseph Addison (whom he called the "divine Addison"). His best-known work is "Sally in Our Alley." There is evidence that he wrote "God Save the King," published anonymously in 1742, but that evidence is slim and Carey's claim to the song is somewhat doubtful. The best known of his comic farces are *Chrononhotonthologos* and *The Dragon of Wantley*.

Poverty was Carey's constant enemy, and he was made especially bitter because he often was unable to receive credit for the writing that he did and most of his successful plays were pirated by other companies. He died suddenly in London on October 4, 1743, at the height of his career; most sources confirm that he hanged himself, and some assert that he took the life of his small child at the same time. A son later claimed that Carey was the author of "God Save the Queen," a claim that has been discredited.

George Saintsbury summarizes Carey's life and writings thusly: "little as is positively known about him, accumulates an unusual assemblage of interesting details round his personality and work. [He is the] reputed son of the great Marquis of Halifax; ancestor, it seems, of Edmund Kean, creator in the farce-burlesque of *Chrononhotonthologos*, of many quaint names and some actual lines of verse which have stuck in literary memory; inventor of Ambrose Phillips' nickname [i.e., Namby Pamby] and of a rare set of skittish verses attached to it; musician, playwright and (it would seem, almost as much in gaiety of heart as on any other occasion in his life) suicide."[2]

Literary Analysis
Carey's importance in literary history rests primarily on his burlesque-farces. Of the seven examples included in Samuel Macey's *The Plays of Henry Carey*, the two best and best known are *Chrononhotonthologos* and *The Dragon of Wantley*. Many of his other plays follow stock plot lines and present stereotypical characters in

amusing, but not particularly interesting ways. Still, *Chronon* and *Wantley* are very funny even today. They burlesque the heroic drama of Carey's time and join John Gay's *The Beggar's Opera* in spoofing Italian opera. Carey was regarded primarily as a musician by his contemporaries, but most of his music has been lost, so we must rely on the words only to convey his wit and humor. Macey laments this loss and asserts that reading Carey without the music is equivalent to reading "Gilbert without his Sullivan."[3] V.C. Clinton-Baddeley opposes satire and burlesque in a way which clearly describes the tone of Carey's plays: "Satire is the schoolmaster attacking dishonesty with a whip. Burlesque is the rude boy attacking pomposity with a peashooter. Satire must laugh not to weep; burlesque must laugh not to burst."[4] The tone of Carey's plays is effervescent, bursting with laughter.

Chrononhotonthologos (1743) is full of extravagant word play. Just the list of some of the characters shows Carey's love of language: Chrononhotonthologos, King of Queerummania; Bombardinian, his General; Aldiborontiphoscophornio and Rigdum-Funnidos, Courtiers; Fadladinida, Queen of Queerummania; Tatlanthe, her favorite. Frederick Bateson describes the play as "happy nonsensicality."[5] It continually pokes fun at bombastic language and melodramatic episodes. When the king approaches, one of his courtiers comments:

But, lo! the King his Footsteps this Way
    bending
His cogitative Faculties immers'd
In Cogibundity of Cogitation:
Let Silence close our Folding Doors of
    Speech,
'Till apt Attention tell our Heart the Pur-
    port
Of this profound Profundity of
    Thought.[6]

When the Queen falls madly in love with the King of the Antipodes, or the "topsy-turvy king" as he is called in the play, she exclaims:

That's he! that's he! that's he!
I'd die ten Thousand Deaths to set him
    free:
Oh!, my Tatlanthe! have you seen his
    Face,
His Air, his Shape, his Mien, his ev'ry
    Grace,

In what a charming Attitude he stands,
How prettily he foots it with his Hands!
Well, to his Arms, no to his Legs I fly,
For I must have him, if I live or die.[7]

The gaiety and absurdity of this play keep it fresh, and it has had significant influence on subsequent dramatists. For example, George Bernard Shaw borrowed from it in *The Admirable Bushville*.[8]

The Dragon of Wantley (1737) is more tightly structured than *Chronon*, but it is not as extravagant in its use of language. Bateson prefers *Chronon*, as most modern readers do, because of its absurdity: "The rough-and-tumble of *Wantley* is about as easy as winking, but it must have required an exceptionally sensitive and intelligent audience in the eighteenth century to relish the aimless absurdities and the finely flavoured imbecility of Queerumania."[9] Again the parody of heroic drama is obvious: the dragon must be killed; the fair maiden must be rescued. In the argument the author states, "Wantley in Yorkshire, and the adjacent Places, being infested by a huge and monstrous Dragon, the Inhabitants, with Margery Gubbins at their Head, apply to Moore of Moore-Hall, a Valiant Knight, for Relief; he falls violently in Love with Margery, and for her Sake undertakes the Task; at which Mauxalinda, a Cast-off Mistress of his, is so enrag'd, that she attempts to kill Margery, but is prevented by Moore, who reconciles the Contending Rivals, kills the Dragon, and has Margery for his Reward."[10] Moore kills the dragon by a kick on the backside and has his beloved Margery to whom he had earlier sung:

Pigs shall not be
So fond as we;
We will out-cooe the Turtle Dove.
Fondly toying,
Still enjoying,
Sporting Sparrows we'll out-love.[11]

Wantley is a simpler, more direct burlesque of heroic drama than was *Chronon*; it was very popular on the London stage, being performed sixty-seven times in 1737.[12] Its sequel, *The Dragoness, A Burlesque Opera* (1738), was given twenty-one performances at Covent Garden. In it the problems with the love triangle of Moore, Margery, and Mauxalinda continue, but the play concludes happily with Moore and Margery reconciled after Mauxalinda marries

Gubbins, Margery's father. Carey's other burlesques include *Hanging and Marriage* (1722), *The Contrivances* (1729), *Betty or The Country-Bumpkins* (1732), and *The Honest Yorkshire-Man* (1735). Carey also wrote English opera in a more serious vein: *Amelia* (1732), "a heroic drama of love and honor," and *Teraminta* (1732?), "a Cuban pastoral."[13]

Frederick T. Wood's edition of the poems of Carey contains about 200 poems. The quality of these is uneven, and few of them exhibit the inventive and creative humor found in Carey's best plays. Often they seem conventional and even mechanical imitations of popular forms. Carey published several editions of his poems from 1713 to 1743, but he stated in the preface to the 1729 edition of his poems that poetry was his "amusement," not his "profession."[14] He viewed himself primarily as a musician. Addison praised Carey's poetry, especially "Sally in Our Alley" because it was a "plain, simple copy of Nature."[15] In a ballad form, this poem tells of the love of an apprentice for the daughter of a man who makes cabbage nets:

> My master and the neighbours all
> Make game of me and Sally,
> And, but for her, I'd better be
> A slave, and row a galley;
> But when my seven long years are out,
> O, then I'll marry Sally;
> O, then we'll wed, and then we'll bed,
> But not in our alley.[16]

This poem strikes a modern reader as sentimental with a rhyme which is forced; but it is still a popular ballad in England, perhaps a little like the American "Yankee Doodle."

Some of Carey's poetry that has a sting to it is more appealing to the modern taste. His attack on Phillips reveals the humorist's play with language along with his bitterness because he was not recognized as one of the real poets of the time. He attacks Phillips, calling him "Namby Pamby":

> All ye poets of the age,
> All ye witlings of the stage,
> Learn your jingles to reform,
> Crop your numbers and conform.
> Let your little verses flow
> Gently, sweetly, row by row;
> Let the verse the subject fit,
> Little subject, little wit.[17]

Carey never received the patronage that he needed to become a successful poet or playwright. He was always struggling with financial difficulties and with various writers who either did not recognize his talent or pirated his texts. In "Of Stage Tyrants," he complains that the critics tell him some of his work is not acceptable. Then if a play of his is recognized, they deny that he wrote it: "Because 'twas good, 'twas thought too good for mine."[18]

In addition to the plays and poems discussed above, Carey may be the author of *A Learned Dissertation on Dumpling* (1726) and *Pudding and Dumpling Burnt to Pot, or, A Compleat Key to the Dissertation on Dumpling* (1727). These works were published anonymously, but Macey argues in his 1980 publication of the texts that they are the work of Carey. These satiric pieces attack both the political figure Robert Walpole and the writer Jonathan Swift. The dumpling eaters are the sycophants of eighteenth-century political and literary figures: "Sir John, tho' he was no very great Scholar, yet had a happy way of Expressing himself; He was a Man of the most Engaging Address, and never fail'd to draw Attention: Plenty and Good-Nature smil'd in his Face; his Muscles were never distorted with Anger or Contemplation . . . ; he thought nothing too good for himself, all his Care was for his Belly; and his Palate was so exquisite, that it was the perfect Standard of Tasting."[19] There is some controversy about the authorship of this work, although its similarity to "Namby Pamby" and "Of Stage Tyrants" supports the accuracy of Macey's claim.

Summary

Henry Carey has written humorous works of various kinds, including prose satire and light-hearted poetry. However, his greatest contribution to the tradition of British humor lies in his burlesques, especially *Chrononhotonthologos* and *The Dragon of Wantley*. In these two works he writes a delightful kind of nonsense which foreshadows that of Lewis Carroll in his *Alice* books. The ingenious word play and the rollicking mockery of sentimental and bombastic heroism confirm Carey's place in this tradition of nonsense literature.

Notes

1. Samuel L. Macey, ed., *The Plays of Henry Carey* (New York: Garland, 1980), p. xxv.

2. Quoted in Stanley J. Kunitz and Howard Haycraft, eds., *British Authors Before 1800: A Biographical Dictionary* (New York: H.W. Wilson, 1952), p. 86.
3. Macey, p. vii.
4. V.C. Clinton-Baddeley, *The Burlesque Tradition in the English Theatre after 1660* (London: Methuen, 1952), p. 2.
5. Frederick W. Bateson, *English Comic Drama, 1700–1750* (Oxford: Clarendon Press, 1929), p. 109.
6. Quoted in Macey, pp. 158–59.
7. Quoted in *ibid.*, p. 171.
8. Clinton-Baddeley, p. 71.
9. Bateson, p. 114.
10. Quoted in Macey, p. 91.
11. Quoted in *ibid.*, p. 104.
12. *Ibid.*, pp. v, vii.
13. *Ibid.*, p. xvi.
14. Frederick T. Wood, *The Poems of Henry Carey* (London: The Scholartis Press, 1930), p. 21. Subsequent references to the poems refer to this edition.
15. *Ibid.*, p. 24.
16. *Ibid.*, p. 153.
17. *Ibid.*, p. 112.
18. *Ibid.*, p. 107.
19. Henry Carey, *A Learned Dissertation on Dumpling* and *Pudding and Dumpling Burnt to Pot* (UCLA: The Augustan Reprint Society, 1970), p. 16.

Selected Bibliography

Primary Sources

All of these sources contain very helpful introductory essays by the editors.

A Learned Dissertation on Dumpling and *Pudding and Dumpling Burnt to Pot, or, A Compleat Key to the Dissertation on Dumpling* (1727). UCLA: The Augustan Reprint Society, 1970.

The Plays of Henry Carey. Samuel L. Macey, ed. New York: Garland, 1980.

The Poems of Henry Carey. Frederick T. Wood, ed. London: The Scholartis Press, 1930.

Secondary Sources

Bateson, Frederick W. "Henry Carey." In *English Comic Drama, 1700–1750.* Oxford: Clarendon, 1929, pp. 104–14. In the short chapter on Carey in this work Bateson emphasizes *Chronon* and *Wantley*; Carey's plays are placed in their literary context, especially in relation to Joseph Addison and Samuel Foote.

Clinton-Baddeley, V.C. "Henry Carey." In *The Burlesque Tradition in the English Theatre after 1660.* London: Methuen, 1952, pp. 65–71. Clinton-Bladdeley compares Carey to Henry Fielding and John Gay; discusses the plays' extravagance and occasional lack of structure.

Dane, Henry James. "The Life and Works of Henry Carey." *Dissertation Abstracts,* 27 (1967): 1782–A. University of Pennsylvania. Dane argues that Carey was not the son of George Savile, the first Marquis of Halifax, and emphasizes the central role of music in his works.

Hudson, William H. "Henry Carey: The Author of 'Sally in Our Alley.'" In *A Quiet Corner in a Library.* New York: Books for Libraries rpt., 1965. Hudson argues that the work is not great but that it is "humanly interesting."

Kunitz, Stanley J., and Howard Haycraft, eds. "Henry Carey." In *British Authors Before 1800: A Biographical Dictionary.* New York: H.W. Wilson, 1952, pp. 85–86. A good clear overview of Carey's life and writing.

Martha Rainbolt

C

Carlyle, Thomas

Born: Ecclefechan, Scotland, December 4, 1795
Education: Edinburgh University, 1809–1814
Marriage: Jane Welsh, October 17, 1826
Died: Chelsea, London, February 5, 1881

Biography

Victorian sage and historian Thomas Carlyle was shaped by the conflicting values of his strict Calvinist home life and the transcendentalism that he absorbed from his study of German philosophers. He was born in Ecclefechan, Scotland on December 4, 1795, the second of ten children of James Carlyle, a master stonemason, and his wife Margaret. His stern parents, shrewd but almost illiterate, allowed few books other than the Bible into their home—no works of fiction, not even the poems of their countryman Robert Burns. But, with their encouragement, in 1809 fourteen-year-old Thomas walked one hundred miles from his home in southwest Scotland to Edinburgh to attend the university. He intended to become a minister and survived four years there (eating mostly oatmeal), but he lost his religious faith through reading David Hume, Voltaire, and Edward Gibbon and he dropped out of the university in 1814. His studies prepared him to tutor mathematics and write encyclopedia articles on science.

Religious doubts, the beginning of lifelong bouts with dyspepsia, and the poverty that denied him the hand of attractive Jane Welsh all plagued the young Carlyle and resulted in his dour and irascible character. He found partial answers in Johann Goethe, Emmanuel Kant, and German transcendentalism, which taught that the individual can become an active participant in structuring his universal beliefs. Through these he nullified both the empty posturing of a religion that he perceived as being dead and the materialism of eighteenth-century mechanistic philosophy. Finally, Jane consented to marriage, and the wedding took place on October 17, 1826; they were to have no children. The couple lived their first six years together on her remote farm at Craigenputtock. No fame, no university positions were coming his way.

Twice Carlyle set out for London armed with his manuscript of *Sartor Resartus* ("The Tailor Re-tailored"), which was eventually published in *Fraser's Magazine* (1833–1834). His reputation was little enhanced, and it was in America, after Ralph Waldo Emerson hailed the work, that it was first published in book form.

Carlyle turned his focus exclusively to the travails of England, now plagued with widespread individual poverty amidst great national wealth. Initially allied in temper with John Stuart Mill and the Radicals yet always opposed to the materialism of the Utilitarians and laissez-faire economics, Carlyle watched with horror as England pioneered the industrial age with its exploding urban population, new poor laws, and election reforms. *The French Revolution* (3 vols., 1837) established the author as a prophet crying out in a singular voice. Like *Sartor*, the style of the work was eccentric but intriguing, especially with its focus on interiority rather than "dry-as-dust" facts (see Professor Dryasdust in *Past and Present*). Wealth and fame followed, and the Carlyles' home in Chelsea, London, became a mecca for England's notables, including Alfred, Lord Tennyson, Charles Dickens, John Ruskin, and Robert Browning.

Carlyle's solution to the "condition of England question" focused on the hero who would lead the country: his biographies of Oliver Cromwell (2 vols., 1845) and Frederick the Great (6 vols., 1865) supported his often-read but shallow *On Heroes and Hero-Worship* (1841). Of greater interest today are *Past and Present* (1843), *Chartism* (1839), "The Nigger Question" (1849), and *Latter-Day Pamphlets* (1850), of which only the first rises in literary merit and escapes his growing, shrill reactionary politics. The thematic and literary brilliance of *Sartor* is partially revived in *Past and Present* and then is found no more.

The writer who labeled economics "the dismal science" and challenged his readers ("What art thou afraid of? Wherefore, like a coward, dost thou for ever pip and whimper, and go cowering and trembling? Despicable biped!") was a humorist in both senses: as the creator of *Sartor* and *Past and Present*, and as a bilious, hortatory character himself, much lionized and easily parodied. Carlyle lived a long life, dying in Chelsea on February 5, 1881, fifteen years after the death of Jane, whom many regarded as a brilliant conversationalist and letter writer. He was buried in Ecclefechan. James Anthony Froude's posthumous revelations (*My Relations with Carlyle*, 1903) of Carlyle's sexual impotence and of a crippled marriage dampened admiration for the man and his works immediately after his death.

Literary Analysis

Still poor and virtually unknown as the author of essays on Goethe, Johann Schiller, and Jean Paul Richter in the middle 1820s and of "Signs of the Times" in 1829, Carlyle slowly crafted *Sartor Resartus*, a fantasy biography of a transcendentalist philosopher adrift in a world of materialism and superficiality. *Sartor* was part spiritual autobiography and part diatribe against conditions in England. This satire was Carlyle's only exclusively literary publication, although his adaptation of similar fictive devices in *Past and Present* distinguishes these two works as his lasting successes. The initial reading public did not understand *Sartor* at all, yet by the end of the 1830s Carlyle was hailed as the Victorian sage.

Sartor is both earnest and comic at once, with multiple levels of incongruity as its basis. Formulations of the humor of incongruity were available to Carlyle from several sources, namely fellow-Scotsman James Beattie's *An Essay on Laughter and Ludicrous Composition* (1776) and from Germany, Kant's *Critique of Judgment* (1790) and Arthur

Schopenhauer's *The World as Will and Idea* (1818). However, Carlyle was especially familiar with this theory of humor from Richter and Goethe, both German Romantics. For Richter, humor was the contrast between the finite (perceived by the Understanding) and the infinite (perceived by Reason), resulting in an inverse sublimity. This additional profundity corresponded to Goethe's pronouncement that "true humour springs not more from the head than from the heart." From these guidelines, Carlyle fashioned *Sartor* as a comedy of incongruity, not the social corrective humor later enunciated by George Meredith.

The difficulty in categorizing *Sartor* is that it is not a novel (or even bildungsroman) in any normal sense. Its bizarre narration, which became famous as "Carlylese," is filled with neologisms, Germanisms, off-spellings, congeries of appositions, inversions, biblical injunctions, and a violent and imperative rhetoric that parallels its torrent of ideas and combative spirit. Carlyle called it "a kind of Didactic Novel: but indeed properly like nothing yet extant . . . a kind of Satirical Extravaganza on Things in General."

The story purports to be the biography of Professor Diogenes Teufelsdrockh (translates "god-born devil's-excrement") at the University of Weissnichtwo ("Know-not-where"), who has written a philosophical treatise on the history of clothes, a thinly disguised allegory comparing clothes to philosophical creeds: both must be shed when new apparel suits the times. The skeptical narrator/editor relies on six bags of random notes and miscellany, and so jumbled are they that even he complains of their stylistic "graces and terrors of the Imagination," including "sheer sleeping and soporific passages; circumlocutions, repetitions, touches of pure doting jargon."

Can truth about the "condition of England" be garnered in an "epoch when Puffery and Quackery have reached a height unexampled in the annals of mankind, and even English Editors, like Chinese Shopkeepers, must write on their door-lintels, *No Cheating Here*"? The narrator's response reflects the influences of Laurence Sterne and Jonathan Swift—*Tristram Shandy* for its insistence that truth is inexorably complex and incapable of being rendered in a linear procession, *A Tale of a Tub* for the metaphor that outer garments reveal the inner character. A third influence was Daniel Defoe, who insisted on the veracity of his recorded plagues and castaways. The result in *Sartor* is a prose style, an allegory on clothes, and a parody of scholarship that achieve a mock-heroic tone.

The humor of *Sartor* is rendered in its structure, language, and tone. The reader must work through the disorganized story pieced together from unreliable sources by a skeptical editor. The structure becomes its own transcendental argument of appearance versus reality; it is a hoax, where earnest warnings contrast with the ludicrous weave of events. To top off the hoax, Carlyle had presented Teufelsdrockh in two previous essays, and here he was again! Letters to the *Times* and *Fraser's* protested this odd authority, Teufelsdrockh.

Always bombastic, Carlylese often presents a gallows humor where an aristocrat is a "double-barrelled game-preserver" and the Utilitarian economics of James and John Stuart Mill is "the arithmetical Mill" and the "Mill of Death," or it follows up on the Mill-image by calling the utilitarian a Gerund*grind*er. The results are forceful phrases, such as "the Everlasting No" and "the Everlasting Yea," "despicable biped," "Natural Supernaturalism" (*Sartor*, chapters 7, 8, and 9 of book 2, chapter 8 of book 3) and "Captains of Industry," "Plugson of Undershot," "the Gospel of Dilettantism," "the Gospel of Mammonism," "Millocracy" (*Past and Present*, chapters 1, 2, 3, and 10 of book 3, chapter 4 of book 4), along with outrageous images, such as the Duke of Windlestraw addressing a naked House of Lords (*Sartor*, chapter 9, book 1), and the Pope, whose head protrudes through a kneeling stuffed figure so that, hidden, he may sit at his ease: "this amphibious Pope, with the wool-and-iron back, with the flesh head and hands" practicing only "the scenic theory of worship" (*Past and Present*, chapter 1, book 2).

Along with Windlestraw, who reappears in *Past and Present*, England's fumbling, irresolute leaders read like the cast of a Dickens novel. They include Sir Jabesh Windbag, Mr. Facing-both-ways (borrowed from *The Pilgrim's Progress*), and Viscount Mealymouth. Sir Windbag is "a Columbus minded to sail to the indistinct country of Nowhere" (chapter 14, book 3). Carlyle's images continue the attack on the "Puffery" of English productivity that is no better than its leaders: "The hatter in the Strand of London, instead of making better felt-hats than another, mounts a huge lath-and-plaster hat, seven-feet high, upon wheels; sends a man to drive it through the streets; hoping to be saved thereby. He has not attempted to make better hats, as he was appointed by the universe to do, and as with this ingenuity of his he could very probably have done; but his whole industry is turned to persuade us that he has made such! He too knows that the Quack has become God" (*Past and Present*, chapter 1, book 3).

Carlylese stirred readers with alliterations, double negatives, and literary allusions to Sterne, Swift, and Goethe, among others (for instance, one chapter, titled "Sorrows of Teufelsdrockh," recalls Goethe's *Sorrows of Young Werther*). The author's use of German phrases, some real, some obviously phony ("thatkraft"), are further parodies of scholarship.

Even the tone is unsettling, from its Biblical rhythms and injunctions ("For the night cometh wherein no man can work"; see *John* 9:4) to irony ("Is it possible to have god-ordained priests?") and sarcasm ("his university the worst, except of course England's"). In contrasting all of science and culture with the history of clothes, the book's opening paragraph initiates the mock-heroic parody of scholarship. In forcing the reader to unravel the validity of views put forth by the editor and those of Teufelsdrockh, the irony becomes a complicated double vision. This comedic disarray represents the world which in the transcendentalist view of the universe can be created and re-created (clothed and re-clothed) by the active participation of the reader. The editor warns us that *Sartor*, like life, is not a book where "the truths all stand in a row."

After *Sartor*, Carlyle wrote histories that continued many of his eccentricities but which are seldom read today. It is often suggested that he became his own best parody—living, speaking, and writing Carlylese for the rest of his life. *Past and Present*, his most readable attack on political and economic injustices, also relies on fragmented source materials, the editor persona, and vivid imagery. After *Past and Present*, Carlyle lost sight of his comedic promise that the universe, as well as ourselves, contains both the problem and the solution, Teufelsdrockh's Everlasting Yea.

From his 1832 "Biography" essay onward, Carlyle—puritanical and earnest—denounced fiction, and he urged Tennyson, Dickens, Browning, and Meredith to give up their poetry and fiction for "real" writing. Ironically, in spite of the great popularity of his histories in his time, only *Sartor* and *Past and Present* are re-garded as successful today, largely because he surrendered a factual approach to a comedic view with shadow characters, no verisimilitude, and virtually no plot. These satires allowed the reader to weave everything out of nothing: a perception of order out of chaos that makes us god-like.

The impact of Carlyle on his century was enormous. Ruskin and Dickens were manifest disciples (Dickens's *Hard Times* is dedicated to Carlyle), and in 1855, George Eliot wrote, "there has hardly been an English book written for the last ten or twelve years that would not have been different if Carlyle had not lived." His success continued: in 1882, over 70,000 copies of *Sartor* were sold, and nine editions of *Sartor* were issued in 1900 alone. The sage was parodied in *Punch* magazine and as Dr. Pessimist Anticant in Anthony Trollope's *The Warden* (1855); Carlylese has been best parodied in the "Oxen of the Sun" episode in James Joyce's *Ulysses*. Certainly many of Dickens's eccentrics took their voices from Carlyle in sympathy with what the editor in *Sartor* calls "this piebald entangled hyper-metaphorical style of writing, not to say of thinking."

Summary
Through his distinctive literary experiments, Thomas Carlyle dominated the British literary scene for over a quarter of a century. *Sartor Resartus* and *Past and Present*, in which his comedic vision ridiculed the "vast Blockheadism" of mid-Victorian England, have achieved lasting value. The author's stern solutions to England's problems are often repugnant to moderns, but his stimulating attacks followed his own prescription: "Populations of stern faces, stern as any Hebrew, but capable withal of bursting into inextinguishable laughter on occasion." Carlyle combined the ridiculous with the sublime to achieve a humor of incongruity.

Selected Bibliography
Primary Sources
Past and Present. London: Chapman and Hall, 1843. Modern edition, New York: New York University Press, based on Riverside edition (Houghton Mifflin), 1965.
Sartor Resartus. Serialized in *Fraser's Magazine*, 1833–1834. First book form, *Sartor Resartus: The Life and Opinions of Herr Teufelsdrockh*, Boston, 1836,

with preface by Emerson. First edition in England, *Sartor Resartus*, London: Saunders and Otley, 1838. Modern edition, *Sartor Resartus*, New York: Oxford University Press, 1987.

Secondary Sources

Biographies

Froude, James Anthony. *My Relations with Carlyle*. London: Longmans, Green, 1903. Froude defends Carlyle against charges made by his heirs. Most important biography, by Carlyle's young friend, to whom he gave his memoirs, "Yours to publish or not publish, as you please." The initial result was the four-volume *Life*, the first two volumes titled *Thomas Carlyle: A History of the First Forty Years of His Life, 1795–1835,* and the second two titled *Thomas Carlyle: A History of His Life in London, 1834–1881* (London: Longmans, Green, 1882 and 1884 respectively).

Kaplan, Fred. *Thomas Carlyle, A Biography.* Ithaca, NY: Cornell University Press, 1983. Balanced academic biography that relies on letter and other records, instead of the works that he created. Forty-nine illustrations.

Books and Articles

Bloom, Abigail. *Humor in the Major Works of Thomas Carlyle.* Dissertation, 1988, New York University (*DAI* 49:1147A).

Brookes, Gerry. *The Rhetorical Form of Carlyle's Sartor Resartus.* Berkeley: University of California Press, 1972.

Buckler, William. "*Past and Present* as Literary Experience." *Prose Studies*, 1, iii (1978): 5–25.

Ford, George. "Stern Hebrews Who Laugh: Further Thoughts on Carlyle and Dickens." In *Carlyle Past and Present.* Ed. K.J. Fielding and Rodger Tarr. New York: Barnes & Noble, 1976, pp. 112–26.

Ikeler, A. Abbott. *Puritan Temper and Transcendental Faith.* Columbus, OH: Ohio State University Press, 1972. Carlyle's literary ideals seen as being based on his Scottish Calvinism combined with German Romanticism.

Kingsmill, Hugh. "Some Modern Light-Bringers, as They Might have been Extinguished by Thomas Carlyle."

Bookman, 12 (1932): 766–68.

Levine, George. "*Sartor Resartus* and the Balance of Fiction." In *The Boundaries of Fiction: Carlyle, Macaulay, Newman.* Ed. George Levine. Princeton: Princeton University Press, 1968, pp. 19–78. Rpt. in *Thomas Carlyle.* Ed. Harold Bloom. New York: Chelsea House, 1986, pp. 55–75.

———. "The Use and Abuse of Carlylese." In *The Art of Victorian Prose.* Ed. George Levine and William Madden. New York: Oxford University Press, 1968, pp. 101–26.

Rundle, Vivienne. "'Devising New Means': *Sartor Resartus* and the Devoted Reader." *Victorian Newsletter*, 82 (1992): 13–22. Analysis of *Sartor's* contentious textual interaction with readers.

Tennyson, George. "Parody as Style: Carlyle and His Parodists." In *Carlyle and His Contemporaries.* Ed. John Clubbe. Durham, NC: Duke University Press, 1976.

———. "*Sartor*" Called "*Resartus.*" Princeton: Princeton University Press, 1965. Detailed composition history and structure of *Sartor* as literature, not as philosophy or biography.

Joel Athey

C

Carroll, Lewis

Born: Daresbury, Cheshire, on January 27, 1832

Education: Richmond Grammar School, Yorkshire, 1844–1845; Rugby School, 1846–1849; Christ Church College, Oxford University, B.A., 1854

Died: Guildford, January 14, 1898

Biography

Lewis Carroll, born as Charles Lutwidge Dodgson on January 27, 1832, in the parsonage of Daresbury, Cheshire, was the third child and the eldest son of the eleven children of the Reverend Charles Dodgson and Frances Jane Lutwidge. He was descended from two North Country families with a long tradition of service to church and state. Despite his good family name, all the world has come to know Charles Dodgson as Lewis Carroll, a pseudonym that he chose in 1856 for his fictional and poetical works (he reserved his family name for his academic books and essays).

When he was eleven years old his family moved from Daresbury to the rectory at Croft, just inside the Yorkshire boundary, where his father assumed his new duties as rector. During his years at Croft, Carroll revealed his early genius for nonsense by editing and writing for a series of family magazines entitled *The Rectory Umbrella* and *Mischmasch*. He received his early schooling at the Richmond Grammar School (1844–1845) and later at Rugby School (1846–1849).

Shortly after his graduation from Rugby, Carroll matriculated at Christ Church College, Oxford, on May 23, 1850. At the end of four years of study he distinguished himself by taking first class honors in the Final Mathematical School and he received his B.A. in 1854. That same year he published his first poem and story, in the *Whitby Gazette*. Although he was ordained a deacon in 1861, Carroll decided not to go on to take holy orders but instead to teach mathematics at Oxford, where he was to spend the rest of his life.

In 1856, Carroll purchased a camera and soon developed into one of the foremost portrait photographers of his day. His work includes numerous photographs of children as well as of such famous contemporaries as Alfred, Lord Tennyson, John Ruskin, the Rossetti family, Michael Faraday, John Everett Millais, and Holman Hunt. He has been acknowledged as a pioneer in British amateur photography and the most outstanding photographer of children in the nineteenth century.

It was also in 1856 that Carroll first met the children of Henry George Liddell, the dean of Christ Church. He not only immortalized these children—Alice, Edith, and Lorina—in his photographs but in his classic story *Alice's Adventures in Wonderland*. Alice was the inspiration for the story and her two sisters appear in the tale as the Eaglet (Edith) and the Lory (Lorina). On July 4, 1862, Carroll, accompanied by his friend Robinson Duckworth, made a rowing expedition up the river Isis to Godstow with the three Liddell sisters. It was during this trip that he told them the story of Wonderland. He later wrote out the story and illustrated it with his own drawings. In February 1863, he completed this original version of the story, which he entitled *Alice's Adventures under Ground*. Two years later he published an expanded version of the original story as *Alice's Adventures in Wonderland*, illustrated by the *Punch* artist John Tenniel.

In 1869, Carroll published a collection of his comic and serious verse under the title *Phantasmagoria*, the title poem being about a charming ghost who haunts a country gentleman. He then followed up the success of *Alice's Adventures* with the publication of *Through the Looking-Glass and What Alice Found There* in 1871. His long nonsense poem *The Hunting of the Snark*, illustrated by Henry Holiday, was published in 1876, followed by his last collection of comic verse *Rhyme? Reason?* in 1883.

Despite his innovative excursions into the world of nonsense and the absurd, Carroll did not neglect his traditional studies. He continued to publish a number of serious and traditional studies in mathematics and logic, including *Euclid and His Modern Rivals* (1879), *The Game of Logic* (1887), *Curiosa Mathematica, Part 1* (1888), *Curiosa Mathematica, Part 2* (1893), and *Symbolic Logic, Part 1* (1896).

In 1889, Carroll published an experimental novel entitled *Sylvie and Bruno* which he completed in a second volume called *Sylvie and Bruno Concluded* in 1893. These volumes failed to win the large audience that his two Alice books had.

On January 14, 1898, Carroll died at his sisters' home in Guildford and is buried there. A memorial plaque has subsequently been placed in the floor of Westminster Abbey to honor this remarkable man. *Three Sunsets and Other Poems*, a collection of his serious verse, was published posthumously in 1898.

Literary Analysis

In his serious poetry, collected in *Phantasmagoria* and *Three Sunsets and Other Poems*, Carroll allows us to glimpse some of his heart-felt emotions of grief, anxiety, and love, but not without maintaining a firm control over those emotions. By writing in conventional poetic forms, by alluding to established poets such as Samuel Taylor Coleridge, John Keats, and Alfred, Lord Tennyson, and by modeling his poems upon theirs, and by adopting an accepted sentimental tone, Carroll carefully modulated, refined, and made socially agreeable to his audience and to himself the raw emotions that threatened his sense of order and psychological integrity. He was especially attracted to and influenced by such poems as Coleridge's "The Rime of the Ancient Mariner," Keats's "La Belle Dame Sans Merci," and Tennyson's "In Memoriam" and "Mariana," all of which dwell upon such disturbing themes as guilt, depression, or sexual temptation. In short, Carroll attempted to shape his anxieties within a poetic tradition and to sanctify them against the riotous swirl of fear, chaos, and despair.

Carroll's nonsense verse, on the other hand, is much more complex and paradoxical than his serious poetry. As much as he relaxed and allowed his imagination to blossom in the presence of his young girl friends, Carroll ignored and even challenged some of the conventional literary constraints in writing his comic poetry. The poetry in the two *Alice* books, such as "Twinkle, Twinkle, Little Bat," "Speak Roughly to Your Little Boy," "Turtle Soup," "Jabberwocky," and "The Walrus and the Carpenter," are rebellious in the way that children are.

Cast in the form of the traditional ballad, "Jabberwocky" relates the story of a young boy who slashes the head off a terrifying monster and then carries off the head to show to an awaiting adult, who praises the boy for his brave deed. Besides embodying the David and Goliath story whereby the child becomes the hero in an adult world, the poem is an eloquent testimony to Carroll's linguistic innovations. The poem opens with the haunting lines: "'Twas brillig, and the slithy toves / Did gyre and gimble in the wave: / All mimsy were the borogroves, / And the mome raths outgrabe." Carroll's use of portmanteau words, that is, words comprised of two other words ("brillig" = "brilliant" and "light," and "slithy" = "slimy" and "lithe") set the literary stage for such authors as James Joyce and Vladimir Nabokov.

"Speak Roughly to Your Little Boy," on the other hand, exhibits Carroll's distaste for young boys, parodies G.W. Langford's popular poem "Speak Gently," and mocks the nineteenth century's sentimental glorification of the child. The poem opens with the stark advice: "Speak roughly to your little boy, / And beat him when he sneezes: / He only does it to annoy, / Because he knows it teases." The child in question, of course, is sneezing because the room is full of black pepper, but in the topsy-turvy world of Wonderland, the relationship between one's actions and motives is always in question.

These nonsense poems are visceral, instinctive, and free in their confrontation with authority and convention. While they assume the poetic forms and meters of traditional English poetry, they undermine that tradition by their comic tone, bizarre logic, and unsettling assumptions. Carroll's nonsense verse embodies his primal feelings about the possible meaninglessness of life, his repressed violence and sexuality, and his growing awareness that order and meaning within the context of a poem do not necessarily reflect a corresponding order in the terrifying void of cosmic reality.

Carroll's long poem *The Hunting of the Snark* is his comic defense against the unthinkable idea of the meaninglessness of life and his fear of annihilation after death. Under the leadership of the Bellman, a madcap crew sets forth to hunt the Snark. The hero of this mock epic is the Baker, who has been warned that he will be annihilated if the Snark turns out to be a Boojum. As the center of authority and truth, the Bellman constantly rings his bell (which is depicted in every illustration), reminding the crew of the passage of time and of their mortality. He defines truth by announcing at the outset that whatever he repeats three times is true. Carroll's questors, therefore, design their own world, for that is all that they have. The mythical Snark in the poem turns out to be a booby trap, a Boojum, and the Baker vanishes away forever, thus destroying all order, all hope, and all meaning, and ending the poem.

The author's strong Christian faith, however, would never allow him consciously to think along these lines. There was a God, a clear purpose in life, and an afterlife awaiting the righteous. But even as the Snark hunters manufactured some form of order as a buffer against madness, Carroll created a comic ballad with the bravado of an English adventurer in order to contain his greatest fear.

Although he wrote *Alice's Adventures in Wonderland* explicitly to entertain children, it has become a treasure to philosophers, literary critics, biographers, clergymen, psychoanalysts, and linguists, not to mention mathematicians, theologians, logicians, and the general public, children and adults alike. There appears to be something in *Alice* for everyone, and there are almost as many explanations of the work as there are commentators.

"Curiouser and curiouser," Alice's dream becomes her nightmare. A novelty at first, Wonderland becomes increasingly oppressive to Alice as she is faced with its fundamental disorder. Everything here, including her own body size, is in a state of flux. She is treated rudely, bullied, asked questions with no answers, and denied answers to asked questions. Her recita-

C

tions of poems turn into parodies, a baby turns into a pig, and a cat turns into a grin. The essence of time and space is called into question and her romantic notion of an idyllic garden of life turns out to be a paper wasteland. Even Alice's language and its assumed meanings come under attack at the mad tea party. After the March Hare interrupts to tell Alice to say what she means, she replies, "at least I mean what I say—that's the same thing, you know." But the Hatter retaliates with "Not the same thing a bit! Why you might just as well say that 'I see what I eat' is the same thing as 'I eat what I see!'"

Whether Alice, as some critics argue, is an alien who invades and contaminates Wonderland or an innocent contaminated by it, one important fact remains the same: she has a vision that shows the world to be chaotic and meaningless, a terrifying void. In order to escape that oppressive and disorienting vision, she denies it with her outcry that "You're nothing but a pack of cards!" and happily regains the morally intelligible and emotionally comfortable world of her sister, who sits next to her on the green banks of a civilized Victorian countryside.

Through the Looking-Glass abandons the fluidity and chaos of *Alice's Adventures in Wonderland* for artifice and strict determinism. In the first book the emphasis is upon Alice's adventures and what happens to her on the experiential level. In the sequel the reader accepts Alice and with detachment examines nature transformed in Looking-Glass Land's chess-board landscape. The voyage has shifted from the Kingdom of Chaos, with its riotous motion and verbal whirlpool, to the land of stasis, where the landscape is geometrical and the chessmen are carefully manipulated by the rules of a precise game. In Wonderland everybody says and does whatever comes into their heads, but in the Looking-Glass world, life is completely determined and without choice. Tweedledum and Tweedledee, the Lion and the Unicorn, the Red Knight and the White must fight at regular intervals, whether they want to or not. They are trapped within the linguistic web of the poems that give them life and their recurrent actions are forever predestined.

Whereas *Alice's Adventures in Wonderland* undermines Alice's sense of time, space, and common sense logic, *Through the Looking-Glass* questions her very reality. Tweedledum and Tweedledee express the Berkeleyian view

that all material objects, including Alice herself, are only "sorts of things" in the mind of the sleeping Red King (God). If the Red King were to wake from his dreaming, they warn Alice, she would go out like a candle. Alice, it would seem, is a mere fiction shaped by a dreaming mind that threatens her with annihilation.

The ultimate question of what is real and what is dream, however, is never resolved in the book. In fact, the story ends with the perplexing question of who dreamed it all—Alice or the Red King? Presumably, Alice dreamed of the King, who is dreaming of Alice, who is dreaming of the King, and so on. The question of dream versus reality is appropriately set forth in terms of an infinite regression through mirror facing mirror. The apprehension of reality is indefinitely deferred and the only reality may be one's thoughts and his or her well-ordered expression. Were Alice to wake the Red King, she would share the Baker's fate in *The Hunting of the Snark*. The cool geometry of Looking-Glass Land offers only a temporary oasis in a mutable, biological, and moral wasteland. Carroll recognized that the machinery of conventions and customs, mathematics and logic, reality and dreams, helped to define by contrast and momentarily sustain and comfort the frightened, imperfect, and comic adventurer.

Carroll's sense of the absurd anticipates the work of the Existentialists and Surrealists. The trial of the Knave of Hearts in *Alice's Adventures in Wonderland*, for example, points to Franz Kafka's *The Trial*. The decapitating Queen calls for the Knave of Hearts to be sentenced before the jury submits its verdict. The only evidence brought against him for stealing the tarts is a nonsense poem that is impervious to interpretation. In *The Hunting of the Snark*, Carroll presents another absurd trial in which a pig is sentenced to transportation for life for leaving its pen. By the time the sentence is handed down it is discovered that the pig has long been dead. The blank map that the Snark hunters use in their quest for the Snark also anticipates the Existentialist view of the human will seen in Jean-Paul Sartre's counsel to "leap before you look." Finally, given the fluidity of time and the dream-like atmosphere of Wonderland, it is not surprising that Salvador Dali chose to illustrate *Alice's Adventures in Wonderland* and that other Surrealists find Carroll's illustrations and prose a fertile ground for their own productions.

The great humor of the two *Alice* books, however, is what gives them their energy and immortality. It is a humor that transcends parody, satire, social wit, and slapstick—though to be sure all of those elements are there—in order to fend off the terrifying and incomprehensible issues of time, space, injustice, violence, self-identity, death, and the cosmic void. Rather than face these Medusa-like issues head-on, Carroll circles and jabs at them with his comedy. His Christian faith gave a structure and meaning to his conscious life and his humor protected that meaning from the threatening fears and uncertainties of his unconscious.

In his two-part novel, *Sylvie and Bruno* and *Sylvie and Bruno Concluded*, the writer combines the notions of spiritualists with his Christian belief in the supernatural and with his view of innocent children as emblems of angelic purity. Believing the actual world to be only a shadow of a greater spiritual reality (a belief which, as has been seen, came into serious question in his earlier works), in his novel Carroll attempts to demonstrate how one's ordinary life is shaped and controlled by invisible forces of innocence and love.

The novel is organized in such a way as to illustrate the interaction between two seemingly disparate realms, the actual world and fairyland. In depicting the former, Carroll adopts the form of the romance novel with its conventional love story ending of marriage and happiness ever after. In portraying the latter, he draws upon the conventions of the folk tale, with its rich array of fairies, secret gardens, and magical transformations. He develops his two plots simultaneously and brings them into focus through the Narrator, a London lawyer who suffers from heart trouble that induces states of semi-consciousness (or "eeriness," as Carroll calls it) and trances in which he visits the spirit world called Outland.

Summary

In contrast with the seeming placidity and orderliness of his life at Oxford, Lewis Carroll's writings exhibit considerable violence and disorder and a powerful struggle to control and contain those forces underground. This contrast, which gave rise to his two masterpieces—*Alice's Adventures in Wonderland* and *Through the Looking-Glass*—marks a fundamental conflict within Carroll himself, a ruthless battle between emotion and reason, sentiment and satire, chaos and control. Carroll was sometimes an intensely lonely man who needed the non-threatening company of children to buoy his spirits and to distract him from thoughts of death and the void. The riddles, games, and stories that he created for his child friends helped to bridge their disparate worlds. God may have been Carroll's savior but the countless children to whom he devoted the greater part of his life were his salvation. His books on mathematics and logic, which document the life of his mind, pale in comparison with his two Alice books and nonsense poetry, which document his obsession with the child girl and his unique comic battle with the great human fears that possess us all. If the puzzle of life could not be solved, at least he could create his own comic universe, complex but regulated, puzzling but engaging. Recognizing his modernity and influence, James Joyce has thus appropriately addressed Carroll in *Finnegans Wake* as "Dodgfather, Dodgson and Coo," Dodgson as Father, Son, and Holy Spirit.

Selected Bibliography
Primary Sources

Nonsense (prose)
Alice's Adventures in Wonderland. London: Macmillan, 1866.
Through the Looking-Glass, and What Alice Found There. London: Macmillan, 1871.
Alice's Adventures under Ground, Being a Facsimile of the Original Ms. Book Afterwards Developed into "Alice's Adventures in Wonderland." London and New York: Macmillan, 1886.
The Nursery Alice. London: Macmillan, 1889.
Sylvie and Bruno. London and New York: Macmillan, 1889.
Sylvie and Bruno Concluded. London and New York: Macmillan, 1893.
The Wasp in a Wig: A "Suppressed" Episode of "Through the Looking-Glass and What Alice Found There." Ed. Martin Gardner. New York: The Lewis Carroll Society of North America, 1977.

Poetry
Phantasmagoria and Other Poems. London: Macmillan, 1869.
The Hunting of the Snark. London: Macmillan, 1876.
Rhyme? Reason? London: Macmillan, 1883.
Three Sunsets and Other Poems. London: Macmillan, 1898.

C

Scholarly Works

Euclid and His Modern Rivals. London: Macmillan, 1879.

A Tangled Tale. London: Macmillan, 1885.

The Game of Logic. London: Macmillan, 1887.

Curiosa Mathematica, Part 1. A New Theory of Parallels. London: Macmillan, 1888.

Curiosa Mathematica, Part 2. Pillow Problems. London: Macmillan, 1893.

Symbolic Logic, Part 1. London and New York: Macmillan, 1896.

Diaries, Journals, and Letters

A Selection from the Letters of Lewis Carroll to His Child Friends. Ed. Evelyn Hatch. London: Macmillan, 1933.

The Russian Journal and Other Selections from the Works of Lewis Carroll. Ed. John Francis McDermott. New York: Dutton, 1935.

The Diaries of Lewis Carroll. Ed. Roger Lancelyn Greene. London: Cassell, 1953. 2 vols.

The Letters of Lewis Carroll. Ed. Morton N. Cohen. New York: Oxford University Press, 1979. 2 vols.

Lewis Carroll and the Kitchens. Ed. Morton N. Cohen. New York: The Lewis Carroll Society of North America, 1980. Twenty-five letters, nineteen photographs.

Lewis Carroll and the House of Macmillan. Ed. Morton N. Cohen and Anita Gandolfo. New York: Cambridge University Press, 1987. Carroll's letters to his publisher.

Secondary Sources

Biographies

Clark, Ann. *Lewis Carroll*. London: J.M. Dent, 1979. A thorough, well-researched biography, sympathetic but lacking in analysis.

Collingwood, Stuart Dodgson. *The Life and Letters of Lewis Carroll*. London: T. Fisher Unwin, 1898. The standard family biography, by Carroll's nephew.

Hudson, Derek. *Lewis Carroll: An Illustrated Biography*. New York: New American Library, 1978. The best biography to date, despite its defensive attitude towards psychological interpretations of Carroll's life and work.

Lennon, Florence Becker. *Victoria through the Looking-Glass: The Life of Lewis Carroll*. London: Cassell, 1947. A somewhat disorganized study that contains much information found in no other biography and offers some excellent literary criticism and psychological insights.

Pudney, John. *Lewis Carroll and His World*. London: Thames and Hudson, 1976. A brief biography enriched with many illustrations and photographs.

Books

Gattegno, Jean. *Lewis Carroll: Fragments of a Looking-Glass*. Trans. Rosemary Sheed. New York: Crowell, 1976. A potpourri of analytical snippets that probe Carroll's psychology. Stimulating, though highly speculative, readings.

Gernsheim, Helmut. *Lewis Carroll: Photographer*. New York: Chanticleer Press, 1949. A comprehensive study of Carroll's photographic art, with sixty-four photographic plates.

Greenacre, Phyllis. *Swift and Carroll: A Psychoanalytic Study of Two Lives*. New York: International Universities Press, 1955. The most intelligent and provocative psychoanalytic study of Carroll to date.

Guiliano, Edward, ed. *Lewis Carroll Observed*. New York: Clarkson N. Potter, 1976. A collection of unpublished photographs, drawings, and poetry by Carroll, and fifteen essays about his work.

————, ed. *Lewis Carroll: A Celebration*. New York: Clarkson N. Potter, 1982. Fifteen essays on the occasion of the 150th anniversary of Carroll's birth.

Hancher, Michael. *The Tenniel Illustrations to the "Alice Books."* Columbus: Ohio State University Press, 1985. Hancher traces the artistic roots of Tenniel's illustrations of the *Alice* books to his work for *Punch*, the paintings of various artists, photographs, and Carroll's own drawings.

Kelly, Richard. *Lewis Carroll*. Boston: Twayne, 1990. Kelly examines Carroll's life and writings and demonstrates the intimate relationship between the two. Views Carroll's humor as the author's means of combating his fears of disorder and death.

Phillips, Robert, ed. *Aspects of Alice: Lewis Carroll's Dream-child as Seen Through the Critics' Looking-Glasses*. New York: Vanguard, 1971. The largest single collection of critical essays; includes a useful bibliography of items from 1865 through 1971.

Sewell, Elizabeth. *The Field of Nonsense*. London: Chatto and Windus, 1952. An influential study of the principles of nonsense, based upon logical and linguistic considerations.

Taylor, Alexander. *The White Knight*. London: Oliver and Boyd, 1952. Relates the *Alice* books to contemporary religious controversies.

Articles

Auerback, Nina. "Alice and Wonderland: A Curious Child." *Victorian Studies*, 17 (September, 1973): 31–47. Auerback emphasizes Alice's oral aggressiveness and sees her to be implicated in the "troubled human condition."

Kincaid, James R. "Alice's Invasion of Wonderland." *PMLA*, 88 (January 1973): 92–99. Alice is seen as bringing death, predation, and egoism into the comic harmony of Wonderland.

Madden, William A. "Framing the Alices." *PMLA*, 101 (May 1986): 362–73. Madden argues that the framing poems and prose of the *Alice* books and the text of the stories are mutually dependent.

Morton, Lionel. "Memory in the *Alice* books." *Nineteenth-Century Fiction*, 33 (December 1978): 285–308. Morton views Alice as a mediating figure between Carroll and the mother hidden in memory, comprising elements of both.

Rackin, Donald. "Alice's Journey to the End of Night." *PMLA*, 81 (October 1966): 313–26. An existential reading of *Alice's Adventures in Wonderland* in which Alice's experiences represent a person's search for meaning in a meaningless world.

Richard Kelly

Cary, Joyce

Born: Londonderry, Ireland, December 7, 1888
Education: Hurstleigh Preparatory School, Tunbridge Wells, 1900; Clifton College,
Bristol, 1903–1906; Board of Manufacturers School of Art, Edinburgh, 1907–1909; Trinity College, Oxford University, 1909–1912, Fourth Class place in Law
Marriage: Gertrude Margaret Ogilvie, June 1916; four children
Died: Oxford, March 29, 1957

Biography

George Cary, the grandson of Sir Robert Cary, Clovely Court, Devonshire, left England to become Recorder of Derry, Ireland in 1613, married the sister of Sir Tristram Beresford, bart., built a country mansion, Redcastle, near Derry, and began a line of Ascendency landowners which continued in Inishowen for 300 years until Joyce Cary's grandfather lost two castles and the family estate through the Land Act of 1881.

Arthur Joyce Lunel Cary was born in Londonderry, Ireland on December 7, 1888. The family history, with its lost lands and castles, provided the young Joyce with an aristocratic background, romantically lost but still available to wander through on holidays as well as use for settings for *Castle Corner* (1938) and *A House of Children* (1941). The Irish family debacle forced the boy to see the confrontations of religion, economics, and politics, and to recognize that things happen in human affairs which are neither fair nor any particular person's fault.

The son of Arthur Pitt Chambers Cary, an engineer, and Charlotte Louisa Joyce, the nine-year-old Arthur Joyce Lunel Cary lost his beloved mother in 1898 and in 1900 began to attend Hurstleigh Preparatory School, Tunbridge Wells, where he and his brother Jack became the butt of Irish jokes. Jack, who was athletically inclined, was invulnerable, whereas Joyce, slight of stature and with poor sight, could only find refuge in reading, writing, and drawing. The situation was even worse at Clifton College on the outskirts of Bristol, where he matriculated in 1903. Preparing students for Sandhurst and the army, the college was primarily military and athletic. Oddly enough, Joyce developed a taste for the military life which later led him to service in the Balkans and Nigeria. On the other side of his personality, he developed narrative skills by telling long, serial tales in the dormitory after lights-out. His college classmate, later Sir William Heneage Ogilvie, became a lifelong friend whose sister married Cary in early June, 1916.

At the age of seventeen, on the strength of a £300 annual bequest from his grandmother, Helen Joyce, the youth went off to study art at Edinburgh (with occasional visits to Post-Impressionist Paris). Unhappy with his artistic progress, he turned to writing, and a volume of juvenile verse under the name Arthur Cary was published in Edinburgh by Robert Grant in 1908. Later, as a novelist, Cary's art training in observation and organization would permit him to make a rough sketch of the whole and to happily work on any section of the novelistic canvas that interested him, often producing 300,000-word manuscripts which had to be pared to less than one third of that length for publication.

In 1909, Cary was in residence at Trinity College, Oxford University, reading law (he took fourth place in the 1912 examinations), although his real interests were religion and philosophy. During his third year, he shared a room with Middleton Murry.

In his final Oxford year he met his college friend's sister, Gertrude Margaret Ogilvie. He fell in love; she was dubious, and her family wondered, with good cause, if Cary would ever be able to support a wife.

From 1912 to 1913 he served as a medical orderly under the auspices of the British Red Cross in the Balkan Wars (his *Memoir of the Bobotes* was published posthumously in 1964). After considerable bravery on the field, he worked for several months with Sir Horace Plunkett's co-operative Irish Agricultural Organization Society. Having exercised both his military training and his Irish interests, he turned to his legal education by joining the Nigerian political service late in 1913, but from 1915 to 1917, he was once again in the military with the Nigerian Regiment in the Cameroons, interrupted only by his marriage to Gertrude in June 1916, a devoted love affair that continued until her painful death in 1949. The Nigerian legal-military involvement provided settings for four African novels between 1932 and 1939, one play, several short stories, and two political essays.

In 1920, the Carys left the Nigerian service and settled for the rest of their lives, a literary family with four sons (Michael, Peter, Tristram, George) at 12 Parks Road, Oxford. There followed rich and beautiful years of family life, but the first ten were also a trying time of many authorial starts, with nothing finished, nothing major published in 1920 (ten of his short stories appeared in the *Saturday Evening Post* under the name Thomas Joyce). But by 1932, Cary began a lifelong literary flow that produced sixteen novels, many short works of fiction, two long poems, political treatises, philosophical essays, and autobiographical fragments.

His African novels were followed by two studies of children: *Charley Is My Darling* (1940; working-class waifs evacuated from wartime London) and *A House of Children* (a glorious 1941 summer holiday at grandmother Joyce's estate), which won the James Tait Black memorial prize.

Still writing until the day of his death in Oxford on March 29, 1957, Cary remained devoted to family and friends and committed to a well-ordered presentation of life.

His strong sense of topical form shaped the great central structure of three major trilogies: the first was on art (1941–1944); the second was on politics (1952–1955); and the third was on religion. His recognition in 1956 that time was running out led him to subsume the religion trilogy into a single unfinished volume, posthumously published in 1959.

Literary Analysis

It is doubtful that Cary could be called a humorist in the sense of constantly injecting humor into his narratives. The humor is certainly there, but it emerges from a larger sense of a cosmic comic structure of life. The ironic divergence between the official record and the actual event is the arena in which he performs his dramas of contradiction. In his great trilogy, a single person describes two other persons, but in the descriptions we are forced to recognize the discrepancy between one man's point of view and the private views of those described. The objective truth (if it exists) differs wildly and comically from the subjective view. An actor seems to himself far different from the way others see him, and therein lies his comic dilemma. Most hilarious and pathetic is the divergence between the official record and the actual event. Abundant examples are provided by *Aissa Saved*, the first of the African novels (1932) and his first commercial success.

Aissa, a Christian missionary convert, is eaten alive by soldier ants after she has been maimed, her infant beheaded, and her husband slain. So how can the book be named *Aissa Saved*? Of course, she is "saved" in the evangelical sense and has been listed in London as a triumphant missionary convert. The comic divergence between fact and reporting is everywhere in the novel. Cary, the mildest and most benevolent of men, endlessly patient with family and friends, filled his books with violence, disaster, and horrible death. In the midst of these horrors, the author writes calmly, patiently explaining, like Pangloss in Voltaire's *Candide*, that this is all to be expected and, indeed, could not occur otherwise. The setting is incorrigibly comic, with its planting of genteel British missionaries in Nigerian bush villages. Comic, too, is the built-in divergence between what the missionaries think they are saying when they witness and what the natives hear them saying. In the book's "Prefatory Essay," Cary admits that "Some correspondents took the book for an attack on the Missions. It is not so. African missions have done good work in bringing to Africa a far better faith than any native construction. But it does try to show what can happen to the religious ideas of one region when they are imported into another." How can the twentieth-century missionary who believes in the omnipotence of God explain to primitive animists that this doctrine operates only in the ultimate sense; it does not mean what the native convert understands, that "He can do anything," or that "He'll give me anything I ask for." Obviously there are at least four levels of data here: the meaning to the ancient Jew, to the New Testament Christian, to twentieth-century Britons, and to primitive Nigerians. Even more changes can be played: the meaning of omnipotence when I am good, when I am bad, when I am young, when I am old, when drunk, and when sober. The result is the most savage misunderstandings treated as part of a cosmic comedy built into the very nature of the universe.

In the central body of Cary's work, the three great trilogies, the author addressed the overwhelming topics of art (*Herself Surprised* [1941], *To Be a Pilgrim* [1942], *The Horse's Mouth* [1944]), politics (*Prisoner of Grace*, [1952], *Except the Lord* [1953], *Not Honour More* [1955]), and religion (*The Captive and the Free* [1959]). These modern triptychs by their very structure proclaim that life has form and that that form has meaning. Thus, in the trilogy on art, voluptuous cook Sara Monday, conservative lawyer Thomas Wilcher, and rebellious cook artist Gulley Jimson insist that art draws its power from life and must never suffer divorce. The second trilogy, on politics, starts with the idea of freedom as simple absence of restraint but moves rapidly to the complex concept of freedom as the area of operation of individual creative power which must be preserved by all of the institutions of society and all of the plural interest groups of a modern state. And in his essay *Power in Men* (1939), Cary claimed that, although the power to create was the basic moral absolute for the individual, a constantly expanding political freedom must also be assured by the wise state. Along with the early George Orwell, he thought that in the Soviet experiment he had found a state that was revolutionary in origin and assured of final world mastery. All of his novels were set in the end of the nineteenth century up to World War II, a period that he described as "progress into liberty."

The Horse's Mouth, the third novel in the trilogy about the nature of art and the artist's role in society, is Cary's most widely read work. The first novel shows us Sara as a woman whose flesh and appetites always defeat the platitudes that she utters, and it is exactly her vital flesh which becomes the Muse to inspire the artist Jimson. Son of an Academy painter, Jimson has the misfortune to encounter Impressionism through an Édouard Manet painting: "that lovely vibrating light, that floating tissue of colour" (chapter 13). It is thus clear that art, as are politics and religion, is an expression of epistemology, the sensations that vibrate, the colors that float, transferred by the individual eye to the canvas.

If Impressionism is a theory of sensation, a possibility of knowledge, then Jimson stands right beside Mr. and Mrs. Carr, the missionaries who converted Aissa. All three see an individual vision; is it true, is it shared by others, is it standard? But, for Gulley Jimson, Impressionism is only a phase, albeit his most successful epoch. William Blake's Job drawings knocked Manet out of Jimson's mind and studio, replacing Manet with romantic classicism of line and symbolism of meaning. Studies of the nude Sara are put away; great religious murals on "Adam and Eve," "The Raising of Lazarus," and "The Creation" take her place. Jimson's clientele drops off, canvases are used to patch roofs, left unfinished, or completed just in time for the chapel wall to be demolished, but these accidents are of no importance. The eye has moved from sensation to significance and the reaction of patrons is irrelevant. The works are unappreciated, but the individual vision has been rep-

C

resented. The murals are incomplete or demolished, but the work is of no importance, only the life of creativity. Jimson neglects father, mother, wife, and child. He shoplifts paint; he steals canvas; he robs his protege; he spends time in jail. All of these things occur not because the artist is immoral but because the state has not yet recognized its responsibility for the nurture and expansion of human creative freedom. As every man makes his own world out of chaos, so a study of the artist is also an analysis of Everyman. Of all of the confrontations of divergent views celebrated in Jimson's work, the central tension lies between the traditional and the conservative on the one hand, and the dynamic and creative on the other. As he hyperbolically pronounces in his soliloquy on government, "the only good government . . . is a bad one in the hell of a fright; yes, what you want to do with government is to put a bomb under it every ten minutes" (chapter 32). What a drastic technique for turning the conservative tradition into the dynamic creative!

In 1958, the year after Cary's death, a film version of *The Horse's Mouth* was released. Directed by Ronald Neame and starring Alec Guinness, the marvelous movie, from a screenplay by Guinness, ends differently than the novel—Jimson destroys the chapel wall, claiming that only the artist has the right to destroy his art. The shift in responsibility is interesting, and the concluding scene of Jimson on his houseboat floating down the River Thames and considering the hulls of ships as possible canvases is more "Hollywood" and uplifting than was his death at the close of the novel.

William Van O'Connor accused Cary of "refusing to plot . . . insisting on giving his demon its way." Perhaps it is precisely the wayward demon that gives Cary his verve and breathless forward haste. Andrew Wright paid particular attention to Cary's comedic style: "The Smollettesque dialogue, the Shandean capital letters, the Dickensian names, the brackets (and brackets within brackets), the historical present tense, the abrupt chapter divisions, above all the picaresque structure." Still, L.A.G. Strong makes the most comprehensive summary when he claims that Cary was everywhere and always engaged in "the Comedy of Freedom."

Summary

Joyce Cary is the master of the unexpected simile, a fantastic plot structure slowed down by the intrusive author lecturing on everything, hyperbole unlimited, and the basic assumption that justice is a mental concept unknown in actual experience. As Giles Mitchell says, Cary's style may be comedic, but his moral responsibility to art is very serious—Gulley Jimson is the innocent artist determinedly claiming the freedom to create in an "unholy society." Cary finds on the earth no other kind of society and insists that free creativity is the only worthwhile activity for mankind.

Selected Bibliography
Primary Sources
Aissa Saved. London: Ernest Benn, 1932.
An American Visitor. London: Ernest Benn, 1933.
The African Witch. London: Victor Gollancz, 1936.
Castle Corner. London: Victor Gollancz, 1938.
Mister Johnson. London: Victor Gollancz, 1939.
Charley Is My Darling. London: Michael Joseph, 1940.
A House of Children. London: Michael Joseph, 1941.
Herself Surprised. London: Michael Joseph, 1941.
To Be a Pilgrim. London: Michael Joseph, 1942.
The Horse's Mouth. London: Michael Joseph, 1944.
The Moonlight. London: Michael Joseph, 1946.
A Fearful Joy. London: Michael Joseph, 1949.
Prisoner of Grace. London: Michael Joseph, 1952.
Except the Lord. London: Michael Joseph, 1953.
Not Honour More. London: Michael Joseph, 1953.
The Captive and the Free. New York: Harper, 1959.
First Trilogy. New York: Harper, 1958.
In addition to his novels, Joyce Cary wrote three political treatises, two long poems and three short poems, twenty-seven essays in literary criticism, and twenty-nine miscellaneous essays.

Secondary Sources

Biographies
Foster, Malcolm. *Joyce Cary: A Biography*. Boston: Houghton Mifflin, 1968. A full

study of Cary's life and family. More chatty than informative about individual works.

Books
Allen, Walter. *Joyce Cary*. London: Longmans, Green, 1953. Writers and Their Work series, No. 41. The pioneer study and still a concise and reliable criticism.
Hoffman, Charles G. *Joyce Cary: The Comedy of Freedom*. Pittsburgh: University of Pittsburgh Press, 1964. Thoroughly detailed study of the novels, always intellectually stimulating and pertinent.
Mahood, M.M. *Joyce Cary's Africa*. London: Methuen, 1964. Nigerian scholar's view of the relationship of Cary's African service and his African writing.
Modern Fiction Studies, Joyce Cary Issue, 9, 3, Autumn 1963. This special issue gives both broad coverage and detailed analysis of individual work by a variety of commentators.
Noble, R.W. *Joyce Cary*. New York: Harper and Row, 1973. Modern Writers Series. Considering Wright's study too heavy on metaphysics and social philosophy, Noble concentrates on language and form.
Wright, Andrew. *Joyce Cary: A Preface to His Novels*. New York: Harper and Brothers, 1958. Based on full access to British letters and manuscripts and frequent interviews with Cary, quite ideological, with nine pages of Cary's Preliminary Notes, nine pages locating William Blake quotations in *The Horse's Mouth*, and full bibliography.

Elton E. Smith

Chapman, George

Born: Hitchin, Herfordshire, 1559
Education: Attended Oxford University, 1574
Died: London, May 12, 1634

Biography
In 1559, George Chapman was born in the small town of Hitchin in Herfordshire to Thomas and Joan Chapman. The poet's father was a copyholder and a very rich man. His mother was the daughter of a member of King Henry VIII's court. Despite his father's wealth, Chapman suffered the constraints of poverty throughout his entire life. He was the second son in the Chapman household, and, therefore, his elder brother Thomas inherited the estate. George did attend Oxford University in 1574, but the length of his sojourn is not known, and he did not receive a degree from the institution. He was a servant in the household of Ralph Sadler between 1583 and 1585, and, in 1591 and 1592, he saw military service on the continent. In 1594, he became a member of Walter Ralegh's "School of Night," a group of intellectuals dedicated to the exploration of science and the occult. Chapman began his literary career during this period, a successful vocation that, paradoxically, would bring him continued poverty and occasional disgrace. The poet was imprisoned for debt in 1599 after being defrauded by John Wolfall, an infamous usurer. The poet's greatest hope of prosperity was swept away with the death of King James's son Henry, who sponsored a portion of Chapman's translation of the *Iliad*. However, when the prince died, his father would not continue the patronage. The poet was jailed once again in 1605 when his collaborative dramatic effort *Eastward Ho* offended the King. Chapman died in London on May 12, 1634.

Chapman's poetic career includes his greatest successes as a writer. Approximately eighty of his poems were published in Robert Allot's anthology *The English Parnassus* (1600). He completed Christopher Marlowe's *Hero and Leander* in 1598. However, his most celebrated achievement was his translation of Homer's *Iliad* (1611) and *Odyssey* (1614–1615).

The author's dramatic career began in 1595 with the production of his play *The Blind Beggar* by the Lord Admiral's men at the Rose theater. His drama *An Humorous Day's Mirth* was staged in 1597 at the same location. In 1599, Chapman began writing plays for the Children of the Blackfriar, and here he had a string of successful comedies: *All Fools* (1599), *Sir Giles Goosecap* (date unknown), *May Day* (1601), *The Gentleman Usher* (1602), *Monsieur d'Olive* (1604), *The Widow's Tears* (1605), and *Eastward Ho* (1605).

During the Jacobean period, the playwright wrote a series of six tragedies, five of which were based on French history. Chapman's *Bussy D'Ambios* (1604) was his most renowned dramatic venture, and this was followed by a sequel, *The Revenge of Bussy*, several years later. In the same period, he composed his controversial two-part drama *The Conspiracy and Tragedy of Byron* (1608). When the French Ambassador complained of the play's content, Chapman only narrowly escaped another jail term. The final two tragedies are currently undated; these include *Chabot*, another play based on French chronicles, and *Caesar and Pompey*, a Roman tragedy believed to have been written around the same time as *Bussy*.

Literary Analysis

Chapman was an innovator in the development of dramatic comedy. His play *Blind Beggar* is believed to be the first comedy of humors, a dramatic form later popularized by Ben Jonson, and Chapman also participated in the development of the romantic comedy later perfected by other Jacobean dramatists. However, neither of these styles fully represents the humor of Chapman's plays. The characteristic that seems fundamental to most of his comedies is the struggle between the forces of riot and moderation, a comedic formula termed saturnalian by C.L. Barber. Commonly, Chapman's humorous plays involve the antics of a good-natured intriguer determined to expose folly and to remove the obstacles to mirth and romance, thereby liberating the conservative and inhibited characters from their pretensions and preoccupations. Thus, much of Chapman's comedy involves situational humor, and this discussion will be focused on the amusing and intricate circumstances that arise when one individual tries to reveal the foolishness of others.

The central figure of *The Blind Beggar* is easily the most cunning manipulator in the galaxy of Chapman's characters. He assumes so many disguises that it is difficult to determine his correct title. He is Irus the blind visionary, Cleanthes the banished Duke, Leon the notorious usurer, and the ill-tempered Count. He uses his many personalities to dominate and exploit the other characters in the drama, and the convolutions of his schemes become quite amusing despite the often destructive ramifications of his actions. Posing as Irus, he predicts the future romances of Elimine and Samathia, telling them which husbands to choose, and then, in the same personas that he foretold, woos them himself. He courts Elimine while he is disguised as the Count and Samathia while he poses as Leon. Then later in the drama, he successfully cuckolds himself by reversing the roles. The women are not the only victims of his amusing, yet destructive, pranks. Masquerading as Leon, he loans £4,000 to Antithenes, who offers his lands as collateral; when the debtor repays his obligation, though, Leon refuses to return the deed to the lands. After the debtor seeks justice from the king, the intriguer appears in three different disguises to act as a witness in his own defense, arguing that Antithenes never paid his debt. Consequently, Leon is allowed to retain the property. Clearly, in this drama, the blind beggar represents the spirit of riot and disorder; however, contrary to the plays that follow, the intriguer works his plots only for his own pleasure and advancement, very aptly proclaiming "The joys of many I in one enjoy." His actions do not serve to liberate others from inhibition. Instead, paradoxically, they are both harmful and amusing.

Lemot, the comic manipulator of Chapman's *An Humorous Day's Mirth* (1597), causes the many rigid and self-tormented characters in the drama to recognize the folly of their behavior. His first task is to expose the hypocrisy of Florila, the self-proclaimed puritan whose conspicuous display of virtue is intended to liberate her from the tyranny of her overly jealous husband, Labervele. Lemot attempts to seduce Florila after convincing Labervele that the effort will not corrupt her but instead will constitute a reaffirmation of her virtue when she repels the affront. Labervele agrees to permit the rogue an audience with Florila. However, Lemot soon finds that she is a willing participant who seeks ways to reassure her husband, while at the same time plotting an act of adultery. She wantonly agrees to a rendezvous with Lemot away from her husband's watchful eye, but finds that the rogue merely wants to strip her of her pretensions to virtue. When they meet, Lemot courts the lady roughly, biting her hand, and when she complains, he advises her to return to her husband and to put off her puritanical pose, for she has "discredited . . . [her] religion for ever." Ironically, when she returns, she once again assumes the posture of a puritan and upbraids her husband for his mistrust, soliciting an apology from the unsuspecting man.

In many ways, the predicament of Martia is similar to that of Florila: Martia is a maid who cannot escape her overly protective father and his ever-vigilant servant, Labesha, who is also a hopeful suitor to the young maid. Manipulating Martia, Lemot creates jealousy and confusion in the drama. He lures her away from her father, promising that Labesha will watch her, and then he distracts Labesha with flattery so that the guardian neglects his office. When Martia is free, Lemot uses her to create friction among other characters, telling the jealous Countess Moren and the Queen that their husbands are keeping the company of the young maid and providing an opportunity for them to actually see Martia in the men's company. The conflicts are eventually resolved when Martia is betrothed to the overly melancholy Dowsecer, a match that promises to brighten the young man's sullen disposition. At the same time, the many strife-ridden characters are purged of their jealous humors and experience a return to mirth and romance. Thus, Lemot's roguish and amusing activities create a playful confusion that forces the characters to confront and address their own limitations and that ends as do all Renaissance comedies, in marriage and harmony.

Chapman's drama *All Fools* also involves the schemes of a master intriguer who manipulates everyone in the drama, but who—contrary to Lemot—is eventually exposed as a fool as well. The central conflict of the drama lies in the restrictions imposed by the older generation and the efforts to circumvent those restraints by the young. Rinaldo selflessly intercedes on behalf of his brother Fortunio and a friend, Valerio, both of whom are in love but are forbidden to marry without parental approval. However, Valerio has already married Gratiana without his father's knowledge, and Fortunio is in love with Gostanzo's daughter, Bellanora.

Much of the humor in the play surrounds Rinaldo's ability to deceive the worldly and politic Gostanzo, father of Valerio. He creates an opportunity for all four lovers to be housed under one roof, telling Gostanzo that Fortunio has married Gratiana without permission and asking that the two be allowed to stay in Gostanzo's house to give Fortunio's father time to overcome his wrath. When Gostanzo concedes, both pairs of lovers are united under one roof. Still, their indiscretions create additional problems. Gostanzo witnesses his son kissing Gratiana, the woman whom he believes is Fortunio's wife, so he expels the lovers from the house, not wanting adultery to be carried out under his supervision. The clever and amusing Rinaldo once again rectifies the situation, this time disguising the truth as a lie. He asks Gostanzo to get Valerio and Gratiana admitted as husband and wife into Marc Antonio's home.

Thinking the ploy a ruse staged solely for Marc Antonio, Gostanzo feigns anger at his son's actions, but eventually forgives him. Ironically, he does not realize that his false actions constitute a commitment to endure his son's actual marriage when it is exposed. His reaction is a rehearsal for events at the end of the drama. The humor of the situation lies in Gostanzo's foolish belief that he understands and controls his son. He believes that Valerio is inexperienced in the art of love, while in reality the young man has already married in secret.

Rinaldo's manipulations are not confined to Gostanzo alone. He also fuels Cornelio's jealous rage against his wife, hoping that if the husband divorces her, she will be available for the amorous advances of someone else, but Cornelio recoils from divorce at the last moment, and instead of losing his wife, he manages to gull Rinaldo. He tells the young manipulator that Valerio has been arrested and that Rinaldo must inform Gostanzo. When the father arrives at the designated location, though, he finds his seemingly virtuous son involved in drinking and dicing. Valerio's true character is revealed, and Rinaldo is exposed as a rogue. This playful inter-generational conflict between fathers and sons is truly saturnalian comedy. The young men and women represent the riotous spirit of fun, while the fathers constitute the obstacles to pleasure and romance. Through his actions, Rinaldo circumvents the impediments to mirth, undermining the foolish constraints of the fathers and promoting the progressive values of the sons.

In Chapman's *Sir Giles Goosecap*, comic trickery is not as fundamental to the central action of the drama as it is in the three above-mentioned plays. The gulling of Sir Giles and his two ill-humored companions, Foulweather and Rudesby, actually constitutes a subplot, yet it contains all of the truly amusing events in the drama. The roguish young pages, Jack, Bullaker, and Will, decide to expose the foolishness of the three elder knights. Knowing that the knights are fond of Eugenia, Hyppolita, and Penelope, the pages send the gentlemen on a wild-goose chase to meet the ladies. The pages indicate that Eugenia and her companions have requested the knights' company for breakfast in Barnet, about ten miles from town. Of course, the women are aware of no such plans. Excited, the gentlemen decide to ride to Barnet in the dark in order to ensure their prompt arrival. As one would expect, the nocturnal trip of three

C

fools results in slapstick mishaps such as Sir Giles's falling into a ditch. The comic potential of three doltish knights wandering in the dark can only be fully realized in the production of the drama. Naturally, the fools are curious when the ladies do not arrive for breakfast, and in order to continue the prank as well as to save themselves from punishment, the pages suggest that the ladies are merely trying to test the gentlemen's patience and that Eugenia and her friends hope to determine which knight will prove himself most indulgent by not mentioning the slight. With this comic twist, the pages manage to prevent the discovery of their deception.

The stupidity of Sir Giles is the source of laughter later in the drama as well. When he is invited to Eugenia's for dinner, he becomes the entertainment, demonstrating his rather unmanly skill at sewing and his inaccurate observations of the natural world: as he sews an image of the sea onto a garment, he suggests that the water is so "lively" that the ladies will hear it "rore" with their eyes, and later he creates the image of a camel with horns. He also brags of his skill in lighting tobacco with glow worms. The amusing ignorance of Sir Giles is intensified by his obvious belief that he is a serious and respectable man. Thus, when he becomes the object of laughter, he unwittingly participates in the saturnalian revels and ironically constitutes an undermining of solemnity as restraint gives way to mirth.

In *Monsieur d'Olive*, Chapman once again satirizes folly, suggesting that those who take themselves too seriously are ultimately humorous. The masterful manipulator of the drama is Vandome, who strives to liberate others from grief and melancholy. Count Vaumont unjustly accuses his wife of adultery with Vandome. Recognizing his mistake, he apologizes, but not before his wife locks herself in a tower, vowing never to emerge to create more suspicion. At the same time, the countess of St. Anne, Vandome's sister, has died; her husband, refusing to accept her loss, will not surrender her body for burial. Vandome attempts to intercede in both of these cases. Initially, he visits Count St. Anne and convinces him to release his wife's body, thereby liberating the nobleman from inordinate grief and clearing the way for his happiness. The handling of Vaumont's wife requires more guile. To trick her into quitting her solitary life, Vandome tells her that her husband is involved in an adulterous affair. She emerges, cursing

Vaumont and promising to end his adultery. When she leaves her cell, she breaks her vow of isolation, and Vandome suggests that reconciliation with her husband must then follow, since she is now guilty of the same accusation by which her husband injured her—the wrongful charge of adultery.

The most humorous aspect of the play lies in the satiric subplot that parallels Vandome's actions. Monsieur d'Olive, an upstart courtier, is clearly a malcontent who is excessively critical of others. Upon his introduction, he attacks many of the common objects of satire, such as corrupt courtiers, lawyers, and women. However, as is predictable, this satirist becomes the object of ridicule himself. He is given a commission by Duke Philip to retrieve the body of Countess St. Anne from her grief-stricken husband. In a parody of the pomp and circumstance of courtly life, d'Olive involves himself in such a mighty preparation for his task that Vandome is able to rescue the body and return before d'Olive and his legion of followers are ready to depart on their mission. The lampooning of this self-important and overly serious upstart demonstrates a predominance of the spirit of revelry in the drama. The more that d'Olive tries to be a correct courtier, the more doltish he becomes, while Vandome remains the example of correct, responsible, and deft action. Here again, those characters perceived as the inhibitors of sport and pleasure are forced either to capitulate to the playful members of the cast or to remain an obstacle to fun and the butt of everyone's ridicule.

Chapman once again employs his comic formula in *The Widow's Tears*. In this play, the lusty young courtier Tharsalio decides early in the drama that he will henceforth devote himself to the "patroness of all good spirits, Confidence," whom he believes will make him prosper. Tharsalio's amusing boldness leads him to court the widowed Countess, Eudora, a woman of superior social standing who has vowed never to marry again after her husband's death. However, the young man does not let the lady's rank and conviction daunt him. He has arrived at the humorous conclusion that a woman's vow of chastity after her husband's demise is a pretense that can be easily fractured, so he vigorously courts Eudora, even in the face of rejection and humiliation. His first few assaults are repelled by the haughty and imperious lady, who is offended by the courtier's presumption. She calls him a dog and instructs him to "kennel without" with the other canines. Her insults do not deter Tharsalio, who even employs the assistance of a panderess—a considerable affront to Eudora's dignity and virtue. Eventually, he prevails through commitment and consistency. Thus, he breaks her obstinate resistance to happiness and romance and releases her from the considerable restrictions of her vow and her social station.

Tharsalio's work is not done once he achieves his marriage to Eudora. He seeks to purge his brother Lysander of his jealous humor. Lysander does not trust his wife Cynthia, who has vowed never to marry again after his death. Tharsalio therefore instructs Lysander to feign his own demise and observe his wife's reaction. This time Tharsalio is convinced that the woman will remain upright, and, initially, she locks herself in her husband's tomb, refusing to eat or drink. However, posing as a cemetery guard, Lysander woos his own wife, testing her oath, and eventually she submits to his advances. Stunned by Cynthia's frailty, Tharsalio informs her of her husband's machinations, and she is able to tell Lysander that she knew from the outset that it was he posing as the guard. Thus, the marriage and the lady's reputation are saved. The humor of the drama lies not only in the comic intrigue of Tharsalio but also in the amusing inconstancy of the female characters who cannot maintain their vows of fidelity to their husbands' memory.

Summary

George Chapman was devoted to the saturnalian comedic formula in which the playful forces of disorder attempt to overwhelm the conservative spirit of restraint, thus creating a lively atmosphere of revelry and romance. In each of the dramas, Chapman creates a cunning character, devoted to celebration and determined to make the other characters lead unrestrained and fulfilling lives. This legion of comic Iagos is the pivot upon which most of Chapman's humor turns.

Selected Bibliography

Primary Sources
The Plays of George Chapman: The Comedies. Ed. Allan Holaday. Urbana, IL: University of Illinois Press, 1970.
The Poems of George Chapman. Ed. Phyllis Brooks Bartlett. New York: Russell and Russell, 1962.
The Tragedies of George Chapman. Ed. Thomas Marc Parrott. London: Routledge & Kegan Paul, 1910.

Secondary Sources
Dean, William. "Chapman's *May Day*: A Comedy of Social Reformation." *Parergon*, 16 (1976): 47–55.
De Gerenday, Lynn Antonia. "The Word as Actor: Chapman's Lemot." *Cahiers Elisabéthain*, 32 (1987): 3–11.
Grant, Thomas Mark. *The Comedies of George Chapman: A Study in Development*. Salzburg: Institut Für Englische Sprache und Literatur, 1972. A comprehensive analysis of Chapman's comedies.
Hogan, A.P. "Thematic Unity in Chapman's *Monsieur D'Olive*." *Studies in English Literature, 1500–1900*, 11 (1971): 295–306.
Kaufman, Helen Andrews. "*The Blind Beggar of Alexandria*: A Reappraisal." *Philological Quarterly*, 38 (1959): 101–06.
Kreider, Paul. *Elizabethan Comic Character Conventions as Revealed in the Comedies of George Chapman*. Ann Arbor: University of Michigan Press, 1935.
Preussner, Arnold W. "Chapman's Anti-Festive Comedy: Generic Subversion and Classical Allusion in *The Widow's Tears*." *ISJR*, 59 (1985): 263–72.
Rees, Ennis. "Chapman's *Blind Beggar* and the Marlovian Hero." *Journal of English and Germanic Philology*, 57 (1958): 60–63. Rees argues that Chapman's play is a structural parody of the Marlovian hero.
Schoenbaum, Samuel. "*The Widow's Tears* and Other Chapman." *Huntington Library Quarterly*, 23 (1960): 321–38. This discussion examines the comedy and satire of Chapman's drama.
Smith, John H. "The Genesis of the Strozzo Subplot in George Chapman's *The Gentleman Usher*." *PMLA*, 83 (1968): 1448–53.
Spivack, Charlotte. *George Chapman*. New York: Twayne, 1967. A comprehensive examination of the poet's life, poetry, and drama.
Tricomi, Albert H. "The Focus of Satire and the Date of *Monsieur D'Olive*." *Studies in English Literature, 1500–1900*, 17 (1977): 281–94.
———. "The Social Disorder of Chapman's *The Widow's Tears*." *Journal of English*

and Germanic Philology, 72 (1973): 350–59.

———. "The Date of the Plays of George Chapman." *English Literary Renaissance* (1982): 242–66.

Weidner, Henry M. "The Dramatic Uses of Homeric Idealism: The Significance of Theme and Design in George Chapman's *The Gentleman Usher*." *English Literary History*, 28 (1960): 121–136.

———. "Homer and the Fallen World: Focus of Satire in George Chapman's *The Widow's Tears*." *Journal of English and Germanic Philology*, 62 (1963): 518–32.

James R. Keller

Chaucer, Geoffrey

Born: London, perhaps in the wealthy Vintry Ward, ca. 1340
Education: Uncertain
Marriage: Philippa Pan, ca. 1366; four children
Died: London, October 25, 1400

Biography

Geoffrey Chaucer was born in London in about 1340 to a wealthy family who had been vintners and customs employees for several generations in Ipswich, which is about seventy miles north of London. Chaucer's paternal great-grandfather, Andrew de Dinnington, his son, Robert Malyn le Chaucer, and Robert's son, John Chaucer, complete the paternal line of descent. Grandparents Mary and Robert Malyn le Chaucer moved to London in the late thirteenth century while remaining landowners in Ipswich. After their son John, a vintner like his father, married Agnes Copton, the couple continued to accumulate property, including twenty-four shops and two gardens, through inheritance. One Chaucer property lay in prestigious Thames Street, home of the wealthiest cosmopolitan European merchants and location of Queen Philippa's Tower Royal. Nearby were located three schools, including St. Paul's Cathedral School, which offered Latin, theology, music, and classics, and the Inner Temple, one of the Inns of Court; however, it is not known whether Chaucer was a student at these schools.

A fragmentary household account book contains the earliest mention of Geoffrey Chaucer, son of John and Agnes, as receiving a short jacket, a pair of red and black hose, and shoes in 1357 from Elizabeth de Burgh, Countess of Ulster, perhaps for use as a page in her employ. Subsequently, Chaucer followed the Countess's husband, Prince Lionel, into the army and was temporarily captured by the French near Reims in 1360. Later safe-conduct documents suggest that Chaucer traveled through Navarre, and was possibly sent by the Black Prince to recall English mercenaries from Henry of Trastamara, against whom the prince was mounting an expedition.

Chaucer, courtier, diplomat, and civil servant by occupation, emerging from the social class that produced the most notable writers in England, managed a distinguished literary career in addition to his civil service appointments. In about 1366, he married Philippa Pan, daughter of Sir Gilles, called "Paon" de Roet (a shortened form of "Panneto"), a knight of Hainault. Philippa's sister, Katherine Swynford, married John of Gaunt, son of King Edward III. Chaucer probably had four children, Thomas, Lewis, and Agnes Chaucer, and Elizabeth Chaucy.

Chaucer is recorded as being a member of the royal household in 1367 as *valettus* and *esquier*, one of some forty youths sent about England on the king's service, for which he received summer and winter robes, daily wages, annuities, appointments to office, and liveries of mourning for Queen Philippa in 1369. He may have studied among the lawyers of the Inner Temple at this time, as suggested by an Inner Temple record indicating that Chaucer was fined two shillings for beating a Franciscan Friar on Fleet Street. This would account for Chaucer's knowledge of Chancery hand and French and Latin legal formulas which prepared him to be controller of the customs and clerk of the king's works later in his career.

In 1368, Chaucer was absent from England for about 106 days, perhaps acting as a messenger to Lionel in Milan. The following year he accompanied John of Gaunt to Picardy and traveled with two Italian merchants to Genoa as a military and political negotiator. His 1373 visit to Florence no doubt introduced him to Giovanni Boccaccio and Francesco Petrarch, who would have discussed Dante Alighieri, deceased fifty years, but still influential there. The next year Chaucer was made financially independent and awarded a gallon of wine daily for life from King Edward III (worth about $6,000 today). He was also given a rent-free home over Aldgate, one of the six city gates, near the customhouse where he worked for the next twelve years, although it appears that Philippa did not live with him the entire period. At this time he was appointed controller of the export tax on wool, sheepskins, and leather; in 1382, he received an additional controllership of wine and other merchandise. In the meantime, Chaucer was sent abroad on royal business several times to Paris, Flanders, Montreuil, Lombardy, and elsewhere, once attempting a marriage negotiation between the ten-year-old Prince Richard and the eleven-year-old Marie, Princess of France.

In 1389, King Richard II appointed Chaucer clerk of the king's works, with responsibility for construction and repair of ten royal residences and other holdings (such as the Tower of London, Westminster Palace, Canterbury Cathedral, and Castle of Berkhamsted). As forester, Chaucer oversaw hunting lodges in the royal forests, mews at Charing Cross, hunting preserves, gardens, mills, pools, fences, pasturelands, fields, and villages and their churches, as well as forests.

That Philippa Pan was referred to in her own right and was granted a life annuity of ten marks as a damoiselle in attendance upon Queen Philippa suggests that Chaucer married above his station. No doubt her court connections helped his career. As esquire at court at this time, he would have kept company with musicians, song writers, intellectuals talking of the Chronicles of Kings, and other entertainers, as well as those interested in his literary services.

In 1380, a legal record freed Chaucer from the charge of *raptus* against one Cecily Chaumpaigne, which might have meant actual rape or simply abduction. Legal opinion holds that it was likely the first, and he had to seek legal acquittance. At the same time, several tradesmen released Chaucer of all actions of law, presumably for debts which he might have settled out of court. It is also possible that Chaucer was acting on behalf of one of these tradesmen who was the actual principal in the rape case; in any event, all settlement was resolved at the several dismissals of charges. This episode occurred about the time that Philippa was living in Lincolnshire.

The following year, four days after the Peasants' Revolt, Chaucer quit-claimed his father's holdings on Thames Street to a wealthy merchant named Henry Herbury. He may have been severing London connections to move to Kent, where he held two lucrative wardships. By 1385, he had been appointed to a sixteen-member commission of peace in Kent and held

this position as justice of the peace for four years. In 1386, Chaucer was elected to Parliament representing Kent, and he delivered a deposition that his friends, the Scrope family, had long held the coat of arms that the Grosvenors were attempting to usurp.

At about the same time, Chaucer received his first accolades from the French poet Eustache Deschamps, whose poetic praise extolled Chaucer's brevity, wisdom, practical learning, and translation successes. Thomas Usk, John Gower, and others concurred in their own poetry. By the late 1380s, Philippa disappeared from the records, presumably having died, and Chaucer gave up his Aldgate home of twelve years. Although he survived the King's enemies who dominated Parliament when three of his co-workers were executed, Chaucer had reached a low in his career and sustained several suits for debt. Withdrawing from some official duties, he devoted more time to the "General Prologue" of The Canterbury Tales and to some of the tales themselves.

In 1390, Chaucer was robbed and wounded three times in four days while traveling from one royal manor to another with the payroll. The beatings and injuries may have accounted for his resignation of the clerkship the following year when he was appointed forester. He is thought to have lived at Park House in Petherton Park, Somersetshire, but he remained in contact with the court until 1399 when he took a fifty-three-year lease of a house near the Lady Chapel of Westminster Abbey. Although in the late 1390s Chaucer had trouble collecting his annuities from both King Richard and King Henry IV and as a result was sued for debts, he was collecting several royal grants at the time of his death in London on October 25, 1400. He was buried in Westminster Abbey where his tomb began what subsequently became the Poets' Corner.

Literary Analysis

The chronology of Chaucer's works is uncertain, but John Fisher's edition suggests the following: Book of the Duchess, 1369; Romaunt of the Rose, 1370 (or before); Parliament of Fowles and Second Nun's Tale, 1377; Monk's Tale and Anelida and Arcite, 1376–1377; House of Fame, 1380 or 1381; Boece, 1381–1385; Troilus and Criseyde, 1382–1385; Legend of Good Women, 1385 or 1386; The Canterbury Tales begun in 1386, although some tales may have been written earlier; *Miller's Tale* and *Reeve's Tale*, 1389; *Wife of Bath's Tale*, *Friar's Tale*, *Summoner's Tale*, *Merchant's Tale*, *Clerk's Tale*, and *Franklin's Tale*, 1390–1394.

It is impossible to delimit the numerous influences and authors shaping Chaucer the writer. As a man of his times, he was versed in Scripture and the Patristic writings; he knew the work of Italian authors such as Petrarch (the source of the *Clerk's Tale*), Boccaccio (with whom he shares three tales and much other work in common), and Dante; he was familiar with French poets such as Guillaume de Lorris and Jean De Meun (who wrote the *Roman de la Rose*), Jean Froissart, and Machaut (who provided a model of the elegiac form and many lines in the *Book of the Duchess*). He borrowed beast fables (such as the Reynard story in the *Nun's Priest's Tale*) and fabliau-material from the French analogues. He knew the classics: the story of Theseus which appears in the *Knight's Tale*; Greek and Roman gods and goddesses who regularly intrude into the affairs of men, as in the *Merchant's Tale*; the Roman persecutions that contextualize the *Second Nun's Tale*; and traditional tales that comprise the *Monk's Tale*. As John Fyler says in introducing the *House of Fame* in *The Riverside Chaucer*, "Chaucer exhibits a remarkable range of reading, as he alludes to and adapts Virgil and Ovid, other classical and medieval Latin authors, the Bible, Boethius, and the French love poets" (347); he is also familiar with the many characters that Dante had described. In short, Chaucer was an educated man who drew upon his vast storehouse of knowledge but marketed it in his own special bottles, with a taste and flair all his own.

Noting that the "definition of the terms of comic techniques for Chaucer is sparse and . . . [attempting] to point up areas of research for others" (193), Paul Ruggiers nevertheless warned that "Clearly no system can do justice to any of the great geniuses of comic writing, their wit and irony, the special flavor of license, their power to challenge staid opinion, that peculiar innocence that allows them to escape defilement even in the relating of the obscene" (194). This is particularly true of Chaucer's works. Derek Pearsall is right that "Comedy of one kind or another is present in a large number of *The Canterbury Tales*, and pervasive in the links between the tales" (125). The Chaucerian canon is justly known for its humorous spirit, sparked, no doubt, by that inimi-

table, jocular narrator, affable and lovable, who unfailingly pops up, a poppet in anyone's arms, a jovial, year-round Santa. A master manipulator of time, place, circumstances, and particularly attitude and mood, this round, smiling cherub most often turns his narrative power to comedy.

Both the humorous and the comedic, generously infused into the Chaucerian corpus, are pleasurable. Humorous elements are local—funny, clever, surprising (in reversals and unmaskings), appealingly deceptive, light-hearted, and jovial. They include clever linguistic word play (puns and double entendres) as well as funny events, and occur in plot episodes (rather than the entire plot pattern) and dialogue within the links. Comedic elements are more global, encompassing the whole structure of the tale or story, and culminate in a satisfying resolution of an ending, situation, or milieu. Thus, dark, non-humorous comedies, sinister, dignified, or painful, yet with an ultimately happy ending, may result. Although serious thematic content may permeate the entire gamut of Chaucerian comedy, segments of the canon—*The Canterbury Tales* and some short works—display the humorous strain most representatively. In both humorous and comedic pieces, a triumph over mischance or an opponent in agonistic or phallic contention is often the occasion for rejoicing.

Although the Chaucerian canon may be carved into any number of configurations to display its comedy, examining the operation of time (and timing), place (or locus), circumstance (action or plot), discourse (monologue and dialogue), and tone (mood or disposition) offers a practical method to observe Chaucer's comic structure.

The coalescence of seemingly dissimilar motifs in a surprisingly appropriate confluence is often the source of humor. This congruence of two events at two places occurring simultaneously produces what Susan Wittig calls the "meanwhile-back-at-the-ranch" motif (60). The element of surprise is often the result of perfect, or unexpected, timing. According to E.M.W. Tillyard, "The surprise, the sudden union of the two themes is sublime [in the *Miller's Tale*]. It is as if, for a fraction of a second, the heavens opened and we saw all the gods watching the trivial and ridiculous human comedy below" (90). Also speaking of the *Miller's Tale*, Joseph Dane finds that it is the "sudden coalescing of these identical structures [carpenter John in a washtub awaiting waters of the flood and the cuckolding Nicholas demanding water to cool his burned bum] and the opposing imagery that lends the denouement the sense of logical inevitability and utter surprise" (216).

Appropriate timing, both a slowing down or freezing of time, and rapidly accelerating time, can also trigger humor. As David Wallace points out about the *Merchant's Tale*, "Damyan is poised to do business in the pear tree; and yet Chaucer's Merchant finds time to shift his scene with studied (almost elegant) deliberateness. Such a shift undoubtedly gains in comic effect by echoing similarly deliberate transitions at similarly awkward moments in numerous popular compositions" (*Wallace,* 148).

In some of Chaucer's works, inappropriate places for certain activities or misplaced objects are funny because of their incongruity or even their ironically surprisingly apt congruity. Ribald humor in the fabliaux often plays on misplaced or well-placed obscenity. Whether or not we accept Laura Kendrick's suggestion that the three washtubs, two round and one long, decorating the *Miller's Tale* represent God's giant "privitee," they nevertheless make a ridiculously funny sight hanging from the rafters. No less humorous is the misplaced kiss Absolon smacked on the wrong end of the laughing Alison, who is unable to resist her "Tee-hee."

In the *Reeve's Tale*, the unbridled horses who escape their harness to the freedom of the meadow inspire humor because of their symbolic reference to the free young clerks who become equally unbridled with the sunset—in the miller's house! When we envision the baby's crib, what T.W. Craik calls a "shifting landmark" (35), moved from the foot of one bed to that of another, we laugh at this unexpected "musical beds" plot device and its complications. Most shocking is the vision of Allen crawling into bed next to the snoring Miller Symkin to gloat over his rollicking love-making—with the miller's daughter. In the *Merchant's Tale*, May and Damien precariously perched in a pear tree in violently shaking *flagrante delicto* is so extraordinary as to provoke laughter for its impossible incongruity. Similarly, January's ridiculous dawn song wafting from his bed is matched only by his erect carriage as he springs up to yodel and, in contrast, his wagging, flaccid neck, not unlike the wattle or dewlap that waggles under the chin of a rooster. Which action symbolizes his sexual-

ity is not hard to determine. The marriage bed has become a humorous fiasco, a place of mockery.

Where the Friar in the *Summoner's Tale* finds his buried "inheritance" is so appropriately punitive, but equally unexpected, that the audience must laugh with old Thomas, the perpetrator. In a similar vein, where the Summoner locates those unfortunate Friars who failed to reach heaven (in an undesirable part of the devil's anatomy) is so startlingly repulsive as to jolt the observer into laughter. The place where the Pardoner's three rioters find Death, at the foot of a tree which distracts its visitors with its gold bushels, is deadly funny in a perverse sort of way.

More lighthearted in tone is the *Nun's Priest's Tale*, full of the priest's "safe" humor by which he counteracts Harry Bailly's obscene innuendoes that he is a treadfowl fit for procreating. Chaunticleer's feathering his twenty wives on a tree-branch is only slightly less jocose than Damien's precariously doing the same to Alison in their pear tree. Pertelote offers her share of mirth, perhaps in exchange for what Chaunticleer dishes out in calling women man's confusion—or is it his bliss and joy? Her retaliation, in the potent laxative she prescribes for Chaunticleer, may be said to have a local effect. But, the humorous vision of him, caught in Reynard's mouth, with arms flailing for release, is most powerful, even superseding the fear that we experience for his safety.

Craik points to the humor of place in the *Shipman's Tale* by envisioning a stage: "the poetic effect is one of stage farce: the unsuspecting cuckold ambles off the stage in one direction, and the bold seducer swaggers in from the other. The effect is to be repeated in reverse almost immediately, for the monk's business with the wife is rapidly dispatched" (63). Proper place and time, then, facilitate the farce.

In addition, proper placing or judicious juxtaposition of events or tales highlights both, adding humorous contrast. Craik says that in the *Miller's Tale*:

> Chaucer's object is, of course, the variety which comes from contrast, a "cherles tale" after a "noble storie"; but he makes the contrast more amusing by showing why the Miller insists on interrupting the Host's orderly scheme . . . The comedy results not merely from rebellious drunkenness but also from mis-

understanding: the Miller really does believe that his own tale is a worthy counterpart to the Knight's . . . The contrast and the parody are the funnier because the Miller is unaware of them. (1)

Furthermore, many of the tales gain a comic dimension, perhaps not uproarious jocularity, but a comic satisfaction, by their apropos juxtaposition with contrary or opposing tales. Fabliau quitting tales—the *Miller's* and *Reeve's*, the *Friar's* and *Summoner's*, and even the serious comedies of the *Second Nun's* and *Canon's Yeoman's* tales—most obviously reveal this phenomenon. Personal invective between the first two pairs heightens their parallel tales; contrasting plot-lines of the last adds to the comic richness by the ironic reverberation echoing in both directions. As Craik notices, "The Miller's tale follows the Knight's as a kind of unintentional parody or antimasque, and for this reason precedes the Reeve's" (31). No doubt the *Wife of Bath's Tale* and especially her humorously revealing Prologue generate the irate retort from the Clerk, notwithstanding the intervening paired fabliaux by the Friar and Summoner. An apropos sense of place, either disruptingly congruous or incongruous, within and between tales, thus engenders comedy.

Most often, details of plot or event, apart from character or tone, are simply funny. The action itself is ridiculous, incongruous, surprisingly "on target," or smacks of a sense of superiority in which the audience can join. Chaucer enthusiastically delights in mental gymnastics or clever constructs. Fabliaux action typically exemplifies this type of humor. A. Booker Thro suggests that in the *Miller's Tale* Nicholas unfolds his design in a step-by-step procedure, gradually creating a structure of apparently irrelevant materials for which we can see no final construct. When the confusion is dispelled, and "the clerk fashions coherence and relevance out of perplexity, our curiosity and bewilderment alter to a profound appreciation" (99). Thus, when foolish John crashes to the floor from his perch in the washtub, the fall and resulting clamor culminate a series of cleverly planned maneuvers and simultaneously parody the fulfillment of both the Annunciation and Noah stories. This recreation of biblical history through the contraption of hanging washtubs at the heart of the poem, which Nicholas engineers and John builds, evidences exuberant mental and physical vitality. Thro finds the comic celebration of creativity, the process and product in the *Miller's Tale*, an all-pervasive element, for its ingenious and elaborate mental constructions monopolize our attention (99). Triumphant wit wins. Farce, the expression of destructive impulses and deflation of pretension, plays a secondary role to creative ingenuity.

With somewhat different effect, when the rampant horses escape and gallop recklessly through the *Reeve's Tale*, we are caught up in their chaos and that of the clerks chasing them. In the slapstick denouement, a farcical battle in which the greedy miller is once again undone, this "gnopf" is beaten and humiliated by his wife as well as the clerks. For his stupidity, boorishness, and dishonesty, we greet his noisy demise with our own vocal laughter.

Action in the serious *Knight's Tale* may be funny because of its surprising incongruity. According to Edward Foster, "We cannot avoid the comic irony of the newly victorious Arcite falling off his charger . . . Even Arcite's funeral pyre is made of wood whose cutting comically dispossesses the woodland gods" (92). Analogously, Chaunticleer of the *Nun's Priest's Tale* falls into the mouth of the teasing fox; as Craik notes, "the cock shuts his eyes when he should keep them open, the fox opens his mouth when he should keep it shut" (71).

Furthermore, certain tales are funny because tellers, or occasionally characters, inadvertently reveal their inner character or motivation. The audience then feels "Let in on the joke, or 'privitee,'" gaining some sense of superiority, as Henri Bergson's theory of comedy describes it, over the naive or unself-aware but self-revelatory person. No doubt the Wife of Bath, the Canon's Yeoman, the Pardoner, and the Merchant unwittingly reveal their secrets in their prologues and tales, and in so doing surprise their fellow pilgrims and their audience. The Wife's marital activity—she is truly a WIFE—is humorous in its excess. Her philosophy of unbounded vitality is refreshingly humorous: five husbands at the Church door and welcome the sixth when he arrives. The circumstances of her life with each of them are equally jocose in their vivid, even bombastic, quest for life. Culminating in the slapstick routine with Jankin, when Dame Alice feigns death to frighten her assailant, this incident highlights her dramatic play; she surprises the audience no less than her unwitting competitor. Not without pathos, this rehearsal of the Wife's intimate emotions and her singularly variegated mood transformations leads to a tale of comedic resolution.

In an otherwise serious tale, the Second Nun tells of a young boy who incongruously and inexplicably sits bolt upright after being slain and surprises his awe-struck witnesses with his determined singing. Motivated in a different fashion from January's similar canticle from his bed, the action is yet funny in its unexpected response to death. Equally abrupt is his final expiration when the grain is removed from his tongue, ending the scene in an unceremonious plot conclusion.

Occasionally the circumstance, demeanor, or personality of a character may itself be funny. The Wife of Bath seems, for example, to enjoy her "center stage" role, making fun of herself and inviting the same from others. She parades herself out before the audience for the sheer joy of the attention and basks in the regard that they offer. Yet, her portraiture never draws ridicule from her observers, for she simultaneously exudes a dignity emerging from her *sprezzatura*. Foster finds the caricature of the Knight equally entertaining: "The description of the Knight's appearance in rusted and spattered armor is the perfect emblem of the way reality intrudes on his ideals but cannot destroy them. If he looks comic, the comedy is the most generous possible, always in a tone of admiring sympathy" (91). Humor is for either character not a function of moral or psychological superiority.

The circumstances of the *Shipman's Tale*, as Craik enumerates them, are set up for the fabliau genre: "the merchant so preoccupied with his business that the wife's lover may court her under his nose, the unfaithful wife who offers her favours for sale, the opportunist monk who disregards his vow of chastity" (49–50). When the self-important merchant leaves his wife with his "cosyn," the Monk Daun John, the humorous and seductive banter makes us anticipate and relish the climax. If the Monk seeks sex, the Wife seeks money. Thro finds the wife's persuasion of the monk illustrative of "how Chaucer depicts creativity as a psychologically cogent, realistic life process" (106). Craik discovers "an amusing fitness in her thinking to use [the Monk] for her own convenience, only to find at last that he has used her for his" (59). When Daun John borrows money from the merchant to give to the wife, he never intends to repay it; rather, he shamelessly, but humorously, contrives against her by revealing that she has received the francs. Only her fast-talking excuse saves her from discovery. As she paid the monk off with sex for the hundred francs, so she pays her husband off—for the same hundred francs and again with sex.

Pilgrims also tell tales that reveal much self-consciousness, an awareness that their speech reveals their character, or that they consciously intend to be understood humorously. Chaucer the Pilgrim intends a comic tale of mirth when he relates the *Tale of Sir Thopas*, funny in a way different from that of the fabliaux. Here the circumstances, pricking through the forest to seek adventure, and the unusual characters—the fairy queen and Sir Oliphant—are delightfully laughable. The birthday-party setting, jovial and childlike, creates few expectations for Thopas's valor. Indeed, the entire setting is jovial, but the circumstances are particularly amusing precisely because they are so anti-climactic. As Walter Scheps notes, "Chaucer achieves the illusion of action where none is present in two ways; first, by juxtaposing references to future time . . . with words or phrases that suggest immediacy, and, second, by enjambment which forces one line into another as though the action were proceeding at a rapid pace" (37).

This sense of timing, that the tale is progressing when indeed it is not, sets up unmet expectations, which, it becomes clear, is intentional. Scheps lists some humorous anti-climaxes such as Thopas *climbing* instead of jumping into his saddle; the giant (an elephant!) intending to slay not Sir Thopas but his horse (and this he cannot do); Thopas's not arming himself until he takes sweet wine and delectables; the narrator failing to tell of battle, chivalry, or lady's love; his promise of deeds, heroic or otherwise, never materializing. Comic incongruity, opposing the heroic and bourgeois ethos, results in absurdity: Thopas is fair and gentle *on the battlefield*, not exactly appropriate demeanor there, is born in the mercantile center of Flanders, not a noble habitat, and partakes of the unknightly sports of archery and wrestling. Finally, as Scheps points out, "The tale breaks off with the ludicrous picture of the minuscule knight drinking water continuously" (36). The entire context is established to spotlight that foolish little character. Other comic elements infuse this tale as well, from puns and wordplay to the exaggerated metrics which Chaucer is satirizing. But, the last laugh, as Scheps notes, is Chaucer's: "By characterizing himself as a minstrel who is so unskilled that he cannot retain either the attention or forbearance of his audience, Chaucer enjoys a cosmic laugh at his own expense; by characterizing his knight as a bourgeois hero he enjoys one at the expense of his fellow pilgrims" (40).

Both monologues, from an authoritative, or at least individualist point of view (including linguistic manipulation and puns), and dialogues, fostering tension between two voices, can evoke the comic spirit. Additionally, Donald MacDonald points to "comic contradiction between authoritative assertions of wisdom and misguided or otherwise inappropriate premises" (465) as a significant source of humor. The inimitable January of the *Merchant's Tale* surveys his friends' opinions about a bride, but accepts only the authority of those with whom he agrees. Justinus, who rightly warns the sixty-year-old not to marry a twenty-year-old, is ignored. Thus, when January meets his fate, we laugh at the cuckolded old bird's naive expectations that anything else would occur.

Perhaps the most apparent verbal jocularity in *The Canterbury Tales* erupts in the roughhousing, competitive, phallic, and agonistic debate between pilgrims—both good-natured and testy—in the tale-links. According to Craik, "mirth is the prevailing mood of the prologues and epilogues which link the stories together, and the comic tales often derive added power from the way in which they are introduced" (xiii). Some such as Bertrand Bronson (86) and Paul Beichner (170–72) find the interchange between Host and Pardoner an insult to the pilgrims or an elaborate joke, the nadir of humorous degradation.

Edward Foster points to the "courtly disputation between Palamon and Arcite, after the manner of Capellanus and the French romances, [which] swiftly degenerates into bickering. . . . Such humor has grim implications since departure from the forms can have brutal consequences" (91). This is pointedly true in the *Knight's Tale* and elsewhere as well. MacDonald suggests that alone among English authors, Chaucer "recognizes the possibilities for comic incongruity that arise when an expression of ostensible wisdom, which in another context would be highly respectable intellectual coin, is enlisted in support of a flagrantly erroneous premise" (455).

Straight narration or monologue likewise may be broken with witty, clever, ironic, or incongruously funny language. Speaking of wordplay in the *Knight's Tale*, Foster notes:

[the] ambiguous possibilities of the repetition of "queynte" four times in five lines . . . especially apparent since the scene is the shrine of the virgin goddess and Emily is asking that her virginity be preserved. . . . With these puns in mind it does not take an especially dirty mind to notice the frequency of the word "harnys," which does mean *armour* but is also a curiously appropriate complement to the puns on the female organs. Such a pun adds a realistic dimension to the courtly combat Palamon and Arcite plan. (89, 90)

If bawdy puns qualify the idealistic, courtly, chivalric view of *amor*, the humor lies in the tonal disparity between the two registers. Wordplay in the *Shipman's Tale* adds to the fun as well. Craik notes two ironic puns: the departing merchant advises his wife to be pliant and agreeable to all, and to take care of the household goods; ironically, she complies. His words, in this unexpected context, become humorous. Similarly, Daun John offers well-wishes, promising anything that will do him good. What he gives is the opposite. Finally, the merchant begs his wife to tell him "If any dettour hath in myn absence / Ypayead thee" (397–98), not suspecting Daun John's payment of his own marriage debt (60–66).

In speaking of the *Nun's Priest's Tale*, MacDonald states:

The comic effect of a fable of even the most primitive kind derives from the basic incongruity in the spectacle of animals behaving like humans and, in particular, using human speech; this incongruity is increased in proportion to the degree in which animals not only use the language of humans but, in so doing, display impressive erudition and a mastery of rhetorical forms. (464)

In this regard, many pilgrims and their creations vie for the laurels—the smooth-talking Wife, the suave clerks in the *Miller's Tale*, the carver who solves the verbal crux (how to divide the "inheritance") in the *Summoner's Tale*, old Mabley with the mouth in the *Friar's Tale*, the Old Man introducing Death in the *Pardoner's Tale*—the list goes on; Chaunticleer and Pertelote, however, win the fast-talking prize.

At the end of *Troilus and Criseyde*, Chaucer's "litel tragedye," he announces that he will henceforth re-create comic visions rather than tragic or epic ones. True to his word, from that point on his work veers in a comedic direction, *The Canterbury Tales* being the apotheosis of his plan. A number of tales—the *Knight's*, *Man of Law's*, *Clerk's*, *Franklin's*, *Second Nun's*, and *Wife of Bath's*—properly fit the Aristotelian definition of comedy: serious matter with a successful, happy closure to a difficult dilemma, yet lacking humorous or funny incidents. This contrasts with the more modern definition of comedy requiring lighthearted matter and tone, humorous events, and a cheerful ending. But, sometimes Chaucer's serious matter depicts disastrous events affecting characters, seeing them as victims, though comic victims. Morton Bloomfield describes the phenomenon this way: "Now, curiously enough, the continual victim tends to arouse not our pity but rather our amusement. There is something funny in a perverse way about victims. The tragedy of victimization always hovers perilously near to laughing comedy. Yet it is always sad and never really comic" (386). To various degrees, Chaucer's serious tales with successful "comic" resolutions lie in this nebulous intermediary ground between comedy and tragedy. As such, they cannot be ignored in discussions of comedy.

In the *Knight's Tale*, a balanced, stately journey through ancient Athens, Chaucer depicts monumental issues of war and justice overriding particular plot issues. The serious tone and momentous events are so dominant and all-pervasive as to preclude excessive lightness or laughter. Still, Craik finds that "cheerfulness is always breaking in, the fabric of the whole poem is shot through with Chaucer's characteristic humour and good sense" (x). Foster concurs, pointing to jocular moments, perhaps unconscious, ranging from the bawdy to the grimly ironic. Foster lists the following instances of consciously intended humor: "the Knight's delicate refusal to discuss Emily's whole ritual, the mixture of catastrophe and trivia in the temple of Mars, Saturn's speech about his qualifications to restore order, the displacement of the woodland gods for Arcite's pyre, and the Homeric comedy in the behavior of the gods" (89). The complications reside in the relationship between Palamon and Arcite, representing love and war respectively, as they vie for Emily, the courtly ideal who prefers chas-

tity to either of them. This harmoniously structured work, the longest of the tales, matches these seekers with their triad of patrons—Venus, Mars, and Diana—each promising victory. But, only in the winner's death can a resolution occur; although he wins the battle, Arcite does not live to win the prize. After much lamentation and grieving, then, a comedic ending anticlimactically evolves from a fatally tragic encounter. The serious matrimonial denouement between Palamon and Emily follows from a dignified but humorless epic, for the most part markedly devoid of laughter, yet this tale qualifies as comedic, for its final resolution is appropriate and even joyful despite its tragic climax.

In the religious narrative *Man of Law's Tale*, Chaucer extols the virtues of the forbearing Custance, who is forced to withstand much anguish and pain, finding victory in survival and reclamation of her lost life. No humorous tone or witty puns enliven the serious matter or mitigate the unwanted marriage journey from Rome to Syria on which Custance must go. Space and displacement in space function in reverse fashion here—as dangerous and harmful elements—unlike the function of place in the humorous, lighter tales of mis-placement. Like her male counterpart Job, she is sent travails unending from treacherous mothers-in-law, a would-be rapist, a false accusation of murder, and a cruel sea. Repeatedly cast out to sea, flung first from her home and then from her husband, Custance finds no joy or happiness, no reprieve from her agony. Words such as "cruel," "unhappy," "woeful," and "iniquity" reinforce the persistently oppressive tone.

Nevertheless, as Morton Bloomfield contends, this tale is a comedy, a Christian comedy, because it has a happy ending (388). Lacking all playfulness, it is ultimately resolved successfully, with the adulation of a heroic saint, a type of Christ who never lost faith with her God. Unlike the *Knight's Tale's* climax of tragedy, the first climax here is miraculous: supernatural intervention proclaiming the innocence of this steadfast victim. Perhaps the shocking sound of human speech booming from the clouds is humorous in its unpredictability.

When the Deity's voice exonerates Custance of the Queen's murder, she is freed from human oppression, offered marriage and security by the widowed Sultan, and bears a son, Maurice. But, once again, a wicked mother-in-law casts her net, falsely calling Maurice a devil, and hurling mother and son into the sea. Only the grace of God preserves the pair, returning them to the bosom of the Sultan. Even this anticlimactic rescue after the untold hardship heaped upon Custance is moderated, for we are told that the Sultan soon dies, bringing their joy to an end. Only the spiritual success of the steadfast Custance throughout her ordeals can justify calling this tale of weariness and woe a comedy, for even its conclusion offers only qualified happiness.

Likewise ponderous is the *Clerk's Tale*, the story of faithful Griselda, snatched from the poor but loving bosom of her father to the glory of marquise by the ever-testing Walter. This tale of trials offers no comic relief, no humorous dialogue or action, but it does provide a comic resolution, however unequal to the protagonist's pain. When Griselda promises complete obeisance to the bullying Walter, she never expects that this will entail submission to the murder of her daughter and then her son. The tone is dramatic and serious, admitting no humor or levity. Audience patience grows thin when Griselda, supplanted by a younger surrogate, is expected to prepare the new bride for her faithless husband. This model of submission and faithfulness successfully passes trial after endless trial. Her heroic victory which the obdurate Walter must finally acknowledge prompts the return of the children, whose murders were only feigned to test her submissiveness. The conclusion thus celebrates Griselda's steadfast obedience and the reunion of the family, a joyous, comic resolution to a serious, emotional tale.

The Breton Lai *Franklin's Tale*, a concise Celtic romance of poetry and magic set in Brittany, contains moments of levity and joy interspersed with those of anguish and indecision, and finally concludes with a satisfying resolution perhaps worthy of the generous Franklin. A joyful wedding begins this fairy-tale story, but the husband Arveragus's departure puts Dorigen in jeopardy. Fending off the would-be lover Aurelius, she playfully retorts that she will accede to his demands only if he makes the treacherous coastal rocks vanish. When they in fact seem to disappear, the shocked, dismayed wife is caught between two promises. Anguishing over her plight, she confesses her dilemma to Arveragus, who generously sends her to fulfill her promise. But magnanimity finds its match, first in the lover who refuses to take advantage of such a generous husband, and then in the magician who refuses to accept pay-

ment from the equally generous lover. Although critics have questioned the wisdom and helpfulness of a husband who sends his wife on an unwanted encounter, his motives cannot be impugned. The conclusion is unambiguously happy, for unlike the previous serious comedic tales, this tale depicts no one injuring or taking advantage of another. By kindness and generosity, an harmonious resolution satisfies both the characters and the audience in a comedic and joyful victory.

A serious and determined tone marks the *Second Nun's Tale*, the legend of a busy St. Cecilia converting her husband, brother-in-law, and citizens of Rome during the persecutions. Little outright laughter breaks the solemnity of this tale, although moments of humor intrude, perhaps unintentionally. The business of conversion is a weighty one and brooks no interference. When in fact Cecilia audibly laughs, her gesture marks the power of God now fortifying her. Cecilia's moral and religious victory is paid for with her life, but the ethos of the tale and its resolution locates it as comedic—a grand celebration—for the souls won to Christ, before her captors end her mission and her life, have gained salvation. Thus, a joyous closure smack in the face of physical death concludes a comic tale of success.

The *Wife of Bath's Tale*, a fairy-tale romance, begins with rape and a thoughtful reparation of the damage done to an innocent maid. Throughout the tale, until the culmination, the tone is one of anxious quest and resolute acceptance, not joyful celebration. Although circumstances occasionally are lighthearted—the fairies dancing out of the magical fairy mound—they conspicuously contrast the deadly serious business being enacted. Clearly the rapist-knight feels impending doom if he fails to discover what women most want. The answer from the hag (a woman not pleasantly humorous, but grotesquely so) initiates the turning-point in the story, though not without further anguish for the criminal.

Chaucer's early works, the *Book of the Duchess, House of Fame*, and *Parliament of Fowles* being the most well known, are more subtly and gently humorous than the rollicking plot contrivances or comic resolutions of serious narratives. The *Book of the Duchess* is a lament for the deceased Blanche, ostensibly a consolation to her husband, John of Gaunt, a sorrowful recollection of her beauty and goodness. Within its parameters are the most striking images which can only be called funny. Envision for example, the shock of a horse patiently waiting in the Dreamer's room, ready for action at his awakening. Further, the Dreamer's ploy to bribe the god Morpheus with a feather pillow so that he can get some sleep is a marvelous stroke. His obtuse and painstaking questioning of the Black Knight whom he meets crying by a tree is itself funny. However, none of the humor detracts from the serious and respectful commemoration which this charming poem offers.

The *House of Fame* introduces us to that jolly narrator with a hearty sense of humor. Book 2 depicts Geoffrey being swooped away by a golden eagle with long sharp nails who carries him to the heights in his claws "as lyghtly as I were a lark." The frightened and astonished narrator, finally brought to his senses by a squawking bird, is told that he is a troublesome burden to carry. Fantasizing first his demise and then that Jove will make him a heavenly star, Geoffrey is finally distracted by his conversation with the eagle about his love poetry. The humorous construct of visiting the House of Fame is the means to inform this naive eagle-rider.

The *Parliament of Fowles* likewise offers a joyful garden setting and humorous interaction between the Valentine's Day participants. As Francis J. Smith says:

> The manner and spirit of *The Parliament of Foules* is light and gay; such a mirthful approach is immediately delivered by the title itself, which is essentially mock-serious, as well as the opening line "The lyf so short, the craft so long to lerne," which is, with deliberate comedy, distorted to fit a context of love matters. In other words, Chaucer did not save his fun for the chatter of birds in the last fourth of the poem but only allowed the comedy to rise gradually to a full climax in that part of it. (16–17)

The humorously verbose avians arguing among themselves give rise to the orderly Parliament, an attempt at a comic resolution which, however, is forestalled by the formal eagle herself. According to Smith, "the very situation of choosing a mate on a given date is farcical, as silly as the gondoliers in Gilbert and Sullivan's romp of marriage who choose blindfolded or as whimsical as Palamon's contention that Emily is his true love because he saw her first" (20).

Several of the short lyrics are written in a jocular vein, or contain humorous elements, especially those comic requests for patronage such as "The Complaint of Chaucer to His Purse." The "Lenvoy de Chaucer a Bukton" on marriage humorously invites the Wife of Bath to read the poem. In "To Rosemounde," Chaucer claims never was pike more steeped in Galatine sauce than he is steeped in love for the lady, a surprisingly funny image preceding the humorous appellation with which he styles himself—"the second Tristam." Taken together, these short works are one more indication, in yet another mode, of the Chaucerian sense of humor for which the master is so well known.

Summary

The concept of comedy is complicated and multifaceted. The most obvious definition, and recognizable characteristic, no doubt includes the humorous and funny, established on a local and limited scale. Time, place, circumstance, and discourse can all be manipulated for effect by one with an ironic or simply wry sense of the world. A second, perhaps more sophisticated aspect of comedy finds embodiment in satisfying closure, denouement, and completion: reestablishment of some social or physical harmonious order. Geoffrey Chaucer uses his wry sense of humor in both ways. As Foster points out, "consistent with his role as human comedian, Chaucer does not stop with the comfort of a philosophical resolution" (93). Such a comic resolution accompanies and reinforces his expansive vision of the ironic, the witty, the incongruous, the surprising. No doubt Andreas is right in calling *The Canterbury Tales* the greatest comic poem in western literature (58). The balance of Chaucer's corpus, the short works and lyrics, while not principally or exclusively humorous, reiterate the ever-prevalent Chaucerian sense of humor in wry content, densely reverberating texture, and philosophical resolution. No doubt this jovial poppet of a man, as Harry calls him, like his Troilus, is somewhere out there in the eighth sphere laughing at these mere mortals obsessed with dissecting and evaluating his methodology and categorizing his brands of humor instead of enjoying their comic resonances.

Selected Bibliography

Primary Sources
Geoffrey Chaucer: The Works, 1532, with
    Supplementary Material from the Edi-

tions of 1542, 1561, 1598, and 1602. Ed. William Thynne. Berkeley, CA: Scolar Press, 1969; rpt. 1976.

The Canterbury Tales, 1775–78. Ed. Thomas Tyrwhitt. London: Pickering, 1830. 5 vols.

The Complete Works of Geoffrey Chaucer. Ed. Walter W. Skeat. Oxford: Clarendon, 1894–1897. 7 vols.

The Book of Troilus and Criseyde, Edited from All the Known Manuscripts. Princeton: Princeton University Press, 1926.

The Canterbury Tales. Ed. John M. Manly. New York: Holt, 1928.

The Works of Geoffrey Chaucer. Ed. F.N. Robinson. Boston: Houghton Mifflin, 1933; 2nd ed. 1957. (3rd. ed. by Larry D. Benson. See below under *Riverside Chaucer*).

The Text of the Canterbury Tales, Studied on the Basis of all Known Manuscripts. Ed. John M. Manly and Edith Rickert. Chicago: University of Chicago Press, 1940. 8 vols.

The Tales of Canterbury. Ed. Robert A. Pratt. Boston: Houghton Mifflin, 1974.

Chaucer's Major Poetry. Ed. Albert C. Baugh. New York: Appleton-Century Crofts, 1963.

Chaucer's Poetry: An Anthology for the Modern Reader. Ed. E. Talbot Donaldson. New York: Ronald, 1975. 2nd ed.

The Complete Poetry and Prose of Geoffrey Chaucer. Ed. John H. Fisher. New York, Chicago, etc.: Holt, Rinehart and Winston, 1977; 2nd ed. 1989.

The Canterbury Tales by Geoffrey Chaucer Edited from the Hengwrt Manuscript. Ed. N.F. Blake. London: Arnold, 1980.

The Variorum Edition of the Works of Geoffrey Chaucer. Ed. Paul G. Ruggiers. Norman: University of Oklahoma Press, 1982–. Each tale is edited in a separate volume with complete critical apparatus by individual scholars under the general editorship of Ruggiers.

The Riverside Chaucer. Ed. Larry D. Benson. Boston: Houghton Mifflin, 1987. Based on Robinson's edition. This is the standard edition, most often used.

Secondary Sources

Bibliographies

Allen, Mark, and John H. Fisher. *The Essen-* *tial Chaucer: An Annotated Bibliography of Major Modern Studies.* Boston: G.K. Hall, 1987. Covers 1900–1984.

Baird-Lange, Lorrayne Y. *Bibliography of Chaucer 1964–73.* Boston: G.K. Hall, 1977.

Crawford, William R. *Bibliography of Chaucer 1954–63.* Seattle: University of Washington Press, 1967.

Giaccherini, Enrico. "Chaucer and the Italian Trecento: A Bibliography." In *Chaucer and the Italian Trecento.* Ed. Piero Boitani. Cambridge: Cambridge University Press, 1983.

Griffith, Dudley D. *Bibliography of Chaucer 1908–53.* Seattle: University of Washington Press, 1955.

Hammond, Eleanor P. *Chaucer: A Bibliographical Manual.* New York: Peter Smith, 1933.

Leyerle, John, and Anne Quick. *Chaucer: A Bibliographical Introduction.* Toronto Medieval Bibliographies 10. Toronto: University of Toronto Press, 1986.

Mills, David, and J. David Burnley, eds. *Year's Work in English Studies.* London: The English Association, 1921–.

Peck, Russell A. *Chaucer's Lyrics and Anelida and Arcite: An Annotated Bibliography 1900–1980.* Toronto: University of Toronto Press, 1983.

Spurgeon, Carolyn F.E. *Five Hundred Years of Chaucer Criticism and Allusion, 1357–1900.* Cambridge: Cambridge University Press. 2nd. ed., 1925. 3 vols.

Studies in the Age of Chaucer. Norman: University of Oklahoma Press, Pilgrim Books, 1979–. Annotated bibliography.

Biographies

Baugh, Albert C. "Chaucer the Man." In *Companion to Chaucer Studies.* Ed. Beryl Rowland. New York: Oxford University Press, 1979.

Bland, D.S. "Chaucer and the Inns of Court: A Reexamination." *English Studies,* 33 (1952): 145–55.

———. "When Was Chaucer Born?" Times *Literary Supplement* (April 26, 1957): 264; Amplifications: Margaret Galway (May 10, 1957): 289; C. Warner and C.E. Welch (May 17, 1957): 305; G.D.G. Hall (June 28, 11957): 397; Margaret Galway (July 12, 1957): 427.

Brewer, Derek. *Chaucer and His World.* New

York: Dodd, Mead, 1977.

Crow, Martin M., and Clair C. Olson, eds. *Chaucer Life Records*. Oxford: Clarendon, 1966. From materials compiled by John M. Manly and Edith Rickett.

Gardner, John Champlin. *The Life and Times of Chaucer*. New York: Knopf, 1976.

Howard, Donald R. Chaucer: *His Life, His World, His Works*. New York: Dutton, 1987.

Hulbert, James R. *Chaucer's Official Life*. Menasha, WI: 1912; New York: Phaeton Press, 1970.

Kern, Alfred. *The Ancestory of Chaucer*. Baltimore, MD: Lord Baltimore Press, 1906.

Rudd, Martin B. *Thomas Chaucer*. Research Publications of University of Minnesota 9, Minneapolis: University of Minnesota Press, 1926.

Books and Parts of Books

Bronson, Bertrand. *In Search of Chaucer*. Toronto: University of Toronto Press, 1960.

Corsa, Helen S. *Chaucer: Poet of Mirth and Morality*. Notre Dame: University of Notre Dame Press, 1964. Corsa notes that in the *Book of the Duchess*, the gentlemanly obtuseness of the narrator is comic without detracting from the poem's grave simplicity or sad dignity. Finds the *Parliament of Fowles* comic in its subject, happy in its tone, joyous in celebrating nature, and "of good adventure." In *Troilus and Criseyde* comedy is laced into serious love scenes and tragic moments. *The Canterbury Tales*, a comedy of human existence, encompasses various humorous modes. Each portrait displays some tension, a "warring soul" full of comic potential for the "game."

Craik, T.W. *The Comic Tales of Chaucer*. London and New York, 1964. Systematic discussion of comedy in ten humorous tales for those unfamiliar with *The Canterbury Tales*. Plot summaries and comparisons point out humorous elements.

Gibaldi, Joseph, ed. *Chaucer's Canterbury Tales*. New York: Modern Language Association, 1980. Approaches to Teaching World Literature series.

Kern, Edith. *The Absolute Comic*. New York: Columbia University Press, 1980. Kern finds that in the literature of the comic absolute, the scapegoat is not the father blocking young love but "a cuckolded husband who becomes the laughing stock of all concerned, while his adulterous wife triumphs and frequently is the object of tacit or open approval" (40). Compares the *Wife of Bath's*, *Merchant's*, and *Miller's* tales to sixteenth-century charivari, a processional punishment of males whose wives defy their submissive role.

Kendrick, Laura. *Chaucerian Play: Comedy and Control in the Canterbury Tales*. Berkeley: University of California Press, 1988. An exploration of the mechanisms and meanings of medieval mirth, especially of Chaucer's literary play, by analyzing human behavior from modern psychological, psychoanalytic, anthropological, and historical studies. Examines goliardic and other burlesques of sacred Christian texts in paintings and Chaucerian fabliaux.

Leonard, Frances McNeely. *Laughter in the Courts of Love: Comedy in Allegory from Chaucer to Spenser*. Norman, OK: Pilgrim Books, 1981. Chronological tracing of the Chaucerian tradition of comic allegory to its culmination in the *Faerie Queene*. Although Leonard devotes little attention to *The Canterbury Tales*, she claims "From the *Book of the Duchess* through *The Canterbury Tales*, Chaucer is intent upon evoking both serious reflection and laughter" (30).

Payne, F. Anne. *Chaucer and Menippean Satire*. Madison: University of Wisconsin Press, 1981. Payne believes Chaucer combines parody of Boethius and its dialogic unyielding presentations of the world's multifariousness, finding Menippean dialogue the dominant structural feature of his work.

Rodway, Allan. *English Comedy: Its Role and Nature from Chaucer to the Present Day*. Berkeley and Los Angeles: University of California Press, 1975. Rodway notes Chaucer created comedy both skeptical and complex, cosmopolitan and bourgeois, especially obvious in the eagle of the *House of Fame*, the birds in the *Parliament of Fowles*, Pandarus in *Troilus and Criseyde*, and in *The Can-*

C

terbury Tales. Claims Chaucer's great gift is not so much a flair for satire but a quizzical, zestful conveying of a three-dimensional world. Examines the *Miller's, Reeve's,* and *Wife of Bath's* tales, all implicitly satirizing bourgeois churlishness.

Steadman, John M. *Disembodied Laughter: Troilus and the Apotheosis Tradition: A Re-examination of Narrative and Thematic Contexts.* Berkeley, Los Angeles, and London: University of California Press, 1972. Well-informed, wide-ranging. Using classical and contemporaneous European literature and philosophy, Steadman finds Troilus is not a tragic hero but a lover experiencing conventional vicissitudes. Claims "transiency of worldly love rather than loss of worldly dignities and high estate [are] his subject matter, but he has invested this erotic content with the shape and structure of tragedy" (89). Believes Chaucer "gave clearer definition to the comic values already inherent in his poem [than do his predecessors]." Although the tragic sense predominates in the plot, the comic vision overcomes in the end, complementing but not contradicting the tragic.

Tillyard, E.M.W. *Poetry: Direct and Oblique.* London: Chatto and Windus, 1948.

Wittig, Susan. *Stylistic and Narrative Structures in the Middle English Romances.* Austin: University of Texas Press, 1978.

Journal Articles

Ames, Ruth. "Prototype and Parody in Chaucerian Exegesis." *Acta,* 4 (1977): 87–105. Ames finds Chaucer's parody irreverent and his piety sincere. Discusses Old Testament parodies, concluding Chaucer was neither moved by them nor convinced by current exegetical modes. Finds Chaucer's balance between laughter and prayer precarious and his parodies twisting from grossness to subtlety and back again.

Andreas, James R. "The Rhetoric of Chaucerian Comedy: The Aristotelian Legacy." *The Comparatist,* 8 (1984): 56–66. Andreas sees Aristotle's comic theory as the ultimate source for the tradition, assimilated but not superseded by Bergson, Freud, and Bakhtin. Notes that

the early dream visions are shot through with parody, reversal, exaggeration, and elaborate punning, standard comic features. Examines characters, themes, and rhetorical devices of *The Canterbury Tales* in the light of Aristotelian poetic theory.

Bloomfield, Morton W. "The Man of Law's Tale: A Tragedy of Victimization and a Christian Comedy." *PMLA,* 87 (1972): 384–90. "A mixture of the superficially tragic and the slightly comic . . . does not lie easy with us" (384). Interruptions, apostrophes, little characterization, much improbability, and description distance us from emotional involvement in the *Man of Law's Tale.*

Dane, Joseph A. "The Mechanics of Comedy in Chaucer's *Miller's Tale.*" *Chaucer Review,* 14 (1980): 215–24. Dane contends that the denouement's comic effect rests on the tale's formal structure. Discusses static elements (ordering of characters into two stable, parallel sets) and dynamic elements (manipulation of those sets) which heighten the denouement, "one of the most absurdly comic situations in *The Canterbury Tales.*" The Miller sublimates expectations of "low-comedy" by glossing moral deficiencies, thus giving Chaucer license with the aesthetics of comic denouement.

David, Alfred. "Sentimental Comedy in the *Franklin's Tale.*" *Annuale Mediaevale,* 6 (1965): 19–27. David claims that Chaucer's irony includes the Franklin despite sympathy for his bourgeois values. Thus, his tale resembles the bourgeois genre called sentimental comedy: a potentially tragic plot resolved happily through noble behavior.

Falke, Anne. "The Comic Function of the Narrator in *Troilus and Criseyde.*" *Neophilologus,* 68 (1984): 134–41. Falke believes attempts to isolate an identifiable persona for the speaker in the *Troilus* or separate him from Chaucer the poet fail. Rather, discusses the effect of the narrator on the audience and how he converts tragedy to comedy. Finally, both Troilus and the narrator reach a new level of understanding.

Foster, Edward E. "Humor in the *Knight's Tale.*" *Chaucer Review,* 3 (1968): 88–94. Chivalric anachronism reveals the limitations causing unexpected and unconscious humor in the *Knight's Tale.* Surveys puns, dialogue, and incongruous actions and style, concluding that the Knight "is comic in the enviable way that idealists are often made to seem ludicrous by the demands of reality; but that, of course, does not destroy the value of his ideals" (94).

Frank, Robert W., Jr. "The *Reeve's Tale* and the Comedy of Limitation." In *Directions in Literary Criticism: Contemporary Approaches to Literature.* Ed. Stanley Weintraub and Philip Young. University Park: Pennsylvania State University Press, 1973, pp. 53–69. Frank claims that if "the contrast between the Knight and the Miller (and Reeve) is a comedy of class and nurture, the conflict between the Miller and the Reeve arising between members of the same class, is a comic reflection of the absurd clashes created by the limitations of human vision."

Garbaty, Thomas J. "Chaucer and Comedy." In *Versions of Medieval Comedy.* Ed. Paul G. Ruggiers. Norman: University of Oklahoma Press, 1977, pp. 173–90. Garbaty finds Chaucer's comic theory only implied in opposition to his Boethian definition of tragedy in the Monk's Prologue. Although he reworked tradition as he used it, humor of situation, using control and balance, was always one of his strengths.

———. "Satire and Regionalism: The Reeve and His Tale." *Chaucer Review,* 8 (1973): 1–8. Garbaty finds internal humor emerging from the text, and external humor only available to Chaucer's contemporaries who knew the historic context.

Grennen, Joseph E. "*Makyng* in Comedy: 'Troilus and Criseyde,' V, 1788." *Neuphilologische Mitteilungen,* 86 (1985): 489–93. Grennen examines the phrase at the end of the *Troilus* that God might yet send him "myght to make in some comedye." Sees the poet as surrogate for the Creator who "makes" within his world rather than as a shaper working from some external position.

Hira, Toshinori. "Chaucer's Laughter." *Bulletin of the Faculty of Liberal Arts, Nagasaki University,* 20 (1979): 27–42.

Hira examines Chaucer's role of love servant, love-renegade, and spectator, claiming that with age Chaucer gradually rejected courtly love conventions. Considers how the mercantile influence and feudalism affect Chaucer's characters and tellers. Finally, as aristocratic standards are replaced by bourgeois ones, no differences are found between human beings.

Lanham, Richard A. "Game Play and High Seriousness in Chaucer's Poetry." *English Studies,* 48 (1967): 1–24. Lanham uses Matthew Arnold's theory of high seriousness as a touchstone to examine Chaucer as a "great" poet of high seriousness. Discusses game theory in the corpus, claiming Chaucer subconsciously viewed the world *sub specie ludi,* using jokes and games whose rules fix and stylize conflict, thus revealing ambivalence toward seriousness.

Levy, Bernard S. "Biblical Parody in the *Summoner's Tale.*" *Tennessee Studies in Literature,* 11 (1966): 45–60. Levy describes the relationship of Prologue to Tale, the first positing the special kind of grace or wind that the Friars are said to have and the second exemplifying it. The division of the "gift" is a precise parody of the descent of the Holy Ghost upon the Apostles at Pentecost, both being a problem of distribution. Notes that the Pentecost cupola in St. Mark's, Venice, uses a wheel as a central iconographic image to separate the Apostles, much like that of the Summoner's cartwheel.

MacDonald, Donald. "Proverbs, *Sententiae,* and Exempla in Chaucer's Comic Tales: The Function of Comic Misapplication." *Speculum,* 41 (1966): 453–65. Chaucer consciously employed proverbs, *sententiae,* and exempla to enhance comic effect.

Marzec, Marcia Smith. "The *Man of Law's Tale* as Christian Comedy; Or, the Best-laid Schemes." *Proceedings of the Patristic, Medieval and Renaissance Conference,* 12–13 (1987–88): 197–208. Marzec suggests that Chaucer cultivates a dual perspective—from man's, within the world, and from God's, from above, where order and reasonableness can be seen. The plot offers intellectual but not emotional pleasure—a thematic success but dramatic failure.

McCall, John P. "The Squire in Wonderland." *Chaucer Review*, 1 (1966): 103–09. McCall argues that in the Squire, Chaucer has carefully created ambivalence—a teller of youthful, zesty, fantasy yet also a self-conscious narrator craftily using his literary tools—for a delicate, humorous effect.

Nist, John. "The Art of Chaucer: *Pathedy*." *Times Literary Supplement*, 11 (1966): 1–10. Chaucer's genius is in his fusion of tragic and comic visions through the tragicomic art of humility: *pathedy*.

Pearsall, Derek. "The Canterbury Tales II: Comedy." *The Cambridge Chaucer Companion*. Ed. Piero Boitani and Jill Mann. Cambridge, London, New York, etc.: Cambridge University Press, 1986, pp. 125–42. Chaucerian comedy differs from classical, which is socially normative, by correcting behavior through seeing the ridiculousness of vice. Explores the variegated tones that distinguish six fabliaux tales from each other despite their shared comic structure.

Reid, David S. "Crocodilian Humor: A Discussion of Chaucer's Wife of Bath." *Chaucer Review*, 14 (1979): 73–89. The Wife of Bath is not an individual but a comic shrew stock figure of both good fun and woman-evil execration in a pantomime of stock tricks from which she draws vitality for that absurd stock figure. She makes sense only in terms of burlesque and knockabout comedy. Because we are involved in a comic displacement, our response is equivocal or crocodilian: "we enjoy her jolly, hearty nature. On the other, we know her to be, like Falstaff and Long John Silver, common and villainous."

Reiss, E. "Medieval Irony." *Journal of the History of Ideas*, 42 (1981): 209–26. Reiss claims that "Because of the ironic nature of his artistry—because it is a given that the workings of the artist are trivial—Chaucer is able to reveal traditional Christian *doctrina* at the same time as he reveals a literary *poseur*, the Man of Law."

Rudat, Wolfgang E.H. "Chaucer's Spring of Comedy: The *Merchant's Tale* and Other 'Games' with Augustinian Theology." *Annuale Mediaevale*, 21 (1981): 111–20. A discussion of the parodic use of Christian notions and how Chaucer's bawdy manipulation of them are absorbed into the Spring of Comedy permeating *The Canterbury Tales*.

Ruggiers, Paul G. "A Vocabulary for Chaucerian Comedy: A Preliminary Sketch." In *Medieval Studies in Honor of Lillian Herlands Hornstein*. Ed. J.B. Bessinger and R. Raymo. New York: New York University Press, 1977, pp. 193–225. Ruggiers lays out a vocabulary for Chaucerian comedy based on Aristotle's *Nicomachean Ethics* and *Rhetoric*, the Coislinian *Tractate*, and Lane Cooper's re-creation of an Aristotelian theory of comedy. Focuses on plot and character rather than irony; discusses definition, plot elements, the dianoetic function, comic catharsis, reader response, comic characters, and probability.

Sarno, Ronald A. "Chaucer and the Satirical Tradition." *Classical Folia* 21 (1967): 41–61. Sarno explores the classical tradition of satire (Horace, Juvenal, and Jerome) to determine Chaucer's relation to each. While links to Horace are tenuous, Chaucer mentions Juvenal in *The Wife of Bath's* Prologue and *Troilus and Criseyde*. Believes the shrew in Jerome's *Adversus Jovinianium* is the model for the Wife of Bath, concluding that "Chaucer seems to be laughing at all the anti-feminine literature of the past [pointing] out the dangers inherent in a satire which treats women merely as the gate of hell and forgets they are persons with feelings too" (53). Compares Chaucer to Gower and Langland, finding his *double-entendre*, clever wit, and humane understanding to be Chaucer's personal contribution to English satire.

Scheps, Walter. "Sir Thopas: The Bourgeois Knight, the Minstrel and the Critics." *Times Literary Supplement*, 11 (1966): 35–43. *Sir Thopas*, a tail-rhyme in miniature, telescopes description and action, characteristics typical of romance, in detailing flora, birds and beasts, and hunting, all in 207 lines.

Smith, Francis J. "Mirth and Marriage in *The Parliament of Foules*." *Ball State University Forum*, 14 (1973): 15–22. Smith sees irony and sophisticated amusement beginning the *Parliament*. Objects to overly serious treatment of the work's putative design to reconcile apparently conflicting authorities. Emphasizes the dream-vision experience and the joyful affirmation of life and love also found in the Prologue to the *Legend of Good Women*.

Stevens, Martin. "'And Venus Laugheth': An Interpretation of the *Merchant's Tale*." *Chaucer Review*, 7 (1972): 118–31. Stevens believes the *Merchant's Tale* comic and the teller sympathetic but not self-revelatory. Contends the harangue about wife and marriage are delivered with tongue in cheek and absurd exaggeration.

Thro, A. Booker. "Chaucer's Creative Comedy: A Study of the *Miller's Tale* and the *Shipman's Tale*." *Chaucer Review*, 5 (1970): 97–111. In Chaucer's comedy the triumph of wit is often a "creative act" of imaginative, ingenious construction more complex than the situations require. Points out brilliant contriving but rejects Craik's notion of farce as destructive impulses, finding creativity and human constructiveness dominating the *Miller's Tale*. Finds the *Shipman's Tale* presents scenes of "creative persuasion" in the wife's shifting persuasive tactics of "advance-and-retreat" indirection in content and syntax. Concludes Chaucer's idealism and verisimilitude is a "high-Gothic" quality.

Veldhoen, N.H.G.E. "Which Was the Mooste Fre: Chaucer's Realistic Humour and Insight into Human Nature, As Shown in *The Frankelyens Tale*." In *Other Words: Transcultural Studies in Philology, Translation, and Lexicology Presented to Hans Heinrich Meier on the Occasion of His Sixty-Fifth Birthday*. Ed. J. Lachlan Mackenzie and Richard Todd. Dordrecht: Foris, 1989, pp. 107–16. Veldhoen sees the Franklin's ironic excuse for his weak rhetorical skill in his Prologue as justification to defy conventions and offer an imaginative tone unusual in this genre.

Jean E. Jost

Chesterton, G[ilbert] K[eith]

Born: London, England, May 29, 1874
Education: St. Paul's School, 1887–1892;
Slade School (of art), 1892–1895; lec-
tures at University College, London,
while studying at Slade
Marriage: Frances Blogg, June 28, 1901
Died: Beaconsfield, England, June 14, 1936

Biography

Gilbert Keith Chesterton was the son of Edward Chesterton, a house agent, and Marie Grosjean Chesterton, an Englishwoman of French-Swiss descent and herself one of twenty-three children. Edward Chesterton retired early from business to enjoy his family and his hobbies. G.K. Chesterton, born in London on May 29, 1874, was thus raised in a family that provided warmth, attention, and security. He was one of three children; his brother, Cecil, was five years younger, and a sister, Beatrice, died in childhood.

At St. Paul's School (1887–1892), Chesterton was perceived to be a lonely boy with a remarkable memory who showed no interest in ordinary school work, although he could quote from his favorite authors at length. At school, however, he made lifelong and influential friends, the most important of these being E.C. Bentley (later inventor of the comic poetic clerihew and a noted writer of detective fiction). Chesterton, though not at that time a Roman Catholic, won the Milton Prize at St. Paul's for a poem about St. Francis Xavier, a Jesuit missionary to China.

After St. Paul's, Chesterton, intending to be an artist, studied at the Slade School (1892–1895). This period, for him, was a time of deep mental distress which he records in the "How to be a Lunatic" chapter of his *Autobiography*. Causes of this distress were complex: sexual questioning, loneliness, growing doubt about traditional political and religious certainties in which he had been raised. His sense of evil in the world moved him toward an increasingly passionate Christian orthodoxy while the political and social turmoil of his time and the Liberalism of his family simultaneously moved him toward an equally passionate contempt for capitalist industrial society.

During his years at Slade, Chesterton began work as an underpaid assistant to publishers—first Redway, during 1892 and 1893, and later Fisher Unwin from 1893 to 1899. He began writing in earnest to earn income sufficient to permit marriage to Frances Blogg, whom he met in 1896. Although schoolboy efforts had been published, his real career began in 1900 with publication of his first full-length works,

Greybeards at Play and *The Wild Knight*. That same year he met Hilaire Belloc—who would influence his political and religious thinking—and publicly opposed the Boer War, an act that would bring him popular attention.

After marrying Frances on June 28, 1901, he settled into the quasi-bohemian life of Fleet Street journalism, writing prolifically while eating and drinking heavily. With his wife's help he also developed the public image that was to capture the attention of his age: cape, swordstick, wide-brimmed hat, all decorating a large body that was to become increasingly obese. As a writer, speaker, and eccentric, he was highly successful, and his image was also enhanced by his colorful debates with playwright George Bernard Shaw in print, on public platforms, and, later, on radio.

Between 1911 and 1916, Chesterton underwent another period of serious distress. His brother Cecil, now editor of *The New Witness*, was charged with libel after having accused Godfrey Isaacs, a director of the American Marconi Company and brother of Attorney General Sir Rufus Isaacs, of fraud. Even though he might have been imprisoned, Cecil was fined, and even the lesser punishment embittered G.K., hardening his already bitter attitude toward government bureaucracy, his devotion to an economic theory called Distributism (which would have broken up big business and big government), and his sense of an international conspiracy, which he believed was certainly capitalist and probably Jewish in nature. In 1914, suffering under the strain, his health broke down completely; he lay in a coma from November of that year until March of the following year, and he remained convalescent for some months after. Three years later, his beloved brother Cecil, who had volunteered for military service in France during World War I, died of disease shortly after the Armistice.

By 1922, the year of his father's death, many of Chesterton's friends had become converts to the Roman Catholic Church, as had Cecil. Chesterton himself had long been a friend of Father (later Monsignor) John O'Connor, model for the author's fictional detective Father Brown. Chesterton was received into the Roman Catholic Church on July 30, 1922.

In 1909, Chesterton's wife—fearing for her husband's health and longing for a home of her own—had moved them into the country, but Chesterton did not retire there to the dignified life of man of letters, as she had apparently

hoped. Instead, he kept up his arduous regime as a writer and, increasingly, as an editor. After Cecil's death, his deep commitment to his brother's memory kept him editing *The New Witness* until it suspended publication in 1923 and, after that, beginning *G.K.'s Weekly* as a forum for similarly conservative religious ideas and Distributist economics. Much of his own income went toward the publication of these periodicals, and the unceasing work and responsibility placed great strain on his corpulent body. By the 1930s, his health was severely weakened. He had recently visited the shrine at Lourdes when he died at his home in Beaconsfield on June 14, 1936.

Literary Analysis

In his posthumously published *Autobiography* (1936), Chesterton recorded the importance of the toy theater that his father had created for him. With it, Chesterton could act out his fantasies. That theater became for him a symbol of life itself; Chesterton and Shaw shared a sense that life is essentially theatrical, with tiny humans acting out their little dramas against a greater spiritual tapestry of which they are unaware. Acutely aware of that spiritual dimension, Chesterton perceived the world as magical, filled with symbols which were to be painted verbally with the highly visual eye of a man who had once studied painting at the Slade School.

These characteristics inform the best of Chesterton's writing from its beginning. Careless with detail, to the chagrin of his editors when he wrote *Robert Browning* for the "English Men of Letters" series (1903), he nonetheless was so clever in sketching the essence of his subject that the volume was highly successful and brought the writer to the attention of the celebrities of his time, including Max Beerbohm, Shaw, John Masefield, and Algernon Swinburne. Equally successful was his *The Victorian Age in Literature* (1913).

The same elements characterize his early fiction, as in his 1904 novel, *The Napoleon of Notting Hill*, a futuristic story in which men rise against an authoritarian state, select their king from civil service lists, and turn each borough of London into a colorful walled city. This novel is an early vehicle for Chesterton's Distributist economics—a defense of smallness and the individual against the conformity and bureaucracy that he perceived to be the most serious threat of the twentieth century; the writer hoped that each man would once again, as in his vision of an earlier age, farm his own plot of ground and satisfy his own needs with tools from his own workshop. Modern critics have shown the impracticality of this idea without stringent population control, to which Chesterton would have been opposed, and without thorough retraining of the modern man in techniques of efficient farming.

Just as Chesterton was not at his best as a novelist of ideas, so his fiction is not its best when, as in *The Napoleon of Notting Hill*, ideas dramatically control the action. As a literary artist, he reached the height of his powers in *The Man Who Was Thursday: A Nightmare* (1908) and in the Father Brown detective stories.

The Man Who Was Thursday is a melodramatic spy story, a religious allegory, and a fantasy. Gabriel Symes, a poet and undercover policeman, finds himself in a den of anarchists dedicated to the overthrow of all order. Each anarchist takes the name of the day of a week; Symes becomes Thursday. They are led by Sunday, a massive figure seen primarily in terms of light and shadow, as is the figure of the chief policeman who recruited Symes onto the side of the law. As Symes pursues anarchists across London and France, each anarchist, unmasked, turns out to be an undercover policeman. Together, they pursue Sunday, who, himself unmasked, turns out to be nature, existence, Pan, godhood itself.

In this example of Chesterton's writing and wit at their finest, ideas impel and inform the fiction, but the fiction is important for its own sake. Illumining his theme are dramatic and colorful scenes, as when the Anarchists first convene in a subterranean crypt decorated in bombs that look "like the bulbs of iron plants, or the eggs of iron birds"[1] or when Sunday escapes by elephant from the London Zoological Garden, pursued by six detectives in a cab. There is no mistaking the symbolic nature of the novel's ending when each undercover policeman is dressed in the robes symbolizing a day of creation and seated alongside Sunday at a vast masquerade ball with dancers dressed to illumine the oddities of God's creation. Nor is it possible to ignore the symbolic meaning of the book: that evil and goodness are two sides of a coin that man can only dimly apprehend; the paradox of good and evil, seemingly inexplicable in human terms, can be resolved only by an omniscient God whom man can only accept, not explain. At the same time, the plot allows Chesterton to write with a painterly and theatrical vision that also reveals his love of the magical. The final scene, in which Sunday is unveiled, is a tapestry of figures that include "a man dressed as a windmill with enormous sails, a man dressed as an elephant," and one "dressed like an enormous hornbill, with a beak twice as big as himself."[2] "Every couple dancing," Chesterton writes, "seemed a separate romance; it might be a fairy dancing with a pillarbox or a peasant girl dancing with the moon; but in each case it was, somehow, as absurd as Alice in Wonderland, yet as grave and kind as a love story."[3] Toward the end of the novel, the author inadvertently reveals why this book works, as much of his other writing, as art, does not: "The philosopher," he writes, "may sometimes love the infinite; the poet always loves the finite."[4] In this novel, Chesterton is a poet, not a philosopher, and the allegory is invested with great wit and great charm.

The Father Brown stories are equally effective. First collected in *The Innocence of Father Brown* (1911), they had begun to appear in 1910 when "The Blue Cross," the first of the stories, was published in *Storyteller*. Father Brown was modeled on Father John O'Connor; Chesterton, who had imagined himself to be a journalistic man of the world, had assumed that a priest was ignorant of the abysses of human behavior and was shocked when in a conversation with O'Connor he realized the kind of knowledge that came to a priest in the confessional. From this realization came the image of the small, dusty, Roman Catholic priest whose powers of observation and whose understanding of the human heart enable him to solve crimes when more worldly and conventional detectives fail.

As in *The Man Who Was Thursday*, Chesterton's vision is essentially painterly and theatrical. For example, "The Invisible Man," perhaps the most famous of the stories, begins against a backdrop of a confectioner's shop that exemplifies Chesterton's gift for metaphor and visual imagery with its window that "glowed like the butt of a cigar," or, rather, "like the butt of a firework, for the light was of many colours." The list of "rainbow provocations" continues with chocolates "all wrapped in those red and gold and green metallic colours which are almost better than chocolate itself; and the huge white wedding-cake in the window was somehow at once remote and satisfying, just as if the whole North Pole were good to eat."[5] As two men drive through London in a futile attempt to prevent a murder, the backdrop is that of a toy theater: "Soon the white curves came sharper and dizzier; they were upon ascending spirals . . . Terrace rose above terrace, and the special tower of flats they sought, rose above them all to almost Egyptian heights."[6] Similarly, the story ends with a Christmas card image as Father Brown walks "those snow-covered hills under the stars for many hours with a murderer, and what they said to each other will never be known."[7] While much of the humor in this story is thus gentle and charming, here, as in other Father Brown stories, Chesterton also gains witty effect from traditional rhetorical devices, such as the principle of climax: searching for the flamboyant detective Flambeau, the protagonist finds in his exotically decorated chambers "sabres, harquebuses, Eastern curiosities, flasks of Italian wine, savage cooking-pots, a plumy Persian cat, and a small dusty-looking Roman Catholic priest."[8] Typically, paradoxes also abound in a story based upon the paradox that what men see is not necessarily what they look at. Not only did detective fiction give Chesterton a popular audience for his reenactment of the battle of goodness against the deadly sins, but it also, as he noted in his "A Defense of Detective Stories," allowed him to express the romance of life and poetry of the urban landscape.[9]

Illuminated by wit, paradox, verbal play, and intensely visual imagery, these works and much of his poetry—for example, "The Rolling English Road"—illustrate Chesterton at his best in the years before World War I. Although the paradoxes and word play continue after that time, Chesterton's later work considered on the basis of its humor and verbal art is generally of less interest. Often, in his passion to effectively describe his thought and promote his ideas, Chesterton seems to lose control of the formal rhetorical devices (parallelism, alliteration, antithesis) that he used to great effect in his early work; in certain of his later essays and in his posthumous *Autobiography*, such devices are piled upon each other until the effect is cloying.

Scholars differ in their analyses of this later work. Those concerned with Chesterton as a thinker and critic of society see no change between his pre- and post–World War I writing; those scholars, mostly Roman Catholic, who see his life as a spiritual journey toward conversion, prefer that written after the war.

Considered solely on its aesthetic and humorous values, however, there is a marked difference between the pre- and post-war work, and to see Chesterton as British humorist, the reader must go to the poetry, the Father Brown Stories, and the novels—especially *The Man Who Was Thursday*—written before the Marconi scandal, the war, and Cecil's death.

Summary

In the period between 1900 and World War I, G.K. Chesterton wrote a series of stories, novels, and poems that place him among the greatest of British literary humorists. In the world of letters, this is his lasting contribution, and it is an important one. Chesterton also was a serious literary critic, a critic of industrial and capitalist society, and a writer of religious studies; paradox and verbal wit enliven his writings in these fields and make him foremost among early twentieth-century political, social, and religious polemicists.

Notes

1. G.K. Chesterton, *The Man Who Was Thursday: A Nightmare* (1908; New York: Putnam, 1960), p. 19.
2. *Ibid.*, p. 184.
3. *Ibib.*, p. 186.
4. *Ibid.*, p. 183.
5. G.K. Chesterton, "The Invisible Man." *The Father Brown Omnibus* (New York: Dodd, Mead, 1982), p. 82.
6. *Ibid.*, p. 90.
7. *Ibid.*, p. 100.
8. *Ibid.*, p. 93.
9. Chesterton's "A Defense of Detective Stories" (1901) has been called "the best and briefest apology for the short form to be found anywhere" and ranked "among the best things ever written on the subject" by critics such as Jacques Barzun and Wendell Hertig Taylor in *A Catalogue of Crime* (New York: Harper, 1971, p. 454), and David Lehman in *The Perfect Murder: A Study in Detection* (New York: Free Press, 1989, p. 122). Unfortunately, the best lengthy analysis of the Father Brown stories themselves, including a discussion of wit in these stories, is by Anthony Boucher (pseud. of William Anthony Parker White) in a now virtually inaccessible paperback edition entitled

The Adventures of Father Brown (New York: Dell, 1961).

Selected Bibliography
Primary Sources

Autobiographies
Autobiography. London: Hutchinson, 1936; reissued with introduction by Anthony Burgess, 1969.

Essays and Criticism
"A Defense of Detective Stories." *The Defendant*. London: Dent, 1901; rpt. in *The Art of the Mystery Story*, ed. Howard Haycraft, New York: Grosset, 1946, and elsewhere.
Twelve Types. London: Humphreys, 1902.
Robert Browning. English Men of Letters series. London: Macmillan, 1903.
Charles Dickens. London: Methuen, 1906.
George Bernard Shaw. London: John Lane, 1909.
The Victorian Age in Literature. London: Williams, 1913.

Fiction
The Napoleon of Notting Hill. London: Lane, 1904.
The Club of Queer Trades. New York: Harper, 1905.
The Man Who Was Thursday: A Nightmare. London: Simpkin, 1908.
The Innocence of Father Brown. London: Cassell, 1911. Annotated and republished as *The Annotated Innocence of Father Brown*, ed. Martin Gardner, London: Oxford University Press, 1987.
The Flying Inn. London: Methuen, 1914.
The Wisdom of Father Brown. London: Cassell, 1914.
The Incredulity of Father Brown. London: Cassell, 1926.
The Secret of Father Brown. London: Cassell, 1927.
The Scandal of Father Brown. London: Cassell, 1935.
"The Vampire in the Village." In *Twentieth-Century Detective Stories*. Ed. Ellery Queen. New York: World, 1948. Father Brown story not included in collections above.

Poetry
Collected Poems. London: Methuen, 1936.

Secondary Sources

Bibliographies
Sullivan, John. *G.K. Chesterton: A Bibliography*. New York: Barnes, 1958. Scholarly compilation of primary and secondary sources through 1957.
———. *Chesterton Continued: A Bibliographical Supplement*. London: University of London Press, 1968. Supplements and amends earlier work, includes new primary material, latest item dated 1966.

Biographies
Barker, Dudley. *G.K. Chesterton: A Biography*. New York: Stein, 1973. Readable and balanced view of Chesterton's life and all aspects of his writing.
Chesterton, Ada E. *The Chestertons*. London: Chapman, 1941. Cecil's wife's portrayal of family; her biased account of Gilbert Keith's marriage to Frances has been discredited, but the book remains useful.
O'Connor, John. *Father Brown on Chesterton*. London: Muller, 1937. Recollections and commentary by the priest who was the model for Father Brown.
Ward, Maisie. *Gilbert Keith Chesterton*. New York: Sheed, 1943. Despite unscholarly approach, remains most important biography.
———. *Return to Chesterton*. London: Sheed, 1952. Supplements, rather than continues, earlier work.

Books
Canovan, Margaret. *G.K. Chesterton: Radical Populist*. New York: Harcourt, 1977. Analysis of Chesterton's political theory.
Clipper, Lawrence. *G.K. Chesterton*. New York: Twayne, 1974. Twayne's English Authors Series. Thorough and balanced study of Chesterton's ideas with chronology of significant personal events and excellent bibliography, but requires prior knowledge of Chesterton's life and works.
Coates, John. *Chesterton and the Edwardian Cultural Crisis*. Hull, England: Hull University Press, 1984. Coates analyzes Chesterton in cultural context of his early career.
Conlon, D.J., ed. *G.K. Chesterton: A Half Century of Views*. New York: Oxford

University Press, 1987. Short essays, mainly laudatory, by many authors, including W.H. Auden, Graham Greene, and Evelyn Waugh.

Coren, Michael. *Gilbert: The Man Who Was Chesterton*. New York: Paragon, 1990. Analysis includes sensitive handling of Chesterton's anti-semitism.

Furlong, William B. *GBS/GKC Shaw and Chesterton: The Metaphysical Jesters*. University Park: Pennsylvania State University Press, 1970. Examination of personal and intellectual relationship between most famous debaters of their age.

Kenner, Hugh. *Paradox in Chesterton*. New York: Sheed, 1961. Chesterton's paradoxes and analogies are seen as a way of expressing his vision of life.

Lea, F.A. *The Wild Knight of Battersea: G.K. Chesterton*. London: Clarke, 1945. Modern Christian Revolutionaries Series. Lea focuses on Chesterton as a religious figure; good one among many such treatments.

Shaw, Bernard. *Pen Portraits and Reviews*. London: Constable, 1932. Contains "The Chesterbelloc," "Chesterton on Shaw," "Something like a History of England (G.K. Chesterton)," and "Chesterton on Eugenics and Shaw on Chesterton" by a contemporary who understood him well.

Articles and Chapters in Books

Borges, Jorge Luis. "On Chesterton." *Other Inquisitions 1937–1952*. Trans. Ruth L.C. Sims. New York: Washington Square Press, 1966, pp. 88–89. Borges suggests Chesterton's influence.

Gross, John. "Edwardians." *The Rise and Fall of the Man of Letters: A Study of the Idiosyncratic and the Humane in Modern Literature*. London: Weidenfeld, 1969, pp. 211–232. Brief discussion of Chesterton important to understanding of the literary tradition in which he worked.

Lehman, David. "From Paradise to Poisonville." *The Perfect Murder: A Study in Detection*. New York: Free Press, 1989, pp. 117–134. Brief but perceptive analysis places Father Brown within the context of the detective genre.

Teachout, Terry. "Coming to Terms with Chesterton." *American Scholar*, 50 (Winter 1989): 105–112. Balanced reassessment of Chesterton's value for late twentieth-century readers.

Betty Richardson

Churchill, Winston S.

Born: Blenheim Palace, Oxfordshire, November 30, 1874
Education: Harrow (1888–1893); Royal Military College, Sandhurst (1893–1895)
Marriage: Clementine Hozier, September 12, 1908; four children
Died: London, January 24, 1965

Biography

Winston Churchill, Prime Minister of Great Britain during World War II and a giant in world affairs in the twentieth century, authored thirty-two volumes of history and biography plus twenty volumes of speeches, and won the Nobel Prize for Literature in 1953. The voice of Churchill, especially when England stood alone against the Nazi blitz, made him the greatest orator of modern times.

Born at Blenheim Palace, Oxfordshire, on November 30, 1874 and descended from John Churchill, first Duke of Marlborough and hero of the eighteenth-century wars against France, Churchill was largely neglected by his parents, Lord Randolph Churchill and his American wife, Jennie Jerome. Lord Randolph died in 1895, after his political career in Parliament and the Cabinet self-destructed. During these formative years, Churchill was an indifferent student at Harrow (1888–1893), which he had entered as the lowest boy in the lowest form, and he required three attempts before being accepted at Sandhurst, the Royal Military College (1893–1895). He did not attend a university. Only during his boredom as a cavalry officer in India (1896) did he study the influences that mark his intellectual development, particularly the work of Plato, the English historians Edward Gibbon and Thomas Babington Macaulay, and *Bartlett's Familiar Quotations*. Of these studies Churchill wrote: "I approached it with an empty, hungry mind and with fairly strong jaws, and what I got I bit."

In pursuit of fame and glory, the ambitious young Churchill sought danger and warfare, rushing to Cuba to report on the war against Spain (1895), serving in India at the battles of the Northwest Frontier (1896–1897), marching with Lord Kitchener in the Nile campaign at Khartoum (1898), and being captured by the

Boers in South Africa (1899) and escaping as a hero. He returned home to begin fifty-five years service in the House of Commons. In addition, he married Clementine Hozier on September 12, 1908; the couple had four children.

All of his war experiences were converted to journalistic efforts and histories, including *The Story of the Malakand Field Force* (1898) on the India campaign, *The River War* (1899) on the Nile expeditionary force, his only novel, *Savrola* (1900), and numerous reports from the South African war for London's *Morning Post*.

His important histories consist of the life of his father, *Lord Randolph Churchill* (1906), *Marlborough: His Life and Times* (6 vols., 1933–1938), *The Second World War* (6 vols., 1948–1953), and *A History of the English-Speaking Peoples* (4 vols., written in the 1930s, published 1956–1958).

Churchill was supremely aware of the power of language and worked out his theory of the art of rhetoric in his unpublished "The Scaffolding of Rhetoric" (1901). Along with diction, argument, and rhythm, Churchill carefully considered humor and analogy as elements that make the powers of the orator "more durable than that of a great king." He also published *My Early Life* (1930), *Thoughts and Adventures* (1932), and *Painting As a Pastime* (1948).

Plagued throughout life by bouts of depression, which he labeled the "black dog," Churchill used humor and adventure to keep the "dog" at bay. In 1963, he became the only honorary citizen of the United States. On January 24, 1965, he died in London. He had been happily married for fifty-seven years and, though hardly a Christian, is memorialized at Westminster Abbey (he is buried in Bladon churchyard, Oxfordshire). Churchill's long and interesting life has been the subject of numerous studies, and his special gifts as an orator and conversationalist are recorded in Colin Coote's *A Churchill Reader: The Wit and Wisdom of Sir Winston Churchill* and Kay Halle's *Irrepressible Churchill: A Treasury of Winston Churchill's Wit*.

Literary Analysis

All accounts of Churchill as an author and speechmaker refer to his humor. In practice, Churchill blended written and oral traditions because after *The River War* he dictated all of his books and they have the orator's ring to them. This, in large measure, accounts for his scintillating style with its sharp, pungent phrases, although his critics labeled him "overly florid." Churchill studied the eighteenth- and nineteenth-century historians, fusing the stately cadence and balanced sentences of Gibbon with the crisp, forceful antitheses of Macaulay. One reviewer of *The River War* alluded to the author's "having the *Decline and Fall* up his sleeve." Churchill never left out his own personality, as demonstrated in the "Preface" of *The Second World War* when he acknowledged that the volume was not a history itself but "a contribution to history."

Churchill's humor was the result of his philosophy of the individual. Always the Victorian optimist, he opposed determinism and advocated the individual's role in shaping his environment. This spirit of optimism, with its romantic blush of ardor and courage, denied absolutes and required a comic view to delineate the complexity of the world and improve the lot of mankind. Churchill combined this spirit with his penchant for the piercing phrase, as in "The war of the giants has ended; the quarrels of the pygmies have begun" (*The World Crisis*, 1928), or in his derogation of political opponent Clement Attlee: "He is a sheep in wolf's clothing" (1945).

Churchill issued no personal credo on writing or contemporary literature in his Nobel Prize acceptance speech, although the presenters called him "a Caesar who has the gift of Cicero's pen." His acceptance began on a note of levity: "I feel we are both running a considerable risk and that I do not deserve it. But I shall have no misgivings if you have none."

What kind of humor was Churchill's? It was, like Samuel Johnson's, a bluff, masculine humor that confronted the ethics of an individual or the requirements of empire and leadership. The tone of his remarks can readily be associated with the attitudes of empire held by Rudyard Kipling, the Bully spirit of Teddy Roosevelt, the machismo of Ernest Hemingway, and the frontier spirit of Mark Twain. Churchill exhibited various styles of humor but seldom strayed far from ego and conquest. Two episodes illustrate this virility. First, in *The Second World War* (Vol. 2) Churchill describes the 1940 meeting between Germany's foreign minister Joachim von Ribbentrop and Russia's Vyacheslav Molotov: "After supper at the Soviet Embassy there was a British air raid on Berlin. We had heard of the conference beforehand, and though not invited to join in the discussion did not wish to be entirely left out of the proceedings." Second, eager to continue discussions on the draft of the United Nations Pact in 1942, President Franklin Roosevelt wheeled himself into Churchill's chambers at the White House, only to find Churchill "stark naked and gleaming pink from his bath," in the words of presidential advisor Harry Hopkins. To a startled Roosevelt, Churchill proclaimed, "Pray enter— the Prime Minister of Great Britain has nothing to hide from the President of the United States."

In the first example, we see the humor of understatement elevating a somber description of England's "finest hour." It also demonstrates the exuberance of Churchill's histories rather than their exactitude. The second example is a coarser humor though like the first its effect is achieved due to the incongruity between the serious personages and the event at hand. The second story, while it sounds apocryphal, was recorded by Churchill and others.

Churchill's humor may be defined by the social incongruity principle, expressed early by the Scottish philosopher James Beattie in *An Essay on Laughter and Ludicrous Composition* (1776): "Laughter arises from the view of two or more inconsistent, unsuitable, or incongruous parts or circumstances, considered as united in complex object or assemblage, or as acquiring a sort of mutual relation from the peculiar manner in which the mind takes notice of them." Laughter arising from such inappropriateness was also defined by nineteenth-century critic William Hazlitt in "On Wit and Humour" (1819) as "the incongruous, the disconnecting of one idea from another, or the jostling of one feeling against another," and in Immanuel Kant's negative terms, "the sudden transformation of a strained expectation into nothing" (1790). The social corrective in this humor, commended by George Meredith in *On Comedy and the Uses of the Comic Spirit* (1897), excels in the political sphere when noble persons are brought to the level of an everyman. To whatever extent humor endeared Churchill to his constituents, these theoretical explanations diagnose its effects but were not themselves the stimulus for his humor.

Other instances of Churchill's humor emerged in his BBC broadcasts, although the first of the examples below was delivered to a Joint Session of Congress as well. At the time America had just entered the war and dramatically transformed Allied prospects. In his first address to a foreign legislature, Churchill began by characterizing the honor of the invitation:

By the way, I cannot help reflecting that if my father had been American and my mother British, instead of the other way round, I might have got here on my own. In that case, this would not have been the first time you would have heard my voice. In that case I should not have needed any invitation, but if I had, it is hardly likely it would have been unanimous.

A second example, from 1942, replete with the sarcasm of its childlike tone, was not intended to charm his hosts but to demonstrate his superiority and mock his foes:

Then Hitler made his second great blunder. He forgot about the winter. There is a winter, you know, in Russia. For a good many months the temperature is apt to fall very low. There is snow, there is frost, and all that. Hitler forgot about this Russian winter. He must have been very loosely educated. We all heard about it at school, but he forgot it. I have never made such a bad mistake as that!

The wit of Churchill, extensive enough to fill a large volume, is based on social class distinctions which placed him in his situation and in turn became his humorous mode. With his birthright firmly situated in Blenheim Palace and a noble ancestry from the duke of Marlborough to his own father, with his politics linked indissolubly to the British Empire ("I have not become the King's First Minister in order to preside over the liquidation of the British Empire"—1942), Churchill confidently viewed life through an aristocratic lens, à la Kipling's "white man's burden" philosophy of empire. The effectiveness of his wit is grounded on these notions of family, class, history, and empire contrasted with the requirements of his public performance and station, answering to a triple constituency of Parliament, voters, and foreign allies, especially Americans. Just as his histories contrast his dual roles of reporter and participant, there is an underlying irony in many of his spoken expressions.

Consider these examples of humor based on incongruity: "To jaw-jaw is better than to war-war," and "It is a good thing for an uneducated man to read books of quotations." Or, the famous anecdote of his response to a bureaucrat's correction of his placement of a preposition at the end of a sentence: "This is the sort of English up with which I will not put."

Another well-known story attributed to Churchill, even though it is probably apocryphal, helps to understand the man in his humor: "At a social gathering of dignitaries, a patronizing matron admonished the cigar-smoking Prime Minister: 'I am shocked, sir, that you are so drunk.' To which Churchill responded: 'Madam, tonight I am drunk and you are ugly, but tomorrow I shall be sober.'" Although offensive, this story is typical of American frontier humor—rough, coarse, bullying. Note that in its wit the story could be related to either Abraham Lincoln or Twain, but it is never so applied because in Lincoln's case its acrimony violates his kindness and humility and would reinforce, rather than contrast with, his lower class origins, and in Twain's case, it is perfectly believable but irrelevant because Twain is an artist, not a statesman, and hence the remark would smack only of wit and retribution, not of astonishment at upset expectations. In either case, the humor would be mitigated.

Finally, confronted by a matron of opposing politics who stated, "If you were my husband, I'd poison your morning coffee," Churchill replied, "Madam, if I were your husband, I'd drink it." This, too, captures the spirit of the man.

At eighty, Churchill was presented his portrait by the notable British artist Graham Sutherland and jocularly construed it as "a remarkable example of modern art" (he later cremated the work). Ten years later, BBC's "Ninety Years On," scripted by Terence Rattigan and hosted by Noel Coward, celebrated the venerable statesman by featuring his favorite entertainment, music-hall songs, once again reinforcing the contrast of the noble and the common. Churchill's final recorded remark was, "I am bored with it all."

Summary

Winston Churchill, a great leader of the free world against the Nazi and Communist tyrannies, used wit both to resolve his own personal dilemmas and to enhance his public speaking and dynamics as a political leader. "In my belief, you cannot deal with the most serious things in the world unless you also understand the most amusing," he said. His humor depended largely on contrasts, on upset expectations, and the incongruity of a prominent leader and orator issuing ripostes that both instruct and amuse, in language that naturally exploits the emotional climate of the situation.

Selected Bibliography

Primary Sources

Winston S. Churchill: His Complete Speeches 1897–1963. Ed. Robert James. New York: Chelsea House, 1974. 8 vols.

A Churchill Reader: The Wit and Wisdom of Sir Winston Churchill. Ed. Colin Coote. Boston: Houghton Mifflin, 1954.

Secondary Sources

Biographies

Gilbert, Martin. *Winston Churchill*. Boston: Houghton-Mifflin, 1966–1988, 8 vols. The official biography, begun by his son Randolph Churchill and finished by Martin Gilbert.

———. *Churchill: A Life*. New York: Henry Holt, 1991. Gilbert's one-volume, accessible biography.

Manchester, William. *The Last Lion: Winston Spencer Churchill, Visions of Glory*. Boston: Little, Brown, 1983–1990, 3 vols. Manchester's biography is also accessible reading

Pearson, John. *The Private Lives of Winston Churchill*. New York: Simon and Schuster, 1991. A psychological biography that relates Churchill's writings to his actions and attitudes.

Books and Articles in Books

Commager, Henry Steele. "Introduction." In *Marlborough: His Life and Times* by Winston Churchill, Vol. 1. Ed. Henry Steele Commager. New York: Scribner's, 1968. Excellent treatment of Churchill as author and historian.

Halle, Kay. *Irrepressible Churchill: A Treasury of Winston Churchill's Wit*. Cleveland, OH: World Publications, 1966.

Miller, Amos. "Winston S. Churchill." In *British Winners of the Nobel Literary Prize*. Ed. Walter Kidd. Norman, OK: University of Oklahoma Press, 1973. A full treatment of Nobel requirements and Churchill's literary merits.

C

Willans, Geoffrey, and Charles Roetter. *The Wit of Winston Churchill*. London: Parrish, 1956.

Joel Athey

Cleese, John

Born: Weston-Super-Mare, England, October 27, 1939
Education: Clifton College, 1953–1958; Downing College, Cambridge University, M.A. in Law, 1963
Married: Connie Booth, February 20, 1968; divorced 1978; one daughter; Barbara Trentham, February 15, 1981; divorced 1990; one daughter; Alyce Faye Eichelberger, December 1992

Biography

John Marwood Cleese, comedic actor and screenwriter, is most famous as a member of the Monty Python group of television and movie fame. His wacky sense of humor permeates all of his performances, even those decades beyond *Monty Python's Flying Circus*.

Born on October 27, 1939 in Weston-Super-Mare, and raised in a relatively normal household, Cleese was the only child of insurance salesman Reginald Cleese (whose own father changed the family name from Cheese when he went off to World War I) and Muriel Cleese. As a day boy at Clifton College (1953–1958), he was a solitary youth who learned to make fellow students laugh. He taught for two years before entering Downing College, Cambridge as a law student; he would receive an M.A. in law in 1963. Tall, bright, and energetic, Cleese was already in possession of his special off-the-wall humor.

At Cambridge the Footlights Club engaged as much of his attention as his legal studies did, and he joined future Monty Pythons, Graham Chapman and Eric Idle, as well as David Frost, in their revues. The 1963 Footlights show, *A Clump of Plinths*, was subsequently mounted off-campus at the Lyric Theatre in London's West End, with its name changed to *Cambridge Circus*. The show toured New Zealand, then Broadway for three weeks, and was telecast on *The Ed Sullivan Show*. In New York, Cleese met cartoonist Terry Gilliam, a future Python.

Success followed rapidly. He first wrote professionally as a student, for Frost's *That Was The Week That Was*; afterwards, he contributed to *The Frost Report* and Marty Feldman's *Comedy Machine*. He wrote and performed in two successful BBC radio shows: *At Last, the 1948 Show* (1967), and the BBC's longest-running comedy, *I'm Sorry, I'll Read That Again* (1965–1974). The latter thrived on puns and groans from the audience, and Cleese soon tired of it.

Meanwhile, the seed for Monty Python was sown, and the Cambridge three joined the Oxford two, Terry Jones and Michael Palin, plus Gilliam, to become Monty Python's Flying Circus, a name culled from a long list (not surprisingly, "circus" appeared in many of the candidate titles). The BBC turned them loose on a series of thirteen half-hour television shows, which was extended to forty-five shows (1969–1973 in England, 1974 and after in the United States). They complemented these with three movies, *Monty Python and the Holy Grail* (1975), *The Life of Brian* (1979), and *The Meaning of Life* (1983).

With Chapman, Cleese worked on the screenplay of *The Magic Christian*, a Peter Sellers vehicle in which Cleese appeared as the Sotheby auctioneer. With his wife, Connie Booth, whom he married on February 20, 1968 (the couple had one daughter), Cleese co-wrote *Fawlty Towers* (1975, 1979). In the television series he played Basil Fawlty and Booth played Polly. They continued their joint efforts even after their 1978 divorce.

There was meaning in life after Monty Python for Cleese. *Fawlty Towers* ran for only twelve episodes (six in 1975, six in 1979) but was highly regarded. He formed his own company, Video Arts, to produce industrial training films, over fifty in all, with titles such as *How to Lose Customers Without Really Trying*. These were purchased by corporate decision-makers to the tune of over sixteen million dollars in 1988. He sold the company in 1989. For Amnesty International the humorist wrote and starred in *The Secret Policeman's Other Ball* (1982), *The Secret Policeman's Private Parts* (1984), and two other Policeman films with similar titles. With psychologist Dr. Robin Skynner, he coauthored *Families and How to Survive Them* (1983) and *Life and How to Survive It* (1993), which blends counsel with humor, just as his training videos do.

Cleese played Petruchio in the BBC production of William Shakespeare's *The Taming of the Shrew* (1980), he won an Emmy for his performance on an episode of the American television hit *Cheers* (1987), and he cameoed in *The Great Muppet Caper* (1981). His first non-Python feature film, *Privates on Parade* (1982), was less than successful—he was Major Flack—but served as a learning experience for him. In 1988, he rebounded with great success by writing and starring in *A Fish Called Wanda*. The film earned him an Oscar nomination for his writing and the British Academy of Film and Television Arts best actor award. In 1994, Cleese was featured in Kenneth Branagh's *Mary Shelley's Frankenstein*, and his current screenplay, which has the working title *Death Fish II*, was released in 1995.

Enormous energy and diversity have propelled Cleese into many activities, and probably out of them too. He left the Pythons when he perceived their innovativeness abating. He refrained from creating a Fawlty Towers movie for the same reason. The profitability of his management film company he embraced with vigor and his usual irreverence: "Sincerely, I was after a fast buck." His personal life has reflected a propensity for change, too. On February 15, 1981, the writer married Barbara Trentham, with whom he had a daughter. Like his first marriage, this union ended in divorce (1990), and he entered into a third marriage, to Alyce Faye Eichelberger, in December 1992. All of his wives are American.

Literary Analysis

The comedy of Cleese and his fellow–Monty Pythons was innovative and anarchic, based on slapstick and repartee that border on the surreal. Their motto, a Cleese/Chapman sketch signature, became "And now for something completely different."

This style was an outgrowth of the revues that they performed at their respective universities. Cleese's *At Last, the 1948 Show* was an early incarnation of the Monty Python format. With the hilariously madcap, seemingly illogical antics of Spike Milligan and Peter Sellers in the 1950s as their model, the Pythons added the optimism and energy of the late 1960s and early 1970s. They got away with irreverence and naughty words because BBC executives ignored them at the beginning and were confounded by precedents when they did notice.

The Pythons influenced, Cleese acknowledges, practically nobody in the subsequent era. Whether this was due to a return to reality in the post-Vietnam 1970s and economic hard times, or whether it was the normal aftermath of innovation that became popular, there were few emulators. *Saturday Night Live*, the weekly NBC television show whose creators admired the Pythons, followed a similar format with an occasional foray into the surreal, but the American show's effect centered on topical issues and mimicry of celebrities and presidents rather than the Python's target of human behavior and television itself.

The six would-be Monty Pythons had known each other in the 1960s through BBC projects. In 1969, when BBC offered Cleese a series, he telephoned the others and they ended up with carte blanche for thirteen late-night spots on BBC2.

From the beginning, all six Pythons agreed on the show's structure, modeled after Milligan and Sellers' *The Running, Jumping, Standing Still Film* (1960), Milligan's *The Goon Show*, which aired on BBC radio in the 1950s, and the stream-of-consciousness approach in Milligan's television show *Q5*. The forty-five Monty Python television shows were composed of short skits, sometimes loosely connected by a word or recurring motif. In order to upset viewers' expectations, the Pythons wanted to push television beyond its customary form and content.

Typically, creativity followed form: Cleese and Chapman, united since their Cambridge days and *At Last, the 1948 Show*, focused on overturning expected formats, namely conventional plots with beginnings, middles, and endings, serious announcers, and stage-revue closings; theirs was a verbal send-up of television itself. The Oxford twosome, Palin and Jones, who had worked on *Do Not Adjust Your Set* (1967), focused on stream-of-consciousness techniques and the circus atmosphere of their Bonzo Dog Doo Dah Band; theirs was visual humor. Animation by Gilliam was featured in this latter effort. Idle, although a Cambridge cohort, was a swing man who most often generated ideas on his own. As Pythons, they insisted on breaking their medium away from the traditional limitations of stage and cinema.

The Cleese signature sketch is an absurdity based on strict rationality, in contrast to non sequiturs from Jones. He learned this from Feldman: "When I first met Marty, he went on at great length about what he used to call the internal logic of a sketch, which is that you could have everybody sitting in dustbins or dressed as carrots, but if somebody walks into the room who isn't dressed as a carrot or who isn't wheeled in in a dustbin, then you have to explain why not . . . it's got to be founded on that, on solid logic. It's all got to fit internally."

C

At times the writing partnerships were deliberately shifted, but invariably they returned to Cleese and Chapman, Jones and Palin, Idle doing his own thing, and Gilliam showing up on taping days with animated surprises for all of them. As might be expected, there were temperamental differences, with the main split between Cleese and Jones. The group recognized this dichotomy, which did not mend until the third movie, *The Meaning of Life*, as a disharmony that generated dynamics for much of their communal creativity.

Chapman describes Cleese as brilliant, punctual, forgetful. When struck by a creative blank, they would thumb through a thesaurus, Bible, or other reference book to hit upon ideas. Then, as Chapman tells it, Cleese would write down their sketch, lose it, and they would rewrite it, all at home.

Python skits were absurd, in the way that the Coneheads on NBC's *Saturday Night Live* appeared in the United States; their cartoons were bizarre, much like the rock videos on MTV. There was, however, an intellectual element in Python skits that is rare in either of these foster children.

The humor was not always intellectual, though; witness the number of men-in-drag skits or Cleese performing The Silly Walk—picture an English barrister with briefcase and bowler hat, strutting so that his feet rise above waist-high (this is the act that fans pester Cleese to repeat on stage, and which he came to dislike). Nor was the quiz show parody intellectual: he emceed "Spot the Brain Cell" in order to browbeat contestants, mostly addled old ladies. This sketch evolved into a celebrity event wherein the guest celebrity beats up a blindfolded contestant whose task is to identify the star.

Some general recognition was required to upset viewer expectations in Cleese's situation comedy skit "The Attila the Hun Show," which was complete with a wife, children, and a black butler. Even less recognition is evident with the Pepperpots—two old dames played by Cleese and Chapman—who, in one scene, listen to "The Death of Mary, Queen of Scots" until the radio explodes, then the television comes on and the announcer warns them that the penguin on top of their TV will explode, which it does. The segue into this skit was the show's motif, "How to Recognize Different Parts of the Body," where Part #22 was the nipple, and the viewer saw a radio dial. There

was no intellectualism in the famous Spam scene, in which every item catalogued by the annoying waitress is Spam—Spam salad, and so on, until it is finally "Spam, Spam, Spam, Spam"—certainly the inspiration of *Saturday Night*'s John Belushi sketch about cheeseburgers and Pepsi.

One Python newscast showed a coal miners' brawl, which the audience learns erupted over the correct date of the Treaty of Utrecht. Their pique was heightened, one miner claims, because just last week his disputant lied about the binomial theorem. In patented BBC monotone, the newsman reveals that the strikers have increased their demands to thirty reasons why Henry III was a bad king.

Panel discussions supplied more inanity, as when the question of "Is There Life After Death?" is discussed by three dead people plus a professor and a priest, and in a trivial pursuit game show for Vladimir Lenin, Karl Marx, Mao Tse Tung, and Che Guevera—on the category of sports. One interview spot had three guests: one who spoke only the beginnings of words (Cleese), another the middles, the third the ends; finally they utter a collective sentence. In another segment Cleese narrates a documentary on the Royal Clinic for Overacting, where viewers spy on inmates muting their deliveries of "To be, or not to be" and "A horse, a horse, my kingdom. . . ."

The Pythons were good visual actors, and Cleese's strength lay in playing authority figures—the tall, decent, stiff-upper-lip Englishman. In one episode the Pythons are pigeon fanciers who have been collected, and their every movement mimics the stutter-motions of pigeons themselves, except that these are English gentlemen who hop out of baskets and flit across the plaza. Another popular skit was the Bruces, which stereotyped Australians who wear khaki shorts, bush shirts, Aussie hats; they drink a lot and are all named Bruce, except for the new man: "Mightn't this be confusing, you being named Michael and all?"

The Monty Python show took hold slowly, but the actors won over their audience and it became a smash hit. Before the fourth, and final, season, Cleese left the Flying Circus, dissatisfied with what he perceived as repetitiveness, together with some personal disagreements. In Cleese's absence, the name of the show was shortened to Monty Python. It was the fourth series that the ABC network bought and edited in 1975, which initiated a legal battle won by the Pythons and set a precedent regarding copyright laws.

Subsequently, Cleese played the cantankerous hotel owner in *Fawlty Towers*. Even the writer/actor was surprised by the success of this situation comedy, with its regular plot complications and adversaries, namely a wife, hotel guests, and employees who infuriate the apoplectic Basil Fawlty. In some ways the show's lunacy resembled antics on *I Love Lucy*, including the physical humor for which Cleese was never at a loss: his hurried Groucho Marx walk in panic has been adapted by Kramer on American television's *Seinfeld*, and Basil's agitated flapping of his arms or pounding of his head against the floor, only to be witnessed and embarrassed, is reminiscent of Lucille Ball's Lucy.

But, there is more verbal humor in *Fawlty Towers* than in the other shows mentioned. When a stuffy, partly deaf matron demands a refund because she can see only the town from her room, the irritable Basil responds, "When one looks out the window of a Torquay hotel, what does one expect to see other than Torquay? The Sidney Operahouse? The Hanging Gardens of Babylon? Herds of wildebeests sweeping majestically across the horizon? Are you disappointed because Krakatoa isn't erupting within your view?"

In another episode, his wife, always a worthy temperamental match, hints at their anniversary. "Anniversary of what?" he teases, "The battle of Agincourt? Crecy? Trafalgar?" In every episode the irascible Basil conflicts with his English-as-a-second-language assistant, Manny, who is from Barcelona. In a fit of pique Basil demands comprehension from Manny: "This is not a proposition from Wittgenstein!"

Unlike the Monty Python shows, which were based on bizarre ideas and upset expectations about what television should be concerned with, in *Fawlty Towers* Cleese presented human behavior and emotions. The show's success, he suggests in his description of Basil, "embodied the kind of thing that the English feel sometimes—which is because they can't say 'I'm sorry, this food is not good enough' or 'I bought this pair of shoes and I want you to replace them'—because they can't do these simple acts of self-assertion, they tend to become on the surface a kind of brittle politeness and underneath a lot of seething rage." Its audiences were larger than those of the Pythons, although not in America, possibly because there was no follow-up movie.

The three Monty Python movies continued the comic anarchy, and each has become a favorite of select fans. The weakness in each is their unevenness, very funny moments followed by lulls.

Produced on a slim budget (£229,000, or $500,000), *Monty Python and the Holy Grail* included music from Led Zeppelin and Pink Floyd. Most viewers remember the knights with no horses, hopping along, clopping coconut halves to simulate the sounds of horses' hooves. Soldiers debate whether a five-ounce European swallow could have transported a one-pound coconut to England, or was the African swallow, larger but non-migratory, needed, or perhaps two swallows in tandem. The attack of the Killer Rabbit, written by Cleese/Chapman, is one of the funniest visual jokes in the movie.

The movie quickly became a cult favorite in America, but for television in 1977 CBS edited out its blood and suggestive language. Later the Pythons regained their film, and PBS showed it uncut.

The Life of Brian dropped its initial, uninviting parody of Christ and turned to an attack on blind followers of religion. Brian was "just a bloke in Judea in 33 A.D.," says Cleese. Ultimately, the mob that follows Brian splits into shoe, sandal, and gourd factions, or "the entire history of religion in two minutes." At the local stoning-to-death scene where Roman soldiers allowed no women, four women appear disguised as men, played, of course, by Pythons: hence, a scene where men play women who are pretending to be men. At the filming in Tunisia, Python hero Milligan showed up and they wrote him into a scene. The film was banned in some southern states in America.

The last Python film, *The Meaning of Life*, provided a greater variety of social targets because in it the group reverted to sketches in the mode of classic Python irreverence. Its two great scenes are "Every Sperm is Sacred" (with Cleese as the headmaster who, with his wife, demonstrates sex techniques to bored schoolboys) and the enormously obese Mr. Creosote (Jones) at his gross-out best.

With Monty Python finally behind him, Cleese wrote and starred in his most successful non-Python film, *A Fish Called Wanda*. In this complicated jewel-heist and seduction film, Cleese again plays the respectable authority figure, a barrister unwittingly involved in farcical intrigues. He once again ends up caught and embarrassed (this time, naked) by decent but bewildered strangers. But, it is all in fun, and the barrister escapes with Wanda (definitely not a fish, but a beautiful amoral American thief played by Jamie Lee Curtis) to Rio.

Other Cleese performances include the voice of Cat R. Waul in Steven Spielberg's *An American Tail 2: Fievel Goes West* (1991), the audiotape of C.S. Lewis's *The Screwtape Letters* (1988), his own 1986 film *Clockwise* (successful in the United Kingdom), and Robin Hood in Gilliam's *Time Bandits* (1981). Topping all of these is his lucrative career as a television pitchman for Sony, Schweppes, American Express, Magnavox, and others: "The sillier the activity, the more they seem to pay," says Cleese.

His video arts training films are even more profitable (earning over $20 million in 1992). Cleese writes and stars in most of these half-hour segments with titles like *Decisions, Decisions*; *Meetings, Bloody Meetings*; *The Importance of Mistakes*; and *How Am I Doing?* Combining humor with instruction, he dredges up historical examples such as Brutus, Ivan the Terrible, and Ethelred the Unready.

Summary

John Cleese is a world-famous writer and actor for stage, television, and cinema. His wit is zany and unpredictable, with a large measure of the absurd. His style upsets viewer expectations. For English fans, he captures comic elements of the human situation, including despair at what television has wrought and how the hotel manager or the gentleman is treated or ought to be treated. For American fans he epitomizes the eccentric Englishman, intellectual but daft. He is most famous for his antics as a member of the Monty Python troupe, but in this and all of his other shows he has proven to be both a consummate actor and an innovative humorist. This is true not only for *Monty Python's Flying Circus*, but for *Fawlty Towers* in the 1970s and *A Fish Called Wanda* in 1988 as well.

Selected Bibliography

Primary Sources
Fawlty Towers. CBS/Fox Video, 4 tapes, 12 episodes; BBC recordings, soundtracks to 8 shows; *The Complete Fawlty Towers*, scripts to all 12 episodes. London: Methuen, 1988.
A Fish Called Wanda. 1988. CBS/Fox Video: *A Fish Called Wanda* (book), London: Methuen, 1988.
Monty Python's Flying Circus. Paramount Home Video, 22 tapes, 45 episodes.
Monty Python and the Holy Grail. 1974. RCA/Columbia Pictures Home Video.
The Life of Brian. 1979. Paramount.
Monty Python's The Meaning of Life. 1983. MCA Home Video.

Secondary Sources

Biographies
Margolis, Jonathan. *Cleese Encounters*. New York: St. Martin's Press, 1992. Unauthorized biography.

Books and Articles
Dwyer, Paula. "John Cleese's Flying Business Circus." *Business Week* (June 21, 1993): 104 ff.
Johnson, Kim. *The First 20 Years of Monty Python*. New York: St. Martin's Press, 1989. A detailed look at the Pythons and each television episode and movie, with commentary, by a friend and fan. Good photos.
———. *Life Before and After Monty Python: The Solo Flights of the Flying Circus*. New York: St. Martin's Press, 1993. A second caring description of the individual performances by the six Pythons, with commentary. Good photos.

NB. Thanks to Ms. Kate Herbert at David Wilkinson Associates (Mr. Cleese's agent), London, and to Ms. Chuck Bartelt at Garland Publishing, New York, for current reference materials.

Joel Athey

Coleridge, Samuel Taylor

Born: Ottery St. Mary, October 21, 1772
Education: Christ's Hospital School, London, 1782–1791; Jesus College, Cambridge, October 1791
Marriage: Sara Fricker, October 1795; four children
Died: Highgate, July 25, 1834

Biography

Samuel Taylor Coleridge was born to the Reverend John and Ann Bowdon Coleridge in the small Devonshire town of Ottery St. Mary on October 21, 1772. The son of a rural vicar and schoolmaster and the youngest of ten children, Coleridge began his formal education at age three. At age six he transferred to his father's grammar school, and there he laid the groundwork for a lifetime of extensive reading.

After their father's death in 1781, the family left Devonshire, and in the spring of 1782 Coleridge was enrolled in Christ's Hospital School, London, where he began his friendship with Charles Lamb. In his nine years at Christ's, Coleridge was affected not only by his reading in philosophy, medicine, and classical literature, but also by the dramatic shift between rural and urban living that he experienced. His reflections on his own schooldays in "Frost at Midnight"—and (erroneously) on Lamb's in "This Lime-Tree Bower My Prison"—reveal the poet's abiding preference for his early years in the country.

By any standard, Coleridge's college career was unenviable. He entered Jesus College, Cambridge in 1791, and there his regimen of study often gave way to what he called "the empty gratification of the moment." On December 4, 1793, in a fit of desperation, Coleridge left the university and enlisted in the Light Dragoons under the pseudonym of Silas Tomkyn Comberbache. He soon failed as a soldier, and through his brothers' efforts was returned to Cambridge in less than four months. He quit school by the end of 1794, however, having devoted much of his creative energy to his new plan of establishing an ideal community in America—a "pantisocracy," as he called it, in which a dozen couples would settle in Pennsylvania to live in unselfish, unsuperstitious community.

Coleridge developed his utopian ideas with his friend Robert Southey, whom he met on a trip to Oxford in June of 1794. Both were young poets and radical liberals sympathetic to what they perceived as the spirit of the French Revolution. In the interest of their liberal pantisocracy, Coleridge became engaged to Sara Fricker, the sister of Southey's fiance, Edith Fricker, whom he married in October 1795 and with whom he had four children. To Coleridge's disappointment, the plans for an ideal society on the banks of the Susquehanna River fell through; nonetheless, he went ahead with his pantisocratic marriage.

In 1796, still brimming with enthusiastic liberalism, Coleridge began work on a periodical, *The Watchman*, which failed after ten issues. He then published his first collection of poetry, *Poems on Various Subjects*. In September, his first child, David Hartley Coleridge, was born, and by the end of the year the family moved to Nether Stowey to be near Coleridge's friend and early patron Thomas Poole. The year was marred only by Coleridge's first use of opium to treat his worsening physical ailments.

At Stowey, in 1797 and 1798, Coleridge established his collaboration with William Wordsworth and wrote most of his best-known poetry: "The Rime of the Ancient Mariner," "This Lime-Tree Bower My Prison," "Kubla Khan," "Frost at Midnight," and "Christabel." His wife gave birth to a second son, Berkeley, in May of 1798, four months before the publication of *Lyrical Ballads*.

In September of 1798, Coleridge left his family to tour Germany with William and Dorothy Wordsworth. He was away eleven months, during which time his son Berkeley died (February 10, 1799). In April, he wrote an epitaph on an infant who died before baptism; speaking of the poem, he wrote to his wife, "Ah, my poor Berkeley! . . . When I wrote it, my heart with a deep misgiving turned my thoughts homeward." He returned to England in July, and for a few years thereafter most of what he wrote was somber.

Wordsworth and his sister Dorothy moved to the Lake District at the end of 1799, and in the summer of 1800 Coleridge followed. In September, another son, Derwent, was born to the Coleridges, and Samuel busied himself with the printing of the second edition of *Lyrical Ballads* and its revolutionary preface. During the winter of 1800–1801, Coleridge's health deteriorated, and he developed a critical addiction to opium that would plague him for the rest of his life.

That winter began a difficult sixteen-year period marked by ill health, drug addiction, and failed relationships. In 1800, he met and fell in love with Sarah Hutchinson, Wordsworth's sister-in-law, for whom he wrote "Dejection: An Ode" in September of 1802. Their platonic relationship would be a continual source of conflicting feelings for Coleridge. In December, he had a daughter, Sara Coleridge, who after his death would edit his work. In spite of the birth, however, his family life irrevocably deteriorated.

In 1808, Coleridge permanently separated from his wife and began working on a series of essays, *The Friend*, which he published from June of 1809 to May of 1810. Then, in October 1810, Sarah Hutchinson moved from Grasmere, and shortly afterward Coleridge broke off his friendship with Wordsworth. For the next six years he wrote little. Although his early play *Osorio* (1797) was revised and produced, his intellectual production was primarily lectures on literature and aesthetics. In 1812, he reconciled with Wordsworth, but their relationship was never fully reestablished.

In April 1816, Coleridge was taken in by the Highgate physician James Gillman, under whose care he lived until his death in 1834. By the end of 1816 he published "Kubla Khan," "Christabel," and "The Pains of Sleep." A year later, he wrote and published all of *Biographia Literaria*, arguably the most important work of literary criticism of the nineteenth century, and he also published *Lay Sermons*; a play, *Zapolya*; and a collection of poetry, *Sibylline Leaves*.

In 1818, Coleridge's life as an influential conversationalist began. By 1822, a group of listeners regularly gathered in his parlor on Thursday nights to hear "the sage of Highgate" expound in Johnsonian depth, breadth, and wit on virtually any topic. Among the many literary figures influenced by Coleridge's conversations in this period were John Keats, Ralph Waldo Emerson, Walter Scott, Thomas Carlyle, James Fenimore Cooper, and William Hazlitt.

His last publications were two prose works: *Aids to Reflection* (1825) and *On the Constitution of the Church and State* (1829). He died at Highgate on July 25, 1834, as renowned a conversationalist as he was a writer.

Literary Analysis

Coleridge is clearly one of the most multifaceted of British writers. A gifted poet, a towering figure as a literary critic, and an influential philosopher and theologian—Coleridge has been claimed over the years by many different schools of thought. Reasonably enough, his great achievements as a writer of serious poetry and philosophy have obscured his work as a humorist. Nevertheless, he did sporadically produce a significant body of light verse and epigrams from the beginning through the end of his career, and he left in his letters and in the written record of his conversations a long testament to his comic wit.

Coleridge's earliest poetry is peppered with comic inflations and terse witticisms. His 1789 poem "The Nose," for instance, concludes with the following neoclassic rapture:

Proboscis Fierce! I am calcined! I die!
Thus, like great Pliny, in Vesuvius' fire,
I perish in the blaze while I the blaze
    admire.

In 1790, he composed his "Monody on a Tea-Kettle" to mark the passing of his kitchen's "sooty swain" tossed in the garbage to "rust obscure midst heaps of vulgar tin." A year later, while still only nineteen, Coleridge wrote his epigramatic poem "On Imitation," which ends "Tho' few like Fox can speak—like Pitt can think— / Yet all like Fox can game—like Pitt can drink." That year he also wrote a series of three odes, two on uncomfortable carriage travel and one on the "scrape and blow and squeak and squall" of the Tiverton Church choir ("Inside the Coach," "Devonshire Roads," and "Music"). These poems, all more than simple doggerel, show the early development of Coleridge's eighteenth-century wit. The humor is expressed in hyperbole, wordplay, and the pleasing shock of irreverence.

The most abrasive, if not abusive, of his youthful poetry is the poem "Written After a Walk Before Supper," which Coleridge included in a letter to his brother, the Rev. George Coleridge, on August 9, 1792. The poem describes the Rev. Fulwood Smerdon, who replaced Coleridge's father as the vicar at Ottery St. Mary in 1781. It depicts as well the vicar's wife and portrays the couple as Jack and Mrs. Sprat: the wife, "Vulgarity enshrin'd in blubber"; the husband, "a meagre bit of littleness." The vicar is indeed so thin and the wife so fat that "In case of foe, he well might hide / Snug in the collops of her side." Were the author unknown, one would sooner ascribe this hyperbolic caricature to Lord Byron than to Coleridge.

In 1797, the year that his friendship with Wordsworth began and the same year he wrote most of his best poetry, Coleridge published his "Sonnets Attempted in the Manner of Contemporary Writers" in the *Monthly Magazine*. Here, in a rare instance, we see Coleridge parodying himself. In a November letter to his friend and publisher Joseph Cottle he wrote the following revealing description of the poems:

> I sent to the *Monthly Magazine* (1797) three mock Sonnets in ridicule of my own Poems, and Charles Lloyd's and Lamb's, etc., etc., exposing that affectation of unaffectedness, of jumping and

misplaced accent in common-place epithets, flat lines forced into poetry by italics (signifying how well and mouthily the author would read them), puny pathos, etc. etc . . . . I think they may do good to our young Bards.

Evidently, Coleridge saw as early as 1797 the need for "young" poets not to take themselves too seriously. Ironically, part of the high comedy of the situation is that at age twenty Coleridge no longer considered himself a young poet, although only three years had passed since he had left the Light Dragoons. Twenty years later, however, he reprinted the four sonnets in chapter 1 of *Biographia Literaria*, and his critique of his own (and Wordsworth's) style remained largely unaltered.

In 1798, in the summer before the publication of *Lyrical Ballads*, Coleridge published his satire "Recantation" in the *Morning Post* (July 30). Like his unpublished poem "The Madman and the Lethargist," "Recantation" is an indirect political satire. In the introduction, the poet calls the work "a very humorous description of the French Revolution, which is represented by an Ox." Although the *degree* of the humor is a question, Coleridge's allegory is clear enough.

The revolutionary ideal, here pictured as an ox, is driven to violent madness by a country mob while an elderly Protestant man tries to tell them that the ox was merely happy. One of the bumpkins then turns to the old man and says, "To slit your windpipe were good fun, / 'Od blast you for an *impious* son / Of a Presbyterian wh—re!" A footnote Coleridge included in later versions of the poem (*Annual Anthology*, 1800; *Sibylline Leaves*, 1817) accounts for the expression "Presbyterian whore" in exceptionally Horation style: "One of the many fine words which the most uneducated had about this time a constant opportunity of acquiring, from the sermons in the pulpit and the proclamations in the — corners." In the urbanity of that comment, the reader discovers a seldom-discussed side of Coleridge: the deep irony of his invective satire. When he took up the satiric form, Coleridge chose an incongruous balance of urbanity and seething sarcasm; amid the calm, Virgilian tone of the satire, we can detect the bitter, self-superior voice of Juvenal.

As the Sage of Highgate, Coleridge spoke much more than he wrote, but the poetry that he did produce was often lighthearted and witty. Of especial interest is "The Reproof and Reply" (1823), one of four "Lightheartednesses in Rhyme" first published in *Friendship's Offering* (1834). Coleridge prefaced the poem with the following motto: "I expect no sense, worth listening to, from the man who never does talk nonsense." Again, like his parodic sonnets, this poem warns against an excessive seriousness.

The purely comic narrative recounts how Coleridge was caught stealing flowers from someone's garden on a Sunday morning in May. Coleridge would have been fifty years old. The poem begins with a twelve-line reproof—"Fie, Mr. Coleridge!—and can this be you? / Break two commandments? and in church-time too!" It turns then to forty-seven lines of neoclassic posing, and concludes with the following absolution from the wronged gardener:

> "Poor youth! he's but a waif! The spoons
> all right? then hen and chickens safe?
> Well, well, he shall not forfeit our re-
> gards—The Eighth Commandment was
> not meant for Bards!"

Here again we find the complex woof of Coleridge's humor. The brevity and wit of the epigram appears in tandem with the hyperbole of the early doggerel. Moreover, we should keep in mind that this poem is fundamentally ironic. It is a study in the largely purposeless satire known as the burlesque.

Two other of the "Lightheartednesses" that Coleridge published in *Friendship's Offering* are companion poems that he wrote in 1828 on the foul odors of a certain German city: "Cologne" and "On My Joyful Departure from the Same City." Walking the streets of what he calls "the body-and-soul-stinking town," he counts "two and seventy stenches, / All well defined, and several stinks!" In a footnote then he ponders the irony that such a town could ever have given the world perfume. As the most coarse, indeed grotesque, of Coleridge's humorous poems, these are remarkable in that they come at the end, not at the beginning of his career.

Coleridge's last poem is his own epitaph, one of over eighty epigrams that he published in his lifetime. As has long been known, most of them are unacknowledged translations of German works, but the early and the late epigrams (those not written for newspaper deadlines) are apparently wholly original. A good

C

example of the wit demonstrated in these epigrams is his oft-quoted "On a Volunteer Singer" (1800):

> Swans sing before they die—'twere no
> bad thing
> Should certain persons die before they
> sing.

Few epigrams in English better illustrate the blend of brevity and surprise that continues to make this poetic form so widely pleasing. That same wittiness is applied in the poet's own epitaph, which he completed on November 9, 1833, eight months before his death. The light, casual tone of the poem, in tandem with the gravity of the content, evokes a Renaissance sense of the good death reminiscent of John Donne and George Herbert:

> Stop, Christian passer-by!—Stop, child
> of God,
> And read with gentle breast. Beneath this
> sod
> A poet lies, or that which once seem'd
> he.
> O, lift one thought in prayer for S. T. C.;
> That he who many a year with toil of
> breath
> Found death in life, may here find life in
> death!
> Mercy for praise—to be forgiven for
> fame
> He ask'd, and hoped, through Christ. Do
> thou the same!

Coleridge's humor has received very little attention over the years outside of the biographies and the recollections of the poet's friends and acquaintances. One critic of the 1960s went so far in her dismissal of the light verse as to say that Coleridge wrote "two kinds of poetry that really mattered: the conversation poems and the poems of high imagination."[1] Nevertheless, Coleridge's light verse, his epigrams, his satires, and his conversational witticisms were not merely the juvenilia of a developing poet—they were the lifelong products of one of the most complex and diverse wits of the nineteenth century. Coleridge was more than the poet of the "Dejection" ode; he was also the high-spirited Sage of Highgate who, having drunk too much claret, tossed his glass through a closed window and then declared a fellow window breaker "as true a genius as Dante."[2]

For those readers who admire only the solemn Coleridge, the poem in the "Lightheartedness" series—"Lines: to a Comic Author, on an Abusive Review"—may be most appropriate:

> What though the chilly wide-mouth'd
> quacking chorus
> From the rank swamps of murk Review-
> land croak:
> So was it, neighbor, in the times before
> us,
> When Momus, throwing on his Attic
> cloak,
> Romp'd with the Graces.

Summary

Samuel Taylor Coleridge is best known as a serious poet of the "high Imagination," a concept that he helped define as one of the most influential literary critics of the nineteenth century. As a humorist, however, and as a witty conversationalist, he also left a smaller, though still pleasing mark on the Romantic period. His invective satires reinforce his opinion that the French Revolution was a noble idea gone wrong; the light verse and epigrams demonstrate the urbane and dispassionate wit of a classical comedy as well as the irreverence, the incongruity, and the hyperbole of the burlesque; and "Sonnets Attempted in the Manner of Contemporary Writers," later reprinted in *Biographia Literaria*, show a gift most unusual among Romantic poets: that of self-parody.

Notes

1. Virginia L. Radley, *Samuel Taylor Coleridge*. New York: Twayne Publishers, 1966.
2. This reference to William Jerdan's account of Coleridge's spirited vandalism appears in David Perkins's introduction to Coleridge in *English Romantic Writers* (New York: Harcourt Brace Jovanovich, 1967), pp. 388–89.

Selected Bibliography

Primary Sources
With Robert Southey. The Fall of Robespierre. An Historic Drama. Cambridge: Printed by Benjamin Flower for W.H. Lunn and J. & J. Merrill, 1794. Act 1 by Coleridge, Acts 2 & 3 by Southey.
Christabel: Kubla Khan, A Vision; The Pains of Sleep. London: Printed for John

Murray by William Bulmer, 1816.

With William Wordsworth. Lyrical Ballads, with a few Other Poems. Bristol: Printed by Biggs & Cottle for T.N. Longman, 1798.

With Charles Lamb and Robert Southey. Poems on Various Subjects. London: C.G. & J. Robinson, and Bristol: J. Cottle, 1796.

Biographica Literaria; or Biographical Sketches of My Literary Life and Opinions. London: Rest Fenner, 1817.

With Robert Southey. The Devil's Walk. A Poem. London: Marsh & Miller, and Edinburgh: Constable, 1830.

The Collected Works of Samuel Taylor Coleridge. Ed. Kathleen Coburn. Princeton: Princeton University Press, 1971 (ongoing). When completed, the full collection will be twenty-six or twenty-seven volumes of meticulously edited text. The following is a list of titles and editors: *Lectures 1795: On Politics and Religion,* ed. Lewis Patton and Peter Mann; *Essays on His Times,* ed. David V. Erdman; *The Friend,* ed. Barbara E. Rooke; *Lectures 1808–1819: On Literature,* ed. Reginald A. Foakes; *Lay Sermons,* ed. R.J. White; *Biographia Literaria,* ed. James Engell and Walter Jackson Bate; *Lectures 1818–1819: On the History of Philosophy,* ed. Owen Barfield; *Aids to Reflection,* ed. John Beer; *On the Constitution of the Church and State,* ed. John Colmer; *Shorter Works and Fragments,* ed. J.R. de J. Jackson and H.J. Jackson; *Marginalia,* ed. George Whalley; *Logic,* ed. J.R. de J. Jackson; *Table Talk,* ed. Carl R. Woodring; *Opus Maximum,* ed. Thomas McFarland; and *Poetical Works,* ed. J.C.C. Mays.

Complete Poetical Works of Samuel Taylor Coleridge. Ed. E.H. Coleridge. Oxford: Oxford University Press, 1912. 2 vols. Until Mays's three-volume *Poetical Works* becomes available, readers should be able to find this standard collection of the poetry, dramas, epigrams, juvenilia, and fragments.

The Collected Letters of Samuel Taylor Coleridge. Ed. Earl Griggs. Oxford: Oxford University Press, 1956–1971. 6 vols. More useful as an insight into Coleridge's humor than are the biogra-phies, the letters show the continuous ebb and flow of Coleridge's wit throughout his adult life.

Coleridge's Notebooks. Ed. Kathleen Coburn. Princeton: Princeton University Press, 1957 (ongoing). Like the letters, Coburn's enormous collection of Coleridge's notebooks—close to seventy in all, when the five projected volumes are all complete—offers those interested in the poet's humor a wealth of information, not the least of which being the mention of a yet-undiscovered essay, "An Apology for Puns" (#3762).

Coleridge the Talker: A Series of Contemporary Descriptions and Comments. Ed. Richard W. Armour and Raymond F. Howes. Ithaca: Cornell University Press, 1940. This volume pulls together the recollected conversations of seventy-six of Coleridge's contemporaries. Like Woodring's edition of *Table Talk,* it accounts admirably for Coleridge's continued reputation as a Johnsonian conversationalist.

Secondary Sources

Bibliographies

Jordan, Frank, ed. *The English Romantic Poets: A Review of Research and Criticism.* New York: MLA Press, 1985. Max F. Schultz's 124-page chapter on Coleridge in this exhaustive annotated bibliography of the period offers students an extraordinarily useful tool of research. He organizes and briefly discusses the historical, literary, and the sociopolitical criticism of the poetry and the prose, as well as Coleridge's artistic and intellectual influences and indebtednesses. For books and articles after 1984, the *MLA Annual Bibliography* must suffice.

Biographies

Bate, Walter J. *Coleridge.* New York: Macmillan, 1968.

Wiley, Basil. *Samuel Taylor Coleridge.* New York: Norton, 1992.

Books and Articles

Abrams, M.H. *The Mirror and the Lamp.* Oxford: Oxford University Press, 1953. Coleridge as critic.

Hodgson, John A. "Coleridge, Puns, and Donne's First Poem: The Limbo of Rhetoric and the Conceptions of Wit." *John Donne Journal*, 4, 2 (1985): 181–200.

Lowes, J.L. *The Road to Xanadu*. Boston: Houghton Mifflin, 1927, rev. 1930. A classic investigation of the sources and compostion of *The Ancient Mariner* and *Kubla Khan*.

Newlyn, Lucy. "Parodic Allusion: Coleridge and the 'Nehemiah Higgin-Bottom' Sonnets, 1797." *Charles Lamb Bulletin*, 56 (1986): 255–59. Newlyn's is the only article-length study of the parodic sonnet sequence.

Radley, Virginia L. *Samuel Taylor Coleridge*. New York: Twayne Publishers, 1966. Introduction to the poet's life and works.

Shawcross, John T. "Opulence and Iron Pokers: Coleridge and Donne." *John Donne Journal*, 4, 2 (1985): 201–24. These are the first articles to deal seriously with the poet's indebtedness to the Renaissance poet.

Robert A. Prescott

Collier, John Henry Noyes

Born: London, May 3, 1901
Education: Privately educated
Marriage: Harriet Hess, May 25, 1954; one child
Died: Pacific Palisades, California, April 6, 1980

Biography

John Collier was born in London on May 3, 1901. John George and Emily Mary Noyes Collier could not afford a genteel education for their son because the father had become responsible for his own sixteen younger siblings. Educated at home by tutors, principally by his uncle, the novelist Vincent Collier, John determined to become a poet. Though dismayed at first by this decision, his father managed to provide him with a small allowance which afforded his son a chance to work as a reviewer and journalist and to bring out *Gemini*, a book of poems. He remained in London in the 1920s, savoring the bohemian life of the city. His first novel, *His Monkey Wife*, though controversial, established his literary reputation. Other novels and short stories followed, and tiring of city life he moved to rural France. In 1935, needing $500 to buy a sailboat, he impulsively accepted an offer to write a screenplay and went off to Hollywood. Continuing to write short stories, but principally employed as a screenwriter, Collier moved between Hollywood, England, and France before finally settling in Hollywood in 1942. Though considered over-scrupulous and slow as a scenarist, Collier worked for most of the major studios and achieved considerable success with scripts for *Sylvia Scarlett*, *I Am a Camera*, and *The War Lord*. He was responsible, too, for much of the development of the film version of *The African Queen*. Returning from a trip to Mexico in 1953, he was stopped at customs and subjected to a searching inquisition which revealed that the FBI had compiled a considerable dossier on him. In part, this unwelcome attention resulted from his being confused with another John Collier, a suspect bureaucrat. Graylisted himself and indignant over the blacklisting of many of his fellow screenwriters during the McCarthy era, the author moved first to Mexico and then in 1955 to France, which remained his home until he returned to California a year before his death, of a stroke, on April 6, 1980. Few realized that the John Collier who wrote witty pieces for *Playboy*, *Esquire*, and the *New Yorker*, and teleplays for *Alfred Hitchcock Presents*, was the same John Collier whose novels had satirized London society in the 1930s. In his last years he attempted a major philosophical work, a new version of *Paradise Lost* in the form of a reader's film script, an effort that found few readers. He is remembered mainly for fifty light, elegant, and witty short stories which are widely anthologized and frequently dramatized.

Literary Analysis

Collier was surprised when journalists and biographers approached him to write about his life and work. He considered his work to be minor. One of a generation of talented writers who guiltily "sold out" their art for easy money in Hollywood, Collier was, nevertheless, a scrupulous craftsman and an author who aspired to make serious statements about life. In 1932, he coauthored *Just The Other Day: An Informal History of Great Britain Since the War*, and even his book of poems *Gemini* (1932) is a serious reflection on the Dionysian and the Apollonian embodied in the vital but uncouth Orson and the refined and dandiacal Valentine. Though the central proposition of his first novel, *His Monkey Wife* (1930), seems lighthearted and preposterous, like *Just The Other*

Day (1932) and *Gemini* it analyzes civilization and its discontents. The story concerns an Englishman who returns from Africa with a monkey bride who fascinates British society; he eventually returns with her to her home. Emily, a sensitive, warm, compassionate, and highly educated chimpanzee, is contrasted to the hysterical women and neurasthenic men of London society. Collier's next novel, *Tom's A-Cold* (1933), continues Collier's examination of society. In a post-apocalyptic world his characters discuss the natural relationship between aristocrats and workers. Unleavened by Collier's wit, this piece of conservative philosophizing was an embarrassment to the author in his later years. Collier's last novel, *Defy the Foul Fiend* (1934), is a picaresque following of the fortunes of a naive young man, and, in the process, satirizes many aspects of modern life. Willoughby, the hero, passes through phases of romantic love, radicalism, and decadent hedonism, and finally becomes a Tory. His enthusiasms are all doomed to ironic outcomes, and his final incarnation as a country squire is essentially a defeat. Despite the serious intent of this satiric novel, Willoughby anticipates the dopey young men who are taught grisly lessons about life in many of Collier's short stories. Collier's novels are the work of a serious moralist with a taste for the absurd and an audacious wit. These traits are more ebulliently manifested in his short works.

Many humorists darken in their later years as they contemplate more seriously matters that seemed merely absurd to them in their youth. In Collier's case the serious works came first and it was not until the period from 1937 through 1939 that he wrote most of the stories for which he is remembered as a humorist. Of all of his works these came most easily. They were written offhandedly, quickly, and to pay bills. He said that the major problem was framing the first sentence, and that when he had done that the story more or less wrote itself. "The Devil, George and Rosie" opens: "There was a young man who was invariably spurned by the girls, not because he smelt at all bad, but because he happened to be as ugly as a monkey." In the story, George finds an opportunity to achieve revenge on the female gender when he is appointed chief persecutor of women in hell. Rosie is in hell by accident, but agrees to stay so as not to create a fuss, and George falls in love with her. Fleeing to earth with George on Charon's boat, a sort of cruise ship, Rosie is tempted by passing images of film stars and high fashions to look back at hell, but she perseveres more successfully than Lot's wife or Eurydice and the very next day she and George go shopping for furniture on Oxford Street.

Collier pitches headlong into his tales, and like this one, they frequently involve the romantic misadventures of somewhat limited young men, supernatural elements, grisly episodes, social satire, and parody of myth, fairy tale, or serious literature. Their chief appeal is their style. His stories are usually very short, averaging about 3,000 words. The short-short form demands ingenious economy, lightness of touch, and carefully contrived but nonetheless surprise endings. If first lines were Collier's major challenge, it is last lines that remain in the reader's memory. In "The Chaser," his shortest and probably most familiar tale, Alan, a young man, buys a love potion guaranteed to produce absolute lifelong adoration. He is surprised to find that the price is much less than that of an untraceable poison, but the old herbalist from whom he buys the potion assures him that his beloved will dote on him ceaselessly and unrelentingly. At the end of the story, the young man is exultant, and the old man explains that he does not mind doing business for a pittance. His customers return later when they are wealthier for more expensive items: "Thank you again," says Alan. "Goodbye." "Au revoir," says the old man.

The narrator of "Are You Too Late Or Was I Too Early" is a dreamy recluse who one day finds the footprint of a woman on his shower mat. More and more he becomes aware of her presence in his apartment—her breath on the mirror, flowers parting their petals for her unseen face, her breathing in his bed. He senses her presence with increasing vividness until finally, by an intense effort of will, he is able to hear her voice: "I heard in a full opening of the sense, the delicate intake of her breath, the very sound of the parting of her lips. Each syllable was clear as a bell." The last words in the story are hers: "Oh, it's perfect. It's so quiet for Harry's work. Guess how we were lucky enough to get it! The previous tenant was found dead in his chair, and they actually say it's haunted."

In "Bottle Party" a young man decants a genie who brings him a bottle containing the most beautiful girl in the world. Pleased with her, but suspecting that she has a secret lover concealed in her bottle, he has his genie put him in the bottle, only to find himself corked in and watching the genie and the girl cavorting outside. The bottle is returned to the bottle shop and resold as still containing the most beautiful girl in the world to sailors. The conclusion here is that when the sailors opened the bottle at sea "their disappointment knew no bounds, and they used him with the utmost barbarity."

Collier's verbal mastery puts his surprise-ending stories in a different category from O'Henry's. The macabre and fantastic plots, contrasting with the refined and elegant style, are characteristic of an approach which one critic has called a strictly British genre of humor. Lord Dunsany and H.H. Munro (Saki) were earlier practitioners, Roald Dahl a later. Collier cited Lawrence Sterne, Tobias Smollett, and Henry Fielding as his influences, insisted that he had not read Saki until 1939, and that "Thus I Refute Beelzy" (1939) was a direct extrapolation on Saki's "Sredni Vashtar" (1911), his only story influenced by his predecessor. (Similarly, Roger Zelazny's story "A Museum Piece" [1962] is a sort of *hommage* to Collier, going his "Night, Youth, Paris and the Moon" one better.) This genre of short stories has attracted the peripheral attention of critics, usually those interested in horror and the supernatural.

Summary

John Collier achieved mastery of the demanding and entertaining short grotesque tale in a period in which world problems shifted serious literary attention to more momentous works. Elusive and peripatetic, Collier did not court fame, but his work has survived through its own merits, its deft plotting, its economical characterization, its satire, and its style. Though he worked in other media and genres, his short stories are what survive, not only frequently anthologized, but also adapted for films, television, and the musical theater.

Selected Bibliography
Primary Sources

Short Stories
Fancies and Goodnights. Garden City: Doubleday, 1951.
The Devil and All. London: Nonesuch Press, 1954.
The Best of John Collier. New York: Pocket Books, 1975.

Novels
His Monkey Wife or, Married to a Chimp.

London: Peter Davies, 1930.
Tom's A-Cold. London: Macmillan, 1933.
Defy the Foul Fiend, or The Misadventures of a Heart. London: Macmillan, 1934.

Screenplays
Sylvia Scarlett, 1936.
Elephant Boy, 1937.
Her Cardboard Lover, 1942.
Deception, 1946.
Story of Three Loves, 1953.
Equilibrium, 1953.
I Am a Camera, 1955.
The War Lord, 1955.

Miscellaneous Works
Gemini. London: Ulysses Press, 1932.
Milton's Paradise Lost: Screenplay for Cinema of the Mind. New York: Knopf, 1973.

Secondary Sources
Gawsworth, John. *Ten Contemporaries: Notes toward Their Definitive Bibliography.* Second series. London: Joiner and Steele, 1933, pp. 109–17. Contains Collier's personal essay on his withdrawal to country life, "Please Excuse Me, Comrade."
McCarty, John, and Brian Kelleher. *Alfred Hitchcock Presents.* New York: St. Martin's Press, 1985. Includes synopses of shows adapted from stories written by Collier.
Milne, Tom. "The Elusive John Collier." *Sight and Sound*, 45 (Spring 1976): 104–08. Discussion of Collier's screenwriting career and interview material.
Richardson, Betty. *John Collier.* Boston: Twayne, 1983. Biography and critical analysis—the sole and definitive book on Collier, this volume includes material from two long interviews.
Updike, John. "Milton Adapts Genesis, Collier Adapts Milton." *The New Yorker*, 49 (August 20, 1973): 84–85, 89. Collier held this review as responsible for the failure of his version of *Paradise Lost*.

William Donnelly

Congreve, William
Born: Bardsey, England, January 24, 1670
Education: Kilkenny College, 1681–1686; Trinity College, Dublin, 1686–1688; Middle Temple, London, 1691–1695

Marriage: Never married; one known child
Died: London, January 19, 1729

Biography

The son of William and Mary Browning Congreve, the future dramatist, William, was born at Bardsey, Yorkshire, on January 24, 1670. Four years later, when William Congreve, Sr., received a lieutenant's commission to serve in Ireland, the family moved to Youghal, where the younger William began his formal education. In 1678, the family relocated again, to Carrickfergus, and in 1681 the elder Congreve joined the Duke of Ormond's regiment in Kilkenny.

All who served the duke could send their children to Kilkenny College free of charge, and young William entered the college in 1681. It was at Kilkenny that he met his lifelong friend Joseph Keally, and Jonathan Swift was enrolled at the school at the same time. In 1686, Congreve matriculated at Trinity College, Dublin, but his academic career was interrupted by the political upheavals preceding the Glorious Revolution. In 1688, the school closed and the youth's father lost his commission. The family returned to England, where on March 17, 1691 the young man enrolled in London's Middle Temple to study law. However, like Richard Steele's literary Templar in *The Spectator*, like the playwrights Sir George Etherege, William Wycherley, Thomas Shadwell, and Thomas Southerne, Congreve found the Theatre Royal in nearby Drury Lane more congenial than the Inns of Court. As Giles Jacob wrote, "Mr. Congreve was of too delicate a Taste, had Wit of too fine a turn to be long pleas'd with a crabbed unpalatable Study . . . This concurring with his natural Inclination to Poetry, diverted him from the Bar to the declining Stage."

John Dryden, quickly recognizing Congreve's talent and learning, invited him to assist in translating the works of Juvenal; Congreve supplied the English version of the eleventh satire for Dryden's 1693 edition. The former Poet Laureate was also impressed with the draft of a play that Congreve had brought with him to London. Together with Arthur Manwayring and Thomas Southerne, Dryden helped the young man revise *The Old Batchelor*, which opened at the Theatre Royal on March 9, 1693 and ran for a remarkable fourteen nights. Though his second play, *The Double Dealer* (premiered 1693) pleased the public less, *Love for Love* (1695) was so successful that the newly formed acting company at Lincoln's Inn Fields offered Congreve a share in the theater in return for a play a year, if health permitted. Troubled by gout and problems with vision throughout his life, Congreve could not prepare another piece until 1697, but *The Mourning Bride* proved immensely popular. Charles Gildon's 1699 edition of Gerard Langbaine's *The Lives and Characters of the English Dramatic Poets* included the comment, "This play had the greatest Success, not only of all Mr. Congreve's; but indeed of all the Plays that ever I can remember on the English Stage."

The Way of the World (1700), Congreve's last serious dramatic effort, did not fare well. Despite its brilliance, it was caviar to the general public and earned only a tepid response from audiences; the playwright thereafter went into semiretirement. In 1705, he received his first substantial government sinecure when he became one of the commissioners of wines. With the arrival of the Hanoverians in 1714, Congreve's Whiggish politics were rewarded: he received the post of Secretary to the Island of Jamaica, which brought him a salary of £700 a year. Congreve hired a deputy to do the work while he himself enjoyed most of the income in retirement among his friends.

A genial man, Congreve is described by Giles Jacob in the *Poetical Register* (1720) as abounding "with Humility and good Nature. He does not shew so much the Poet as the Gentleman: he is ambitious of few Praises, tho' he deserves numerous Encomiums; he is genteel and regular in his Oeconomy, unaffected in Behaviour, pleasing, and informing in his Conversation, and respectful to all." He retained the esteem of such diverse figures as Alexander Pope and Steele, Lady Mary Wortley Montagu and Henrietta, Duchess of Marlborough. He probably met Henrietta in 1703; twenty years later she gave birth to his daughter, Mary, who would inherit his £10,000 estate. On his tomb in Westminster Abbey, Henrietta had inscribed her memory of "the happiness and Honour she enjoyed in the Sincere Friendship of so worthy and Honest a Man." Her mother, the acerbic Sarah, remarked of the inscription, "I know not what 'pleasure' she might have had in his company, but I am sure it was no 'honour.'" After his death Henrietta had a statue made of him; rumor claimed that she talked to it and fed it at table. If her love was extreme, it was not unique; Lord Cobham erected a monument to Congreve in his garden at Stowe, and Dryden, who called Congreve William Shakespeare's equal, named the young man his own successor. When Congreve left the stage in 1700, England lost a great playwright. When he died at his house in Surrey Street, London on January 19, 1729, all who knew him lost even more, a friend.

Literary Analysis

Although Congreve writes in the tradition of the Restoration dramatists who preceded him, his ideas of comedy go back to Aristotle. As he states in his *Amendments of Mr. Collier's False and Imperfect Citations* (1698), such plays depict the worst sort of people, not "in respect to their Quality, but in respect to their Manners." Comedy for Congreve must first of all delight, but it should also instruct. Thus, "as vicious People are made asham'd of their Follies or Faults, by seeing them expos'd in a ridiculous manner, so are good People at once both warn'd and diverted at their Expense." Three years earlier, the prologue to *Love for Love* expressed admiration for William Wycherley's *The Plain Dealer*, with its "manly rage." In a letter to William Walsh, Dryden claimed that *The Double Dealer* failed to please because "the Women think he has exposed their Bitchery too much; and the Gentlemen, are offended with him; for the discovery of their Follyes: and the way of their Intrigues, under the notion of Friendship to their Ladyes Husbands." Similarly, in 1708, John Downes attributed *The Way of the World*'s cool reception to its being "too Keen a Satyr."

Among Congreve's earliest publications is his translation of Juvenal's eleventh satire, and satire constitutes an important facet of his humor. Yet, his primary quality is wit, exemplified in the brilliant repartee of even his first comedy and in *The Way of the World* attaining a standard unequaled until *The Importance of Being Earnest*. Congreve's language and action delight in paradox that provokes laughter and thought, that points a moral even as it adorns a tale.

The primary object of Congreve's attacks is affectation. In his eleventh satire Juvenal comments on the foolish attempts of middle-class and even poor Romans to present feasts rivaling the banquets of the rich in luxury. The same theme informs Congreve's poem "Of Pleasing; an Epistle to Sir Richard Temple":

All Rules of Pleasing in this one unite,
Affect not any thing in Nature's Spight
. . .

None are, for being what they are, in
Fault,
But for not being what they wou'd be
thought.

In a letter to John Dennis (July 10, 1695), Congreve objects to ridiculing defects over which one has no control such as blindness or old age. Only when a lame person, for instance, pretends to be a dancing master does he become a fit object for comedy.

The Old Batchelor abounds with impostors, beginning with the title character, Heartwell. "I am for having everybody be what they pretend to be," he says (1.1), but as the *dramatis personae* states, he pretends "to slight Women" while being "secretly in love with Silvia." His feigned misogyny is one source of absurdity; another is his pursuit of a woman much his junior. So besotted is he that he easily falls prey to Silvia's cunning. Having slept with both Bellmour and Vainlove and been rejected by both, she seeks a husband to provide for her. By assuming the guise of innocence she seduces Heartwell into proposing marriage. Masquerading as the dissenting minister Tribulation Spintext, Bellmour performs the ceremony; then, together with Sharper, Vainlove, and Belinda, he reveals Silvia's past. Heartwell suffers so much from their taunts that his tormentors begin to pity him and explain that he is not married to the woman after all.

Though he suffers for his folly, Heartwell is more fortunate than the play's greatest fools, Sir Joseph Wittol and Captain Bluffe, whose names reveal their characters. Sir Joseph has such a high opinion of himself that he is gulled into thinking that Araminta, a fine lady, has fallen in love with him. Under this delusion he is married to Silvia, and thus each is punished with the other. Her maid, Lucy, who had been the mistress of Vainlove's servant, Setter, is married to Bluffe, a pretender to valor. She deserves no better because she tried to spoil the match between Vainlove and Araminta.

The Puritan banker Fondlewife earns cuckoldom for doing what Heartwell is saved from—marrying someone very much his junior. At the beginning of the fourth act he catechizes himself:

Tell me, Isaac, why art thee jealous? why art thee distrustful of the wife of thy bosom?—because she is young and vigorous, and I am old and impotent. Then, why didst thee marry, Isaac?—because she was beautiful and tempting, and because I was obstinate and doting, so that my inclination was, and is still, greater than my power . . . She's fonder of me than she has reason to be; and in the way of trade, we still suspect the smoothest dealers of the deepest designs—and that she has some designs deeper than thou canst reach, th' hast experienced, Isaac.

As the concluding double entendre reveals, Laetitia Fondlewife remains sexually unsatisfied. She has, therefore, arranged an assignation with Vainlove, who commissions Bellmour as his surrogate. Even though Fondlewife discovers Bellmour in his wife's bed, the old man allows himself to be deceived into believing that she is innocent. As he says, "I won't believe my own eyes . . . As long as I believe it, 'tis well enough" (4.6).

Even Vainlove endures some unquiet moments when Lucy sends him a letter, supposedly written by Araminta, expressing love for him. Vainlove adores only those who are coy; when he reads the letter, which he believes is authentic, he declares Araminta lost and behaves rudely to her even though he really loves her. Happily, he learns of the deceit and can at least partially regain her affection, though at the end of the play she refuses to marry him immediately.

In contrast to these affected characters is Bellmour, the traditional Restoration hero. "A cormorant in love," as he describes himself (1.1), his promiscuity is acceptable because it is natural for the young, at least the young men. His pursuit of pleasure does not, however, leave him indifferent to others. When Fondlewife discovers him with Laetitia, Bellmour defends her honor and so prevents a divorce. He again displays generosity when he saves Heartwell from marrying Silvia, and he provides appropriate husbands for Silvia and her maid. More intelligent than the pretenders, he proves his wit in both speech and action, controlling conversations and events.

In many ways *The Old Batchelor* offered nothing new. Congreve claimed to have written the piece in 1689, before he was familiar with the London stage. Smock Alley Theatre, Dublin, was, however, active while Congreve was at Trinity College, and his frequent absences from school on Saturday afternoons suggest that he was attending the company's productions. *The Old Batchelor* satirizes the standard butts of Restoration ridicule—dissenters, "cits," country bumpkins, old men—and rewards the witty couple with marriage at the end of the fifth act. Also indicative of the author's lack of experience in writing plays is the absence of a plot. The cuckolding of Fondlewife, the gulling of Sir Joseph and Bluffe, and Heartwell's supposed marriage have nothing to do with each other, nor do they relate to the marriage of Bellmour and Belinda, which could just as easily occur in the first scene of the play as the last.

While obviously an apprentice piece, the play shows promise. The opening dialogue between Bellmour and Vainlove exemplifies the brilliant language that pervades Congreve's comedies. Thus Bellmour greets his friend, "I thought a contemplative lover could no more have parted with his bed in a morning, than he could have slept in't" (1.1). The witty paradoxes continue: "Come, come, leave business to idlers, and wisdom to fools: they have need of 'em: wit, be my faculty, and pleasure my occupation; and let father Time shake his glass," Bellmour declares. The sentiments are those of dozens of Restoration comic heroes, but the speech is uniquely Congreve's. As the scene continues, Bellmour maintains that Silvia has remained true to Vainlove even though Bellmour has slept with her, for she imagined that she was with Vainlove. Vainlove is not convinced, but his friend persists: "Why, faith, I think it will do well enough, if the husband be out of the way, for the wife to show her fondness and impatience of his absence by choosing a lover as like him as she can; and what is unlike, she may help out with her own fancy." If anyone is abused here, it is the lover, not the husband, "for 'tis an argument of her great zeal toward him, that she will enjoy him in effigy."

As typical of Congreve as the clever speeches is the insight that the characters have into themselves. Pope wondered whether Congreve created any fools, not only because the playwright gives good lines to everyone but also because even a Sir Joseph has moments of enlightenment. When Sharper and Setter are gulling Sir Joseph and Bluffe into marriage, Sharper allows the pair to overhear his apparent distress at Araminta's falling in love with the knight: "Death, it can't be!—an oaf, an idiot, a wittol!" Sir Joseph remarks, "'Tis I, my own individual person." Sharper continues, "A wretch, that has flown for shelter to the lowest shrub of mankind, and seeks protection from a blasted coward." Sir Joseph then tells Bluffe, "That's you, bully back" (5.2). Heartwell and Fondlewife know that they are foolish in loving younger women, and Vainlove recognizes the folly of his beginning affairs for Bellmour to consummate.

Such self-knowledge makes these objects of satire sympathetic. When Belinda and Bellmour taunt Heartwell for marrying a whore, Vainlove urges them to stop, and even Belinda soon declares that she is beginning to feel sorry for him. Heartwell replies to his attackers in a powerful speech which concludes with his asking Belinda whether she mocks him because he refused to sleep with her. Belinda is offended, but Araminta tells her that she is justly served. There is a touching as well as a humorous element to Fondlewife's belief in his wife's innocence. Even Sir Joseph and Bluffe may fare better than they deserve in marrying Silvia and Lucy. Silvia tells her husband, "The worst of me is, that I am your wife" (5.5). John Gay described Congreve as an "unreproachful" friend; that generosity extends to Congreve's characters.

In the dedication to the printed version, Congreve gave to the actors much of the credit for the work's success; still, he gave them not only clever lines but also fine opportunities to show their skills. When Fondlewife and Laetitia are reconciled, she puts her arms around his neck—and so provides Bellmour with the chance to kiss her hand behind Fondlewife's back. Heartwell's inability to move from Silvia's doorway, Silvia's pretense of innocence, and Bluff's of bravery (as soon as danger vanishes) are entertaining spectacles.

Dryden called *The Old Batchelor* the best first play that he had ever seen. Commenting on Congreve's next play, *The Double Dealer*, the former Poet Laureate wrote:

> Thy first attempt an early promise made,
> That early promise this has more than
>   paid;
> Heaven that but once was prodigal be-
>   fore,
> To Shakespeare gave as much; she could
>   not give him more.

Though the praise of the comedy is excessive, *The Double Dealer* reflects greater artistic control than its predecessor. In his dedication Congreve observed, "I designed the moral first, and to that moral I invented the fable." The moral is, he continued, "To paint the vices and follies of humankind," and the work is indeed darker than *The Old Batchelor*. By confining the action to Lord Touchwood's house, Congreve effectively uses setting to mirror the closed social world that he portrays, and by limiting the play to the night before Mellefont's marriage to Cynthia the dramatist adds significance to the action. The tension remains artificial, though. Because Cynthia controls her own fortune, she and Mellefont could elope; only her insistence on his outwitting his opponents forces the couple to remain in the world of the play. While the plot has more coherence than that of the dramatist's first comedy, Brisk and the Froths are superfluous, however funny their behavior may be.

The play's title derives from the character of Maskwell, Lady Touchwood's servant and lover. Both want to prevent the marriage of Cynthia and Mellefont—Maskwell because he loves Cynthia, Lady Touchwood because she has loved Mellefont, her nephew, and now hates him for rejecting her. Lady Plyant, Cynthia's mother, also opposes the match because she wants Mellefont for herself. Mellefont's task is to secure the approval of his uncle and future in-laws. Careless, by making love to Lady Plyant, gains her consent to the match and thus her husband's as well, since she controls him. Maskwell supposedly is helping Mellefont with the Touchwoods, but actually he is double dealing. He almost succeeds in preventing the match. He fails only because he overreaches himself when he attempts to betray Lady Touchwood as well as Mellefont.

In *A Short View of the Profaneness and Immorality of the English Stage* (1698) Jeremy Collier notes that three of the four women in the play are unchaste, with Cynthia, as her name suggests, being the lone exception. Seeing no example of marital felicity, she asks Mellefont whether they should abandon their wedding plans. He replies that the game of marriage "depends entirely upon judgment" (2.1), but his view remains questionable. Even in the last scene he admits that he trusted and loved Maskwell, despite warnings from Careless. Lord Touchwood concludes the piece with a warning against secret villainy, and both

Maskwell and Lady Touchwood are to be punished. Yet, the liaisons between Brisk and Lady Froth and between Careless and Lady Plyant are likely to continue unexposed. This is not the triumph of wit and innocence but rather the self-destruction of an over-ambitious villain.

As in *The Old Batchelor*, the play contains much witty dialogue and several enjoyable scenes. In the second act Lady Froth wants her husband to show Cynthia how he bowed when he was rewarded with a picture of his future wife. Handing him a mirror, Lady Froth asks that he imagine it her picture. The stage direction reads, "He bows profoundly low, then kisses the glass" while he remarks, "I saw myself there, and kissed it for your sake" (2.1). He seems so fond of the image which he finds there that his wife begins to grow jealous.

Careless's offer to help Sir Paul beget a son, like Brisk's encounters with Lady Froth, is filled with sexual innuendo. When Lady Froth, a would-be poet, speaks of her work, her husband asks, "Have you nothing about you to show him, my dear?" She replies, "Yes, I believe I have.—Mr. Brisk, come . . . into the next room, and there I'll show you what I have" (2.1). Later Lord Froth finds the two embracing. She pretends that they are practicing a dance and invites her husband to join. "No, my dear, do it with him," Lord Froth says, and his wife readily consents: "I'll do it with him, my lord, when you are out of the way" (4.2). Mellefont's description of Lady Plyant's refusal to have sex with her husband—the only man whom she rejects—provides a comic set piece: "She has him swathed down, and so put to bed; and there he lies with a great beard, like a Russian bear upon a drift of snow" (3.2).

Commenting on a 1959 revival of the piece, the *Tatler* praised the "many brilliantly entertaining scenes" and the "dialogue which in its easy volubility and exquisite precision is unlike the dialogue of any other Restoration playwright." Nevertheless, the tone of the piece is dark. The targets of satire are no longer the marginal characters of *The Old Batchelor* but society itself; London's lords and knights appear as foolish as the Wittols and Fondlewifes. Dryden probably was correct to attribute the play's failure to the audiences' objection to the satire, for Congreve was hitting very close to home.

Love for Love marks a major advance over Congreve's first two plays. Though the prologue notes that the piece offers variety, it correctly states, "And for the thinking party there's a plot" which deals with Valentine's efforts to win the rich Angelica. The two lovers could marry immediately, but Angelica must be certain that Valentine wants her, not her fortune. She knows that she lives in a world of tickling commodity where exchanges are based on self-interest. Valentine's father, Sir Sampson Legend, will pay his son's debts, but only if Valentine will in return renounce his right as first born to the Legend estate. In return for protecting Tattle's relationship with Mrs. Frail, Scandal insists that his supposed friend reveal the names of other mistresses. Mrs. Frail will not step into another room without some recompense, and she retains her interest in Ben Legend only as long as he is likely to inherit a fortune. Thinking that he could buy her love, Valentine has squandered his money in pursuing Angelica. Scandal, too, believes that money rules all, and he tells Valentine, "You have little reason to believe that a woman of this age, who has had an indifference for you in your prosperity, will fall in love with your ill-fortune" (1.2).

The two lovers prove themselves exceptions to the ways of this world, though, both in their generosity and their intelligence. To save himself from signing over his fortune to his father, Valentine feigns madness. He also hopes to trick Angelica into expressing sympathy for him and so expose her true feelings, but she is too clever to fall for the ruse. She has, moreover, devised an effective way to help Valentine. Pretending to love Sir Sampson, she secures from the old man the bond that he had made his son sign and in which Valentine promised to surrender his birthright in return for £4,000. Valentine believes that she really wants to marry the old man and proves his generosity by ending his charade of lunacy. He will give up his claims to the Legend estate so that she or her children can inherit it. Certain at last of Valentine's integrity, Angelica tears up the bond, declaring, "I'll use it, as I would everything that is an enemy to Valentine" (5.2). In this selfish world the true wits have made the proper exchange, love for love, thus earning the happiness—and incidentally the fortune—that they deserve.

In this and the following two plays Congreve reenacts the Glorious Revolution, depicting the triumph of Lockean reason over Hobbesian appetite and oppression. In his *Two Treatises on Government* (1689), John Locke describes tyranny as "the exercise of power beyond right, which nobody can have a right to;

and this is making use of the power any one has in his hands, not for the good of those who are under it, but for his own private, separate advantage." Sir Sampson behaves like James II, maintaining his absolute power. He says to his son, "Are you not my slave? Did I not beget you?" (2.1). He would strip Valentine naked and send him into the world unhoused, unprovisioned; he would even take away from him the woman whom he loves. This cruelty to his son and pretension to Angelica prove Sir Sampson's undoing. As Scandal tells Angelica in the penultimate speech of the play, "Well, madam, you have done exemplary justice, in punishing an inhuman father, and rewarding a faithful lover" (5.2).

Although the theme of the play is serious, the tone is lighter than that of *The Double Dealer*. Sir Sampson's evil intentions are opposed by two intelligent characters, and the old man lacks the cunning of Maskwell. The sharpest satire is confined to the fourth act, when Valentine pretends to think himself Truth. His comments here are harsh indeed. He asks a lawyer, "Does thou know me?" When the lawyer says yes, Valentine retorts, "Thou liest, for I am Truth. 'Tis hard I cannot get a livelihood amongst you" (4.2). Thinking that Valentine can foretell the future, Foresight asks what will happen at court. Valentine responds, "I am Truth, I never come there" (4.3). Because Valentine supposedly is mad, though, such speeches have less sting than if they were pronounced by a sane character.

Again unlike *The Double Dealer*, where the good Lord Touchwood appears as gullible as Lord Froth, only pretenders are punished. The ironically named Foresight, an astrologer, cannot tell who is in conjunction with his wife. He is foolish not only because he believes in fortune-telling but also because he has married a "young and sanguine" woman despite his gray hairs. Tattle, who would like to be thought a fashionable rake, and Mrs. Frail, a promiscuous woman who wants to marry Valentine, are wed to each other.

Even further removed from the social norms are Prue, a country girl, and Ben, a sailor. Tattle's initiating Prue into the art of love is doubly funny, first because he points out how lovers dissemble, and second because Prue is so adept a pupil. Tattle asks whether she will kiss him. Having mastered his instructions she says, "No, indeed; I'm angry at you." At the same time she runs and kisses him. He tells her that she has done "pretty well" but should have let him kiss her; she eagerly replies, "Well, we'll do't again." By the end of the scene she announces that she will hide from him behind her bed curtains, and he shall have to push her down to get into her room (2.2).

Ben, whom Angelica calls "an absolute sea-wit" (3.3), speaks a nautical jargon that has its own humor, but he is more honest than most of those who are better socialized. He recognizes that Prue and Mrs. Frail are flawed, and when Tattle and Mrs. Frail marry by mistake he observes rightly, "Why, there's another match now, as tho'f a couple of privateers were looking for a prize, and should fall foul of one another" (5.2). He is not mercenary and will happily return to sea, which is his element, as Prue would marry honest Robin the butler, who truly loves her. Whereas the typical Restoration comedy would satirize such misfits as Prue and Ben—Congreve himself did so in *The Old Batchelor*—they fare better here than do the pretenders. Their lack of social grace raises a laugh, but they are spared the worst consequences of their naivete.

Using Collier's arithmetic, two of the three principal women are unfaithful in *Love for Love*, and the London social realm is flawed. Nevertheless, Valentine and Angelica demonstrate that with the intelligence and generosity of true wit one can master that world, as Mellefont and Cynthia seem unable to do, without succumbing to its follies, as Belinda and Bellmour may. Congreve's art would continue to mature, but the author of *Love for Love* was already closer to *The Way of the World* than to *The Old Batchelor*.

In every way Congreve's masterpiece, *The Way of the World* is the most unified of his works. Though the plot is complicated and relies on flashbacks to enlighten the audience, it is a single plot. As in *Love for Love*, the truewits seek to marry, but for the first time in Congreve a serious obstacle must be overcome. Millamant will forfeit half of her fortune if she marries Mirabell without the consent of her aunt, Lady Wishfort. Formerly in love with Mirabell herself, Lady Wishfort opposes the match, especially after she learns that he was courting her to gain access to her niece. To win Lady Wishfort's blessing, Mirabell has devised another plan that plays on the old lady's desire for an "iteration of nuptials" (4.2). Disguising his servant, Waitwell, as the rich Sir Rowland, Mirabell seeks to secure a marriage contract between the two. Mirabell will then release Lady Wishfort from the agreement if she will permit Millamant to marry.

Complicating this scheme and eventually frustrating it is Marwood, who, like Lady Wishfort, once loved Mirabell but has become his enemy because of his indifference to her. She is carrying on an affair with Fainall, who is married to Lady Wishfort's daughter and Mirabell's ex-mistress. Fainall hopes to secure the forfeited half of Millamant's fortune and the widow's entire estate, threatening to divorce his wife for infidelity if Lady Wishfort does not comply with his demands. In the end, greed and selfishness succumb to generosity and trust, depicted here by an actual deed of trust that Mrs. Fainall gave to Mirabell before she married. Since her estate belongs to Mirabell, and since Fainall has no money of his own, Fainall cannot abandon his wife. Lady Wishfort is so pleased at this outcome that she gives her consent to the Mirabell-Millamant union.

Every character is drawn into this confrontation, which begins with the opening lines. Fainall has just beaten Mirabell at cards, and their dialogue continues the sparring. Fainall declines to play any more because Mirabell is indifferent to the game: "I'd no more play with a man that slighted his ill fortune than I'd make love to a woman who undervalued the loss of her reputation" (1.1). The observation is well phrased and clever; in his dedication Congreve remarked that some people had trouble distinguishing the truewits from the pretenders in the play, and one recalls Pope's questioning whether Congreve's fools were fools indeed. Fainall is witty and intelligent, but his comment demonstrates that he is also malicious. As the discussion turns to Marwood, Mirabell emerges as both the better man and keener wit. Fainall suspects that Marwood's hatred of Mirabell stems from the pangs of despised love. Mirabell denies the charge, and Fainall replies, "You are a gallant man, Mirabell; and though you may have cruelty enough not to satisfy a lady's longing, you have too much generosity not to be tender of her honour. Yet you speak with an indifference which seems to be affected, and confesses you are conscious of a negligence." Mirabell's retort shows that he is more intelligent than his antagonist: Fainall wants to learn the nature of Mirabell's relationship with Marwood, but Mirabell knows what Fainall and Marwood are doing. Moreover, Mirabell's generosity, even to a Marwood or Lady Wishfort, stands in sharp contrast to the selfish malice of Fainall: "You pursue the argument with a distrust that seems to be unaffected, and confesses you are conscious of a concern for which the lady is more indebted to you than is your wife" (1.1).

This opposition of Mirabell and Fainall extends to their treatment of the public and private spheres of life. As the play's title indicates, Congreve is anatomizing society, and he finds four ways of dealing with a flawed world. One possibility is retreat from London's pleasures and problems, an option that Lady Wishfort proposes to Marwood: "Let us leave the world, and retire by ourselves and be shepherdesses" (5.2). Fainall also suggests retirement to Marwood. This is the choice made by Sir Wilfull Witwoud, a country squire too innocent and ignorant of urban wiles to fit into sophisticated society. Like Ben in *Love for Love,* he is a comic figure; he mistakes Millamant's allusion to the poet Suckling as a reference to a young pig, and he behaves inappropriately in the drawing room, but his simplicity is better than the false modishness of his half-brother, who thinks that it is unfashionable to acknowledge a relative.

Sir Wilfull's aunt, Lady Wishfort, though she may speak of abandoning society, has no life outside the public sphere. She remarks to Foible, "I look like an old peeled wall" (3.1), indicating that she is all facade. There is a humorous double significance in this image in that she stands between Mirabell and Millamant, and that (proving that she is too old for the young man) her vanity causes her to cover her wrinkles by caking on makeup so thickly that it cracks and peels like old paint. Appropriately, Congreve introduces her at her toilet, reflecting her emphasis on appearances. Her chief concern about her upcoming meeting with Sir Rowland is how to receive him: "In what figure shall I give his heart the first impression" (4.1). She is so concerned with her image that she will not endure the publicity of a trial to prove her daughter's innocence of Fainall's charge of adultery; whatever the outcome, public discussion would be too embarrassing. She would rather sacrifice her fortune and her niece's.

Witwoud and Petulant, two of the false wits of the play, demonstrate a similar concern for appearances. The former memorizes clever sayings so that he will be deemed intelligent, and Petulant pays people to call on him so that he will be thought to be popular. He has gone so far as to leave a gathering, disguise himself, and return to "call for himself, wait for himself; nay, and what's more, not finding himself, sometimes [leave] a letter for himself" (1.2).

Congreve recognizes that servants, too, lack a private life. Waitwell and Foible may love each other, but they marry for Mirabell's convenience, not their own recreation. Mirabell sends a footman to tell them that they must "adjourn the consummation till further orders" (1.1); even this most private of actions is subject to others' wills. Waitwell's very identity is subject to his master's whim; he becomes Sir Rowland when Mirabell wants him to.

Fainall and Marwood have private lives, though they abuse these personal relationships. Fainall has married to get his wife's money, and at the end of the play he tries to kill her for thwarting his plot. Mirabell rightly characterizes him as "an interested and professing friend, a false and designing lover" (2.2). Marwood professes friendship to Lady Wishfort, but she uses the older woman to revenge herself on Mirabell and to extort money. Even the Fainall-Marwood relationship is flawed. She claims that he has injured her "fame and fortune"; he accuses her of infidelity (2.1).

As in *Love for Love*, Congreve demonstrates that a Lockean compact can defeat Hobbesean malice. Fainall's limitless greed is overcome by his wife's deed of trust, and Mirabell and Millamant make a compact that will allow private integrity without renunciation of public amenities. In the deservedly famous proviso scene of the fourth act Mirabell accedes to Millamant's request for dominion over her sphere: "To have my closet inviolate; to be sole empress of my tea-table," to visit whom she pleases, to dine when she wants, and to wear what she pleases. She in turn agrees neither to be ruled by foolish fashion nor to attempt to usurp his province. As true wits, they can function in society without losing their independence. They know, however, that they need money to have both worlds. Mirabell is not mercenary in seeking all of Millamant's fortune. He does not want to be outwitted by Fainall or Lady Wishfort, who do not deserve the £6,000, but he also knows that with only half of his wife's fortune the couple cannot live well in London.

The proviso scene also introduces the theme of time. Millamant is upset when Mirabell speaks of her having children, but Congreve recognizes that the coquette will be-come a mother. She will never, one hopes, be-come a Lady Wishfort, although someday she, too, may have to paint her face to look as good as her portrait. The past in this play affects the present; Mirabell's affair has driven his former mistress into an unhappy marriage—it also provides the means to guarantee Mirabell a happy one. *The Way of the World* is not an artificial comedy but a vision of reality. Even its conclusion defies convention. The true wits are united, the false wits exposed, the villains driven from the stage, yet Mrs. Fainall is still married to a man who has just tried to run her through with a sword. Mirabell's sententious conclusion about marriage frauds offers an ambiguous moral—each Fainall deceived the other—to a play that has its shadows as well as its sunshine.

Summary
William Congreve was not only a master writer of comedies. His poetry is at least competent, often rising above that level. His tragedy, *The Mourning Bride*, contains much fine writing and at least two memorable passages: "Music has charms to soothe a savage breast" (1.1) and "Heaven has no rage, like love to hatred turned, / Nor hell a fury, like a woman scorned" (3.2). *Semele*, written in 1707 and later orchestrated by George Frideric Handel, is the first English libretto.

Congreve's great gift to English letters, however, was the four comedies that he produced before the age of thirty. He had said that comedies should delight and instruct, and his do both. His direct reply to Collier's charges of immorality makes some telling points, but his best answer lies in the plays themselves, which offer an ideal of generosity, intelligence, urbanity. In these works one can trace many debts to other seventeenth-century dramas, but Dryden was right to say that they surpass their predecessors in brilliance of dialogue, keenness of observation, and capaciousness of spirit. Congreve was the best, as he was the last, of the Restoration dramatists, and the successful revivals of *Love for Love* and *The Way of the World* demonstrate that he was, like Shakespeare, not for an age but for all time.

Selected Bibliography
Primary Sources

Drama
The Old Batchelor. London: Peter Buck, 1693.

The Double Dealer. London: Jacob Tonson, 1694.

Love for Love. London: Jacob Tonson, 1695.

The Mourning Bride. London: Jacob Tonson, 1697.

The Way of the World. London: Jacob Tonson, 1700.

The Judgement of Paris: A Masque. London: Jacob Tonson, 1701.

Poetry

The Mourning Muse of Alexis. A Pastoral Lamenting the Death of Queen Mary. London: Jacob Tonson, 1695.

A Pindarique Ode, Humbly Offer'd to the King on His Taking Namure. London: Jacob Tonson, 1695.

The Birth of the Muse: A Poem. London: Jacob Tonson, 1698.

A Hymn to Harmony, Written in Honour of St. Cecilia's Day. London: Jacob Tonson, 1703.

A Pindarique Ode, Humbly Offer'd to the Queen. London: Jacob Tonson, 1706.

Poems upon Several Occasions. London: Jacob Tonson, 1710.

Fiction

Incognita: or, Love and Duty Reconcil'd. A Novel. London: Peter Buck, 1692.

An Impossible Thing. A Tale. London: J. Roberts, 1720.

Non-Fiction

Amendments of Mr. Collier's False and Imperfect Citations . . . London: Jacob Tonson, 1698.

Secondary Sources

Bibliographies

Bartlett, Laurence. *William Congreve: A Reference Guide.* Boston: G.K. Hall, 1979. A chronological listing of criticism from 1729 through 1977. Annotated. Indexed to allow users to locate specific items or commentary on specific works.

Biographies

Hodges, John C. *William Congreve the Man: A Biography from New Sources.* New York: Modern Language Association of America, 1941. The standard biography.

Lynch, Kathleen M. *A Congreve Gallery.* Cambridge, MA: Harvard University Press, 1951. Lynch discusses Congreve's early friendships and his relationship with Henrietta, Duchess of Marlborough.

Books

Fujimure, Thomas H. *The Restoration Comedy of Wit.* Princeton: Princeton University Press, 1952. An important study of the subject in general, with a good discussion of Congreve's work as the "culmination of the comedy of wit."

Loftis, John. *Comedy and Society from Congreve to Fielding.* Stanford: Stanford University Press, 1958. Loftis relates the plays to the society reflected in them.

Love, Harold. *Congreve.* Totowa, NJ: Rowman and Littlefield, 1974. Discussion of each of the comedies in a separate chapter. Love argues that for Congreve wit "is not simply a verbal skill but a mode of personal interaction" and that his characters mirror real life.

Markley, Robert. *Two-edg'd Weapons: style and ideology in the comedies of Etherege, Wycherley and Congreve.* Oxford: Clarendon, 1988.

Morris, Brian, ed. *William Congreve.* London: Ernest Benn, 1972. A collection of nine fine essays on the plays; includes two pieces on staging of the works.

Novak, Maximillian E. *William Congreve.* New York: Twayne, 1971. A critical survey of Congreve's oeuvre, with individual chapters on each of the plays. Includes a helpful annotated bibliography of twentieth-century criticism.

Van Voris, William H. *The Cultivated Stance: The Design of Congreve's Plays.* Chester Springs, PA: Dufour Editions, 1967. Van Voris concentrates on Congreve's treatment of time but also examines his Lockean outlook.

Williams, Aubrey. *An Approach to Congreve.* New Haven, CT: Yale University Press, 1979. Williams sees Congreve's plays as providential rather than secular.

Articles

Kronenberger, Louis. "Congreve." In his *The Thread of Laughter: Chapters on English Stage Comedy from Jonson to Maugham.* New York: Hill and Wang, 1952, pp. 117–45. Congreve is seen as presenting "the civilized point of view."

C

Leech, Clifford. "Congreve and the Century's End." *Philological Quarterly*, 41 (1962): 275–93. Congreve's plays are indebted to their predecessors but also anticipate the sentimentality and morality of the next age.

Muir, Kenneth. "The Comedies of William Congreve." In *Restoration Theatre*. Ed. John Russell Brown and Bernard Harris. London: Edward Arnold, 1965, pp. 220–37. Stratford-upon-Avon Studies, no. 6. A defense of Congreve that ranks him as the greatest writer of comedies between Shakespeare and Shaw.

Novak, Maximillian E. "Love, Scandal, and the Moral Milieu of Congreve's Comedies." In *Congreve Considered*. Los Angeles: William Andrews Clark Library, 1971, pp. 23–50. "If Congreve's comedies can be reduced to anything as blatant as a message, it is that in a world of general levity, corruption, and public scandal, private love between men and women of genuine wit is the only hope for happiness on earth."

Wertheim, Albert. "Romance and Finance: The Comedies of William Congreve." In *Comedy from Shakespeare to Sheridan: Change and Continuity in the English and European Dramatic Tradition*. Ed. A.R. Braunmuller. Newark, DE: University of Delaware Press, 1986, pp. 255–73. Examines Congreve's treatment of love and marriage in relation to money.

Joseph Rosenblum

Coren, Alan

Born: London, June 27, 1938

Education: Wadham College, Oxford University, B.A., 1960; M.A. 1970. Also attended University of Minnesota, Yale University, and the University of California

Marriage: Anne Kasriel, October 14, 1963; two children

Biography

Born in London on June 27, 1938, to Samuel and Martha Coren, members of the middle or lower-middle class, and given a good secondary education, Alan Coren sometimes seems to exaggerate his humble origins: he describes his younger self as "a natural oik, given to finking deep foughts abaht making sunnink of meself and only using an aitch when I used the word haitch" and claims to have been to "a state school hung with the secondhand trappings of a private school where kids from working-class homes had grafted onto them the paraphernalia and mores" of the upper classes (*Sanity Inspector*, 12–14).

At any rate he went on to Oxford and received a B.A., with first-class honors, from Wadham College in 1960. Afterward he spent some time in the B.Litt. program at Oxford, then, making use of a Harkness Commonwealth Fellowship for study in the United States, he visited the University of Minnesota, Yale University, and the University of California at Berkeley. At the time his "plan was to get an American Ph.D. and then get an academic job" ("Humor's Death," 35). His educational background may help to explain both the frequent erudition of his humor and his comfort with American literature and culture coupled with a "desire throughout my working life to be able to commend myself to both cultures" (James, 149).

Since 1963, Coren has been a full-time—in fact, very busy and active—writer. In that year he became assistant editor of *Punch*, the venerable humor magazine; he was afterwards the literary editor (1967–1969), the deputy editor (1969–1973), and the editor from 1978–1987. During most of that time, he wrote weekly columns for *Punch* which were published as the anthologies that make up most of his books of humor for adults, and his position there also accounts for his editorship of miscellaneous collections such as *The Punch Book of Kids*.

In 1963, Coren also became a scriptwriter for the BBC television show, *That Was the Week That Was*, a trend-setting satirical revue. He has also written for *Not So Much a Programme* (1965–1966), *At the Eleventh Hour* (1967), *The Punch Review* (1976–1977), all on BBC-TV, as well as television plays and situation comedies, television documentaries, and radio plays. In addition, he has written extensively for newspapers, serving as the television critic for *The Times* and then *The Mail on Sunday*, and maintaining a column, at one time or another, in the *Daily Mail*, the *Evening Standard*, and most recently *The Times*, where he became a regular "diarist" in 1988. In 1988, he also became editor of *The Listener*, a weekly miscellaneous magazine published by the BBC; he was sacked from that position for exercising editorial independence in 1989.

Coren has found time to write ten children's books and at least one novel, too, though the novel apparently has not been published. From 1973 to 1976 he was the Rector of St. Andrews University in Scotland.

A born Londoner, Coren continues to live there, in a less than fashionable part of north London. His columns give an undoubtedly exaggerated but detailed account of his tribulations as homeowner, taxpayer, and gardener. He writes in a more disguised way of his family; his wife Anne, whom he married on October 14, 1963, is a doctor but appears in his humor as a somewhat stereotyped wife, and his two children are the occasion for some comedy about odd clothing and musical tastes, frightening taste in friends, safety pins through the cheeks, and so on.

Literary Analysis

Coren is a very versatile writer, turning his hand to fiction, children's stories, and scripts for television and radio; he is a successful editor, who in his nine years editing *Punch* increased its circulation, lowered the average age of its readers (it had grown stodgy), and increased its concentration on humor. His output falls into three classes of work: children's books, special books on a single topic or with a single purported author, and miscellaneous collections of comic columns.

In the first category are his ten children's books about a recurring character, Arthur. These have such titles as *Arthur the Kid* (1976), *Arthur's Last Stand* (1977), and *Arthur and the Bellybutton Diamond* (1979). These have proved quite popular, having been published in the United States as well as in Britain and in French and Spanish as well as in English.

The second category includes his two books about Idi Amin, *The Collected Bulletins of Idi Amin* (1974) and *The Further Bulletins of Idi Amin* (1975), and *The Peanut Papers* (1977), which is "about" the Jimmy Carter administration and pretends to be "by" Miz Lillian Carter. That these are even more timebound than his other books is obvious from their topics; satire of the Carter family, particularly their more trivial follies, dated very rapidly.

All three of these books are somewhat unsatisfactory. For one thing, they rely for their effect on what is supposed to be Coren's talent for mimicry. In *The Peanut Papers* he writes in what he thinks is the style of an old Southern woman, incorporating many of the features of spoken southern English into her written account. Too often this is either inaccurate, betraying a bad ear for Southern dialect, or simply an illustration of the stereotype that an old Southern woman must write ignorantly. The stereotyping carries over into the content where he assumes attitudes on behalf of both Miz Lillian and her son the President that are very different from those which they actually held. To enjoy the humor of this book very much would probably require reading it as if it were about entirely fictional people rather than real human beings unfairly mocked for attitudes and educational deficiencies that were never theirs.

It is difficult to feel any sympathy for Idi Amin, however, or to wish that Coren had been more "fair" to him in his two collections of bulletins supposedly from the African dictator. The problem with these two volumes is that the things of which Amin actually was guilty are too horrible for laughter. So, Coren falls back on stereotypical "African" behavior and language, including a dialect that seems based more on nineteenth-century minstrel shows than on any real Africa. This form of humor was slightly shocking in the 1970s, and it soon gets old in any case.

Coren's major accomplishment as a writer is the series of books that reprint short humorous pieces which first appeared in magazines—usually, though not always, in *Punch*. His first such book, *The Dog It Was That Died*, appeared in 1965. In it the pieces, which are reprinted from *The Atlantic Monthly* and *The Listener* as well as from *Punch*, are divided into sections called "Us," "Them," and "Me." In the "Us" section, he writes about Britain, while the "Them" pieces are about America and Americans. Coren had spent a good deal of time in the United States in the early 1960s, and he has explained that "educated in both countries, and loving both countries equally, I have always wanted to have a part in what one might call the CisAtlantic tradition" (James, 149). The third section, the pieces collected under "Me," shows a strong tinge of S.J. Perelman, featuring a persona in which physical haplessness, frustrated elegance, and linguistic playfulness coincide.

His next collection, *All Except the Bastard*, published in 1969, is like *The Dog It Was That Died* in being divided into thematically arranged sections and having an explicit geographical focus. There is a series of articles on parts of England; a section called "American Dreams" is mostly about the war in Vietnam;

"Behind the Curtains" is about Communist countries; "The Chronicles of Magoon" is a collection of heavy-handed satires, not without easy racist jokes, about a newly independent African country. It is the same vein later mined in the Idi Amin books.

With *The Sanity Inspector* (1974) Coren's books start to take on what has become their characteristic shape and tone and strength. The book contains thirty-one pieces reprinted from *Punch* and a foreword explaining the title. Included are essays about urban and suburban life; pretended articles on literary subjects ("Once I Put It Down, I Could Not Pick It Up Again"); and others. "All You Need to Know About Europe," apparently meant to help Britons adjust to the Common Market, includes such facts as, "Like the Germans, the Dutch fall into two quite distinct physical types: the small, corpulent, red-faced Edams, and the thinner, paler, larger Goudas," and "The median Italian, according to the latest figures of the Coren Intelligence Unit, is a cowardly baritone who consumes 78.3 kilometres of carbohydrates a month and drives about in a car slightly smaller than he is, looking for a divorce" (*Sanity Inspector*, 73–75).

Like Robert Benchley and Perelman, from whom he learned much, Coren often takes off from something he has read in the papers. For instance, the news that Sotheby's plans to auction some of Lord Byron's hair leads him to "Ear, Believed Genuine Van Gogh, Hardly Used, What Offers?" A news report predicting that soon the salesgirls at Woolworth's will have degrees stimulates "Counterweight," in which Doreen and Vera, a philologist and a biologist, discuss Arnold Schönberg, the architecture of All Souls College, the Norwegian Eddas, and Spinoza: as Doreen says, "I've always liked Spinoza. You know where you are with the *Tractatus Theologico-Politicus*. He's never flash, is he? If there's one thing I can't stand, it's a flashy determinist" (155).

In two other essays in the collection Coren demonstrates his skill as a parodist and his recurring animosity to the more dogmatic ideas of the British Labor Party. "Suffer Little Children" contains samples of children's literature as they might have been written by Feodor Dostoyevsky, William Shakespeare, and Ernest Hemingway. In "The Worker's Bag is Deepest Red" he reacts to the Scottish Labor Party's plans to nationalize Highland estates and salmon fisheries with a fantasy of a man trying to get a fishing license, frustrated by two stupid bureaucrats who think that you hunt salmon with ferrets, use flies to catch grouse, and shoot trout—which must be retrieved by cats.

The pattern established in *The Sanity Inspector* is followed in *Golfing for Cats* (1975), *The Lady from Stalingrad Mansions* (1977), *The Rhinestone as Big as the Ritz* (1979), *Tissues for Men* (1981), *The Cricklewood Diet* (1982), *Bumf* (1984), *Something for the Weekend* (1986), *Bin Ends* (1987), and *The Best of Alan Coren* (1980), which is collected from all of these books through *Tissues for Men*.

Coren's practice in choosing titles is usually self-deprecating. Sometimes he pretends that only a deceptive title will sell the book, so he gives a misleading one drawn from a more popular kind of book entirely; *Golfing for Cats* is explained by the British public's fondness for books about golf and books about cats; a swastika is displayed on the cover because the public also likes books about the Third Reich. *The Cricklewood Diet* is so named for obvious reasons; with a number of other titles he goes beyond books entirely (as bookstores more and more make their money by selling non-book items): *Tissues for Men*, *Bumf* (a British term for toilet tissue), *Something for the Weekend* (a slang reference to condoms), and *Bin Ends* (wine).

A reading of these books confirms the high level of Coren's achievement and his versatility. He continues to create sharp parodies, both of individual writers—his "The Short Happy Life of Margaux Hemingway" is a fine parody of the actress's grandfather—and of genres of writing: detective fiction, political prose, diet books, gardeners' advice columns, even chess problems and crossword puzzle clues.

There is continued satire on the state of Britain. Here the targets are often the decline of education, both on the secondary level and at Oxbridge; the increasing inefficiency, bureaucratization, and acceptance of failure in English life; the silliness of television; the pretentiousness of the "chattering classes" of leftish intellectuals; and the vulgarity of popular tastes. Coren weighs in fairly often against American targets, including the stupidity of American presidents (he is particularly sharp against Gerald Ford and Ronald Reagan) and the smug ignorance of Americans as they appear to Europeans. One continuing series features a cast of regulars in a pub, whose conversation (on subjects like the royal family, science, and economic issues) combines ignorance, complacence, and intolerance in roughly equal portions. Their discussion of the possible second coming of Christ includes this exchange:

"I got an enamel tray from Viareggio one year," said the man in the herringbone overcoat, firmly, "with the last dinner on it."

"What did you have?" enquired the QPR supporter.

"Not my last dinner, you prat," said the man in the herringbone overcoat, "*The* Last Dinner. A picture of it. They are all tucking in, and He is in the middle, and they all have goblets. You cannot tell me it is water. First off, you cannot trust the water out there, second off, we have already debated about where He waves His wand and Lo! a couple of crates of red." (*Something for the Weekend*, 55)

Much of what he writes is not really satire, however, but more fantasy. A typical piece begins with something in the press. It may be a mistake. For instance, a classified advertisement in which an *Encyclopedia Britannica* is offered for sale, containing a misspelling of *Britannica*, sends him off on a tour-de-force about a self-miseducated man who complacently teaches his children comically wrong facts—"explaining one or two of the basics to Nigel, to wit, how Father Bee lies down beside Mother Bee and puts ovary in her stamen and so forth" (*The Cricklewood Diet*, 51–52). Or, it may be something like the reference in an American news story to "a 70-year-old James Bond," that leads to his story, "Doctor No will see You Now," which begins with Bond tensing in the darkness and reaching for his teeth (*Rhinestone*, 53). "A Little Learning," based on a news article revealing that "headmasters today are giving their bad teachers glowing references in order to get rid of them," causes Coren to ask where they are all ending up, and then imagine a school which employs all of them. He suggests that the result might be evident in the conversation in the Staff Room:

"Wasn't it T.S. Eliot," murmured a pale elderly man in a wine-spattered linen jacket, "who said *Neither a lender nor a borrower be?*"

"You tell us," snapped Mr. J.D. Hobley, who was in fact somewhat relieved to have the subject changed, since Dr. Edwin Stokes [the mathematics master] had now taken off his socks and was calculating furiously, "you're supposed to be Head of English."

"Our greatest novelist," said the Head of English, quietly, "after Shaw." (*The Lady from Stalingrad Mansions*, 98–99)

These pieces, several hundred of them collected in eleven books, are the heart of Coren's achievement as a humorist. The level of the humor is quite high, though this is partly a result of his extraordinary productivity over a long period of years. Since each book contains thirty or so pieces from a period of two or three years during which Coren filled his column at *Punch* every week, these are the best of his work. His best is very good.

Coren left *Punch* in 1987 and since then has had no regular outlet for the kind of short, humorous piece which has been his specialty. He appears frequently on radio and television, and his work as a diarist for *The Times* resulted in his book *Seems Like Old Times: A Year in the Life of Alan Coren* (1989), *More Like Old Times* (1990), and *A Year in Cricklewood* (1991). His contributions to this column have been not so much comical as whimsical: lighthearted explorations of events in his life (his car needs repairs; his garden is a problem) and things which have come to his attention in public life or through his reading. The diary form seems to have inhibited somewhat the writer's tendencies toward fantasy, coruscating satire, and the uses of more literary forms such as short plays, mock opera, parodic fictions, and so on; in general this book, though not without interest, does not match Coren's accomplishments as a humorist in his best works.

Summary

Despite Alan Coren's many accomplishments as an editor, versatile newspaper columnist, and author of children's books, his central achievement is as the author of short, humorous columns covering a very wide range of types, subjects, and generic variations. He is a conscious follower of American periodical humorists such as Benchley and Perelman (with whom he was close and to whom his *Tissues for Men* is dedicated). He is skilled at the personal essay that makes ordinary life and its problems the subject of comic treatment, the outward-looking or issue-oriented essay (sometimes very politically engaged as well as funny), and the humorous fantasy, including parodies of both popular and *recherche* kinds of writing. His books bear the tribute "the funniest writer in Britain today" from the *Sunday Times* and this valuation is very likely accurate.

Selected Bibliography
Primary Sources
The Dog It Was That Died. London: Hutchinson, 1965.

All Except the Bastard. London: Robson, 1969.

The Sanity Inspector. London: Robson, 1974; New York: St. Martin's Press, 1975.

The Collected Bulletins of Idi Amin. London: Robson, 1974.

Golfing for Cats. London: Robson, 1975; New York: St. Martin's Press, 1976.

The Further Bulletins of Idi Amin. London: Robson, 1975.

The Lady from Stalingrad Mansions. London: Robson, and New York: St. Martin's Press, 1977.

The Peanut Papers. London: Robson, 1977; New York: St. Martin's Press, 1978.

The Rhinestone as Big as the Ritz. London: Robson, and New York: St. Martin's Press, 1979.

Tissues for Men. London: Robson, 1981; New York: Parkwest, 1989.

The Best of Alan Coren. London: Robson, 1980; New York: St. Martin's Press, 1981.

The Cricklewood Diet. London: Robson, 1982.

Bumf. London: Robson, 1984.

Something for the Weekend. London: Robson, 1986.

Bin Ends. London: Robson, 1987.

Seems Like Old Times: A Year in the Life of Alan Coren. London: Robson, 1989.

More Like Old Times. London: Robson, 1990.

A Year in Cricklewood. London: Robson, 1991.

As editor
Present Laughter: A Personal Anthology of Modern Humour. London: Robson, 1982.

The Punch Book of Kids. London: Robson, 1983.

The Penguin Book of Modern Humour. Harmondsworth, Penguin, 1983. A new edition of *Present Laughter*.

Children's Books
Buffalo Arthur. London: Robson, and Boston: Little, Brown, 1978.

The Lone Arthur. London: Robson, and Boston: Little, Brown, 1978.

(There are eight additional Arthur books.)

Secondary Sources
Anonymous. Review of *The Lady from Stalingrad Mansions*. *The New Yorker*, 53 (December 19, 1977): 151–52. Brief review.

Dunlap, Benjamin. Review of *Golfing for Cats*. *The New Republic*, 175 (October 23, 1975): 24–26. Fullest and most penetrating review.

"Humor's Death and Other Exaggerations." *World Press Review*, 27 (November 1980): 35–37. Interview with Coren. His attitude toward his work, toward America, his friendship with S.J. Perelman, etc.

James, Clive. "Alan Coren." In *Contemporary Authors*. Ed. James A. Bowden. Detroit: Gale Research, 1978. Vol. 69–72, pp. 148–49. Biography, bibliography, some criticism.

Lasson, Robert. Review of *Golfing for Cats*. *New York Times Book Review* (March 21, 1976): 14–15. Brief review.

Merritt Moseley

Coward, Sir Noel Pierce
Born: Teddington on The Thames, Middlesex, December 16, 1899

Education: Chapel Road School, Clapham; Italia Conti Academy (acting school), Liverpool

Died: Jamaica, March 26, 1973

Biography
Noel Pierce Coward was born in Teddington on The Thames, in Middlesex, on December 16, 1899. His father was Arthur Sabine Coward (a clerk, aged thirty-four when this second son was born), and his mother, Violet Agnes Veitch (the daughter of a captain in the Royal Navy). Both sides of the family were musical: Grandfather Coward was a professor of music and all ten of

his children sang in the choir at St. Alban's except Jim, who played the organ. It was in the choir that Violet, who was also very interested in the theater, met Arthur. Their first child, named Russell Arthur Blackmore Coward (after his godfather R.D. Blackmore, author of *Lorna Doone*) died of meningitis at the age of six. Eighteen months later Noel was born, too close to Christmas, he always objected, to get a proper share of presents. He also grew up to dislike his middle name; his godmother was Jessie "Flower" Pierce, and she had not even given him a christening present.

As early as age seven, according to his earliest extant letter, Coward reports that he "had some little boys over . . . to tea and I dressed up in a short dress and danced to them and sung to them." In 1911, he went on the stage as one of Lila Field's "wonder children," and by age fourteen he had appeared professionally in *Peter Pan*. His desire to star may have gotten a boost from the birth of his brother Eric (who later spelled his name Erik) in 1905, which challenged five-year-old Noel's supremacy in the household. At the age of seven he saw that the stage was the way to prominence.

He learned a little about theatrics at Chapel Road School in Clapham and a bit more at Italia Conti Academy, a second-rate acting school in Liverpool, but Coward really learned to play comedy by appearing with Sir Charles Hawtrey and other dashing actors. Bit by bit he developed a style of his own, part of which depended on his meticulously clear delivery, said to have been adopted because his dear mother was rather hard of hearing. Like Colley Cibber (a famous comic actor and theater director of the late Restoration and eighteenth century), Coward decided early on that if he wanted leading parts that suited him perfectly he would have to write them himself. *I'll Leave It to You* was his first major success as a dramatist, but it was with *The Vortex* which premiered in London on his birthday in 1924 and played to full houses for a year that he proved the wisdom of that decision and, following up with great success in *Hay Fever* (which also starred the inimitable Marie Tempest), he established himself as a matinee idol and the principal comedy writer of the 1920s in Britain. In fact, by June 1925 these two plays together with *Fallen Angels* and his revue *On with the Dance* were all running in the West End simultaneously. In the 1930s, he launched his "big play on a big scale," *Cavalcade* (1931), and enjoyed a series of personal triumphs with his hit plays and musicals. He became an international superstar and a leading figure among the Beautiful People of both the theatrical and society worlds. He started the vogue of calling everyone "darling"—it helped when one could not remember all of the names of all of the people who flocked around in his professional and private life. He was himself regarded as a darling of the stage, the movies, cabaret—the all-around celebrity. He was a performer, a dramatist, a creator of immensely popular light music, a writer of film scripts and short stories and autobiographies and more. Devotees affectionately and respectfully called him "The Master." In 1970, he was given a rather belated knighthood (perhaps his flamboyant private life delayed this recognition, as it did in the case of several other theater personalities), and he received an honorary doctorate two years later from the University of Sussex. By then he had reveled in decades of fame, universal applause, the compliment of imitation insofar as was possible (though no one else seemed to be able to embody an era as well as Coward did, nor to wear the mantle of achievement with such flair).

There is a monument to him in Westminster Abbey: "A Talent to Amuse." Coward, however, is buried in Jamaica. He retired to Jamaica in his later life and died there on March 26, 1973.

The author's life and work were joyfully interconnected and his writing does seem to lack something when separated from his distinctive style of presentation. Still, many of his works in various *genres* are so attractive that successors manfully keep them alive. Some have attempted to equal his success in playwriting but generally they achieve at most his speed, not his brilliance. His "blithe spirit" as a suave actor is also much imitated, but not often well. "*Hay Fever*," he wrote, "is far and away one of the most difficult plays to perform that I have ever encountered."

There were many glamorous women in Coward's life and a few adoring ones, none of whom he married. Coward's longtime companion, Cole Lesley, tells the whole story in his *The Life of Noel Coward* (1976). "I have sometimes thought of marrying," Coward told Ward Morehouse in an interview in 1956, "but then I've thought again." Coward's many works in many fields are his children.

What Sir John Betjeman, then Poet Laureate, said at Coward's memorial service is true

C

about the relationship between Coward's personal style and the works that the public knew and loved:

> We can all see him in our mind's eye
> And in our mind's ear
> We can hear his clipped decided
>   voice!. . .

Literary Analysis

The most extraordinary thing about Coward's monumental success in popular entertainment may be the fact that St. John Irvine noted in *Essays by Divers Hands* that Coward, the sly sophisticate who was dismissed by the envious as "tenuous" or "trivial," was really "a Savonarola in evening dress." Beneath Coward's scintillating and disarmingly slick surface lies (as in the case of Oscar Wilde) the outsider's yearning for morality and the contrivances for battling a bitter disillusionment. Coward put on a brave and occasionally flippant front, but he faced facts. His credo was, "the fewer illusions that I have about me or the world around me, the better company I am for myself." He seldom lost his poise—or his poison. He prided himself on seeing things clearly, even unpleasant things, but the fact that he liked his *Bitter Sweet* best may indicate his tendency to sugar-coat now and then. He was aware even of that tendency. One of the reviews out of the mountain of reviews that he most wished "proudly to keep" was that in which Walter Bolitho (*New York World*) spoke of what Coward termed "semi-nostalgic sentiment": "You find it faintly when you look over old letters the rats have nibbled at, one evening you don't go out; there is a little of it, impure and odorous, in the very sound of barrel organs, in quiet squares in the evenings, puffing out in gusts that intoxicate your heart." Near the end of his life Coward sang at a private party that Patrick Garland noted in *Vogue* "with a sense of both regret and pain":

> Night after night
> Have to look bright
> Whether you're well or ill,
> People must laugh their fill . . .

Keep it crisp.

Coward knew that depressing thoughts or overt malice would spoil the fun. He never abandoned his faith in satire ("a sly dig at the right moment can work wonders") or his brave *hauteur* and cheering charm. Nevertheless, Desmond McCarthy, when he reviewed *Private Lives* at its opening in London in the Fall of 1930, saw something beneath the dazzling wit: "It is proof of Mr. Coward's adroitness that he has managed to conceal the grimness of his comedy, and to conceal from the audience that his conception of love is desolate and false."

Coward's comic vision derives from a hate-love relationship with the world as it is and a disappointment that that world is not as it should or could be. Longing for and missing full connection with that world, the writer is by turns flip, cruel, romantic, realistic, gay, and *gay*. He is attracted to the glitter of the trivial present, nostalgic for an imagined past, sometimes wry and sometimes riled about how foolish mortals are. He can rise into high comedy and descend into camp. He hates cynical and self-absorbed people and derides them; but, with his practiced contrarian aplomb, he admires their courage and partly agrees that when life hands you lemons you should make lemonade. Out of sadness, like Heinrich Heine, he "makes little songs," and if anger enters into the comedy, "heigh-ho." He is at heart a moralist and an idealist; he takes the essentials (if not always himself and the traveling companions that he is not quite sure are worthy of him) very seriously indeed.

His ambition to make life a stage upon which he can enter as an unknown and exit as a star made the theater the obvious choice both as a pattern for self-fashioning and an arena for personality and celebrity. Indeed, his greatest talent was for the theatrical in all things. His plays are actable in a way that only someone who played a part himself, brilliantly, continuously, off and on stage, could make them. His comic dialogue is quotable as "zingers" but its *raison d'être* is to be spoken from the stage, given gesture as well as voice, said in situations that underline its effectiveness. It loses in the reading; it blossoms in the playing. Absent performance, it lacks all of its music, and everything that Coward wrote was set to some melody in his brain, whether an operatic waltz or a Jazz Age syncopation, a taunting tune of derision or a haunting melody of love.

Mrs. Patrick Campbell snapped that his characters "talk like typewriters." It is true that they chatter on in an unnaturally smart and staccato speech, which owes a lot to natural speech but is theatrical, in apparently casual abandon. They can sound—as Coward was annoyed to hear himself dismissed by the sillier critics—"brittle" and "thin" and "shallow." Gilda in the profound (and profoundly depressing) comedy *Design for Living* slashes at Leo's play: "He flips along with easy, swift dialogue, but doesn't go deep enough." This condemnation is not applicable to The Master. Coward often goes very deep. However, he permits his people to be sophisticated and debonaire. They cannot always go deep because they live on the surface of things, are often on very thin ice. They must "laugh, laugh, laugh" or fall into a crying jag. Part of the reason that they are so comic is that they cannot let their tragedy show, whether they are lost souls or just mislaid.

Into his characters' mouths Coward puts some of the sharpest and most scintillating dialogue ever written, full of the concise and telling wit of his devastating song lyrics and employing the same poetic devices of alliteration, assonance, impudent and caustic wit, ingenious rhymes, and captivating rhythms. His practical poetry makes rich use of reference to contemporary events and celebrities such as Cecil and Grace and Elsie—that's De Wolfe and not Maxwell at that Riviera "wonderful party"—which dates and for some moderns destroys his jokes. Similarly, ill-educated moderns do not understand many of his historical and literary allusions. He can make the single word "cellophane" hilarious in its time. He is at his best when his squabbling spouses are something more lasting than post-war or post-debutante, just humans in domestic difficulties. To appreciate the cartooning of *Sail Away* and similar plays, it helps to have a sense of time and place, but everywhere there must be stage mothers of one sort or another worth discouraging (*Don't Put Your Daughter on the Stage, Mrs. Worthington*), or up-to-date equivalents of leftovers from the *Raj* (*I Wonder What Happened to Him*) and the Empire (*Mad Dogs and Englishmen*) or Mayfair before Britain became defeated, drab, and sullen. It helps to know that World War I created a craze for mediums and a lot of manic/depressive bliss ninnies, how High Society used to get high, what the party of the 1920s and the hangover that eventually followed were like, and how the world was from about 1910 to about 1970. If you know about Judyism (the Judy Garland cult), *Why Must the Show Go On?* strikes you as devastating, but if you don't know, it still asks an impertinently pertinent question. Comedy often asks the audience to be better informed and smarter than most people. Coward rewards intellect—but he can also convulse the unthinking with farce that would "make a cat laugh," to use a phrase from another writer.

Coward is not comic caviar for the general. Lots of people not of his time or his temperament find him funny. They love to enter, if only vicariously, his world of wit. They wish that they could talk like his characters and joke like he does. In real life Coward was as amusing as in his work; real life was part of his work, as it was with Wilde. When "Lawrence of Arabia" tried to hide as an enlisted man (his dog tag was 338171), Coward wrote to him, "Dear 338171 (may I call you 338?)." He sent hilarious telegrams to friends. When Gertrude Lawrence married, he celebrated in doggerel:

Dear Mrs. A,
Hooray, hooray,
At last you are deflowered.
On this as every other day
I love you. Noel Coward.

How pleasant it would be to be able to erase the dullness of life or face disaster with the insouciance of Coward characters! How pleasant to imagine that we could be as bohemian and care-free or blithely unaware as they! How pleasant it would be if everything were fun and things were "organized better"! How pleasant it would be if his "talent to amuse" were still alive, even to perpetuate "a personal issue of adipose tissue" or "a roll in the hey-nonny-nonny" or "West Point cadets forming fours do it." Wouldn't it be nice if we, too, could be out of sympathy with our times and yet in the swim, full of "present laughter" in spite of the hand that we are dealt in a game that we cannot win? In the most professional playwriting, for over half a century, Coward lit up the stage with a comedy that was his way of being a rebel while making The Establishment, along with everyone else, take him to their hearts. Through his comedy he expressed a brave and bold and artistic approach to the tragedy of alienation and accident and final meaninglessness. As Amanda remarks in *Private Lives*, a comedy that may prove perdurable after Eugene O'Neill and Bernard Shaw are only names in obscure histories, "Extraordinary how potent cheap music is."

Characteristically, the writer never quite admitted to his sentimental streak, though he permitted pathos to surface in some haunting short stories. He liked to talk of surfaces, not secrets, to stress reception. Of one important play he wrote: "It was described in the papers variously as being 'tenuous,' 'thin,' 'brittle,' 'gossamer,' 'irridescent [sic],' and 'delightfully daring.' All of which connoted, to the public mind, 'cocktails,' 'evening dress,' 'repartee,' and irreverent allusions to copulation, thereby causing a gratifying number of respectable people to queue up at the box office."

Making some rather unpalatable content generally acceptable by means obvious and not so obvious was the playwright's stock in trade. He sold what another author once referred to as the artist-educator's "pot of message" by deftly stirring in some exotic spices. He even got people to accept this creed of his:

> I believe in doing what I can,
> In crying when I must,
> In laughing when I choose.
> Heigh ho, if love were all
> I should be lonely.
> I believe the more you love a man,
> The more you give your trust,
> The more you're bound to lose.
> Although when shadows fall
> I think if only—
> Somebody splendid really needed me,
> Someone affectionate and dear,
> Cares would be ended if I knew that he
> Wanted to have me near.
> But I believe that since my life began
> The most I've had is just
> A talent to amuse.
> Heigh ho, if love were all!

Coward found love eventually (with [Leonard] Cole Lesley), but money and fame came earlier and easier while he soldiered on (like his heroine in "Alice Is at It Again"):

> The curious secrets that nature revealed
> She refused to allow to upset her
> But she thought when observing the
>   beasts of the field
> That things might have been organized
>   better.

Coward's acceptance of his sex drives (never seriously "thinking of taking the veil") was not unrelated to his outlook on other people's lives in all of their complexity. He liked to comment on those lives in a flip yet serious, cynical and whimsical, blase and sometimes stinging, sometimes sad way—"I'm world weary"; "The party's over now."

He plays with self-criticism and self-pity, fashionable ennui and foolish optimism, stuck-up pretension and sticky sentiment, home truths and homosexual "camp." He asks questions such as "What Is Love?" and "Why Does Life Get in the Way So?" He ranges from "Why Is It the Woman Who Pays?" to "Why Do the Wrong People Travel?" He challenges tradition: "Why Must the Show Go On?" His answer to that last question is courage, professionalism. He deplores Judy Garland's approach:

> We know that you're sad,
> We know that you've had
> A lot of storm and strife
> But is it quite fair
> To ask us to share
> Your dreary private life?

Laugh and the world laughs with you; cry, and you smear your mascara *and* drive away your friends, like Louisa, the Movie Queen:

> When friends came to visit, their hands
>   she would clutch
> Crying, "Tell me, why is it I suffer so
>   much?
> If only, if only, if only
> My life wasn't quite such a strain."
> And soon after that she was terribly
>   lonely,
> All over again.

Coward, less blithely gay than bravely *gay*, made his set his family and his audiences his rewards. He decided to be true to his talent and content with enormous celebrity. He created a sophisticated mask and wore it cheerfully and to cheers from those who likewise wore masks and others who had no idea about talent or sophistication or culture.

His professional persona may belong more to sociology than to literature to the extent that it led to a certain elegant *gay* role model as well as to theatrical imitations. Coward was *sui generis*, yet we cannot but compare him to numerous other public personalities such as the waspish aesthete that Clifton Webb played in the film version of Somerset Maugham's *The Razor's Edge*, not to mention "Somerset and all the Maughams" in real life. The persona had many literary antecedents, among them Lord Henry Wotton in Wilde's *The Picture of Dorian Gray*. There were also real-life examples, even heterosexual ones such as the provincial from Omaha who made himself into Fred Astaire. The persona was one with dash and decadence between the wars. It was not as extreme as Quentin Crisp. It was ante-*out* if not anti-*out*, paradoxically both furtive and flamboyant by turns. Proud to be sensitive if eccentric, those who dared this pose were not likely to "come out of the closet" in those times. Rather, they furnished the closet as a kind of boudoir (awesome Louis XIV or awful Art Deco) and invited the rest of us to peek in and admire.

Society was expected to take this pose as talent's prerogative, to accept banter about deviation if not (as the title of a Cole Porter song had it) to "Experiment." The avant-garde was allowed to be bohemian. It was bourgeois to be censorious. It was chic to be amused. It was *de rigeur* to keep up with the latest as well as with the classics. The latest might shock: "People's behaviour / Away from Belgravia" might "leave you aghast," but that was titillating and not threatening ("I couldn't have liked it more"). For Coward life was "a marvellous party," and some strange people dropped in, inevitably, entertainingly. So what? Coward described all of this, shockingly or sentimentally ("Some Day I'll Find You"). It was delightful. The entertainers were always pure fun (on-stage).

Coward's plays were so witty and charming and well-constructed (even *Hay Fever*, which scarcely can be said to have a plot) that they always worked. His musicals were clever and tuneful and the books were no sillier than what P.G. Wodehouse and Guy Bolton were writing. His comic songs were hilarious. His short stories could be very deft, very touching.

Today the short stories are neglected (except as television fodder). The comic songs are perhaps distanced by contemporary references, once fresh. What was the CLV and the PAVO? Who were Ramon Navarro and Richard Dix? Worse, allusions to the former core curriculum of the educated classes may today fall on ignorant ears. Nonetheless, even those who lack a familiarity with standard authors and old British show-biz histories, even those far too young to recall the gossip of the 1920s and 1930s, can listen with pleasure to these songs. The lyrics are lively, the lilting waltz tunes and other melodies are captivating, the occasional rowdy songs ("Finiculi, finicula, finic' yourself") are tame by

modern standards. There is skill and there is bite in "Don't Let's Be Beastly to the Germans," "There Are Bad Times Just around the Corner," "Uncle Harry," "A Bar on the Piccola Marina," and "Mad Dogs and Englishmen." Many people love these songs, even if they do not "get" all of the words. At a World War II meeting, President Franklin Roosevelt and Prime Minister Winston Churchill took time off from more pressing matters to debate who remembered correctly a line from "Mad Dogs and Englishmen."

The catty jabs and debonair, suggestive comments about such things as "a roll in the hey-nonny-nonny" do not demand excessive background. The punchlines of the comedies have the actors to help get them across. The recordings of Coward himself singing (*Noel Coward at Las Vegas*, *Noel Coward in New York*, *The Master Sings*, and so on) have made his personal style well known, and stage farragoes such as *O Coward!* and *Cowardy Custard* have brought to audiences slighter bits than in the plays that amateurs especially are so tempted to stage. Part of the memories of many older folk are linked to songs such as "I'll See You Again," "A Room with a View," "Poor Little Rich Girl," "Zigeuner," "I'll Follow My Secret Heart," and "Nothing Can Last Forever." It may be that the cleverest songs are such light pieces as "Nina," "The Stately Homes of England," or "Saturday Night at The Rose and Crown," once heard, never forgotten. Benny Green did not overstate the case when he described Coward as "the best British composer of the last fifty years . . . the best lyricist this country has produced, certainly since Wodehouse, perhaps since Gilbert."

It may be that Coward is better than Gilbert, if only because his cruelty can surface better (like Dorothy Parker's). Coward is the British peer of Cole Porter. He carries the same punch, the iron fist in the velvet glove. All of Coward's humor has an element of *attack* in it, a nastiness that saves it from the two great vices of British humor: whimsicality and sentimentality. It is not beside the point to mention that Coward always showed a mean streak in film roles and that he once turned down the part of Professor Higgins in *My Fair Lady*. The professor was played by Rex Harrison, despite the fact that Harrison's accent was hopelessly wrong *and* the fact that "Sexy Rexy" lacked the streak of nastiness that the professor's part, maybe the most off-putting of all leads in musicals, demands. Coward would have etched deeper. He had more acid.

Coward's biting tongue in lines and lyrics is famous but, like Wilde and others of the type, he put a good deal of his genius into his life, too, and Coward's *mots* deserve to be better known. He told actress Evelyn Laye (who was prone to wave her arms about) that she played "like a windmill." He said of actor A.E. Matthews, who was shaky in his lines, that he "ambled through" a play "like a charming retriever who has buried a bone and can't quite remember where." When Shaw rejected complimentary tickets to a Coward premiere, Coward was livid but said nothing. For his *next* opening Coward sent Shaw tickets to a stage box that seated four: "bring *all* your friends." When a dimwit Hollywood actor blew out his brains, Coward remarked, "He must have been a wonderful shot."

He pilloried affectations and even afflictions (if not courageously borne), but he was ready to scourge himself as well as others. His *Design for Living* as a movie, he claimed, contained only a few of his original lines, notably "Pass the mustard." He was a patriot, even a spy for his country, but he hated knee-jerk jingoism: a Lady Mayoress in New Zealand chided him for being disrespectful of The Empire. In fact, Coward was disrespectful of almost everything and everyone except little old ladies; they tended to remind him of his mother. A perfectionist, he detested sloppiness. He polished his works and performances to a dazzling finish, and he demanded complete dedication and effort from his colleagues. He could be a difficult person. He thought that pursuing one's talent almost guaranteed that.

By the time that he went to Hollywood, Coward could get away with playing himself. His bit part in *Around the World in Eighty Days* was described in the film script as "superior and ineffably smug." Coward joked that it was typecasting. There is a quality in his comedy in particular of *de haute en bas*: he, as Shaw said of himself, "specialized in being right when other people are wrong." Often the shock of recognition as the unsaid is finally spoken is the trigger for laughter; the "not done" done, the thrill.

Those who find mischief malevolent and perfectionism artificial rather than artistic may dislike Coward's work. Those who think cynicism and satire are unconstructive may call him brittle or sadistic. Those who believe technical virtuosity must be at odds with sincerity may dismiss him as trivial. Many Americans may see in Coward what Pauline Kael in her book of film reviews, *Hooked*, ticked off: "the curse of the British, a terrible empty brilliance."

Americans are serious about comedy. Even when what is called for is perfect timing and other evidences of precision, Americans tend to value the hard punch and dislike tricky footwork. Few of the leading American writers excel in comedy and many serious writers cannot write well: Herman Melville, Theodore Dreiser, William Faulkner, O'Neill, Arthur Miller, et al. are clumsy, too reckless or romantic to do the seven drafts in pencil before going to the typewriter that gave the prose of Truman Capote its perfection. We admire writers who refuse to revise, like Jack Kerouac. "That ain't writin'," crooned Capote, "that's *typin'*!"

Coward's plays are beautifully crafted, his lyrics delightfully deft, his short stories economical and effective. All of his work has a polish, a perfection of style that it is hard to see in any American writers since Perelman. And, no one at all in America has had in so very many different aspects of popular entertainment so powerful and lasting a talent to amuse as did The Master.

Coward was the kind of prolific and popular dramatist who could have several plays running at once in London's West End, but did not earn the contempt that has been shown to more recent successes such as Andrew Lloyd Weber. Even in his own time Coward's hits were regarded as classics of the theater and expected to remain to represent his period to later times. He wrote charming light music for his operetta *Bitter Sweet* and his extravaganza *Cavalcade* and more, not to mention a series of revues that included *This Year of Grace* (1928), *Words and Music* (1932), and *Sigh No More* (1945). After a couple of forgettable collaborations with Esme Wynne in 1917 and some slight sketches for *Tails Up!* (1918), Coward hit his stride with *I'll Leave It to You* (1920) and then, until *Nude with Violin* (1965) or *The Girl Who Came to Dinner* (1963), to note but a few theatrical milestones, he enjoyed decades and decades of fame in the theater.

Multitalented, he also created a ballet (*London Morning*, 1959) and half a dozen film scripts. Remarkable among the film scripts were two based on his own plays: *In Which We Serve* (1942) and *Brief Encounter* (1946). *In Which We Serve* was a tribute to the Royal Navy and to British doggedness. No less British was *Brief*

Encounter, which film historian Leslie Halliwell called "one of the great post-war British films . . . a discerning script . . . Its stiff Britishness has caused it to be unfairly revalued, but it will certainly be cherished in a more tender age." In these mass-market materials Coward's sentimental strain proved a real advantage. Millions loved the movies.

Perhaps less noticed is the contribution that he made to comedy in his sentimental *and* funny short stories and his witty popular songs. Coward carried a thesaurus and a rhyming dictionary on all of his extensive travels and would dash off a song whenever he had a spare minute during his wartime entertaining of the troops or his peacetime diverting of the sophisticated classes. Some he wrote to sing himself in his inimitable style; others he wrote for performers such as Bea Lillie to revel in.

Coward spent half a century acting in films, from *Hearts of the World* (1918) to the caper comedy of *The Italian Job* (1969). Mostly he played suave if caddish gentlemen. He also created a superior spy and, in *Bunny Lake Is Missing* (1965), a sinister pervert, wrapped for once not in a sleek silk dressing gown but a seedy bathrobe. In the 1930s, moviegoers saw his films of *Private Lives* (1931), *Cavalcade*, *Tonight Is Ours*, and *Bitter Sweet* (all 1933), and *Design for Living* (1934). Coward starred in *The Scoundrel* (1935) as a roué who both attracted and repelled. In the 1940s, he was general factotum for *In Which We Serve* and he also gave the public *We Were Dancing* (1942), *Blithe Spirit* and *This Happy Breed* (both 1945), and *The Astonished Heart* (1949). In the 1950s, Coward moved to the West Indies but continued to wear his comic mask in cameo parts in *Meet Me Tonight* (1950) and *Around the World in Eighty Days*, and as a British spy in *Our Man in Havana* (1959). In the 1960s, he was seen in *Surprise Package* (1960) and *Paris When It Sizzles* (1964). His most characteristic film appearance of the 1960s involved scene-stealing from Elizabeth Taylor in a bomb named *Boom*, a Hollywood revision of Tennessee Williams's *The Milk Train Doesn't Stop Here Anymore*. For *Boom*, despite Coward's failing health, the part of a bitchy countess was rewritten so that he could play it. He played on his by then world famous cool, clipped, camp, and condescending comic persona. He was rather valetudinarian, ready to die rather than "stagger on into the nineties." "I have never been one for staying up too late," he claimed.

Coward left the scene but his plays remain. *Blithe Spirit*, for example, in which Charles Condomine contends with two wives, one living (Ruth) and one a ghost (Elvira). There is plenty of vivacious and sometimes sharp dialogue and some of Coward's best characters, including that acted by the unforgettable Margaret Rutherford (that rare medium, so well done in the film version) in evening dress on a bicycle. Eccentricity also provides plenty of scope for bravura acting in the more farcical *Hay Fever*. Judith (an actress) is married to David (a novelist) and they have a couple of madcap children, Sorel and Simon. Each invites a weekend guest into the family's midst, and before the bohemian hijinks drive all of the guests away there is plenty of motion and emotion. *Hay Fever* is very much of its period but the crazy family gives the piece continuing appeal. More among what Shaw might have called Coward's "unpleasant plays" is *Design for Living*, crafted as a vehicle for the Alfred Lunts and Coward himself. Coward said that *Design for Living* was "liked and disliked, and hated and admired, but never, I think, sufficiently loved by any but its three leading actors." He added in introduction to *Play Parade* (1933): "I never intended for a moment that the design for living suggested in the play should apply to anyone outside its three principal characters, Gilda, Otto, and Leo. These glib, overarticulate, and amoral creatures force their lives into fantastic shapes and problems because they cannot help themselves. Impelled chiefly by the impact of their personalities each upon the other, they are like moths in a pool of light, unable to tolerate the lonely outer darkness, and equally unable to share the light without colliding constantly and bruising one another's wings."

Design for Living is less likely to be revived today than some Coward comedies. However, it does underline the fact that all of his carefully constructed plays, for all of the opportunities for eccentric and stand-out performances, involve the close interaction of characters in a tangled web of relationships; they demand the most subtle ensemble acting as well as "glib, overarticulate" and other characteristics not very frequently found in today's actors. Coward called modern actors "the scratch-and-mumble school" and deplored "the squalid and monotonous" social problems they went on about in "political or social propaganda in the theatre." For those who can stand the actors being smooth and the content of the play less than theological (say, about ecology or some other new religion), possibly the best Coward choice is *Private Lives*.

Tallulah Bankhead (who played Amanda in *Private Lives* for "over two hundred weeks") says in her autobiography of this reliable vehicle: "I played it for an entire summer in Chicago, while racked with neuritis, and for an entire season in New York. I played it in summer theatres, in Shrine mosques, in school auditoriums, in a blizzard in Minneapolis, in a coma in Westport. I played it in Passaic, in Flatbush, in Pueblo, in Cedar Rapids, in Peoria, in the Bronx, in Joplin, in 'thunder, lightning and in rain' . . . in towns known but to God and Rand McNally." With colorful enough leads, *Private Lives* can still be played in all of these places and more, but it demands great skill in execution. This might be deduced by the cast of the first production: Coward, Gertrude Lawrence, Olivier, and Adrianne Allen.

Just as one is tempted to try to sound like Coward to sing his songs, just as one hears his voice as one reads his fiction, one is tempted to try to imitate his stage personality. That is difficult. The character had a touch of the cad in it (rather like George Saunders) and of the low comic as well (rather like Edward Everett Horton).

In a television biography filmed in Switzerland near the end of his life, Coward was asked for a summing up. He said: "Sum up? Well, now comes the terrible decision as to whether to be corny or not. The answer is in one word, Love. To know that you are among people whom you love, and who love you. That has made all the success wonderful . . . That's it."

Coward's best work is *Bitter Sweet*. "It combines my talents in almost perfect balance," he said. Love or the lack of it often informs the best of his short stories, wry but sometimes exploiting pathos, bitter with a twist, and it colors his portraits of old age in two late plays, *Waiting in the Wings* (1960), in which the playwright deals with retired actresses in a home, and *A Song at Twilight* (1965), in which a famous author's declining years are spoiled by a long-hidden homosexual past which suddenly returns to threaten him. *A Song at Twilight* is light years away from the frivolity of *I'll Leave It to You*. It is, as one critic has said, "the first convincing, completely serious well-made play in the British theatre for more than half a century."

Summary

"A Coward play," wrote J.C. Trewin, "has always been highly theatrical and glossily professional," and that is the way that both the writer and his works will always be remembered. Sir Terence Rattigan has testified that Noel Coward always spoke and wrote with wit, "and wit is a quality that does not date." "He is interested not only in humanity, its quirks and foibles," Rattigan added, "its vanities and idiocies, its prejudices and pomposities, and these things, as Congreve and Sheridan have taught us, are changeless" (3). That is why Coward was able to create in Madame Arcati a character as deathless as Mrs. Malaprop. Coward wrote operettas as permanent as those of Richard Strauss, the best comedy of bad manners since *The Importance of Being Earnest*, the best of the bitter and cynical reactions to World War I (*The Vortex*), some of the greatest stage successes of the twentieth century, and work that will live long after playwrights and songwriters more highly regarded now are long gone. Edward Albee wrote in introduction to *Three Plays by Noel Coward* (1965): "A man I know and like and whose opinion I respect, a man involved with the theatre, a man who has produced the work of such playwrights as Beckett, Ionesco, Pinter, Arrabal and Ugo Betti, said to me not long ago that he greatly admired Noel Coward's plays, that he thought Coward a better playwright than Bernard Shaw and that Coward's plays would be on the boards long after most of the men writing today had been forgotten" (5).

Selected Bibliography
Primary Sources

Collections
Three Plays. London: Ernest Benn, 1925.
Collected Sketches and Lyrics. London: Hutchinson, 1931.
Play Parade. London: Heinemann, 1933–1962. 6 vols.
The Coward Song-Book. New York: Simon and Schuster, 1953.
The Lyrics of Noel Coward. London: Heinemann, 1965, 1983.
Short Stories, Short Plays, and Songs. Ed. Gilbert Millstein, 1955.
The Wit of Noel Coward. Ed. Dick Richards. London: Leslie Frewin, 1968.
Collected Short Stories. London: Heinemann, 1969.
Cowardy Custard. Ed. John Hadfield. Lon-

don: Heinemann, 1973.
Collected Verse. Ed. Graham Payne and Martin Tickner. London: Methuen.

Plays
Ida Collaborates, produced 1917, written with Esme Wynne.
Woman and Whisky, produced 1917, written with Esme Wynne.
I'll Leave It to You. New York: Samuel French, 1920.
Bottles and Bones, produced 1921.
The Better Half, produced 1922.
The Young Idea. London and New York: Samuel French, 1922.
The Vortex. London: Ernest Benn, 1924.
The Rat Trap. London: Ernest Benn, 1924; produced 1926.
Hay Fever. London: Ernest Benn, 1925.
Fallen Angels. London: Ernest Benn, 1925; revised production 1967.
Easy Virtue. London: Ernest Benn, 1926.
The Queen Was in the Parlour. London: Ernest Benn, 1926.
This Was a Man, produced 1926, New York.
The Marquise. London: Ernest Benn, 1927.
Home Chat. London: Martin Secker, 1927.
Sirocco. London: Martin Secker, 1927.
Bitter Sweet (with music by the author). London: Martin Secker, 1929.
Private Lives. London: Heinemann, 1930.
Post-Mortem. London: Heinemann, 1931.
Cavalcade. London: Heinemann, 1932.
Design for Living. London: Heinemann, 1933.
Conversation Piece. London: Heinemann, 1934.
Point Valaine. London: Heinemann, 1935.
Tonight at 8:30. London and Toronto: Heinemann, 1936. One-acts produced in three programs, 1935.
Operette (with music by the author). London: Heinemann, 1938.
Blithe Spirit. Garden City, NY: Doubleday, Doran & Co., 1941; London: Heinemann, 1942.
Present Laughter. London: Heinemann, 1943.
This Happy Breed. London: Heinemann, 1943.
Pacific 1860 (with music by the author). 1946.
Peace in Our Time. London: Heinemann, 1947; London: Samuel French, 1949.
Ace of Clubs (with music by the author). Produced 1950.

Relative Values. London: Heinemann, 1952; London: Samuel French, 1954.
Island Fling. London: Heinemann, 1954. Produced 1951, as *South Sea Bubble,* produced 1956.
Quadrille. London: Heinemann, 1952.
After the Ball (with music by the author). London: Chappell, 1954.
Nude with Violin. London: Heinemann, 1957.
Look after Lulu. London: Heinemann, 1959.
Waiting in the Wings. London: Samuel French, 1960.
Sail Away (with music by the author). Produced 1961.
The Girl Who Came to Dinner, produced 1963, music and lyrics by Coward.
Suite in Three Keys. London: Heinemann, 1966. Three plays produced in two programs, 1966.
Come into the Garden, Maud. London: Samuel French, 1967.
A Song at Twilight. London: Samuel French, 1967.
Semi-Monde, produced 1977.

Screenplays
In Which We Serve, 1942.
This Happy Breed, 1944.
Blithe Spirit, 1945.
Brief Encounter, published in *Three British Screen Plays.* Ed. [Arnold] Roger Manvell. London: Methuen with British Film Academy, 1950.
The Astonished Heart, published with other screenplays, 1950.
Meet Me Tonight, 1952.

Radio Plays
The Kindness of Mrs. Redcliffe, 1951.

Revue Sketches in
Tails Up! produced 1918.
The Co-Optimists, produced 1922; revised production 1924.
London Calling!, written with Ronald Jeans; produced 1923; revised productions 1923 and 1924; some parts printed in *Collected Sketches and Lyrics,* 1931, and *The Noel Coward Song-Book,* 1953.
Charlot's London Revue, 1924.
Yoiks! 1924.
Charlot's Revue of 1926, produced 1925.
On with the Dance, music by Philip Braham, produced March 17, 1925, Manchester

Palace, and April 30, 1925, London Pavilion; some parts printed 1931 and 1953.

White Birds, produced 1926.

This Year of Grace, produced 1928, in *Play Parade II*, 1939; some lyrics in *The Lyrics of Noel Coward*, 1965, 1983.

Charles B. Cochran's 1928 Revue. London: Chappell & Co.

Charles B. Cochran's 1931 Revue. London: Chappell & Co., produced 1931.

The Third Little Show, produced 1931.

Weatherwise, pb. 1931. Produced September 8, 1932, Malvern Festival.

Words and Music, produced 1932; revised and produced as *Set to Music* 1938; printed in *Play Parade II*, 1939.

All Clear, produced 1939.

Sigh No More, produced 1945; some lyrics printed 1953, 1965, 1983.

The Lyric Revue, produced 1951.

The Globe Revue, produced 1952.

The Noel Coward Revue. New York: Studio Duplicating, 1968.

Fiction

To Step Aside: Seven Short Stories. London and Toronto: Heinemann, 1939.

Star Quality: Six Stories. London: Heinemann, 1951.

Pomp and Circumstance. Garden City, NY: Doubleday, 1960.

Seven Stories. Garden City, NY: Dolphin Books, 1963.

Pretty Polly Barlow and Other Stories. London: Heinemann, 1964; rpt. as *Pretty Polly and Other Stories*, 1965.

Bon Voyage and Other Stories. London: Heinemann, 1967.

Spangled Unicorn: An Anthology. London: Hutchinson, 1932.

Not Yet the Dodo and Other Verses. London: Heinemann, 1967.

Poems. As by "Hernia Whittlebot." London: Hutchinson, 1923.

Chelsea Buns. As by "Hernia Whittlebot." London: Hutchinson, 1925.

Autobiographies

Autobiography. London: Methuen, 1986. Introduction by Sheridan Morley. Contains *Present Indicative*, *Future Indefinite*, and uncompleted *Past Conditional*. Da Capo Press (New York) reprinted the first two in 1980.

"In Which He Served." *Sight & Sound*, 59 (Summer 1990): 183–84. Coward as film adviser to the Royal Navy in World War II, with his report.

The Noel Coward Diaries. Ed. Graham Payn and Sheridan Morley. Boston: Little, Brown, 1982.

Miscellaneous

A Withered Nosegay: Imaginary Biographies. London: Christophers, 1922; revised as *Terribly Intimate Portraits*, 1922.

Present Indicative. London and Toronto: Heinemann, 1937.

Australian Broadcast. London: Heinemann, 1941; also as *Australia Visited 1940*.

Middle East Diary: July to October 1943. London: Heinemann, 1944.

Future Indefinite. London: Heinemann, 1954.

London Morning. London: Chappell, 1959. (Score.)

The Last Bassoon. New York: Clark, Irwin, 1960. Editor of diaries of Fred T. Bason.

Secondary Sources

Albee, Edward. "Introduction." In *Three Plays by Noel Coward*. New York: Dell, 1965.

Braybrooke, Patrick. *The Amazing Mr. Noel Coward*. Philadelphia: R. West, 1977. One of several reissues of an early appreciation first published in London by Archer in 1933.

Briers, Richard. *Coward and Company*. London: Robson Books, 1987.

Castle, Charles. *Noel*. London: Abacus (W.H. Allen) and Garden City, NY: Doubleday, 1972. [F]resh, lively, well illustrated with pictures, many of which are new, and supported with dozens of interviews with his friends" (London *Evening News*).

Catsapias, Helene. "Noel Coward et la France." *Revue d'Histoire du Theatre* (January-March 1981): 83–96. Coward loved France, and *vice versa*.

Citron, Stephen. *Noel and Cole: The Sophisticates*. London: Sinclair-Stevenson, 1992.

Davies, Russell. "Doing without the Music." *Times Literary Supplement*, 4215 (1984): 33. A survey of *The Lyrics of Noel Coward* (Woodstock, NY: Overlook, 1983) and Coward's contribution to popular music compared to Cole Porter, *et al.*

England, D. "Peter Pringle, No Cowardly Lion." *Performing Arts in Canada*, 25, 1 (1988): 46. Review of Peter Pringle in *Noel Coward: A Portrait. O Coward!* and *Cowardy Custard* surpassed all one-man-show attempts. Only Coward in Las Vegas or anywhere could do it *alone.*

Gay, Frances [B.] *Noel Coward*. Basingstoke (Hants.): Macmillan, 1987.

Greacen, Robert. *The Art of Noel Coward.* Philadelphia: R. West, 1978. Reprint (earlier editions include: Folcroft Library Edition, 1974, and Norwood Edition, 1976) of important early criticism first published in England (Hand and Flower Press) 1933, when Coward reigned over the London theater world.

Hadfield, John, ed. *Cowardy Custard*. London: Heinemann, 1973. "The World of Noel Coward by John Hadfield: based on the Mermaid Theatre [London] entertainment by Gerald Frow, Alan Strachan and Wendy Toye." One of several farragoes of Coward material seen on stage and television.

Kiernan, Robert F. *Noel Coward*. New York: Ungar, 1986. Better than Levin.

Lahr, John. *Coward, The Playwright*. London: Methuen, 1982. Better than Kiernan.

Lesley, Cole. *The Life of Noel Coward*. London: Jonathan Cape, and as *Remembered Laughter*, New York: Knopf, 1976; New York: Penguin, 1978. By the man who knew him best. A must.

———, Graham Payn, and Sheridan Morley. *Noel Coward and His Friends*. New York: Morrow, 1979.

Levin, Milton. *Noel Coward*. Boston: G.K. Hall, 1968; rev. ed. 1989. Typically pedestrian, workmanlike Twayne's English Authors Series coverage. Useful, but see Morley and Lahr.

Loss, Archie K. "Waiting for Amanda . . ." *Journal of Modern Literature*, 11, 2 (July 1984): 299–306. Connects Coward with The Theatre of the Absurd.

Mander, Raymond, and Joe Mitchenson. *Theatrical Companion to Coward*. London: Rockliff, 1957; London and New York: Macmillan, 1974. A stage-struck gay couple's delightful theater scrapbook.

Marchant, William. *The Privilege of His Company*. London: Weidenfeld and Nicolson, and Indianapolis: Bobbs-Merrill, 1975. Appreciation of "The Master."

Moore, John Rees. Review of *The Collected Short Stories of Noel Coward* (New York: Dutton, 1983). *Studies in Short Fiction*, 21 (Fall 1984): 409–10. Also compares other such reviews, including J. McCourt's in *New York Times Book Review*, 88, 51 (1983): 96. The short stories deserve a book-length study.

Morley, Sheridan. *A Talent to Amuse*. London: Heinemann, and New York: Doubleday, 1969; Boston: Little, Brown, 1985. The all-around best evaluation of Coward. See also Morley's theater reviews.

———. *Out in the Midday Sun*. New York: Philosophical Library, 1988. Appreciative study of Coward's paintings.

Morse, Clarence R. "Mad Dogs and Englishmen: A Study of Noel Coward." *Emporia State Research Studies*, 21, 4 (1973): 5–50. Shows Coward is known even by the faculties of teachers' colleges; Coward is not taken seriously enough in serious universities, a survey of scholarly publications reveals.

Richards, Dick. *The Wit of Noel Coward*. London: Ferwin, 1988. A compilation not to be read straight through, any more than one would eat a whole box of chocolates at a sitting.

Russell, Jacqui. *File on Coward*. London and New York: Methuen, 1987. Useful more than insightful.

Rutherford, Malcolm. "Fat Plays, or Thin?" *Encounter*, 72, 4 (1989): 74–75. One of few good magazine articles on Coward; Rutherford considers the perennial question of whether he is a substantial, serious artist.

Trewin, J.C. *Dramatists of Today*. London: Staples Press, 1953.

Wynne-Tyson, Jon. "Noel Coward." *Times Literary Supplement*, 4150 (1982): 1132.

Leonard R.N. Ashley

Crisp, Quentin

Born: Sutton, Surrey, December 25, 1908
Education: Boarding school in Derbyshire, 1922–1926; King's College, London University, 1926

C

Biography

Quentin Crisp has written that he was "reluctantly" born as Denis Pratt to middle-class, middlebrow, and middling parents in Sutton, Surrey, a suburb of London on December 25, 1908. Close to his mother, whom he characterized as the model of British tact, grace, and respectability, Crisp recalled in *The Naked Civil Servant* that he did not require love so much as unconditional obedience from her. He had two brothers who aspired to be ship's captains and firemen, but his own vocation was to be a chronic invalid. In *Manners from Heaven*, Crisp remembers that he "was extremely plain as a child, physically very weak, timid, dreamy, sickly" (14) and "the only time I felt united with my brothers and my sister was when someone was present who attracted more ridicule than I" (43). In *How to Become a Virgin*, Crisp writes that "The only member of my family who did not heap ridicule upon me was my father and that was because he never spoke" (44). For four years (1922–1926) Crisp attended a Derbyshire boarding school that was a cross between a monastery and a prison, but he writes that at fifteen he "had reached the limit of [his] educability . . . For my final two years I sat in a Nissen hut and read trashy novels by Susan Glaspell" (15–16). He attempted to take a degree in journalism at King's College in London in 1926 but left without being graduated.

The forty years between 1926 and 1966 were filled with poverty, ridicule, and misery, according to the autobiographical *The Naked Civil Servant*. Forcing others to notice him with his mincing, make-up, and henna rinsed hair, Crisp was subject to derision, physical violence, and certain failure in both his professional and personal life. He lived a hand-to-mouth existence as an always-inept commercial artist, a tap dancing teacher, an occasional writer, and an artist's model, legitimate jobs at which he never earned more than $25 a week. At times he could eat only by stealing meals from restaurants; he argues that he did not "object to these felonies because they were against the law. My very existence was illegal. I was embarrassed by their pettiness . . . I couldn't really afford virtue, so I settled for indignation with vice. It served roughly the same purpose and was much cheaper" (38).

Crisp's life changed completely after 1968. *The Naked Civil Servant* was not an immediate success as a book, but Crisp became an international celebrity after the Thames Television production aired in England and America. Since then, Crisp has become a talk-show circuit regular, has contributed to various periodicals, and has written six more books, including a second autobiographical account, *How to Become a Virgin*. He has had success as an actor (he appeared as Lady Bracknell in *The Importance of Being Earnest*) and in touring America with his one-man question and answer show, *An Evening with Quentin Crisp*. In the introduction to *The Wit and Wisdom of Quentin Crisp*, the author objectively wrote, "These public appearances are his humble attempt to thank the human race for having to some extent revised the condemnatory opinion it has held of him for so long" (xv). Crisp immigrated to the United States in 1977, and he currently resides in New York City as a resident alien.

Literary Analysis

In *Laughter* (1921), his long essay on the meaning of the comic, Henri Bergson wrote that society "will be suspicious of all inelasticity of character, of mind, and even of body, because it is the possible sign of a slumbering activity as well as of an activity with separatist tendencies, that inclines to swerve from the common centre round which society gravitates: in short, because it is the sign of an eccentricity" (19). In his character, mind, and body, Crisp has a unique center of existence. Since—in Crisp's own words—acting the part of England's "second reigning queen" and being a "stately homo" did not destroy him, despite his best attempts to have these actions do so, they eventually made him a celebrity. In *Manners from Heaven*, Crisp writes that both habit and strategy were necessary for him to survive as an effeminate, passive, homosexual man: "Having been the butt of mockery and abuse almost from birth I became well acquainted with humility and her twin, irony, even before my compulsory miseducation began in earnest" (90).

It is both Crisp's humility and irony that best describe his humor. In *The Naked Civil Servant* he writes that "I now know that if you describe things better than they are, you are considered to be romantic; if you describe things as worse than they are, you will be called a realist; and if you describe things exactly as they are, you will be thought of as a satirist" (177). If this be so, then Crisp uses a traditional method of satire. He creates a persona whose good sense is always at odds with a chaotic and unsympathetic world. The persona in his prose is a humble, disarming, and charming man who, alienated from any nation and any social convention, can offer shrewd, wise, and witty observations about the human animal.

There is no subject about which Crisp has no opinion. In his essay "Camping Out," the writer observes that "I do not believe in politics, thinking of them as the art of making the inevitable appear to be a matter of wise human choice" (187). In "Taste Be Damned," he remarks that "A boutique is merely a shop in which the goods are more expensive than elsewhere" (91). In "Sex and the Single Bed," Crisp tells of a famous English romance novelist and her husband who maintained separate residences for their entire lives, the arrangement ensuring that "both parties always knew they were guests in the home of the other and, presumably, were therefore on their best behavior. No wonder she could write about romance" (180). In his review of Donald Soto's life of Marlene Dietrich, *Blue Angel*, Crisp praises the book for its completeness and style, but questions Soto's implied judgment about the loneliness inherent in a life of world touring. He ends his review by asking, "Would anyone in her right senses prefer a life of mere domestic bliss to 11 curtain calls a night?" (10).

As a resident alien in America, Crisp may best be seen in the tradition of Englishmen such as Charles Dickens and Oscar Wilde who travel to America to perform public readings and to offer social criticism. He has remarked in *How to Become a Virgin* that "Everything in America is on wide screen" (152). The American media do not have the power to change minds, he notes, but "they can reorient the dithers" (81). In his essay "Going Out in New York," Crisp claims that "Americans have the greatest respect for a gimmick" (137), and in "Reflections off the City of Angels," an essay about a visit to Los Angeles, Crisp observes that "the Los Angeles airport, like so much in America, is in a chaos of improvement" (93).

Crisp will even mock the persona that he has created. When he talks about his first long-distance flight from London to Toronto in *How to Become a Virgin*, he writes, "I found air travel less exciting than the movies had led me to expect. No one became hysterical, no one near me was handcuffed to anyone else and I couldn't glance nervously at the ice forming on the wings because I couldn't see the wings. You eat, you sleep and you go to the movies. You're hardly better off than on earth" (128).

For a man who spent the first sixty years of his life defying convention, there may be some irony inherent in his writing a book on manners. If *Manners from Heaven* is cynical, it is also a shrewd guide for getting along in a world populated with rude people living in an impolite society. Crisp's wonderful sense of the absurd is illustrated no better than in his closing remarks in the "Foreword": "The fact that someone may drop The Bomb in the middle of our mad tea party should in no way deter us from serving the best tea and best conversation in our best manner—for ever" (12).

When Jean W. Ross interviewed Crisp in 1983, she observed that *Doing It with Style*, the humorist's book on lifestyles, contained both humor and good sense, to which Crisp remarked, "Yes, well, it's the essence of humor that it's true. In fact, nothing can be funny that isn't at least partially true" (91). And in spite of his insistence that one should "never, ever work," Crisp has compiled a large body of writing that has won him recognition in contemporary culture. The best of it will remain as a valuable and valiant contribution to humor in the twentieth century.

Summary

Daring to be flamboyantly effeminate, Quentin Crisp follows his own injunction that having a style is, quite simply, having the courage to be what one is. He has found a cult following as a social arbiter and a wider audience as a touring personality and talk show guest. In his writing, Crisp may sometimes be too much aware of his own cleverness, but his prose style is delightfully aphoristic. If his books and essays are cynical, they are, at least, full of good sense and free from the bitterness found in most satire.

Selected Bibliography
Primary Sources

Books
Color in Display. London: Blandford Press, 1938.
Little Reviews Anthology. Baker, Denys, ed. London: Methuen, 1949.
The Naked Civil Servant. Jonathan Cape, 1968; London: Cecil Woolf, 1975; New York: Methuen, 1979.
Love Made Easy. London: Duckworth, 1977.
Chog: A Gothic Fable. London: Methuen, 1979.
How to Have a Life Style. New York:

Methuen, 1979.

Doing It with Style. With Donald Carroll. London: F. Watts, 1981.

How to Become a Virgin. London: Duckworth, 1981; New York: St. Martin's Press, 1984.

How to Go to the Movies: A Guide for the Perplexed. New York: St. Martin's Press, 1989.

Quentin Crisp's Book of Quotations: 1000 Observations on Life and Love By, For, and About Gay Men and Women. New York: Macmillan, 1989.

Manners from Heaven: A Divine Guide to Good Behavior. With John Hofess. New York: Harper, 1985.

Kettelhack, Guy, ed. *The Wit and Wisdom of Quentin Crisp*. New York: Harper, 1984.

Uncollected Essays

"Theatre." *New York* (January 22, 1979): 64.

"I Visit the Colonies." *New York* (January 29, 1979): 34–36.

"Tallulah Bankhead." *After Dark* (December 1980): 82.

"Greta Garbo." *After Dark* (January 1981): 82.

"Mae West." *After Dark* (February 1981): 82.

"Marlon Brando." *After Dark*, March 1981, p. 82.

"Reflections off the City of Angels." *Esquire* (February 1983): 93–94.

"Going Out in New York." *Vanity Fair* (September 1983): 137–39.

"Talk About Talk Shows." *Channels of Communication* (May/June 1983) 45–47.

"Your Show of Shows." *Village Voice* (April 16, 1985): 33.

"Anti Hero." *Spin* (April 1987): 70.

"Taste Be Damned." *House and Garden* (August 1989): 90–91.

"Camping Out." *House and Garden* (October 1989): 184–87.

"Sex and the Single Bed." *House and Garden* (May 1990): 178–82.

"A Place Where Love Becomes a Chronic Invalid." Rev. of *Paris Is Burning*. *New York Times* (April 7, 1991) Sec. 2, p. 20.

"In Praise of Censorship." *UTNE Reader* (November/December 1991): 118.

"Insight." *Elle* (January 1992): 32.

Interviews

Lague, L. "Interview." *People Weekly* (August 26, 1985): 92–94.

Lavin, Cheryl. "'Never, ever work.'" *Chicago Tribune* (June 19, 1990): Sec. 5, p. 3.

Ross, Jean W. "Contemporary Authors Interview." *Contemporary Authors*. Vol. 116. Ed. Hal May. Detroit: Gale Research, 1986, 89–92.

Secondary Sources

Braddell, Maurice. "Quentin Crisp and the Elements of Style." *The Washington Post Book World* (February 17, 1980): 5. Review of *Chog: A Gothic Fable* and *How to Have a Life Style*. A review of Crisp's attitudes and humor from a fellow Englishman.

Dirda, Michael. Review of *How to Become a Virgin*. *The Washington Post Book World* (February 14, 1982): 8. High praise of Crisp's second autobiography.

Kempley, Rita. "'Quentin Crisp': Gay Abandon." *The Washington Post* (April 18, 1992) Sec. C, p. 3. Review of *Resident Alien: Quentin Crisp in America*. Kempley offers her sincere comments about Jonathan Nossiter's documentary film of Crisp's later life.

Liebman, Roy. Review of *How to Go to the Movies*. *Library Journal* (December 1989): 126. Liebman calls this book important for its analysis of movies, their audiences, and theaters.

Nelson, Alix. Review of *The Naked Civil Servant*. *New York Times Book Review* (September 18, 1977): 16. Nelson ironically calls this the first how-to book for losers, how to self-destruct with style.

Shales, Tom. "The Unlikely Hero gets his Reward." *The Washington Post Book World* (October 1978): Sec. D, p. 1. Review of the Thames Television film *The Naked Civil Servant*. Shales quotes Crisp as saying that the world now rewards him for what it had previously beaten him for. Crisp finds the situation humorous.

Watts, Franklin. Review of *Doing It with Style*. *The Washington Post Book World* (November 8, 1988): 11. Watts writes that Crisp's advice is always good.

Yardley, Jonathan. "Quentin Crisp's Golden Rules." Review of *Manners from Heaven*. *The Washington Post Book World* (March 17, 1985): 3. Yardley praises the good sense in Crisp's non-snobbish book of etiquette.

Randall Calhoun

D

Dahl, Roald

Born: Llandaff, Wales, September 13, 1916
*Education: Graduated from the Repton
School, 1932*
*Marriage: Patricia Neal, July 2, 1953; di-
vorced 1983; five children; Felicity Ann
Crosland, 1983*
Died: Oxford, November 23, 1990

Biography

Roald (pronounced Roo-aal) Dahl was born in
Llandaff, Wales on September 13, 1916. His
father, Harald Dahl, was an immigrant Norwegian shipbroker who died when his son was
four. Roald attended public school at Repton,
where he proved an indifferent scholar and accomplished athlete at football, squash, and
handball. After his graduation in 1932, instead
of entering a university, he embarked upon a
commercial career with Shell Oil in East Africa,
an experience that he later described as "a silly
young man in charge of twenty Indian clerks."

When war broke out Roald joined the
Royal Air Force, cramming his six-foot-six
frame into the cramped cockpit of fighters. His
plane crashed in north Africa, nearly killing
him, and he flew in the air war over Greece. By
1941, he was assigned to Washington, D.C. As
a genuine RAF hero, Dahl and his anecdotes
were much in demand. C.S. Forester came to
Washington to interview him for the *Saturday
Evening Post* but instead had Dahl write his
own account. (Dahl says he lost the $1,000 fee
playing poker with Senator Harry Truman at
the University Club.) Eleanor Roosevelt invited
him to the White House. Bernard Baruch was
an acquaintance, and in New York Dahl stayed
at the home of Mrs. Ogden Reid. With his war
years in vogue and contacts like these, the

young man was better placed to succeed in the
United States than he might have been at home.
He did return to Britain briefly after the war but
by 1947 he was back in New York City, an eli-
gible bachelor who cut a social swath as "the
New Yorker's odd Englishman."

Dahl's war stories were collected in 1946
under the title *Over to You: Ten Stories of Flyers and Flying*. Having discovered his vocation
as a writer by what he called "a pure fluke,"
Dahl began to write stories in the vein that established his reputation. His second collection,
Someone Like You, came out to excellent reviews in 1953. On July 2 that same year he
married actress Patricia Neal (who was on the
rebound from her affair with Gary Cooper),
with whom he would have five children. Neal
had been hailed on Broadway as "the new
Tallulah Bankhead" in 1946, but her Hollywood career had gotten off to a disappointingly
slow start. While their respective talents established solid reputations for each, Pat and Roald
also became a famous couple, articles about one
often highlighting the other. Tragedy and misfortune beset the Dahl family—a daughter died
of a sudden illness, a son suffered a terrible head
injury when his stroller was struck by a New
York City taxicab, and Pat was struck down by
a nearly fatal stroke. Her heroic recovery was
given much attention in the press, which tended
to portray Dahl as a sort of saintly curmudgeon
whose affectionate nagging helped restore his
wife's vitality.

Dahl added books for young readers (nineteen in all, including *The BFG*) and screenplays
to his repertoire in the 1960s, enhancing both
his fame and his financial security. He liked to
restore old paintings, collect antique furniture,
and grow roses. An inveterate gambler, he even

played "razor golf," a game which consisted of shaving in the fewest possible strokes; he kept track of his best scores, once claiming to have broken twenty half a dozen times. He took special pride in having helped invent a shunt for hydrocephalic children, the Wade-Dahl-Till Valve.

The media which had created Dahl's plaster saint image during Pat's recovery tended to trash their own creation during the nasty and protracted separation and divorce. Pat was making a Maxim commercial when she befriended fashion coordinator Felicity Ann Crosland, who was soon more intimately befriended by Roald. The marriage dragged on for several years, ending in a 1983 divorce with a lot of bad press for Roald. He married Crosland that same year.

Pat's portrayal of her ex-husband in her 1988 autobiography *As I Am* is savage to the point of character assassination. Dahl told his own story through 1941 in two well-received reminiscences, *Boy: Tales of Childhood* and *Going Solo*. Having suffered at the hands of highbrow critics, he got some of his own back in 1989 when he blasted the Booker Awards as elitist.

Dahl died in Oxford on November 23, 1990.

Literary Analysis

A *New York Times* reviewer once noted that "Mr. Dahl could be a cult without half trying." Dahl has his cult following, but he has also been subjected to enormous amounts of damnation by faint praise. The jury is still out. If his enthusiasts are lavish in their admiration, his detractors are stinging in their attacks. Much of this may be a matter of taste: *de gustibus non est disputandum*. Dahl's carefully wrought stories for adults employ a tone reminiscent of Saki and endings so cleverly unexpected that they evoke O. Henry. Neither Saki nor O. Henry enjoys great status among the literati, though their stories certainly entertained vast readerships. Perhaps because his stories blend the commonplace with the macabre (or because so many appeared in the *New Yorker*), Dahl is often likened to the cartoonist Charles Addams, another icon of modern pop culture.

A meticulous craftsman who worked hours daily writing in "spidery longhand" to produce about three stories a year, Dahl's narrative flair is unquestioned. Still, the reservations of his more scathing critics are daunting.

Victoria Glendinning said, "It is all perhaps a little slick." J.D. O'Hara wrote that "As *Playboy* neutralizes pornography with an airbrush, so Dahl sweetens nastiness into mild amusement." Paul Levy accused Dahl of writing in "a rare dialect of English—publisher's Mid-Atlantic." Joyce Carol Oates called his stories "professional in form and execution—smooth and seamless and totally undisturbing . . . almost frightening and almost amusing, crafted along old-fashioned lines of 'suspense,' peopled with characters who are given proper names and one or two characteristics."

Dahl's admirers seem to be reading another writer entirely. One insists that he "is incapable of the pornographic, the second-rate. What he *is* capable of is so shattering that I cannot find a word for it, but it is always in excessively good taste—which makes it worse!" Writing in the *Kenyon Review*, James P. Degnan said that Dahl's stories are, "despite their lack of pretension, a great deal more profound in their insight into human nature than much fiction passing as profundity today."

There is a middle view, too, typified by the complaint of Granville Hicks that the plot tricks tend to deteriorate into "mere formula" but that Dahl remains "an uncommonly entertaining writer." Some of the difficulty in evaluating Dahl's accomplishment is related to the fate of his genre in the post-war marketplace. With fewer and fewer places to publish short stories, an enormous abyss developed between the handful of commercial magazines that paid very well and the handful of literary magazines that paid only in prestige and a couple of contributor's copies. Dahl confronted the commercial pressures to conform in his story "The Great Automatic Grammatisor." In it, an author with nine starving children can have a "golden contract" if only he agrees to put his name on mechanically-produced drivel which will be as popular as it is mediocre. This story does not have a trick ending. Instead, it ends with an ironic plea for artistic integrity: "Give us strength, oh Lord, to let our children starve."

Dahl invented the word "gremlin" for a juvenile story that he wrote during World War II (a gremlin being an imp who delighted in creating mechanical problems in fighter planes). Fearing that he might go stale if he wrote only stories for adults, Dahl began to write children's books in the early 1960s. Millions of young readers were enchanted by *James and the Giant Peach*, *Charlie and the Chocolate Factory*, and their many successors. Adult reaction was yet more violently mixed than it had been in evaluations of his stories for grownups. The wit was often wickedly macabre, and the language occasionally less than genteel. Some reviewers, librarians, and educators expressed outrage. While Dahl's many works for young readers are not as consistent as his tales for adults, at their best they are so delightful that they will certainly endure to be read as long as children can be enticed away from the television long enough to crack the covers of a book, and they remain very popular with his young audience.

The electronic age has been kind to Dahl in several ways. Disappointed, perhaps embittered by the failure of his play *The Honeys* in 1953, Dahl was to enjoy much greater success as a screenwriter. His first produced script was an adaptation of Ian Fleming's James Bond adventure *You Only Live Twice* (starring Sean Connery) in 1967. It was Dahl's first non-original work, but it had many of his own inventions, including the volcano missile bunker, at the time reputed to be the most expensive single set ever built. In the curious way of the Hollywood marketplace, Dahl was paid more for this one script than his Oscar-winning wife had earned in all her movies. He went on to adapt Fleming's juvenile *Chitty Chitty Bang Bang* (1968) and his own *Willy Wonka and the Chocolate Factory* (1971).

Television has also been good for Dahl and vice versa. A series based on twenty-two of his stories was produced under the title *Tales of the Unexpected*. His marvelous *Danny: The Champion of the World* was made as a sort of family affair with Jeremy Irons, his son, and his father-in-law.

Dahl's non-fiction includes two volumes of reminiscences—*Boy: Tales of Childhood*, and *Going Solo*, about his experiences working for Shell Oil in East Africa and flying in combat in the early years of the war. About *Boy*, Dahl made a precise distinction: "This is not an autobiography. I would never write a history of myself." Instead, he wrote about his most vivid memories, discarding everything else as tedious until he came to the war when "there was no need to select or discard because every moment was, to me at any rate, totally enthralling." Each volume of memories includes snapshots.

Summary

A most perceptive observation about Roald Dahl's writing was made by a writer for the *Spectator*: "Dahl exhibits a conscience without being sanctimonious about it." His satiric wit redeems his morality tales from any taint of the merely didactic. Naomi Lewis in the *New Statesman* put it this way: "These really are moral tales. Go wrong and you get some very peculiar deserts." Defending his works for young people, Dahl insisted that "my nastiness is never gratuitous. It's retribution. Beastly people must be punished." A fan like Barry Farrell makes rather more ambitious claims about Dahl's literary achievement: "The short stories were all sculpted from large ideas, and their structure imposed a fine tension between humor on the one hand and grinning-skull horror on the other, a tension kept alive by the texture of the language and the subtle, inevitable tone of the secret moralist; they were stories of truth and consequence."

Selected Bibliography
Primary Sources

Short Story Collections
Over to You: Ten Stories of Flyers and Flying. London: Reynal, 1946.
Someone Like You. New York: Knopf, 1953.
Kiss, Kiss. New York: Knopf, 1960.
Switch Bitch. New York: Knopf, 1974.
Taste and Other Tales. London: Longman, 1979.

Juveniles
The Gremlins. New York: Random House, 1943.
James and the Giant Peach. New York: Knopf, 1961.
Charlie and the Chocolate Factory. New York: Knopf, 1964.
The Magic Finger. New York: Harper, 1966.
Fantastic Mr. Fox. New York: Knopf, 1970.
Danny: The Champion of the World. New York: Knopf, 1975.
The Enormous Crocodile. New York: Knopf, 1976.
The Twits. Jonathan Cape, 1980.
Revolting Rhymes. Jonathan Cape, 1983.
The Witches. Farrar, Straus, and Giroux, 1983.
The BFG. Clio Press, 1989 (reprint of 1982 edition).

Novels
Sometime Never: A Fable for Supermen. New York: Scribner's, 1948.
My Uncle Oswald. London: M. Joseph, 1979.

Screenplays
You Only Live Twice. United Artists, 1967.
Chitty Chitty Bang Bang. United Artists, 1968.
The Night-Digger. Metro-Goldwyn-Mayer, 1970.
Willy Wonka and the Chocolate Factory. Paramount, 1971.

Memoirs
Boy: Tales of Childhood. London: Farrar Straus Giroux, 1984; New York: Penguin, 1988.
Going Solo. London: Farrar Straus Giroux, 1986; New York: Penguin, 1987.

Secondary Sources
Farrell, Barry. *Pat and Roald.* New York: Random House, 1969.
"Gipsy House." *House and Garden* (January 11, 1988).
Neal, Patricia. *As I Am.* New York: Simon and Schuster, 1988.
"Not a Chivalrous Affair." *The New Republic* (October 31, 1983): 7.
People (June 27, 1983).
"Roald Dahl." *Contemporary Authors.* Vol. 1. Ed. James M. Ethridge and Barbara Kopala. Detroit: Gale, 1967, pp. 223–24.
"Roald Dahl." *Contemporary Literary Criticism.* Vol. 1. Ed. Carolyn Riley. Detroit: Gale, 1973, p. 71.
"Roald Dahl." *Contemporary Literary Criticism.* Vol. 6. Ed. Carolyn Riley and Phyllis Mendelson. Detroit: Gale, 1976, pp. 121–22.
"Roald Dahl." *Contemporary Literary Criticism.* Vol. 18. Ed. Sharon Gunton. Detroit: Gale, 1981, pp. 108–109.

Ken Lawless

D'Arcy, Ella

Born: London, August 4, 1857
Education: Formal education in English and Continental schools, and at the Slade School of Art, 1880–1881
Died: London, September 5, 1937

Biography

A daughter of Anthony Byrne D'Arcy and Sophia D'Arcy, Constance Eleanor Mary Byrne D'Arcy was born in London on August 4, 1857. Few particulars of her life are known. She re-ceived a formal education at English and Continental schools, and she trained for a career in painting at the Slade School of Art (1880–1881), but defective eyesight forced her to seek other means of livelihood, so she turned to literature. She published short stories in many of the best-known magazines of her day, including *Blackwood's, Temple Bar,* the [London] *Argosy, Good Words, Century,* and *The English Review.* Interestingly, many of these pieces were published under the pseudonym Gilbert H. Page. D'Arcy's greatest renown resulted from her connection with *The Yellow Book,* that famous, or notorious, hardcover quarterly (1894–1897) published by John Lane at the Bodley Head, edited by Henry Harland and, for the first several volumes, with covers and illustrations by Aubrey Beardsley. D'Arcy worked as a sub-editor for this publication, assisting with design and layout. She died in London on September 5, 1937.

Literary Analysis

D'Arcy's initial ventures into fiction writing—that is, in the stories that she published between 1890 and April 1894, when "Irremediable" caused outcries from staid readers and reviewers of the first volume of *The Yellow Book*—offer much in the way of a fairly genial humor centered mainly in Anglo-Irish urban life, with which she was familiar at first hand, or else in contrasts between urban and rural situations. Her later works also feature comic touches, although frequently the mirth comes with an absolute razor edge of irony in order to make more pointed the tragedies involved. Interestingly, her one published, and brief, novel, *The Bishop's Dilemma* (1898) appeared years after she first began work on it. The reader's report, prepared in 1892 for the Scottish firm of Blackwood, commented on the fine humor in that piece and endorsed publication, but why D'Arcy elected to delay remains a mystery.[1]

High quality humorous writing was hard to come by during this era, according to L.F. Austin, who in reviewing Ella Hepworth Dixon's much touted novel, *The Story of a Modern Woman* (1894), lamented the dearth of "real humour, the blessed thing which is so casual a visitant in women's novels" (*Illustrated London News* [August 25, 1894]: 238). Specific influences upon D'Arcy's writings are difficult to pinpoint, although her contemporaries and a few later literary historians were quick to remark that she followed in the footsteps of the Guy de Maupassant school or in those of Henry James (whose style she missed no opportunity to lambast). Just how strong the Maupassant impact was upon English fiction writers during the 1890s has been questioned by some critics. In her fiction and letters we find D'Arcy alluding to O.W. Holmes, Emil Zola, Edgar Allen Poe, Thomas Carlyle, and Maupassant.[2] D'Arcy might have indeed learned much from Maupassant's biting ironies concerning humans' interactions; her own stories frequently highlight such ironic conditions.

What may now be seen as D'Arcy's predilections toward foregrounding ill-starred love matches and other ironic and tragic circumstances appeared at the outset of her literary work. Granted, tragedy is minimal in "An April Folly," her first *Argosy* piece (April 1891), which presents a deft case of working an April Fool's Day joke into an amusing story in diary form. The plot reversal is well handled. Katherine, the narrator's beloved, tells him on April 1, 1890 that she doesn't "like" him, and, on a rebound, he retreats into the country where, for a time, he inveighs against the wiles and thoughtlessness of urban women. Charmed by Annie, the attractive daughter in his host's farm family, he mentally weighs the pro's and con's of marrying her, betraying his egotism and priggishness throughout:

> [She would be] an amiable and adoring little wife, who would forestall my slightest wish, who would warm my slippers for me, for whom I should be the Alpha and Omega of existence—she would give into my keeping, as a good wife should, the key of her smiles and of her tears. But of course I should wish her to laugh. I should wish the dear little creature to remain as merry and thoughtless as possible. (341)

He is shocked when he discovers that she is engaged to a neighboring farmer, a young man whom she has known all her life. His discomfiture rapidly vanishes, however, when a note from Katherine informs him that although she had teased about not liking him she actually loves him dearly—and so he prepares to return to marry her. The diary structure suits the narrator's shifting emotions; the comedy arises from our realizing the disparities between his outward demeanor of calm and stoicism and his inner turmoil.

Equally satisfactory in the end, "Unqualified Assistance" (*Argosy*, July 1892) features a first-person narrator, Arthur Goodchilde, whose hopes for a high-ranking medical career are dashed, and whose emotional intensities instead become channeled toward marriage with a governess for the family of the doctor who employs him as an assistant. The governess, Miss Merriman, is supposed to marry before she reaches age twenty-one or forfeit a substantial inheritance. She rapidly comes to prefer Arthur to her cousin Robert—who wishes to marry her, she says, only because he does not wish her godmother's legacy to escape her. Matters come to a head when Arthur's hitherto domineering Aunt Laetitia writes, requesting him to come home and prevent annoyances from housebreakers. Since he cannot leave Madge—Miss Merriman—behind, they both give notice to their employers and move to his home, where his aunt also dowers him handsomely. Other, similar stories of comedy amidst servant life in urban households are "Kensington Minor" (*Argosy*, April 1893) and "Kathleen: Maid of All Work" (*Good Words*, November 1894). In the former a secretary who pretends that he is master and that his employer is his servant is unmasked and his hopes for a good marriage frustrated. The latter numbers among the most cheerful of D'Arcy's works, sketching the vicissitudes besetting a strong-willed, not-too-intelligent, Irish girl who works in a London household. By the neighbors, a phonograph salesman, and even the family dog, Kathleen is propelled into hilarious reactions. Her dialect intensifies the comic substance in this tale, a trademark of much humorous writing on both sides of the Atlantic during the 1890s.

A kind of sad companion to these pieces exists in the more tragically oriented story, "The 'Elegie,'" originally in *Blackwood's Edinburgh Magazine* (November 1891), later collected in *Monochromes* (1895). This tale outlines the German Schoenemann's egotistical career as a music composer, to which he willingly sacrifices his family life, all friendship, and his one great love affair. This account of an artist-protagonist falls well within mainstreams of character and situation presentations in fiction at the turn of the century. Like a story by James, "The 'Elegie'" delineates the ironies consequent upon the principal character's undertaking an artis-

D

tic life at the expense of his humanity. Touches of humor are bleak in the portrayal of ever more stark incongruities between Schoenemann's indifference to his family and friend, who experience variations of death-in-life because of his coldness, on through his fiancee's emotional and physical isolation from normal life to her actual death. The Graf Dittenheim's cynical remarks during his interview with Schoenemann as a prospective son-in-law are amusing. The Graefin accuses her husband of viewing life as a stage play, and indeed the motifs of masking that pervade this story contribute that kind of dramatic aura to it. Smug in the thought that Marie, the young daughter of Graf Dittenheim, will unswervingly await his return after seven years separation as stipulated in the Graf's bargain with him, Schoenemann is astounded to learn, as the time concludes, that Marie has agreed to marry another, albeit by this time he no longer wishes to marry her. He is shocked far more severely when he goes to upbraid her, only to discover that she has died. These emotional upheavals provide the inspiration for his greatest musical work, the "Elegie." Marie's father's prediction, that the waiting period will cool the youthful and that passionate romance (he dislikes the notion of his daughter's marrying a commoner and measures young Schoenemann's powers of faithfulness accurately) will terminate before any marriage takes place proves to be true with an ironic event that he did not foresee, that is, his child's dying. The division numerals indicate shifts in mood and direction as Schoenemann's life unfolds.

Another type of humor, that found in names, also makes for amusement, albeit of an astringent kind, in D'Arcy's fiction. An *Argosy* story, "A Modern Incident" (November 1891) centers on an ocean voyage, a shipwreck, and the aftermath, to point up the isolation and indifference frequently encountered in contemporary society. The first mate's name, appropriately, is Fleet, a transparency of no great imagination. The supercargo (or officer who handles commercial concerns), Tennyson Tupper, bears names that hit satirically at two extremely influential Victorians, the Poet Laureate, Lord Tennyson, and Martin Farquar Tupper, another popular poet of the times. D'Arcy's Tupper, we quickly divine from his conversation, resembles the actual Tupper (and the conception of Tennyson among his hostile critics) in loftily offering platitudes concerning spiritualizing the conduct of everyday life and

in offering second-rate verse as a panacea for the world's trials. In line with these allusions to well-known writers, it may be no accident that the cook's name is Blake, after the poet whose work had sustained a renaissance during the later nineteenth century because of the enthusiasm of writers like the Rossetti brothers and Algernon Swinburne. Tupper and another passenger, Dr. Macnab, exchange wisecracks during dinner, most of them centering on the plight of a pitiful stowaway revealed to the captain, whose wrath knows no bounds. The miserable stowaway is ill, and the captain predicts that he will not enjoy a long life. Suddenly the ship runs aground on a reef, confusion ensues, the limited number of life preservers go to all but the captain, and ironically only Tupper and the stowaway survive—ironically because they seem least fitted for survival. Exchanging "glances of contempt and hatred, [they] crept off in different directions . . . And there, like certain noxious plant-growths, each in his separate sphere thrives apace to this day" (386). Thus, we behold the quick dropping of masks as we as seeming individuals confront life's grim realities. We might also wonder whether D'Arcy's story may in part have inspired Stephen Crane's "The Open Boat" (1898), whatever his personal experiences involving being cast adrift on frightening seas may have been.

Similar humor occurs in "Unqualified Assistance." The narrator's name, Arthur Goodchilde, along with his activities, suggests the questing of the legendary King Arthur, and because the names of children in another story, "At Twickenham" (*The Yellow Book*, January 1897; rpt. *Modern Instances*, 1898), are Lancelot, Hugo, and Guinevere—two of them, to be sure, hinting at the author's acquaintance with Arthurian lore—we cannot overlook the possibilities of D'Arcy's intentionally having fun with this kind of naming. Moreover, a marriage between persons named Goodchilde and Merriman suggests a deft blending of personality traits. Here and elsewhere the name Laetitia for one who remains unadmired and that of Willoughby in "Irremediable" (*The Yellow Book*, April 1894; rpt. *Monochromes*, 1895) alert us to D'Arcy's familiarity with George Meredith's famous comic novel, *The Egoist* (1879), which she did not hesitate to quarry for her own purposes in humor.[3]

A variant on this type of comedy appears in a later story; "Sir Julian Garve" (*The Yellow Book*, April 1897) includes a caricature of

Henry Harland, editor of *The Yellow Book* and a good friend of D'Arcy's, in the young American Francis Underhill whose features closely resemble Harland's, notably as D'Arcy would later describe them in her reminiscences, "Yellow Book Celebrities," written in the 1920s.[4] The distinction between the non-fiction essay and the story is that in the latter Underhill, who has discovered Garve's cheating at the gaming table, is shot by the gambler without warning to prevent exposure of his duplicity. "Sir Julian Garve" and "A Modern Incident" align with *roman à clef* fiction popular during the 1890s such as Robert Hichens's lampooning of Oscar Wilde and Lord Alfred Douglas in *The Green Carnation* (1895) and James's gentler takeoff upon the popular, if notorious, woman writer, "George Egerton" (Mary Chavelita Dunne Bright), as Guy Walsingham in his story "The Death of the Lion" (1894).

Mirth of sharper acridity than encountered in most of the stories mentioned above is far more customary in D'Arcy's writing, however. *The Bishop's Dilemma*, one of her earliest experiments though not published till 1898, represents this mordant humor. Young Father Fayler, a Catholic priest, is assigned by his bishop to a country chapel dominated by elderly and bigoted Lady Welford, and he rapidly, although not without anguish because of his calling, falls in love with her ward, Mary. Detecting their feelings, the mean-spirited old lady sends Mary away and requests that the bishop relocate Father Fayler. The young priest appears to be one of D'Arcy's typically emotionally overwrought and physically weak characters, and he is unlikely to live long in his new post in an unhealthy area where his duties will be severely taxing. His name may be yet another of D'Arcy's well-chosen ironic transparencies. The cruel ironies that ruin the young lovers are balanced by comedy in the drunken antics of another priest with whom Fayler had earlier worked and who visits him in his country residence. Nonetheless, Catholicism is depicted unsympathetically in this novelette of grim realism.

An offset to such unremitting tragedy may be found in D'Arcy's only altogether humorous story of the Channel Islands, "White Magic," from *The Yellow Book* (October 1894), collected in *Monochromes*. Mr. Mauger, a canny pharmacist, comments to his off-island friend that nineteenth-century science is no match for lingering, but strong, island superstitions, citing as a case in point his duping of a young woman, whose thoughtless, but harmless, playfulness at a Sunday school picnic had alienated her proud, imperious lover. The girl asks Mauger for a preparation which, according to local lore, will be useful in determining her future with the angry young man. Mauger gives her a harmless preparation but tells her to apologize to her wounded swain. She does, and the story concludes with Mauger and his friend beholding the young pair, obviously reunited and happy with each other, returning from an afternoon's pleasurable sailing. A kindred story of restored love after a season of uncertainty, "Our Lady of Antibes" (*Century Magazine*, November 1899), emphasizes two significant encounters. In the first a girl and her mother journey to a religious shrine in hopes of determining the girl's future husband—which determination is presumably revealed to the girl alone. In the second, which concludes the piece, the girl and her lover discuss the future, she angers him by seeming to prefer another, and, quite surprisingly, the long-suffering man, who has endured overmuch from his coquettish mistress, flings a bouquet of flowers into her face, tells her to marry another if she wishes, and the outcome is that she flings herself upon him, protesting that she has loved him greatly all along and has been foolish enough to resist her destiny.

Far more biting ironies enliven some of D'Arcy's other, perhaps better known, stories. Her most famous, "Irremediable" (*The Yellow Book*, April 1894; rpt. *Monochromes*) delineates an ill-starred marriage between young Willoughby, on holiday in the country, and Esther, a girl from a lower social class who is temporarily residing with her aunt and thus far removed from her London place of employment, an unpleasant tailoring establishment. Willoughby's initial impulses to improve Esther's lot and ensure their married happiness (in which, for him, at least, sexual attraction appears to play a strong part) soon come to grief. Esther will not adapt to his notions of social graces or intellectual companionship, and at the end of the story Willoughby is soured by dislike and yet unable to free himself from the destructive circumstances. His earlier sureness about the good in the upcoming marriage has wholly disappeared.

Another rendering of similar circumstances, "A Marriage" (*The Yellow Book*, October 1896), collected in *Modern Instances*, 1898) illustrate the linear progression of an af-

D

fair between Catterson and his lower-class mistress through their marriage to a point at which his death (from tuberculosis) seems near. All of his former boasts to his cynical, worldly-wise friend, West, regarding Nettie's dependence upon him, her ardent love, and her domestic abilities, give way in the face of her increasing social climbing, her officious displays of their wealth, her detestation for their son (who will inherit Catterson's estate) and preference for their first child, Gladys, born out of wedlock, and her hostility toward her husband.

A pendant story, "An Engagement" (*The Yellow Book*, January 1896), collected in *Modern Instances,* chronicles the fortunes of the aggressive Dr. Owen, newly come to the Channel Islands, indifferent to his patients' plights and needs, and not at all loath to break an engagement to young, pretty, and innocent Agnes Allez, whom he had supposed to be an heiress but whose uncertain prospects quickly make her unattractive in his eyes. His crassness ultimately brings about the girl's death from sunstroke, leaving her widowed grandmother with a mentally deficient grandson as her sole companion. Several attendant bits of humor occur in this story. Owen's predecessor taunts him sarcastically about his relationship with Agnes, reminding him about Margo, his sexually rampant mistress. The doctor and the girl had appeared in D'Arcy's first Channel Island story, "Poor Cousin Louis" (*The Yellow Book*, July 1894, collected in *Monochromes*), in which Margo's sadistic propensities for playing horrifying jokes upon a feeble and senile old man assist in bringing about his death. Her red hair and rampant sexuality mark her out as a devil figure, although D'Arcy characterizes the girl such that her realistic psychological makeup rather than any supernatural qualities are made frightening. Her obvious physical intent toward Owen and his past willing responses are emphasized as part of their inhumane activities. Owen departs to let old Louis Renouf's servants murder him, and we are confident that Margo will have no small part in causing that death. Ironically, anyone not intimately connected with the Renouf household would think that both were trying to serve the old man's best interests. Overriding irony infuses the progression from a sunny, edenic opening—in which the viewpoint of Louis Poidevin, Renouf's imperceptive cousin, prevails—on through a series of psychological reversals to the horrifying night scene (dominated by Owen's inhumane viewpoint about the death of old Renouf) that closes the tale.

"The Pleasure-Pilgrim," a story that occasioned considerable comment in the press when it first appeared in *The Yellow Book* (April 1895) may serve as a final example of D'Arcy's deft artistry as an ironist. This tale of an American girl abroad, thematically much like many of James's works, is structured around the counter-views of Lulie Thayer, the wealthy young American traveler, presented by two other visitors to the German resort where they meet. Campbell, a British writer who has returned to this spot for respite from his work, is simultaneously astonished by Lulie's forward behavior toward him (he is painfully shy) and attracted to her physical charms (notably her red hair and her eyes). His boon companion, Mayne, married, cynical, and clearly antagonistic toward Lulie, manages to persuade Campbell that she's little more than an adventuress, one who likes to count up the men who have been her lovers without any reciprocal feeling toward any of them. We are left to wonder if the girl is actually a product of what Europeans would have considered American openness, with the freedom and boldness that they discerned in such a background, or if she genuinely cares for Campbell. We are left to wonder, too, if her shooting herself is deliberate or unwitting. Since she had been characterized as a New Woman out of the West (i.e., an American version of a strong feminist), additional ambiguities surround her portraiture. The story ends with Mayne's theorizing about Lulie, confident that her primary traits were those of an actress. In such a context the masking motifs central to so much artistic expression during the 1890s are subtly employed by D'Arcy to create an open-ended story in the Jamesian manner, despite her caveats about his style. Lulie's red hair and her forwardness with men may mark her out as a sensualist—if not such a devil-figure as Margot—but we are left to ponder the probabilities of her genuine, if sudden, affections for Campbell and the disparities arising out of his misunderstanding them. Mayne's flippant, off-handed dismissal of Lulie's emotional makeup marks a final high peak of irony in this chronicle of ill-starred love, a theme that invites ironic presentations.

Summary

Ella D'Arcy's humorous touches are not at all like those uproarious passages created by Mark

Twain, one of the most widely known comic writers of her time. In her use of unheroic character types and colloquial speech she bears rather closer kinship to the New Humorists of the 1890s, although she never mentioned any acquaintance with them or their works. Her mirth never achieves the belly-laugh stage; instead, she adds ironic touches to what are usually tragic stories. Thus, she resembles Thomas Hardy in treating life's ironies, just as she reminds us of Florence Farr, an actress whose novel, *The Dancing Faun* (1894), was likened in John Lane's Keynotes Series to the astringent comedy in Oscar Wilde's plays, as D'Arcy's *Monochromes* was, and of Evelyn Sharp, another of Lane's coterie, whose comic underpinnings for harsh situations were repeatedly noticed. Many of D'Arcy's contemporary readers ignored the comic touches in her fiction, although now and then a reviewer was wont to notice them. In fact, "The Pleasure-Pilgrim" was repeatedly thought to be a satiric thrust at James or as a hit at the New Woman figure so popular at the time. Overall, though, D'Arcy created reasonably straightforward stories of Anglo-Irish life in which comic upsets would have been a recognizable literary stereotype, and she comprehended the concept of dramatic relief and thus used ironic comedy to leaven the otherwise overwhelming senses of dislocation and isolation in her stories.

Notes

1. This report is in the Blackwood papers in the National Library of Scotland—to which institution I render thanks for permitting me to examine this document and D'Arcy's correspondence with the firm. I also acknowledge debts of gratitude to Mr. Alan Anderson of Loanhead, Scotland, and to Dr. G. Krishnamurti of London for their graciously supplying me with information concerning D'Arcy.
2. D'Arcy specifically alludes to Maupassant in a supernatural story, "The Villa Lucienne," *The Yellow Book*, 10 (July 1896): 274–84; rpt. *Modern Instances* (London and New York: John Lane, 1898): 183–98. See Benjamin Franklin Fisher, "Ella D'Arcy: A Commentary with a Primary and Annotated Secondary Bibliography," *English Literature in Transition* (August 30, 1992): 4; and George J. Worth, "The English 'Maupassant School' of the 1890's: Some

Reservations," *Modern Language Notes*, 72 (May 1957): 337–40.
3. Fisher, "Ella D'Arcy," p. 187.
4. "Yellow Book Celebrities" is incorporated into Benjamin Franklin Fisher, "Ella D'Arcy Reminisces," *English Literature in Transition*, 37 (January 1994).

Selected Bibliography
Primary Sources

Uncollected Stories
As Gilbert H. Page
"An April Folly." *Argosy*, 51 (April 1891): 334–44; rpt. *Living Age* (May 30, 1891): 506–12.
"The Smile." *Argosy*, 52 (October 1891): 348–51.
"A Modern Incident." *Argosy*, 52 (November 1891): 381–86.
"Unqualified Assistance." *Argosy*, 54 [Summer Supplement No. 76] (July 1892): 76–87.
"In a Cathedral." *Argosy*, 54 (December 1892): 532–36.
"Kensington Minor." *Argosy*, 55 (April 1893): 345–52.
"Kathleen: Maid of All Work." *Good Words*, 35 (November 1894): 779–84.
As Ella D'Arcy
"Our Lady of Antibes." *Century Magazine*, 59 [n.s. 37] (November 1899): 51–57.
"In Normandy." *Temple Bar*, 130 (December 1904): 690–712.
"Agatha Blount." *English Review*, 2 (June 1909): 435–70.
"From the Chronicles of Hildesheim." *English Review*, 3 (November 1909): 619–28.
"Every Day Brings a Ship." *English Review*, 4 (February 1910): 429–55.
"An Enchanted Princess." *English Review*, 5 (December 1910): 30–46; rpt. *Living Age* (January 28, 1911): 232–42; *Turn-of-the-Century Women*, 3 (Summer 1986): 3–14.

Books
Ella D'Arcy: Some Letters to John Lane. Ed. Alan Anderson. Edinburgh: Tragara Press, 1990.
Monochromes. London: John Lane, and Boston: Roberts Brothers, 1895; New York: Garland, 1984.
The Bishop's Dilemma. London and New York: John Lane, 1898.

Modern Instances. London and New York: John Lane, 1898; New York: Garland, 1984.

Ariel, the Life of Shelley. London: John Lane; New York: D. Appleton, 1924; New York: Frederick Ungar, 1952.

Secondary Sources

Anon. "Our Short Story Writers. II." *Pall Mall Gazette* (August 30, 1895): p. 4. The variety in contemporary short story, uses of tragic, comic, dramatic, and pictorial elements are noted.

Austin, Louis F. "Art is One Volume." *Illustrated London News* (August 25, 1894): p. 238. Evaluates Ella Hepworth Dixon's popular novel treating women's issues, *The Story of a Modern Woman*, and applauding its humor.

Fisher, Benjamin Franklin IV. "Ella D'Arcy: A Commentary with a Primary and Annotated Secondary Bibliography." *English Literature in Transition*, 32, 2 (1992): 179–211. Amplest bibliographical treatment of D'Arcy to date, listing uncollected and pseudonymously published items and considerable secondary materials. "Commentary" outlines her life and career, along with terse analyses of her writing. She's not intent on theme alone, as were many of her contemporaries, but, like Hubert Crackanthorpe, she devotes much art to structure and, in the trend of short-story writing at the turn of the century, she creates prose poems. Readers should also be alert to her humor.

———. "Ella D'Arcy, First Lady of the Decadents." *The University of Mississippi Studies in English*, n.s. 10 (1992): 238–49. Brief overview of D'Arcy's personal and career situations, with more extensive critiques of her fiction.

———. "Ella D'Arcy Reminisces." *English Literature in Transition*, 37 (January 1994).

Mix, Katherine Lyon. *A Study in Yellow: The Yellow Book and Its Contributors.* Lawrence: University of Kansas Press, 1960. Reminiscences and critical-historical evaluations by one who knew D'Arcy in her last years.

Worth, George J. "The English 'Maupassant School' of the 1890's: Some Reservations." *Modern Language Notes*, 72

(May 1957): 337–40. Questions the attribution of large debts of British fictionists to the Frenchman.

Benjamin F. Fisher

Deloney, Thomas

Born: Norwich (?), ca. 1560
Education: Not known
Marriage: Probably married; one probable child
Died: Perhaps at Newbury, late in 1599 or early in 1600

Biography

Nothing is known of Thomas Deloney before he began his public career as a pamphleteer and ballad monger. He is thought to have been born in Norwich not much later than 1560 and perhaps considerably earlier. There is no record of a formal education, but since he knew Latin he presumably attended grammar school, and he must have been apprenticed as a silk weaver because he is known to have been employed at that trade. From his name, his strong anti-Catholic views, and his occupation, it seems probable that he belonged to a family of Flemish refugees who settled in East Anglia to escape French persecution of Protestants. Several of his works show a familiarity with French books that had not been translated in his day, so he may well have picked up a knowledge of French at home. He also seems to have been married, since on October 16, 1586, a Richard Deloney, son to Thomas, Weaver, was christened at St. Giles, Cripplegate.

The earliest work attributed to Deloney is a 1683 translation of the Latin broadside in which the Archbishop of Cologne announced his intention to marry and to allow the "free exercise of the preaching of the Gospel" in his Electorate. Deloney wrote one other extant religious work, an epic poem *Canaans Calamitie: Jerusalems Misery; or, The Dolefull Destruction of the Faire Jerusalem by Titus, the Sonne of Vaspasian Emperour of Rome in the Year of Christs Incarnation 74*; this is sometimes erroneously attributed to Thomas Dekker.

Although Deloney appears to have begun his writing career with a religious treatise, he shortly afterward turned to humorous ballads. Unfortunately, most of these have perished, although his early ballads on contemporary murder cases have survived—*The Garland of Good Will* is a collection of these early ballads. His murder case ballads were so characteristic that in 1589 a satirist was able to write that "Deloney . . . mourningly doth speake" when he writes "hempen tragedy" in which "massacre's made of . . . balladry." Deloney was quickly acknowledged as the most popular balladeer of his day, a successor to William Elderton, whose career was just drawing to an end at this time.

Deloney's ballads became the standard by which others were judged, and in 1592 in *The Defence of Conny Catching,* Robert Greene seems to refer to Deloney with his glancing reference to "Such triviall trinkets and threedbare trash" as is produced by "T.D. whose braines [are] beaten to the yarking up of Ballades." His work as a balladeer was commented on more favorably by such formidable literary figures as Gabriel Harvey and Michael Drayton, who called his rhymes "full of state and pleasing." Thomas Nashe said of him, "Thomas Deloney, the balleting silke-weaver of Norwich, hath rime inough for all myracles." On the other hand, in 1596 Deloney was cited before the Lord Mayor as the maker of a "scurrilous Ballad" (which does not survive) complaining about the scarcity of corn (i.e., wheat). He had obviously become the English François Villon.

His novellas do not seem to have excited literary or political commentary in his own day, although in 1600 he was described by the actor Will Kempe in *Nine Daies Wonder* as having presented in his novels the lives of "honest men, omitted" by the chronicles. In the same work Kempe notes that Deloney had recently "died poorly" and been "honestly buried, which is much to be doubted of some" ballad writers. The exact date and place of Deloney's death are unknown, though he obviously died in late 1599 or early 1600, perhaps in Newbury.

Literary Analysis

Deloney's original popularity and primary reputation in his own day were the result of his work as a balladeer. Many of his ballads have disappeared, literally read to pieces, but a large and heterogeneous body of his work remains to show that Deloney was representative of his age in both style and subject. He is least successful with historical subjects (*Strange Histories of Kings, Princes, Dukes, Earls, Lords, Ladies, Knights, and Gentlemen* is a book-length collection of these tales) but very effective when writing about contemporary domestic tragedies, a staple of the genre since in the Renais-

sance the ballad served much the function that the supermarket tabloid plays today.

Although some of Deloney's surviving ballads are written with a light touch (many of his explicitly humorous ballads have perished), his humorous voice is much more evident in his fiction, and his enduring reputation is based on his work in this genre. His fiction is often called realistic but is so categorized primarily because of his depicting the language and some of the social conditions of middle-class life. His plotting is not realistic, nor is it novelistic.

A major development of prose as a medium for fiction occurred in the sixteenth century, and the novel (or novella) of this period is a necessary prelude to the modern novel. There was no direct conversion of the verse tale to the short story. Instead, the romance was first prosed, as in Sir Philip Sidney's *Arcadia,* and then closure (a sense of ending) was brought to this newly identified genre of prose romance. The intuition that there was a popular interest in narrative works with closure is probably the explanation of why the fiction of this period is often so short: the authors of the period apparently felt an urgency to bring their stories to a close.

Together with Nashe and Greene, Deloney is in the first generation of writers adapting the romance to the new requirements of prose and closure, and as in any period of innovation, new paradigms are sometimes aspired to with only indifferent success. Deloney in particular has a tendency to interrupt his narrative with ballad digressions, and he often leaves some elements of plot inadequately resolved. However, he is in advance of the other writers of his period in introducing realistic descriptions of the contemporary scene and in creating satire and humor from character and incident rather than just from wit and word play.

He is obviously struggling to find his genre even in his best work, *Thomas of Reading; or, The Sixe Worthie Yeomen of the West.* Here, as elsewhere in his fiction, the engaging realism of the history of the clothier's trade is intermingled with traditional romance material in which the heroine Margaret, daughter of the disgraced and exiled Earl of Shrewsbury, disguises herself as a serving girl and is wooed and won in this guise for her merit alone by the fallen Duke of Normandy. Even with such familiar romance elements, Deloney takes a novelistic turn toward psychological realism since even though the lovers are united at the end of the story it is

D

only with the qualification that the Duke's eyes are sewn closed by order of his brother the king to keep him out of further mischief. Yet, *Thomas of Reading* is Deloney's most carefully constructed plot. Even the digressive ballads so common in his other novels are kept to a minimum here. Furthermore, the ending shows a fully modern sense of closure with all of the various plot elements resolved satisfactorily and the subsequent careers of the various characters convincingly foretold just as they would be in the novels of Henry Fielding or Charles Dickens. Despite the heterogeneous material here and elsewhere, Deloney manages a uniformity of style and tone that always make him easy to read.

The key is that in all of his works Deloney is selecting romance materials that are compatible with middle-class tastes. He glories in the frankness of his adaptations of romance themes. While the Elizabethan period was an age of limited social mobility and Queen Elizabeth refused to create new peers, a merchant's daughter could marry a duke. Here was material for Deloney's new middle-class romance precisely because while such a thing did not happen very often in real life, it was a highly unlikely but just barely possible middle-class dream. Deloney must have had all of the fascination for his original readers that playing the lottery has for some people today. The establishment was not charmed by Deloney's possible if improbable middle-class success stories and preferred the traditional romance represented by Sidney's *Arcadia* with its princes disguised as shepherds wooing shepherdesses who are, correspondingly, princesses in disguise. Class tells in the traditional romance, but Deloney sends class distinctions on a "Shoemaker's Holiday" (Thomas Dekker's play of this name is based on one of the middle-class romance stories in Deloney's work *The Gentle Craft*; 1597).

Jack of Newbery (in full *The Pleasant Historie of John Winchomb, in His Yonguer Yeares Called Jack of Newbery, The Famous and Worthy Clothier of England; Declaring His Life and Love, Together with His Charitable Deeds and Great Hospitalitie;* 1597) features a hero, Jack of Newbery, who is so coy that he must be wooed by his mistresses. The novel is episodic in its construction, each of the eleven chapters telling what is essentially a self-contained humorous anecdote. Deloney's central theme in this loose chain of plotting is a tracing of a double rise of fortunes out of the work-

ing class which are a result of merit and unprompted by unsavory ambition. Jack the apprentice marries his master's widow. Of course, he proves fully worthy of the position thrust upon him. For him to have proved unworthy would have been to satirize or even condemn the dreams and aspiration of the working class.

Deloney is just as unrealistic and just as romantic in temperament as Sidney, although with very different fantasies to aspire to. When Jack's wife dies leaving him sole master of the looms, he does not take as his second wife any of the rich widows of the county but instead chooses a girl from his own staff of weavers. The image that perhaps best sums up Deloney's special combination of realistic detail with wistful improbability is that of Jack surrounded by all of the rich widows of the town offering themselves to him in vain.

In the real world of the sixteenth century and in the genuinely realistic writing of any age, what happens to a girl who has an affair with a knight? First she gets pregnant and then she is abandoned. The last story in *Jack of Newbery* is about just such a situation. Jack, however, takes care of his workers. He sets the girl up in London as a rich but enceinte young widow, and she drives her seducer, Sir George Riley, to a passion with her inaccessibility. Sir George cannot even get a good look at her, since she goes about veiled all the time in supposed token of her mourning. The plan works beautifully. Sir George becomes so obsessed by the unseen prize that he marries her. Then, when he discovers he has been tricked into marrying his discarded mistress, he has the good grace to accept the situation.

There is a fine indication of Deloney's eye for social detail in the last few lines of the work. When the newlyweds come to visit, Jack and his wife give precedence to them at table since the seduced and abandoned Joan is now a lady and she and her husband outrank them.

While Deloney is not a socialist, he is a middle-class apologist. He supports the common middle-class feeling that the social order is basically right and should be kept—although it would be nice to have a somewhat better place in it. Perhaps his chief trait is that he teaches good-humored acceptance of the way things are. He is a romantic because his heroes always find the possible if not particularly probable loopholes that exist in the system. Deloney's heroes are always generous and always good—generous to a fault, though never to a fall. Naturally, they can afford to be so because they live in a world in which good cheer triumphs.

Summary

While primarily famous in his own day as a balladeer, Thomas Deloney is today remembered for his short fiction. Though the short novels of the sixteenth century are in general suggestive precursors of the modern novel rather than direct antecedents, Deloney's works have more of a claim to a position in the line of development than those of his fellows. Deloney's novels show not only the plot closure characteristic of Elizabethan fiction but also the realistic depiction of contemporary manners, particularly middle-class manners, that is so much a part of the texture of the novel as it developed in the eighteenth and nineteenth centuries. He is also one of the few prose writers of the sixteenth century who is still accessible to the general reader. Because Deloney describes everything with a light satiric touch, Merritt E. Lawlis concludes that "Surely no other English writer of prose fiction of the sixteenth and seventeenth centuries can entertain us so well, and no other before Dickens gives us so many well-conceived and fully satisfying characters."

Nevertheless, Deloney is not really a novelist in the modern sense. He has exactly the right understanding of middle-class values and knows how to describe the options offered by the world realistically while at the same time calling attention to one-in-a-million opportunities of beating the odds. What he does not do is bring all of his plot elements to a neat resolution. In fact, his approach is exactly the opposite of that taken by his prose-writer contemporaries such as Thomas Lodge and Greene. These writers discover how to end a romance and thus bring a neat sense of conclusion to the sprawling works of medieval narrative, but they retain the full range of medieval hierarchical sensibilities, including the suggestion that it is never possible to change social conditions or to move from one social class to another. More than a century later, when Daniel Defoe, Samuel Richardson, and Fielding finally come to understand how to combine these two discoveries—narrative closure and the middle-class dream of upward mobility—the novel is born. Deloney's contribution was the dream. This is his importance in the history of the novel. He continues to be read not so much for his themes as for his rollicking good humor and engaging realistic style in presenting the middle-class dream of success.

Selected Bibliography

Primary Sources

The Novels of Thomas Deloney. Ed. Merritt E. Lawlis. Bloomington: Indiana University Press, 1961.

The Works of Thomas Deloney. Ed. Francis Oscar Mann. Oxford: Clarendon, 1912.

Thomas Deloney and The Mirrour of Mirth and Pleasant Conceits. Ed. O[le] R. Reuter. Helsinki: Soc. Scientiarum Fennica, 1982. Edition of English translation of *Nouvelles Recreations et joyeux devis* by Bonaventure des Periers, attributed to Deloney on linguistic grounds.

"Two Emendations of the Text of Merritt E. Lawlis's Edition of *The Novels of Thomas Deloney* (1961)." In Iiro Kajanto, Inna Koskenniemi, Esko Pennanen, and Hikka Aaltonen, eds. *Studies in Classical and Modern Philology.* Helsinki: Soumala Inen Tiedeakatemia, 1983, pp. 129–31.

Secondary Sources

Bache, William B. "'The Murder of Old Cole': A Possible Source for *Macbeth.*" *Shakespeare Quarterly*, 6 (1955): 358–59. Deloney may have been the source for Shakespeare's version of the murder of Duncan.

Bowers, Frederick. "A Transformational Description of the Elizabethan *be* + V-*ing.*" *Orbis*, 17 (1968): 23–33. Bowers uses Deloney for case study in linguistic analysis of the development of progressive verb forms because of his popular appeal and common origins.

Camp, Charles W. *The Artisan in Elizabethan Literature.* New York: Columbia University Press, 1924. Deloney provides important evidence of the lives and working conditions of artisans in the sixteenth century.

Chandler, W.K. "The Sources of the Characters in *The Shoemaker's Holiday.*" *Modern Philology*, 27 (1929): 175–82. A study of the adaptation of Deloney's book *The Gentle Craft* by Thomas Dekker.

Chevalley, Abel. *Thomas Deloney: Le Roman des metiers au temps de Shakespeare.* Paris: Nouvelle Revue Française [1926]. A study of Deloney emphasizing his realistic depiction of the lives of artisans.

Dahl, Torsten. *Linguistic Studies in Some Elizabethan Writings, I: A Inquiry into Aspects of the Language of Thomas Deloney*. Copenhagen: Munksgaard, 1951. Deloney is used for a case study in linguistic analysis because of his popular appeal and common origins.

———. *Linguistic Studies in Some Elizabethan Writings, II: The Auxiliary "Do."* Copenhagen: Munksgaard, 1956. Dahl uses Deloney for case study in linguistic analysis because of his popular appeal and common origins.

Davis, Walter R. *Idea and Act in Elizabethan Fiction*. Princeton: Princeton University Press, 1969. Deloney's work is a special instance which shows that realism and romance in Elizabethan fiction differ only in reportorial technique, not in plotting or theme.

Devine, Paul. "Unity and Meaning in Thomas Deloney's *Thomas of Reading*." *Neuphilologische Mitteilungen*, 87 (1986): 578–93. A description and appreciation of the artistry of *Thomas of Reading*.

Domnarski, William. "A Different Thomas Deloney: *Thomas of Reading* Reconsidered." *Renaissance and Reformation*, 6 [old series 18] (1982): 197–202. Praise of Deloney's penetrating social analysis.

Dorsinville, Max. "Design in Deloney's *Jack of Newbery*." *PMLA*, 88 (1973): 233–39. A description and appreciation of the artistry of *Jack of Newbery*.

Dunn, Charles W. "Weaver of Silk, Spinner of Tales: A Study of Thomas Deloney, Novelist." *McMaster University Quarterly* (April 1946): 49–55. A description and appreciation of the realistic depictions of artisan life in Deloney.

Ebbsworth, John Woodfall. "Deloney, Thomas (1543?-1600?)." *The Dictionary of National Biography*. Ed. Sir Leslie Stephen. 21 vols. London: Oxford University Press, 1885–90. Vol. 5, pp. 777–78. Brief scholarly biography and pioneering bibliography of original works.

Enrle, Rowland Esmund Prothero, Lord. *The Light Reading of Our Ancestors: Chapters in the Growth of the English Novel*. London: Hutchinson, 1927. A study of popular authors, including Deloney.

Garke, Esther. *The Use of Songs in Elizabethan Prose Fiction*. Bern: Francke, 1972. Includes an examination of Deloney's use of songs in his fiction.

Howarth, R[obert] G[uy]. *Two Elizabethan Writers of Fiction: Thomas Nashe and Thomas Deloney*. Cape Town: University of Cape Town Press, 1956. Despite the same attention to everyday life, Deloney's fiction is characterized by apparent artlessness, natural comedy, and respect for class and tradition in contrast to Nashe's, which is self-conscious, vehement, and sensational.

Jordan, Constance. "The 'Art of Clothing': Role-Playing in Deloney's Fiction." *English Literary Renaissance*, 11 (1981): 183–93. Over the course of Deloney's career, his fictional characters become increasingly disengaged from role-playing; the ineffectuality of his romantic characters suggests that he could not find—or make—the matter of romance interesting.

Lawlis, Merritt E. *Apology for the Middle Class: The Dramatic Novels of Thomas Deloney*. Bloomington: Indiana University Press, 1960. Lawlis argues that Deloney is the most entertaining fiction writer in English and that he has the most various characterization of any writer before Charles Dickens.

Mustazza, Leonard. "Thomas Deloney's *Jack of Newbury* (1596?): A Horatio Alger Story for the Sixteenth Century." *Journal of Popular Culture*, 23 (1989): 165–77. *Jack of Newbery* is seen as an exemplum of the Protestant work ethic.

O'Connell, Laura Stevenson. "The Elizabethan Bourgeois Hero-Tale: Aspects of an Adolescent Social Consciousness." In Barbara C. Malament, ed. *After the Reformation: Essays in Honor of J.H. Hexter*. Philadelphia: University of Pennsylvania Press, 1980, pp. 267–90. Deloney's Protestant work ethic and world view are found to be naive.

Parker, David. "*Jack of Newbery*: A New Source." *English Language Notes*, 10 (1973): 172–80. *Jack of Newbery* is modeled on the popular ballad "A Gest of Robyn Hode."

Patzold, Kurt-Michael. "Thomas Deloney and the English Jest-Book Tradition." *English Studies*, 53 (1972): 313–28. Deloney in the jest book tradition.

Reuter, Ole [R]. "Some Aspects of Thomas

Deloney's Prose Style." *Neuphilologische Mitteilungen*, 40 (1939): 23–72. A rhetorical study.

Reuter, O[le] R. *Proverbs, Proverbial Sentences and Phrases in Thomas Deloney*. Helsinki: Soc. Scientiarum Fennica, 1986. A rhetorical study of Deloney's proverb lore.

———. "Thomas Deloney's *Thomas of Reading* and *The Pinder of Wakefield*: An Attempt at Determining their Relative Chronology." *Neuphilologische Mitteilungen*, 77 (1976): 599–607. Questions the direction of the influence.

Roberts, Warren E. "Folklore in the Novels of Thomas Deloney." In *Studies in Folklore in Honor of Distinguished Service of Professor Stith Thompson*. Ed. W. Edson Richmond. Bloomington: Indiana University Press, 1957, pp. 119–29. A study of folkloric themes in Deloney's writing.

Rollins, Hyder E. "Deloney's Sources for Euphuistic Learning." *PMLA*, 51 (1936): 399–406. The influence of John Lyly on Deloney.

Schlauch, Margaret. *Antecedents of the English Novel, 1400–1600 (from Chaucer to Deloney)*. London: Oxford University Press, 1963. Deloney as the culminating author in the proto-history of the novel.

Schwegler, Robert A. "The Arthur Ballad: From Malory to Deloney to Shakespeare." *Essays in Literature* (Macomb IL), 5 (1978): 3–13. Source study of Malory in Deloney and Deloney in Shakespeare.

Simmons, John. *Realistic Romance: The Prose Fiction of Thomas Deloney*. Winchester: King Alfred's College, 1983. A study of realism and romance in the works of Deloney.

Wagenknecht, Edward. *Cavalcade of the English Novel, from Elizabeth to George VI*. New York: Holt, 1943. Deloney's important place in the proto-history of the novel.

Wright, Eugene P. *Thomas Deloney*. Boston: Twayne, 1981. Clear general survey of the life and works.

Edmund Miller

Dickens, Charles

Born: Landport, Portsmouth, February 7, 1812

Education: First lessons from his mother, then a "dame's school" in Rome Lane, followed by attendance at a school kept by William Giles, 1821–1823; several years at Wellington House Academy, Hampstead Road

Marriage: Catherine Hogarth, April 2, 1836; ten children

Died: Gad's Hill Place, June 9, 1870

Biography

On Friday, February 7, 1812, Charles John Huffam Dickens was born at 13 Mile End Terrace, Landport, Portsmouth, the second of eight children of John Dickens, a clerk in the Navy Pay Office, and Elizabeth Barrow Dickens. The next year, the family moved to London lodgings (possibly 10 Norfolk Street) because John had been transferred from Portsmouth to duties at Somerset House. In 1817, John moved again to Chatham, Kent where he made extensive and finally disastrous personal loans. Beginning in 1821, while living in a smaller house, Charles, who had his first lessons from his mother and later at a "dame school" in Rome Lane, attended a school kept by William Giles, son of the minister of the Baptist Chapel next to Dickens's home. In spite of enduring the death of an infant brother and sister and the indebtedness and imprisonment of his father, Charles, small, sickly, but brilliantly imaginative, enjoyed being taken to theatrical performances by Dr. Matthew Lamert (his aunt's husband) and the doctor's son, James. All of these experiences provided recurring motifs for Charles's short stories, novels, and amateur theatricals.

A cluster of misfortunes assailed the family in 1823. John's salary dropped from £400 to £350. Elizabeth unsuccessfully attempted to start a neighborhood school. The family could no longer afford to keep Charles in school, but James Lamert got him a job at Warren's blacking-warehouse, Hungerford Stairs, Strand. The next year, John was arrested for debt and imprisoned in the Marshalsea, Borough High Street. Mrs. Dickens and three of the children moved into the prison and Charles went into lodgings. Even when John's mother died, leaving a £450 legacy, it went entirely to creditors. After a quarrel between John (now released under the Insolvency Debtor's Act) and his son's employer, Charles was withdrawn from Warren Blacking and sent for the next several years to Wellington House Academy, Hampstead Road.

In 1825, John retired with the meager pension of £145 per annum. He supplemented his income by occasional journalism. Two years later, after the family had once more been evicted for non-payment of rent, fifteen-year-old Charles went to work as a clerk to solicitors and mastered the Gurney System, "that savage stenographic mystery." After becoming a freelance reporter at the Doctors' Commons, Charles felt able to propose marriage to Maria Beadnell, daughter to a banker, but her parents, unimpressed by the eighteen-year-old suitor's prospects and dismayed by his father's insolvency, sent her to finishing school in Paris. Having become a court stenographer at seventeen, and rapidly advancing to parliamentary reporter for the *Morning Chronicle*, Charles began submitting sketches of London life. These were published in 1836 as *Sketches by Boz* (a title that was derived from Dickens's brother Angustus's nickname, "Moses," which had been childishly pronounced "Boses").

In 1833, Dickens wrote an operatic burlesque *O'Thello* and performed it privately for and with his family and friends. Three years later he wrote the libretto for *The Village Coquettes* and read it aloud to friends before it was published by Bentley. These were the beginnings of his infatuation with the theater which would periodically exhaust him, make him especially predisposed to using melodramatic plots in his fiction, and (in the form of great public readings) contribute to his demise.

On April 2, 1836, Dickens married Catherine Hogarth, the daughter of the journalist and music critic George Hogarth. *The Posthumous Papers of the Pickwick Club* was published periodically in the *Times* and Charles Dickens and his creations Sam Weller and Mr. Pickwick became famous.

When on August 11 of the same year he agreed to write a Christmas book (which was never written), he began a more profitable drain on his novelistic energies that would produce such popular masterpieces as *A Christmas Carol*, *The Chimes*, and the *Cricket on the Hearth*.

After *Pickwick,* Dickens's readers were eager and ever more numerous and it was for this audience, cherished and beloved by the journalist, that his great novels were written. Characteristically, the pieces appeared first in monthly installments which were then collected into books (usually the first two were published together, as were the last two chapters). *Oliver Twist* (1838) was followed by *Nicholas Nickleby* (1839), then by two works originally intended to begin a series called "Master Humphrey's Clock" but which came out as *The Old Curiosity Shop* (1841) and *Barnaby Rudge* (1841). The former stenographic reporter wrote rapidly, occasionally working on two novels simultaneously, and he boasted that he always had the next installment ready just as the type was to be set on the current installment. The loosely plotted narratives incorporating scores of persons and places made him the most popular writer of a day in which Edward Bulwer-Lytton, Thomas Hardy, William Makepeace Thackeray, the Brontës, Anthony Trollope, and George Eliot were writing.

His visit to America in 1842 received a triumphal ovation which was marred by his demand for copyright protection and his sympathy with abolition. Accustomed to admiration, he replied with sharp criticism in *American Notes* (1842) and in his novel *Martin Chuzzlewit* (1844).

Dombey and Son (1848) was the beginning of a string of successful novels including *Bleak House* (1853), *Hard Times* (1854), *Little Dorrit* (1857), *A Tale of Two Cities* (1859), and *Our Mutual Friend* (1865). These were interspersed with the autobiographical studies which were his favorites: *David Copperfield* (1850) and *Great Expectations* (1862).

In 1856, Dickens bought a long-desired country home at Gad's Hill, but the domestic harmony of Charles, Catherine, and their ten children was broken by Charles's admiration of and attention to an actress, Ellen ("Nelly") Lawless Ternan, who was twenty-seven years his junior. The relationship of husband and wife had long been strained and uncomfortable, and Charles, the great "family writer," tended to greet each new child with groans of dismay. All told, Catherine bore him ten children. Although his wife obtained a formal separation, Charles nevertheless maintained his tender memories of Mary Hogarth, Catherine's sister who had died young, and another sister, Georgina, remained with Charles to care for the household and for the younger children. The Ternan relationship continued; the pair made every effort to be discreet, leaving England on different schedules to meet abroad, for example, but the elder children and close friends were fully cognizant of the relationship.

Dickens was frantically engaged at work, editing and contributing to *Household Words* from 1850 to 1859 and to *All the Year Round* from 1858 through 1870. Added to this frenetic activity, he continued to follow his first love for managing and acting in amateur theatricals. His platform readings from his novels and Christmas books having become enormously popular and very profitable, he made three tours in the British Isles, in 1858, from 1861 to 1865, and from 1866 to 1867, followed by an exhausting but triumphant American tour (1867–1868). When he undertook another British tour in 1869 and 1870, his health finally broke under the strain.

In Chester, Dickens probably suffered a minor stroke and dyslexically reversed syllables and slurred consonants as a result. In Preston, where he was scheduled for a performance that evening, Dr. Beard told him that he had to cancel the engagement and return to London for consultation with a heart specialist. It was enormously difficult for the British bundle of energy to give up his immediate contact with a live audience. After a Dickens reading in 1863, Thomas Carlyle had marveled: "Charlie, you carry a whole company of actors under your own hat." At the magazine offices he smoked incessantly and at home he turned to cigars, port, sherry, brandy, and, in company, champagne to maintain his public image as a paragon of good cheer. His final readings, however, were melodramatic rather than comic. For instance, in his reading version of Bill Sikes's murder of Nancy (*Oliver Twist*) he was memorializing the actual and fictional young women who had stirred him deeply: Mary and Georgina Hogarth, his sister Fanny, and his daughter Katie, as well as Little Nell and Little Em'ly. The Nancy of the readings thus became both the pure maiden who helps the helpless child and the horrible women of his life, his mother and his wife, who must be eliminated. Indeed, when he read "The Murder of Nancy" in Cheltenham, W.R. Macready pronounced it the equal of "two Macbeths!"

Ill or not, in 1870 Dickens was busily planning a glass conservatory extension of the dining room at Gad's Hill, organizing London "farewell readings," and writing the first two numbers of *The Mystery of Edwin Drood* for late summer and early fall. The twelve final readings drew overflow crowds to St. James's Hall. A private audience with Queen Victoria on March 9 was followed by his formal presentation at court. On March 15, the exhausted celebrity made his final platform appearance,

his four hundred seventy-second, with his left foot giving him great pain. The program consisted of *A Christmas Carol* and the trial scene from *Pickwick*. The writer finished the fifth *Drood* installment and directed Mamie and Kate's performance of *Prima Donna* (with scenery designed by John Everett Millais). Then, after dinner at Gad's Hill, he collapsed and died of a brain hemorrhage at 6:00 p.m. on June 9, 1870. He was survived by his estranged wife Catherine and eight of their ten children. His will, covering an estate of approximately £93,000, instructed that his funeral should be inexpensive, unostentatious, and private, with no black hatbands "or other such revolting absurdity." Georgina died in 1916. Ellen Ternan, whose financial security Dickens had arranged, married a clergyman-schoolmaster six years later; her relationship with the author did not come to public attention until twenty years after her death in 1916.

Dickens was, indeed, a whole cast of characters: the meticulous editor (with his friend and biographer John Forster), the shrewd businessman, the clan father, the writer of genius, the earnest philanthropist (along with Angela Burdett-Coutts), a man of the theater, the public lecturer and performer, an international celebrity, a cosmopolitan city-dweller, and the country squire with dogs and walking stick.

Literary Analysis

Dickens's trenchant criticisms of Chancery, Poor Houses, boys' boarding schools, the lack of education for women, the tyrannies of family life, the reliance upon alcohol, and the effects of poverty link him with the other writers of the age who were devoted to reform. His frequent depiction of the suffering and death of children and the elderly endeared him to a sentimental age that reveled in pathos. His narrative construction, so episodic yet intricate, so full of wonderful coincidences, *fausse denouement*, and total reversal, and always emphasizing the ultimate triumph of goodness, mark his indebtedness to the well-wrought French drama of Ernest Legouve, Augustin Scribe, and Victorien Sardou and to the English melodrama of Dion Boucicault and Charles Reade.

Finally, however, it was not indignation, pathos, ingenuity, or farce that made him the most popular writer of his era; rather than tears, it was his ability to evoke laughter that created his enormous readership. In the *Fortnightly Review* for December 1882, Mowbray Morris reported that 4,239,000 volumes of Dickens's works had been sold in England in the twelve years after his death. His gift for portraying the funny side of Sam Weller and Mr. Pickwick continued from the beginning to the end of his career.

In 1969, George Wing wrote about Dickens's great emphasis in his first six novels on the ridiculous and absurd aspects of the human comedy. The critic raised the question of whether this emphasis was exaggeration or sober truthfulness. John Carey, in 1973, decided against exaggeration and talked about Dickens's ability to see through pretense. More exhaustively, in 1971, James Kinkaid claimed that Dickens's "rhetoric of laughter" was simply a technique of persuasion.

It is appropriate to think of Dickens's comedy as a form of hyperbole, that figure of speech in which conscious exaggeration has no intention of literal persuasion. Thus, Jonathan Swift does not insist upon the existence and dimensions of Lilliputians, Brobdingnagians, Laputans, noble Houyhnhnms, or filthy Yahoos. Instead, Gulliver always takes his measure by the most extreme of standards and ends up feeling at home only in a stable. Presumably this is the reason that Dickens's pathos and social criticism are often blunted by the extremities of perfection or the monsters of hypocrisy against which they are measured.

His varied humor is verbal, situational, farcical, and melodramatic. His verbal magic extends from simple mispronunciations of individual words, as in Weller Senior's comments about nonconformist theology in *Pickwick Papers*:

She's got hold o' some inwention for grown-up people being born again, Sammy, the new birth I thinks they call it. I would wery much like to see that system in haction, Sammy. I should wery much like to see your mother-in-law born again.

Dickens also utilizes metaphors by which people become the thing that they are called, so that the Veneering's butler in *Our Mutual Friend* is not simply like something, he is "the Analytical Chemist," and Mr. Wilfer is not simply cherubic, he is a cherub. This transformation works in reverse too. As much as Dickens loved the stage and theatrical imposture, he could still deflate a Crummles Family set:

There was a gorgeous banquet, ready spread for the third act, consisting of two pasteboard vases, one plate of biscuits, a black bottle, and a vinegar cruet; and, in short, everything was on a scale of the utmost splendour and preparation. (*Nicholas Nickleby*)

His metaphors can even swallow up the human, as in the case of a Podsnap soiree (*Our Mutual Friend*) when the haunch of mutton produces such a steam-bath of moist odors that the diners are described as bathers.

Dickens's situational humor is bound up with his love not only for describing a multitude of characters but of playing all of the roles himself as well. Such virtuosity in role-playing can even be rewarded with connubial bliss, as witnessed by Crummles's first sight of his wife-to-be "on the butt-end of a spear surrounded with blazing fireworks." The smitten swain confesses: "Such grace, coupled with such dignity! I adored her from that moment!" (*Nicholas Nickleby*). Dickens might have depicted Dotheboy's Hall, in that great attack upon the Yorkshire schools, with the tones of Arnoldian "high seriousness" as a school where unwanted children, bastards, and inconvenient heirs might be abandoned, forgotten with every assurance that brutality and neglect would shovel the problem into the grave. Still, in order not to "disgust and weary the reader," instead of arousing indignation, he elicits laughter as the freezing barracks of Dotheboy's Hall becomes a situation-comedy set with the new boys and the new master the butts of savage humor and fantastical jokes. This is the way that great satire makes us laugh at situations too painful to consider seriously.

With Dickens, these situation-comedies often degenerate into popular nineteenth-century farces. On the one hand, after a ferocious administration of brimstone and treacle, Ms. Squeers casually calls upon a boy to come forward so that she may wipe her sticky fingers on his curly hair, evidence of her casual, even callous, insensitivity. On the other hand, when Vincent Crummles lovingly details the talents of his dramatic troupe, he does not omit the pony's mother who was famous for eating apple pies, firing pistols, and going to bed in a night-cap; "in short, [she] took the low comedy entirely" (*Nicholas Nickleby*).

The farcical and popular portions of the novels are all built around empty-headed, hollow-hearted caricatures who, being totally bloodless, feel no pain and never think. The central characters can feel and think, but, alas, not with us. Instead, in the heroic-tragic style of W.R. Macready (to whom *Nicholas Nickleby* was dedicated with "admiration and regard"), they declaim pious platitudes and clutch their hearts and lose the modern audience. When Nicholas discovers the villainous plans of his uncle, he declaims in high style to his mother, "Your own honour and good name demand that, after the discovery of his vile proceedings, you should not be beholden to him one hour, even for the shelter of these bare walls." This may be what the noble son is supposed to say to his mother, but it is neither moving nor convincing. There is delight, though, from the literal application of an old cliché by his totally bloodless mother: "the walls are very bare, and want painting too, and I have had this ceiling whitewashed at the expense of eighteen pence, which is a very distressing thing, considering that it is so much gone into your uncle's pocket." The caricature mother neatly dismisses the abstractions of her own honor, her son's pride, and her daughter's virtue to lament the needless expenditure of eighteen real pence.

The division of characters into histrionic, cliché-ridden leads and wonderfully funny supports can be expanded into types of character-humor. The first type is composed of the perfect innocents at whom we may not laugh. Into such a category certainly would fall Little Nell, Oliver Twist, Smike, Kate Nickleby, Mr. Wilfer, and Mrs. Boffin. Their perfect innocence is invulnerable to violence, theft, hunger and seduction—in short, to experience. We may suffer with them, weep for them, but we know from chapter 1 that they will die closing innocent blue eyes upon a world that taught them nothing.

Obviously, the next category is the innocents at whom we may laugh. The dividing line here seems to be the character's capacity for knowledge of the world and the self as well as a potential for growth. Into this group fall David Copperfield and Pip. David can be betrayed by Steerforth and enamored of a child-wife, but just about the time that we have given up on him, Dora dies and the angelic Agnes finally becomes his companion-wife. Pip, who longs for gentility, can be teased by Miss Haversham, adopted by a convict, and disdained by Estella, but he finally comes to recognize that blacksmith Joe is the finest gentle-man that he has ever met and Magwitch is his most generous benefactor.

The most disquieting of Dickens's humorous character categories is composed of the villains at whom we are expected to laugh. Scrooge may mistreat employees, but he is scared into reformation by ghosts. Wackford Squeers beats boys with great relish, but his hypocritical sense of his great scholarship and his innate respectability are hilarious. Jew Fagin victimizes children, but he performs remarkably as a surrogate parent. Uriah Heep's villainy is endless, but who can forget the assumption of humility and those twined, double-jointed legs? Silas Wegg specializes in biting the hands that feed him, but he keeps bursting out irrepressibly into an idiot survey of British poetry to adorn his villainy.

If he does not hesitate to draw laughter from villainy, Dickens even more distressingly asks us to laugh at monsters: the physically, mentally, and emotionally handicapped: the miniature Miss La Creevy, dressing up ordinary citizens in splendid uniforms in order to reduce them to her own dimensions as miniatures; Mr. Lillyvick, whose giant self-esteem sees him through a humiliating and disastrous marriage and abandonment; the little dolls' dressmaker, Jenny Wren, who is pathetically crippled but irresistibly funny when she not only calls her drunken father her "bad child" but actually sustains that kind of relationship to him. All of these monsters share invulnerability with the perfect innocents who are so insulated within their own vision that nothing can really get at them. Life cannot teach anything to the little madman who woos Mrs. Nickleby so alluringly from the garden wall: "I have estates, ma'am . . . jewels, lighthouses, fish-ponds, a whalery of my own in the North Sea, and several oyster-beds of great profit in the Pacific Ocean."

Caricatures and stereotypes fit together. The Veneerings are givers of dinners at which each guest immediately becomes "one of our oldest and dearest friends." Their regular guests, Boots and Brewer, are never even identified by personal names, they are always known only by their vocations. Mr. Pickwick is an "affable host" and the Cheeryble Brothers are "imperturbable figures of philanthropy." In *Little Dorrit*, the rent-collector, Panks, is grimy, puffs and blows off steam, so every time he appears he is likened to a steam-engine. The pretensions of the nouveau-riche are comfortably ensconced in Mrs. Wititterly, who oscillates between the hysteria of social glitter and the total exhaustion of collapse—there seem to be no intermediate facets to her personality.

There are also the pathetic for whom Dickens extracts both tears and laughter. The gem of the Vincent Crummles Travelling Players is their own daughter who is always referred to as "the Infant Phenomenon." The maiden is a marvel of ballet twirls, leaps, entrechats, poising on one leg, always flutteringly in action. Advertised as ten, she is short of stature but with a comparatively aged face. Upon investigation it appears that her proud, loving parents, always more appreciative of drama than life, kept her up late every night, fed her little, and gave her an unlimited allowance of gin-and-water from infancy to protect the Infant Phenomenon from the blight of growth. Dickens states it candidly through the lisp of Mr. Sleary: "People mutht be amuthed." So Gamfield, the chimney-sweep overseer, makes us laugh in *Oliver Twist* by lighting dry straw fires while the boys are in the chimneys: "Boys is wery obstinit, and wery lazy, gen'lmen, and there's nothink like a good hot blaze to make 'em come down with a run. It's humane too, gen'lmen, acause, even if they've stuck in the chimbley, roasting their feet makes 'em struggle to hextricate theirseves."

In all of the categories of dramatic presentation and all of the classes of characters who make us laugh, it is undeniable that hyperbole reigns supreme. Everyone is larger than life or smaller than life but never just life-size. Every situation is darker than doom and every odd character is impossibly ludicrous. It is almost as if the son of the imprisoned debtor who had a job that he despised beneath Hungerford Stairs, immersed in the hideous crowd of beggars, drunks, rogues, and the deformed, discovered that the way to handle disgust and pity is through distance achieved by the comic vision. Humor can be a social weapon, and Dickens used it as such, but it can also serve as the final refuge of the vulnerable heart. So, the boy who learned to survive by humor became the enormously successful writer who prospered by the power of laughter.

Summary

Charles Dickens's great achievements were to depict a London full of human oddities and danger and to neutralize both by hilarity. His London is unmistakably real, Kent is idyllic, and the sea a place for dying. His sharp reportorial eye saw all of the social injustices, but his depictions always lead us to laugh or to cry, and neither response lends itself to social amendment. He revered haughty aristocrats like Lord Dedlock, Sir John Chester, the Marquis de St. Evremond, and Eugene Wrayburn, and he depicts them blunderingly. He adored success and loathed failure—were not the lower classes that he had known from birth all failures? His men are shrewd, villainous, or noble beyond bearing; his women are overwhelming, or childlike, or noble and self-effacing wives.

His passion for amateur theatricals suggests that the performer and the entertainer were of paramount importance and that he considered the installment of a novel as essentially equivalent to a scene from a cosmic melodrama. Every loose end gets knitted into the fabric in his works, and Providence rewards goodness and punishes evil. Beneath all the caricatures and stereotypes who people his pages there flows a mighty Thames of genius which leavens and lifts the lumps of humanity into luminous and unforgettable stature.

Selected Bibliography
Primary Sources

Novels
Many fine editions of Charles Dickens's works are available, most notably *The New Oxford Illustrated Dickens*. Ed. Walter Bagehot. London and New York: Oxford University Press, 1948. The following is a list of the original publications in periodical and/or book form.

The Posthumous Papers of the Pickwick Club. London: Chapman & Hall, 1837. Monthly numbers, April 1836–November 1837.

Oliver Twist; or The Parish Boy's Progress. London: Richard Bentley, 1838. Monthly numbers in *Bentley's Miscellany*, February 1837–March 1839.

Life and Adventures of Nicholas Nickleby. London: Chapman & Hall, 1839. Monthly numbers April 1838–October 1839.

The Old Curiosity Shop. London: Chapman & Hall, 1841. Weekly numbers in *Master Humphrey's Clock*, April 1840–February 1841.

Barnaby Rudge: A Tale of the Riots of 'Eighty. London: Chapman & Hall, 1841. Weekly numbers in *Master*

Humphrey's Clock, February–November 1841.

Life and Adventures of Martin Chuzzlewit. London: Chapman & Hall, 1844. Monthly numbers January 1843–July 1844.

Dealings with the Firm of Dombey and Son, Wholesale, Retail and for Exportation. London: Bradbury and Evans, 1848. Monthly numbers October 1846–April 1848.

The Personal History of David Copperfield. London: Bradbury and Evans, 1850. Monthly numbers May 1849–November 1850.

Bleak House. London: Bradbury and Evans, 1853. Monthly numbers March 1852–September 1853.

Hard Times for These Times. London: Bradbury and Evans, 1854. Weekly numbers in *Household Words*, April–August 1854.

Little Dorrit. London: Bradbury and Evans, 1857. Monthly numbers in *Household Words*, December 1855–June 1857.

A Tale of Two Cities. London: Chapman & Hall, 1859. Weekly numbers in *All the Year Round*, April–November 1859.

Great Expectations. London: Chapman & Hall, 1862. Weekly numbers in *All the Year Round*, December 1860–August 1861.

Our Mutual Friend. London: Chapman & Hall. Monthly numbers May 1864–November 1865.

The Mystery of Edwin Drood. London: Chapman & Hall, 1870. Monthly numbers April–September 1870 (six of the anticipated twelve).

Poetry
The Poems and Verses of Charles Dickens. Ed. F.G. Kitton. New York and London: Harper and Brothers, 1903.

Drama
Complete Plays and Selected Poems. London: Vision Press, 1970. Includes *The Lamplighter, A Farce* (London: 1879); *The Village Coquettes* (London: 1836); *Is She His Wife? or Something Singular* (London: 1837); *The Strange Gentleman* (London: 1837).

Christmas Books
Christmas Books. Ed. G.K. Chesterton. London: J.M. Dent and Sons, 1907.

Christmas Books and Pictures from Italy. Ed. Edward Everett Hale. New York: P.F. Collier and Son, 1911.

Other Prose
Sketches by Boz. Published 1836 by John Macrone; London: Oxford University Press, 1957. Monthly numbers in *Monthly Magazine* and *Morning* and *Evening Chronicle*, 1835.

American Notes for General Circulation. London: Chapman & Hall, 1842. 2 vols.

American Notes and Pictures from Italy. London: Oxford University Press, 1957.

A Child's History of England. London: Bradbury and Evans, 1852–1854. 3 vols. Weekly numbers in *Household Words*, January 25, 1951–December 10, 1853.

The Uncommercial Traveller and Reprinted Pieces, etc. London: Oxford University Press, 1958. *The Oxford Illustrated Dickens*.

The Speeches of Charles Dickens. Ed. K.J. Fielding. Oxford: Clarendon, 1960.

The Public Readings of Charles Dickens. Ed. Philip Collins. Oxford: Clarendon, 1975.

Heart of Dickens. Ed. Edgar Johnson. New York: Duell, Little, 1952. Letters to philanthropist Angela Burdett-Coutts.

Selected Letters of Charles Dickens. Ed. David Paroissien. Boston: Twayne Publishers, 1985.

The Letters of Charles Dickens. Ed. Madeline House, Graham Storey, KathleenTillotson, Nina Burgis, and Kenneth J. Fielding. Oxford: Clarendon, 1988. 6 vols. The Pilgrim Edition.

Secondary Sources

Biographies
Forster, John. *The Life of Charles Dickens*. London: Chapman & Hall, 1872–1874, 3 vols.; New York: Charles Scribner's Sons, 1899. The authorized biography by a longtime friend and editorial associate. Obviously admiring in tone but containing a wealth of detail both private and public.

Johnson, Edgar. *Charles Dickens: His Tragedy and Triumph*. New York: Simon and

Schuster, 1952. 2 vols. Long, highly detailed biography, some literary analysis, strongly related to the nineteenth-century milieu, with previously unpublished account of liaison with Ellen Ternan.

Kaplan, Fred. *Dickens: A Biography*. New York: Morrow, 1988. Presents a picture of Dickens as "a driven, work-obsessed artist . . . astonishingly generous and heartlessly cruel . . . reformer and bitter anti-democrat."

Page, Norman. *A Dickens Chronology*. Boston: G.K. Hall, 1988. A very useful outline of biography and publication history.

Books

Ackroyd, Peter. *Dickens*. New York: Harper Collins, 1990. Enormous book, badly bound. Reads like a novel but makes almost no new contributions.

Carey, John. *The Violent Effigy: A Study of Dickens' Imagination*. London: Faber, 1973. Carey concentrates on seven aspects of Dickens's novels: violence, order, humor, corpses and effigies, symbols, children, and sex.

Chesterton, G.K. *Charles Dickens: A Critical Study*. London: Methuen, and New York: Dodd, Mead, 1906; rpt. as *Appreciation and Criticism of the Works of Charles Dickens*. London: Dent, 1911. Genial author makes Dickens the model British humorist and invites us to the Gargantuan feast.

Cockshut, A.O.J. *The Imagination of Charles Dickens*. London: Collins, 1961. Cockshut attempts to answer two invidious questions: How did a man with "such a coarse mind" become a master of his art, and is it possible for a book to be a best-seller and a true classic simultaneously?

Davis, Earle. *The Flint and the Flame: The Artistry of Charles Dickens*. Columbus: University of Missouri, 1963. Contains an eminently tolerant and abbreviated survey of Dickens criticism.

Dolby, George. *Charles Dickens as I Knew Him*. London: T. Fisher Unwin, 1885. The story of the reading tours in Great Britain and America (1866–1870).

Dunn, Richard J., ed. *Dickens' David Copperfield*. New York: Modern Language Association, 1984. Approaches to Teaching World Literature series.

Ford, George H. *Dickens and His Readers*. Princeton: University Press, 1955. Ford moves beyond a listing of reviews to a general study of Dickens's readership: politicians, society ladies, magazine editors, aesthetes, as well as the populace.

Garis, Robert. *The Dickens Theatre*. Oxford: Clarendon, 1965. The theatricality and mimicry intrinsic to Dickens's life and artistry are emphasized. The great entertainer claims attention and love for what he does, not for what he is.

Gissing, George. *Charles Dickens: A Critical Study*. New York: Dodd, Mead & Co., 1898; London: Graham, 1903. Gissing discusses many aspects of Dickens's authorship that will be dominant in later criticism.

Hardy, Barbara. *The Moral Art of Dickens*. London: Athlone Press, 1970. A general introduction to Dickens's moral concerns, including patterns of change and the conversion experience, focusing on *Pickwick, Chuzzlewit, Copperfield*, and *Great Expectations*.

House, Humphry. *The Dickens World*. London: Oxford University Press, 1941. Strong study of Dickens's relationship with his times, particularly interested in exploring his attitudes on reform and employer-employee relations.

Johnson, E.D.H. *Charles Dickens: An Introduction to His Novels*. New York: Random House, 1969. A book for the general reader plus some background material.

Kincaid, James R. *Dickens and the Rhetoric of Laughter*. Oxford: Clarendon, 1971. Kincaid discusses Dickens's use of laughter as a tool toward audience persuasion in eight novels: *Pickwick, Twist, Curiosity Shop, Rudge, Chuzzlewit, Copperfield, Dorrit*, and *Mutual Friend*.

Leavis, F.R. and Q.D. Leavis. *Dickens the Novelist*. London: Chatto and Windus, 1970. Husband and wife reevaluate their previous estimates of Charles Dickens, F.R. with bullying criticism and dismissal of other critics, Q.D. with careful scholarship and measured decorum.

MacKenzie, Norman and Jeanne MacKenzie. *Dickens: A Life*. New York: Oxford University Press, 1979. Best at describing

Dickens's restless, energetic, driven personality; poorest in the area of literary criticism.

Mankowitz, Wolf. *Dickens of London*. London: Weidenfeld and Nicholson, 1976; New York: Macmillan, 1977.

Miller, J. Hillis. *Charles Dickens: The World of His Novels*. Cambridge, MA: Harvard University Press, 1952. Very influential study; Dickens's imaginative, not his sociopolitical world is explored. Symbolic reading, ponderously scholarly and often palpably biased. Illuminating glimpses of the authorial mind at work.

Monod, Sylvere. *Dickens the Novelist*. Norman: University of Oklahoma Press, 1968. Trans. of *Dickens romancier*. Paris Hachette, 1953. Learned discussion of the actual Dickens manuscript texts to show increasing care in stylistics and composition structure.

Nisbet, Ada. *Dickens and Ellen Ternan*. London: Cambridge University Press, 1952. 62 pages of discussion, 12 pages of documents. Foreword by Edmund Wilson.

Sucksmith, H.P. *The Narrative Art of Charles Dickens: The Rhetoric of Sympathy and Irony in His Novels*. Oxford: Clarendon, 1970. Sucksmith finds in Dickens's vision of life "an ironic tragi-comedy of deception." Points out Dickens's stylistic successes and excesses, but ends with the kind of determinism more often associated with Thomas Hardy and George Eliot.

Wilson, Angus. *The World of Charles Dickens*. London: Secker and Warburg, 1970. A "Studio Book." Stimulating study of how Dickens's imagination fed on his public and private life.

Wilson, Edmund. *The Wound and the Bow*. London: W.H. Allen, 1941; London: Methuen, 1961. First exposure of Dickens to psychological investigation and the deadly earnest lines of intensive academic research.

Wing, George. *Dickens*. Edinburgh: Oliver and Boyd, 1969. Examines the comedy of the first six novels, the mood of the middle novels from *Dombey* to *Dorrit,* and infatuation in the later novels. Excellent final chapter, "Patterns of Criticism."

Elton E. Smith

D'Israeli, Isaac

Born: Great St. Helen's, London, May 11, 1766
Education: Private school in Enfield; private tutor in Amsterdam in 1780
Marriage: Maria Basevi, February 10, 1802; five children
Died: Bradenham, Buckinghamshire, January 19, 1847

Biography

Isaac D'Israeli is probably known to the twentieth century as the father of the British Prime Minister, Benjamin D'Israeli, but in the early nineteenth century he was a well-known author respected by his peers, most notably Lord Byron.

Born in Great St. Helen's, London, on May 11, 1766 to Benjamin D'Israeli and his second wife Sarah, Isaac was destined for the family import business, founded in 1757 by his father, a Jewish immigrant from Italy. Soon after he was born the family moved to a country house in Enfield that had been designed by Christopher Wren (and later used as a school where John Keats was a pupil). Educated at a private school in Enfield run by a Scotsman named Morison, all that Isaac learned was a little Latin. His attendance became increasingly erratic and his propensity for literature increasingly enthusiastic, much to his father's dismay.

Isaac was sent to Amsterdam in 1780 and, supervised by his father's agent, he studied with a private tutor. He made little progress in the classics, but he read widely in the modern languages and developed a lasting affinity for French literature and writers such as François Voltaire and Jean Jacques Rousseau. He returned home in 1782, determined to be a poet. When his father, haunted by images of literary penury, counselled him to join a commercial house in Bordeaux, Isaac replied with the poem "Against Commerce which is the Corruption of Mankind." His parents agreed to let him follow his own course in life.

For the young Jew, impulsive and volatile, there followed the struggle for recognition. Abroad again in 1788 he studied in Paris, made notes on antiquities in Italy, and at the outbreak of the French Revolution he returned home to re-engage the literary controversies of his day. In 1791, an inheritance from his maternal grandmother, Esther Shiprut, secured his independence, and he moved to Adelphi, London. That same year he published *Curiosities of Lit-*

erature, which established him as a popular author.

From 1794 to 1796, he recuperated in Exeter from what Benjamin called "a mysterious illness" characterized by "lassitude and despondency," which nevertheless did little to stem the variety of his writings. On February 10, 1802, he married Maria Basevi and between then and 1813 they had five children, four of whom survived, including Benjamin (in 1804), who was to become Prime Minister. The marriage, a very happy one, hardly altered his routine: mornings spent studying in the British Museum, evenings in his library at home. The flow of writings continued throughout his life.

The remaining non-literary event of significance was Isaac's break with the Bevis Marks Synagogue. Although not a practicing Jew (French rationalism had made him wary of bigotry and superstition), he had maintained an association with the synagogue. A break in relations in 1813, compounded in 1817 by the Wardens' obduracy, led to Isaac severing all formal ties. On a friend's advice his four surviving children were baptized as Christians, making possible Benjamin's political career.

Following his wife's death in the previous summer, Isaac died on January 10, 1847 in Bradenham, and was buried beside her in the local churchyard.

Literary Analysis

When D'Israeli was thirty, in 1796, an anonymous reviewer wrote, "He is a rare instance of a person of (Jewish) origin acquiring any literary reputation."[1] He had fulfilled his first ambition, to be a poet. His verse defense of the Poet Laureate, "On the Abuse of Satire," had created a minor scandal, however. This and other poems were failures, and his authorial "reputation" was based on contributions to periodicals, the *Curiosities of Literature* (1791), and *An Essay on the Literary Character* (1795). Still, these works were seen as "mere compilations" of interesting literary and historical anecdotes, and D'Israeli yet yearned for recognition as a creative writer. For another fifteen years he persevered as poet and novelist. *The Tale of Mejnoun and Leila, a Persian Romance* from *Romances* (both 1799) may have influenced Edgar Allen Poe's "Ligeia"; his satirical novels *Vaurien, or Sketches of the Times* (1797) and *Flim-Flams! Or the Life and Errors of My Uncle, and the Amours of My Aunt!* (1805) were both a *succes de scandale,* incorporating

fairly obvious portraits of living people and events, but little more.

Then, from 1812 onward, D'Israeli concentrated on the literary and political explorations for which he was best known and most popular, *Calamities of Authors* (1812) and *Quarrels of Authors* (1814), and a work on James I, *An Inquiry Into the Literary and Political Character of James the First* (1816). In 1821, he was elected a Fellow of the Society of Antiquaries. In 1828, he published his five volume *Commentaries on the Life and Reign of Charles I* for which Oxford awarded him an honorary Doctor of Civil Law (D.C.L.). By 1839, he was partially blind; even so, with the help of his daughter Sarah, he worked on his history of English Literature, *Amenities of Literature* (1841).

D'Israeli lived through the cultural shift from the Enlightenment into romanticism. Two influences from his youth were paramount in his writing: Voltaire, who ruled his head and Rousseau, who ruled his heart. This ensured that, although he exercised a skeptical detachment in his desire to get to the truth of things, he never lost his fascination with the particularities of the individual. It was his investigations of the genius and creativity of the literary character that led Lord Byron to name him the "Bayle of literary speculation." Among English poets his defense of Alexander Pope in the Bowles controversy and his remarkably modern view of John Skelton testify to his taste for the witty and satirical. An influence not always acknowledged in one so wary of religious cant and hypocrisy was that of "the third Moses," Moses Mendelssohn, a philosopher of the Jewish Enlightenment. D'Israeli, the proponent of "A cheerful, a tolerating and an active benevolence," is the inheritor of Mendelssohn who wrote, "Love man and you please God."

For one who did so much to pioneer new forms of literary study, it is ironic that D'Israeli's own reputation should have fallen so low. During his lifetime, his compendium of quirky information, ranging from "Anecdotes of Errata" to "Of Literary Filchers," called *Curiosities of Literature*, went through various expansions and revisions, expanding from one volume to three and going through thirteen editions. This was the cornerstone of his popularity and while it had many imitators it was never superseded. After his death, eleven more editions appeared, most recently a one-volume paperback selection (1964). It is essentially the work of a literary antiquary.

Far more interesting was D'Israeli's study of the psychology of literary men of genius. First published as *An Essay on the Literary Character* (1795), it too went through a constant process of revision and expansion to two volumes. The later editions incorporated extensive comments and interpolations made by Byron in the margin of his personal copy. The subject matter was of intense interest to the Romantics, with their belief in individuality. Similarly dealing with the literary character were *Calamities of Authors* (two volumes) and *Quarrels of Authors* (three volumes). The two works consist of a series of essays about writers now both known and unknown, such as Pope in "Pope and his Miscellaneous Quarrels" and John Dennis, who figures in "Influence of a Bad Temper in Criticism." These are compilations of historical information rather than original works. More original is his *Amenities of Literature*, which is an exercise in literary history wherein D'Israeli investigates many new sources and returns to neglected ones. His essay on "The Origin of the English Language," describing the transition from Old English to post-Conquest English, still repays study, as does his estimate of Skelton.

In all of this extensive and varied output of scholarship certain themes emerge. Perhaps most important of these is the spirit of the works: a desire for truth, combined with a flair in presenting the subject under scrutiny. His books on King James I and King Charles I, unlike most history of the time, were characterized by his attempt to be fair to his subjects—to conduct, as he said himself, an "affair of literary conscience." Part of the writer's method was to investigate primary sources wherever he could, a practice common now in historiography, but not so at that time. His enthusiasm often may have led him to over-value so-called secret histories and documents; however, his creative gifts lent color and vitality to his subjects.

D'Israeli's scholarly integrity stemmed partly from Voltaire and partly from his belief, expressed in *Literary Character*, that men of genius with their intelligence, detachment, and benevolence stand between the governors and the governed. The question, then, is how does genius arise? The answer lies in the unique predisposition of the individual: a combination of Voltaire's intelligence and Rousseau's belief in natural goodness and man's individual character.

One wonders how D'Israeli, the detached seeker after truth, the "amiable and upright man of letters,"[2] managed to be involved in so many controversies, minor literary scandals, and even threatened libel actions. The reason is that his work falls into two distinct parts, nonfiction and fiction. His non-fiction is enlivened by a witty, capricious, and ironic style, but in the fiction these pleasant features are supplemented by an altogether grosser humor, sarcasm, and outright personal attacks.

In D'Israeli's non-fiction, the humor is a supplement to the intellectual content, both enlivening it for the reader and being expressive of the enthusiasm of the writer. From the *Curiosities*, for instance, we learn of Rabbi Benjamin of Tudela that "He describes a journey, which if he ever took, it must have been with his night cap on, being a perfect dream." In the article "On the Custom of Saluting after Sneezing" he skeptically cites three explanations for the custom: those of a Catholic writer, the rabbis, and Aristotle, who thought that the sneeze coming from the head was saluted to distinguish it from two other eruptions of air, "which are never accompanied by any benediction from the bystanders."

The fictional works are different, however, particularly the satirical novels. *Vaurien* was an attack on those in England who still sympathized with the French Revolution, which had turned so bloody in the early 1790s. The protagonist travels to England to foment a revolution; he fails because the English revolutionaries are so busy quarreling that they cannot unite. Characters modeled after the major figures of the day, Mr. Subtile for William Godwin and Mr. Reverberator for Thomas Holcroft, are included and the fun that D'Israeli had at their expense gained plaudits from the traditionalists but displeasure from supporters of Godwinian philosophy.

D'Israeli's other satire, *Flim-Flams*, similarly deals with contemporary notables and events, though it is more humane, explicitly acknowledging Laurence Sterne in its opening. The plot follows the progress of My Uncle through his scientific experiments and explorations. Central are the Philos, a group formed for the pursuit of knowledge ("in their hearts they would ridicule the pursuits of each other, yet each felt he wanted a support"), who are a source of foils or companions in satires on landscape gardening, inventions, and philosophy. There is Miss Eleanor, "Better known as an inventor than for her inventions themselves," who knows more of the body of man "than was thought decent." There is also Dr. Della Lena, "the crafty Italian [who] humiliated his ear close to the key-hole," and Contour, the landscape gardener. Finally, after many adventures, such as bleaching his Negro servant, My Uncle marries Miss Eleanor who as My Aunt gives birth to an ape. While the book is a constant stream of satires on everything and the character of everybody, some people found the book gross and offensive. The character of My Aunt, based on Caroline Herschel (an astronomer), was found particularly offensive, while others such as Edmund Cartwright, inventor of the power loom, took the joke at his expense in good humor. From the perspective of time the book is fun—sometimes cruel, sometimes coarse—but many of the particular references are lost.

The name Isaac itself means laughter and the core of D'Israeli's humorous technique is the incongruous, or what Immanuel Kant termed "frustrated expectation." In *Vaurien,* Charles, the conventionally innocent country lad come to town, is shocked to find a prostitute who is a virtuous and affectionate parent, an elderly thief who is an official justice, and a pickpocket who is an esteemed gentleman. But the book has an underlying seriousness where *Flim-Flams* is altogether lighter in vein. In this book incongruity is demonstrated through parody, satire, and farce as well as the sly wit and humor characteristic of his non-fiction work.

In form, *Flim-Flams* is a parody of the excesses of scholarship. The book purports to be a serious account of the intellectual and personal history of My Uncle, an avid scholar who, "whatever the world knew least and wished to know less, this great man knew most, and wished to know more." The book has not one but four prefaces, addressed to various readerships, and a veritable cornucopia of footnotes. While parody normally works through an incongruity of means and goals, or subject and objective, satire is usually a manifestation of the satirist's superior understanding. However, this is not so with D'Israeli's works, in which even satire is mediated by his sympathetic understanding emphasizing what he sees as the foibles of humanity rather than his own superiority. When satirizing, for example, scientific method, My Uncle "kept mercury in digestion for fifteen years, with a constant heat of 100 degrees . . . things remained just as they were: however it

was a great satisfaction to the scientific world that My Uncle laboured fifteen years to demonstrate the whole affair." Even with the landscape gardener Kent, striving for the picturesque, we sense the incongruous rather than the critical when "to secure an effect he planted a dead tree!"

Only with farce does D'Israeli's invention sometimes go adrift by continuing an unfunny scene too long or by betraying a grossness which even some inhabitants of the robust eighteenth century found objectionable. The example of Herschel, who was fifty at the time and of impeccable character, giving birth to an ape was both gratuitous and cruel, as is the climax of book three in which My Uncle cures her of "hankering after illicit venery" by locking her in her room and bleeding her. Still, these lapses are few from a writer whose wit did not except himself: "I sent my Memoir to the Royal Society: a set of unbelieving Jews! they crucify my genius, and circumcize my papers!"

In *The Times* of January 9, 1849, it was written that "Isaac Disraeli [*sic*] belongs to the aristocracy of literature." It was not his creative work that earned him generous plaudits but rather his historical investigations of literature and politics. He writes best when his mind is controlled by the need to interpret real events in a just and equitable manner and his capricious and artful pen invokes a shared enthusiasm in the reader. He was a pioneer in the field of literary history and the psychological study of authors; he contributed to the genre of Eastern Gothic; above all he contributed considerably to the political ideas of his Prime Minister son, Benjamin. Unfortunately, history has not been so kind to a pioneer of historiography and a charming and amusing writer.

Summary

Isaac D'Israeli, in spite of coming from a nonliterary background, became a literary encyclopedist of considerable talent. He wore his scholarship with a detached irony, humor, and modesty that brought him friends and readers from among the notables of his day. His Voltairian satires are deeply rooted in the issues of the day, in style linking him with Sterne and Thomas Love Peacock, as well as influencing his son, Benjamin D'Israeli. It is sad that with time the son's political career has all but overshadowed the father's literary career.

Notes
1. Anonymous, *Monthly Mirror* (December 1796).
2. Anonymous, *Blackwood's Edinburgh Magazine*, 13 (February 1823): 165.

Selected Bibliography
Primary Sources
Curiosities of Literature. London: Murray, 1791; Vol. 2, London: Murray, 1793; London: Murray, 1817, 3 vols.
A Second Series of Curiosities of Literature. London: Murray, 1823. 3 vols.
An Essay on the Literary Character. London: Cadell and Davies, 1795.
The Literary Character of Men of Genius. London: Murray, 1818. 2nd ed. enlarged.
Vaurien, or Sketches of the Times. London: Cadell and Davies, 1797. 2 vols.
Romances. London: Murray, 1799. Contains *Mejnoun and Leila*.
Flim-Flams! Or the Life and Errors of My Uncle, and the Amours of My Aunt! London: Murray, 1805. 3 vols.
Calamities of Authors. London: Murray, Edinburgh: Blackwood, and Dublin: Cumming, 1812. 2 vols.
Quarrels of Authors. London: Murray, 1814. 3 vols.
An Inquiry into the Literary and Political Character of James the First. London: Murray, 1816.
Commentaries on the Life and Reign of Charles I. London: Colburn and Bentley, 1828–1831. 5 vols.
Amenities of Literature. London: Moxon, 1841. 3 vols.
The Works of Isaac Disraeli [*sic*]. Ed. Benjamin D'Israeli. London: Routledge, Warnes, and Routledge, 1858–1859.

Secondary Sources
Bleiler, Everett. Preface to *Curiosities of Literature*. New York: Dover, 1964. Good general portrait.
D'Israeli, Benjamin. "On the Life and Writings of Mr. Disraeli" [*sic*]. memoir prefacing *Curiosities of Literature*, 14th ed., 1849. A marvellously sympathetic portrait that makes Isaac more of a scholar and less of a literateur and controversialist. Isaac mirrors Benjamin himself.
Jerman, B.R. *The Young Disraeli* [*sic*]. Princeton: Princeton University Press,
1960. Much original material on Benjamin, good on father's circle of friends.
Lee, Sir Sidney. "D'Israeli." *Dictionary of National Biography*, Vol. 15, 1888. Rather general, sometimes inaccurate in detail.
Lipkind, Goodman. "D'Israeli, Isaac." *The Jewish Encyclopedia*, IV. Ed. S. Singer. New York: Funk and Wagnalls, 1904, pp. 621–622. General account, repeats story of Isaac attending the opening of the Jewish Reform Synagogue in 1839.
Ogden, James. *Isaac D'Israeli*. Oxford: Oxford University Press, 1969. The best, most balanced, and most accurate account, encouraging enthusiasm for its subject.
West, Muriel C. "Poe's 'Ligeia' and Isaac D'Israeli." *Comparative Literature*, 16 (1965): 19–28. West discusses D'Israeli's influence on Edgar Allen Poe.

Dissertations
Calcott, Emily S. "The Influence of Isaac D'Israeli on Edgar A. Poe." University of Virginia, 1931.
Hayes, Michael J. "Duty to Self and to Society in the Early Writings of Benjamin Disraeli." University of London, 1984. Early part deals with influence of Isaac on Benjamin.
Kopstein, Sarah. "Isaac D'Israeli." University of Jerusalem, 1939.

Michael Hayes

Donne, John

Born: London, sometime between January 24 and June 19, 1572
Education: Hart College, Oxford, and possibly Cambridge University, 1584– 1589?; begins legal studies at the Inns of Court, 1591
Marriage: Ann More, December 1601; twelve children (including two stillbirths)
Died: March 31, 1631

Biography

John Donne was born during an age when a person's religion was as much a political fact as a matter of faith. At the time of his birth England was officially a Protestant country, and the social position of a Catholic family like Donne's was uncertain and potentially dangerous. His father and namesake was a wealthy ironmonger; shortly after his father died in 1576, Donne's mother, Elizabeth, married John Syminges, a distinguished physician. Donne's mother descended from a family of prominent Catholics, and two of her brothers were in fact Jesuit priests. One of them, Jasper Heywood, was captured, imprisoned, and sentenced to death in 1583–1584, although in 1585 he was exiled to France.

In 1584, Donne and his younger brother, Henry, had begun studying at Hart College, Oxford, but they left before finishing their degrees and before being required to take the Anglican Church's Oath of Supremacy. Dr. Syminges died in July 1588, and in 1588 and 1589 Donne may have studied at Cambridge, while in 1589 and 1591 he may have traveled on the continent. In 1590 or early 1591, his mother remarried again, this time wedding Richard Rainsford. In 1591, Donne began his legal studies at Thavies Inn, then in 1592 he transferred to Lincoln's Inn where he continued to study law but did not take a degree. In June 1593, having become twenty-one, he received his share of his father's estate. That same year his brother Henry died of the plague after having been imprisoned for harboring a Catholic priest (who was brutally executed early in 1594).

Later in 1594 Donne was chosen, but declined to serve as, Steward of Christmas at Lincoln's Inn, where he had already served as Master of the Revels in 1593. Dating Donne's poems is often difficult, but his years at the Inn were productive. While there he seems to have written many of his elegies, two of his *Satyres*, several of the prose *Paradoxes and Problems*, and perhaps a number of the *Songs and Sonets* on which his modern reputation largely depends. None of these poems were published; like most of the verse that Donne wrote throughout his life, these works circulated in manuscript. Donne composed poetry as an amateur, not a professional—as a gentlemanly sideline, not as a career. His growing reputation for learning and wit, however, helped set him apart from the other aspiring young men of his day, and his decision to volunteer in 1596 and 1597 for service with Queen Elizabeth's favorite, the Earl of Essex, in naval campaigns against Catholic Spain indicates not only the influential circles in which he had begun to move but also some estrangement from the religion of his youth. Certainly by the late 1590s Donne seems to have accommodated himself to

the state religion, as is suggested by his appointment as secretary to Sir Thomas Egerton, the Lord Keeper who was himself a former Catholic and whose son Donne had met during his voyages with Essex. By the turn of the century Donne's political career seemed promising; through Egerton's influence he served in Parliament in the fall of 1601, but by the end of that year Donne committed an act that undercut his hopes of future advancement. Without permission, he secretly married Ann More, the sixteen-year-old niece of Egerton's wife and, like Donne, once a resident in Egerton's household. Ann's father, Sir George More, was outraged when Donne informed him of the marriage early in 1602; Donne was briefly imprisoned and, at Sir George's insistence, was dismissed from Egerton's service. The young couple then went to live at the estate of Francis Wolley, Ann's cousin, at Pyrford.

For Donne, the next few years were socially frustrating but not unproductive. By the time Queen Elizabeth died in March 1603, he had already written many of his most important secular poems, including all of his *Satyres* and *Epigrams*, many of his verse epistles, and more of the poems posthumously published in the collection of *Songs and Sonets*. The new king, James I, may have met Donne when he visited Pyrford in August 1603, the same year in which Donne's first child probably was born. More children followed, at almost yearly intervals, for the next fourteen years; the third, a son, seems to have been born in 1605, when Donne was traveling on the continent. When he returned to England in 1606, he moved his family to Mitcham, closer to London and potential employment, although his attempt in 1607 to win a position in the Queen's household was unsuccessful. It may have been in 1607 or 1608 that he composed *Biathanatos*, an unpublished prose "paradox" defending suicide in certain limited cases. In 1607, Donne was encouraged by Thomas Morton, an Anglican theologian, to take holy orders. Donne declined, however, either because he felt unprepared or (more likely) because he still hoped for secular employment. In 1608, for instance, he unsuccessfully sought a post as secretary in Ireland, while in 1609 he failed in his attempt to become a secretary with the Virginia Company. These first few years of James's reign were disappointing for Donne the courtier, but they provided ample time to work on his various writings, including more lyrics, more verse epistles, more *Paradoxes and Prob-*

lems, and many prose letters to friends. Interestingly, many of his explicitly religious poems, including *A Litany*, the sonnet sequence entitled *La Corona*, and the first of the *Holy Sonnets* may also date from these years.

Donne's interest in religion bore fruit in other ways, too, including the prose tract *Psuedo-Martyr* (published in 1610), which defended the King's right to require Catholic subjects to take an Oath of Allegiance, and *Ignatius His Conclave* (published in 1611, in Latin and English), a witty indictment of the Jesuits. In 1610, Donne was awarded an honorary M.A. from Oxford University, and within the next two years he published two poems commemorating Elizabeth Drury, the deceased young daughter of Sir Robert Drury, who invited Donne to travel with him and his wife in Europe. Returning in 1612, Donne moved his family into a house in Drury Lane, London, provided by his patrons. In 1613, he published poems lamenting the death of Prince Henry and celebrating the marriage of Princess Elizabeth, and he also won the patronage of the Earl of Somerset, James's favorite. He celebrated Somerset's marriage in a poem in 1614 and served in the short Parliament held that year, but other efforts to obtain secular employment failed. The King was determined to make Donne a minister, and by 1615 Donne agreed. From this point on his rise was steady, and he became an increasingly prominent figure in the Anglican church. In the period shortly before or after his decision to enter the church, he composed the prose *Essays in Divinity*, a collection of meditations and prayers.

Ordained a deacon and priest in January 1615, Donne was soon appointed a royal chaplain and, by royal decree, was made a Doctor of Divinity by Cambridge University. The next year he was granted two rectories and was selected Divinity Reader at Lincoln's Inn. He preached at all three sites as well as at court, and the bulk of his writing after his ordination consisted of a series of highly eloquent sermons. The death of Donne's wife at age thirty-three in August 1617, shortly after a stillbirth, seems to have inspired one of his last *Holy Sonnets*, and in general from this point on Donne wrote poetry less and less. An official visit to Germany in 1619 provoked his beautiful *Hymn to Christ*, and other occasional poems would follow from time to time. By the time of his return to London in 1620, however, Donne was thought of chiefly as priest, not as a courtier or poet, and

his eminence was confirmed by his election, in late 1621, as Dean of St. Paul's Cathedral. In the early 1620s his sermons began to be published, and 1624 saw the publication of his prose *Devotions upon Emergent Occasions* in which he meditated on the serious illness that he had suffered in 1623. This affliction may also have provoked two of his best (and last) religious poems, the "Hymn to God My God, in My Sickness" and "A Hymn to God the Father."

Early in April 1625, a month after King James's death, Donne delivered the first court sermon to the new monarch, Charles I. For the last five years of his own life, Donne was occupied chiefly by his official duties in the church, including the delivery of regular sermons. More and more of these were published, both during Donne's life and after his death, and at the time he died in March 1631, Donne was known mainly as one of the leading priests and preachers of the Anglican faith. Even then, though, he was recognized as having been one of the greatest poets of his age, and in our century that reputation has become steadily more secure.

Literary Analysis

Although it is uncommon to think of Donne as chiefly a humorous poet, it is not at all uncommon to regard him as a "wit." Indeed, this noun—and its adjective, "witty"—turns up repeatedly in analyses of Donne's writing; it was no accident that J.B. Leishman called his extremely helpful study of Donne *The Monarch of Wit*. Yet "wit" in the seventeenth century meant something more than it tends to mean today. It was closely allied to ideas of *wisdom*, and true "wit" required more than flippant cleverness. It demanded knowledge, discrimination, mental agility, and verbal skill. Donne had these in abundance, and they helped make his poetry more than merely funny (though it is often that); they helped make it challenging, exhilarating, and delightful.

Donne's poems in general, and his humorous poems in particular, are best approached by remembering that their speakers are not necessarily spokesmen for Donne. Distinguishing between "author" and "speaker" (or between "poet" and "persona") is usually helpful, but it is especially useful when dealing with Donne. Recognizing that he often wrote in a voice not his own is crucial to appreciating many of his poems, and this is especially the case with his "humorous" poems. Donne can be an extremely playful poet, and half of the fun of some verses comes from recognizing how he plays with situations, tones, and speakers. In some poems he invites us to identify the speaker with himself; in fact, in some of his most serious poems he seems to demand it. But, with most of Donne's poems it is simplest, and safest, to speak of a "speaker."

It is also worth remembering that Donne wrote in a wide variety of genres, or poetic *kinds*. An epigram differed from an epistle; a satire differed from a sonnet. Most of Donne's readers knew these generic differences, and Donne knew how to exploit such distinctions for his own poetic purposes. He could observe the rules or break them; he could repeat past practices or transform them. Generic expectations provided one standard by which his performance—including his wit and originality—could and would be assessed.

The traits of Donne's speakers and the meanings of his various poems have been described quite differently by various critics. Donne has been one of the most studied poets in the twentieth century, and his poems have provoked an avalanche of varying interpretations. One of the most difficult problems that critics have faced has been deciding how seriously individual poems should be taken. This is especially true of *The Songs and Sonets*; poems that some critics have read as serious statements of romantic love have been read by others as comic or ironic, and indeed the issue of irony frequently becomes crucial in reading Donne. It is often difficult to say for certain how seriously he meant a particular poem to be read, or how closely he meant the speaker's feelings to reflect his own. Donne is universally regarded as a witty and often humorous poet, but the nature, purpose, and presence of his wit and humor are oftentimes disputed when particular poems are discussed. Different readers have found Donne funny for different reasons, and poems that some people have read as humorous have been taken quite seriously by others, sometimes for conflicting reasons.

Nonetheless, most commentators would agree that certain traits typify Donne's wit and humor, even though they might disagree about the uses made of those traits in particular poems. Certainly a highly developed sense of *drama* is a characteristic of many of Donne's lyrics. His poems typically start by dropping us into the midst of an implied situation; suddenly we find ourselves listening to a voice that sounds authentic and that takes its own reality

for granted. Donne had a gift for creating the impression of an actual speaking voice, of a "real" person addressing the reader or another character in vigorous, colloquial diction. His poems usually involve or imply a dramatic situation in which the speaker does not so much meditate privately as speak to an audience inside or outside the poem. Tone of voice may therefore be a source of Donne's humor; his speakers can be either self-consciously witty and clever or implicitly mocked and satirized by the poet himself, and sometimes both possibilities seem involved. Speakers proud of their own glibness and wit often seem the butts of Donne's irony. Since many of his speakers love to argue, and since many of the poems attempt persuasion of one sort or another, much of the humor of a number of his poems derives from the real or presumed cleverness of a speaker's logic. Donne thus seems to display his own wit by implicitly undercutting the self-conscious wit of his speakers.

The "logical," argumentative structures of many of Donne's poems could be used to show up the illogic of a speaker's arguments; in this manner the poet displays his own wit and tests the wit of his readers by exhibiting the smug cleverness of speakers who fail to recognize their own error, pride, and folly. From this perspective, even Donne's funniest and wittiest poems can be seen to have the fundamentally moral purpose of exposing the shallow conceit of their self-consciously "clever" speakers. Such speakers may seem funny in ways that they themselves do not realize. Of course, the implicit nature of irony can make its presence and importance in any particular work debatable, but most critics agree that irony of some sort frequently characterizes Donne's writing.

Paradox is another trait that often contributes to Donne's humor. Often his poems attempt to prove cases that seem at first preposterous by offering arguments displaying the speaker's ingenuity or clever boldness. The arguments normally depend on witty, unexpected, and elaborately developed analogies, and their tone tends to be hyperbolic or whimsical. The poems are frequently full of puns or other forms of word play, and the imagery can range from the homely and familiar to the abstract and outlandish. The language and development of the poems are rarely predictable, and our anticipation of the unexpected keeps us on our toes and contributes to the freshness, cleverness, and wit of Donne's works. The poems tend to develop not in any predetermined or conventional fashion but in ways that reflect the stops and starts, the shifts and turns, of a thinking mind. Donne's speakers may be argumentative, but their arguments are usually dense and tightly packed, and the humor of many of the poems depends on unusual twists of ideas, diction, or imagery. These traits, combined with an often crabbed, rough meter, enhance the drama and the colloquial vigor of Donne's works, and keep his humor from seeming pretty, petty, or light. In even his funniest poems there is an intelligent mind at work, either within or behind the speaker. In addition, humor could be used by Donne not as a frivolous device but as a method of detachment, criticism, and control; the humor of many poems checks or balances any tendency toward sentimentality, giving his works their characteristic intelligence and toughness. Donne always seems to have known what he was doing (even if we cannot always agree on what that was), and the wit of his poems is one measure of his self-conscious control. The poems contain an urbanity and sophistication that prevents their humor from seeming untutored or naive.

Donne's poems can reflect a wide range of comic moods, and the moods may shift and combine even within single works. Cynicism is a frequent tone, but the extent to which Donne's cynical personae speak for Donne himself is a matter of debate. At times the poet seems to mock or undercut the bitter, disillusioned wittiness of various speakers whose cynicism frequently reveals more about their own limits and defects than about the faults or failings which they attack. Contrarily, a gentle, teasing humor that suggests mutual understanding and shared values between speaker and audience (either inside or outside the poem) is another aspect of Donne's comic tone. Usually this tone is present in poems celebrating a satisfying mutual love, but even in these poems the speaker's ability to express himself humorously prevents the poems from becoming saccharine or sentimental. The lover's ability to joke with his beloved suggests the intimacy which they share so that the flippant wit often underscores the depth of their affection.

Donne could use humor for other purposes, too. In "The Relique," for instance (one of his most powerful poems), a cynical speaker begins by imagining that someday his grave will be broken up:

Some second guest to entertain,
(For graves have learned that woman-head
To be to more than one a bed) . . .

He prophesies that the credulous will regard the bone of his arm, and the "bracelet" of his beloved's "bright hair" wrapped around it, as religious relics, and he mockingly predicts that "All women shall adore us, and some men." His joking, however, gives way in the third stanza to a more serious tone in which he celebrates the innocent (and for that reason nearly miraculous) love that he and his beloved have shared. Then the poem shifts gears again when the speaker confesses in the final lines that

now alas
All measure, and all language, I should
    pass,
Should I tell what a miracle she was.

Not until the poem's very last word do we discover that the woman whom the speaker loves is dead. Immediately all of the earlier joking about graves and all of the apparent cynicism about women is placed in a new perspective: we realize that the speaker's humor is less biting than poignant, less flippant than a means of coming to terms with genuine loss and grief. Left alone, bereft of the woman he loved, the speaker feels dead in a deeper sense than he had earlier joked about. He himself is now a living relic—something left behind. In this poem as in others by Donne, humor is used to cope with pain, to complicate and intensify more "serious" feelings. By mixing tones, Donne deepens them.

One of Donne's most famous witty poems, "The Flea," illustrates many characteristics of his writing and humor. The poem's speaker tries to persuade a lady to go to bed with him by comparing various aspects of their relationship to a flea he has discovered on her body:

Mark but this flea, and mark in this,
How little that which thou deny'st me is;
It sucked me first, and now sucks thee,
And in this flea, our two bloods mingled
    be;
Thou know'st that this cannot be said
A sin, or shame, or loss of maidenhead,
    Yet this enjoys before it woo,
    And pampered swells with one
    blood made of two,

And this, alas, is more than we would
do.

Oh stay, three lives in one flea spare,
Where we almost, nay more than mar-
    ried are.
This flea is you and I, and this
Our marriage bed, and marriage temple
    is;
Though parents grudge, and you, we are
    met,
And cloistered in these living walls of jet.
    Though use make you apt to kill me,
    Let not to this, self murder added be,
    And sacrilege, three sins in killing
        three.

Cruel and sudden, has thou since
Purpled thy nail, in blood of innocence?
In what could this flea guilty be,
Except in that drop which it sucked from
    thee?
Yet thou triumph'st, and say'st that thou
Find'st not thyself, nor me the weaker
    now;
    'Tis true, then learn how false fears
        be;
    Just so much honour, when thou
        yield'st to me,
    Will waste, as this flea's death took
        life from thee.

Although the idea of drawing analogies
between a flea and a romantic relationship
might seem startlingly unique, in fact there was
a long tradition of similar poems. Still, Donne's
own treatment of the theme seems fresh and
original, and this poem exemplifies many of his
most typical techniques. The poem is explicitly
an argument; it plunges us into the midst of a
dramatic situation and involves direct address
to a silent (but not unresponsive) listener. The
speaker is proud of his "logic," of his ability to
prove a case, but his means of arguing seems
outrageously odd and impudent, and Donne
may be having as much fun with the speaker as
the speaker seems to be having in making his
case. This poem illustrates the extended development of a single image (or "conceit")—a
technique typical in many poems by Donne. It
also illustrates his characteristic use of paradox,
hyperbole, and vigorous speech.

Part of the wit in the poem involves the
speaker's ability to sustain his analogy for three
whole stanzas, moving from one unexpected

analogy to the next. His talent for exploiting the
poem's basic comparison for all it is worth, and
the mental agility with which he does so, illustrate the cleverness of the speaker's creator
without necessarily implying that the speaker
speaks for Donne. Although extended, the development of the comparison never seems mechanical or belabored; despite its "logical" progression, the poem illustrates the suppleness of
an active, responsive mind. The work is "dramatic" not only because it involves direct address but also because action is implied: the lady
apparently picks up the flea in the gap between
the first two stanzas, and then she kills it in the
gap between stanzas two and three. For all of
the speaker's self-conscious cleverness, the
woman remains unpersuaded, but the speaker
remains undeterred. Instead, he attempts to turn
even her act of killing the flea into a refutation
of her concerns about preserving her "honor."
We have a sense of how the woman thinks and
reacts even though we never hear her speak, and
although the poem ends on a note of self-satisfied triumph (the speaker, at least, is convinced
that he has won the argument), we note that he
is no closer to bedding the lady by the end of the
poem than he was at the beginning.

The speaker's smugness may be as much an
object of fun as his outlandish analogy, and
those readers who interpret the poem ironically
can point to the religious language embedded in
all three stanzas. Such language may remind
readers of standards of value and conduct that
the speaker seeks to violate but that the virtuous lady upholds, so ultimately the poem may
illustrate the poet's witty morality by showing
up the speaker's shallow wit. Donne often seems
to make his witty speakers use language whose
full implications may subvert the arguments
that they so cleverly attempt to make. In any
case, the use of religious language in erotic contexts is another trait typically found in many of
Donne's poems. At the very least, such usage
provides an excellent example of the poet's ability to draw together realms of experience that
might normally seem distinct. If such language
does actually provide an ironic context for interpreting the arguments of apparently "flippant" speakers, then it exemplifies the ethical
and religious seriousness that may underlie
many of Donne's most apparently humorous
poems.

The distinction between speaker and poet
seems especially clear in Donne's elegies, which
are indebted to the witty precedents set by the

Roman poet Ovid. "Elegy 6: The Perfume" provides a wonderful example of Donne's ability to exploit humorous situations and language. Once again the poem is dramatic: an indignant speaker complains about having been caught carrying on a secret affair with the daughter of a rich citizen. Because the girl's parents were suspicious, the speaker had taken all sorts of precautions to escape detection, but in the end it was his potent cologne (or "perfume") that allowed him to be apprehended. The situation itself is funny, but what Donne does with it is even funnier. Few poems illustrate more effectively his zestful language and vigorous description. The annoyed, agitated speaker resents being "catechized" by the girl's "hydroptic father," whose "glazed eyes" made him look (at least to the speaker) as if he had come "to kill a cockatrice." The girl's "immortal mother . . . doth lie / Still buried in her bed, yet will not die." She sleeps during the day so that she can keep watch on her daughter's activities at night. Fearing that her daughter may be pregnant, she carefully scrutinizes her "paleness, blushings, sighs, and sweats." The list is funny (particularly the last word), yet it also helps to characterize the comically exasperated speaker. Donne's inventive, colloquial, often hyperbolic diction, as well as his ear for effective rhythms, are evident in the speaker's description of one of the girl's monitors, a "grim eight-foot-high iron-bound serving-man, / That oft names God in oaths, and only then," but this is only one of several passages that may remind us of values the speaker himself transgresses. He speculates that even "if in hell no other pains there were," the serving-man "Makes me fear hell, because he must be there." The thought is funny, though the words may have more serious implications than the speaker himself realizes. Again, one often suspects that Donne is taking witty advantage of self-consciously witty speakers.

The poem's humor becomes progressively more outrageous. The speaker laments that his "loud perfume . . . cried / Even at thy father's nose," the mixed metaphor suggesting both the speaker's wit and his frustration. He speculates that if the suspicious father had detected "some bad smell, / he would have thought / That his own feet, or breath, that smell had wrought." Such grossness provokes laughter, but it also helps characterize the speaker. Part of the poem's humor springs from the speaker's tendency to describe inanimate objects as if they

were willful or alive, as when he mentions teaching his "silks, their whistling to forbear," or when he notes that "Even my oppressed shoes, dumb and speechless were," or when he attacks the perfume as if it were a person and complains that it "me traitorously hath betrayed." The language here illustrates Donne's comic capacity to exploit unexpected comparisons and to joke by seeming to take metaphors too literally, while his love of paradox and word play is exemplified when the speaker complains that his perfume "At once [immediately; simultaneously] fled unto him [the father], and stayed with me." The poet's ability to mix and complicate the tones of his work is illustrated by the speaker's complaint that through the disguise permitted by perfume, "the silly amorous sucks his death / By drawing in a leprous harlot's breath."

This and other language darkens the elegy's concluding atmosphere and suggests the serious implications that may underlie the poet's presentation of his comically exasperated speaker. When the speaker alleges that perfume is "much loved in the prince's hall" because "There, things that seem, exceed substantial," one senses that Donne sympathized with this satire on courtly superficiality, but it may also be noted that the speaker himself is deceitful, perfumed, decked out in silk, and fundamentally insubstantial. His satire seems to boomerang, although his comment on the court is no less cogent for being hypocritical. Here, as so often elsewhere, the writer wittily exploits a speaker's wit, and nowhere is his ability to shift tones more evident than in this poem's final couplet: "All my perfumes, I give most willingly / To embalm thy father's corse [corpse]; What? will he die?" If the idea seems grotesque and repugnant, it may be only the last stroke in Donne's increasingly unattractive portrait of his cocky speaker—a portrait all the more clever for being delivered as a self-portrait from the speaker's own mouth.

Whatever else Donne's speakers describe, they inevitably depict themselves, and the frequent ironies of their self-presentations seem to lie at the heart of much of the poet's humor. Although this speaker's reference to the "father's corse" is all the more forceful because it is unexpected, and although the poem's abrupt ending emphasizes the impression of an active mind and actual speaking voice, the reference to the corpse simultaneously illustrates the structural and thematic sophistication of Donne's poems, even those that might at first seem merely light and humorous. Images of death, after all, have pervaded this work; the sudden return to direct address in the final couplet presents only the most shocking of many references to physical corruption. While "The Perfume" is one of Donne's funniest poems, in some ways it also is one of his most ironic, probing, and disturbing. Indeed, his humor here as elsewhere is not without an edge. That edge is perhaps most apparent in his five satires, in which his wit is most obviously deployed to attack contemporary follies and corruption, but it is present in many of his other writings.

Donne's poems often combine mingled seriousness and humor; the mixed tones suggest the complexities of the speakers and situations which the author presents. A random sampling from a few of *The Songs and Sonets* illustrates some of the methods and meanings of his comic writing. In "The Good Morrow," for instance, the speaker uses humor to contrast the fulfilling love that he and his mistress now enjoy with their experiences before they met. It is as if they are only now fully awake; it is as if, in the past, they simply "snorted" in "the seven sleepers' den." Here a single word, "snorted," comically underscores how distant and foreign the speaker's past experiences now seem to him, how changed he feels. The word highlights the delicate, gentle humor implicit in the rest of the poem, in which the speaker happily celebrates a love so fulfilling that it "makes one little room, an everywhere."

Humor is used to different effect in the famous "Song" beginning, "Go, and catch a falling star." As the first line suggests, the poem is chiefly a catalogue of comic impossibilities, all leading up to the assertion that "Nowhere / Lives a woman true, and fair." The speaker claims that even if such a woman could be located next door, "Yet she / Will be / False, ere I come, to two, or three." Here the humor derives not only from the speaker's teasing cynicism but also from the cleverness with which Donne exploits the rhythm of the lines. The crucial word, "False," is skillfully delayed and then metrically emphasized, while the way in which the words "or three" are added, almost as an incidental afterthought, gives the end of the line the same kind of surprise and emphasis found at its beginning, underlining the speaker's confident cynicism.

Donne's humor often works by this kind of subtle surprise, as when, for instance, he opens "Woman's Constancy" by asking, "Now thou hast loved me one whole day, / Tomorrow when thou leav'st, what wilt thou say?" Not "*if*," but "*when*": the phrasing catches us off guard, and even though the assumption seems funny, we realize, too, that the speaker's humor serves partly as a kind of defense or self-protection against the inconstancy that is described in the poem. Behind the joke lies an atmosphere of distrust that is foreign to the mutual assurance celebrated in "The Good Morrow." The sudden shift in tone between the first and second lines of "Woman's Constancy" illustrates the quickness of Donne's wit, but it also emphasizes the theme of mutability so central to the poem. The assonance and heavily accented monosyllables of "one whole day" suggest duration, but this mood is immediately undercut. In all of these ways Donne's lines are witty and clever, yet in all of these ways the wit and cleverness also contribute to the poem's thematic unity and deeper meaning. Donne is often witty but rarely superficial. His humor works in several senses, almost always contributing to the moral, thematic, and structural integrity of his poems. The humor helps create convincingly vivid and memorable speakers even as it suggests the wit of the man who created them.

Take, for instance, the famous opening of "The Sun Rising," in which the speaker, lying in bed with his mistress, chastises the sun as a "Busy old fool" and a "Saucy pedantic wretch." He orders it to "go chide / Late schoolboys, and sour prentices," and threatens to "eclipse and cloud" the sun's beams "in a wink." Or, take "The Canonization," which opens with the exclamation, "For God's sake hold your tongue, and let me love," and in which the speaker's passion is later justified by the question, "What merchant's ships have my sighs drowned? / Who says my tears have overflowed his ground?" The last lines in particular demonstrate Donne's ability to draw on and parody the conventions of Petrarchan love poetry, but both works also exhibit other characteristic devices: direct address; jumping into the midst of a dramatic situation; hyperbole; paradox; impudence; spontaneity; argument; and vigorous, colloquial action. The poems are performances, displays, not only by the speakers for their internal audiences, but by the poet for us. Whether we imagine Donne identifying with or mocking his speakers, the one indisputable impression that we usually take away from such poems is an impression of the poet's cleverness and creative facility. However the humor of the poems leaves us feeling about their speakers, it almost inevitably leaves us feeling good about Donne. This claim seems worth stressing, since Donne's poems—perhaps especially the funny ones—can be seen from one perspective as instruments of self-advertisement and self-promotion. His wit is disarming in several senses; his comedy could help him compete. His cleverness was one measure and tool of his intellectual and social power, one means of self-assertion.

This is most obviously true in his satires, but it also seems to be the case in nearly all of his poems, particularly in his epistles in verse and prose, and especially in the epistles to various patrons. The wit of such poems is ambiguous: on the one hand it reflects the poet's personal endowments, his unique gifts and autonomous genius, but on the other hand it demonstrates his need to prove appealing, to make his mark in others' eyes. For this and other reasons, the wit that underlies so many of Donne's poems is rarely simple or uncomplicated. The humor of his writing may seem playful, yet it is often deeply involved with matters of the utmost seriousness, including his senses of personal identity and social status.

The fact that humor sometimes appears even in Donne's most clearly sincere and serious poems, those addressed to God, suggests just how deeply ingrained his humor was, how much his wit was an integral part of his personality. In the "Hymn to God my God, in my Sickness," for example, the speaker anticipates the day when he will die and be made part of God's "music." His sickness gives him the opportunity to "tune the instrument here at the door, / And what I must do then, think now before." The speaker's wit implies his trust in God's goodness and mercy; the fact that he can joke about his death suggests that he does not entirely fear it. His humor implies strength as well as humility. He describes how his "physicians by their love are grown / Cosmographers, and I their map, who lie / Flat on this bed. . . ." Both the ironic distancing exhibited in these lines and the speaker's unexpected analogy typify Donne's wit, and both suggest the assurance that God's love provides. The mood becomes more serious as the poem develops, evolving from a witty self-description into a plangent appeal; the mingled seriousness and humor of the hymn exemplify Donne's complex sensibility.

Similar complexity is evident in his "Hymn to God the Father." Here the poet plays repeatedly with his own name, arguing that even when God "hast done" with forgiving the speaker's various sins, He "hast not done [Donne], / For I have more." This refrain is spoken twice, but the poem concludes by asking God to swear that He will be forever merciful: "Having done that, thou hast done, / I fear no more." The poem is playful in any number of ways, not only in its punning on Donne's name but also in its teasing tone and because it alludes to an earlier, secular love poem (with a similar refrain) by the sixteenth-century wit Sir Thomas Wyatt. Even in addressing God, Donne could exploit his own (and his readers') familiarity with literary tradition. The fact that he can be so humorously familiar with God suggests the trust that his "Father" inspires, and the poem certainly displays the kind of comic affection that one might expect to find between an impetuous child and his sometimes stern but dependably loving parent. Donne's humor both offsets and emphasizes the "fear" that he confesses in the last stanza—the fear that he will "perish on the shore." By the end of the hymn he seems certain that God will forgive all of his sins, even "that sin which I did shun / A year, or two: but wallowed in, a score." Here the joke (with its precisely effective final verb) makes fun of the speaker, but the fact that he *can* joke is ultimately a tribute to God's love.

Donne's good humor and wit made and make him one of the most appealing poets of his time, and his many works in numerous genres testify to the variety, pervasiveness, and importance of his comic touch. His humor displays an intellectual agility and artistic control, and it helps make his voice distinctive, no matter which persona he happens to adopt.

Summary

John Donne was one of the most significant poets and prose writers of the late sixteenth and early seventeenth centuries. His humor is typically "witty," and his poems are often simultaneously dramatic, argumentative, colloquial, and intellectual. He frequently uses paradoxes, analogies, hyperbole, irony, striking imagery, and unexpected juxtapositions or twists of thought. His playfulness conveys a sense of intellectual alertness and of spontaneity combined with disciplined artistry. His best poems are both serious and clever.

Selected Bibliography

Primary Sources
A variorum edition of Donne's poems is due to be published shortly (general edi-

D

tors: Gary A. Stringer and John R. Roberts). This should be an invaluable resource for students and scholars. A scholarly edition of Donne's letters is being prepared by Robert Parker Sorlein; it should also prove extremely helpful.

Biathanatos. Ed. Ernest W. Sullivan, Jr. Newark: University of Delaware Press, 1984.

Devotions upon Emergent Occasions. Ed. Anthony Raspa. New York: Oxford University Press, 1987.

The Divine Poems. Ed. Helen Gardner. 2nd ed. Oxford: Oxford University Press, 1978.

The Elegies and the Songs and Sonnets. Ed. Helen Gardner. Oxford: Oxford University Press, 1963.

The Epithalamions, Anniversaries and Epicedes. Ed. Wesley Milgate. Oxford: Oxford University Press, 1978.

Essays in Divinity. Ed. Evelyn M. Simpson. Oxford: Oxford University Press, 1952.

Ignatius His Conclave. Ed. T.S. Healy, SJ. Oxford: Oxford University Press, 1969.

Paradoxes and Problems. Ed. Helen Peters. Oxford: Oxford University Press, 1980.

The Satires, Epigrams, and Verse Letters. Ed. Wesley Milgate. Oxford: Oxford University Press, 1967.

The Sermons. Ed. George R. Potter and Evelyn M. Simpson. Berkeley: University of California Press, 1962. 10 vols.

The Songs and Sonets. Ed. Theodore Redpath. 2nd ed. New York: St. Martin's Press, 1983.

Secondary Sources

Bibliographies

Keynes, Geoffrey. *Bibliography of Dr. John Donne*. Oxford: Clarendon Press, 1973. 4th ed.

Biographies

Bald, R.C. *John Donne: A Life*. Oxford: Oxford University Press, 1970. Still the standard scholarly biography.

Gosse, Edmund. *The Life and Letters of John Donne, Dean of St. Paul's*. 2 vols. London: Heinemann, 1899. Still useful although untrustworthy.

Walton, Izaak. *The Life and Death of Dr. Donne*. London, 1640. Subsequently revised and enlarged. A standard early source.

Books

Dennis Flynn is at work on what promises to be a major new biography of Donne; many of Flynn's articles are already in print. The *John Donne Journal* (first volume: 1982) publishes many important essays. Other valuable biographical and critical resources include the following:

Alvarez, A. *The School of Donne*. London: Chatto and Windus, 1961. Donne's realism, logic, and original coterie audience are stressed.

Andreasen, N.J.C. *John Donne: Conservative Revolutionary*. Princeton: Princeton University Press, 1967. Andreasen stresses the morality of Donne's wit.

Carey, John. *John Donne: Life, Mind, and Art*. Oxford: Oxford University Press, 1981. Provocative and controversial.

Eliot, T.S. "The Metaphysical Poets." In *Selected Essays of T.S. Eliot*. 2nd ed. New York: Harcourt Brace Jovanovich, 1951. Influential but controversial; stresses how Donne unites mind and emotion.

Guss, Donald L. *John Donne: Petrarchist: Italianate Conceits and Love Theory in the Songs and Sonets*. Detroit: Wayne State University Press, 1966.

Hester, M. Thomas. *Kinde Pitty and Brave Scorn: John Donne's Satyres*. Durham, NC: Duke University Press, 1982. Detailed analysis of themes and contexts.

Leishman, J.B. *The Monarch of Wit: An Analytical and Comparative Study of the Poetry of John Donne*. 5th ed. New York: Harper and Row, 1965. Still one of the best introductions.

Marotti, Arthur. *John Donne, Coterie Poet*. Madison: University of Wisconsin Press, 1986. Marotti reads the poems autobiographically; stresses the influence of Donne's small original audience of friends and patrons.

Miner, Earl. *The Metaphysical Mode from Donne to Cowley*. Princeton: Princeton University Press, 1969. Miner emphasizes the private aspects of the poetry, its definitional, dialectical wit, and its satire and affirmations.

Pinka, Patricia Garland. *This Dialogue of One: The Songs and Sonnets of John Donne*. University, AL: University of Alabama Press, 1982. Analyses of the poems' varying speakers or personae.

Roberts, John R., ed. *Essential Articles for the Study of John Donne's Poetry.* Hamden, CT: Archon Books, 1975. Very comprehensive anthology.

———. *John Donne: An Annotated Bibliography of Modern Criticism 1912–1967.* Columbia: University of Missouri Press: 1973. Extremely useful.

———. *John Donne: An Annotated Bibliography of Modern Criticism 1968–78.* Columbia: University of Missouri Press, 1982. Exceptionally detailed.

Roston, Murray. *The Soul of Wit: A Study of John Donne.* Oxford: Clarendon Press, 1974. Roston discusses Donne's mannerisms and serious wit.

Simpson, Evelyn. *A Study of the Prose Works of John Donne.* 2nd ed. Oxford: Clarendon Press, 1948. Emphasizes biographical contexts.

Stein, Arnold. *John Donne's Lyrics: The Eloquence of Action.* Minneapolis: University of Minnesota Press, 1962. Stein studies Donne's style and wit.

Tuve, Rosemond. *Elizabethan and Metaphysical Imagery.* Chicago: University of Chicago Press, 1947. Emphasizes Donne's links with contemporary styles of writing and thought.

Robert C. Evans

Douglas, Norman

Born: Falkenhorst, Thuringen, Austria, December 8, 1868
Education: Uppingham School, England, 1878–1883; Karlsruhe Gymnasium, Germany, 1883–1888
Marriage: Elizabeth Louisa Fitzgibbon, 1898; divorced, 1903; two sons
Died: Capri, February 7, 1952

Biography

"My generation grew up on *South Wind*," Graham Greene wrote in his preface to *Venus in the Kitchen*, a volume of aphrodisiac recipes collected by Norman Douglas and Giuseppe Orioli under the pseudonym of Pilaff Bey and published just after the death of Douglas in 1952. A friend of Joseph Conrad, Ford Madox Ford, Charles Doughty, and other luminaries of the early twentieth-century British literary scene, Douglas was romanticized by Muriel Draper in her *Music at Midnight* (1929), vilified as Argyl by D.H. Lawrence in *Aaron's Rod* (1922), and eulogized in the British press by Greene and V.S. Pritchett. Still, for all of his early fame and apparent influence, Douglas is so little remembered today that even Penguin Books, which has published his comic masterpiece *South Wind* since 1935, has for some time listed him under Australian writers in its literature catalogue.

In fact, Douglas was born in Austria, not Australia, at the Tyrolean village of Falkenhorst, Thuringen, on December 8, 1868, to a prominent family with local and Scottish connections. His paternal grandfather immigrated to Austria from Scotland for business reasons; his maternal grandfather was an Austrian baron and his maternal grandmother was the daughter of a Scottish lord. The death of his father in a hunting accident when the boy was only six seems to have affected him profoundly, and biographers have often suggested that Douglas's own peripatetic interests derived in part from emulating a father whose recreational pursuits included mountain climbing, archeology, and geology. In his autobiographical collection *Looking Back* (1933), Douglas expresses tremendous affection for the father that he barely knew, as well as a love for the Tyrolean backdrop of his boyhood.

In 1878, however, at the age of nine, Douglas was sent to school in England where he spent an unhappy five years in several educational settings, including the Uppingham School. At the age of fourteen, Douglas began five rather better years at the gymnasium in Karlsruhe, Germany, but the English experience seems to have colored his opinions regarding education. In *South Wind* (1917), for example, the talkative Mr. Keith claims that "our English system of education is all wrong,"[1] and rails against "Mathematics . . . . And Euclid—that frowzy anachronism . . . . And the hours spent over history! What on earth does it matter who Henry the Twelfth's wife was? Chemistry! All this, relatively speaking, is unprofitable stuff" (37–38). Douglas himself chose the Foreign Service over a university education and was posted to the British Embassy in St. Petersburg in 1894. A social entanglement, purportedly with a married woman, caused him to end his diplomatic career and leave Russia in 1896.

For the next eight years, Douglas traveled widely in Europe, North Africa, and Asia. During that time (in 1898), he married a cousin, Elizabeth (Elsa) Fitzgibbon, and they used his villa in Italy as the home base for their journeys.

Douglas supported that lifestyle with income from the family holdings in Austria, but when the collapse of his marriage in 1903 was followed by financial reverses, he decided to turn to writing to supplement his greatly reduced income.

Douglas had already published a number of scholarly studies and, in collaboration with his wife, a book of stories entitled *Unprofessional Tales* (1901), under the pseudonym of Normyx. According to Ralph D. Lindeman, "eight copies of *Unprofessional Tales* were sold, the remainder were pulped, and the book is now a curiosity" (20). Beginning in 1904, after settling on Capri, Douglas wrote a number of studies of Roman antiquities and early Italian history, especially as related to Capri. Some of these privately printed papers were reused by him in two subsequent books on Italy, and all of them were later collected and reprinted by Giuseppe Orioli as *Capri: Materials for a Description of the Island* (1930). Despite some success in placing magazine articles on travel and literature, most of Douglas's early writings contributed a great deal more to his reputation than to his bank account. In 1910, at age forty-one and having spent the first three months of the year in Tunisia, Douglas moved to London in search of a steady job and a publisher for a book of sketches about Capri and southern Italy, including some that had already been printed privately. That book was *Siren Land* (1911), Douglas's first critical success, which nevertheless met about the same fate as his earlier attempts: its first edition, too, according to Ian Greenlees, "was mostly sold as waste paper" (7). Douglas next published *Fountains in the Sand* (1912), an account of his time in Tunisia, but it was not until his second book of Italian travels, *Old Calabria*, appeared in 1915 that Douglas can be said to have established himself as a writer. By then, he was working as an assistant editor on the *English Review*, under Ford Madox Hueffer (later Ford Madox Ford), as well as publishing essays and reviews there. This period of stability was to prove temporary, though. According to some accounts, in part because of his openly homosexual lifestyle Douglas lost the indulgence of Joseph Conrad, who had been his friend and benefactor, and he may also have been under the threat "of facing arrest on a certain charge" of immorality (Aldington, 148). Douglas had also grown dissatisfied with his position on the *English Review* once Ford resigned as editor. As a conse-quence, he returned to Capri in 1916 to finish his current book and then moved to an impoverished life in Paris.

When that book was published as *South Wind*, Douglas's satiric masterpiece, the timing of its appearance had a great deal to do with its reception for more than a decade. Its light and witty tone contrasted starkly with the dark days of World War I, when it first appeared, and its apparently hedonistic irreverence attracted an entire generation of disaffected writers throughout the 1920s—the generation of Greene and Pritchett. The success of *South Wind* made Douglas something of a cultural icon—the Epicurean—but it also helped free him, if slowly, to live the life of epicurean delights that he desired. In the years before World War II, Douglas traveled frequently throughout the Mediterranean basin, in Europe, Africa, and the Near East. He published more than a dozen books during this time, many based on his travels or personal recollections. Only two were fiction: the strange *They Went* (1920), set in a fantasized Middle Ages, and the stranger *In the Beginning* (1927), a mythological attack on religious and social conventions. These long out-of-print works are rarely even mentioned today, though Lindeman describes the former as "an odd little book of fiction which some critics have preferred to *South Wind*" (29). Similarly, Douglas's travel books have never received much attention in the United States, but they have long since eclipsed the popularity of his novels in Britain. Indeed, Greenlees has argued that "*Old Calabria* is the masterpiece of Douglas" and "his finest work" (11, 22).

The years between the wars were not only Douglas's most productive but his most stable. He settled in Florence in 1922 and began a relationship with Orioli that was to last the rest of his life. After the success of *South Wind*, Douglas found it financially rewarding to return to his earlier practice of privately printing his works before later selling the rights to a commercial publisher. Orioli published Douglas's work privately in his Lungarno Series and subsequently became so inseparable from Douglas that the title of Richard Aldington's biography, *Pinorman*, is "a portmanteau word used by themselves and friends for Pino (Orioli) and Norman (Douglas)" (Aldington, 1). Orioli and Douglas remained close for the rest of the latter's life, and the posthumously published *Venus in the Kitchen* is a collaborative effort between them.

Douglas left Florence in 1937 and spent the early part of the war in the south of France and Portugal before arriving in London in 1941. Nearing eighty, he returned to his beloved Capri in 1946 at the first opportunity following the armistice; he died there on February 7, 1952.

Literary Analysis

Despite occasional claims for the importance of his travel writings and his other fiction, Douglas's reputation and the influence that he exerted on younger British modernists in the period between the wars rest almost entirely on his most widely read work, *South Wind*. The adulation that *South Wind* originally inspired has subsequently been tempered with the recognition of its similarity, if not indebtedness, to the conversational novels of Thomas Love Peacock. If the oblivion to which *South Wind* increasingly has been consigned since Douglas's death contrasts markedly to the literary persistence of the other great, if more subtle, British satirical novel that appeared during the war years, Ford Madox Ford's *The Good Soldier* (1915), perhaps the reason can be found in the manic quality of Douglas's fiction. While Ford's novel concentrates on four or five characters at most and directs its satire against the British upper class, Douglas peoples his satire with a Dickensian cast and tilts at a multitude of social and cultural windmills simultaneously.

Set on the Capri-like Mediterranean island of Nepenthe, the novel begins with the visit of Mr. Heard, the English Bishop of Bampopo, in Africa—a genial and intelligent man, among whose initial sins, for Douglas, is the strength of his faith. The bishop arrives in Nepenthe to serve as escort to a married female cousin on her way from India to England, and later he watches as that cousin pushes a man (who turns out to be her first husband) off a cliff. "How to make a murder palatable to a bishop: that is the plot" of *South Wind*, Douglas wrote in a reverie during his Italian travels in *Alone* (1921), and indeed the bishop is finally willing to accept that murder in terms of "the insignificance of a human life . . . . One dirty blackmailer more or less; what on earth did it matter to anybody?" (308). The bishop attains that understanding on the heels of a revelation about his own religion: "His sympathies had outgrown the ideals of that establishment; a wave of pantheistic benevolence had drowned its smug little teachings. The Church of England! What was

it still good for? A stepping-stone, possibly towards something more respectable and humane; a warning to all concerned of the folly of idolizing dead men and their delusions. The Church? Ghosts!" (304).

But, if the bishop is brought to see Douglas's light, some of the author's own traits and ideals are also scrutinized under it. Actually, many of the residents of Nepenthe seem to share something of Douglas's own personality. One is a loquacious epicure, another a Jewish geologist, a third is an antiquarian and a con-man, and so on. These characters are mixed with others fulfilling more symbolic functions, like the inebriated and often undressed Miss Wilberforce or the Russian immigrant sect known as the Little White Cows. In fact, there is something for almost everyone to make fun of in Douglas's overpopulated little paradise.

There is a lot of fun to be made, too, not only in the endlessly satirical conversations that dominate the book but in the atmospherics and set-pieces of the work as well, items such as the eruption of the island's volcano or the chapter-long parody of "history of Saint Dodekanus, and the origin of his cult on Nepenthe" (20). A Cretan monk, according to that history, Dodekanus grew restless after repeated "visions" of "a young woman of pleasing exterior . . . and whether it was a woman of flesh and blood, or merely an angel, was never discovered, for he seems to have kept his brother monks in ignorance of the whole affair." Subsequently, Dodekanus set sail for Libya, was shipwrecked en route, and became an African missionary, "preaching to black nations and converting tribes innumerable" (20):

> For three-and-thirty years he wandered till, one evening, he saw the moon rise on the right side of his face.
>
> He had entered the land of the Crotalophoboi, cannibals and necromancers who dwelt in a region so hot, and with light so dazzling, that their eyes grew on the soles of their feet. Here he laboured for eighty years, redeeming them to Christianity from their magical and bloodthirsty practices. In recompense whereof, they captured him at the patriarchal age of 132, or thereabouts, and bound him with ropes between two flat boards of palmwood. Thus they kept the prisoner, feeding him abundantly,

until the old equinoctial feast drew near. On the evening of that day they sawed the whole, superstitiously, into twelve separate pieces, one for each month of the year; and devoured of the saint what was to their liking. (20)

Douglas's spoof of religion in general, and the lives of saints in particular, continues in the same arcane manner, including a lengthy quotation from the Antiquities by Monsigneur Perelli, "the learned and genial historian of Nepenthe" (22), and a brief account of the debate over the origins of the name Dodekanus—whether "from the Greek word *dodeka*, signifying twelve and alluding to the twelve morsels into which his body was superstitiously divided" or from "Do dekanus: give us a deacon" (21), the cannibals' purported plea in bad Latin for someone to convert them.

The efficacy of the Nepenthe islanders' faith in Saint Dodekanus is confirmed for them when showers of ash from a mainland volcano cease with its eruption. Saved from the ashes, the islanders are indifferent to the fate of the mainland villagers now threatened by the lava flow.

> The fact that villages were being overwhelmed under a deluge of flame, vineyards scorched and hundreds of innocent folk, their retreat cut off by fiery torrents, were even then being roasted to death, was of no concern to the islanders. It only proved what every one knew: that the jurisdiction of their Patron Saint did not extend to the mainland.

> Each of those villages had its own Saint, whose business it was to forestall accidents of this kind. If they failed in their duty through incapacity or mulishness, nothing was easier than to get rid of them; there were others to choose from—dozens of others, waiting for the job! Thinking thus, the islanders gave vent to an immense sigh of relief. They wished long life to their Patron Saint, with whose services they had reason to be satisfied. Their own crops and lives were safe from harm, thanks to the martyr Dodekanus. He loved his people, and they loved him. He was a protector worthy of the name—not like those low-bred bastards across the water. (26)

Douglas's humor ranges easily, as in the history of Saint Dodekanus and, later, of Saint Eulalia, from the silly to the scholarly, but always within the context of the novel's themes. The bishop's motto before arriving in Nepenthe is simplistic: "Be perfect of your own kind, whatever that kind may be." In Africa, Heard himself "had been so perfect of his kind, so exemplary a pastor, that there was small chance of a return to the scene of his episcopal labours" (5). As a corrective, Douglas sends the bishop to Nepenthe, to meet all sorts of perfection—perfect fools, perfect villains, even a perfect murderess. And, ironically, instead of overturning the bishop's motto, the novel confirms it. A combination of brilliant social satire and verbal slapstick, *South Wind* is nothing short of a tongue-in-cheek modernist tour-de-force which has been neglected for too long.

Summary

Norman Douglas and his satiric novel *South Wind* had a tremendous influence on British writers coming of age in the aftermath of World War I but were later unfairly dismissed as hedonistic, in the one case, and derivative, in the other. The witty style of his fiction is also to be found in his many travel books, which attained great popularity in England, though not in the United States. Personally praised by Conrad and attacked by Lawrence, Douglas should be studied as a major personality on the British literary scene in the early decades of this century and the author of one of the great comic creations in the history of the modern British novel.

Notes
1. Norman Douglas, *South Wind* (Harmondsworth: Penguin, 1976), p. 36. Subsequent references are to this edition.

Selected Bibliography

Primary Sources
Normyx (pseudonym). *Unprofessional Tales.* London: Unwin, 1901. Short stories written with Elsa Douglas.
Siren Land. London: Dent, and New York: E.P. Dutton, 1911. Travels in Italy.
Fountains in the Sand: Rambles Among the Oases of Tunisia. London: Secker, 1912; New York: Dodd, Mead, 1921. Travels in Tunisia.
Old Calabria. London: Secker, and Boston: Houghton Mifflin, 1915. Travels in Italy.

London Street Games. London: St. Catherine Press, 1916. Descriptions of and comments on popular children's games.

South Wind. London: Secker, 1917; New York: Dodd, Mead, 1918. Satirical novel about Nepenthe.

They Went. London: Chapman & Hall, 1920; New York: Dodd, Mead, 1921. Novel about magical medieval Brittany.

Alone. London: Chapman & Hall, 1921; New York: McBride, 1922. Travels in Italy.

Together. London: Chapman & Hall, and New York: McBride, 1923. Travels in Austria.

Experiments. London: Chapman & Hall, and New York: McBride, 1925. Essays, stories, reminiscences, and reviews.

In the Beginning. Florence: Privately printed, 1927; New York: John Day, 1928. Novel.

Birds and Beasts of the Greek Anthology. London: Chapman & Hall, and New York: Jonathan Cape and Harrison Smith, 1928.

How About Europe? Some Footnotes on East and West. London: Chatto and Windus, 1930. American title: *Goodbye to Western Culture.* New York: Harper, 1930.

Capri: Materials for a Description of the Island. Florence: Orioli, 1930.

Three of Them. London: Chatto and Windus, 1930. Includes *One Day, Nerinda,* and *On the Herpetology of the Grand Duchy of Baden.*

Paneros: Some Words on Aphrodisiacs and the Like. London: Chatto and Windus, and New York: McBride, 1931.

Summer Islands: Ischia and Ponza. London: Harmondsworth, and New York: Colophon, 1931.

Looking Back: An Autobiographical Excursion. London: Chatto and Windus, and New York: Harcourt Brace Jovanovich, 1933.

Late Harvest. London: Drummond, 1946. Reprinting of *Summer Islands,* with essays on Douglas's own books.

Footnote on Capri. London: Sidgwick and Jackson, 1952. Text to accompany photographs.

Pilaff Bey (pseudonym). *Venus in the Kitchen, or Love's Cookery Book.* London: Heinemann, 1952; New York: Viking Press, 1953. In collaboration with Giuseppe Orioli. Introduction by Graham Greene.

Secondary Sources

Aldington, Richard. *Pinorman: Personal Recollections of Norman Douglas, Pino Orioli, and Charles Prentice.* London: Heinemann, 1954. Chatty, anecdotal, sometimes mean-spirited biography based on a friendship apparently gone sour.

Cunard, Nancy. *Grand Man: Memories of Norman Douglas.* London: Secker and Warburg, 1954. Personal reminiscences and appreciations by Cunard and others, of little literary value.

Dawkins, Richard M. *Norman Douglas.* London: Hart-Davis, 1952. 2nd ed. Short, philosophical essay.

Greenlees, Ian. *Norman Douglas.* London: Longmans, 1957.

Holloway, Mark. *Norman Douglas: A Biography.* London: Secker and Warburg, 1976. The most recent and most complete biography of Douglas.

Leary, Lewis. *Norman Douglas.* New York: Columbia University Press, 1968.

Lindeman, Ralph D. *Norman Douglas.* New York: Twayne, 1965. Well-balanced and thorough introduction to both the life and the works.

Tomlinson, Henry M. *Norman Douglas.* London: Chatto and Windus, 1952. 2nd ed.

Woolf, Cecil. *A Bibliography of Norman Douglas.* London: Hart-Davis, 1954. Includes notes by Douglas.

David Mesher

D

Dryden, John

Born: Northhamptonshire, August 8, 1631
Education: Westminster School in London; graduated from Trinity College, Cambridge, January 1654
Marriage: Lady Elizabeth Howard, December 1, 1663; three children
Died: London, May 1, 1700

Biography

Widely considered the finest author of the late seventeenth century, John Dryden was born in the parsonage house of Aldwinkle All Saints in Northhamptonshire on August 8, 1631. His parents, Erasmus Dryden and Mary Pickering, were both Puritans with strong anti-monarchal sympathies. Although Dryden was a public figure for most of his career, surprisingly little is known of his private life, and less still is known of his youth and young adulthood. It is recorded that he attended Westminster School in London and graduated from Trinity College Cambridge, in 1654, and that his marriage to Lady Elizabeth Howard on December 1, 1663, produced three sons.

After his arrival in London in 1657, Dryden turned to a career of writing for the stage. For the next twenty-four years, his reputation as both an author and a critic grew steadily in London. Politically, it appears that he dropped his hostility toward the monarchy after the Restoration (as many in England did at that time) in return for the stability which it offered. His popularity with the theatergoing public and with Charles II brought about Dryden's commission as Poet Laureate and Historiographer Royale in 1670. His career was essentially unchanged by the appointment until the intrigues of the Popish Plot in 1681.

In the political maelstrom that followed the fictitious plot to reinstate a Roman Catholic monarchy in England, Dryden wrote a series of superb satires, notably "Absalom and Achitophel" and "Mac Flecknoe." After the Popish Plot, Dryden appears to have taken another step toward conservatism by converting to Catholicism. After the Glorious Revolution of 1688, Dryden was stripped of his royal offices and forced to return to writing for the theater to earn his living.

Dryden's later efforts at theater were not particularly successful, largely because the taste for his rhymed tragedies had waned. During the last decade of his life, he turned to translations of the classics, where he found renewed success. His primary translations were *Ovid's Epistles*, *Works of Virgil*, and *Fables, Ancient and Modern*.

Late in his life, Dryden gained a good deal of respect as the grand old man of literature, holding forth regularly at Will's Coffee House with a group of writers that included, on various occasions, William Congreve and a young Alexander Pope. He died nearly penniless in London on May 1, 1700. Dryden's many friends provided him with a splendid funeral, and he was laid to rest in the Poets' Corner in Westminster Abbey.

Literary Analysis

It would be difficult to overvalue Dryden's contribution to literature in the English language. "Perhaps no nation ever produced a writer that enriched his language with such a variety of models," Samuel Johnson wrote in his *Lives of the Poets: Dryden*—"What was said of Rome, adorned by Augustus, may be applied by an easy metaphor to English poetry embellished by Dryden . . . He found it brick, and he left it marble." As a playwright, poet, and critic, few individuals (such as Dr. Johnson himself) have left such an imprimatur on the literature of their time as did Dryden.

Still, as a writer of Restoration comedies, Dryden enjoyed only limited success. Of his several works, *Marriage à la Mode* (1671) is considered his best effort at capturing the wit and gaiety of the Restoration theater. His greatest success in drama, however, came as a result of his work in heroic tragedy, Dryden's attempt to bring to the theater the nobility and grandeur of epic poetry. Although *The Conquest of Granada* (1672) was probably his greatest commercial success, *All For Love* (1678) is regarded as the best example of the genre from any author.

A revision of William Shakespeare's *Antony and Cleopatra*, *All For Love* is a textbook example of Dryden's adherence to the classical unities of time, place, and action; the broad reach of the Shakespearean original is reduced to the final fateful day. The spirit of the play is modeled after the style of Jean Baptiste Racine, with its emphasis on psychological analysis. Torn between his love for Cleopatra and his duty to Ventidius, Dryden's Antony marches grandly off to his death. While Shakespear's lovers are swept along by forces that they can never master, in Dryden's play their love assumes center stage as historical events shrink to the background.

Dryden's most enduring literary success came almost accidentally, as the result of a long-forgotten political intrigue. In 1678, the Earl of Shaftesbury sought to exclude the Duke of York (the brother of Charles II and later James II) from ascending the throne. In York's stead, Shaftesbury sought to promote the Duke of Monmouth, one of Charles II's illegitimate children. Dryden, in his role as Poet Laureate, embarked on a series of political satires on behalf of the Tories, and these remain classic examples of the mock-heroic.

The first was "Absalom and Achitophel" (1681) in which Dryden refuted Monmouth's claim to the throne and in the process parodied the principles of the Whig cause. Dryden saved particular venom for George Villiers, Duke of Buckingham, who had skewered Dryden ten years earlier in his play *The Rehearsal*. There is little plot to the satire, loosely based on the Biblical story of Absalom's revolt against King David. The similarities between the political situation and the story of Absalom were particularly fortuitous for Dryden's purposes, but it should be remembered that the idea itself was not new; authors had been drawing parallels between London and Jerusalem and between the reigning monarch and David for generations. What sets Dryden's use of the story apart is the sharpness of his satire, including the immortal line (in reference to Shaftesbury): "Great wits are sure to madness near allied / And thin partitions do their bounds divide."

A dominant theme that runs throughout "Absalom and Achitophel" is the idea of turbulence or unsettledness. Dryden, like many of his contemporaries, valued the stability that the monarchy provided, and he feared the return of civil war. Indeed, it should be noted that the desire for stability was particularly strong in Dryden, as we will see later in "Religio Laici" (1682). In nearly every satirical portrait in "Absalom and Achitophel," a key psychological trait is instability. Dryden's depiction of Zimri is typical of the poet's humor and his characterization of his opponents:

A man so various, that he seem'd to be
Not one, but all mankind's epitome
Stiff in opinions, always in the wrong
Was everything by starts, and nothing long.
But, in the course of one revolving moon,
Was chymist, fiddler, statesman, and buffoon:
Then all for women, painting, rhyming, drinking,
Besides ten thousand freaks that died in thinking.
Blest madman, who could every hour employ,
With something new to wish, or to enjoy!

The immediate occasion of the poem was to publicly disgrace Shaftesbury, who had been imprisoned in the Tower of London. Charles II hoped to have his rival indicted on charges of treason, and in that respect Dryden's poem was a failure because the grand jury failed to hold Shaftesbury for trial. In fact, when Shaftesbury was released from the Tower, his supporters struck a special commemorative medal in his honor. That was the occasion for Dryden's second great satire, "The Medal" (1682). "The Medal" was again a satire upon the Whigs and their leader, and although the poem is somewhat lacking in the variety of its satire, in many places it is equal to "Absalom and Achitophel" in its vigor and wit. Dryden describes, for example, the engraving and casting of the medal itself:

Five days he sate for every cast and look;
Four more than God to finish Adam took.
But who can tell what essence angels are,
Or how long Heav'n was making Lucifer?
O could the style that copied every grace,
And plow'd such furrows for an eunuch face,
Could it have form'd his every-changing will,
The various piece had tir'd the graver's skill!

What Dryden carries over into "The Medal" from "Absalom and Achitophel" is the idea of monarchal stability versus the chaos of mob rule. Shaftesbury is depicted as a potential despot who was once a loyal subject, but "even in the most sincere advice he gave; he had a grudging still to be a knave." Dryden exhibits some finesse in this poem when he chides the English nation for being dissatisfied with a relatively comfortable life: "Too happy England, if our good we knew / Would we possess the freedom to pursue / The lavish government can give no more / Yet we repine and plenty makes us poor." Also significant (and characteristic) in the poem is Dryden's ability to explain points of political philosophy in rhymed couplets. The poet seeks to reassure the English nation that Charles II poses no threat to liberty: "Our temp'rate isle no extremes sustain / Of pop'lar sway or arbitrary reign."

Dryden's career made a significant turn with the publication of these two satires. As a popular playwright, he was naturally going to be subject to a certain amount of scorn from those who did not care for his heroic tragedies or his wit. But, with "Absalom and Achitophel" and "The Medal," Dryden became a political figure as well, and the pens of the Whigs, many of whom had not cared for Dryden's dramatic works in the previous decade, turned furiously upon the Poet Laureate. Among them was Thomas Shadwell, a onetime Dryden friend, now a bitter enemy. Shadwell's attack on Dryden, "The Medal of John Bayes" (1682), is little more than a diatribe. Dryden's response, *Mac Flecknoe* (1682), was both swift and crushing. It remains one of the best verse satires in the English language.

Richard Flecknoe was a minor author who wrote several plays, poems, and volumes of travel literature. He was not quite the dullard that Dryden made him out to be, but it has become his lot to be remembered to the world as the monarch of dullness who, in his old age, resolves to settle the question of succession (in a devastating parody of current events) by crowning his son, Shadwell, as heir to the throne. The satire is at once sharp, rollicking, and slightly vulgar. In the opening lines, Mac Flecknoe is nearing the end of his reign over the "realms of Nonsense" and trying to determine who shall follow him. He chooses Shadwell:

> And, pond'ring which of all his sons was
>   fit
> to reign, and wage immortal war with
>   wit,
> Cried: "'Tis resolv'd; for nature pleads,
>   that he
> Should only rule, who most resembles
>   me.
> Sh_____ alone my perfect image bears,
> Mature in dulness from his tender years:
> Sh_____ alone, of all my sons, is he
> Who stand confirm'd in full stupidity.
> The rest to some faint meaning make
>   pretense,
> But Sh_____ never deviates into sense."

Dryden simply uses a "Sh_____" to represent Shadwell, but a close reading of the poem reveals that in many cases "Shadwell" would not fit the rhyme scheme of the heroic couplet—the common word for excrement, however, would fit.

Even though Charles II survived the Popish Plot, the Stuart monarchy did not last long. Having lived with distant relatives in France during the Interregnum, Charles had been exposed to Catholicism during his formative years, and he long harbored—even in strongly Protestant England—sympathies toward the Catholic cause. He probably practiced the religion in private (as did many Catholics), and on his deathbed he converted. James II, who was openly Catholic, ascended the throne in 1685, and this was cause for considerable tumult among the English (ostensibly, the Popish Plot was devised to prevent the ascension of a Catholic monarch). During these years, Dryden was apparently going through a crisis of faith himself.

Like many Englishmen, throughout his life Dryden had been seeking a sense of stability and continuity. He indirectly described this search in "Religio Laici" (1682), the first of two poems in which he makes a rare personal statement of belief. In this work the poet purports to take up "the sword of Goliath" in the battle against impiety. Against the Deists he levels the charge that they have taken away "the pillars of our faith, and [propped] it only with a twig." Admitting that he is by nature a skeptic in philosophy, the author cannot concede that mankind can gain an understanding of God: "How can the less the greater comprehend / Or finite reason reach Infinity / For what could fathom GOD were more than he."

What is significant in "Religio Laici" are Dryden's relative attitudes toward Papists and Dissenters. While he believes both are threatening, Dryden clearly favors Catholicism. He absolves Catholics from any part in the Popish Plot when he says, "I will grant their behavior in the first to have been as loyal and brave as they desire; and will be willing to hold them excused." He also states his belief that Catholicism is not fundamentally opposed to the state. Regarding the Dissenters, the writer is far less charitable. He contends that "the doctrine of king-killing and deposing . . . have been espoused, defended and are still maintained by the whole body of Nonconformists."

In 1685, Dryden converted to Catholicism. His new expression of faith is contained in "The Hind and the Panther" (1687). The poem was the occasion for a good deal of derision among the wits and Whigs of London, but their literary conclusions are obviously colored by religious bias, which Dryden expected. In this poem, he sketches his own religious development and argues in favor of the scriptural authority of the Catholic Church. Whereas in "Religio Laici" the poet appears to be content to ignore the more particular questions of religious doctrine ("For points obscure are of small use to learn / But common quiet is mankind's concern"), in "The Hind and the Panther" he appears to be seeking a definite authority. Dryden's change in religions, when viewed in light of his intellectual development, is clearly not a change in fundamental philosophy.

For those who have since claimed that Dryden was merely a spineless time-server, it should be noted that Dryden, already an old man, made no attempt at reconciliation with the new government after the Glorious Revolution of 1688. He returned to writing for the theater in order to earn his living, but he met with little success. As a translator of classics, though, he not only received a decent living in his old age, but he also acquired a great deal of lasting respect from both contemporary and later critics. For nearly three years he toiled away at a complete translation of Virgil, which was published by subscription in 1697. Although his *Virgil* is not literal by any standard, it bears the unmistakable mark of its translator, including some sly satires on current political leaders.

Summary
John Dryden's stock as a literary figure has risen and fallen over the centuries since his death. Aside from a fervent desire for political stability, he expressed no redeeming social aspirations, and he seemed unwilling or unable to write about the aspirations of the human soul. He was an anathema to the Romantic poets, and many in the twentieth century have found his work politically reactionary. Yet throughout the years, critics have returned to Dryden's style, for few poets in the English language have had his facility with rhyme and numbers. Few, if any, could so clearly express ideas and abstractions and at the same time so devastatingly satirize and parody. "It is hardly too much to say," wrote T.S. Eliot, "that Dryden found the English speechless, and he gave them speech."

Selected Bibliography

Primary Sources
Works. Ed. E.N. Hooker and H.T. Swedenborg. Berkeley: University of California Press, 1956–.

Secondary Sources

Bibliographies
MacDonald, Hugh. *John Dryden: A Bibliography of Early Editions and of Drydeniana.* Oxford: Clarendon, 1939. A good source of information concerning attacks on Dryden by his contemporaries.

Biographies
Johnson, Samuel. *Lives of the Poets: Dryden.* Ed. G. Hill. Oxford: Oxford University Press: 1905.
Ward, C.E. *Life of John Dryden.* Chapel Hill, NC: University of North Carolina Press, 1961. Still considered one of the best biographies of Dryden, the volume is formidable in its scholarship.

Books
Bredvold, Louis. *The Intellectual Milieu of John Dryden.* Ann Arbor: University of Michigan Press, 1934. Bredvold examines the effects of seventeenth-century skepticism in general and on Dryden's philosophy in particular.
Eliot, T.S. *John Dryden: The Poet, The Dramatist, The Critic.* 1932; rpt. New York: Haskell House, 1966. Eliot praises Dryden for creating standards for the language of both poetry and prose.
Miner, Earl. *Dryden's Poetry.* Bloomington: Indiana University Press, 1967. Miner examines Dryden as a Christian humanist. He believes that Dryden's poetical virtues far outweigh the faults.
Van Doren, Mark. *The Poetry of John Dryden.* New York: Haskell House, 1969. Originally published in 1920, this book was part of the Dryden renaissance in that decade. Van Doren attempted to reclaim critical respect for Dryden by a close examination of his verse.

Jeffrey Ritchie

Du Maurier, George
Born: Paris, March 6, 1834
Education: Pension Froussard, Paris; University College, London, 1851; atelier of Charles Gleyre, Paris, 1856; Antwerp Academy of Fine Arts, 1857
Marriage: Emma Wightwick, January 3, 1863; five children
Died: London, October 7, 1896

Biography
Born in Paris on March 6, 1834, George Louis Palmella Busson Du Maurier was the son of ex-

patriate parents; his father was Louis-Mathurin Busson Du Maurier, an impecunious Englishman of French extraction and a failed inventor; George's mother was the former Ellen Clarke, daughter of Mary-Anne Clarke, the notorious mistress of the Duke of York, brother of King George III.

Known all his life by his boyhood nickname, Kicky (or Kiki), Du Maurier attended a boarding school, Pension Froussard, in Paris and later studied chemistry without much enthusiasm in London at University College (1851). Having failed at scientific enterprises, Du Maurier went back to Paris in 1856 to study painting in the atelier of Charles Gleyre. Fellow students included James McNeill Whistler and Tom Armstrong, who were to become Du Maurier's lifelong friends, although he and the former were to have a characteristically Whistlerian falling out many years later. While studying at Antwerp Academy of Fine Arts in 1857, Du Maurier suffered the loss of sight in his left eye. He thought that he would have to give up art altogether and fell into a deep depression. However, his remaining eye proved strong enough that he could still draw well, black on white. He returned to London in 1860 and supported himself with free-lance drawings for periodicals such as the *Illustrated London News*, *Once a Week*, and *Cornhill Magazine*. His earliest drawings in *Punch* appeared in the early 1860s; the following year, at age thirty, Du Maurier was named the permanent replacement for the late John Leech on the staff of the venerable humor magazine.

In *Social Pictorial Satire*, his tribute to *Punch* cartoonists Leech and Charles Keene, Du Maurier describes their work and his own as "The craft of portraying, by means of little pen-and-ink strokes, lines and scratches, a small portion of the world in which we live; such social and domestic incidents as lend themselves to humorous or satirical treatment; the illustrated criticism of life, of the life of our time and country, in its lighter aspects" (1). The targets for his satire came largely from the middle and upper classes: "We [Du Maurier and Keene] hated and despised the bloated aristocracy . . . without knowing much about them; and the aristocracy, to do it justice, did not pester us with its obtrusive advances" (13).

On January 3, 1863, Du Maurier married Emma Wightwick, who bore him five children: three girls and two boys. The younger son, Gerald, became a noted actor-manager and the father of the novelist Daphne Du Maurier. Daphne writes, in her introduction to *The Young George Du Maurier*: "Even when pulling jokes . . . [he] was never malicious or unkind. He mocked at many, but with a twinkle in the eye . . . He laughed at people because he loved them, because he understood and shared their little weaknesses, their foibles; their snobbery, their sudden social gaffes and faux pas were misfortunes committed all too often by himself, a bohemian on the fringe of High Society" (ix).

In addition to drawing his cartoons, Du Maurier illustrated the novels of a number of late nineteenth-century authors, including Elizabeth Gaskell, William Makepeace Thackeray, and Thomas Hardy, as well as his own literary works. Late in life Du Maurier, who had frequently entertained Henry James with stories told on their evening walks, began writing, at his friend's urging, the first of his three novels, *Peter Ibbetson*, which appeared in 1891. More than for his humorous drawings, it is for his second novel, *Trilby*, an 1894 international best-seller, that Du Maurier may be best remembered, having created in it the memorable characters of the transformed Trilby and the spellbinding Svengali.

Du Maurier remained unaffected by his fame and sudden, late-day fortune. A *Punch* cartoon reprinted in the May 1883 issue of *Century Magazine* demonstrates his attitude toward success: an elderly man and woman are seated on a park bench, and the caption reads:

EVANS EVANS, R.A., the famous artist, Knight of the Order of Merit in Germany, Office of the Legion of Honor in France, &c., &c., &c., &c . . . . visits his native place in Wales, and meets his first and only love, who married (alas!) the village doctor.

SHE: "Dear me! To think of our meeting again after so many years! How well I remember you! . . . you used to go in for painting, and sketching, and all that . . . and do you go in for it still?" (60)

After spending the years of his greatest success and raising his family in Hampstead, Du Maurier and his wife moved to a house in Oxford Square in London, where he died shortly thereafter of congestive heart failure on October 7, 1896.

Literary Analysis

In addition to cartoonists Leech and Keene, Du Maurier says in *Social Pictorial Satire* that he very much admired William Hogarth, "For he was not merely a light humorist and a genial caricaturist; he dealt also in pathos and terror, in tragic passion and sorrow and crime" (99). By contrast, at *Punch* Du Maurier was "allotted the social and domestic dramas, the nursery, the schoolroom, the dining and drawing rooms, and croquet-lawns of the more or less well-to-do" (75).

The objects of Du Maurier's wit were inhabitants of what Richard Kelly calls "high society trying its best to be highly civilized" (30). During his thirty-year career, Du Maurier created such recurring cartoon characters as the aesthetes Maudle, the painter, and Jellaby Postlewaite (who bears a striking resemblance to Oscar Wilde), the artistically pretentious Mrs. Cimabue Brown and the socially ambitious Mrs. Ponsonby de Tompkyns, and the vulgar, nouveau-riche Sir Gorgius and Lady Midas.

Favorite subjects for Du Maurier's parody were the affected medievalisms of the Pre-Raphaelites and the preciousness of the followers of the Aesthetic Movement. For example, "The Six-Mark Tea-Pot" (*Punch*, October 30, 1880) presents a young couple examining a piece of the blue-and-white china fashionable among the followers of the Movement:

> Aesthetic Bridegroom: "It is quite consummate, is it not!"
> Intense Bride: "It is indeed! Oh, Algernon, let us live up to it!"

Although some of Du Maurier's social commentary still brings a smile, the difficulty with satire is its dependence upon context. For today's reader, lacking a full knowledge of the time in which the cartoons were published, the humor of some pieces may not be immediately evident. In order to measure the wit of their creator, it is necessary to accept the evaluation of his contemporaries.

In "George Du Maurier: English and American Criticism on His Life and Works," an article from the *London Times*, Du Maurier's work is called "refined to the point which is quite incompatible with the noisier and more boisterous forms of British fun. The humor is always there, and it is always genuine. It is not tinged with melancholy, as a rule, nor is it subtle and difficult to seize. It bubbles up very naturally, and even when a little malicious, very sweetly as a rule, is never loud" (77).

An unsigned Biographer's Note in *Pictures of English Society* reads: "It is not too much to say that the principal attraction of 'Punch' for many readers has been the exquisite social satires from the pencil of Du Maurier . . . English life and character have never been more faithfully depicted, never presented with keener insight into peculiarities of types either by English novelists or artists; and this striking fact gives to Du Maurier's drawings a permanent charm wholly independent of their humorous or satirical element" (3–4).

Henry James found Du Maurier "full of soft irony"; in the May 1883 *Century Magazine*, James writes that "No one has rendered like Du Maurier the ridiculous little people who crop up in the interstices of that huge and complicated London world . . . the snob, the cad, the prig, the duffer—Du Maurier has given us a thousand times the portrait of such specialties" (55). If James has any fault to find with Du Maurier's cartoons, it is that they are so beautifully drawn that "We forget the joke, but we remember the scene" (56). With Du Maurier's fondness for beauty, "English society makes pictures all around him, and he has only to look to see the most charming things, which at the same time have the merit that you can always take the satirical view of them" (59).

In the novels, which are late-Victorian romances, love stories spiced by something of the supernatural, Du Maurier uses humor for comic relief. He creates Dickensian minor characters whose exaggerated appearances and behaviors contrast with the trials and triumphs of the good-looking lovers. His descriptions sound very much like directions to himself for making the accompanying illustrations or his satirical drawings for *Punch*.

In *Peter Ibbetson*, for example, the eponymous hero is, as a child, instructed by a schoolmaster who is a send-up of the type: "With his green tail coat, his stiff shirt collar, his thick flat thumbs stuck in the armholes of his nankeen waistcoat, his long flat feet turned inward, his reddish mutton-chop whiskers, his hat on the back of his head, and his clean, fresh, blooming, virtuous, English face" (50). The English face is further caricatured (as only an Englishman might) as having "prominent front teeth, a high nose, a long lower lip, a receding jaw . . . dull, cold, stupid, selfish green eyes, like a pike's, that swerved neither to right nor left, but looked steadily over people's heads as it stalked along in its pride of impeccable self-righteousness" (51).

In *Trilby*, Taffy and Sandy (called the Laird) are a jolly couple of penniless British painters sharing a studio in Paris with the young hero; they provide a humorous contrast to the love-sick little Billee and his beloved, their model Trilby. In describing the appearance of the villain Svengali, Du Maurier takes another subtle jab at his countrymen: "He was very shabby and dirty, and wore a red beret and a large velveteen cloak, with a big metal clasp at the collar. His thick, heavy, languid, lustreless black hair fell down behind his ears on to his shoulders, in that musicianlike way that is so offensive to the normal Englishman" (11–12).

Du Maurier also satirized his friend Whistler as the idle apprentice Joe Selby; when *Trilby* was serialized in *Harper's Monthly Magazine*, Whistler failed to see the humor and threatened legal action. The novelist revised the text and before the book appeared he removed one illustration that unmistakably resembled the painter.

Du Maurier's last novel, *The Martian*, while its narrator exhibits occasional whimsy and an ironic attitude towards himself, contains few instances of the comic. The theme is the evolutionary perfection of the human race; its seriousness may account for its having been Du Maurier's least successful work of fiction, unintentionally funny, with what Richard Kelly calls "a farcical and melodramatic conclusion" (132).

Summary

George Du Maurier was for thirty years the leading satirical cartoonist for *Punch*, poking gentle fun at the pretensions of the middle and upper classes. Only in his late fifties did he become a novelist, publishing *Peter Ibbetson* (1891), *Trilby* (1894), and *The Martian* (1896). He is perhaps best remembered for having created the fictional characters of Trilby and Svengali.

Selected Bibliography

Primary Sources
Pictures of English Society. New York: D. Appleton, 1884.
Social Pictorial Satire: Reminiscences and Appreciations of English Illustrators of the Past Generation. New York: Harper and Brothers, 1898; rpt. *Harper's New Monthly Magazine*, 96 (Feb.–Mar. 1898): 331–44, 505–21.
The Young George Du Maurier: A Selection of His Letters, 1860–67. Ed. Daphne Du Maurier. Garden City, NY: Doubleday, 1952.

Secondary Sources

Books
Kelly, Richard. *George Du Maurier*. Boston: Twayne, 1983. Illustrated, with a bibliography. Kelly discusses the cartoons in relationship to the later novels.
Ormond, Leonee. *George Du Maurier*. Pittsburgh: University of Pittsburgh Press, 1969. Illustrated, with a bibliography. Ormond covers early years as source of late fiction; examination of career as social satirist for *Punch*.

Articles
"George Du Maurier: English and American Criticism on His Life and Works." *Book News*, 15, 171 (Nov. 1896): 77–82. Unsigned short pieces reprinted from the *London Times*, *New York Post*, *Philadelphia Press*, *Philadelphia Star*, *New York World*, *London's Publishers' Circular*, *Philadelphia Ledger*, *New York Sun*, and *Publishers' Weekly*.
James, Henry. "Du Maurier and London Society." *Century Magazine*, 4 (May 1883): 49–65. The novelist's personal reflections on *Punch* and Du Maurier's social satire.
Matthews, Roy T. "George Du Maurier." In *The 1890s, An Encyclopedia of British Literature, Art, and Culture*, ed. G.A Cevasco. New York and London: Garland Publishing, 1993, pp. 177–80. Brief overview of life and career.

P.B. Parris

Dunbar, William

Born: ca. 1460
Education: He may have been the William Dunbar mentioned as taking a bachelor's degree at St. Andrew's University in 1477 and a master's degree in 1479. By 1504, he had taken priest's orders.
Died: Before 1522

Biography

Factual details about William Dunbar's life are few and derived from entries in the manuscript records of The Faculty of St. Andrew's University in Edinburgh as well as entries of the Accounts of the Lord High Treasurer of Scotland. Beyond these, much of what is known about Dunbar is surmised from his poems. He was born about 1460 (possibly as early as 1456) and most likely descended from the earls of Dunbar and March of ancient Scottish lineage. It is assumed that he took a bachelor's degree at St. Andrew's University in 1477 and a master's degree in 1479. There is little concrete evidence concerning his life between 1479 and 1500. He may have been a Franciscan novice and traveled in Europe as a preaching friar and later as an emissary of James IV of Scotland. He may have been part of the delegation sent to England in 1501 to make arrangements for the marriage of James to Margaret Tudor, daughter of Henry VII. By 1504, he had taken priest's orders and clearly by then was a part of the court of James IV. Court records show him having been granted various pensions within the first decade of the sixteenth century. It is not known whether he followed James to the disastrous battle of Flodden in 1513, although some scholars think that he died in that year. It is assumed that he died by 1522, based on poetic references to him as dead before that time.

Literary Analysis

Dunbar writes within the courtly tradition of medieval France and England. Dunbar himself acknowledges his poetic masters to be Geoffrey Chaucer, John Gower, and John Lydgate. Yet like all of the English and Scottish poets of the late fifteenth-early sixteenth century, he was also greatly influenced by French poetic forms. Much of his poetry is devotional and panegyric, but one of his most distinctive traits as a poet is his comic or satiric mode. His technical virtuosity and originality in using poetic forms for his own purposes distinguish him from the other Scots makars. The verse forms and metres which Dunbar uses include rhyme-royal and shorter stanzas as well as the couplet and the alliterative line. He is perhaps best known for his mastery of the Chaucerian nine-line stanza in his *The Goldyn Targe* (1503). The poetic modes that he uses include allegory and dream vision, panegyric, moralizing, comic narrative, and satire. Except for those poems clearly composed for particular occasions, it is difficult to arrange the poems chronologically.

The subject matter of Dunbar's poetry is primarily the events and interests of the court of James IV, King of Scotland. The court of James was a prosperous one, filled with gaiety and music and rich pageantry. Dunbar's poetry, in its subject matter and range in diction, reveals a court audience with a wider range of tastes than a modern reader might expect. The poet writes in at least three different styles, which have traditionally been called "high," "middle," and "low." Poems in the high style are mostly occasional poems. For instance, *The Thrissill and the Rois* (*The Thistle and the Rose*, dated May 9, 1503), written on the occasion of James IV's marriage to Margaret Tudor, daughter of Henry VII of England, is a dream vision clearly indebted to Chaucer's *Parliament of Fowles* in both content and stanza form (the French *chant-royal*). Another example of a poem in the high style is *The Goldyn Targe*, which employs the conventions of the love allegory. Poems in this style are characterized by courtly subject matter and Latinate diction. The poems in the middle style are mostly devotional and involve moralizing about the subject matter. A good example of this middle style is *Timor Mortis conturbat me* (published 1508), sometimes called "Lament for the Makars," a meditation on death which includes a catalogue of the poets who have died before Dunbar and a recognition that he may be the next to die. The diction is plain and homely, without the preponderance of Latin-derived words of the poems in the high style. Finally, it is with poems in the low style that Dunbar exhibits the wild, satiric humor which is one of his most distinctive qualities. These poems often illustrate Dunbar's play with the conventions of courtly love and the romance tradition, while frequently the diction is coarse and "low" and derived from Scots Gaelic.

In "Ane Ballat of the Fenyeit Freir of Tungland" (1507), Dunbar uses the dream allegory, a popular medieval poetic form, to burlesque John Damian's attempt to fly from the heights of Stirling Castle. An alchemist and a charlatan, Damian had been appointed Abbot of Tungland by James IV. Dunbar employs heavy alliteration to ridicule Damian, describing the hapless fellow as he is attacked by the birds and falls in disgrace at the foot of the castle:

> And evir the cuschettis at him tuggit,
> The rukis him rent, the ravynis him druggit,
> The hudit crawis his hair furth ruggit:
> The hevin he micht not bruke. (69–72)

Another poem that burlesques the conventions of the dream vision as well as conventions of chivalric romance is *Fasternis Evin in Hell*, especially the first and second parts, "The Dance of the Sevin Deadly Sins" and "The Turnament." "The Dance of the Sevin Deadly Sins" presents a procession of personified sins in Hell, each personified figure described as behaving in a way that embodies the sin. Each figure is surrounded by dancers who exhibit in their appearance and behavior symptoms of the sin and who writhe and twitch in a scene that is lurid and painfully comic. This poem perhaps best exhibits a characteristic often identified with reference to Dunbar's comic and satiric poetry: *eldritch* (which means "exuberant," "frightful," "weird"). The horror of the dance is mixed with the comedy of the figures, as may be seen in the portrait of the followers of Avarice, who vomit hot molten gold on each other, while the devils immediately pour more gold down their throats:

> Out of their throttis they schot on udder
> Hett moltin gold, me thocht a fudder,
> As fyreflawcht maist fervent;
> Ay as they tomit thame of schot
> Feyndis fild thame new up to the thrott
> With a gold of allkin prent. (61–66)

Using the kind of excretory jokes that were common in medieval humor, in the poem which follows, "The Turnament," Dunbar parodies chivalric romance and derides those people of the trades who are not equal to the heroic ideal.

Other poems which satirize the conventions of courtly love and the romance tradition are "In Secreit Place" and "Schir Thomas Norny." "In Secreit Place" is a dialogue overheard by a poet-narrator between a foul-mouthed man-about-town and a foolish kitchen girl. Although the poem begins in the courtly manner, the true nature of the participants is quickly revealed, their conversation degenerating to animal metaphors and reduplicative baby talk, as is illustrated in the girl's calling her suitor "My belly huddroun, my sweit hurle bawsy, / My honygukkis, my slasy gawsy" (38–39), phrases which mean "big bellied glutton, clumsy fellow, sweet idiot," with the meaning of the last phrase being obscure. "Schir Thomas Norny," a parody of courtly romance, uses tail-rhyme stanzas and conventional romance diction, as Chaucer does in *The Tale of Sir Thopas*,

to ridicule a character at the court of James IV, perhaps the court fool.

Dunbar also parodies the liturgy of the Church. "The Dregy of Dunbar Maid to King James The Fowrth being in Strivilling" is a parody of the Office of the Dead, a type of parody common in the later Middle Ages. In this poem addressed to James IV at Stirling, Dunbar contrasts the ascetic life that James is leading at the Franciscan monastery in Lent with the delights of life at court in Edinburgh. "The Tesment of Maister Andro Kennedy" is a satiric testament, a form popular in medieval France. Dunbar's intent is comic as he writes alternating lines in Scots and Latin, with Andro Kennedie, a drunken court physician, revealing his weaknesses in self-incriminating language.

Finally, Dunbar's manipulation of form matched with a novel handling of theme is most evident in his longest poem, *The Tretis of the Tua Mariit Wemen and the Wedo (The Treatise of the Two Married Women and the Widow)*. Composed in the old alliterative line, *The Tretis* parodies several different genres. The poem begins with the convention of the eavesdropping narrator overhearing a conversation among three lovely, elegantly-dressed women. Yet as the women speak, the coarseness of their speech seems to contrast with their outward loveliness. The widow takes charge of the conversation and makes a request to the others to tell their true opinions of wedded life. As their tales unfold, the women are revealed as lecherous and cruel, offering a pleasant face to their husbands in public but being demanding and cruel in their private lives. The widow instructs the other two with regard to how to manage their husbands for their own benefit, and in so doing, she is found to be even more hypocritical, lecherous, and greedy than they are. Dunbar's use and control of the alliterative line in this poem contributes much to its success. This is evident in the "piling up" of sounds which contribute to the meaning in the speech of the first wife as she laments the old husband that she has:

> I have ane wallidrag, ane worme, an auld
>   wobat carle,
> A waistit wolroun no worth bot wordis
>   to clatter,
> Ane bumbart, ane dron bee, ane bag full
>   of flewme,
> Ane scabbit skarth, ane scourpioun, ane
>   scutarde behind. (89–92)

In this series of epithets, the wife's scorn is apparent even to those without a full understanding of the words. The widow of this poem is clearly related to Chaucer's Wife of Bath, although the figure of the older woman who is worldly-wise is a stock figure in the anti-feminist writing of the Church fathers and in other writing of the time. In *The Tretis*, Dunbar is clearly interested in the contrast between appearance and reality, the lovely appearance of the women clashing with their base nature. The alliterative line is used successfully to create the effect of loveliness as well as ugliness.

Summary

William Dunbar is a poet whose flawless craftsmanship far exceeds that of the other Middle Scots poets, but whose interests and philosophical depth are rather limited. Although his poetry lacks depth, Dunbar reveals in his comic and satiric work a wild imagination, the "eldritch" quality so often mentioned by scholars, and a delight in the play of sounds which contributes to that quality. Working well within the traditions of poetry to which he was heir, Dunbar offers a fresh handling of forms and takes an obvious delight in the effects that he can achieve through language.

Selected Bibliography
Primary Sources

Manuscripts and Early Prints
Chepman and Myllar Prints (ca. 1508). Edinburgh. Ed. G. Stevenson. Scottish Text Society 12. Edinburgh: Blackwood, 1918. Photofacsimile. Ed. William Beattie. Bibliographical Society, 1950. Contains six poems by Dunbar.
Asloan Manuscript (ca. 1515). Auchinleck, Ayrshire. Ed. W.A. Craigie. Scottish Text Society 16–17. Vols. 1–2. Edinburgh: Blackwood, 1924. Contains three poems by Dunbar and part of a fourth.
Bannatyne Manuscript (ca. 1568). Edinburgh; National Library of Scotland. Ed. W. Tod Ritchie. Scottish Text Society 22–25. Vols. 1–4. Edinburgh: Blackwood, 1928–34. Contains sixty poems by Dunbar.
Maitland Folio Manuscript (ca. 1570–86). Pepysian Library, Magdalene College, Cambridge. Ed. W.A. Craigie. Scottish Text Society 7. Vols. 1–2. Edinburgh: Blackwood, 1919 and 1927. Contains sixty-one poems attributed to Dunbar.
Redpeith Manuscript (1622–23). Cambridge University Library. Mainly a copy of Maitland, contains forty-seven poems by Dunbar, twelve of which are printed in Vol. 2 of Craigie edition of Maitland Folio, Scottish Text Society 20 (1927), pp. 40–58.

Modern Editions
The Poems of William Dunbar. Ed. John Small. Edinburgh: Blackwood, 1883–1893. Scottish Text Society 2, 4, 16, 21, 29. 3 vols. Introduction and appendices by A.J.G. Mackay and notes by W. Gregor and Mackay.
The Poems of William Dunbar. Ed. J. Schipper. Vienna: Kaiserliche Akademie der Wissenschaften, 1891–94. 5 parts. Gives most textual variants, written in English.
The Poems of William Dunbar. Ed. W. Mackay Mackenzie. London: Faber & Faber, 1932; rpt. 1960, with corrections by Bruce Dickins. Standard available text.
The Poems of William Dunbar. Ed. James Kinsley. Oxford: Clarendon, 1979. Will become the standard.

Secondary Sources

Books
Bawcutt, Priscilla. *Dunbar the Makar.* Oxford: Oxford University Press, 1992. Bawcutt discusses all of Dunbar's poems thoroughly, acknowledging Dunbar's technical virtuosity and wide range of styles; supersedes earlier book-length studies in its detail and thoroughness.
Baxter, J.W. *William Dunbar: A Biographical Study.* Edinburgh: Oliver and Boyd, 1952. Baxter summarizes and discusses most of Dunbar's poems, relies heavily on poems for information about his life.
Hope, A.D. *A Midsummer Eve's Dream: Variations on a Theme by William Dunbar.* Canberra: Australian National University Press, 1970. Hope focuses exclusively on *The Tretis of the Tua Mariit Wemen and the Wedo*, discussing its origins in folklore and legend.
Reiss, Edmund. *William Dunbar.* Boston: Twayne, 1979. All of the poems are discussed. Dunbar is seen as essentially a

D

moral poet, with the values of his faith permeating all of his poetry.

Ross, Ian Simpson. *William Dunbar*. Leiden: Brill, 1981. Ross discusses most of Dunbar's poems; gives a convincing account of what Dunbar's education, culture, and ambitions must have been.

Scott, Tom. *Dunbar: A Critical Exposition of the Poems*. New York: Barnes, 1966. Scott discusses most of Dunbar's poems. Especially effective discussion of diction and versification; some interpretations of poems rather idiosyncratic.

Articles and Chapters in Books

Fox, Denton. "The Scottish Chaucerians." In *Chaucer & Chaucerians: Critical Studies in Middle English Literature*. Ed. D.S. Brewer. University, AL: University of Alabama Press, 1966, pp. 164–200. Very good introductory study.

Lewis, C.S. "The Close of the Middle Ages in Scotland." In *English Literature in the Sixteenth Century, Excluding Drama*. Oxford: Clarendon, 1954, pp. 90–100. Important and influential study. Lewis discusses Dunbar's poetry by categories.

Leyerle, John. "The Two Voices of William Dunbar." *University of Toronto Quarterly*, 31 (1961): 316–38. A distinction between Dunbar's "aureate" and his "eldritch" voices.

Morgan, Edwin. "Dunbar and the Language of Poetry." *Essays in Criticism*, 2 (1952): 138–58. Morgan discusses the influence of the alliterative tradition on Dunbar's poetry.

Pamela K. Shaffer

E

Ewart, Gavin

Born: London, February 4, 1916
Education: Wellington College, 1929–1933;
Christ's College, Cambridge University,
B.A., 1937; M.A., 1942
Marriage: Margo Bennett, March 24, 1956;
two children

Biography

Gavin Buchanan Ewart was born in London on February 4, 1916; his parents were George Arthur Ewart, a surgeon, and Dorothy Turner Ewart, a surgeon's daughter.[1] He was educated at Wellington (1929–1933), where he was introduced to the poetry of W.H. Auden, and Christ's College, Cambridge, where he read classics and English and was taught by F.R. Leavis and I.A. Richards. He received a B.A. from Cambridge in 1937 and an M.A. in 1942. In 1938, Ewart worked briefly as a salesman of contemporary lithographs. From 1940 to 1946, he served in the army (the East Surreys and the Royal Artillery), mainly in North Africa and Italy. Then, after a short stint in publishing, he worked from 1946 to 1952 with the British Council as an assistant in the book-review department, and from 1952 to 1971 as a copywriter in advertising agencies. On March 24, 1956, Ewart married Margo Bennett; the couple has two children. Since 1971, he has supported himself and his family as a free-lance writer. He currently lives in Putney, a part of South London, very close to Putney Bridge.

Ewart's first book, *Poems and Songs*, was published in 1939; his second, *Londoners*, was not published until 1964. Since 1964, he has published more than twenty-five books and edited several others, most notably *The Penguin Book of Light Verse* (1980). *The Collected Ewart 1933–1980* contains all of the poems in his books prior to 1980, with the exception of *All My Little Ones* (1978). Books since 1980 include *The New Ewart: Poems 1980–1982*, *The Young Pobble's Guide to His Toes* (1985), *Late Pickings* (1987), *Penultimate Poems* (1989), and *Collected Poems 1980–1990* (1991). Ewart's first American book, *The Gavin Ewart Show: Selected Poems 1939–1985*, was published in 1986; a second American book, *Gavin Ewart: Selected Poems 1933–1988*, appeared in 1988.

Literary Analysis

In a review of *The New Ewart* (May 1982), Philip Larkin observed: "The most remarkable phenomenon of the English poetic scene during the last ten years has been the advent, or perhaps I should say the irruption, of Gavin Ewart."[2] Stephen Spender has referred to Ewart as "compulsively readable," a writer who "from a rather bitter isolation makes devastatingly funny comments on contemporary manners."[3] Andrew Motion has called him "unflaggingly entertaining and inventive"; Anthony Thwaite wrote that he is "a clever and funny poet who gets cleverer and funnier as the years go by." Although he is by no means solely a humorous writer, Ewart is certainly that. He himself has remarked: "All writers (Shakespeare included) are, in the last analysis, in the entertainment business." His poem "Modest Proposal" begins:

> Good light verse is better than bad heavy
>   verse
> any day of the week.
> Of course it's not the greatest thing in
>   the universe

but it's able to speak
clearly of the ironies—not dull or solemn
        or
proud or stuck-up . . .

"Sonnet: Afterwards," the final poem in *The Collected Ewart*, concludes with a sort of epitaph: "They'll say (if I'm lucky): / He wrote some silly poems, and some of them were funny."

Ewart's strong affinity for the comic began early: "As a lad I always enjoyed comedy: P.G. Wodehouse, Gilbert, and the very unhighbrow and rather Philistine poetry and prose writers of *Punch*, who in the Twenties and Thirties produced some very childish work."[4] His first published poem, "Phallus in Wonderland," was written shortly after his seventeenth birthday and printed by Geoffrey Grigson in *New Verse*. Its title alone suggests his satirical bent, irreverence, predilection for word play and allusiveness, and attraction to the theme of sexuality. An early and persistent influence has been Auden, whose poetry Ewart characterized as a "wonderful hybrid rose that crossed the comic with the tragic," a description that applies equally well to Ewart's own cosmopolitan, conversational style.

"Office Friendships," published in the mid-1960s, is representative of the flavor of Ewart's writing. He vivifies what could have been regarded as a mundane situation and setting, treating it with exuberance and gusto:

Eve is madly in love with Hugh
And Hugh is keen on Jim.
Charles is in love with very few
And few are in love with him.
Myra sits typing notes of love
With romantic pianist's fingers.
Dick turns his eyes to the heavens above
Where Fran's divine perfume lingers.
Nicky is rolling eyes and tits
And flaunting her wiggly walk
Everybody is thrilled to bits
By Clive's suggestive talk.
Sex suppressed will go berserk,
But it keeps us all alive.
It's a wonderful change from wives and
        work
And it ends at half past five.

Ewart gives the impression of being a writer for whom nothing is too commonplace or insignificant to write about and who is ca-

pable of saying just about anything. What has been called his "unabashed sexual relish" is evident in the opening stanza of "To a Plum-Colored Bra Displayed in Marks & Spencer":

The last time I saw you, as like as two
        pins,
you were softly supporting those heavenly twins
that my hands liberated before the gas
        fire
in the mounting impatience of driving
        desire.

The crossing of "the comic with the tragic" may be seen in the blend of bitter experience and easy-going rhythm at the conclusion of "Hurried Love":

Making love against time is really
the occupation of all lovers
and the clock-hands moving
point a moral:
not crude, but clever
are those who grab what soon is gone
        for ever.

It can also be seen in the sextet of "Sonnet: The Last Things," which is of interest formally because Ewart has made frequent use of the "unrhymed sonnet" as a vehicle for meditations and comment on a wide range of topics:

Then there are last words, variously reported,
such as: Let not poor Nelly starve. Or:
I think I could eat one of Bellamy's veal
        pies.
If there were time I'd incline to a summary:
Alcohol made my life shorter but more
        interesting.
My father said (not last perhaps): Say
        goodbye to Gavin.

Other characteristics of Ewart's verse which bear resemblance to Auden's are technical proficiency and inventiveness. Ewart not only writes in an extraordinary array of forms, but he often adapts the manner of other poets, sometimes for the purposes of parody, sometimes as a tribute, commonly as a combination of the two. A partial listing of writers who undergo his high-spirited reworkings includes Samuel Pepys, Lord Byron, Alfred, Lord Tennyson, Robert Browning, Thomas Hardy, Rudyard Kipling, Philip Larkin, and John Betjeman. "William Wordsworth (1770–1850)" is composed in the manner of Ogden Nash:

> Most modern Nature Lovers have a personal
> scale of values that tells them what each
> tree, hill or bird's worth;
> But this doesn't apply to Wordsworth.
> For Wordsworth, as it were, believing
>   was
> much the same as seeing—
> he thought natural phenomena were the
>   guardians
> of his heart and soul of all his moral
>   being . . .

"The Meeting," perhaps the ultimate word on its subject, is in the trochaic tetrameter of "Hiawatha," considered by Ewart the most boring of all meters:

> In the long and boring meeting,
> in the hot and boring meeting,
> there was shouting by the Chairman,
> bullying almost by the Chairman,
> people rose on points of order,
> caused chaos with points of order . . .

The poem continues this way for fifty-four more lines! "The Importance of Being Earnest" sums up the plot of Oscar Wilde's play in nine limericks, and "The Pilgrim's Progress" provides a slangy précis of John Bunyan's allegory in twenty-five (Christian is alluded to as Chris). Jargon of any sort incites Ewart's penchant for mimicry. He updates Sir Thomas Wyatt's "They Flee From Me That Sometime Did Me Seek":

> At this moment in time
> the chicks that went for me
> in a big way
> are opting out:
> as of now, it's an all-change situation.

Byron's "So We'll Go No More A-Roving" becomes:

> So we won't go wandering about any
>   more
> into the wee small hours,
> though I'm still terrifically keen on you
> and the moon still looks very shiny.

And, throughout his poetry there are allusions as well to classical and foreign authors and to fiction writers.

In his lightest vein, Ewart can be determinedly, indeed, outrageously, humorous, delighting to give mischievousness free rein. One entire poem, "Love in a Valley," consists of Los Angeles Valley Girl "Valspeak." All forty-one lines of "The Owl Writes a Detective Story" end-rhyme with "who," Ewart explaining in a note: "This poem was written to be read aloud, and the 'oo' sounds at the ends of lines should be intoned like the call of an owl." He has embraced "the semantic limerick," a form in which *Oxford English Dictionary* definitions are substituted for the words of well-known bawdy limericks:

> There existed an adult male person who
> had lived a relatively short time, belonging or pertaining to St. John's, who desired to commit sodomy with the large
> web-footed swimming birds of the genus
> *Cygnus* or subfamily *Cygninae* of the
> family *Anatidae* . . .

He has written clerihews, and edited a book entitled *Other People's Clerihews*; in his "Introduction" he credits *Chambers Dictionary* with perhaps the best short definition of the clerihew: "a jingle in two short couplets purporting to quintessentialise the life and character of some notable person." He has edited a book of light verse for children, and written three of his own, *The Learned Hippopotamus*, *Caterpillar Stew*, and *Like It Or Not*. He has written a great many very short poems, including one-liners, and numerous parodies of popular song lyrics, as well as spoofs based on news items, advertising slogans, and overheard remarks. In short, anything that he comes across, in whatever guise, written or spoken, is fair game for Ewart's wit.

Finally, however, though not averse to being remembered for his "funny" poems, Ewart's intent is usually satirical and ultimately serious. A clue to what he wishes his legacy to be is furnished in his eulogy, "In Memoriam Sir John Betjeman (1906–84)":

> you were good, and very British.
> Serious, considered "funny,"
> in your best poems, strong but sad, we
>   found
> a most terrific pleasure.

A less somber summing-up of his rationale and method appears in the lilting poem on the back cover of *The Complete Little Ones* (1986):

> Lightly (as lightly they're written)
> just kiss the Joy as it flies
> and read them for nothing but pleasure
> with uncensorious eyes
> The world's a horrific enigma,
> it's serious and sad—
> it could be a good sense of humor
> that stops us going mad.

Summary

Since the 1960s, Gavin Ewart, author of more than twenty-five books of poems, "has become perhaps Britain's most prolific poet . . . and is generally regarded as being one of the most influential seriocomic writers of verse in this country."[5] His work exemplifies technical virtuosity and inventiveness, and is frequently allusive, even erudite in its range of references. Yet, Ewart's poems are conversational in style, genial in tone, and often funny as well as sardonic. They are usually immediately accessible, and almost invariably entertaining.

Notes

1. More extensive biographical detail, as well as a chronological critical overview of Ewart's work and its importance, may be found in Peter Reading's essay, "Gavin Ewart," *The Dictionary of Literary Biography Vol. 40: Poets of Great Britain and Ireland Since 1960*, ed. Vincent B. Sherry, Jr. (Detroit: Gale Research, 1985).
2. From *Quarto*, quoted in Reading's essay.
3. The quotations from Spender, Motion, and Thwaite appear on the back cover of *The Collected Ewart, 1933–1980*.
4. From a November 15, 1990 letter by Ewart to the author.
5. From Reading's essay.

Selected Bibliography

Primary Sources

Poems and Songs. London: Fortune Press, 1939.

Londoners. London: Heinemann, 1964.

Throwaway Lines. London: Keepsake Press, 1964.

Pleasures of the Flesh. London: Alan Ross, 1966.

Two Children. London: Keepsake Press, 1966.

The Deceptive Grin of the Gravel Porters. London: London Magazine Editions, 1968.

Twelve Apostles. Belfast: Ulsterman, 1970.

The Gavin Ewart Show. London: Trigram, 1971.

Alphabet Soup. Oxford: Sycamore Press, 1971.

An Imaginary Love Affair. Belfast: Ulsterman, 1974.

Be My Guest! London: Trigram, 1975.

No Fool Like an Old Fool. London: Victor Gollancz, 1976.

A Question Partly Answered. Knotting: Sceptre Press, 1976.

On Where a Young Penguin Lies Screaming. London: Victor Gollancz, 1977.

The First Eleven. Hatch End, Middlesex: Poet & Printer, 1977.

All My Little Ones. London: Anvil Press, 1978.

The Collected Ewart, 1933–1980. London: Hutchinson, 1980. Contains all of the poems from Ewart's books prior to 1980, with the exception of *All My Little Ones* (1978).

The New Ewart: Poems 1980–1982. London: Hutchinson, 1982.

The Young Pobble's Guide to His Toes. London: Hutchinson, 1985.

The Complete Little Ones. London: Hutchinson, 1986. Contains *All My Little Ones*, *More Little Ones* (1982), and sixty-seven new poems, comprising all the short poems to date Ewart thought fit to preserve.

The Gavin Ewart Show: Selected Poems 1939–1985. Cleveland: Bits Press, 1986. Ewart's first American book publication.

Late Pickings. London: Hutchinson, 1987.

Gavin Ewart: Selected Poems 1933–1988. New York: New Directions, 1988. Includes some of the poems from the Bits Press *Selected Poems*, but is essentially a different collection.

Penultimate Poems. London: Hutchinson, 1989.

Collected Poems 1980–1990. London: Hutchinson, 1991.

Children's Books

The Learned Hippopotamus. London: Hutchinson, 1986.

Like It Or Not. London: The Bodley Head

Children's Books, 1992.

Caterpillar Stew. London: Hutchinson, 1990.

As Editor

The Batsford Book of Children's Verse. London: Batsford, 1976.

The Batsford Book of Light Verse for Children. London: Batsford, 1978.

The Penguin Book of Light Verse. Harmondsworth: Penguin, 1980.

Other People's Clerihews. Oxford: Oxford University Press, 1983.

Secondary Sources

Bennett, Bruce. "From Rueful to Raucous." *New York Times Book Review* (August 17, 1986): 26. Reviews of *The Young Pobble's Guide to His Toes* and *The Gavin Ewart Show: Selected Poems 1939–1985.*

Reading, Peter. "Gavin Ewart." *The Dictionary of Literary Biography Vol. 40: Poets of Great Britain and Ireland Since 1960.* Ed. Vincent B. Sherry, Jr. Detroit: Gale Research, 1985, pp. 110–16. Reading provides an excellent brief critical introduction to Ewart's life and work, evaluating his development, reputation, and contribution to contemporary British poetry. Includes references to the most important reviews of Ewart's books—virtually the only other secondary sources available.

"'Witverse': An Interview with Gavin Ewart." Edited by Stan Sanvel Rubin from a Brockport Writers Forum videotape. Published in *Light,* 2 (Summer 1992): 31–34. In this interview, conducted by Professors Stan Rubin and Bruce Bennett on October 12, 1988, Ewart speaks about influences on him, the sources of his poetry, his ideas about form and technique, and the nature and place of "witverse," which he prefers to the term "light verse."

Bruce Bennett

F

Farquhar, George

Born: Londonderry, Ireland, ca. 1678
Education: Attended Trinity College, Dublin,
1694–1696
Marriage: Margaret Pemell, early 1703 (?);
two children
Died: May 20 (?), 1707

Biography

George Farquhar, the most popular playwright of his day, was at once the last of the Restoration comic dramatists and the first of the new sentimental comic dramatists of the eighteenth century. His two major comedies, *The Recruiting Officer* and *The Beaux' Stratagem*, were performed more often in his own century and in subsequent periods than any other Restoration or eighteenth-century drama. Farquhar wrote eight plays and "A Discourse Upon Comedy."

Letters uncovered in this century indicate that Farquhar was the son of an Anglican clergyman, Thomas Farquhar; other details, such as a reference to seven siblings, are very sketchy. Born in Londonderry, Ireland circa 1678, Farquhar witnessed the siege of Londonderry in 1689 and claimed to have participated in the Battle of Boyne in 1690. While attending Trinity College in Dublin (1694–1696), he turned to the theater, but in 1697, as a young actor at Smock Alley, Dublin, Farquhar forgot to use a blunted foil and skewered his fellow actor during a performance. The victim recovered, but Farquhar's acting career did not. London gained a playwright instead.

In London he was the quintessential, handsome Restoration man-about-town. Farquhar's first play, *Love and a Bottle* (1698), enjoyed success enough to support the author for a year. His rapid success was due to his working

knowledge of the theater, his appreciation of new actors, and an inherent grasp of public tastes. Serendipitously, Robert Wilks, Farquhar's friend from his short-lived Dublin acting days, moved to London and became its foremost actor. In 1699, *The Constant Couple, or the Trip to the Jubilee*, with the showcase role of Sir Harry Wildair written for Wilks, was the hit of the town. At twenty-two, Farquhar was on top of London's theater scene.

Subsequent plays—the sequel *Sir Harry Wildair* (1701), *The Inconstant* (1702), and *The Twin Rivals* (1702)—each missed its season's mood. In addition, early in 1703 Farquhar married Margaret Pemell, a widow ten years older than himself, who he thought had money but instead had two children (the couple later produced two children of their own). To compensate for this setback, Farquhar joined the army for £54.15 a year and served as a recruiter.

Success and satire returned in 1706 with *The Recruiting Officer*. Both major theaters, Drury Lane and Lincoln's Inn Fields, featured the play. In 1707, *The Beaux' Stratagem* opened at the Queen's Theater, and for most of the season the three theaters ran these two plays and *The Constant Couple* in various combinations.

Farquhar, though, was already dead of tuberculosis, having lived his last weeks, as legend has it, in a back garret with scarcely a shilling in his pocket. The bon vivant spirit that infused his plays hid his true state, and although supposedly he died on the third night of *The Beaux' Stratagem*, it is more likely that he died around May 20, a month after it opened.

Literary Analysis

Farquhar arrived in London when Restoration comedies of manners, filled with intrigues and ridicule, still held center stage. These plays by George Etherege, William Wycherley, John Vanbrugh, and William Congreve aimed their intrigues, wit, and polished satire at the dandies, coquettes, prigs, and dullards of fashionable drawing-room society. To achieve spicy amusement and shock effect, they often subordinated plot to witty dialogue and intellectualized licentiousness to outrage middle-class morals.

However, just at this time public tastes were changing away from the brittle wit of ridicule toward an emotional release of sentiment, from favoring exemplary characters who were no longer just a "type" suitable for pity or ridicule to those with whom the audience identified. The comedy of wit and farce, of wooing and social-climbing, continued, but the problems and mind of a "sentimental" character appealed to the heart as well as the intellect. Sentimental comedy became the new stage morality, which Farquhar helped institute. Such shifts into and out of sentiment are as old as English drama, but the shift was particularly pronounced at this time.

Love and a Bottle is derivative of earlier plays by Wycherley (*Love in a Wood*, 1671), Aphra Behn (*The Rover*, 1677), and Colly Cibber (*Love's Last Shift*, 1696). Farquhar disguised his heroine, Leanthe, as a boy and outdid his predecessors in mock marriages by using three. His hero, Roebuck, was an Irish rake newly come to London, and thereafter critics searched for autobiography in every Farquhar play. The limited success of the play was due to the coarseness of Roebuck, a rake in both practice and principle, and to the disunity in the plot. Perhaps the play is a burlesque on Restoration comedy itself, but, in any case, the audiences attended for its "wickedness." They ignored Farquhar's integration of John Locke's argument on virtue and self interest, a type of intellectual application that he would use in later plays.

Farquhar's second play, *The Constant Couple, or the Trip to the Jubilee*, showed significant advances in his dramatic technique and ran an unprecedented fifty-three performances at Drury Lane. Lady Lurewell, a jilt, was too callous, but the urbane and graceful rake, Sir Harry Wildair, played by Wilks, was the success of the London season. With its satire directed at pedants, marriage, and a society that encourages scandalous behavior, character development and plot superseded mere wit and the perfunctory reform of a rake.

In spite of this coming-of-age for the young dramatist, his next three years were unsuccessful. A sequel, *Sir Harry Wildair*, was merely fashionable. Farquhar had yet to modify his wit and initiate comedy that would move away from manners and into sentiment, an attitude which would reign for the next half century. This change, in part, corresponded to Jeremy Collier's assault upon the theater in "A Short View of the Immorality and Profaneness of the English Stage" (1698).

During this period, Farquhar published two volumes of poems and witty epistles on various topics. "A Discourse upon Comedy" (1702) dismissed the unities of classical dramatic theory by advocating audience tastes: "to make the moral instructive, you must make the story diverting . . . let him do it by what rules he pleases." With few critics holding opposing views at this time—Jean Baptiste Molière had already issued similar views, and even strict John Dennis allowed laxity for comedy—Farquhar's purpose is unclear. Perhaps he was defending his own plays in general, once again attacking pedants, or responding to Collier's broad impeachment of Restoration dramas. By attacking Aristotle's limited experience in dramatic modes and empirically supporting practicing dramatists, his methodology, not his ideas, set the tone for Joseph Addison and later eighteenth-century critics.

The Recruiting Officer, suggested by the playwright's experience in the army, became the first of Farquhar's lasting successes. The military theme is a satire on impressing/bribing recruits; other plots revolve around romantic intrigues of rakes who in the end turn out to be less than rakish after all. This began a new morality that still squared with Restoration motifs. It reflects why Congreve's *The Way of the World* (1700) failed in its own time when Richard Steele's *The Funeral* (1701) succeeded. However, many elements enabled *The Recruiting Officer* to be sprightly rather than funereal.

The satire is directed not only against recruiting but military life and, in turn, society itself, with its shams and hypocrisy. All of Farquhar's plays feature officers who "receive your pay and do no duty" while they are more likely to "debauch us at home than they do us good by defending us abroad." The soldiers are no better: "Pray, gentlemen, let me have one honest man in my company, for the novelty's sake" (5.5.86–88). Twice, Captain Plume, the central figure, maintains that "my company is a perfect representative of the whole commons of England" (5.7.45–46).

Captain Plume is himself the sauciest recruiter. At one point he admonishes his subordinate for signing a lawyer: "An attorney! Wer't thou mad? List a lawyer! Discharge him, discharge him this minute" (1.1.84–85). And, his tactics are cunning: "So kiss the prettiest country wenches, and you are sure of listing the lustiest fellows. Some people may call this artifice, but I term it stratagem, since it is so main a part of the service—Besides, the fatigue of recruiting is so intollerable, that unless we cou'd make our selves some pleasure amidst the pain, no mortal man wou'd be able to bear it" (4.1.140–46). In between, he is lusty: "I tell'e what, I'll make love like a platoon." When asked how this occurs, he responds, "I'll kneel, stoop and stand, Faith; most ladies are gain'd by platooning" (3.2.105–09).

The play's openly bawdy behavior contrasts sharply with the conventional intellectualized games of the Restoration. Plume supposes that "we lampooned all the pretty women in town," and he says to his recruiting officers, "I thought 'twas a maxim among them to leave as many recruits in the country as they carried out" (1.1.225–26). Silvia, who performs the breeches role by dressing up as a soldier and in doing so reverses roles by recruiting both her father (civilian) and Plume (military), is androgynous from the start. Not recognizing Silvia as a *she*, Sergeant Kite kisses her: "What, men kiss one another! . . . 'tis our way; we live together like man and wife, always kissing or fighting" (3.2.234–36). Plume kisses her / him in two scenes, saying, "You shall be with me, you young rogue." But the chaste Silvia selects Rose to bed with, an ostensible conquest of her own.

The realistic rural setting is Farquhar's unmitigated contribution to the comic tradition. By removing the action from London's drawing rooms and no longer caricaturing provincials as fools, Farquhar broadened the canvas of Restoration comedy and began the shift away from the tired pleasures of stylishness to behavior and nature.

The concept of the play is original, although it employs many conventions, including the metaphor of sex as war. Both activities require adjustments in order to preserve the stability of society, and Farquhar works these out in masterly parallels. For the next seventy-three years, London never had a season in which *The Recruiting Officer* was not on the boards. It was the first professional play performed in the American and Australian colonies, and in 1963 it was part of London's National Theatre opening season.

In early 1707, sick and impoverished, Farquhar was urged by Wilks to energize himself by writing; the result was his masterpiece, *The Beaux' Stratagem*. Focused on romantic intrigues and the theme of divorce, this play employed wit in both modes—manners and sentiment. Again the scene is a country inn, where two impoverished rakes pose as a peer and servant. One falls in love with a wealthy daughter, the other with the unhappily married Mrs. Sullen. After saving their lovers from robbery, the two rakes reveal their true status, their fortunes are restored, and all is harmonized, including the agreeable departure of boorish Mr. Sullen.

In contrast to other sentimental plays, notably Vanbrugh's *The Relapse* (1696), where the rake reforms only after the seduction, here the two gentlemen hunters of love and fortune—Archer and Aimwell—are heroes with conviction. When Mrs. Sullen cries out "thieves" to save her house from invasion by Hounslow and Bagshot, she also alters the invasion of virtue by Archer and Aimwell; hence the two plots are united.

The play's thematic statements on divorce and poverty attack society's preference for appearance over reality. "Nature is the first lawgiver," announces Mrs. Sullen, elevating social values above mere dogma or legalisms. However, with the play's Prologue promising only comedy, the divorce issue was not analyzed until 1840 when Leigh Hunt attended to it in the introduction to his edition of *The Dramatic Works of Wycherley, Congreve, Vanbrugh, and Farquhar*. Only in 1924 were the echoes from John Milton's *Doctrine and Discipline of Divorce* demonstrated: "instead of beeing one flesh, they will be rather two carkasses chain'd unnaturally together; or, as it may happ'n, a living soule bound to a dead corps." In act 3, Sullen announces: "One flesh! rather two carcasses join'd unnaturally together," and Mrs. Sullen replies: "Or rather a living soul coupled to a dead body." Poverty as a theme is no less evident: "there is no scandal like rags, nor any crime so shameful as poverty" (1.1.132–33). This application of authority was a technique that Farquhar used from his early plays on. In this play he is perhaps doubly convincing due to his own unhappy marriage and poverty.

The play's comedy operates on various levels, from farce to wit, in developing the themes.

One level is plain ribaldry, such as in the famous "Love's catechism" scene between Archer, who is pretending to be a footman, and Cherry, the country lass. In part, the scene satirizes Cherry's novel-reading background, but their repartee ends with, "And now, my dear, we'll go in, and make my master's bed." However, she is not finished and presses him to acknowledge that he's not what he pretends to be, which he accedes to but sticks to his design, "And then we shall go make the bed" (2.2.201). In a later scene, Mrs. Sullen describes her passion for Archer: "Tho' to confess the truth, I do love that fellow;—And if I met him drest as he shou'd be, and I undrest as I shou'd be—Look'ye Sister, I have no supernatural gifts;—I can't swear I cou'd resist the temptation,—tho' I can safely promise to avoid it; and that's as much as the best of us can do" (4.1.460–65). In her speech the ribaldry blends with the melancholy of an afflicted wife and impending divorce; it also infuses sentiment because in truth she does resist temptation, an action which signified the new mode of comedy.

The play incorporates the standard practice of symbolic names, such as Freeman, Sullen, Bellair, Lady Bountiful (used here for the first time); Aimwell is not only a fortune hunter, but one who is decent and aims for the good. It also features husband-wife bickering, as when Mrs. Sullen describes her marriage to a sullen mate: "There's some diversion in a talking blockhead; and since a woman must wear chains, I wou'd have the pleasure of hearing 'em rattle a little . . . He came home this morning at his usual hour of four, waken'd me out of a sweet dream of something else . . . he comes flounce into bed, dead as a salmon into a fishmonger's basket; his feet cold as ice, his breath hot as a furnace, and his hands and his face as greasy as his flannel night-cap.—Oh matrimony!" (2.1.60–70). A similar scene, with Sir John Brute, occurred earlier in Vanbrugh's *The Provok'd Wife* (1697).

But there is intellectual wit too, literary allusions and keen ripostes, particularly in the famous picture gallery scene that is used to mock eloquence as well as to show off wit. Language underscores the thematic deceptions of the play, as the two fortune hunters mock their station (e.g., 3.3.156–253) at the same time they exhibit it. Farquhar's characters can change their tone of address to suit the objectives of ridicule for different scenes.

The play echoes other works, as when Archer describes their situation: "So—we're like to have as many adventures in our inn, as Don Quixote had in his" (2.2.238–39). The robbery scene is reminiscent of Falstaff and his motley highwaymen (*Henry IV, Part 1*) in league with the innkeeper. And, much of the farce and dialogue of the robbers in act 4 parallels the low comedy of Dogberry in *Much Ado About Nothing*. The tradition continued more than half a century later, when Kate Hardcastle in Oliver Goldsmith's *She Stoops to Conquer* (1773) asks, "Don't you think I look something like Cherry in *The Beaux' Stratagem*?"

The humor of *The Beaux' Stratagem* reflects a very original view, more than simply a transition from comedy of manners to moralizing sentiment. The comedy is broader because its focus is no longer on artificial wit to exhibit individuals and their consequent punishment or reform. As in *The Recruiting Officer*, in this play the dramatist emphasizes relationships that need to be righted, and this occurs in a country inn using "low dialogue," as it was then labeled. The humor thus produced realism that audiences identified with and also gave some degree of complexity to the characters; few are held up to complete ridicule.

The Beaux' Stratagem was popular both on stage and in publication, with nine editions being published in 1707 alone. Written in six weeks as its author lay dying of tuberculosis, the play never betrays its vivacity. It has as many choice parts as any other English play, and, in general, Farquhar's women characters are the most interesting created by any Restoration or eighteenth-century playwright.

Because the genre of dramatic comedies faded temporarily, Farquhar's immediate influence was not profound: opera became the rage, Steele left the theater for journalism, and Congreve abandoned playwriting. However, the open-air wholesomeness of his plays produced prototypes of humane characters and settings seen later in the novels of Henry Fielding and Tobias Smollett and in Goldsmith's *She Stoops to Conquer*. These characters are no longer targets of satire but have become lovable eccentrics. Similar characters appear in John Gay's *The Beggar's Opera* (1728) and Richard Sheridan's *The School for Scandal* (1777).

Farquhar's comedies have played well over the years, starring David Garrick in the eighteenth century and Sir Laurence Olivier, Trevor Howard, Dame Edith Evans, and Maggie Smith, among others, in modern times. Even his early plays—*The Twin Rivals* and *The Constant Couple*—played in the 1980s. *The Recruiting Officer* was revived in another version as Bertolt Brecht's *Pauken und Tromptin*. In 1988, the Royal Court Theatre ran *The Recruiting Officer* in repertory with Timberlake Wertenbaker's *Our Country's Good* (1988), which is about convicts in Australia performing the earlier play. *The Beaux' Stratagem* remains one of the most frequently performed Restoration plays on both professional and academic stages and is generally considered the epitome of its genre.

Summary

George Farquhar began with the conventions of the comedy of manners and ended by developing the comedy of sentiment. He transported comedy out of the drawing rooms of high society and into country inns. In undercutting the comedy of manners, he both shaped and reflected public tastes.

Farquhar relied on far more than autobiography to create his plays. This is evidenced by the conventions that he employed and by the genial characters which he created that influenced later eighteenth-century novelists and dramatists. His untimely death has left critics wondering what more he would have accomplished, but, nevertheless, his final plays are works of maturity.

As the only major playwright before the twentieth century who was also an actor and a university man, Farquhar brought an unusual range of experiences to his productions and developed social themes that did not reappear on the English stage until George Bernard Shaw's problem plays approximately 200 years later.

Selected Bibliography

Primary Sources

The Works of George Farquhar. Ed. Shirley Kenny. 2 vols. Oxford: Oxford University Press, 1988. Line numbers for quotes vary among editions.

Secondary Sources

Biographies

James, E. Nelson. *George Farquhar A Reference Guide*. Boston: G.K. Hall, 1986. Chronological listing of secondary sources to 1980, amply annotated. Excellent overview of biographies, criticisms, and editions in introduction.

Books

Connely, Willard. *Young George Farquhar, The Restoration Drama at Twilight*. London: Cassell & Co., 1949. Connely argues for autobiographical element in every Farquhar play. In spite of title, book covers all of Farquhar's life.

James, E. Nelson. *The Development of George Farquhar as a Comic Dramatist*. The Hague: Mouton, 1972. James presents Farquhar as conscious literary artist following his own theories on comedy. Most thorough treatment.

Kenny, Shirley. "Perennial Favorites: Congreve, Vanbrugh, Cibber, Farquhar, and Steele." *Modern Philology*, 73, 2 (May 1976): S4–S11. Statistics given on frequency of performances.

Kimball, Sue. "Ceres in Her Harvest: The Exploded Myths of Womanhood in George Farquhar's *The Beaux' Stratagem*." *Restoration and 18th-Century Theatre Research*, 3, 1 (1988): 1–9.

Larson, Milton. "The Influence of Milton's Divorce Tracts on Farquhar's *Beaux' Stratagem*." *PMLA*, 39 (1924): 174–78.

Milhous, Judith, and Robert Hume. "*The Beaux' Stratagem*: A Production Analysis." *Theatre Journal*, March 1982, pp. 77–95. Rpt. in *Producible Interpretation, Eight English Plays 1675–1707*. Carbondale: Southern Illinois University Press, 1985.

Rothstein, Eric. *George Farquhar*. New York: Twayne, 1967. Good overview that sees Farquhar as a moralist.

Joel Athey

Fergusson, Robert

Born: Edinburgh, Scotland, September 5, 1750

Education: The High School, Edinburgh, 1758–1762; Dundee Grammar School, 1762–1764; University of St. Andrews, 1764–1768

Died: Edinburgh, Scotland, on October 16, 1774

Biography

Robert Fergusson was born in Edinburgh on September 5, 1750, the second son (and one of four children) of William Fergusson and Elizabeth Ford. William Fergusson had been an apprentice merchant in his native city of Aberdeen but was forced, for reasons now obscure, to find employment as a clerk in the Scottish capital in 1746.

Robert's parents paid to have him educated from the age of six at a small private school where, despite a continuously weak constitution, he performed well. He continued his education at the High School of Edinburgh but left for the city of Dundee when he won a bursary to the grammar school there. He entered St. Andrews University in 1764 at the age of thirteen, again on a bursary, to undertake the Arts degree. At St. Andrews, Fergusson gained a reputation as a poet (his accomplished satire, "Elegy on the Death of Mr. David Gregory," dates from these teenage years), a singer, and a bon viveur, narrowly avoiding, according to some traditions, being expelled for his riotous behavior. He left St. Andrews in 1768, without taking a degree, a not unusual or untoward occurrence in an eighteenth-century Scottish university.

Following an attempt to find employment through the sponsorship of a wealthy uncle who lived near Aberdeen went wrong, he walked all the way back to Edinburgh. He was soon afterwards employed as a clerk in the office of the Commissary-clerk of Edinburgh, part of the Scottish capital's great legal system. In Edinburgh, Fergusson threw himself into the lively cultural life of the capital, establishing a close friendship with the famous Italian opera singer Giusto Tenducci (who was a resident in the city through 1769), contributing poetry regularly to Thomas Ruddiman's *Weekly Magazine or Edinburgh Amusement* (his first poem in Scots to be published, "The Daft Days," appeared in the magazine in January 1772), and in participating in the debating/drinking club culture then prevalent in Edinburgh—he joined the Robinhood Society and later, in 1772, the Cape Club. His only collection to be published in his lifetime, *Poems*, appeared in January 1773.

His decline into death has been variously ascribed to his weak constitution, drunkenness, and/or sexual dissolution and madness, the latter with perhaps a morbidly religious turn. Whatever the reality of his disability, his widowed mother did not have the financial means to prevent his dying in the Edinburgh asylum on October 16, 1774 at the age of twenty-four.

Fergusson's biography has been appreciated in several ways in his native Scotland. He has been seen as an archetypally dissolute poet by Calvinist Scotland, as an important forerunner of Robert Burns, and, most generously, as a symbol of the neglect of native vernacular genius in bourgeois and puritanical classical Edinburgh.

Literary Analysis

Along with Allan Ramsay and Robert Burns, Fergusson is generally regarded as one of the three most important poets in the eighteenth-century Scots vernacular revival. Avowedly though not consistently nationalistic in reacting against the Union of Parliaments of Scotland and England in 1707, the revival movement sought to highlight the traditional poetic form and language of Scotland. This led to the utilization of the energetic "Habbie Simson" and "Christis Kirk" stanzaic forms and a strident Scots diction in the most dominant mode of the revival, as Scottish poets sought satirical force to counter the puritanism of the Calvinist church and Anglicisation of the Scots language and Scottish culture.

Fergusson's poetic achievement lies in two main areas. First, he extended the range of eighteenth-century Scots poetry, creating for it a new lyricism and a new "high" register. This is apparent in four of his greatest poems: "The Daft-Days" (1772), "The Farmer's Ingle" (a poem often recognized as a forerunner of Burns's "Cottar's Saturday Night" but a far superior work to that of Burns; 1773), "Ode to the Gowdspink" (1773), and "Auld Reikie" (1773). Second, Fergusson was responsible for writing some of the most effective satire in Scots in any period. This satire is directed, usually with an Edinburgh context, against cultural encroachments by the Whig political establishment, the "polite" sensibility of the eighteenth century and, to a lesser extent, against puritanical religion. Often his poetry conforms to ideas of an anarchistic literature as a means of social protest. This strain of Fergusson's work is most apparent in his poems "The King's Birth-Day in Edinburgh" (1772), "Hallow Fair" (1773), and "Leith Races" (1773), where riotous demotic revelry occurs in the face of social vacuum.

The author frequently features festive release in his poetry. The communal function of eating and drinking in Edinburgh taverns and the threat to community, manifested by the "black banditti" (the highland militia employed by the Edinburgh council to police the town), is dealt with in the relatively high-style poem, "The Daft Days," but in later poems these ideas are used to produce a rather sinister form of the carnivalesque. In "The King's Birth-Day in Edinburgh," the most obvious poem in this category, George III, the Hanoverian king who is the cause for the celebrations, is not explicitly mentioned. There is, then, a festivity ripped from its context—which is one expression of the carnivalesque principle of "misrule." Written in the sprightly "Standard Habbie" stanza, the poem is explicitly parodic from the start as the Muse is characterized as a serving-wench who cannot inspire singing in her own right but must provide whiskey to instill the inspiration. The Muse herself is so drunk as to be an appropriate witness to the scenes of disorder being recounted. Thus, the scene is set for the comic ineptitude of the celebrations and a saluting cannon explodes. Fergusson demonstrates his talent for the grotesque as he addresses the cannon as a woman:

> What black mishanter gart they spew
> Baith gut and ga'
> I fear they bang'd thy belly fu'
> Against the law.

Along with the farcical, almost cartoon-like depiction here, there is a much darker note. The reason for this darkness becomes apparent as Fergusson goes on to satirize the Edinburgh magistrates, who are seen to be socially detached from the people, and the highland militia, who are grotesquely caricatured but who are still an effective means of social control. The townspeople play with fireworks and cause the wigs of some of the more affluent citizens to catch fire and, for good measure, they assault their superiors with drowned cats. This poem highlights the farcical surface of much of Fergusson's poetry, but underneath there lies a serious point arising from the poet's eighteenth-century Tory sensibilities: the bad behavior of the lower orders is made possible by the unsociableness of officialdom.

Along with Fergusson's surprisingly oblique mode of satire, given that this occurs within the context of farce, there is a range of more explicitly sighted satirical targets. "The Rising of the Session" (1773) and "The Sitting of the Session" (1773) are satires on the Edinburgh legal system within which the author worked. In these poems he again complains of social detachment, this time of the legal system which the writer argues should stand in a more mutualistic relation to the commerce and general well-being of the capital that it is licensed by.

With "The Election" (1773), the first political satire to be written in the "Christis Kirk" stanza, Fergusson shows the way for Burns and John Galt as he sneers at the corruption of "rotten borough" practices.

"An Eclogue" (1772) is a very earthy usurpation of more stylized eighteenth-century pastoral expectations, as Fergusson creates a dialogue about shrewish women between two realistically drawn Scottish peasants. Here, as is often the case, Fergusson's family knowledge of the Buchan country dialect, an integral part of his low-style register along with his mastery of urban Edinburgh parlance, is invaluable. There is more explicit sociocultural comment in "To the Principal and Professors of the University of St. Andrews, on their superb treat to Dr. Samuel Johnson" (1773), a counter to Johnson's disparagement of Scottish cuisine and culture in general wherein Fergusson imagines changes in the menu of the banquet St. Andrews held in Johnson's honor so that the Englishman is fed haggis, sheep's head, and other Scottish delicacies.

Fergusson's close alliance of verbal energy and the grotesque is also evident in "Mutual Complaint of Plainstones and Causey" (1773), a reworking of the old Scottish "flyting" mode as an energetically humorous debate is contrived between the sidewalk and the road, and in "To the Tron-kirk Bell" (1772), which features a personified church-bell. In both the personification of inanimate objects and in the beginnings of a serious critique of Calvinism, Fergusson again points the way for some of the most famous later achievements of Burns:

> Wanwordy, crazy, dinsome thing,
> As e'er was fram'd to jow or ring,
> What gar'd them sic in steeple hing
> They ken themsel',
> But weel wat I they couldna bring
> War sounds frae hell.

Something of the frequent onomatopoeia, alliteration, and assonance, devices which Fergusson employs to capture the energy of his urban settings and to enhance his pointed comment, are seen in this stanza.

"Braid Claith" (1772), "On Seeing a Butterfly in the Street" (1773), and "To My Auld Breeks" (1773) are three of Fergusson's most general social satires. In each of these poems he is concerned with attacking the shallow construction of status by materialism, and in all three he is specifically concerned with the effect of clothes upon mental perceptions in a way that is most pertinent to the social transformations occurring in the Britain of his day and which looks toward the critique of materialism of Thomas Carlyle. In "Braid Claith" Fergusson says:

> Braid claith lends fock an unco heese,
> makes mony kail-worms butter-flies,
> Gies mony a doctor his degrees for little
>   skaith:
> In short, you may be what you please
> Wi' gude Briad Claith.
>
> For thof ye had as wise a snout on
> As Shakespeare or Sir Isaac Newton,
> Your judgement fouk wou'd hae a doubt
>   on,
> I'll tak my aith,
> Till they cou'd see ye wi' a suit on
> O' gude Braid Claith.

These lines clearly evidence the hallmark of Fergusson's comedic output, poetry that is both farcically funny and culturally pointed.

Summary

Robert Fergusson is a key poet in the eighteenth-century Scots vernacular revival. He utilizes a range of Scots registers, including urban working-class Scots and peasant dialects, and works in the most energetic Scottish stanzaic traditions to produce slanted, sardonic, sneering comment on the socio-cultural condition of Scotland.

Selected Bibliography

Primary Sources
The Poems of Robert Fergusson. Ed. Matthew P. McDiarmid. 2 vols. Edinburgh and London: Scottish Text Society, 1954.
The Works of Robert Fergusson. Edinburgh: The Mercat Press, 1970.
Poems by Allan Ramsay & Robert Fergusson. Ed. Alexander M. Kinghorn and Alexander Law. Edinburgh: Scottish Academic Press, 1985. The most readily available selection of Fergusson's poetry.

Secondary Sources
Daiches, David. *Robert Fergusson*. Edinburgh: Scottish Academic Press, 1982. A good introduction to Fergusson.
Freeman, F.W. *Fergusson and the Scots Humanist Compromise*. Edinburgh: Edinburgh University Press, 1984. The most scholarly study of Fergusson, which is particularly good on the poet in his socio-cultural context.
MacLaine, Allan H. *Robert Fergusson*. New York: Twayne, 1965. An excellent introduction to Fergusson which is particularly helpful on the technicalities of his poetic form.
Smith, Sydney Goodsir, ed. *Robert Fergusson, 1750–1774: Essays by Various Hands to Commemorate the Bicentenary of the Birth*. Edinburgh: Nelson, 1952. Many of the essays are a little dated in their approach but the enthusiasm of the contributors makes for stimulating reading.

Gerard C. Carruthers

Fielding, Henry

Born: Sharpham Park, Somerset, April 22, 1707
Education: Eton, 1719–1724; University of Leiden, 1728–1729
Marriage: Charlotte Cradock, November 28, 1734; two children; Mary Daniel, November 27, 1747; five children
Died: Junqueira, Portugal, October 8, 1754

Biography

The son of Edmund and Sarah Fielding, Henry Fielding was born on April 22, 1707, probably at Sharpham Park, Somerset, the home of his maternal grandfather, Sir Henry Gould. When he was three, his family moved to Dorset, where Sarah had inherited a comfortable estate in East Stour. Just before Henry's eleventh birthday his mother died, leaving Edmund with six children: Henry, Catharine, Ursula, Sarah, Beatrice, and Edmund. Fielding's father, who had already depleted the family fortune by gambling, soon married again. His new wife was a Roman Catholic from Italy, a fact that occasioned a violent quarrel between him and his mother-in-law, Lady Gould. Gould started legal proceedings against Edmund, partly to get what little was left of the estate out of his clutches and partly to shield the children from the Roman Catholicism of their stepmother. She won her case.

At the age of twelve Fielding was sent to Eton. He remained there until he was eighteen, after which he went to London. There, with the encouragement of his cousin Lady Mary Wortley Montagu, his first play, *Love in Several*

Masques, was produced in 1728. A short while later Fielding left to study literature at the University of Leiden in the Netherlands.

The next year, however, his father, who had never provided more than meager support, was not able to pay him an allowance, and Fielding returned to London. Despite his education and family connections, he had limited options. As he said, he had "no choice but to be a hackney-writer or a hackney-coachman." Choosing the former option, he proceeded to write and produce plays for the next eight years and achieved great success with high-spirited farces like *Tom Thumb* (1730–1731).

Salisbury was the home of his grandmother, and it was there that he fell in love with Charlotte Cradock, a beautiful woman whom he courted for four years. She was his one great love; indeed, his deep affection for her is commemorated in Sophia and Amelia, for whom she was the model. They eloped and were married on November 28, 1734. The couple settled in the house at East Stour where he had spent his boyhood, but within a year they returned to London.

There Fielding resumed his dramatic career. He formed a company of actors, which he named "The Great Mogul's Company of English Comedians," and wrote and produced more plays, including the two political satires *Pasquin* (1736) and *The Historical Register for the Year 1736* (1737). The latter contained biting attacks on the government of Sir Robert Walpole, who retaliated with the Licensing Act of 1737, effectively forcing Fielding out of the theater.

With two infant daughters and a wife to support, the thirty-year-old author began a hasty search for another means of livelihood. He entered the Middle Temple to study law and was admitted to the bar in 1740, completing in three years a program that normally took six or seven. To supplement his scanty income during this period, Fielding returned to writing as the editor of *The Champion* (1739–1741), an Opposition journal dedicated to overthrowing Walpole.

Early in 1741, Fielding produced *Shamela*, a bawdy and boisterous parody of Samuel Richardson's *Pamela* (1740), and in February 1742 he published *Joseph Andrews*, the first great comic novel in English. However, during this productive literary period, his personal life was filled with tragedy. In March 1742, Charlotte, his favorite daughter, died, and in 1744

his wife, whom he had taken to Bath for the waters, passed away in his arms after a long illness. His friends feared that he would go mad. A few years later (on November 27, 1747), to the derision of London society, he married her servant, Mary Daniel, with whom he was to have two sons and three daughters.

Fielding returned to journalism in 1745, writing anti-Stuart-and-Popery articles in *The True Patriot* (1745–1746). He did the same in *The Jacobite's Journal* (1747–1748), a paper that had such propaganda value that the government distributed 2,000 copies of each issue free in inns and alehouses. His reward from the government came in 1748: after several years of practicing law on the Western Circuit, he was appointed Justice of the Peace for the city of Westminster and later for the county of Middlesex as well.

When Fielding took the post, it was one of small honor and of only such profit as could be made from bribes. Fielding, however, refused to be a "trading justice." He took his work very seriously, considerably reducing the position's lucrativeness by his honesty, and he spent the last five years of his life performing great and sometimes thankless public service. Among other accomplishments, he produced the rudiments of an effective police force by recruiting a small band of active and able "thieftakers," the Bow Street Runners.

Throughout it all, Fielding kept writing. In 1749, *Tom Jones* appeared, and in 1751 *Amelia* was published. A month later, in January 1752, he returned to journalism in *The Covent-Garden Journal*. However, his strenuous efforts took their toll on his health. By April 1754, his ailments and backbreaking exertions in the courts forced him to resign as a justice. Exhausted and fatally ill, he sailed in June for Portugal with his wife and daughter to seek a more congenial climate. He died in Junqueira near Lisbon in October at the age of forty-seven and was buried in the English cemetery. His *Journal of a Voyage to Lisbon* was published a year after his death.

Literary Analysis

Fielding was a highly versatile author who worked successfully in several different genres, including drama, journalism, and the novel. As a playwright, he had a short career which lasted only the nine years from 1728 to 1737. During that period, though, he wrote no fewer than twenty-six plays. All were comedies, but they ranged in form from farce to ballad opera to burlesque to comedy of manners. Indeed, he had such a ready gift for drama that in 1732 alone he had five new plays staged, one of which he wrote and produced in three weeks.

His initial aim was to follow in the tradition of William Congreve. However, the characterizations in his high comedies are often flat and undistinguished; deservedly, these plays met with only moderate success. Fielding's real dramatic talents lay in the broader forms of humor where he could freely indulge his high spirits. He wrote two popular farces, *The Mock Doctor* (1732) and *The Miser* (1733), both adapted from Molière, who was one of his five favorite authors. Also included on his list were Jonathan Swift and Lucian, so it comes as no surprise that he excelled at satire and parody as well.

Indeed, Fielding's best and liveliest plays are farcical, almost plotless mixes of song, dance, and parody, written with verve and a distinct satiric edge. Farce in his hands becomes a moral medium as he uses it to undercut such deserving figures as corrupt politicians, conniving lawyers, and incompetent doctors. This is certainly his method in his most memorable play, *Tom Thumb*—his first overwhelming theatrical success and a masterpiece of dramatic burlesque. A year after the original version appeared, Fielding revised and expanded the play as *The Tragedy of Tragedies: or The Life and Death of Tom Thumb the Great* (1731), a travesty so amusing that it made Swift laugh for only the second time in his life.

Among Fielding's other notable plays are: *Love in Several Masques* (1728), his first drama; *The Author's Farce* (1730), a good-humored satire in which the playwright provides an amusing view of the relations between booksellers and the hack-writers whom they employed; *The Covent-Garden Tragedy* (1732), a blank-verse parody of the neoclassical drama then becoming popular; and *Don Quixote in England* (1734), which contains Fielding's two best-known songs, "The Roast Beef of Old England" and "The Dusky Night Rides Down the Sky."

Fielding was the most successful dramatist of his era, and his plays were intensely in touch with the times. This can present serious difficulties for the modern reader since a complete understanding of them requires specialized knowledge of the period's personalities and problems. However, in their own day, the topicality of the plays was a major source of their success as they lambasted contemporary "pollitricks," as Fielding used to call it, especially as practiced by the prime minister, Walpole.

With plays like *Pasquin* and *The Historical Register for the Year 1736*, Fielding in fact became the Opposition's principal satirist. These two comedies are patterned on Lord Buckingham's *The Rehearsal* (1671) and feature the framing device of a play-within-a-play. This allows Fielding ample opportunity to accompany the action with critical comments—comments critical of Walpole in particular. Incensed and uneasy over the immense popularity of these farces, the government passed the Theatrical Licensing Act of 1737 which placed the playhouses under the Lord Chamberlain's strict control. Indeed, Walpole saw to it that three days after the Licensing Act became law, Fielding's Little Theatre in the Haymarket was closed.

Thus ended Fielding's dramatic career, but it had not gone for nought. While most of his plays are of limited interest today, the lessons that he learned from them were many. He had learned how to write entertaining dialogue tailored to the individual speaker, how to present a succession of lively and contrasting scenes, and how to construct a plot that builds to a climax in which all is resolved. These lessons were to bear fruit in the novels that lay ahead.

However, the defrocked dramatist first turned to another genre, journalism. He edited *The Champion*, the chief Opposition paper, which appeared three times a week from 1739 to 1741. In it Fielding followed in the footsteps of Joseph Addison and Richard Steele and wrote under an assumed persona, that of Captain Hercules Vinegar, whose business it was to discuss the issues of the day, aided and abetted by his wife Joan and their two sons.

Fielding was involved in journalism sporadically for the rest of his life. In 1745, when the Jacobite Rebellion broke out, he came to the defense of the establishment in *The True Patriot*, which he wrote almost singlehandedly until it ceased publication on the defeat of Prince Charles Edward at Culloden. He reinforced his position as the government's most effective apologist when he again supported the Hanoverians in another one-man weekly, *The Jacobite's Journal* (1747–1748). As its title suggests, the journal took an ironic approach to current affairs. Finally, in 1752, he edited the biweekly *Covent-Garden Journal* under the pseudonym of Sir Alexander Drawcansir.

Fielding's most important achievement, though, lay elsewhere. Early in 1741, he had interrupted his work as a journalist to write *Shamela*, the first and by far the best of the satires of Richardson's *Pamela*. Filled with bite and purpose, this ribald and remarkably clever parody undercuts what Fielding saw as Richardson's spurious morality while revealing the "sham" of Richardson's heroine, who is exposed as a calculating hussy, utterly without morals although always ready to talk for "a full hour and a half about my vartue."

In its exposure of disguise and pretense, *Shamela* is very much in the mainstream of Fielding's works. His first publication was a satiric poem called "The Masquerade," and if Richardson could trust in the appearances of a Pamela, Fielding consistently took delight in the exposure of those who wear false masks. Truly, the unmasking of sham and affectation is his most enduring comic theme, as he reveals the discrepancy between what we claim to be and what we are.

When he published *The History of the Adventures of Joseph Andrews, and of His Friend Mr. Abraham Adams Written in Imitation of the Manner of Cervantes*, he discussed this directly. If Aristotle believed in a tragic catharsis, Fielding in the preface to *Joseph Andrews* argues for a comic one:

> Mirth and Laughter . . . are probably more wholesome Physic for the Mind, and conduce better to purge away Spleen, Melancholy and ill Affections, than is generally imagined. Nay, I will appeal to common Observation, whether the same Companies are not found more full of Good-Humour and Benevolence, after they have been sweeten'd for two or three Hours with Entertainments of this kind, than when soured by a Tragedy or a grave Lecture.

He goes on to argue that comedy has its source in affectation, which proceeds from vanity or hypocrisy. Consequently, it is the role of the humorist to show that the vain man lacks the quality that he professes and that the hypocrite is not what he pretends to be. In Fielding's view, this process of unmasking not only entertains the reader but may lead him to correct similar faults of his own. Indeed, Fielding always regarded his comedy as serving a moral end. He satirizes genially, not savagely, hoping to laugh sinners out of their follies. Humor in Fielding has an ethical purpose.

It is in this spirit that the sweeping social comedy *Joseph Andrews* is presented, as Fielding unmasks uncharitable clergymen, grasping innkeepers, and affected fops. Nonetheless, there is more than simply satire here. The novel is also filled with a benevolent humor that centers on the gullible Parson Adams. On the title page it is announced that the novel was "written in imitation of the manner of [Miguel de] Cervantes," and Adams, a new Don Quixote, is in his Christian innocence one of the great figures of comic literature. Moreover, the novel owes a debt to more than just *Don Quixote* (1605–1615). It incorporates elements of romance, burlesque, drama, the epic, and picaresque fiction. The result is a new amalgam which Fielding describes as "a comic epic-poem in prose."

In 1743, the author issued by subscription three volumes of his *Miscellanies*. Fielding's poetry is of little interest when compared with his other work, and such is true of the poems in these volumes. However, also included in these volumes are two plays, some essays, *A Journey from This World to the Next*, and *Jonathan Wild*. The latter is a devastating political satire on Walpole written in the form of a mock-heroic biography of Wild, a notorious criminal of the day.

As a matter of fact, while Fielding made much use of the mock-heroic throughout his career, in *Jonathan Wild* it is especially pervasive, whether in the form of inflated rhetoric, Homeric similes, or mock battles. For example, the writer burlesques the high style of heroic drama and romance in his presentation of Wild's execution (4, 14):

> The day now drew nigh when our great man was to exemplify the last and noblest act of greatness by which any hero can signalize himself. This was the day of execution, or consummation, or apotheosis (for it is called by different names) . . . A completion of greatness which is heartily to be wished to every great man; nothing being more worthy of lamentation than when Fortune, like a lazy poet, winds up her catastrophe awkwardly, and bestowing too little care on her fifth act, dismisses the hero with a sneaking and private exit, who had in the former part of the drama performed

F

such notable exploits as must promise to every good judge among the spectators a noble, public and exalted end.

The result of Fielding's satire on the confusion of greatness with goodness is an ironic moral fable that Samuel Taylor Coleridge felt was superior even to Swift's *Gulliver's Travels* (1726) and *A Tale of a Tub* (1704).

Nevertheless, Fielding's masterpiece is *The History of Tom Jones, a Foundling*. Considered by some scholars to be the greatest novel in British literature by any standards, it is a remarkable achievement. Fielding carefully planned the work, which is a marvel of literary engineering. Despite its vast gallery of characters and its many varied and counterpointed scenes, its sense of structure gives it a unity that was new to the novel form. Also unifying the book is Fielding's intrusive narrator, who guides his protagonists through the intricate complications of the plot.

The presence of Fielding with his healthy high spirits is strongly felt as he chats with his readers genially and entertains us with several types of humor. There is mock-epic burlesque as well as out-and-out farce and buffoonery made all the more effective by their contrast with the sophistication of the style. There is the satire that one would expect of a man who admired Swift and William Hogarth. There is the warm-hearted comedy of the good-natured characters like Tom who, though they sometimes go wrong, are filled with a predisposition to do right. And, throughout it all there is the irony that is a mainstay of the novel, as in this brief digression on the upper classes (14, 1):

> Now it happens that this higher Order of Mortals is not to be seen, like all the rest of the Human Species, for nothing, in the Streets, Shops, and Coffeehouses: Nor are they shewn, like the upper Rank of Animals, for so much a Piece. In short, this is a Sight to which no Persons are admitted, without one or other of these Qualifications, *viz.* either Birth or Fortune; or what is equivalent to both, the honourable Profession of a Gamester.

Fielding writes with a grace and assurance that make him among the most companionable of authors. He fills the novel with witty allusions, apt quotations, and rhetorical flourishes but is never pretentious or pedantic. Rather, his style is urbane and yet playful, as he infuses *Tom Jones* with an infectious blend of gusto and good humor. His odyssey of the road overflows with comic energy and offers a vivid panorama of society high and low, urban and rural, in eighteenth-century England.

Fielding, though, is not simply the historian of his age; he is its critic as well, as he unmasks the vain and hypocritical of all ranks. However, as in *Joseph Andrews*, his satire is clearly different from that of the Scriblerians. While he certainly admired them—he published both *The Author's Farce* and *Tom Jones* under the name Scriblerus Secundus—his satire has a more benign tone than that of Swift and Alexander Pope. He believed that scorn and contempt were less likely to effect reform than were good-natured raillery and banter. Consequently, his satire is combined with a generous tolerance and large-hearted openness of soul that imparts a great sense of humanity and understanding.

Fielding followed *Tom Jones* with *Amelia*. The somberness of the opening scenes set in Newgate Prison establish the tone of this far darker novel. While his concerns are in part unchanged, with Fielding showing an acute awareness of masks and sham, the mood is bleaker with a new earnestness and a graver attitude toward human folly. The novelist's satire is more bitter as well, as he attacks both social and political abuses. Given his painfully deteriorating health and constant exposure as a magistrate to the worst of human life, it is not surprising that the world now seemed to him a much less comic place than in his youth.

His *Journal of a Voyage to Lisbon*, which describes in detail his final trip, was published posthumously in 1755. In it Fielding approaches his end with his intellectual vigor undiminished by the sufferings that crippled his body. His powers of observation and characterization did not desert him, as he describes his last weeks with dignity and courage.

The man may have died, but his influence did not. Writers such as Sir Walter Scott, William Makepeace Thackeray, and George Eliot held him in high esteem. Scott actually called him the father of the English novel, and Fielding did do much to shape the future course of the genre. Whereas epistolary novels and pretended autobiographies had hitherto been regarded as more legitimate, Fielding's works contributed to the ascendancy of acknowledged fictions narrated by the author. Indeed, he was the first to devise a fully developed theory of the novel.

Moreover, the artistic unity of *Tom Jones* set the structural standard for the genre in England, while his panoramic surveys of contemporary society, complete with ironic social commentary, became the norm for English fiction until the end of the nineteenth century. A twentieth-century author like John Barth owes a debt to Fielding as well since *Tom Jones* and *Joseph Andrews* may be credited with introducing into English the self-reflexive novel in which its own artificiality is displayed.

Summary

Henry Fielding's contemporary reputation rests primarily on his comic novels. In them his genial and strongly felt presence helps unify the various types of humor, such as satire, burlesque, and farce, that he incorporates into his bustling plots. The unmasking of vanity and hypocrisy was his special province, and he used his comedy for a moral end. Fielding chose, as he variously put it, to speak truth with a smiling countenance, to laugh humankind out of its favorite follies. If he did his best to remedy injustice as a judge, he did the same in his writing, championing the innocent and downtrodden while exposing the villainous and corrupt. In both his fiction and his life, he applied his energies in the service of what he knew to be the right. Fielding was not merely a humorist of the first order; he was a humanitarian as well.

Selected Bibliography

Primary Sources

Novels

The History of the Adventures of Joseph Andrews, and of His Friend Mr. Abraham Adams Written in Imitation of the Manner of Cervantes. London: Millar, 1742.

The Life of Mr. Jonathan Wild the Great. London: Millar, 1743.

The History of Tom Jones, a Foundling. London: Millar, 1749.

Amelia. London: Millar, 1751.

Plays

Love in Several Masques. London: Watts, 1728.

The Temple Beau. London: Watts, 1730.

The Author's Farce; and the Pleasures of the Town. London: Roberts, 1730.

Tom Thumb. London: Roberts, 1730 (rev. and enlarged as *The Tragedy of Tragedies.* London: Roberts, 1731).

Rape upon Rape. London: Watts, 1730 (reissued as *The Coffee-House Politician.* London: Watts, 1730).

The Letter-Writers. London: Roberts, 1731.

The Welsh Opera. London: Rayner, 1731.

The Grub-Street Opera. London: Roberts, 1731.

The Lottery. London: Watts, 1732.

The Modern Husband. London: Watts, 1732.

The Covent-Garden Tragedy. London: Watts, 1732.

The Old Debauchees. London: Watts, 1732.

The Mock Doctor. London: Watts, 1732.

The Miser. London: Watts, 1733.

The Intriguing Chambermaid. London: Watts, 1734.

Don Quixote in England. London: Watts, 1734.

An Old Man Taught Wisdom. London: Watts, 1735.

The Universal Gallant. London: Watts, 1735.

Pasquin. London: Watts, 1736.

Tumble-Down Dick: or, Phaeton in the Suds. London: Watts, 1736.

Eurydice. London: Roberts, 1737.

The Historical Register for the Year 1736. London: Roberts, 1737.

Miss Lucy in Town. London: Millar, 1742.

The Wedding-Day. London: Millar, 1743.

Eurydice Hiss'd. London: Watts, 1745.

The Fathers: or, The Good-Natur'd Man. London: Cadell, 1778.

Periodicals

The Champion: or, British Mercury. London: Cooper, Graham, Huggonson, 1739–1741.

The True Patriot: and The History of Our Own Times. London: Cooper, 1745–1746.

The Jacobite's Journal. London: Strahan, Cooper, 1747–1748.

The Covent-Garden Journal. London: Dodd, Sharp, 1752.

Other Writings

The Masquerade, a Poem. London: Roberts, 1728.

Of True Greatness. London: Corbet, 1741.

The Veroniad. London: Corbet, 1741.

An Apology for the Life of Mrs. Shamela Andrews. London: Dodd, 1741.

F

The Crisis: A Sermon on Revel. xiv. 9–11. London: Dodd, 1741.

The Opposition, A Vision. London: Cooper, 1742.

A Full Vindication of the Dutchess Dowager of Marlborough. London: Roberts, 1742.

Plutus, the God of Riches (trans. from Aristophanes). London: Waller, 1742.

Concerning the Terrestrial Chrysipus. London: Roberts, 1743.

Miscellanies. London: Millar, 1743.

A Serious Address to the People of Great Britain. London: Cooper, 1745.

The History of the Present Rebellion in Scotland. London: Cooper, 1745.

A Dialogue between the Devil, the Pope, and the Pretender. London: Cooper, 1745.

The Female Husband. London: Cooper, 1746.

A Dialogue Between a Gentleman of London . . . and an Honest Alderman of the Country Party. London: Cooper, 1747.

A Proper Answer to a Late Scurrilous Libel. London: Cooper, 1747.

Ovid's Art of Love Paraphrased, and Adapted to the Present Time. Book I. London: Millar, 1747.

A Charge Delivered to the Grand Jury, at the Sessions, the 29th of June, 1749. London: Millar, 1749.

A True State of the Case of Bosavern Penlez. London: Millar, 1749.

An Enquiry into the Causes of the Late Increase of Robbers. London: Millar, 1751.

A Plan of the Universal Register Office. London: n.p., 1752 (with John Fielding).

Examples of the Interposition of Providence in the Detection and Punishment of Murder. London: Millar, 1752.

A Proposal for Making an Effectual Provision for the Poor. London: Millar, 1753.

A Clear State of the Case of Elizabeth Canning. London: Millar, 1753.

The Journal of a Voyage to Lisbon. London: Millar, 1755.

Secondary Sources

Bibliographies

Morrissey, L.J. *Henry Fielding: A Reference Guide.* Boston: G.K. Hall, 1980. An annotated bibliography of works from 1755 to 1977.

Stoler, John A., and Richard D. Fulton.

Henry Fielding: An Annotated Bibliography of Twentieth-Century Criticism, 1900–1977. New York: Garland, 1980.

Biographies

Battestin, Martin. *Henry Fielding: A Life.* London: Routledge, 1989. Supersedes all previous biographical studies.

Cross, Wilbur L. *The History of Henry Fielding.* New Haven: Yale University Press, 1918. Long the standard critical biography, with a valuable bibliography.

Dudden, F. Homes. *Henry Fielding: His Life, Works, and Times.* Oxford: Clarendon, 1952. Dudden covers much of the same ground as Cross but can be helpful on the historical background.

Rogers, Pat. *Henry Fielding, A Biography.* New York: Charles Scribner's Sons, 1979. Rogers presents some valuable material, especially on Fielding as dramatist and magistrate.

Books

Alter, Robert. *Fielding and the Nature of the Novel.* Cambridge, MA: Harvard University Press, 1968. Alter discusses the style, the structure, and the handling of character in the novels.

Battestin, Martin. *The Moral Basis of Fielding's Art: A Study of "Joseph Andrews."* Middletown, CT: Wesleyan University Press, 1959. *Joseph Andrews* is intended as a moral work in the Latitudinarian and benevolist traditions.

Blanchard, Frederic T. *Fielding the Novelist: A Study in Historical Criticism.* New Haven: Yale University Press, 1926. The standard survey of Fielding's changing literary reputation.

Butt, John. *Fielding.* London: Longmans, Green, 1954. A solid and succinct introduction.

Digeon, Aurelien. *The Novels of Fielding.* London: Routledge, 1925. The pioneering textual study.

Ehrenpreis, Irvin. *Fielding: "Tom Jones."* London: Edward Arnold, 1964. A discussion of the novel under the headings of author, story, doctrine, meaning and form, and comedy.

Golden, Morris. *Fielding's Moral Psychology.* Amherst: University of Massachusetts Press, 1966. Golden examines Fielding's relationship to Lord Shaftesbury.

Irwin, Michael. *Henry Fielding: The Tentative Realist*. Oxford: Clarendon, 1967. Irwin argues that Fielding's fiction is essentially non-realistic.

Johnson, Maurice. *Fielding's Art of Fiction: Eleven Essays on "Shamela," "Joseph Andrews," "Tom Jones," and "Amelia."* Philadelphia: University of Pennsylvania Press, 1961. Essays on Fielding's use of literary devices, stressing his craftsmanship and his use of literary parallels.

Paulson, Ronald, ed. *Fielding: A Collection of Critical Essays*. Englewood Cliffs, NJ: Prentice-Hall, 1962. Includes essays by Ian Watt, Maynard Mack, Andre Gide, John Middleton Murry, and William Empson, among others.

Paulson, Ronald, and Thomas Lockwood, eds. *Henry Fielding: The Critical Heritage*. New York: Barnes & Noble, 1969. Eighteenth-century commentaries on Fielding.

Rawson, Claude J. *Henry Fielding and the Augustan Ideal under Stress*. London: Routledge & Kegan Paul, 1972. The style and form of Fielding's works demonstrate a sense of stress, reflecting the threats to the Augustan ideal of harmony that were surfacing at the time.

Trainor, Charles. *The Drama and Fielding's Novels*. New York: Garland, 1988. A detailed study of the influence of the theater on the novels.

Watt, Ian. *The Rise of the Novel: Studies in Defoe, Richardson, and Fielding*. Berkeley: University of California Press, 1957. Watt examines Fielding in the context of the history of fiction and contrasts his type of realism with Richardson's.

Wright, Andrew H. *Henry Fielding: Mask and Feast*. Berkeley: University of California Press, 1965. Wright studies Fielding's comic methods and techniques, arguing that he intentionally emphasizes the artificiality of his novels.

Charles Trainor

Finch, Anne

Born: Sydmonton in the county of Hampshire, April 1661
Education: Little known, probably educated at home
Marriage: Heneage Finch, May 15, 1684
Died: London, August 5, 1720

Biography

In April 1661, Anne Kingsmill was born into a very old, aristocratic family; the family of her father, Sir William Kingsmill, had been closely connected to the British monarchy since the twelfth century. The family of her mother, Anne Haslewood, was also very wealthy and aristocratic. Unfortunately, both of Anne's parents died when she was very young. Her father died when she was only five months old; her mother died when Anne was three, and her stepfather died when she was ten. The records show that Anne was left well provided for financially by her family, but most of the details of her early life and upbringing have been lost. The 1992 biography by Barbara McGovern does supply some more information.

There are records in 1682 which show that Kingsmill was one of the six maids of honor to Mary of Modena, the wife of James, Duke of York. Of the other maids of honor the best known is Anne Killigrew, the poet and painter about whom John Dryden wrote an ode. A contemporaneous account states that both Annes were "much beloved by her [Mary of Modena], were ladies of irreproachable virtue, members of the Church of England, and alike distinguished for moral worth and literary attainments."[1] At Court, Kingsmill met Heneage Finch, the gentleman to the bedchamber of James. Despite her assertion early on that she would not marry, she married Finch on May 15, 1684. The marriage was a very happy one; Heneage was her friend and lover as well as her husband; he encouraged her writing of poetry, even "requir'd her rhymes"; they enjoyed and eagerly sought quiet time together. There were no children.

When James was exiled in 1688, Anne and Heneage Finch refused to take the oath of allegiance to William and Mary because of their loyalty to James. After about two years of living with various friends, they were invited by Charles, the Earl of Winchilsea, to live with him at his country estate at Eastwell Park, where they lived for the rest of their lives. Heneage was retired from public life and spent his time in scholarly activities, especially mathematical drawing and antiquarian pursuits, related especially to antique manuscripts; Anne wrote her poetry, conversed with her friends, and took long walks on the estate. In 1712, upon the death of the Earl of Winchilsea, Heneage succeeded to the title, and Anne thus became the Countess of Winchilsea.

F

The Finches spent most of their winters in London, so Anne was a part of the London literary circle. She corresponded with Alexander Pope about his treatment of women and female hypochondria in *The Rape of the Lock*; Jonathan Swift was a friend and supporter of her writing—he refers to her in his *Journal to Stella*. She knew Nicholas Rowe and wrote an epilogue to *Jane Shore*. The work of Aphra Behn and Katherine Philips had a major influence on her writing. In 1713, she published, with the encouragement of her husband, a small volume of some of her poetry, *Miscellany Poems on Several Occasions, Written by a Lady*, but most of her poems were not published during her lifetime. She left a manuscript with the works carefully arranged, but the collected poems were not published until 1903, although several of the individual pieces had been anthologized and were praised by William Wordsworth, Leigh Hunt, and other nineteenth-century British writers and literary historians. Finch, the Countess of Winchilsea, died in London on August 5, 1720.

Literary Analysis

The critical analysis of Finch's poetry has focused primarily on two areas: initially she was studied as an Augustan writer and placed in the tradition with John Dryden and Andrew Marvell; more recently she has been studied by the feminist critics, especially for her comments about women and writing. So, while her poetry encompasses several modes, Finch has not been regarded primarily as a humorist. Myra Reynolds divides her works into nine, somewhat overlapping categories: translations, dramas, songs, religious poems, pindaric odes, fables, verse criticism, satiric work and nature poetry.[2] Finch's satiric and humorous work, depending upon how those terms are defined, includes about one-half of her writing. The serious love poetry, songs, poetic drama, religious poetry, and nature poetry make up the rest of her canon. Her best-known poem, "A Nocturnal Reverie," was greatly admired by Wordsworth and has been studied as a precursor of Romanticism; Ann Messenger compares and contrasts her "To the Nightingale" to some Romantic poems on the same subject.

Finch's humorous work can be grouped into three types: the playful, whimsical poems about loving, writing, and living as a woman; the fables with their light satiric edge; and the humorous satires especially about women and

fashion. The tone of the majority of Finch's poetry is light and playful. She does not have the biting edge that most of us associate with late seventeenth- and early eighteenth-century British satire. For instance, in her poem "To Mr. F. Now Earl of W." she describes all of her endeavors to enlist the muses' help in writing a poem for him. However, all of them refuse because expressing love for a husband is unthinkable:

> A *Husband!* eccho'd all around:
> And to *Parnassus* sure that Sound
> Had never yet been sent;
> Amazement in each Face was read,
> In haste th'affrighted Sisters fled,
> And unto Council went.[3]

Finch is forced to use only her own devices for expressing love for a husband; no self-respecting muse could help her to do such a thing. This playful idea of no one being willing to help her, which paradoxically underlines her independence of the tradition, reveals her joy in her love for her husband and her joy in writing about it.

Finch wrote several works of verse criticism, but none of them resemble either Dryden's "Mac Flecknoe" or Pope's "An Essay on Criticism." Her tone is light, comic, even mocking the inflated seriousness of some poets' judgments about literature. In "The Circuit of Apollo," she satirically examines the question: who is the greatest woman poet. Finch, or "Ardelia" (the poetic name that she gave herself), describes Apollo traversing the world in reviewing contemporary women poets. Ardelia presents all of the poets positively. There is none of the criticism that would be expected in such a mode. No Colley Cibber is ridiculed; no Thomas Shadwell is despised. All of the women are praised, including "Ardelia" Finch. Unlike Paris, Apollo decides not to determine one winner, but to award the prize to all four:

> Since in Witt, or in Beauty, itt never was
>   heard,
> One female cou'd yield t'have another
>   preferr'd,
> He changed his dessign, and devided his
>   praise,
> And said that they all had a right to the
>   Bay's,
> And that t'were injustice, one brow to
>   adorn,

With a wreath, which so fittly by each
    might be worn. (74)

In this passage, Finch gently chides poets for
their jealousy of one another, though the tone
of the whole poem is generous and accepting.

Ardelia also mocks the Lydia Languish
mentality of some seventeenth- and eighteenth-
century women. In *La Passion Vaincue,*" she
describes a "desperate Maid" who is contemplating suicide because her beloved has betrayed
her, "Since his Vanity lives, whilst my Character dies." However, the maid decides against
suicide because of her pride: "Why this Strife, /
Since the *Swains* are so Many, and I've but *One*
Life?" (125). The pastoral setting of the poem,
its French title, and its serious subject set up the
final line which is pragmatic but also comic.

This use of allusions and the literary tradition for comic effect is also seen in "Adam
Pos'd." In this poem Ardelia asks how Adam,
who gave the names to all other creatures, could
possibly find a name for a "vain Fantastick
Nymph . . . in all her antick Graces, / Her various Fashions, and more various Faces." In the
last line the only label that Finch can give to this
Nymph is "Thing": how could Adam have
"giv'n this Thing a Name" (149). If this poem
were read outside the context of her other poetry, a reader might think that Finch was expressing an attitude similar to that of Pope in
"To a Lady." The "Thing" is woman, a chameleon-like creature with low standards and little
intelligence. Still, the tone and stance of many
other poems by the writer refute this possibility; the Nymph "thing" of this poem may be
some women, but she is not *woman*. Woman
should be and could be much more than this
teasing flirt. She can and should rise above the
"dull manage of a servile house." Certainly
Finch is concerned about the quality of women's
lives and their writing. At the same time she
often laughs about it and mocks herself and
other women in a whimsical and generous way.

Finch did not seem to regard her fables as
highly as her other poetry, even though they
constitute about one-third of her poetry. She
describes them as "childish tales," although a
modern reader can see them as "vignettes of
social satire."[4] These fables follow most of the
conventions of beast fables: owls, eagles, sows,
and cats talk and act in funny but disastrous
ways and the poems often conclude with a two-
line aphorism. Again Finch's voice is a whimsical one; she chides but does not pontificate. Her
"lessons" focus on the domestic life, rather than
the public one. Her fable, "The Goute and the
Spider," is written to her husband when he suffers from that disease. In the poem she describes
Goute coming up from Hell to dwell with them,
and she promises that she will stay by him and
offer "tender and officious care." She ends with
lines which express her joy in marriage:

> Since heaven does in the Nuptial state
>   admitt
> Such cares but new endearments to
>   begett
> And to allay the hard fatigues of life
> Gave the first Maid a Husband, Him a
>   Wife. (32)

Eve is now the "first Maid," an unusual and apt
descriptive phrase.

Most of the other fables are more directly
moralistic. In "The Owl Describing Her Young
Ones," the poet tells the story of a Mother-Owl
who was fearful that His Highness, the Eagle,
would destroy her young ones, so she describes
them to him as "pretty Souls," "Heiresses," and
"Beauties . . . / Whose Eyes outshine the Stars
by Night." When the eagle does see the owlets,
they do not look like "an enchanting, beaute-
ous Race." Instead, they appear as ugly things
who look like vultures and have no "brightness
in their eyes." Since he does not recognize them
from Mother-Owl's description, he eats them
for his dinner. Finch ends the poem:

> Faces or Books, beyond their Worth
>   extoll'd,
> Are censur'd most, and thus to pieces
>   pull'd. (181)

The humor of this fable and the many others
similar to it illustrate the satiric quality which
is present in various forms in most of the
author's lighter poetry.

Her best known satiric poem, "Ardelia's
Answer to Ephelia," is a more sustained piece
of writing. In this poem Finch criticizes the
women in her society who live with a superficial and frivolous set of values and expectations.
As Katharine Rogers has pointed out, Ardelia
is an outsider, a visitor to the city; Ephelia belongs. Ardelia says that she will never fit into the
fashionable world because she will not "pass a
gen'rall censure on mankind." She also ridicules
Ephelia's insincere flattery, her obsessive concern with her appearance and that of others, the

preening and parading of the "nymph" with "various faces." According to Rogers, "In her satire on women, the satirist is not a censor scolding or instructing an inferior class, but a right-minded person criticizing other human beings for degrading themselves below the standards which all should meet."[5] Finch judges a woman not merely against other women but against a human standard. In "The Introduction," she reminds her reader that women are "Education's, more than Nature's fools."

At times Finch's satire resembles that of other Augustan wits; she hates the affectation and insincerity of the people in her world and ridicules it in poems like "Sir Plausible":

> Sir Plausible, as 'tis well known,
> Has no opinions of his own;
> But closes with each stander by,
> Fast as chameleons change their dye;
> Has still some applicable story
> To gratify a Whig or Tory,
> And even a Jacobite in tatters
> If met alone he smoothly flatters;
> Greets friend and foe with wishes fervent,
> And lives and dies your humble servant.[6]

Summary

Anne Finch writes in many different modes, but much of her work is comic and satiric. She is an Augustan with strong affinities to Pope and John Gay, but the tone of her satire differs markedly from theirs. Reynolds concludes that "Her antipathies were lively and her insight acute, yet her satire was seldom personal, and seldom really acrimonious. Much of it is in the fables and even those with the most caustic morals are often marked in the narrative portions by a gayety, a humorous lightness of touch, and a tolerance far enough removed from a genuinely pessimistic view of human nature."[7] Finch sees clearly the problems of women's lives in the eighteenth century and especially of women writers, but she can and does laugh at those problems, at the men, and at herself in a witty, intelligent way.

Notes

1. Myra Reynolds, ed., *The Poems of Anne, Countess of Winchilsea* (Chicago: University of Chicago Press, 1903), pp. 23–24.
2. *Ibid.*, pp. 94–110.
3. Katharine M. Rogers, ed., *Selected Poems of Anne Finch, Countess of Winchilsea* (New York: Frederick Ungar, 1979), p. 29. Subsequent references in the text refer to this edition.
4. Reynolds, pp. 90, 91.
5. Rogers, "Anne Finch, Countess of Winchilsea: An Augustan Woman Poet," in *Shakespeare's Sisters: Feminist Essays on Women Poets*, ed. Sandra M. Gilbert and Susan Gubar (Bloomington: Indiana University Press, 1979), p. 46.
6. Denys Thompson, ed., *Anne Finch, Countess of Winchilsea: Selected Poems* (Manchester, England: Fyfield Books, 1987), p. 79.
7. Reynolds, pp. 120–21.

Selected Bibliography

Primary Sources
The Poems of Anne, Countess of Winchilsea. Ed. Myra Reynolds. Chicago: University of Chicago Press, 1903.
Selected Poems of Anne Finch, Countess of Winchilsea. Ed. Katharine M. Rogers. New York: Frederick Ungar, 1979.
Anne Finch, Countess of Winchilsea: Selected Poems. Ed. Denys Thompson. Manchester, England: Fyfield Books, 1987.

Secondary Sources

Biographies
McGovern, Barbara. *Anne Finch and Her Poetry: A Critical Biography.* Athens and London: University of Georgia Press, 1992. The first book-length critical and biographical study of Anne Finch. Focuses on her historical place, her relationships with other women writers and her construction of a poetic identity as a woman and a royalist.

Books and Articles
Brower, Reuben A. "Lady Winchilsea and the Poetic Tradition of the Seventeenth Century." *Studies in Philology*, 42 (1945): 61–80. Brower argues that Finch's poetry is not pre-Romantic but part of the Augustan tradition.
Gilbert, Sandra, and Susan Gubar. *The Madwoman in the Attic: The Woman Writer and the Nineteenth-Century Imagination.* New Haven: Yale University Press, 1979, pp. 7–14, 60–63. Discussion of Finch's idea of women as cyphers and "powerless intellectual eunuchs."
Mallinson, Jean. "Anne Finch: A Woman

Poet and the Tradition." In *Gender at Work: Four Women Writers of the Eighteenth Century*. Ed. Ann Messenger. Detroit: Wayne State University Press, 1990, pp. 34–76. Extensive biographical and critical discussion of the life and writings of Finch.

Mermin, Dorothy. "Women Becoming Poets: Katherine Philips, Aphra Behn, Anne Finch." *English Literary History*, 57 (1990): 335–55. Mermin describes the similarities among the three poets: their friendship with other women as a source of support, their strong sense of themselves as women writers in a female poetic tradition.

Rogers, Katharine M. "Anne Finch, Countess of Winchilsea: An Augustan Woman Poet." In *Shakespeare's Sisters*: *Feminist Essays on Women Poets*. Ed. Sandra Gilbert and Susan Gubar. Bloomington: Indiana University Press, 1979, pp. 32–46. Discussion of Finch as "both a woman and an Augustan." Emphasis on her distinctively female kind of satire.

Salvaggio, Ruth. "Anne Finch Placed and Displaced." In *Enlightened Absence*: *Neoclassical Configurations of the Feminine*. Urbana: University of Illinois Press, 1988, pp. 105– 26. Finch had a special fondness for shade which is suggestive of her sense of displacement and her "disease" in the male dominated society of her time.

Wordsworth, William. "Essay, Supplementary to the Preface of the Second Edition of the *Lyrical Ballads*" (1815). Wordsworth sees Finch's poetry as one of the few examples where "it can be inferred that the eye of the Poet had been steadily fixed upon his object." He praises her nature poetry and describes her as "one poetess to whose writings I am especially partial."

Martha Rainbolt

Firbank, Ronald

Born: Mayfair, January 17, 1886
Education: Privately; Trinity Hall, Cambridge University, 1906
Died: Rome, May 21, 1926

Biography

Arthur Annesley Ronald Firbank—a name that he shortened to Arthur Firbank before settling, in his twenties, on Ronald Firbank—was born into a quintessential middle-class Victorian family. His grandfather was Joseph Firbank, a celebrated railroad contractor whose lines, tunnels, and viaducts crisscrossed the Midlands and made him a hero of Victorian capitalism. Ronald's father, Thomas, was a Conservative Member of Parliament for East Hull; he belonged to all of the proper Tory clubs, gained inclusion in *Burke's Landed Gentry* for 1898, and was knighted in 1902. On the maternal side, Lady Firbank was the daughter of an Anglo-Irish cleric from County Carlow. However, these roots of Victorian capitalism, religion, and politics could not have produced a more unlikely flower in the grandson and son.

Born in Mayfair on January 17, 1886, Firbank grew up in the south London suburb of Chislehurst. Times there were interrupted by therapeutic trips to warmer climates in an effort to improve the poor health that plagued him all of his life. The comings and goings of his childhood also established what Brigid Brophy, in her biography of Firbank, has called "the pattern for the non-pattern, the international nomadism, of his adult life" (123).

In 1906, Firbank went to Cambridge University where a friend and classmate was Vyvyan Holland, Oscar Wilde's youngest son. Firbank's time at Cambridge was not academically auspicious, and he came down without taking a degree. During his years at the university, however, Firbank wrote the first short story to exhibit the traits and motifs of his later work, "Lady Appledore's Mesalliance" (1907). Also while at Cambridge, he became a member of the Roman Catholic Church after receiving instruction from the novelist and well-known cleric, R.H. Benson.

Slight, effeminate, and painfully shy, Firbank spent much of his adult life in voluntary exile. His favorite places were the fashionable watering holes of the Continent and North Africa, where homosexuality was condoned or openly practiced. When in London, he mixed with the habitues of the Cafe Royal. His friends were such well-known aesthetes or enemies of the orthodox as Lord Berners, Augustus John, and Osbert Sitwell. Often thought of as the last of the decadents of the 1890s, Firbank himself sported painted fingernails and begrudged spending money on all but flowers—and his own writing. He financed the publication of most of his novels and left provisions for his estate to assume the costs of posthumous publications.

Firbank died in the Quirinale Hotel in Rome on May 21, 1926, and was buried in the Protestant Cemetery, where John Keats is also interred and where Shelley's heart lies buried. Firbank's sister, aware of her brother's conversion to Catholicism, had the body exhumed and reburied in the Catholic cemetery at Verano.

Literary Analysis

Scant critical attention has been paid to Firbank's writing in the decades since his death. When critics do comment about him, the tendency is to see him as the heir apparent to Wilde. Characteristics of Firbank's fiction that owe no small debt to Wilde are the outrageous circumstances of plot, the comic names of his characters, and the camp repartee and sexual innuendos. Cyril Connolly, an early admirer of Firbank, labeled him one of "the breed of the permanent giggle."

But, in his novels the giggle leads to a certain liberation of subject matter, to a belief that anything is fair game for the novelist. This freedom sees its greatest expression in the proliferation of homosexual concerns in Firbank's novels—from lesbian nuns to pederastic priests. It is seen too, however, in Firbank's exploration of the black cultures of the Caribbean (*Prancing Nigger* and *Valmouth*), Harlem (*Prancing Nigger*), and North Africa (*Santal*).

Firbank also deserves credit for his innovations with dialogue, which makes up much of the bulk of his short novels. In a typical Firbank novel there is little in the way of authorial commentary or interior monologue. Instead, dialogue prevails. It is responsible for narrative thrust and character development, and because of the reliance on dialogue, Firbank's novels are highly dramatic, reading almost like theatrical scripts. Dialogue is also the source for much of the humor in his fiction. What is not said by Firbank's characters is often as funny as what is said, as the following exchange among the courtiers in *The Flower Beneath the Foot* (1923) illustrates:

"Did you hear what the dear King said?"

"No."

"It's almost *too* appalling . . . " Lady Something replied . . . "Fleas," she murmured, "have been found at the Ritz."

". . . . ! . . . . ? . . . !!"

At a time in the development of early twentieth-century British fiction when James Joyce, Virginia Woolf, Ford Madox Ford, and others were freeing the novel from nearly all structural constraints imposed on it by earlier novelists, Firbank added to the Modernist revolution by insisting that narrative need not be bound by the rules of cause and effect. Plot, as a series of actions and appropriate reactions, is almost nonexistent in Firbank's fiction. Instead, his novels tend to be a series of tableaux or vignettes, often with only the barest common thread. However, as E.M. Potoker has pointed out (37), Firbank plants subtle hints and references, perhaps pages apart, that gradually link one scene to another. In the posthumously published *Concerning the Eccentricities of Cardinal Pirelli* (1926), for example, the odd behavior of the title character includes the baptizing of a German shepherd puppy named Crack, an ecclesiastical faux pas with serious consequences for the Cardinal. Both Pirelli and his unusual gesture are only obliquely mentioned throughout much of the novel. In the closing scene, though, the focus returns to the cardinal, who has been summoned to the Vatican to hear of his punishment for the canine baptism. But before he can make the trip to Rome, he drops dead of a heart attack, brought on by his ardent chase after a much desired choirboy named Chicklet. The result of this circuitous or oblique storytelling is similar, Potoker claims, to that of cinematic montage, which was enjoying a vogue among the continental filmmakers of the same era.

Even his admirers, however, have failed to comment sufficiently on Firbank's contributions to black humor. His best fiction illustrates his ability to express through comedy the malaise and futility of modern life brought on by the failure of hope—and all without the slightest sentimentality. Firbank's most widely read novel, *The Flower Beneath the Foot*, offers the best example of this loss and despair hidden beneath the manic humor common to his fiction. In *Flower* he depicts, among other things, the hagiography of St. Laura de Nazianzi in the kingdom of Pisuergia, where fleas at the Ritz signal a national scandal and cold potatoes are "tres gutter." Offering a stark contrast to the wackiness preceding them, the final scenes of the novel depict Laura on the walls of the Flaming Hood convent, heartbroken at losing Prince Josef to another. She mortifies herself with broken glass as the haunting voice of a beggar calls out, "For the Love of God . . . in the name of

Pity . . . of Pity." Parallel sufferers in the novel are the English exiles of the diplomatic colony who are doomed to a life of perpetual isolation. All are rootless flowers crushed beneath the foot of an unforgiving history. And despite the novel's scatological jokes and frivolity, clearly present is the sense of apocalyptic gloom that covered much of Europe after World War I.

Summary

Although Ronald Firbank has always had a small but loyal following, most critics have viewed his fiction as narrow, dandyish, and inconsequential. Such an evaluation, however, fails to grant Firbank his rightful place among the notable eccentric comic writers of British fiction. More comment is needed on the influence of Henry Fielding and Laurence Sterne on Firbank's fiction; similarly, the debt that Firbank owes to Lewis Carroll for the use of twisted logic and nonsequiturs in dialogue has not been sufficiently examined.

Among those whom Firbank's fiction in turn influenced is certainly Ivy Compton-Burnett, whose short novels rely heavily on dialogue. A sufficient study has yet to be done on the effect of Firbank on the comic visions of Evelyn Waugh and Kingsley Amis, as well as on the strange anti-worlds of surrealists and absurdists such as Irish writer Flann O'Brien. One could even argue that a great deal of British popular comedy of the 1950s and 1960s is Firbankian in tone. For example, much of the humor of the Cambridge Footlight Players, some of whom would evolve into Monty Python, and of the Radio Prune Crew—Peter Sellers, Spike Milligan, et al.—seems to have come straight from Firbank's pages.

Selected Bibliography

Primary Sources
Vainglory. London: Grant Richards, 1915.
Inclinations. London: Grant Richards, 1916.
Caprice. London: Grant Richards, 1917.
Valmouth. London: Grant Richards, 1919.
The Princess Zoubaroff. London: Grant Richards, 1920.
Santal. London: Grant Richards, 1921.
The Flower Beneath the Foot. London: Grant Richards, 1923.
Prancing Nigger. New York: Brentano's, 1924. (Published in Britain as *Sorrow in Sunlight*.)
Concerning the Eccentricities of Cardinal Pirelli. London: Grant Richards, 1926.
The New Rhythm and Other Pieces. London:
Duckworth, 1962.
Complete Short Stories. Ed. Steven Moore. Elmwood Park, IL: Dalkey Archive Press, 1990. The title is misleading; this is largely juvenilia.

Secondary Sources

Bibliographies
Benkovitz, Miriam J. *A Bibliography of Ronald Firbank*. 2nd ed. Oxford: Clarendon, 1982.

Biographies
Benkovitz, Miriam J. *Ronald Firbank: A Biography*. New York: Knopf, 1969.

Books
Brooke, Jocelyn. *Ronald Firbank*. London: Arthur Barker, no date. Brooke's remains one of the best analyses of Firbank's style.
Brophy, Brigid. *Prancing Novelist: In Praise of Ronald Firbank*. London: Macmillan, 1973. Brophy's biography is regarded by many as being too "Firbankian" itself; its eccentric approach and organization lessen its usefulness.
Potoker, E.M. *Ronald Firbank*. New York: Columbia University Press, 1969.

Articles and Chapters in Books
Barnhill, Sarah. "Method in Madness: Ronald Firbank's *The Flower Beneath the Foot*," *English Literature in Transition*, 32 (Fall 1989): 291–300.
Connolly, Cyril. *Enemies of Promise*. New York: Persea Press, 1983, pp. 33–38.
———. *The Condemned Playground*. London: Hogarth Press, 1985, p. 115.
Sitwell, Osbert. "Introduction," *Five Novels by Ronald Firbank*. Norfolk, CT: New Directions, 1949, pp. xi–xii.
Wilson, Edmund. *The Shores of Light: A Literary Chronicle of the Twenties and Thirties*. New York: Farrar, 1952, pp. 69–72.

Sarah Barnhill

Fletcher, John

Born: Rye, Sussex, December 1579
Education: Bene't College (Corpus Christi) Cambridge University, B.A. (?) 1591–1595; M.A. (?) 1595–1598
Marriage: (?) Joan Herring, 1612; one child
Died: August 1625, probably in London

Biography

John Fletcher came from a family of high social stature, apparently was educated at Cambridge, and spent a lengthy professional life in London as a reliable and admired playwright. Still, biographical data about Fletcher is surprisingly thin, especially in the light of his fame and productivity; indeed, the biographical facts about William Shakespeare seem rich and detailed by comparison with the scanty information available about Fletcher's personal life.

It is known that Fletcher's father was Richard Fletcher, who enjoyed a successful career as a clergyman; as a dean, he gave the official prayer at the execution of Mary, Queen of Scots, and he rose to become bishop first of Bristol and then of Worcester, before attaining the rank of bishop of London in 1594. However, the elder Fletcher's second marriage in 1595 offended Queen Elizabeth I, whose favor he had enjoyed in his rise to prominence in the Anglican Church. Richard's political decline was brief because he died in 1596.

At any rate, John, the second son and fourth child of Bishop Fletcher, was born in Rye, Sussex, in December 1579 (he was baptized on December 20 of that year) and is thought to have taken a B.A. (1595) and an M.A. (1598) from Cambridge University's Bene't College, but not much is known about his life before he began his long and prosperous career as a professional dramatist. He could claim to be from a literary family: his uncle was Giles Fletcher the elder, a diplomat and minor Elizabethan poet, and his cousins, Giles Fletcher the younger and Phineas Fletcher, are remembered as allegorical poets in the tradition of Edmund Spenser. Fletcher himself surfaced as a playwright in 1606, writing for the private theaters. His famous collaboration with Francis Beaumont began in that year with a comedy, *The Woman Hater*, and lasted until Beaumont's retirement in 1612, though tradition has made their names almost inseparable in subsequent literary history.

During this time, Beaumont, the older of the two, is usually considered the stronger author in the collaboration which produced a number of works, including a brilliant, satiric comedy in *The Knight of the Burning Pestle* (1607), a popular sentimental tragicomedy in *Philaster* (1610), and a tough and ironic Jacobean tragedy in *The Maid's Tragedy* (1611). However, Fletcher's youthful romanticism found expression in *The Faithful Shepherdess* (ca. 1608), one of the few unsuccessful pastoral comedies in Elizabethan and Jacobean drama.[1]

By 1610, Beaumont and Fletcher had become leading dramatists for the King's Men, Shakespeare's company. After the retirement of Beaumont from writing for the stage, Fletcher turned to other collaborators. His most distinguished coauthor was the semiretired Shakespeare, who is believed to have collaborated with him on *Henry VIII* and *The Two Noble Kinsmen* (1612–1613). Thereafter, Fletcher worked with other playwrights, although he also wrote many of his plays alone, especially some of his numerous comedies. Undoubtedly, his most frequent collaborator after Beaumont was Philip Massinger, a dramatist of limited poetic talent but admired for the social realism of his mature comedy, *A New Way to Pay Old Debts* (1625–1626). Fletcher's partnership with Massinger probably began around 1616 when, following the deaths of Beaumont (1616) and Shakespeare (1616), he became the chief playwright for the King's Men.

A tradition accepted by Alexander Dyce, a nineteenth-century editor of Fletcher's works, was that the playwright married Joan Herring in 1612 and a son, John, was born in 1619. Twentieth-century scholars, especially Gerald Eades Bentley, have been skeptical of this tradition.

Fletcher may have written as many as forty-two plays, either working alone or with a collaborator, between 1609 and 1625, according to Bentley, the best twentieth-century authority on the stage history of Jacobean plays. At any rate, Fletcher's popularity during his lifetime was considerable. With Massinger, he apparently produced sixteen plays, including *The Custom of the Country* (1620) and *The Beggars' Bush* (1621). His other collaborators probably included the ubiquitous journeymen playwrights Nathan Field and William Rowley.

Several of Fletcher's lively comedies have been attributed unassisted authorship. These include: *The Woman's Prize, or The Tamer Tamed* (1611), a light-hearted and somewhat feminist "sequel" to *The Taming of the Shrew* (and perhaps influenced by Aristophanes' *Lysistrata*); *The Wild-Goose Chase* (1621), in which a rake is reformed; and *Rule a Wife and Have a Wife* (1624), a comic struggle over power in a marriage.

During his lifetime, Fletcher's tragicomedies, which usually offered sentimental or romantic happy endings, were generally popular, and the reputation of the "Beaumont and Fletcher plays" (the title usually given to the canon of Fletcher and his collaborators), continued into the Restoration when John Dryden praised the works for their realism in depicting the behavior of young gentlemen.

Fletcher died unexpectedly at the height of his fame in August 1625, evidently as a result of an attack of the plague in London's summer heat. A playwright with strong royalist and aristocratic sympathies, he was spared from witnessing the political disintegration of King Charles I's reign and the Puritan closing of the theaters in 1642.

Though his reputation (along with that of Beaumont) was high in the early years of the Restoration, it began to wane in the later seventeeth century, the age of neoclassicism. While the reputation of the Beaumont and Fletcher plays was revived a bit during the Romantic Era, modern scholars have, for the most part, only grudgingly conceded some value to Fletcher's work.

Literary Analysis

Fletcher probably deserves a higher reputation for some of his lively and exuberant comedies than he currently enjoys. Because of his collaborations, and the problems of attribution that this practice has created, his work has frequently been slighted, or, as in the case of *The Knight of the Burning Pestle* (which drew upon Miguel de Cervantes's masterpiece, *Don Quixote*), much of the credit has been given to his collaborator, Beaumont. Fletcher's commercial exploitation of romantic tragicomedy has also been considered a fault, and clearly his rapid and prolific production lowered the overall quality of his work. Nevertheless, his works contain a rich vein of comic imagery and invention, and he had a sharply satirical eye for social behavior and an impressive command of the comic possibilities in numerous variations on the theme of the war between the sexes.

Fletcher's satirical bite is demonstrated early in *The Knight of the Burning Pestle*, with its spirited parody of the middle-class infatuation with naive chivalric romance, when the collaborators bring a middle-class London housewife on the stage and allow her to direct the action into foolish by-ways of knight errantry. The chief comic technique used is broad parody embodied in the form of a burlesque of the romantic conventions of popular Elizabe-

than drama, as they are exhibited in pastoral and chivalric romances of the 1580s and 1590s, including the romantic comedies of John Lyly and Shakespeare. But, the comedy's irony is double edged: not only are chivalric conventions mocked in the comedy's farcical enactments of a romantic plot, but when the housewife insists that her husband's apprentice play the hero of the play, the authors seem to satirize middle-class aspirations to gentility of taste and manners.

It is customary nowadays to attribute this amusing play almost entirely to Beaumont on the reasonable grounds that it may have been staged before the collaboration between Beaumont and Fletcher began; but, even if this is so, Fletcher could have contributed to revisions of the original acting script, and thus have exercised an influence on the first published version (1613). (Fletcher is thought to have revised another early Beaumont comedy, *The Woman Hater*, ca. 1606.) At any rate, the satirical humor of this famous comedy is very likely in large part the product of Beaumont's imagination; still its extravagant humor and loving parody of theatrical convention are similar to the features displayed in some of the comic works attributed mainly to Fletcher. While some have argued that the comedy merely mocks romantic conventions and treats the middle class with a patronizing affection, its satirical tone clearly reflects the increasingly cynical and pessimistic mood of the Jacobean era.

Fletcher's genial and ribald humor appears more distinctively in the comic gusto of an early solo work, *The Woman's Prize, or The Tamer Tamed*. In this play a saucy young wife named Maria turns the tables on her overbearing bridegroom Petruchio, who is supposed to be the Petruchio of Shakespeare's earlier farce, *The Taming of the Shrew*, but now a former widower living in London for no clear reason. Maria battles for women's rights and dignity by withholding sexual pleasure from her arrogant husband, until he displays a more humble temperament and a willingness to reform from his overbearing manners.

Much of the play's action develops in a mode of broad slapstick: a scene in which Petruchio and his male friends assault Maria's house which Maria and her friends have barricaded against the men clearly requires pratfalls and comic physical mishaps. Partly because of this scene, and the play's overall theme, scholars have frequently invoked parallels with

Aristophanes' classic celebration of feminine power, *Lysistrata*. Indeed, *Lysistrata* is probably one of the influences on Fletcher's play, but its energetic gusto also reflects the broad sexual humor of Latin and Italian comedy (which contributed much to the farcical tone of Shakespeare's *Taming of the Shrew* as well). The earthy and ribald tone of the play appears most noticeably in the dialogue which displays an impressive array of humorous metaphors with sexual implications. A typical example is this exchange of wedding night badinage between Petruchio and his friends:

> *Petronius:* . . . Will you to bed sonne?
> This pride will have a fall.
> *Petruchio:* Upon your daughter:
> But I shall rise again,
> if there be truth
> In Egges, and butter'd Parsnips.
> *Petronius:* Wil you to bed son, & leave
> talking;
> Tomorrow morning we shall have you
> looke,
> For all your great words, like St. George
> at Kingston,
> Running a foot-back from the furious
> Dragon,
> That with her angry tayle belabours him
> For being lazie.
> *Sophocles:* His warlike launce
> Bent like a crosse bow lath, alas the
> while. (act 1, scene 3, lines 12–23,
> Ferguson edition)

As this passage suggests, the play is dominated by an exuberance of comic metaphor and invention: the humorous possibilities of the plot are constantly depicted in a spirit of exaggeration which tends to be more important than the story or characters themselves. As a result, it scarcely matters that Fletcher's Petruchio is more of a Jacobean rake than the clever and worldly rogue of Shakespeare's farce, for *The Woman's Prize* remains one of the more Rabelaisian comedies of the Jacobean era.

Although Fletcher had produced a putative sequel to Shakespeare's *Taming of the Shrew* in *The Woman's Prize*, this action did not prevent him from apparently collaborating with Shakespeare in *The Two Noble Kinsmen* and some other works which are assigned to the waning days of Shakespeare's career. It is notable that Fletcher was evidently capable of writing plays devoted mainly to romantic sentiment, as in the tragicomedy of *The Two Noble Kinsmen* (1613), or in his youthful romantic pastoral drama, *The Faithful Shepherdess* (ca. 1608). It was in his preface to *The Faithful Shepherdess* that Fletcher's famous definition of tragicomedy appeared, the new type of play with which his name is associated: "A tragicomedy is not so called in respect of mirth and killing, but in respect it wants deaths, which is enough to make it no tragedy, yet brings some near it, which is enough to make it no comedy." In his later career, Fletcher showed the ability to turn out numerous comedies and comic scenes dominated by ribald humor.

Surprisingly, the playwright is sometimes portrayed as an early advocate of women's rights, but this point of view would have surprised Dryden and other authors of Restoration comedy who imitated his depiction of the sexual attitudes of young gentlemen, and went much further in describing their amatory pursuits and successes. Fletcher certainly was not a consistent supporter of feminist principles in his comedies, despite the theme of *The Woman's Prize* and the feminine triumphs in certain other plays. Instead, he tended to portray the persistent and shifting nature of the conflict of the constant struggle for power between men and women. Perhaps the comic variations of this struggle were more interesting to him than any particular result. Moreover, as a serious professional dramatist, he was capable of depicting sympathetically the feelings and attitudes of both genders involved in this perennial battle for dominance.

Indeed, the various stratagems and duplicities employed in the battle of the sexes provides the source for much of the humor in Fletcher's comedy. For instance, *The Scornful Lady* (1616), probably another collaboration with Beaumont, reverses the formula of *The Woman's Prize* by heaping comic embarrassments on an arrogant heiress. In this comedy, moreover, Fletcher modifies his comic techniques: the action tends to be focused on comic intrigue, while the central figure is depicted as a kind of Jonsonian humors character.

Read without reference to the Fletcher canon as a whole, the tightly controlled *Scornful Lady* could be taken as a work of heartless misogyny; but, as one of Fletcher's more perceptive critics has observed, taken in the context of Fletcher's other work it shows Fletcher as an urbane ironist and observer of human behavior.

The same point is illustrated by some of the writer's other comedies in the same tone, such as the much later and more spirited comedy, *Rule a Wife and Have a Wife* (1624). Here, as in several other Fletcher plays, a series of stratagems is used to establish male dominance over a wife, but the apparent masculine dominance is offset by the wife's gaining the love of her husband. Here, as elsewhere, Fletcher's heroines sometimes express an enthusiasm for sexual experience which is almost as great as that of his male characters.

Fletcher's comedies show unflagging enthusiasm for a youthful rake's pursuit of a woman, as in his frenetic *The Chances* (1624), in which he portrays the misadventures of two Spanish gentlemen in Bologna, and the drama is notable mainly because of one of its womanizing leads, Don John, who claims to be an expert in amatory pursuits. He complains ruefully after one nocturnal adventure:

> What have I got by this now? What's the
>   purchase?
> A piece of evening Arras work, a child
> Indeed an infidel: this comes of peeping:
> A lump got out of laziness; good white
>   bread
> Let's have no bawling with ye: 'sdeath,
>   have I
> Known wenches thus long, all the ways
>   of wenches,
> Their snares and subtleties? have I read
>   over
> All their School learnings, div'd into
>   their quiddits,
> And am I now bum-fidled with a Bas-
>   tard?
> Fetch'd over with a Card of five and in
>   mine old days,
> After the dire massacre of a million
> Of Maidenheads . . . (act 1, scene 6,
>   Cambridge English Classics edition)

This speech illustrates one of Fletcher's stronger traits as a humorist, the ability to deal with a foolish character's sense of comic exasperation. Incidentally, though Don John has enjoyed a past like his more celebrated Spanish namesake, the play involves an intrigue plot of mistaken identity and the successful testing of a woman's love. The plot may have been suggested by a Spanish original, like *Rule a Wife and Have a Wife*, another drama of sexual conflict. But its chief humor arises from Fletcher's inventive treatment of Don John's escapades, which verge on the ludicrous.

However, the playwright also gained some comic effects from reversing the formula of masculine pursuit of a desirable woman by having a charming but wily woman pursue a rascally young gallant, as in *The Wild-Goose Chase* (1621). This is a rather primitive precursor of George Bernard Shaw's *Man and Superman*, in which the hero tries to escape from a marriage that a determined young woman wants. In Fletcher's comedy, Mirabel, a rebellious young gentleman, rejects an arranged marriage but is pursued by the virtuous Oriana, an apparently helpless and ingenuous young woman who loves the irresponsible youth, despite his reputation for wildness, his inclination to pursue other women, and his hostility to marriage.

Nonetheless, Oriana turns out to be more clever than she appears. After attempts to win Mirabel through appeals to his pity fail, she dazzles him by appearing in disguise as a wealthy and perhaps unattainable lady. While Mirabel has rejected the actual Oriana because he can have her with a minimum of effort, and because the pressure to marry her is imposed by sober friends and the older generation, he falls in love with her when she appears as a mysterious woman embodying a male fantasy. This clever stratagem is a tactic that is more subtle and appealing than the clever "bed trick" performed by Shakespeare's Helena in *All's Well That Ends Well*, one of the earlier comedies dealing with feminine pursuit of a rake and a probable influence on *The Wild-Goose Chase*.

Although much of the amusement provided in the play results from the audience's growing admiration for Oriana's craftiness, no doubt some of the laughter also resulted from the persistent complaints of Mirabel about the evils of matrimony:

> Pray, sir, your pardon;
> For I must travel. Lie lazy here,
> Bound to a wife? Chained to her subtle-
>   ties,
> Her humors, and her wills, which are
>   mere fetters?
> To her today pleased, tomorrow peevish,
> The third day mad, the fourth rebellious?
> You see before they are married, what
>   moriscoes,
> What masques and mummeries they put
>   upon us:

To be tied here and suffer their lavoltas!
(act 5, scene 2, Fraser and Rabkin
edition)

In general, despite a persistent comic tone of sexual liberalism, in his humorous plays Fletcher often resorts to a sentimental resolution, and avoids the more coarse and amoral seduction scenes of Restoration comedy. No doubt the romantic expectations of Fletcher's audience, however, and the limitations of censorship prevented him from depicting a more amoral world of sexual experience, such as would be presented in the plays of William Wycherley and William Congreve fifty or sixty years later. Indeed, the sentimental reformation of the wild young gallant in *The Wild-Goose Chase* (brought about by the love and charm of its innocent but clever heroine) runs counter to the dominant tendency of the comedy of the time of Charles II, and Restoration observers such as Samuel Pepys indicated their disappointment with this play. (In the more sentimental early eighteenth century, George Farquhar revived the play in a slightly adapted version.) But, it also should be noted that Fletcher himself, despite his tolerant spirit and his indebtedness to Latin comedy, probably felt a certain faith in the professed values of his audience, which was becoming increasingly restricted to the aristocracy and gentry by the end of the reign of James I.

At its best, Fletcher's comedy displays a forceful command of comic imagery and a language drawn from the vigorous London colloquial speech of his time. In *Wit Without Money* (1614), Valentine, an idealistic and foolish young heir who believes that wealth is vulgar and that when his estate is squandered he will be able to live on the good will of others, defends his position in a veritable whirlwind of words:

Means? Why all good men's my means.
My wit's my Plow, the Town's my stock,
Tavern's my standing-house, and all the
world knows there's no want; all Gentlemen that love Society, love me; all Purses
that wit and pleasure opens, are my Tenants; every mans Cloaths fit me, the next
fair lodging is but my next remove, and
when I please to be more eminent and
take the Air, a piece is levied, and a
Coach prepared, and I go I care not
whither, what need state here? (act 1,

scene 1, Cambridge English Classics edition)

Valentine ignores the counsels of prudence and worldly wisdom because he is a pedant, an eccentric gentleman whose education has made him believe in Renaissance idealizations of friendship. Like many other pedants in the world of drama, he can never be content with a simple statement of his ideals; every defense of his conduct must display his ferocious verbal exuberance. When he learns that his companions are only fair weather friends who are ready to abandon him after his money is gone and his debts are mounting, he displays the same kind of tumultuous verbal tirade in denouncing them.

Actually, nothing that Valentine does can be accomplished without an explosive barrage of comic metaphors and allusions, in amusing contrast to his brother who lives a Spartan life and speaks in a terse and laconic prose style. Though Valentine is the nominal hero of the play, he is a character modeled on a Jonsonian humors type, and it is the energy with which he expresses his eccentric nature that makes the changes he undergoes appear risible. As the plot unwinds, Fletcher saves Valentine's reputation by allowing his prudent uncle to manipulate him into a marriage with a wealthy widow; but his gradual and reluctant acceptance of a match that will mend his fortunes provides some sprightly comic scenes.

As *Wit Without Money* demonstrates, the dramatist was often successful at entertaining his audiences because of the unceasing fertility of his invention and his seemingly tireless ability to produce a series of theatrical surprises. Fletcher was especially effective in preparing his audience for a dramatic transformation in a character, as in the sudden reversal in the lead character of *The Elder Brother* (1624), another play in which he deals with the troubles of a foolish young heir.

In this spirited comedy (which scholars believe was written partly by Massinger, or perhaps revised by Massinger), Charles, the older brother—and apparently a bookish milksop—is about to lose his inheritance and his fiancee to his jealous and amoral younger brother until he suddenly recognizes the perils in his situation and undergoes a metamorphosis into a robust defender of his rights. The transformation of the retiring Charles from a tiresome pedant into a decisive man of action—and a masterful lover who astonishes his bored fiancee—is amusing to observe, not only because of the comic embarrassments heaped on the treacherous brother and his henchman, but because of Charles's dawning realization that he thoroughly enjoys his new role as a man who takes charge of his own destiny.

Throughout his career, Fletcher was fond of sudden and unexpected reversals in the behavior of his characters, but in this play the turnabout is a little more credibly motivated than usual. The plot of *The Elder Brother* suggests an early anticipation of the more decorous comedy of P.G. Wodehouse in the twentieth century; as in some of the farces of Wodehouse, much of the humor results from the sudden transformation of a timid protagonist into a forceful and assertive hero. Another appeal of this play, like that of *Wit Without Money*, is that it tended to reinforce the values of the aristocracy and the gentry of Fletcher's time, much as the novels of Henry Fielding in the eighteenth century tend, despite their satire, to support the values of the squirearchy. At any rate, *The Elder Brother*, which benefits from a rural setting, probably deserves to be better known than it is.

When Fletcher's importance is assessed, it is obvious that his comedies exercised a considerable influence on later playwrights, especially James Shirley, who dominated the Caroline stage and refined some of Fletcher's plots and characters in his own work. Indeed, Shirley's clever heroines, although in part inspired by Shakespeare's brilliant ingenues like Rosaline, also owe something to some of Fletcher's clever heroines, like Celia of *The Humorous Lieutenant* (1619), whose charm and whimsical stratagems tend to entertain herself as well as the audience. As has been noted already, Fletcher similarly provided models of the rake and of sexual conflicts for the Restoration playwrights. Finally, Fletcher followed the lead of Jonson and Roman comedy by depicting, in the representative plays discussed here and in such comedies as *Monsieur Thomas* (1610–1622?) a gallery of comic types. These include lecherous older men, egotistical gentlewomen, absent-minded family retainers and chaperones, befuddled pedants, improvident young heirs, and rascally servants.

Nevertheless, Fletcher's reputation continues to be lower than it deserves to be. He has been criticized with some justice for creating synthetic pathos in his tragedies and tragicomedies and of relying too much on sentimental resolutions in the comedies. Nor can it be denied that the cost of his prolific output was frequently hasty and careless work. In fact, it has sometimes been alleged that Fletcher's plays are effective as a progression of entertaining scenes, but lack coherence viewed as complete units. There is some merit in this complaint, especially in regard to those plays that are obviously thrown together too hastily—though even in these cases Fletcher's sure sense of his audience's attitudes is usually impressive.

Summary

John Fletcher deserves respect as a humorist and satirist, and the strength and vitality of the language in his comedies, as well as his sure and professional portraits of enduring comic character types, guarantee him an enduring position as a dramatic humorist.

Notes

1. As was the case with *The Knight of the Burning Pestle*, this play was so novel that it failed on stage. However, it was immediately published in a volume that included commendatory verses by dramatists Beaumont, George Chapman, and Ben Jonson.

Selected Bibliography

Primary Sources

Comedies and Tragedies "written by Francis Beaumont and John Fletcher, Gentlemen." London: Humphrey Robinson & Humphrey Moseley, 1647. This is the first collected edition of the "Beaumont and Fletcher" canon of plays, and it had the honor of being edited by one of Fletcher's chief admirers, James Shirley, the Caroline dramatist. Seventeenth-century standards of editing, however, were woefully below those of modern scholarship.

The Works of Beaumont and Fletcher. Ed. Alexander Dyce. 11 vols. London: Edward Moxon, 1843–1846. The chief nineteenth-century edition still is useful.

The Works of Francis Beaumont and John Fletcher. Variorum Edition. Ed. A.H. Bullen, et al. 4 vols. London: G. Bell & Sons, 1904–1912. Useful, though somewhat dated.

The Works of Francis Beaumont and John Fletcher. Ed. Arnold Glover and A.R. Waller. Cambridge English Classics. 10

vols. Cambridge: Cambridge University Press, 1905–1912. An edition that provides relatively easy reading, but the texts of many of the plays may be studied more reliably in later editions.

The Dramatic Works in the Beaumont and Fletcher Canon. Ed. Fredson Bowers, et al. 7 vols. to date. Cambridge: Cambridge University Press, 1966–. This modern edition provides the best texts, but it is unfortunately not complete.

Note: Some excellent modern text editions of individual plays have been published. One such edition is: *The Woman's Prize, or The Tamer Tamed.* Ed. George Ferguson. The Hague and London: Mouton, 1966.

Secondary Sources

Appleton, William. *Beaumont and Fletcher: A Critical Study.* London: Allen and Unwin, 1956. One helpful modern study, though later research has gone beyond some of Appleton's conclusions.

Bentley, Gerald Eades. *The Jacobean and Caroline Stage.* 7 vols. Oxford: Oxford University Press, 1940–1968. Indispensable aid to the stage history of the Fletcher plays.

Bradbrook, M.C. *The Growth and Structure of Elizabethan Comedy.* London: Chatto and Windus, 1955. A good general study of both Elizabethan and Jacobean comedy, with a short, interesting, but mostly negative chapter on Fletcher.

Danby, John. *Elizabethan and Jacobean Poets.* London: Faber & Faber, 1964. Unusual but helpful because Danby relates Fletcher to Elizabethan poetic traditions.

Finkelpearl, Philip J. *Court and Country Politics in the Plays of Beaumont and Fletcher.* Princeton: Princeton University Press, 1990. As the title suggests, in this study the critic examines the political attitudes of the plays closely.

Hensman, Bertha. *The Shares of Fletcher, Field, and Massinger in Twelve Plays of the Beaumont and Fletcher Canon.* 2 vols. Salzburg: Institute for English Language and Literature, 1974. A helpful attribution study.

Hoy, Cyrus. "The Shares of Fletcher and His Collaborators in the Beaumont and Fletcher Canon." *Studies in Bibliography,* 8, 12 (1956–1962) pp. 129–46 (vol. 8), pp. 143–62 (vol. 9), pp. 85–106 (vol. 11), pp. 91–116 (vol. 12). Important work on the collaborations of Fletcher with other playwrights.

Kirsch, Arthur. *Jacobean Dramatic Perspective.* Charlottesville: University Press of Virginia, 1972. A stimulating study of Jacobean drama, with a helpful discussion of Fletcher. Still contemporary in outlook.

Leech, Clifford. *The John Fletcher Plays.* London: Chatto and Windus, 1962. A sensible and well-written assessment of Fletcher's work by a respected English scholar.

Pearse, Nancy Cotton. *John Fletcher's Chastity Plays: Mirrors of Modesty.* Lewisburg, PA: Bucknell University Press, 1973. Pearse examines the romantic and sexual attitudes in the plays and shows Fletcher's differences from Restoration playwrights.

Squier, Charles L. *John Fletcher.* Boston: G.K. Hall, 1986. A fresh and well-balanced recent assessment of Fletcher's career.

Edgar L. Chapman

Foote, Samuel

Born: Truro, Cornwall, England, 1721
Education: Worcester College, Oxford, 1737–1740
Marriage: Mary Hickes, January 10, 1741
Died: Dover, October 21, 1777

Biography

Samuel Foote's parents, Samuel and Eleanor Goodere Foote, were important members of the community of Truro in Cornwall. Samuel senior held many civic offices, including that of mayor. Eleanor was the only daughter of Sir Edward Goodere and inherited from him a considerable fortune. In later years, however, she lost all of her money and frequently called on her son Samuel for financial help. Samuel was the youngest of three surviving children in the family. His eldest brother, Edward, was educated as a clergyman. A second brother, John, probably changed his name to Dinely in order to inherit his uncle's estate. Samuel was baptized on January 27, 1721. Even in grammar school he was notorious for pranks and buffoonery. One of his classmates recollects that Foote dismissed all of the students for a day, without approval from the schoolmaster.

At Worcester College, Oxford, to which he was admitted in 1737, Foote continued to build his reputation as a prankster, but he was very proud of his Oxford education, incomplete though it was. He was asked to leave the college in 1740 because of persistent absences: the college record states that he had "a course of many irregularitys and lying out of the College."[1] After leaving college, Foote seems to have spent some of his time studying law in an unofficial capacity but most of the time he lived the life of a beau and a wit. Predictably, this life exhausted his financial resources, so he married Mary Hickes, on January 10, 1741, to gain her fortune. According to all reports, he neglected his wife and, though she remained loyal to him, he finally deserted her; they had no children.

In 1744, Foote made his acting debut, playing Othello to Charles Macklin's Iago at the Haymarket Theatre. From this time until he sold his interest in the Haymarket Theatre because of his health in 1777, Foote's life and living centered upon the stage. He was an actor, a director, a manager, and a playwright. Little else seems to have mattered very much to him. Foote began writing about the stage and for the stage in 1747. His first publications were two essays: "A Treatise on the Passions, so far as they regard the Stage" and "The Roman and English Comedy Consider'd and Compared." In that same year his first play, *The Diversions of the Morning*, was produced at the Haymarket Theatre. He continued to write—over twenty plays in the next thirty years—and to be constantly engaged in conflict with individuals whom he attacked in those plays. Two of his best-known plays were *The Minor* (1760), which includes an attack on Methodism and especially George Whitefield in the character of Mr. Squintum, and *The Mayor of Garratt* (1763), in which Foote mocks politicians and election practices.

In February 1766, Foote fell from the Duke of York's very spirited horse while at a weekend party at the country house of Lord and Lady Mexborough. As a result of this accident, he had to have his leg amputated. It took him about a year to recover, but, as a kind of recompense for the accident, the Duke of York granted him a Royal patent for the Haymarket Theatre, although only for the summer season. (At this time, all theaters in London had to be patented in order to present plays, and there were only two patented theaters: Drury Lane and Covent Garden. David Garrick and James Lacey, the owners of these theaters, certainly did not want to share their audiences with Foote and the Haymarket or with any other manager.) Foote continued to write and perform; he even wrote plays for himself as a one-legged actor, among them *The Devil Upon Two Sticks* (1768). He also continued to mock the life and living of lawyers, doctors, nabobs from India, and others. In *The Trip to Calais* (1775), he ridiculed the powerful Duchess of Kingston in the character of Lady Kitty Crocodile. The Duchess persuaded the Lord Chamberlain to censor the play, but Foote revised it and changed its title to *The Capuchin* (1776). The Duchess then framed Foote on a charge of homosexual assault. He was acquitted of the charge in December of 1776, but his health, fragile because of his profligate lifestyle, was broken by the tension and fear which the trial created for him. He began having fainting fits and convulsions and so was unable to act. His doctor recommended a winter in the south of France, but Foote died in Dover on October 21, 1777, on his journey to a kinder climate. He is buried in Westminster Abbey.

Literary Analysis

Foote's biographer, Simon Trefman, describes him as "the most notorious wit and prodigal of his day."[2] Several times James Boswell describes Samuel Johnson's varied responses to Foote in his *Life of Johnson*. In one section Johnson mentions that Foote is "not a good mimic." Still, Johnson continues, while Foote is a buffoon, he "has wit too, and is not deficient in ideas, or in fertility and variety of imagery. . . . Then he has a great range for his wit; he never lets truth stand between him and a jest, and he is sometimes mighty coarse."[3] Each critic who writes about Foote emphasizes the inextricable connection between his personality and his writing; more than most writers, he *is* what he wrote. Thus, there is a personal, even quarrelsome tone in some of his writings which mars their effectiveness as drama and can even make some scenes seem petty.

The question about a narrow or personal content as opposed to a broad or comic aspect is central in any analysis of Foote's work. Most modern critics would agree that his humor is primarily in the mode of farce, not of comedy. In the eighteenth century, though, farce was a pejorative term, and Foote would not have considered himself a writer of farce in any way.

F

He defined farce as "a sort of hodge-podge dressed by a Gothic cook, where the mangled limbs of probability, common-sense, and decency are served up to gratify the voracious cravings of the most depraved appetites."[4] In the dedication to *Taste* (1752), Foote writes:

> It may be thought presumptuous of me to have dignified so short a Performance with the Name of a Comedy; but when my Reasons why it cannot be called a Farce are considered, the Critics must indulge me with the Use of that Title; at least till they can furnish me with a better. As the Follies and Absurdities of Men are the sole Objects of Comedy, so the Power of the Imagination (Plot and Incident excepted) are in this Kind of Writing greatly restrained. No unnatural Assemblages, no Creatures of the Fancy, can procure the protection of the Comic Muse; Men and Things must appear as they are. To Farce greater Liberties are permitted. I look upon Farce to hold the same Rank in the Drama, that Burlesque does in other Poetry. It is employed either in debasing lofty Subjects, or in raising humble Ones. (iv–v)

Johnson does not concur, however, with the playwright's assessment of his own works. He agrees that Foote has "a great deal of humour" but denies Boswell's assertion that Foote has a "talent for exhibiting character." Johnson concludes that "It is not a talent; it is a vice; it is what others abstain from. It is not comedy, which exhibits the character of a species, as that of a miser gathered from many misers: it is farce, which exhibits individuals." Johnson continues by saying that Foote will not attack him, because he knows that if he does, Johnson will cut off his other leg.[5] Certainly many of Foote's contemporaries agreed with Johnson that the dramatist attacked the individual, not the species, that he was writing farce, not comedy.

The quality of Foote's plays is uneven. One of his early works, *The Englishman in Paris* (1753), seems to Trefman to be "stodgy, dull, and heavily didactic."[6] Even Foote was probably aware of the problems with this play which mocks the Englishman abroad who refuses to modify his behavior in order to accommodate a more refined set of customs and manners. Trefman thinks that the problems lie in Foote's didacticism in this play which is a departure from his normal pattern of attacking rogues and fools with incisive and sometimes vicious caricature. Conversely, in *The Minor,* Foote had a great success in every sense of that word. The play was very popular in London (thirty-five performances in the first year), and it still reads well today. The work was a rewriting of an unsuccessful production in Dublin and is an attack on religious hypocrisy in general and especially Whitefield, the Methodist preacher. Foote describes his subject as "those itinerant field orators, who, tho' at declared enmity with common sense, have the address [*sic*] to poison the principles, and at the same time pick the pockets of half our industrious fellow subjects."[7] The depth of his attack on religious hypocrisy is especially evident in the character of Mrs. Cole (who was played by Foote). She professes to be a deeply religious woman, yet she is also a bawd and entices young women to prostitution by advertising for servants under seventeen in rural newspapers. As she says to Sir George Wealthy and Loader:

> There had I been tossing in a sea of sin without rudder or compass; and had not the good gentleman [the itinerant preacher] piloted me into the harbour of grace, I must have struck against the rocks of reprobation, and have been quite swallowed up in the whirlpool of despair. He was the precious instrument of my spiritual sprinkling.—But, however, Sir George, if your mind be set upon a young country thing, to-morrow night, I believe, I can furnish you. (*Minor*, 44)

The Minor was a success, but even more so when Foote himself acted in it. His broad comic style was extremely appealing to the London audience.

Another of his very successful plays which attacked the villains and vices of his time was *The Mayor of Garratt*. In it he focuses "on corrupt politics, on the fickleness of the mob, and on the trials of married life."[8] Jerry Sneak is a caricature of the henpecked husband whose wife is affectionate to other men but cold, haughty, and shrewish to her spouse. A conversation between Major Sturgeon and Sneak reveals Sneak's complete subservience to his wife:

> *Major:* And you must not think of disobliging your lady.

Sneak: I never does: I never contradicts her, not I.

Major: That's right: she is a woman of infinite merit.

Sneak: O, a power: And don't you think she is very pretty withal?

Major: A Venus!

Sneak: Yes, werry like Wenus—Mayhap, you have known her some time?

Major: Long.

Sneak: Belike, before she was married?

Major: I did, Master Sneak.

Sneak: Ay, when she was a wirgin. I thought you was an old acquaintance, by your kissing her hand; for we ben't quite so familiar as that— But then, indeed, we han't been married a year.

Major: The mere honey-moon.

Sneak: Ay, ay, I suppose we shall come to it by degrees. (*Mayor,* 20–21)

In addition to the satire of married life, political corruption and the stupidity of the mob are objects of Foote's ridicule. The electorate vacillates from one candidate to another on the slightest provocation—the parallels to contemporary political ads on television are rather striking. Indeed, the tone of this play is gentler than that of most of his satires. It is foolishness and ignorance that are mocked here, not viciousness and manipulation.

The first play which Foote wrote and performed after the amputation of his leg was *The Devil upon Two Sticks.* In this play the devil is called by two lovers to help them elope from Spain to England. They also ask the devil to help them learn a profession. After ridiculing several occupations, the devil suggests that they become actors at the Haymarket Theatre. The plot of the play is primarily a vehicle for the devil, played by Foote, to satirize the bluestockings and other aspects of contemporary English life. The central part of the play ridicules the medical profession, especially in its debate about which universities could train the doctors who would be admitted to the Royal College of Physicians. Each performance concluded with a monologue by Foote on the current happenings; these monologues are no longer extant, but they were very popular with the London audience.

In one of his last plays, *The Cozeners* (1774), Foote attacks Lord Chesterfield's idea of grace as delineated in his posthumously pub-

lished letters. Chesterfield had encouraged a successful libel suit against Foote by George Faulkner in regard to *The Orators* (1762). With the character of Mrs. Aircastle, Foote satirizes the ideas of manners without morals and grace without substance. When Mr. Aircastle questions his son Toby's upbringing, his wife responds:

> Nothing but grace! I wish you would read some late Posthumous Letters; you would then know the true value of grace: Do you know that the only way for a young man to thrive in the world, is to get a large dish of hypocrisy, well garnished with grace, an agreeable person, and a clear patrimonial estate? . . . Toby, be mindful of grace! and do'ye hear? don't laugh! you may grin, indeed, to show your teeth and your manners. (*Cozeners,* 37–38, 39)

The Cozeners, like Foote's other strong plays, reiterates the central concerns of mid-eighteenth century England. It attacks, as do several of the major satires of the period, show without substance, hypocrisy, selfishness, and greed.

Upon hearing of Foote's death, two of the representative figures of the age, Garrick and Johnson, responded in very different ways. Garrick wrote, "Mr. Foote dy'd a few days ago . . . . He had much wit, no feeling, sacrific'd friends & foes to a joke, & so has dy'd very little regretted even by his nearest acquaintance."[9] Johnson, with his characteristic generosity and forgiveness, wrote to Mrs. Thrale about Foote, "He was a fine fellow in his way: and the world is really impoverished by his sinking glories."[10]

Summary

As a British humorist, Samuel Foote does not have the dramatic strengths of Henry Fielding and Garrick. The plots of his plays are often derivative and sometimes loosely developed. Critics also cite his "inability to delineate emotion" and "a heavy reliance upon mimicry of individuals."[11] But, for a period of thirty years Foote's plays and his presence were an integral part of the British theater. The themes and the characters which he drew are clear and fascinating evidence of the quality and tone of eighteenth-century life. Through the twenty comedies that he wrote the modern reader can see the manners, the vices, and the foolishness of Georgian England.

Notes

1. Simon Trefman, *Sam. Foote, Comedian, 1720–1777* (New York: New York University Press, 1971), p. 7.
2. *Ibid.*, p. 1.
3. G.B. Hill and L.F. Powell, eds., *Boswell's Life of Johnson* (Oxford: Clarendon, 1934–1964), III, p. 69.
4. Quoted in Elizabeth N. Chatten, *Samuel Foote* (Boston: G.K. Hall, 1980), p. 29.
5. *Life of Johnson*, II, p. 95.
6. Trefman, p. 61.
7. Paula R. Backscheider and Douglas Howard, eds., *The Plays of Samuel Foote* (New York: Garland, 1983), I, *The Minor*, p. 8.
8. Chatten, p. 79.
9. Quoted in Trefman, p. 263.
10. Quoted in Trefman, p. 264.
11. Chatten, p. 142.

Selected Bibliography

Primary Sources

The Roman and English Comedy Consider'd and Compared. London, 1747.

A Treatise on the Passions, so far as they regard the Stage. London, 1747; New York: Benjamin Blom, 1971.

The Plays of Samuel Foote. Ed. Paula R. Backscheider and Douglas Howard. 3 vols. New York: Garland, 1983.

Bon Mots of Samuel Foote and Theodora Hook. Ed. Walter Jerrold. London: Dent, 1894. A collection of the witty and acerbic comments of Foote.

Secondary Sources

Biographies

Cooke, William. *Memoirs of Samuel Foote.* 3 vols. London: Richard Phillips, 1805. The earliest biography. Written by a friend of Foote, anecdotal and uncritical.

Fitzgerald, Percy H. *Samuel Foote, A Biography.* London: Chatto, 1910. Clear narrative, but regarded as somewhat unreliable.

Books and Articles

Belden, Mary Megie. *The Dramatic Works of Samuel Foote.* Yale Studies in English, no. 80. New Haven, CT: Yale University Press, 1929. A detailed and thorough examination of Foote's works.

Chatten, Elizabeth N. *Samuel Foote.* Boston: G.K. Hall, 1980.

England, Martha. "Apprenticeship at the Haymarket?" In *Blake's Visionary Forms Dramatic.* Ed. David V. Erdman and John E. Grant. Princeton: Princeton University Press, 1970, pp. 3–29. England argues that Blake's *An Island in the Moon* is heavily influenced by the writings of Foote.

Forster, John. "Samuel Foote." In *Historical and Biographical Essays.* 2 vols. London: John Murray, 1858. A positive analysis of Foote's skill as a dramatist.

Hill, G.B., and L.F. Powell, eds. *Boswell's Life of Johnson.* 6 vols. Oxford: Clarendon, 1934–1964. Many generous, as well as some devastating, references to the character of Foote and to the dramatic quality of his plays.

Trefman, Simon. *Sam. Foote, Comedian, 1720–1777.* New York: New York University Press, 1971. The most recent extended treatment of Foote's life and writings. Good analysis of the plays in the context of eighteenth-century life, with special emphasis on the theater.

Wilkinson, John Wells. "The Life and Works of Samuel Foote. Part One." British Museum Cup. 504 b.5. 1936. 5 typescript vols. Copies are also in the Huntington Library and the University of Bristol Library. A carefully documented collection of materials essential to any thorough study of Foote's life and writing.

Martha Rainbolt

Ford, Ford Madox

Born: Merton, Surrey, December 17, 1873
Education: Attended University College School of London in 1889; honorary doctor of letters degree from Olivet College, Michigan, 1937
Marriage: Elsie Martindale, May 17, 1894; separated in 1910; three children (two with Martindale, one with Stella Bowen)
Died: Deauville, France, June 26, 1939

Biography

Ford Hermann Hueffer, who changed his name to Ford Madox Ford in 1919, was born in Merton, Surrey, on December 17, 1873. Both of his parents had connections with the art world: Dr. Francis Hueffer was a music critic for the London *Times* and Catherine Madox Brown was the daughter of the Pre-Raphaelite painter Ford Madox Brown, so it was only natural that Ford took up the study of music at University College School in London in 1889.

In 1891, however, his literary ambitions emerged with the publication of *The Brown Owl*, a children's fairy tale. At this time he also converted to Roman Catholicism, and his religious sentiments can be detected throughout much of his writing.

Successive years saw a string of publications; his first novel, *The Shifting of the Fire*, appeared in 1892, and a collection of poems entitled *The Questions at the Well* came out in 1893 under the pseudonym Fenil Haig.

On May 17, 1894, Ford eloped with Elsie Martindale, a former classmate, and their first daughter, Christina, was born in 1897. Ford's romantic life has been described as a "mess"; after the birth of his second daughter, Katherine, in 1900, Ford suffered a nervous collapse (1904), left his wife, and lived with Violet Hunt from 1908 to 1915. In 1910, he officially separated from his wife and sought a divorce in Germany; she refused to agree to the divorce and the subsequent legal expenses bankrupted Ford. In 1918, Ford met the painter Stella Bowen, a friend of Ezra Pound, and in 1919 Ford and Stella took up farming in Sussex. Their daughter, Esther Julia Ford, was born in 1920, and the three moved to Paris in 1922. However, Ford separated from Stella in 1927, and in 1930 he met the painter Janice Biala, with whom he lived for the rest of his life.

Regardless of this romantic turmoil, Ford maintained an impressive artistic output throughout his life, writing, among other works, thirty novels. His biography of his grandfather, Ford Madox Brown, appeared in 1896, and his meeting in 1898 with English novelist Joseph Conrad began a ten-year collaboration that saw the publication of three novels. In 1906, the first novel of the "Katherine Howard" trilogy, *The Fifth Queen*, came out, and his art criticism on *The Pre-Raphaelite Brotherhood* was published the next year.

From 1908 to 1910, Ford edited the famous *English Review*, which he founded; he later became editor of the *Transatlantic Review* (1923–1924). Through his work on these two journals he published pieces by writers such as H.G. Wells, D.H. Lawrence, John Galsworthy, Henry James, James Joyce, Wyndham Lewis, Pound, and William Carlos Williams, among a host of others.

Despite the heavy schedule and time constraints imposed by publishing literary magazines, Ford continued to write novels, and *The Good Soldier*, published in 1915, established him as a major talent. His experiences in World War I as a second lieutenant in the Welsh Regiment (he was "shell-shocked" during the Battle of the Somme in 1916) led to his massive and ambitious tetralogy, *Parade's End*. The four novels comprising the work were all written during the 1920s: *Some Do Not* (1924); *No More Parades* (1925); *A Man Could Stand Up* (1926); *The Last Post* (1928).

In the 1930s, Ford continued to publish novels and his *Collected Poems* appeared in 1936. In 1937, he was appointed lecturer in comparative literature at Olivet College, Michigan, where he also received an honorary doctor of letters degree.

In the midst of a hectic schedule and frequent travels to the Continent, Ford died in Deauville, France on June 26, 1939.

Literary Analysis

Although Ford's voluminous output consists of such varied works and genres as poems, art criticism, children's stories, and autobiographical sketches, it is primarily on his work as a novelist that his fame and reputation rest. His first novel, *The Shifting of the Fire*, was published when the author was only twenty years old, but his real development as a writer began with his collaboration with Conrad from 1898 to 1908. Together they produced three novels: *The Inheritors* (1901), *Romance* (1903), and *The Nature of the Crime* (1924). Conrad, an established Polish-English writer and author of such famous books as *Lord Jim*, *The Heart of Darkness*, and *Nostromo*, wrote novels about human relationships, the failure of idealism, and the psychology of the human heart, the novels often being set in exotic lands or on the high seas. His ideas about the novel influenced the young Ford and were important for the younger writer's development of the technique of impressionism, which involves attention to detail, imagery, symbolism, and shifts in point of view. Conrad often being used multiple points of view to suggest the complexity of the human experience, and Ford adopted this impressionistic technique in his exploration of human interactions.

Other early influences were James's essay, "The Art of Fiction" (1888) and the French novelist Gustave Flaubert's concept of "le mot juste." James, one of the master American psychological novelists of his time, was also a proponent of impressionism and he was deeply interested in delving into the recesses of the human heart and uncovering our psychic motivations. Flaubert, the famous French realist, is notable for his unflagging devotion to the search for "just the right word." A master stylist, Flaubert's work impressed Ford with the importance of matching the content of a story with its form.

These influences led Ford to reject much of the Pre-Raphaelite and aesthetic tendencies of the late nineteenth century which were primarily concerned with the senses and an exploration of the artificial nature of art. Instead, Ford sought a more realistic portrayal of life, one that would be both representative of life and demonstrate the special vision of the artist. For Ford, the complexity of human relationships was a central concern, and his use of impressionism, with its shifts in narration and perspective, helped him express some of that complexity. Thus, Ford is best seen as a contemporary of the modernists—writers and artists of the first half of the twentieth century who undertook experimental explorations of the inner human self. Additionally, he rejected John Ruskin's view that art had to have a moral purpose; Ford's primary interest lay in defining the parameters of human affairs, not moralizing on them.

These concerns and influences find expression in Ford's second novel, his first mature effort after the association with Conrad. Published in 1905 and subtitled "A Tale of a Small Circle," The Benefactor revolves around the interaction of a few characters and their dealings with George Moffat, the principal figure. The tension in the story comes from the foiled attempt to mesh Moffat's late Victorian honor and idealism with reality. Ford explores the clashes in Moffat's affairs with other people arising from the breakdown of his idealism, and the author thus suggests the complex nature of human interrelationships.

Ford continues this exploration in his "Katherine Howard" trilogy, consisting of The Fifth Queen, Privy Seal (1907), and The Fifth Queen Crowned (1908). The novels derive from a biography of Henry VIII that the author was working on at the time, and, although flawed by a good deal of historical inaccuracy, they demonstrate Ford's continuing interest in the pathways of human relationships and the theme of an idealist brought down by human meanness. In its historic scope and thematic concerns, the trilogy anticipates Ford's later tetralogy, Parade's End, a more ambitious and controlled study of the fall of idealism.

A string of novels followed as Ford continued to sharpen his skills as a novelist: An English Girl (1907), a "romance"; Mr. Apollo (1908), a social satire; The Half Moon (1909), a return to the historical novel and a study of Jacobean England with references to Henry Hudson; and The Portrait (1910), a mild satire on the late seventeenth century.

With A Call, published in 1910, Ford returned to an analysis of human affairs similar to his exploration in The Benefactor. A more controlled novel, the story revolves around a married couple, Dudley Leicester and Pauline Lucas, and Dudley's former lover, Etta Stackpole. A mysterious phone call interrupts Dudley and Etta as they spend the night together, and Ford weaves a complex narrative out of the ensuing romantic entanglements. Although flawed by a lack of full character realization, A Call looks forward to Ford's masterpiece, The Good Soldier, an exploration of a similar affair.

Before that landmark novel, Ford produced a string of other books, a few of which are worth mentioning as they exhibit the development of the novelist and his concerns: The Simple Life Limited (1911), an anti-Utopian novel; Ladies Whose Bright Eyes (1911), an analysis of the chivalric ideal of the fourteenth century; The Panel (1912), a comedy of modern times with a satire on literary tastes; The New Humpty-Dumpty (1912), a weak satire set in the fictional republic of Galizia; Mr. Fleight (1913), a satire on English party politics; and The Young Lovell (1913), a historical romance. Unfortunately, most of these books are now out of print, but it can be deduced from the above summary that their emphasis on satire suggests a comic vision of the world as falling short of an ideal. Indeed, Ford saw much of the clash of human affairs arising from the failure of an individual's idealism to withstand the essential rottenness of other people.

In The Good Soldier, Ford reveals these concerns in what has been called a stylistically perfect novel. His undisputed masterpiece, The Good Soldier ties together Ford's earlier thematic concerns and techniques and gives them their fullest expression. Charles G. Hoffman states that The Good Soldier is "so closely interwoven in theme, character, structure, and technique that it reaches Flaubert's ideal of the perfect fusion of form and subject matter" (47). Ford himself, perhaps recognizing his own achievement, called the book his "great auk's egg," and he intended that it be his last work.

Essentially, the story concerns a British and an American couple and their complex interrelationships. Edward Ashburnham, the moral, upper-class Englishman, complicates matters with his passion for a younger woman. As with other Ford novels, the central focus is on the problems arising from the affairs of the people involved. The genteel, pre-war society, represented by the two couples, is seemingly on a collision course with the passions that play just below the surface of social reality. The plot, almost too difficult to describe, meanders through the murkiness that is the meeting point between surface reality and the underlying desires which complicate that reality.

Ford's unique narrative style highlights the complexity of the interrelationships. The narrator, John Dowell, the husband in the American couple, impressionistically retells the story in four parts, though not chronologically. The narration jumps around between the years 1902 and 1914, and the events are related as they are remembered. Thus, the shift in perspective of the narration itself invokes a sense of the complexity of human psychology and personal affairs.

One aspect of the novel that has drawn much critical attention, especially from critics interested in humor and comedy, is the book's ironic tone, which saturates both the story and the narration. For instance, Dowell's shifting perspective reveals an unsure grasp of the situation, while the reader can deduce much more quickly what has transpired (i.e., who is being unfaithful to whom), thereby producing many ironic moments in the reading of the book. The irony lends itself to a comic uneasiness as readers are tempted to laugh at the short-sightedness of the narrator, but this purely comic enjoyment is tempered by the realization that we are simultaneously being drawn into the tangle of adulterous affairs playing themselves out in the text. Ann Barr Snitow comments that "[t]he collapse of the comic into nightmare, pathos, or grief is an increasing tendency as the novel proceeds" (180); indeed, the novel's initial mixing of potentially comic with potentially tragic elements turns by the conclusion into a meditation on "private desperation" (Snitow, 183)—the comic eclipsed by personal grief and pain.

Critics often ask if Ford's exploration of the two couples is intended to impart any message. Many critics, however, maintain that *The Good Soldier* has no *moral* message. Dowell, perhaps speaking for Ford, anticipates the questions of meaning and intention. At the beginning of the novel he says, "You may well ask why I write. And yet my reasons are quite many. For it is not unusual in human beings who have witnessed the sack of a city or the falling to pieces of a people to desire to set down what they have witnessed for the benefit of unknown heirs or of generations infinitely remote; or, if you please, just to get the sight out of their heads." The text is meant as a representation of the destructiveness which seems to reside at the core of mankind. Idealism fails and human relationships break down, but Ford seems unwilling to moralize on the sins of a particular person (or people); his goal is to trace their demise.

But, is the book simply nihilistic? Some critics think not. The characters in the novel play their parts, letting their jealousies, hatreds, fears, and passions dominate, and each seems trapped in his or her own perspective. It is the refusal to attempt to overcome the limitedness of the *individual* point of view that seems to be the problem. Hoffman says of Dowell, "What is 'appalling' ultimately—the final effect to which the novel has progressed in its last words—is that Dowell, Ashburnham's pale American image, is unable to say anything, even something sentimental, for fear of breaching 'English good form'" (60). Sondra Stang supports this view in her assessment of Dowell: "His periodic claims to nothingness—being nothing, doing nothing, knowing nothing, feeling nothing, thinking nothing, believing nothing—and the pervasive nihilism of his attitudes are his camouflage for his shrinking from conclusions, his fear of experience and his failure to deal with it" (76). The self-entrapment in one's own point of view and the failure to escape the neutrality which that entrapment implies is perhaps what Ford finds to be truly evil. Stang concludes, "If [the novel] left a good deal unresolved, as some of [Ford's] critics have pointed out—where, for example, to place one's sympathy once and for all, or how exactly to interpret matters of tone—it also left the reader with the sense of having had the experiences under scrutiny turned to every kind of light" (92–93).

Ford's next novel, *The Marsden Case* (1923), was published eight years after *The*

Good Soldier and is considered a failure. A pale imitation of *The Good Soldier*, it remains out of print and entirely overshadowed by Ford's ambitious tetralogy, the first volume of which came out the following year. In fact, *Parade's End* remains one of Ford's grandest achievements. Flawed in parts, the novels are a testament to the author's stylistic innovation, and there is nothing quite like them in English literature.

Essentially, *Parade's End* revolves around Christopher Tietjens, described as the last English Tory. As with other Fordian novels, the protagonist's naive idealism comes under frequent attack, and his affairs and relationships with his wife and a host of other characters provides the dramatic tension for the work.

Unlike *The Good Soldier*, however, the concerns of *Parade's End* are not limited to just a handful of characters but are also tied to larger social issues—specifically World War I. The reader is called upon to examine the individual problematics of human relationships and the over-arching social concerns not as two separate spheres but as interrelated areas of conflict. The juxtaposition of the two is ambitious and compelling as *Parade's End* becomes both a personal saga and a social history.

In *Parade's End* Ford continues to explore the meanness and cruelty of the human heart as Tietjens is variously betrayed and misunderstood. Some critics even consider Tietjens to be a modern Christ figure, but if he is, then he is a Christ figure who, as Hoffmann points out, "does not understand his role" (85). Ultimately, *Parade's End* is not specifically about the war but rather it is about the breakdown of society and social norms as the various characters explore and test the limits of their own and others' psychological endurance. As Robie Macauley says in his introduction to *Parade's End*, "Ford saw the war as simply a dramatic heightening of the inevitable process of ruin. . . . The telling thing, Ford thought, was not that the world had changed physically to any great extent, but that the lines of communication had broken down . . . The traditional modes of relationship among people had disappeared and there were no new ones to take the place" (ix).

Such heady subject matter, however, is constantly tempered throughout *Parade's End* by the work's prevalent comic sketches and undertones. In her highly illuminating book on Ford and comedy, *Ford Madox Ford and the Voice of Uncertainty* (1984), Ann Barr Snitow main-

tains that "for all the suffering and despair [that Ford] presents [in *Parade's End*, it] is essentially a comic work" (217). As with *The Good Soldier*, Ford's brilliance lies in his ability to mix both comedy and tragedy, creating a multifaceted if paradoxical panorama of the human condition in all its irony and ambiguity. But unlike *The Good Soldier*, the tetralogy sustains a comic tone throughout, even as tragic events, such as the war, are being described. With this sustained use of comedy, Ford is able to create a sense of life affirmation and hope in the face of seemingly overwhelming social and personal upheaval and destruction.

Snitow comments upon several passages from the work which reveal an essentially comic tension between a potentially tragic morality or situation and a lapse into an affirmative humor. In the following exchanges from *Some Do Not*, the participants of an afternoon tea party become fodder for Ford's comic and satiric appetite:

> "Chaste!" [Mr. Duchemin] shouted. "Chaste, you observe! What a world of suggestion in the word . . . " He surveyed the opulent broadness of his table-cloth; it spread out before his eyes as if it had been a great expanse of meadow in which he could gallop, relaxing his limbs after long captivity. He shouted three obscene words and went on in his Oxford Movement voice: "But chastity . . . "

> Mrs. Wannop suddenly said:

> "Oh!" and looked at her daughter, whose face grew slowly crimson as she continued to peel a peach.

> "When my revered preceptor," Mr. Duchemin thundered on, "drove away in the carriage on his wedding day he said to his bride: 'We will live like the blessed angels!' How sublime! I, too, after my nuptials . . . "

> Mrs. Duchemin suddenly screamed:

> "Oh . . . *no*!"

> As if checked for a moment in their stride all the others paused—for a breath. Then they continued talking with

polite animation and listening with minute attention. To Tietjens that seemed the highest achievement and justification of English manners! (*Some Do Not*, 99–100; commented upon by Snitow, 220–221)

The tensions between the vulgar Mr. Duchemin and the other terribly polite and proper guests creates a comedy of manners reminiscent of Wilde's *Importance of Being Earnest*. Tietjens praises the maintenance and saving graces of "English manners," but the reader gets the impression that these "manners" are only barely holding together a societal fabric being ripped apart by pressures from below; the Edwardian social tapestry of the early twentieth century is steadily unraveling.

Other social pressures, such as World War I, prove a greater strain, but the comic elements do not diminish; instead, the close proximity of tragedy seems to intensify Ford's humorous touch. Note this hysterical sketch of Tietjens's encounter with a German soldier in the trenches:

The Hero arrived. Naturally, he was a Hun. He came over, all legs and arms going, like a catamount; struck the face of the parados, fell into the trench on the dead body, with his hands to his eyes, sprang up again and danced. With heavy deliberation Tietjens drew his great trench-knife rather than his revolver. Why? The butcher instinct? Or trying to think himself with the Exmoor staghounds. The man's shoulders had come heavily on him as he had rebounded from the parados-face. He felt outraged. Watching that performing Hun he held the knife pointed and tried to think of the German for *Hands Up*. He imagined it to be *Hoch die Haende*! He looked for a nice spot in the Hun's side.

His excursion into a foreign tongue proved supererogatory. The German threw his arm abroad, his—considerably mashed!—face to the sky.

Always dramatic, Cousin Fritz! Too dramatic, really.

He fell, crumbling, into his untidy boot. Nasty boots, all crumpled too, up the calves! But he didn't say *Hoch der Kaiser*, or *Deutschland uber alles*, or anything valedictory. (*A Man Could Stand Up*, 559)

With all of the springing up and dancing, the passage is practically literary slapstick. The horror of meeting the enemy face to face becomes an Abbott and Costello romp—an essentially comic encounter between two fumbling fools lost in an overwhelming situation.

Other passages contain recognizable comic elements, but their humor is somewhat strained, as in this description of a dead body in the trenches:

. . . When they removed him a little to make room for Tietjens's immensely larger boots his arms just flopped in the mud, the tin hat that covered the face, to the sky. Like a lay figure, but a little less stiff. Not yet cold. (*A Man Could Stand Up*, 559)

The phrases "immensely larger boots" and "just flopped," along with the references to "lay" people, seem comically out of place in this description, lending the scene a sense of bizarreness. Other war writers, such as the poet Wilfred Owen and the novelist Richard Aldington (*Death of a Hero*), expressed the horror and carnage of the war as essentially tragic and psychically devastating. But Ford's description, like Evelyn Waugh's satire about World War II in his *Sword of Honor* trilogy, points to the potentially humorous in all human activity, even death. Not all will find such comic exaggeration funny or amusing, and it is easy to recognize Ford as a precursor to the tragic absurdity of Samuel Beckett's work (*Waiting for Godot*, *Endgame*). Nevertheless, Ford's use of humor, albeit hyperbolic and often satiric, is important; laughter, even strained laughter, may be the best way to maintain personal control and perspective in a world falling apart—in a world whose parade has come to an end.

Ford continued writing after *Parade's End*, producing such novels as *No Enemy* (1929), *A Little Less than Gods* (1928), and *Vive Le Roy* (1936, his last published novel), but critics generally agree that these works represent a decline in his power as a novelist. The latent disillusionment and cynicism of these works overcome the clever mixing of comedy and tragedy which characterizes his greatest literary achievements, *The Good Soldier* and *Parade's End*.

Summary

Ford Madox Ford, editor, poet, and novelist, occupies a firm place in English letters as a master writer. Prolific in output, his reputation rests mostly on two works, *The Good Soldier* and *Parade's End*, the former book considered an almost perfect expression in the genre of the novel. Influenced by the major novelists of his day (Conrad, James), Ford continued their development of the psychological novel by his adherence to impressionism and his almost unfailing devotion to the exploration of human affairs and relationships. Pessimistic at times but generally refusing to moralize, his often comically and ironically expressed tragicomic vision of life gave him both a unique style and a special artistic viewpoint, ensuring his place in twentieth-century English letters.

Selected Bibliography

Primary Works

Novels

Most of Ford's novels are out of print; among those available are:

The Good Soldier. London: Bodley Head, and New York: Lane, 1915.

The Last Post. New York: Albert and Charles Boni, 1928.

No Enemy. New York: Macaulay, 1929.

Parade's End. New York: Knopf, 1950. Introduced by Robie Macauley.

Poetry

Available editions include:

Collected Poems. London: Goschen, 1913.

On Heaven, and Poems Written on Active Service. London, New York: John Lane, 1918.

Collected Poems. New York: Oxford University Press, 1936.

Selected Poems. Ed. Basil Bunting. Cambridge: Pym-Randall Press, 1971.

Critical Writings and Analyses

Critical Writings. Ed. Frank MacShane. Lincoln: University of Nebraska Press, 1964.

The English Novel, from the Earliest Days to the Death of Joseph Conrad. Philadelphia and London: J.B. Lippincott, 1929.

Henry James, a Critical Study. New York:

A. & C. Boni, 1915.

A History of Our Time. Ed. Solon Beinfeld and Sondra J. Stang. Bloomington: Indiana University Press, 1988.

Letters. Ed. Richard M. Ludwig. Princeton: Princeton University Press, 1965.

Rossetti: A Critical Essay on his Art. London: Duckworth, 1914.

The Ford Madox Ford Reader. Ed. Sondra J. Stang with a foreword by Graham Greene. Manchester: Carcanet, 1986. A useful text providing an omnibus collection of Ford's work.

Secondary Sources

Biographies

Judd, Alan. *Ford Madox Ford*. London: William Collins Sons, 1990. A recent, highly readable biography with some biographical attention to the literary works.

Moser, Thomas C. *The Life in the Fiction of Ford Madox Ford*. Princeton: Princeton University Press, 1980. Mostly a biographical study.

Books

Cassell, Richard A. *Critical Essays on Ford Madox Ford*. Boston: G.K. Hall, 1987. A collection of essays on various aspects of the author's writings.

Green, Robert. *Ford Madox Ford: Prose and Politics*. Cambridge: Cambridge University Press, 1981.

Hoffmann, Charles G. *Ford Madox Ford*. Boston: Twayne, 1990. Rev. ed. One of the best critical texts on Ford, this updated version gives special attention to all of the major and most of the minor novels.

Lid, R.W. *Ford Madox Ford: The Essence of His Art*. Berkeley: University of California Press, 1964.

Snitow, Ann Barr. *Ford Madox Ford and the Voice of Uncertainty*. Baton Rouge: Louisiana State University Press, 1984.

Stang, Sondra J. *Ford Madox Ford*. New York: Ungar, 1977. An excellent study of Ford by one of the experts on the novelist, Stang provides some particularly useful commentary on Ford's autobiographical writings, his critical writings, and the last novels.

Weiss, Timothy. *Fairy Tale and Romance in Works of Ford Madox Ford*. Lanham,

MD: University Press of America, 1984.

Jonathan Alexander

Forster, E[dward] M[organ]

Born: London, January 1, 1879
Education: King's College, Cambridge University, 1897–1901
Died: June 7, 1970

Biography

E.M. Forster, one of the great British novelists of the twentieth century, was born in London on January 1, 1879, to Edward Morgan Llewellyn Forster and Alice Clara Whichelo. His father, an architect, died a year and a half after the son's birth, leaving the family with limited financial resources which made Forster's mother turn to her relatives for support and nurture. One important stabilizing factor for the young boy and his mother was the family residence at Rooksnest, a country home in Hertfordshire that was later to become the model for the house in *Howards End*. There the young boy was the center of attention for several loving and protective female relatives who helped him to have a sheltered and happy boyhood that was lived close to nature.

A totally new experience awaited him when he enrolled at King's College, Cambridge University, in 1897. His years in preparatory and public schools had been unhappy because of the stress on discipline and correctness in ideas and conduct with little attention given to the emotional needs of the boys, but Cambridge was different. There he discovered art, literature, liberal studies, and a congenial atmosphere that encouraged his friendships with other young men who had similar interests. One of his closest friends was H.O. Meredith, who helped to liberate his mind and to realize his homosexual feelings. Although their friendship remained on a platonic level, Meredith became the inspiration for Clive Durham in *Maurice*. Both Meredith and Forster were members of the Apostles, a private university society that met weekly to read papers and discuss ideas. Forster broadened his circle of friends and began to liberate his spirit and develop the humanistic ideas that were to be a distinguished mark of his later writings. The Apostles and some of his professors were instrumental in encouraging him to become a writer, as well, and he began first to write essays for undergraduate magazines and then short stories.

The decade following his graduation in 1901 was the most productive in Forster's literary life. It began with a year's travel with his mother to Italy, Sicily, and Austria, a very significant trip because from it he collected materials which were to form the settings for two of his novels, *A Room With a View* and *Where Angels Fear to Tread*. Once back in London he began to reestablish contact with some of his old Cambridge friends and fellow members of the Apostles. This diverse group of intellectuals and artists included many who later became famous: Lytton Strachey, historian and biographer; John Maynard Keynes, economist; Leonard Woolf, political theorist; Roger Frye and Clive Bell, art critics. The group soon expanded to include non-Apostles such as the Stephen sisters, Vanessa and Virginia—the latter married Leonard Woolf. Since many of them lived in the Bloomsbury section of London close to the British Museum which they used for their writing and research, they later became known as the Bloomsbury Group, with Virginia Woolf as the center. This informal group of friends met frequently and shared their ideas on politics, religion, sex, art, and literature. There was an openness in the group that alternated between high seriousness and lighthearted humor, and Forster caught this spirit and used it in his novels.

In 1905, Forster published his first novel, *Where Angels Fear to Tread*, which appears on the surface to be a domestic romance set in Italy where an English woman marries an Italian with disastrous results, but the book is actually more of an account of a journey toward understanding. His second novel, *The Longest Journey* (1907), is the story of the trials and education of Rickie Eliot, a sensitive young man somewhat similar to Forster, who struggles to discover order and value in a disorderly world. In his third novel, *A Room with a View* (1908), he found his voice as a novelist. He returns to Italy as the setting for a story of a young English lady who feels that her view of life is as cramped as is her view of Florence until a young man gives her his room and opens her eyes to a life of freedom and love. Two years later (in 1910) Forster published *Howards End*, his finest novel to that point. Using as his epigram the words "Only connect," he reveals to the reader two families, the Schlegels and the Wilcoxes, who are very different in their views of life. Margaret Schlegel and her sister Helen are full of passion for art,

F

ideas, reform, for life itself, but Henry Wilcox is a man of prose. He is a businessman—practical, efficient, domineering, and highly successful—though Forster shows that it is possible to,connect the passion with the prose and produce something that is exalted.

Howards End was widely accepted, and Forster was praised as one of the leading novelists of his age, but the writer did not publish another novel for fourteen years. After four novels in the space of five years it is, perhaps, understandable that he needed to step away from his material and view it from a different perspective. India offered him this new experience when he visited it for the first time in 1912 and 1913. During his six months in India, he observed closely the Englishmen serving abroad and how they dealt with their Hindu and Moslem brothers. Once he returned to England he began writing the "Mosque" section of *A Passage to India*, but he had to put this aside during the years of World War I.

Throughout the war years, Forster wrote some essays for newspapers and magazines, which showed that he could have had a successful career as a literary journalist had he desired it, but he preferred to write only about things that interested him. Since he had a private income and his novels had produced royalties, he did not have to do anything that he did not choose to do. He did work with the Red Cross for three years in Alexandria helping to locate missing soldiers, and there he learned more about the difficulties that exist when men from different cultures and races attempt to be friends.

In 1921, he returned to India as the private secretary to the maharajah of an Indian state, and he reestablished his friendships from his earlier visit. He also witnessed the festival of the Birth of Krishna. His experiences as an Englishman living in India caused him to return to his earlier manuscript, and in 1924 he published *A Passage to India*, one of the great novels of the twentieth century. It is the most elaborate statement of his essential theme that human beings have to try to understand and accept one another, despite any social pressure or censure that may result from it. The fact that his main characters do not effect such a passage in the novel does not negate Forster's deep belief that it is possible.

Following the successful completion of five novels, in 1927 the author was elected Fellow at his alma mater, King's College, and he delivered the Clark Lectures that year—these were later published as *Aspects of the Novel* (1927). This classic critical study provides us with many of our definitions of the fundamentals of the novel. He explains the difference in flat and round characters where the latter is "capable of surprising in a convincing way." He clarifies the distinction between a story and a plot with the emphasis resting on causality: "'The king died and the queen died' is a story. 'The king died, and the queen died of grief' is a plot."

Such critical writing, and some short stories, provided Forster's main outlet for the remaining years of life. He was the champion of liberal political and social ideas and defended the writer's need for freedom from censorship. He was one of the witnesses speaking in favor of the publication of D.H. Lawrence's *Lady Chatterley's Lover* at the trial in 1960. His concern for freedom of expression caused him to return to his early manuscript of a young man who discovers that he is a homosexual. The first version of the novel, *Maurice* (1971), was completed in 1914, but he laid it aside only to take it up years later and complete a revision. He felt, however, that the social climate would still not allow the reading public to accept a story of a homosexual who was not exposed and condemned and who did not repent of his perversion. Since he could not accept such a judgment of himself or his protagonist, he chose just the opposite conclusion in which Maurice finds happiness with Alec Scudder, a gamekeeper. The ending, however, caused him to withhold publication during his lifetime.

In the latter part of his career, Forster produced a number of volumes that include biographies, travel books, literary essays, and even the libretto to Benjamin Britten's opera *Billy Budd*. Two of his prose works require special mention. *Abinger Harvest* (1936) is a collection of eighty articles, essays, reviews, poems, etc. which express his views of the English character, his assessments of the literary accomplishments of his contemporaries, and his view of the past. *Two Cheers for Democracy* (1951) is a collection of later essays, articles, and radio broadcasts that reveal his beliefs about the terrors of war and civilization's need for art and culture. His title stems from a friend's joke, which he decided had some merit, as he explained: "One because it admits variety and two because it permits criticism. Two cheers are quite enough; there is no occasion to give three." Included in the section on art is his essay "What I Believe," which is perhaps his best brief expression of his humanistic view of life.

In all of his writings, both fiction and non-fiction, Forster has been an important voice in affecting our culture and our literature, especially in upholding the role of the intellectual as one who has to probe the minds and consciences of his readers. In 1969, he was awarded the Order of Merit by Queen Elizabeth II, and he died on June 7, 1970 while visiting friends in Coventry, England.

Literary Analysis

To understand what Forster thought about the novel, it is best to look at his Clark Lectures. There one can see that he has a great love and respect for the novel, but he also views it with some detachment and humor. Although he sees the writing of novels as serious work, he also believes that it can be fun. He describes the novel as "a formidable marsh occasionally degenerating into a swamp." He explains the importance of plot but then he scoffs at it, calling it "a sort of higher government official" telling the author what to do. Such a light-hearted attitude in such a formal setting as Cambridge University perhaps will assure us that Forster, who is normally thought of as a very serious writer and proponent of liberal humanism, can be fun to read.

His own novels are based on lofty ideas and develop meaningful themes, but his humor plays a central part in each of them. Sometimes he creates comic characters to amuse the reader or to vary the tone. Sometimes he devises humorous situations or employs satire to poke fun at some of the characters who have allowed their estimate of themselves to get out of hand. It is the interplay of the serious and the comic that provides the special charm of his writing and perpetuates his lofty reputation as one of England's finest novelists.

A Room with a View is one of Forster's earliest and least intricate novels. It gives the reader an introduction to some of his favorite themes, and it is an excellent example of his use of humor. The book is a simple story of the heroine, Lucy Honeychurch, meeting in Italy George Emerson, the young man whom she will eventually marry, but not before she has to overcome a number of complications, including a disastrous engagement to a man whom she does not love. Lucy is a typical Forsterian character who is searching for the potential that life has to offer but who is afraid to allow her natural passion to break out. She is finally able, however, to overcome her scruples and to attain the love that she seeks.

Because *A Room with a View* is a domestic romance, it contains some of Forster's best humor. He even creates a character, Miss Lydia Lavish, who is writing a novel about her countrymen visiting Florence, which will include "some humorous characters." She gives warning that she intends "to be unmerciful to the British tourist." Forster's novel is not in the same genre as Mark Twain's *Innocents Abroad*, but it is in the same vein. One snobbish character, the Rev. Mr. Eager, the head of the English colony in Florence, scoffs at such tourists as they go from city to city and pension to pension until they are thoroughly confused. It reminds him, he says, of the American girl in *Punch* who says, "'Say, poppa, what did we see at Rome?' And the father replies: 'Why I guess Rome was the place where we saw the yaller dog.'"

Similar to Miss Lavish, Forster has little mercy for his fictional countrymen. The English tourists abroad have as their first consideration finding a hotel as similar to London as possible. This they find in the Pension Bertolini, complete with a Cockney landlady. The guests include Charlotte Bartlett, Lucy's chaperon, who has a superior attitude not just toward the Italians but her own countrymen as well. She especially finds Mr. Emerson and his son George ill bred because they have the impertinence to speak to them on the first day rather than waiting a day or two to find out if they would "do." Emerson is also so indelicate as to offer her and Lucy their rooms, which have a view. She is totally nonplussed because her natural response is to snub such a person, but it is "impossible to snub any one so gross."

Even Lucy is held up for ridicule, but this ridicule is based on her lack of education and her innocence. She is caught particularly off guard when she finds herself at Santa Croce without her Baedecker and without a guide. She knew that the church was noted for its frescoes and architecture but it was difficult for her to be enthusiastic about monuments when she did not know the authorship or date. She might praise one only to find that John Ruskin had singled out another for its beauty and purity.

Forster is even harsher in his treatment of the other British tourists. Miss Lavish is effusive, untrustworthy, and unthinking. After she offers to serve as Lucy's chaperon, she gets them both lost and abandons her charge to go off in

F

search of "local colour." The Rev. Eager is a snob, the male counterpart of Charlotte, who is anxious to snub anyone who does not live the life of privileged leisure that he does. The Rev. Beebe is more caring than the others, but we later discover that he is basically superficial.

Forster's use of such comic characters is common in comedy of manners novels, although normally these characters are satirized because they do not measure up to society's standards. In *A Room with a View* the characters take society's and others' expectations of them far too seriously.

Forster also uses humor in the development of his characters. Emerson is presented as comic, ill-bred, even childish at the beginning of the novel. He speaks too quickly and too frankly, but we later learn that he speaks from the heart. In response to a lecturer's praise of the faith that built the medieval churches, he remarks, "Built by faith indeed! That simply means the workmen weren't paid properly." Our understanding of him, however, changes as we get to know him better. By the end of the novel we see him as the most important character in the novel who can direct both his son and Lucy toward the happiness they both seek. The Rev. Beebe is the opposite in that originally he appears to be sensitive and wise, but his less attractive qualities are revealed as the plot develops.

Cecil Vyse is another comic character who seems to grow as the novel progresses. Cecil is society's choice, and thus Mrs. Honeychurch's choice, for Lucy to marry. To the world he is the ideal bachelor, yet to the author he is medieval, "like a Gothic statue." He insists on propriety and finds it difficult to relate to other people. His way of getting close to others is to play a joke on them. One of his gestures is finding two strangers whom he thinks stupid in the National Gallery and talking them into renting an empty villa near the Honeychurch's house. To him it is "a great victory for the Comic Muse," but he later finds, to his dismay, that the two are Mr. Emerson and George. In the eventual confrontation when Lucy has to tell Cecil that she cannot marry him, he begins to realize that he is the sort of person who cannot be intimate with anyone. He thanks her for showing him his true character, and the reader feels that there is some hope for him in the future.

In *A Room with a View,* Forster is having fun with the characters. He is amused by them, but the reader knows that he likes them. The structure of the novel rests heavily on improvisation and coincidence, yet because the tone is light and fanciful it is all right—everything works toward the happy ending where George and Lucy are married and celebrating in Florence, where their eyes were first opened.

Forster began work on *Howards End* in 1908, the year that he published *A Room With a View*, and when he finished it two years later, it gave him world-wide recognition. Again he chose the subject of marriage, using it as his vehicle to address one of his central themes, the need for us all to make meaningful connections. He wished to see how a marriage would work between Margaret, a wife who was deeply committed to art and ideas, and her husband, Henry, who was committed to business and finance. In the novel the author also explores the the differences between the two sisters and the differences between the upper and lower classes, as the two sisters try in different ways to help Leonard Bast, a clerk with aspirations to high culture.

Howards End is a serious novel about the merging of several important aspects of English life, but in it Forster uses social comedy in many important ways. Once again he creates comic characters as counterparts to the more serious characters. Aunt Juley Munt, one of his most successful comic characters, always has good intentions, but she bungles everything that she does. Whether she is giving advice on weddings, vacations, or investments, her nieces have to use extreme caution to protect their best interests and to protect Aunt Juley's feelings.

The novel opens with Aunt Juley on a mission of mercy which ends almost disastrously because of a case of mistaken identity. After receiving a telegram from Helen, who is visiting at Howards End, saying that she is engaged to Paul Wilcox, Aunt Juley rushes there to assess the situation. At the station she mistakenly meets the older brother, Charles, and she has a humorous conversation with him which ends with the revelation that she knows that he is to be Helen's husband. This is most shocking to Charles, since he is engaged to another lady and since he knows nothing of Paul's plans. By now Helen and Paul have decided that it was only an infatuation, but the meeting of the Schlegels and the Wilcoxes proved disastrous.

Bast is another important character who gains our sympathy but who is also comical. He is poor, but he is striving to improve himself through self-education and participation in the arts. Forster makes him a much more complex character by presenting him as both a hero and a clown. The Schlegel sisters meet him after a concert because Helen takes his umbrella home by mistake. Although he readily recognizes that they are superior to him in class, nevertheless, he suspects that they are running a confidence game of some kind. Even after he secures his umbrella, he still has doubts about them because they invite him to tea. This certainly casts doubt upon their status because, he reasons, why would "real ladies" have invited someone like him to tea?

Throughout the novel Leonard is a Don Quixote-type character, idealistic, comic, and yet tragic. He reads John Ruskin's *Stones of Venice* rather than heeding his live-in mistress's call to come to bed. He walks all one night in order to get back to the earth, as Richard Feverel did, but he has to confess that it was boring and the dawn very ordinary and not worth the trouble. He goes to Henry Wilcox's daughter's wedding and brings his wife, who happens to be Henry's former mistress, which almost destroys Margaret's engagement. The most pronounced example of mixed heroism and comedy, however, is Leonard's death. He goes to Howards End hoping to find Margaret and to confess that he has wronged the Schlegels, but Charles catches him there. In a parody of the ceremony of knighthood, Charles grabs old Mr. Schlegel's sword and strikes Leonard with the flat of the blade. As Leonard stumbles, a bookcase falls on him, causing his heart to fail. Thus, Leonard is clearly a victim of the very culture that he sought so desperately as a means to a rich and better life.

The most important union in the novel is that of Henry and Margaret, two people who seem vastly different. He is steady, successful, conservative, and proper. He has difficulty in relating to other people and thus he maintains a very proper and passionless attitude at all times. He decides not to kiss Margaret in the car because it is noon and they are passing Buckingham Palace. She, on the other hand, is liberal in her ideas and in her relations with others. She loves to do the unconventional thing and is always very outgoing because of her kindness and love for others. Still, there is nothing weak in her character. She shows her strength most when she confronts Henry about Helen's illegitimate child. She forces him to see the double standard that he is trying to use, excusing his own infidelity while condemning

Helen's. After Leonard's unfortunate death, Margaret brings Helen and Henry together at Howards End, where she can help them both to recover and adjust to their new lives.

While *Howards End* has many humorous elements in it, the theme of the novel is serious. The marriage of Margaret and Henry demonstrates that two different people and two different philosophies of life can come together. In the famous dictum of Matthew Arnold, Henry is one who sees life steadily and Margaret is one who sees life whole. Margaret brings all of the various factions together at the end, and Forster even shows promise of a connection between the classes because Helen and Leonard's son will be the heir to Howards End.

After publishing four novels in six years, the author began what was to be his greatest novel in 1913, right after his first trip to India, but he was not to complete it until 1924, fourteen years after *Howards End*. He had to make another journey to India, where he spent ten months serving as private secretary to a local maharajah and attending the Hindu celebration of Shri Khrisna, which he re-created as the conclusion of the book.

The beginning of *A Passage to India* is similar to those of his other novels which include a domestic romance. Adela Quested goes to India to see if she will marry Ronnie Heaslop, but midway through the narrative the focus shifts from a wedding of an English couple to a metaphysical union of different races, cultures, religions, and approaches to life. As in Walt Whitman's poem, from which Forster takes his title, he wishes "passage to more than India." He wishes to explore the possibilities of bridging the great gaps which separate us from each other and from the universe.

In *Aspects of the Novel* Forster defined two distinct types of novels, fantasy and prophecy. Both of them are concerned with human beings and their problems, but in fantasy a more humorous look at reality is presented. Fantasy has an improvised air about it, and it involves "slips of the memory, all verbal coincidences, Pans and puns." Prophecy, on the other hand, takes as its theme the universe or something universal. Even though it may not "say" anything definite or recommend any particular attitude, it does imply the need for unity. It is like the song of the bard that pushes the reader beyond the barriers and differences that separate. Surprisingly, one quality which he says that prophecy demands is the suspension of the sense of humor. Even though he considers humor as "that estimable adjunct of the educated man," he feels that in the novel of prophecy it must be laid aside.

There appears to be a contradiction here because most critics view Forster as a prophetic novelist and *A Passage to India* as his most perfect work in that genre. Yet, in the novel he certainly does not lay aside his use of humor. In fact, many of its major points are made by using humor.

Deeply imbedded in the novel is a satirical treatment of characters that holds them up to ridicule. One of the most obvious themes is the division between the Anglo-Indian administrators and their native subjects, the rulers and the ruled. Forster's humanistic ideals would not allow him to present the arrogance and inhumanity of the rulers without showing them in their true light. He abhors their sense of superiority and condescension. Mrs. Turton, the wife of the head of the British colony, assures a newcomer that the English, because they are English, are superior to everyone in India. She learns a few words of Urdu, but only to give orders to her servants. Thus, she knows none of the politer forms and only the verbs in the imperative mood. Mrs. Callendar, the wife of the Chief Surgeon, offers additional advice: "Why, the kindest thing one can do to a native is to let him die." The Turtons host a Bridge Party to introduce Adela and Mrs. Moore to the Indian community, though as an attempt to bridge the gulf between East and West, it is a total failure. The Indian guests stay together at one end of the lawn and their hosts stay together on the English side of the lawn while each group talks about the other group in unflattering terms.

A Passage to India is also full of ironic situations which are humorous to the reader but which reflect very unfavorably on the characters. Some of these situations involve minor characters like the subaltern who condemns the depraved Indian accused of attacking Miss Quested and wishes that all Indians were like the one who played polo with him, not knowing that the two are the same man, Dr. Aziz. Police Superintendent McBride is a rational man who appears to be a competent and fair administrator until he begins explaining his theory that the dark races are criminals at heart and, therefore, are prone to succumb to their sexual drives. The irony is that Aziz, the widower, is innocent, but McBride is having an extramarital affair.

Forster ridicules the Anglo-Indian officials because they are so provincial. He once said that the Englishmen's difficulties abroad are due "to an underdeveloped heart, not a cold one!" The officials are unwilling to challenge their own accepted patterns and behaviors and open themselves to new experiences, to new friendships, and to new approaches to life. They refuse to admit that there is mystery and absurdity all around them. Their rationality demands an answer to every question. Everything must have a name (the green bird, the hairy animal), and every event must have a recognizable cause (the confrontation in the Caves). The English may have brought order and progress to India, but they often left as personally impoverished as when they came.

Even though the novel has many satirical portraits of characters who fail to fulfill their human potential, it is not just a sociological indictment of the failures of colonialism. Forster's purpose is much more encompassing. He wishes to explore a metaphysical passage and say something about the universe. To do so he divides the novel into three symbolic sections and uses one character to represent each. The first section, "Mosque," features Dr. Aziz, a Muslim who is dominated by his emotions. "Caves" is dominated by the English couple, Cyril Fielding and Adela Quested, who stand in the Christian tradition and who approach life through the intellect. "Temple" is dominated by Professor Godbole, the Brahman Hindu whose approach to life is spiritual. According to Glen Allen, each section also represents a different attitude toward life as Islam practices the Way of Works; Christianity, the way of Knowledge; and Hinduism, the Way of Love. Each, separate from the others, is inadequate.

Forster uses humor as one way to show the inadequacy of each of the main characters and, thus, the inadequacy of their attitudes toward life. Aziz has many endearing qualities. He is full of vitality; he is spontaneous, direct, concerned for the immediate, whether it is food or success at the Caves. Because he allows his emotions to dominate him, he often is irrational and inconsistent. He resents being snubbed by the English, but he snubs Dr. Lal, the Hindu, and ridicules Professor Godbole. He is concerned about others, but at the same time he is self-centered. He claims that "all men are my brothers," but because of a rumor that he does not bother to validate, he turns his back on Fielding, who tries desperately to be his brother.

He may be innocent of the charges that the English bring against him, but he is guilty of many weaknesses as a human being.

Fielding is treated much more sympathetically than the other Anglo-Indians. He appears to be the kind of liberal humanist that Forster himself was while he lived abroad. Fielding believed that the world is "a globe of men who are trying to reach one another and can best do so by hope of good will plus culture and intelligence." Yet, he finds that his sympathetic kindness is not enough. Had he not waited for Godbole to finish his prayers the episode at the Marabar Caves probably would not have happened. Nor is his culture and intelligence sufficient to aid Aziz in his defense or to prevent Aziz from believing that Fielding had betrayed him by marrying Adela.

Professor Godbole's spiritualism is presented as a flawed approach partly through the humorous portrayal of him and the Hindu ceremony. There is something ludicrous about him whether he is taking tea and "encountered food by accident" or interrupting Fielding on the day of Aziz's arrest to secure suggestions for the name of a nonexistent school that he hopes to found. Even in the final chapter during the Birth of Khrisna festival, he dances, twisting his head as if it didn't belong to his body, clanging cymbals and shouting. He, along with the whole ceremony, is "a muddle . . . a frustration of reason and form." The sacred ceremony itself consists of practical jokes—stealing lumps of butter from another worshipper's forehead, drawing chairs out from under others, or stealing articles of clothing—because man's humor has to coincide with the divine sense of humor. The Hindu ceremony emphasizes the belief that "there is fun in heaven," but it does not, of itself, bring about unity. The Muslims and the Christians are excluded and have to watch it from a distance.

The final resolution in the novel is made symbolically through the person of Mrs. Moore and through the accident that causes all of the major characters to fall into the sacred tank of Mau. Mrs. Moore, although English and Christian, shares the emotional spontaneity of Aziz and the spiritual sensitivity of Godbole. She dies midway through the novel and becomes a sort of Hindu demigoddess, Esmiss Esmoor, who lives in the minds of Aziz and Godbole. While she was alive, she believed that "God is love," and at the Hindu ceremony one inscription reads, "God si love," a slip of the draughts-man's hand, but a statement that love is possible, even if it is not perfect love here on earth. Her two children offer promise for the future because they can bring together all three disparate attitudes toward life. Aziz, when he meets Ralph and recognizes the same kindness and sensitivity in him that he saw in Mrs. Moore, pronounces him to be "an Oriental." Stella, like her brother, is interested in the spirit of Hinduism but not in its forms.

The boating accident that comes during the Birth ceremony is another symbolic way that Forster shows the possibility of unity. Aziz, the child of emotion and Islam, is in one boat with Ralph; Fielding, the child of Christianity and the intellect, is with Stella in another. Godbole is standing in the waves attempting to float the God of Love away upon the sacred water as "an emblem of passage; a passage not easy, not now, not here." It is then that the boats collide and all of the separateness is dissolved as the characters fall into each others' arms. The journey toward the unity of man is achieved in the spirit of love.

After *A Passage to India* Forster did not publish any other novels. He did, however, continue to write, but the stories were on homosexual themes and were published, along with *Maurice*, only after his death. *Maurice* was written as early as 1914, but Forster revised it extensively in 1959–1960. The novel is the story of Maurice Hall's inward struggles to accept who he is, knowing that he is normal in all ways except in his sexual preference. Once he becomes aware of his true nature, he tries to change in order to conform to the values of his society. He discovers, however, that it is not a passing phase with him, as it was for Clive Durham, his initial lover at Cambridge. His eventual acceptance of his homosexuality and his choice of a lover from the lower class, Alec Scudder, a gamekeeper, mark him an outcast from his family, his profession, and his friends.

As sensitive as the subject was for Forster, he was still able to employ his sense of humor. Most of the treatment of Clive is very serious, but there is also an element of satire, especially in the way that Clive glorifies homosexuality in literature but hedges at the borders of lasting commitment in real life. He realizes his true sexual nature after reading Plato's *Symposium* and adopts homosexuality in an idealized way for a brief time, but then he puts away these boyish notions, marries, and settles down to run the family estate.

There is also some ironic humor in one attempt that Maurice makes to develop his heterosexuality. Feeling that he only needed to find the right girl, he escorted Miss Tonks to a concert which featured Peter Tchaikovsky's *Symphonic Pathétique.* He was more moved by the music than he was by the young lady, and he began to understand his own situation when he discovered that Tchaikovsky had fallen in love with a nephew and had written and dedicated his masterpiece to him. Instead of moving Maurice toward heterosexuality, the evening only confirmed him even more in his homosexuality.

Forster uses satiric humor in his treatment of the liberal, intellectual, and scientific communities as they are represented in Dr. Barry. When Maurice is in total despair with no one to whom he can talk, he decides to see a doctor in the hope of being cured. His first overture is to a young friend who is a doctor who tells Maurice "the unspeakables of the Oscar Wilde sort" are only dealt with "in the asylum work." Maurice then decides to consult an old family friend, now in retirement. Dr. Barry is very liberal in most areas of his life but he is very conservative in sexual matters and is very slow in reading Maurice's symptoms. His first guess is that Maurice has venereal disease, and when Maurice breaks down and begins to cry, he guesses impotence. After Maurice tells him his true problem, Dr. Barry's reply is "Rubbish . . . evil hallucination, that temptation from the devil." Forster is expressing the frustration of an age when most either would avoid the subject completely or, if forced to confront it, would condemn it.

Maurice is not one of Forster's best novels, but it is important because of the subject matter and his honest attempt to confront a personal problem that he felt was "unspeakable." This confusion and uncertainty continued to affect his writing in the years following *A Passage to India.* We know from his diaries and from the large corpus of unpublished works that he continued to write fiction, but he could not get inspired to write about the subject that he felt he was permitted to write about—the love of men for women and women for men. Most of his creativity, therefore, was poured into stories that he believed were not respectable and which were dangerous to his career as a novelist. When he showed these stories to his closest friends, they mostly disapproved and, thus, he published no fiction at all.

Summary

In virtually every study of twentieth-century British fiction, one will find E.M. Forster. The lists will vary, with some names added or some dropped, but Forster is nearly always there, along with Conrad, Joyce, Lawrence, and Woolf. His inclusion in such select company is due to his novels, but one should not overlook his later prose writings. His essays on society, politics, and travel reveal a wise, articulate, perceptive observer of mankind. His literary criticism likewise helps to increase the reader's sensitivity and to explore the fraudulent and the pretentious as it champions his humanistic view of life.

The novels, however, are the reason for his lofty reputation. They range from broad social comedy to metaphysical speculation in the vein of prophecy. His major characters are caught in a battle between happiness and unhappiness and between meaning and nonmeaning, and they have to choose on the basis of their values. Important as the issues are, Forster uses humor to show that life, although serious, is not a vale of tears. The issues often involve life and death but the characters, despite their flaws and weaknesses, are capable of making life-fulfilling decisions. His novels are memorable not only because of the weighty themes but also because they are enjoyable. Forster never lost his sense of humor.

Selected Bibliography
Primary Sources

Collections
The Abinger Edition of E.M. Forster. Ed. Oliver Stallybrass and Elizabeth Heine. 14 vols. London: Edward Arnold, 1972–1984; New York: Holmes and Meier, 1972–1984.

Novels
Where Angels Fear to Tread. London: William Blackwood, 1905; New York: Knopf, 1920.
The Longest Journey. London: William Blackwood, 1907; New York: Knopf, 1922.
A Room with a View. London: Edward Arnold, 1908; New York: Putnam's, 1911.
Howards End. London: Edward Arnold, and New York: Putnam's, 1910.
A Passage to India. London: Edward Arnold,

and New York: Harcourt Brace, 1924.

Maurice. London: Edward Arnold, and New York: Norton, 1971.

Arctic Summer and Other Fiction. London: Edward Arnold, 1980; New York: Holmes and Meier, 1981.

Short Stories

The Celestial Omnibus and Other Stories. London: Sidgwick and Jackson, 1911; New York: Knopf, 1923.

The Eternal Moment and Other Stories. London: Sidgwick and Jackson, and New York: Harcourt Brace, 1928.

The Collected Tales of E.M. Forster. New York: Knopf, 1947; republished as *Collected Short Stories of E.M. Forster*. London: Sidgwick and Jackson, 1948.

The Life to Come and Other Stories. London: Edward Arnold, and New York: Norton, 1972.

Other Prose Works

Alexandria: A History and Guide. Alexandria: Whitehead Morris, 1922; Garden City, NY: Doubleday, 1961.

Pharos and Pharillon. Richmond, England: Leonard and Virginia Woolf, and New York: Knopf, 1923.

Aspects of the Novel. London: Edward Arnold, and New York: Harcourt Brace, 1927.

Goldsworthy Lowes Dickinson. London: Edward Arnold, and New York: Harcourt Brace, 1934.

Abinger Harvest. London: Edward Arnold, and New York: Harcourt Brace, 1936.

England's Pleasant Land, a Pageant Play. London: Hogarth Press, 1940.

Nordic Twilight. London: Macmillan, 1940.

Billy Budd: An Opera in Four Acts. Libretto by E.M. Forster and Eric Crozier. London and New York: Boosey and Hawkes, 1951.

Two Cheers for Democracy. London: Edward Arnold, and New York: Harcourt Brace Jovanovich, 1951.

The Hill of Devi. London: Edward Arnold, and New York: Harcourt Brace Jovanovich, 1953.

Marianne Thornton (1797–1887): A Domestic Biography. London: Edward Arnold, and Harcourt Brace Jovanovich, 1956.

Commonplace Book: E.M. Forster. London: Scolar Press, and Stanford: Stanford University Press, 1985.

Secondary Sources

Biographies

Furbank, P.N. *E.M. Forster: A Life*. New York: Harcourt Brace Jovanovich, 1978. Authorized biography and an indispensable source for information on Forster's life and career.

Books and Articles

Allen, Glen O. "Structure, Symbol, and Theme in *A Passage to India*." *PMLA*, 70 (1955): 934–54. One of the most insightful articles that helps to explain some of the puzzles that the novel presents.

Beer, John B. *The Achievement of E.M. Forster*. London: Chatto and Windus, 1962. A close reading of the novels, stressing Forster's romantic heritage.

Bell, Quentin. *Bloomsbury*. London: Weidenfeld and Nicholson, 1968. An excellent discussion of Bloomsbury and Forster's role in the group.

Bell, Vereen M. "Comic Seriousness in *A Passage to India*." *South Atlantic Quarterly*, 66 (Autumn 1967): 606–17. A consideration of the importance of social and psychological comedy in exploring the source and effects of human conduct.

Bradbury, Malcolm, ed. *Forster: A Collection of Critical Essays*. Englewood Cliffs, NJ: Prentice Hall, 1966. Fifteen essays on the life, style, technique, and theme of Forster's fiction.

Brower, Reuben A. *The Fields of Light: An Experiment in Critical Reading*. New York: Oxford University Press, 1951. Contains a standard essay on the image patterns in *A Passage to India*, stressing the triumph of disillusion over affirmation.

Brown, E.K. *Rhythm in the Novel*. Toronto: University of Toronto Press, 1950. An application of Forster's concept of rhythm in analyzing his narrative technique.

Colmer, John. *E.M. Forster: The Personal Voice*. London: Routledge & Kegan Paul, 1975. A comprehensive study of Forster's life and writings, including his novels, short stories, and criticism.

Crews, Frederick C. *E.M. Forster: The Perils*

of *Humanism*. Princeton: Princeton University Press, 1962. A critique of Forster that stresses his resistance to the twentieth century, preferring the humanistic values of the past.

Gardner, Philip, ed. *E.M. Forster: The Critical Heritage*. London: Routledge & Kegan Paul, 1973. A collection of contemporary criticism since 1905 of Forster's novels and criticism to help the reader to understand the writer's historical situation and immediate reception.

Johnstone, J.K. *The Bloomsbury Group: A Study of E.M. Forster, Lytton Strachey, Virginia Woolf and Their Circle*. New York: Farrar, Straus, 1978.

Kelvin, Norman. *E.M. Forster*. Carbondale: Southern Illinois University Press, 1967. A sound critical study of the five major novels with an emphasis on Forster's humanism.

Leavis, F.R. "E.M. Forster." *Scrutiny*, 7 (1938): 185–202. Leavis criticizes Forster's violations of realistic fiction.

Lebowitz, Naomi. *Humanism and the Absurd in the Modern Novel*. Evanston: Northwestern University Press, 1971. Contains one chapter on *A Passage to India* as an example of humor in the absurdist novel.

McDowell, Frederick P.W. *E.M. Forster*. Rev. ed. Boston: Twayne, 1982. An excellent introduction to Forster, providing a brief review of his life and perceptive critiques of his major works.

McConkey, James. *The Novels of E.M. Forster*. Ithaca: Cornell University Press, 1957. An interesting study of Forster's use of characters and his technique.

Rutherford, Andrew, ed. *A Passage to India: A Collection of Critical Essays*. Englewood Cliffs, NJ: Prentice-Hall, 1970. Ten essays on Forster's most intricate novel.

Stallybrass, Oliver. *Aspects of E.M. Forster*. London: Edward Arnold, 1969. An interesting and informative collection of essays and recollections.

Stone, Wilfred. *The Cave and the Mountain: A Study of E.M. Forster*. Stanford: Stanford University Press, 1966. A comprehensive review of the life and major novels, written with the assistance of E.M. Forster.

Thomson, George H. *The Fiction of E.M. Forster*. Detroit: Wayne State University Press, 1967. Thomson concentrates on the mythology and symbolism that is central in Forster's major novels.

Trilling, Lionel. *E.M. Forster*. 2nd ed. Norfolk, CT: New Directions, 1965. One of the earliest major studies (1943), which helped to establish Forster's reputation; a critical-biographical introduction.

Wilde, Alan. *Art and Order: A Study of E.M. Forster*. New York: New York University Press, 1964. A study of the importance of aesthetics and order in the fiction of Forster.

———. *Critical Essays on E.M. Forster*. Boston: G.K. Hall, 1985. A collection of seventeen essays offering a variety of approaches to Forster's achievement.

Edwin W. Williams

Frayn, Michael

Born: Mill Hill, North London, September 8, 1933

Education: Emmanuel College, Cambridge University, B.A., 1957

Marriage: Gillian Palmer, February 18, 1960; divorced, 1989; three children

Biography

Michael Frayn was born in a North London suburb, Mill Hill, on September 8, 1933. The son of Violet Alice Lawson and asbestos salesman Thomas Allen Frayn, he grew up in the nearby suburb of Ewell—an area subject to frequent bombings by the Germans during World War II. Frayn's recollections of such bombings, however, are of pure entertainment without any sense of danger. This very early example of the confusion between subjective and objective reality may have been thematically influential on his writing.[1]

Frayn's formal education began at Kingston Grammar School in Surrey. There he began to develop his interest in music, poetry, and Russian culture. Before entering Emmanuel College, Cambridge University in 1954, he served two years in the Royal Artillery and Intelligence Corps (1952–1954) as a Russian interpreter.

Frayn recalls Cambridge as a microcosm of the outer world; indeed, he majored in the "moral sciences," or philosophy, and his Cambridge years provided him with social and aesthetic underpinnings from which he would develop his writing. He became a columnist for the university newspaper and wrote comic sketches for theatrical revues. In spite of a childhood passion to write for the theater, however, Frayn did not go to work in the theater upon graduation in 1957. Instead, he became a newspaper reporter, making his name as a satirical columnist first for the *Guardian* (1959–1962) and then for the *Observer* (1962–1968). He continued to contribute foreign news features to the *Observer* as he traveled to such countries as Cuba, Israel, Japan, and Sweden. On February 18, 1960, Frayn married Gillian Palmer, with whom he had three daughters. The couple separated in 1980 and were divorced in 1989.

During the 1960s and 1970s, Frayn's ongoing interest in fiction led him to explore such new genres as the comic novel, farce, translation, and the screenplay (both fiction and documentary). Of his six novels, the first, *The Tin Men*, won the 1966 Somerset Maugham award. He also won the 1967 Hawthornden Prize for Fiction for *The Russian Interpreter*, as well as a National Press award in 1970. By the mid-1970s, Frayn had turned his attention almost entirely to playwriting and the translation and adaptation to the stage of works by Anton Chekhov.

Frayn received recognition for his play *Alphabetical Order* in 1976 with the Evening Standard Award; this play was soon followed by *Clouds* (1976), *Donkeys' Years* (1976), and *Balmoral* (1978). During the 1980s and first part of the 1990s, Frayn continued to write plays, translations for the stage, screenplays, and novels. Of his plays, *Noises Off* (1982) and *Benefactors* (1984) have been produced as commercial successes on both sides of the Atlantic, and his stage adaptation of Chekhov's *Platonov* (entitled *Wild Honey*) as well as his farcical screenplay for the 1986 film *Clockwise* (starring John Cleese) played to both London and New York audiences. More recently, in the United States, Peter Bogdanovich directed a film adaptation of *Noises Off* (1992) which features both British and American comic actors. Starring Michael Caine and Carol Burnett, the supporting Anglo-American cast also included Denholm Elliot, Christopher Reeve, Julie Hagerty, and John Ritter. Bogdanovich relocated Frayn's typically British farce-within-a-farce to the United States, focusing on a predominantly American troupe of actors led by a British director (Caine). Frayn's *Look Look* (1990) premiered on the London stage to mixed reviews. His latest novelistic ventures have been

A Landing on the Sun (1991) and *Now You Know* (1992).

Literary Analysis

Frayn has been described as a "contemporary Renaissance man,"[2] a humorist whose versatility in writing includes satirical journalism, documentary, the novel, metaphysical musings (*Constructions*, 1974), and philosophical farces for the stage. He is known at home and abroad for his adaptations and translations of Chekhov. Furthermore, a BBC television production of *First and Last* (1989), as well as television and radio projects to revive his television plays such as *Jamie's on a Flying Visit* and *Birthday* (1968), attest to the author's success and flexibility in writing for media beyond the theater.

In addition to the more direct influences of philosophers Bertrand Russell and Ludwig Wittgenstein, Frayn's preoccupation with language and communication in the modern world in part may be attributed to the social landscape of post-war Europe. His penchant for social satire began, perhaps, when he chronicled the adventures of the fictitious undergraduate, John Plod, for the Cambridge University newspaper; it is also possible that Frayn's service as a Russian language interpreter may have led him to the work of Chekhov, who became one of the most crucial influences on his writing.

Frayn's literary career has encompassed three distinct genres, several media, and several phases of writing: journalism, 1959–1968; novels, 1965–1974; and, although he began to write plays in 1968, it only has been since 1975 that he has devoted his attention primarily to the stage, in addition to occasional screenplays and novels.

Several volumes of Frayn's writings for *The Guardian* exist: *The Day of the Dog* (1962); *Never Put Off to Gomorrah* (1964); *On the Outskirts* (1964). *At Bay in Gear Street*, a compilation of articles from the *Observer*, was published in 1967. In the witty writings he satirizes such archetypes of British society as the clergy ("The Bishop of Screwe") or ambitious *parvenu* couples from the suburbs like "Horace and Doris Morris."

In his novels, Frayn develops his interest in social commentary as he stresses the theme of man in modern society. His first novel, *The Tin Men* (1965), for example, features an institute for automation research. Amid clever jokes, Frayn shows how computers represent the

F

mechanization of culture. While commenting on culture, however, Frayn also incorporates his experiences as an interpreter and a student in his autobiographically tinged novels, *The Russian Interpreter* (1966), *Towards the End of the Morning* (1967), *A Very Private Life* (1968), and *Sweet Dreams* (1973). The last two merge fantasy with social critique: the characters of *A Very Private Life* inhabit an Orwellian universe, complete with windowless houses, mood drugs, and a three-dimensional "holovision." In *Sweet Dreams*, a middle-aged man finds himself in Heaven, discovers that he can fly and change his age, and that God is a student whom he had admired at the university. Frayn continues to explore modern society and man's relationship to it in his most recent novels, *The Trick of It* (1989), *A Landing on the Sun* (1991), and *Now You Know* (1992).

While British audiences may know Frayn for his talent as a novelist, screenwriter, and a dramatist with a "philosophical bent,"[3] Americans are most familiar with Frayn as a playwright with a flair for comedy, but also as a translator of Chekhov's plays. Frayn's interest in the development of characters and their interrelationships, in fact, may stem from his early admiration of Chekhov's ability to present people "coolly and objectively from the outside."[4] Frayn claims Chekhov as an influence particularly in the Russian's ability to absent his authorial voice from his work; referring to Chekhov, Frayn says, the "best thing for a writer to be is transparent and just refract the world through him."[5] In his desire to experiment with the presentation of various points of view, Frayn turned from the novel to playwriting where he, too, would strive to absent his own voice from the text.

His earliest produced plays belonged to an evening of playlets about the state of marriage, *The Two of Us* (1970). In spite of the poor reception of these pieces, two characteristics still evident in Frayn's work were present even then: his knack for witty dialogue and a detailed score for physical action, in *Black and Silver* and *Mr. Foot* especially. In both of these two-person plays repetition serves to enhance the humor. The couple on their second honeymoon in *Black and Silver* spend a night attempting to communicate with one another only to be repeatedly interrupted by the cries of their baby. They rush about their hotel room between their bed and the baby bassinet, unable to quiet the baby. In *Mr. Foot*, the protagonist's chronic, un-

controllable tic—his jiggling foot—asserts itself as if it is a self-generating being. The wife goes so far as to admit to an imaginary conversation partner that she is jealous of the intrusive body part: "it's just that I think it's getting a *hold* over him . . . which I don't think it's right for a foot to have over a man." In both of these short plays, the humor not only stems from the characters' thwarted communication but also from their repeated attempts to control that which is out of their control, whether a baby or a twitching foot.

As is typical of many modern comedies, Frayn's plays juxtapose order and disorder. His characters tend to be at odds with the worlds which they inhabit. And, it is often the efforts that they make toward ordering the confusion around them which instigates both poignancy and humor. Such is the case with *Alphabetical Order* (1975), which marked Frayn's first stage success in Britain. The semi-autobiographical play is set in a provincial, antiquated newspaper cuttings office. A young female librarian takes over the office, transforming it from a den of disorder into an efficient, albeit sterile working environment—much to the dismay of the old workers.

Donkeys' Years and *Clouds*, both produced in 1976, represent two further examples of what Frayn terms "the way we impose our ideas on the world around us."[6] The first play features a comic reunion night at a university where old graduates indulge in antics reminiscent of their school days. Although the men have changed over the years, their reunion causes them to replay old roles which they have outgrown, resulting in somewhat grotesque behavior. Their behavior corresponds to their memories of themselves as undergraduates, as well as to how they *think* their former classmates may remember them. *Clouds*, on the other hand, examines the impact of an alien culture (Cuba) on an American and two British journalists. Their contact with the foreign country represents a shift in their perspectives on the world and its values, including their sexual attitudes.

Frayn relies on irony in his last two plays of the decade, the social satires *Balmoral* (1978) and *Make and Break* (1980). The first of these plays juxtaposes capitalist and socialist viewpoints; it takes place in a castle during 1937 in the "Soviet Republic of Great Britain" at a state-run writer's collective. The second play provides a grimmer portrayal of capitalism and industrialism and the emphasis on consumerism. The setting is a German trade fair where the workaholic protagonist, who makes doors and walls, exploits all of those around him.

Within the past decade or so, Frayn has written several additional plays. Two of these, *Noises Off* (1982) and *Benefactors* (1984), were commercial successes in London's West End and on New York's Broadway. *Noises Off* features a provincial touring company of actors who rehearse a sex farce, *Nothing On*, during the first act; Acts II and III feature two matinee performances of the farce. The interaction and confusion of the touring actors' offstage lives with their onstage lives as actors provide humor as the farce-within-the-farce's conventional misunderstandings merge with unexpected misunderstandings. For example, the leading man in the company—as play character and as real actor—suspects his real-life mistress (an actress with the company) of having an affair with another company actor. As he performs in the farce, the leading man's suspicions mount, which ultimately leads to utter chaos as the backstage world spills onto the stage, and the offstage worlds of the actors collide with their roles as characters.

Contrary to the frenetic action of this farce-within-a-farce, the action in *Benefactors* remains subdued and cerebral. This situation comedy deals with man's attempts to perceive and transform the world. The irony of the play suggests that while man seeks to change the world, that world is changing on its own—out of our control. This concept is exemplified by the life of the architect, David, who is forced to design a modern high-rise housing complex—precisely the kind of development that he despises.

Frayn employs an array of humorous techniques in both plays. Nevertheless, it is *Noises Off* that especially marks Frayn's talent for comedy. In addition to the farce-within-a-farce framework, manic entrances, exits, and pratfalls provide humor as do the actors' repeated use and misuse of props in *Nothing On* (a ubiquitous plate of sardines is continually referred to, mislaid, stuck to an actor's hand, and stepped on). There are also the traditional plot complications characteristic of farce which Frayn further compounds by incorporating the complications of the actors' offstage lives into the play's play. Alongside a non-verbal score of such slapstick moments as a half-clad woman stuck in a linen closet, a doorknob that comes off, a backstage axe-wielding jealous lover who brandishes his anger onstage, or the actress who loses her contact lens amid the scene, Frayn's talent for verbal wit and quick repartee is also evident in the script. For example, one actor continually refers to the housekeeper, Mrs. Clackett, as Mrs. Blackett, Crockett, Clockett, but never Clackett. And, in the playbill in the program for *Nothing On/Noises Off*, Frayn provides more humor with his fictitious biographies, such as for the farce's author, a former "unsuccessful gents hosiery wholesaler whose first play, *Socks Before Marriage* ran for nine years in the West End."

The silly fun inspired by the first two acts of *Noises Off* continues in the third act, but the mishaps and plot complications are not resolved in the expected manner of traditional farce. Instead of the climax unraveling toward resolution, the last act of *Noises Off* features the actors in the height of confusion during their performance of the sex farce. The offstage dramas interfere with their performance, which they try to cut short. But even their final curtain gets stuck, making them forcibly seize it to drag it down. Thus ends Frayn's serious farce in which the "everyday" life of a troupe of actors not only becomes theatricalized but also incorporated into their play performances.

In the one-act play *Audience* (first performed in 1987), later expanded by an act into *Look Look* (1990), Frayn switches the comic focus from actors to spectators. The play fuses both physical and mental planes of action as actors enact a theater audience that is supposedly viewing a play, which by act 2 turns out to be a play about themselves as individual audience members. To further complicate the use of differing levels of reality, the play-within-the-play incorporates doubles of the actor-characters, who watch themselves, as the audience too looks on. The self-referential play derives much of its humor from the writer's portrayal of the group of self-conscious spectators. These theater-goers are recognizable comic types: the pretentious theater buff, the doddering old man who sleeps through the first act, the innocent youth who finds romance with the girl seated beside him, the lovers whose secret affair becomes public, and the play's author himself who cannot help but manipulate and orchestrate audience response to his play, evident in such lines as, "Laugh coming up here, by the way." Frayn also provides comic physical business, typical of a theater-going experience: the late-

F

comer who sits in the wrong seat, the loud coughers, sneezers, paper rustlers, and those whose digital watch alarms beep at inopportune times (in this play, the beeping watch belongs to the playwright). Finally, the actors-as-spectators wittily comment on the play they watch. Nonplussed, they look down from the stage at us in the real audience with such remarks as, "I wish they'd stop staring! I hate plays where they peer out at you!" Ultimately, these "spectators" onstage try to make sense of their unsettled lives much as we—whom they see "peering" at them—do as we view or read Frayn's work.

Frayn's comedies are about perception and misperception—the actor's perception about a character, an audience's perception of a performer, or a human being's perception of his or her place in the world. Drawing on the theme of philosophy, Frayn illustrates the dilemma of existence and our personal relation to an objective world:

> The world plainly exists independently of us—and yet it equally plainly exists only through our consciousness of it. We are circumstantial specks . . . amidst the vast structured fabric of the objective universe. And yet that universe . . . has structure only in so far as we give it expression in our perception and language—has objective form only in so far as we conceive it from our single standpoint in space and time.[7]

The dramatist interweaves shifting points of view in his plays to suggest how human beings structure reality based on their singular points of view. The characters, then, make up the reality of existence as they "see" it. As does Chekhov, Frayn crafts his plays using two simultaneous levels of reality: his drama reveals an existent "subtext" beneath the superficial "reality" of action and dialogue. This is often evident as a separate physical score of action—alongside language—particularly noticeable in the author's most recent plays in which he emphasizes his philosophy through theatrical convention.

Frayn belongs to the new group of postwar British farceurs which includes Joe Orton, Tom Stoppard, and particularly Alan Ayckbourn. These dramatists rely on commercially popular conventions of comedy to convey their ideas. Moreover, they strive to exploit a theatricality unique to the stage in redefining the relationship of audience to the stage. This attempt includes the use of non-traditional performance spaces, nonrepresentational settings, and stylistic conventions such as breaking the illusory "fourth wall" as characters directly address the audience.

In *Clouds*, for example, Frayn's setting consists of various stage levels: "an empty blue sky," and occasional masses of cumulus. The required props are a table and six chairs which will be arranged to suggest everything else, including the car in which the travelers tour Cuba. *Benefactors* calls for three entrances on stage, "left, right, and centre," which indicate three separate loci for the play's four characters. The left and right sides of the stage demark two households whose boundaries are only suggested through convention. The alternating retrospective narration with conversational dialogue in the characters' monologues establishes the fact in performance that the action spans fifteen years. And, again, *Noises Off* and *Look Look* feature a play-within-the-play, while in *Look Look*, a stage audience attends the play's play. In *Noises Off*, the stage setting offers a backstage view as well as a setting for the play's farce. And in *Look Look*, an usherette shows spectators to their seats in an onstage auditorium featured behind a reverse proscenium arch. All of these theatrical and self-referential devices emphasize the author's dramatic aims to demonstrate varying points of view about the world while indicating the existence of the potential chaos that underlies language.

Frayn's interest in language and what language masks is evident in his work as a translator from Russian to English. While he has adapted Leo Tolstoy's work to the stage (1979), it is his translations of Chekhov's major plays for which he is known. Besides his most recent *Uncle Vanya* adaptation for the stage (1988) which starred Jonathan Pryce, Frayn has worked on lesser-known Chekhov scripts. These include the adaptation of *Platonov* (entitled *Wild Honey*, starring Ian MacKellan, 1984), along with a staged production of four one-acts based on *The Sneeze* and other short stories (1988).

Frayn's popularity has been long proven in England. Especially because of his most recent works, North American scholars and audiences are becoming more familiar with his work as a playwright and translator. The recent film adaptation of *Noises Off* has reached an even wider American audience. Frayn continues to write for film, television, and the stage. He also believes that it is essential to continue his journalistic reporting so as not to forget what the real world is like.

Summary

A "philosophical farceur" of arts and letters, Michael Frayn is a versatile writer whose work includes humorous articles, novels, plays, and screenplays, as well as translations and stage adaptations of Chekhov's works. While he began his career as a journalist and novelist, he is also known increasingly for his plays and translations.

His admitted affinity with Chekhov suggests Frayn's preoccupation with individual characters and the separate points of view which symbolize the characters' separateness. In addition to a thematic focus on perception and misperception in modern society and on order versus disorder, in his plays Frayn incorporates the farcical and the dramatic in his reliance on comic dialogue and highly physical action.

Notes

1. Benedict Nightingale, "The Entertaining Intellect." *New York Times Magazine* (December 8, 1985): 126.
2. *Ibid.*, p. 124.
3. *Ibid.*, p. 67.
4. Quoted in Nightingale, p. 128.
5. Michael Lawson, "The Mark of Frayn," *Drama*, 169, 3 (1988), p. 8.
6. Quoted in Introduction to *Plays: One* (London: Methuen, 1985), p. xiii.
7. Quoted in Introduction, *Plays: One*, p. xiv.

Selected Bibliography

Primary Sources
Never Put Off to Gomorrah. New York: Random House, 1964.
The Tin Men. London: Collins, 1965.
The Two of Us. London: Collins, 1968.
Balmoral. London: Methuen, 1978.
Benefactors. New York: Samuel French, 1984.
Plays: One, Alphabetical Order, Donkeys' Years, Clouds, Make and Break, Noises Off. London: Methuen, 1985.
The Trick of It. New York: Viking, 1989.
Trans. and adapt. *The Sneeze: Plays and Stories by Anton Chekhov*. New York: Samuel French, 1989.
Jamie's on a Flying Visit and Birthday. London: Methuen, 1990.
Look Look. London: Methuen, 1990.
Audience. New York: Samuel French, 1991.
A Landing on the Sun. New York: Viking, 1991.
Now You Know. New York: Viking, 1992.

Secondary Sources
Cave, Richard Allen. *New British Drama in Performance on the London Stage: 1970–1985*. Gerrard's Cross, Buckinghamshire: Colin Smythe, 1987, pp. 61–64, 103–04. Cave discusses contemporary British drama on stage and provides views on Frayn's brand of farce, and focuses on the dramatic devices used in *Benefactors*.
Hewison, Robert. "A Last Look." *London Times*, 6 (May 1990): E1. In this review of Frayn's play, *Look Look*, Hewison incorporates the playwright's own comments on why his recent (and innovative) drama—which is about a playwright who eavesdrops on his audience's reactions—failed on stage.
Lawson, Mark. "The Mark of Frayn." *Drama*, 169, 3 (1988): 7–9. Based on his interview with Frayn, the author presents the playwright as a translator of Anton Chekhov, drawing parallels between the works and interests of both writers. A good source for understanding Frayn's writing process.
Jack, Ian. "Frayn, Philosopher of the Suburbs." *Sunday Times* (April 13, 1975): 43. Brief biographical account of Frayn with an emphasis on his love for the suburbs.
Nightingale, Benedict. "The Entertaining Intellect." *New York Times Magazine* (December 8, 1985): 67, 125–128, 133. An extensive treatment of Frayn's life and an overview of his work. The author includes Frayn's own words on his life and his work.
Rusinko, Susan. *British Drama 1950 to the Present: A Critical History*. Boston: Twayne, 1989. Overview of British drama and dramatists. Useful in placing Frayn in his theatrical times. Pages 180–184 provide general information of Frayn's work as a playwright.
Turner, John. "Frayn: Desperately Funny." *Plays and Players*, 375 (December 1984): 8–10. This article, written by Frayn's

F

cousin, also a drama critic, focuses on the more intimate details of Frayn's life and work.

Worth, Katherine. "Farce and Michael Frayn." *Modern Drama*, 26, 1 (1983): 47–53. This is a useful in-depth analysis of the 1982 farce, *Noises Off*.

Rebecca Rovit

Friel, Brian

Born: Omagh County, Tyron, Northern Ireland, January 9, 1929

Education: St. Collumb's College, Derry, 1941–1946; St. Patrick's College, Maynooth, 1946–1948; St. Joseph's Teacher Training School, Belfast, 1949–1950

Married: Anne Morrison, December 27, 1955; 5 children

Biography

Brian Friel was born in a Catholic family in Omagh, County Tyrone, in rural Northern Ireland on January 9, 1929. His childhood was dominated by the powerful presence of his mother, Christina MacLoone Friel, and his six aunts. His father, Patrick Friel, was a school principal. Brian married Anne Morrison on December 27, 1955; they have one son and four daughters. In the manner of small towns in Ireland, Friel's family and his wife's family were close friends and they had known each other since they were 16, and they still live close to where they were born.

Friel studied for the priesthood before switching to education and later to writing. He attended St. Collumb's College, Derry (1941–1946), St. Patrick's College, Maynooth (1946–1948), and St. Joseph's Teacher Training School, Belfast (1949–1950). He was a teacher until he became a full-time writer in 1960. He began this second career by writing short stories and became a regular contributor to the *New Yorker*. He has published two collections of short stories, *The Saucer of Larks* (1962) and *The Gold in the Sea* (1966), and a compendium volume called *The Saucer of Larks: Stories of Ireland* (1969). As a result of the publication of one of these short stories, Friel began a correspondence with Tyrone Guthrie. When Guthrie was opening a new theater in America, he suggested that Friel might like to come with him. Thus, in the spring of 1963, Friel became an unpaid observer during the first season of the Guthrie Theatre in Minneapolis and, as a result, changed direction as a writer. Being at Guthrie's side gave Friel an understanding of stagecraft that was to enable him to become one of the most versatile and at the same time most poetic playwrights working today.

Friel served briefly and without distinction in the Irish Senate in 1987. However, his understanding of the workings of the Irish government is explored in his play *The Mundy Scheme* (1970), a brilliant and cutting satire about governmental corruption and treachery. His plays are not usually overtly political, although *The Freedom of the City* (1974) is set in Londonderry during the time of the civil rights marches in 1970. The play is about three demonstrators who take shelter in town hall and are mistaken for terrorists and shot.

Friel is not a very accessible man and does not often appear in public. When a special performance of *Dancing at Lughnasa* (1990) was being given in Glenties, the site of the events described in this autobiographical play, Friel was most reluctant to attend. He claimed to feel like "the ghost at the feast."[1] Nevertheless, he eventually decided to attend and did address the audience before the production.

The author is a cofounder of the Field Day Theatre Company (1980), a company that tours Ireland with productions of original works by Northern Irish writers. He has been a member of the Irish Academy of Letters since 1972 and of Aoesdana (the Irish Academy of Arts) since 1983. He holds honorary D.Litt degrees from the University of Chicago, the National University of Ireland, and Queen's University, Belfast. His play *Translations* (1981) won the Ewart-Biggs Memorial Prize and the British Theatre Association Award; *Making History* (1989) won the New York Drama Critics Award for Best Foreign Play; *Dancing at Lughnasa* (1990) won the Oliver Award in London and in the United States it won a Tony Award, the Outer Critics Award for Best Broadway Play, and the New York Drama Critics Circle Award for Best Play.

Literary Analysis

One of Ireland's most respected contemporary dramatists, Friel is at the forefront of the movement to rediscover the images and myths that define the culture of the northern part of that country. In many ways the writer sees the problem of finding an Irish identity for Northern Ireland as being caused by the usurpation of

Irish culture by the English. This "lost" culture has been displaced, he feels, by a romantic vision of Ireland that is essentially an English construct. It was part of the process of the rediscovery of an authentic culture for Northern Ireland that Friel became a cofounder, along with actor Stephen Rae, of the Field Day Theatre Group.

The aims of the Field Day group are to tour original plays throughout Ireland and to publish materials that deal with all aspects of Irish language and culture and, by so doing, to raise the level of political consciousness wherever they go. When Friel talks about raising a "political consciousness," of course, he is talking about the raising of an Irish consciousness. This process, by its very nature, is inherently political—especially in the murky, sectarian waters of Northern Irish politics. Rather than becoming directly involved in politics, Field Day provides a means of dealing "with issues that affect the *polis* of Ireland, past and present."[2] Friel, Rae, and the cross-denominational board of Field Day bring together northern writers in a celebratory union that seeks to redefine the culture of their country, a culture that has often sought to hide behind English, or American, versions of a mythic "Irishness."

The playwright's central concern in his own writing is to redefine and celebrate a national heritage that is to be seen, primarily, through Irish eyes. However, Friel's definition of a national heritage as expressed in his writing is an unavoidably limited one. D.E.S. Maxwell has pointed out that in a land that is defined by sectarian issues, "the environment of [Friel's] stories is a Catholic one. He is not an artist of the whole community, Protestant and Catholic. It is likely impossible that he could be."[3] Friel is not explicitly anti-English in his writing, though his plays frequently provide a cutting critique of the history of the complex relationship between England and Ireland.

In his play *Translations*, for example, he deals with the outlawing of the Irish language and, by extension, the Irish culture by the English. Set in 1833, the play follows the activities of the British army in its successful attempt to replace the Irish language with English and thereby bring Ireland once and for all under the domination of England. Still, Friel does not always take a consistently anti-English stance. In *Making History* (1989), he considers the historical figure of Hugh O'Neill, a man who is neither hero nor traitor but who struggles with the inevitable dichotomy created by the clash between his Ulster homeland and his English education. O'Neill eventually leads an ill-fated uprising in alliance with Spain against the English. Yet, O'Neill is married to the sister of the famed "Butcher of Bagenal," a British soldier notorious for murdering Irish peasants. O'Neill is also an admirer of the English queen and feels a personal loyalty to her. When faced with his failure, the "hero" O'Neill lapses into drunkenness even as his biographer proceeds to create the myth of an Irish hero.

While Friel is deliberately ambiguous about his feelings toward O'Neill, an ambiguousness that might reflect the dramatist's own search for a reasoned response to the troubles of Northern Ireland, his plays frequently have a dominantly autobiographical emphasis. The use of autobiography as a starting point in his plays can be seen, for instance, in the way that the seven sisters of his upbringing become the five sisters in *Lughnasa*. In fact, the sisters in the play even have the same first names as his real-life aunts. Through his picture of these unmarried sisters whose sparse existence is transformed by the music of their radio into a pagan, ecstatic celebration of the festival of Lughnasa, Friel shows his deep compassion for the people and the land of his native Northern Ireland.

Most of Friel's plays are set in the mythical town of Ballybeg; a composite of the region in which he was born and still lives. Because of his association with a particular landscape, there is a unique sense of place in Friel's work. His plays present a worldview that is deeply committed to the Ireland that Ballybeg represents. This sense of place does not lead to a sameness in the plays; instead, there is a progression in his work in the way in which each new play seems to counter any dogmatic reading that might have been given to his previous work. Interestingly, the town allows him to focus on purely isolated and regional issues yet gives him an opportunity to furnish his plays with a sense of the universality of human concerns. Ballybeg speaks of the "Irishness" of Northern Ireland in the same way that Dylan Thomas's Llareggub speaks of the "Welshness" of South Wales.

While Friel celebrates the land, he does not present a Romantic view of pastoralism. In his play *Communication Cord* (1983), a companion piece to *Translations*, the author writes about a remote Donegal peasant's house that has been converted into a weekend cottage for

F

the wealthy urban elite. In this play the contemporary rape of the Irish countryside and culture is explored for its farcical and comic potential, and the Irish middle classes are shown to be as guilty of destroying Irish culture through sentimentalizing the peasant society as the English were in their linguistic and military tyranny. This image of a dispossessed middle class is further explored in his *Wonderful Tennessee* (1993), in which three couples embark on a journey to the remote island of Oilean Draoichta, off the remote northwest coast of County Donegal. The island comes to represent something spiritual that is missing in the lives of these middle-class couples. However, in this play Friel does not seem to be condemning the middle classes for their destruction of the mythical life of Ireland but rather he writes with understanding of their need for a spiritual harmony with their lost environment.

In *Communication Cord*, Friel depicts the members of a closed community whose relationship to the landscape is challenged by outsiders, but often the characters in his plays are trapped by their environment while the rest of the world is in turmoil. In many ways this image is reminiscent of Anton Chekhov's writing. Friel had adapted Chekhov's *Three Sisters* (1981) as well as Ivan Turgenev's *A Month in the Country* (1992) and *Fathers and Sons*. Friel's most Chekhovian play to date is his *Aristocrats* (1979). In this play a large Catholic family is gathered for the wedding of their youngest daughter. In a deliberate echo of *The Cherry Orchard*, Friel contrasts the decaying Georgian mansion, Ballybeg Hall, with the surrounding abundant farmland. In this setting Friel emphasizes character rather than plot. The large house encompasses a wide range of eccentric characters including a dying patriarch, a dotty Uncle, an American academic, illegitimate children, and drunken wives. The dramatist takes these potentially stereotypical characters and creates a very funny, but moving play.

As in Chekhov's plays, the characters explore the crises of their lives through language. Indeed, language is the central defining characteristic of Friel's work and his language is by turn lyrical and brutal. His dramas provide a commentary on and a criticism of the power of language to ambush and confound his audience. Friel sees language as simultaneously the cause and the solution of his characters' problems (and by extension, of the problem of Irish identity). In *Translations* the characters talk in English, accented English, and Irish-accented English, depending on to whom they are talking. Some characters even talk in Irish, Latin, or Greek. Language literally becomes a point of conflict for both the characters and the audience members—who may not understand what is being said. In addition, Friel attempts to create a different dramatic language for each play. In *Dancing at Lughnasa*, for example, he creates a very physical and ritualistic climax for the play that transcends the spoken language. In *Translations* the lovers find that they do not have a common spoken language with which to communicate; therefore, they create a physical language that is unique to them.

Friel's central themes of dispossession, dreams of departure, and lost illusions are frequently focused on individuals who are alone in the claustrophobic Catholic family and thus on the claustrophobic relationship between England and Ireland, and between Ireland and America. In his plays people are frequently coming and going. The image of emigration and return is at the center of his drama *Philadelphia, Here I Come!* (1964), the play that established him as a leading playwright. On the eve of his emigration to Philadelphia, Gareth O'Donnell reruns his past life; he plans to carry this mental "film" of the old country with him. He is represented on stage by both his public and private self, a device that provides much of the humor of the piece.

The suspicion that the author stands within as well as without the narrative of his plays is a recurrent one. In *Dancing at Lughnasa*, the figure that represents the playwright as a boy is played by an adult who thus is able to comment on both the past and the future. In this way Friel places the audience in a matrix in which he explores the notion that the individual represents his or her society just as he or she also represents the history of the society. At the same time, the character is capable of representing the relationship between the artist and the audience in the very process of creation. Friel concurrently has his characters represent the world of the play and the world of the artist.

The role of the artist in society is perhaps most intimately explored in *Faith Healer* (1979). In this play the life of an itinerant faith healer is explored through a series of four monologues. Friel compares the faith healer to the artist in what Mel Gussow has called "an eloquent metaphorical study of the artist's life and death struggle . . . his most personal statement about art and faith" (56). Friel sees the role of the artist as one of raising up the hopeless to a point of faith. The faith healer does not fully understand the process by which his "talent" sometimes works, but it is clear that Friel is a playwright with a clear and inventive grasp of the language of the theater. The "doubt" expressed by Friel's hero, Frank Hardy, spurs him on to ever more dangerous manifestations of "this gift, this craft, this talent." It is, perhaps, this sense of danger that makes Friel one of the most exciting playwrights to come out of Ireland in recent years.

Summary

Brian Friel is one of the most successful and inventive Irish playwrights working today. His primary concern as a dramatist is to rediscover an Irish identity through an exploration of that country's mythic past. The collective nature of the Field Day group allows Friel to present his work without having to be associated with any one theater or director. He is thus able to spread his focus over the whole of Ireland. He writes about his native Northern Ireland in a way that opens up the universal themes of his work to a wider audience, and his work has been highly successful in both England and America.

His plays are multilayered, from the point of view of character, atmosphere, and ideas. The distinctive texture of his work comes from his ability to use language in a way that seems both real and surreal at the same time. The world that he creates in his plays appears real, but in a nonnaturalistic, highly stylized, and theatrical way, and he is able to find bold theatrical devices that shift the focus away from a stereotypical "Irish" reading of his linguistic virtuosity. Friel uses humor in a distinctively Irish way, through character and language, yet he avoids the anglicized notion of Irish humor typified by George Bernard Shaw and Oscar Wilde by clearly focusing his characters and language on the task of demythologizing the images and myths that have created a false view of Irish culture. By so doing Friel hopes to rediscover a mythic past that is free of post-colonial overtones.

Notes

1. Quoted by Mel Gussow in "From Ballybeg to Broadway," *New York Times Magazine*, September 29, 1991, p. 59.
2. "Field Day in London: Through Irish Eyes," *The Economist*, vol. 309, no. 7579 (December 3, 1988): 104.
3. D.E.S. Maxwell, *Brian Friel* (Cranberry, NJ: Bucknell University Press, 1973), p. 46.
4. Gussow, "From Ballybeg to Broadway," p. 56.

Selected Bibliography
Primary Sources

Short Stories
The Saucer of Larks. New York: Doubleday, 1962.
The Gold in the Sea. New York: Doubleday, 1966.
The Saucer of Larks: Stories of Ireland. New York: Doubleday, 1969.

Plays
The Doubtful Paradise. Produced in Belfast, 1960.
The Enemy Within. Produced in Dublin, 1962. Ontario: Proscenium Press, 1975.
Three Blind Mice. Produced in Dublin, 1963.
Philadelphia, Here I Come! First published in Dublin at Gaiety Theatre, September 28, 1964; produced on Broadway at Helen Hayes Theatre, February 16, 1966. London: Faber & Faber, 1965. New York: Farrar, Straus and Giroux, 1967.
The Loves of Cass McGuire. First produced on Broadway at Helen Hayes Theatre, February 16, 1966. New York: Farrar, Straus and Giroux, 1967.
Lovers. Two one-acts, *Winners* and *Losers;* first produced in Dublin at Gate Theatre, 1967; produced on Broadway at Vivian Beaumont Theatre, June 25, 1968. New York: Farrar, Straus and Giroux, 1968.
Crystal and Fox. First produced in Dublin, 1968; produced in Los Angeles at Mark Taper Forum, February 1969; produced in New York, March 1972. New York: Farrar, Straus and Giroux, 1970.
The Mundy Scheme. First produced in Dublin at Olympia Theatre, June 11, 1969; produced on Broadway at Royale Theatre, December 11, 1969. New York: Farrar, Straus and Giroux, 1970.
The Gentle Island. First produced in Dublin at Olympia Theatre, 1971. London: Davis-Poynter, 1973.
The Freedom of the City. First produced in Dublin at Abbey Theatre, 1972; pro-

duced in Chicago at Goodman Theatre, 1974; produced on Broadway, 1974. New York: S. French, 1974.

Volunteers. First produced in Dublin at Abbey Theatre, 1975. London: Faber & Faber, 1978.

Living Quarters. First produced in Dublin at Abbey Theatre, 1977. London: Faber & Faber, 1978.

Aristocrats. First produced in Dublin, 1979. Essex, CT: Gallery Press, 1980.

Faith Healer. Produced in New York, 1979. London: Faber & Faber, 1980.

Translations. Produced in Derry, 1980. London: Faber & Faber, 1981.

Three Sisters. Trans. of Anton Chekhov play; produced in Derry, 1981. Essex, CT: Gallery Press, 1981.

The Communication Cord. Produced in Derry, 1982. London: Faber & Faber, 1983.

Fathers and Sons. Adaptation of Ivan Turgenev novel; first produced in London, 1987; produced in New Haven, CT, 1988.

Making History. Produced in London, 1988.

Dancing at Lughnasa. Produced in London, 1990. London: Faber & Faber, 1991.

The London Vertigo. After Alys E. Macklin.

A Month in the Country. Adaptation of Ivan Turgenev novel. New York: Dramatists Play Service, 1993.

Wonderful Tennessee. Produced in 1993. London: Faber & Faber, 1993.

Molly Sweeny. Produced in London, 1994.

Selected Plays of Brian Friel. London: Faber & Faber, 1984. Washington, D.C.: Catholic University Press, 1986.

Secondary Sources

Books and Parts of Books

Deane, Seamus. *Celtic Revival: Essays in Modern Irish Literature, 1880–1980.* New York: Faber & Faber, 1985.

Leary, Daniel. "The Romanticism of Brian Friel." In James D. Brophy and Raymond J. Porter, eds., *Contemporary Irish Literature.* Boston: Iona College Press, 1983, pp. 127–41.

Maxwell, D.E.S. *Brian Friel.* Cranbury NJ: Bucknell University Press, 1973.

O'Brian, George. *Brian Friel.* Boston: Twayne, 1990.

Pine, Richard. *Brian Friel and Ireland's*

Drama. London: Routledge, 1990.

Zach, Wolfgang. "Brian Friel's *Translations:* National and Universal Dimensions." In Richard Wall, ed., *Medieval and Modern Ireland.* Gerrards Cross: Smythe, 1988, pp. 74–90.

Articles

Ahrens, Rudiger. "National Myths and Stereotypes in Modern Irish Drama: Sean O'Casey, Brendan Behan, Brian Friel." *Fu Jen Studies*, 21 (1988): 89–110.

Binnie, Eric. "Brecht and Friel: Some Irish Parallels." *Modern Drama*, 31 (September 1988): 365–70.

Deane, Seamus. "Introduction." In *Friel: Selected Plays.* Washington: Catholic University of America Press, 1984, pp. 11–22.

"Field Day in London." *The Economist*, 309, 7579 (December 3, 1988): 104–05.

Gussow, Mel. "From Ballybeg to Broadway." *New York Times Magazine,* September 29, 1991, Sec. 6, p. 30, col. 1.

Hughes, Eamonn. "To Define Your Dissent: The Plays and Polemic of the Field Day Theatre Company." *Theatre Research International*, 15 (1990): 67–77.

Kearney, Richard. "Friel and the Politics of the Language Play." *Massachusetts Review*, 28 (1987): 510–15.

Lojek, Helen. "Brian Friel's Plays and George Steiner's Linguistics: Translating the Irish." *Contemporary Literature*, 35, 1 (Spring 1994): 83–99.

McGrath, F.C. "Language, Myth and History in the Later Plays of Brian Friel." *Contemporary Literature,* 30 (1989): 534–45.

Maxwell, D.E.S. "Northern Ireland's Political Drama." *Modern Drama*, 33 (1990): 1–14.

O'Grady, Thomas B. "Insubstantial Fathers and Consubstantial Sons: A Note on Patrimony and Patricide in Friel and Leonard." *Canadian Journal of Irish Studies*, 15, 1 (1989): 71–79.

Rollins, Ron and Nita. "*The Loves of Cass McGuire*: Friel's Wagnarian Music Drama." *Canadian Journal of Irish Studies*, 16, 1 (1990): 24–32.

Smith, Robert S. "The Hermeneutic Motion in Brian Friel's *Translations.*" *Modern Drama*, 34 (1991): 392–409.

Streifeld, David. "On Being and Irishness."

Washington Post, December 8, 1991, Sec. WBK, p. 16, col. 1.

Throne, Marilyn. "Brian Friel's *Faith Healer*: Portrait of a Shaman." *Journal of Irish Literature*, 16, 3 (1987): 18–24.

White, Harry. "Brian Friel, Thomas Murphy and the Use of Music in Contemporary Irish Drama." *Modern Drama*, 33 (1990): 553–62.

Wiley, Catherine. "Recreating Ballybeg: Two Translations by Brian Friel." *Journal of Dramatic Therory and Criticism*, 1, 2 (1987): 51–61. Friel translates imagined and material events in Ireland's history into present time; Wiley focuses on *Aristocrats* and *Translations*.

Winkler, Elizabeth H. "Eejitin' about: Adolescence in Friel and Keane." *Eire/Ireland*, 16, 3 (1981): 138–44.

Wolf, Matt. "Brian Friel's Ireland: Both Private and Political." *New York Times*, April 30, 1989, Sec. 2, p. 7, col. 1.

Anthony R. Haigh

Fry, Christopher

Born: Bristol, December 18, 1907

Education: Bedford Modern School, 1918–1926

Marriage: Phyllis Marjorie Hart, December 3, 1936; one child

Biography

One of the two most important writers of verse drama in English in the twentieth century (along with T.S. Eliot), Christopher Fry has pursued a number of other careers as well, some of them directly related to the theater (actor, director, translator of plays from the French and adaptor of a play from the Norwegian, writer of screenplays and radio plays and of the lyrics and music for musicals), some indirectly related to the theater (composer, secretary to a songwriter), some of them unrelated to theatrical pursuits (teacher, schoolmaster, cartoonist, lecturer, editor of school's magazine).

He was born Christopher Fry Harris, on December 18, 1907, in Bristol, the second son of Charles John Harris and Emma Marguerite (Daisy) Fry Hammond Harris, whose mother was Emma Louise Lowe Fry Hammond. His father, who was never very successful, had been a builder and a builder's clerk; his parents had tried a brief, highly unsuccessful emigration to Australia (from May 1896 to November 1897),

but returned to England where, in 1902, Christopher's only sibling, Charles Leslie Harris, was born. In 1904, when Charles was eighteen months old, his father's building business failed, and the elder Harris, an active member of St. Luke's Church, New Brompton (Gillingham), studied for the spring, took "an examination in simple theology and Bible knowledge," and received the bishop's license to serve as a lay reader, a poorly paid position in the Church of England serving pastoral functions but under the supervision of an ordained priest. This career Christopher's father pursued for the last six years of his short life, first in Marwood, in Devon (for eighteen months), then in Bristol in the West Country, where Christopher was born.

Fry later described his father as "what was then called a Christian socialist, or something very like it." The Bristol into which Fry was born was marked by poverty, unemployment, and unrest. Poor and harried himself, Charles Harris worked earnestly and diligently among his Bristol parishioners, but fell subject to bouts of drinking, left his family briefly for a "walking tour," and died suddenly of heart failure in May 1911. Christopher was three. "The easy acceptance of life which had carried me through my first three years began to dwindle after my father died," he said, "My father made no will. There was nothing to be willed." Shortly after his father's death, young Christopher awoke in the night to see his father standing at the foot of his bed. It was in this image that he recalled his father, rather than in any living episode of his first three years.

His mother had only the small income from her mother's estate. She moved with her two young sons to Homedale to live with her husband's parents, John and Sarah Ann Skinner Harris. By the end of January 1912, she and her older, unmarried sister, Ada Louise, had pooled their incomes and moved into their own house in Gillingham. Reading to him from the Bible and from John Bunyan's *Pilgrim's Progress*, Ada, severely religious, devoted, and hypochondriacal, was to become, along with his own mother, a significant and powerful influence upon Fry.

By the age of five, Fry had composed a "Pharaoh's March" for the piano. (The biblical Egyptian theme recurs in his plays and is central in his early *The Firstborn* and Caedmon's proof-song in *One Thing More*.) When he was six he played the role of King Alfred in a civic school pageant; still very young, he composed a piano piece, "The Lovers' Quarrel," which he described as being made up wholly of accidentals, "notes of chromatic alteration." Then on March 31, 1913, the household of two women and two boys moved to Bedford, where Fry grew up. He always referred to Bedford as "Bunyan's town."

On September 19, 1913, Fry started school at Froebel Kindergarten in The Crescent, with Mrs. Harris taking in a boarder in order to pay his fees. At this time, the child began to experience a recurring nightmare in which he was escaping from a doomed city about to be destroyed by a mighty explosion, using as his path the keyboard of a piano. When, in 1914, World War I broke out, soldiers were frequently quartered in the Harris household; eventually, the Harrises lost a cousin in the War, another cousin in a prison camp, and a cousin's fiancée, a nurse, drowned when her ship was torpedoed. Through all of these losses, young Christopher continued his studies. Toward the end of 1915 (near his eighth birthday), Fry was given his first press notice. The *Bedfordshire Times* wrote that at the school Christmas party "a little and shapely lad of tender years danced the hornpipe as cleverly as we have ever seen it done."

At Froebel Training College, Christopher (not yet eleven) wrote a school play, a farce, and acted in another, took private elocution lessons, and acted out a scene from Charles Kingsley's *Water Babies* from which their teacher was reading stories to the children. "What stories she read us as we sat at her feet I don't remember (they are not in Kingsley's book), but suddenly words were not only sentences but individuals. She gave each word so exactly its proper weight and meaning, yet so lightly, I felt I could hold the words like coloured stones in my hand."

At twelve, Fry wrote his first poem; at fourteen, his first verse-play, never published or produced. The play foreshadows themes to be found in the mature Fry—the depicting of an aging uncle confronted and disturbed by the sudden presence of his exuberant nephew who kidnaps his uncle and cousin to take them on a two-day search for the Elixir of Youth. The uncle returns, having accepted, as will the Duke of Altair later in *Venus Observed*, the inevitability, even the wisdom, of his own aging.

In 1918, Fry left Froebel Training College, "coming home with an honours certificate in drawing"; two of his uncles had made their careers in Australia as drawers or painters. In September, he sat for his entrance examination for Bedford Modern School. He was admitted and started the next day in the fifth form of the Juniors, pleased to be in the same school as his older brother, Charles Leslie. Fry was to remain a student in Bedford Modern School for eight years after the end of the war. Among his other studies there, he took Greek, as a preparation for a possible calling as an Anglican priest.

Young Fry often ranked at the bottom of his class in formal studies in English, but his literary talents began to be conspicuous in more creative ways. By the time he was seventeen, he had written a play called *Armageddon*. In it a group of men and women flee a ravaged world to find refuge on a rocky island—his recurring *Pilgrim's Progress* City of Destruction nightmare, perhaps with additional overtones from World War I. He also wrote by 1924 his first play eventually to see production, *Youth and the Peregrines*, to be produced ten years later by the Tunbridge Wells Repertory Players when he was directing them. It would be characterized by the local reviewer then as "a modern comedy with a strong vein of fantasy"; Fry himself called it "A fantastic triviality."

Shortly after his leaving Bedford Modern School at the age of eighteen, Christopher changed his name to Fry, explaining much later that "I took the name Fry by deed-poll when I started working in the theatre: largely because at the time I knew the Fry part of the family more intimately than my father's side; and was much helped and encouraged by my mother's cousin John Fry and his wife Nancy (to whom I dedicated *Curtmantle*)." At another point he said, more briefly, that the name change was "a matter of euphony."

After leaving Bedford Modern School, Fry accepted a position as master of Bedford Froebel Kindergarten, an experimental school that made a special point of stressing creativity in its students. He taught there for a year, tutoring the nephew of Lord Ampthill at about the same time. Then he left to accept his first theatrical position, becoming for six months general assistant at Citizens House Theatre, a social center and small repertory company in Bath, doing both acting and office work there.

Fry subsequently turned back to teaching, as schoolmaster at Hazelwood Preparatory School in Limpsfield, Surrey, from 1928 to 1931. He managed to save £10 in his years there and promptly quit his job, his last stint of schoolteaching. In the spring of 1930, he had taken a walking tour of the Cotswolds with Robert Gittings, a poet, verse playwright, and biographer. That same year that Fry wrote the libretto and Michael Tippett the music for *Psalm in C*. In the summer of 1932, Fry and Gittings moved into an abandoned country rectory at Thorn St. Margaret, Somersetshire, under the Quantocks. The two took with them one hundred books, two typewriters, a crate of digestive biscuits, and a large barrel of beer, and set out to write intensely and undisturbed. They finished the beer and the biscuits, but Fry produced only a comedy never staged, *Siege*. Nevertheless, he was later to recall that summer as having for him sharp literary significance, for it "increased in me the hope that one day the words would come." At this time (1931–1932), Fry served as secretary to a novelist and a popular songwriter. During this period, he also worked sporadically as a cabaret entertainer and as an actor's understudy.

In 1932, Fry became the Founding Director of the Tunbridge Wells, Kent, Repertory Players, serving in that capacity until the company failed in 1935. The most important dramatic contribution of this experience (besides the added familiarity it gave him with the practical performance of a variety of plays—by William Shakespeare, George Bernard Shaw, Oscar Wilde, James Barrie, Noel Coward) was the first professional public performance of his play *Youth and the Peregrines*, written when he was seventeen but revised for this occasion and put on as a curtain-raiser to the English premiere of Shaw's "comediettina for two voices in three conversations," *Village Wooing*, in which Fry played the principal role. Fry also produced both plays, used his previously written *Tempest* music as the overture, and wrote the incidental music to go with *Youth and the Peregrines*. Reviews of Fry's work were favorable, though he was praised at greater length as an actor than as a playwright.

In 1934, Fry and Ronald Frankau wrote the lyrics for *She Shall Have Music*, a revue by Andre Charlot, with book by Frank Eyton, and music by Fry and Monte Crick. The revue was produced in London, opening August 3, 1934. In 1935, he wrote for a second revue, *To Sea in a Sieve*, produced in Reading.

During the years 1934 through 1939, Fry also served as a touring lecturer for Dr. Barnardo's Homes for Children, a charitable organization caring for orphaned and abandoned children, and an editor of the school's magazine. In 1936, he wrote a commissioned play, *Open Door*, in aid of the Homes, about the life of Dr. John Barnardo, the British social reformer who had founded them. The play was produced in London, and Fry toured England with it for the next two years.

The *Who's Who* entry on Fry says of those years that his life was "too complicated for tabulation," and these years were indeed complex (and itinerant) ones. On December 3, 1936, he married Phyllis Marjorie Hart, a journalist who became his wife for more than fifty years; the next year their only child, Tam, was born. Fry also directed and toured in *How-Do, Princess?* by Ivor Novello, and in the year of Tam's birth, he acted in plays in touring repertory and in Bath. But, things went badly for the newlyweds financially. The Tunbridge Wells Repertory Players had collapsed without funds in 1935; despite Fry's efforts in the interim, his financial situation became increasingly desperate. By 1937, he had moved his family to the little Sussex village of Colman's Hatch and was writing vaudeville lyrics and touring all of England as a lecturer, doing cartoons, and editing a magazine, but the combined pay for all of these activities was insufficient for the Frys' needs. By 1938, he recalled, "we finally got to the point that we had no money at all." Then, a cousin died and left the Frys a small legacy: "It wasn't very much, but it tided us over till other things turned up."

The things that were turning up increasingly grew from his playwriting. In 1937, Fry had written his first published play, *The Boy with a Cart*, based on the early life of St. Cuthman, the patron saint of Sussex, a miracle play first performed by local amateur groups, notably by village actors at Colman's Hatch in celebration of the anniversary of the village church. The play was important to Fry not only because it evinced an increasingly mature playwright's hand but because it served to introduce him to the Religious Drama Society of Chichester and to the bishop there. It was also the first clear instance of a yoking that Fry would recurringly favor throughout his dramatic career between a play and a specific church, and it shows Fry's special blending of prose and verse, the comic, and the religious. (Its greatest importance, though, may have come eleven years later, when it was staged in London, giving Richard Burton his first leading London part.)

F

Much of Fry's writing during these years was directed toward children. In 1938, he wrote the libretto for *Robert of Sicily: Opera for Children*, with music by Michael Tippett; in 1939, the libretto for *Seven at a Stroke: A Play for Children*, with music again by Tippett. In 1939, he wrote a series of radio plays for the *Children's Hour*. His first notable London success came in 1939, when his *Thursday's Child: A Pageant* (with music by Martin Shaw) was produced in London at Albert Hall, with Queen Mary in attendance; it was printed that year by the London Girls' Friendly Society. In the same year he wrote another pageant play, *The Tower*, on the history of Tewkesbury Abbey. The play impressed T.S. Eliot, almost a generation older than Fry and already writing highly publicized verse dramas. At about this same time, Fry came to the attention of Charles Williams, a poet, novelist, and theological writer, who worked for many years with the Oxford University Press and who expressed high expectations for Fry's future in the playwriting world.

In 1939, at the beginning of World War II, Fry moved his family to Shipton-under-Wychwood, Oxfordshire. He bought a tiny laborer's cottage on the edge of a farm, built a shed on the back of the cottage, and did most of his writing there, from 10:00 p.m. or midnight to dawn, by candlelight or oil lamp. From 1939 until he was called up for the National Service in 1940, he served as Director of the Oxford Repertory Players, becoming friends with Pamela Brown, then just a rising young actress but the one for whom he would ultimately write his most successful play.

Called up in 1940, Fry, as a conscientious objector, was assigned to the Pioneer Corps (the Non-Combattant Corps) and sent to clear away bomb damage in various parts of England and to fight blitz fires on the docks of Liverpool in 1941. His role in the Pioneer Corps became that of an entertainer as well. He tapdanced, devised charades, stage-managed shows, and became a section leader. Before the war had broken out, he had begun his tragedy, *The Firstborn*, about Moses and Pharaoh, perhaps his most pure iambic pentameter play. Although he attempted to complete the tragedy during the War, he found that he could not, though parts of it were performed in Liverpool twice during this period, and Fry wrote short poems printed in *New Road*, *Life and Letters*, and other vanguard publications and in Geoffrey Grigson's *Poetry of the Present*. During this same period, he wrote a still-unprinted long poem, *Fourth Month Elegy*. He remained in the Pioneer Corps for four years, until he was hospitalized and then mustered out in 1944.

In the late summer of 1944, Fry returned to the Oxford Repertory Players to serve for two years as their visiting director. In 1945, he became director of the Arts Theatre Club in London as well; he became staff dramatist in 1947. He achieved particular success at this club in his direction of James Laver's *The Circle of Chalk* and of Richard Brinsley Sheridan's *The School for Scandal*.

It was in mid-1946 that Fry suddenly made his name as a playwright, as distinguished from director or actor, with his one-act play, *A Phoenix Too Frequent*, based on a story that he traced back from Jeremy Taylor to Petronius, with a title that he said he took from Robert Burton quoting Martial. The play made Fry's dramatic reputation; within a year, he turned away from directing, producing, acting, and writing of Tin Pan Alley-like tunes to concentrate upon playwriting. Yet, Derek Stanford recalls that even in the years from 1945 to 1950 the Frys continued to live very simply: "Every Tuesday morning one could see him riding his bicycle into the village laden with the weekly laundry gathered together in a white knotted sheet."

In the mid-1940s, the author also completed his tragedy *The Firstborn*, but his most impressive single dramatic feat was writing, in eight months of 1947–1948, his most popular and best-known play, *The Lady's Not for Burning*. As was usual, Fry had not made up the plot but had found it, he reported, in an old German short story. The play opened in March 1948 in London, directed by Jack Hawkins. Enormously popular from its first performance, it moved in May 1949 to the Globe Theatre for a nine-month run (294 performances), directed by John Gielgud, with an impressive cast: Gielgud as Thomas Mendip, Richard Burton as Richard, Claire Bloom as Alizon Eliot, and Pamela Brown. Gielgud helped make the play; it in turn reestablished his reputation as an actor. Brown commented of her part in it: "I approached this part with joy and with fear because Christopher Fry had written the part of Jennet for me—which adds a terrible personal responsibility to your author. It is also a great relief for me as an actress not to have to go mad or die or kill somebody in act 3, which I seem to have got into the bad habit of doing lately."

The Friends of Canterbury Cathedral commissioned Fry to write another miracle play for performance at the Cathedral Festival, so in June 1948, his *Thor, with Angels* was first performed at the Canterbury Festival, Chapter House, with the dramatist once again linking a play on religious history with a specific church setting for its performance. This play, a tragedy with comic overtones, dealt with the conflict between the Jutish religion with Thor and Woden and their fellows and the defeated Britons imperfectly recalling their earlier Christianity.

In the summer of 1948, Fry had taken a long journey down the Rhine at the invitation of the BBC; in November he broadcast his observations on that trip as a radioplay, *Rhineland Journey*.

In 1948, the dramatist won what was to be the first of a series of public drama prizes, the Shaw Prize Fund Award, with the naming of *The Lady's Not for Burning* as the best play of the year. Despite his sudden fame, he continued to take walking trips through England, Scotland, and Wales, and to do his playwriting in his unelectrified Oxfordshire. At other times he wrote outdoors, on Shipton Barrow or elsewhere. "I think writers should work more out of doors," he commented, "the way landscape painters do." But, he could no longer escape his skyrocketing reputation as a dramatist. In 1949, still another commission came, this one from Sir Laurence Olivier, who commissioned him to write a play specifically for Olivier's lead performance. Fry would give him *Venus Observed*, Fry's own favorite among his plays.

By January 1950, four of Fry's plays were running simultaneously on the London stage: *The Lady's Not for Burning, Venus Observed, The Boy with a Cart,* and *Ring Round the Moon: A Charade with Music* (Fry's translation of Jean Anouilh's *L'Invitation au chateau*, the first of his very successful translations of French plays). Directed by Peter Brook, so popular was this Fry translation that it ran for eighteen months at the Globe Theatre and established Anouilh's reputation in England. Fry had first refused Brook's request that he translate the play, then did it only in an interim when he had written the first act of *Venus Observed* but for a while could not devise what was to happen next. In this same year Fry directed a revival of *A Phoenix Too Frequent* at Brighton and wrote a BBC television play, *The Canary*. Starting on January 18 of that year, *Venus Observed* was first performed in London.

Also in 1950, the playwright soared into prominence in the United States. In April *A Phoenix Too Frequent* had failed in New York, shutting down after only five performances, but on November 8 *The Lady's Not for Burning* scored an impressive American success, opening at the Royale Theatre in New York, directed by Gielgud (who called its direction perhaps the most difficult task of the five plays that he had directed), with Gielgud and Brown in its leads, and running for 151 performances. In March it was televised; a month later it was broadcast over the BBC Home Service. Soon it would be performed in Holland and Denmark as well. On November 23, *Ring Round the Moon* opened at the Martin Beck Theatre in New York and ran for sixty-eight performances. Late in 1950 Catholic University in Washington, D.C. staged *Thor, with Angels*. Evidence of Fry's sudden grip on the American imagination was perhaps best given by the highly favorable and lengthy cover story on him in *Time* magazine for November 20, 1950.

By 1950, the Frys had surrendered to his immense popularity to the extent of adding an indoor bathroom to their Oxfordshire cottage and renting a town house in London in Maida Vale, on Bromfield Road, facing Regent's Park Canal, "Little Venice." Fry affixed to it a warning pun, "Beware of the doge."

Despite his sudden great success as a playwright, Fry had not abandoned his interest in music. In 1951, he composed the music that Leslie Bridgewater scored for him for Brook's production of Shakespeare's *The Winter's Tale*, which opened at the Phoenix Theatre in June and was recorded by Caedmon.

In 1951, Fry also brought out his most important play written specifically to be performed within a church structure, *A Sleep of Prisoners* (commissioned by the Religious Drama Society), in which the lives and dreams of the four prisoners are interwoven with the Old Testament accounts of Cain and Abel, Joab and Absalom, Abraham and Isaac, and Shadrac, Meshac, and Abednego. In the play Fry eschews killing of any type—sacrifice, murder, war—and suggests an answer in any level of forgiving love. In April 1951, the play premiered at the Oxford University Church of St. Mary's as part of the programme for the Festival of Britain; later that same year it was performed in London and in New York.

In 1951, the author was awarded the Foyle Poetry Prize and the New York Drama Critics

Circle Award, winning the latter prize again in 1952 and in 1956. His dramatic reputation was spreading quickly to non-English-speaking European countries as well; by 1952 his plays had been translated into German and performed in Sweden, Holland, and Germany. He was also gaining stature as a literary theorist, making critical statements in *The Listener*, *Adelphi*, and *Adam*. Probably his four most important essays—always moving from dramatic specifics to philosophical inquiry—came out at this time: "An Experience of Critics" (an address to the Critics' Circle at the Arts Theatre, London, April 1952), "How Lost, How Amazed, How Miraculous We Are" (1952), "Why I Write in Verse" (1954), and "Why Verse?" (1955).

Fry's two most important productions of 1953 were screenplays. He added lyrics for the film of *The Beggar's Opera*, with Denis Cannan, and he wrote the film commentary for *The Queen Is Crowned*, a documentary on the coronation of Elizabeth II.

A new Fry play, *The Dark Is Light Enough*, opened in April 1954 in London at the Aldwych Theatre after first being performed in Edinburgh. Dame Edith Evans played Countess Rosmarin. The play moved in February 1955 to New York City.

The most important dramatic events of 1955 for Fry were productions of two more of his translations of contemporary French playwrights. In May, a Brook production of Anouilh's *The Lark* opened at the Lyric Theatre, Hammersmith, London, with Dorothy Tutin as Joan, in a play that Fry described as having a happy ending: "The true end of the story is a kind of joy." In November *The Lark* moved to New York. In a similar pattern, in June 1955, *Tiger at the Gates*, Fry's translation of Jean Giraudoux's *La Guerre de Troie n'aura pas lieu*, opened at the Apollo Theatre in London, with Michael Redgrave playing Hector; this play too moved to New York City.

A third French translation was to follow much the same pattern on March 3, 1958, when the Theatre Royal in Newcastle-upon-Tyne brought out Fry's translation of Giraudoux's *Pour Lucrece*, a study of chastity, fidelity, sexuality, and honor, which Fry titled *Duel of Angels*, and which starred Vivien Leigh as Paola and Bloom as Lucile; in April the production moved to the Apollo Theatre in London, and in April 1960, it opened in New York City.

On March 1, 1961, Fry's historical drama, *Curtmantle*, opened in Tilburg, Holland, pre-

sented by the Ensemble Company. The play was Fry's study of Henry II and his conflict with Thomas à Becket, with his Queen, Eleanor of Aquitaine, with his sons, with France, and with the Church. The state/church conflict between Becket and Henry II had attracted many playwrights, but unlike Eliot or Alfred, Lord Tennyson or Anouilh, Fry put his emphasis on Henry II, not on Becket; the play does not end until Henry's death. A mixture of verse and prose, *Curtmantle* has Henry speaking either, according to mood and occasion, rather than the assignment of speech-types by classes, as Fry had tended to do in his earlier plays. In *Curtmantle* the prose sometimes has the bite that Fry had formerly given to his poetry. When Henry dies, the First Refugee comes over to be sure that he is dead, then proceeds to strip his body, saying, "I wouldn't come close to a great king, but what we have here is a dead man. You've seen fifty like it, or more."

June 20, 1962, saw the first London performance of Fry's third translation of a Giraudoux play, *Judith: A Tragedy in Three Acts*, with Sean Connery as Holofernes, but the play failed in its English translation, as it had failed Giraudoux in its first Paris production in 1931. In September of the same year, *Curtmantle*'s first performance in English was at the Edinburgh Festival; its London premiere followed in October. In 1962, Fry also adapted Par Lagerkvist's novel, *Barabbas*, as a screenplay. He received two major awards in that year: the Queen's Gold Medal for Poetry and the Royal Society of Literature Heinemann Award, the latter specifically for *Curtmantle*.

Fry's chief literary activity in 1964 was the translating of Sidonie Colette's story, *L'Enfant et les Sortileges*, as *The Boy and the Magic*. Her story had in turn been based on Maurice Ravel's opera about a destructive little boy in Normandy, lazy, vandalous, and cruel to animals. When the things that he has vandalized and tormented come alive and turn on him in his house, he flees to his garden, only to face there the accusations of his victims: "Now it's your turn to be beaten, and shot at, and pinned to the wall." The boy redeems himself by a single impulsive act of kindness to an injured squirrel—"it is a wise child that they give back to his mother, as welcome and warm and friendly as the light from the windows." This story has two of the same themes to be found in Fry's stage writings: the emphasis on children and on Quaker-like gentleness as a means of regaining Eden.

The emphasis on children recurred a year later when, in 1965, Fry brought out a children's book, *The Boat That Mooed*, published in New York by Macmillan. The story is about Tom Crunch, a young boy who lives on a boat with his Uncle Jack, who says only "Good morning" and "Good night" to the boy—"It was hard to tell if he were awake or asleep." A heavy fog isolates Tom still further, but in the course of it he encounters a second boat, with an equally lonely child, Ann, who tells him of her father, "He hasn't got time to say much because of all the singing. Oh, and this is my dog Dan." The children, dog, finally even the father, manage to blow the fog away, so that "They felt as warm as toasted muffins. And the sky was as blue as a blue hyacinth." The two boats stay side by side, with the children visiting each other on alternate days, finding "so much to do, and so much to see." The world about them is not a particularly cheerful one, and the adults are little help and less companionship, but the children have learned to sustain and support each other.

In the next year Fry, assisted by Jonathan Griffin, wrote the screenplay for *The Bible: In the Beginning*. In it Fry reworked a number of the most familiar Genesis stories, choosing to retain the language of the King James Version but adding materials, dialogue, and scenes of his own. It was an approach that Fry had used fifteen years earlier in *A Sleep of Prisoners*; one of the dream stories (Cain and Abel) reappears. Fry (who had never gone to college) also received the first of many university academic honors to follow: the D.A. degree from Manchester Polytechnic.

In 1968, there were major revivals of two of his play-translations and his creation-adaptation of a new television play. *Tiger at the Gates* was revived in New York, *Ring Round the Moon* in London. Fry wrote as a television play his adaptation of Anne Brontë's *The Tenant of Wildfell Hall*, the first notable instance of his continuing interest in the Brontës.

In May 1970, at Chichester Festival Theatre, Fry's adaptation of Henrik Ibsen's *Peer Gynt* was performed, based upon the Johan Fillinger translation. In July of the same year the writer's last major stage play, *A Yard of Sun*, was produced by the Nottingham Playhouse; it moved on August 10 to the Old Vic.

The Candida Plays production of *The Lady's Not for Burning* came in 1971, and Fry himself directed and toured with the play. In

1973, the BBC put on Fry's extraordinary four-play series studying that extraordinary literary family, *The Brontës of Haworth*, that concludes with Mr. Brontë, having outlived all of his gifted children, speaking, as though to Mrs. Gaskell, "I do not deny that I am somewhat eccentric. Had I been numbered amongst the calm, sedate, concentric men of the world, I should not have been as I now am, and I should in all probability never have had such children as mine have been." The four plays are a disturbing evocation of the forces that produced the Brontës and of the personalities themselves.

Two years later (May 14, 1975) Fry brought out yet another of his translations of recent French drama into English, in the Festival Theatre, Chichester, production of Edmond Rostand's *Cyrano de Bergerac: A Heroic Comedy in Five Acts*, directed by Jose Ferrer and starring Keith Mitchell as Cyrano. In that same year, Charles E. and Jean G. Wadsworth brought out in Cambridge and Boston the collection *Root and Sky: Poetry from the Plays of Christopher Fry*.

In 1976, Fry wrote another television play for the BBC, *The Best of Enemies*, and in the next year another, *Sister Dora*, based upon the book by Jo Manton. Also in 1977, Chichester Cathedral had a series of three lectures under the general title of *Our Basic Concerns*. Fry gave the second of these lectures in November with the title "Death Is a Kind of Love." The talk, when printed in 1979 by Charles E. Wadsworth, bears an epigraph taken from itself: "Death is a part of life; it is included in the terms of the contract by which we take over the lease of our living." Early in the talk Fry declares that his purpose "is to talk of death in what I suppose we must call a secular way, if anything in this world can really be called secular; of the part it plays in all our lives, of whatever faith or persuasion or unpersuasion we may be."

In 1978, Fry brought out *Can You Find Me: A Family History*, often called his autobiography. But, it is scarcely that, as its subtitle indicates. It stops when the author is eleven and pays much more attention to a number of his relatives than to himself. The title is a half-comic allusion to a postcard that his mother had sent to his Aunt Ada in 1906, almost eighteen months before Fry was born—a photo of a sheep-shearing that said at the bottom, "Can you find me." The statement seemed to Fry an archetypal one, as he explores the experiences and the personalities of those kin to him, long

F

past and present, to try to find out where he fitted into their pattern of life and death, of fulfillment and disappointment, of mirth and tragedy.

In 1978, an opera version of *Paradise Lost* was produced in Chicago, an adaptation by Fry, with music by Penderecki.

If *Can You Find Me* had been in part an act of familial piety, even more so was Fry's 1980 edition and introduction to *Charlie Hammond's Sketch Book*, a collection of the Australian sketches of his mother's brother. In 1981, Fry wrote another BBC television play, *Star Over Bethlehem*. Two years later in London *Tiger at the Gates* was revived, this time under a literal translation of Giraudoux's title, *The Trojan War Will Not Take Place*. In 1985, *The Brontës of Haworth* was performed for the first time onstage; in 1986, at the age of seventy-nine, Fry produced another original play, titled with deliberate ambiguity, *One Thing More: or, Caedmon Construed*, produced at Chelmsford, Essex. Like much of his earlier work, *One Thing More* takes an early church figure, an unlikely saint, Caedmon, an elderly, unlearned herdsman who in a vision receives the power of song, and whose story Fry links to a liturgical celebration.

In 1987, Fry delivered a lecture at King's College, University of London, on "Genius, Talent, and Failure: The Brontës." In this same year his wife Phyllis died.

In 1988, Fry was made an Honorary Fellow of Manchester Polytechnic and was awarded a D.Litt. from Lambeth. He had already been made a Fellow of the Royal Society of Literature. His pacifist convictions he continued to express by becoming a signatory of the Authors World Peace Appeal. He currently lives at East Dean, near Chichester, West Sussex.

Literary Analysis

If Fry is a key entry in an *Encyclopedia of British Humorists*, it is because humor encompasses more than the ludicrous or the incongruous or even the merely comic. For Fry, humor is near allied to tragedy and springs from the same perceptions and the same sources. He wrote the manifesto of this kind of humorous writing in a 1952 article in *Adelphi*: "Comedy is an escape, not from truth but from despair: a narrow escape into faith. It believes in a universal cause for delight, even though knowledge of the cause is always twitched away from under us. . . . In tragedy every moment is eternity; in comedy

eternity is a moment. . . . Somehow the characters have to unmortify themselves: to affirm life and assimilate death and persevere in joy . . . not by a vulnerable optimism but by a hard-won maturity of delight. . . . Joy (of a kind) has been all on the devil's side and one of the necessities of our time is to redeem it."

It is this sense of comedy snatched out of the jaws of despair that marks even Fry's non-religious dramas. His are tragicomedies more than comedies, made of the same cloth as Shakespeare's dark comedies. His characters are all articulate, witty, metaphorically gifted, full of allusions (especially to the classics and to the Bible) but not of illusions. The world in which they find themselves is absurd, in the modern sense of the term: unnatural, illogical, even mad. In this world they are trapped as Christian existentialists, passionately aware that they are dependent upon others for existence and menaced by death, forced to make hard choices, half-blindly, yet to accept the responsibility and the guilt for those choices if they produce tragedy. In one sense, all of Fry's plays are about what the twentieth century has come to call its search for identity; the characters must discover who they are by the end of even Fry's lighter comedies. The final act of a traditional comedy reveals the nature of its comic protagonist to others in the play; the end of a typical Fry comedy reveals the natures of the characters mainly to themselves.

In 1950, four Fry plays were being presented simultaneously on the London stage; almost a half century later, despite a continued strain of critical disparagement or dismissal, his plays continue to be revived as stage successes on both sides of the Atlantic. The sturdy success of his staged plays may be explained by six qualities in these comedies.

First, like Shakespeare and Jean Baptiste Molière, Fry had a great deal of experience with the theater in ways other than the writing of plays. As an actor and director, he had gained a practical sense of stagecraft—devices and stratagems that would attract and interest a theater audience. (Though he owed much to Eliot's verse dramas, it was this sense of stagecraft that Eliot appears to have learned from Fry by the time he wrote *The Cocktail Party*.)

Second, in a century not much given to description of Nature, in the sense of the countryside, Fry often focuses on the natural setting of his plays, and like the Renaissance dramatists, he presents these settings not in stage directions but in the lines of the characters themselves. When Perpetua returns from America in *Venus Observed*, she is struck especially by the moist greenness of the England to which she has come back: "this green and pleasant aquarium" (a line containing a Shakespearean allusion).

Third, there is the author's much-praised sense of language. In "An Experience of Critics" he ruefully points out that the critical view of him as "a man reeling intoxicated with words; they flow in a golden—or perhaps pinchbeck—stream from his mouth; they start out his ears; they burst like rockets and jumping crackers and catherine-wheels round his head" is in sharp contrast to his own experience of himself, sitting for hours in front of his typewriter, finally typing a word, as "the night wears dumbly on towards dawn." Nevertheless, however painful for its playwright its actual construction was, when staged a Fry comedy gives us characters who speak articulately, volubly, metaphorically, who are never at a loss for words, who can respond vividly, even when surprised or threatened, when silly or when dying. A Fry character may use words malapropistically, as Old Skipps does in *The Lady's Not for Burning*, and the pyrotechnics of the verse Fry himself called "sliced prose" may be set off against passages of deliberate colloquialness or journalistic flatness and prosiness, but the words come; no character ever finds himself with nothing to say, inarticulate, fumbling helplessly for speech. A word for Fry always has more than one edge. As Reedbeck remarks in *Venus Observed*, "A spade is never so merely a spade as the word / Spade would imply." George Jean Nathan reports that Eliot once said of Fry, "If the young man wants to be a poet, he must first learn to be less poetical." Although the diction in the later Fry plays is more austere, less extravagant, Eliot's was a lesson that Fry never really chose to learn—and it marks one of the distinctions between the verse plays of the two dramatists.

Fourth, Fry has created some of the most memorable female characters of the twentieth-century British stage. Granted, he was fortunate to have his heroines played by some of the outstanding actresses of mid-century England—Bloom, Leigh, Brown, Dame Edith—but it is difficult to separate cause and effect; in part, these great women of the stage chose to play Fry women because the roles were so attractive. A Fry heroine has the same command of words (and of plot-line) as does her male counterpart;

moreover, she is witty and wise and sensitive without making that male counterpart any less so. Fry was lavish in the roles that he made for women, sometimes including several dazzling female roles in a single play, as with the two in *The Lady's Not for Burning* and the four in *Venus Observed*.

Fifth, Fry comedies have taken two archetypal human themes, love and death, and bound them inextricably together. If in the comedies love seems to be winning at the end, it is doing so only temporarily, and the characters acknowledge the transitory nature of its triumph. At the end of *The Lady's Not for Burning*, Jennet reminds Thomas that she is asking for "only another / Fifty years or so and then I promise / To let you go," and the author closes his penultimate lines with "my ultimate friendly death." This *liebestod* theme runs throughout Fry's work and saves it from shallow optimism. When he was seventy and gave his Chichester Cathedral lecture, "Death Is a Kind of Love," Fry was quoting himself in his title. It is Tegeus's line from Fry's first acclaimed stage success, *A Phoenix Too Frequent*, written when he was thirty-nine. The love-death binding spans his lifetime.

Finally, Fry's comedies continue to succeed because of their paradox and irony. Both of these devices reinforce his sense of the complexity of language and of human beings. Words never operate to a single purpose; they are always glancing off into a pun, a *double entendre*, an imprecision. Likewise, human lives in his plays never move directly to their intended goals but instead reverse themselves in mockery upon the intender. It is this haunting sense of multi-leveled paradox and irony that gives depth to Fry's plays over fifty years after their creation.

Perhaps how Fry's comedies work may be illustrated best by looking at the four that he designated as his seasonal comedies: *The Lady's Not for Burning*, *Venus Observed*, *The Dark Is Light Enough*, and *A Yard of Sun*. Despite their spanning twenty-two years of the writer's dramatic career, the four plays have several things in common. All four are verse tragicomedies related to a particular season; all explore questions of self-identity, family relationships, guilt, responsibility, love, and death; all center on some sort of public observance or ceremony.

The earliest and most perennially popular of the four seasonal comedies, *The Lady's Not for Burning*, is set in "A room in the house of Hebble Tyson, Mayor of the small market-town of Cool Clary . . . 1400 either more or less exactly." The ostensible public ceremony about which it centers is the engagement ball of Alizon Eliot and Humphrey Devize, but behind this pleasantry loom two less winning possible ceremonies: the hanging sought by Thomas Mendip by his false confessions to murder, the stake-burning shunned by Jennet Jourdemayne—"I am such / A girl of habit. I had got into the way / Of being alive." It is an April-time of lovers still young and flexible enough to learn. Two pairs leave at the end of the play; in each pair, each lover has had to learn lessons from the other, to make accommodations, before any such joint departure is possible. It is also an April play in that act 1 is punctuated by the April rains. And it is symbolically (like Eliot's *Waste Land*) April too. When Alizon, just out of her convent-rearing, puzzles, "Men are strange. It's almost unexpected / To find they speak English," Richard, who has fallen in love with her, responds, "Things happen to them." "What things?" asks Alizon, and Richard replies, "Machinations of nature. / As April does to the earth." "I wish it were true!" Alizon retorts. "Show me daffodils happening to a man!" "Very easily," says Richard, but Thomas the cynic adds, "And thistles as well. And ladies' / Bedstraw and deadly nightshade and the need / For rhubarb." Later in the same act, Nicholas calls love "An April anarchy." The imagery continues throughout the play, with April suggesting the Shavian life force that figures so strongly in Fry's plays, a creative impulse that opposes itself to law and reason and age and death.

Shortly after he had finished *The Lady's Not for Burning*, the dramatist called it his spring play and announced his intention of bringing out three other plays to celebrate the other seasons. The second, *Venus Observed*, was not slow in coming. It is his autumn (October) play, set in Stellmere Park in contemporary England; its public ceremonies center about Halloween imagery, about the group observation of an eclipse of the sun by the moon, and about a public conflagration, perhaps suggestive of the Guy Fawkes bonfires on November 5. Its protagonist, the middle-aged Duke of Altair, has decided to thrust on his son Edgar the Judgment of Paris, a choice among the Duke's three former mistresses as to which shall be Edgar's stepmother in what the Duke calls his "resignation of monogamy." The choice is complicated by young Perpetua, who returns

from ten years in America to find herself loved by both Edgar and his father. Again, the chronological references are frequent. Act 1 identifies its date specifically as October 29, and the Duke adds:

> The leaves transfigured by the thought
>   of death,
> The wind south-west, a blue sky
>   buffaloed
> By cloud, the sun approaching
>   its eclipse.

And because the season is autumn, the Duke cannot have the springlike Perpetua, whom he loves, but must take instead his middle-aged former mistress, Rosabel Fleming (who has just set fire to his mansion in a retributive act of thwarted love). Toward the end of the last act the Duke accepts with resignation his aging, his approaching death, even "A sudden illumination of lumbago," and looks once more with combined self-pity and affection at the autumnal world around him:

> Branches and boughs,
> Brown hills, the valleys faint with brume,
> A burnish on the lake; mile by mile
> It's all a unison of ageing,
> The landscape's all in tune, in a falling
>   cadence,
> All decaying. And nowhere does it have
>   to hear
> The quips of spring, or, when so nearing
>   its end
> Have to bear the merry mirth of May
> How fortunate to grow in the crow-
>   footed woods.

Fry's winter comedy is *The Dark Is Light Enough*. As befits the season of winter and death, this play is the most nearly tragic of the four; we should not have called it a comedy except that its author does. It is set in an Austrian country-house near the Hungarian border in the winter of 1848–1849, a year of revolutions, and in it the playwright is concerned particularly with the Hungarian revolution of that year. The play opens with the Countess Rosmarin Ostenberg missing, having been heard by one of the servants driving away alone, before daybreak,

> The great sleigh making for the Thierick
>   gate.

But now the snow's so deep there's no
way of telling.

The public ritual about which this play is constructed is, in one sense, the Thursday evenings
at which the Countess gathers her friends for
an intellectual and social exchange; in quite
another sense, it is the later dance of the Hungarian revolutionist soldiers who occupy the
country-house. But, winter is the season of
death, and at the end of the play the Countess
dies, saying:

That was a roundabout drive in the
snow,
Owing to my eccentric sense of direction!

Richard Gettner, whom she has died to save and
whom she did not expect to stay with her, remains with her to face the capture and death
that he has been attempting to avoid throughout the course of the play. Indeed, it is a winter
play, but Fry insists that its dark light is enough.

The last of the four seasonal comedies, *A
Yard of Sun*, is subtitled *A Summer Comedy*
and set in Siena in July 1946. World War II is
recently over; prisoners are still returning to
Italy. One of Fry's few plays without a plot-
source, in *A Yard of Sun* he tells a story of re-
assembling two Italian families in a ward; the
Brunos, to whom the son Edmondo returns as
a great worldly success, and the Scapares, to
whom the young horse-racer, Alfio, comes to
meet his father's other family and to whom the
father, Cesare, returns from a concentration
camp. It is July and hot and stormy, yet there
is no water because it has been turned off at the
mains. The public ceremony is the Palio, the
horse race between ten of the Sienese wards
which has been held since medieval times on
July 2 and August 16. There are references
throughout the play to the heat and the sunshine, and recurrences of Fry's themes of self-
knowledge and of guilt and responsibility.
(Whose lapse led to capturing the hidden Cesare
and sending him to the concentration camp?)
Returned from the concentration camp, Cesare
comments, "A good idea, the sun," and his
mistress Giosetta concurs, "Yes, it helps."

Fry's four seasonal comedies remind us of
a Frye with a different spelling, the Canadian
Northrop Frye, who was writing at this same
time in *The Archetypes of Literature* of the four
seasons and how they appear philosophically in
literature and in folklore: the dawn, spring, and
birth phase; the zenith, summer, and marriage
or triumph phase; the sunset, autumn, and
death phase; the darkness, winter, and dissolution phase. Both Fry(e)s had arrived at the same
conclusion: in the natural seasons we find original patterns that underlie all human experience
and human storytelling. Fry's four seasonal
comedies have survived for almost a half-cen-
tury as a dramatic embodiment in language and
stagecraft of this archetypal theory.

Summary
During a career in writing professional drama
that spanned over sixty years (1924–1986),
Christopher Fry served the theater in many capacities—playwright, actor, translator, director,
adapter, writer of radio plays, screenplays, and
television plays, and of lyrics and music for
musicals. In addition to all of these dramatic
forms, he produced a number of essays and lectures as well as children's plays and musicals
and a story book.

Throughout his life many of his dramatic
productions were linked to specific church performances, Biblical stories, saints legends, or
religious themes. Despite the metaphysical
depth and complexity of those topics, however,
in an age that was neither deep nor complex,
Fry always was witty and cheerful in his language and often even in his content. Probably
the most popular British playwright of the mid-
twentieth century, he nevertheless ran counter
to many of the tendencies of his age. Alien
among playwrights who were often either naturalistic (Osborne and the kitchen sink school)
or surrealistically absurd (Beckett and Pinter),
Fry wrote comic verse drama (as only Eliot, a
generation older, having come later in his own
career to playwriting, was doing).

Even in his tragedies, Fry is always the
humorist. He finds language a source of perpetual delight, funny and illuminating in itself.
He calls most of his plays comedies; we should
more likely have called them tragi-comedies, for
his comedy is snatched from the jaws of despair.

Fry contradicted many of the dominant
dramatic traits of his time and has had no immediate successors, but in being highly atypical
he has kept alive possibilities for humor and
poetry on the British stage. Only he and Eliot
insisted through their witty, articulate stage
comedies on serious metaphysical themes that,
although the world in which we find ourselves
may be absurd, the riddles that it poses may

have some possible answers and that we may find these answers partly through the wit of language, through characters who, discovering their identities by the end of the plays, speak much more wittily and charmingly than we are able to do but reveal to us beneath their pyrotechnic wit those truths that we recognize but did not have the words for. For years Fry reminded the British stage that it was possible to be simultaneously funny and poetic and religious.

Selected Bibliography
Primary Sources

Plays
Youth and the Peregrines. Produced 1934.
She Shall Have Music. Book by Frank Eyton, music by Fry and Monte Crick. Produced 1934.
To Sea in a Sieve. Produced 1935.
Open Door. Produced 1936.
Robert of Sicily: Opera for Children. Libretto by Fry, music by Michael Tippett. Produced 1938.
The Boy with a Cart: Cuthman, Saint of Sussex. London: Oxford University Press, 1939; New York: Oxford University Press, 1951.
Seven at a Stroke: A Play for Children. Libretto by Fry, music by Michael Tippett. Produced 1939.
Thursday's Child: A Pageant. Music by Martin Shaw. Produced 1939.
The Tower. Produced 1939.
A Phoenix Too Frequent. London: Hollis & Carter, 1946; New York: Oxford University Press, 1949.
The Firstborn. Cambridge: Cambridge University Press, 1946; New York: Oxford University Press, 1950.
Thor, with Angels. Canterbury: Goulden, 1948; London: Oxford University Press, 1949.
The Lady's Not for Burning. London and New York: Oxford University Press, 1949; rev. 1973.
Venus Observed. London and New York: Oxford University Press, 1950.
Ring Round the Moon: A Charade with Music, adapted from Jean Anouilh's *L'Invitation au chateau.* London: Methuen, and New York: Oxford University Press, 1950.
A Sleep of Prisoners. London and New York: Oxford University Press, 1951.
The Dark Is Light Enough. London and New York: Oxford University Press, 1954.
The Lark, adapted from Jean Anouilh's *L'Alouette.* London: Methuen, 1955; New York: Oxford University Press, 1956.
Tiger at the Gates, adapted from Jean Giraudoux's *La Guerre de Troie n'aura pas lieu.* London: Methuen, 1955; New York: Oxford University Press, 1956.
Duel of Angels, adapted from Jean Giraudoux's *Pour Lucrece.* London: Methuen, 1958; New York: Oxford University Press, 1959.
Curtmantle. London and New York: Oxford University Press, 1961.
Judith: A Tragedy in Three Acts, adapted from Jean Giraudoux. London: Methuen, 1962.
Peer Gynt, based on Johan Fillinger's translation of Henrik Ibsen. London and New York: Oxford University Press, 1970.
A Yard of Sun: A Summer Comedy. London and New York: Oxford University Press, 1970.
Cyrano de Bergerac: A Heroic Comedy in Five Acts, adapted from Edmond Rostand. London and New York: Oxford University Press, 1975.
Paradise Lost, music by Penderecki, from the poem by Milton. Produced 1978.
One Thing More; or, Caedmon Construed. London: King's College London, 1986; New York, 1987.

Screenplays
The Beggar's Opera, adapted by Fry and Denis Cannan from John Gay. British Lion, 1953.
The Queen Is Crowned, documentary by Fry. Universal, 1953.
Barabbas, adapted from Par Lagerkvist. Columbia, 1962.
The Bible: In the Beginning, by Fry, Jonathan Griffin, Ivo Perilli, and Vittorio Bonicelli. Twentieth Century–Fox, 1966.

Radio Plays
Children's Hour series. BBC, 1939–1940.
The Firstborn. BBC, 1947.
Rhineland Journey. BBC, 1948.

Television Plays
The Canary. BBC, 1950.

The Tenant of Wildfell Hall. BBC, 1968.

The Brontës of Haworth. BBC, 1973; published, 2 vols. London: Davis-Poynter, 1975.

The Best of Enemies. BBC, 1976.

Sister Dora, from the book by Jo Manton. BBC, 1977.

Star Over Bethlehem. BBC, 1981.

Verse

Root and Sky: Poetry from the Plays of Christopher Fry. Ed. Charles E. Wadsworth and Jean G. Wadsworth. Cranberry Isles, ME: Tidal, 1975.

Essays

"Cock in a Shower." *London Mercury*, 38 (August 1938): 307.

"The Artist Views the Critics." *Atlantic*, 191 (March 1943): 52–55.

"The Author Explains." *World Report*, 4 (June 1949): 18–21.

"A Playwright Speaks." *Listener*, 42 (February 1950): 331–32.

"The Play of Ideas." *New Statesman and Nation*, 22 (April 1950): 458.

"Drama in a House of Worship." *New York Times* (October 14, 1951): sec. 2, p. 2.

"How Lost, How Amazed, How Miraculous We Are." *Theatre Arts*, 36 (August 1952): 27.

"Comedy." *Adelphi*, 27 (November 1952): 27–29.

"Letters to an Actor Playing Hamlet." In *Shakespeare Survey*. Ed. Allardyce Nicoll. Cambridge: Cambridge University Press, 1952, pp. 58–61.

"Poetry in the Theatre." *Saturday Review* (March 21, 1953): 18–19.

"Author's Struggle." *New York Times* (February 6, 1955): sec. 2, p. 3:1.

"Why Verse?" *World Theater*, 4, 4 (Autumn 1955): 51–61.

"On Keeping the Sense of Wonder." *Vogue*, 127 (January 1956): 122–23.

"Christmas Transformation." *Vogue*, 128 (December 1956): 106–07.

"Enjoying the Accidental." *Vogue*, 130 (October 1957): 92.

"Talking of Henry." *Twentieth Century*, 169 (February 1961): 186–90.

"Theatre and History." *Essays and Studies*, 30 (1977): 86–87.

"Looking for a Language." *Adam International Review* (1980): 428–30.

Children's Books

The Boat That Mooed. New York: Macmillan, 1966.

Lectures

"An Experience of Critics." In *An Experience of Critics and The Approach to Dramatic Criticism*. Ed. Kaye Webb. London: Perpetua, 1952.

"Death Is a Kind of Love." With drawings by Charles E. Wadsworth. Cranberry Isles, ME: Tidal, 1979.

"Genius, Talent, and Failure: The Brontës." Adam Lecture, 1986; London: King's College London, 1987.

Autobiography

Can You Find Me: A Family History. London: Oxford University Press, 1978.

Secondary Sources

Bibliographies

Schear, Bernice Larson, and Eugene G. Prater. "A Bibliography on Christopher Fry." *Tulane Drama Review*, 4, 3 (March 1960): 88–98. The best (though still incomplete and sometimes inaccurate) bibliography on Fry to date.

Wiggins, Kayla June. "American, British, Irish, and Commonwealth Verse Drama: An Annotated Bibliography, 1935–85." Diss. Texas Christian University, 1990. Pays only brief attention to Fry.

Books

Leeming, Glenda. *Christopher Fry*. Boston: Twayne, 1990. Leeming moves from a biographical portrait to an accessible interpretation of Fry's major works, from *The Boy With a Cart* to *One More Thing*, to a selective bibliography of primary and secondary sources.

Roy, Emil Lawrence. *Christopher Fry*. Carbondale: Southern Illinois University Press, 1968. Roy examines Fry's contemporary critical reception, explores the nature of his imagery, and analyzes in depth his major plays from *The Boy With a Cart* to *Curtmantle*, blending literary history with explication. Roy contends that all of Fry's plays reveal his preference for "the romantic, the philosophical, and the oddly unique lying behind surface fragmentation."

Stanford, Derek, ed. *A Christopher Fry Album*. London: Nevill, 1952. A detailed but anecdotal (and at times inaccurate) account of Fry's life with descriptions of early productions.

———. *Christopher Fry: An Appreciation*. 2nd ed. London: Nevill, 1951. A 222-page compilation of Fry's biography, a study of his dual role as poet and playwright, a comparison of his work with that of his contemporaries, and an analysis of the corpus of his work exploring the mystery of existence and the riddle of human metaphysics in each.

———. *Christopher Fry*. London: Longmans, Green, 1954; rev. ed., 1962. A mixture of biography and criticism, Stanford posits that Fry cannot be appreciated in any single play but must be examined holistically in order to understand his genius that balances necessity and possibility couched in mystery, fantasy, and rich poetic language.

Wiersma, Stanley M. *Christopher Fry: A Critical Essay*. Grand Rapids: Eerdmans, 1969. A good source of critical commentary on Fry's plays.

———. *More Than the Ear Discovers: God in the Plays of Christopher Fry*. Chicago: Loyola University Press, 1983. One of the best Fry studies to date, focusing more on the plays and less on the productions.

Portions of Books

Gassner, John. *The Theatre in Our Times*. New York: Crown, 1954, pp. 383, 411, 420–21, 429. Often negative to Fry, Gassner uses Fry only to provide examples to support generalizations about modern English drama.

Highet, Gilbert. "The Poet and the Modern Stage: Christopher Fry." In *People, Places, and Books*. New York: Oxford University Press, 1953, pp. 61–68. A brief biographical portrait and condescending view of Fry's style, dialogue, imagery, and plots, dismissing him as a thoughtful playwright but not a serious dramatist.

Kerr, Walter. *Pieces at Eight*. New York: Simon and Schuster, 1957, pp. 134–49. Kerr's piece is both narrative and review: while writing a short biography of Fry's literary career, he also evaluates his plays but rarely offers any interpretive criticism.

Kunitz, Stanley J., ed. *Twentieth Century Authors*. First Supplement. New York: Wilson, 1955, pp. 346–47. A brief, literary dictionary portrait of Fry, including a selected bibliography of primary and secondary sources.

Kurdys, Douglas Bellamy. *Form in the Modern Verse Drama*. Salzburg: University Salzburg, 1972, pp. 92–142. After positing that language and not theme is "the most important element" in Fry's works, Kurdys analyzes how Fry's "verbal devices" contribute to developing the overall tone and structure of his plays.

Leeming, Glenda. *Poetic Drama*. London: Macmillan, 1989. Leeming devotes an entire chapter to Fry's poetic language and governing philosophy as they have developed through his plays.

Nathan, George Jean. *Theatre Book of the Year, 1949–50*. New York: Knopf, 1950, pp. 274–79. A favorable review of O'Shaughnessy's production of *A Phoenix Too Frequent* in New York, though finding it not as strong a play as *The Lady's Not For Burning*.

———. *Theatre Book of the Year, 1950–51*. New York: Knopf, 1951, pp. 87–94, 126–29. Favorable reviews of Gielgud's production of *The Lady's Not For Burning* and of Miller's production of *Ring Round the Moon*, both in New York.

———. *The Theatre in the Fifties*. New York: Knopf, 1953, pp. 124–131. Disparaging reviews of MacOwan's production of *A Sleep of Prisoners* and of Olivier's production of *Venus Observed*.

Scott-James, Rolfe A. *Fifty Years of English Literature, 1900–50*. 2nd ed. London: Longmans, Green, 1957, pp. 224, 234–39. Scott-James admires Fry's gift for poetry and language, as evidenced in plot summaries and brief interpretations of several plays.

Spanos, William V. *The Christian Tradition in Modern British Verse Drama*. New Brunswick, NJ: Rutgers University Press, 1967, pp. 304–24. Spanos reexamines *A Sleep of Prisoners* with respect to what Fry meant by the word "comedy," arguing that of all of his plays it comes closest to integrating "the Incarnation as the agency of the redemption of time" into religious verse drama.

Vos, Nelvin. "The Comic Victim-Victor: His Passionate Action in the Drama of Christopher Fry." In *The Drama of Comedy: Victim and Victor*. Richmond, VA: Knox, 1966, pp. 74–99.

Whiting, Frank M. *An Introduction To The Theatre*. New York: Harper, 1954; rev. ed., 1961, pp. 81–82, 134.

Wilder, Amos N. *Modern Poetry and The Christian Tradition*. New York: Scribner, 1952.

———. *Theology and Modern Literature*. Cambridge, MA: Harvard University Press, 1958, pp. 25, 32, 44.

Williamson, Audrey. *Contemporary Theatre, 1953–1956*. London: Rockliff, and New York: Macmillan, 1956, pp. 26, 30–32, 147–48.

———. *Theatre of Two Decades*. London: Rockliff, 1951, pp. 145–55.

———, and Charles Landstone. *The Bristol Old Vic: The First Ten Years*. London: Miller, 1957, pp. 87–88, 102, 112.

Articles

Adler, Jacob H. "Shakespeare and Christopher Fry." *Educational Theatre Journal*, 11 (May 1959): 85–98. Adler assesses Fry's comedies and explores why and how they remind audiences of Shakespeare and what is gained and lost by such a comparison.

Anderson, B.W. "The Poetry of Mr. Fry." *Spectator*, March 31, 1950, p. 432. A favorable account of Fry's poetic style.

"Another Language." *Time* (April 24, 1950): 112. Review of *The Lady's Not for Burning* as a literary work, claiming that it moves Fry into a select circle of playwrights.

Arrowsmith, William. "Notes on English Verse Drama: Christopher Fry." *Hudson Review*, 3, 2 (Summer 1950): 203–16. Arrowsmith finds in interpreting several of Fry's plays that his greatest achievement is his verse and not his dramaturgy.

Bak, John S. "'little death-watch beetle': Nicholas as Satan in Fry's *The Lady's Not for Burning*." *Notes on Contemporary Literature*, 23, 5 (November 1993): 6–8. Nicholas Devizes's metaphorical tropes connect him to the elements—blood, death, and fire—which reflect Fry's intention of making him kin to the

underworld.

Barnes, Lewis W. "Christopher Fry: The Chestertonian Concept of Comedy." *Xavier University Studies*, 2 (March 1950): 30–47. Barnes attempts to resolve the apparent conflict between Fry's metaphysical poetry and untraditional comedy by claiming that his "metaphysical comedy" closely aligns itself to G.K. Chesterton's.

Becker, William. "Reflections On Three New Plays." *Hudson Review*, 8, 2 (Summer 1955): 258–63. Severe criticism of *The Dark Is Light Enough* after its Broadway debut, claiming that it lacks plot and character development and adds nothing new to what Fry had said in previous plays.

Bewley, Marius. "The Verse of Christopher Fry." *Scrutiny*, 18 (June 1951): 78–84. A critical attack upon Fry's poetic style of writing, finding it vacuous.

Brown, John Mason. "Seeing Things: Poets and Players." *Saturday Review of Literature* (December 2, 1950): 44–46, 68–69. A narration on how hearing a bizarre reading of Shakespeare's *Macbeth* by Edith Sitwell led Brown to appreciate *The Lady's Not for Burning,* most notably its metaphoric use of language.

———. "Seeing Things: Yes and No." *Saturday Review of Literature* (March 1, 1952): 20–22. After extolling Fry as having a "nimble and original" wit, an "agile and unpredictable" mind, as "playful as it is probing," Brown calls *Venus Observed* a disappointment because it tires the audience's ears with overwhelming verbiage.

"Christopher Fry." *Theatre Arts*, 34 (November 1950): 21. Caption attributes the start of twentieth-century renaissance poetry to Fry.

"Christopher Fry's Sermon for Peace." *New York Times Magazine* (May 20, 1951): 58–59. Summary of Fry's "four-soldier show," *A Sleep of Prisoners,* his contribution to the Festival of Britain.

Clurman, Harold. "Theatre: In Contrast to Fry." *New Republic* (August 20, 1951): 21–22. Clurman contrasts Fry with the French and American playwrights of his time, finding Fry to be more "humorous," "gentle," "sweetly ironic," "undisturbed," and "personal" than his foreign

F

counterparts' stolid or melodramatic material.

Collins, J.A. "Poet of Paradox: The Dramas of Christopher Fry." *Literary Half-Yearly*, 12, 2 (July 1971): 62–75. Collins attempts to reverse the trend of dismissing Fry as a careerist by exploring the paradoxical nature of his plays as manifested in their imagery and poetic language.

Corrigan, Robert W. "Christopher Fry and Religious Drama." *Ivory Tower*, May 1953, pp. 8–12.

Davis, Earle. "Christopher Fry: The Twentieth Century Shakespeare?" *Kansas Magazine* (1952): 10–15. Comparison of *The Lady's Not for Burning* and *Venus Observed* with Shakespeare's comedic tradition, saying that in language (blank verse and metaphor) and in plot they are very Shakespearean, but that Fry has not yet "challenged Shakespeare in tragic utterance."

Dobree, Bonamy. "Some London Plays." *Sewanee Review*, 63 (Spring 1955): 270–80. A caustic review of Fry's *The Dark Is Light Enough,* arguing that whereas its stucture is tighter than any of Fry's previous plays, its language is "less exuberant."

Donoghue, Denis. "Christopher Fry's Theatre of Words." *Essays in Criticism*, 9 (January 1959): 37–49. By examining the language in Fry's plays, Donoghue castigates critics for admiring Fry as a major poetic talent, concluding that Fry is careless with words and that his "permanent contribution" to drama "will be slight."

Eliot, T.S. "The Aims of Poetic Drama." *Adam International Review*, 200 (1950): 10–16. Argues the use of verse over prose in drama, mentioning Fry and a handful of other poets who have taken up the challenge of writing poetry for the stage.

"Enter Poet, Laughing." *Time* (November 20, 1950): 58–64. A literary biography and cursory analysis of Fry's plays in anticipation of his arrival on Broadway.

Ferguson, John. "The Boy with a Cart." *Modern Drama*, 8 (December 1965): 284–92. Ferguson argues that in choosing the story of Cuthman, Saint of Sussex, Fry "naturally accepted an episodic pattern for the drama," then proceeds to analyze how the play's characters, language, and chorus nevertheless give it unity.

———. "Christopher Fry's *A Sleep of Prisoners.*" *English*: *The Journal of the English Association*, 10 (1954): 42–47. Ferguson finds *A Sleep of Prisoners* "one of the most interesting examples of contemporary religious drama" but, because of its emphasis on symbolic message rather than on characterization, with dramatic limitations.

Findlater, Richard. "The Two Countesses." *Twentieth Century*, 156 (August 1954): 175. A criticism of *The Dark Is Light Enough*'s first production.

Fulks, Wayne Mahlon. "The Image of Dance in Christopher Fry's Seasonal Tetralogy." *Wascana Review*, 17, 1 (Spring 1982): 37–54. Unity to the seasonal comedies is found in the metaphor/image of the dance—a "cluster of symbols" that represents the dance of life (existence) and its pairing off of partners—and in the dance as an event that helps to establish and resolve the plays' tensions.

Gibbs, Wolcott. "The Theatre: The House of Bondage." *New Yorker* (May 10, 1958): 83–84. A review of Fry's *The Firstborn,* calling it a discouraging contribution to the theater because it is "dull, pretentious, and often largely incomprehensible," its failure lying in its misrepresentation of characters and highfalutin' language.

Gillespie, Diane Filby. "Language as Life: Christopher Fry's Early Plays." *Modern Drama*, 21 (September 1978): 287–96. Gillespie expounds on Fry's statement that poetry is a "twentieth-century need for a new realism" that communicates human complexities "more successfully than prose"; therefore, the recent criticism that says Fry's language supplants his thought is errant since "Fry's thought is his language."

Gillett, Eric. "The Poet's for the Theatre." *National Review* (May 1950): 388–96. Gillett defends, through an analysis of his plays, Fry's stature as a dramatist amidst current critical attacks, concluding (contrary to what Stephen Spender asserted) that Fry is good poetry, good drama, and good entertainment.

Gittings, Robert. "The Smell of Sulphur."

Encounter, 50 (January 1978): 73–78. Fry's main source for the characters, dialogues, and theme of *The Lady's Not for Burning* is Charles Williams's 1941 book, *Witchcraft.*

Green, Anne. "Fry's Cosmic Vision." *Modern Drama,* 4 (December 1962): 355–64. An extension of Derek Stanford's assertion that Fry's "antitheses grow out of . . . the elusiveness of truth" and that Fry's plays take the "form of moral dilemmas," concluding that Fry's cosmic vision of life as explored in his canon is a "total" one—he sees "joy, grief, madness, hope, love, fear" at once—all of his plays being "products of the same vision."

Hewes, Henry. "Fry in the Belfry." *Saturday Review of Literature,* 1 (March 1952): 22. Review of *A Sleep of Prisoners,* stating that Fry poorly "exhibits the endless slippery metaphor" and "eternal pun"; readers of Fry know his work better belongs on the stage because there at least his words have a "mysterious evanescence."

Hobson, Harold. "Christopher Fry's Other World." *Drama,* 132 (Spring 1979): 13–17. Review of Fry's autobiography *Can You Find Me?,* finding it as enigmatic as Fry himself.

———. "London Hails Mr. Fry, Playwright." *New York Times Magazine* (March 12, 1950): 24–25, 61–63. Hobson praises Fry for his "romantic tales clothed in splendid language and laced with wit" in *Venus Observed, The Boy With a Cart,* and *The Lady's Not for Burning;* describes Fry's stage collaboration with Gielgud; and discusses why Fry is a good playwright, mainly because of unique use of language.

Hunor, Mary. "Theatre Letter." *Kenyon Review,* 18 (Winter 1956): 128–30. A review of Clurman's production of Fry's *Tiger at the Gates* that talks more about the production than about Fry, but does credit Fry with a superior translation of Giraudoux's play.

Igoe, W.J. "Sketch of a Portent." *America* (July 5, 1952): 357–59. Igoe asserts in a brief literary biography that as a skilled craftsman Fry frees the English audience from its provincialism by writing plays that, although set centuries ago, address issues of humanity that are timeless.

Julie, Sister. "Do We Dare Try Medieval Plays?" *America* (July 21, 1951): 399–401. Because of their connection to Christianity and the spiritual, *The Firstborn, Thor, with Angels,* and *The Boy With a Cart* are affirmative answers to Father Gardiner's probing question from an earlier *America* article, "Do we dare try medieval plays?"

Kerr, Walter. "The Lady's Not for Burning." *Life* (November 27, 1950): 141–42. A favorable review of Gielgud's production of *The Lady's Not for Burning,* but finds that the play's strength lies in its rich language and not in its dramatic powers.

Kulisheck, Clarence L. "Christopher Fry and 'It's Greek to Me.'" *Notes and Queries,* 197 (June 1952): 274–75. Considering the paucity of Greek scholars and texts in England in 1400 (the time of action in this play), Kulisheck finds the chaplain's comment "legal matters and so forth / Are Greek to me" to be one of several anachronisms in *The Lady's Not for Burning.*

Lecky, Eleazer. "Mystery in the Plays of Christopher Fry." *Tulane Drama Review,* 4, 3 (March 1960): 80–87. The sense of mystery in Fry's plays is "an awareness that every experience is unique," an experience that elicits three responses from his characters: wonder, amazement/amusement, and belief/doubt. Lecky then analyzes these elements of mystery in each of Fry's poetic dramas.

Lewis, Robert C. "Christopher Fry—Exponent of Verse Plays." *New York Times* (April 23, 1950): sec. 2, pp. 1, 3. Lewis argues in this literary portrait that Fry is a playwright who appeared in just "the right place at the right time" because his poetry gives people what they lack during wartime—"richness and reaffirmation." The popularity of his plays proves that poetic drama is not just a fad.

"London Acclaims Fry for State Successes." *New York Times,* January 24, 1950, p. 27:4. *Venus Observed*'s opening night extolled for successfully directing attention away from the American hits *A Streetcar Named Desire* and *Death of a Salesman.*

MacArthur, Roderick. "The Dark Is Light Enough." *Theatre Arts,* 39 (February 1955): 72–75. Pictorial synopsis (with lengthy accompanying captions) of *The Dark Is Light Enough.*

McLaughlin, John J. "The disenthroned muse." *America* (November 3, 1951): 128–30. Comparing *The Lady's Not for Burning* with Eliot's *The Cocktail Party,* McLaughlin declares the two to be "polar extremes from each other in poetic and dramatic technique" but still achieving "remarkable success" in rekindling poetic drama.

Mandel, O. "Theme in the Drama of Christopher Fry." *Etudes anglaises,* 10 (October–December 1957): 335–49. An early and complete study of the major dramatic theme in Fry's canon: Life, or the Bergsonian Life-force, as the "perpetual miracle" of mankind.

Maura, Sister M. "Christopher Fry: An Angle of Experience." *Renascence,* 8, 1 (Autumn 1955): 3–11, 36. The title *The Dark Is Light Enough* suggests a way of evaluating Fry's "angle of experience" in all of his plays, namely his faith in the divine order of things in a disordered universe.

Morgenstern, Charles. "Fantastical Bouquet." *Theatre Arts,* 35 (January 1951): 26–30. An analysis of Fry's "banquet" of plays, including *A Phoenix Too Frequent, The Lady's Not for Burning,* and *Venus Observed,* focusing on the successful integration of Fry's comical vision with his poetical language.

"Muse at the Box Office." *Time* (April 3, 1950): 50–51. Praise for Fry (and Eliot) for making poetic drama sizzle, declaring that all of his plays are "witty and rich in imagery, scant of plot, roundly romantic in temperament . . . and steeped in the religious quality of his Quaker's faith."

Nathan, George Jean. "Theatre: Young Man Named Fry." *New American Mercury,* 72 (February 1951): 220–24. A review of *The Lady's Not for Burning* and a defense of Fry's dramatic techniques against American critics who claimed that Fry amounted to little or nothing in *A Phoenix Too Frequent,* though Nathan agrees that Fry tries too hard to be "literary."

"New Play in Manhattan." *Time* (November 20, 1950): 58. A review of Gielgud's production of *The Lady's Not for Burning* in New York, calling it a gem whose "forte," however, is "fireworks, not illumination."

Nichols, Lewis. "A Visit with Mr. Fry." *New York Times* (April 27, 1958): sec. 2, p. 1, 3. An interview with Fry on the occasion of Fry's visit to New York for the performance of *The Firstborn.*

Prater, Eugene G. "Christopher Fry: Reconsidered." *Ball State University Forum,* 6, 3 (Autumn 1965): 69–79. Prater finds Fry's "preoccupation with the 'mystery' of the universe . . . refreshing" (albeit static from play to play) but sees Fry's "pyrotechnic use of puns and language" in his dramatic treatment of man and the mystery of existence a serious fault.

Redman, Ben Ray. "Christopher Fry: Poet-Dramatist." *College English,* 14, 4 (January 1953): 191–97. Fry's experience as actor/director gives him "knowledge of stagecraft" plus an "understanding of the relationship of dramatist, director, and actors"; therefore, his plays read and play well, indicative of his skills as a poet and as a dramatist.

Roy, Emil Lawrence. "Archetypal Patterns in Fry." *Comparative Drama,* 1, 2 (1967): 93–104. Fry's repetitive use of archetypal patterns (such as the quest or the journey and the phoenix and fire) more clearly defines him as an artist, "opposed to that of arranger or maker."

———. "Christopher Fry as Tragicomedian." *Modern Drama,* 11 (May 1968): 40–47. According to Roy, all of Fry's plays save *Curtmantle* "belong to the tradition of tragicomedy"—tragedy with a happy ending or a serious theme with light overtones.

———. "Imagery in the Comedies of Christopher Fry." *Modern Drama,* 7 (May 1964): 79–88. By studying the imagery of Fry's comedies, we discover how close Fry is in theory and practice to the dialectical traditions that give meaning to ideas only by their relationship to opposites; yet his "image-world" constitutes "interlinked, subordinate polarities" that often reverse these traditional metonomic associations, where light portends evil and dark good.

Scott, W.T. "The Literary Summing Up." *Saturday Review of Literature* (December 30, 1950): 6–8, 28–29. Reviews of the best publications of 1950, including Fry's

The Lady's Not for Burning and *Venus Observed* because they are as exciting in print as they are on stage.

Scott-James, R.A. "Christopher Fry's Poetic Drama." *Nation* (October 7, 1950): 315–16. A review in praise of Fry's poetic versification and perspective on life antipathetic to the despair and renunciation currently popular on the British stage.

Spanos, William V. "Christopher Fry's *A Sleep of Prisoners*: The Choreography of Comedy." *Modern Drama*, 8 (May 1965): 58–72. Spanos sets out to refute the "conventional interpretation" that Fry's *A Sleep of Prisoners* is a departure from the "'secular' season comedies" by showing how Fry's definition of "comedy" as a "sacramental world" like Dante's is "more applicable to *Sleep*" than to any of the seasonal comedies.

Spears, Monroe K. "Christopher Fry and the Redemption of Joy." *Poetry*, 78, 1 (April 1951): 28–43. Fry is seen as a possible means of restoring audience desire for poetry but calls Fry's romantic immaturity—evidenced in his penchant for fantasy, his nonfunctional poetic language, and his "unwillingness to subordinate himself to his dramatic medium"—his central weakness.

Spender, Stephen. "Christopher Fry." *Spectator* (March 24, 1950): 364–365. A discussion of Fry's colorful but "bloodless" imagery, finding that "sentences are more important to Mr. Fry than any other reality."

Stamm, Rudolf. "Christopher Fry and the Revolt Against Realism in Modern Drama." *Anglia*, 72, 1 (1954): 78–109. After fifty years of realism on the London stage, Fry (through T.S. Eliot) adapted a new type of play based primarily on imagery.

Stanford, Derek. "Christopher Fry." *Contemporary Review*, 188 (September 1955): 174–77. A defense of Fry's dramatic prowess disguised as a chatty portrait of the playwright and his works seen through the eyes of a friend.

———. "Comedy and Tragedy in Christopher Fry." *Modern Drama*, 2 (May 1959): 3–7. Stanford argues that, although Fry's comedies are very close to being tragedies, *The Firstborn*, a timely study of how the "tyranny of power" drives a man to thoughts of imperialization, is Fry's only true tragedy and finest work.

———. "God in the Drama of Christopher Fry." *London Quarterly and Holborn Review* (April 1957): 124–30. A search through the Fry canon for a stronger understanding of Fry's definition of and belief in God.

Trewin, J.C. "The Plays of Christopher Fry." *Adelphi*, 27 (November 1950): 40–45.

———. "The World of the Theatre: Make-Believe." *Illustrated London News* (February 11, 1950): 228. Trewin admires Fry's lively language, lack of pretention, and use of the stage as a "place for sophisticated make-believe" in *Venus Observed*; finds *The Boy With a Cart* dull; and likes Fry's adaptation of Anouilh in *Ring Round the Moon*.

Vos, Alvin. "Christopher Fry's Christian Dialectic in *A Phoenix Too Frequent*." *Renascence*, 36, 4 (Summer 1984): 230–42. Vos explains how the design of a wine bowl in *A Phoenix Too Frequent* is key to understanding Fry's "daring claims about the religious essence" of his comedy.

Wiersma, Stanley M. "Christopher Fry's *A Phoenix Too Frequent*: A Study in Source and Symbol." *Modern Drama*, 8 (December 1965): 293–302. A "probable and hitherto unnamed source" for the plot of *A Phoenix Too Frequent*: a combination of a pagan, Roman joke and St. Paul's letter to the Romans.

———. "Fry's *A Phoenix Too Frequent*." *Explicator*, 37, 2 (Winter 1979): 29–31. Bacchus's wine goblet in *Phoenix* adds to the existing evidence of the "sacramental imagery," proving that *Phoenix* is Fry's adaptation of the pagan joke by Petronius. Fry "turned it into our world's wittiest commentary on the Epistle of Paul to the Romans."

Williamson, Audrey. "Christopher Fry." *Dictionary of Literary Biography 13. British Dramatists Since World War II. Part 1. A–L.* Ed. Stanley Weintraub. Detroit: Bruccoli Clark/Gale Research, 1982, pp. 185–92.

Woodfield, James. "'The Figure of a Dance': Christopher Fry's *A Phoenix Too Frequent*." *Ariel*, 9 (July 1978): 3–19.

F

Woodfield discusses death and resurrection archetypes that underscore the play's structure and Fry's shift from the distinctly tragic to the comic mode of writing—his movement away from a secular drama and final statement that is essentially religious.

———. "'A Unity of Difference': Christopher Fry's Quest for Meaning." *English Studies in Canada*, 2 (1976): 97–108. Discussion of how in all of Fry's plays the general secular message is that an individual exists only in relation to another; the substructure of each play, however, is a religious covenant to communicate the complex meanings of the "diversity, paradoxes, and polarities" of life.

Frances Mayhew Rippy

G

The Gawain/Pearl Poet

Dates: Middle to late fourteenth century
Locale: North West Midlands

Biography

The anonymous "Gawain Poet" (or "Pearl Poet") composed the verses now attributed to him in the second half of the fourteenth century, working somewhere, if the dialect of his poems may be used as evidence, in the North West Midlands of England. Although a number of nineteenth- and earlier twentieth-century scholars have attempted to provide him a name, profession, and family, and to elucidate other details of his life,[1] no specific biographical information can be determined with any certainty. Indeed, the tenuousness of such "clues" as his writings may hold has convinced recent critics to abandon the quest. Even the assertion that the same individual was responsible for all four English poems uniquely contained in the Cotton Nero A.x, art. 3. manuscript remains open to question, though most scholars now accept stylistic, linguistic, and thematic similarities as sufficient to posit a single author for at least *Gawain* and *Pearl*.

Despite the lack of a positive identification, much can be said of the Gawain Poet, even based upon evidence from only the two longer poems. That the writer was intimate with the household of a great lord is indicated by the detailed descriptions of courtly life and activities (dress, feasting, jousting, hunting) and by the preoccupation with such aristocratic concepts as *cortaysye*; the emphasis on masculine aspects of this life (e.g., arming for combat), the gender of the protagonists, and the anti-female bias surfacing in such instances as Gawain's misogynist rantings of fytte five suggest a male author. Moreover, much in his works identifies the poet as a member of the nobility. His education, for example, seems to have included a broad base in the humanities as well as business: his sources range from the Vulgate Bible and general tenets of the patristic tradition to contemporary French and Italian literature, while his diction owes much to the legal and lapidary vocabularies in addition to that of courtly love. He employs the forms of classical rhetoric and argument. He delights in the rituals of the hall, hunt, and boudoir. But, perhaps the most important key to his sensibilities and background—and to the interpretation of his works—lies in his treatment of the received views of Church and court. Here, while he explores the intricacies and possible internal contradictions of both orthodox Church doctrine (*Pearl*) and the various aspects of the chivalric code (*Gawain*), he ends by firmly supporting these interdependent ideologies.[2]

The Gawain Poet, then, was the product of a privileged class in the high Middle Ages. His writings (produced in a time which witnessed the growth of English patriotism and the initial breakdown of the old social paradigms, by a man living in the orbit of the powerful, conservative, independent northern barons) reflect the tensions between the old and the new orders. In the native alliterative tradition, itself rooted in Anglo-Saxon heroic verse, he frames a thorough questioning of contemporary institutions and the vision of humanity supported by those institutions. Still, the Gawain Poet, however critical his eye, ultimately embraced the concerns and sympathies of the fourteenth-century establishment.

Literary Analysis

The Gawain Poet's presumed canon serves as a compact survey of Middle English literary forms and themes. *Patience* and *Cleanness* are homilies, sermons illustrating the virtues identified in their titles through *exempla*. In contrast, *Pearl* frames a medieval *debat* and a classical *consolatio* in the dream-vision form, while all major aspects of the courtly romance find expression in *Sir Gawain and the Green Knight*. The manuscript containing the poems dates from the very late fourteenth century, but sources and possible topical references give them a composition date range from 1365 to 1390. If it is accepted that they are the work of a single author, the order of execution is generally believed to be *Patience*, *Cleanness*, *Pearl*, and finally *Gawain*, a judgment based mainly upon thematic complexity and poetic sophistication.[3]

The homilies *Patience* and *Cleanness*, straightforward and relatively short, offer little grist for the interpretive mill. Their plan is simple. Both begin by defining the virtue under consideration and its value in Christian life. One or more scriptural *exempla* follow, further elucidating the quality through its absence in others. Finally, the poems offer explication of the exempla and exhort the audience to practice the virtue. *Patience*, the more simple of the two, draws upon the tale of Jonah and the whale as its sole example; the longer *Cleanness* (also known as *Purity*) includes three sets of *exempla*, each consisting of a major and two or three minor illustrations and illuminating different aspects of cleanness. These are united by transitional passages discussing its application to human existence. Neither poem strays from or builds upon the biblical accounts beyond the expansion of description and dialogue. Both are completely orthodox in their vision. The only notable features setting them apart from other medieval sermons are the poet's use of *negative* examples to illustrate his topic, and the gently mocking view of humanity that he evinces.

The much more complex *Pearl* continues to stimulate considerable debate as to its basic nature and purpose, its symbolism, and its central theme. Some scholars subscribe to the early interpretation of the poem as an elegy for the author's two-year-old daughter, a working out of his grief and reconciliation to Divine Will. Others view it as an allegory in which the "precious perle wythouten spot" may represent lost and regained innocence, the human soul redeemed, the possibility of salvation, Church ritual, the kingdom of Heaven itself, or a combination of these and/or other spiritual values. Taking the debate to a formal level, John Conley argues convincingly for *Pearl* as a traditional Christian *consolatio* built upon "the sovereign theme of the Christian tradition, as of life itself: the nature of happiness, specifically false and true happiness" (63). Whatever the original motivation, none of these readings necessarily precludes the others. All, moreover, pivot upon the relationship of the worldly to the spiritual life, about which the poet reaches a conclusion as orthodox as those presented in *Patience* and *Cleanness*.

Pearl's difficulty stems from its very sophistication, that is, the multiple facets of the pearl symbol itself and the undefinable relationship between the dreamer and the pearl-maiden. The result is a kaleidoscope of meanings, one moving into focus as another fades, each dependent upon the others for its fullest realization while at the same time appearing to negate them. For example, the depth of the narrator's sorrow seems excessive for a lost gem, but not so for a lost child—until his (and the reader's) perspective expands to include the scheme of birth, death, and heavenly reward expounded by the maiden. As the representation of lost innocence (individual or, through Adam's fall, of the race) or of the human soul itself, the pearl may not be over-valued; but the dreamer's immoderate grief approaches dangerously close to despair, and hence the necessity of the maiden's lecture on Divine Grace. The complexity of the poem increases as the relative positions of dreamer and pearl-maiden change to reflect the shifting symbolism. As child, the maiden uses her own history to expound on the doctrine of the salvation of innocents; as courtly mistress, she embodies the chastity and other virtues which qualify her as a bride of Christ; and as divine teacher, resembling Boethius's Dame Philosophy, she may scold the jeweler for his attachment to earthly values and instruct him in the proper attitude for Christian living. Thus, no linear development of symbol or dreamer-maiden relationship appears in the poem, but rather there is a sphere of translucent layers, each shining through the next with a different shade of meaning.

Underlying all discussion in *Pearl* are the dreamer's dogged but futile attempts to understand the complex position of his pearl. He seems driven to explain logically the apparently contradictory doctrines of salvation through acts versus faith, of the child's innocence versus original sin, of heavenly equality versus hierarchy. But, puny human reason is incapable of understanding the maiden's simple answer to these dilemmas: the Grace of God is in itself sufficient to explain and justify all things. The best that the dreamer, or any human being, can do is humbly to accept that mystery and get on with life as best he can.

With *Sir Gawain and the Green Knight*, the poet moves into the secular arena to challenge its tenets, embodied in the chivalric code, much as the dreamer challenges points of doctrine in *Pearl*. While there remain those who would see this romance as primarily a vegetation myth or an allegory for a clash between Christianity and older fertility religions, most scholars agree that the testing of Gawain's ideals is the crux of the poem. And, as with Church teachings in *Pearl*, the evaluation of chivalry involves an exposure of its apparent contradictions which cannot be satisfactorily resolved.

From the moment that he rides into Arthur's great hall, the Green Knight concerns himself with disproving the ideal court's claim to chivalry. He tests courtesy with his rudeness, courage with his fierce challenge, troth with the commitment to seek him out for a return blow. The real testing, however, arrives when Gawain is expected not merely to uphold one virtue of his creed at a time but to remain true to all of its major components simultaneously.

The chivalric code comprises three major aspects—true knighthood (honor, courage, prowess at arms, *cortaysye*, hospitality), Christian virtue, and courtly love—all of which find ample representation in Gawain's trappings and reputation. The Green Knight's game is devised to bring the three into conflict. In behaving as the ideal courtly lover toward the lady of the castle, Gawain is encouraged to break his troth with his host and thereby also to abuse the hospitality offered him. Granted, he does manage to keep his chastity and conceal the source of the kisses, but these triumphs, while not strictly breaking the rules, do not seem quite honorable even before he conceals the green girdle. Once he hides the girdle, Gawain becomes trapped between two aspects of the code, the more so since he is motivated by his survival instinct rather than the lady's honor, in essence taking advantage of her devotion. His knighthood is further compromised by the lapse in courage itself as well as by the tacit breech of his prom-

ise not to defend himself from the Green Knight's return blow. Lastly, placing his faith in the magic girdle represents a clear betrayal of his Christian faith, symbolized by the icon on the inside of his shield. In the final analysis, no one aspect of the chivalric ideal has been upheld at the expense of another; all are equally betrayed.

At first glance, all of Gawain's troubles stem from the incompatibility, overtly demonstrated or implied, of the various tenets of his behavioral paradigm. Courtly love, with its sensual basis and often illicit consummation, runs counter to a number of Christian virtues. Certainly, too, making love to a friend's wife is a breach of honor and etiquette on all counts. Similarly, the expected pride in one's knightly honor may contradict Christian humility, and so forth. However, nothing in Gawain's testing really made it necessary for him to break his troth to lord, lady, or deity: his fear of death, his attachment to his own mortal state, alone underlies his failures. Thus, despite potential conflicts, the chivalric ideology remains an admirable standard for human behavior, and although even the most perfect of knights cannot fulfill it, his greatest honor lies in the attempt.

The Gawain Poet, then, exhibits an acute awareness of the potential weaknesses in the established ideologies of his class and of the impossibility of adhering to the standards set thereby. Jonah time and again misunderstands God's treatment of sinners; the dreamer of *Pearl* repeatedly misses the maiden's point and attempts the forbidden river crossing; Gawain sacrifices his most sacred principles in an effort to save his skin. The resulting vision would be bleak indeed were it not for the sympathetic humor with which the author treats the plights of his various protagonists and, by extension, the human condition itself.

All four *Pearl*-manuscript poems embody a strong comic strain, but that in *Gawain* differs considerably from the other three. The religious poems generate their humor from the depiction of the protagonist as absurd, attempting to escape the inevitable through childish means (e.g., Jonah hiding from his responsibility) or appearing so impossibly thick-headed that he cannot understand the simplest of lessons (notably the dreamer in *Pearl*). The result is what W.A. Davenport calls the "two voices" of the poems: one serious and reserved, that of the "teacher" figure, whether that be God himself or the pearl-maiden in his stead; the other of the unwilling human pupil who must learn the lesson of obedience, patience, humility, or some other Christian virtue. The use of humor rather than moralistic condemnation of the erring protagonists fulfills a number of functions. First, it suggests that disobedience is not only sinful but contrary to logic, simply not worthy of consideration as a course of action. Second, it implies a positive view of human nature in that it finds well-meaning error more readily than deliberate sin. Finally, and most importantly, it suggests the insignificance of petty worldly concerns and of puny human apprehension in the light of the divine. This last function places the poems securely in a well-established medieval literary subgroup.

The diminishment of the undesirable through its association with the ridiculous is a literary commonplace, but its specific application to support a Boethian vision of the universe and of humanity's place within it had become something of a tradition by the fourteenth century. It dominates such continental works as Petrarch's *My Secret*, in which a slow-witted and hapless persona undergoes instruction by St. Augustine to learn the insignificance of love poetry in comparison to the pursuit of heavenly knowledge.[4] The technique makes its appearance in English shortly later, notably with Geoffrey Chaucer who uses it in *The House of Fame* to illustrate the gulf between Geoffrey's imperfect knowledge and the heavenly eagle's omniscience, and to justify the ironic laughter of the ascended Troilus as he gazes down upon this "litel spot of erthe" at the end of *Troilus and Criseyde*. The silly heroes of certain of the cycle plays, such as the Wakefield *Second Shepherds' Play*, who despite their thick-headedness are capable of finding God's grace through the mystery of faith, are born of the same tradition, itself doubtless related to the older stereotype of the "holy innocent." While the motif never completely disappears from English literature, it suffers a significant decrease in popularity with the displacement of faith by high Renaissance humanism.

In contrast to the Gawain Poet's religious works, the comedy of his romance derives mainly from the French burlesque tradition.[5] True, the protagonist of *Sir Gawain and the Green Knight* is made to appear ridiculous, but his absurd position in the bedroom scene does not stand out against that of any exalted teacher nor does it illuminate a failing on the hero's

part. Instead, the comedy here is of situation, of role reversal between the reticent knight and the amorous lady of Bercilak's castle. Nonetheless, the Gawain Poet adapts the burlesque to his own purposes, and the result is once again the reduction of earthly concerns to the ridiculous in the light of greater Christian truths.

As D.D.R. Owen points out, the character of Gawain had always been suspect in the French romances as one willing to sacrifice principle to amorous interest and one continually defeated by his own uncontrolled libido. However, the Gawain Poet adapts the stereotype to his own purposes. He is not interested in exposing Arthur's nephew as a rake but, in concert with his view in the earlier poems, in reducing him to human status in this imperfect and foolish world. By portraying the courtly love play of Gawain and the lady as an undignified absurdity, the ideal is exposed as a petty, self-interested ploy with no real value in the light of Gawain's (or humanity's) greater purposes. Later, when the Green Knight exposes Gawain's error with the girdle, the hero behaves childishly and churlishly as he blames women for his undoing, appearing (as does Jonah in *Patience*) as the ungracious butt of a joke. Once again, his dignity as a knight is undercut, his aspirations deflated. The final blow comes in Gawain's immoderate remorse. While both Bercilak and Arthur's court are willing to laugh at the insurmountable odds which the protagonist has attempted to overcome, and to recognize his considerable achievement in doing so, Gawain continues to take himself and his ideals much too seriously, attempting to make even his failure overly profound. The poet will not allow him even this, though, for the green baldric becomes a symbol of honor in which the nobility of the goal and the embarrassment of failure are equally immortalized. With it, the poet has not diminished Gawain's heroic status but merely accorded him some human failings. And, only Gawain has missed the point.

All of the Gawain Poet's protagonists, like Gawain himself, stand at the end of their tales with lessons only partly learned, despite an earnest desire to behave in an exemplary fashion. No condemnation attaches itself to those whose natural condition dooms them to positions half-heroic and half-absurd, for as long as humans remain attached to this world of insignificant aspirations and imperfect understanding, they will continue to fail.

Summary

The Gawain Poet's vision, with one eye drawn to Heaven by faith and the other critically fixed on the aspirations and doings of humans on earth, is very much a product of the period in which he lived. On the one hand, it embodies the belief that humans should disassociate themselves with the longings of this world and place their faith in the mystery of God's grace whereby they will find joy in the world to come. On the other, it asserts that their behavior on earth is key to attaining that reward. It accepts the necessity of behavioral standards that may be impossible to meet and which themselves may contain instances of faulty human logic. Rather than face the paradox with despair, the Gawain Poet chose to embrace its absurdity, and he encourages his readers to accept the mysterious condition of humanity by engaging in gentle and good-natured laughter at themselves.

Notes

1. Henry L. Savage's *The Gawain-Poet* (Chapel Hill University of North Carolina Press, 1956) provides the most thorough and convincing attempt at biographical investigation, although based partly on coincidences and not without its weaknesses, suggesting the identification of the seventh Sire de Coucy (also Earl of Bedford), who was married to Edward III's daughter Isabella.

2. Early twentieth-century arguments that the views expressed in *Pearl* were heretical precursors of early Protestantism have since been disproved. Refer to Marie Padgett Hamilton's and John Conley's 1955 essays for summaries.

3. There are differences of opinion on this matter. For example, A.C. Spearing asserts that *Cleanness* preceded *Patience* based on what he perceives as a development in perspective. Much rarer are scholars who assert that *Pearl* and/or *Gawain* preceded the shorter, simpler poems. All of these composition sequences differ from the works' order of presentation in the manuscript.

4. Other works in the tradition include Petrarch's *Ascent of Mount Ventoux* and Boccaccio's last works in Latin.

5. D.D.R. Owen's 1968 article thoroughly explores the connection of Gawain to the burlesque in its French analogues and sources.

Selected Bibliography

Primary Sources

Andrew, Malcolm and Ronald Waldron, eds. *The Poems of the Pearl Manuscript*. Berkeley: University of California Press, 1978. An excellent standard text in Middle English, with minimal normalization.

Gardner, John, trans. *The Complete Works of the Gawain-Poet*. Chicago: University of Chicago Press, 1965. A good standard translation.

Secondary Sources

Brewer, D.S. "Courtesy and the *Gawain-Poet*." In *Patterns of Love and Courtesy*. Ed. John Lawlor. Evanston: Northwestern University Press, 1966, pp. 54–85. Brewer reviews the language and imagery of chivalric courtesy as a means of expressing the central concepts of the poems.

Burrow, J.A. *Ricardian Poetry*. New Haven: Yale University Press, 1971. Burrow places the work of the Gawain Poet in the context of his Ricardian contemporaries.

Conley, John. "*Pearl* and a Lost Tradition." *Journal of English and Germanic Philology*, 54 (1955): 332–47. Rpt. in *The Middle English Pearl: Critical Essays*, ed. John Conley. Notre Dame: University of Notre Dame Press, 1970, pp. 50–72. The *Pearl* is analyzed in terms of Christian consolation.

Davenport, W.A. *The Art of the Gawain Poet*. London: Athlone, 1978. A study of all four poems as tragicomic works juxtaposing the ideal to the real. The most successful study of them as the work of a single poet with a developing style.

Hamilton, Marie Padgett. "The Meaning of the Middle English *Pearl*." *Publications of the Modern Language Association*, 70 (1955): 805–24.

Miller, Miriam Youngerman, and Jane Chance, eds. *Sir Gawain and the Green Knight*. New York: Modern Language Association, 1986. Approaches to Teaching World Literature series.

Moorman, Charles. *The Pearl-Poet*. New York: Twayne, 1968. A good contextual and stylistic analysis, useful for its summary of earlier views.

Owen, D.D.R. "Burlesque Tradition and *Sir*

Gawain and the Green Knight." *Forum for Modern Language Studies*, 4 (1968): 125–45. An examination of the comic roots of *Gawain* in the French romances written in the burlesque mode.

Savage, Henry L. *The Gawain-Poet*. Chapel Hill: University of North Carolina Press, 1956. The most thorough of attempts at reconstructing a biography of the Gawain Poet through his works.

Spearing, A.C. *The Gawain-Poet*. London: Cambridge University Press, 1970. A good general study of the Gawain Poet's style, within the context of alliterative revival, and its development, mainly in the areas of perspective and relative positions of man and supernatural forces.

Wilson, Edward. *The Gawain-Poet*. Leiden: E.J. Brill, 1976. Wilson places the poems in the context of other medieval traditions, such as the cycle plays, courtly love, and so forth.

Gwendolyn Morgan

Gay, John

Born: Barnstaple, Devon, June 30, 1685
Education: Barnstaple Grammar School, possibly between 1695 and 1702.
Died: London, December 4, 1732

Biography

John Gay was born on June 30, 1685, in Barnstaple to parents of established gentility in Devonshire. By 1694 his father, William Gay, and his mother had died, and John was reared by an uncle, Thomas Gay. Educated in the Barnstaple Grammar School, probably from 1695 to the turn of the century, Gay was apprenticed to a silk mercer in London in 1702, but he returned to Barnstaple in 1706. In London the next year he became secretary to schoolboy friend Aaron Hill, already an established author. Gay's first publication, the poem *Wine*, appeared in 1708. Although his pamphlet *The Present State of Wit* received favorable attention in 1711, his farce, *The Mohocks*, was refused by the playhouse in 1712. Gay took a post as domestic steward for his first aristocratic patron, the Duchess of Monmouth. The next year brought greater literary success: publication of the poems "Rural Sports" and "The Fan" and production of a dramatic comedy, *The Wife of Bath*. At the end of 1713 Gay, with

his friends Alexander Pope, Jonathan Swift, John Arbuthnot, and Thomas Parnell, formed the short-lived Scriblerus Club.

After this literary apprenticeship Gay's reputation grew. His popular pastorals, *The Shepherd's Week*, appeared in 1714, when he was also appointed secretary to a diplomatic mission to Hanover, which ended abruptly after Queen Anne's death. In 1715, Gay began to enjoy the patronage of Lord Burlington and wrote *The What D'Ye Call It*, a successful farce. In 1716, his satirical poem *Trivia* was published to critical acclaim. Between the performance of *Three Hours after Marriage* (a comedy co-authored with Pope and Arbuthnot) in 1717 and the publication of *Poems on Several Occasions* (including the tragedy *Dione*) in 1720, Gay made two trips to the continent with wealthier friends. Unfortunately, he invested the large income from subscriptions to his *Poems* in South Sea Company stock which collapsed in the infamous Bubble.

Gay's later years mingled greater literary fame with disappointment. In 1721, he became increasingly friendly with new patrons, the Duke and Duchess of Queensberry, in whose residences he spent more and more time nearer the end of his life. He received a government position as Commissioner of the State Lottery in 1723. His tragedy *The Captives* was produced the next year. Still seeking court preferment, Gay wrote a series of *Fables* for young Prince William. The year after their publication in 1727, he was offered the position of gentleman-usher to Princess Louise, which he declined. In 1728, Gay's masterpiece, *The Beggar's Opera*, was very successful on the stage, with sixty-two performances (a record number at that time), but the Lord Chamberlain refused to permit production of its sequel, *Polly*. Gay's short opera *Acis and Galatea*, with music by George Handel, had its first London performance in 1731.

Gay died in London on December 4, 1732 and was buried in Westminster Abbey near a poet whom he admired greatly, Geoffrey Chaucer.

Literary Analysis

"With native Humour tem'pring virtuous Rage, / Form'd to delight at once and lash the age," wrote Pope of Gay in one couplet of the epitaph for his friend's monument in Westminster Abbey.[1] Gay's "My own Epitaph" (published twelve years before his death) is less solemn and more ironic: "Life is a jest; and all things show it, / I thought so once; but now I know it."[2] Pope's antitheses—humor / rage, delight / lash—are complemented by Gay's single word "jest," which nicely identifies his achievement as the author of burlesque, mock pastoral, mock georgic, fable, farce, comedy, and ballad opera. Gay's own antithesis of thought and knowledge reflects a maturing vision that separates the humorous works written before his tragedies from those written afterward. Although now known primarily as the author of a single play, *The Beggar's Opera*, and as the friend of better-known authors, Pope and Swift, Gay was an important humorist in early Georgian England.

Much of Gay's poetry at the outset of his career explores differing styles for comic effects. In *Wine*, a burlesque in blank verse, he parodies John Milton by using a sublime style for a trivial subject; the poet celebrates the pleasures of the beverage by imitating two popular burlesques by John Philips, *The Splendid Shilling* (1701) and *Cyder* (1708). In *Rural Sports* (1713; revised extensively 1720), Gay uses the iambic pentameter couplets characteristic of most of his longer poems and follows a classical model, Virgil's *Georgics*, in creating a mock pastoral. In *The Fan*, he attempts to fashion a mock epic ridiculing the *beau monde*; in the poem the goddess Venus presents a fan to Strephon, enabling him to win the heart of the vain Corinna through his gift. In these poems Gay experiments with varieties of the mock form that Martin Price calls "the most distinctive contribution of the age" because of the way it "plays off a pure 'view'—heroic, tragic, pastoral—against the befuddling reality from which it makes a sharp selection."[3] The ironic perspectives inherent in these mock forms generate much of the humor in Gay's best poetry and drama.

In *The Shepherd's Week* (1714), a mock pastoral, the poet consolidates these early experiments in six poems intended to parody the supposed realism of Ambrose Philip's *Pastorals* (1709) and, to some extent, the artifice of Virgil's *Eclogues*. The Chaucerian animal imagery of shepherds and shepherdesses so homely named (Lobbin Clout, Cuddy, Marian, Sparabella, Hobnelia, Bumkinet, Grubbinol, and Bowzybeus) presents a humorous world that is suprisingly realistic in its manners and settings, especially in the use of country superstitions and proverbs. The comic incongruity of language and action is nowhere clearer than in "Wednesday," in which Sparabella, lamenting her abandonment by her lover, postpones suicide until a more convenient time. Her "moanful Notes" include these:

> Farewel, ye Woods, ye Meads, ye
>   Streams that flow;
> A sudden Death shall rid me of my Woe.
> This Penknife keen my Windpipe shall
>   divide.—
> What, shall I fall as squeaking Pigs have
>   dy'd!
> No—To some Tree this Carcass I'll sus-
>   pend.—
> But worrying Curs find such untimely
>   End![4]

Sparabella's descent from the opening Virgilian echo to farm imagery typifies Gay's ridicule of the artificiality of pastoral poetry, both ancient and modern. Her search for a death more dignified than penknife or hanging mocks her and her literary antecedents.

Gay's shepherds are antiromantic fictions rather than real laborers or idyllic swains. So, it is easy for Bumkinet and Grubbinol in "Friday" to forget their lengthy lamentations for deceased Blouzelinda when they see the handsome Susan. Nevertheless, this poem captures, in its comic mixture of styles, the more homely kind of dirge that an eighteenth-century shepherd might plausibly compose, if shepherds composed poems:

> Lament, ye Fields, and rueful Symptoms
>   show,
> Henceforth let not the smelling Primrose
>   grow;
> Let Weeds instead of Butter-flow'rs ap-
>   pear,
> And Meads, instead of Daisies, Hemlock
>   bear;
> For Cowslips sweet let Dandelions
>   spread,
> For Blouzelinda, blithesome Maid, is
>   dead!
> Lament ye Swains, and o'er her Grave
>   bemoan,
> And spell ye right this Verse upon her
>   Stone.
> Here Blouzelinda lyes—Alas, alas!
> Weep Shepherds,—and remember Flesh
>   is Grass.[5]

G

No pastoral elegy, this charming pastiche conveys one shepherd's conventional regret. With his English flowers and biblical morality Bumkinet comically transcends parody.

Gay's *Trivia: or, The Art of Walking the Streets of London* is a mock-georgic, a poem of Hogarthian detail dependent on Virgil's depiction of rural life in the *Georgics* to survey the disorder of eighteenth-century urban existence. The term "palimpsest" has been used to describe this poem.[6] In fact, the idea of one work written over another partially erased is very suggestive for Gay's poetry in general. With the example of Swift's city poems also before him, Gay wrote a work of greater scope, in three books, "Of the Implements for walking the Streets, and Signs of the Weather," "Of Walking the Streets by Day," and "Of Walking the Streets by Night." Although there is no unified action, the "art" of the poem is humorously presented through vignettes of place or character within London. For example, the walker is warned to avoid chimney-sweeper, dust-man, chandler, and butcher by day and pick-pocket, ballad-singer, whore, watchman, and rake by night. He is taught to know the day of the week by detecting the smells of tradesmen. He is alerted to the daytime dangers of Watling Street or the evening perils of the Strand. Though *Trivia* includes the reminder that "Pride corrupts the lavish Age,"[7] Gay's satire proceeds through the anatomy of daily incongruities of London life.

Gay evoked Virgil in another group of humorous eclogues collected in *Poems on Several Occasions.* Several of these he called town eclogues—"The Toilette," "The Tea-Table," and "The Funeral"—poems written to ridicule the affectations of upper-class London women. Like *The Fan*, they re-create the world also found in Pope's satires of women. "The Espousal," on the other hand, is a "sober" eclogue that mocks the supposed piety of Quaker lovers betrayed by their flesh. The best of the eclogues is a true country poem, "The Birth of the Squire," an imitation of Virgil's "Pollio" that takes an ironic view of an heir destined to a life of recreation—hunting and drinking—rather than to re-creating a Golden Age.

Gay's most popular poems during his lifetime were the *Fables*, a collection of fifty poems in tetrameter couplets which were written for and dedicated to four-year-old Prince William near the end of Gay's pursuit of preferment. These poems were so successful that Gay began

a second series before his death; those sixteen fables were published posthumously in 1738. An ancient form given new prestige by the French poet Jean de La Fontaine in the late seventeenth century, the fable proved an apt vehicle for Gay's ridicule of human folly. Not only did the mostly animal or inanimate characters allow Gay comic distance to ridicule general human traits such as ambition, hypocrisy, and greed, but this perspective also enabled him to satirize the Court which had ignored him for many years, all under the guise of gentle instruction for the young prince.

While many of the *Fables* have a charm suitable for their dedicatee, others have more bite. For example, in "The Elephant and the Bookseller" a sneering animal tells his human auditor that the spaniel and the fox still have much to learn in servility or cunning from human beings and offers this viewpoint: "But is not man to man a prey / Beasts kill for hunger, men for pay."[8] As in another work of Gay's maturity, *The Beggar's Opera*, the image of man as predator is a repeated one in the *Fables*. The main character in "The Monkey who had seen the World" returns to his native habitat with lessons that lead his species to increased mischief as a result of imitating human manners. A pheasant in "The Philosopher and the Pheasants" judges human ingratitude peculiar to this worst of animals which is less trustworthy than hawk or vulture. The most famous of the *Fables*, the autobiographical "The Hare and many Friends," takes a final disillusioned look at nominal friendship in public places.

In addition to his satiric and narrative poetry, Gay wrote a dozen mostly humorous plays. These include four farces, two comedies, and three ballad operas, as well as two tragedies and a short pastoral opera. His initial two plays are not notable. Gay called the first *The Mohocks* (1712), a "Tragi-Comical Farce." An experiment in mingling dramatic forms, this brief, topical play presents a comic confrontation between street bullies called Mohocks, swaggering in blank verse, and a Shakespearean group of watchmen, easily intimidated by them. Gay's second play, *The Wife of Bath* (1713; revised extensively in 1730), is a five-act prose comedy of sexual intrigue employing several characters from Chaucer's *The Canterbury Tales*, including the Wife of the title and Chaucer as the play's protagonist. A Franklin wishes his daughter to marry the poet Doggrell, although she loves Merit. Chaucer courts

Myrtilla, also pursued by Doggrell, who is tricked into bed with the Wife and into marriage with a servant.

More indicative of Gay's developing talent than these plays are two farces, *The What D'Ye Call It* (1715) and *Three Hours after Marriage* (1717). In the first, a two-act play, Gay experimented with a mixture of genres that he called "a Tragi-Comi-Pastoral Farce." A parody of seventeenth- and early eighteenth-century tragedy, *The What D'Ye Call It* includes a framing action to present a holiday play at Sir Roger's country house, a play used by the steward to trick Squire Thomas into marrying the woman whom he has seduced, the steward's daughter Kitty. In this play-within-the-play, written in pentameter couplets, these young lovers act out characters about to be separated by his military service. Their sentimental parting in act 1 is followed by ghosts accusing several justices of injustice. In act 2, Peascod, a deserter about to be hanged, is reunited with his daughter and receives a last-minute reprieve, while the distracted Kitty contemplates suicide and sings a melancholy ballad before her reunion with Thomas. As in other parodies of high forms of literature, Gay exposes the inadequacy of tragedy to represent the experience of ordinary characters.

While *The What D'Ye Call It* shows the influence of the Scriblerus Club's learned wit, *Three Hours after Marriage* is a collaboration of Gay with Pope and Arbuthnot, though exact contributions are uncertain. In this three-act prose comedy the eccentric Fossile, an aging antiquarian (satirically modeled after a well-known contemporary), marries a young wife whom two rakes plot to seduce, even disguising themselves as an alligator and a mummy to gain entrance into her house. In addition to this farcical cuckoldry plot, there is a satiric subplot involving Fossile's literary niece, an aspiring tragic dramatist. All of the main characters—the virtuoso, the town lady, the rakes, the female author, and the critic—are ridiculed.

Gay wrote no more comic dramas for a decade, concentrating instead on other kinds of plays, *Acis and Galatea* (a brief pastoral opera written about 1718, though not performed in London until 1731), *Dione* (a five-act pastoral tragedy in pentameter couplets published in 1720), and *The Captives* (a five-act tragedy in blank verse which was performed in 1724). When he returned to playwriting after publication of the *Fables*, Gay created a new comic

genre, the ballad opera, and wrote three plays of this type, each in three acts. The first, *The Beggar's Opera*, was so successful and controversial that its much anticipated sequel, *Polly* (published in 1729), was banned by the government. At the time of his death Gay had completed a third ballad opera, *Achilles*, which was mounted the following year, in 1733. However, two other plays, *The Distress'd Wife* (a five-act prose comedy staged in 1734), and *The Rehearsal at Goatham* (a brief farce published in 1754), show that Gay turned to other forms at the end of his life.

The best of all of his plays, *The Beggar's Opera* parodies Italian opera, English tragedy, and sentimental comedy as it satirizes the moral disorder resulting from human self interest and politicians who take advantage of that vice. The play's theatrical parody takes several forms. To begin with, the author gives voice to lower-class characters—highwaymen and prostitutes, fences and prison keepers—in a contemporary urban setting. Since these characters are hypocrites, their songs of love and honor create a mock-heroic effect. The play also parodies opera through the kind of music that these characters sing, airs based on popular melodies, many taken from Thomas D'Urfey's collection *Wit and Mirth: or, Pills to Purge Melancholy*. For example, Gay transforms conventional operatic images of flowers into an ironic song about feminine virtue bought and sold in Covent Garden (Air VI); but his juxtaposition of charming melodies with sordid content often provides humor to temper his satiric tone. Moreover, in *The Beggar's Opera* he ridicules tragedy through the heroic posturing of its protagonist, the highwayman Macheath, and ironic allusions to tragic plays, such as John Dryden's *All for Love*. (In the last act Macheath finds himself masquerading as Dryden's Antony, torn between devotion to his versions of Cleopatra and Octavia.) Finally, Gay satirizes the sentimental comedy of Richard Steele and other contemporaries by undermining its optimistic assumptions about human nature and middle-class virtue.

The fence Peachum and his wife, incarnations of self-interest in the guise of tradesmen's values, dominate act 1. "Through all the Employments of Life / Each Neighbour abuses his Brother," sings Peachum in the play's first air, as he asserts that his "Employment" is as honest as any man's.[9] Mrs. Peachum, outraged at her daughter's marriage, expresses this complaint in mockery of middle-class expectations: "If she had had only an Intrigue with the Fellow, why the very best Families have excus'd and huddled up a Frailty of that Sort. 'Tis Marriage, Husband, that makes it a Blemish."[10] Both of the elder Peachums effectively incarnate the play's satire: the value system that operates at this low level of Georgian society operates at all levels. This position is rationalized by another of the play's tradesmen, Lockit the keeper of Newgate Prison, in terms of human nature: "Of all Animals of Prey, Man is the only sociable one."[11] Unfortunately for these tradesmen, their daughters are in love with the play's gentleman, Macheath, who mimics the pleasures of the aristocracy along with other highwaymen and their ladies (actually prostitutes), a set of characters prominent in act 2. The mock-tragic rivalry of Polly Peachum and Lucy Lockit over the imprisoned Macheath, who is disillusioned by his gang's betrayal, intensifies in the Newgate scenes of act 3 until, finally, the beggar satisfies popular taste by granting the condemned highwayman a reprieve.

The "similitude of Manners in high and low Life,"[12] as the Beggar calls his method, has another purpose. Through these characters Gay satirizes the politics of the Court, especially the corrupting leadership of the prime minister, Robert Walpole, who is ridiculed both in the figure of the scheming Peachum, who is interested only in his own profit and survival, and in the self-aggrandizing Macheath. Macheath himself ridicules the corruption emanating from the top of society in a song that evokes the play's complex ironies:

The Modes of the Court so common are
    grown
That a true Friend can hardly be met;
Friendship for Interest is but a Loan,
Which they let out for what they can
    get.[13]

His confident invective is undercut when Macheath discovers that the values of his part of the underclass have also been spoiled by the prevalence of interest; the gentlemen of the road are not better, or worse, than the gentlemen of the court. Such irony, which erases social and political difference, also keeps Gay's play from despair. In this scene Macheath postures and sings to the popular satirical melody of "Lillibullero." His song is one of many in a parody of Italian opera and other dramatic forms. The elaborate artifice provides the distance necessary for laughter in *The Beggar's Opera*. Like Swift's *Gulliver's Travels* (1726), Gay's satire functions on several levels, employing the mock form for literary, political, and moral purposes, all to unsettle the audience's complacency about human life and contemporary society.

Polly Peachum, the heroine of *The Beggar's Opera*, is either a romantic fool or a character of some integrity. She interested Gay enough that he made her the title character of the sequel, *Polly*, in which she pursues the transported Macheath to the West Indies. However, act 1 of this play focuses on the wealthy Ducat, who attempts to make Polly his mistress, and his fashionable wife in a satire of marriage. When Polly escapes disguised as a boy, she encounters both pirates and Indians in act 2. The pirates are captained by Macheath, disguised as the black Morano, again torn in mock-heroic fashion between love and honor. The Indians are noble savages whose virtue contrasts with self-interested Europeans whose vices are now exposed as custom rather than nature. In act 3, after Polly frees a captured Indian Prince, she discovers Macheath's disguise at the moment of his execution and recognizes her attraction to the prince.

Each of Gay's three other comic plays turns to new material. *Achilles*, his last ballad opera, puts the Greek hero in the disguise of a young woman because his mother, the goddess Thetis, wants to keep him out of the Trojan war. The plot is both a burlesque and a modernization of its mythical subject. As in *Polly*, the young "woman" becomes a source of comic conflict— in this case between King Lycomedes and his jealous wife, who plans for "her" to marry a warrior. While Achilles resists these claims, he is soon torn in a familiar mock-heroic conflict between his love for Deidamia and the honor demanded by his fellow Greeks. Through this farcical action Achilles functions as a satire of marriage and courtiers. *The Distress'd Wife*, on the other hand, is Gay's one comedy of manners written in the style of the preceding age. In the play Sir Thomas Willit, a country gentleman, finds himself and his wife in financial ruin because of her extravagantly fashionable life, and he compels her to return to the country. Sir Thomas acts with the aid of the merchant Barter, a figure superior to the corrupt ladies and gentlemen of the court. *The Rehearsal at Goatham* (which adapts an episode from

Miguel de Cervantes' *Don Quixote* in light of Gay's own recent experience) ridicules the gentlemen of a town's corporation when they suppress a puppet show out of fear that it may satirize them. As a character rehearses the puppet play for them, these gentlemen expose the sins that they use their power to conceal. The puppet master's final words are a fitting end to Gay's career as a dramatist: "The Drift of Plays, by *Aristotle's* Rules, / Is, what you've seen— Exposing Knaves and Fools."[14]

Summary

As a poet and dramatist, John Gay both exploits the double perspectives of irony and experiments with form. In his best early poems, the mock pastoral *The Shepherd's Week* and the mock georgic *Trivia*, Gay mingles high form and low subject matter to represent the satiric reality of rural and urban existence, respectively. In his best later poems, the first series of *Fables*, he uses a more traditional genre to anatomize foolish and predatory qualities in human society. Gay also experiments with form for comic effect in his early plays. In the most notable of these, a farce entitled *The What D'Ye Call It*, he parodies tragedy in representing the more ordinary loves of his characters. Gay's most original achievement was the invention of a new kind of drama, the ballad opera, as a vehicle for parody and satire. In *The Beggar's Opera*, his masterpiece, he presents the world of criminals to ridicule the self interest pervasive in Georgian society. In the midst of the gaiety of the play's songs its predators appear— the mercenary fence Peachum and the amorous highwayman Macheath. The increased moral seriousness of Gay's later plays is also reflected in his other ballad operas, *Polly* and *Achilles*, and his comedy of manners, *The Distress'd Wife*. As his friend Pope remarked in his epitaph, Gay used humor to satirize the age in which he lived.

Notes

1. *The Poems of Alexander Pope: A Reduced Version of the Twickenham Text*, ed. John Butt (New Haven: Yale University Press, 1963), p. 818.
2. *John Gay: Poetry and Prose*, ed. Vinton A. Dearing with the assistance of Charles E. Beckwith (Oxford: Clarendon, 1974), Vol. 1, p. 253.
3. Martin Price, *To the Palace of Wisdom: Studies in Order and Energy from Dryden to Blake*. (New York: Doubleday, 1964), p. 250.
4. *Gay: Poetry and Prose*, Vol. 1, p. 108.
5. *Ibid.*, p. 116.
6. Arthur Sherbo, "Virgil, Dryden, Gay, and Matters Trivial," *PMLA*, 85 (1970): 1063.
7. *Gay: Poetry and Prose*, Vol. 1, p. 138.
8. *Gay: Poetry and Prose*, Vol. 2, p. 315.
9. *John Gay: Dramatic Works*, ed. John Fuller (Oxford: Clarendon 1983), Vol. 2, p. 4.
10. *John Gay: Dramatic Works*, Vol. 2, p. 16.
11. *Ibid.*, p. 46.
12. *Ibid.*, p. 64.
13. *Ibid.*, p. 48.
14. *Ibid.*, p. 371.

Selected Bibliography

Primary Sources

Drama

The Mohocks. A Tragi-Comical Farce. London: Bernard Lintot, 1712.

The Wife of Bath. A Comedy. London: Bernard Lintot, 1713.

The What D'Ye Call It: A Tragi-Comi-Pastoral Farce. London: Bernard Lintot, 1715.

Three Hours After Marriage. A Comedy. London: Bernard Lintot, 1717. Co-authored with Alexander Pope and John Arbuthnot.

The Captives. A Tragedy. London: Jacob Tonson, 1724.

The Beggar's Opera. London: John Watts, 1728.

Polly: An Opera. London: Printed for the Author, 1729.

Acis and Galatea: An English Pastoral Opera. London: John Watts, 1731.

Achilles. An Opera. London: John Watts, 1733.

The Distress'd Wife. A Comedy. London: Thomas Astley, 1743.

The Rehearsal at Goatham. London: Thomas Astley, 1754.

Poetry

Wine. A Poem. London: William Keble, 1708.

Rural Sports. A Poem. London: Jacob Tonson, 1713.

The Fan. A Poem. London: Jacob Tonson, 1714.

The Shepherd's Week. In Six Pastorals. London: Ferd. Burleigh, 1714.

Trivia: or, The Art of Walking the Streets of London. London: Bernard Lintot, 1716.

Poems on Several Occasions. London: Jacob Tonson; Bernard Lintot, 1720.

Fables. London: Jacob Tonson; John Watts, 1727.

Fables. By the Late Mr. Gay. Volume the Second. London: J. & P. Knapton; T. Cox, 1738.

Modern Editions

Burgess, C.F., ed. *The Letters of John Gay.* Oxford: Clarendon, 1966. Annotated edition of eighty-one letters.

Dearing, Vinton A., ed. with assistance of Charles E. Beckwith. *John Gay: Poetry and Prose.* Oxford: Clarendon, 1974. 2 vols. Standard edition of Gay's twelve plays with thorough annotations and a detailed introduction.

Secondary Sources

Biographies

Irving, William Henry. *John Gay: A Favorite of the Wits.* Durham: Duke University Press, 1940. The best account of Gay's life and literary background.

Books

Armens, Sven M. *John Gay: Social Critic.* New York: King's Crown Press, 1954. Argument for a moral seriousness in Gay's work generated by the contrast of rural and urban perspectives.

Calhoun, Winton. *John Gay and the London Theatre.* Lexington: University Press of Kentucky, 1993. A study of Gay's career as a dramatic author in relation to the London stage between 1705 and 1733.

Forsgren, Adina. *John Gay, Poet "of a Lower Order."* Stockholm: Natur och Kultur, 1964–1971. 2 vols. An analysis of Gay's achievement in "lower" forms, rural poems (Vol. 1) and urban and narrative poetry (Vol. 2).

Spacks, Patricia Meyer. *John Gay.* New York: Twayne, 1965. A survey of Gay's works with attention to their personae and complexity.

Articles and Chapters in Books

Battestin, Martin C. "Gay: The Meanings of Art and Artifice." *The Providence of Wit: Aspects of Form in Augustan Literature and the Arts.* Oxford: Clarendon, 1974, pp. 119–140. Discussion of Gay's affirmation of art and the metamorphosis of nature in his poetry.

Bronson, Bertrand. *"The Beggar's Opera." Studies in the Comic.* University of California Publications in English, Vol. 8, No. 2, 1941, pp. 197–231. Analysis of thematic and musical contexts.

Donaldson, Ian. "'A Double Capacity': *The Beggar's Opera." The World Upside-Down: Comedy from Jonson to Fielding.* Oxford: Clarendon, 1970, pp. 159–182. Analysis of Gay's comic leveling, disclosure of human interchangeability.

Empson, William. *"The Beggar's Opera:* Mock-Pastoral as the Cult of Independence." *Some Versions of Pastoral.* London: Chatto & Windus, 1935, pp. 195–250. Discussion of the play's irony and deflection of the heroic and the pastoral.

Erskine-Hill, Howard. "The Significance of Gay's Drama." In *English Drama: Forms and Development. Essays in Honour of Muriel Clara Bradbrook.* Ed. Marie Axton and Raymond Williams. Cambridge: Cambridge University Press, 1977, pp. 142–163. Discussion of Gay's restless experimenting with forms, idioms and subjects.

Gale, Steven H. "The Function of 'Air #1' in John Gay's *The Beggar's Opera." English Dance and Song,* 44, 2 (1979): 11.

James E. Evans

Gibbons, Stella Dorothea

Born: London, England, January 5, 1902
Education: North London Collegiate School, 1915–1921; University College, London, 1921–1923
Marriage: Allan Bourne Webb, April 1, 1933; one child
Died: London, December 19, 1989

Biography

Novelist and poet Stella Gibbons was born in London on January 5, 1902, the daughter of Telford Charles Gibbons, a physician in a poor section of the city, and Maud Williams Gibbons. Stella was tutored by governesses until she was thirteen; she entered North London Collegiate School for Girls in 1915 and then took the two-year journalism course at University College, University of London (1921–1923). After World War I she began her writing career as a cable decoder for British United Press. She worked as a journalist, most notably for the London *Evening Standard*, between 1920 and 1930. In 1930, she published her first book of poems, *The Mountain Beast*, and embarked upon a successful literary career which stretched to 1970 when, as she says, she retired as a novelist. She also contributed pieces to *Punch*, the *Tatler*, and other British periodicals.

Gibbons married Allan Bourne Webb, an actor and operatic baritone, on April 1, 1933; the couple had one daughter. In 1950, Gibbons was elected a Fellow of the Royal Society of Literature. Webb died in 1959, and Gibbons died in London on December 19, 1989.

Literary Analysis

Gibbons's primary reputation as a humorist comes from her early novel *Cold Comfort Farm*. Called by Marya Mannes "one of the most brilliantly funny books ever written,"[1] it has been a minor cult classic since its publication in 1932. It is the story of orphaned Flora Poste's six-month stay with her Starkadder relatives in the gloomiest imaginable reincarnation of a Sussex peasant farmhouse dating back to a swineshed of Edward the Sixth. Perhaps, she thinks, "one or two of the relations will have messes or miseries in their domestic circle which I can clear up."[2]

Cold Comfort Farm is one of the best specimens in the English language of parodic satire. Flora tidies up the remarkably untidy lives of her cousins in a deliciously vicious parody of the romance novel of the 1930s. Brooding, sensual Seth, who is loved by girls but who loves only the Talkies, is lured to Hollywood by Flora's producer friend who is looking for a new Clark Gable. Flora transforms artsy Elfine into an elegant young woman who prates of Marie Laurencin and marries the neighborhood squire. Urk, who marked Elfine for his own with a cross of water-vole blood on her nursing-bottle, takes second-best hired girl Meriam, who has been pregnant every summer since puberty, and becomes a doting daddy to her babies. Flora convinces patriarch Amos to take his hell-fire preaching on the road in a Ford van, thus clearing the way for Reuben, the only sensible Starkadder, to begin buying fertilizers and plows with the egg money that he has se-

cretly withheld from Aunt Ada. Melancholy Cousin Judith, Amos's wife, transfers her gloom to Flora's psychiatrist friend, who shifts the transference to a love of old cathedrals. Most delightfully, Aunt Ada, who has ruled the family ruthlessly because she saw something nasty in the woodshed as a child and now refuses to allow anyone to leave the farm, succumbs to Flora's blandishments and flies away to Paris in a new leather trousers suit from *Vogue*, leaving the remaining sons free to bring their clandestinely acquired wives to live in the farmhouse. In the end Flora falls in love with her cousin Charles and literally flies off into the sunset with him.

In addition to the obvious satire on the British pastoral novel of the turn of the century and on the ponderous gloominess of Lawrencian virility, Gibbons pokes gentle fun at literary pretension by transforming Heathcliffish Urk into a paterfamilias and literary critic Mr. Mybug into an anachronistic advocate of the Branwell-Brontë-wrote-all-of-his-sisters'-novels school. The 1930s delight in Victorian novels is undercut by Flora's observation that they were the only books that one could read while eating an apple. Gibbons even marks "the finer passages" with asterisks in the style of Baedecker guides as she laughs at herself.

Charming as this is, if there were nothing more, *Cold Comfort Farm* would be forgotten today. Its lasting appeal to Anglophiles lies in its use of satire to develop a clear-eyed analysis of British nature as it is projected into an envisionable future. (Few readers today realize that the novel is set in the future, complete with picture-phones and other as yet uninvented devices.) Flora is a paragon of cheerful British common sense, and her managing nature creates order in the world of the future as the British Empire did in the world of the past. After she has invaded and civilized them, "life at the farm-house was much pleasanter for the Starkadders than it had ever been before; and they had Flora to thank for it" (199). At Elfine's wedding reception, they reached the height of civilization by having a "nice time . . . in an ordinary human manner. Not having it because they were raping somebody, or beating somebody, or having religious mania or being doomed to silence by a gloomy, earthly pride, or loving the soil with the fierce desire of a lecher, or anything of that sort . . . She had accomplished a great work" (217). Yet even this blessed normality is undercut by Flora's vision of what it would have been like had Aunt Ada not relented but instead descended on the wedding party "in her usual clothes and with her usual manner, and tried to stop the wedding, and . . . been defied by the Starkadders in a body. That *would* have been worth seeing" (221). This whisper of discontent with the beatitude of civilized life is repeated when Flora asks to be taken home, saying "there's nothing left for me to do here" (228). The work is valuable, but savagery too has its joys, not the least of which is the providing of new continents to civilize.

This vague unrest leads to Gibbons's only other "Cold Comfort" novel, *Conference at Cold Comfort Farm* (1949). Flora, married sixteen years to the Rev. Charles Fairford and the mother of five, goes to *Cold Comfort Farm* to help Mr. Mybug coordinate a conference of the International Thinkers' Group and ends up reuniting the Starkadder men whom Gibbons sent off to South Africa in the interregnum. The Farm has been redone, with every room labeled in pseudo-Middle-English (Lytle Stille-Roome, Greate Scullerie) and the farm implements shined and hung as decorations. Graceless, Feckless, and Aimless, the cows who lost horns and hoofs and legs in *Cold Comfort Farm*, are gone. Toby jugs, peasant pottery, window-seats, and other figments of the imagination of those nostalgic for farm life have made the farm into a historic site "exactly like being locked in the Victoria and Albert Museum after closing time" (46).

Into this museum Gibbons places the leading thinkers of post-war Europe. The delegates draw up a Bill of Human Rights, which one ancient delegate actually believes in, "suffering from the delusion that the promulgation would have practical results" (54). The art exhibit draws wails from the Starkadder females—it is not the pictures themselves but "th' poor souls as made 'em as we be weepin' for . . . Fancy wantin' to make sich things, Miss Poste! . . . Yon things must ha' taken weeks to fashion! Th' poor souls as made 'em must ha' had to look at 'em all that long time! Fair breaks me heart to think o't!" (81). Modern music is satirized by Bob Flatte's latest opera, *The Flayed*, which portrays a tanner torn between passion for his craft and for his girl. The grotesquely Freudian relationship between the tanner and his hides climaxes with an aria sung by his mother "in which she confesses that Stan is the illegitimate son of a taxidermist who seduced her in early youth, thus accounting for her son's sadistic obsession; Stan symbolically attempts to skin her and they both become insane. The opera then ends. It was to represent English music at the International Music Festival in the following year" (105).

Philosophy and asceticism are satirized in the form of the Sage, who walks everywhere and is intent upon resisting the lure of Monkey, which animates machinery and guides all human strivings and plottings. The hypocrisy of asceticism is revealed when the Sage refuses to decide not to partake of what the conferees offer him and thus ends up enjoying Monkey's food and pleasures while retaining his own purity. The conference attendees, meanwhile, take revenge on his superiority by asking him to tell their fortunes. The upper class takes its lumps in the form of a depressed girl chauffeur, the daughter of an impoverished Lord, who, in order to earn money, has gone to school to learn a Cockney accent and acquire tackiness. She considers herself fortunate to have made the move toward downward mobility, which spells success in the form of employment. Gibbons even satirizes her own humor in the form of a novel apparently about a camel but in fact an allegory of "Man's" relation to the universe.

After such a display of the frailty and fatuity of human nature, Gibbons is able to reevaluate the British orderliness that she postulated fifteen years earlier. The farm has become a caricature of itself and can only be saved by a reinstitution of Starkadderness. The seven remaining Starkadder cousins and brothers are lured home and at once set about destroying the Victoria-and-Albert retreat and returning the farm to the original fen-like state that Flora had found it in. The perfection which concluded *Cold Comfort Farm* cannot be maintained; civilization must lose the battle between order and chaos for only then is there room for the talents of the Flora Postes (and the Britains) of the world. Non-Britishness must exist, even thrive, in order for Britishness to assert itself eternally. It would be unreasonable and romantic to expect that the Starkadders would value, or even want, cleanliness or decor. The chaos which their nature entails cannot tolerate the sort of superficial niceness which preservation demands. And, as that niceness has been shown to be a veneer as antihuman as the other artifacts of British culture, the reinstatement of Starkadder humanity, depraved though it may be, is the only possible answer to the conferees that Gibbons has so roundly satirized and dismissed. Finally, all this works because Gibbons uses humor to undercut the pretensions which underlie social "principle."

Gibbons wrote only one other novel that is "funny" in the same way as the Cold Comfort novels. *Ticky* (1943) is darker than the Farm novels, counterbalancing human needs for control and autonomy. Control is represented by the nineteenth-century British army, whose officers live in luxury and whose rules give those officers the illusion of both physical and mental control over the "waiters," servants who diligently eke out freedom between the inevitable cracks in the rules. The novel's plot grows out of the Colonel's desire to appropriate the waiters' Pleasure Ground, a muddy acre deeded to the waiters by means of a Charter. Since the Charter can no longer be located, the Colonel prepares his unwilling troops to invade and occupy the Pleasure Ground. At the last moment the Charter is found—serving as a dishcloth. The balance of power between upper-class control through ownership and working-class freedom through autonomy is uneasily restored, but the issue remains unsettled, and perhaps, for Gibbons, unsettleable. Both the nineteenth-century setting and the militaristic framework imbue the book with a closed-ended determinism which at best can be used to ridicule pomposity and smile warmly on the simplicity of human feelings. But, the simple people literally retire to rose-covered cottages at the end while the Colonel returns to his attempts to find a way around the Charter.

In her other early novels the author employs a far gentler humor. While *Miss Linsey and Pa* (1936) skewers, in passing, butch lesbianism and the artsy downward mobility of the young intelligentsia, its charm resides in its loving treatment of a slightly silly and anachronistic old maid trying to survive in contemporary London. We chuckle over the naivete of Miss Linsey's cousin Len because he truly believes that he can find the girl he left behind in France two decades ago, and even over the impotent rage of Dorothy Hoad when her tantrums fail to convince Edna Lassiter to stay with her. *Bassett* (1934) shows the cooperative union of an impoverished and flighty aristocrat and a doughty pattern-cutter fired from her job as the two create a new life as boarding-house owners. Gibbons has a humorist's vision which sees both the sad realities and the golden hopes of ordinary people, and we learn as we laugh at them that we must, as she does, also appreciate their kind souls.

As a humorist, Gibbons is mistress of the exact word or description. Many of her characters are likened to animals: "He looked like a saucy but well-meaning adolescent chicken."[3] Nature is often anthropomorphized: "the iron table [was] set in the scanty shade of a discouraged birch."[4] Ordinary language undergoes comic scrutiny: of the phrase "little baby," Nancy Leland in *The Wolves Were in the Sledge* says, "why do people call them little, by the way? They always are, and surely it could be taken for granted by now?" (102); and "undies" is "a word which ought, were proper control exercised in such matters, to be publicly banned by the BBC, the Bishops and the senior Universities and the use of it forbidden on pain of the instant liquidation of the user."[5] She captures the sitcom tone of youth: "I often think it must be nice to be elderly and frivolous. Such small things seem to excite them."[6]

Relations between the sexes is for Gibbons a constant source of humor. She believes firmly in a woman's place—and approves of it: "Frenchwomen . . . are much more free to be proper women—afraid of loud bangs, and ready to forgive people, and that kind of thing,"[7] or "Men! Why need there be any? . . . of course, you had to have them for other things, like looking at bodies when people were murdered, but if there weren't any men probably no one would get murdered."[8]

These gently humorous ways of viewing language and life permeate all of Gibbons's novels. Her humor is both more savage and more outrageous in the early books, up until about 1940. After the war, however, her stories are more serious explorations of human nature, sympathetic rather than skewering. In her three novels dealing with World War II, *White Sand and Grey Sand* (1958), *The Bachelor* (1944), and *The Matchmaker* (1949), she shows directly the effects of the war on the lives of working-class people living through bombings, exile, separations, and uncertainty. These books are much underrated as a necessary supplement to historical accounts. Young love is the topic of several novels (*My American* [1939], *Westwood* [1946], *Here Be Dragons* [1956], *The Weather at Tregulla* [1962], *The Wolves Were in the Sledge* [1964]). Her heroines long for romance but rarely find it. When they do, it comes in unexpected forms, as in *The Wolves Were in the*

Sledge, in which Nancy Leland, whose only concern is to live well and have pretty clothes, finds herself and her adored husband passionately involved in the education of orphans. The failure of romance often leads to a clear-eyed, if chastened, view of self, as in Margaret Steggles's disillusionment with the self-centered romanticism of the Challis family in *Westwood* or Nell Sely's eventual disenchantment with her dissolute, demanding cousin John in *Here Be Dragons*. The women who *do* find romance are invariably ecstatic—novelist Amy Lee in *My American*, or Edna Lassiter in *Miss Linsey and Pa*—perhaps in imitation of Gibbons's own very happy marriage.

A final strand in Gibbons's literary work is the occult. *Starlight* (1967) begins with a sympathetic portrait of elderly London slum residents and ends with a startling exorcism. In *The Shadow of a Sorcerer* (1955), the eerily charming hero might be the devil himself. Amy Lee in *My American* (1939) has premonitory visions, and in *The Charmers* a man who died in World War II is heard playing the piano in the parlor. In all cases, Gibbons makes the supernatural appear as ordinary as satire did in *Cold Comfort Farm*. We have only ourselves to fear.

Summary

Despite the variety of her topics and protagonists, Gibbons is not a "problem" novelist and does not move far from the lives of inarticulate working-class people, sincere and unsophisticated and *nice*, whose voices we have not heard before. She has a rare ability to enter into the feelings of the uncommunicative and to bring to life the emotions of the unremarkable. Her comic genius has been recognized in the timeless popularity of *Cold Comfort Farm*, which won the Femina Vie Heureuse Prize for 1933 and is still in print. In 1968, it was serialized by BBC2, and in 1971 Masterpiece Theatre televised it in a production which won raves from New York critics. The novel has also been translated into French. *Here Be Dragons*, *The Matchmaker*, and *The Weather at Tregulla* were reprinted by White Lion in 1972, and *Ticky* was reissued in 1984 as part of Sutton's "Classics of Humor" series. Gibbons's death in 1989 warranted obituaries in the *New York Times*, the *London Times*, and the *Los Angeles Times*.

Notes

1. Marya Mannes, "What *Did* Aunt Ada See?" *New York Times* (December 26, 1971): sec. II, 19:1.
2. Stella Gibbons, *Cold Comfort Farm* (London: Longmans, Green, 1932), p. 21.
3. Gibbons, *Here Be Dragons* (London: Hodder and Stoughton, 1956), p. 301.
4. Gibbons, *The Weather at Tregulla* (London: Hodder and Stoughton, 1962), p. 65.
5. Gibbons, *My American* (London: Longmans, Green, 1939), p. 183.
6. Gibbons, *The Wolves Were in the Sledge* (London: Hodder and Stoughton, 1964), p. 187.
7. *Ibid.*, p. 79.
8. Gibbons, *The Charmers* (London: Hodder and Stoughton, 1965), p. 206.

Selected Bibliography

Primary Sources

The Mountain Beast (poetry). London: Longmans, Green, 1930.
Cold Comfort Farm. London: Longmans, Green, 1932; New York: Penguin, 1977.
Bassett. London: Longmans, Green, 1934.
The Priestess (poetry). London: Longmans, Green, 1934.
The Untidy Gnome (children's book). London: Longmans, Green, 1935.
Enbury Heath. London: Longmans, Green, 1935.
Miss Linsey and Pa. London: Longmans, Green, 1936.
The Roaring Tower (stories). London: Longmans, Green, 1937.
Nightingale Wood. London: Longmans, Green, 1938.
The Lowland Venus (poetry). London: Longmans, Green, 1938.
My American. London: Longmans, Green, 1939.
Christmas at Cold Comfort Farm (stories). London: Longmans, Green, 1939.
The Rich House. London: Longmans, Green, 1941.
Ticky. London and New York: Longmans, Green, 1943; London: Sutton, 1984.
The Bachelor. London: Longmans, Green, 1944.
Westwood, or The Gentle Powers. London: Longmans, Green, 1946.
Conference at Cold Comfort Farm. London: Longmans, Green, 1949.
The Matchmaker. London: Longmans, Green, 1949; London: White Lion, 1972.

Collected Poems. London: Longmans, Green, 1950.

The Swiss Summer. London: Longmans, Green, 1951.

Fort of the Bear. London: Longmans, Green, 1953.

Beside the Pearly Waters (stories). London: Peter Nevill, 1954.

The Shadow of a Sorcerer. London: Hodder and Stoughton, 1955.

Here Be Dragons. London: Hodder and Stoughton, 1956; London: White Lion, 1972.

White Sand and Grey Sand. London: Hodder and Stoughton, 1958.

A Pink Front Door. London: Hodder and Stoughton, 1959.

The Weather at Tregulla. London: Hodder and Stoughton, 1962; London: White Lion, 1972.

The Wolves Were in the Sledge. London: Hodder and Stoughton, 1964.

The Charmers. London: Hodder and Stoughton, 1965.

Starlight. London: Hodder and Stoughton, 1967.

The Snow Woman. London: Hodder and Stoughton, 1969.

The Woods in Winter. London: Hodder and Stoughton, 1970.

Secondary Sources

Ariail, Jacqueline. "Cold Comfort from Stella Gibbons." *Ariel: A Review of English Literature*, 9, iii, pp. 63–73. Review and analysis.

English Study Group, Birmingham University. "Thinking the '30s." In *Practices of Literature and Politics*. Ed. Francis Barber, Jay Bernstein, John Coombes, Peter Hulme, David Musselwhite, and Jennifer Stone. Colchester: University of Essex, 1979, pp. 1–20. Analysis of social commentary in *Cold Comfort Farm*.

Cooke, Judy. "Stella Gibbons." In *Contemporary Novelists*. Ed. James Vinson and Daniel Kirkpatrick. New York: St. Martin's Press, 1986, pp. 336–38.

MacPike, Loralee. "Stella Gibbons." In *British Women Writers*. Ed. Janet Todd. New York: Garland, 1988, pp. 190–91. Biography and criticism.

Mannes, Marya. "What *Did* Aunt Ada See?" *New York Times* (December 26, 1971): sec. II, 19:1. Review of December 26,

1971, BBC production of *Cold Comfort Farm*.

Moorman, Charles. "Five Voices of a Dragon." *Southern Quarterly*, 16 (1978): 139–50. Folklore of dragons in Gibbons, Mary Webb, three other writers.

"Stella Gibbons." In *Contemporary Authors*. Ed. Clare Kinsman. Detroit: Gale, 1965. Vol. 13–16, p. 314.

Obituaries

New York Times (December 20, 1989): sec. IV, 22:6.

London Times (December 20, 1989): 18:4.

Los Angeles Times (December 21, 1989): A47:6.

Loralee MacPike

Gilbert, W[illiam] S[chwenck]

Born: London, November 18, 1836

Education: Boulogne, France, 1842; Western Grammar School, Brompton, 1846–1849; Great Ealing School, 1849–1852; King's College, Cambridge University, 1853–1857 (B.A., 1857). Entered Inner Temple, 1855.

Marriage: Lucy Blois Turner, August 6, 1867

Died: Grim's Dyke, Harrow Weald, Middlesex, May 29, 1911

Biography

William Schwenck Gilbert, called the "king of Victorian jesters" and the master of what he himself called "Topsy-turvydom," once answered a request from the *Strand Magazine* with the following: "Date of birth 18 November 1836. Birthplace, 17 Southampton Street, Strand, in the house of my grandfather, who had known Dr. Johnson, Garrick and Reynolds, and who was the last man in London, I believe, who wore Hessian boots and a pig-tail." His father, William Gilbert, had been a naval surgeon who retired at the age of twenty-five when he inherited a small but comfortable fortune. The elder Gilbert married Anne Morris and set up housekeeping in Hammersmith where he attempted, unsuccessfully, to establish a literary career. As he complained, "From my earliest childhood, the ridiculous has thrust itself into every action of my life. I have been haunted through my whole existence by the absurd." His son, William Schwenck Gilbert, likewise was to be haunted by the absurd, but he was clever and fortunate enough to turn this into a considerable fortune.

A notorious early incident has become part of the legend of W.S. Gilbert. While traveling with his parents, at the age of two or three—the time of this event varies among sources—Bab (as he was called by his family) was kidnapped by what his biographer Hesketh Pearson called "two courteous Italians" who stopped his nurse one day and informed her that "the English gentleman" had sent them to fetch the baby. After being carried through some "fine mountain scenery," he was redeemed for the equivalent of twenty-five pounds sterling. This abduction was frequently recalled in his later years. Not only was the abduction of "Bab" the subject of at least one of the humorist's cartoons, but he was later to use this event as a plot element in *The Pirates of Penzance*. All of life's topsy-turvy events were potential material for the humorist.

In 1842, Gilbert was sent to school at Boulogne, France, and from 1846 to 1849 he attended the Western Grammar School at Brompton, London. From 1849 to 1852, he attended Great Ealing School where he became Head Boy in his last year.

At Great Ealing School the clever and domineering Gilbert showed a gift for art and developed an interest in the theater. At the age of fifteen he played Guy Fawkes in a school melodrama and, after seeing the famous Charles Kean in *The Corsican Brothers*, presented himself to Kean with the intention of going on the stage professionally. Kean wisely suggested that the aspiring young thespian return to school.

After finishing his schooling at Ealing, Gilbert entered King's College, London in 1853. At King's he began to show an interest in literature and writing, and he contributed verse to the college magazine. He also became interested in the army and attempted to enter the Royal Artillery with the intent of going to the Crimea, but the end of the war there forestalled his embarking upon a military career. His continued interest in military affairs is reflected later, particularly in the "Bab Ballads" and in the cartoons that he drew in conjunction with these poems which were published in the magazine *Fun*.

In 1857, Gilbert received his B.A. degree from King's College and entered the civil service as assistant clerk in the Education Department

of the Privy Council offices at a salary of £120 a year, "one of the worst bargains any government ever made," he said. He hated the job and stayed only until 1862 when he was able to procure an adequate income from other sources.

Between 1857 and 1883, he served first in the 5th West Yorkshire Militia and later in the Royal Aberdeenshire Militia, in which he fulfilled at least part of his aspiration to be a soldier. According to one source, in 1855, while still at King's College, Gilbert entered the Inner Temple as a law student, though he later said that he had entered the Middle Temple. There are many inconsistencies in the biographical record, especially of Gilbert's early life. He was finally called to the Bar in 1863.

During these years, he was also writing and drawing and attending the theater, for which he had a continuing passion. Aside from student publications, his first work to appear in print was a translation of the "Laughing Song" in Daniel François Auber's operatic version of Abbe Prevost's *Manon Lescaut*; Gilbert's translation was sung by Euphrosyne Parepa-Rosa at a Promenade Concert in Covent Garden in 1858. Gilbert ironically said of the occasion, "I went to those concerts to enjoy the intense gratification of standing at the elbow of any promenader who might be reading my translation, and wondering to myself what that promenader would say if he knew that the gifted creature who had written the very words he was reading was at that moment standing within a yard of him?"

From 1861 to 1871, Gilbert contributed regularly to the humor magazine *Fun*, and occasionally to *Punch*, the *Illustrated Times*, and other publications. In 1862, he inherited £300 and resigned his civil service position. "With 100 pounds," he said about this event, "I paid my call to the bar (I had previously entered myself as a student at the Middle Temple), with another 100 pounds I obtained access to a conveyancer's chambers, and with the third 100 pounds I furnished a set of chambers of my own, and began life afresh as a barrister-at-law." He did not prosper in this new profession, though he used his knowledge of law and of the proceedings of the courts to advantage in his later writing, both before and after his successful association with Arthur Sullivan.

He was not particularly successful at the practice of law, but he continued to gain some income from his writing and his comic drawings. In October 1863, his first identified play, *Uncle Baby*, was performed at the Lyceum Theatre. In 1865, he illustrated his father's novel, *The Magic Mirror*, and continued his parallel writing and legal careers. In 1866, he joined the Northern Circuit as a barrister, but he was already leaning more toward the theater than the court. On December 29, 1866, *Dulcimara*, his first acknowledged piece for the theater, was produced at the St. James's.

On August 6, 1867, he married Lucy Blois Turner, "Kitty," at St. Mary Abbot's, Kensington, and set up house at Eldon Road, Kensington. In 1868, the couple (who never produced any children) moved to 8 Essex Villas, Kensington. A short piece called "Trial By Jury," later to be the seed of the light opera with music by Sullivan, was published in *Fun*.

In 1869, The *"Bab" Ballads* was published. This was a collection of comic poems, subtitled "Much Sound and Little Sense" and illustrated by the author with his characteristic cartoons. These poems had originally been published in *Fun*, when that periodical was under the editorship of Tom Hood. Gilbert also illustrated his father's novels *King George's Middy* and *The Seven League Boots*. In March his play *No Cards*, "A Musical Piece in One Act for four characters," was performed at Mr. German Reed's Gallery of Illustration. This was his first work in his long and successful association with Reed's company.

Gilbert served as a war correspondent for the *Observer* newspaper during the Franco-Prussian War in 1870; he was briefly detained by French police as a possible Prussian spy because of his "Prussian" middle name, Schwenck—given to him, as he explained, without his permission, by his god-parents at his christening. This event he later used as the basis for a short story.

The same year *The Palace of Truth*, his first "fairy play," was produced at the Haymarket Theatre, and a year later his *Pygmalion and Galatea* was performed there.

Gilbert's name has been associated with that of Arthur Sullivan for a long time, but as a matter of fact they had both established reputations in their respective fields before they met— Gilbert as a writer of comic poems and a cartoonist, as well as a playwright and lyricist, Sullivan as a composer, performer, and conductor. Both had been involved with the writing of comic musical plays, each with other collaborators.

Sullivan's first musical comedy, *Cox and Box*, performed on May 11, 1867 at the Adelphi Theatre, was a great success. Although the two men did not meet on that occasion, Gilbert, a critic from *Fun* magazine, was in the audience. He complained that Mr. Sullivan's music was "too high class" for the "absurd plot to which it was wedded." On December 26, 1871, *Thespis*, Gilbert's first collaboration with Sullivan, was produced at the Gaiety Theatre.

In 1873, Gilbert unsuccessfully sued the *Pall Mall Gazette* for calling parts of his play *The Wicked World* "coarse and obscene." It is difficult for most people today to see what all the fuss was about, but at the time it was quite a serious matter to Gilbert. In any case, *The Wicked World* was produced at the Haymarket. In that year Gilbert also published *More Bab Ballads*.

His *Sweethearts* was produced at the Prince of Wales's Theatre in 1874. That December "Rosenkrantz and Guildenstern" was published in *Fun*; this was his last contribution to that periodical. During this period, he was being drawn into a closer association with Sullivan, and this association was to dominate the rest of his professional life.

Trial By Jury, with music by Sullivan, was produced in 1875 at the Royalty Theatre. This was Gilbert's first association with Richard D'Oyly Carte, the businessman and theater manager whose name also became closely linked with the Gilbert and Sullivan team. In the following year, Gilbert's *Original Plays* was published, and he and Kitty moved to a mansion in Kensington that was visible evidence of their growing prosperity. In this year, too, D'Oyly Carte formed the Comedy Opera Company with himself as managing director. In October, Gilbert's *Princess Toto*, with music by Frederic Clay, opened at the Strand.

In 1877, another volume of poems, *Fifty Bab Ballads*, was published, the satirical farce *Engaged* was produced at the Haymarket, and *The Sorcerer*, by Gilbert and Sullivan, was produced by the Comic Opera Company at the Opera Comique, which was leased for the production.

From this point onward Gilbert and Sullivan were to become inseparably associated in establishing a new form of English comic opera. In 1878, *HMS Pinafore*, which was to become one of their most popular comic operas, was presented at the Opera Comique, and in the following year a partnership was formed between Gilbert, Sullivan, and D'Oyly Carte in which profits from their productions were to be divided equally.

Because of the lack of copyright protection, books and plays were freely pirated in America, and in order to protect their property and also to show American audiences how their works should be produced, Gilbert, Sullivan, and D'Oyly Carte traveled to New York for a premiere of an "authorized" performance of *HMS Pinafore* and the premiere of *The Pirates of Penzance*, which was presented in London at the Opera Comique the following year.

Although Sullivan usually kept the composing and conducting of his "serious" music separate from his work with Gilbert, the two did collaborate in producing the oratorio *The Martyr of Antioch*, adapted by Gilbert from a work by H.H. Milman and set to music by Sullivan. This was performed in October 1880, at the Leeds Festival, with Sullivan conducting. It was not well received by the music critics, but Gilbert declared that he liked it very much indeed.

In 1881, Gilbert's *Original Plays*, second series, was published. In April, Gilbert and Sullivan's *Patience* was produced at the Opera Comique, and on October 10, D'Oyly Carte opened his new Savoy Theatre and leased it to the D'Oyly Carte Opera Company, which was to handle Gilbert and Sullivan productions in the future. Five days later a revival of Gilbert's *Princess Toto* opened at the Opera Comique.

In October 1881, the Gilberts moved again, to another address in Kensington, and the following month *Iolanthe* was produced at the Savoy. In February 1882, Gilbert, Sullivan, and D'Oyly Carte signed a new five-year agreement under which they would share profits equally after expenses. That May, Sullivan was knighted, but Gilbert was not, evidence that serious music was more highly regarded by the crown than comic writing. Over the next several years, a number of new Gilbert and Sullivan works appeared at the Savoy: *Princess Ida* in 1884; *The Mikado* in 1885; *Ruddigore* in 1887; *The Yeomen of the Guard* in 1888; *The Gondoliers* in 1889. There were also revivals of *The Sorcerer* in 1884, *HMS Pinafore* in 1887, *The Pirates of Penzance* in 1888, and *The Mikado* in 1888. In 1889, the Garrick Theatre opened, financed by Gilbert, and *The Gondoliers* was produced at the Savoy.

Gilbert quarreled with D'Oyly Carte in 1890 and withdrew from the partnership. His *Foggerty's Fairy and other Tales* was published, and Gilbert moved to his final home, Grim's Dyke, Harrow Weald, Middlesex.

In 1891, his *Songs of a Savoyard* was published, and there was a Command Performance of *The Gondoliers* before the Queen at Windsor. Gilbert was also awarded the honorary title of Deputy Lieutenant for the County of Middlesex, and his *Rosenkrantz and Guildenstern*, "A tragic episode in three tableaux," was performed at the Vaudeville. In September, another Command Performance, this time of *The Mikado*, was presented before the Queen at Balmoral.

Gilbert was reconciled with D'Oyly Carte and resumed collaboration with Sullivan in 1893, but their major work together had already been finished. *Utopia Limited* and *The Grand Duke* were produced at the Savoy, but *The Grand Duke* collapsed after 123 performances, the shortest run of any Gilbert and Sullivan opera since their first joint work, *Thespis*, twenty-two years earlier. *The Mikado* was revived and was immensely successful.

In November 1900, Sullivan died at the age of fifty-eight, and the following April, D'Oyly Carte died at the age of fifty-six. In 1905, Gilbert entered into an agreement with Mrs. D'Oyly Carte, granting her the exclusive performing rights in Gilbert and Sullivan operas.

On June 30, 1907, Gilbert was knighted by King Edward VII at Buckingham Palace. On a fine May afternoon in 1911, Sir William took two young ladies to swim in his lake at Grim's Dyke. One of them got out of her depth and started to struggle, so the elderly knight dove into the water, fully clothed, to save her. The two young women survived, but Sir William was dead when he was pulled from the water, apparently the victim of a heart attack.

Literary Analysis

It is unfortunate that the ghost of Sir William Gilbert could not observe and comment on his own death, or at least draw a cartoon similar to the one that the much younger W.S. Gilbert drew of his own kidnapping as a small child— he would have enjoyed the humor of it. The kidnapping cartoon depicts a Venetian in a large turban tossing a baby wearing a dress (and upside down in the air at the moment of the picture) from the end of a gondola to a man in a tall hat on the shore. In real life the child in such circumstances might be in great danger; in a cartoon, especially if the drawing is as whimsical as Gilbert's, the sense of danger is replaced by a sense of absurdity. Thus, the horror of death by beheading or any of the other frightful misadventures that befall the characters in Gilbert's works, are relieved by laughter. In *The Mikado*, for example, Ko-Ko and the chorus sing about the kinds of people who should be beheaded and others who are minor irritants.:

As some day it may happen that a victim
    must be found,
I've got a little list—I've got a little list
Of society offenders who might well be
    underground
And who never would be missed—who
    never would be missed!
There's the pestilential nuisances who
    write for autographs—
All people who have flabby hands and
    irritating laughs—
All children who are up on dates, and
    floor you with 'em flat—

Beheading is, to a monarch, no great thing. The "humane" Mikado, a "true philanthropist," sings:

My object all sublime
I shall achieve in time—
To let the punishment fit the crime—
    The punishment fit the crime;
And make each prisoner pent
Unwillingly represent
A source of innocent merriment
    Of innocent merriment!

And, he goes on to suggest specific tortures such as that of:

The advertising quack who wearies
With tales of countless cures,
His teeth, I've enacted,
Shall all be extracted
By terrified amateurs.

The effect of these verses is, of course, dependent upon the music supplied by Sullivan, which heightens the contrast between the meaning and the lighthearted mode of expression.

Humor always has its base in something that is potentially shocking. A central incongruity, or absurdity, however, releases the tension and gives rise to laughter. A young knight saving a damsel in distress is romantic; an elderly one (especially one whose knighthood is gained

for his work in the comic theater) leaping theatrically into the cold water for the same purpose can, if viewed as Gilbert often saw the world, give rise at least to a smile at the irony of the situation.

Gilbert was noted for his ready wit and sharp remarks. One often repeated anecdote is of him standing in a hall waiting for a friend when a shortsighted gentleman, thinking him one of the servants, told him "Call me a cab!" Gilbert looked at him carefully and said, "You're a four-wheeler." "How dare you, sir! What do you mean?" the old gentleman said wrathfully. "Well," Gilbert retorted, "you asked me to call you a cab—and I couldn't call you 'hansom.'"

When Gilbert and Sullivan visited America in order to put on the premiere of *The Pirates of Penzance,* they attended many formal dinners, at one of which a lady asked him, "Oh, Mr. Gilbert, your friend Sullivan's music is really too delightful. It always reminds me of dear Batch [meaning Bach]. Do tell me, what is Batch doing now? Is he composing anything?" "Well, no," Gilbert replied seriously, "just now, as a matter of fact, Batch is by way of decomposing."

According to another story, Gilbert was standing outside his club when a man approached him and said, "I beg your pardon, sir, but do you happen to know a gentleman, a member of this club, with one eye called Matthew?" "I can't say I do," Gilbert replied. Then, after a pause, he continued, "And what was his other eye called?" Gilbert's conversation was studded with impromptu remarks that suggest the way that his mind worked. He was always sensitive to the potential absurdities of language and of situation, and these carried over into his poems, his cartoons, his stories, and his works for the stage. It is fortunate that he was able to match up with a composer whose musical wit could complement his verbal one.

The Victorian period is noted for its love of nonsense: Edward Lear, Lewis Carroll, and Gilbert all contributed to that reputation and probably could have done what they did at no other period. This was the time of the rise of such magazines as *Punch* and the even more nonsensical periodical *Fun,* and the seriousness with which Victorian society took itself made everything all the more open to parody and light satire. Gilbert admired the army and the navy, yet he could at the same time poke fun at the absurdities and pomposities of the services. He

G

was a barrister with a great respect for the English concept of law, but he could see how the law could be distorted and the affinities between the drama of the courtroom and that of the comic stage.

In an early short story, "My Maiden Brief," apparently based on the author's own experience in the practice of law, a young barrister defends a "respectable old lady" on the charge of picking a pocket on a bus. In court, the barrister, who is the first-person narrator, is shocked by a number of things. First, the prosecutor is not there, so "the junior counsel present," who happens to be the narrator's friend and sharer of chambers, Polter, is assigned by the judge to prosecute. Polter destroys the narrator's case with the help of a policeman, who testifies that the "respectable old lady" is really a well-known thief. When she is convicted, the old lady pulls off a heavy boot, flings it at her barrister's head, and assaults him with "a torrent of invective" against his abilities as a counsel—"The language in which her invective was couched was perfectly shocking." Polter afterward got plenty of briefs and went on to a flourishing practice, while the narrator remained "as briefless as ever."

This "topsy-turvy" world is characteristic of the situations in which Gilbert's characters find themselves. Sometimes they gravely state facts which sound like impossibilities. In one of the Bab Ballads, "The Yarn of the 'Nancy Bell,'" an "elderly naval man," who somewhat resembles Samuel Taylor Coleridge's ancient mariner, tells the narrator that "I am a cook and a captain bold, / And the mate of the *Nancy* brig, / And a bo'sun tight, and a midshipmite, / And the crew of the captain's gig."

In a long verse dialogue the seaman answers the narrator's questions and in rollicking verse explains how he became all of the persons he lists: after a shipwreck, they turned to cannibalism until finally he was the sole survivor and therefore contained within himself all of the others.

> And then we murdered the bo'sun tight,
> And he much resembled pig;
> Then we wittled* free, did the cook and
>   me, [*vittled, ate]
> On the crew of the captain's gig.

The cook then boils a kettle of water for the captain-narrator, who has other plans:

> And he stirred it round and round and
>   round,
> And he sniffed at the foaming froth;
> When I ups with his heels, and smothers
>   his squeals
> In the scum of the boiling broth.
> And I eat that cook in a week or less,
> And—As I eating be
> The last of his chops, why, I almost
>   drops,
> For a wessel* in sight I see! [*vessel,
>   ship]

This is not a new story—Lord Byron used a similar anecdote in his *Don Juan*—but Gilbert manages to keep the situation acceptable by his use of absurd rhyme and meter. This is typical of what he does in all of the Bab Ballads.

The plot of babies switched at birth is very ancient and is used in many serious stories. It has, however, its obvious comic potential, which Gilbert utilizes on more than one occasion. In the Bab Ballad "General John" he plays on the hereditary class distinction that underlies military rank: General John is an officer because of his high birth. Likewise, Private James is a private because of his low birth, but he has a "glimmer" that he and the general were "cruelly changed at birth." The general sneers at this, and Private James reproves him with the observation that no true gentleman would sneer at his inferior's "glimmer." General John then concludes that, "being a man of doubtless worth," Private James must be right if he feels "certain quite," and they change places and ranks. The general, being a gentleman, cannot do otherwise, and so they become "General James" and "Private John." Such events occur over and over again in Gilbertian plots. This is the world of Topsy-turvydom, in which everything is capable of being turned upside down without making any more—or less—sense. Gilbert's works reflect the world in which he and his audience lived and still live. They are like the trick, distorting mirrors that simultaneously reflect and distort. His works are not at all realistic, yet they portray a real world, however magically distorted.

Gilbert's delightful comic drawings accompany his poems in the periodicals in which they appeared and in the volumes of the Bab Ballads. They are such an integral part of the poems that it is difficult to discuss the poems in the absence of these illustrations. They carry into a visual dimension the exaggeration of detail that gives

Gilbert's poems, stories, and plays their distinctive quality. They often portray horrible scenes, as for example three men impaled on the three points of a grappling hook (in "Brave Alum Bey"), yet their hand gestures and their silly smiling faces make it difficult for the reader to be shocked.

Tragedy, in Gilbert's view, is merely comedy turned upside down—and vice-versa—and wit, the soul of humor, is the ability to see this and to comment on it appositely. A good example of this principle appears in his parody of *Hamlet*, "Rosenkrantz and Guildenstern," which was first published in *Fun* in December 1874 (during the run of Irving's *Hamlet* on the stage) and eventually performed publicly in 1890. The king, Claudius, is guilty of having, as a young man, written a five-act tragedy. It was received with extreme hilarity, and although Claudius could have tolerated hisses, he cannot stand laughter and thus makes any reference to the play a capital offense. Hamlet, who seems actually to be Claudius's son, is addicted to giving long, dull soliloquies expressing his very boring melancholy. The "merry courtiers" Rosenkrantz and Guildenstern, with the aid of Ophelia (who is in love with Rosenkrantz and vice versa), steal the single surviving copy of the king's banned play from Polonius (who as Chamberlain has the duty of censoring plays and therefore has a copy). Hamlet puts on the play, himself reciting silly soliloquies, to the amusement of everyone but the king, who is furious. For putting on the play, Hamlet is guilty of a capital offense, but the king commutes his sentence to banishment to Engle-land, where people might tolerate such stuff, and the play ends with Rosenkrantz embracing Ophelia.

This is, of course, broad parody, but it is also good fun and contains some clever comic verse. It does all of the things that Gilbert's other dramatic pieces do, in a form that is easily grasped by anyone who is interested in how Gilbert's humor works. He uses meters and rhymes that clash with potentially serious statements which are couched in words that are pompously apropos but undermine any serious implication. In all of the plays that Gilbert wrote for the musical theater, including those for which Sullivan composed the music, the same principles apply. This is what makes the texts so easily identifiable as "Gilbertian" and the music of those plays which he did with Sir Arthur so obviously Sullivan's. The two complemented each other's work admirably. Gilbert always wrote the complete text first, and Sullivan composed music to fit the words and meters, rarely needing to consult the author. Indeed, the two never actually worked together, but each plied his own trade in his separate place.

No one familiar with the style of Gilbert and Sullivan ever mistakes their joint works for anything else. What distinguishes one work from another thematically is the subject that Gilbert chooses to treat in a humorous fashion. *Thespis*, the first work on which they collaborated, made fun both of classical myth and the current conventions of the stage. *Trial by Jury* pokes fun at the English court system, and *HMS Pinafore* focuses on the absurdities of the Royal Navy, as *The Pirates of Penzance* does on those of the army and the police. It would be difficult for any of these targets of ridicule to be offended, however, since the criticism is always leveled with such good humor. Gilbert never intended, in fact, to undermine the persons and institutions at which he aimed his humor but only to point out their absurdities and excesses.

Summary

W.S. Gilbert is primarily known to audiences now for the works that were set to music by Arthur Sullivan, but he had made a name for himself as a humorist well before they met. Early in his career he wrote poems, mainly published in the magazine *Fun*, for which he also drew delightful cartoons. He also wrote short stories, which were published in magazines, and he wrote comedies for the theater, not all of them with music. He is principally remembered, however, for his collaboration with Sullivan, and it is that work for which he was knighted by King Edward VII and for which he is principally noted today.

Selected Bibliography

Primary Sources
Plays and Poems of W.S. Gilbert with a Preface by Deems Taylor. New York: Random House, 1932. Includes the complete texts of the fourteen Gilbert and Sullivan operas, three other plays, and all of the Bab Ballads, with illustrations by the author.
The "Bab" Ballads: Much Sound and Little Sense. New York: George Routledge and Sons. A total of 215 illustrations by the author.

G

Lost Bab Ballads. Ed. Townley Searle. London and New York: Putnam, 1932.

Gilbert Before Sullivan. Ed. Jane W. Stedman. Chicago: University of Chicago Press, 1967.

Plays by W.S. Gilbert. Ed. with introduction and notes by George Rowell. Cambridge: Cambridge University Press, 1982.

The Lost Stories of W.S. Gilbert. Ed. Peter Haining. London: Robson Books, 1982.

Asimov's Annotated Gilbert & Sullivan. Ed. and annotated by Isaac Asimov. New York: Doubleday, 1988.

Secondary Sources

Bailey, Leslie. *Gilbert and Sullivan: Their Lives and Times*. London: Thames and Hudson, 1973.

Dark, Sidney and Rowland Grey. *W.S. Gilbert: His Life and Letters*. London: Methuen, 1923.

Jones, John Bush, ed. *W.S. Gilbert: A Century of Scholarship and Commentary*. New York: New York University Press, 1970.

Pearson, Hesketh. *Gilbert and Sullivan: A Biography*. New York: Harper, 1935.

Searle, Townley. *Sir William Schwenck Gilbert: A Topsy-Turvy Adventure*. London, Alexander-Ouseley, 1931.

Donald R. Swanson

Goldsmith, Oliver

Born: Pallas, County Longford, Ireland, November 10, 1730 (?)

Education: Trinity College, Dublin, B.A., 1750; University of Edinburgh, 1752–1754; University of Leyden, Holland, 1754–1755

Died: London, April 4, 1774

Biography

The fifth child of the Reverend Charles Goldsmith and Ann Jones, both of Anglo-Irish descent, Oliver Goldsmith was probably born on November 10, 1730, most likely at their farmhouse in Pallas, County Longford, Ireland. Soon the Goldsmith family moved to the village of Lissoy, nearer the parish in County Westmeath where Charles was Curate-in-charge. Oliver attended the village school there, the Diocesan School at Elphin, and other schools at Athlone and Edgeworthstown, County Longford before entering Trinity College, Dublin in 1745 as a sizar, obliged to earn his tuition through service. An undistinguished student, impoverished after his father's death in 1747, Oliver earned his B.A. in 1750.

Goldsmith's life between 1750 and 1757 was, in his own phrase, that of a philosophic vagabond. For a short time a tutor after failing to obtain ordination as a clergyman, Goldsmith left Ireland to study medicine at the University of Edinburgh in 1752; there he stayed, without receiving a degree, until early 1754. Departing for Europe, he studied medicine briefly at the University of Leyden in Holland and traveled, in poverty, through France, Germany, Switzerland, and Italy. Journeying to London in 1756, he held such jobs as apothecary's assistant, usher at a boy's school, and physician. He remained a resident of London for the rest of his life. He never married.

Goldsmith began his literary career in 1757 by reviewing books for the *Monthly Review*. The next year, while serving temporarily as master of a school, he published his first book, a translation. Disappointed in his hopes for a medical position in India, Goldsmith was compelled to write for money; in 1759 he contributed essays to various periodicals and authored *An Enquiry into the Present State of Polite Learning in Europe* and his own weekly magazine, *The Bee*. In 1760, he began a series of "Chinese Letters" for John Newbery's *Public Ledger*, collected as *The Citizen of the World* in 1762. A generous publisher, Newbery recognized Goldsmith's talent and guided his career for several years. Also in 1762, Goldsmith completed *The Life of Richard Nash* and sold the manuscript of a novel to pay his debts. During this period of hack writing, the author developed the friendships with writers and artists— Samuel Johnson, Sir Joshua Reynolds, Edmund Burke—who made him a charter member of The Club in 1764.

The Traveller, a poem published in 1764, finally brought Goldsmith the fame that he sought and initiated a decade of considerable literary achievement. The work's critical success led to the publication of Goldsmith's collected *Essays* in 1765 and his novel, *The Vicar of Wakefield*, in 1766. The poem's reputation also resulted in Goldsmith's meeting his only patron, Lord Clare. His first play, *The Good Natur'd Man*, was performed at Covent Garden in 1768. In 1769, he was appointed Professor of Ancient History at the Royal Academy. Goldsmith published his poem *The Deserted Village* in 1770 and *The History of England, from the Earliest Times to the Death of George II*, his third historical compilation, in 1771. His second five-act comedy, *She Stoops to Conquer*, and a one-act farce, *The Grumbler*, were performed at Covent Garden in 1773. After the writer's death in London on April 4, 1774, several works were published posthumously, including the poem *Retaliation*. In 1776, Goldsmith was honored with a monument in Westminster Abbey.

Literary Analysis

Goldsmith, like his more celebrated friend, Johnson, was an eighteenth-century man of letters. Poet, essayist, reviewer, biographer, historian, novelist, and dramatist, he made important contributions to the literary genres of his period. As Johnson fondly recalls in his epitaph for Goldsmith, he "touched almost every kind of writing, and touched none that he did not adorn."[1] His best works—the essays in *The Citizen of the World*, the two long poems, *The Traveller* and *The Deserted Village*, the novel, *The Vicar of Wakefield*, and the two comedies, *The Good Natur'd Man* and *She Stoops to Conquer*—made Goldsmith a significant figure in literary London of the 1760s and 1770s. In addition to displaying such variety and artistry, Goldsmith appealed successfully to the taste of the town and the time. No author of these decades more effectively blended the satire and the sentiment that different parts of his audience expected in imaginative writing.

Early evidence of Goldsmith's art and humor can be found in the essays that constitute his literary apprenticeship which concluded with *The Citizen of the World*. In the weekly magazine *The Bee* (Goldsmith contributed essays for eight issues in late 1759), many pieces demonstrate his propensity for humor. While writing about miscellaneous topics such as eloquence or luxury, he occasionally paused to laugh at folly. For example, the essay "On Dress" in the second number gently ridicules affectation through the humorous experience of two older characters displaying their fine clothes in the Mall. "A Reverie" in Number V mocks the pretensions of several contemporary authors seeking a coach ride to the temple of fame. This essay's allusion to a more famous periodical, the *Spectator* (1711–1712) of Joseph Addison and Sir Richard Steele, is a reminder of one important influence on Goldsmith's prose. Several humorous essays appeared in others' periodicals; the best is "A Reverie at the Boar's-head-tavern in Eastcheap," a survey of human folly over time which was published in the *British Magazine* (1760).

Goldsmith displayed his talent as an essayist more fully in *The Citizen of the World*, the series of 123 essays that appeared irregularly as a column in a newspaper, the *Public Ledger*, from January 1760 until August 1761 and which he collected and revised in 1762. In these letters Goldsmith employed the persona of Lien Chi Altangi, supposedly a philosopher from China, to comment on English life. Among the influences on this technique are the Baron Charles Louis de Secondat de Montesquieu's *Lettres Persanes* (1721), Lord Lyttleton's *Persian Letters* (1735), and *Lettres Chinoises* (1739) by the Marquis D'Argens. As in those works, the perspective of an oriental spectator of European folly created an ironic distance responsible for much of the humor in *The Citizen of the World*. Even more an outsider in England than his Irish author, Lien Chi is also the first of Goldsmith's philosophic travelers taught by experience "to laugh at folly alone, and to find nothing truly ridiculous but villainy and vice."[2]

Lien Chi's letters, mostly directed to the president of the Ceremonial Academy in Peking, remark on diverse aspects of English society, sometimes humorously, as in his visits to the law courts in Westminster Hall or the races at Newmarket, and sometimes more solemnly, as in his visit to Westminster Abbey. Among the topics of ridicule, for example, are the rivalry of the two London theaters, the fashion in funeral elegies, and the absurdities of characters attending a visitation dinner or constituting a club of authors. The latter essay, which sketches comic figures such as Dr. Nonentity and Tim Syllabub, includes a ridiculous poem read by a vain poet. Since he satirizes the pretensions of authors, Goldsmith occasionally lets Lien Chi behave foolishly, as when he mistakes London prostitutes for hospitable ladies.

Goldsmith diversified *The Citizen of the World* by including an occasional letter from Lien Chi's son Hingpo and by introducing two recurrent characters, the Man in Black and Beau Tibbs. Hingpo's pursuit of a beautiful captive introduces a note of sensibility and romance into the series. The Man in Black, however, is "an humourist in a nation of humourists."[3] Affecting misanthropy, though in reality being full of good nature, he exhibits an incongruity that is a source of benevolent laughter. As Lien Chi's guide to London's sites, the Man in Black also introduces him to Beau Tibbs, a shabby character whose affectation of gentility is comical. In Letter LXXI, for instance, Lien Chi observes Tibbs and his foolish wife at the pleasure gardens of Vauxhall with detached amusement. The final letter, in which Hingpo is united with the captive, herself the niece of the Man in Black, and all are entertained at a dinner held by Mr. and Mrs. Tibbs, shows Goldsmith organizing characters in a way that anticipates his later work as a novelist and dramatist.

Goldsmith developed the benevolent character who is both ironic observer and fool in the title character of his novel *The Vicar of Wakefield*. The Reverend Charles Primrose demonstrates more completely than Lien Chi the amiable humor characteristic of the middle third of the eighteenth century. Though he has antecedents in a character such as Sir Roger de Coverley in the *Spectator*, the amiable humorist is fully realized in the novels of Henry Fielding and Laurence Sterne. Parson Abraham Adams in *Joseph Andrews* (1742) and Uncle Toby in *Tristram Shandy* (1760–1767) are the two most famous previous examples of the character who combines good nature and folly in nearly equal proportions. Despite Goldsmith's objection, in the "Advertisement" prefacing the novel, to those who "mistake ribaldry for humour,"[4] his parson resembles these ribald novelists' characters more than he would have admitted. But, while Primrose is a poor country clergyman with a family like Fielding's Adams, he has the additional function of narrating his adventures, like Goldsmith's Lien Chi.

Primrose is wise enough to mock the affectation of his wife and daughters, who desire to imitate the gentry, but he is not always effective in preventing the consequences of the affectation. The family portrait too large for the Primrose house in chapter 16 is a comic instance. The Vicar, while genuinely concerned for the well-being of his family, is himself guilty of affectation, as in the ridiculous obsession with a theological controversy that initially puts the family in distress. Although he can see how easily others are deceived by appearances, Primrose is no better a judge of character. Like Lien Chi, he mistakes London prostitutes for ladies. An inexperienced rural character, he is no match for superior cunning. He cannot properly distinguish between Squire Thornhill, the fine gentleman who plans to seduce his younger daughter, and Sir William Thornhill, a true gentleman, disguised as a poorer man, who loves his older daughter. While the squire reprises the stereotype of the rake, Sir William is another good-natured humorist whose benevolence provides a happy ending for the novel. The Vicar's narration of these events displays the mixture of wisdom, good nature, and folly found in his character.

Such comic ironies are more obvious in the first half of the novel, which also provides another kind of humor through the attention to picturesque rural life that adds an idyllic charm to the story. In the second half, including the daughter's seduction and betrayal and Primrose's journey and imprisonment, Goldsmith focuses more on his protagonist's family as victims; thus, there is a resemblance to the romantic fiction that the writer criticized in his own early book reviews. To some extent, the novel also retells the story of Job in a comic form, showing the Vicar's complacent faith being tested by adversity and having providence ultimately release this imperfect character from suffering. But, Goldsmith situates his Job in a highly self-conscious fiction that parodies such narrative conventions of his time as sentimental reunions and happy endings with multiple marriages. To diversify this novel, Goldsmith includes the picaresque adventures of the Vicar's son, George, who narrates his history as a philosophic vagabond. As in the comic novels of Fielding and Sterne, in this one the styles of various genres are mixed into a distinctive hybrid of laughter and feeling. As did Johnson in *Rasselas* (1759), Goldsmith represents the difficulties of human experience within a framework of comic irony. It is Goldsmith's "high benevolent irony" that the German poet Johann Wolfgang von Goethe praised.[5] In the nineteenth century William Hazlitt, Washington Irving, and William Makepeace Thackeray also commented approvingly on Goldsmith's humor, which influenced Irving the more noticeably.

By the time that he published *The Vicar of Wakefield* Goldsmith had also written a considerable amount of poetry. His novel, in addition to the sentimental song "When lovely woman stoops to folly" and the tender ballad of Edwin and Angelina, contains the ironic "An Elegy on the Death of a Mad Dog," a poem that burlesques the elegaic style as Goldsmith had done earlier in "An Elegy on that Glory of her Sex, Mrs. Mary Blaize" in *The Bee* and "On the Death of the Right Honourable ***" in *The*

Citizen of the World. The source of Goldsmith's satiric quatrains in each poem was the French poet Bernard La Monnoye. Another influence, that of Jonathan Swift's satiric poetry, can be seen in several early minor poems, "The Double Transformation: A Tale," "The Description of an Author's Bedchamber," and "A New Simile. In the Manner of Swift."

In his own time Goldsmith's reputation was secured by the publication of two long poems, *The Traveller* and *The Deserted Village.* Written in heroic couplets in the manner of John Dryden, Alexander Pope, and Johnson, these poems do not contribute much, however, to Goldsmith's development as a humorist. Although *The Traveller* is a Horatian epistle, Goldsmith does not use the form for satire as Pope did. The speaker, like Lien Chi Altangi or Charles Primrose, is a philosophic wanderer whose general ironic observations on human happiness in Italy, Switzerland, France, Holland, and England lack the particularity needed for humor. In *The Deserted Village,* Goldsmith includes humorous sketches of a preacher, a schoolmaster, and an inn within his nostalgic evocation of the village of Auburn. While the poem's focus, the threat of economic change to an older way of life, affords some scope for satire on luxury, it is not a subject for gentle humor.

Two posthumously published poems, addressed to friends and written in anapestic couplets, demonstrate more of Goldsmith's characteristic humor. *The Haunch of Venison,* written about 1771 but not published until 1776, is a Horatian epistle to his patron Lord Clare. Influenced by Swift and the French satirist Nicolas Boileau-Despreaux, the poet first imagines the dinner with his literary friends that will follow the Lord's gift of venison, then describes in comic detail his disappointing meal at the house of an ill-bred acquaintance. In the unfinished *Retaliation,* published a few weeks after Goldsmith's death in 1774, he responds to the friendly mockery of his club at St. James's Coffee House. Provoked to answer a comic epitaph, Goldsmith retaliates in humorous sketches of nine friends.

When Goldsmith decided to write for the theater, he responded to the sentimental comedy of his time (written by Richard Cumberland, Hugh Kelly, and others) by striving to write comedy in the more humorous style prominent at the turn of the eighteenth century in the plays of Sir John Vanbrugh, William

Congreve, and George Farquhar. Both *The Good Natur'd Man* and *She Stoops to Conquer* reflect this goal. In his "Preface" to the first play Goldsmith regrets that refinement threatens to elevate English comedy so much that it will lose its humor; he also defends the necessary lowness of humor by recalling the period before such genteel comedy when "little more was desired by an audience, than nature and humour."[6] He elaborated this position in the *Westminster Magazine* for January 1773 in "An Essay on the Theatre; or, a Comparison between Laughing and Sentimental Comedy," a piece designed to prepare a proper reception for his second play. Invoking the classical authority of Aristotle to criticize the mingling of genres in recent plays, Goldsmith provides a pithy definition of comedy, "that natural portrait of Human Folly and Frailty." He faults his contemporaries for lacking *vis comica,* comic force, in attempting to make characters admirable. Comedy, he argues, "should excite our laughter by ridiculously exhibiting the Follies of the Lower Part of Mankind."[7]

While Goldsmith's plays evoke laughter at human folly, they also assimilate some aspects of the sentimental comedy that he criticized, especially its benevolism. The protagonist of *The Good Natur'd Man* ridicules the sentimental hero through the distresses that arise when his good heart is unchecked by a sound head. The immature Honeywood must learn to restrain the benevolence that leads him into debt and prevents him from declaring his love out of fear of offense. However, the value of his charity is never questioned, and Sir William Honeywood's unannounced return to London only teaches him a dramatic lesson about its excess. The more sensible heroine, Miss Richland, must confront two other suitors, Leontine and Lofty, before she can marry Honeywood. The former, a conventional romantic lover, wants to marry Olivia, the young woman whom others believe to be his sister. His deceived father, the ridiculously pessimistic Croaker, insists that he marry Miss Richland, who is also courted by the affected Lofty. The resulting misunderstandings lead to a humorous denouement at an inn in act 5. But, while the play's action causes laughter at these characters' folly, its final speeches reaffirm the importance of good nature.

In *She Stoops to Conquer,* Goldsmith blends laughter with sentiment even more effectively. The play's subtitle, *The Mistakes of a*

G

Night, indicates from the outset the comic misunderstandings that are fundamental to the action. When Tony Lumpkin tricks two gentlemen from London into believing that his stepfather's country house is an inn, he enables his stepsister Kate Hardcastle to play the part of a maid and to test the young man whom her father has chosen for her to marry. Influenced by George Farquhar's *The Beaux' Stratagem* (1707), this play is both more farcical and more sentimental than its predecessor. Tony Lumpkin is Goldsmith's final example of the amiable humorist, a good-natured jokester whose deception lets Goldsmith ridicule the affectation of Marlow and Hastings. As was Honeywood in the earlier play, Marlow is an immature character who is brought closer to maturity by the dual embarrassment of mistaking his host's house and his daughter. Kate, a more active agent for comic change than Miss Richland, consciously deceives the reluctant suitor whose good nature she recognizes. The play's other pair of lovers, Hastings and Miss Neville, are involved in a more conventional comic subplot to outwit the foolish Mrs. Hardcastle, who wants Miss Neville to marry her son Tony. Her humorously eccentric husband, Mr. Hardcastle, allows his daughter Kate to marry the man of her choice.

Goldsmith ridicules sentimental comedy in *She Stoops to Conquer* most effectively during the lovers' comical first meeting in act 2 when Marlow stammers out sentiments that Kate must complete. However, the heart is crucial to Marlow's maturation. Frightened by the idea of courting a woman of his own class, he learns to trust his feelings when the disguised Kate pretends to weep in act 4. In a scene that delicately blends the ironic and sentimental aspects of this comedy, he is touched by her simplicity and refuses to pursue the woman whom he believed to be a maid and whose true identity he does not yet know. As their fathers hide behind a screen in the last act, Kate finally laughs Marlow out of his folly as he learns who she is and who he ought to be. Goldsmith's friend Johnson identified the comic pleasure that arises while watching these characters: "I know of no comedy for many years that has so exhilarated an audience, that has answered so much the great end of comedy—making an audience merry."[8]

Summary

Although Oliver Goldsmith was a man of letters who wrote in many genres popular in the 1760s and 1770s, his finest achievements as a humorist were the essay series *The Citizen of the World*, the novel *The Vicar of Wakefield*, and two plays, *The Good Natur'd Man* and *She Stoops to Conquer*. These four works, along with a few other essays and poems, show his skill as an ironist ridiculing the folly of mankind or the foolish conventions of more romantic or sentimental forms of literature while also celebrating the good nature of many characters. In *The Citizen of the World* and *The Vicar of Wakefield* Goldsmith focuses on an older humorous character—a Chinese philosopher in London and an English clergyman in the country—who narrates his comic adventure. In *The Good Natur'd Man* and *She Stoops to Conquer* he presents a young English gentleman involved in comic misunderstanding of himself and others. No work better demonstrates the "natural portrait of Human Folly and Frailty" that Goldsmith sought in comedy than *She Stoops to Conquer*. No character better incarnates his comic wisdom than its heroine, Kate Hardcastle.

Notes

1. James Boswell, *Life of Johnson*, rev. ed. (London: Oxford University Press, 1953), p. 779, translated from the Latin epigraph.
2. *Collected Works of Oliver Goldsmith*, ed. Arthur Friedman (Oxford: Clarendon, 1966), Vol. 2, p. 22.
3. Goldsmith, *Collected Works*, Vol. 2, p. 109.
4. Goldsmith, *Collected Works*, Vol. 4, p. 13.
5. Quoted in G.S. Rousseau, ed., *Goldsmith: The Critical Heritage* (London: Routledge, 1974), p. 278.
6. Goldsmith, *Collected Works*, Vol. 5, p. 13.
7. Goldsmith, *Collected Works*, Vol. 3, pp. 209–10.
8. Boswell, p. 525.

Selected Bibliography
Primary Sources

Prose
An Enquiry into the Present State of Polite Learning in Europe. London: R. and J. Dodsley, 1759.
The Bee. Being Essays on the Most Interesting Subjects. London: J. Wilkie, 1759.
The Citizen of the World; or Letters from a Chinese Philosopher, Residing in Lon-

don, to his Friends in the East. 2 vols. London: John Newbery, 1762.

The Life of Richard Nash, of Bath, Esq. Extracted Principally from His Original Papers. London: John Newbery, 1762.

Essays. By Mr. Goldsmith. London: W. Griffin, 1765.

The Vicar of Wakefield: A Tale. Supposed to be Written by Himself. 2 vols. London: F. Newbery, 1766.

The History of England, from the Earliest Times to the Death of George II. 4 vols. London: T. Davies, 1771.

Poetry

The Traveller, or A Prospect of Society. A Poem. London: John Newbery, 1765 [1764].

The Deserted Village, A Poem. London: W. Griffin, 1770.

Retaliation: A Poem. London: G. Kearsly, 1774.

The Haunch of Venison, A Poetical Epistle to Lord Clare. London: G. Kearsly & J. Ridley, 1776.

Drama

The Good Natur'd Man: A Comedy. London: W. Griffin, 1768.

She Stoops to Conquer: or, The Mistakes of a Night. A Comedy. London: F. Newbery, 1773.

Modern Editions

Balderston, Katherine C., ed. *The Collected Letters of Oliver Goldsmith.* Cambridge: Cambridge University Press, 1928. Annotated edition of fifty-three surviving letters.

Friedman, Arthur, ed. *Collected Works of Oliver Goldsmith.* 5 vols. Oxford: Clarendon, 1966. Standard edition with thorough annotations; includes complete texts of poems, plays, novel, essays, reviews, biographies, and excerpts from various other works.

Lonsdale, Roger, ed. *The Poems of Thomas Gray, William Collins, Oliver Goldsmith.* London: Longmans, Green, 1969. Useful introductions and annotations to Goldsmith's poems.

Secondary Sources

Biographies

Wardle, Ralph M. *Oliver Goldsmith.*

Lawrence: University of Kansas Press, 1957. Best overview of Goldsmith's life and career, with little analysis of his works.

Books

Backman, Sven. *This Singular Tale: A Study of "The Vicar of Wakefield" and Its Literary Background.* Lund: Gleerup, 1971. Backman examines the novel in relation to traditions of prose fiction, the periodical essay, and drama.

Bevis, Richard. *The Laughing Tradition: Stage Comedy in Garrick's Day.* Athens: University of Georgia Press, 1980. Examination of the comic genres and comic authors contemporary with Goldsmith's plays and places the dreams in that context.

Dixon, Peter. *Oliver Goldsmith Revisited.* Boston: Twayne, 1991. A survey of Goldsmith's writing in various genres with attention to the paradoxical qualities of his humor.

Hopkins, Robert H. *The True Genius of Oliver Goldsmith.* Baltimore: Johns Hopkins Press, 1969. Hopkins examines the major works from the viewpoint that Goldsmith is primarily an ironist.

Jeffares, A. Norman. *A Critical Commentary on Goldsmith's "She Stoops to Conquer."* London: Macmillan, 1966. Brief analysis of theme and technique.

Quintana, Ricardo. *Oliver Goldsmith: A Georgian Study.* New York: Macmillan, 1967. A survey of Goldsmith's works with emphasis on his Georgian context.

Rousseau, G.S., ed. *Goldsmith: The Critical Heritage.* London: Routledge, 1974. Responses to Goldsmith's work in the eighteenth and nineteenth centuries.

Swarbrick, Andrew, ed. *The Art of Oliver Goldsmith.* London: Vision, 1984. Collects ten new essays on various aspects of Goldsmith's work.

Articles and Chapters in Books

Dussinger, John A. "Oliver Goldsmith, Citizen of the World." *Studies on Voltaire and the Eighteenth Century,* 55 (1967): 445–61. The basis for Goldsmith's ironic perspective is in his intellectual cosmopolitanism.

Helgerson, Richard. "The Two Worlds of Oliver Goldsmith." *Studies in English*

Literature, 13 (1973): 516–34.
Helgerson locates in the relationship of
the village and the city a basis for
Goldsmith's irony.

Hume, Robert D. "Goldsmith and Sheridan
and the Supposed Revolution of 'Laughing' against 'Sentimental' Comedy." In
*The Rakish Stage: Studies in English
Drama, 1660–1800*. Carbondale:
Southern Illinois University Press, 1983,
pp. 312–55. Reassessment of
Goldsmith's criticism of contemporary
comedy and description of a strong
comic tradition.

James E. Evans

Grahame, Kenneth

Born: Edinburgh, Scotland, March 8, 1859
*Education: St. Edward's School, Oxford,
    1868–1876*
*Marriage: Elspeth Thomson, July 1899; one
    child*
Died: Pangbourne, July 6, 1932

Biography

Kenneth Grahame, the third child in his upper-
class Scottish family, was born on March 8,
1859 in Edinburgh, Scotland, where his father,
James Cunningham Grahame, a descendant or
collateral relative of many of the ancient Scottish families, was an advocate. His mother was
the former Bessie Ingles of Hilton, Lasswade,
who had married her lawyer husband in 1853.
In the year following Kenneth's birth James received the appointment of Sheriff Substitute for
Argyllshire, and the family moved to Inverary.
It was here that Kenneth's younger brother was
born and his mother contracted scarlet fever,
dying when Kenneth was five years old. The
four Grahame children were sent to their maternal grandmother in Cookham Dene, Berkshire. Although they rejoined their father in
Scotland during the summer of 1866, he had
evidently been completely demoralized by his
wife's death and had become an alcoholic; he
sent the children back to their grandmother,
resigned his post, and went to France to live.
From 1867 to his death in 1887, he had no
contact with his children. Although they were
physically well cared for by their relatives and
enjoyed living in the beautiful countryside of
southern England, the children grew up in an
austere world of impersonal adults.

In 1868, Kenneth and his older brother
Willie were sent to the newly founded St.
Edward's School in Oxford. Kenneth was a
model schoolboy who excelled in both sports
and scholarship and who was head of the
school in his final year. He expected to continue
on at Oxford University, as other boys in his
social position would have done after such a
successful school experience, but his older relatives decided that he would have to begin a
business career; his disappointment over this
occasioned many complex emotions which influenced his later writings. For two years he
worked in the Westminster offices of his uncle,
John Grahame, a parliamentary agent; in January 1879, Kenneth entered the Bank of England
as a Gentleman-Clerk, serving an apprenticeship that enabled him to learn the banking profession on a level which brought him into an
executive position.

Grahame's business career at the Bank of
England might well have been the source of the
cliché about "Banker's hours": he went to the
Bank late in the morning, left early in the afternoon, and enjoyed vacations measured not in
days or weeks, but in months. During this period, he wrote the personal essays which first
established his literary reputation. Although he
was remembered by his colleagues as something
less than the ideal man of business, he achieved
success; at the age of thirty-nine he became the
youngest-ever Secretary to the Bank, and in his
later years he enjoyed a secure and comfortable
financial situation. In 1908 (he was then forty-
nine years old), he resigned his post and lived
the rest of his life as a gentleman of leisure.

Grahame never considered himself a professional author, and the nature and quantity of
his writings were directly related to the circumstances of his life. Until he married in 1899 he
maintained a bachelor establishment and enjoyed the society of his male friends, among
whom were the literary scholar F.J. Furnivall,
the prominent editor and poet William Ernest
Henley, the novelist and academic Arthur
Quiller-Couch, and others, either gentlemen of
the rentier class or of the literary establishment.

In July 1899, Grahame married Elspeth
Thomson, a thirty-seven-year-old spinster from
a wealthy family with many literary connections. In May 1900, she gave birth to their only
child, Alistair. From 1898 to 1908, Grahame
published nothing. Both husband and wife had
unrealistic expectations of their marriage, and
both were equally disappointed. Their son fur-

ther complicated their relationship, for in their frustration with one another they attempted to live out their fantasies through him and completely spoiled him. Yet, it was one of the father's gifts to his son that has become Grahame's major literary achievement. *The Wind in the Willows* (1908) originated in the letters which Kenneth wrote for Alistair's amusement. Alistair was later sent to Rugby and Eton and was miserable at both; he was then tutored at home and finally won admission to Oxford University. At the age of twenty he was severely handicapped by failing eyesight and beset by psychological and religious problems; during the night of May 7, 1920, he was run over by a railway engine. Although the verdict was accidental death, the evidence suggested suicide. With Alistair's death, the elder Grahames became ever more reclusive, though they traveled extensively in Europe. Kenneth's death in Pangbourne on July 6, 1932 from a cerebral hemorrhage and cardiac problems was hastened by his gourmandizing and sedentary life.

Literary Analysis

The quantity of Grahame's writings was so limited in comparison to that of his contemporaries such as H.G. Wells, Arnold Bennett, and George Moore that he must be referred to as a minor figure, yet his writings could be used as textbook examples of their time and genres. His literary output falls into three phases: the early personal essays collected in *Pagan Papers* (1893); the stories of *The Golden Age* (1895) and *Dream Days* (1898); and the beast fable (or, as I shall argue, the mock-epic novel) *The Wind in the Willows* (1908).

The product of the first of these phases, the personal essays, are so typical of English writing in the early 1890s as to be inaccessible to readers of later periods. In them the writer concerns himself with style to the almost complete exclusion of content which, in any case, comes from contemporary themes. Grahame's language epitomizes the classical education of the upper classes in late Victorian England: Latin and Greek tags, even puns, appear on almost every page, as do allusions to classical literature. French, the second language of the English upper classes, is used with such frequency as to leave no doubt as to the social standing of both the writer and the expected reader, although the essays are never far from the heritage of English literature. Yet, there are subtle expansions of this literary tradition, for, as Peter Green notes, Grahame also refers to writers outside the accepted Victorian pale.[1] In "The Romance of the Road," for example, he begins by quoting Rabelais.

The titles of the personal essays in *Pagan Papers* indicate some of the themes: "Loafing," "Of Smoking," "The Lost Centaur," "Marginalia." Green identifies these "stock themes" as "food and drink, tobacco, sleep, travel, walking, nature-mysticism."[2] Similar topics appear in the writings of other nineteenth-century essayists such as Robert Louis Stevenson, Lionel Johnson, C.S. Calverley, and (perhaps the source of all who followed him) Charles Lamb. The twenty-four pieces in *Pagan Papers* had all been published in either the *St. James's Gazette* or the *National Observer* when Grahame offered them to John Lane for publication as a volume. The title selected—something of a misnomer considering the innocuous nature of the essays—alluded to the most contemporary of literary movements, the "neo-paganism" which was manifesting itself in the theosophical and anti-Christian movements of the time. Grahame had little to do with such matters, and "paganism" seems to have meant to him merely a relaxing of the Calvinistic doctrines which had influenced his early life along with an emphasis on the life of classical Greece. In this respect Grahame's attitude can be seen as anticipating the early short stories (as well as various scenes in the novels) of E.M. Forster. These personal essays embody the reflections and gentle humor of a sensitive writer who, although aspiring to say "what oft was thought, but ne'er so well expressed," never establishes an identifiable persona for himself.

At the same time, there are six pieces in *Pagan Papers* (five of them were written between March and September 1893, just before the volume was published in October) which show Grahame moving away from the personal essay into a form which, for want of a better term, can be called the short story. These pieces—"The Olympians," "A Whitewashed Uncle," "The Finding of the Princess," "Young Adam Cupid," "The Burglars," and "Snowbound"—were gathered, along with twelve others, in the volume *The Golden Age*. In these stories Grahame expresses a personal point of view in a voice that is clearly his own. To a certain extent the style is determined by the point of view; the stories concern a group of children whose activities and outlooks are reported by one of the children who, while using the vocabulary of the adult as well as the subsequent experiences of the adult, nevertheless retains the child's first instinctive response. Unlike other nineteenth-century authors who wrote about children, Grahame presents the children as complete individuals whose feelings, emotions, and even physical responses are completely true to themselves. This point of view allowed him to show up the pretensions of adult life in a way that might be compared to Voltaire's practice in *Candide*, were it not that Grahame restrains himself to a domestic scene that realistically mirrors late nineteenth-century England. In addition, rather than satirizing or attempting to reform or change the situation, Grahame achieves an almost elegiac tone by his control of the distance between the experiences recounted and the point of view of the adult who seemingly has total recall of the event.

These "anecdotes" or "humorous reminiscences" concern the childhood experiences of five brothers and sisters—Charlotte and Selina, Edward and Harold, and the unnamed narrator. Grahame found his tone in the early essay "The Olympians," published in the *National Observer* in 1891 and later used as the "Prologue" for *The Golden Age*. It begins:

> Looking back to those days of old, ere the gate shut to behind me, I can see now that to children with a proper equipment of parents these things would have worn a different aspect. But to those whose nearest were aunts and uncles, a special attitude of mind may be allowed. They treated us, indeed, with kindness enough as to the needs of the flesh, but after that with indifference (an indifference, as I recognize, the result of a certain stupidity), and therewith the commonplace conviction that your child is merely animal. At a very early age I remember realizing in a quite impersonal and kindly way the existence of that stupidity, and its tremendous influence in the world; while there grew up in me, as in the parallel case of Caliban upon Setebos, a vague sense of a ruling power, willful and freakish, and prone to the practice of vagaries—"just choosing so": as, for instance, the giving of authority over us, to these hopeless and incapable creatures, when it might far more reasonably have been given to ourselves over them.

The essay is written in a nondramatic style, but as Grahame continued to work with this seemingly autobiographical material he learned to dramatize it and to use dialogue to report events and create character. Thus, in "The Burglars" the children's sexual innocence and scorn for adult life are shown in such an exchange as this between the narrator and his brother Edward:

"What's spooning?" I asked meekly.

"Oh, I dunno," said Edward, indifferently.

"It's—it's—it's just a thing they [grown-ups] do, you know."

Grahame establishes the innocent, yet knowing, character of the narrator by allowing him at the end of the story to tease his Aunt Maria and her suitor, the curate, as the latter makes "a mild curatorial joke about the moral courage required for taking the last piece of bread-and-butter[;] I felt constrained to remark dreamily, and as it were to the universe at large, 'Mr. Hodgitts! you are brave! for my sake, do not be rash!'"

While "Et in Arcadia ego" is the prevailing sentiment, there is an occasional asperity in the narrator's manner that foreshadows the more blatant cynicism of "Saki" (H.H. Munro). As the volume title suggests, there is little sense of time in this ageless world of childhood; incident follows incident with only occasional hints that time is passing, and the concluding story, "Lusisti Satis," concerning Edward's departure for school, shocks the reader into realizing that the children cannot remain in the "golden age." The narrator, carefully manipulating his recollections of the event, writes: "Fortunately I was not old enough to realize, further, that here on this little platform [of the train station] the old order lay at its last gasp, and that Edward might come back to us, but it would not be the Edward of yore, nor could things ever be the same again."

Throughout *The Golden Age* Grahame values the child's world of the imagination as equal to the adult's world of reality, and indeed through his gentle wit and humor persuades the reader that it may even be more valuable. This extolling of the imagined world and the dream life (which is very similar to George du Maurier's point of view in *Peter Ibbetson*) reaches a high point in the appropriately named

Dream Days. In the volume's eight pieces Grahame concentrates on the narrator's daydreams of wish fulfillment. Having established the character and voice of the narrator in *The Golden Age*, the author in effect omits dramatization and returns to the form of the personal essay, yet because these daydreams are the uninhibited expressions of a child, he achieves a more universal quality than was seen in the earlier *Pagan Papers*. Thus, "A Saga of the Seas" is a boy's fantasy of romantic adventure on the high seas—a concentrated summary of just such deeds as Grahame's cousin Anthony Hope [Hawkins] expanded upon in his bestselling romance *The Prisoner of Zenda*. The exception is "The Reluctant Dragon" in which, using the device of a story told by a character within a larger framework, Grahame revises the legend of St. George and the dragon. While an obvious example of Victorian whimsy, the story also has satiric intentions, with national and cultural ideals being the subject of the author's humor.

In the following decade (1898–1908) Grahame married, fathered his son, and retired from the Bank of England. But, he published nothing until 1908, when, after some difficulty in locating a publisher, he persuaded Methuen in London and Scribner's in New York to issue *The Wind in the Willows*, an outgrowth of letters and stories that he originally wrote for his young son. Although the publishers were uncertain as to the potential audience, it was accepted as a children's book and soon became—and remained throughout the twentieth century—a bestseller. Like other beast fables, it concerns the activities of a group of animals: Rat, Mole, Toad, Badger, and Otter. Although they originate in Grahame's observations of the natural world, they coexist (sometimes as peers) with the human world and in a relationship to one another that bears little resemblance to that between actual animals. Much of the charm of the work indeed lies in Grahame's unique blend of anthropomorphism and naturalism.

One clue to the writer's intention lies in the form of the work, which also shows that Grahame holds an important—and generally unacknowledged—place within the emerging modernist movement. *The Wind in the Willows* consists of twelve chapters, arranged not so much in terms of sequential action as in time periods. Each chapter establishes its precise time in the introductory paragraphs: chapter 1 is set in the spring, and the story progresses to mid-summer of the following year by chapter 7. Chapter 8 continues the story of chapter 6, although "many weeks" have passed. Chapter 9 jumps to the end of the summer, but chapters 10, 11, and 12 continue the story of chapters 6 and 8.

If chapter 1 is considered to be a prologue, an introduction to the cast of characters as well as an invocation to the springtime, then chapter 7 functions as the central chapter, with five chapters preceding and five following it. The time sequence then is summer to summer, chapter 1 being the only chapter set in the spring. The first half of the novel consists of clock and calendar time and moves from season to season. In the second half, Grahame creates a sort of mythical, perpetual, ideal summer. The two are linked by chapter 7, the midsummer chapter, so that "The Piper at the Gates of Dawn" brings the reader into the mythical world.

This organization of the novel in twelve units links the work with the classical epic, the functions of chapters 1 and 7 resembling the invocations at the beginning and at the middle of the epic. Grahame appears to have deliberately aimed at reproducing the epic structure and, through his invocations of the spring and midsummer together with his use of the animal kingdom, at thrusting the unsuspecting reader into the world of eternal verities demonstrated in the life of nature. Further evidence of Grahame's intentions may be seen in his use of generic names for his characters; in spite of their engaging personalities, they do not have personal names. Grahame does not want readers to think of one animal, limited in time and space, but rather of creatures from a world outside the boundaries of time who, having escaped individuality, have also escaped mortality.

Still, *The Wind in the Willows* is obviously not a tale of great, heroic figures upon whom the fate of nations depends. Rather, it is a tale of the humble and simple who are ignored or looked down upon by the mass of humanity. It is actually the epic turned upside down, the mock epic. Grahame does not belittle his characters by putting them in such a framework; instead he forces the reader to reexamine real-world values and to awaken to the heroic in nature. At the same time, as in traditional mock epics, the characters are presented in terms of a satiric scheme. The mock-epic form also helps to explain the wide-ranging forms and styles, for the traditional epic incorporates all sorts of

G

different writing. In *The Wind in the Willows* the author uses both prose and poetry to attain his wide-ranging literary goals which include, among others, farce (Toad in his motor cars), potential tragedy (references to the deaths of small animals in traps), pathos (Mole's longings for his home), and satire (Toad's experiences in the courts of law).

The humor of *The Wind in the Willows* depends chiefly upon the stylistic incongruities that the mock-epic demands: the tradition requires that great matters be treated with nonchalance, and minor events with the most inflated language. Since Toad epitomizes the mock-epic hero, Grahame frequently uses this stylistic device in referring to him, especially in his trial and subsequent escape from prison. Thus, although Toad is ignominiously disguised as a washerwoman and humiliatingly hurled overboard by the barge-woman, Grahame describes him as finding that "The water . . . proved quite cold enough for his taste, though its chill was not sufficient to quell his proud spirit, or slake the heat of his furious temper"— the adjectives apply rightly to the epic hero in a moment of triumph and increase the humorous incongruities of the situation. Later, the hungry Toad encounters a gypsy caravan on the common; an iron pot hangs over a fire, and:

[O]ut of that pot came forth bubblings and gurglings, and a vague suggestive steaminess. Also smells—warm, rich, and varied smells—that twined and twisted and wreathed themselves at last into one complete, voluptuous, perfect smell that seemed like the very soul of Nature taking form and appearing to her children, a true Goddess, a mother of solace and comfort. Toad now knew well that he had not been really hungry before. What he had felt earlier in the day had been a mere trifling qualm. This was the real thing at last, and no mistake, and it would have to be dealt with speedily, too, or there would be trouble for somebody or something.

To make sure that the reader understands how inappropriate such language is for Toad, the author continues with the horse-dealing scene. The gypsy offers to buy the horse at a "'Shillin' a leg,' and Toad responds: 'A shilling a leg? . . . If you please, I must take a little time to work that out, and see just what it comes to.'

He climbed down off his horse, and left it to graze, and sat down by the gypsy, and did sums on his fingers, and at last he said, 'A shilling a leg? Why, that comes to exactly four shillings, and no more.'" The length of time that Toad takes to comprehend such a simple proposition accentuates the distance between the style of the author and the subject of his writing. In fact, Grahame completely captures the mock-epic style in the passage, to the point that, as in his earlier essays, style and content are perfectly balanced.

Grahame's concern with achieving humor through his expression manifests itself in the numerous parodies found throughout *The Wind in the Willows*. They range in length from almost complete chapters to sentence-long echoes of classical or traditional writings. One particularly amusing parody is that of the Sherlock Holmes detective stories which Sir Arthur Conan Doyle began publishing about the same time that Grahame began his writing career. In chapter 3, when Rat and Mole are lost in the Wild Wood, Grahame casts Mole in the role of Dr. Watson, with Rat as Holmes. Mole has cut his shin in the snow: "'It's a very clean cut,' said the Rat, examining it again attentively. 'That was never done by a branch or a stump. Looks as if it was made by a sharp edge of something in metal. Funny!'" From this observation he is able to search for a door-scraper, which in turn leads to a door-mat, and finally to the brass plate beside the door that says "MR. BADGER." Mole's Watson-like doubts are vanquished: he "fell backwards on the snow from sheer surprise and delight. 'Rat!' he cried in penitence, 'you're a wonder! A real wonder, that's what you are. I see it all now! You argued it out, step by step, in that wise head of yours, from the very moment that I fell and cut my shin, and you looked at the cut, and at once your majestic mind said to itself, 'Doorscraper!'" And so Mole continues, providing the reader with an unmistakable impression of Conan Doyle's verbose doctor and demonstrating Grahame's talent for mimicking the popular writer.

Although Grahame shows here and in other passages his knowledge of contemporary writing, the parodies based on classical literature naturally bring him closest to the genuine mock-epic level. Perhaps the most unmistakable of these is the account of the retaking of Toad Hall in the final chapter, significantly entitled "The Return of Ulysses." Grahame particularly enjoys manipulating sound effects (a fact that makes the work so suitable for reading out loud) as he describes how Badger, Rat, Mole, and Toad spring upon the weasels in the banqueting-hall:

> What a squealing and a squeaking and a screeching filled the air!
>
> Well might the terrified weasels dive under the tables and spring madly up at the windows! Well might the ferrets rush wildly for the fireplace and get hopelessly jammed in the chimney! Well might tables and chairs be upset, and glass and china be sent crashing on the floor, in the panic of that terrible moment when the four Heroes strode wrathfully into the room! The mighty Badger, his whiskers bristling, his great cudgel whistling through the air; Mole, black and grim, brandishing his stick and shouting his awful war-cry, "A Mole! A Mole!" Rat, desperate and determined, his belt bulging with weapons of every age and every variety; Toad, frenzied with excitement and injured pride, swollen to twice his ordinary size, leaping into the air emitting Toad-whoops that chilled them to the marrow!

While *The Wind in the Willows* may well be read and enjoyed solely on the merits of its story and style (and generations of readers have been content to do so), it gains additional richness and meaning when considered in relationship to its author's life and possible intentions. Grahame developed the work between 1904 and 1908 when he was at middle age and making tremendous adjustments to married life and parenthood; moreover, he was living in a place with many personal associations, for in 1906 he had moved from London to Cookham Dene, his childhood home. Green declares that Grahame's "inner purpose throughout [the novel] was threefold: to satirize contemporary society, to sublimate his personal life, and to construct an ideal model of the Good Life."[3] Writing in this pre-Freudian age (and consistently maintaining that the work had no ulterior motives—"it is only an expression of the very simplest joys of life as lived by the simplest beings," he declared to his admirer President Theodore Roosevelt[4]), he draws a picture of the males of the privileged upper bourgeoisie. They are the upholders of law and order who expect—and in this ideal world receive—the respect due them from the lower classes. (The only females in the entire work are the bargee's wife and the gaol-keeper's daughter, both humans of the lower classes.) Like Grahame himself, Mole, Rat, Toad, and Badger represent a social class threatened from within and from without. Some members of this social group fail to uphold the standards of their class: Toad allows his passion for novelties to gain the upper hand, and—most heinous of crimes—he wastes the patrimonial fortune. At the same time there is the constant presence of the hoi-polloi and the rabble from the Wild Wood—the stoats and weasels who take over Toad Hall. Only the physical force of the superior class can conquer the lower and force its members to clean up Toad Hall. Once the upper bourgeoisie regain power, the idyll of the long summer resumes. Although this satiric level may appear to be at odds with the almost century-long acceptance of *The Wind in the Willows* as a harmless children's story, it is confirmed by biographical accounts of Grahame and of his friends and contemporaries. This fable of harmless little animals puts forward the not-very-gentle, certainly sexist, and possibly even fascistic, social and political ideals of a late-Victorian reactionary.

Grahame's satire is not limited to political matters, for *The Wind in the Willows* also includes such matters as Toad and his imprisonment (a reference, understood even by Grahame's contemporaries, to Oscar Wilde's jail sentence) and the Sea Rat and his bohemian existence. With these incidents Grahame moves away from conscious satire into a region that he undoubtedly suspected but, given his psychological make-up and social background, could never have verbalized. In the heart of this conservative author there is a strong longing for the opposite way of life: the life of the artist, a disdain for the limitations imposed by polite society, a Dionysian spirit that yearns for a freedom of mind and body not unlike that which D.H. Lawrence writes about in his stories and novels. Grahame's divided loyalties are most obvious in his creation of Badger, the epitome of the strong father figure who does not allow himself to be held in by the limitations of polite society, and in the story of Toad's brushes with the law. Such tensions between opposing psychological concepts provides an important level of meaning in the work, yet Grahame does not allow it to become a dominant force. It is controlled within the novel's own structure, specifically in the figure of Rat. When he longs to throw aside his domestic world, to follow after the Sea Rat, and to visit distant lands, he suppresses such longings by letting Mole persuade him to write verses. Thus, aesthetic expression holds destructive psychological forces in check. If Grahame offers a moral lesson in the work, it may well lie here, for he balances his own fears, unhappinesses, and attitudes through the characters and actions of this novel. What appears to be absolute fiction ultimately reveals itself to be a self-portrait of its author disguised in the fantastic characters that he creates. Mole is the domestic, home-loving side of his nature; Rat is the artist who sublimates his longings in the act of artistic creation; Toad is the unrepressed, boisterous child still living in the man; Badger is the ideal, strong male, the archetypal father-figure who is at once both longed for and feared; Otter is the loving father, who is also the clever provider. Together they might be considered to form Grahame's ideal male figure.

While Grahame wrote various occasional pieces after 1908 and even edited the *Cambridge Book of Poetry for Children* in 1916, thereby acknowledging the role of children's author which the success of *The Wind in the Willows* had thrust upon him, he never published another book or major piece of writing.

Summary

Although known first as an essayist and the creator of idylls of childhood, after 1908 Kenneth Grahame was associated with *The Wind in the Willows* and considered to be primarily a writer of children's literature. However, while the characters, incidents, and setting of this work can appeal to any age level, it is essentially a serious satire that sets forth the political ideals of a late Victorian, couched in forms that anticipate the structural and satiric practices of several of the early modernist authors.

Notes

1. Peter Morris Green, *Beyond the Wild Wood. The World of Kenneth Grahame, Author of The Wind in the Willows* (New York: Facts on File, 1983), p. 81.
2. *Ibid.*, p. 85.
3. *Ibid.*, p. 141.
4. Patrick Chalmers, *Kenneth Grahame: Life, Letters and Unpublished Work* (London: Methuen, 1933), p. 138.

Selected Bibliography
Primary Sources
Pagan Papers. London: Elkin Matthews and John Lane, 1894 [1893].
The Golden Age. London: John Lane, 1895.
The Headswoman. London: John Lane, 1898. Bodley Booklets, No. 5.
Dream Days. London: John Lane, The Bodley Head, 1899 [1898].
The Wind in the Willows. London: Methuen, and New York: Scribner's, 1908.

Secondary Sources
Chalmers, Patrick. *Kenneth Grahame: Life, Letters and Unpublished Work*. London: Methuen, 1933. Port Washington, NY, and London: Kennikat Press, 1972. The "official" biography, written in the customary adulatory style, and providing many hitherto unreprinted writings, as well as letters by and to Grahame.
Graham, Eleanor. *Kenneth Grahame*. London: Bodley Head, 1963. A short study of Grahame as a writer of children's literature.
Green, Peter Morris. *Kenneth Grahame, 1859–1932: A Study of His Life, Work and Times*. London: John Murray, and New York: World, 1959. Rpt. in an abridged form with extensive illustrations as *Beyond the Wild Wood: The World of Kenneth Grahame, Author of The Wind in the Willows*. Exeter, England: Webb and Bower, 1982; New York: Facts on File, 1983. The standard biography and critical study of Grahame. The 1959 edition provides the most complete checklist of his writings, as well as a general list of secondary material, while the 1982 revision is based on manuscript documents preserved by Lord Courtauld-Thomson, the brother of Mrs. Elspeth Grahame, and provides many important photographs in both color and black-and-white.
Kuznets, Lois. *Kenneth Grahame*. Boston: Twayne, 1987. Twayne's English Authors Series No. 449. Working within the TEAS format, Kuznets provides summaries of the primary writings while noting influences upon Grahame and the judgments of his critics. The focus is generally on Grahame as a writer of children's literature. Includes a usefully annotated list of contemporary periodical criticism.
Elgin W. Mellown

Gray, Simon

Born: Hayling Island, Hampshire, October 20, 1936

Education: Westminster School; Dalhousie University, B.A. (honors in English), 1958; Cambridge University, B.A. (honors in English), 1963

Marriage: Beryl Mary Kerven, August 20, 1964; two children

Biography

The son of physician James Davidson and Barbara Celia May Holliday Gray, Simon James Holliday Gray was born on Hayling Island, Hampshire, England, on October 20, 1936. To escape the hostilities of World War II, in 1940 he and his brother were sent to stay with their grandparents in Montreal, Canada. Gray's first diary details the feelings of displacement and acts of mischief that occurred during that period. At the age of nine he returned to London where he barely met the admission criteria of Westminster School. However, after he matriculated, his talent for essay writing and his keen interest in games became apparent. Once he was nearly expelled for an escapade which involved defrauding the London Transport system. In order to gain both a ticket and some loose change, he substituted Georgian pennies for the required fare. Chastened by this event, Gray settled into the life of the school and excelled in the classroom and on the playing field.

The pattern of moving back and forth between Britain and Canada continued. In 1953, he returned to Canada where he won a place at Dalhousie University, Halifax, Nova Scotia. Upon completion of the B.A. degree with honors in English in 1958, he accepted a lectureship at the University in Clermont-Ferraud, France. Returning to England in 1963 to study at Cambridge University, Gray earned a second B.A. in English, with honors. He stayed on at Cambridge as a research fellow. During this time, the first of three satiric novels, *Colmain* (1963), was published. This was followed by *Simple People* (1963) and *Little Portia* (1967).

His university degrees completed in 1964, Gray accepted an offer to return to Canada where he joined the faculty of the University of British Columbia as a lecturer in English. He married Beryl Mary Kerven, a picture researcher, on August 20. Eventually, they would have two children. Gray's understanding of the publishing field began here while he served as an editor for *Delta Magazine*.

Next, Gray returned to Cambridge as a supervisor in English in 1965. He published his second novel and in 1966 took a lecturer's position at Queen Mary College, London. Thus, Gray's claim that he went to the university at seventeen and never left continued to be accurate for some twenty years. He had embarked on a career which ultimately offered him many roles as professor, playwright, novelist, scriptwriter, editor, and stage director. The Oxford and London productions of *Butley* in 1971 firmly established his reputation as a playwright; the subsequent New York production in 1972 secured him international recognition.

Until 1984, he continued as a lecturer in English Literature at Queen Mary College while writing for both stage and screen. His television plays include *Death of a Teddy Bear* (1967), for which he won the Writers' Guild Award, as well as adaptations from his stage plays of *The Rear Column* (1980), *Melon* (1990), *Quartermaine's Terms* (1987), and *The Common Pursuit* (1990). The screenplays include *After Pilkington* (1987), *Butley* (adapted from the stage play, 1975), and *A Month in the Country* (1987). He adapted *The Common Pursuit* for film in 1993.

Gray has also turned to directing his own works. The revivals of *The Common Pursuit* (1988) at the Phoenix in London and the Promenade in New York and *The Holy Terror* (1992) at the Promenade as well as the original London production of *Hidden Laughter* were under his direction.

Literary Analysis

Gray is best known as a popular, commercial playwright. People and scenes from academic and literary life provide the objects for his satiric critiques. With great verbal and visual wit, he writes about middle-aged men who are adrift and who metaphorically war with the social mores and conventions that both define and confine them. The bureaucracies of school, government, and church and the suffocation of marriage and the office are all subject to scathing verbal attacks. The work is excellently crafted; Gray's education has given him a deep understanding of literature and dramatic form which he often uses to parody past traditions and to reveal the shallowness of present social conventions.

The author's early plays *Wise Child* (1967), *Dutch Uncle* (1969), and *Spoiled* (1970) stem from the tradition of Georges Feydeau farces and Agatha Christie mysteries. With wildly funny suspense and fast-moving turns of plot, the dramatist plays on ambiguous sexual identity, exploiting both visual and verbal humor. *Wise Child*, originally written as a television script, was considered unsuitable for family viewing. Produced in London in 1967, its black humor and complex farcical plot, which starred Alex Guinness in drag, caused something of a scandal. With a classic farce setting of two adjoining bedrooms, the plot revolves around two robbers who are hiding out in the seedy hotel, one disguised as the mother of the other. The hotel owner is a middle-aged homosexual who falls for the younger crook. Playing on this lust, the crooks plot to steal the hotel bankroll. Critics suggested that the audience was uncertain as to the sexual identities and relationships of the characters; similar ambiguities show up in the later plays.

Dutch Uncle provides an excellent example of the visual jokes made through the relationships of characters to objects. On stage there is an oversized wardrobe, which Godboy has bought and prepared especially for the purpose of murdering his wife. Getting rid of May Godboy will allow him to have an affair with his neighbor's wife and gain notoriety which will attract the male Inspector Hawkins, whom he idolizes. His efforts to get his wife into the cupboard end in an amusing reversal of the situation. The play suggests Gray's themes of marital estrangement and uncertain sexual identity. (The later *Stage Struck* [1979] demonstrates Gray's more mature craft as he has skillfully perfected his farcical techniques.)

With the abolition of stage censorship in Britain, these first plays flirt with once taboo subjects. *Spoiled* lays the groundwork for an exploration of erotic relationships between teachers and students.[1] Howarth has invited Donald home for the weekend to study French. Teaching becomes a seductive act. The characters use humor to gain power over one another.

While a number of the playwright's interests are indicated in these early plays, the true originality and refinement of themes and comic devices are found in Gray's artistically and commercially successful school plays: *Butley* and *Quartermaine's Terms*. These are his best works aesthetically; they are also his most representative plays. Although *Butley* opened initially to mixed critical reviews, audiences embraced it enthusiastically. It offered a stellar role for Alan Bates and was directed by Harold Pinter; it be-

gan an important and continuing theatrical alliance among the playwright and this actor and director.

Set in a university office replicating Gray's own, in the play the dramatist details Ben Butley's bad day. Butley's wife has left him, and his former prize student Joey, now both his office and apartment mate, has taken a new lover.[2] With great wit and needling perseverance, Butley pries and probes to confirm his suspicions and to exact the details of Joey's new relationship with Reg, a London publisher. During his interrogation, Butley is constantly and comically interrupted by students who seek tutorials, administrators and colleagues who have complaints, and his wife, Anne, who wants a divorce so that she can marry "the most boring man in London."

Butley is a consummate game player, as is Gray.[3] Butley skillfully competes and wins a number of rounds only to lose finally the professional and personal relationships which were after all perhaps not worth having. He tells Joey, "All our games together are going a trifle stale, Reg and I may be able to find some new ones."[4] In the taunting culminating scene, Butley goads Reg by mimicking his northern dialect and denigrating his class origins. He is finally decked by Reg, who refuses to continue to play.

Butley then performs for Joey a replay of their first T.S. Eliot tutorial. Gardner, a new student, whom Butley has commandeered from one of his colleagues, seems a possible replacement for Joey. However, Joey leaves and Butley gives up the game:

> Ben: Go away Gardner . . . I don't want to start again. It's all been a ghastly mistake . . . You're not what I mean at all, not what I mean at all. I'm too old to play with the likes of you. (74)

The complexity of Gray's intriguing central character has stirred considerable critical debate. Katherine H. Burkman places the character of Butley in the tradition of the fool figure whose fooling reveals the "aridity of life around him."[5] Verbal and gestural *double entendre* mock university pedantry, literary and theatrical conventions, and the characters' current situations. Literary allusions from John Donne, Lord Byron, Eliot, John Milton, John Suckling, and William Shakespeare, among others, coupled with Beatrix Potter's middle-class nursery rhymes operate as linguistic games which Butley uses to dominate or to secure relationships with the other characters.

These verbal games also make a game for the audience who can puzzle out the parallels of past verse to current circumstances. Sophia B. Blaydes argues that the use of this intersexuality simultaneously reveals character and satirizes academics.[6] Laughter can come from a fresh framing. Butley often gives a sexual turn to the allusions. For example, Joey is trying to prepare a lecture on William Blake; Butley, seeking to discover the intimate facts of Joey's sexual alliance, queries him with a Blake quotation: "Did he who made the lamb make thee?"

In the clown tradition Butley takes a squashed banana from his pocket and throws its peel on Joey's desk. He is at war with an object in the best of such traditions: he tries to get the lamp on his own desk to light; he exchanges it for Joey's. When Joey enters, he, of course, turns on the malfunctioning desk light without trouble. Butley foolishly wears a cotton wad on his chin from a shaving mishap. These silent actions come from the *Auguste*[7] clown tradition and from cinema comedian's shtick.

In his verbal games of oneupmanship, Butley's opponents ultimately lose because they try to play by the rules of their past relationships only to find that Butley, as master improviser, has changed the game. The result is a triple game—one within the play, another which parodies social, literary, and theatrical traditions, and yet another which the playwright is simultaneously playing with his audience:

> Ben: . . . Does Reg's mother work in the shop, too?
> Joey: No.
> Ben: Oh. Where is she then, in the daytime?
> Joey: Out.
> Ben: Out where?
> Joey: Just out.
> Ben: She has a job then?
> Joey: Yes.
> Ben: And where does she do this job? On the streets?
> Joey: You could put it like that, yes.
> Ben: What does she do? Sweep them?
> Joey: No.
> Ben: She walks them?
> Joey: Yes, in point of fact.

> Ben: The precise suburb is irrelevant. (pause) So Reg's mother is a prostitute.
> *Joey giggles, checks himself.*
> Joey: No, she's a—traffic warden. (18/19)

Rhythms of the music hall and a traditional joke structure are apparent. The audience-players and character-players are presented with a mystery, sufficient clues for successfully finding its solution, and a pause where if they knew the proper frame, they might offer the correct answer; then the winner delivers the scoring punch line.

Butley loses this particular round to Joey. By a series of topic changes, he eventually finds out what he seeks to know. It is the one who knows who has the power. All of the central characters withhold information from one another or refuse to recognize a truth when confronted by it.

Parodying the structure of Greek tragedy while maintaining the classical unities, Gray creates a complex anti-hero. The fun lies in the repartee among True Wits, Would-be Wits, and the Witless, in the play's mocking of theatrical form and academic pretensions, and in the self-conscious awareness of this double game:

> Joey: Well then—well then—I can't keep it from myself any longer. I've been trying to keep you and Reg apart because I knew this would happen. But I've been longing for it, all the same. (Pause) I'm sorry it had to be today, what with Anne and Tom. I would have waited . . .
> Ben: (in senile professional tones) Which shows you have no sense of classical form. We're preserving the unities. The use of messengers has been quite skillful. (70)

Where Oedipus puts out his eyes, Butley, who has seen himself in Joey's mirror, once again tries to turn on the desk lamp.

Gray's humor is made manifest not only in the verbal pyrotechnics and visual pictures created within the comic situation of a teacher who tries not to teach, but also in the parodic relationship between the play and its audience. These stratagems provide clear examples of Gray's comic techniques, which are found at play in all of his other texts as well.

Quartermaine's Terms, thought by many critics to be Gray's best dramatic achievement, offers the second paradigm for studying Gray's comic techniques. The naming of St. John Quartermaine for the desert saint and Rider Haggard's explorer hero is an example of Dickensian irony. (Charles Dickens is Gray's special scholarly subject, and a writer who has much influenced him.) In an inversion of the brilliant, sarcastic, and often cruel characterization of Butley, Quartermaine is a submissive and mediocre but lovable teacher whose task is to teach English to foreign students. The play takes place in the school's staff room and the focus is on the relationships among its inhabitants. Its structural game follows the model of Anton Chekhov's *The Cherry Orchard*. In a nonlinear use of time, the major events in the characters' lives occur between the scenes, and what is not said is often more important than what is actually stated. The comedy in the language lies in social pleasantries and in the inadequacies of words to express true feelings. Language fails to connect people. Speech conceals rather than reveals. The limitations of language and the conventions of politeness are part of the joke:

> *Quartermaine:* I say, how's old Camelia?
> *Sackling:* (barks out a laugh) Oh fine! just—fine!
> *Quartermaine:* Terrific, and little Tom too?
> *Sackling:* Tom too, oh yes, Tom too.
> *Quartermaine:* The last time I saw him he was teething, standing there in his high chair dribbling away like anything, while Camelia was sitting on old Mark's lap making faces at him with orange peel in her mouth—
> Sackling bursts into tears. Anita goes to Sackling, puts her hand on his shoulder.
> *Quartermaine:* What? Oh—oh Lord!
> (214)

Sackling's wife has left him. He laments that if she had not left him just as he was to read her part of the novel that he was writing, she would have known his true feelings. Sackling can write sentiments; unfortunately, he cannot say aloud the words that truly express them.

The playful Gray has great fun not only formally but also topically with *The Cherry Orchard*, which is presumably playing at the nearby theater. References to it provide a running joke and one of the staff says about it, "All that Russian gloom and doom and people shooting themselves from loneliness and depression and that sort of thing. But then mother says I don't understand comedy" (238). Ending as does *The Cherry Orchard* with the new order replacing the old, Quartermaine like the Chekhovian servant is left alone on stage. Time and his colleagues have passed him by. The suffering of lost career hopes, the loss of love, and the breakdowns of loved ones are the bittersweet portrayals of little people who are utterly isolate in Gray's creation of this very human comedy.

The ghosts—those characters who are absent on stage but present in conversation—serve as devices that provide comic texture. They are used as an important thematic idea in *The Common Pursuit* (1984). One, most particularly, exists in references to F.R. Leavis and his "Great Tradition." Leavis, an influential critic and renowned university don, believed that the study of great books would provide models of high standards which his students (Gray, among them) could use as a basis for leading significant and productive lives. A character gets a fictional letter from this now deceased real person:

> Good God, there's a letter here from old Leavis! (Reads out.) "Can't persuade myself that in the current literary and indeed cultural climate, when the decline in our Cambridge values . . . ." (293)

Gray's story, a postmodern morality play, centers on five Cambridge graduates who plan to start a literary magazine to be named *The Common Pursuit* in Leavis's honor. The play, originally entitled *Partners*, provides the culmination of a number of themes evident in prior works but makes an important formal change and portrays a fragmented contemporary environment. In creating a technological world, similar to the one indicated in *Otherwise Engaged* (1975) but more fully critiqued here, the playwright presents some would-be literary careerists who verbally subscribe to Leavis's great tradition; however, as Gray explores the patterns of their lives from graduation through middle age, they often fall short of their ideals—to establish their critical standards and to demonstrate that they are serious (traditionally, seriousness was that prized Victorian quality of earnestness and commitment):

Stuart: What we need to talk about now isn't simply what we want for our first few issues but our whole future. One very important thing . . . is that, above all, we've got to be very careful. Take into account all the things that could go wrong, all the traps that other people have fallen into when starting out on something like this. That's the only way we'll survive. By knowing what it is we are about to give the world precisely.

Marigold: Absolutely.

Martin: Yes. Absolutely. (353)

Developing themes that reveal today's world as chaotic, hostile, and chancy, Gray creates characters who have no center; they are merely role players, often dislocated. Identity is only a set of relationships, a facet of where the character is located in timespace. In *Quartermaine's Terms*, one of the teachers quotes his daughter: "she suddenly insisted that we couldn't prove that other people existed—and that perhaps when we thought about them or remembered them or saw and heard them even—we were actually just making them up—and of course I took her up on this and attempted to explain how it is we do know that other people exist including people we don't know exist, if you follow—(Laughing.) and she kept saying 'But you can't prove it, Daddy, you can't actually prove it!'" (240–42).

While Gray always provides connections between the comic and the serious considerations and ideas lying beneath the surfaces, his demands on the audience's sympathies for evaluation of the characters' behaviors are most important and more fully developed in this play. The characters are in pursuit of "true judgement" and the audience is also asked to join with them in the search. Although the many laughter-provoking devices are those previously established, in this play Gray's use of time and space is very contemporary. The first scene is interrupted and then finished at the end of the piece. The audience, Janus-like, can judge the characters' lives in the process of their becoming, yet it is finally reminded of the promise, mostly unfulfilled, for their leading the important lives predicted in their youthful primary scene.

The dramatist also plays one of his literary games, this time with Oscar Wilde's *The Impor-*

tance of Being Earnest. Characters use the social etiquette which is also social restriction to find various freedoms, usually sexual. Peter, whose marital location is in the country, pretends to have meetings with Martin in the city where he can easily meet his mistress. Marigold, who lives with Stuart, claims a visit to sick parents in the country which frees her eventually to replace Stuart with Martin. The homosexual Humphry creates the illusion of heterosexuality for his parents through weekend visits to a woman in the country. These characters are literally and metaphorically dislocated. Moving from place to place and from alliance to alliance, they cannot seem to find out who they really are:

> *Martin:* But why on earth don't you come and stay with me? You can have either of the spare rooms. Or both of them. I can move old Samantha [the cat] back to my bed. There she longs to be anyway, and would be, if she didn't make me sneeze. So why don't you move in? Tonight if you want.
>
> *Stuart:* Thanks. But I'm here from strategy, too, you see. I have an odd feeling. To do with territory. That after seven years it would be harder to get me out of here if I've made this completely mine at last. If Giorgio does try to evict me, he'll get nervous if he finds I'm sleeping here. He'll start imagining me as some animal defending his lair. A threatened lion or a trapped tiger. Or a bankrupt rat. Anyway, something savage with teeth and jaws. (302)

The playwright claims that there is no plot, only a set of happenings, which he describes as "the routine stuff of English social comedy."[8] Those material acts, which frequently are associated with genres like the Well-Made Play or Comedy of Manners, are played out discontinuously here. The temporal patterns shift the audience's attention away from the characters' psychological development and toward a cultural and social critique.

Gray writes two diaries—*The Unnatural Pursuit and Other Pieces* (1985) and *How's That for Telling 'Em, Fat Lady?* (1988)—about the writing process and his London and California production experiences with this play. These companion pieces with the play make a double fiction, one which is self-revealing about Gray's own personal pursuits. For example, the author has frequently been asked if he based the character of Butley on himself. In the introduction to *Plays: One*, he says, "I now realize that it was far more likely that, for a time at least, I based myself on Butley—or more precisely, Alan Bates's performance of it" (ix). In the creation of a performing self in his writing acts, Gray also functions as an astute chronicler of his times.

Perhaps as the playwright faces his own mortality in whatever midlife crises that he experiences, he seeks to face and, possibly, to defeat death through laughter in *Close of Play* (1979), *Melon* (1987), and *Hidden Laughter* (1990). These are his family plays. The exploration of the meaning of existence and the search for some kind of truth on which to base a life still plague Gray's characters. For instance, *Melon* takes place in memory; its simultaneous setting shows four rooms: the psychiatric room, Melon's publishing office, Melon's bedroom, and Melon's sitting room. The story is of mental breakdown, and in it Melon is both narrator and character. He opens the play directly:

> I'll tell you what happens. This is what happens. One day—one perfectly routine—perfect in its routineness, routine in its perfectness because one thing you discover when what happens—and it might! Why shouldn't it? That's the point after all—when what happens to me happens to you . . . One Day. There you'll be, walking along on the surface, as always. One foot placing itself casually, unthinkingly, thoughtlessly, unwatchfully—hah! above all, unwatchfully in front of another, strolling coolly along you are, possibly, humming. Or humming eagerly along to where you go for your pleasures, or because you're late for work, when suddenly—yes, quite suddenly without the slightest warning—the ground opens at your feet.[9]

Bates gave a *tour de force* performance making Gray's portrayal of a man trapped in existential despair both comic and tragic.

In the introduction to *The Holy Terror and Tartuffe* (1990), a revision of *Melon*, Gray reveals his continuing, nagging feelings of dissatisfaction with the original play. He decided to revisit the earlier play, and the result is an extensive revision. The changes demonstrate Gray's comic techniques as well as a legacy of British humor. Its comedy lies not in the story (of psychological breakdown) but in the complexity of its central character, its social satire, its events, and its funny lines. The first monologue, rewritten in a more playful and energetic voice, still belongs to Mark Melon, who now is speaking to the Women's Institute in Cheltenham, England. Melon, the terror of the publishing world, both regales them with commentary and reenacts the story of his rise and fall. He seems to be a character in his own play. Melon's name, like those of his medieval comic ancestors, designates his excess: melancholy. Moving from success to success, Melon initially encounters some hilarious publishing proposals: a manuscript in made-up language and a comedy of contemporary manners written in heroic couplets. He solicits a novel that he considers "ill natured pornography" in order to bed its author. His clothes come off for a quick "lunch" with his smart and sexy secretary, who wants help with her preparation on Shakespeare for her university exams, and he finds himself in his underwear addressing the ladies' club. Melon speaks of his work at the office as "sport" and his colleagues as "playmates." In continued clowning, he literally stands on his head. Suspicion and jealousy cause him to accuse his wife of infidelity; his Comedy-of-Manners fear of cuckoldry causes his downfall and eventually drives him to a sort of Groucho Marx psychiatrist named in the cast list as Shrink.

The explanation for Melon's problem, like that in *The Importance of Being Earnest*, is related to sibling rivalry. Melon protests that he never had a brother:[10]

> *Shrink:* Don't worry. Doesn't matter in the slightest. In fact quite the contrary. Not having an actual sibling to rival meant you had to make one up. Having made him up, you had to assault him for not existing. Which is precisely what you did to the friend of yours who was *not* having an affair with your wife. His not having an affair was the treachery of the brother who didn't exist. If he had existed, he would have affirmed the rivalry and thus his

siblingness by actually having an affair with your wife, and would have eventually required psychiatric help himself. As it is, you've had to come in his place. In other words *you* are your nonexistent brother. (66)

Gray directed the New York production, as he had done with the New York revival of *The Common Pursuit*. He also directed his most recent work, *Hidden Laughter*. This play takes its title from Eliot's "Burnt Norton," the beginning of the "Four Quartets." In it, Gray's concern is with the spiritual and moral responsibility of his characters, which makes for an interesting thematic development. A middle-class family, which includes three generations, acquires a weekend cottage that they call "Little Paradise." Gray works into the comedy an allegory of contemporary life and evidences a nostalgia for the past of the great tradition, a past in a more stable world. The most interesting character is the vicar Ronnie, who is the family's neighbor and serves both literally and metaphorically as their gardener. Though they are not his parishioners, he acts as their friend and confessor. Ben, a recent widower, expresses difficulty in believing in "a God who condones madness, death . . . "[11] The vicar agrees:

Ben: Well, do you or don't you believe in God?

Ronnie: I don't know—well, who can say—but . . . but . . . the point is— you see, there's no point in believing in him unless it's impossible to believe in him, if you follow, because if he existed, and we all knew he existed there'd be no difficulty at all in believing in him and what'd be the point in *that* . . . fair is . . . a matter of believing what's impossible to believe. Do you, um, see? Otherwise it's not faith. It's certainty. If you follow. (10)

The vicar himself is an unsure spiritual mentor. The Edenic garden contrasts ironically with the contemporary social problems (abortion, care for the elderly, homosexuality, adultery) with which the play is concerned. The characters engage in illusive searches for happiness, a state that is ever present, though these foolish mortals cannot find it.

Summary

Novelist, professor, stage director, and script writer, Simon Gray is most recognized for his witty and urbane work as a playwright. A master of comic situations, he is admired for his development of complex antiheroic protagonists, which many critics suggest are autobiographical. His clever use of language and literary allusions as well as his parodic dramatic structures connect the comic play to serious thought. He stands as a chronicler of his class and times. With biting observations of the social scene, Gray creates intriguing protagonists who engage in either verbal pyrotechnics or who, as sounding boards for other characters, seek for themselves peace and quiet order amid the chaos of the contemporary, technological world. Gray writes not only for the stage but also for film and television. *Otherwise Engaged*, *Quartermaine's Terms*, and *Melon* are cited with *Butley* as his best and most representative works.

Notes

1. See, for example, Judith Roof, "Simon Gray and the Pedagogical Erotics of Theatre," in *Simon Gray: A Casebook*, ed. Katherine H. Burkman (New York: Garland, 1992), pp. 25–39.

2. See John M. Clum, "Being Took Queer": Homosexuality in Simon Gray's Plays," in Burkman, pp. 61–83.

3. For a discussion of literature as game playing and authors as games players, see, for example, *Auctor Ludens: Essays on Play in Literature*, ed. Gerald Guinness and Andrew Hurley (Philadelphia: John Benjamins, 1986); Peter Hutchinson, *Games Authors Play* (London: Methuen, 1983); Richard Poirier, *The Performing Self: Compositions and Decompositions in the Language of Contemporary Life* (New York: Oxford University Press, 1971).

4. Simon Gray, *Butley*, in *Plays: One* (London and New York: Methuen, 1986), p. 47. Further references to *Butley* are from this text, as are the references from *Quartermaine's Terms* and *The Common Pursuit*.

5. See Katherine H. Burkman, "The Fool as Hero: Simon Gray's *Butley* and *Otherwise Engaged*," *Theatre Journal*, 33 (1981): 163–72.

6. See Sophia B. Blaydes, "Literary Allusion as Satire in Simon Gray's *Butley*," *Midwest Quarterly*, 18 (July 1977): 374–91.

G

7. Named for its 1860 originator, this clown character is a descendent of the Vice character in Medieval plays. The *Auguste* clown is an untidy buffoon who shows up at inappropriate times to spoil his partner's tricks. Generally, he thoroughly enjoys fouling situations up.

8. Gray, *The Unnatural Pursuit and Other Pieces* (New York: St. Martin's Press, 1985).

9. Gray, *Melon* (London: Methuen, 1987).

10. Gray, *The Holy Terror and Tartuffe* (London and Boston: Faber and Faber, 1990).

11. Gray, *Hidden Laughter* (London: Faber & Faber, 1990), p. 10.

Selected Bibliography
Primary Sources

Collected Works
The Definitive Simon Gray. 2 vols. London: Faber & Faber, 1992.

Plays—Publications
Dutch Uncle. London: Faber & Faber, 1969.
Spoiled. London: Methuen, 1971.
Butley. London: Methuen, 1971; New York: Viking, 1972.
Otherwise Engaged. London: French, 1976.
Close of Play and Pig in a Poke. London: Eyre Methuen, 1979.
Quartermaine's Terms. London: Eyre Methuen, 1979; New York: French, 1983.
Stage Struck. London: Eyre Methuen, 1979; New York: French, 1979.
The Common Pursuit. London: Methuen, 1984.
Plays: One. London and New York: Methuen, 1986. Includes *Butley, Otherwise Engaged, The Rear Column, Quartermaine's Terms, The Common Pursuit.*
Wise Child. New York: French, 1974; London: Faber & Faber, 1986.
Melon. London: Methuen, 1987.
Hidden Laughter. London and Boston: Faber & Faber, 1990.
The Holy Terror and Tartuffe. London and Boston: Faber & Faber, 1990.

Novels
Colmain. London: Faber & Faber, 1963.
A Comeback for Stark, under the pseudonym Hamish Reade. London: Faber & Faber, 1969.

Non-Fiction
How's That for Telling 'Em, Fat Lady? London: Faber & Faber, 1988.
The Unnatural Pursuit and Other Pieces. New York: St. Martin's Press, 1985.

Secondary Sources

Books
Burkman, Katherine H., ed. *Simon Gray: A Casebook.* New York: Garland, 1992. Eleven essays "range over Gray's dramatic career, discussing all of his plays from *Wise Child* (1967) to *Hidden Laughter* (1990)." Contains an excellent chronology of his life and works including television, screen, and radio plays, as well as a carefully annotated bibliography.

Articles and Chapters in Books
Blaydes, Sophia B. "Literary Allusion as Satire in Simon Gray's Butley." *Midwest Quarterly,* 18 (July 1977): 374–91. Blaydes demonstrates the revelation of character through the satiric use of allusions as laugh-producing attacks and defenses: an intersexuality that subverts the academy.

Burkman, Katherine. "The Fool as Hero: Simon Gray's *Butley* and *Otherwise Engaged.*" *Theatre Journal,* 33 (1981): 163–72. Burkman reveals the ritual pattern of the plays and places their central characters within the fool tradition.

Cornish, Roger, and Violet Ketels. "Introduction" to *Quartermaine's Terms.* In *Landmarks of Modern British Drama.* Vol. 2. London: Methuen, 1985, pp. 445–50. The play in relationship to Anton Chekhov's work. Includes biographical data and some references to earlier plays.

Gale, Steven H. "Simon Gray." In *Critical Survey of Drama.* Vol. 2. Ed. Frank Magill. Englewood Cliffs, NJ: Salem Press, 1985, pp. 804–13. Useful evaluation and description of Gray's plays up to *Quartermaine's Terms.*

———. "Simon Gray's *Butley*: From Stage to Screen." In *Simon Gray: A Casebook.* Ed. Katherine H. Burkman. New York: Garland, 1992, pp. 85–100.

Imhof, Rudiger. "Simon Gray." In *Essays on Contemporary British Drama.* Ed. Hedwig Bock and Albert Wertheim. Munich: Max Hueber Verlag, 1981, pp.

223–52. In addition to brief discussions of the early plays, Imhof provides in-depth criticism of *Butley*, *Otherwise Engaged*, and *The Rear Column*.

Mills, John. "Old Mr. Prickle-Pin: Simon Gray's *Butley*." *American Imago*, 45, 4 (1988): 411–29. A psychoanalytic investigation of Butley's self-destructive urges and repressed homosexuality.

Nothof, Anne. "Simon Gray's Comedy of Bad Manners." *Essays in Theatre*, 6, 2 (May 1988): 109–22. Nothof locates the plays in the tradition of Restoration comedy.

Shafer, Yvonne. "Aristophanic and Chekhovian Structure in the Plays of Simon Gray." *Theatre Studies*, 31/32 (1984–86): 32–40. Structural analyses in which Aristophanes and Chekhov are used to illuminate the actions in *Otherwise Engaged* and *Quartermaine's Terms*.

Smith, Carolyn. "Simon Gray and the Grotesque." In *Within the Dramatic Spectrum*. Ed. Karelisa Hartigan. New York: University of American Presses, 1986, pp. 168–76. A look at the Grotesque in *Butley*, *Otherwise Engaged*, and *Quartermaine's Terms*, applying Wolfgang Kayser's *The Grotesque in Art and Literature* (1963) and Mikhail Bakhtin's *Rabelais and His World* (1948) as critical strategies.

Marya Bednerik

Greene, Graham

Born: Berkhamsted, Hertfordshire, October 2, 1904

Education: Berkhamsted School, 1912–1922; Balliol College, Oxford University, 1922–1925

Marriage: Vivien Dayrell-Browning, 1927; two children

Died: Vevey, Switzerland, April 3, 1991

Biography

Henry Graham Greene was born on October 2, 1904, the fourth of six children, in Berkhamsted, Hertfordshire, just northwest of London. His parents, Charles Henry and Marion Raymond Greene, were first cousins and could trace their lineage back through centuries of successful Greenes; perhaps of more eventual importance to her son, Graham Greene's mother was also a first cousin of Robert Louis Stevenson. For Greene's first six years, the family lived at St. John's house, Berkhamsted School, where his father taught; the family moved into the village proper in 1910, to live in the more comfortable and private surroundings of the headmaster's house when his father assumed that position. Berkhamsted School, however, was to figure largely in Greene's rite of passage. In one sense, this was because he found himself among both the teachers and students in the delicate situation of the headmaster's son, "like the son of a quisling in a country under occupation," as Greene anachronistically described it, but, in a greater sense, it was because at the school "one met for the first time characters, adult and adolescent, who bore about them the genuine quality of evil."[1]

Greene's unhappiness at Berkhamsted, which he attended from 1912 to 1922, was no doubt exacerbated by two classmates who tormented him, and critics have found echoes of these childhood enemies in several of his works. Still, those cruel boys only exploited an ongoing condition in Greene, a *malaise de vivre* born of fear and boredom, which took the form not only of truancy and running away from home, but of repeated attempts at suicide. It is ironic that Greene once claimed that "the psychoanalysis that followed my act of rebellion" as a seventeen-year-old runaway "had fixed the boredom as hypo fixes the image on the negative" because his first suicide attempt (some five or six years earlier) involved drinking "a quantity of hypo under the impression that it was poisonous." There followed numerous other tries at self-annihilation: "the blue glass bottle of hay fever lotion which as it contained a small quantity of cocaine had probably been good for my mood: the bunch of deadly nightshade that I had eaten with only a slight narcotic effect: the twenty aspirins I had taken before swimming in the empty out-of-term school baths."[2] Indeed, Greene's methods showed not just determination, but a perverse imagination; according to a letter by his mother, he once "tried to poison himself with eye-drops."[3]

Greene's suicidal tendencies persisted after analysis, but they took a particularly ominous form. As he later recounted in several places, beginning with "The Revolver in the Corner Cupboard" in *The Lost Childhood* (1951), Greene experimented with Russian roulette during his last months at Berkhamsted and first months at Balliol College, Oxford. He had read about the "game" as an antidote for boredom among White Russian officers. Thirty years later, in *The Lost Childhood*, the author continued to miscalculate that "the chance, of course, was six to one in favour of life" (173); in fact, the odds are only five to one, though the players of this particular game of chance must be particularly oblivious to the odds. Greene used the "game" as a drug that banished his own sense of *ennui*: "I remember an extraordinary sense of jubilation. It was as if a light had been turned on. My heart was knocking in its cage, and I felt that life contained an infinite number of possibilities" (175). Nevertheless, the boredom quickly returned, and Greene used the revolver repeatedly, until "as I took my fifth dose it occurred to me that I wasn't even excited: I was beginning to pull the trigger about as casually as I might take an aspirin tablet" (176).

The importance of these suicide attempts and games is made clear by the title of Greene's autobiography, *Ways of Escape* (1980). According to *The Lost Childhood*, as he walked out to the Common that first time with the revolver in his pocket, Greene was determined "to escape in one way or another" (174). Like Herman Melville's Ishmael, then, Greene first considered suicide, but opted for an escape from boredom through travel and writing.

Greene's public career as a writer began at Oxford University, where he studied from 1922 until 1925, when he took a second in Modern History. He organized a reading by Oxford student-poets for the BBC in 1923, with himself, Harold Acton, and A.L. Rowse taking part, among others, and began publishing poems in local newspapers like the *Weekly Westminster* and the *Oxford Chronicle*. Greene's first book was a volume of these derivative poems, *Babbling April* (1925). His first novel, *The Man Within* (1929), ended a stint as a journalist for *The Times*, and appeared two years after his marriage in 1927 to Vivien Dayrell-Browning. His relationship with Vivien, a convert to Catholicism with whom he had a son and a daughter, had prompted Greene's own conversion in 1926—an act that was to have a profound effect on his later writings. After the mild success of *A Man Within*, Greene produced two novels, *The Name of Action* (1930) and *Rumour at Nightfall* (1931), which he later described as being "of a badness beyond the power of criticism properly to evoke."[4] As Norman Sherry

explains, "there is too much self-love, too little self-criticism in these early portraits of pleasant, anguished young men built up from Greene's own notion of himself as a young man romantically caught in the toils of love" (411).

Deeply in debt to his publisher and with his career going nowhere, Greene re-created himself as a writer with *Stamboul Train* (1932; published in the United States as *Orient Express*), a thriller that takes place on the famous train as it travels through Europe. It is the first of his "entertainments," a class of short, fast-paced fictions that Greene kept separate from his more serious novels through most of his career. And, where his three earlier novels are too self-conscious to contain much comedy, *Stamboul Train* also contains Greene's first attempts at humor. One of these had a nearly disastrous consequence—J.B. Priestley's threatened lawsuit over the character of Mr. Savory. Priestley was the most successful novelist then writing for Heinemann, Greene's own publisher. Although Greene long denied that Priestley was the target of his satire, according to Sherry, Greene's diary indicates otherwise.[5] At any rate, Greene had to dictate over the telephone to the publisher the changes demanded by Priestley and share in the costs of unstitching more than a thousand copies already bound for the first edition of *Stamboul Train*, of reprinting twenty pages of the text, and of replacing those pages and rebinding the books. Greene's discovery of the failings of self-absorption in his first three novels and the dangers of outwardly directed satire in his fourth were eventually to lead him to use his own weaknesses as material for his fiction and especially his humor.

One of the secrets of the writer's success with *Stamboul Train* was his use of changing scenery. By uniting his love of travel with his vocation for fiction, the peripatetic author hit upon a formula that would be sustained throughout his long career. In fact, *Stamboul Train* seems originally to have been concocted by Greene to finagle a free ticket through Europe. When he was refused a free pass, he decided that he would write the novel anyway, but he could only afford a ticket on the train as far as Germany. "The reader will probably notice more details on this first stretch of the line than I had the confidence to include later," Greene admitted later in *Ways of Escape* (he had returned to England while the train continued on through the Balkans). The popularity of *Stamboul Train* and a second entertainment, *A*

Gun for Sale (1936; American title *This Gun for Hire*), was not matched by Greene's other work in the early 1930s, work which included two more novels, a travel book, and a collection of short stories. That situation changed with the publication of *Brighton Rock* (1938), the first work to establish Greene as a major writer and, as he declared in *Ways of Escape*, "perhaps it is one of the best I ever wrote" (82). *Brighton Rock* is the story of Pinkie, a small-time gangster who throughout the course of the novel tries to cover up a murder that he has committed. But it is also an allegory about good and evil, and as such the first book with what some critics have decided is an explicitly Catholic theme.

Greene's wanderlust and Catholicism combined in his next major success, *The Power and the Glory* (1940), a novel that he conceived of while traveling in Mexico to investigate the anti-Catholic nature of the Mexican revolution. Those investigations were published as *The Lawless Roads* (1939; entitled *Another Mexico* in the United States), but Greene's imagination was struck by stories of a drunken priest that he had heard. *The Power and the Glory*, which pits a whiskey priest against Mexican officials bent on his destruction, is perhaps Greene's most important work, though its reception on publication in the early days of World War II would not have indicated that.

Success, however, brought a new set of problems. Greene's marriage to Vivien was failing; they separated at the end of the war never to reconcile but, as Catholics, never to divorce. The novelist's doubts about his faith grew stronger, even as Catholicism became an increasingly central feature of his fiction. Furthermore, he was involved in a number of personal and legal disputes. In one, as he recounted in *Ways of Escape*, child-star Shirley Temple brought a libel action against him over his review of the film *Wee Willie Winkie*, in which he accused "Twentieth Century–Fox of 'procuring' Miss Temple 'for immoral purposes' (I had suggested that she had a certain adroit coquetry which appealed to middle-aged men)" (63). However, World War II allowed him to escape from those problems in both art and life. At first an air-raid warden, Greene managed to secure a post in the British Secret Services' counterintelligence unit, MI6. He was the operative in Freetown, Sierra Leone, for two years, beginning in 1941. Later Greene worked in London under Kim Philby, whom he befriended. He had already written a spy story

in *The Confidential Agent* (1939), an entertainment about a British academic who, sent abroad to undertake economic negotiations, becomes involved with foreign agents. Greene's personal experiences in the intelligence service also provided much more detailed information and served as the basis for several of his later novels, beginning with *The Ministry of Fear* (1943), in which a man who has murdered his wife becomes involved in an unrelated espionage plot. Africa, espionage, and Catholicism are all involved in Greene's thematically related next novel, *The Heart of the Matter* (1948), which brought Greene his greatest critical and popular success. For R.W.B. Lewis, *The Heart of the Matter* formed the third leg of a "trilogy," together with *Brighton Rock* and *The Power and the Glory*, which "managed to release the special energy and 'vision' that would characterize Greene as a writer of stature."[6]

In fact, *The Heart of the Matter* seems to have much more in common with the works written shortly before and after it, especially *The Ministry of Fear* and *The End of the Affair* (1951). Indeed, the triangles at the heart of *The Heart of the Matter* and *The End of the Affair* seem mirror images of each other: in the former, the focus is on Scobie, the cuckolded husband, while the main protagonist of the latter is Bendrix, the unmarried lover. Still, in his first novel of the 1950s he attempts to break new ground in both content and style. As the title indicates, *The End of the Affair* takes up pretty much where *The Heart of the Matter* left off, and it does so, as A.A. DeVitis has pointed out, using "many of the devices of the modern novel: the emotionally involved narrator, the stream-of-consciousness technique, the flashback, the diary, the letter, the inner reverie, and the spiritual debate."[7]

The decade proved to be full of experiments for Greene. He took a prestigious position as a director of The Bodley Head, his publisher, and traveled the world on journalistic assignments for *Life*, *The Sunday Times*, *Le Figaro*, and other major newspapers and magazines. His next novel, *The Quiet American* (1955), set in Saigon and detailing American involvement in Indochina before the fall of the French, seems to replace Catholic concerns with political or existential ones in the work's central ethical crisis. Having dabbled in film scripts in the 1940s[8]—including, most notably, the Orson Welles–Joseph Cotten thriller entitled *The Third Man* (published as a novella in 1950)—Greene wrote his first three plays in the 1950s. The plays are mostly significant as comedies, a medium that Greene began transferring to fiction in the last two works that he termed entertainments: *Loser Takes All* (1955), a light romance about a honeymoon in Monte Carlo, and the satiric masterpiece *Our Man in Havana* (1958), about the absurdities of life and espionage during the waning days of the Batista regime in Cuba.

After the achievements of the past twenty-five years, which had arguably made Greene the preeminent post-war British novelist, the 1960s were a decade of disappointment. *A Burnt-Out Case* (1961), his first novel since the immensely successful *Our Man in Havana*, was greeted with scathing reviews by critics of almost every religious and political stripe. Frank Kermode, for example, began his review with a telling question: "Mr. Graham Greene's new novel is so far below one's expectation that the questions arise, was the expectation reasonable, and has there been any previous indication that a failure of this kind was a possibility?"[9] Greene rejected such criticism as shortsighted, claiming later, in *Ways of Escape*, that such reviewers "were too concerned with faith and no faith to notice that in the course of the blackest book I have written I had discovered comedy" (267). But at the time, Greene felt himself to be a burnt-out case, at least as far as the writing of novels was concerned.

Two years later, the greatest spy scandal in Britain's Cold War period broke and Greene's friend Philby, a high-ranking member of the British intelligence service and a classic Soviet double-agent, defected to Moscow. Greene managed to alienate almost everyone, publicly avowing his friendship for Philby while just as publicly supporting Soviet dissidents. His health, too, began to suffer, as he experienced a bout of pneumonia on a trip to the Soviet Union and a bronchoscopy for suspected lung cancer. Determined to leave England permanently, in 1966 he settled in France and two years later resigned from The Bodley Head as a director. As for his writing during this period, what sort of comedy he had discovered in *A Burnt-Out Case* is not clear. Still, Greene did devote himself to comedy of one sort or another for most of the decade: first, in two essentially humorless works, *A Burnt-Out Case* and *The Comedians* (1966); then, in the stories collected in *May We Borrow Your Husband? And Other Comedies of the Sexual Life* (1967). Once in

residence in France, though, Greene again re-created himself as an author, as he had done in 1932 with *Stamboul Train*, and again he used a similar vehicle for his fiction—a long journey, including a train ride through Europe. This time the story was driven by humor, not suspense, in what Greene described in *Ways of Escape* as "the only book I have written for the fun of it" (296), *Travels with My Aunt* (1969).

The re-creation seems not to have taken at first, and Greene spent the entire decade of the 1970s looking backward over old territory, albeit often with a more humorous vision. As if sensing his end was close, he compiled "scraps of the past" into a volume of autobiography entitled *A Sort of Life* (1971), followed by collections of his stories and film criticism. His next novel, *The Honorary Consul* (1973), which seems a more ironic version of his own *The Power and the Glory* by way of Malcolm Lowry's *Under the Volcano* (1947), was, according to Greene, "one of the novels I found hardest to write" (*Ways*, 305). *Lord Rochester's Monkey* (1974), Greene's only foray into biography, was resuscitated from a decades-old manuscript that he had never quite finished. *The Return of A.J. Raffles* (1975) is another of Greene's plays based on a comedy of manners.

The Human Factor (1978), yet another presentation of the absurd world of intelligence services, gains a certain interest from its Philby-like protagonist, Maurice Castle. After defecting to Moscow, Castle discovers that he has been used by both sides as a minor player in a senseless exercise: the British, knowing that Maurice is spying for the Russians, have been feeding him false information which he has unwittingly passed on to his contact in Moscow; but that contact is himself a false British double-agent who in turn supplies London with two different sets of false intelligence—the London-originated misinformation that Castle is reporting to him and the Moscow-originated misinformation that the KGB wants passed on to MI5. *The Human Factor*, too, was a resurrected project, resumed more than ten years after Greene had originally begun it. In *Ways of Escape*, he recounts Philby's reaction to the copy of the novel which Greene had sent to Moscow for him: "I had made Castle's circumstances in Moscow, he wrote, too bleak. He himself had found everything provided for him, even to a shoehorn, something he had never possessed before. (It was true, he added, that he was a more important agent than Castle.)" (309).

Once more, after the lackluster reception of *The Human Factor*, Greene thought that his career as a novelist might be over. "Nearly twenty years before," he recounts in *Ways of Escape*, "I had assumed, after *A Burnt-Out Case*, that my writing days were finished—at any rate, as far as the novel was concerned—and I assumed the same again now, but a writer's imagination, like the body, fights against all reason against death" (310). The final decade of his life did, indeed, hold surprises for his art. The black humor of *Doctor Fischer of Geneva, or the Bomb Party* (1980), the astute autobiography *Ways of Escape* (1980), and the philosophical humor of *Monsignor Quixote* (1982) are full of Greene's charm and inventiveness. His last completed novel, *The Captain and the Enemy* (1988), falls back on the familiar terrain of intrigue. Greene died on April 3, 1991, in Vevey, Switzerland.

Literary Analysis

Readers may have been caught by surprise when Greene published *Travels with My Aunt*. Those familiar with the seedy, fly-specked grimness of the world of his imagination, often dubbed Greeneland, were suddenly confronted with lighthearted, sometimes slapstick comedy. According to the reviewer for *Time* magazine, "It is as if Shakespeare, after the tragedies, had chosen to write not *The Tempest* but *Charley's Aunt*." But, like Shakespeare, Greene had previously found room for comic scenes and characters even in his darkest works, and the humor of *Travels with My Aunt* and his later fiction is best appreciated in relation to the earlier comic creations that have enlivened the population of Greeneland.[10]

What Greene meant when he wrote that he "had discovered comedy" in *A Burnt-Out Case* is difficult to determine. One could make the case that the discovery had taken place several years earlier, with the writing of *Loser Takes All* and *Our Man in Havana*. As Paul O'Prey suggests, "comic scenes and characters are scattered throughout all Greene's books, but *Loser Takes All* is his first attempt at a sustained piece of humorous writing. What follows it is a truly comic masterpiece: *Our Man in Havana*."[11] But, Greene finds evidence of comedy in his earlier works, too. In *Ways of Escape* he recounts how he began by thinking that the plot of *The Ministry of Fear* (1943) was "a funny one: a man acquitted of the murder of his wife by a jury (though he knows his own guilt), who finds himself pursued for a murder of which he is entirely innocent but which he believes he has committed." Long before he finished the book, however, Greene realized that "the story was not after all very funny, though it might have other merits" (99). Indeed, where Greene intended to generate "carefree humor" (101) in such a paranoid thriller is more of a mystery than the novel itself.

There are, though, reasons for accepting Greene's assessment of the importance of *A Burnt-Out Case*. Whatever the humor of particular passages and works, as John Spurling has noted, "people don't laugh much in Greene's novels."[12] Yet, there are two particularly memorable—and climactic—laughs. One of these comes at the end of Greene's short story, "The Destructors" (1954), first published seven years before *A Burnt-Out Case*, in which a gang of boys literally deconstruct the house of their elderly adversary, Mr. Thomas. They lock Thomas, or "Old Misery," as the boys call him, in his outhouse overnight while they dismantle the house from the inside so that the touch of a truck the next morning will bring it crashing down. Seeing the destruction, the lorry driver "began to laugh . . . . He said, 'I'm sorry. I can't help it, Mr. Thomas. There's nothing personal, but you got to admit it's funny.'"[13] The "nothing personal" repeats a phrase that one of the boys has used with Old Misery earlier (345), and one of the grim ironies of the story is its impersonality and barrenness—from its setting around "an impromptu car-park, the site of the last bomb of the first blitz" (327–28), and the gang calling its leader T. instead of Trevor "because otherwise they had no excuse not to laugh at it" (327) to the senseless battle between T. and Old Misery himself.

Greene reshaped that ending for the climax of *A Burnt-Out Case*, where Querry, the dubious hero who has come to an African leper colony for refuge, not salvation, also dies laughing or, more accurately, dies for laughing. Facing the barrel of a gun held by Rycker, his lover's husband, "Querry made an odd awkward sound which the doctor by now had learned to interpret as a laugh, and Rycker fired twice."[14] Dying, Querry explains that he was not laughing at Rycker but at himself, before experiencing something of an existential recognition: "'Absurd,' Querry said, 'this is absurd or else . . .' but what alternative, philosophical or psychological, he had in mind they never knew"

(244). *A Burnt-Out Case* is not a funny novel, and what the doctor says about Querry is equally true of the reader: "He doesn't laugh easily" (244).

In a sense, Greene's first period of comedy falls between these two extremes of strained laughter, neither of which is very funny: the witness to absurdity, who can laugh because the destruction does not touch him; and the victim of absurdity, who laughs at himself because of the destruction he has caused. Three intervening works of this first comic period—*Loser Takes All*, *Our Man in Havana*, and *The Complaisant Lover* (1959): a play and Greene's last two "entertainments"—achieve their humor by retaining their distance: though their world is no less absurd, the protagonists manage to prosper by becoming adept at those very absurdities. In each, the author uncovers the human reality beneath a familiar cliché, but not before a good deal of fun has been had.

Loser Takes All is, as Peter Wolfe noted, the only one of Greene's "entertainments" that "bypasses the terror of the thriller in favor of light romantic comedy."[15] The scenes of *Loser Takes All* are familiar enough: the comedy of errors (and, ultimately, disappointment) as bride and groom, after going "together now for years and years and years,"[16] spend their first night together on the eve of their wedding; the frustrated husband's sudden passion for gambling, leading to a quarrel on their honeymoon; and finally the stratagem of taking a lover to make one's spouse jealous, a plan that is comically complicated because both spouses adopt it simultaneously until a surprise encounter leads to their reconciliation and a happy ending. Greene's absurdities arise not only from the clichéd process itself but also from elements involving the groom's job and his system at roulette.

If *Loser Takes All* surprises by being so different from the author's previous works, *Our Man in Havana* is even more remarkable for being similar in all but one way: the last of Greene's "entertainments," *Our Man in Havana* is also one of his two comic masterpieces. The absurdities of international espionage, which he had already used in *The Ministry of Fear* and would use again in *The Human Factor* in more serious ways, is presented here as the backdrop for humor as insightful as it is outrageous. Gags in this spy spoof range from puns like "Wormold," the name of the vacuum-cleaner salesman in Cuba who becomes a Brit-ish operative, to visual humor, such as the drawings of vacuum-cleaner parts that he passes off as giant secret weapons, to pure slapstick, including the famous game of checkers between Wormold and the sinister Captain Segura in which the pieces are replaced by souvenir shot-sized bottles of liquor, and each player must drink down every man that he captures. In the rubber match of the evening, Wormold, playing Scotch, offers Segura, playing Bourbon, a draw:

> "No drawn game. Look. I take your king." He opened the little bottle of Red Label and drank it down.

> "Two bottles for a king," Wormold said and handed him a Dunosdale Cream.

> Segura sat heavily in his chair, his chin rocking. He said, "Admit you are beaten. I do not play for pieces."

> "I admit nothing. I have the better head and look, I huff you. You could have gone on." A Canadian rye had got mixed with the Bourbons, a Lord Calvert, and Wormold drank it down. He thought, it must be the last. If he doesn't pass out now, I'm finished. I won't be sober enough to pull a trigger. Did he say it was loaded?

> "Matters nothing," Segura said in a whisper. "You are finished anyway." He moved his hand slowly over the board as though he were carrying an egg in a spoon. "See?" He captured one piece, two pieces, three . . .

> "Drink this, Segura." A George IV, A Queen Anne, the game was ending in a flourish of royalty, a Highland Queen.

> "You can go on, Segura. Or shall I huff you again? Drink it down." Vat 69. "Another. Drink it, Segura." Grant's Stadfast. Old Argyll. "Drink them, Segura. I surrender now." But it was Segura who had surrendered. Wormold undid the captain's collar to give him air and eased his head on the back of the seat, but his own legs were uncertain as he walked towards the door. He had Segura's gun in his pocket.[17]

The novel is played out with two casts of characters: the neatly stereotyped comic figures of Wormold's world, such as his daughter Milly, a teenager who has nearly spent Wormold into bankruptcy, and his friend Dr. Hasselbacher, the good German, and the even funnier "agents" that Wormold invents to increase his funding from London.

As in *Our Man in Havana*, in his play *The Complaisant Lover*, which trumpets its humor in its subtitle, *A Comedy*, Greene uses materials familiar from his more serious works. In this case the love triangle which goes awry in *The Heart of the Matter*, *The End of the Affair*, and *A Burnt-Out Case* goes only wry in *The Complaisant Lover*, as Clive Root remains complaisant in the face of his lover's husband's demands. Root, not coincidentally suffering from tooth-decay, is ordered by the cuckolded Victor Rhodes, the dentist, to remain his wife's lover at the play's end, and Clive, complaisant as ever, agrees for the time being. After all, as Clive has told Mary Rhodes earlier, "We aren't allowed a tragedy nowadays without a banana skin to slip on and make it funny. But it hurts just the same."[18]

Certainly it hurt more when a triangle tragedy was again presented sans peel in Greene's next work, *A Burnt-Out Case*, in which the author claimed to have discovered comedy, not lost it. Though the title of his subsequent, almost equally bleak novel, *The Comedians* (1966), suggests that Greene was pursuing this discovery of comedy, that pursuit apparently did not lead him to write especially humorous novels. *The Comedians* was only published five years later, after a period, as we have noted, in which Greene considered his career as a novelist over. Many critics have explained the title of the novel on the basis of one of its narrator's observations: "Life was a comedy, not the tragedy for which I had been prepared, and it seemed to me that we were all . . . driven by an authoritative practical joker towards the extreme point of comedy."[19] As Richard Hauer Costa has suggested, the title can also be understood to refer not "to conscious laughter but rather to the rituals of the *commedia dell'arte* in which the principals either play parts thrust on them by circumstances or enact roles meant to cover their true selves."[20]

Biographical factors, such as his permanent move to France and later retirement from the board of The Bodley Head, may have influenced Greene's perception of his own work.

Whatever the cause, a major transition occurred after *The Comedians*. Sandwiched between volumes of collected essays, stories, film criticism, and autobiographical recollections—the sort of thing that one might expect from a writer gracefully summing up his life and work—Greene published two books that indicated a radically new direction for him in comedy: *May We Borrow Your Husband? And Other Comedies of the Sexual Life* and *Travels with My Aunt*. This major shift is perhaps best indicated by the rearrangement of the list of the author's published volumes facing the title page of *Travels with My Aunt* where for the first time Greene's thirty-three-year-old distinction between novels and entertainments is dropped. Previous to that, Greene had taken pains to distinguish between the two, as he explained to Walter Allen in a 1955 radio interview: "In one's entertainments one is primarily interested in having an exciting story as in a physical action, with just enough character to give interest to the action, because you can't be interested in the action of a mere dummy. In the novels I hope one is primarily interested in the character and the action takes a minor part."[21]

The distinction between novels and entertainment was not always as clear as the writer proposed. *Brighton Rock*, for example, was published as a novel in England, but it appeared in the United States as an entertainment at first, before finding its permanent place back among Greene's novels on both sides of the Atlantic. The reason for this change may have as much to do with the novel's popularity as with Greene's own belated recognition of what he had achieved in it. Similarly, having completed *Travels with My Aunt*, Greene must have realized that it fit comfortably into neither category. The entertainments were mostly thrillers and mysteries, though sometimes humorous ones; the novels were more philosophically demanding tales of life, love, and values. Although the reviewer in *Time* may have intended only a facetious comparison, many of Greene's last works, like those of Shakespeare, defy easy categorization and may rightly be called "problem novels." This is especially true of the explicit comedy of *Travels with My Aunt*, the black humor of *Doctor Fischer of Geneva*, and the literate wit of *Monsignor Quixote*.

Travels with My Aunt is the story of Henry Pulling, a retired bank manager who is reunited with his eccentric Aunt Augusta at his mother's funeral only to discover in the course of a series

G

of trips with Augusta which provide the background for the novel that she is his real mother. Both are in search of themselves, albeit Henry at first unwittingly. Augusta uses their trips to review her life, this time with her son included—and what a sexually rollicking life it must have been, Henry and the reader can surmise as they seemingly face brief reprises of Aunt Augusta's past at every terminal and port-of-call. Inevitably, Henry learns not only about her, but about himself as well. By the end of the novel he has embarked upon a new life in the new world of South America, with his newfound mother nearby—leaving behind a lifetime of inadequacy and frustration:

> "My darling boy," she said, "all that is over now," and she stroked my forehead with her old hand as though I were a school-boy who had run away from school and she was promising me that I would never have to return, that all my difficulties were over, that I could stay at home.

> I was stuck deep in my middle age. All the same I laid my head against her breast. "I have been happy," I said, "but I have been so bored for so long."[22]

Like the younger, Russian-roulette playing Greene, Henry is rescued not from unhappiness, but from boredom. Henry receives what might be called abundant recompense for his tedious past, including a new career and a beautiful sixteen-year-old bride. If not literally reborn, he nevertheless ends his adventures in better shape than any other denizen of Greeneland.

Much of the significance of this happy ending lies in the protagonist's name. As Philip Stratford has argued, Greene's "marked antipathy for his own Christian name" has caused him "to bestow it, with playful malice, on rather unpleasant characters in his fiction."[23] The uncharacteristically affirmative end of Henry Pulling, then, may be read as the author's own belated acceptance of himself, Henry Graham Greene. And, Aunt Augusta's itinerary is interesting in this context, as the "sort of life" into which Henry is being initiated. Greene admitted in *Ways of Escape* that he was aware that the trips seem "a kind of resume of my literary career—a scene in Brighton, the journey on the Orient Express" (298). Both characters, then, can be seen as projections of the author's own

personality: boring Henry is the despised, middle-class self left behind, while Aunt Augusta is one way of escape from boredom, through social and sexual liberation.

The destructive self-absorption of Greene's earliest novels, and even what Gwenn R. Boardman has somewhat misleadingly termed his later "excursions in self-mockery," including *Our Man in Havana*,[24] can thus be seen to lead to this integration of self through comedy which is not completely realized until *Travels with My Aunt*, and only after Greene's own escape from England itself. Not surprisingly, then, Greene continued to set most of his fiction outside England, as he had done for much of his career. Yet, more than a decade was to pass before the publication of his next and last great comic novel. The intervening years saw a return to familiar territory in his writing, though with a greater insistence on irony and satire, in such novels as *The Honorary Consul*, *The Human Factor*, and *Doctor Fischer*. Against this background, the surprisingly delicate and reflective humor of *Monsignor Quixote* represents a final reworking of Greene's most important themes as well as a last departure in his comedy.

Greene's Quixote is the village priest of El Toboso, in the La Mancha of post-Franco Spain. Like the great Don himself, from whom he is directly descended, this Quixote is poor, his clothes threadbare, his steed (a Seat 600 jalopy he calls "in memory of his ancestor, 'My Rocinante'") little better than scrap.[25] The Bishop of Motopo, who drives a Mercedes, wonders (irreverently, of course, in a novel), "How can he be descended from a fictional character?" (16). The answer is to be found in the novel's epigraph from *Hamlet*, "There is nothing either good or bad but thinking makes it so."

Thinking is important for this modern Quixote. Although he updates several of his ancestor's most famous adventures—jousting with the Guardia instead of windmills, for example, and freeing the galley slaves in the person of a fugitive robber—the action and humor of *Monsignor Quixote* are more philosophical than physical. An early instance of this in the novel is the discussion of the parable of the Prodigal Son by Father Quixote and his sidekick, the ex-Mayor of El Toboso:

> "A very beautiful parable," Father Quixote said with a note of defiance. He felt uneasy about what was to come.

"Yes, it begins beautifully," said the Mayor. "There is this very bourgeois household, a father and two sons. One might describe the father as a rich Russian kulak who regards his peasants as so many souls whom he owns."

"There is nothing about kulaks or souls in the parable."

"The story you have read has been probably a little corrected and slanted here and there by the ecclesiastical censors."

"What do you mean?"

"It could have been told so differently, and perhaps it was. Here is this young man who by some beneficent trick of heredity has grown up against all odds with a hatred of inherited wealth. Perhaps Christ had Job in mind. Christ was nearer in time to the author of *Job* than you are to your great ancestor, the Don. Job, you remember, was obscenely rich. He owned seven thousand sheep and three thousand camels. The son feels stifled by his bourgeois surroundings—perhaps even by the kind of furniture and the kind of pictures on the walls, of fat kulaks sitting down to their Sabbath meal, a sad contrast with the poverty he sees around him. He has to escape—anywhere. So he demands his share of the inheritance which will come to his brother and himself on their father's death and he leaves home."

"And squanders his inheritance in riotous living," Father Quixote interrupted.

"Ah, that is the official version. My version is that he was so disgusted by the bourgeois world in which he had been brought up that he got rid of his wealth in the quickest way possible—perhaps he even gave it away and in a Tolstoyan gesture he became a peasant."

"But he came home."

"Yes, but his courage failed him. He felt very alone on that pig farm. There was no branch of the Party to which he could look for help. *Das Kapital* had not yet been written, so he was unable to situate himself in the class struggle. Is it any wonder that he wavered for a time, poor boy?" (55–56)

Father Quixote's Catholicism collides at times with his Sancho's Communism, but balancing between them is that other "C"—Cervantes, whose great romance is discussed or alluded to on almost every page. Greene's own quixotic spirit of humanism softens both characters' creeds, making of one "a Catholic in spite of the Curia," of the other "a Communist who is still alive in spite of the Politburo" (179). Literature, religion, and politics, those consistent concerns of Greene's life, all find closure in the humor of *Monsignor Quixote*.

Summary

Though he dominated English letters for more than four decades, Graham Greene's comic achievements are often ignored by those for whom Greeneland is unrelievedly shabby and depressing. In fact, an interest in comedy can be seen in many of his works, both fiction and drama, not only in his three comic masterpieces, *Our Man in Havana*, *Travels with My Aunt*, and *Monsignor Quixote*, but in others, such as *A Burnt-Out Case* and *The Comedians*, for which comedy is more of a subject or theme than a description.

Notes

1. *A Sort of Life* (London: Bodley Head, 1971), p. 72; *The Lawless Roads* (London: Longmans, Green, 1939), p. 4.
2. *The Lost Childhood* (New York: Viking Press, 1952), pp. 174–75.
3. Quoted in Norman Sherry, *The Life of Graham Greene, Volume 1: 1904–1939* (New York: Viking Press, 1989), p. 87. The letter from Marion Greene also helps to confirm the accuracy of Graham Greene's account of his own suicidal tendencies. This is particularly important in view of the suspicions cast upon it by Philip Stratford, who has warned that "this account has been swallowed uncritically by every one of Greene's serious critics. Advised of Greene's passion for practical joking, however, before making any neat biographical equation, one should at least entertain the possibility that the confessional essay is pure fantasy" ("Unlocking the Potting Shed,"

Kenyon Review, 24 [1962]: 131–32).
Much of what Stratford says can be dismissed as critical cleverness and unsub-
stantiated speculation. There is, however,
enough apparent substance in his assertions—including the disturbingly parallel
"green baize door" passages from
Gwendolyn Greene's *Two Witnesses*
(1930) and Graham Greene's own *The
Lawless Roads* ("Unlocking," p. 138)—
to warrant a good deal of skepticism
when dealing with the self described in
the novelist's autobiographical writings.

4. *Ways of Escape* (New York: Simon and
   Schuster, 1980), p. 19.
5. *The Life of Graham Greene, Volume 1:
   1904–1939*, pp. 436–37.
6. R.W.B. Lewis, *The Picaresque Saint*
   (Philadelphia: Lippincott, 1959), p. 239.
7. A.A. DeVitis, *Graham Greene* (New
   York: Twayne, 1964), p. 104.
8. Many of Greene's works have been
   filmed: *The Power and the Glory* (1933),
   dir. William K. Howard, starring Spencer
   Tracy; *Ministry of Fear* (1944), dir. Fritz
   Lang, starring Ray Milland, Dan
   Duryea, and Hillary Brooke; *Confidential Agent* (1945), dir. Herman Shumlin,
   starring Charles Boyer, Lauren Bacall,
   and Peter Lorre; *Brighton Rock* (1947),
   dir. John Boulting, starring Richard
   Attenborough; *The Fallen Idol* (1948),
   dir. Carol Reed, starring Ralph
   Richardson and Jack Hawkins; *The
   Third Man* (1949), dir. Carol Reed, star-
   ring Orson Welles and Joseph Cotten;
   The Heart of the Matter (1954), dir.
   George More O'Terrall, starring Trevor
   Howard, Elizabeth Allan, Maria Schell,
   and Denholm Elliott; *Our Man in Ha-
   vana* (1960), dir. Carol Reed, starring
   Alec Guinness, Burl Ives, Maureen
   O'Hara, Ernie Kovacs, Noel Coward,
   and Ralph Richardson; *The Comedians*
   (1967), dir. Peter Glenville, starring
   Elizabeth Taylor, Richard Burton, Alec
   Guinness, Peter Ustinov, Paul Ford,
   Lillian Gish, Raymond St. Jacques,
   James Earl Jones, and Cicely Tyson;
   Travels with My Aunt (1972), dir.
   George Cukor, starring Maggie Smith
   and Alec McGowen; *England Made Me*
   (1973), dir. Peter Duffell, starring Peter
   Finch, Michael York, and Michael
   Hordern; *The Human Factor* (1975), dir.
   Edward Dmytryk, starring George
   Kennedy, John Mills, Raf Vallone, Rita
   Tushingham, Barry Sullivan, and Arthur
   Franz; *The Tenth Man* (1988), dir. Jack
   Gold, starring Anthony Hopkins, Derek
   Jacobi, Cyril Cusack, and Paul Rogers.
9. Frank Kermode, "Mr. Greene's Eggs and
   Crosses," *Encounter*, 16 (April 1961), p.
   69.
10. "Hamlet's Aunt." *Time*, 95 (January 19,
    1970), p. 68.
11. Paul O'Prey, *A Reader's Guide to Gra-
    ham Greene* (New York: Thames and
    Hudson, 1988), p. 110.
12. John Spurling, *Graham Greene* (London:
    Methuen, 1983), p. 48.
13. Greene, *Collected Stories* (New York:
    Viking Press, 1973), p. 346.
14. Greene, *A Burnt-Out Case* (New York:
    Viking Press, 1961), p. 243.
15. Peter Wolfe, *Graham Greene the Enter-
    tainer* (Carbondale: Southern Illinois
    University Press, 1972), p. 133.
16. Greene, *Loser Takes All* (New York: Vi-
    king Press, 1957), p. 37.
17. Greene, *Our Man in Havana*, Collected
    Edition (New York: Viking Press, 1981),
    pp. 215–16.
18. Greene, *The Complaisant Lover* (New
    York: Viking, 1961), p. 48.
19. Greene, *The Comedians*, Uniform Edi-
    tion (New York: Viking Press, 1981), p.
    30.
20. Richard Hauer Costa, "Graham
    Greene," *Dictionary of Literary Biogra-
    phy 15: British Novelists 1930–1959*, ed.
    Bernard Oldsey (Detroit: Gale, 1983),
    Vol. 1, p. 162.
21. Quoted in David Pryce-Jones, *Graham
    Greene*, 2nd ed. (Edinburgh: Oliver and
    Boyd, 1973), p. 62. Philip Stratford
    warns specifically against taking this in-
    terview too seriously, as well, when he
    reports that one commentator wrote,
    "One got the impression . . . Greene
    didn't like being interviewed, and even
    that he didn't like Mr. Allen" ("Unlock-
    ing the Potting Shed," pp. 130–31).
22. Greene, *Travels with My Aunt* (New
    York: Viking Press, 1970), p. 236.
23. "Unlocking the Potting Shed," p. 133,
    n. 2.
24. Gwenn R. Boardman, *Graham Greene:
    The Aesthetics of Exploration*
    (Gainesville: University of Florida Press,

1971), p. 119.

25. Greene, *Monsignor Quixote* (New York: Simon and Schuster, 1982), p. 15.

Selected Bibliography

Primary Sources

Novels

The Man Within. London: Heinemann, and Garden City, NY: Doubleday, 1929.

The Name of Action. London: Heinemann, 1930; Garden City, NY: Doubleday, 1931.

Rumour at Nightfall. London: Heinemann, 1931; Garden City, NY: Doubleday, 1932.

Stamboul Train. London: Heinemann, 1932; as *Orient Express.* Garden City, NY: Doubleday, 1933.

It's a Battlefield. London: Heinemann, 1934; Garden City, NY: Doubleday, 1935.

England Made Me. London: Heinemann, and Garden City, NY: Doubleday, 1935; rpt. as *The Shipwrecked.* New York: Viking Press, 1953.

A Gun for Sale. London: Heinemann, 1936. American title: *This Gun for Hire.* Garden City, NY: Doubleday, 1936.

Brighton Rock. London: Heinemann, and Garden City, NY: Doubleday, 1938.

The Confidential Agent. London: Heinemann, and New York: Viking Press, 1939.

The Power and the Glory. London: Heinemann, 1940. American title: *Labyrinthine Ways.* New York: Viking Press, 1940; rpt. as *The Power and the Glory.* New York: Viking Press, 1946.

The Ministry of Fear. London: Heinemann, and New York: Viking Press, 1943.

The Heart of the Matter. London: Heinemann, and New York: Viking Press, 1948.

The Third Man and The Fallen Idol. London: Heinemann, 1950. American title: *The Third Man.* New York: Viking Press, 1950. Novella and story related to screenplays.

The End of the Affair. London: Heinemann, and New York: Viking Press, 1951.

Loser Takes All. London: Heinemann, 1955; New York: Viking Press, 1957.

The Quiet American. London: Heinemann, 1955; New York: Viking Press, 1956.

Our Man in Havana. London: Heinemann, and New York: Viking Press, 1958.

A Burnt-Out Case. London: Heinemann, and New York: Viking Press, 1961.

The Comedians. London: Bodley Head, and New York: Viking Press, 1966.

Travels with My Aunt. London: Bodley Head, 1969; New York: Viking Press, 1970.

The Honorary Consul. London: Bodley Head, and New York: Simon and Schuster, 1973.

The Human Factor. London: Bodley Head, and New York: Simon and Schuster, 1978.

Doctor Fischer of Geneva, or the Bomb Party. London: Bodley Head and New York: Simon and Schuster, 1980.

Monsignor Quixote. London: Bodley Head, and New York: Simon and Schuster, 1982.

The Tenth Man. London: Bodley Head and Anthony Blond, and New York: Simon and Schuster, 1985. "Rediscovered" novel from 1944.

The Captain and the Enemy. London: Reinhardt, 1988; New York: Viking Press, 1988.

Stories

The Basement Room and Other Stories. London: Cresset, 1935.

Nineteen Stories. London: Heinemann, 1947; New York: Viking Press, 1949.

Twenty-One Stories. London: Heinemann, 1954; New York: Viking Press, 1962.

A Sense of Reality. London: Bodley Head, and New York: Viking Press, 1963.

May We Borrow Your Husband? And Other Comedies of the Sexual Life. London: Bodley Head, and New York: Viking Press, 1967.

Collected Stories. London: Bodley Head and Heinemann, 1972; New York: Viking Press, 1973.

Plays

The Living Room. London: Heinemann, 1953; New York: Viking Press, 1954.

The Potting Shed. New York: Viking Press, 1957; London: Heinemann, 1958.

The Complaisant Lover. London: Heinemann, 1959; New York: Viking Press, 1961.

Carving a Statue. London: Bodley Head, 1964.

The Return of A. J. Raffles. London: Bodley

G

Head, 1975; New York: Simon and
Schuster, 1976.

Travel

Journey without Maps. London: Heinemann,
and Garden City, NY: Doubleday, 1936.
Liberia and Sierra Leone.

The Lawless Roads. London: Longmans,
Green, 1939. American title: *Another
Mexico.* Garden City, NY: Doubleday,
1939. Essays on Mexico.

In Search of a Character. London: Bodley
Head, 1961; New York: Viking Press,
1962.

Miscellaneous

Babbling April. Oxford: Blackwell, 1925.
Poems.

The Bear Fell Free. London: Grayson, 1935.
Juvenile.

British Dramatists. London: Collins, 1942.
Criticism.

The Little Train. Norwich: Jarrold, 1946;
New York: Lothrop, 1958. Juvenile.

The Little Fire Engine. Norwich: Jarrold,
1950; rpt. as *The Little Red Fire Engine.*
New York: Lothrop, 1953. Juvenile.

The Lost Childhood and Other Essays. London: Methuen, 1951; New York: Viking
Press, 1952.

The Little Horse Bus. Norwich/London:
Jarrold/Parrish, 1952; New York:
Lothrop, 1954. Juvenile.

The Little Steamroller. London: Parrish,
1953; New York: Lothrop, 1955. Juvenile.

Collected Essays. London: Bodley Head, and
New York: Viking Press, 1969.

A Sort of Life. London: Bodley Head, and
New York: Simon and Schuster, 1971.
Autobiography.

The Pleasure-Dome. London: Secker and
Warburg, 1972. American title: *Graham
Greene on Film.* New York: Simon and
Schuster, 1972. Collected film criticism,
1935–1940.

Lord Rochester's Monkey. London: Bodley
Head, and New York: Viking Press,
1974. Biography.

Ways of Escape. London: Bodley Head, and
New York: Simon and Schuster, 1980.
Autobiography.

Getting to Know the General. London:
Bodley Head, and New York: Simon and
Schuster, 1984. Account of Greene's rela-
tionship with Panamanian strongman
Omar Torrijos Herrera.

Yours Etc. London: Reinhardt, and New
York: Viking Press, 1989. Letters to the
press.

Secondary Sources

Bibliographies

Cassis, A.F. *Graham Greene: An Annotated
Bibliography of Criticism.* Metuchen,
NJ: Scarecrow, 1981. Well-annotated
bibliography of Greene criticism, to
1979.

Wobbe, R.A. *Graham Greene: A Bibliography and Guide to Research.* New York:
Garland, 1979. Excellent bibliography of
primary sources, including some manuscripts, and secondary sources, through
1976.

Books

Boardman, Gwenn R. *Graham Greene: The
Aesthetics of Exploration.* Gainesville:
University of Florida Press, 1971.

Costa, Richard Hauer. "Graham Greene."
*Dictionary of Literary Biography 15:
British Novelists 1930–1959.* Ed. Ber-
nard Oldsey. Detroit: Gale, 1983. Vol. 1,
pp. 146–69. Good, brief overview of
Greene's work.

Couto, Maria. *Graham Greene: On the Frontier.* New York: St. Martin's Press, 1988.
Excellent study of political themes in the
novels.

DeVitis, A.A. *Graham Greene.* New York:
Twayne, 1964.

Kermode, Frank. "Mr. Greene's Eggs and
Crosses." *Encounter,* 16 (April 1961):
69–75. A blistering retrospective, from *A
Burnt-Out Case* backward.

Lewis, R.W.B. *The Picaresque Saint.* Philadelphia: Lippincott, 1959. Includes his essay
on Greene's "trilogy."

Lodge, David. *Graham Greene.* New York
and London: Columbia University Press,
1966. Columbia Essays on Modern
Writers, No. 17.

Miller, R.H. *Understanding Graham Greene.*
Columbia: University of South Carolina
Press, 1990. Good introduction to the
variety of Greene's work.

O'Prey, Paul. *A Reader's Guide to Graham
Greene.* New York: Thames and
Hudson, 1988.

Pryce-Jones, David. *Graham Greene*. Edinburgh: Oliver and Boyd, 1973. 2nd ed.

Sharrock, Roger. *Saints, Sinners, and Comedians: The Novels of Graham Greene*. Notre Dame: University of Notre Dame Press, 1984. A post-modern reading of an essentially modernist writer.

Sherry, Norman. *The Life of Graham Greene, Volume 1: 1904–1939*. New York: Viking Press, 1989. Massive but very readable and well-documented biography of Greene.

Spurling, John. *Graham Greene*. London: Methuen, 1983.

Stratford, Philip. "Unlocking the Potting Shed." *Kenyon Review*, 24 (1962): 129–43. Challenging but largely speculative review of Greene's autobiographical and other sources.

———. *Faith and Fiction: Creative Process in Greene and Mauriac*. Notre Dame: University of Notre Dame Press, 1964. Focus on the religious themes and imagery.

Thomas, Brian. *An Underground Fate: The Idiom of Romance in the Later Novels of Graham Greene*. Athens: University of Georgia Press, 1988.

Wolfe, Peter. *Graham Greene the Entertainer*. Carbondale: Southern Illinois University Press, 1972. A study of the seven works that Greene originally termed "entertainments," though this volume was not published until after Greene had stopped making that distinction.

NB. Since 1987, Peter Wolfe has also edited a journal called *Essays on Graham Greene: An Annual*.

David Mesher

Greene, Robert

Born: Norwich, July 1558 (christened July 11, 1558)

Education: St. John's, Cambridge University, B.A., 1580; Clare Hall, Cambridge University, M.A., 1583; Oxford University, M.A., 1588

Marriage: Isabel Beck (?), 1579 (?); one child

Died: London, September 3, 1592

Biography

Of all of the University Wits none was a more prolific writer or a more profligate individual than Robert Greene. Ironically, about him only the fewest hard facts are known. This lack of hard facts has made Greene's life as tantalizing to scholars as is his work. The problem with Greene's life is that in one respect we know too much; contemporary accounts are plentiful. Greene wrote much about himself as well. The difficulty lies in separating the fiction from the truth.

Greene was born in Norwich in 1558. A baptismal record shows that Robert Greene, son of Robert Greene, was christened on July 11. The father may have been a saddler or a cordwainer turned innkeeper. Whether young Robert spent his entire youth in Norwich remains unknown. It is known that a Robert Greene matriculated as a sizar (a student receiving an allowance from his college toward his expenses) at St. John's College, Cambridge University, in November 1575. He received the B.A. in 1580. This Robert Greene then changed colleges, moving to Clare Hall, Cambridge, where he took an M.A. in 1583. He also received an Oxford M.A. in 1588. Virtually no details of his university years exist. Something is known, however, about the universities in the late sixteenth century. The sons of clerks and bricklayers (who may have entered as sizars) mingled with the sons of the nobility, all pursuing the new humanism. This environment might account for some of the tension between the aristocrat and the commoner in Greene's later work.

Greene may have traveled to the Continent. He did apparently marry (possibly to Isabel Beck in 1579) and have a child. Although once again there are few hard facts, the number of references to a wife and child and accounts of Greene's asking her forgiveness for his having deserted them lend credence to this possibility.

Accounts of Greene's London life suggest that he was the prodigal *par excellence*. He lived, drank, gambled, wore his hair long, wenched, fathered a bastard, ran with the notorious cutpurse Cutting Ball, and took his sister as his mistress. In all he seems to have lived the life depicted in his prose. Again, though, how much is true it is difficult to say. While his prose evinces a lived reality about it, he may have been merely a keen observer of London life. This "lifestyle" provoked differing accounts of him in life as well as death. While Thomas Nashe (who wrote the preface to Greene's *Menaphon* [1589]) found him a talented and decent fellow, Gabriel Harvey vilified him.

The circumstances of Greene's death seem to be as much fiction as fact. The author wrote a number of repentance pamphlets about the time that he died. They do suggest his being in poverty, and they do make appeals to his wife for forgiveness. Greene's death allowed Harvey to attack further his old antagonist. From Harvey and others we get the oft repeated notion that Greene died after overindulging on a meal of Rhine wine and pickled herring. A more realistic view, yet far less romantic and prodigal, is that he died of plague in London on September 3, 1592.

Unfortunately, what Greene is most known for is neither his life nor his work, which stands on its own merits. His fame lies in a rather small work written near the time of his death, *A Groatsworth of Wit Bought with a Million of Repentance* (1592). It contains the earliest known written reference to William Shakespeare. Greene refers to the dramatist as an "upstart crow," a "*Johannes factotum*" of the theater, and as "the only Shake-scene in the country," all suggesting Shakespeare's rising star to Greene's falling one.

Literary Analysis

When thinking of "comedy" and "the comic" in Renaissance literature, the modern reader must consider what was defined as comedy in the sixteenth and seventeenth centuries. In its broadest sense, comedy is that which ends happily regardless of whether deaths occur. Comedy is also corrective; that is, it addresses questions of loyalty, friendship, loving outside of one's station in life, and other consequences of violating decorum. And while broad comedy exists, as a general rule much of what the Renaissance deemed comic does not seem humorous to a contemporary audience. At the same time, a number of comic devices exist in those works; Greene's prose falls into this category.

Although Greene was a prolific writer, the authorship of much of what is attributed to him is uncertain. Even his role in the creation of the infamous *A Groatsworth of Wit* has come under question.

The writer's prose works begin with *Mamillia* (1580), which is Greene's contribution to the *querelle de femmes*. Cast as a narrative in the debate mode, *Mamillia*, contains the author's presentation of the faithless Pharicles, who repeatedly proves that men are far more fickle than women. Written as his response to John Lyly's *Euphuese*, Greene employs the euphuistic style throughout.

In his letter to the "gentlemen readers," Greene mocks his fellow authors whose own prefatory letters are self-deprecating and disavow any value in the volume. With characteristic playfulness, Greene acknowledges his betters who have claimed their work poor when he has found them highly skilled and perfectly polished and then denigrates what follows by saying that he "cannot find one [word] bad enough" to apply to his own writing since others have already preempted him. By so disclaiming, however, he more highly praises his own work through satirizing the extremes of his predecessors.

In the body of the work Greene is a master of euphuism. He is at no loss for the balanced construction or flights of alliteration: "yea the concord of their nature was such, as no sops of suspicion, no mists of distrusts, no floods of fickleness, could once foil their faith: their friendship so firmly founded on the rock of virtue: for this straight liking was not fleshly fancy, but a mere choice of Chastity." Not only does this passage illustrate the pattern followed in the rest of the work but it also sets the comic tone for exploring the question of who is more fickle—man or woman. The Italian setting allows Greene to satirize that country's citizens and by implication those "Italianate" Englishmen who ape Continental fashions. The men who seek to woo Mamillia would "correct nature" via dress to improve their narrow shoulders, thin bellies, crooked legs, small shanks, and—most importantly—their two faces. Faulty in figure, they are duplicitous in nature as well.

Greene employs irony throughout. His narrator, commenting on and raising rhetorical questions about the various debates that arise, calls the gentlemen readers' attention to the trifling nature of male love and pronounces Pharicles the "Archcaptain" of all such false lovers, those who flatter and deceive for their own gain. As the plot turns from good fortune to bad, Greene announces the change in a flurry of alliteration that contributes comic diminution to the scene: the couple who are "now flowing in floods of felicity are by the falsehood of Pharicles soused in the seas of sorrow." Despite Pharicles's bad behavior, Mamillia remains wholly faithful, and it is she who, ironically yet appropriately, effects Pharicles's rescue in part

2. Given the debate-narrative form, the characters remain types rather than being fully realized. At the same time, Greene has his fun in proving womankind superior in loyalty in the all-too-human comic debate on love.

Pandosto (1588) and *Menaphon* (1589) are both excellent examples of the English prose pastoral romance. Even the modern reader can appreciate Greene's talent and the popularity that he enjoyed as a result of these volumes. The primary convention of the pastoral world is that it provides a respite from the world of the Court and its inherent corruption and deviousness, yet at the same time that respite is temporary, for both evils spill over into the pastoral world. That spillover is usually a consequence of a court member having to flee the Court by being exiled or becoming "Fortune's football." Once in the pastoral landscape, that individual adopts the pastoral life and lives harmoniously among the native inhabitants. The exile either knowingly disguises herself/himself and assumes a pastoral role or has that role imposed upon her/him if the exile is abandoned or exposed as an infant. Tranquility never lasts, however; other courtly intruders arrive in the pastoral world and disrupt the harmony by vying for the affection of the exiled individual. In pastoral romances, like appeals to like. Despite the exile's assumed humble manner and pastoral garb, the sojourning courtier(s) gravitate automatically to the inherent grace and goodness in her/him.

Pandosto was one of Greene's most popular works, running to nine editions by 1632. While its fame today rests in its being Shakespeare's primary source for *The Winter's Tale*, the work stands on its own merits. Again, there is a tale of Nature, love, and Fortune. Again, like attracts like. The drama also ends as comedy in the broad sense—despite the fact that in Greene's work Pandosto, the model for Shakespeare's Leontes, dies out of remorse for his incestuous lust. The reconciliation takes place and the erstwhile shepherds and shepherdesses return to their courts and marry happily.

In *Pandosto*, Greene relies primarily on irony. Early on when Egistus arrives for his lengthy stay at Pandosto's court, Pandosto greets his friend, "protesting that nothing in the world could have happened more acceptable to him than his coming" only to be plotting to poison Egistus in the space of a few pages. Another irony that various characters give voice to throughout the work is that those who might be the subject of envy are actually those most given to care. The ultimate ironies lie in the fact that (1) Fawnia knows nothing of her royal lineage, although her deportment conveys it loudly, and (2) that Pandosto lusts incestuously for Fawnia.

Greene is not beyond the pun and sexual bawdry in an otherwise rather refined work. As his jealousy grows, Pandosto "was assured . . . that his friend Egistus had entered a wrong point in his tables, and so had played him false play." The reference is to backgammon, yet the play on "point" and the game alluded to imply sexual misconduct. Similarly, the shepherd's wife, on seeing her husband carrying home an infant, wonders "that her husband should be so wanton abroad, since he was so quiet at home" and with a cudgel threatens metaphorically "to make clubs trumps, if he brought any bastard brat within her doors."

Modern readers have difficulty with *Pandosto*'s ending, given Dorastus's imprisonment, Egistus's desire for his own son's death, and Fawnia's being "joyful that she had found such a father" who had earlier ordered her put to death. One wishes, perhaps, that the irony that occurs throughout had surfaced here. Reconciliation however, is the key to this form of comedy. As Greene reminds his audience at the very end of *Pandosto*, the shepherd (Fawnia's surrogate father) returns to Sicilia and relates the entire "comical event" to Egistus.

The plot of *Menaphon* is typically complex and irony is the primary comic device. When Menaphon, an Arcadian shepherd, is first encountered he scorns Venus and her bastard son and the shepherds who are their victims. Immediately after his song, he spies the banished and shipwrecked Sephestia, her uncle, Lamedon, and her infant son, Pleusidippus. Menaphon falls in love with Sephestia, who hides her noble background. In the pastoral world she does find love, but once more it is among kind. The author compounds the irony. Sephestia falls in love with Milcertus, who is actually her husband, Maximus (that neither recognizes the other strains modern credulity). In time, Pleusidippus is kidnapped and taken to Thessaly where he is reared. Again Greene compounds the irony: major disharmony occurs when Pleusidippus and Democles, Sephestia's father, arrive in Arcadia and fall victim to her beauty. She rejects them both, neither of whom recognizes her, although she recognizes her father. Democles sets Pleusidippus and Milcertus at single combat. Both being noble, they cannot defeat one another. When they tire, Democles springs an ambush, massacres the shepherds, imprisons Pleusidippus and Milcertus, and woos his daughter. Because Sephestia refuses Democles's advances, he brands her an adulteress, orders her and Milcertus to their deaths, and releases Pleusidippus out of fear of reprisal from the king of Thessaly. On the scaffold neither Sephestia nor Milcertus will reveal their identity to save their lives—Greene leaves this to a *deus ex machina* prophetess who sorts out the relationships. By Renaissance standards and despite the massacre, the work ends comically. All ironies are resolved, and the courtly company, revitalized by the pastoral experience, returns to the court world.

Greene's romantic comedies stand out among his works, and it is they which have prompted the most comparisons with Shakespeare's. The comedies show a line of development from *Alphonsus, King of Aragon* (1599) to *James IV* (1598; accurate dating for these works is difficult). *Alphonsus* is Greene's least skillful and most imitative work. The playwright patterns Alphonsus on Christopher Marlowe's Tamburlaine, and this play serves more as a training exercise for what follows than as successful drama.

Orlando Furioso (1594) is possibly a parody of *Tamburlaine*. Less refined than *Friar Bacon and Friar Bungay*, *Orlando Furioso* is overtly comic. The comedic center of the play pits the title character against Sacrapant as they pursue the fair Angelica, whom Greene changes from the capricious character in Ariosto to a loyal and constant woman. He creates a bombastic fool in Sacrapant, thereby satirizing the theatrical excesses of his fellow, albeit lesser, playwrights. In what is perhaps a self-referential pun to his attacks on the poor conceits of poetasters, Greene has Sacrapant observe:

> Sweet are the thoughts that smother
>   from conceit;
> For when I come and set me down to
>   rest,
> My chair presents a throne of majesty;
> And when I set my bonnet on my head,
> Me thinks I fit my forehead for a Crown;
> And when I take my truncheon in my
>   fist,
> A scepter then comes tumbling in my
>   thoughts;
> My dreams are princely, all of diadems.

> Honor: me thinks the title is too base:
> Mighty, glorious, and excellent,—aye
>   these,
> My glorious genius, found within my
>   mouth. (254–64)

Greene deflates both bombast and conceit with base language.

That Orlando easily falls victim to Sacrapant's plot to make him believe Angelica unfaithful allows the writer to satirize woman's inconstancy. Ironically, Angelica, as is typical of Greene's heroines, is a model of virtue. When her father exiles her, believing her unfaithful to Orlando and thus the cause of his madness, she quietly accepts her situation and patiently waits.

The bulk of the comedy in *Orlando Furioso* is the result of Orlando's madness. When Orlando mistakes his servant, Orgalio, for Angelica's supposed lover, Orgalio shifts the blame to a shepherd whose leg Orlando tears off and bears for a club. The "shepherd" merely receives his due, for as Sacrapant's man it was he who assured Orlando that womankind (i.e., Angelica) is false. Furthermore, clowns spice the cause of comedy, the weapons that he provides are spits and dripping pans, and when they discover a woman in the company of enemies, the clown Thomas offers to allow Orlando to "strike . . . down the men, and then let me [Thomas] alone to thrust in the woman" (980–81). Later, cross-dressed as Angelica, Thomas demands eighteen pence payment from Orgalio, which causes Orlando to brand "her" a strumpet, a Cressida. Thomas's reply that he will leave if he is not used "like a gentlewoman" creates a multilevel pun for which Orlando beats him. Orgalio employs Thomas one more time, this time as a fiddler. Orlando mistakes the fiddler for a soldier and the fiddle for a sword. Given the subject of woman's inconstancy, the phallic punning—is the "sword's temper" good, will it "hold," and Orlando's discovery/complaint that "the blade is curtal short"—is a comment on Orlando's obsession.

Ultimately, through an enchantress's aid Orlando learns the truth. The plot returns to the chivalric romance, and the play ends with reconciliation between father and daughter, Orlando and Angelica.

Friar Bacon and Friar Bungay (1594) and *James IV* are Greene's finest dramatic works. In *Friar Bacon and Friar Bungay* the author intertwines the felicity of the landscape with the reality of human passion. He draws on themes established in his prose romances: men and women who dwell in an idyllic landscape—not unlike the depiction of Fressingfield—and who, acting in accord with human nature, encounter the problems of frustrated love and the reality of death.

In spite of such a melancholy-sounding theme, the play is comic. The clowns in the dual plots mock their masters in various ways. Rafe, the king's jester, makes bawdy yet ironically appropriate puns about the "love" that Prince Edward professes for the humble Margaret. Rafe suggests that Friar Bacon, the necromancer, change Edward into either a silken purse or a smock, for the one she will place in her placket (punning on the female pudenda) and the other she will put on for bed. Since Edward merely lusts after her, the puns truly reflect on his purpose. Bacon's poor scholar Miles is a satirization of learning and the pretensions thereof—through Miles's physical and verbal bungling, we see Bacon and his learning laid low. Greene employs physical as well as verbal comedy in presenting Miles. Assigned to watch the great Brazen Head that will enable Bacon to accomplish great feats such as ringing England all round with a brass wall, Miles bangs his head, falls down, and trembles at great noises. At the same time his pun on the Pope's nose satirizes the Roman Catholic church and his remonstrance with the head proves him the fool he is. For Miles's reward Greene, relying on a stock comic device from the morality plays, has Miles packed away to hell on a devil's back.

The playwright employs dramatic and situational irony as well. To try and seduce Margaret, the Prince has Lacy, the earl of Lincoln, spy on her in disguise to win her love. Lacy ironically states, "I will, my lord, so execute this charge / As if that Lacy were in love with her," and Lacy not only falls in love with but ultimately marries Margaret. Situational irony occurs when the young scholars, Serlesby and Lambert, appeal to Friar Bacon to use his glass perspective to allow them to see how their fathers fare. What they witness is their fathers dueling to their deaths over Margaret, which provokes a fight between the scholars and their own deaths.

In *James IV* the writer focuses on the theme of national corruption due to lust. James himself, as with Oedipus, is the source of social upheaval. As in *Friar Bacon*, Greene achieves comic resolution by having James recognize his folly, reject his former behavior, rue his agreeing to kill his queen Dorothea, and reconcile himself with her. In the play, on the occasion of his marriage to the English Princess Dorothea, James spies Ida, after whom he immediately lusts. Ida, in the tradition of Greene's heroines, would rather die than live unchaste. Dorothea flees the court for fear of her life, is wounded, and is left for dead. Ultimately, her presumed death provokes her father to declare war against Scotland. Dorothea returns disguised as a squire and forgives James, thereby stopping the war. James repents and Scotland is restored. Thus, Greene deals with a theme common in his work—the idea that true love creates harmony in society while lust corrupts it. At the same time, Dorothea's wholehearted forgiveness and advocacy for the sanctity of wedding vows strain modern belief.

The pure comedy in the play originates in the framing device that Greene employs. In it Bohan, a disaffected Scot who has found court, city, country, and married life all corrupt and has turned hermit, encounters Oberon, the king of the fairies. Bohan's sons perform a jig for Oberon, and the fairy king rewards one with a quick wit and the other, Slipper, a wandering life. In return, Bohan offers to show Oberon why he has turned hermit, and the play ensues with Slipper and his brother involved in the action. Slipper is a typical witty servant akin to Shakespeare's Launcelot Gobbo in *Two Gentlemen of Verona*. Slipper offers to keep his master's "stable when it is empty, and his purse when it is full and has many qualities worse than these" (515–17). Merrily he cozens a countess to give him meat and drink. And, when asked to steal letters from his master for monetary reward, he cheerfully understates, "why were it to rob my father, hang my mother, or any such like trifles, I am at your commandment, sir" (1294–96). Slipper disappears about two-thirds through the play after being cheated out of his reward. He provides the comic elements of dance and witty commentary on corruption.

The main plot of *James IV* affords Greene another opportunity to satirize foreigners. While Italians were his targets in *Mamillia*, here he takes on the French. Jaques, the would-be assassin of Dorothea, speaks in badly broken English—"me will homa to France, and no be hanged in a strange country" (2188–90)—and mixes his bad English with French in macaronic dialogue.

G

In his final period, Greene produced the cony-catching and repentance pamphlets. They, too, have their comic moments. The former employ card tricks, diversions, and "bait and run" dodges as common on today's streets as they were in the late sixteenth century. We laugh at the gulls and know that we could not possibly fall victim to such schemes. Greene seems to laugh at us as well. The repentance pamphlets have a brittle comedy. In *A Groatsworth of Wit* the university-educated Roberto's legacy of a groat to buy some wit leads him to cozen his brother out of his legacy. The courtesan whom Roberto employs as his accomplice cheats him in turn, and he follows a dissolute life as a player, writer, and gambler. The laughter is at Roberto's expense. This work, however, ends on a serious note. Greene admonishes his fellow University Wits—especially the playwrights—to use their wits to better purpose. The work concludes with a letter to his wife acknowledging his profligacy and stating that their son is with him in London. There is question about the letter's authenticity.

Summary

Robert Greene's literary significance has long been burdened with the fact that he was not Shakespeare. Today, scholars are giving more due to the man and his work. His earliest work was licensed in 1580, and from that time he wrote continuously until his death in 1592. His canon includes prose pastoral romance (including poetry and song), cony-catching pamphlets, repentance pamphlets and moral dialogues, and romantic comedies. A talented writer, he was among the first to attempt to live by his pen.

Selected Bibliography

Primary Sources
Mamillia, 1580, published 1583.
Pandosto, 1588.
Menaphon, 1589.
A Groatsworth of Wit, 1592.
Orlando Furioso, 1594.
Friar Bacon and Friar Bungay, 1594.
James IV, 1598.
Alphonsus, King of Aragon, 1599.
Note: The exact dates of Greene's works are difficult to ascertain. Often works were entered in the Stationer's Register and not published until much later. Sometimes they were not entered and we have late editions as with the plays. The above dates are the dates of publication. Consult Collins, below.

Editions
Brockbank, Philip, and Brian Morris, gen. eds. *Complete Works of Robert Greene*. London: Ernst Benn, 1969.
Collins, J. Churton, ed. *The Plays & Poems of Robert Greene*. 2 vols. Oxford: Clarendon, 1905. Although flawed, the standard edition.
Dyce, Alexander, ed. *The Dramatic and Poetical Works of Robert Greene & George Peele*. London: Routledge, 1861.
Grossart, Alexander B., ed. *The Life and Complete Works in Prose and Verse of Robert Greene*. 15 vols. London: Huth Library, 1881–1886.

Secondary Sources

Bibliographies
Hayashi, Tetsumaro. *Robert Greene Criticism: A Comprehensive Bibliography*. Metuchen, NJ: Scarecrow, 1971. Builds on Tannenbaum's work.
Tannenbaum, Samuel A. *Robert Greene (A Concise Bibliography)*. New York: S.A. Tannenbaum, 1939.
———, and Dorothy R. Tannenbaum. *Supplement to a Bibliography of Robert Greene*. New York: S.A. Tannenbaum, 1945.

General Studies
Braunmuller, A.R. "The Serious Comedy of Greene's *James IV*." *English Language Review*, 3 (1973): 335–50. Examines Greene's use of various dramatic conventions.
Carroll, D. Allen. "Who Wrote *Greene's Groats-worth of Witte* (1592)?" *Renaissance Papers* (1993): 69–77. Summarizes the history of authorship and argues for Henry Chettle as author.
Clemen, Wolfgang. *English Tragedy before Shakespeare*. Trans. T.S. Dorsch. London: Methuen, 1961, pp. 178–191. Discusses Greene's plays as examples of the general move away from set speeches.
Crupi, Charles W. *Robert Greene*. Boston: Twayne, 1986. A valuable study. Unscrambles the truth and myth of Greene's life and offers an assessment of the work that makes us take the work seriously on its own terms.
Davis, Walter R. *Idea and Act in Elizabethan Fiction*. Lawrenceville, NJ: Princeton

University Press, 1969. Davis examines Greene's place as a fiction writer.

Ellis-Fermor, Una. "Marlowe and Greene: A Note on Their Relations as Dramatic Artists." In *Studies in Honor of T.W. Baldwin.* Ed. Don Cameron Allen. Urbana: University of Illinois Press, 1958, pp. 136–49. Ellis-Fermor finds the *Orlando* the key to Greene's more sophisticated later dramas.

Empson, William. *Some Versions of the Pastoral.* London: Chatto, 1935. An important commentary on the relationship between love and magic in *Friar Bacon and Friar Bungay.*

Helgerson, Richard. *The Elizabethan Prodigal.* Berkeley: University of California Press, 1976. An important study that explores the relationship between art and life in the portrayal of these men.

Hunter, Robert Grams. *Shakespeare and the Comedy of Forgiveness.* Irvington, NY: Columbia University Press, 1965. A study of the influence of Greene's work on Shakespeare.

Jordan, John Clark. *Robert Greene.* Irvington, NY: Columbia University Press, 1915. A beginning point for Greene studies; emphasizes Greene's narrative skills.

Lascelles, Mary. "Shakespeare's Pastoral Comedy." *More Talking about Shakespeare.* Ed. John Garrett. London: Longmans, Green, 1959, pp. 70–86. Lascelles compares Greene's techniques in the use of the pastoral with Shakespeare's.

Lavin, J.A. Introduction. *Friar Bacon and Friar Bungay.* In *Complete Works of Robert Greene.* Gen. ed. Philip Brockbank and Brian Morris. London: Ernst Benn, 1969. Lavin focuses on Margaret and sees the double murders as the means of drawing our attention back to her.

Seltzer, Daniel. Introduction. *Friar Bacon and Friar Bungay.* Regents Renaissance Drama Series. Gen. Ed. Cyrus Hay. Lincoln: University of Nebraska Press, 1963. Seltzer dwells on Margaret's inherent nobility which provides her with the steadfastness and felicity to withstand and triumph over her various trials.

Senn, Werner. *Studies in the Dramatic Construction of Robert Greene and George*

Peele. Bern: Francke, 1973. Swiss Studies in English 74. Margaret is seen as an unwholesome influence and concludes that the play is really a study of "Edward's decisive growth in moral stature" (147).

Towne, Frank. "'White Magic' in *Friar Bacon and Friar Bungay?" Modern Language Notes,* 67 (1952): 9–13. Towne argues against the view that Bacon's magic is innocent.

Mary Free

Grossmith, George

Born: London, December 9, 1847
Education: North London Collegiate School, completed in 1866
Marriage: Emmeline Rosa, 1873; four children
Died: Folkestone, Kent, March 1, 1912

Grossmith, Walter Weedon

Born: London, June 9, 1854
Education: Royal Academy schools and Slade [Art] School
Marriage: May Lever Palfrey, 1895; one child
Died: London, June 14, 1919

Biography

The Grossmith brothers were two versatile theatrical and literary artists active in the late Victorian period. George, the elder of the two, was born in London on December 9, 1847; Walter Weedon, six years his junior, was born on June 9, 1854, also in London. Their father, George Grossmith, was a lecturer and police-court reporter, and son George began assisting his father at the police courts when he was seventeen. After schooling at the North London Collegiate School, he followed this profession until 1877 and briefly resumed it in 1880. In the meantime, he married Emmeline Rosa in 1873, and they had four children.

In 1864, George also began to give performances—readings, songs, and impersonations—for private parties; in 1870, he began doing the same work professionally, and he traveled, performing sketches either alone or with actresses or his father, until 1877.

In that year he was cast as John Wellington Wells in W.S. Gilbert and Arthur Sullivan's *The Sorcerer,* and this became his main activity for some time. He created important roles in many of the best-known of the Savoy Operas, including the part of Bunthorne in *Patience* and the Lord Chancellor in *Iolanthe*. In 1899, he left the Savoy and devoted himself, until his retirement in 1909, to "humorous and musical recitals" in England, Canada, and the United States.

George was a composer and playwright; he provided the music for Gilbert's opera *Haste to the Wedding* and wrote several plays which were produced in the 1870s and 1880s, and he wrote two books of reminiscences, *A Society Clown* and *Piano and I*.

His younger brother, Weedon, studied art at the Royal Academy and the Slade School, and exhibited his paintings at the Royal Academy and the Grosvenor Gallery. In 1885, he turned to what was something of a family specialty, public performing, and he appeared on the London stage for many years. According to H.W.C. Davis and J.R.H. Weaver in the *Dictionary of National Biography*, he excelled in "acting 'dudes' and small, underbred, unhappy men," both in his own plays and in those written by others (Davis, 231). In 1895, Weedon married May Lever Palfrey; the couple had one child. Weedon wrote several plays, the most successful of which was *The Night of the Party* (1901), and a novel, *A Woman with a History* (1896). Davis and Weaver assert (oddly, in view of his artistic activities) that "his artistic taste showed itself best in his *flair* for old furniture" (231). His reminiscences were published in 1913 as *From Studio to Stage*.

George died at Folkestone in Kent on March 1, 1912; Weedon died in London on June 14, 1919.

Literary Analysis

Though the Grossmith brothers were the authors of plays, novels, and books of memoirs, and though they were certainly recognized in their own time as popular performers, they are now best known—almost *exclusively* known—for their book *The Diary of a Nobody*. Written by George and Weedon and illustrated by Weedon, it was first published as a serial in *Punch* and then appeared in book form in 1892.[1] *The Diary* seems to have been popular from the beginning; it is regularly referred to in terms such as "masterpiece" and the "immortal *Diary of a Nobody*" (Priestley, 94). Evelyn Waugh called it "the funniest book in the world" (85), and Hilaire Belloc is quoted on the dust-jacket of the

book as calling it "one of the half-dozen immortal achievements of our time."

The Diary of a Nobody is the record of fifteen months in the life of Mr. Charles Pooter, a nobody. He begins his record with his move to a new home, extravagantly named "The Laurels," Brickfield Terrace, Holloway (suburban London), and many of the things that he records have to do with his home—the dissatisfactions of living by the railroad tracks, his difficulties getting the garden to grow, humiliations with tradesmen, failures in home repair, and his and his neighbors' minor snobberies. Pooter's wife, the long-suffering Carrie, is another constant; so are his two good friends, Mr. Cummings and Mr. Gowing, and his son Willie, a swell who renames himself Lupin.

That nothing very important happens to the Pooters in these fifteen months is, of course, the point of the book. They enjoy little domestic parties; they spend a holiday at the seaside; they endure minor domestic arguments. Mr. Pooter makes bad jokes, of which he is inordinately proud, and Carrie dutifully laughs at them.

The mundane level of life is varied by two categories of incident. One is the Pooters' occasional foray into high life—an invitation to the Lord Mayor's Ball at the Mansion House, attendance at the Volunteers Ball given by the East Acton Rifle Brigade, dinner with a celebrated visiting American journalist, Mr. Hardfur Huttle. Each of these nights turns out to be less impressive than the Pooters had anticipated. For instance, they get into a tizzy of excitement about the Lord Mayor's Ball. Carrie sends the invitation to her mother for inspection and is horrified when it comes back stained with wine. But when they get to the Mansion House, they find that almost anybody can come. The severest blow is finding their ironmonger among the guests.

In each of these cases the Pooters are humiliated in some way. Having drunk too much champagne, Pooter crashes to the floor with Carrie while dancing at the Mansion House; dining with the American journalist, they are forced to listen in silence while he denounces exactly the kind of people that they are and the life that they live.

The other running series of events out of the ordinary is provided by son Lupin. He loses several positions, invests and makes money, becomes engaged twice, and generally lives at a much higher speed than his father. His flashy clothing, slang, show-business aspirations, and uncouth friends affront the Pooters, who are "respectable" above all else. Lupin's refusal to settle down to a safe life as a clerk, combined with his annoying ability to make much more money than his father without any work habits to speak of, makes him a continual reproach to his parents.

The quality of *The Diary of a Nobody* which makes it distinctive is its delicacy of attitude toward the Pooters. The Grossmiths were sophisticates, West End performers, even (at least in Weedon's case) aesthetes. Their attitude toward a small clerk living in a grubby suburb and consoling himself with such pleasures as "Jackson Freres" champagne and games of charades could be expected to be severe. And it is true that Pooter, as the narrator of his own story, is always an unreliable narrator. The reader is always invited to recognize the shortcomings of the Pooters, to feel superior to their ideas and their aspirations. As J.C. Squire comments, "there is at once a record and a criticism; for amongst other things the Grossmiths were admirably sound on aesthetics, lampooning bad architecture, bad music and bad furniture with equal certainty" (11).

They also lampoon the Pooters. George Orwell notes that Pooter "is a true Englishman both in native gentleness and his impenetrable stupidity" (280). He and his wife are certainly common people, they think that their ugly house is handsome, they do not know much, and they take pride in the wrong things. Pooter often does (or suffers) things which make him look foolish. The following is a description of a completely typical event (typical even in being low-key):

> Things might have become rather disagreeable but for Gowing . . . suggesting they should invent games. Lupin said: "Let's play 'monkeys.'" He then led Gowing all round the room, and brought him in front of the looking-glass. I must confess I laughed heartily at this. I was a little vexed at everybody subsequently laughing at some joke which they did not explain, and it was only on going to bed I discovered I must have been walking about all the evening with an antimacassar on one button of my coat-tails. (112)

However, this selection only suggests the tone of the book. After all, it cannot be very hard to make jokes about a man like Pooter. The more difficult part is to produce sympathy for him. In part this is accomplished by making the problems that he faces recognizably universal. For instance, though we may not ever paint our bathtubs because we have leftover paint in an attractive color, then turn ourselves red because the paint is water-soluble, still the requirement of adjustment to life's indignities, the disparity between what we would like to be and what we are often reminded that we are, the steady refusal of life to fulfill our dreams of it—these are all the current of every life. Roger B. Henkle comments:

> Certainly we are laughing *at* Pooter, whose ineptitude transcends whatever ours might have been, but we are also registering our sense that he is playing out the very social traumas that most of us endure. The kind of comedy in *The Diary of a Nobody*, which treads such familiar home ground, and in which we feel an affectionate identification with the comic characters, is brought into the area of our own emotional experience. Its virtue, its great appeal, is its ability, through obliquity and a light touch, to insinuate us into that inner awareness and release into laughter. (230)

Our laughter is partly predicated on our assurance that Pooter's ineptitude transcends ours: this may not be true, but at least ours is locked in our bosoms, not exposed in a published diary. Most of the readers of this book are themselves not exalted personages, but the comforting reflection that at least we have not made public our personal diary of a nobody is a key to the Grossmiths' inspired comic invention.

The diarist, Charles Pooter, has given the English language the eponym "a Pooter" and the adjective "Pooterish." British humorist Keith Waterhouse has published *Mrs. Pooter's Diary* (1983) and *The Collected Letters of a Nobody* (1986), and the genre of diary humor runs from the Grossmiths through such recent popular books as Sue Townsend's *The Secret Diary of Adrian Mole* (1984).

Summary

George and Weedon Grossmith were both very active in the Victorian theater, but today they are best known for a single volume—*The Diary of a Nobody*. The comic effects of the book are

G

produced in a slow and cumulative way. There is nothing sensational about its humor. Instead, there is a seductive combination of homely truths, slightly exaggerated embarrassments, and honest emotion. Weedon's illustrations are an essential part of the action that this book has exercised on readers for nearly a hundred years. Particularly in view of its origins in periodical humor, this durability justifies the often-repeated claims that the Grossmiths' book is a class of British humor.

Notes

1. There is a difficulty with the date of first book publication. The date is given as 1892 in Ousley, Vinson, and the original dedication (reprinted in the 1963 Everyman reprint); but in the *Dictionary of National Biography*, Roger B. Henkle, and J.C. Squire (in his Introduction to the same Everyman reprint) that date is given as 1894. The 1912 reprint, which includes laudatory letters and a quotation from Hilaire Belloc as prefatory material, dates the first edition in 1892.

Selected Bibliography

Primary Sources

The Diary of a Nobody. Bristol: J.W. Arrowsmith, 1892; London: J.M. Dent, 1963.

Secondary Sources

Davis, H.W.C. and J.R.H. Weaver. *The Dictionary of National Biography (1912–1921)*. London: Oxford University Press, 1927. Brief biographical sketches.

Henkle, Roger B. *Comedy and Culture: England 1820–1900*. Princeton, NJ: Princeton University Press, 1980. The most extended discussion of *The Diary of a Nobody*.

Orwell, George. *The Collected Essays, Journalism and Letters of George Orwell: As I Please 1943–1945*. Ed. Sonia Orwell and Ian Angus. New York: Harcourt, Brace & World, 1968. Brief reference and comparison to Soviet literature.

Ousley, Ian, ed. *The Cambridge Guide to Literature in English*. Cambridge: Cambridge University Press, 1988. Brief reference.

Priestley, J.B. *English Humor*. New York: Stein and Day, 1976. Brief reference.

Squire, J.C. Introduction to *The Diary of a Nobody*. London: J.M. Dent, 1963. Good explanation of background, assessment of strengths.

Vinson, James, ed. *Novelists and Prose Writers*; Vol. 2 of *Great Writers of the English Language*. New York: St. Martin's Press, 1979. Brief account.

Waugh, Evelyn. *The Essays, Articles and Reviews of Evelyn Waugh*. Ed. Donat Gallagher. Boston: Little, Brown, 1984. *The Diary of a Nobody* mentioned almost in passing.

Merritt Moseley

H

Haliburton, Thomas Chandler

Born: Windsor, Nova Scotia, December 17, 1796

Education: King's College, Windsor, B.A., 1815

Marriage: Louisa Neville, May 28, 1816; eleven children; Sarah Harriet Owen, September 30, 1856

Died: Isleworth, Middlesex, August 27, 1865

Biography

Although most of his life was spent in Nova Scotia, Thomas Chandler Haliburton felt strongly attached to Britain and more at home in his mother country than he did in the colony of his birth. Moreover, the majority of his works were conceived and written for a British audience. An affinity for Britain was acquired from his grandfather, William Haliburton, whose interest in genealogy fostered Haliburton's pride in his British heritage. Despite the absence of legal proof, William was convinced that the Nova Scotia branch of the family shared maternal ancestors with Sir Walter Scott. Although he was an immigrant to British North America from Newport, Rhode Island, William was a loyal Tory whose political beliefs influenced three generations of Haliburtons. He was the first family member to enter the legal profession, initially as a justice of the peace and later as a Nova Scotia judge. His son, William Hersey Otis Haliburton, was a lawyer, a member of the Nova Scotia legislature, and subsequently a judge of the Inferior Court of Common Pleas, a position later held by his own son, Thomas Chandler Haliburton.

Thomas Chandler Haliburton was born on December 17, 1796 in Windsor, Nova Scotia, the only child of William Hersey Otis Haliburton and Lucy Chandler Grant. In 1810, he graduated from King's Collegiate School, Windsor and continued on to King's College, Windsor, where he took a B.A. in 1815. Both were Anglican, Tory institutions; the latter in particular resisted the influence of the United States on the political and cultural ideologies of the province and upheld the values of the monarchy. Haliburton's education reinforced the Tory attitudes instilled by his parent and grandparent.

In 1816, on a second visit to Britain, Haliburton met Louisa Neville and married her on May 28 of that year. They had eleven children, three of whom died in infancy. Haliburton was admitted to the bar of Nova Scotia in 1820 and began a successful law practice at Annapolis Royal. His political career began in 1826 with his election to the Nova Scotia Legislative Assembly as the member for Annapolis Royal. During his period of tenure in the assembly, Haliburton championed several causes, among them the subsidization of a public school system for Nova Scotia, the provision of permanent funding for Pictou Academy, and the equitable treatment of the province's Roman Catholic population. However, Haliburton was an outspoken orator who soon alienated his fellow members. Upon the death of his father in 1829, he was elected First Justice of the Inferior Court of Common Pleas. In 1841, he was appointed Judge of the Supreme Court of Nova Scotia. On November 29, 1841, Haliburton suffered the tragic loss of his wife of twenty-five years. Louisa's death influenced his decision in 1856, upon retiring from the bench at the age of sixty, to move to England permanently.

In England, Haliburton lived in Isleworth, Middlesex. On September 30, 1856, he married his second wife, Sarah Harriet Owen, a widow.

Despite increasing ill health, Haliburton's retirement years in England were productive and enjoyable. In 1861, as the first chairman of the Canadian Land and Emigration Company, he negotiated the purchase of land for settlement purposes in Haliburton and Victoria counties, Canada West. The following year he became a member of the first board of the British North American Association of London which disseminated information about the colony and encouraged a union of the provinces. With his election in 1856 to the British House of Commons, the Judge resumed his political career. Haliburton's performance as Member of Parliament for Launceston was disappointing, though. His Tory beliefs and his concern for colonial affairs were not of interest to fellow members and when his term concluded in 1856 he did not seek reelection. He died on August 27, 1865, and was buried in Isleworth-on-Thames.

In addition to his career in law and politics and his writing, Haliburton was successful in business. In Windsor he was the proprietor of a gypsum quarry, six retail shops, and wharf facilities, and he was a partial owner of the bridge which crossed the Avon River. Haliburton's various professional endeavors provided the material comfort which he relished throughout his life. He indulged a sensual appetite for food, liquor, horses, and conversation; his gustatory pleasures contributed in large part to the gout which plagued his later years. In spite of his outmoded political beliefs, his contradictory nature, and his extravagant pleasures, Haliburton was universally recognized as a gifted writer. In 1858, he was awarded an honorary DCL by Oxford University for his contribution to literature, the first colonial to be so honored. Haliburton continues to be known primarily as an author whose works attracted international acclaim throughout the nineteenth century.

Literary Analysis

Haliburton's diverse interests were reflected in an oeuvre that included history, political writing, and fiction. His first books were histories. In 1823, at the young age of twenty-six, he published *A General Description of Nova Scotia*, previously attributed to Walter Bromley and now known to be the work of Haliburton. The author was displeased with the effort, however, and in 1829 he published a two-volume study, *An Historical and Statistical Account of Nova-Scotia*, which is said to be the first history of the province. Haliburton won public acclaim for this work and his compelling description of the Acadian expulsion inspired Henry Wadsworth Longfellow's poem, *Evangeline, a Tale of Acadie*. *The English in America*, published in 1851, was less successful, due largely to Haliburton's blatant plagiarism of Richard Hildreth's *The History of the United States of America* (1848–1852).

Two political works appeared in 1839 which were described by Fred Cogswell as the "least considerable of Haliburton's longer writings" (351). Both *The Bubbles of Canada* and *A Reply to the Report of the Earl of Durham* were ill-conceived and poorly written. In the latter, Haliburton saw the appointment of Lord Durham as Governor General to British North America as undermining Tory policy. In addition, two of Haliburton's speeches were published as pamphlets: *An Address on the Present Condition, Resources and Prospects of British North America, Delivered by Special Request at the City Hall, Glasgow, on the 25th March, 1857* (1857) and *Speech of the Hon. Mr. Justice Haliburton, M.P. in the House of Commons, on Tuesday, the 21st of April 1860, on the Repeal of the Differential Duties on Foreign and Colonial Wood* (1860).

Haliburton was best known, however, as a humorist, the creator of Sam Slick whose "wise saws" and "soft sawder," combined with a keen grasp of "human natur'" ensured his instant popularity. On September 23, 1835, the *Novascotian, or Colonial Herald*, the Halifax newspaper owned and published by one-time premier of the province, Joseph Howe, included the first of a series of twenty-two sketches entitled "Recollections of Nova Scotia." The sketches ran until February 11, 1836 and were so admired that Howe decided to issue the series in book form. Although its title page was dated 1836, the first series of *The Clockmaker; or The Sayings and Doings of Samuel Slick, of Slickville* in all likelihood appeared in January 1837. The immediate appeal of Slick was an unprecedented literary success for a nineteenth-century British North American writer. In fact, Slick proved so popular that within three months of publication a pirated edition was brought out by the London publisher Richard Bentley. From that point forward Haliburton regarded himself as a British author and wrote for a British audience. Despite a similar success in the United States, due to numerous American piracies of *The Clockmaker* series, Bentley became Haliburton's principal publisher. Two further series of *The Clockmaker* were issued by the London firm in 1838 and 1840 respectively. Incredible as it may seem today, Sam Slick's popularity with nineteenth-century readers rivaled that of Charles Dickens's Sam Weller of *The Posthumous Papers of the Pickwick Club* (1836–1837).

Each of *The Clockmaker* volumes was a series of episodic sketches in which the author adopted humor, satire, and irony to develop a moral point. As a sequence of adventures, the structure of *The Clockmaker* was borrowed from the picaresque novel. Haliburton was familiar with the work of fellow Nova Scotian Thomas McCulloch, whose ironic "Letters of Mephibosheth Stepsure" were serialized in Halifax's *Acadian Recorder* between 1821 and 1822. He was also influenced by the frontier humor of the anonymously published *Sketches and Eccentricities of Col. David Crockett of West Tennessee* (1833) and by Seba Smith's (alias Jack Downing) *The Life and Writings of Major Jack Downing of Downingville, Away Down East in the State of Maine* (1833), which made similar use of Yankee vernacular. That these and other sources were elements in the creation of a highly original work was later confirmed by Charles Farrar Browne, alias Artemus Ward, who described Haliburton as the father of American humor.

As a series, *The Clockmaker* did not sustain a unified plot; rather, the author employed eccentric characters, regional dialect, anecdote, and a sophisticated narrative technique to entertain and engage his readers. At the center of each sketch was the shrewd Yankee, Sam Slick, an independent and outspoken character. Slick's speech was consistently framed by one of two foils, Squire Poke or Reverend Hopewell, who articulated the imperialist views of their creator. Never before had Nova Scotians been either charmed or offended by the likes of Slick. An American traveling through the Maritime provinces peddling his clocks to the credulous Blue Noses, Slick occupied the privileged position of an outsider. He could visit Nova Scotia, offer scathing commentary, partake in controversial political discussion, temper it with flattery, and leave comfortably to return upon his next whim.

Slick's character was built on contradictions and sly witticisms. In his wide-ranging discourse, he favored the use of aphorisms, epigrams, and metaphors to make what was so often a political point:

> The English are the boys for tradin' with; they shell out their cash like a sheaf of wheat in frosty weather; it flies all over the thrashin' floor: but then they are a cross-grained, ungainly, kickin' breed of cattle, as I e'enamost ever seed. Whoever gave them the name of John Bull, knew what he was about, I tell you; for they are bull-necked, bull-headed folks, I vow; sulky, ugly-tempered, vicious critters, a-pawin' and a-roarin' the whole time, and plaguy onsafe unless well watched. They are as headstrong as mules, and as conceited as peacocks.

The international success of *The Clockmaker* can be attributed in part to the ideological position from which it was written. Despite its criticism of Britain and her colony, the series upheld the virtues of imperialism. In the first half of the nineteenth century the population of Nova Scotia included Loyalists and British immigrants who would regard the imperialist subtext of *The Clockmaker* as just. Although implicated by Slick's affronts, Nova Scotian readers were finally engaged by the work's imperialist bias.

Similarly, *The Clockmaker* beguiled the English with its praise of their country. While British readers would feel superior to the Nova Scotians whom Slick derided, they could enjoy the entertainment and elucidation provided by the work. Conversely, American readers would take a certain pride in Slick's ambition and intelligence. They, too, would feel superior to their colonial neighbors and would not loathe Slick's exploitation of the Nova Scotians.

Slick also figured in *The Attaché; or, Sam Slick in England*, first and second series (1843 and 1844), *Sam Slick's Wise Saws and Modern Instances; or, What He Said, Did, or Invented* (1853), and *Nature and Human Nature* (1855). These books, however, were less successful than *The Clockmaker* series; by the early 1840s Slick and his mischief had been overplayed. Haliburton's other humorous works included *The Letter Bag of the Great Western; or, Life in a Steamer* (1840) and *The Season-Ticket* (1860). The former, an epistolary record of a steamship voyage, was influenced by Tobias Smollett's *The Expedition of Humphry Clinker* (1771). *The Season-Ticket* consisted of articles which Hali-

H

burton contributed to the *Dublin University Magazine* between 1859 and 1860.

The Old Judge; or, Life in a Colony (1849) is perhaps the most overlooked of Haliburton's works. Like *The Clockmaker*, it consisted of a series of sketches but its nostalgic tone, quiet understatement, and somber realism distinguished it from the earlier work. Stephen Richardson, a native Nova Scotian, replaced Sam Slick as the central figure of the series and was no less intriguing a character:

> . . . one of the oddest fellows in this country, [is] Stephen Richardson, of Clements, in the County of Annapolis. There is some drollery about him, inexhaustible good humour, and, amid all the nonsense he talks, more quickness of perception and shrewdness than you would at first give him credit for. Take him altogether, he is what may be called a regular character.

Soon after the early success of *The Clockmaker*, first series, Haliburton was rejected by his fellow Nova Scotians for the harsh assessment of them in the pages of his narrative, the same assessment that gained him popularity abroad. Ironically, today he is regarded by Canadian scholars as the foremost nineteenth-century writer of histories, political tracts, and fiction whose genius created *The Clockmaker* series. In his day, however, Haliburton enjoyed the privilege of British publication, strove to win the favor of British readers, and was feted as a British humorist.

Summary

Thomas Chandler Haliburton, the British North American author of *The Clockmaker* series, won international acclaim for his character Sam Slick, the Yankee clock peddler whose popularity during the nineteenth century rivaled that of Dickens's character, Sam Weller.

Selected Bibliography

Primary Sources

A General Description of Nova Scotia; Illustrated by a New and Correct Map. Halifax: Royal Acadian School, 1823.

An Historical and Statistical Account of Nova-Scotia. 2 vols. Halifax: Joseph Howe, 1829.

The Clockmaker; or The Sayings and Doings of Samuel Slick, of Slickville. First series. Halifax: Joseph Howe, 1837.

The Clockmaker; or The Sayings and Doings of Samuel Slick, of Slickville. Second series. London: Richard Bentley; Halifax: Joseph Howe, 1838.

The Bubbles of Canada. London: Richard Bentley, 1839.

A Reply to the Report of the Earl of Durham: By a Colonist. London: Richard Bentley, 1839.

The Clockmaker; or The Sayings and Doings of Samuel Slick, of Slickville. Third series. London: Richard Bentley, 1840.

The Letter Bag of the Great Western; or, Life in a Steamer. London: Richard Bentley, 1840.

The Attache; or, Sam Slick in England. First series. 2 vols. London: Richard Bentley, 1843.

The Attache; or, Sam Slick in England. Second series. 2 vols. London: Richard Bentley, 1844.

The Old Judge; or, Life in a Colony. 2 vols. London: Henry Colburn, 1849.

The English in America. 2 vols. London: Colburn, 1851. Rpt. as *Rule and Misrule of the English in America.* 2 vols. New York: Harper, 1851.

(Ed.) *Traits of American Humor, by Native Authors.* 3 vols. London: Colburn, 1852.

Sam Slick's Wise Saws and Modern Instances; or, What He Said, Did, or Invented. 2 vols. London: Hurst & Blackett, 1853.

(Ed.) *The Americans at Home; or, Byeways, Backwoods, and Prairies.* 3 vols. London: Hurst & Blackett, 1854.

Nature and Human Nature. 2 vols. London: Hurst & Blackett, 1855.

An Address on the Present Condition, Resources and Prospects of British North America, Delivered by Special Request at the City Hall, Glasgow, on the 25th March, 1857. London: Hurst & Blackett, 1857.

The Season-Ticket. London: Richard Bentley, 1860.

Speech of the Hon. Mr. Justice Haliburton, M.P. in the House of Commons, on Tuesday, the 21st of April 1860, on the Repeal of the Differential Duties on Foreign and Colonial Wood. London: Edward Sanford, 1860.

The Letters of Thomas Chandler Haliburton. Ed. Richard A. Davies. Toronto: University of Toronto Press, 1988.

Secondary Sources

Chittick, V[ictor] L[ovitt] O[akes]. *Thomas Chandler Haliburton ('Sam Slick'): A Study in Provincial Toryism.* 1924. Rpt. New York: AMS, 1966. A comprehensive biography of Haliburton, with an extensive bibliography.

Cogswell, Fred. "Haliburton, Thomas Chandler." In *Dictionary of Canadian Biography*, ed. Francess G. Halpenny. Toronto: University of Toronto Press, 1976. Vol. 9, pp. 348–57. A biographical and critical essay on Haliburton and his works.

Davies, Richard A., ed. *On Thomas Chandler Haliburton: Selected Criticism.* Ottawa: Tecumseh, 1979. Tecumseh Critical Views. A selection of reviews and articles on Haliburton, including essays by V.L.O. Chittick, Northrop Frye, and Robert L. McDougall.

Gibson, Dyanne. "Thomas Chandler Haliburton." In *Profiles in Canadian Literature 1*, ed. Jeffrey M. Heath. Toronto: Dundurn, 1980, pp. 9–16. An essay on Haliburton which consists of five sections: critical overview and context, chronology, comments by Haliburton, comments on Haliburton, and selected bibliography.

McMullin, Stanley E. *Thomas Chandler Haliburton and His Works.* Toronto: ECW, 1989. An essay on Haliburton which consists of five sections: biography, tradition and milieu, critical overview and context, Haliburton's works, and selected bibliography.

Panofsky, Ruth. "A Bibliographical Study of Thomas Chandler Haliburton's *The Clockmaker*, First, Second, and Third Series." Dissertation, York University, 1991. An analysis of the complex composition and publication of *The Clockmaker* series, with detailed bibliographical descriptions.

Tierney, Frank M., ed. *The Thomas Chandler Haliburton Symposium.* Ottawa: University of Ottawa Press, 1985. Reappraisals: Canadian Writers 11. A collection of conference papers on Haliburton, including essays by Gwendolyn Davies, Richard A. Davies, Stanley E. McMullin, Bruce Nesbitt, and George L. Parker.

Ruth Panofsky

H

Hall, John

Born: Durham, August 1627
Education: Palace Green School; St. John's College, Cambridge University, 1645–1647; legal studies at Gray's Inn 1647–1650 (admitted to the Bar 1650)
Marriage: 1647
Died: Durham, August 1, 1656

Biography

John Hall, the son of Michael Hall, "gent.," was born in Durham in August 1627. He attended Palace Green School and then matriculated at Cambridge University in 1645. Hall began his writing career while still a student at St. John's College, Cambridge, with the publication of a collection of essays in the Baconian style called *Horae Vacivae* (1646 as by J.H.). The volume was said by his friend John Davies of Kidwelly to have "amazed not only the University but the more serious part of men in the three nations." The Cavalier Poet Richard Lovelace exclaimed, "At nineteen, what essays have we beheld!"

Within a year, Hall followed up this promising beginning with *Poems* (1646). The following year, he edited *In aliquot Sacrae Paginae loca Lectiones* by Robert Hegge. Some of Hall's divine poems were also reprinted in 1647. His translations of Latin works by Johann Valentin Andreae as *A Modell of a Christian Society* and *The Right Hand of Christian Love Offered* also appeared in 1647, as did *An Account and Character of the Times* (as by N. LL.). Around this time Hall also completed the manuscript of a prose romance called "Leucenia" that he considered his masterpiece. Unfortunately, the manuscript was mislaid by a friend and never printed. Also around this time Hall seems to have developed a grievance against the University for failing to advance him to a fellowship or professorship. At any rate, in 1647 he left Cambridge without taking a degree.

Between May and August of 1647, Hall married, perhaps in an attempt to repair his fortunes. He seems not to have had the knack for the married state, however, and, if his detractors are to be believed, soon sent his wife home to her father. A feud between the two families ensued.

Fleeing this domestic imbroglio, Hall settled in London, where he entered Gray's Inn in 1647 to read law while resuming the vocation of scholarly writer. His first London work, published in 1649 as by J.H., was a polemic—

although a well-reasoned and temperate one again showing the influence of Francis Bacon in both thought and style. This work, *An Humble Motion to the Parliament of England Concerning the Advancement of Learning and Reformation of Universities*, intimates that the revenues of the universities were being misspent and that the curriculum was too restrictive. Curiously, for someone already known as a humanist, Hall argues for the introduction of experimental science into the curriculum, faulting the preponderance of linguistic and philosophical study.

Hall was admitted to the Bar in 1650. That same year *Paradoxes* was published, and an expanded edition appeared in 1653—oddly enough this time under a pseudonym, J. de la Salle, even though a new preface by Davies of Kidwelly reiterated Hall's authorship. Preparing translations of Longinus's *The Height of Eloquence* (1652), Michael Maierus's *Lusus Serius; or, Serious Passe-Time* (1654 as by la Salle), and Procopius's *Secret History* (unfinished at Hall's death) occupied some of his time, as did preparing an edition of *Hierocles upon the Golden Verses of Pythagoras; Teaching a Vertuous and Worthy Life*, which was published posthumously in 1657.

While pursuing these academic interests, Hall began a second career as a government propagandist. In 1648, as a person of well-known Commonwealth sympathies, Hall was asked by the astrologer William Lilly to edit a newspaper. The result was *Mercurius Britannicus*. His work on this, together with *A Satire against Presbytery* and *An Answer to the Scots Declaration* (both 1648), brought him to the attention of Oliver Cromwell, the future Lord Protector.

Established as a pensioner, he wrote a *Serious Epistle to Mr. Prynne* and was invited by the Council of State to accompany Cromwell in the pacification of Scotland. Hall was probably very willing to be involved in this campaign since he and his family had suffered during the Scottish occupation of Durham. His contribution to Cromwell's Scottish campaign was the antimonarchical tract *On the Grounds and Reasons of Monarchy Considered* (1650). He went on to write other tracts in support of actions taken by the government during the Commonwealth. *A Letter to a Gentleman in the Country, Touching the Dissolution of the Late Parliament*, published in 1653 as by N. LL. and at one time attributed to John Milton, for example, attempts to justify Cromwell's dissolution of the Rump Parliament. Other such propagandistic works are *A Gagg to Love's Advocate; or, An Assertion of the Justice of the Parliament in the Execution of Mr. Love* (1651), *Answer to the Grand Politick Informer* (1653), and *Confusion Confounded* (1654). Hall also brought out an edition of several earlier tracts accusing the Dutch of cruelty, explicitly doing so to incite public enmity in the war then being waged against the United Provinces.

Despite a reputation for writing with great rapidity and his enviable record of productivity, Hall was a man of pronounced inactivity in all other aspects of life. Indeed, ill health kept him bedridden throughout much of the early 1650s, and his salary was actually stopped in 1655 because he was not producing his full quota of propaganda. His ill health may have had its origin in personal habits. His friend Davies notes that Hall found elements of grooming "tedious torment" and describes him as constitutionally "inclined to pursinesse & fatnesse," and he is even reported to have adopted the practice of swallowing pebbles to weight himself down and increase his immobility. In notes on the life of the philosopher Thomas Hobbes, Anthony à Wood quotes Hobbes as being of the opinion that had not Hall's "debauches & intemperance diverted him from the more serious studies, he had made an extraordinary person; for no man hath ever done so great things at his age" (460). He died in Durham in 1656 from the exertion of a trip home to visit his ailing father. It cannot but be supposed that his death at an early age was in some measure the consequence of his preposterously sedentary habits. His friend Davies of Kidwelly saw to the posthumous publication of a number of his works. The *Hierocles*, which he had just finished, and an early work called *Of the Advantageous Reading of History* were printed for the first time in 1657. The *Emblems with Elegant Figures: Sparkles of Divine Love* (1658) are a redaction of Michael Hoyer's *Flammulae Amoris S.P. Augustini*, reprinting a selection of the plates (there may have been a prior edition of which no copy survives).

Literary Analysis

Although Hall described himself modestly as "of the unfittest making for a Translatour" in the preface to his Longinus, a substantial proportion of his work consists of accurate and gracefully written translations of relatively obscure works. Of the authors he translated, only

Longinus is likely to find any but specialist readers today, and there are many later translations available. Hall's was, however, the first, and, although superseded, it should perhaps be remembered for its apt title, *The Height of Eloquence*.

Hall's importance in his own day was primarily as an essayist serving the Commonwealth. While not striking enough to bear comparison with the prose works of Milton (whose significance as a writer in his own day is exactly similar) or with those of the period's other great masters of style, Hall's prose works are always both elegant and clear. His work on *The Advancement of Learning* has, in addition, a modest historical place as an early document in the debate of the Ancients and the Moderns, a debate which was to gain increasing importance as the century progressed.

In his own day, Hall's reputation was greatly colored by the notice given his youthful publication of a volume of poetry. Among his poems are a dozen devotional lyrics in English and two in Latin. Although the editor George Saintsbury thinks that one of the English devotional poems, "On an Hour-Glass," illustrates the intensity of the best of the Metaphysical Poets, the theme of the poem is the commonplace one of "My life is measur'd by this glass." The general standard of these divine poems is merely competent.

Justifiably more prominent in contemporary comments on Hall's reputation as a poet is his secular verse, particularly the satiric material. In a commendatory poem to Hall's collected verse, the Neo-Platonic philosopher Henry More, for instance, praises Hall as a "Young monster! born with teeth"; ironically, More's poem, by beginning thus, rewards the reader with a measure of surprise that Hall himself never achieves.

Actually, the most characteristic of Hall's English secular poems (two of which are in Latin) are not particularly satiric but are rather witty lists illustrating simple observations. "Upon the King's Great Porter," for example, is a series of hyperbolic exclamations noting how small all other things seem in comparison to Evans the Porter: he must use the Rhine River for a looking glass; he wears his wife's bracelet as a thumb ring; his breath is a whirlwind. "Upon T.R., a Very Little Man, but Excellently Learned" is a catalogue of surprising conjunctions of big and little such as "This giant and this dwarf in one." "An Eunuch" is a series of exclamations over the ambiguity of androgyny:

> How doth Nature quibble, either
> He, or she, boy, girl, or neither;
> Thou may serve great Jove instead
> Of Hebe both and Ganymede.

Even making allowances for changes in the sound system of English since the seventeenth century, as the citation from "An Eunuch" illustrates, Hall has something of a tin ear for rhyme.

Perhaps the author's most affecting list poem is "Home Travel" on the theme "That who would travel here might know / The little world in folio." The poet presents a list of all of the things for which others "ransack Africk" and the rest of the world while the poet "may / More choicer wonders" at home in England "survey." Simple and unpretentious, the poem has a special poignancy as an autobiographical statement from an author who physically weighted himself down so that he could not move.

There are a number of poems with more depth than the list poems. When an image works in one of these, as in "We'll talk Narcissus to a flower again" from the aubade "The Call," the effect is to raise the level of the whole activity. But despite an understandable celebration of Hall's precocity, there is no justification for Lovelace's hyperbole: "thy undown'd face mov'd the Nine to shake, / And of the Muses did a decade make."

Hall is not particularly funny. He does make droll choices of subject matter, but his wry detachment in the absence of outright humor makes it difficult to point to anything actually amusing in his poetry. In addition, he writes occasional verse that was undoubtedly more engaging to those who knew "T.R., a Very Little Man," the "Deformed X.R.," and "M.W. the Great Eater" than they can be to us at this distance in time. Still, the forced rhymes of Hall's poetry were perhaps a necessary prelude to the humorous, multisyllabic rhymes of Restoration and Augustan poets. In particular, despite Hall's failure to write any sustained satires, both his satirical thrust and his unusual rhymes have long been acknowledged as specific influences on Samuel Butler in the composition of *Hudibras*. Although Hall usually writes in decasyllabic couplets while Butler uses octosyllabic couplets for *Hudibras* (tightening the humorous effects by bringing the rhymes closer together and showing more inventiveness in feminine endings), without Butler's sustained wit Hall does show the full development of the other distinctive characteristics of Hudibrastic rhyming: two words rhymed with one ("press" and "ne'ertheless") and off-rhymes that surprise as they unexpectedly unite difference with sameness ("prescription" and "confusion," "produce" and "diaphanous"). Ricardo Quintana has suggested that beyond the specific influence on the development of the Hudibrastic couplet, Hall was even more substantively influential in the development of the verse satire of the next century since he shows not only the aesthetic of rhyming and a general taste for mockery but also gives an early indication of eighteenth-century philosophical ideas of the hierarchy of intellectual values.

Summary

History has not sustained the judgment of such a contemporary as Robert Herrick about John Hall, "That none hereafter sho'd be thought, or be / A Poet, or a Poet-like but Thee." Hall's secular poems are in general sharp but somewhat studied, although they contain touching lines and forceful images. Saintsbury suggests that Hall had caught the "poetic measles" that were epidemic in a century thronged with poets—good, bad, and indifferent. Even when he is at his best there is something parochial about Hall that will keep his poetry from ever attaining the interest for which his precocity and the not inconsiderable literary productivity of his short life might otherwise make a claim. As a poet, he must be remembered chiefly as a forerunner of eighteenth-century satirical standards of both hierarchal decorum and surprising rhyme, specifically as practiced by Butler, whom Hall influenced in the development of the Hudibrastic couplet.

Selected Bibliography

Primary Sources
Emblems. Ed. J. Horden. Menston: Scolar, 1970.
An Humble Motion to the Parliament of England Concerning The Advancement of Learning and Reformation of Universities. 1649. Ed. A.K. Croston. Liverpool: University Press of Liverpool, 1953.
Paradoxes (1650). Ed. Don Cameron Allen. Delmar: Scholars' Facsimiles and Reprints, 1956.

Poems. Minor Poets of the Caroline Period. Ed. George Saintsbury. 3 vols. Oxford: Clarendon, 1906. Vol. 2, pp. 175–225.
de la Salle, J. (pseud.). "To the Translator of Rabelais." Prefatory poem. Thomas Urquhart, trans. *Translation of Rabelais*. London: for Richard Baddeley, 1653.

Secondary Sources
Brown, Huntington. *Rabelais in English Literature*. Cambridge, MA: Harvard University Press, 1933, pp. 31–32, 35, 69, 73, 77–79, 86. Hall prefatory poem cited as indicating that he was one of the first English writers to appreciate Rabelais.
B[rydges], [Sir] S[amuel] E[gerton]. "Life of the Author." *Poems of John Hall*. London, 1816. Brief biography.
Bullen, Arthur Henry. "Hall, John (1627–1656)." In *The Dictionary of National Biography*. Ed. Sir Leslie Stephen. 21 vols. London: Oxford University Press, 1885–1890. Vol. 8, pp. 955–56. Brief scholarly biography and pioneering bibliography of original works.
Davies of Kidwelly, John. "Account of the Author of This Translation, and His Works." *Hierocles upon the Golden Verses of Pythagoras*; *Teaching a Vertuous and Worthy Life* by John Hall. London: by John Streater for Francis Eaglesfield, 1657. Eulogistic biographical reminiscence by friend and literary executor; notes in passing that Hall is the author of *A Letter to a Gentleman in the Country*.
Firth, [Sir] C[harles] H. "A Tract Attributed to Milton." *Athenaeum*, 3615 (February 6, 1897): 183–84. Letter to the Editor noting that Hall is the author of *A Letter to a Gentleman in the Country*.
Freeman, Edmund L. "Bacon's Influence on John Hall." *Publications of the Modern Language Association of America*, 42 (1927): 385–99. Hall seen as very consciously adopting Bacon's style.
Haller, William. "Two Early Allusions to Milton's *Areopagitica*." *Huntington Library Quarterly*, 12 (1949): 207–12. One of these allusions is to Hall's *Advancement of Learning*.
Havens, P.S. "A Tract Long Attributed to Milton." *Huntington Library Bulletin*, 6 (1934): 109–14. Havens notes that Hall is the author of *A Letter to a Gentleman*

in the Country, apparently unaware that Davies of Kidwelly and Firth have already done so.

Herrick, Robert. "To His Worthy Friend Master *John Hall*, Student of Grayes-Inne." *The Complete Poetry of Robert Herrick*. Ed. J. Max Patrick. New York: New York University Press, 1963, p. 393. Celebratory poem.

Howell, James. Letter of December 3, 1646. *Epistolae Ho-Elianae*. Ed. J. Jacobs. London: Nutt, 1889. Vol. 1.2, pp. 432–33. Familiar letter of literary appreciation and advice.

Jones, R[ichard] F[oster]. *Ancients and Moderns: A Study of the Rise of the Scientific Movement in the Seventeenth Century*. 1936; St. Louis: Washington University Press, 1961. Jones treats Hall's *Advancement of Learning* as an early document in the debate.

Lovelace, Richard. "To the Genius of Mr. John Hall: On His Exact Translation of Hierocles His Comments upon the 'Golden Verses of Pythagoras.'" *Minor Poets of the Seventeenth Century*. Ed. R.G. Howarth. London: Everyman's Library, 1969, pp. 359–60. Celebratory poem.

Mullinger, J[ames] B[ass]. *The University of Cambridge*. Cambridge: Cambridge University Press, 1911. Vol. 3. *From the Election of Buckingham to the Chancellorship in 1626 to the Decline of the Platonist Movement*. Mullinger considers Hall's early academic fame.

Quintana, Ricardo. "John Hall of Durham and Samuel Butler: A Note." *Modern Language Notes*, 44 (1929): 176–79. Hall examined as an innovator whose off-rhymes provided a pattern for eighteenth-century verse satire.

Thompson, Elbert N[evins] S[ebring]. *The Seventeenth-Century Essay. University of Iowa Humanistic Studies*, 3, 3 (1926): 8, 49–50, 103–04. Thompson places Hall in the Baconian tradition.

Turnbull, G[ordon] H[enry]. *Hartlib, Dury, and Comenius: Gleanings from Hartlib's Papers*. London: University Press of Liverpool, 1947, p. 39. Discusses Hall's contribution to the debate of the Ancients and Moderns.

———. "John Hall's Letters to Samuel Hartlib." *Review of English Studies*, 4 (1953): 221–33. Private correspondence in the debate of the Ancients and Moderns.

Wood, Anthony à. "Thomas Hobbes." *Athenae Oxonienses*. Ed. Philip Bliss. Vol. 2. 1691–92; London: for the Ecclesiastical Society, 1815, p. 460. Hobbes's opinion of Hall quoted.

Edmund Miller

Hall, Joseph

Born: Ashby-de-la-Zouch, July 1, 1574
Education: Ashby Grammar School; Emmanuel College, Cambridge University, B.A., 1592; Fellow, 1595; M.A., 1596; B.D., 1603; D.D., 1612
Marriage: Elizabeth Winiffe, 1603; eight children
Died: Higham, September 8, 1656

Biography

Joseph Hall, born at Bristow Park, Ashby-de-la-Zouch on July 1, 1574, to John and Winifred (Bambridge) Hall, was one of twelve children. His father was steward to the third Earl of Huntingdon. His mother was a strict Puritan, and the domestic environment in which Hall was reared was notable for its intense religiosity.

Hall was educated at Ashby Grammar School and, at fifteen, was on the point of entering the service of a local lecturer to be trained as a minister. On the very day that the articles binding him for seven years were to be signed, his father was persuaded by one of Hall's uncles to permit the boy to enter Emmanuel College, Cambridge, which had been established only five years earlier specifically to educate Puritans for the clergy (Hallett Smith, 232). Hall seems to have been a brilliant student. He received his B.A. degree in 1592 and was soon elected Fellow (1595) and appointed reader in rhetoric.

In 1597, at age twenty-three, he published the first three books of *Virgidemiarum*, "Toothlesse Satyrs," followed in 1598 by the final three books, "Byting Satyres." Hall's satires ignited a controversy which grew so bitter that, by order of Whitgift, Archbishop of Canterbury, and Bancroft, Bishop of London, his books were consigned to be publicly burned along with other books regarded as scurrilous or pornographic. Included in this general roundup were works by Hall's fellow satirists John Marston and Edward Guilpin, whose works were, in fact, burned, though the order was rescinded in Hall's case.

Hall entered holy orders around 1600 and took up the benefice of Halsted, Suffolk in 1601. His patron was Sir Robert Drury, known to literary scholars as the patron of John Donne, to whose *First and Second Anniversaries* Hall provided prefatory verses. Hall was a fervent supporter of King James I, whose accession to the throne in 1603 provided the occasion for Hall's last effort in verse, "The King's Prophecie or Weeping Joy." In the same year, Hall married Elizabeth Winiffe. She bore him two daughters and six sons, four of whom entered holy orders.

In 1605, Hall traveled on the Continent and was particularly struck by the evidence that he encountered of the devastation wrought by religious zealotry: "Along our way how many churches saw we demolished, nothing left but rude heaps to tell the passenger, there hath been both devotion and hostility. Oh, the miserable footsteps of war!" That year a work of Hall's in Latin appeared, published anonymously, under a Frankfort imprint, and without his authorization. This work, *Mundus Alter et Idem*, was translated into English and published, still without attribution, as *The Discovery of a New World* in London in 1608. The confusions over the date, place, and authorship are typical of Lucianic satire (imaginary voyages), and Hall's authorship of the work was sufficiently well known by the time of the "Smectymnuus controversy" of the 1640s for John Milton to make it part of his attack on Hall.

Hall's *Epistles in Six Decades* and *Characters of Vertues and Vices* also appeared in 1608. In the former, sixty "familiar letters," the author treats a broad range of contemporary topics informally and displays his characteristic fluency, rhetorical refinement, and conventionality of thought. The *Characters* represent the first extended effort in a modern language to adapt the Theophrastan character to contemporary society. "Character writing" had been part of any education in rhetoric, but until Hall no one had attempted either to present such sketches as an independent work or to organize a group of them in a coherent moral order. Following this lead, a number of character books were written in the seventeenth century.

The *Meditations*, which he wrote while abroad and which were also published in 1608, marked a new, more serious direction for Hall's literary efforts. These reflections brought the writer to the attention of Henry, Prince of Wales, who appointed him one of his twenty-four chaplains. The stipend for such responsibility being insufficient to support a family, Hall was permitted to take up the ministry of Waltham, Essex, through the gift of the Earl of Norwich. In subsequent years Hall undertook several errands abroad for King James, traveling as chaplain to Lord Doncaster in his embassy to France (1616) and representing the King, by then as Dean of Worcester, at the Synod of Dort (1618), where he particularly distinguished himself. In 1624, Hall declined the offer of the bishopric of Gloucester, but in 1627 he accepted King Charles's offer of the bishopric of Exeter.

Hall's reputation as a staunch supporter of episcopacy made him a valuable ally to the King's party, but his insistent moderation meant that he was constantly being suspected by his own party of insufficient zeal while constantly being attacked by the Parliamentary party. The later years of Hall's long life were clouded by controversy, poverty, imprisonment, and illness and illustrate "the misfortunes of the conventional moderate man in a revolutionary age" (Hill). The story of these years is related with a touching simplicity and freedom from rancor in Hall's own *Hard Measure* (1647), written at the point when he retired from public life. The rest of his writing (a considerable bulk: Hall was relentlessly productive, and his collected *Works* run to ten substantial volumes) is, when not devoted to controversy, primarily made up of meditations, sermons, or other devotional efforts.

He spent his last years in the village of Higham, near Norwich, the city to which he had been translated as bishop in 1641, just before the disestablishment of episcopacy. There he died on September 8, 1656, having spent a retirement of undiminished productivity in creating new or revising earlier controversial and devotional works.

Hall tried to uphold a Senecan ideal of Stoical moderation and detachment during one of the most turbulent periods of British history, and although he succeeded in this task, his very success placed him at the margin of the great upheavals of the time. His conciliatory posture was simply an inadequate response to what the times demanded. His "standpoint . . . is none the less narrow because it is midway between two extremes. And his benign platitudes inveighing against extremism satisfy neither party and do nothing to advance us closer to agreement" (Craik).

Literary Analysis

Hall is not a humorous writer in any generally recognized sense of the term, nor is he a comic writer in any sense at all. Although best known during his life as the writer of meditative and controversial works, Hall is remembered today, and is of interest to scholars of British humor, for a series of remarkably innovative works published early in his literary career, works which pioneered in the development of several genres that proved fertile ground for later comic writers, the *Virgidemiarum*, *Mundus Alter et Idem*, and the *Epistles in Six Decades* and *Characters of Vertues and Vices*.

Virgidemiarum (which might be translated "harvest of switches") begins with the bold claim that it founds a new genre:

> I first adventure: follow me who list,
> And be the second English satirist.

The claim was disputed at the time, as it continues to be, but Hall probably meant merely to indicate that, in good Renaissance fashion, he was reviving a long-disused classical model, in this case formal verse satire. There had been verse satires in English before *Virgidemiarum*—in the sixteenth century alone, John Skelton, George Gascoigne, and Thomas Lodge had produced them—along with a flourishing literature of moral criticism deriving from *Piers Plowman*. But, Hall was the first English author to adopt the tone, subject matter, and style of the Roman satirists Persius, Juvenal, and Horace and then to embody this approach in a long and internally coherent series of poems.

The strict derivation of Hall's satiric practice from Roman models gives his writings an antiquated tone to the modern ear, since the conception of satire to which they subscribe has been largely abandoned. The satiric tradition that remains vital derives from Greek comedy—especially the so-called Old Comedy of Aristophanes—and instead of discharging its energy in ferocious denunciation (as in Juvenal) or explicit mockery (as in Horace), proceeds by way of mock-heroic narrative or fantasy. This "vernacular" tradition, sometimes called Menippean satire, embraces the work of Francois Rabelais, Miguel Cervantes, Alexander Pope, Jonathan Swift, Francois Voltaire, and, in the twentieth century, George Orwell

(see Lewis). English formal verse satire, on the other hand, following Hall's example, tended to rely on personal ridicule and the affectation of bitter anger.

It must be remembered that not until the eighteenth century was there widespread recognition that the very word "satire" derived from the Latin "satura"—"full." In the late Elizabethan period, some believed that the word had come into the language by way of "satyr," others traced it to "Saturn / saturnine," while others followed it to its proper origin. A conflation of these etymologies permitted a conception of satire to develop that included all three possibilities: satire was, like the satyr, rough, rude, shaggy, and riddling; like the saturnine temperament, gloomy and solitary; and like the "satura" or fruit salad, crammed with all variety of matter. Hall's satires indeed are notably less smooth in versification than the verses of his contemporaries and are characterized by unexpected and abrupt changes of subject. That Hall believed formal satire required an enigmatic ruggedness is clear from the way that he apologizes for his own satires' failure to be sufficiently difficult in sense and prosody:

> Some say my satyrs over-loosely flow,
> Nor hide their gall enough from open
>   show:
> Not riddle-like obscuring their intent,
> But pack-staff plain, uttering what thing
>   they meant;
> Contrary to the Roman antients,
> Whose words were short, and darksome
>   was their sense.

But, in the satires of *Virgidemiarum* the poet primarily subscribes to the "saturnine" or gloomy conception of satire:

> The satire should be like the porcupine,
> That shoots sharp quils out in each angry line,
> And wounds the blushing cheeke, and
>   fiery eye,
> Of him that hears, and readeth guiltily.
>   (5, 3)

Elizabethan satire is not lighthearted. Hall and his successors adopted a bitter, lacerating persona, that of the man ruled by melancholy and discontent with the human condition and the state of the world. This persona actually became a recognized personality type, the Malcontent, and was used both to comic and serious effect by dramatists and pamphleteers. The Malcontent satirist was supposed to be enraged by the badness of the world and missed no opportunity to antagonize the reader. Since satire, like the epigram, was asserted to be impersonal in its ridicule, to take offense at the harshness of the satirists was to confess to the faults attacked and objections would be met with an inescapable dilemma: "Art thou guilty? Complain not, thou art not wronged. Art thou guiltless? Complain not, thou art not touched" ("Postscript" to *Virgidemiarum*). The satirist was performing a grim but necessary public service and warranted gratitude. Thus, while we normally associate satire and comedy, to the Elizabethans, satire was no laughing matter.

The first book of *Virgidemiarum* is still of considerable interest as one of the few extended attempts at literary criticism produced during the late Elizabethan period. In these nine poems, plus the first two of book 2, Hall finds grounds for complaint or alarm in almost every manifestation of a popular, nonacademic spirit in contemporary writing—anything, that is, that would not have been produced by a university-trained humanist. Hall targets plays, bad classical imitations (particularly heroic verses and Ovidian erotic poetry), the use of erotic imagery in religious verse, and the exaggerated claims of love poets. He deplores the loss of standards that has encouraged production of so much bad poetry, and the folly of writing for money.

Hall's literary criticism is ultimately disappointing, however. Except for his deferential attitude toward Edmund Spenser, he only knows how to attack and, again except for Spenser, he directs his attack against anonymous writers (thereby avoiding legal action). In addition, even his severest criticism of fellow poets is almost surely suggested by and modeled after similar attacks in Juvenal and Persius rather than representing a personal response to contemporary writing (Campbell).

Book 2 of *Virgidemiarum* criticizes the professions (writers again, scholars, lawyers, physicians, clergymen, teachers, and astrologers), while book 3 considers general moral issues. These poems deal with features of Elizabethan daily life that we would give much to know more about: hiring and work, rents, enclosures, teaching, inheritance, social climbing, dressing up, public behavior (at the theater, in church), and other pastimes and occupations. They offer intriguing anticipations of modern

concerns: Hall might be proposed as a precursor of environmentalism when he asks, "O Nature was the world ordained for nought, / But fill man's maw, and feed man's idle thought?" (3.1.6–57). Yet here again, less is delivered than is promised. The unremitting tone of grievance and the self-conscious imitation of Roman models (a product of "the humanistic passion for reviving all ancient kinds," according to Lewis) mean that even the most ferocious of his denunciations are not free from conventionality. The satires therefore suffer from two seemingly contradictory vices: as written by a twenty-three-year-old, they tend to be jejune and unconvincing ("Nothing is easier or less interesting than to proclaim with raucous conviction that whores are unchaste, misers ungenerous, and hypocrites insincere" [Lewis]). At the same time, satiric force is vitiated by the fact that the objects of attack are essentially fixed by convention. A careful reader of Hall's satires will wish to discriminate between those in which he imitates classical models, those in which he reprehends specifically Christian vices, and those in which he inveighs against new-fangled ways.

Mundus Alter et Idem is another serious satire, though at least one reader capable of untangling its macaronic puns and jokes found it "inordinately amusing" (Salyer, "Renaissance," 321). In it the author purportedly reports on a voyage of "Mercurio Britannico" to "Terra Australis Incognita," a previously undiscovered continent at the South Pole where almost all familiar European laws, customs, and values are turned upside down. Thus, in the province of Ivronia (drunkenness) in the country of Crapulia (gluttony), there are penalties for public sobriety and for refusing to drink when a toast is proposed. In Viraginia, where women rule, men must perform domestic chores, endure frequent beatings, and obey their wives in everything. Moronia is inhabited by fools, while the denizens of Lavernia live by fraud and theft.

The humor of *Mundus* is that of an extended academic *jeu d'esprit* relying largely on puns accessible only to someone familiar with a dozen or more modern and ancient languages. Other similarly donnish humor is wrung from burlesque, parody, and imitation of models both respected (Lucian, Erasmus) and deplored (Rabelais, travelers' tales), and rarely do the humorous elements mingle with the satiric; the harsh bits are not funny and the funny bits are not harsh. The work alternates between simply mocking European vices by presenting them as virtues and attacking vices by showing the dire consequences of their exaggerated form in the New World. The complete topsy-turvyness of the New World can leave it unclear just who or what is being satirized. Thus, the women in Viriginia are monstrous, which might seem to imply that so are European men whose normal behavior is being parodied. At the same time, the jokes (about women wanting to wear the pants, and about their talking all the time), and the stipulated results of gynocracy (barren fields, crumbling cities, general squalor), echo traditional antifeminist propaganda and satire.

Again, as with *Virgidemiarum*, we find in Hall fresh and strikingly modern insights alongside thoroughly conventional moral judgments and satiric thrusts that were already old in classical times. Many of his targets still draw the fire of satirists: the low salaries paid to academics and the pressure on them to publish novelties; the decline of civility; sudden and steep increases in rent; the choosing of political leaders for their cosmetic appeal. Critical opinion has varied widely on *Mundus*. Sandford Salyer finds the work "delightful" and "superior to *Utopia*" in literary craftsmanship, while for Christopher Hill, "nothing is more dreary than the balanced nullity of sensible men. Such persons are boring enough in the present, but even worse in the past, since the wicked extremes they pillory are either today's commonplaces, or else they are so antiquated as to lack even historical interest. A good prose style may freshen past platitudes: but not in translated Latin" (432).

"Theophrastan" character writing had been a traditional rhetorical and educational method well before the seventeenth century. Hall's innovation in *Characters of Vertues and Vices* was to make the technique serve for more than just detached amusement and local effect, as in Ben Jonson or, in fact, Theophrastus himself. As with all of Hall's writing, the object was moral awareness, according to Leonard D. Tourney.

Hall's characters depart from those of Theophrastus in representing virtues as well as vices, in having a specifically Christian emphasis, and, unfortunately, in lacking humor (Huntley, *Essays in Persuasion*). Although the idea of an extended description of a personality type derives from Theophrastus, the tone and form of Hall's vices owe little to the source, while the virtues are in an entirely different tradition—that of the "Solomonic" books of the Old Testament (Song of Songs, Ecclesiastes, and Proverbs)—sources that would have been familiar in Hall's day even to an unlettered audience as a consequence of attendance at sermons. What finally distinguishes Hall's characters from those of Theophrastus is their insistent moral emphasis. All of Hall's rhetorical skills are bent to the task of arousing "ravishment" or, alternatively, "loathing" in the reader.

Character writing enjoyed a spectacular but relatively brief vogue among English authors. Even though Hall's were the first fully realized essays in the form, they were not themselves responsible for establishing its popularity. Credit for this rests with Sir Thomas Overbury, whose name actually designates the work of a group of authors which includes Overbury himself as well as the dramatists John Webster and Thomas Dekker and the poet and divine Donne. Their characters, appended in ever-increasing number to successive editions of Overbury's enormously popular poem *A Wife*, abandoned the didactic, moralizing tone of Hall, adopting in its place a witty, epigrammatic style. Whereas Hall's portraits could be traced to classical and sermon literature, those of the wits derived from the plays of Jonson and from personal observation of court behavior.

Summary

Joseph Hall's achievement is uncomfortably ambiguous, and twentieth-century critics have approached him with mingled respect and distaste. Hall distinguished himself both as an author and as a divine during a long career. He was a skilled if not particularly brilliant controversialist, resolutely Puritan in outlook. His meditative writings are still read with enjoyment.

Though his literary innovations mark him as a writer of independent spirit, the substance of his writing and thought was undeviatingly conventional. The genres he founded—formal verse satire, the familiar letter, and the character—neither loom very large in literary history nor continued to develop along the lines that he inaugurated. Hall's sort of verse satire could not accommodate a major talent; John Dryden, for example, had to develop the mock-heroic approach to express his satiric vision. Epistolary writing either lapsed back into the informal essay or burst its boundaries and became the novel. Character writing emerged as a popular genre only after it shed its didactic focus and moved into psychology and social criticism. Hall had, in the harsh but fair characterization of Hill, "the fatal gift of being fluent but with nothing novel to say." His reputation survived into the mid-eighteenth century when it was, indeed, at its height, but it faded rapidly thereafter. There have been periodic attempts to resuscitate his fame, usually by tracing a relationship between his accomplishments and those of authors with more viable reputations such as Erasmus and Thomas More (some of whose temper survives in Hall), Donne and Isaak Walton (as prose stylists), Pope (who admired Hall's work), and Swift (whom Hall may have influenced). These attempts have generally been unpersuasive, and Hall remains a figure more interesting to read about than to read. He is primarily important for innovating genres in which greater writers produced enduring works, Hall's own appearing rather wooden in comparison.

Selected Bibliography

Primary Sources

The Works of Joseph Hall. Ed. Josiah Pratt. 10 vols. London, 1808.

The Works of Joseph Hall. Ed. Peter Hall. 12 vols. Oxford, 1837–1839.

Works of the Right Reverend Joseph Hall, D.D. Ed. Philip Wynter. 10 vols., 1863; New York: Facsimile AMS, 1969.

Virgidemiarum, Six Bookes. First Three Bookes of Tooth-lesse Satyrs. London, 1597.

Virgidemiarum, Six Bookes. The Three Last Bookes of Byting Satyres. London, 1598.

As "Mercurio Britannico." *Mundus Alter et Idem, sive Terra Australis ante hac semper Incognita*. [Frankfort?, 1605?]; trans. as *The Discovery of a New World*. Trans. J[ohn]. H[ealey]. London, 1608(?); Ed. H.J. Anderson. London, 1908.

The Discovery of a New World (Mundus Alter et Idem). Ed. Huntington Brown. Cambridge: Harvard University Press, 1937. An edition of the Healey translation.

Another World and Yet the Same: Bishop Joseph Hall's Mundus Alter et Idem. Trans. and ed. John Millar Wands. New Haven: Yale University Press, 1981. A new translation from Hall's Latin.

Characters of Vertues and Vices. In Two Bookes. London, 1608.

Epistles in Six Decades. London, 1608–1611.

Heaven Upon Earth and Characters of Vertues and Vices. Ed. Rudolph Kirk. New Brunswick: Rutgers University Press, 1948. Introduction is good on Hall's Christian Stoicism.

The Complete Poems of Joseph Hall. Ed. A.B. Grosart. Manchester, 1879.

The Collected Poems of Joseph Hall. Ed. Arnold Davenport. Liverpool: University of Liverpool Press, 1949. Standard modern edition with full apparatus.

Secondary Sources

Books and Parts of Books

Alden, Raymond MacDonald. *The Rise of Formal Satire in England Under Classical Influences*. Philadelphia: University of Pennsylvania Press, 1899 [1961], pp. 97–129. Still-useful summary and analysis.

Anselment, Raymond A. "John Milton *contra* Hall." In *'Betwixt Jest and Earnest': Marprelate, Milton, Marvell, Swift & the Decorum of Religious Ridicule*. University of Toronto Press: 1979. About Milton's attack on Hall—forty years after the satires had been written.

Bloom, Edward, and Lillian Bloom. *Satire's Persuasive Voice*. Ithaca, NY: Cornell University Press, 1979. Hall as originator of the satirist's "image of holy rage well barbed."

Boyce, Benjamin. *The Theophrastan Character in England to 1642*. Cambridge: Harvard University Press, 1947. Strong statement of Hall's influence on character writing.

Bush, Douglas. *English Literature in the Earlier Seventeenth Century 1600–1660*. 2nd ed. Oxford: Clarendon, 1962, pp. 192–220. Bush analyzes and accounts for the popularity of character writing.

Campbell, O.J. "The Prevailing Forms of English Satire, 1588–1599." In *Comicall Satyre and Shakespeare's Troilus and Cresida*. San Marino: Huntington, 1938, pp. 15–53. A subtle analysis of interplay of conventional satirical *persona*, classical models, and contemporary mores.

Cazamian, Louis. *The Development of English Humor*. Durham: Duke University Press, 1952, pp. 367–70. Cazamian finds humor in Hall's epigrammatic brevity, realism, and "cynical flings."

Chalmers, Alexander. *The Works of the English Poets from Chaucer to Cowper*. London, 1810. Vol. 5, pp. 221–86. Complete *Virgidemiarum* plus Warton's analysis of Hall's satires.

Craik, Henry. *English Prose Selections*. New York: Macmillan, 1894, pp. 133–55. Lively, harsh assessment of Hall.

Fischer, Hermann, ed. *English Satirical Poetry from Joseph Hall to Percy B. Shelley*. Tubingen: Niemeyer, 1970. Anthology.

Gordon, G.S., ed. "Theophrastus and His Imitators." *English Literature and the Classics*. Oxford, 1912.

Gransden, K.W., ed. *Tudor Verse Satire*. London: Athlone, 1970. Introduction helpful on classical background.

Greenough, Chester N. and J. Milton French. *A Bibliography of the Theophrastan Character in English with Several Portrait Characters*. Cambridge: Harvard University Press, 1947.

Harris, Bernard. "Men Like Satyrs." In *Elizabethan Poetry*. Ed. John Russell Brown and Bernard Harris. London: Arnold, 1961, pp. 175–201. On Hall-Marston.

Huntley, Frank Livingstone. "Joseph Hall, John Marston, and *The Returne from Parnassus*." In *Illustrious Evidence: Approaches to English Literature of the Early Seventeenth Century*. Ed. Earl Miner. Berkeley: University of California Press, 1975, pp. 3–22. On Hall's partial authorship of *The Returne* and its role in the Hall-Marston controversy.

———. *Bishop Joseph Hall, 1574–1656: A Biographical and Critical Study*. Cambridge: D.S. Brewer, and Totowa, NJ: Rowman & Littlefield, 1979. Full-length study.

———. "King James as Solomon, the Book of Proverbs, and Hall's *Characters*." In *Essays in Persuasion on Seventeenth Century Literature*. Chicago: University of Chicago Press, 1981, pp. 48–56. On the literary and political background of Hall's characters.

Kernan, Alvin. *The Cankered Muse: Satire of the English Renaissance*. New Haven: Yale University Press, 1959. Kernan discusses *persona*.

Kinloch, Tom Fleming. *The Life and Works of Joseph Hall, 1574–1656*. London:

Staples, 1951. Full-length study.

Lewis, C.S. *English Literature in the Sixteenth Century Excluding Drama*. Oxford: Clarendon, 1954, pp. 468–78. "The shapeless Roman model was a fatal encouragement to the Elizabethan love of facile moral ferocity."

McCabe, Richard A. *Joseph Hall: A Study in Satire and Meditation*. Oxford: Oxford University Press, 1981. Full-length study.

Milton, John. Milton's attack on Hall occupies parts of three pamphlets: *An Apology for Smectymnuus* (London, 1641); *Animadversions upon the Remonstrant's Defense, Against Smectymnuus* (London, 1641); and *An Apology Against a Pamphlet Call'd A Modest Confutation* (London, 1642).

Miner, Earl. "In Satire's Falling City." In *The Satirist's Art*. Ed. H. James Jensen and Malvin R. Zirker, Jr. Bloomington: Indiana University Press, 1972, pp. 3–27. Examines a crucial *topos* in late Elizabethan satire.

Patterson, Annabel. *Hermogenes and the Renaissance: Seven Ideas of Style*. Princeton: Princeton University Press, 1970. Patterson attempts to show influence of second-century Greek rhetorician on Renaissance literary criticism and poetry, especially satire and epic.

Paylor, W.J. *The Overburian Characters*. Oxford: Blackwell, 1936.

Peter, John. *Complaint and Satire in Early English Literature*. Oxford: Clarendon, 1956, pp. 138–43. Hall seen as a "decisive break . . . with the traditional mode of Complaint and with the earnestness and scrupulousness of the Middle Ages."

Smith, Hallett. "Satire: The English Tradition, the Poet and the Age." *Elizabethan Poetry: A Study in Conventions, Meaning, and Expression*. Cambridge: Harvard University Press, 1952, pp. 194–256. Judicious assessment of Hall, Marston.

Tourney, Leonard D. *Joseph Hall*. Boston: G.K. Hall, 1979. Full-length study.

Warton, Joseph. *The History of English Poetry from the Close of the Eleventh to the Commencement of the Eighteenth Century*. London, 1774. Admiring analysis.

White, Harold Ogden. *Plagiarism and Imitation During the English Renaissance: A*

H

Study in Critical Distinctions. Cambridge: Harvard University Press, 1935.

Worcester, David. *The Art of Satire*. New York: Russell, 1960. "With Hall, satire comes of age."

Articles

Baldwin, Edward Chauncey. "The Relation of the Seventeenth Century Character to the Periodical Essay." *Publications of the Modern Language Association of America*, 19 (1904): 75–114. Contains chronological list of Character-books, 1605–1759.

Beckwith, E.A. "On the Hall-Marston Controversy." *Journal of English and Germanic Philology*, 25 (1926): 84–89. Beckwith traces origin of this literary feud.

Clausen, Wendell. "The Beginnings of English Character Writing in the Early Seventeenth Century." *Philological Quarterly*, 25 (1946): 32–45. Hall and his predecessors in the genre.

Corthell, Ronald J. "Joseph Hall's *Characters of Vertues and Vices*: A 'Novum Repertum.'" *Studies in Philology*, 76 (1979): 28–35. Hall's *Characters* represent "a new use of an old form" based on biblical models and consistent with Renaissance literary theory.

———. "Beginning as a Satirist: Joseph Hall's *Virgidemiarum Sixe Bookes*." *Studies in English Literature 1500–1900*, 23 (1983): 47–60. Corthell sees Hall's satires as part of a conscious effort to build a literary career.

———. "Joseph Hall and Seventeenth-Century Literature." *John Donne Journal*, 3 (1984): 249–68. Review article.

Davenport, Arnold. "Interfused Sources in Joseph Hall's Satires." *Review of English Studies*, 18 (1942): 208–13. Hall's use of his sources went far beyond simple imitation.

———. "The Quarrel of the Satirists." *Modern Language Review*, 37 (1942): 123–30. Davenport carefully distinguishes roles of Hall, John Marston, Guilpin, and Weever in satirists' war.

Day, W.G. "A Borrowing from Bishop Hall in *Tristram Shandy*." *Notes & Queries*, 22 (1975): 496.

Dinshaw, Fram. "Two New Epigrams by Joseph Hall." *Notes & Queries*, 29 (1982): 422–23.

Gill, R.B. "A Purchase of Glory: The Persona of Late Elizabethan Satire." *Studies in Philology*, 72 (1975): 408–18. Both fictional *persona* and personal voice are present.

Gottlieb, Sidney. "Sterne's Slawkenbergius and Joseph Hall." *Cahiers Elisabéthains*, 30 (1986): 79–80.

Hall, H. Gaston. "Moliere, Chevreau's *Ecole du Sage* and Joseph Hall's *Characters*." *French Studies*, 29 (1975): 398–410.

Hall, Joseph H. III. "Joseph Hall, The English Seneca and Champion of Episcopacy." *Historical Magazine of the Protestant Episcopal Church*, 21 (1952): 62–99.

Hill, Christopher. Review of Hall's *Another World and Yet the Same*, ed. and trans. Wands. *Times Literary Supplement* (April 16, 1982): 432. "A good prose style may freshen past platitudes: but not in translated Latin."

Jensen, Ejnar J. "Hall and Marston: The Role of the Satirist." *Satire Newsletter*, 4 (1967): 72–83.

Kane, Robert J. "Joseph Hall and *Work for Chimney-Sweepers*." *Publications of the Modern Language Association of America*, 51 (1936): 407–13. Hall may have been author of first antitobacco tract.

Latham, Jacqueline E.M. "'Standing Water' in *The Tempest* and Joseph Hall's *Characters*." *Notes & Queries*, 21 (1974): 136.

Limouze, Henry S. "Joseph Hall and the Prose Style of John Milton." *Milton Studies*, 15 (1981): 121–41.

McCabe, Richard A. "Fulke Greville and Joseph Hall." *Notes & Queries*, 28 (1981): 45–46.

McNeir, Waldo F. "Hall's 'Fortunio' and 'Raymundus' Once More." *Notes & Queries*, 6 (1959): 255–57. McNeir recapitulates and resumes argument over identification of Hall's eponymous satiric targets.

Muller-Schwefe, Gerhard. "Joseph Hall's *Characters of Vertues and Vices*: Notes Toward a Revaluation." *Texas Studies in Language and Literature*, 14 (1972): 235–51. Hall's characters are truly Theophrastan in being based on "observation and verisimilitude."

Perry, George Gresley. "Hall, Joseph (1574–1656)." In *The Dictionary of National*

Biography. Ed. Sir Leslie Stephen. 21 vols. London: Oxford University Press, 1885–1890.

Platt, J.E. "An Early Autograph Poem by Joseph Hall." *Notes & Queries*, 26 (1970): 407–09.

Randolph, M[ary] C. "The Medical Concept in English Renaissance Satiric Theory: Its Possible Relationships and Implications." *Studies in Philology*, 38 (1941): 125–57. Renaissance satirists presented themselves as physicians purging, bleeding, and scourging a sick society.

———. "The Structural Design of the Formal Verse Satire." *Philological Quarterly*, 21 (1942): 368–84. Primarily concerns Augustan satire.

Salyer, Sanford M. "Renaissance Influences in Hall's *Mundus Alter et Idem*." *Philological Quarterly*, 6 (1927): 321–34. Enthusiastic reading of *Mundus* tracing its ideas back to Rabelais, More, and Erasmus and ahead to Swift.

———. "Hall's Satires and the Harvey-Nashe Controversy." *Studies in Philology*, 25 (1928): 149–70. Suggests that *Virgidemiarum*, which led to the Hall-Marston controversy, was an aftermath of the Harvey-Nashe pamphlet war.

Sitter, John E. "Pope and Hall: A New Manuscript." *Scholia Satyrica*, 1 (1975): 41–44. Pope's admiring revision of Hall.

Smith, Philip A. "Bishop Hall, 'Our English Seneca.'" *Publications of the Modern Language Association of America*, 63 (1948): 1191–204. Hall and the stoicism of Seneca.

Stein, Arnold. "The Second English Satirist." *Modern Language Review*, 38 (1943): 273–78. On the Hall-Marston controversy.

———. "Joseph Hall's Imitation of Juvenal." *Modern Language Review*, 43 (1948): 315–22. Stein argues that Hall was more original than has been supposed.

Tourney, Leonard D. "Joseph Hall and the *Anniversaries*." *Papers on Language and Literature*, 13 (1977): 25–34. Corrective analysis of Hall's prefatory poems.

Turner, Paul. "Hall's 'Byting Satyres': A Double Tooth?" *Notes & Queries*, 4 (1957): 190–91.

Wands, John Millar. "The Early Printing History of Joseph Hall's *Mundus Alter et Idem*." *Publications of the Bibliographical Society of America*, 74 (1980): 1–12. Wands sorts out the (often deliberately) obscure bibliographical data on author, place, date, and printer.

———. "Antipodal Imperfection: Hall's *Mundus Alter et Idem* and Its Debt to More's *Utopia*." *Moreana*, 18 (1981): 85–100.

———. "A Borrowing of W.S. Gilbert." *Notes & Queries*, 29 (1982): 320–22.

Williams, Melvin G. "The Bishop's Not a Preacher: A Reading of Joseph Hall's *Virgidemiarum*." *Christianity and Literature*, 24 (1975): 36–41.

Martin Beller

Hankin, St. John

Born: Southampton, Hampshire, September 25, 1869
Education: Merton College, Oxford University, B.A., 1890
Marriage: Florence Routledge, 1901
Died: Llandrindod Wells, Wales, June 15, 1909

Biography

Edward Charles St. John (pronounced "Sin-Jin") Hankin was born in Southampton on September 25, 1869. His father, Charles Wright Hankin, was the headmaster of the King Edward VI Grammar School in that city, and his mother, Mary Louis Perrot, was a published poet who came from a family of Worcestershire landowners. Hankin attended Merton College, Oxford after completing his public school education at Malvern. He left Oxford in 1890, having completed a second-class degree in classics.

Hankin was engaged for a time as a private tutor, but eventually found his vocation in journalism. After writing for the *Saturday Review* and the *Westminster Review*, the author went to India in 1894 to join the staff of the *Indian Daily News* in Calcutta. He quickly contracted malaria, however, and returned to London within the year. In the second half of the decade Hankin became a regular drama critic for *The Times* and contributed satires and parodies of contemporary stage plays, novels, and poetry to *Punch* and the *St. James's Gazette*. A collection of Hankin's satiric pieces was published in 1901 as *Mr. Punch's Dramatic Sequels* and the literary parodies were collected as *Lost Masterpieces and Other Verses* in 1904.

Hankin was married in 1901 to Florence Routledge, the daughter of the publisher George Routledge. By 1902, Hankin had assumed a prominent role in the running of the Stage Society, a group dedicated to promoting the development of English drama outside the confines of contemporary commercial theatrical practices. In the last years of his life, Hankin's energies were devoted almost entirely to the management of the Stage Society and to writing plays. *The Two Mr. Wetherby's*, Hankin's first full-length play, premiered under the auspices of the Stage Society in February of 1903. Four more full-length plays were produced within Hankin's lifetime, all by the Stage Society or the repertory theater project managed by J.E. Vedrenne and Harley Granville-Barker at the Court Theatre.

Hankin's anxiety over his health led to an early retirement to the country in 1904. By all accounts, the writer suffered from the nervous condition described as "neurasthenia" by contemporary doctors, and he feared that he would gradually slide into the life of an invalid as had his father. Hankin's bouts with illness continued, and by 1908 he could produce little new imaginative work. On June 15, 1909, Hankin committed suicide by drowning while visiting the small Welsh spa of Llandrindod Wells.

Literary Analysis

Hankin's topical satires and parodies of well-known plays, novels, and verse are perhaps typical of the mainstream turn-of-the-century material published in *Punch*, the bastion of British humor. Hankin's satires on subjects such as the dress regulations of the Royal Navy, the inefficiencies of the London telephone exchanges, scholarship, motor racing, and West End theatrical practices are playful mockery and goodhearted fun rather than exposes of vice and perniciousness. The manner of Hankin's satire is quite similar to the burlesque mode adopted by William Schwenck Gilbert for the comic operas that he wrote in collaboration with the composer Arthur Sullivan.

The two volumes of Hankin's humor published in his lifetime, *Mr. Punch's Dramatic Sequels* and *Lost Masterpieces and Other Verses*, contain what might be the best of his contributions to *Punch* and the *St. James's Gazette*. *Mr. Punch's Dramatic Sequels* is a collection of fourteen of the author's dramatic parodies, all of which burlesque prominent new plays or noteworthy revivals from the decade of the 1890s. Hankin's method for most of the parodies is to provide a brief continuing scene that ironizes and deflates the manner and theme of the original play. For example, his parody of William Shakespeare's *The Tragedy of Hamlet*, "The New Wing at Elsinore," finds that Horatio, not Fortinbras, has taken possession of the throne of Denmark and is busily supervising renovations of the castle by the grave-digging clowns. Horatio refers to them as his "Master-Builders," introducing a satiric note about the notoriety of the plays of the Norwegian dramatist Henrik Ibsen in late-Victorian theater through the reference to one of Ibsen's major plays. Hankin's piece begins with a burlesque of the ghost scene. The ramparts of Elsinore are still haunted, but this time by the ghost of Shakespeare, who resents the additions and rebuilding to his castle:

> Horatio. [Furious.] Here, I can't stand this. I'll cross it though it blast me. Stay, Illusion! [The figure stops.] Are you aware, Sir, that you are trespassing? This is a private house.
> Ghost. [In a sepulchral voice.] My private house!
> Horatio. Oh, come, you know, you can't mean that! Your house? Considering that I'm building it myself—Of course assisted by an architect—I think that you must admit there's been some mistake.
> Ghost. [Turning and advancing towards them.] Pooh! What do I care for your architect? It's mine, I say, my house, my plot, my play. I made them all![1]

Hankin's burlesque of Shakespeare develops into a satiric comment on the late-Victorian and Edwardian actor-managers' propensity for revising and adding to Shakespeare's plays for their own lavish productions. The humorist's parodies of contemporaneous plays include Arthur Wing Pinero's *The Second Mrs. Tanquery* and *The Notorious Mrs. Ebbsmith*. In "The Third Mrs. Tanquery," Hankin envisions Aubrey Tanquery marrying yet again, this time to a reform-minded feminist who dominates Aubrey and alienates him from his friends. "The Unfortunate Mr. Ebbsmith" is presented as a prologue to the original play in which the circumstances of Agnes Ebbsmith's eight years of married life before the beginning of the action of Pinero's play show her to be a feminist zealot and an embarrassing hindrance to her husband's career as a solicitor. The antifeminist note of these parodies is perhaps typical of *Punch*, where turn-of-the-century feminists and suffragists were frequently lampooned with unfavorable caricatures.

Lost Masterpieces and Other Verses con-tains verse parodies and light verse that origi-nally appeared in either *Punch* or the *St. James's Gazette*. The verse parodies include the major figures in Romantic poetry (William Words-worth, Lord Byron, Percy Bysshe Shelley, and Robert Burns) as well as the prominent Victo-rians (Alfred, Lord Tennyson; Robert Brown-ing; Gabriel Rossetti; Arnold Swinburne; Mat-thew Arnold). The parodies function in much the same manner as the dramatic burlesques, depending on an ironic deflation of theme and manner. Perhaps typical of the verse parodies is "Home Thoughts from at Home," which takes Browning's nostalgic poem about the beauties of springtime in England, "Home Thoughts, from Abroad," and reduces it to a suburban complaint about the dismal weather of England in the fall.

Hankin's talent for parody and satire greatly influenced his writing for the stage. The irony and wit of his *Punch* parodies runs throughout the author's five full-length plays, and the same dissatisfaction with the outmoded conventions of late-Victorian theater expressed in the parodies informs their structure and themes. In *The Cassilis Engagement*, for instance, Hankin in essence parodies Victorian plays, such as Tom Taylor's *New Men and Old Acres* and T.W. Robertson's *Caste*, where the plots convention-ally and sentimentally resolve the conflicts brought about by misalliances between the social classes. *The Last of the De Mullins* reverses the usual outcome of the fallen woman motif in Vic-torian drama, while *The Two Mr. Wetherby's* reads like a parody of Oscar Wilde's *The Impor-tance of Being Earnest*.

Summary
St. John Hankin's humor covers a wide variety of subjects, including political, military, eco-nomic, social, and literary issues. On the whole, his writing shows a preference and a talent for parody and goodhearted satire. Hankin's satires belong to the mainstream of late-Victorian and Edwardian humor, as his regular contributions to *Punch* demonstrate. His most noteworthy comic writings are the parodies of plays, nov-els, and verse which he first published in *Punch* and the *St. James's Gazette*, and which provide an interesting contemporary insight into the forces behind the dramatic and literary changes in late-Victorian and Edwardian England.

Notes
1. St. John Hankin, "The New Wing at Elsinore," collected in *Mr. Punch's Dra-matic Sequels* (London: Bradbury, Agnew, 1901), pp. 22–36.

Selected Bibliography
Primary Sources
Mr. Punch's Dramatic Sequels. London: Bradbury, Agnew, 1901.
Lost Masterpieces and Other Verses. London: A. Constable, 1904.
The Dramatic Works of St. John Hankin. John Drinkwater, ed. 3 vols. London: Martin Secker, and New York: M. Kennerly, 1912.

Secondary Sources
McDonald, Jan. "St. John Hankin." In *The "New Drama" 1900–1914*. New York: Grove Press, 1986. A sound commentary on Hankin's major plays.
Phillips, William H. *St. John Hankin: Edwardian Mephistopheles*. London and Teaneck, NJ: Associated University Presses, 1979. Phillips concentrates on Hankin's career as a dramatist, but in-cludes a useful selected bibliography of his satires and parodies published in *Punch* and the *St. James's Gazette*.

Peter C. Hall

Hardy, Thomas

Born: *Upper Bockhampton, near Stinsford in Dorset, June 2, 1840*
Education: *Village school; school in Dorchester; self-educated in Greek; articled to John Hicks, an ecclesiastical architect, in 1856*
Marriage: *Emma Lavinia Gifford, September 17, 1874; Florence Emily Dugdale, Feb-ruary 19, 1914*
Died: *Max Gate near Dorchester, January 11, 1928*

Biography
Thomas Hardy, the son of Thomas Hardy II and Jemima Hand, was born on June 2, 1840,

in the small hamlet of Upper Brockhampton, near an untamed wilderness in Dorsetshire which he called Egdon Heath. From early childhood, he was apparently influenced by primitive ideas and superstitions in addition to Saxon and Celtic influences. He was impressed by native folklore, and much of what he was exposed to found its way into his writings. His schooling took place first in the school in his village and then at a school in Dorchester. He taught himself Greek, and in 1856 he was articled to John Hicks, an ecclesiastical architect.

Influenced by his father's trade of master builder, Hardy intended to follow the architectural profession which he later pursued in London. While articled to Hicks, he continued to follow his literary interests, influenced intellectually by his friend Horace Moule, son of the Vicar of Fordingbridge. On September 17, 1874, he married Emma Lavinia Gifford.

Hardy eventually received the accolades that were due him, both from the people at large and the literary society in particular. In July 1910, he received the Order of Merit. Somewhat unusually, though not an unknown situation, he was recognized in literary circles as a superior practitioner in both the genres of novel writing and poetry, not to mention his great three-part epic-drama, *The Dynasts*, which established his literary excellence in a third genre. Emma died in November 1912; two years later Hardy married Florence Emily Dugdale, a writer of children's books and periodical articles.

Hardy retired to Max Gate, a residence near Dorchester, which he built himself in 1883. It was here that he received further accolades, both on his seventieth and eightieth birthdays, from many segments of the English-speaking world. His death on January 11, 1928 closed the curtain on the Victorian era.

Literary Analysis

Hardy's literary career can be divided into three periods: the first period encompasses his accomplishments as a novelist ending with *Jude the Obscure*; his second period consists of his heralded epic poem, *The Dynasts*, perhaps his single greatest work; and finally, to the third period can be assigned his lyric poetry which began with "Times Laughing Stocks" in 1909. Indeed, it is through the mastery of his lyric expression that the rustic humor of the Dorset villagers emerges.

Among those who exerted an influence on Hardy, one must not overlook Herbert Spencer (1820–1903) whose essay, "First Principles," presented a picture of the universe with specific attention to force, motion, and matter. This stimulated Hardy's interest in First Causes and human destinies. Algernon Swinburne, too, strongly inspired Hardy.

Hardy's humor, evident mostly in his early writings, pertains to the country life and his perspective concerning urban existence compared with its more rustic counterpart. His humor is most evident in *Under the Greenwood Tree* (1872) and *Far from the Madding Crowd* (1874). In later years his humor was not so apparent, though it was rekindled in *A Few Crusted Characters* (1894).

One can appreciate the Wessex clowns and wits of his early novels even though, to some extent, they are stock characters akin to William Shakespeare's Bottom, the gravedigger, and Dogberry. According to Annie Macdonell, Hardy "has his eye always on the comedy of circumstances. Some of the novels, like *Two on a Tower* (1882), lack humor in the detail, but have it in the central conception" (130). His humor is less evident in *The Return of the Native* (1878), except, perhaps, in its overall conception in which circumstances doth make fools of the human condition.

Humor in Hardy's novels was neither the author's goal nor a major accomplishment. Nevertheless, it was a concomitant ingredient of several of his works in this genre. The shepherd hero, Gabriel, in *Far from the Madding Crowd* is presented in "a comic-realistic perspective," according to Noorul Hasan (15). Even the description of his watch appears to Hasan to be a "deliberate comic deflation" (15). Indeed, the entire first chapter is one of humorous design. The pastoral setting of the novel along with its rustic characters pits amusing conditions against a more serious tale. The analogy of Gabriel's hut to Noah's Ark strengthens the comic aspect of the tale. Gabriel's lack of tact is another humorous element, particularly in his romantic encounters with Bathsheba. Certainly, no one can doubt the humor of Bathsheba throwing milk on the unconscious Gabriel to bring him back to life.

Further, Gabriel and Bathsheba's inability to communicate with each other is a comic element, though not necessarily the thematic purpose of the novel. Bathsheba, herself, is amusing in her oxymorons: "I *hate* to be thought men's property in that way, though possibly I shall be had some day," she says, and "I shouldn't mind being a bride at a wedding, if I could be one without having a husband." Part of the humor, therefore, rests in the antithetical behavior of the two protagonists. She, the saucy misogamist; he the conventional swain.

Another element of humor in the novel is the character of Boldwood, who can best be categorized as a humorous character. Hasan describes him as being "so dominated by a single 'humor' that he seems a kind of pasteboard figure of sexual obsession unable by definition to attain full tragic stature while carrying about him a portentous air of tragedy" (35).

Though satire is a more acerbic form of humor than most of its brethren, nevertheless it qualifies as a valid entry into the genre. In this respect, then, some of the writer's novels with their rustic setting are worthy of attention. In *The Poor Man and the Lady* (1867–1868), the author's first attempted novel, the focus of the satire is centered on the more affluent urban populace. The book was not an immediate success. In fact, three publishers turned it down unceremoniously. Hardy's surgery on the novel resulted in an abridged version, *An Indiscretion in the Life of an Heiress* (1878). This novelette included one section of its unfortunate progenitor. Additional sections found their way into several of the writer's other novels with the original meeting a similar fate to that of James Joyce's *Stephen Hero*. Both manuscripts were sacrificed to the literary "Phoenix," though segments of both are extant.

Hardy's first novel, *Desperate Remedies* (1871), was published anonymously. This was followed the next year by *Under the Greenwood Tree*. Revealed in this novel is Hardy's penchant for creating artful female characters. Indeed, the heroine, Fancy Day, lacks the romantic qualities one might suspect of her position. Referring to her love, Dick Dewy, she says, "I like Dick, and I love him; but how plain and sorry a man looks in the rain, with no umbrella, and wet through." Here, too, the humor is revealed in the novel's rustic setting. Following this novel was *A Pair of Blue Eyes* (1873). In this romantic tragedy Hardy once again employed rustic humor, this time represented by provincial characters acting out a drama that was both humorous and macabre. Once again, the female character, Elfride Swancourt, provides much of the humor. Expecting a gentleman caller with whom she was not acquainted, she asked her father to come downstairs and introduce the man to her. Her father, suffering from gout in his big toe, indicated that this would be impossible. To this, Elfride replied, "What! sit there all the time with a stranger, just as if I knew him, and not anybody to introduce us?" She is also much concerned about what to serve the man when her father indicates that she has to give him some food. The following dialogue speaks for itself:

Must he have dinner?

Too heavy for a tired man at the end of a tedious journey.

Tea, then?

Not substantial enough.

High tea, then?

Yes, high tea.

Must I pour out his tea, papa?[1]

Perhaps Hardy's greatest novel, *The Return of the Native*, boasts little, if any, humor. Only in the scenes in which Diggory Venn, the Reddleman, appears can one find traces of humor, and then, for the most part, it is only implied.

There followed a series of novels that, like Shakespeare's *Titus Andronicus*, would probably have been interred in a literary graveyard had it not been for the fame of their respective authors. These include such works of Hardy's as *The Hand of Ethelberta* (1876), *The Trumpet Major* (1880), *A Laodicean* (1881), *Two on a Tower* (1882), and *The Romantic Adventures of a Milkmaid* (1883).

There is no humor, even of the subtle variety, in *The Mayor of Casterbridge* (1886). The novel is stark and unrelenting, lacking the amiable enchantment of his lesser works. In 1887, Hardy wrote *The Woodlanders*. Perhaps he needed this novel as a counterpoint to *The Mayor*. Here, he returns to his rustic setting in a tender story of sylvan characters.

Hardy wrote several short stories, none of which would have established him as a leader in that genre. Nevertheless, they contain elements of humor, irony, and satire that justify their inclusion here. The first set of stories was assembled under the title *Wessex Tales* (1888).

A Group of Noble Dames (1891) followed, as did Life's Little Ironies (1894) and A Changed Man and Other Stories (1913). The tales for the most part are anecdotal and trivial to the extent that they never transcended the local milieu. In fact, some of them appeared to be outlines for longer works.

Though not distinguished for his short stories, Hardy wrote several tales that were notable. "The Three Strangers" contains comic episodes, particularly the scene in which the escaped convict sings a counterpart to the hangman's grisly song while waving cups with him.

One would be remiss, humor notwithstanding, if Hardy's two great novels were omitted from this study. Tess of the d'Urbervilles was published serially beginning in 1891. The serialization was bowdlerized to cater to Victorian prudery. When it appeared in book form, though, with all of the original text restored, Hardy came under tremendous criticism for its sexual theme and for its stand against social prejudice. Nevertheless, the publishing of Jude the Obscure (1895) attests to the fact that Puritan attitudes in Victorian society were declining, even though its publication created a scandal in an era that had not yet cast off all of its prudery.

It was in the realm of poetry that Hardy often vented his humor—sardonically, even gruesomely at times. He authored over 900 poems, many of which were of little consequence poetically. On other occasions, his poetry exhibited a regal style as in his sonnet "At a Lunar Eclipse." Most notable among his collections of poetry are Wessex Poems (1898),[2] Poems of the Past and the Present (1902),[3] Time's Laughing Stocks (1909),[4] Satires of Circumstance (1914),[5] Moments of Vision (1917),[6] Late Lyrics and Earlier (1922),[7] Human Shows (1925),[8] and Winter Words (posthumous, 1928).[9]

In Satires of Circumstance, Hardy demonstrates his lyric competence in a slim volume of poetry exhibiting a satiric humor sometimes gentle and often piquant. The heroic couplet in "The Sweet Hussy" contradicts, almost sonnet-like, the earlier sentiment that the woman in question was compromised and blameless. He concludes, with a touch of wry humor, that years later he understood that he was the good one and she the wicked.

Many critics have felt that the poetry of Hardy has had greater influence than that of W.B. Yeats, T.S. Eliot, D.H. Lawrence, or Ezra Pound. Donald Davie states that "Pound, to be sure, unlike the others named [Yeats, Eliot, and Lawrence], has declared himself among the beneficiaries of Hardy" (3).

In what might be considered his own epitaph, Hardy negates his poetic efforts as "Assessing minds, he does not need."[10] He concludes rather lightheartedly by saying:

Whatever his message—glad or grim—
Two bright-souled women clave to him;
Stand and say that while day decays;
It will be word enough of praise. (228)

The author's humor is most evident in "In the Room of the Bride-Elect" where a young lady who is about to be wed chides her parents for not insisting that she marry her former suitor who was the right beau whereas the current one is a "dolt" (62).

Hardy's poems after the death of his first wife, though certainly without humor, must be mentioned for their beauty and poignancy. In particular "The Walk" (1912) epitomizes this loss. He reflects, "And I went alone, and I did not mind, / Not thinking of you as left behind."

Hardy's great poetic drama of the Napoleonic conflicts, The Dynasts (1903–1908), and England's role in that drama, is monumental in scope. Conceived on a grand scale, it traverses the human condition from pathos to satiric realism. However, what it achieves in grandeur it often lacks in diction, though passages involving the mad King George III, Admiral Horatio Nelson, and Sir John Moore transcend the lesser elements. Humor is most evident in the satiric realism of the Prince Regent. Humor is evident, too, in the conversations of the servants. When Josephine falls ill, they speculate on a successor for her. She must have certain qualities, among them:

First Servant: She must be young.
Second Servant: Good. She must. The country must see to that.
First Servant: And she must be strong.
Second Servant: Good again. She must be strong. The doctors will see to that.
First Servant: And she must be fruitful as the vine.
Second Servant: Ay, by God. She must be fruitful as the vine. That, Heaven help him, he must see to himself,

like the meanest multiplying man in Paris.[11]

Summary

Thomas Hardy's fame rests with his major novels, with their rural settings and rustic characters. Hasan states that "Hardy's status as a major novelist is assured" (ix). It is in this genre with the peasants in their Wessex environment (which Hardy only occasionally left) that one finds the humor rivaled only by Shakespeare's bucolic peasants. In addition to his novels, Hardy was remarkable in his enormous poetic output and in his great literary contribution, *The Dynasts*. Though not distinguished for his poetry, his efforts in this genre apparently had great influence on other writers of his own and subsequent eras.

It was the Wessex setting that distinguished Hardy's novels. In the rustic heaths and fields of furze, humans were often at the mercy of nature or fate, surviving only by their own inner strength and indomitable spirit. The rural settings, therefore, were both the matrix of his humor and the source for his heroic characters.

Notes

1. Thomas Hardy, *A Pair of Blue Eyes* (New York: Macmillan, 1960), p. 3.
2. Hardy, *The Complete Poems of Thomas Hardy* (New York: Macmillan, 1976), pp. 6–81.
3. *Ibid.*, pp. 84–187.
4. *Ibid.*, pp. 190–299.
5. *Ibid.*, pp. 303–423.
6. *Ibid.*, pp. 427–553.
7. *Ibid.*, pp. 556–698.
8. *Ibid.*, pp. 701–831.
9. *Ibid.*, pp. 834–930.
10. Hardy, "A Poet," *Satires of Circumstance* (London: Macmillan, 1925), p. 228.
11. Hardy, *The Dynasts* (London: Macmillan, 1915), pp. 263–64.

Selected Bibliography

Primary Sources

Desperate Remedies: A Novel. London: Tinsley, 1871; New York: Macmillan, 1960.

Under the Greenwood Tree: A Rural Painting of the Dutch School. London: Tinsley, 1872; London: William Collins Sons, 1958.

A Pair of Blue Eyes: A Novel. London: Tinsley, 1873; New York: Macmillan, 1960.

Far from the Madding Crowd. London: Smith, Elder, 1874.

The Hand of Ethelberta: A Comedy in Chapters. London: Smith, Elder, 1876; London: Macmillan, 1960.

The Return of the Native. London: Smith, Elder, 1878; New York: W.W. Norton, 1969.

The Trumpet-Major: A Tale. London: Smith, Elder, 1880; New York: Macmillan, 1962.

A Laodicean: A Novel. New York: Harper, 1881; New York: Macmillan, 1962.

Two on a Tower: A Romance. London: Low, Marston, Searle, & Livington, 1882; London: Macmillan, 1960.

The Mayor of Casterbridge: The Life and Death of a Man of Character. London: Smith, Elder, 1886; New York: Harper and Brothers, 1922.

The Woodlanders. London and New York: Macmillan, 1887; New York: Macmillan, 1963.

Wessex Tales: Strange, Lively, and Commonplace. London and New York: Macmillan, 1888; London: Macmillan, 1960.

Tess of the d'Ubervilles: A Pure Woman Faithfully Presented. London: Osgood, McIlvaine, 1891; New York: W.W. Norton, 1976.

A Few Crusted Characters. London: Osgood, McIlvaine, 1894.

Jude the Obscure. London: Osgood, McIlvaine, 1895; New York: Knopf, 1985.

The Dynasts, Part First. London and New York: Macmillan, 1904.

The Dynasts, Part Second. London and New York: Macmillan, 1906.

The Dynasts, Part Third. London and New York: Macmillan, 1908.

Satires of Circumstance: Lyrics and Reveries with Miscellaneous Pieces. London: Macmillan, 1914.

The Complete Poems of Thomas Hardy. Ed. James Gibson. New York: Macmillan, 1976.

Secondary Sources

Brown, Douglas. *Thomas Hardy*. London: Longmans, Green, 1961.

Davie, Donald. *Thomas Hardy and British Poetry*. New York: Oxford University

Press, 1972.

Hasan, Noorul. *Thomas Hardy, The Socio-logical Imagination*. London: Macmillan, 1982.

Macdonell, Annie. *Thomas Hardy*. New York: Dodd, Mead & Co., 1895.

Millgate, Michael. *Thomas Hardy A Biography*. New York: Random House, 1982.

Ross Brummer

Herbert, A[lan] P[atrick]

Born: London, September 24, 1890
Education: Winchester College; New College, Oxford University, 1910–1914
Marriage: Gwendolen Harriet Quilter, January 1915; four children
Died: London, November 11, 1971

Biography

The eldest of three sons of Patrick Herbert, a clerk of Irish extraction in the India Office, and Beatrice Eugenie Selwyn, granddaughter of the founder of Selwyn College, Cambridge (a fact never emphasized by Herbert, who was a devoted Oxonian), A.P. Herbert spent his early years in Kensington, not far downstream from Hammersmith on the north bank of the River Thames, where he was to live all his adult life. Herbert's two brothers, Owen and Sidney, were both killed in action, Owen in 1914 and Sidney in 1941. His mother died when he was eight, an occurrence which might be "the source of the peculiar private reticence that baffled those who most closely shared his life and affections, and was liable to disconcert those who did not" (Pound, 21).

Following an educational pattern typical of the upper middle classes, he attended Winchester College until 1909, and then went up to New College, Oxford, from 1910 to 1914, where he gained "a not very good Second" in Honours Moderations (i.e., Classics), followed by "a very good First" in Jurisprudence. He had shown a facility in writing light verse even in his schooldays, and his first contribution to the humorous weekly, *Punch* (a connection that was to continue for sixty years), appeared on August 24, 1910, when he was not yet twenty. In the summer of 1914, he met and fell in love with Gwendolen Quilter; they married in January 1915, and in February 1916 they leased the house at 12 Hammersmith Terrace, overlooking the Thames, where they were to live for the next fifty years.

But, these events took place in the intervals of his active service in the First World War. In September 1914, Herbert enlisted as an Ordinary Seaman in the Royal Naval Volunteer Reserve and after being commissioned sub-lieutenant early in 1915 was sent out to Gallipoli, to take part in the disastrous attempt, masterminded by First Lord of the Admiralty Winston Churchill, to establish a bridgehead against the Turks. In July 1915, he was invalided home with virulent enteritis but returned to active service in France in the summer of 1916. In April 1917, he was once again invalided home, and during his convalescence he wrote a novel, *The Secret Battle*, based on a court-martial and execution that had occurred in the Division.

The Secret Battle was published in 1919 and admired by Lloyd George, who commended it to Churchill and Bernard (later Field-Marshal) Montgomery, both of whom remained lifelong friends of Herbert's. However, the public wanted amusement, as perhaps he did also: "The dark side of life had been too much with him in recent times, instilling in him a mistrust of the imagination, with a consequent loss of creative force. Laughter was a solvent of fear, humorous journalism an antidote to the terrors of the night"; as literature, however, *The Secret Battle* "was and remains APH's best book" (Pound, 65).

Following the War, though he was called to the Bar, he abandoned the idea of a legal career after a few months, devoting himself to writing a crime novel, *The House by the River* (1920), which was heavily dependent on the setting of his own house and the adjacent Thames. Above all, though, when this novel attracted little critical attention, he worked at building up his links with *Punch*, still under the editorship of Owen Seaman, who had encouraged his first efforts. Both his light verse and the quizzical sidelights on legal peculiarities in the form of mock court-reports under the general heading of *Misleading Cases* continued to appear until the 1960s and were regularly collected and published in book form. He turned his hand to writing plays and musical-comedy libretti too.

Still, Herbert was not content with merely providing amusement. The *Misleading Cases*, mostly civil lawsuits instigated by his fictional *alter ego*, Albert Haddock, had the serious purpose of highlighting legal abuses and absurdities, as had also, in a broader political and social context, his lifelong habit of writing letters to the London *Times*—by the end of his life about 1,000 had been published.

He thus had the means of promoting his favorite causes. The Entertainment Duty, which was imposed on all theaters and similar places of entertainment in 1916 as a temporary wartime measure and then remained in force for forty years, infuriated him as an example of ministerial mendacity. In 1934—becoming Albert Haddock in reality—he took the House of Commons to the High Court on the grounds that it was flouting the Licensing Laws by allowing alcoholic liquor to be on sale in its bars outside licensing hours. Though he lost the case, the Lord Chief Justice was sufficiently amused not to require him to pay his opponents' costs. It is typical of his ambivalence toward power that what may have begun in resentment at watching the members enjoy their out-of-hours drinks on the terrace as he sailed by in his boat, the *Water Gipsy*, ended in a claim that "through my rash act the liberties of the faithful Commons were proclaimed and freed from doubt by the High Court of Justice, and established for ever" (*Independent Member*, 21).

The following year, he was able to drink on the terrace in his own right. At that time, the British universities returned twelve members to the House of Commons, of which Oxford University returned two, elected by its 22,000 M.A.'s. A chance word dropped to him on a railway journey put the idea of standing into his head. At least this is what he claimed, though in the 1920s he had written a series for *Punch* (collected under the title of *Topsy MP* [1929]) where the flapper, Topsy, the improbable wife of Albert Haddock, becomes even more improbably an MP when Haddock is unseated "owing to some weasel of a man who gave beer to the populace" (*Topsy MP*, 5), which may imply that Herbert had already dreamed of that role. At all events, with a very small band of helpers he put together and mailed out an election address as an Independent, and, to general astonishment, beat the Labour candidate into third place.

Though he was to be an MP for fifteen years, his most remarkable achievement occurred in the year following his entry. In his maiden speech, which by convention should be uncontroversial, he had announced to derisive laughter that he intended to bring in a bill to reform the divorce laws. The following year he did so and, against all the odds, steered it through to the Statute Book by July 1937, a process that he described in detail in *The Ayes Have It* (1937). The new act allowed divorce on grounds other than adultery and thus eliminated, among other things, the elaborate charade of the wronged husband chivalrously providing incriminating evidence against himself. Evelyn Waugh's *A Handful of Dust* (1934) includes a graphic example of this practice. Herbert continued to show wit in his speeches, on one occasion addressing the House in verse (on the subject of population statistics), and on another provoking the prime minister, Neville Chamberlain, to growl: "Say it in *Punch*!"

When the Second World War broke out, Herbert's boat was commandeered for service in the Royal Naval Auxiliary Patrol, with himself as Master of what had now become HMS *Water Gipsy*. During the war years, he patrolled the River Thames on a full-time basis, from which vantage-point he watched the Battle of Britain. He also went ashore at Westminster to attend debates in the Commons, though, since Private Members' Time had been suspended for the duration of hostilities, backbenchers no longer had the opportunity to take initiatives. At the end of the war he received a knighthood, on Churchill's recommendation.

In the 1945 election, however, though Herbert himself was once more returned by the Oxford University electors, Churchill was voted out of office in favor of a Labour government under Clement Attlee. Herbert was profoundly out of sympathy with this government—and hardly less so with the Conservative governments of the 1950s which sought to consolidate rather than dismantle the Welfare State that Attlee had brought into being. Moreover, he had the very specific grievance that Attlee effectively abolished the University seats from the 1950 election (though he still came to watch the Oxford and Cambridge Boat Race from the windows of Herbert's house), and Churchill was never able to fulfill his promise to restore them. Since Herbert could never have operated within the confines of even the Conservative Party, and since the idiosyncrasies so appealing to Oxford graduates could never have induced a majority of electors of an ordinary constituency to vote for him, his parliamentary career came to an end.

In the 1950s and 1960s, he fought many battles for middle-class individualism. As a self-

H

employed writer with a vacillating income, he was in permanent conflict with the Internal Revenue and bitterly attacked the high taxation (especially the surtax imposed on above-average incomes) required by the Welfare State. One of his judges in *Misleading Cases* remarks: "We love and honour Her Majesty, we love and serve our country: but we find it difficult to conceal our loathing for the State" (*Punch*, Vol. 229, p. 494). He attacked British Summer Time on the grounds that, since the British had given the world the Greenwich Meridian, they were honor bound to observe Greenwich Mean Time, the universal measure for mariners and astronomers. He attacked metrication and the replacement of Fahrenheit by Celsius. He wrote pamphlets defending the use of public libraries without fee, and advocating the Public Lending Right—his phrase for the right of authors to receive royalties on their books borrowed from such libraries.

The English have always loved an eccentric, and though he was by now going against the main current of the time, he received many honors. In 1958, he was awarded an honorary degree by Oxford University, in the inappropriate company of Lord Beveridge, the architect of the Welfare State, of whom he declared, in his speech of thanks in verse:

> Boy Beveridge you duly decorate,
> The Archimedes of the Farewell State,
> Who did so well distributing the gravy
> That poor Britannia can't afford a Navy.
> (quoted in Pound, 254)

In 1966, he was elected chairman of the British Copyright Council. In 1967, he was elected president of the Society of Authors. In 1970, the year of his eightieth birthday, the Borough of Hammersmith made him a freeman, and the queen made him a Companion of Honour. In August of the same year *Punch* marked his sixtieth year as a contributor with a special issue and enacted a joke from *Misleading Cases* by writing out a check payable to him on a cow, which was led into the bank and duly honored. (Herbert himself had written checks on champagne-bottles and restaurant napkins.) His hastily written autobiography was published in time for his birthday. Following a seizure at the end of 1970, he never recovered his health: his very last letter to the *Times* was published in August, and he died in London on November 11, 1971.

Literary Analysis

Herbert's output—especially his contributions to *Punch*—was prolific, and he boasted, with reason, that no living Briton had written so much verse as he. But, when his *alter ego* in *Misleading Cases*, Albert Haddock, sued the newspapers for libel on the basis of obituaries published while he was missing and believed dead off the coast of Labrador (Herbert had been active in supporting Newfoundland's unsuccessful attempt to remain independent of Canada), "he objected to the suggestion that, though a careful observer and recorder, he was lacking in imagination" (*Codd's Last Case*, 59).

The implied self-criticism is just, and the lack is particularly noticeable in his novels. What is most vivid in *The House by the River* and *The Water Gipsies* is neither the characterization nor the plotting but the very recognizable surroundings: his own house with its garden running down to the Thames at Hammersmith; the river explored upstream towards Richmond and Teddington and downstream as far as the Pool of London; and, in the latter novel, the Grand Union Canal (the "Cut"), as well as the skittle-alley at the local pub ("Under his patronage, skittles at the Black Lion developed into a Hammersmith cult" [Pound, 120]). Also characteristic were his *romans à these* that function similarly to the letters to the *Times* and *Misleading Cases*, as in *Holy Deadlock* (1934), in which he demonstrates the absurdities of the existing divorce laws ("Nowhere did it show penetrating insight into the realities of the married state" [Pound, 116]), and *Made for Man* (1958), in which Herbert himself appears, under the thinnest of disguises, as Sir Ewan Harker, to argue against the refusal by the Church of England to remarry divorcees in church.

The long series of *Misleading Cases*, which is Herbert's most original form of humorous writing and almost certainly his most lasting claim to fame, appeared in *Punch* between 1924 and 1970 and was collected under the titles *Misleading Cases in the Common Law* (1927), *More Misleading Cases* (1930), *Still More Misleading Cases* (1933), all of which were gathered into the omnibus volume, *Uncommon Law* (1935), *Codd's Last Case* (1952), and *Bardot MP?* (1964). For Herbert, the law was a touchstone for the absurdities of life, both those that it exposed and those that it embodied. In his volumes the underlying principle, as stated by one of his fictitious judges, is that "the way to remove a fantastic measure from the Statute Book is not to evade or ignore but to enforce it" (*Uncommon Law*, 313). What occasions this comment is a Victorian statute of 1869 levying an annual tax of fifteen shillings on all male servants, which the judge now requires to be paid on a male civil servant who is constantly in attendance upon his minister and carries out various personal and domestic duties.

Herbert turned his logic onto other governmental and parliamentary practices: he charged the Chancellor of the Exchequer and the Postmaster-General with living off immoral earnings, because the government levied income tax on the earnings of prostitutes and provided them with the telephones through which they contacted their clients (*Punch*, Vol. 229, pp. 493–94); he put all the members of Parliament in the dock, on the grounds that they were guilty of bribery because they had induced electors to vote for them by promising to reduce unemployment and find them jobs—which also laid them open to further charges of using deceit and false pretenses (*Uncommon Law*, 275–78). He ridiculed the application of the law to marriage. Answering the question: "Is Marriage Lawful?," the president of the divorce court feels obliged to pronounce that "in all matrimonial transactions . . . the element of skill is negligible and the element of chance predominates. This brings all marriages into the category of gaming . . . and therefore I hold that the Court cannot according to law assist or relieve the victims of these arrangements, whether by way of restitution, separation, or divorce. Therefore it will be idle for married parties to bring their grievances before us, and, in short, this Court will never sit again" (*Uncommon Law*, 99).

As a trained barrister but one who had never practiced, Herbert was well equipped to mimic the polished lucidity of legal language while pursuing its logical outcomes into absurdities, remarking at the end of his life that, though he was never "one of the brotherhood that serve the laws of England . . . at least for fifty years I have saluted them as a loyal guerrilla, prancing in the woods, salutes the regular troops" (*APH: His Life and Times*, 145).

This curious image (what function does a guerrilla have, if he is on the same side as the regular forces?) is unwittingly revealing: Herbert was simultaneously the boatrocking outsider and a part of the establishment. At first glance, the series was an intellectual game, but underlying it was Herbert's sense of outrage at the power held by the government and the state over the individual. The device enabled him to apply his knowledge of the law in a fictional context and to amuse the public without running the risk of causing irritation through litigiousness. The collections thus accumulated as dedicatees and writers of introductions a glittering group of high-ranking legal luminaries, such as past and present lord chief justices and lord chancellors. Herbert was immensely proud that "the Cases have been quoted on the Bench of the Supreme Court of the United States, in our own High Court, and in the House of Lords" (*APH: His Life and Times*, 138).

His light verse, however, has been less kindly affected by the passing of time. From the age of sixteen, he discovered a natural aptitude for writing humorous poetry, and his talents were encouraged by Seaman, the editor of *Punch*, with the result that his second contribution was a celebration of his imminent twentieth birthday. The verses that he produced in large quantities during the 1920s—he had the privilege of sending his copy directly to the printer, so the editor saw it for the first time in proof—reflect the outlook and preoccupations of English middle-class society of the inter-war years: light flirtations; a stylization of pretty young women that would now be considered offensively patronizing; housemaids with their simple pleasures of half-days off spent with boyfriends at the cinema; comic charladies with hearts of gold; a distaste for socialism, claimed by the working classes to be felt with no less force; a slightly sardonic appreciation of Britain as being stodgy but dependable, and a corresponding mild xenophobia toward America and Continental Europe; and a mild philistinism toward arty Bohemians and even toward the national bard, William Shakespeare. The same political attitudes emerge as in all of his writings: an underlying belief in the rightness and stability of British middle-class life and a consequent hostility toward any outside force, whether the Labor Party or the League of Nations, that tries to change it.

The verse-forms are extremely varied, even within single poems: "He was always trying new forms and he mastered nearly every one he tried, with a mastery unspoiled by ostentatious effort" (Price, 240). A stanza from "The White Wine Election," on the predominance of the Prohibition issue in the 1928 United States presidential election, will serve to illustrate both his verbal skills and his perceptual limitations:

> Abraham Lincoln sits in the sky
> With good George Washington and one
>   or two mates,
> And "Abe," says Washington, "I can't
>   think why
> There's all this noise in the United
>   States."
> And Abraham says
> "When I was Pres.,
> Nobody could say we'd no ideels,
> But we didn't much mind
> How Americans dined,
> And we never had elections all about
>   meals."
> And George said, "Father told me it was
>   rude,
> To talk in company about one's food,
> And I never knew it mattered such a lot
> If Americans drank white wine or not."
>   (*A Book of Ballads*, 452)

The frequent appearance of choruses is a reminder that he was also producing libretti for a dozen musical comedies in the 1920s, though the climax of his career as a librettist came after the Second World War when he collaborated with composer Vivien Ellis in a series of musicals produced by impresario Charles Cochrane: *Big Ben* (1946), *Bless the Bride* (1947), which was the most commercially successful, and *Tough at the Top* (1949)—sugary confections that suited his own, and popular, taste in this second post-war period of his life.

Summary

A.P. Herbert's novels have probably had their day. His verse will always be admirable in its sheer linguistic facility, though the attitudes it expresses are colored by his class and time. The *Misleading Cases*, despite expressing the same attitudes, are sufficiently original in concept to possess enduring appeal, based as they are upon a genuinely humorous insight into the disparity between the manic unruliness of life and the desperate attempts to master it through the lucidity of legal language, a disparity which reflects Herbert's own position as the licensed jester of the English middle classes.

Selected Bibliography

Primary Sources
The Secret Battle. London: Methuen, 1919.

The House by the River. London: Methuen, 1920.
Misleading Cases in the Common Law. London: Methuen, 1927.
Topsy MP.* London: Ernest Benn, 1929.
More Misleading Cases. London: Methuen, 1930.
The Water Gipsies. London: Methuen, 1930.
A Book of Ballads, being the Collected Light Verse.* London: Ernest Benn, 1931. (Contains *Laughing Ann* [1925], *She-Shanties* [1926], *Plain Jane* [1927], and *Ballads for Broadbrows* [1930].)
Still More Misleading Cases. London: Methuen, 1933.
Holy Deadlock. London: Methuen, 1934.
Uncommon Law.* London: Methuen, 1935.
The Ayes Have It. London: Methuen, 1937.
Bless the Bride. London: Samuel French, 1948.
Independent Member. London: Methuen, 1950.
Codd's Last Case, and other Misleading Cases.* London: Methuen, 1952.
Made for Man. London: Methuen, 1958.
Bardot MP?, and other Modern Misleading Cases.* London: Methuen, 1964.
APH: His Life and Times. London: Heinemann, 1970.
*Collections of pieces that first appeared in *Punch*.

Secondary Sources
Pound, Reginald. *A.P. Herbert: A Biography*. London: Michael Joseph, 1976. A sympathetic and judicious account by a fellow journalist.
Price, R.G.G. *A History of "Punch."* London: Collins, 1957.
Thomas, W.K. "Satire for Those over Thirty: 'A Herbert Come to Judgement.'" *Dalhousie Review*, 55 (1975): 405–18. An analysis of the satirical strategies employed in *Uncommon Law*.

David M. Jago

Herbert, George

Born: Montgomery Castle, Wales, April 3, 1593
Education: Westminster School; Trinity College, Cambridge University, B.A., 1613; minor fellow, October 1614; major fellow, March 1616; M.A., 1617

Marriage: Jane Danvers, March 5, 1629; two adopted children
Died: Bemerton, Wiltshire, March 1, 1633

Biography

George Herbert was born at Montgomery Castle, Wales on April 3, 1593, the fifth son of Richard Herbert, who died when George was four, and Magdalen, a woman reportedly of great beauty, care, refinement, and virtue, and a patron of the poet John Donne, with whom Herbert also developed a friendship. After Richard's death, Magdalen married Sir John Danvers, who was twenty years her junior. Her influence on George appears to have been great and lasting. Privately tutored for several years, George entered Westminster School at age twelve and matriculated as King's Scholar at Trinity College, Cambridge, on December 18, 1609. He became a Bachelor of Arts in 1613, a minor fellow in October of 1614, a major fellow in March of 1616, and a Master in 1617. While at Cambridge, Herbert wrote Latin satiric verses in defense of the English Church and the universities in reply to the satirical *Anti-Tami-Cami-Categoria* of Andrew Melville, a reforming Presbyterian minister much in conflict with James I.

From 1620 to 1628, Herbert held the post of Public Orator to the University. Partially through this position and his familial connection, he became closely associated with the court from this time and until the death of James I. According to Izaak Walton in his *Life of George Herbert* (1670), Herbert enjoyed "court-conversation," a taste for fine clothes, and pleasure. From this chrysalis of "wit" would emerge the great religious beauties of his later poetry.

Herbert led an active public life from 1620 through 1628. With the favor of James, he received the living at Whitford, with a yearly income of £120. He was returned to Parliament from Montgomery in 1624 and 1625. He became canon of Lincoln Cathedral in 1626 and in July of that year, prebendary at Leighton Bromswold, where he rebuilt the church and moved the landowners to lend money through what Walton described as "witty and persuasive letters."

In 1627, Herbert's mother, who had been a constant advisor, died, and he published *Memoriae matris sacrum*, which also contains Donne's sermon on her death. His health, always fragile, now failed, and he resigned his posts at the university, something which he had long wished to do. On March 5, 1629, Herbert married Jane Danvers, his stepfather's cousin, the eldest daughter of Charles Danvers of Bainton, Wiltshire. They adopted two nieces of Herbert's who had been orphaned. Within a year Herbert took deacon's orders and installed himself at Bemerton, from whence comes the verse for which he is best known. Three years later, on March 1, 1633, the poet died of consumption in Bemerton. He had often referred to his fragile health, saying, according to Walton, that he had "a wit like a penknife in too narrow a sheath, too sharp for his body."

Literary Analysis

From the beginning, Herbert's writing dealt almost exclusively with religion. Yet, Herbert's early Greek and Latin poetic exercises, as well as his epistles, testify to his acquaintance with classical forms of humor. One of his first important collections, Latin verses in response to Andrew Melville's *Anti-Tami-Cami-Categoria*, contain many satirical pieces, including one mocking Melville's vocabulary. Herbert was, in fact, known by contemporaries for his wittiness and humor.

Because of the supposed smoothness of his verse (compared with Donne's rough style), his religious themes, and his saintly last years, Herbert is thought of as saint-like. But, like his younger contemporary, John Milton, Herbert enjoyed mirth, and contemporaries found in his style a mixture of quaint quirks and pranks, of twisted, extended metaphors known as "conceits," as well as of gentle, elevated, and virtuous thought. Later critics, from T.S. Eliot and Sir Herbert Grierson, have characterized Herbert's writing as displaying "metaphysical" wit which is noted for its odd distortions of language such as its reliance on surprise or paradox, its novel and far-fetched images, and its blend of a simple and direct speaking voice with compelling emotions and mind-stretching ideas.

Most of Herbert's poetry appeared in the posthumous *The Temple* (1633). Although a religious work, *The Temple*, like other "metaphysical" poetry, shows a stylistic capriciousness in harmonic tension with its serious message. This tension produces a sense of what may be called "surprising fitness." The volume's plan itself shows ingenious design, for the individual poems elaborate the architecture of a church; moreover, based on the symbol of the body as a building, the poems simultaneously elaborate on the idea that the Christian life that leads to salvation. The playful ambiguity of the title suggests the sources of humor in Herbert's project: first, Herbert considers "mirth" and play central to making meaning; second, from the standpoint of salvation, he considers life a comedy.

The first poem of the volume makes the central role of mirth clear. In "The Church Porch," he writes that his verses will be "a bait of pleasure" that may "turn delight into a sacrifice." That first poem characterizes the worldly as witty and mirthful, and it recounts the purification required of those who enter the temple. Still, reaching salvation is a process full of humor. And, in this introductory poem, Herbert advises the worldly not to give up their humor, but to purify it: "when thou dost tell another's jest, therin / Omit the oaths, which true wit cannot need" (11); "Laugh not too much; the witty man laughs least" (39):

> Pick out of mirth, like stones out of thy
>   ground,
> Profaneness, filthiness, abusiveness;
> These are the scum, with which coarse
>   wits abound;
> The fine may spare these well, yet not go
>   less.
> All things are big with jest; nothing that's
>   plain
> But may be witty, if thou has the vein.
>   (40)

This cleansed wit, the property of "plain" things, becomes the characteristic humor of Herbert. "The Church Porch" has such wit. In that poem seventy-seven interlocking but independent verses, like the one above, show the impact of epigrammatic forms of humor. Each verse comprises three sections, roughly marked by two lines each: a general proposition, a witty comparison, and a pointed aphorism. At the very entrance to the temple, the writer illustrates in his own verse how elements of humor may be yoked to a spiritual design.

Various types of mirth play conspicuous roles throughout *The Temple*. The titles of numerous poems suggest this—"Parodie," "Paradox," "Quidditie," "Quip," "Charms and Knots"—although the point may be, as in "Parody," that certain types of humor are not mirthful—as, for instance, sin's parody of virtue. Certainly the novel "metaphysical" com-

parisons often show a good deal of humor: "Look on meat, think it dirt, then take a bite" ("Church Porch" XXII); or when he speaks of the "natural delights" as God's "glorious household-stuff" ("Affliction"). In both cases the comparison surprises. Yet each displays a different humor. The former instances a sharpness of satire that Herbert could have found in Juvenal, while the latter employs a Horatian tone to mock Herbert's own previous view.

In particular, Herbert makes contributions to the history of "whimsy" through his experimentations with form. There are obvious examples such as "Easter Wings," a precursor of Lewis Carroll's "Mouse's Tale," an emblematic or pattern poem shaped like wings, its lines and ideas expanding and contracting accordingly. His "Ana[mary / army]gram" or his "JESU," which takes apart J-ES-U to form I Ease You, rely on a play with letters. So too in "Paradise" he dices up the endings in each stanza, taking off the first letter of the previous rhyme to create the next—"start," "tart," "art." Playfulness becomes a mark of many poems, from "Prayer [I]," with its plethora of metaphors, to the more serious "Church Monuments."

In the middle poems of *The Temple*, Herbert exploits the various devices of humor most. "Avarice," for instance, ends with an epigrammatic couplet: "Man calleth thee his wealth, who made the rich; / And while he digs out thee, falls in the ditch." In "Conscience" Herbert lampoons conscience as a boor: "Peace, pratler, do not lour; / Not a fair look but thou dost call it foul, / Not a sweet dish but thou dost call it sour; / Music to thee doth howl." "The quip" burlesques the world as a pack of gallants who tweak the poet for his lack of fashion until God has the last laugh. Nor are "jests" missing. In "Time" he complains that Time allows people to live too long and that a good Christian seeks early death in order to have a speedier resurrection: "Thus far Time heard me Patiently; / Then chafing said: 'This man deludes; / What do I here before his door? / He doth not crave less time, but more.'"

Like the volume's introductory poem, the volume itself moves from mirth to deep and nearly mirthless seriousness at the end and back to mirth for the finale. Of the last poems, "Heaven" contains the whimsical echo form for its rhymes and the tone of "Love" is light, funny, and idiomatic. After all, as Herbert writes, God is "mirth" that purges all earthly sorrow ("The Glance").

Summary

Humor and wit are at the heart of the works of many of those known as "metaphysical" poets. Herbert not only exemplifies this, but in *The Temple* self-consciously demonstrates the possibility of yoking a "purified" mirth to a spiritual purpose, as he had done in his Latin satires and his witty requests for church monies. Although one rarely connects Herbert with humor, his twelve years at university and court in a brilliant circle of acquaintances added their witty leavening to the quirky, calm, brilliant, intensely personal poetry of his last three years. Herbert, an important "metaphysical humorist," helped develop and disseminate a wide variety of whimsical poetic structures and spiritual forms of humor.

Selected Bibliography

Primary Sources

The Poems of George Herbert. Ed. Arthur Waugh. London: Oxford University Press, 1913.

The Works of George Herbert. Ed. Francis Ernest Hutchinson. Oxford: Clarendon, 1964.

Secondary Sources

Books

Summers, Joseph. *George Herbert, His Religion and Art*. Cambridge: Harvard University Press, 1954. A general overview of Herbert's craft and ideas.

Tuve, Rosemond. *A Reading of George Herbert*. Chicago: University of Chicago Press, 1952. In "Wit" (pp. 137–58). Tuve discusses the way that the subtleties of Herbert's wit rest on an understanding of the tradition behind his simple images.

Walton, Izaak. *Lives of Donne & Herbert*. Ed. S.C. Roberts. Cambridge: Cambridge University Press, 1957. An intimate glimpse of the lives and temperaments of Walton's great contemporaries.

Articles

Merrill, Thomas F. "Sacred Parody and the Grammar of Devotion." *Criticism*, 23, 3 (Summer 1981): 195–210. Merrill uses the poem "A Parodie" to show the relationship between parody and Herbert's utilization of the languages of love and religion.

Nardo, Anna K. "George Herbert Pulling for Prime." *South Central Review*, 3, 4 (Winter 1986): 28–42. On the relationship of the treatment of God to game and play.

Randall, Dale B.J. "The Ironing of George Herbert's 'Collar.'" *Studies in Philology*, 81, 4 (Fall 1984): 473–95. Randall discusses the connection between figurative language and punning in Herbert.

Ray, Joan Klingel. "Herbert's 'Easter Wings.'" *Explicator*, 49, 3 (1991 Spring): 140–42. A discussion of Herbert's use of puns.

David Rosen

H

Hoffnung, Gerard

Born: Berlin, March 22, 1925
Education: Highgate School; Hornsey College of Art (expelled)
Marriage: Annetta Bennett, November 1, 1952; two children
Died: London, September 28, 1959

Biography

Gerard Hoffnung was born at a very early age (as he was wont to say). Unfortunately, he also died at one, of a brain hemorrhage at age thirty-four. In that short span he was able to cultivate an extraordinary range of comedic talents—as a cartoonist, raconteur, and impresario. Above all he was a personality, an amazing blend of sophistication and innocence, a fount of gentle but exquisite humor, a man of boundless good cheer, a Santa Claus, a rather large pixie, a creation virtually indistinguishable from his caricatures of himself.

The only child of Ludwig Hoffnung, a well-to-do grain merchant, and Hilde Hoffnung, Gerard, a quintessentially British humorist, was born in Berlin, Germany on March 22, 1925, a twentieth-century German Jew. Consequently, his early upbringing occurred under some of the least humorous circumstances the world has known. He was enrolled at a little day school for "undesirable" (i.e., "non-Aryan") children—located next to Heinrich Himmler's residence! But, even at this time Hoffnung was Hoffnung (and how better to underscore the title of one of his records: "The Importance of Being Hoffnung"?): "his face like a firm apple, rich blond hair, blue eyes: a little angel—from a distance! If one looked closer, a most un-angelic bonfire of mischief sparkled in those eyes."[1] At an early age he was drawing caricatures,[2] playing every musical instrument he could get his hands on (especially percussion), and in general making himself the antic center of attention.

As a child with a loving mother in a well-to-do family, the young Hoffnung was certainly to some degree insulated from the horrors going on around him. He was exposed to high culture as a youth, and he was already a fan of opera and Igor Stravinsky before his teens. He lived in his own world, a world that contained elements of the macabre (as evidenced by some of his earliest childhood drawings). It is likely, though, that this interest had more to do with the films that he loved and his natural attraction to the hyperbolic, the outlandish, and the grotesque than anything in the world of politics.[3] It is important to note, however, that the mature Hoffnung was far from indifferent to social issues. His outlook on race relations, homosexuality, nuclear disarmament, the treatment of animals (especially hunting), and, for that matter, the music of Béla Bartók and Arnold Schönberg, is liberal and impassioned. He joined the Society of Friends in 1955, and he became active in a prison visitation program.

Hoffnung's family left Germany in 1938, when Gerard was thirteen, and he was enrolled at Highgate School in London the following year.[4] As might be expected, Gerard was a cutup, chafing at the rules. Three years later he finally persuaded his mother to let him go to art school, but even here he wanted his own way too much for the comfort of school authorities: he was expelled from Hornsey College of Art. Ineligible for military service because of his German birth, he found work cleaning milk bottles at a dairy until being hired to teach art at Stamford School in 1945 at the age of twenty.

Hoffnung's accelerated life did not leave him teaching for long. His first published drawing appeared in *Lilliput* when he was only fifteen. By the age of twenty-two he was a regular in many periodicals and could at last devote himself fully to cartooning . . . and just being Hoffnung, with the Hoffnung persona soon coming to the fore. A talk entitled "Fungi on Toast" was accepted by the BBC in 1950. Soon Hoffnung was appearing on the Sunday afternoon radio show "One Minute Please" and he became a national personality.

During the decade of the 1950s, Hoffnung made his mark. He was a frequent guest on radio and the new television and continued to be published widely, including in *Punch*, the *Daily Express*, and the London *Evening News*. The year 1952 saw the first of several "comic oratory performances" at the Cambridge Union and Oxford Union and also his first book of cartoons (*The Right Playmate*). In 1953 came *The Maestro*, the first of six cartoon books on musical subjects. And in 1956 and 1958, Hoffnung achieved his *clowning* glory: two comedy musical festivals at the Royal Festival Hall in London, featuring such works as "Concerto for Hosepipe and Strings" and "Let's Fake an Opera" and involving such legitimate musical luminaries as Malcolm Arnold, Dennis Braine, and Aaron Copland.

Perhaps not coincidentally, the decade of the 1950s was also the period of Hoffnung's courting and marrying Annetta Bennett (November 1, 1952) with whom he had two children. The couple appears to have enjoyed a close and productive relationship. In fact, fully half of the Hoffnung bibliography is posthumous, having been brought to fruition by his widow after his death in London on September 28, 1959. She has exerted the same meticulous care on these projects that one would expect of Hoffnung himself. Mrs. Hoffnung has also overseen the production of over one hundred Hoffnung Music Festivals worldwide, in which both she and their children sometimes participate.

Literary Analysis

Hoffnung was his own grandest creation. The preceding biography gives evidence of his being a definite *character*. To what degree was it a put-on? The available literature suggests that the public Hoffnung known and loved by millions was no mere *role*; by all accounts this is the way he really was: jolly, concerned, highly observant, fastidious, whimsical, cherubic, arch, a superb mimic, a whirlwind. All in all, he was a precocious child in not only an adult's body but, curiously, an old man's.[5] Nonetheless, he did create as well a truly artistic comedic product in two genres: especially cartooning and oratory.

Hoffnung once remarked that his musical friends thought that he was a very good artist, and his painter friends thought him a very good musician. Despite his own expansive view of himself, Hoffnung was here for once being rather modest. While perhaps best described as an amateur in the world of music (although one skilled enough to be the soloist for Vaughan Williams's *Tuba Concerto*), Hoffnung was surely an outstanding practitioner of the art of drawing, especially cartooning.

His talent arrives full-blown on the book scene; there is no more sophisticated work in the Hoffnung corpus than his first book, *The Right Playmate* (1952). Words by the American James Broughton relate the story of a lonely boy whose growing up is both typical and exceedingly odd. The opening frame, captioned "To begin with, I was a perfectly normal boy," shows a forlorn-looking chap skipping rope, except that instead of a rope he appears to be holding barbed wire. The book is worldly wise, utterly bizarre, and hilarious.

The remaining cartoon books brought out during his lifetime are on musical subjects.[6] They begin with *The Maestro*, whose humor, unlike *The Right Playmate*, is straightforward, though certainly farcical and witty. The definitive caricature of the orchestral conductor is seen in all of his emotings and contortions. While no doubt owing some of its inspiration to the German cartoonist Wilhelm Busch's vignette, "The Virtuoso" (1865), the style has a lightness, both graphic and in spirit, that is unmistakably Hoffnung.

In rapid succession there appeared *The Hoffnung Symphony Orchestra* (1955), *The Hoffnung Music Festival* (1956), *The Hoffnung Companion to Music* (1957), *Hoffnung's Musical Chairs* (1958), and finally, in the year of his death, *Hoffnung's Acoustics* (1959). In all of these books we are introduced to the truly extraordinary instrumentation of Hoffnung's musical world: from the saxophone stuffed with tobacco whose player is lighting up for a puff, to the cor anglais that lays an egg; from the Vacuum Quartet in A Flat ("the Hoover"), to the jazz drummer sweeping dust into a dustpan; from accordion caterpillars to bagpipe octopi and elephantine alphorns; from the electric guitar cum pop-up toaster to the kettledrum filled with boiling oil (reserved for the conductor, of course). Both the graphic art and the musical ideas increase somewhat in inventiveness, culminating in *Acoustics*, where sheer sound becomes the subject of imaginative sketches. And, again, one can trace influences. Surely, for example, there is a relationship with some of the work of *New Yorker* cartoonist Saul Steinberg, but to the visual wit of the latter, Hoffnung brings a measure of sheer charm.

The rest of the Hoffnung cartoon books are posthumous, consisting of various collections compiled by Mrs. Hoffnung. While little

new ground is broken, there is a great deal to be found among them, on both musical and nonmusical subjects, that the Hoffnung aficionado will treasure. Of particular note are Hoffnung's color rendition of Maurice Ravel's opera *L'Enfant et les Sortileges* in *The Boy and the Magic* (1964) and his sketches for Glyndebourne Festival Opera programs and designs for the Chelsea Arts Ball in *Hoffnung's Encore* (1968).

Hoffnung was also a master of the spoken use of language for comedic effect. The Hoffnung wit, abundantly in evidence from his drawings, proved to be linguistic as well. Indeed, it could be luxurious, as in the letter ("read" at his celebrated Oxford Union speech in 1958) from a Tyrolean innkeeper: "Having freshly taken over the proprietary of this notorious house, I am wishful that you remove to me your esteemed costume. Standing among savage scenery, the hotel offers stupendous revelations. There is a French widow in every room, affording delightful prospects." The author's very name could be the vehicle of humor; introducing himself to the audience of the Oxford Union, he explained that he was called "Gerard" after a cousin and "Hoffnung" after "Gerard."

But, as with the drawings, there was always more than wit that made Hoffnung's work distinctive. Timing and emphasis are usually considered important elements of spoken humor, and of these Hoffnung had the keenest sense. It is instructive to compare Hoffnung's rendition of the Bricklayer story to that of the comedy act Bert & I (its origin predates both). The latter rushes to a comedic conclusion, yet Hoffnung savors every moment and extends a paragraph of text into a veritable novella and concludes with a lightning quick denouement.

Of that which has been preserved on recordings, perhaps the most extraordinary Hoffnung performance is the series of interviews conducted by Charles Richardson for the BBC beginning in 1957. There were fifty or more of these brief chats, but apparently most have been lost except for a dozen preserved by accident; these are precious indeed. In them Hoffnung speaks about a typical working day ("I rather like to sleep in the morning"), his hobby of collecting knives ("The woman in the shop suggested I buy another knife to open the first one with. That's how it all started"), his childhood housekeeper ("She was very small; that was the only odd thing about her. I never forget the first day she came to me—I could see her through the window—she was *jumping* up at the bell"), his attitude toward hunting ("O, I don't hunt animals. I shoot people. I like to shoot those people who hunt, you know"), his diet ("I just have a suckling pig now for breakfast"), his exercise regime ("I don't crawl. I *swim*!"), his distaste for traveling by air ("They had a nanny goat sitting next to me on the seat") and his preference for the train ("I like to go in one of those sleepers. I like to go up that little velvet ladder. I just go up that little velvet ladder, up and down all the time, all night long"), his pets ("We've got another puss now . . . actually, it's an octopus. Of course it didn't start off as an octopus; he started off as a duopuss . . . you know, with two tentacles. Then later they become a triopuss, and so it goes on. It takes them about eight years"), and his speculations on spaceflight ("I wonder if they've got any monkeys on the Moon"). Astonishingly, according to Richardson (whose dry style is the perfect foil to Hoffnung), the interviews were largely unrehearsed.

Summary

Gerard Hoffnung, a refugee from the Nazis who thrived in England in the 1950s, lived a brief but productive, and by all accounts, jolly life. Before his death in 1959 at the age of thirty-four, this multitalented individual left his comic mark as an illustrator, a raconteur, and an impresario. Hundreds of cartoons, mainly on musical subjects, exhibit artistry, wit, and charm. The Music Festival Concerts that he organized display flamboyance, irreverence, and a love of fun. His many public speaking appearances reveal a master of the language and of comic performance. In the end all of his art was an expression of Hoffnung, the personality: unique, endearing, profoundly funny; in his own words, "probably a lunatic, but not one of the dangerous type."

Notes

I would like to thank Mary Coykendall, Rochester Public Library, Rochester, New York, and Richard Warren, Curator, Historic Sound Recordings, Yale University, for their research assistance. Mrs. Annetta Hoffnung has also been very generous in leading me to sources.

1. Reminiscence of a teacher; from *O Rare Hoffnung: A Memorial Garland* (London: Putnam, 1960) p. 99.

2. Over 1,000 of his early drawings (beginning in his sixth year) are extant and have served as the subject of a scholarly study by S.M. Paine of London University's Institute of Education. See her article, "Gerard Hoffnung: Development as an Artist in Childhood and Adolescence," in *The Hoffnung Festschrift*, ed. Joel Marks (*Essays in Arts and Sciences*, 21 [October 1992]).

3. Just before he died Hoffnung was planning a Festival of Horror at the National Film Theatre. His drawing for the festival program's cover shows a vampire drinking a glass of blood through a straw.

4. Hilde took Gerard to England for the educational opportunites; Hoffnung's father went to Palestine to seek his fortune in the family banking business. The war made the separation inadvertently permanent.

5. A neighbor notes that in 1945, when Hoffnung was only twenty, "He seemed an old man" (*O Rare Hoffnung*, 148). Mrs. Hoffnung remarks in her biography of her husband, "I do not know why Gerard's appearance should have been at such variance with his age" (45). On recordings he sounds like a man in his sixties. The misperception persists: in a review of a posthumous Hoffnung Festival Concert in Canada in 1986, Mrs. Hoffnung is referred to as "Hoffnung's daughter, Annetta."

6. Although his cartoons adorn several books on other subjects, see Marks (1992) for a complete bibliography.

Selected Bibliography
Primary Sources

Cartoon Books
Note: Except as indicated, the following are black-and-white and are now published by Souvenir Press, Ltd., 43 Great Russell Street, London WC1B 3PA, England.
The Right Playmate. Words by James Broughton. New York: Farrar, Straus, & Young, 1952.
The Maestro. London: Dennis Dobson, 1953.
The Hoffnung Symphony Orchestra. London: Dennis Dobson, 1955.
The Hoffnung Music Festival. London: Dennis Dobson, 1956.

The Hoffnung Companion to Music. London: Dennis Dobson, 1957.

Hoffnung's Musical Chairs. London: Dennis Dobson, 1958.

Hoffnung's Acoustics. London: Dennis Dobson, 1959.

Ho Ho Hoffnung. London: Dennis Dobson, 1959.

Birds, Bees and Storks. London: Dennis Dobson, 1960.

Hoffnung's Little Ones. London: Dennis Dobson, 1961.

Hoffnung's Constant Readers. London: Dennis Dobson, 1962.

The Boy and the Magic. Words by Colette (trans. Christopher Fry). London: Dennis Dobson, 1964.

Hoffnung's Encore. London: Dennis Dobson, 1968. Souvenir title: *Hoffnung in Harmony.*

Hoffnung's Humoresque. London: Souvenir Press, 1984.

The Penguin Hoffnung. London and Baltimore: Penguin Books, n.d.

Recordings—Monologues and Interviews

Note: All of the following are currently available in various reissues, collections, and formats.

Hoffnung. BBC Records REF 157M (1973). Two-disc set of the above two LPs, with some omissions; contains in addition "Talking About Music" (*Music Club*, November, 1954).

Hoffnung, A Last Encore. BBC Enterprises. An amalgam of *Hoffnung* and *Timeless Hoffnung.*

The Importance of Being Hoffnung. BBC Records. REB 21M (1968). The Richardson/Hoffnung interviews (1957).

Timeless Hoffnung. BBC Records. REB 87M (1970). Contains "Life Begins at 38" (Speech Day, Oxford Union, December, 1958; includes "The Bricklayer"); letters by Hoffnung read by his wife Annetta; "My Life" (*Woman's Hour*, December, 1953); "The Film Fan" (*Talking About Films*, December, 1955); "Blowing Up Balloons"; and "Tuba."

Recordings—Festival Concerts

Note: All of the following are currently available in various reissues, collections, and formats.

Hoffnung Music Festival Concert (1956). An-gel 35500 (1957). Originally as Columbia (EMI) 33CX1406; reviewed in *Gramophone* (English), January 1957.

Hoffnung's Interplanetary Concert (1958). Angel 35800 (1959). Originally as Columbia (EMI) 33CX1617; reviewed in *Gramophone* (English), January 1959.

Hoffnung's Astronautical Concert (1961; posthumous). Angel 35828 (1962). Originally as Columbia (EMI) SAX2433 (stereo) and 33CX1785 (mono); reviewed in *Gramophone* (English), February 1962.

Hoffnung's Music Festivals. HMV (EMI) SLS.870(3) (1974). Three-record boxed set of the above three LPs with illustrated booklet containing cartoons, photos, and a pop-up cartoon.

The Best of Hoffnung. Selections from 1956 and 1958. Angel S-37028 (1974). Originally as Columbia (EMI) SEL1704; reviewed in *Gramophone* (English), December 1962.

Secondary Sources

Amis, John. *Amiscellany: My Life, My Music.* London and Boston: Faber & Faber, 1985, pp. 111–19. Contains a chapter on Hoffnung.

Hoffnung, Annetta. *Gerard Hoffnung: His Biography.* London: Gordon Fraser, 1988. A treasure trove for any Hoffnung fan; profusely illustrated.

Marks, Joel, ed. *The Hoffnung Festschrift.* Special issue of *Essays in Arts and Sciences,* 21 (October 1992). Contains bibliographies, discography, filmography, articles, reminiscences, and two rare texts by Hoffnung. Black-and-white illustrations and photographs throughout. Available from the author of this entry.

O Rare Hoffnung: A Memorial Garland. London: Putnam (with Dennis Dobson), 1960. A superb collection of reminiscences by friends, family, and colleagues. Black-and-white and color.

Joel Marks

Hogg, James

Born: Ettrick, Scotland, baptized December 9, 1770

Education: At local Ettrick schools

Marriage: Margaret Phillips, April 28, 1820; five children

Died: Altrive, Yarrow, November 21, 1835

Biography

Born in December 1770 (he was baptized December 9), James Hogg spent his childhood in that part of the Selkirkshire region of southern Scotland known as Ettrick Forest, a hilly, sheep-farming district which at that time was isolated and sparsely populated. His parents were Robert Hogg, a tenant farmer, and Margaret Laidlaw. According to his brother William (in a manuscript now in the Beinecke Library at Yale University), Hogg's formal schooling lasted for "only three or four winters," starting when "he was about six years old." For much of his childhood Hogg was employed in farm work of various kinds, often in conditions of physical hardship. In his twenties he was employed as a shepherd by a distant relative, Mr. Laidlaw of Blackhouse. During this particularly happy period, he began the wide-ranging and intelligent reading which continued for the remainder of his life; he also began at this time to earn a reputation as a poet.

While in his thirties Hogg undertook various farming and literary projects (among them supplying material for Sir Walter Scott's *Minstrelsy of the Scottish Border,* 1802–1803), with mixed success, but in 1813 his poem *The Queen's Wake,* about Mary Stuart, brought him considerable fame and the friendship of figures such as Lord Byron, William Wordsworth, and Robert Southey. Other book-length poems followed, and beginning in 1818 he produced a series of four remarkable works of prose fiction which culminated in his magnificent novel *The Private Memoirs and Confessions of a Justified Sinner* (1824).

From 1815 until his death twenty years later, Hogg pursued a dual career as a professional man of letters and a farmer in the Yarrow valley in Ettrick Forest. Known as the "Ettrick Shepherd," he came into vogue as part of the ballad revival connected with the Romantic movement. During this fruitful period of his life, Hogg published extensively in *Blackwood's Edinburgh Magazine* and other Scottish and English periodicals; a usual pattern was that he would send a piece to London for publication if it was rejected in Edinburgh. In addition to his magazine work, Hogg continued to produce volumes of poetry and prose through the 1820s and early 1830s. In the spring of 1832, he visited England and spent three months in London, where his presence aroused considerable interest. After a short illness Hogg died at his Altrive, Yarrow home on November 21, 1835.

Literary Analysis

In the brief autobiographical memoir prefixed to *The Mountain Bard* (1807), Hogg speaks of a play, *The Scotch Gentleman,* which he began in 1795: "on reading it to an Ettrick audience . . . it never fails to produce the most extraordinary convulsions of laughter." Unfortunately, this play does not survive, but laughter plays an important part in many of Hogg's works, including some of the most somber. Thus, the *Justified Sinner* is a chilling story involving murder, diabolic possession, and damnation, but it contains some richly funny scenes. A similar example is provided by *The Three Perils of Woman* (1823). This work is a series of interconnecting stories, each reflecting and commenting on the others as a composite picture is built up, "thereby displaying," as Hogg puts it, "both the lights and shadows of Scottish life." *The Three Perils of Woman* contains harrowing scenes describing devastation and genocide in the aftermath of the battle of Culloden in the 1740s; it also contains an account of the farcical adventures in the 1820s of the farmer Richard Rickleton, who finds himself engaged to several young women at the same time and who fights a series of memorably absurd duels. Other novels by Hogg also contain comic passages: Davie Tait's prayer in *The Brownie of Bodsbeck* (1818) is a particularly striking and well-known example, and there are also memorable comic passages in Hogg's other major novel, *The Three Perils of Man* (1822).

Hogg is generally recognized as one of the great parodists of the English language, largely on the strength of *The Poetic Mirror* (1816). The parodies of Wordsworth in this volume are particularly well known, but Samuel Taylor Coleridge, Byron, and Scott also figure among Hogg's victims. The wickedly accurate, and very funny, parodies of *The Poetic Mirror* demonstrate a remarkable talent for mimicry. This gift is also an important ingredient in Hogg's more serious writings: the ability to catch the individual tone of different voices is one of the glories of his fiction.

While works like the *Justified Sinner* and *The Three Perils of Woman* are highly complex, Hogg also produced many shorter pieces, both in poetry and in prose, which are entirely or predominantly comic in tone. Some of these are pleasant, genuinely funny, but comparatively slight. For example, the prose tale "Willie Wastle and his Dog Trap," published in the

Royal Lady's Magazine for July 1832, is an amusing story about a dancing and talking dog. The author's chief achievement as a humorist, however, lies in a number of remarkable comic poems that combine a mad, high-spirited energy with a vein of wild, fantastic absurdity which at times borders on the sublime. Two well-known examples are "The Witch of Fife" from *The Queen's Wake* and "May of the Moril Glen," which was included in *A Queer Book* (1832). Another poem of this kind from *A Queer Book* is "The Good Man of Alloa," in which a very earthy old man is taken by a mermaid on a treasure-hunt along the ocean floor. All of these poems involve a strong presence of the supernatural, and all are set in a distant past which nevertheless carries strong hints of the present. For instance, we are told that the old man of "The Good Man of Alloa" protects himself from the sea so well that he might have been wearing a mackintosh, a waterproof garment patented by Charles MacIntosh five years before Hogg wrote the poem. "A Few Remarkable Adventures of Sir Simon Brodie," from the collection entitled *Tales of the Wars of Montrose* (1835), is an example of a prose tale by Hogg similar in spirit to poems like "The Good Man of Alloa."

Summary

After a long period of neglect, James Hogg is now generally regarded as one of the key figures of Scottish romanticism. As a humorist, his main claims to fame are as a parodist and as the creator of a number of memorably funny poems that combine the earthy and the fantastic in a way that is very much his own while showing some links with Robert Burns's "Tam o' Shanter." In spite of the recent revival of interest in Hogg, many of his works are still not readily available, but a new multivolume collected edition (to be published by the Edinburgh University Press) is in active preparation.

Selected Bibliography

Primary Sources

Hogg was a prolific author, producing over thirty books and pamphlets as well as numerous contributions to periodicals. Many of his main humorous works are to be found in the following volumes.

The Poetic Mirror. London and Edinburgh, 1816.

Winter Evening Tales. 2 vols. London and Edinburgh: Printed for Oliver & Boyd and G. & W.B. Whittaker, 1820.

The Poetical Works of James Hogg. 4 vols. London and Edinburgh: Printed for Archibald Constable and Hurst, Robinson, 1822.

The Shepherd's Calendar. 2 vols. London and Edinburgh: William Blackwood and T. Cadell, 1829.

A Queer Book. London and Edinburgh, 1832.

Tales of Love and Mystery. Ed. David Groves. Edinburgh, 1985.

Poetic Mirrors. Ed. David Groves. Frankfurt am Main, 1990.

Secondary Sources

Bibliographies

Hughes, Gillian H. *Hogg's Verse and Drama: A Chronological Listing.* Stirling, 1990.

Mack, Douglas S. *Hogg's Prose: An Annotated Listing.* Stirling, 1985.

Books

Gifford, Douglas. *James Hogg.* Edinburgh, 1976.

Groves, David. *James Hogg: The Growth of a Writer.* Edinburgh, 1988.

Hughes, Gillian H., ed. *Papers Given at the First James Hogg Society Conference.* Stirling, 1983.

———, ed. *Papers Given at the Second James Hogg Society Conference.* Aberdeen, 1988.

Mergenthal, Silvia. *James Hogg: Selbstbild und Bild.* Frankfurt am Main, 1990.

Parr, Norah. *James Hogg at Home.* Dollar, 1980.

Smith, Nelson C. *James Hogg.* Boston, 1980.

Articles

Many articles on Hogg are to be found in the periodical *Studies in Hogg and His World.*

Douglas S. Mack

Hone, William

Born: Bath, June 3, 1780

Education: Home- and self-educated; little formal schooling

Marriage: Sarah Johnson, July 1800; twelve children

Died: Tottenham, November 6, 1842

Biography

The son of William Hone, a legal clerk, and Frances Maria Stawell, William Hone was born in Bath on June 3, 1780. He spent most of his childhood in the burgeoning "suburban" communities on the outskirts of London. His early life was dominated by the influence of his father, a deeply religious man and stern disciplinarian, but in the late 1790s Hone was caught up in the spirit of popular radicalism, and he was briefly involved with the French-inspired "New Philosophy" of the London Corresponding Society. In July 1800, Hone married Sarah Johnson and began a varied but usually unprofitable career as a writer, publisher, bookseller, antiquarian, auctioneer, and even banker. Financial difficulties, exacerbated by his rapidly growing family, which eventually included twelve children, forced Hone to change residences as well as occupations frequently, but he continued in various ways to promote such causes as Parliamentary reform, abolition of the slave trade, and relief for the destitute.

Hone came to public prominence in 1817 when he began writing and publishing a short-lived radical weekly called the *Reformist's Register* and, more spectacularly, when he was brought to trial to face blasphemous libel charges for writing three antigovernment squibs, *The Late John Wilkes's Catechism*, *The Political Litany*, and *The Sinecurist's Creed*. Hone was found innocent of all charges, and his courtroom victory was widely celebrated as a demonstration of how an honest and determined citizen, when given a fair chance in a jury trial, could successfully do battle against the entrenched powers of a repressive government. Hone, in short, became a sort of living symbol of the power of a free press, and he took advantage of his notoriety by producing several hugely popular antigovernment satires, many of which were illustrated by the young George Cruikshank.

In the mid-1820s, Hone began to retreat from the public spotlight. He was forced by financial problems to abandon his long-advertised *History of Parody*, and he turned his attention increasingly toward antiquarian works such as the *Apocryphal New Testament* (1820) and *Ancient Mysteries Described* (1823), the latter a synoptic edition of some Middle English mystery plays that Hone had discovered in the British Museum. Later in the decade with some help from his friends Charles and Mary Lamb, Hone produced three works of folklore, *The*

Every-Day Book (1827), *The Table Book* (1828), and *The Year Book* (1832)—works which are still valuable as catalogues of English folk customs, beliefs, and traditions.

In the 1830s, Hone was largely a forgotten man. Plagued as usual by financial worries, he tried several more occupations—including operating a coffeehouse and writing occasional antiquarian pieces for the *Times*. This period also saw a revival of his religious spirit as he joined the enthusiastic followers of Edward Irving and subsequently spent some years as "sub-editor" for an evangelical weekly called *The Patriot*. Hone died in Tottenham on November 6, 1842, after a few months' illness.

Literary Analysis

Though Hone was a prolific writer and publisher, his corpus of specifically comic works consists primarily of a few political parodies and satires published in the late 1810s and early 1820s. These pieces are topical and to present-day readers they often seem dated. They certainly have not ranked high as works of literature or wit. In their time, however, Hone's satires caught the attention of an enormous readership. Between 1819 and 1822 alone, he sold over 250,000 copies of his political squibs, making him the best-selling author in Britain. Like that of most political writers, Hone's technique as a humorist is inseparably bound up with the audience for whom he was writing and the influence which he hoped to have on that audience.

The Regency Period, of course, was noteworthy for the extravagance of the Regent, the desperately repressive policies of the Tory government, and the destitution and consequent discontent of the lower classes. The obvious inequities between the empowered and the disenfranchised led to frequent episodes of social unrest—the Spa Fields Riots (1816) and the "Peterloo Massacre" (1819), for instance—which pitted the vociferous, mass-platform politics of radicals and reformists against the government's repressive machinery of domestic surveillance, censorship, and violence. Hone's political satires played an important role in this class conflict. With simple language that was understandable even by the marginally literate, in his comic works Hone exposed the foibles of the established powers and thereby helped to consolidate his audience's antigovernment leanings. Indeed, Hone's comic technique seems calculated to appeal to an audience of discontented working-class readers as well as to readers associated with the Whig opposition.

The famous parodies of 1817 are typical of Hone's early style. Formally, the works are based on the Catechism, the Litany, and the Athanasian Creed from the *Book of Common Prayer*, but instead of following through on the religious implications of his models, Hone changes the content so as to present a radically critical interpretation of England's political leadership. In *The Late John Wilke's Catechism*, for instance, "Lick Spittle," a fictional government placeman, answers questions put to him by a Ministry official. Having rehearsed his "articles of faith"—a declaration of support for Tory politics—Spittle is asked the set question "What dost thou chiefly learn in the Articles of thy Belief?" He answers, "First, I learn to forswear all conscience, which was never meant to trouble me, nor the rest of the tribe of Courtiers. Secondly, to swear black is white, or white black, according to the good pleasure of the Ministers. Thirdly, to put on the helmet of impudence, the only armour against the shafts of patriotism." Hone recasts the Lord's Prayer (renamed the "Minister's Memorial") in a similar vein. Beginning with "Our Lord who art in the Treasury," the passage describes the greedy aspirations and political negligence of some particularly servile government lackeys, and then concludes, "Turn us not out of our Places; but keep us in the House of Commons, the land of Pensions and Plenty; and deliver us from the People. Amen."

The discursive strategy of the parodies is clear. The base texts would, of course, be thoroughly familiar to Hone's intended audience of politically conscious working-class readers, and this familiarity served crucial rhetorical purposes. It enabled even the most inexperienced readers to comprehend the work, and it set in stark relief the ideological conflict between a repressive government and "the People."

Sensing the political danger of the pamphlets, the Attorney General filed ex officio information charging Hone with blasphemous libel, but in three spectacular and well-publicized trials in December of 1817 Hone defended himself successfully against all counts, arguing that parody does not necessarily impugn the quality or the validity of the original text from which it takes its form. The acquittals were a major embarrassment to the government. Moreover, they effectively earned Hone an immunity from further libel prosecutions. He responded to his hard-won freedom of expression by producing several more parodies. Some of these, like *Buonapartephobia* (1817) and *A Slap at Slop* (1822) were directed against his arch-rival John Stoddart (Hone's "Dr. Slop"), the Tory propagandist and editor of *The New Times*. Others were more pointedly political.

In this latter category the five pamphlets that Hone produced between 1819 and 1821 deserve special notice. *The Political House That Jack Built* (1819) was the most popular of all of Hone's works, selling over 100,000 copies in just one year. As suggested by its title, this work was based on the famous children's story. As he had in his 1817 parodies, Hone fuses the form of the original with a political content. The resulting comic text chastises government actions that threaten to plunder the "wealth" (i.e., the Magna Carta, the Bill of Rights, and Habeas Corpus) that lay in the house that Jack built. But, *The Political House* also shows a significant refinement in the parodic strategy of the earlier works: the pamphlet is extensively and brilliantly illustrated by the author's friend and collaborator, George Cruikshank. No doubt the numerous illustrations made the work even more accessible to and influential upon Hone's working-class readership. Hone adopted the same strategy in two more parodies produced in 1820 during the Queen Caroline affair. *The Queen's Matrimonial Ladder* offers a brief and highly critical reading of the history of the Regent's relationship with his unfortunate consort; it takes its form from a children's toy that Hone had seen in a shop window. *Non Mi Ricordo!* is a parody based on the extensively publicized cross-examination of one of the Italian witnesses whom the government had brought to England to testify against Caroline. Both works served to ridicule the position of King George IV and his Ministry and to chastise the hypocrisy of the English Church as it kowtowed to the demands of political expediency.

The other two pamphlets in this series show different elements of Hone's comic technique. *The Man in the Moon* (1820) is perhaps the most "literary" of his popular humorous works. In a dream-vision poem, the speaker is transported to the moon where he listens to the "Prince of Lunataria" deliver his annual address to the assembled Parliament. The speech itself—a parody of the English Regent's Parliamentary address—takes up most of the poem. Predictably, it is spiked with unmistakable criticism of the political and economic conditions in England:

> Reform, Reform, the swinish rabble
>   cry—
> Meaning, of course, rebellion, blood,
>   and riot—
> Audacious rascals! you, my Lords, and I,
> Know 'tis their duty to be starved in
>   quiet.

In *The Political Showman—At Home!* (1821), Cruikshank's caricatures of prominent political figures are supplemented by Hone's text written in imitation of the language of a carnival barker. The speaker's patter presents the political characters as dangerous zoo animals, "Curiosities and Creatures" exhibited for the horror and fascination of the onlookers. In addition, each caricature is surrounded by excerpts from Michel Montaigne, Edmund Spenser, William Shakespeare, Richard Crashaw, William Cowper, and other literary figures. The excerpts serve consistently to guide readers toward a comic and satirical interpretation of the political characters depicted. Thus, the *Political Showman* shows Hone moving toward the compilation and arrangement techniques that he would use later in the decade in his antiquarian works, *The Every-Day Book*, *The Table Book*, and *The Year Book*. Perhaps the most prominent theme in all of Hone's parodies and satires concerns the political function of the press itself. Appearing frequently, both in Hone's text and in Cruikshank's illustrations, the printing press is celebrated as the ultimate nemesis of the self-aggrandizing schemes of government authorities. The emphasis is crucial, for it underscores the historical significance of Hone's comic publications. The author worked in an era when the popular press was struggling to establish its voice as a free and independent critic of political and religious institutions. His acquittals in the trials of 1817 and the subsequent popularity of his antigovernment squibs played a major part in this process. In effect, his teasing voice of opposition helped to break the stranglehold of libel prosecutions, fines, and prison terms through which the established social powers had sought to smother overt public criticism. Hone's career as a humorist, then, offers a singular example of how the comic writer's tools of satire and parody can so galvanize public opinion that real social and political change become inevitable.

Summary

William Hone's parodies are topical squibs written to expose what he took to be hypocrisy and abuses of power by the government. Hone typically uses simple, straightforward language and bases his parodies on familiar cultural texts, thus making them accessible to an audience of even semiliterate readers. His acquittals on blasphemous libel charges in 1817 and the popularity of his later works helped to consolidate widespread antigovernment feeling, thereby moving England closer to the social ideals of a free press and an equitable representative government.

Selected Bibliography

Primary Sources

[All works published privately in London by William Hone.]

The Late John Wilkes's Catechism, 1817.

The Political Litany, 1817.

The Sinecurist's Creed, 1817.

Buonapartephobia, 1817. A parody based on Laurence Sterne's *Tristram Shandy*.

The Reformist's Register, weekly, February to October, 1817.

The Three Trials of William Hone, 1818. Transcripts of the 1817 trials.

The Political House That Jack Built, 1819.

The Man in the Moon, 1820.

The Queen's Matrimonial Ladder, 1820.

Non Mi Ricordo!, 1820.

The Apocryphal New Testament, 1820.

The Political Showman—At Home!, 1821.

A Slap at Slop and the Bridge-Street Gang, 1822. Parody of John Stoddart's *The New Times*.

Ancient Mysteries Described, 1823.

The Every-Day Book, weekly, 1826; collected edition 1827.

Facetiae and Miscellanies, 1827. A useful collected edition of many of Hone's popular parodies and other comic works.

The Table Book, weekly, 1827; collected edition 1828.

The Year Book, 1832.

Secondary Sources

Books

Hackwood, Frederick W. *William Hone: His Life and Times*. London: T. Fisher Unwin, 1912; New York: Augustus M. Kelley, 1970. The only full-length biography; generally reliable, but omits discussion of some important texts.

Wickwar, William. *The Struggle for the Freedom of the Press, 1819–1832*. London: Allen & Unwin, 1928. An excellent history of the tensions between publishers and politicians; includes considerable commentary on Hone.

Articles

Sikes, Herschel M. "William Hone: Regency Patriot, Parodist, and Pamphleteer." *The Newberry Library Bulletin*, 5 (1961): 281–94. A good survey of Hone's political parodies.

Vitale, Marina. "The Domesticated Heroine in Byron's *Corsair* and William Hone's Prose Adaptation." *Literature and History*, 10 (1984): 72–94. Vitale uses an early Hone work to demonstrate how the popular radical press maintained traditional images of women. Helpful commentary on the social impact of Hone's radicalism.

Kyle Grimes

Hood, Thomas

Born: Poultry, London, May 23, 1799
Education: Errol village school; Prospect House Academy at Clapham; Alfred House Academy; apprentice to an engraver in London
Marriage: Jane Reynolds, May 5, 1825
Died: London, May 3, 1845

Biography

Born in Poultry, London, on May 23, 1799, Thomas Hood was the second son of Thomas Hood, a Scottish bookseller, and Elizabeth Sands. Thomas attended Erroll village school, a private school in Tokenhouse Yard after which he went to a preparatory school in Clapham, where he was not very happy. He then attended the sleep-in academy, Alfred House at Campbell Green. After his father's death in 1811, he was forced to leave Alfred House and return to his home where he entered a more modest day school. Hood's new school, located above a grocery shop, was kept by a decayed Dominie. Though the pedagogue was not himself well educated, he apparently did more for his students than he had done for himself, and Hood's stay at the school was among the happiest and most educationally rewarding of any that he attended.

Reversals in the family fortune made it necessary for Hood to work as a city clerk for a short period of time before he became apprenticed to an engraver. Throughout most of his life he suffered from tuberculosis and effects of a bout with rheumatic fever. He spent time in Dundee, Scotland from 1815 to 1817 in the hope that his ill health (probably rheumatic heart disease which plagued him throughout his life) would improve. With his return to England in 1817, Hood, considerably stronger than when he left two years earlier, returned to the occupation of engraving, resuming his apprenticeship, probably with Robert Sands. His work in his chosen trade left little time for Hood's more creative talents. He wrote little, other than occasional letters. In one such letter to his nephew, he wrote: "In fact, I am now obliged to turn the amusing, if I can, into the *profitable*, not that I am ambitious, or of a very money-loving disposition, but I am obliged to be so." He later became an editor of the *London Magazine* after the death of John Scott, and in this capacity he met many of the men of letters who contributed to its pages. He was also the editor of *The Gem* in 1889, and subsequently was associated with the *Athenaeum and (London) Literary Chronicle* and edited *New Monthly Magazine*.

On May 5, 1825, Hood married Jane Reynolds, the daughter of George Reynolds, the head writing master at Christ's Hospital. Reports that the Reynolds family objected to the marriage of their daughter to Thomas have been refuted by Walter Jerrold who stated that "letters to Jane's mother and sister, which I am enabled to publish for the first time, effectually dispose of that tradition."[1]

Hood died on May 3, 1845, in London after a year-long illness which included heart problems and complications from tuberculosis which were further aggravated by influenza, which he contracted in March of that year. The body of work that he left behind, although not of exceptional quality, was very influential during the nineteenth century, and his humanitarian poems became models for social protest worldwide.

Literary Analysis

According to J.C. Reid, "In Scotland, then, uncongenial though he found most of the people, Hood fell under the spell of literature and became aware of his own power over words."[2] Hood's inclination for the amusing, nurtured in Scotland, became a more forceful initiative, perhaps prompting him to join the literary society that waited on ladies and gentlemen in their own homes. Hood's poetic output thus far had been rather meager. His talents, though emerging, needed additional impetus. In 1821, he left the field of engraving and became an assistant editor and contributor to the *London Magazine*. Some of the contributors to that distinguished journal included Charles Lamb, Thomas Carlyle, William Hazlitt, and of course, Hood. This prestigious chronicle, unfortunately, was short-lived, meeting its demise in 1824.

The move to the *London Magazine* drastically altered Hood's life. Three major changes occurred as a result of his taking this new position. To begin with, he had the opportunity to meet some of the most outstanding authors of the day. In addition, he transferred his abilities from that of engraver to that of author. Finally, he met the woman with whom he would spend the rest of his life.

Though Hood was still virtually unknown to the public at large in 1824, he was recognized for his writing ability by those who followed his contributions to the *London Magazine*. It was in 1825 that he published his first comic compilation, *Odes and Addresses to Great People*. This volume was a collection of pieces that had appeared in the *London* and other magazines. A collaboration between Hood and John Hamilton Reynolds, Hood's brother-in-law and fellow writer, whom Hood met while he was working on the *London Magazine*, the fifteen poems that comprise the book include nine by Hood and five by Hamilton. Notable throughout the selections was Hood's wonderful use of the pun. One poem, "Sally Brown," was written in collaboration, though it is impossible to know how much each writer contributed. Hood, himself, refers to the role that he had in composing the ballad, commenting that he was very vain about the part that he had played in its creation.

Odes and Addresses was followed a year later by *Whims and Oddities*, Hood's first complete book. This, too, included previously published magazine pieces, together with some new ones. The comic verse of this collection soon became his trademark. Though he did make excursions into more serious domains, this genre with the pun, his most potent tool, became synonymous with his poetry. Among the humorous poems included were "Faithless Nelly Gray" and "Faithless Sally Brown." The book was immediately successful and was followed by *Whims and Oddities, Second Series*. Using the standard ballad stanza, the poet satirized the themes of "love" and "death." The usual scenario was the return of a lover who, finding his sweetheart has been unfaithful to him, kills himself. In the ballad of Nelly Gray, the satire of serious themes with Hood's penchant for punning can be seen in these lines:

> Ben Battle was a soldier bold,
> And used to war's alarms:
> But a cannon-ball took off his legs
> So he laid down his arms![3]

The ballad of Sally Brown also contained the usual puns:

> His death, which happened in his berth,
> At forty-odd befell:
> They went and told the sexton, and
> The sexton toll'd the bell.[4]

In addition, however, the writer also made use of ribald humor, with an obvious vulgar reference to Sally's honor, and hypocrisy with regard to her love for Ben, the carpenter. Hood's penchant for combining the grotesque and the humorous is evident in much of his poetry. His themes, in addition to infidelity, also included physical disabilities, family relations, inebriation, and bodily handicaps.

One of Hood's most popular poems, *The Dream of Eugene Aram, the Murderer* was issued separately and was illustrated by William Harvey in 1831. In the work, Hood relates the account of Aram's execution in 1759. Hood's use of the six-line stanza is remarkably reminiscent of Samuel Taylor Coleridge's "The Rime of the Ancient Mariner," which also treats the macabre and the fantastic, themes that fascinated both men.

Perhaps anticipating Edgar Allan Poe in its scenes of death, Hood's "The Last Man" is a ghastly science-fiction view of the end of the world as described by a hangman-narrator. Appearing in *Whims and Oddities*, "The Last Man" was described in a review in *Blackwood's Edinburgh Magazine* as "a sort of absurd sailor-like insolent ruffian, sitting with arms a-kimbo, cross-legged and smoking his pipe on the cross-tree of a gallows."[5] This poem anticipates the more modern black, or sick, humor popular in America today.

"The Lay of the Labourer" demonstrates Hood's deep concern with social problems (as does "The Bridge of Sighs" and other poems). Published in October 1845 in *Hood's Magazine*, the poem is an appeal on behalf of unemployed workers in England. A personal letter to the Home Secretary, along with a copy of the magazine in which the poem appeared, apparently was ignored by the Secretary. Prime Minister Robert Peel was more receptive. He was very much affected by Hood's writings and granted Mrs. Hood an annual stipend of 100 pounds a year, approved by Queen Victoria.

In February 1827, *National Tales* was published. It is sufficient to say that this work was not well received. The tales were anecdotes set in England, Venice, Persia, and Arabia. They were written in imitation of the Italian *novella* and were plodding and unimaginative. Also, in 1827, Hood's volume, *The Plea of the Midsummer Fairies*, was published with the title poem dedicated to Lamb. Though some of the thirty-seven poems were written as early as 1821, new ones were added too. It was Hood's hope that this volume would establish him as a serious poet. The longest poem in the volume, "Lycus the Centaur," was dedicated to his brother-in-law. Many of the poems show the unmistakable influence of Percy Bysshe Shelley and John Keats. Hood was particularly influenced by Keats. Indeed, it has been speculated that Keats and Hood knew each other, though that is probably unlikely; Keats died four years before Hood's marriage. Still, Hood loved Keats's work and it inspired his more serious poems. It also "encouraged him to branch out into a form of light verse that he practiced for the rest of his life."[6]

"Lamia," published after the author's death, was a dramatization of the Keats poem. William Jerdan, editor of the *Literary Gazette*, published Hood's piece in his own *Autobiography*. This rendering of Keats's poem, though exaltedly conceived, was poorly done and was the low water mark of Hood's career—which may be the reason that he never had it published during his lifetime.

The Comic Annual (1830–1839, 1842), one of the earliest humor journals initiated in the nineteenth century, contained a great volume of Hood's work. The successor to this journal, *Hood's Own*, was widely popular, apparently influencing many authors and their comic output. Among the most successful humorous progeny of these magazines (extant until 1992) was *Punch*, which was originally edited by Hood.

Hood's popularity, growing steadily, even reached America, influencing such writers as Oliver Wendell Holmes, John Greenleaf Whittier, Henry Wadsworth Longfellow, and James Russell Lowell. Several of Hood's poems were translated into German, including *The Dream of Eugene Aram, the Murderer, The Song of the Shirt*, "The Bridge of Sighs," "Up the Rhine," and "A Paternal Ode." Even Goethe was influenced by Hood, praising his inventiveness and humanity. His popularity extended to Russia, where his biographical sketch appeared in the *Literaturnaya Gazetta* in 1848, shortly after his death. The revolutionist and poet Mikhail Mikhaylov translated *The Song of the Shirt*, "The Death Bed," and other poems and essays as well.

Perhaps Hood's greatest success, although not in this instance humorous, came from his poem, "The Song of the Shirt," published in *Punch* in the December 16, 1843, issue. It was inspired by the story of a seamstress who was tried for pawning articles belonging to her employer. Her plight, brought on by a salary so small that she and her two children could not survive on it, prompted several periodicals to take up her cause, including the *London Times* and *Punch*. It was then that an incensed Hood wrote his *Song*, which editor Mark Lemon of *Punch* printed anonymously. Its immediate popularity caused *Punch*'s circulation to triple. Many journals and newspapers reprinted the poem, notably among them the *Times* (London). Translations followed in several languages, including German, Russian, French, and Italian. It inspired poets and social reformers in many parts of the world. The English were particularly stunned by the poem, many committing it to memory. Lines such as "Sewing at once, with a double thread, / A Shroud as well as a Shirt,"[7] stirred the multitude and even inspired church sermons.

Indeed, Hood was prolific in his choice of subjects. In a satiric poem, "A Discovery in Astronomy," the poet humorously destroys the astronomers of his day, whom he will not name precisely, whether the person were South, Herschel, or Baily:

> But one of those great men who watch
> the skies,
> With all their rolling, winking eyes,

Was looking at that Orb whose ancient
　　God
Was patron of the Ode, and Song, and
　　Sonnet . . .

He continues by saying that the astronomer
wondered why no other astronomer was able to
tell the reason for the spots on the sun. Hood
concludes by saying that "Lord, master!"
mutter'd John, a liveried elf, / "To wonder so at
spots upon the sun! / I'll tell you what he's
done— / Freckled himself!"[8]

Even the topic of blindness was not exempt
from Hood's pen. Apparently everything was
grist for his mill. In "Tim Turpin," subtitled "A
Pathetic Ballad," Hood, in twenty-two quotations, puns continually on blindness:

Tim Turpin he was gravel blind
And ne'er had seen the skies:
For Nature, when his head was made,
Forgot to dot his eyes.
So, like a Christmas pedagogue,
Poor Tim was forc'd to do—
Look out for pupils, for he had
A vacancy for two.

Hood explains that poor Tim finally got married, and though he was initially happy, his life
took a deviant turn, when a surgeon was able
to restore his sight, and when he looked on his
wife:

But when his eyes were open'd thus,
He wish'd them dark again:
For when he look'd upon his wife,
He saw her very plain.
Her face was bad, her figure worse,
He couldn't bear to eat:
For she was any thing but like
A Grace before his meat.[9]

One final "Pathetic Ballad," entitled
"Mary's Ghost," is the depiction of a woman
whose ghost appears before a "young William."
The ghost laments that her resting place was disturbed by grave robbers who dismembered her
body, supposedly for scientific purposes. The
poet describes how various parts of her body
went to different places and people: a doctor has
her hands; her legs are now in a hospital, and:

The cock it crows—I must be gone!
My William we must part!
But I'll be your's in death, altho'

Sir Astley has my heart.
Don't go to weep upon my grave,
And think that there I be;
They haven't left an atom there,
Of my anatomie.[10]

Hood's penchant for the macabre and the
grotesque might stem, suggests Jeffrey, from the
poet's own pain.[11] He expresses this pain in humor with puns as the modus operandi. This can
be seen in such poems as "The Supper Superstition," "Ode to H. Bodkin, Esq." (1825),
"Pompey's Ghost" (1840), "Sally Simpkin's Lament" (1829), and many others. Whether one
appreciates Hood's bizarre humor is a matter of
individual taste. Many find this type of punning
on human frailties somewhat distasteful, e.g., the
one-armed beggar in "Ode to H. Bodkin, Esq.":

Poor Jack is gone, that used to doff
His batter'd tatter'd hat
And show his dangling sleeve, alas!
There seem'd no *arm* in that![12]

It is questionable whether the name of
Thomas Hood would be remembered today if
his fame rested solely on his prose contributions
to literature. Most of his prose writings were
first published in one or another of the journals
to which he was connected.

His first published prose work was "A Sentimental Journey from Islington to Waterloo
Bridge, in March, 1821." The title itself suggests the influence of Laurence Sterne's *Sentimental Journey through France and Italy by Mr.
Yorick (1768).* In Sterne's *Sentimental Journey,*
the author implores his readers to understand
that his philosophical message "was to teach us
to love the world and our fellow creatures better than we do." Hood's "Sentimental Journey"
follows the same prescript as Sterne's, with the
hero, on one occasion, settling an argument
between two lovers, and philosophizing on the
equality of the sexes. The work is amusing, if
not of great consequence.

Literary Reminiscences followed in 1839.
This autobiographical piece was more serious
than "Journey" and contained Hood's penchant
for the fantastic (as was seen in his poetry, in
particular, "The Last Man"). The reminiscences
of this work take on a rambling style which,
given the structural premise of a journey, is acceptable. The work is pleasant, witty, and light.

Hood's prose works, on the lighter side,
include "Johnsoniana" (1883), and two earlier

essays, "Queries in Natural History" and "Speculations of a Naturalist" (both 1839). Puns are rampant in these essays, including one on the oyster in which the humorist observes that "an Oyster is very anomalous" because "you must take it out of its bed before you can tuck it in!"

Somewhat autobiographical in content are two additional prose works: "The School-mistress Abroad: An Extravaganza" (1839) and "Fishing in Germany" (1840). Both works contain ample morsels of Hood's humor, though "The Schoolmistress" has its serious side as well. In this volume the tourist-narrator is a bigoted person who hates everything and finds her own knowledge of the continent, specifically foreign languages, seriously lacking. She concludes by observing that this lack makes her rather unsuited to be a governess.

Besides these works, Hood also wrote *The Happiest Man in England* (1839), *The Undertaker* (1839), three letters published in the *Athenaeum and (London) Literary Chronicle* in 1837, and "Copyright and Copywrong," a thirty-six-page protest and plea concerning the rights of authors. In 1839, Hood wrote "The Black and White Question" in which he called attention to the biased treatment of Negroes in the society, specifically with regard to the unjust conditions of apprenticeship.

He ventured into the realms of the short story with such works as "The Apparition" (1839), "A Tale of the Great Plague" (1839), "The Grimsby Ghost" (1844), and "A Tale of Terror" (1844). These stories, in the Gothic mode, again occasionally show the influence of Sterne (particularly "The Grimsby Ghost"). They are, nevertheless, not the substance upon which Hood's fame rests.

Literary criticism was another interest of Hood's. He assayed to evaluate Charles Dickens's *A Christmas Carol* in 1843, which was an appreciatory piece rather than true criticism. More substantial was his review in the *Athenaeum* in 1840 of part of Dickens's *Master Humphrey's Clock*.

Hood's most ambitious prose work was *National Tales*. The stories contain examples of Gothic, romantic, tragic, comic, and moralistic concepts, with characters poorly developed and themes ill conceived. The two volumes, containing twenty-five stories, were not well received by the public who, for the most part, just ignored the "Tales."

In 1834, he published his novel, *Tylney Hall*. It was generally well liked, but more for its humorous content than for the serious elements as he would have hoped. In 1840, he wrote *Up the Rhine*. This was a novel, of sorts, that was very popular when it came out, but generally is ignored today by literary critics. Finally, Hood attempted his last novel, *Our Family*, which was abandoned in 1845. The novel, often quite humorous, marked the end of his literary career.

Summary

Thomas Hood's literary contributions present a dichotomy. He wrote poetry about the macabre and grotesque, emphasizing man's defects and woman's unfaithfulness, epitomized in such works as *Whims and Oddities*, *The Plea of the Midsummer Fairies*, and *Odes and Addresses to Great People*: "If Thomas Hood had died in 1835, he would be classified today as another minor romantic poet, like Darley and Beddoes, illustrative of the transition from the romantic to the Victorian era."[13] The additional ten years of life presented a different perspective for him, in which there "ran a gradually heightening awareness of the distressed condition of English society and of his fellow man."[14] He became much concerned with social reform. Works such as "The Bridge of Sighs," "The Lay of the Labourer," and *The Dream of Eugene Aram, the Murderer* are decidedly not humorous but do represent his deep concern with the social climate. For the most part, these poems were without his usual signature punning. Nevertheless, his penchant for punning is what made Hood stand out from his contemporaries. He wrote humorously for profit and seriously for posterity. His attempts at prose were often unsuccessful, but when they were well received, it was often the humor that attracted both reviewers and public alike.

As a humorist, Hood will be remembered for his contributions to the *London Magazine*, his comic collection in *Odes and Addresses to Great People*, and the comic verse of *Whims and Oddities* which featured "Faithless Nelly Gray" and "Faithless Sally Brown."

He was influenced by many great writers including Keats, Coleridge, Sterne, Poe, and Dickens. He, in turn, influenced others including American writers such as Holmes, Longfellow, Whittier, and Lowell. His influence was felt in other countries, including Germany and Russia. Lloyd Jeffrey[15] sums up the poet as "A Lively Hood for a Livelihood." What better epitaph can one have for a man who, like William Shakespeare, dignified the pun and made it respectable?

Notes

1. Walter Jerrold, *Thomas Hood: His Life and Times* (New York: Greenwood Press, 1969), p. 124.
2. J.C. Reid, *Thomas Hood* (London: Routledge & Kegan Paul, 1963), p. 27.
3. Thomas Hood, *Selected Poems of Thomas Hood*, ed. John Clubbe (Cambridge: Harvard University Press, 1970), p. 81.
4. *Ibid.*, p. 80.
5. Reid, p. 75.
6. *Ibid.*, p. 49.
7. Hood, p. 305.
8. Hood, *Thomas Hood, The Works, Vol. IX* (New York: George Olms Verlag, 1970), p. 143.
9. *Selected Poems of Thomas Hood*, p. 87.
10. *Selected Poems of Thomas Hood*, pp. 84–86.
11. Lloyd N. Jeffrey, *Thomas Hood* (New York: Twayne, 1972), p. 68.
12. *Selected Poems of Thomas Hood*, p. 272.
13. John Clubbe, *Victorian Forerunner* (Durham, NC: Duke University Press, 1968), p. 3.
14. *Ibid.*, p. 3.
15. *Ibid.*, p. 35.

Selected Bibliography

Primary Sources
Selected Poems of Thomas Hood. Ed. John Clubbe. Cambridge: Harvard University Press, 1970.
The Works of Thomas Hood, Vol. IV. Ed. Thomas Hood, Jr., and daughter, Frances Freeling Broderip. New York: 1970.

Secondary Sources
Clubbe, John. *Victorian Forerunner*. Durham, NC: Duke University Press, 1968.
Jeffrey, Lloyd N. *Thomas Hood*. New York: Twayne, 1972.
Jerrold, Walter. *Thomas Hood: His Life and Times*. New York: Greenwood Press, 1969.
Reid, J.C. *Thomas Hood*. London: Routledge & Kegan Paul, 1963.

Ross Brummer

Hook, Theodore Edward

Born: London, September 22, 1788
Education: Attended several schools including Harrow (1804–1805)
Marriage: Never married but had a common-law wife (unnamed in sources); five children
Died: London, August 24, 1841

Biography

Theodore Edward Hook was born in London on September 22, 1788. His father, James Hook, was a well-known musician; his mother, under the name Miss Madden, wrote a farce called *The Double Disguise*; and his older brother, James, wrote fiction and librettos.

Hook attended several schools, including Harrow; among his classmates was Lord Byron. Hook matriculated at Oxford but did not attend. Upon leaving school, he began to write melodramas and farces.

Hook loved to mix with the aristocracy. He was constantly invited to parties where he dazzled audiences with his musical skills and his wit. He was deft at improvising humorous songs on any topic the guests desired. Also a notorious prankster, his most famous prank was the Berner's Street Hoax in 1809, when he arranged for thousands of callers to come to the home of his unsuspecting victim.

Hook gave up playwriting when he received a high-paying appointment as Accountant-General and Treasurer of the island of Mauritius in 1812. However, he had to return to England to stand trial in 1818 when money was reported missing from the treasury in Mauritius.

He focused his attention on the Tory opposition to Caroline, consort to King George IV, while he awaited his trial. He satirized Caroline in the essay *Tentamen*. The periodicals *Arcadian* (1820) and *John Bull*, which Hook edited anonymously from 1820 to 1841, also savagely ridiculed Caroline.

Hook's abilities as a Treasurer were questionable, but, in all likelihood, he was not guilty of embezzlement in the Mauritius episode. Nevertheless, in 1821 he was held to be responsible for £12,000. He then moved to Somers Town and began a relationship with a woman who was to bear him five children. Eventually, he was removed to a debtor's prison in Shire Lane in 1823 where he remained until 1826, a stay which had a serious effect on his health.

He began writing fiction during his time at Shire Lane. Although his novels were generally quite popular, Hook could never get out of debt. When he died in London from a diseased liver on August 24, 1841, his family was left impoverished, and he was said to owe £30,000.

Literary Analysis

Hook's plays *Tekeli* (1806) and *The Fortress* (1807) were among the first melodramas produced in England. His most famous play, *Killing no Murder* (1809), a two-act farce, ran for thirty-five performances. The play proved to be controversial because of its ridicule of Methodists. As a result, it could not be performed until the objectionable lines were omitted. Hook, a fierce Conservative, simply distributed printed copies of the suppressed scene.

His literary reputation, however, lies with his fiction, not his plays. "His novels," as Myron F. Brightfield says, "are filled with minute descriptions of the manners, the things, the outer appearances of contemporary English life" (281). They document in particular the rituals of fashionable dining. Elliot Engel and Margaret F. King, in fact, feel that Hook's series of stories, *Sayings and Doings*, might just as easily have been named *Suppings and Dinings* (122).

The author's fiction achieved a remarkable level of popularity despite their slipshod construction. There is often little semblance of a plot, and the major characters generally lack depth. Still, Hook can create striking "humors" characters. Here, for example, is Mrs. Rodney from "Passion and Principle" (from the second series of *Sayings and Doings*, 1825):

> . . . a lady exemplary and domestic, and as methodical and mechanical in all her movements, as if she had been wound up at seven o'clock in the morning to go through certain evolutions until eleven o'clock in the evening. She was always at the breakfast-table to see the boys fairly served with their plank-like pieces of bread and butter, and jorums of milk. She always carved their dinners, during which ceremony she dressed herself in a peculiarly constructed apron with a bib and sleeves. In the due execution of this office she properly apportioned the fat and the lean, administered with care the lumps of preparatory pudding and produced ninety-two cuts from every shoul-

der of full-grown mutton which was sent to table. (Ch. 1)[1]

Despite his faults as a writer, Hook had a gift for anticipating what would appeal to his readers. He was, for instance, one of the earliest exponents of the "silver-fork novel" of the 1820s. Hook's first successful attempt at fiction was *Sayings and Doings* (1824). All of the stories in this collection illustrate a moral. The motto of "Danvers," for example, is "Too much of a good thing is good for nothing." In this story, a middle-class lawyer comes into a fortune, but misfortune plagues him. The story displays Hook's Conservative belief that people should not aspire above their station. He published two further series of *Sayings and Doings* in 1825 and 1828. Perhaps the best story is "Gervase Skinner," about a man who is ruined by his miserliness, which is reflected in the motto "Penny wise and pound foolish."

Hook also employed his knowledge of the aristocracy in his novels *Maxwell* (1830) and *The Parson's Daughter* (1833) and the stories in *Love and Pride* (1833). However, he saw that the interest in the fashionable novel had peaked. Therefore, his works after 1833 began to utilize farce more heavily, and his emphasis shifted from aristocratic to middle-class characters, whom he generally cast in an unfavorable light.

Gilbert Gurney (1836) is considered his best work. The plot revolves around a protagonist who leaves his study of law to pursue a career in the theater. Gurney's assessment of himself certainly applies to Hook: "any thing that could be done in a hurry, and with little trouble, I did tolerably well—but application I had not" (ch. 1). The book is a string of anecdotes, many of which are autobiographical. Hook relates stories about such real-life figures as Byron and playwright Richard Sheridan. In one scene, for example, Sheridan loses a play sent to him for examination. Sheridan apologizes and then shows the aspiring playwright a drawer stuffed with plays sent to him. He offers the man any three plays that he has been sent as consolation for the lost piece.

Hook never could recapture the popularity of *Gilbert Gurney*. The poorly written sequel, *Gurney Married* (1838), was initially published (as was *Gilbert Gurney*) in the *New Monthly Magazine*, which Hook edited from 1837 to 1841. *Jack Brag* (1837), like "Danvers," is a condemnation of the quest for a higher social status. Hook was working on

Peregrine Bunce (1842) when he died in 1841; the novel was completed by another hand. In his final years, ever in need of money, he allowed himself to be listed as editor to several books in which he probably had little or no part.

Summary

As R.H. Dalton Barham states, "Any estimate of the powers of Theodore Hook, drawn from the writings alone, must be fatally inadequate and erroneous" (2:250). To convey Hook's charm and ability in conversation to an audience that is unfamiliar with him is nearly impossible. All we have left to evaluate him by are his published works, which have serious flaws. He had a sharp wit and could tell a lively story, but he had an extremely limited range.

Almost forgotten today, his works are either out of print or available only in expensive reprint editions. Few libraries contain his books. Nonetheless, Hook was an important figure in his day. He had an intimate knowledge of fashionable London, and his combination of humor and realism influenced Charles Dickens, William Makepeace Thackeray, and Anthony Trollope. Samuel Taylor Coleridge claimed that Hook was "as true a genius as Dante" (quoted in Garnett 14:1170). Nevertheless, Hook, if he is now known at all, is remembered in portraits by other writers, such as Thackeray's unflattering view of him as Mr. Wagg of *Pendennis* and Benjamin D'Israeli's kinder depiction, Lucian Gay in *Coningsby*. Gay, a man who wasted his talent, seems to mirror Hook most.

Notes

1. Since there are several editions of many of Hook's works, I have used chapter rather than page numbers.

Selected Bibliography

Primary Sources

Plays
The Soldier's Return; or What Can Beauty Do? A Comic Opera in Two Acts. London: Longman, Hurst, Rees, and Orme, 1805.
Tekeli; or, The Siege of Montgatz: A Melodrama in Three Acts. London: C. and R. Baldwin, 1806. An adaptation of Pixerecourt's *Tekeli: ou, Le Siege de Montgatz.*
Killing no Murder: A Farce, in Two Acts. London: Printed by W. Flint for S. Tipper, 1809.
Exchange no Robbery; or, the Diamond Ring: A Comedy in Three Acts. London: W. Wright, 1820.

Prose
The Man of Sorrow, a Novel, as Alfred Allendale. 3 vols. London: Tipper, 1808; reissued as *Ned Musgrave; or, the Most Unfortunate Man in the World.* 1 vol. London: 1842.
Tentamen; or, An Essay Towards the History of Whittington, Some Time Lord Mayor of London, as Vicesimus Blinkinsop. London: Wright, 1820.
Sayings and Doings: A Series of Sketches from Life. 3 vols. London: Colburn, 1824.
Sayings and Doings: or, Sketches from Life. 3 vols. London: Colburn, 1825. Second Series.
Sayings and Doings: or, Sketches from Life. 3 vols. London: Colburn, 1828. Third Series.
Maxwell. 3 vols. London: Colburn and Bentley, 1830.
The Parson's Daughter. 3 vols. London: Bentley, 1833.
Love and Pride. 3 vols. London: Whittaker, 1833. Also published under the title *The Widow and the Marquess; or, Love and Pride.* 1 vol. London: Bentley, 1842.
Gilbert Gurney. 3 vols. London: Whittaker, 1836. In briefer form in the *New Monthly Magazine,* 1834–1835.
Jack Brag. 3 vols. London: Bentley, 1837.
Gurney Married: a Sequel to Gilbert Gurney. 3 vols. London: Colburn, 1838. By installments in the *New Monthly Magazine,* 1837–1838, under the title *The Gurney Papers.*
Precepts and Practice. 3 vols. London: Colburn, 1840. A collection of pieces first published in the *New Monthly Magazine.*
Peregrine Bunce: or, Settled at Last. A Novel. 3 vols. London: Bentley, 1842. Completed by another author.

Selected Play Productions
The Soldier's Return; or, What Can Beauty Do?, with overture and music by James Hook. London, Drury Lane Theatre, April 23, 1805.

Tekeli: or, The Siege of Montgatz, with music by James Hook, London, Drury Lane Theatre, November 24, 1806.

The Fortress, with music by James Hook, London, Haymarket Theatre, July 16, 1807.

Killing no Murder, with music by James Hook. London, Haymarket Theatre, August 21, 1809.

Secondary Sources

Baker, Ernest A. *The History of the English Novel*. London: Witherby, 1936. Vol. 7, pp. 206–21. Appreciative overview of the novels.

Barham, R.H. Dalton. *The Life and Remains of Theodore Edward Hook*. 2 vols. London: Bentley, 1849. Source for most of the biographical material on Hook.

Brightfield, Myron F. *Theodore Hook and His Novels*. Cambridge: Harvard University Press, 1928. The best study of Hook.

Engel, Elliot, and Margaret F. King. *The Victorian Novel before Victoria: British Fiction during the Reign of William IV, 1830–37*. New York: St. Martin's Press, 1984, pp. 119–28. Hook's comic fiction written during William's reign.

Garnett, Richard. "Hook, Theodore Edward." *The Dictionary of National Biography*. Ed. Sir Leslie Stephen. 21 vols. London: Oxford University Press, 1921–1922.

[Lockhart, John Gibson]. "Peregrine Bunce." *Quarterly Review*, 72 (May 1843): 53–108. Early biographical sketch.

Parascandola, Louis J. "Theodore Hook." *Dictionary of Literary Biography*. Vol. 116, pp. 151–56.

Schweitzer, Cora May. "Theodore Hook: Novelist of Manners." Ph.D. dissertation. Texas Christian University, 1967. Discusses influence of comedy of manners on Hook's works.

Louis J. Parascandola

Hope, Anthony

Born: Clapton, London, February 9, 1863

Education: Marlborough and Balliol College, Oxford. Literae Humaniores, 1885

Marriage: Elizabeth Somerville, July 1, 1903; three children

Died: Walton-on-the-Hill, Surrey, July 8, 1933

Biography

Sir Anthony Hope Hawkins, born in London on February 9, 1863, was the younger son of the Reverend Edwards Comerford Hawkins and his wife, Jane Isabella Grahame. His first cousin on his mother's side was the novelist Kenneth Grahame, author of the masterpiece of children's fantasy, *The Wind in the Willows*. Hope began his education under the tutelage of his father, who was headmaster at the St. John's Foundation School for the Sons of Poor Clergy. He attended Marlborough from 1876 to 1880, and then was admitted to Balliol College, Oxford. At Oxford he attained a first class in literae humaniores in 1885 and became president of the Oxford Union in 1886.

At the instigation of his father, Hope prepared at university for a career in the law or politics. Subsequently, in 1887, he was called to the bar by the Middle Temple and began a promising law career. In 1892, he stood for Parliament unsuccessfully as a Liberal in a traditionally conservative borough. While beginning to make his mark in law and politics, Hope also pursued his literary inclinations. His first novel, *A Man of Mark*, was privately published in 1890, followed by *Father Stafford* in 1891, *Mr. Witt's Widow* in 1892, *Sport Royal* in 1893, and *The God in the Car* in 1894. While none of his early novels achieved commercial success, he was acknowledged by reviewers as a writer with some promise.

In April 1894, his novel *The Prisoner of Zenda* was published to both critical acclaim and tremendous commercial success. *The Dolly Dialogues*, a collection of delicately witty dialogues reflecting the concerns of the London social scene, followed later in the same year. The fame and financial rewards brought by two popular successes in the course of a few months prompted Hope to give up his legal clients and embark on a literary career.

Although the writer would publish prolifically and profitably for over two decades, he remained typed by the book-buying public as the author of *The Prisoner of Zenda*. The formula for success that he had found in *The Prisoner of Zenda*—a debonair English gentleman reacting with grace and honor when swept into the political turmoil of a fictionalized Balkan kingdom—was easily repeated in *The Heart of Princess Osra* (1896), *Phroso* (1897), *Rupert of Hentzau*, a sequel to the original novel (1898), and *Sophy of Kravonia* (1906). The tremendous popularity of these stories and the continuing success of *The Prisoner of Zenda* in novel, stage-play, and film-play form overshadowed the rest of Hope's literary efforts. Interestingly, the author rated the now long-forgotten *The King's Mirror* (1899) and *Double Harness* (1904) as his best novels.

On July 1, 1903, Hope married Elizabeth Somerville Sheldon, the daughter of an American businessman, whom he first met while in New York on a trip attempting to arrange for an American production of his play *The Adventure of Lady Ursula* (1898). Marriage finally prompted Hope to move out of his father's house, where he had lived for the seventeen years since leaving Oxford. The couple had three children, two sons and a daughter.

With the outbreak of World War I, he joined the Editorial and Public Branch Department (a forerunner of the Ministry of Information) and wrote propaganda pamphlets explaining the position of Britain and its allies. He was knighted for his services in 1918.

The post-war period found Hope largely in semiretirement. His productive period as a novelist ended with the onset of the war. He published a modest volume of reminiscences, *Memories and Notes*, in 1927. He died at his country house, Heath Farm in Surrey, on July 8, 1933.

Literary Analysis

Hope's reputation as humorist stems almost entirely from *The Dolly Dialogues*. The dialogues, which originally appeared in the *Westminster Gazette*, are purportedly the small talk of Lady Mickleham and Mr. Samuel Carter who, in an often elliptical and seemingly trivial manner, comment on the concerns of the London social scene. The dialogues are, in the main, studies of the fine arts of flirtation as practiced in the salons of the upper-class. Lady Mickleham—Dolly to her friends—is a composite sketch of the flirtatious society lady, alternately fishing for a compliment and fending off its import:

"You know, Mr. Carter, that before I was married—oh, how long ago it seems!"

"Not at all"

"Don't interrupt. That before I was married I had several—that is to say, several—well, several—"

"Start quite afresh," I suggested encouragingly.

"Well, then several men were silly enough to think themselves—you know."

"No one better," I cheerfully assented.

"Oh, if you won't be sensible! Well, you see, many of them are Archie's friends as well as mine; and of course, they've been to call."

"It is but good manners," said I.

"One of them waited to be sent for though."

"Leave that fellow out," said I. (*The Dolly Dialogues*, 53)

And while Dolly might wonder about the propriety of receiving in her salon, after marriage, men who were her suitors, she is also quite capable of thinking it bourgeois to go to the theater with her husband, when another gentleman was available:

"Bourgeois," I observed, "is an epithet which the riff-raff apply to what is respectable, and the aristocracy to what is decent."

"But it's not a nice thing to be, all the same," said Dolly, who is impervious to the most penetrating remark.

"You're in no danger of it," I hastened to assure her.

"How should you describe me then?" she asked, leaning forward, with a smile.

"I should describe you, Lady Mickleham," I replied discreetly, "as being a little lower than the angels."

Dolly's smile was almost a laugh as she asked:

"How much lower, please, Mr Carter?"

"Just by the depth of your dimples," said I thoughtlessly.

Dolly became immensely grave. (*The Dolly Dialogues*, 78–79)

During the course of their original serial publication, *The Dolly Dialogues* created enough of a stir to cause them to be parodied in *Punch*. On the surface the dialogues appear quite trifling, but as in Oscar Wilde's "trivial comedy for serious people," *The Importance of Being Earnest* (1895), there is much more of import to be found under the superficial quality of the banter. While the delicate wit of Mr. Carter's conversations with Lady Mickleham does not have the same epigrammatic quality of the dialogue of Lady Bracknell, Gwendolen Fairfax, and Ernest Worthing, it does similarly expose essential truths about the mores of late-Victorian society.

Although Hope's novels are not overtly comic, there is a characteristic humor to be found in his prose, especially in novels written in the same vein as *The Prisoner of Zenda*. That novel was praised by reviewers for its "snap and humor," a quality derived from the characterization of the main character—a suave, nonchalant, and urbane English gentleman. The witty irreverence of the hero in the opening passage of *The Prisoner of Zenda* is typical in Hope's modern adventure-romance novels:

> "I wonder when in the world you're going to do anything, Rudolf?" said my brother's wife.
>
> "My dear Rose," I answered laying down my egg-spoon, "why in the world should I do anything? My position is a comfortable one. I have an income nearly sufficient for my wants (no one's income is ever quite sufficient, you know). I enjoy an enviable social position: I am brother to Lord Burlesdon, and brother-in-law to that most charming lady his countess. Behold, it is enough!"
>
> "You are nine-and twenty," she observed, "and you've done nothing but—"
>
> "Knock about? It is true. Our family doesn't need to do things."
>
> This remark of mine rather annoyed Rose. (*The Prisoner of Zenda*, 1)

The insouciant tone that Hope gives to his hero, Rudolf Rassendyl, is similar to that employed by Wilde in *The Importance of Being Ernest* on the same subject when Lady Bracknell responds to Jack Worthing's admission that he did, indeed, smoke: "I am glad to hear it. A man should always have an occupation of some kind." The flippancy and iconoclasm of Hope's humor is also related to that found in the New Humor of the 1890s. Interestingly, while critics disapproved of the flippancy and iconoclasm in the characteristically lower- and middle-class subject matter of what was labeled New Humor, the same tone applied to upper-class characters and situations was generally well-received.

Summary
Anthony Hope is a relatively minor figure in British humor, notable only for his one immensely popular collection of witty and funny pieces, *The Dolly Dialogues*. Although *The Dolly Dialogues* lacks the timeless quality of acknowledged comic masterpieces, it does provide an interesting and useful insight into the social mores of fashionable late-Victorian scene. In his modern adventure-romances, Hope helped create the enduring stock character of literature, stage, and film of the debonaire English gentleman responding with grace and honor under pressure.

Selected Bibliography
Primary Sources
The Dolly Dialogues. London: James Nesbitt, 1894.
The Prisoner of Zenda. Bristol: J.W. Arrowsmith, 1894.
Comedies of Courtship. New York: Scribner, 1896.
Simon Dale. New York: F.A. Stokes, 1897.
Rupert of Hentzau. New York: Henry Holt, 1898.
The Adventure of Lady Ursula. New York: R.H. Russell, 1898.
The King's Mirror. London: Methuen, 1899.
The Great Miss Driver. New York: McClure, 1908.
Second String. New York: Doubleday and Page, 1910.
Mrs. Maxon Protests. New York and London: Harper and Brothers, 1911.
Memories and Notes. Garden City, NY: Doubleday, Doran, 1928.

Secondary Source
Mallet, Sir Charles Edward. *Anthony Hope and his books; being the authorised life*

of Sir Anthony Hope Hawkins. Port Washington, NY: Kennikat Press, 1968. Rpt. of 1935 ed.

Peter C. Hall

Housman, A[lfred] E[dward]

Born: Fockbury, Worcestershire, March 26, 1859

Education: Bromsgrove School, 1870–1877; St. John's College, Oxford University, 1877–1881

Died: Cambridge, April 30, 1936

Biography

The oldest child of solicitor Edward Housman and his first wife, Sarah Jane Williams, Alfred Edward Housman was born at Valley House, Fockbury, in Worcestershire, on March 26, 1859. Mrs. Housman died when Alfred was twelve, and Edward then married his cousin, Lucy Housman, who became a great influence in Alfred's life. Alfred's excellent training at the Bromsgrove School (1870–1877) motivated his entrance into St. John's College, Oxford, in 1877, where he trained in classics. He roomed with Alfred Pollard and Moses Jackson during his Oxford years, fell hopelessly in love with the latter, and continued to cherish his memory. Jackson never returned Housman's love; instead he married in 1889, then worked in India and Canada for many years.

Although Housman was a brilliant student, apparently his pent-up feelings toward Jackson combined with an arrogance toward studies and the sudden news of his father's serious illness to result in his failing final examinations in 1881, when he left Oxford without taking a degree. He then worked in London in the Patent Office, reading during his spare time at the British Museum and beginning a series of publications in classical journals. In the middle 1890s, he also composed the poems that appeared in *A Shropshire Lad* and many of those later collected in *Last Poems* (1922). Housman's reputation as a classical scholar led to his appointment as Professor of Latin at University College, London, in 1892, where he remained until 1911. His publications and reputation then brought about his appointment as Professor of Latin at Cambridge. He was soon thereafter named Kennedy Professor of Latin, a post he held until his death on April 30, 1936.

Throughout his life, A.E. Housman impressed people in sharply different ways. The creator of some of the most poignant lyrics in English poetry constituted one side of his public image. On the other, Professor Housman's mien conveyed little of the poet or of one who obtained any emotional thrill from the Greek or Latin works in which he engaged for many years. In all walks of life Housman maintained a staunch reserve, cultivated, no doubt, because he was ambivalent about human nature in general and his sexual leanings in particular during an era of great intolerance. Often in their adult lives his own family did not know the details of his everyday activities. Housman was also rather shy, but that shyness frequently suggested an impersonal remoteness in his personality. Nonetheless, those few who braved his apparent standoffishness found him cordial. He was reasonably companionable in the university dining hall, where his expertise in food and wine made him a great favorite. His perceptions of disparities between human aspirations and the obstacles to fulfilling most of them contribute to his humor, which often veers from a wistful wryness to savage irony and acrid wit.

The initial appearance of *A Shropshire Lad* in early 1896 won no immediate accolades for the poet, but Grant Richards's reissue of the volume in late 1898 quickly drew admiration from devotees of poetry. What was then considered the pessimism, the anti-Victorianism, the intense pleasure in Nature, and the exquisite verse techniques made the book popular. Requests for more poems from this author went unsatisfied for many years, during which time his academic career and scholarly publications came to the fore. In 1922, he permitted Richards to announce another collective volume, significantly entitled *Last Poems*, which appeared in October. Many of the pieces in this book had been written much earlier, some of them contemporary with what had appeared in *A Shropshire Lad*, as indicated by similarities in subject matter and verse forms.

Housman's topic for the annual Leslie Stephen Lecture at Cambridge (May 9, 1933), "The Name and Nature of Poetry," occasioned lively debate among lovers of poetry and critics, many of whom considered that the emphasis on emotional inspiration was reactionary. The lecture was published as *The Name and Nature of Poetry* the same year. Housman later directed that his brother, Laurence, as his literary executor, might, if he wished, bring out more of the unpublished poems as long as they matched the quality of what the poet himself had overseen. *More Poems* (1936) and *Additional Poems* (1937) are, however, more uneven than their creator might have wished. Laurence's failure to destroy the literary manuscripts also initiated controversies over privacy and the poet's intents that have long enlivened the reading about his brother.

Literary Analysis

Housman seems to have written verse from a very early age. Several extant works are deliberately comic, types of light verse and parody, including, for example, "The shades of night were falling fast," "Fragment of a Greek Tragedy," "Purple William or, The Liar's Doom," and a lampooning of Salvation Army hymns, all conveniently available in either Laurence Housman's *My Brother, A.E. Housman* (1937) or Christopher Ricks's *A.E. Housman: Collected Poems and Selected Prose* (1989). Others have apparently not seen print, mostly because Housman himself destroyed them or else forbade publication. He wrote such nonsense verse during much of his life and thus takes a place with such late nineteenth-century poets as Edward Lear, "Lewis Carroll" (C.L. Dodgson), C.S. Calverley, and W.S. Gilbert, who turned out humorous verse and were adept parodists.

All of Housman's ventures are cast into simple language and structures, revealing a playful intention. The author's razor wit sounds repeatedly through his writings on classical subjects, too, mainly as it is directed to the deficiencies in other scholars' work. He jotted savage remarks in his notebooks, storing them to bring out on appropriate occasions for demolishing shoddy scholarship;[1] his intent was to attack without quarter. Present-day readers are more familiar with his poetry.

The poems that evince Housman's genuine artistry often contain comic elements of far greater subtleties, even if in passages they seem to sound a playful note. *A Shropshire Lad*, the volume that brought him fame, contains humor in various keys, as do subsequent collections of his verse, although the later collections lack the unification found in the first book. Unmistakable ironies sound from first to last among the sixty-three poems published in *A Shropshire Lad*. Their recurrence furnishes a unifying element in this book, one more evident, perhaps, than found in *Last Poems*. The "lad's" maturing awareness of his place in the world, his notions about military life, as it signally affects the lives of many young persons, his outlook on love, and his perceptions about other conditions which life imposes on us combine to effect a plausible structuring principle. Thus, his vision encompasses oscillations between comic and tragic aspects of life. One wonders, for instance, what Queen Victoria's impression of the opening poem, which alludes to her Golden Jubilee bonfires, might have been, if she had read it. The ironic references to those soldiers who have died in efforts to maintain the British empire might not have been altogether pleasing in her ears.

To take another example, in medium and measure No. IV, "Reveille," suggests a parody of the Christian hymn, "Hark, the Voice of Jesus Crying," which dates from 1868 and therefore could have been familiar to Housman. His quasi-hymn framing of a secular circumstance (military signaling and the thoughts it calls up) is ironic. Considering that many of Housman's poems are cast in ballad forms, which are also forerunners of hymnody in English, and that balladry leans to thematic irony, such an inversion is entirely plausible.[2]

Moving from a quasi-sacred into a wholly worldly context, No. V, in which Housman's typically understated poetic humor is apparent, is the dramatization of an encounter between a would-be seducer and his mistress. She evades his ever more pressing urges that she satisfy his passion. Her offhanded responses to his entreaties, in what amount to refrain conclusions for each stanza, indicate her objectivity regarding their affair, and her ultimate "Good-bye, young man, good-bye" rounds off the poem with an amusing fillip, just as it leaves the lad isolated from human mutuality, as is the case throughout the book.

A sequence incorporating effects of love and lust follows, as is plausible in a youth's experimenting with the freedoms that life apparently holds out, culminating in amusing fashion in No. XVIII. The lover-lad has now ceased to maintain the good behavior that he displayed to impress his mistress, is once again free, and seems to be "quite myself" in the estimate of his acquaintances. The brevity of love recurs thematically in No. XXV, though, as the speaker relates how his inamorata's former lover, Fred, is now dead, leaving him to triumph in Rose's affections. This poem numbers among those in which the rhyme-scheme should alert us as to what is coming, notably in the echoing of "Fred" with "dead," as if to prepare us for the irony in the concluding revelation.

A like technique enhances No. LVI, another of Housman's soldier poems. The speaker ticks off all of the negative possibilities in serving in the military, finally telling his listening comrade: "Stand and fight and see your slain, / And take the bullet in your brain." One is left to ponder whether the deadly bullet is literal or if the emotional impact from witnessing carnage is likened to a shot in the head. The rhymes in poems like these bear kinship with those in Housman's far lighter verse.

Two other poems also subtly revolve around the thoughts and inquiries of one destined to die (XXVI) or of one already dead (XXVII). In both, an aura of the sexual side of relationships is highlighted, as if to press close the implications of "dying" in literal and figurative senses. Number XXVI, especially, sounds a wry note as the living speaker, unavoidably led to answer as he must, says that the dead man's girlfriend is happy, and reveals that "I lie as lads would choose; / I cheer a dead man's sweetheart, / Never ask me whose." Adroitly and amusingly these words stop the questioning and bring the poem to a resounding close.

Equally viable comic undercurrents may be found in one of Housman's most frequently anthologized pieces from *A Shropshire Lad*, No. IX, "The chestnut casts his flambeaux. . . ."[3] Two young men sit drinking while one of them laments at first that life has not substantially rewarded them. The clouds and storm may represent literal unpromising weather and the emotional tempests that one encounters as a matter of course in life. The phlegmatic attitude of the speaker is punctuated in the first, fifth, and seventh (closing) stanzas by his attention to drinking as a sop to his emotional sores. His exhortations to his companion to drink and likewise forget life's severities are amusing in that they are the offhanded, not entirely coherent murmurings of an intoxicated speaker. The listener appears not to be so attentive to his own drinking or to passing the can as the speaker, and so occasionally he must be prompted in regard to manners and morals—and the shifts from exterior phenomena to inner concerns mirror the movement in the poem overall from gorgeous springtime growth to emotional maturing. The uncharacteristic exaggeration in the adjuration to "Shoulder the sky, my lad, and drink your ale" deftly expresses the speaker's intent in that it appeals to his hearer's potential strength, albeit in terms delightfully ambiguous as to physical or psychological reserves.

A student of language as sensitive as Housman could not help perceiving possibilities for diction that runs to innuendo, creating exquisite wordplay, as is evident in No. IX of *A Shropshire Lad*. Meditating about a comrade's approaching execution, the speaker muses: "And Naked to the hangman's noose / The morning clocks will ring / A neck God made for other use." Such fondness for wordplay occurs, too, in *Last Poems*, No. VI. The voice is that of a dead soldier contemplating the responses of those who see the slain bodies in the field or of those who witness funeral ceremonies for these dead. Among the latter, "The girls will stand watching them [the plumes] wave, / And eyeing my comrades and saying / *Oh who would not sleep with the brave?*" The last line serves as a kind of refrain after appearing as line two, whence it intensifies in ironic implications as it echoes from the initial sober querying of the patriot on to the girls' comments in which a Freudian slip betraying sexual impulses may be covertly placed. Numbers XIV and XVI in *Last Poems* also convey such sexual hints, particularly the latter. A young man scorned by the girl he loves awakens to a beautiful morning. A line that seems usual enough—"Half the night he longed to die"—may insinuate his urgent sexual desires or fantasies, however, especially since the stanza, after the comment that there are daytime pleasures to distract him, concludes "Ere he longs to die again," and since the final stanza reveals that during the past night the scornful girl has been sleeping with someone else.

Multiple incongruities, which are after all the foundation for humor, seem to coalesce in the penultimate poem in *A Shropshire Lad*, No. LXII, "Terence, this is stupid stuff," one often quoted and interpreted among Housman's devotees. Terence, the presumed poet who has created the preceding poems, is taunted by a bluff, sensually oriented friend about the depressing elements in his works. The friend suggests that Terence might find relief, and maybe produce more palatable poetry, were he to indulge in worldly pleasures. Terence responds that dancing and drinking may temporarily lull one's perceptions about the bleakness in the world ("malt does more than Milton can / To justify God's ways to man"), as he himself knows from experience, but that his verses express his own preparations to confront the saddening events that life brings. He concludes with recounting the story of King Mithridates, who regularly ingested poison to forestall being assassinated by poisoners, as was the popular custom of those in the East who would effect a new government. In other words, Terence answers a would-be humorist with an astringent irony.

Summary

A.E. Housman certainly does not rank as a wholeheartedly genial humorist, although many of his poems have comic, if often savagely comic, touches, and he elsewhere displays mirthful propensities. Most commentators on his verse have overlooked humor for other features of more serious import, and it was only after Housman's death that substantial allusions to his comic writings appeared in critical interpretations, chiefly because Housman himself minimized and suppressed his endeavors in comedy, instructing his brother Laurence not to foreground his humorous poems. The humor in Housman's poems is not heavy-handed or obvious, as John Bayley recently noted.[4] Rather, its surprise nature gives it strength. It contributes to the unity in *A Shropshire Lad*, and it provides comic relief to his other poetic works.

Notes

1. Norman Page, *A.E. Housman: A Critical Biography* (London: Macmillan, and New York: Schocken Books, 1983), pp. 143–47.
2. Page, p. 148, notes Housman's comic handling of hymn materials.
3. John Bayley comments on mingling of the "weighty and deadpan" throughout the poem in *Housman's Poems* (Oxford: Clarendon, 1992), p. 15.
4. *Ibid.*, pp. 138–39.

Selected Bibliography

Primary Sources

Books: Verse, Poetics, Letters
A Shropshire Lad. London: Kegan Paul & Trench, 1896; New York: John Lane, 1897.
A Shropshire Lad. London: Grant Richards, 1898.
Last Poems. London: Grant Richards, and New York: Henry Holt, 1922.
The Name and Nature of Poetry. Cambridge: Cambridge University Press, and New York: Macmillan, 1933.
More Poems. London: Jonathan Cape, and New York: Knopf, 1936.
Additional Poems. London: Jonathan Cape, 1937; New York: Charles Scribner's Sons, 1938.
The Letters of A.E. Housman. Ed. Henry Maas. London: Rupert Hart-Davis; Cambridge, MA: Harvard University Press, 1971. The most comprehensive collection to date, although many letters do not appear. Housman's wry humor often surfaces in these communications.

Books: Classical Scholarship
Manilius Astronomica. London: Grant Richards, 1903–1930.
Juvenalis Saturae. London: Grant Richards, 1905; 2nd ed. Cambridge: Cambridge University Press, 1931.
Lucani Bellum Civile. Oxford: Basil H. Blackwell; Cambridge, MA: Harvard University Press, 1926.
Platt, Arthur. *Nine Essays*, pref. A.E. Housman. Cambridge: Cambridge University Press, 1927.

Secondary Sources

Biographies
Page, Norman. *A.E. Housman: A Critical Biography*. London: Macmillan, and New York: Schocken Books, 1983. The best biography, with critical assessments of the poems.

Books and Articles
Bayley, John. *Housman's Poems*. Oxford: Clarendon, 1992. A survey of the entire Housman poetic canon, showing his development out of Romanticism and assessing his themes and techniques.
Fisher, Benjamin Franklin IV. "A.E. Housman." In *Research Guide to Biography and Criticism*. Ed. Walton Beacham. Washington, D.C.: Research Publishing, 1985, pp. 590–93. Cites and annotates essential resources for Housman studies.
Haber, Tom Burns. *A.E. Housman*. New York: Twayne, 1967. Synthesizes many of Housman's ideas, evaluates his methods, and provides bibliographical aids. A good introduction.
Leggett, B.J. *Housman's Land of Lost Content: A Critical Study of "A Shropshire Lad."* Knoxville: University of Tennessee

H

Press, 1970. Leggett posits a loose unity, centralized in lost Eden motifs, in Housman's first book of verse.

———. *The Poetic Art of A.E. Housman: Theory and Practice*. Lincoln: University of Nebraska Press, 1978. Housman's poetic practices related to ideas set forth in *The Name and Nature of Poetry*. Good on the later poems, and on links between Housman and T.S. Eliot.

Benjamin F. Fisher IV

Howleglas

Born: Kneitlingen, Braunschweig, early 1300s
Died: 1350

Biography

The English word *Howle-glas*, or "Owl-Mirror," is an attempt to translate the name Dyl Uleynspeygel or Till Eulenspiegel, given to the famous rogue/trickster/fool hero of a collection of humorous German tales that spread throughout Europe in the first decades of the sixteenth century. *Howleglas*, the earliest extant English translation, appears to have been printed in Antwerp around 1509. To appreciate the importance of Howleglas, we must first consider Eulenspiegel.

Before the printing of the stories, the character of Till Eulenspiegel, or something analogous, seems to have existed in Northern European folklore for about two centuries; this figure may have been based on (or confused with) the real life of an idiot savant who lived in Braunschweig in the 1300s. The tales certainly provide a biography. In them Eulenspiegel is born sometime in the early 1300s in the village of Kneitlingen. His father's name is Claus Eulenspiegel, and his mother's is Anna Wibeken ("Nicolas Howleglas and Wipeke" in the English); after a wandering life of roguery and mischief, he dies and is buried in Mölln in 1350. And, indeed, one still can find a gravestone bearing Eulenspiegel's effigy.

In 1591, the English traveler Fynes Moryson wrote of visiting the town of Millen [Mölln], "where a famous Jester Oulenspiegel (whom we call Owly-glasse) hath a Monument erected; he died in the yeer 1350. . . . The Townes-men yeerly keepe a feaste for his memory, and yet shew the apparell he was wont to weare." Clearly, by 1591 Eulenspiegel had become world-famous, enough of an attraction to merit a tourist trap. It is also interesting that

Eulenspiegel had become the subject of a yearly feast; this evolution resembles that of the ancient pagan celebrations of the calendar year. Part folk hero, part pagan religious survival, part reality—there are many sides to Eulenspiegel.

Literary Analysis

Till Eulenspiegel is one of the most important comic characters in all literature. In the form of Howleglas he made a crucial impression on the development of the "fool" character in the English Renaissance. Like the character himself, the name *Eulenspiegel* has several contradictory elements. The word "Eulenspiegel" does indeed mean "Owl-Mirror" in High German, and the owl and the mirror are his satiric insignia, but in lower German dialect the name actually means "Wipe-Ass." So Eulenspiegel/Howleglas is not only a mirror for the truth but also a mordant satirist and player of practical jokes on the entire human race.

His literary origins are quite mysterious. In the 1490s, a Low German version of the tale was collected and perhaps printed; in 1500, a second collection was printed in Middle High German. Both of these versions are now lost. The great edition was printed by Johannes Grieninger of Strassburg in 1515. The teller of the tales calls himself simply "N.," and, judging from his dialect, came from the Braunschweig area of Germany (the same area that Eulenspiegel calls home).

About a third of the ninety-five tales are based on other sources: the tales of Marcolphus (a jester at the court of Solomon); German comic characters such as Father Amis and Father vom Kalenberg; Gonella, an Italian fool figure; the jests of the Italian humanist Poggio Bracciolini; and other Italian tales. But, amazingly, the rest seem to be original. Somehow, somewhere, someone had the idea of organizing all of these stories around a central character.

Who was "N."? Recent research by Peter Honegger and others makes a convincing case for Hermann Bote, who probably wrote a version in High German around 1511. (Bote's native tongue was Low German, explaining the linguistic oddities in the original *Eulenspiegel*.) If it was Bote, he created one of the first great masterpieces of early modern European popular culture. Eulenspiegel became popular throughout Europe; in addition to the 1509 English edition, Eulenspiegel volumes had reached the Netherlands by 1530, France by 1532, Poland by 1566, and Denmark by 1571—and many German editions have been printed from the sixteenth century up to the present.

As for the tales of Howleglas themselves, they contain the adventures of a wandering man who appears to be tirelessly idiotic—except for the fact that he always manages to outwit his social and intellectual superiors. It is this ambiguity—is he an idiot or a sly genius?—that gives Howleglas his special power to create mayhem.

His main comic technique is his penchant for practical jokes that show their targets up as fools. Howleglas persuades a priest to tell him what he heard in confession, then demands the priest's horse in return for staying silent. At times these practical jokes become quite brutal—as in the tale in which Howleglas pays back a nasty innkeeper by flaying her dog and presenting her its skin. In one tale, Howleglas convinces everyone in the town of Mayborough [Magdeburg] that he is about to fly off the top of the town hall. He flaps his arms, and the entire town rushes to see him. When they have gathered, he jeers at them ("a hole town ful" of fools) for having believed him in the first place. The townspeople grant him his point: "Than departed the folke from thence, some blaming him & some laughing, saying: he is a shrewed fole for he telleth us the truth." Howleglas is not exempt from the punishment: he gets his share of kicks, whippings, and tricks, but he also takes it out on everyone, from bakers and innkeepers to the king of Denmark.

A second comic technique is that of taking a turn of phrase, a command, or a word absolutely literally. Because his opponents can never tell whether he is shrewd or merely thick, Howleglas retains a certain authority over the near-mystical disaster that ensues as he takes words at face-value. In one excellent tale, Howleglas comes to an inn where he is informed that the visitors "eate for mony." Disregarding social hierarchy, Howleglas seats himself with the richest men at the table and stuffs himself until covered with sweat. When the hostess demands to be paid, Howleglas makes the same demand, saying that she told him he could eat for money: "Thynkest thou that I wyll eate so much and labour my selfe so sore as I dyd, not to be payd for mi labour?" In a single tale, Howleglas manages to upend both social structure and the entire relationship between labor and sustenance.

Howleglas is full of coarse, excremental humor—even though the English translator deleted some of the filthier tales. Still, many tales end with Howleglas or someone else covered in excrement. Howleglas dies only after he has defecated into his pillbox and all over his room and himself. This pattern, like so much in *Howleglas*, has roots in very ancient forms of comedy. Excrement is the ultimate degradation—yet, as a symbol of what everyone has in common, it recalls our humanity. Many of his readers saw the point, though some others found the tales "dirty." In England, along with widespread popularity, *Howleglas* gained a reputation as a book "to be censured of" and "hurtful to youth."

As these examples make clear, *Howleglas* often enters that transcendent realm of humor in which the very logic of social life is disassembled. That is probably why the character was so popular in the turbulent social context of the 1500s. *Howleglas* began the vogue for "fool" characters that lasted for the entire sixteenth century. Next to Howleglas/Eulenspiegel we can place Sebastianus Brant's *Ship of Fools* (1494), Erasmus's *Praise of Folly* (1509), the work of François Rabelais, English jestbooks such as *Cock Lorel's Boat* (1513?), and early English plays such as *Interlude of Youth* (1510) and *Hick Scorner* (1513). Many pamphlets and jestbooks throughout Europe (Martin Luther's *Liber Vagatorum*; the French pamphlet *La Vie Généreuse*; English pamphlets such as *The Twenty Orders of Callets or Drabs*, *The Twenty Orders of Fools*, Robert Copland's *Highway to the Spittal House*, and John Awdeley's *Fraternity of Vagabonds*) portrayed humanity as a fraternity of fools and sots.

Along with his close relation, the rogue, the fool was the most common figure in sixteenth-century literature. Several of the great comic characters of the Renaissance owe some allegiance to Eulenspiegel. Descendants include Panurge of Rabelais' *Gargantua and Pantagruel*; Lazarillo de Tormes and Guzmán de Alfarache of the Spanish picaresque; the later German characters of Grobius and Simplicissimus; Falstaff in Shakespearean comedy; and even Don Quixote.

Eulenspiegel's most immediate impact, however, was on the nature of European jokebooks. In the 1510s and 1520s, these joke-books are more or less chaotic collections. Thanks to Eulenspiegel, jokebooks increasingly became organized around central fictional characters, creating little proto-novelettes. There is even a German word for such a book: *Schwanken-biographie*, or "jest-biography." In England, jestbook heroes include John Scoggan, John Skelton, Dick Tarlton, the Cobbler of Canterbury, Long Meg of Westminster, Luke Hutton, and Gamaliel Ratsey. Thus, Eulenspiegel can be said to have contributed to the emergence of early modern English fiction.

What was it about the fool that spoke so eloquently to the Renaissance? The subversive voice of the underdog, for one thing: Howleglas always bests those who are supposed to be his superiors. He does so, as we have seen, through the ambiguity of his foolishness. His actions all have opposing meanings: he pollutes as he liberates, baffles as he teaches. Above all, Howleglas is a peasant who refuses the slavery of peasant life: "Howleglas would ever farewell and make good cheare but he would not worke." He simply refuses to hold by the normal ways of determining a person's identity. In this practice, he symbolizes the individual's primacy over the forces that seek to contain him. The Greeks had a special name for such a person: the *idiotes*, the "private person" or "person-to-himself." This is where we get our word *idiot*; Howleglas shows why idiocy sometimes "telleth the truth" more clearly than official wisdom.

Summary

Howleglas started as a little pamphlet published on an overseas press; more than a century later, writers were still quoting and stealing from it. Although Howleglas never proposes any alternatives to social inequity, his adventures clearly challenge society and its assumptions. In a century torn by social strife in every major country in Europe, a century in which a rising middle class and a restive lower class were muddling the old ways of perceiving society and humanity, the message of the fool, merry though it was, was trenchant indeed.

Selected Bibliography

Primary Sources
Oppenheimer, Paul. *A Pleasant Vintage of Till Eulenspiegel.* Middletown, CT: Wesleyan University Press, 1972. This is the only modern English translation of all the original Till Eulenspiegel tales. It is interesting to read the modern translation and compare it to the same tales in *Howleglas.* Oppenheimer also has a detailed and helpful background essay, as well as an introduction and notes.

Zall, P.M. *A Hundred Merry Tales and Other Jestbooks of the Fifteenth and Sixteenth Centuries.* Lincoln: University of Nebraska Press, 1963. This book contains the only modern-spelling edition of the original English *Howleglas.* It also contains several early English jestbooks that were contemporaneous with *Howleglas.* Along with Zall's helpful introductions, the reader can not only read *Howleglas* but can also compare it to its closest English equivalents.

Secondary Sources

Books
Coupe, W.A. *The Continental Renaissance.* Harmondsworth: Penguin, 1971. Contains an excellent chapter on German popular culture in the Renaissance by A.J. Krailshammer, in which the emergence of the Eulenspiegel stories is discussed, as well as their historical milieu.

Herford, C.H. "The Ulenspiegel Cycle." In *Studies in the Literary Relations of England and Germany.* Cambridge: Cambridge University Press, 1886, pp. 242–322. An excellent overview of the Eulenspiegel stories and their relationship to German and English literature of the sixteenth century.

Articles
Blamires, David. "Reflections on Recent 'Ulenspiegel' Studies." *Modern Language Review,* 77 (2): 351–60. This is a very useful overview of the best in contemporary scholarship about the origins and meanings of the Eulenspiegel stories.

John Timpane

Huxley, Aldous Leonard

Born: Godalming, Surrey, July 26, 1894
Education: Eton; Balliol College, Oxford University
Marriage: Maria Nys, July, 1919, one child; Laura Aschera, 1956
Died: Los Angeles, California, November 22, 1963

Biography

Aldous Huxley was born in Godalming, Surrey on July 26, 1894, a member of a family famous for intellectual achievement. His grandfather was Thomas Henry Huxley, Charles Darwin's champion; his father, Leonard Huxley, was a writer and editor; his older brother, the biologist Julian, was a Nobel laureate and a founder of UNESCO. Aldous's mother, Julia Arnold Huxley, was a granddaughter of Thomas Arnold of Rugby School, a niece of poet/critic Matthew Arnold, and sister of novelist Mrs. Humphrey Ward. Huxley attended Eton and then Balliol College of Oxford University. He married Maria Nys in July 1919, and the couple had one child.

Huxley's expectations of a brilliant career as a poet, essayist, and novelist seemed thwarted by the early appearance of an eye disorder that left him nearly blind for much of his life. But he adapted to his limitations and went on to become one of the leading literary figures of his generation. Best remembered for his satiric novels of ideas, he was also notable as an essayist with a wide-ranging and erudite style, as a screenwriter, and a short story writer. Only as a poet did Huxley fail to score a conspicuous success.

After immigrating to California in 1937 Huxley became interested in the utopian philosophy of Gerald Heard, Vedanta—a Western version of Hindu mysticism combined with psychedelic drugs. The satirical brilliance of his earlier work waned as he searched for solutions to man's perennial problems, and he was better known, perhaps, as a guru of utopian mysticism and the author of "Doors of Perception," a vivid and enthusiastic essay about his mescaline experience, than as a Bloomsbury wit.

After Maria's death, the author married Laura Aschera, an Italian violinist (1956). Following a long period of recurrent illness, Huxley died in Los Angeles, California on the day that John F. Kennedy was assassinated, November 22, 1963.

Literary Analysis

Huxley's early novels were in the satiric mode of Thomas Love Peacock: a gathering of challenging, articulate, and distinctive personalities is thrown together for a weekend at a country estate, and their drawing room dialogues are contrasted to their responses to the distractions and seductions of luxury and leisure. Huxley had met T.S. Eliot, Bertrand Russell, D.H. Lawrence, and other luminaries at Lady Ottoline Morrell's Garsington Manor House, so his revival of this form crackled with lively

modern personalities and liberated modern thought. His easy and good-humored erudition, his vividly sketched characters, and his detached, ironic handling of the intrigues of his plots allowed his readers to feel comfortably superior as they were exposed to disquieting contemporary, social, biological, and sexual theories.

In *Crome Yellow* (1921), his first novel, Huxley accompanies his somewhat inadequate poet protagonist on a weekend at the country estate, Crome. A visiting inspirational writer with the unlikely name Barbecue-Smith reveals that his literary success started when he began producing automatic writing in a trance state. We follow the local curate's ruminations on the failure of his prophecies of the Second Coming and are provided with an elaborate and mildly ludicrous tract that he wrote on the subject. We share Crome's current lord's research into the estate's history and hear tales of the misadventures of a former lord, only three feet tall, who gathered a menage of midgets about him and rode to terriers after rabbits. We hear modern young ladies discuss the dangers of sexual repression and watch the disappointments of our protagonist as his self-consciousness thwarts his opportunities with them. Huxley's narrative voice supplies no intrusive judgments as he moves from consciousness to consciousness and the comedy never strives to be funny, relying instead on the reader's sophisticated sensibility to relish its absurdities. Though his later comic works, *Antic Hay* (1923), *Those Barren Leaves* (1925), and *Point Counter Point* (1928), sometimes move out of the country house setting, the pattern of diverse characters discussing their theories of life, of sexual misadventures, of erudition and satire, remains the same.

The original sense of the word "humor" referred to the Hippocratian notion that temperaments were dominated by excesses of one or another of the four basic elemental substances, so that certain people embodied the results of such domination to an absurd extent. Henri Bergson suggested that we laugh at characters who are so dominated by a single trait that they have been dehumanized by "something mechanical engrafted on the living" as a way of freeing ourselves from such domination. Building on that tradition, Huxley referred to his novelistic technique as "musicalization" (illustrated in the title of his novel *Point Counter Point*). His subject is how each eccentric character in a discussion of ideas picks up on a chal-

H

lenging theme and distorts it through the narrowness and obsessiveness of his own solipsistic orientation, like instruments in an orchestra. So, at the same time that we are treated to a many-sided and well-informed discussion of some challenging idea, we are not made to feel stupid because each speaker reveals his own limitations. Sexual tension usually crackles below these dialogues, and as we move from consciousness to consciousness, we see the agony that invalidates the social masks of the participants. It is in the bedroom where the errors in judgments and the lapses in human perception that we have seen exposed in the salon are reduced to their final tragic and comic absurdity. Huxley creates a music with many, many distinct voices but no harmony.

With *Brave New World* (1932) the writer moves into the genre of science fiction. In his earlier novels some of the characters had contemplated H.G. Wells's "open conspiracy" of the scientifically educated to produce an ideal society. In this dystopic novel Huxley used the genre that Wells had invented to create a *reductio ad absurdum* of the scientific utopia— a scientific utopia in which compulsory euphoria and mandatory sex, hypnotic consumerism, and mindless conformity are imposed on the majority of the human race by a cabal of social engineers. The agonies of the novel's inadequate protagonist and his failure to find satisfactory alternatives darken the novel after the satiric comedy of the opening chapters, though its prose style and prophetic insight have made it the novelist's most widely read work.

His later works, with one exception, lack the cynical flippancy of the comic novels. *After Many a Summer Dies the Swan* (1939) is another science-fiction work in which social satire lightens the burden of serious philosophizing. *After Many a Summer*, set in a San Simeon–like millionaire's castle, satirizes Hollywood cemeteries, American science, sexual naivete, British scholarship, etc. Like the earlier comic novels, it flits brilliantly among diverse consciousnesses only to be interrupted by chapters of the serious philosophizing of a character based on philosopher Gerald Heard, who proposes a decentralized small-is-beautiful civilization as an alternative to the excesses of modern capitalism. Although *Ape and Essence* (1948) satirizes a society of near-animal survivors ruled by a bestial priesthood in a post-apocalyptic California, the tone of this novel/screenplay is so bleak that nothing in it quali-fies as humorous. Like many lesser comic writers, Huxley's work darkened as he took his mission as writer more seriously. For a relative of Matthew Arnold and a descendant of Thomas Henry Huxley, that evolution is scarcely surprising. A deepening repugnance for the animal qualities of the human race made the more excruciating by idealistic philosophy had by this time brought a Swiftian despair to the once genial satire of this gifted writer.

Summary

Aldous Huxley brought considerable literary and scientific sophistication to his early satirical novels, creating an unusual amalgam of the comic novel and the novel of ideas. In these brilliant and somewhat cynical novels, he contrasted the inept strivings of their characters to the liberated and eloquent texture of their discourse. A deepening disgust at the human condition overtook his later work, but even in that period *Brave New World* and *After Many a Summer Dies the Swan* retained flashes of the audacious imagination and delight in absurdity that illumined his early work.

Selected Bibliography

Primary Sources
Crome Yellow. London: Chatto and Windus, 1921.
Antic Hay. London: Chatto and Windus, 1923.
Those Barren Leaves. London: Chatto and Windus, 1925.
Point Counter Point. London: Chatto and Windus, 1928.
Brave New World. London: Chatto and Windus, 1932.
After Many a Summer Dies the Swan. London: Chatto and Windus, 1939.
Ape and Essence. New York: Harper and Brothers, 1948.
Doors of Perception. New York: Harper and Brothers, 1954.
The Letters of Aldous Huxley. Ed. Grover Smith. London: Chatto and Windus, 1970.

Secondary Sources

Biographies
Bedford, Sybille. *Aldous Huxley, A Biography*. New York: Knopf, 1975.
    The definitive authorized biography. Contains much material collected espe-

cially for this exhaustive study, though
Bedford attempts to avoid literary
criticism.

Books

Meckier, Jerome. *Aldous Huxley, Satire and
Structure*. London: Chatto and Windus,
1969. Meckier discusses Huxley's failure
to maintain the fusion between satire
and structure that characterized his best
work and cites D.H. Lawrence as the
central influence in his artistic life.

Watt, Donald, ed. *Aldous Huxley, The Critical Heritage*. London: Routledge &
Kegan Paul, 1975. A compendium of
critical responses to Huxley's works. Includes reviews by Virginia Woolf, T.S.
Eliot, D.H. Lawrence, Ernest
Hemingway, George Orwell, and many
other distinguished writers spanning the
years from 1918 to 1965.

William Donnelly

H

I

Isherwood, Christopher

Born: High Lane, Cheshire, August 26, 1904
Education: St. Edmund's School, Hindhead,
  Surrey 1914–1918; Repton School, near
  Derby 1919–1922; Corpus Christi Col-
  lege, Cambridge University on scholar-
  ship 1923–1925; King's College School
  of Medicine, London 1928–1929
Died: January 4, 1986, Santa Monica, Cali-
  fornia

Biography

The life of Christopher William Bradshaw-Isherwood falls neatly into four geographical locations: boyhood and youth in Cheshire and Surrey; early manhood in London; teacher of English in Berlin; scenario writer for Metro-Goldwyn-Mayer in Hollywood and professor at California State College and the University of California.

Not quite an aristocrat, Isherwood was certainly upper-class "county gentry." His father, Lieutenant-Colonel Francis B. Isherwood of Marple Hall in Cheshire left that large Elizabethan mansion to start his married life in Wyberslegh Hall with Kathleen Machell-Smith. Unfortunately, being a second son, he was commissioned into the York and Lancaster Regiment in 1892 when he was twenty-three. A perfectly satisfactory officer, nevertheless he was temperamentally unsuited to military life and preferred to spend his time reading, painting, and playing music. As Isherwood later related in *Kathleen and Frank*, although his mother's father was only a wealthy wine merchant, his daughter became more upper class than the really upper-class family that she had married into at the age of thirty-five (cf. Isherwood's Lily Vernon, *The Memorial*). An

examination of parental diaries later surprised the novelist to discover his father longed to travel, was deeply interested in aesthetic theory, and was fascinated by theosophy. His mother's formidable willpower, shared by the son, created terrible domestic confrontations.

Christopher was born on August 26, 1904 at High Lane, Cheshire. Reared by a nanny, he slept for the first time in a separate room when he was nine and a half. His mother's reverence for the past led the youth to determine to turn his back on the past in all its forms—ancestral home, class distinction, history, Cambridge University, and finally England itself.

In the boy's sixth year his father decided to teach him reading and writing by collaboratively producing an illustrated journal, "The Toy-Drawer Times," maintained somewhat sporadically until Christopher went to St. Edmund's four years later. These skills were immediately applied to writing scripts for the home theatricals in which his father delighted. By 1911, he was attending a local school for one hour a day with four other small boys. This same year his brother Richard was born. Shyer than his elder brother, less rebellious against maternal authority, Richard's refusal to complete his education or ever to earn a living made their mother anxious about her elder son's prospects.

St. Edmund's School in Hindhead was a natural choice because it was operated by his father's cousins—Cyril Morgan Brown, his sister Monica, and his daughter Rosamira. On May 1, 1914, the ten-year-old boy was turned over to Brown at London's Waterloo Station. Paradoxically, the Browns seemed unimpressed and displeased with their irritatingly precocious relative and provided little emotional support when his father was killed May 8, 1915, at the second battle of Ypres. Thereafter, his father was held before him as a hero-figure whom he could never match and the boy first caught the idea of a Test which separates the Truly Strong from the Truly Weak. At St. Edmund's he met Wystan Hugh Auden, won the Divinity Prize Forms I and II, and passed his examinations with honors in 1918.

In January 1919, Isherwood was transferred to Repton School near Derby. There he began his lifelong friendship with Edward Upward (the model for Allen Chalmers, *Lions and Shadows*). His most influential Master was G.B. Smith (Mr. Holmes, *Lions and Shadows*). He became one of the school's brightest scholars, winning the literature, the history, and the Form prizes.

Isherwood followed his friend Upward to Cambridge University one year later, entering Corpus Christi College on scholarship in October 1923, and, like spies entering enemy territory (the "Mortmere" manuscripts), Upward identified with the "hearties" and Isherwood with what his friend called "the Poshocracy." They set up the fictive figure of "The Watcher in Spanish" to keep them loyal to their secret rebellion of two against athletes, aristocrats, the history department, the college, and indeed Cambridge itself—which seemed to them to replace the discipline of Repton by the bribery of ancient charm. The Mortmere chronicle of fantasy and escape that they had begun at Repton continued and spawned an offshoot, "The Other Town," about a sinister and dangerous city which lay behind the decorous Cambridge facade. The episodes flowed copiously, novels were begun, poems written, and diaries religiously kept.

Isherwood had a story published in the *Oxford Outlook*, helped found a literary society in 1925, and then, having done no studying, he answered his Tripos examinations facetiously and was given the privilege of withdrawing from the university. In London, after an unsuccessful attempt to find work in film-making, he became, almost by accident, the part-time secretary to the Mangeot family string quartet (the Cheurets in *Lions and Shadows*). Falling in love with the relaxed, bohemian atmosphere, he made invidious comparisons between Olive Mangeot and his own mother. Unfortunately, he was still financially dependent upon his mother until his Uncle Henry started an inadequate allowance right after his

twenty-first birthday. In the ensuing fray he informed her, as a weapon of aggression, that he was homosexual. Moving out of his home, running off to Wales, threatening suicide, he abruptly announced his intention of going to medical school. With his mother's support he entered King's College School of Medicine in October 1928. His first complete novel, *All The Conspirators*, was published by Jonathan Cape in May that year. About this time, a British poet of nineteen, Stephen Spender, joined the party of his lifelong friends.

The King's College experience was a repetition of his Cambridge experience (an attempt to prove to be a success on his mother's terms), but by Christmas his grades were so poor and he was so engrossed in planning a second novel that when Auden appeared full of a new messiah named Homer Lane as interpreted by his disciple John Layard (Barnard in *Lions and Shadows*), Isherwood was ready to be swept away. It was liberating to hear that the devil practiced unreasonable behavior issuing in disease, whereas the god within counseled unreasonable free response to man's anarchic urgings which lead to health! So, armed with £50 from a forgotten War Loan certificate, Isherwood left medical school to join Auden in Berlin on March 14, 1929.

In the next ten years Isherwood's name would be inextricably linked with Berlin during the expiring days of the Weimar Republic and the opening triumphs of Hitlerian Nazism. The mythic figure of a lonely, beleaguered reporter warning a blind world of coming danger was forged by Isherwood and polished by his friends. But, in his later autobiography, *Christopher and His Kind*, he admits that although intellectually stimulated by the coming struggle, he was emotionally aroused by the boy-bars of Berlin. Here Auden obtained for Isherwood a commission to translate Charles Baudelaire's *Journaux Intimes*. His quarterly allowance quixotically withheld by Uncle Henry, Isherwood returned to England to side with his brother Richard in his struggle against the dominance of their mother.

Upon his return to Berlin he became enamored with a German boy ("Otto" in *Christopher and His Kind* and Otto Nowak in *Goodbye to Berlin*) and roomed in the family flat in Hallesches Tor. When it proved impossible to live and write in so uncongenial an atmosphere, he took a room in the flat of Fr. Thurau and there met the cast of characters of the stories which made him famous. Jean Ross became Sally Bowles and Gerald Hamilton became Mr. Norris.

John Lehmann asked Leonard and Virginia Woolf to publish Isherwood's second novel and *The Memorial* appeared in February 1932 and, like his previous novel, sold poorly. In March 1932, Isherwood met a seventeen-year-old German, "Heinz," and this liaison became more serious than any that preceded it. Through Auden, Isherwood met Gerald Heard, who later introduced him to Hindu meditation, and he also visited E.M. Forster and adopted him as literary mentor. On May 13, 1933, with Hitler coming into power, the writer left Berlin with young Heinz. After flight to Athens and the tiny island of St. Nicholas, he took Heinz home to meet his mother. In England he worked as scriptwriter with Berthold Viertel (Dr. Friedrich Bergmann in *Prater Violet*) at Gaumont-British films, the first of his film-writing activities that paid him considerable sums of money but never resulted in any major artistic achievement. At the instigation of Auden, the two friends wrote the first of their three dramatic collaborations: *The Dog Beneath the Skin; or, Where Is Francis?*; *The Ascent of F6*; and *On the Frontier*. In February 1935, Isherwood's first Berlin novel, *Mr. Norris Changes Trains*, was received with great critical enthusiasm and its author became an important young novelist.

After Heinz's arrest for onanism and draft evasion, Isherwood found numbness in completing his first autobiography, *Lions and Shadows*, on September 15, 1937. Upon its publication in March 1938, Auden's publishers contracted both friends to do a travel book on the Far East. The Japanese invasion gave them a war of their own to cover, and they set out on a four-month trip to Hong Kong and Shanghai. Although their experience with front-line fighting totaled two days, *Journey to a War* was a successful last collaboration for the two writers.

In Isherwood's *Goodbye to Berlin* (1939), the reality of a dehumanized and dying city is symbolized by the frenetic follies of a group of foreign friends. From the novel came John van Druten's popular play, *I Am a Camera*, a musical, and the movie *Cabaret*, all of which boosted Isherwood's income considerably.

The emigration of Auden and Isherwood to the United States in January 1939 was bitterly criticized by some of their British contemporaries (including Cyril Connolly, Sir Jocelyn Lucas, and Harold Nicolson) and tended to darken the critical reception of their subsequent writing. By May, Isherwood applied for citizenship, even though in an August 6, 1939, letter to Upward, he described New York City as a succession of "press interviews, photographs, dinners for Spain, lunches for China, lectures, crooked publishers, long-haired Trotters and stern Reds." Lured by the presence of Heard, Christopher Wood, and Aldous Huxley in California, he and a young friend, "Vernon," took a three-week Greyhound bus trip to Washington, D.C., New Orleans, El Paso, Houston, Albuquerque, Flagstaff, and finally Los Angeles. Loving California and with a $2,000 loan from Wood, Isherwood could catch his breath, decide that he was a pacifist, sick of his "Ego, darling Me," and ripe to be converted to Vedanta by Swami Prabhavananda. Thereafter the sense of the god within (Atman), the god without (Brahma), and a divine vocation (dharma) in the transient world of illusion (Maya) lay as a substructure beneath his writing.

Almost immediately the Hollywood British colony found him work with Samuel Goldwyn at Metro-Goldwyn-Mayer. In January, Gottfried Reinhardt employed Isherwood to write dialogue for M-G-M. Regarding Hollywood as a spectacular version of Maya, Isherwood faithfully produced scripts. When his Uncle Henry died in July 1940, leaving him the two family mansions, he turned them over to his brother and was initiated into discipleship to his guru, Prabhavananda, and began a translation of the *Bhagavad-Gita*. Out of his experience of working with Jewish-German director Berthold Viertel, he wrote *Prater Violet* (1945), a translation of Shankara's *Crest-Jewel of Discrimination* (1946), and after a six-month tour of South America with a Kentucky Irish boy named William Caskey, his travel book *The Condor and the Cows* was published by Methuen and Random House (1949) and enjoyed particular popularity in England. From then until 1953 he worked on *The World in the Evening* and was encouraged by his election as a member of the American National Institute of Arts and Letters.

That winter he met Don Bachardy, an eighteen-year-old college student, the last great amour of his life. After Bachardy's first trip to North Africa and Europe with Isherwood, they planned a round-the-world trip, especially to include India. Together they dramatized *The World in the Evening*, the first of many collaborations. Bachardy became a popular portrait artist and Isherwood became visiting professor at California State College and the University of California, Berkeley. *Down There on a Visit*, in which he returned to the form and excellence of his Berlin stories, was published by Methuen in 1962. The absence of Bachardy at shows in Los Angeles and Santa Barbara may have provided the emotional setting for *A Single Man* (1964) as a study in middle-aged loneliness. *A Meeting by the River* (1967) represents Isherwood's peculiar combination of Vedanta and the gay world, since it consists of the letters between two brothers, one a gay, rich publisher and the other about to take vows as a Hindu monk. From 1968 to 1970, spurred by going over family papers after the death of his mother, he set himself to a revaluation of his parents in *Kathleen and Frank*, which was published in 1971. The fragmentary biographies of his mother and father may well have put him in the frame of mind to continue his *Lions and Shadows*, published when he was thirty-four, and its sequel *Christopher and His Kind*, a much franker and less attractive work, when he was sixty-two. Surprised by excellent initial sales, he wrote to Dodie Smith: "Oh, one always thinks one has dropped an H-bomb, and in fact one is lucky if it isn't mistaken for a burst tyre or a car back-firing."

Diagnosed with cancer in 1981, he died on January 4, 1986, in Santa Monica, California.

Literary Analysis

Isherwood's 1980 valedictory statement perfectly expresses four aspects of his written work: "My life is still beautiful to me—beautiful because of Don, because of the enduring fascination of my efforts to describe my life experiences in my writing, because of my interest in the various predicaments of my fellow travellers on this journey" (Summers, 12). "Because of Don" represents the homosexual orientation of the writer, at first only implied, later quite explicit. "My life experiences in my writing" marks out the autobiographical parameters of most of his work. "Predicaments of my fellow travellers" attests to his keen interest in observing others. "This journey" points to a philosophical interpretation of life strongly indebted to Far Eastern religion.

Isherwood told Michael Davie, "I don't see much difference between an autobiography and a novel," and his writing supports the contention. His mother's November 6, 1909, diary entry contains the notation, "After tea, C dic-

tated a story called *The Adventures of Mummy and Daddy*, chiefly about himself!" So, when he was only five, his mother might have foreseen just how he would sum up her life when he became sixty-six. On September 3, 1976, he candidly admitted that *Kathleen and Frank* "is really autobiography," principally "because it's all explanations about why I am the way I am." After his mother's death, the main reason for his October 1966 visit to England was to leaf through his mother's diaries and his father's letters, which had been kept intact by Richard. When he began to write, he had three chronologies to integrate: the parents whom he remembered with such nostalgia (father) and such anger (mother); the parents whom he discovered in diaries and letters—a "*period* love-story"; and the forced recognition that although much marred by his father's early death and estranged during his mother's long life, they were all of the same weave. His narrative device works brilliantly. Chapter 1 employs Kathleen's spasmodically kept diary for 1883 as an introduction. Chapters 2 through 17 intersperse diary and letters to 1915, when his father was killed at Ypres. Additional diary excerpts show how fixated Kathleen became on Frank (to the exclusion of Christopher and Richard). Chapter 18 sums up the remainder of Kathleen's long life. An afterword is Isherwood's examination of the extent to which his character was inherited. The irrepressible author makes interpolations that jump backward and forward in time.

In *Lions and Shadows: An Education in the Twenties,* Isherwood warns the reader that "it is not . . . an autobiography"—it is often polite, it is not always true, the characters are "caricatures," and it should be read "as a novel." Yet, the volume has great charm as a *Bildungsroman,* and the author handles with bright humor the same elements that James Joyce had handled with such tragic overtones in *Portrait of the Artist as a Young Man*. Indeed, the tone is far more like the ironic observation of the youthful self in Lord Byron's *Don Juan* than the usual Romantic "agony." The subtitle, "An Education in the Twenties," suggests that the neurosis that led the novelist from rebellion to self-exile was meant to symbolize an entire generation of middle- and upper-class intellectuals.

As *Lions and Shadows* took Isherwood from Repton and Cambridge to departure for Berlin, *Christopher and His Kind* (1976) takes him from Germany to the United States. Chapter 1 warns again that *Lions and Shadows* was not truly autobiographical; it concealed much, overdramatized more, and dealt with caricatures. *Christopher and His Kind* "will be as frank and factual as I can make it, especially as far as I myself am concerned," he announced. Because he uses real names, he is often polite about the exposure of friends; but because this is a candid study, he is often extremely, even masochistically, hard on himself. This creates the somewhat strident tone of the avowed gay activist who is determined to bare all. He handles the narrative device in a particularly strange manner. The narration is first person singular, but much of the time he describes Christopher as if he were being examined from the outside and that the observer was not altogether pleased by what he saw.

If biography and autobiography are to be read like novels, then presumably the novels are to be read like autobiography. A face looking over his own shoulder, he seems to regard with curious objectivity his pilgrim's progress from angry young man through the comedy of irony to gay liberation publicist. "With me, everything starts with autobiography," he says. The chief difficulty with this critical observation is that it ignores his midway conversion to Hinduism and his later discipline toward the loss of Ego. Thus, it is useful to discuss the nine novels as four novels of ego and five novels of Vedanta.

All the Conspirators (1928), dedicated to Upward, clearly arises out of the Mortmere saga and "The Other Town" in which two arch anarchists enter enemy territory as spies. Begun when he was twenty-one and completed when he was twenty-three, it is a young man's book. The style is indebted to Joyce and Woolf; the rage is the entrapped youth fighting his own family; the tension centers in The Test that classifies the Truly Strong Man and the Truly Weak. At the end Mother has won—Philip can return to the womb of perpetual invalidism; Joan may lose any chance of a life of her own, and Allen, the sanest of the group, must suffer the ultimate ironic humiliation of Philip's patronizing advice delivered with a waving mittened hand, with feet propped up by sister and mother: "You see, Allen, what I really dislike about your attitude is that it gets you nowhere."

If *All the Conspirators* indicts the Edwardian family, *The Memorial* (1932) considers the whole British establishment as a trap. The Great War is portrayed through its after-

effects upon veterans, those too young to go, and the total civilian population. Three generations of the Vernon family represent the disintegration of England. John, the last squire of the great Hall set in the stability of Victorian England, is now in his second childhood, slobbering like a great baby over his food. Lily represents the Edwardian world, idolizing Victorian order, fixated on brief past happiness stolen away by war. Eric, Maurice, and Anne are victims of their own neuroses and are all consciously or unconsciously in love with death. The chronology (book 1 is 1928, book 2 is 1920, book 3 is 1925, book 4 is 1929) works admirably to show that all present action is paralyzed by memories of the past.

Isherwood's humor is often verbal—"Herr Issyvoo" is his wry Germanization of his own name. His dialogue always sparkles with verve and coruscating wit. His characters are usually innocent undergraduates thrown in sharp relief against a background of middle-aged grotesques. In *The Last of Mr. Norris* the protagonist is a fussy, nervous be-wigged man who spends hours each day perfuming his person. His choicest possessions are a notable collection of whips and a pair of high crimson boots. His days are spent in orgies of luxury with his wealthy young friends, but at night he crouches in squalid cellar-clubs with fellow conspirators plotting the revolutionary overthrow of assorted governments. The central incredibility of plot and character is always stressed rather than defended.

The Berlin stories have continued to be Isherwood's best sellers. *Mr. Norris Changes Trains* (1935; published in the United States as *The Last of Mr. Norris*) and *Goodbye to Berlin* trace the sad last days of the Weimar Republic, the frenetic interval of sexual excitement, and the beginning of the Nazi era. The directionless lives of the protagonists mirror the vacuum into which Adolf Hitler resolutely moved. Mr. Norris, who seems so charmingly amoral, is reluctantly exposed as a jewel thief, blackmailer, and double agent for both the Communists and the Fascists. The entire novel is a detailing of a tissue of deceits from Norris's wig to the relationship of hero and heroine and the actual sexual activities of the narrator. Sally Bowles's highspirited and sad presence gives charm to a cast of doomed young people in a doomed city.

Isherwood called *Goodbye to Berlin* "a loosely connected sequence of diaries and sketches." It includes a brilliant internal counterpoint of the lighthearted early diary and the later doom-laden diary, heterosexual outlaws (Sally) and homosexual deviants ("On Ruegen Island"), and an under-privileged working-class family ("The Nowaks") versus a wealthy Jewish family ("The Landauers"). This is the work from which a single statement—"I am a camera with its shutter open, quite passive, recording, not thinking"—was seized upon by Van Druten in the drama *I Am a Camera*, and later used as the basis of a musical comedy and the movie *Cabaret*. Still, the author's use of first person narrator suggests that the truth he records will be more subjective than objective, not simply a camera clicking at Berlin's misfits in a city of, as he originally entitled the stories, "The Lost."

The year 1939 marked the end of London and Berlin and the beginning of New York and Hollywood, but it also marked the end of the naked Ego and the beginning of *dharma* or vocation. In the next five novels Isherwood wrestles with a transcendental rather than an individualistic sense of life. Realizing that the language of Vedanta would alienate worldly readers, in *Prater Violet* he uses the vocabulary of the movie studio so successfully that he came to prefer it to any of his pre-war novels.

Using a musical frame of reference, in the first movement the writer learns the true nature of art from his guru-father, Bergmann. The second movement forces the protagonist to abandon self-importance to become the servant of art. The coda reveals a narrator ego which blocks artistic maturity. Detachment from the ego alone makes possible the artist's release from fear. The real love that develops between the son, Isherwood, and the adoptive father, Bergmann, presupposes renunciation of the clamant, fearful self.

Although *The World in the Evening* (1954) is narrated by the main character, Stephen Monk, he is entirely unacquainted with himself and thus, once again, splits into a prescient observer and a venal narrator. The novel was published to a generally hostile critical reception; Alan Wilde rightly calls it "less a novel than a fable of redemption." Clearly a novel of conversion, Stephen is stopped from running away from himself in "An End," undergoes forced and prolonged self-examination in "Letters and Life," and sails forth on a new selfless phase in "A Beginning." His prolonged confinement in bed is perfect discipline for self-exami-

nation, the study of his wife's letters, and the recognition of his lifelong evasions. A mystical experience with his Aunt Sarah helps him lose the old egocentricity and join a civilian ambulance unit in North Africa.

Down There on a Visit is a fascinating mixture of both old and new orientations of the author. The narrator is called Christopher; the original title for the novel was "In the Face of the Enemy," with each of four protagonists a lonely, alienated ego fighting desperately against "The Others." The tendency of the volume to fall into four individual novelettes rather than one novel is very much like that in the Berlin stories. All of these are the mannerisms of the past. The new Isherwood deals with attachment and non-attachment: becoming weary of art, the hero throws himself feverishly into politics; finally he makes a commitment to a divine reality underlying lesser commitments. The twenty-three-year-old visitor unwittingly contributes to Mr. Lancaster's suicide; the thirty-six-year-old resident devotes his life to protecting Paul from suicide. *Down There on a Visit* is a brilliant mélange of things old and new, with the vigor of the Berlin stories but the meditativeness of Vedanta.

Published two years later, *A Single Man* is a slight monograph with very large meanings. A middle-aged, expatriate professor remembers his dead lover, Jim, and almost wills his own death. Isherwood's year in medical school pays rich dividends as the protagonist, George, experiences heart failure; Vedanta enlightens him to think that his little land-locked pool, flooded by waves, has now become part of the great sea. Not written in the first person, yet it "is fundamentally about me, at my present age, living right here in the canyon." Astonishingly unified and emotionally compact, both Isherwood and Auden considered it his best work. Although about a sexual minority, Isherwood makes it claim everyone's attention as a prose poem on middle age and death.

As *A Single Man* is explicitly homosexual, *A Meeting by the River* is explicitly Vedanta. On his way back from the celebration of Vivekananda's centenary in Calcutta, Isherwood caught the vision of an occidental, at the point of taking his final vows in a monastery on the Ganges, being visited by a worldly brother, his polar opposite, to carry on the kind of dialogue by which Christ was tempted by Satan in the wilderness. Patrick revels in the flesh, the very personification of ego, and he is an atheist. Oliver believes in God, renounces the world, and views his ego with wry distaste. But, because they are brothers, heredity has bound them together so that their love-hate relationship reveals their similarities more than their differences. Indeed, they come to attribute those differences to roles their mother had imposed upon them. Therefore, Stanley Kauffman read the book as a monodrama—all happening within a single life. As the conclusion of *A Single Man* had indicated, from the viewpoint of Vedanta, the ego prevents the individual from becoming part of the fundamental reality; nevertheless, upon closer scrutiny the detached self is little different from other selves.

The central metaphor of *A Meeting by the River* is brotherhood: formerly the brothers sought it in each other, but they grew apart. Now Patrick seeks it in homosexual union as Oliver seeks it in the spiritual union of a monastery. The style of the narrative is badly flawed by the unnaturalness of a successful publishing editor sustaining a long, confessional, epistolary relationship and by the gushy euphemisms of an initiate in a meditative order. Probably the psychological patterns work out more authentically than the spiritual design. In 1968, Isherwood and Bachardy wrote a dramatic version that seemed to their friends more successful than the novelistic treatment.

During most of the Hollywood period, Isherwood was supported by scenario writing for studios, but the actual results were disappointing. An acknowledged master of dialogue, his work was interrupted, reassigned, and cut; most of it never reached the screen.

Summary

Christopher Isherwood's writing is always remarkably lucid and conversational. Indeed, intellectuals bemoaned his "fatal readability." Dialogue is light, easy, and witty. However, underneath lies a basic irony which arises from the sharp differences between what the characters think and what the reader knows. The characters' lack of self-knowledge and understanding of others makes for constant comedies of error. So notable is this pervasive irony that it has often been classified as relativistic, reductive, romantic, equivocal, and transcendental. The young Isherwood seems to have agreed with Jean-Paul Sartre that there is no human possibility of knowing either the self or others. The older Isherwood always suggests that the ego and human evaluation are invariably in error; both must be surrendered to the greater reality.

Selected Bibliography

Primary Sources

Novels

All the Conspirators. London: Jonathan Cape, 1928.

The Memorial: Portrait of a Family. London: Hogarth Press, 1932.

Mr. Norris Changes Trains (American title: *The Last of Mr. Norris*). London: Hogarth Press, 1935; New York: New Directions, 1954.

Sally Bowles. London: Hogarth Press, 1937.

Goodbye to Berlin. London: Hogarth Press, 1939.

Prater Violet. New York: Random House, 1945.

The World in the Evening. London: Methuen, 1954.

Down There on a Visit. London: Methuen, 1962.

A Single Man. London: Methuen, 1964.

A Meeting by the River. London: Methuen, 1967.

Biographies and Autobiographies

Lions and Shadows: An Education in the Twenties. London: Hogarth Press, 1938.

Kathleen and Frank: The Autobiography of a Family. London: Methuen, 1971.

Christopher and His Kind, 1929–1939. New York: Farrar, Straus & Giroux, 1976.

Drama

Coauthored with W.H. Auden

The Dog Beneath the Skin; or, Where Is Francis? London: Faber & Faber, and New York: Random House, 1935.

The Ascent of F6. London: Faber & Faber, 1936; New York: Random House, 1937.

On the Frontier. London: Faber & Faber, 1938; New York: Random House, 1939.

Travel

Journey to a War. London: Faber & Faber, 1939.

The Condor and the Cows: A South American Travel Diary. London: Methuen, and New York: Random House, 1949.

Vedanta

Bhagavad-Gita: The Song of God (trans. with

Swami Prabhavananda). Hollywood: Vedanta Press, 1944.

An Approach to Vedanta. Hollywood: Vedanta Press, 1963.

Ramakrishna and His Disciples. New York: Simon and Schuster, 1965.

My Guru and His Disciple. London: Methuen, and New York: Farrar, Straus & Giroux, 1980.

Secondary Sources

Connolly, Cyril. *Enemies of Promise and Other Essays*. Garden City, NY: Doubleday, 1960. Extensive commentary on Isherwood's style by a critic who was not always an admirer.

Finney, Brian. *Christopher Isherwood: A Critical Biography*. New York: Oxford University, 1979. Probably the best recent study, tracing the biography with care, making incisive critical evaluations, and suggesting coherent trends in the author's intellectual and creative life.

Heard, Gerald. *The Five Ages of Man*. New York: Julian Press, 1963. Basic for an understanding of Isherwood's later work.

Piazza, Paul. *Christopher Isherwood: Myth and Anti-Myth*. New York: Columbia University, 1978. The world is split into two camps: the Enemy or Others and a conspiratorial clique of the author and his intimate friends. With Vedanta comes the recognition that the enemy is within, not out in the world.

Schwerdt, Lisa M. *Isherwood's Fiction: The Self and Technique*. New York: St. Martin's Press, 1989. A study from the point of view of technique: the search for technique, the namesake narrator, broadening the focus, and trying new approaches.

Spender, Stephen. *World Within World*. London: Hamish Hamilton, 1951. Important to read in conjunction with Isherwood's autobiographies.

Summers, Claude J. *Christopher Isherwood*. New York: Frederick Ungar, 1980.

Wilde, Alan. *Christopher Isherwood*. New York: Twayne, 1971. United States Authors Series, No. 173. Good chronology and selected bibliography. Wilde treats the works as related to two themes, "separateness and aloneness" within an encompassing moral vision.

Elton E. Smith

J

Jacobs, W[illiam] W[ymark]

Born: Wapping, London, September 8, 1863
Education: Private school, London; Birkbeck
*   College until 1879*
Marriage: Agnes Eleanor Williams, 1900; five
*   children*
Died: London, September 1, 1943

Biography

The oldest child of William Gage Jacobs and his first wife Sophia Wymark, W.W. Jacobs was born in Wapping, in the shipping area of London, on September 8, 1863. Jacobs's father was a wharf manager and the boy grew up in the vicinity of the London docks, where he acquired the intimate knowledge of ships and nautical lore that he was to utilize so fruitfully in his humorous stories. He attended one of the London private schools and later Birkbeck College until he joined the Civil Service as a clerk in 1879. Jacobs was to hold this enervating position until 1899, when his authorial success overcame his fear of childhood poverty to the extent that he felt secure enough to try to earn his living by his pen.

Jacobs contributed stories to *Blackfriars* as early as 1885, obtaining further notice when Jerome K. Jerome printed some of his material in *To-day* and *The Idler*. Jacobs's tales began to appear in the *Strand Magazine* (which paid handsomely) in 1895. His first collection of short fiction, *Many Cargoes*, was published in 1896. Over the next thirty years he produced a number of volumes of short stories, novels, and plays.

Essentially shy, withdrawn, and conservative, in 1900 Jacobs married the flamboyant suffragette Agnes Eleanor Williams. Their union was not happy and the constant friction of his domestic situation undoubtedly contributed to the author's constitutional melancholy.

The couple had two sons and three daughters, one of whom, Barbara, became the wife of novelist Alec Waugh. In his last two decades, Jacobs wrote little, concentrating on the dramatization of some of his earlier work. Despite this diminished output, his popularity steadily increased and many of his works were republished. He died in London on September 1, 1943, just short of his eightieth birthday.

Literary Analysis

Jacobs's popularity as a humorist was well established by the turn of the twentieth century. He falls into the ranks of the New Humorists, the unflattering appellation first applied to Barry Pain and Jerome K. Jerome by the prevailing literary establishment. Until the appearance of these writers, noted for their use of the vernacular and lower-class subject matter, British humor had been generally aristocratic. Although Jacobs, Pain, Jerome, and others published extensively and were widely read, they were not accepted as viable members of the literati.

As a short story writer, Jacobs is undoubtedly a master. His ability to work well within the confines of short fiction is evidenced in the brevity and quick unfolding of his tales which develop rapidly and effectively. Jacobs is adept at employing plot reversal, so that the reader receives the opposite of what is expected. His range of plots is, however, limited. He tended to recycle material, employing the same basic story-lines with slightly different accouterments. Even with this drawback, the author's appeal was wide and sustained—his stories appeared regularly in the *Strand Magazine* for over three decades.

Although Jacobs's scope is restricted, he seemed content to remain within the self-imposed geographical boundaries that he had set for himself. Perhaps his innate conservatism kept him from branching out into other areas of literary endeavor. Jacobs's early poverty is another possible explanation for his continued production of comic short fiction; the monetary rewards for this work in time became quite munificent.

Like other New Humorists, Jacobs's short pieces cover a cross-section of English society that was generally neglected by earlier comic authors. In mining this rich source of material, he worked out his own unique style and approach to humorous writing. The majority of his work deals with the dock area of London and with Dickensian ne'er-do-well country characters. His fiction is not realistic in the strictest sense since the more repugnant aspects of life are glossed over: in his narrow world the characters' tragedy is comic; pain is a laughable sensation not to be taken seriously.

Many of the humorist's shorter efforts are narrated by the night-watchman who works on the docks and has many years of maritime experience to draw upon. His style of presentation is dry, matter-of-fact, and flatly comic. Speaking in dialect, the night-watchman gives an accurate picture of the multifaceted life around the London wharves that Jacobs knew so well. Among the collections in which this narrator figures so prominently are *Many Cargoes* (1896), *Light Freights* (1901), *Odd Craft* (1903), and *Short Cruises* (1907). Also notable among Jacobs's creations are Ginger Dick and Peter Russett, two hard-drinking seamen whose escapades ashore provide an ample vehicle for the display of the author's comic skill. In "The Money Box," collected in *Odd Craft*, the night-watchman recounts an episode in which Dick and Peter are outwitted by an aged mariner, Isaac. The two younger sailors ask the more experienced tar to hold their wages when they're on leave and dole out pittances to prevent squandering. The pair's attempts while inebriated to recover their capital from the stolid Isaac all go for naught. However, the two are persistent, despite a thrashing from the old man:

> They stuck to Isaac all day, trying to get their money out of 'im, and the names they called 'im was a surprise even to themselves. And at night they turned the room topsy-turvy agin looking for their money and 'ad more unpleasantness when they wanted Isaac to get up and let 'em search the bed.[1]

Jacobs's accurate use of dialect in this and other stories illustrates his easy familiarity with the ways of seamen. The slapstick comic elements present in the tale stand in marked contrast to the tepid aristocratic humor then current.

In "A Change of Treatment," collected in *Many Cargoes*, Jacobs employs a hearty brand of humor appropriate to the rough sailors concerned. The night-watchman tells the story of a ship's captain who is an amateur physician and who enjoys nothing so much as practicing on his crew. Several of the seamen hit on the idea of malingering, after consulting an old medical text:

> He dragged the book away from the old man, and began to study. There was so many complaints in it he was almost tempted to have something else instead of consumption, but he decided on that at last, and he got a cough what worried the fo'c'sle all night long, an' the next day, when the skipper came down to see Dan, he could 'ardly 'ear hisself speak.[2]

The scheme backfires when the first mate mixes up a vile home remedy that he persuades the captain to let him try on the invalids; they quickly return to work. Jacobs's realistic portrayal of the often coarse manners and language of seamen makes this tale successful.

Jacobs is equally at home, however, with the vernacular and mores of rural England. His country poacher, Bob Pretty, is a seemingly inexhaustible source of humorous material. The blasé, crafty Pretty can fool sheriffs, gamekeepers, and country squires with effortless finesse. Bob's utter manipulation of a company of rural functionaries in "The Persecution of Bob Pretty" (collected in *Odd Craft*) is a prime example of Jacobs's control and dexterity in the development of quality short pieces. In building to a comic denouement, the writer moves the reader through a carefully structured plot which allows for inference rather than passive presentation of narrative events.

Jacobs's novels, unfortunately, are not of the same caliber as his short fiction. These longer efforts are essentially reworked short stories. The quick development and effective unfolding of plot that characterize his briefer works are not evident in his lengthier pieces. Light in tone, the subject matter of the novels is not generally of sufficient substance to sustain their length. *Dialstone Lane* (1904) is a case in point. Although an amusing tale of buried treasure and the people who rearrange their lives in order to find it, the book is structurally weak and develops slowly.

Though his contemporary fame rested almost entirely on his humorous work, Jacobs was also a master of the supernatural story, as "The Monkey's Paw," collected in *The Lady of the Barge* (1902), clearly demonstrates. This much anthologized macabre tale, for which Jacobs is best known today, involves an old couple who receive a talisman that grants them three wishes. One wish for money is realized as compensation for the death of their son. The other two are used in restoring him to life and then killing his resurrected cadaver. *The Brown Man's Servant*, included in *The Skipper's Wooing* (1897), is another masterpiece of horror, showing that Jacobs indeed possessed the ability to move beyond the comic form for which he was best known.

Critical opinion of Jacobs's work was varied.[3] Many critics refused to take him seriously and ignored his output. His unwillingness to venture out of his chosen milieu almost certainly denied him the critical attention afforded less deserving authors.

Toward the end of his life, Jacobs became more and more preoccupied with the theater. His drama is, like his fiction, essentially comic in tone. Dealing mainly with lower middle-class situations and employing accurate dialect, in the plays he gently portrays the harmless foibles of the *comedie humaine*. His characters are usually amiable miscreants, petty domestic tyrants, or lazy seamen who expend considerable energy in avoiding work. He reworked many of his earlier stories into one-act plays, some of which met with a measure of success, notably "The Monkey's Paw."

Jacobs's humor was not refined or esoteric, being rather of a more straightforward variety with the purpose of providing simple entertainment. Although capable of more serious work, he remained within the confines of his chosen field and rarely deviated from it. Since his goal was to amuse, with seemingly little ambition to make a mark as a literary author, Jacobs must be considered a decidedly successful comic writer.

Summary

W.W. Jacobs's approach to comic writing, though formulaic, was effective, as evidenced by the sustained popularity of his fiction during his lifetime. His depiction of the activity around the London docks and in rural Britain is valuable not only for its humorous content but for the insights provided into the lives of working-class people as well. Although Jacobs is not considered a major literary figure, he was a talented writer whose contribution to the development of British humor as one of the New Humorists is significant.

Notes

1. Jacobs, *Odd Craft* (New York: Scribner, 1903), p. 6.
2. Jacobs, *Many Cargoes* (New York: Stokes, 1897), p. 4.
3. J.B. Priestley, in "Mr. W.W. Jacobs," an essay in his *Figures in Modern Literature* (London: Lane, 1924), p. 118, discusses the contemporary comparison of Jacobs to both Tobias Smollett and Charles Dickens. He disagrees with this assessment since Smollett is prone to ribaldry and horseplay while Dickens is best known for his wonderfully comic characters. Priestley considers Jacobs's brand of humor more trim and polished, with verbal dexterity being used for its vehicle as opposed to the flights of a more vivid imagination. Two other noted critics take divergent stances regarding the idea of Jacobs's return to classical comic methods. In his essay "W.W. Jacobs," published in his *A Handful of Authors: Essays on Books and Writers* (London and New York: Sheed & Ward, 1953), pp. 29–32, G.K. Chesterton supports the thesis of classicism by pointing out that Jacobs reintroduces a violent, involuntary aspect to humor which stood in marked contrast to the vapid, more aristocratic fare of the day. He also remarks that Jacobs employs plot as a comic device, his style is characterized by clarity, and his work is an artistic expression of the humor of the general populace, all classical characteristics. However, in "W.W. Jacobs and Aristophanes," from *Books and Persons: Being Comments on a Past Epoch, 1908–1911* (London: Chatto & Windus, 1917) pp. 53–55, Arnold Bennett disagrees largely on the basis of Jacobs's lack of breadth. He maintains that the author shows no interest outside his narrow compass. Bennett rejects Jacobs as a proper successor to Aristophanes, with whom he had

been compared, since the Greek humorist's writing is much more universal and intellectual.

Selected Bibliography

Primary Sources
Many Cargoes. London: Lawrence & Bullen, 1896; New York: Stokes, 1897.
The Skipper's Wooing and *The Brown Man's Servant.* London: Pearson, and New York: Stokes; and McKinlay, Stone & MacKenzie, 1897.
Sea Urchins. London: Lawrence & Bullen, 1898. Published as *More Cargoes.* New York: Stokes, 1898.
A Master of Craft. London: Methuen, and New York: Stokes; Dodge; and McKinlay, Stone & MacKenzie, 1900.
Light Freights. London: Methuen, and New York: Dodd & Mead, 1901.
At Sunwich Port. London: Newnes, and New York: Scribner; and McKinlay, Stone & MacKenzie, 1902.
The Lady of the Barge and Other Stories. London and New York: Harper, 1902.
Odd Craft. London: Newnes, and New York: Charles Scribner's Sons; and McKinlay, Stone & MacKenzie, 1903.
Dialstone Lane. London: Newnes, and New York: Charles Scribner's Sons; and McKinlay, Stone & MacKenzie, 1904.
Short Cruises. London: Hurst & Blackett, and New York: Scribner; and McKinlay, Stone & MacKenzie, 1907.
Ship's Company. London and New York: Hodder & Stoughton, 1911.
The Castaways. London and New York: Hodder & Stoughton, 1917.

Secondary Sources
Bennett, Arnold. "W.W. Jacobs and Aristophanes." In *Books and Persons: Being Comments on a Past Epoch, 1908–1911.* London: Chatto & Windus, 1917, pp. 53–56. Essentially negative criticism of Jacobs for his narrow scope; Bennett disagrees with the contemporary comparison of the humorist to Aristophanes.
Chesterton, G.K. "W.W. Jacobs." In *A Handful of Authors: Essays on Books and Writers.* London and New York: Sheed & Ward, 1953, pp. 28–35. Praise of Jacobs for his return to the classical elements of comic writing.
Priestley, J.B. "Mr. W.W. Jacobs." In *Figures in Modern Literature.* London: Lane, 1924, pp. 103–23. Defense of Jacobs as a popular humorist, skilled in the use of the vernacular.
Pritchett, V.S. "W.W. Jacobs." In *Books in General.* London: Chatto & Windus, 1953, pp. 235–41. Maintains that Jacobs is a master of the comic short story, capable of transforming ordinary material into quality fiction.
Ward, Alfred C. "W.W. Jacobs: *Many Cargoes.*" In *Aspects of the Modern Short Story: English and American.* London: University of London Press, 1924, pp. 227–39. Positive assessment of Jacobs's short fiction, emphasizing his skill in the use of dialogue and characterization.
Whitford, Robert C. "The Humor of W.W. Jacobs." *South Atlantic Quarterly,* 18 (July 1919): 246–51. Whitford deals with Jacobs's unaristocratic approach to humor.

John Cloy

Jellicoe, [Patricia] Ann

Born: Middlesbrough, Yorkshire, July 15, 1927
Education: Polam Hall School in Darlington, County Durham, 1936–1940; Queen Margaret's School in Castle Howard, Yorkshire, 1940–1944; London's Central School of Speech and Drama, 1944–1947
Marriage: C.E. Knight-Clarke, 1950; divorced 1961; Roger Mayne, September 3, 1962; two children

Biography

(Patricia) Ann Jellicoe, daughter of John A. Jellicoe and Frances Jackson Henderson, was born on July 15, 1927, in Middlesbrough, Yorkshire. Her parents separated when she was eighteen months old. Jellicoe was educated at Polam Hall School in Darlington, County Durham (1836–1940) and Queen Margaret's School in Castle Howard, Yorkshire (1940–1944), boarding schools which she found restrictive. As Jellicoe explains, "I didn't like Queen Margaret's at first and was only kept from utter misery by a huge fire which destroyed a substantial part of [the school]. This meant we had ten weeks holiday while they sorted the place out. I didn't start the fire but would have been tempted had I thought of it." In 1944, desiring an acting career, she enrolled in London's Central School of Speech and Drama where her ambitions quickly changed to directing. In 1947, she was awarded the Elsie Fogerty Prize and completed her studies at the Central School.

Jellicoe then set out to tour Europe, studying languages, which led to her later translations of Henrik Ibsen and Anton Chekhov, and theater architecture, which in turn resulted in a commission to study the influence of theater architecture on theater practice. The study interested Jellicoe in the open stage, and she founded the Cockpit Theatre Club in London in 1950 to experiment with the form. During the same year, she married C.E. Knight-Clarke. They divorced in 1961, and she married Roger Mayne on September 3, 1962. She has two children.

In 1953, Jellicoe returned to the Central School to teach acting and direct student productions. She left the school in 1955 to write *The Sport of My Mad Mother* as a means of entering professional theater as a director. *The Sport of My Mad Mother* tied for third place in the 1956 London *Observer* play competition, and because of its placing, the Royal Court Theatre in London chose to produce the play in 1958. Jellicoe co-directed with Royal Court founder George Devine. The production resulted in a commission from the Girl Guides association, for which Jellicoe wrote *The Rising Generation*. The Girl Guides rejected the drama, but it was produced at the Royal Court in 1967.

Between 1959 and 1975, Jellicoe filled numerous roles at the Royal Court Theatre. She translated, adapted, and directed plays by Ibsen and Chekhov. She also wrote and directed several plays, including her two most famous comedies, *The Knack* and *The Giveaway*. Jellicoe co-directed *The Knack* with Keith Johnson in 1962, and in 1965, an outstanding film by Charles Wood based on the play won the Best Picture award at the Cannes Film Festival. *The Giveaway* was staged in 1968. Jellicoe's career at The Royal Court climaxed with her serving as the Literary Advisor from 1973 to 1975.

In 1974, Jellicoe moved to Lyme Regis, where she still lives, and she has since written several children's plays. However, her principal interest has been in community plays, which led her to found the Colway Theatre Trust in 1979. Jellicoe's community plays involve large casts of both theater professionals and community members, and are generally historical in nature. Often, the audience is involved as part of the cast.

Literary Analysis

Jellicoe has occasionally been labeled an Absurdist, but while much of her work reveals Absurdist influences, the term is not truly descriptive. As John Russell Taylor has noted, Jellicoe was "trying . . . to do something quite new in the English Theatre." Her works have an atypical experiential dimension. Rather than appealing purely to her audience's intellect through dialogue, Jellicoe's works function as a "totality": action and dialogue are both integral components. She explains that in her works, "all . . . is directly shown instead of being explained; if you're content to watch it without thinking all the time 'What is the meaning?' so that you don't even see or hear, you're so busy thinking—then you will get what it's about."[1] Jellicoe wants her audience to *experience* what happens, not *think* about what is said.

The Knack is Jellicoe's most successful comedy to date and provides an excellent example of the experiential dimension of her works. Intellectually, the play seems to be a comic account of sexual conquest in the 1960s. However, experientially the play is a satiric comment on learning, teaching, and thought control. The action is centered on a series of attempts to communicate and receive knowledge, with the students, Colin and Nancy, caught in a tug-of-war between their teachers, Tom and Tolen. Sexual knowledge is simply the goal. Tolen intellectualizes all experiences, turning learning into imitation and sex into domination. Tom is, in a sense, Jellicoe. He believes that Colin and Nancy must interact with one another, learn about each other, and come to understand their own sexuality; they must directly experience human interaction without an intellectual intermediary.

The play's humor is derived primarily from this experiential dimension. Throughout, Jellicoe uses contrapuntal dialogue that is designed to convey a distinct musical sensation. At its best, it creates a rhythm reminiscent of the classic Bud Abbott and Lou Costello patter. Often, two conversations will proceed at once, each separate from yet highlighting the other:

> Tom. . . . Colin wishes I wouldn't show off.

Colin. Well, you do show off.

Tom. I don't.

Colin. You do . . .

Tom. Nancy, more left.

Nancy. Oh, sorry . . . What's the difference between an elephant and a letter box?

Colin. They can neither of them ride a bicycle.

Nancy. You knew . . . I can reach higher than you.

Colin. Heard it before.

Tom. I don't show off.

Colin. What? No you can't.

Nancy. I can.

Colin. You can't.

Tom. I do—

Nancy. I can—

Tom.—sometimes—

The words in isolation seem almost nonsensical, but the effect in totality is quite musical and amusing.

Tom's teaching stories and games provide *The Knack*'s whimsical charm. Silly tales about cows who wear brassieres abound, and under Tom's guidance Colin, Nancy, and the audience discover that a mattress is a piano and a headboard is part of a lion's cage. One of the funniest scenes in the play contains a description of a fantastic game concocted by Tom to lure Colin and Nancy into learning about one another. Tolen has been practicing his method of seduction on Nancy in an attempt to "teach" Colin about women by showing him a type of "sample seduction." Tom realizes what is happening and "saves it by covering":

Tom. What do you think of our piano? (Pointing to bed) . . .

Nancy. That's not a piano . . . It's a bed.

Tom. It's a piano, honest, listen: Ping! . . . It's a piano, isn't it, Colin?

Colin. Piano? . . . Oh yes, a piano. Ping. (31)

During the rest of the scene, the dialogue is primarily a series of "pings" and "plongs," but Colin and Nancy have such fun that dialogue is unnecessary for the audience's pleasurable experience.

Tom's fantasy world is, in itself, delightful, but the gentle humor is also a device used to provide a foundation for the play's satiric elements. Tolen begins the play as an almost mes-

merizing Don Juan character, but the audience is so beguiled by Tom's childlike world that Tolen's brutal interruptions of the games are increasingly disturbing and threatening. Jellicoe defuses the tension in a variety of amusing ways that reveal Tom's delightful silliness at the expense of Tolen.

One of the most predominant comedic devices is the satiric barbs that Tom wields to puncture Tolen's inflated ego. At one point in the play, Tom becomes angry at Tolen's treatment of Nancy, so he tells Tolen to leave. Irritated at being forced to leave his conquest, Nancy, Tolen attempts to embarrass Tom but only proceeds in making himself look foolish:

Tom. Well that's that. I need this room, Tolen.

Tolen. . . . Expecting someone?

Tom. Maybe.

Tolen. . . . Man or woman? . . . Are you a homosexual?

Tom. No. (Tolen turns, crosses room; when he reaches door:) Thanks all the same. (50)

Soon Tolen returns to announce a phone call for Tom:

Tolen. It's for you.

Tom. Man or woman?

Tolen. Woman. (Tom rises, crosses L. As he passes Tolen snaps his fingers as if to say, "Darn, I hoped it was a man!")

Another high point in the comedy of *The Knack* is seen in Tom's various machinations as he attempts to keep Colin free of Tolen's influence and to prevent Tolen's seduction of Nancy. Tom tries to draw Colin into another of his teaching games, this time concerning lion training. When Colin refuses, Tom easily draws him in by playing on Colin's obsession with sex. Since Colin won't play the lion, Tom says he will, begins roaring, and then says, "Whew! It makes you feel sexy" (35). Colin immediately agrees to be the lion.

However, Tom's plots against Tolen are even more amusing. An extremely funny scene occurs when Tom decides to play a game solo and frustrate Tolen by blocking the passage to his room. He takes apart his bed, then "wheels off head and foot board as if he were a fat housewife with two children." When he reaches the door, he "says in a high falsetto voice, 'Come along children'" (58). When Tolen attempts to carry Nancy up to his room, he crashes headlong into the barricade.

The funniest comic technique employed in the play is the physical humor at the expense of Tolen and Colin as Colin becomes a potential "Tolen-in-progress," if you will. For example, his attempts to imitate Tolen's walk result in a gorilla-like swagger and "goose stepping gestapo style" (68). Colin plays the fool, but in doing so he reveals Tolen's true nature: brutish and brutal rather than sexy and suave.

Jellicoe's humor has a greater purpose than merely evoking laughter: the audience laughs *with* Tom and *at* Tolen. We experience a sense of camaraderie with Tom; we eventually feel contempt for Tolen. The author's humor leads us to experience the characters, and if we do that, we "get what [the play's] about."

Since Jellicoe's plays are a sensory rather than an intellectual experience, at times they have created difficulties for her audiences. Her *The Giveaway*, which was less successful than *The Knack*, is a good example. In this play, too, the dramatist is more concerned with what happens than with what is said. Intellectually, the play is a simple farce about consumerism. However, experientially *The Giveaway* is about relationships: how we "package" and "advertise" ourselves in order to attract a "consumer" or mate, and how this type of human consumerism is based on tricks and illusions, barriers to true human interaction.

The Giveaway is more aggressively visual than *The Knack*. Jellicoe has left behind some of the verbal techniques that made *The Knack* so appealing. The musical patter of contrapuntal dialogue has been replaced by asides and a greater number of non sequiturs. The asides attempt to draw the audience directly into the play, but they have a tendency to seem a bit forced. The non sequiturs are some of the playwright's finest; they do little to draw in the audience, though:

Mum: Last week's *Radio Times*—Daisy still got it?
Wink: Mm? Last week or the week that's ending today?
Mum: There's a lovely competition.
Wink: Competition?
Mum: 'Your cat's weight in gold.'
Wink: Your cat's weight in gold? Never knew you had a cat, Mrs. B.

Mum: He threw ours away before I had a chance to cut it out.

While the lines are quite funny, none of the characters have Tom's charm, and we tend to laugh at them rather than with them.

One verbal comic technique that Jellicoe does not abandon in *The Giveaway* is the delightfully zany satire that was so effective in *The Knack*. Mum Busby is so obsessed with competition that she invents a grandson in order to win a lifetime supply of cornflakes. Jellicoe introduces satire when Daisy Wink agrees to help Mum and Jim by impersonating the non-existent boy for a television commercial produced by the contest sponsors. Daisy's extemporaneous commercial satirizes virtually every television commercial ever written:

Daisy: Every day they grow a little . . . all that energy! Where does it come from? . . . Ah! Kiddies Kornflakes— the energy from a loving mum— energy plus! . . . It's what they need to grow! . . . It's been a long day—a long hard day—back aching? Put your feet up ah! That's better! You know you deserve something a little special—you've earned it—give yourself a treat—give yourself a cornflake . . .
(woman's voice:) He said she looked pretty in pink, so she washed her pink sweater in Kiddies Cornflakes—in case . . .
(man's voice:) In case of what?
(woman's voice:) Just—in case . . . (72)

Still, while this and the rest of the scene is wildly amusing, the satire is aimed at a concept—advertising—not an individual, so once again the experience may not be as concrete as is necessary.

Perhaps the most visual aspect of *The Giveaway* is the sleight-of-hand tricks played with the boxes. The boxes menace characters, appear and disappear, and seem to take on a life of their own. Eventually, the movements resemble a "now you see it, now you don't" shell game, which highlights the play's satire of both human and commercial advertising, the illusion of desirability. Unfortunately, the audience isn't really prepared for this visual tour de force. We have not been drawn into the play or the characters; thus, we have difficulty experiencing the total effect.

J

Summary

As a humorous writer, Ann Jellicoe is best represented by her plays *The Knack* and *The Giveaway*. Both works are uniquely hers in their experiential dimension: she encourages the audience to experience the play on a sensory rather than an intellectual level. She had greater success conveying this effect in *The Knack* and, as a result, enjoyed greater success commercially than with *The Giveaway*, but both plays introduced English audiences to a new type of theater where both action and dialogue are integral components in creating the play's themes. Jellicoe's theory of theater and theories about life as revealed in her works are quite similar: she encourages her audience to experience learning and living directly. If we can do that, then we might "get what it's about."

Notes

1. John Russell Taylor, *Anger and After* (London: Methuen, 1963).

Selected Bibliography

Primary Sources

Drama

The Sport of My Mad Mother. In *The Observer Plays*. London: Faber & Faber, 1958; rpt. in *Two Plays*. New York: Dell, 1964.
Romersholm. (Adapted from Ibsen.) San Francisco: Chandler, 1960.
The Knack. New York: Samuel French, 1962; rpt. in *Two Plays*. New York: Dell, 1964.
Shelley; or, The Idealist. London: Faber & Faber, and New York: Grove Press, 1966.
The Giveaway. London: Faber & Faber, 1970.
Two Jelliplays. London: Faber & Faber, 1974.
Three Jelliplays. London: Faber & Faber, 1975.
Devon. Co-authored with Roger Mayne. London: Faber & Faber, 1975.

Non-Fiction

Some Unconscious Influences in the Theatre. London and New York: Cambridge University Press, 1967.
Community Plays: How to Put Them On. 1987.

Interviews

Rubens, Robert. "Ann Jellicoe, Interviewed by Robert Rubens." *Transatlantic Review*, 12 (1963): 27–34.
Jellicoe, Ann. "Theatre People Reply to Our Inquiry." *World Theatre*, 14 (January/February 1965): 44–53.

Secondary Sources

Bibliographies

King, Kimball. *Twenty Modern British Playwrights: A Bibliography, 1956 to 1976*. New York and London: Garland, 1977, pp. 65–68.

Biographies

Blain, Virginia, Patricia Clements, and Isobel Grundy. *The Feminist Companion to Literature in English*. New Haven and London: Yale University Press, 1990, pp. 572–73.
Schlueter, June, and Paul Schlueter, eds. *An Encyclopedia of British Women Writers*. New York and London: Garland, 1988, pp. 251–53.
Small, Barbara J. "Ann Jellicoe." *Dictionary of Literary Biography: British Dramatists Since World War II*. Ed. Stanley Weintraub. Detroit: Gale Research, 1982. Vol. 13, pp. 255–61.

Chapters in Books

Alaiz, F.M. Lorda. *Teatro Ingles de Osborne Hasta Hoy*. Madrid: Taurus, 1964.
Gottfried, Martin. *A Theatre Divided; The Postwar American Stage*. Boston: Little, Brown, 1967, pp. 218–25. Gottfried discusses *The Knack* as a "left wing" comedy, a comic form "at the beginnings of invention." He suggests that while the play is not allegorical, parallels can be drawn between "post war international relations" and the power plays between the characters.
Salem, Daniel. *La Revolution theatrale Actuelle en Angleterre*. Paris: Denoel, 1969, pp. 57–60.
Taylor, John Russell. *Anger and After*. London: Methuen, 1963, pp. 65–71. Taylor chronicles Jellicoe's beginnings as a writer/director and analyzes her unique theatrical style in *The Sport of My Mad Mother*, *The Rising Generation*, and *The Knack*.
———. *The Angry Theatre*. New York: Hill and Wang, 1969, pp. 73–83. Reprints the entry from *Anger and After*, with

additional commentary on *Shelley; or, The Idealist* and *The Giveaway*.

Articles

Gascoigne, Bamber. "With a Bare Bedstead." *Spectator*, 208 (April 1962): 445. Gascoigne discusses *The Knack* as a "new wave [drama] . . . about sexual callousness."

Klein, Kathleen Gregory. "*The Knack*." *Theatre Journal*, 36, 2 (May 1984): 272–74. Klein suggests that *The Knack* is a play about "love, sex, and . . . power" which is "finally unconvincing" because of Nancy's naivete and Tom's inability to control the other characters.

Kuna, F.M. "Current Literature 1970–II, New Writing. Drama." *English Studies*, 52, 6 (December 1971): 565–73. Kuna argues that in *The Giveaway* Jellicoe sacrifices plot for style. He concludes that the play "reveals an intellectual preoccupation with well-established techniques and topics rather than a creative response to the contemporary scene."

Simon, John. "Theatre Chronicle." *The Hudson Review*, 17 (1964): 428–29. Simon Discusses *The Knack* as Absurdism that "has been domesticated."

Laura Snyder

Jerome, Jerome Klapka

Born: Walsall, Staffordshire, May 2, 1859
Education: Marylebone Grammar School, Lisson Grove, 1868–1873
Marriage: Georgina Henrietta Stanley, June 21, 1888; one child
Died: Northampton, June 14, 1927

Biography

Jerome K. Jerome was born in Walsall, Staffordshire on May 2, 1859, the son of Jerome Clapp Jerome and Marguerite Jones. The elder Jerome's desire to secure his family's fortune in business led him away from his early calling as a Congregationalist clergyman. In business matters, however, Jerome's father was something of a Dickensian ne'er-do-well, failing successively at farming, coal mining, and wholesale hardware merchandising. Accordingly, Jerome's childhood years from four to fourteen were spent in genteel poverty in the East End of London in a house first rented so that the family could be near their father's dockside ironmongery business. Jerome attended the Marylebone Grammar School for five years after passing scholarship examinations at the age of nine. Financial pressures on the family resulting from his father's death in 1871 induced Jerome to leave school at the age of fourteen. In later years Jerome would supplement his education by studying in the reading-room of the British Museum and engaging tutors among the impoverished scholars living in the Bloomsbury district around the museum.

Through a friend of his late father, Jerome obtained a ten-shilling-a-week position as an errand boy and clerk in the advertising department of the London & North-western Railway. He remained a railway clerk until the deaths of his mother and aunt, along with the marriages of his sisters, released him from family responsibilities. In April 1878, while still working as a clerk, he joined a dramatic company under the management of Murray Wood. The season at the theater that Wood managed lasted from April through November in 1878. At the close of the season Jerome was sufficiently encouraged about his prospects as an actor to leave his position as a clerk and begin a three-year acting career in the second tier of London's theatrical world and with touring companies in the provinces. Unable to break into the fashionable West End theaters, he eventually gave up the stage to pursue his literary ambitions. He worked variously as a penny-a-line journalist, an assistant schoolmaster, a private secretary, and a clerk in a solicitor's office until he began to establish himself as a writer in the mid-1880s. On June 21, 1888, he married Georgina Henrietta Stanley; the couple would have one child.

Jerome's experiences as an actor provided him with the material for his first significant publications, a series of humorous pieces that appeared in a theatrical magazine, *The Play*, published by W. Aylmer Gowling. Collected in book form as *On the Stage—and Off* in 1885, the essays remain a valuable and entertaining record of British theatrical practices in the 1870s and 1880s.

Jerome's humor became a regular feature of the magazine *Home Chimes*, where he contributed his own "Idle Thoughts" section as well as much of the material for the "Gossips' Corner." The enormous popularity of *Three Men in a Boat* (1889) in England and America and, in translation, throughout Europe dominated Jerome's career for the next twenty years.

Authorship of what would become a comic classic created some difficulties for Jerome. In the public's eye, Jerome the writer was indistinguishable from the character of the narrator in *Three Men in a Boat* and the authorial voice that Jerome adopted in the "Idle Thoughts" essays. Readers and critics alike began to assume that everything from Jerome's pen was, or ought to be, humorous, an attitude that adversely affected the critical and public reception of some of his serious fiction and drama.

Even though Jerome had given up on acting as a profession, he remained interested in the theater. After a series of one-act curtain-raisers and matinees in the late 1880s, he scored a major success in the West End in February 1890 with a three-act farcical comedy, *New Lamps for Old*. Several other successes made him a popular dramatist of some note in the course of the 1890s, and he continued to write for the stage until the last years of his career.

From 1892 to 1897, Jerome was the publisher and editor of the monthly review *The Idler* and the weekly magazine *To-Day*. Less spectacular than contemporary reviews such as *The Savoy* or *The Yellow Book*, *The Idler* numbered among its diverse list of contributors Rudyard Kipling, Sir Arthur Conan Doyle, W.W. Jacobs, Bernard Shaw, Mark Twain, Israel Zangwill, Annie Besant, Marie Corelli, and Elizabeth Lynn Linton. The broadening scope of Jerome's literary acquaintances in this period encouraged him to publish fiction in a more serious vein, including *John Ingerfield and Other Stories* in 1894 and his semiautobiographical *Bildungsroman, Paul Kelver*, in 1902.

The turn of the twentieth century saw Jerome working primarily as a dramatist with only occasional forays into novels, short fiction, and humorous essays. In the autumn of 1905 and spring of 1906, Jerome undertook a lecture tour of the United States exploiting his popularity as a humorist with American readers and the success of his plays on the New York stage. *Idle Ideas in 1905* and *The Angel and the Author—and Others* were Jerome's final collections of original humorous material, the latter volume clearly showing the strain of a middle-aged man's sensibility working within the style of facetious commentary on everyday life developed by a much younger man.

At the outbreak of World War I Jerome was split between an ingrained pacifism and his distaste for German militarism. In 1915, he traveled to the United States as part of a propaganda mission to explain England's position in the war; he met with President Woodrow Wilson in the White House. Although too old for active military service, Jerome, like other Englishmen in a similar position, found his way to the Western Front by joining the ambulance corps of the French Army in 1916. His health failed him during the winter of 1916/1917, and he returned to London in the spring, joining a group of peace platformists advocating a reasonable, negotiated end to the war.

In the summer of 1917, Jerome resumed writing, working on a dramatization of his pre-war comic short story "His Evening Out," which was produced as *Cook* in the fall of that year. In the immediate post-war years ill health hampered his writing career, and he worked almost exclusively on two novels, *All Roads Lead to Calvary* and *Anthony John*. In 1925, Jerome published his autobiography, *My Life and Times*. He died in Northampton on June 14, 1927, two weeks after suffering a cerebral hemorrhage while driving back to his home in London after a holiday in the country.

Literary Analysis

Jerome's literary reputation as the leading figure in the "New Humor" of the 1880s and 1890s is the result of the enormous popularity of his early humorous books and his editorships of *The Idler* and *To-Day*. The rest of Jerome's career as a popular dramatist and serious novelist is completely overshadowed by his authorship of the classic comic novel *Three Men in a Boat*.

The prominence that Jerome gained with the publication of *Three Men in a Boat* focused contemporary criticism of the "New Humor" on Jerome and his writings. In an ossified Victorian society leery of innovation, the "New Humor" was automatically suspect. The epithet "New" was applied in the late-Victorian era to anything that even remotely appeared to challenge the prevailing standards in society or the arts. The label of "New Woman" referred to both contemporary feminists and to any woman who conducted her life in a fashion that differed from the norms of her mother's and grandmother's generations. Stage plays that strayed from the dramatic and social conventions of mid-Victorian theater were identified as the "New Drama." Jerome's humor earned the label "New" because it deviated noticeably from the norms of Victorian humor. From Charles Dickens's *Posthumous Papers of the*

Pickwick Club through the pages of *Punch* to W.S. Gilbert's librettos for light operas composed in collaboration with Arthur Sullivan, Victorian humor had consisted largely of playful mockery of institutions and individuals such as the Courts of Chancery, marriage and family life, men's clubs, or the pretentious ineffectuality of the House of Lords, and the self-serving qualities of lawyers and politicians, as well as the bumblings of admirals and generals. Superficially, Jerome's humor differed from typically Victorian humor by using contemporary slang and drawing upon everyday middle-class life for its subject matter. But what drew the attention and the criticism of the Victorian literary establishment to Jerome and the other writers of the "New Humor" was the creation of a variety of humor appealing to the growing anti-Victorianism of the 1880s and 1890s. The "New Humor" shared the questioning of established social norms of the other literary and dramatic art of the period that both disturbed and titillated previously complacent late-Victorian readers and audiences.

Jerome's vein of humor, and the style of the "New Humor" as a whole, depended on irreverence and iconoclasm. Writing a letter to the editor of *The Times* was a sign of Victorian earnestness and high-mindedness, and the correspondences printed on particular issues show the tenor of the period. Jerome was determined to have a letter printed in *The Times* and, therefore, he wrote to the editor in the middle of a debate on the propriety of displaying paintings of nude figures at the Royal Academy's Summer Exhibition:

> Sir—I quite agree with your correspondent, "A British Matron," that the human form is a disgrace to decency, and that it ought never to be seen in its natural state.
>
> But, "A British Matron" does not go far enough, in my humble judgement. She censures the painters who merely copy Nature. It is God Almighty who is to blame in this matter for having created such an indelicate object.
>
> I am, Sir, your obedient servant, Jerome K. Jerome.

In his humor Jerome challenges the Victorian sense of propriety by pretending to wholeheartedly accept the values of a decent, Victorian lady. The sly suggestion that in her prudery "A British Matron" is still not Victorian enough and that she inevitably must take issue with the Creator rather than merely the painter thoroughly deconstructs her high moral outrage. This kind of facile mocking of Victorian values and pretentiousness is endemic in the "New Humor." From the perspective of Jerome's contemporary reviewers, who were steeped in traditional Victorian humor, this material was not only considered unfunny but it was also seen as a sign of a poor, narrow, and decidedly vulgar approach to life. The British book- and magazine-buying public enjoyed reading it, however, and the "New Humor" swept through late-Victorian letters like a breath of fresh air.

Jerome's first book, *On the Stage—and Off*, was based on his experiences acting in London and with stock companies touring England in the late 1870s. The narrative style is derived from the familiar essay, being colloquial and friendly, and the story combines broad realism with satire in the manner of the picaresque novel. The structure is essentially episodic, recounting the ambitions, misadventures, and disappointments of, as the book is subtitled, "The Brief Career of a Would-be Actor." The material is in some respects similar to the episode in Dickens's novel *Nicholas Nickleby* involving Vincent Krummel's acting company, but the semiautobiographical quality of the book keeps the characters whom Jerome describes from becoming caricatures as they do in Dickens. Most of the humor comes from the narrator's ironic deflation of his own pretensions as an aspiring actor, while the genuine pathos of the stories comes from the faithful recording of the little incidents of jealousy, grief, and sacrifice among second-rate, but earnest, actors. The book is also of importance as a genuine theatrical reminiscence, supplying a wealth of details about acting methods, rehearsals, costumes and makeup, and management practices in mid-Victorian theater.

Idle Thoughts of an Idle Fellow (1889) includes fourteen essays from Jerome's section in the monthly magazine *Home Chimes*. The essays follow in the tradition of the familiar essays written by Charles Lamb. As did Lamb in his *Essays of Elia*, Jerome exploits his one great subject: himself—his observations of people and the conditions of everyday life.

The charm of *Idle Thoughts of an Idle Fellow* is apparent from the very beginning.

J

Starting with a dedication to "a very dear and well-beloved friend" which turns out to be his pipe, the book proceeds with that irreverence and air of mock-philistinism that is readily identifiable as the "New Humor." What is most striking about *Idle Thoughts of an Idle Fellow* is that it addresses middle-class concerns in a rather middle-class way. The opening of the first essay, "On Being Hard Up," serves to illustrate the vein of self-deprecating wit that is characteristic of Jerome's early writings:

> It is a most remarkable thing. I sat down with the full intention of writing something clever and original; but for the life of me I can't think of anything clever and original—at least, not at this moment. The only thing I can think about now is being hard up. I suppose having my hands in my pocket has made me think about this. I always do sit with my hands in my pockets, except when I am in the company of my sisters, my cousins, or my aunts . . . the chorus of their objections is that it is not gentlemanly. I am hanged if I can see why. I could understand its not being considered gentlemanly to put your hands in other people's pockets (especially by the other people), but how O ye sticklers for what looks this and what looks that, can putting his hands in his own pockets make a man less gentle!

When contemporary critics labeled the book as a specimen of the developing "New Humor," the major objection was that it tended toward the vulgar and dealt with the commonplaces of middle-class life using the language of that very life. But, this was exactly the new note that Jerome brought to the form of the familiar essay that the reading public enjoyed, and it made him immensely popular in spite of critical objections.

In *Stage-Land* (1889), Jerome returned to the theater for his subject-matter. The essays were first serialized in *The Playgoer*, the journal of The Playgoers' Club, a group interested in revitalizing English drama which Jerome had helped organize. Jerome's essays reflect the same concerns for psychological and moral realism in drama that provided the impetus for the development of modern drama—the "New Drama" of the 1890s—on the English stage. With gentle satire, *Stage-Land* explodes the stock characters and shopworn devices of Victorian melodrama. Jerome uses the simple comic device of innocently refusing to separate the stage from reality. The transparently naive assumption behind each essay that all stage life is true allows the author to examine the actions and motives of the characters that populated Victorian melodrama and to show how the idealized plots and characterizations used in the theater were completely divorced from real life. For example, the essay about the Stage Villain begins:

> He wears a clean collar, and smokes a cigarette; that is how we know he is a villain. In real life, it is often difficult to tell a villain from an honest man; but, on the stage, as we have said, villains wear clean collars and smoke cigarettes, and thus all fear of blunder is avoided.

> It is well that the rule does not hold off the stage, or good men might be misjudged. We ourselves, for instance, wear a clean collar—sometimes.

The essays were beautifully illustrated by Bernard Partridge, who would later rise to fame drawing for *Punch*. In addition to being tremendously entertaining, *Stage-Land* is also an important document of stage history that preserves the flavor of Victorian theater and accurately depicts the acting styles and stage effects of melodrama.

Three Men in a Boat is Jerome's most famous work and ranks among the classic comic novels. The story purports to be nothing more than the account of a week spent boating up and down the River Thames by three young men on a holiday. The plot is loosely based on the author's boating excursions with his friends Carl Hentschel and George Wingrave, and much of the book's humor stems from the true-to-life quality of the mishaps and misadventures described. The fourth character in the story, and perhaps most fully developed, is a thoroughly anthropomorphized dog named Montmorency. "J," the narrator, supplies Montmorency's opinions on the events and some of the most amusing episodes involve the dog's preoccupation with chasing rats and fighting with cats. The narrative alternates between exaggeration and understatement as its comic method, and the narrator often supplies a slyly misleading moral commentary on everyday incidents to produce laughter through the patently false conclusions drawn from the facts.

Three Men in a Boat is the epitome of Jerome's "New Humor" style, exhibiting the flippancy of youth that gradually disappeared from his later humorous writings. *The Diary of a Pilgrimage*, published just two years later, attempted to repeat the formula of *Three Men in a Boat*. Unfortunately, the subject matter— a tour of Germany with a friend to see the Passion Play at Oberammergau—does not seem to lend itself as well to Jerome's humor as does a plot line involving three young men larking about on the Thames. As originally published, *The Diary of a Pilgrimage* also included six essays written in the *Home Chimes* fashion and a noteworthy utopian satire. In "The New Utopia" Jerome pokes fun at the late-Victorian vogue for utopian writings, including Samuel Butler's *Erewhon*, William Morris's *News from Nowhere*, and the American Edward Bellamy's *Looking Backwards*. Jerome's satire not only sends up the awkward narrative techniques and creaking plot devices of the fashionable utopian writers, it is also a devastating critique of the authoritarian socialism which underlays most late-Victorian utopian thought. The dystopia that Jerome envisions rivals Kurt Vonnegut's "Harrison Bergeron" in its distrust of egalitarianism and Aldous Huxley's *Brave New World* in its despair of a society in which the State has supplanted all of the functions of the family.

Three Men on the Bummel (1900), written more than a decade after *Three Men in a Boat*, comes closer to recapturing the spirit of the original. The same trio embarks on a bicycle tour of Germany, but this time they are older, more settled men. The instigation of the trip is not the need for a change to shake off a youthful malaise as in *Three Men in a Boat* but rather the desire to escape wives and growing families. The story recaptures much of the sparkle and humor of the original, though the tone often changes as the writer slips into very shrewd analyses of various facets of turn-of-the-century German society.

Jerome's last collections of essays in the "New Humor" style seem to lose some of the freshness and charm of his writing in the late 1880s. The essays in *Tea Table Talk*, *Idle Ideas in 1905*, and *The Angel and The Author—and Others* often slip into a didactic and almost strident mode and at times seem to incongruously impose the manner of the "Idle Thoughts" essay on inappropriate subject matters. Some of the topics that Jerome pursues (the New Woman, socialism, colonialism, the New Drama and the Problem Play, marriage law reform) are just too serious and his own sensibilities are too altered over the years to work in the style of humor that he had developed more than twenty years earlier.

Jerome's work as a humorist greatly influenced his playwriting. His first full-length play, *Woodbarrow Farm* (1888), was a comedy exploiting and satirizing the same stock characters and stage devices that he mocked in the *Stage-Land* essays. In the early 1890s, the writer found farce to be an attractive form for the dramatic expression of his humor. His comedies *New Lamps for Old* (1890) and *The Mac-Haggis* (1896) combine elements of the "New Humor" with the conventional forms of late-Victorian farce. Both plays explore contemporary social concerns in a manner similar to that adopted by George Bernard Shaw in his "Pleasant Plays" later in the decade.

Echoes of the "New Humor" may be found in Jerome's later dramas, too, especially in his depictions of working-class and middle-class characters. The more serious subjects that changed the tone of his humorous essays also appear in his dramatic works. His later plays are social comedies on serious themes analogous to some of the works of Shaw and J.M. Barrie. His most successful play, *Miss Hobbs* (1902), addresses the topical question of the role of the New Woman in late-Victorian society. *Fanny and the Servant Problem* (1909) is concerned with English class-consciousness, *The Master of Mrs. Chilvers* (1911) has a plot rooted in the Suffragist movement, while *The Celebrity* (1926) is a comedy exposing the pretentiousness and hypocrisy of upper-class, socialist reformers. Although popular in their day, Jerome's plays have long since ceased to be performed and are rarely included in studies of late-Victorian and Edwardian theater. Ironically, Jerome, who measured his own career in terms of his development as a dramatist and serious novelist, is now only remembered because of the continuing popularity of his early humorous writings.

Summary
Jerome K. Jerome's humor is best represented in the comic novel *Three Men in a Boat* and his early "Idle Thoughts" essays. The conventions of humor reflect social conventions and have serious social implications. Long after the social

necessities which created Victorian values had passed, humor had remained frozen in the world of Dickens's *Posthumous Papers of the Pickwick Club* and the pages of *Punch*. The irreverence and iconoclasm of the "New Humor" appealed to the emerging anti-Victorianism in the English reading public during the 1880s and 1890s. In his humor, Jerome responded to late-Victorian society's redefinition of customs, attitudes, and ideals as standards of judgment. His writings and the "New Humor" are the manifestation in comic literature of the transition in English society from the Victorian age to the Edwardian period and early modernism.

Selected Bibliography

Primary Sources

On the Stage—and Off. London: Field & Tuer, 1885.

Woodbarrow Farm: A Comedy in Three Acts. London: Samuel French, 1888.

Stage-Land: Curious Habits and Customs of Its Inhabitants. London: Chatto & Windus, 1889.

Idle Thoughts of an Idle Fellow. London: Field & Tuer, 1889; London: Alan Sutton, 1987.

Three Men in a Boat. London: Arrowsmith, 1889; London: Pavilion, 1982.

New Lamps for Old: A Farcical Comedy in Three Acts. Unpublished manuscript 53444 D, dated February 1890 in the Lord Chamberlain's Collection of Plays, Department of Western Manuscripts, British Library.

Told After Supper. London: Leadenhall Press, 1891; London: Alan Sutton, 1985.

The Diary of a Pilgrimage. London: Arrowsmith, 1891; London: Alan Sutton, 1987.

The Prude's Progress: A Comedy in Three Acts. London: Chatto & Windus, 1895.

"*The MacHaggis: A Farce in Three Acts.*" Unpublished manuscript 53625 E, dated March 1896 in the Lord Chamberlain's Collection of Plays, Department of Western Manuscripts, British Library.

The Second Thoughts of an Idle Fellow. London: Hurst & Blackett, 1898; London: Alan Sutton, 1983.

Three Men on the Bummel. London: Arrowsmith, 1900; as *Three Men on Wheels*, New York: Penguin, 1983.

Miss Hobbs: A Comedy in Four Acts. London: Samuel French, 1902.

Tea Table Talk. London: Hutchinson, 1903.

Tommy and Co. London: Hutchinson, 1904; London: Alan Sutton, 1984.

American Wives and Others. New York: Stokes, 1904.

Idle Ideas in 1905. London: Hurst & Blackett, 1905.

The Angel and the Author—and Others. London: Hurst & Blackett, 1908.

They and I. London: Hutchinson, 1909.

Fanny and the Servant Problem: A Quite Possible Play in Four Acts. London: Lacy, 1909.

The Master of Mrs. Chilvers: An Improbable Comedy. London: T. Fisher Unwin, 1911.

My Life and Times. London: Hodder & Stoughton, 1925; London: Alan Sutton, 1984.

The Celebrity: A Play in Three Acts. London: Hodder & Stoughton, 1926.

Secondary Sources

Connolly, Joseph. *Jerome K. Jerome: A Critical Biography*. London: Orbis, 1982. A mostly anecdotal biography drawing heavily from Jerome's autobiography and episodes in Jerome's semiautobiographical *Bildungsroman, Paul Kelver*. Connolly discusses the circumstances of the writing and the inspirations for Jerome's books, but there is no real literary analysis included.

Ruth, Marie. *Jerome K. Jerome*. New York: Twayne, 1974. A basically sound study of Jerome's life and career as a humorist, editor, and novelist. Analyses of Jerome's humorous books are often limited to only appreciative quoting. Treatment of Jerome's career as a dramatist limited to plot summaries of published plays.

Mackgraf, Carl. "Jerome K. Jerome: An Annotated Bibliography of Writings About Him." *English Literature in Transition, 1880–1920*, 26, 2 (1983): 83–132. Useful handlist of contemporary reviews of Jerome's writings. In his annotations Mackgraf is prone to uncritically accept contemporary judgments.

———. "Jerome K. Jerome: Update of a Bibliography of Writings About Him." *English Literature in Transition, 1880–1920*, 30, 2 (1987): 180–211.

Moss, Alfred. *Jerome K. Jerome*. London: Selwyn & Blount, 1928. An appreciation of Jerome's life and writings drawing heavily from Jerome's autobiography.

Peter C. Hall

Jerrold, Douglas William

Born: London, January 3, 1803
Education: Elementary school in Sheerness, thereafter self-educated
Marriage: Mary Ann Swann, August 15, 1824; seven children
Died: Kilburn, June 8, 1857

Biography

Douglas William Jerrold was born in London on January 3, 1803, to a strolling player and provincial theater manager, Samuel Jerrold, and his second wife, Mary Reid, a young actress. Jerrold spent his early years in Kent, first in Cranbrook, then in the port of Sheerness where his father was lessee of the theater. After two years as a naval midshipman he was apprenticed to a printer in London in 1816. It was at this time that he began his literary career, writing plays, prose, and verse. *More Frightened than Hurt* was produced at Sadler's Wells in 1821, the first of many dramas for the minor theaters that he wrote over the next ten years. On August 15, 1824, he married Mary Ann Swann. They were to have seven children, one of whom, Jane Douglas, was to marry Henry Mayhew (best known as a co-founder of *Punch*).

In 1825, Jerrold became the house playwright at Davidge's Coburg Theatre. Moving to Elliston's Surrey Theatre in 1829, he found fame with the production of his immensely popular nautical melodrama *Black Ey'd Susan*. Productions of other plays at Covent Garden and Drury Lane followed, most notably *The Rent Day* in 1832, but a brief venture into theater management in 1836 failed. Jerrold regularly published satiric and humorous prose in the 1820s, his work appearing in the *Athenaeum*, *New Monthly Magazine*, and *Blackwood's Edinburgh Magazine*, among other journals.

By 1835 Jerrold had a wide literary acquaintance, which included Henry Mayhew, Charles Dickens, and William Makepeace Thackeray. From the mid-1830s, he was able to live comfortably from his writings in a succession of houses in and around London, and to vacation in France and Kent as well. His friendships among the liberal literary circles of London led naturally to his involvement with *Punch*, which was founded in July 1841. From the second number of the journal until his death Jerrold contributed features, notes, and reviews to *Punch*, doing much to establish its political and satirical tone. Many of his pieces were reprinted separately, in volumes such as *Punch's Letters to His Son* (1843), *Punch's Complete Letter Writer* (1845), and the very popular *Mrs. Caudle's Curtain Lectures* (1846). Jerrold took on the editorship of the *Illuminated Magazine* from 1843 to 1844; other not wholly successful publishing ventures followed in the 1840s: *Douglas Jerrold's Shilling Magazine* (1845–1848) and *Douglas Jerrold's Weekly Newspaper* (1846–1848). From 1852 until his death he edited *Lloyd's Weekly Newspaper*. However, *Punch* remained an important outlet for his writing. He fought for many liberal causes, particularly for an end to capital punishment. His life was domestic and convivial, enlivened by his literary friendships and clubs. He died on June 8, 1857 at his house in Kilburn.

Literary Analysis

As a young printer from a theatrical background, it is not surprising that Jerrold combined his early attempts at poetry, journalism, and fiction with playwriting, sending his first attempt to the English Opera House at the age of fifteen. Without education or patronage, though, Jerrold faced difficulty making a literary reputation in London through middle-class periodicals, but the immensely vital world of popular theater in the 1820s welcomed his talents. He wrote melodramas for minor theaters such as the Coburg and the Surrey (such theaters concentrated their energies on farce, melodrama, and pantomime because they were legally unable to stage plays without musical accompaniment or a predominance of spectacle). His work satisfied audiences' demands for rapid action, extremes of emotion, and clear-cut characterization. Jerrold wrote with inventive theatricality, creating memorable characters and satisfactory comic situations. In *Mr. Paul Pry* (1827), for example, he transforms a standard comedy by John Poole into an energetic and funny farce by expanding the use of Poole's catch phrase for Paul Pry, "I hope I don't intrude," so that Pry becomes a grotesquely memorable caricature.

As a salaried playwright under Davidge's and Elliston's rapacious managements, Jerrold learned much about influencing the public. His own interests in liberal causes could be linked to the emotional themes that were congenial to spectators—robust patriotism, comic defiance of unreasonable authority, sentimental reconciliation, the triumph of virtue over villainy, grotesque humor, and crime. In 1829, he achieved a triumph with *Black-Ey'd Susan*. Inspired by a famous eighteenth-century ballad of the same name, this melodrama, full of naval vocabulary, marital fidelity, and patriotic enthusiasm, caught the taste of Jerrold's audience perfectly. *Black-Ey'd Susan* is a paradigmatic melodrama in which the innocent are first subjected to malign forces and then reprieved from evil by the intervention of providence. In protecting his virtuous wife from unwelcome advances, William, a jovial sailor in the Royal Navy, hits the unknown assailant, only to find that it is his captain, who is suffering from the effects of drink. However justifiable William's actions, the punishment is death. After he is tried and convicted, the final scene stages the spectacle of a gruesome execution ceremony that at the last moment is interrupted by the revelation that William's discharge from the navy had been granted, but delayed by the villain, so he was not a sailor when he struck the captain and therefore he is not guilty of a capital offense. Order is restored, evil punished, and virtue satisfactorily rewarded. (In his comic prose Jerrold returned frequently to such clashes between law and justice, targeting the failure of social institutions to deliver what they promised.)

The action in *Black Ey'd Susan* is lively, nautical terminology effectively characterizes William, and there is some good comic relief. The play provided the perfect vehicle for T.P. Cooke, an actor whose large following appreciated his role as a combination of mythic "Jolly Jack Tar" and tender, domesticated husband. *Black-Ey'd Susan* became perhaps the first smash hit of the theater; there were 400 performances at six London theaters in the first year that it appeared. The play restored the Surrey's finances and made Cooke a fortune. Jerrold received merely £60 for his work, an unfairness that filled him with bitterness toward theater managers and partly explains his later commitment to campaigns for reform of the theater and copyright laws. On the death, early in the evening, of the notoriously mean Davidge, Jerrold remarked "Humph! . . . I didn't think he'd die before half-price had come in!"[1]

Jerrold wrote other interesting melodramas (and many unremarkable ones) for the minor theaters. *Fifteen Years of a Drunkard's Life* (1828), for instance, a highly moral and emblematic attack on alcoholism, anticipates the methods of Jerrold's writing for *Punch* and exemplifies the social issues with which he remained concerned throughout his life, while *The Mutiny on the Nore* (1830) attempts with some success to apply the formula of *Black-Ey'd Susan* to the politically controversial topic of justified mutiny.

Following his success at the Surrey, Jerrold continued to write melodramas for the up-market "legitimate" theaters. Of these efforts, *The Factory Girl* (1832) is interesting as perhaps the earliest industrial melodrama. Its conventional, conservative reaction to unionism and mob violence and its lack of attention to factory life vitiate what would otherwise be a significant work about the plight of mill-workers. It must surely have disturbed Jerrold's middle-class audience at Drury Lane during the turmoil of the 1830s. In *The Rent Day*, the author claimed to have invented a new genre of "domestic melodrama." Set in a depressed rural community, this play "realized" upon stage two pictures by David Wilkie, with the action faithfully structured around the characters of the paintings.[2] *The Rent Day* has some grossly sentimental speeches, but there are moments of genuine comedy and pathos as well. Jerrold alerts audiences to the social dynamics of the plot through the staged pictures, but he never really comes to grips with the rural unrest caused by agricultural depression in the 1830s. The ending of the play offers not a radical revision of the relations between landlords and tenants but rather the restoration of security and happiness through the intervention of providence and a beneficent paternalistic owner. One genuinely satirical touch running through the play is the comic characterization of Bullfrog, the bailiff, who goes about his job and an unsuccessful courtship alike with the refrain "Business is business" on his lips.

The author's later dramas, which were aimed at the entertainment of more fashionable audiences, lack something of the sharpness of social observation that enlivened his early plays. Their mixture of comedy and sentiment, if more genteel, is less interesting. One exception is the farce, *Bubbles of the Day* (1842), in which he made a sardonically effective commentary on the emptiness of London society, using a series of caricatures, some clever deceptions, and frequent asides. The treacly sentiments and implausible characterization of Jerrold's romantic costume drama, *Time Works Wonders* (1845), are not to modern taste, but contemporaries considered it his finest work: "the wit and the wisdom of it are never asunder," said Dickens,[3] a phrase that summarized his colleagues' attitudes toward Jerrold's work.

While working as a playwright, Jerrold contributed hundreds of articles to a variety of journals in London. Included were comic sketches and reviews, as well as more extended series such as *Men of Character* (1838; serialized 1835). Like Dickens's *Sketches by Boz* and Thackeray's early articles, they are evidence of increasing popular interest in short pieces humorously observing the features and characteristics of contemporary life. A new market for writers was developing as literacy spread and the population of London grew in numbers and sophistication. *Punch*'s foundation by wits, writers, illustrators, and journalists in 1841 was a response to this market. The founders included Jerrold, Mark Lemon, Dickens, Thackeray, and John Leech. They could rely on informed readers who were aware of the politics and cultural events of the time, able to identify parodic and burlesque texts, responsive to the democratic political position of the paper (itself largely a creation of Jerrold in the series of editorials signed "Q"), and who shared in its intolerance of the abuses of power and money in Victorian life.

From 1842 to 1848, Jerrold was, in Richard Kelly's words, "the unrivalled genius of comic journalism."[4] For *Punch,* Jerrold wrote his most biting, inventive, and funniest prose, simultaneously contributing significantly to the running jokes, short parodies, cartoons, reviews, and miscellaneous writing that gave the journal such a distinctive flavor. His fiction, usually episodic, satiric, and with strong fantasy elements, was written not only to amuse but also to direct attention to abuses and injustices. Thus, *The Story of a Feather* (serialized in *Punch* in 1843) is the autobiography of an ostrich plume which journeys from the cradle of the Prince of Wales, through the unfeeling world of the aristocracy and the self-interested, cheating world of commerce, to the virtuous, but poverty-stricken home of a working-girl, exposing vice and hypocrisy on the way. In a later, more grotesque and more interesting story, *A Man Made of Money* (serialized 1848–1849), Jerrold directed his satire against the whole world of consumerism. A moderate man finds himself able to satisfy the demands for money made by his family and society by tearing £100 notes off his body: "Truly he was a Man made of Money. Money was the principle of his being; for with every note he paid away a portion of his life."[5] In *The History of St. Giles and St. James* (1845–1847), a novel which was serialized in his own *Illuminated Magazine* (priced at a shilling and hence aimed at an even more popular readership than *Punch*), Jerrold attacked the enormous gap between the wealthy and the poor of London. Driven by a deep moral seriousness and humanitarian concern for others, Jerrold's comic gifts were used infrequently and, as in his weaker sketches, he subordinated realism and psychological complexity to his social concerns.

Jerrold did not have the narrative skills to develop his fictional sketches into successful novels in the way that Dickens and Thackeray did. He was more comfortable with short squibs, brief moral tales, or series of burlesques or parodies such as *Punch's Letters to His Son* and *Punch's Complete Letter Writer*, in which straining for plot-coherence did not hinder his creation of comic fictional voices. *Punch's Letters to His Son*, which appeared in early numbers of *Punch* in 1842, comprises a witty parody of Lord Chesterfield's *Letters*, satirizing hypocrisy, self-interest, and the worldly wisdom of modern life: "My son, in conclusion, it is well to drink from your own bottle; but it is still better to drink from another man's."[6] At the end the hanging of the son for theft brought up according to these principles is reported. In *Punch's Complete Letter Writer* (serialized in 1844) Jerrold develops the idea of the ironized letter-writer further, using a variety of correspondents, each caught in the act of unconscious self-betrayal. Some letters are primarily comic, like the pair from a home-owner checking the references of a servant and the servant carrying out a similar check on the potential employer. Other letters expose specific abuses, as do those dealing with the employment and exploitation of governesses.

The immediate success of the two series of *Letters* owed much to their comic generality and to their extension of long-existent comic themes. Occasionally the satire deployed by Jerrold was sharper. In the "Jenkins Papers," for instance, he singles out the particularly despicable gossip in *The Morning Post* for ridicule, transposing and mocking whole paragraphs of its pompous reports on fashionable society through exaggeration, burlesque, and heavily ironic commentary. The Royal family was frequently guyed, while Jerrold was at his most cutting when writing about Sir Peter Laurie, an infamously unsympathetic Lord Mayor. Jerrold wrote several burlesques for *Punch* in which humor directed against specific social abuses coexisted with an exuberant elaboration of comic types. He had a cartoonist's ability to represent and exaggerate those aspects of his targets that made their failings most memorable: "As for the member for Muffborough, he is one of those wise philanthropists who, in a time of famine, would vote for nothing but a supply of toothpicks."[7]

The most popular and enduring of Jerrold's comic series was *Mrs. Caudle's Curtain Lectures*, published in *Punch* with great success in 1845. It is comprised of a set of monologues (punctuated by occasional feeble interjections) delivered to the much-suffering Job Caudle by his monstrously tyrannical spouse. They are full of comic inventiveness combined with warmth of sympathy for ordinary human frailties. There are clear parallels to Dickens's monologues, of course, and Mrs. Caudle ranks with his Mrs. Lirriper as a prime example of the humorous possibilities of grotesque ventriloquism.

> All I say is this: I only wish I'd been born a man. What do you say? You wish I had? Mr. Caudle, I'll not lie quiet in my own bed to be insulted. Oh, yes, you did mean to insult me. I know what you mean. You mean, if I had been born a man, you'd never have married me. That's a pretty sentiment, I think? and after the wife I've been to you. And now I suppose you'll be going to public dinners every day! it's no use your telling you've only been to one before; that's nothing to do with it—nothing at all. Of course you'll be out every night now. I knew what it would come to when you were made a mason: when you were once made a "brother," as you call yourself, I knew where the husband and father would be; I'm sure, Caudle, and though I'm your own wife, I grieve to say it. I'm sure you haven't much heart, that you have any to spare for people out of doors. Indeed, I should like to see the man who has! No, no, Caudle; Indeed, I should like to see the man who has! No, no Caudle; I'm by no means a selfish woman—quite the

contrary; I love my fellow-creatures as a wife and mother of a family, who has only to look to her own husband and children, ought to love 'em.

As in so much comic writing, the fun in *Mrs. Caudle's Curtain Lectures* derives from audience prejudices; the complaint made by Anne Marsh-Caldwell in her novel *Emilia Wyndham* that the Mrs. Caudle papers reinforced misogynistic attitudes toward marriage may be valid, for Jerrold elaborates the familiar stereotype of the hen-pecked husband to a readership that he seems to conceive of as primarily male. Many of his jokes are good examples of casual sexism: "Women are all alike. When they are maids they're as mild as milk: once make 'em wives, and they lean their backs against their marriage certificates and defy you"; "He kissed her, and promised. Such beautiful lips. Man's usual fate—he was lost upon the coral reefs."[8] As with Mrs. Lirriper or Geoffrey Chaucer's Wife of Bath, however, the energy of Mrs. Caudle's nightly tirades seems to evoke something more than a mere figure of fun. She is larger than life and in the end her sheer presence makes her memorably triumphant.

The hardest task in any account of Jerrold's canon is to demonstrate what was patently evident to his friends, that in addition to his humor as a writer, he was also one of the wittiest people whom they had ever met. Numerous reminiscences bear witness to his ability to keep gatherings of friends or fellow writers in fits of laughter. The regular editorial meetings of *Punch* were often dominated by Jerrold's flow of witticisms. At the various literary clubs which he founded his conviviality and humor were notorious—and he spared neither friend nor family when the opportunity for verbal wit arose. Planche was discussing the importance of originality of characterization: "Do you remember my baroness in *Ask No Questions?*" he asked; the reply was: "Yes. Indeed I don't think I ever saw a piece of yours without being struck by your barrenness."[9] Quick thinking, verbal felicity, and precise images appear everywhere in Jerrold's writings and recorded sayings: "Dogmatism is puppyism come to full growth"; "[jokes] are the luxury of beggars; men of substance can't afford them"; "Some men get on in the world on the same principle that a sweep passes uninterruptedly through a crowd."[10]

Like the over-determined endings, revelations, and confrontations of his fiction, the distinctive voices and strongly imagined characters that Jerrold invented for *Punch* owed much to his early theatrical experience. Many of the concerns with justice and social fairness are common to his work in the theater and magazines alike. Still, the later flowering of his prose indicates how much his natural talents were confined by the conventions and censorship of stage melodrama. In his prose writing Jerrold used grotesque imagination, fantasy, satire, parody, and sometimes vicious verbal humor with a freedom that the stage did not allow him. His subject matter also broadened. His unceasing attack on the follies of the Royal family, for example, would have been impossible on stage. Jerrold's views on social life are clearly apparent in all his writing. They are not elaborate or thought out; indeed, sometimes they are self-contradictory. But, in his work for *Punch* and other journals, he combined entertainment with a determinedly critical attitude toward contemporary society, an attitude moral rather than political, fired by sentiment rather than analysis. In his work he demonstrated that comedy in journalistic writing could still have the reforming force that it had had in the past, in Jonathan Swift, say, and that comic parody, satire, caricature, and wit remained powerful weapons in the struggle against hypocrisy, poverty, and exploitation. Mrs. Caudle is only the most developed of the masks and voices in his writing through which he ironizes and mocks the attitudes and discourse of his satiric targets with fire and brilliance.

Summary
Douglas Jerrold's most important work is his witty and biting comic journalism for *Punch* which helped establish its characteristic tone and attitudes for a century. His inventive, amusing, but sometimes sentimental fiction, always written "with a purpose," at its best burns with indignation at the hypocrisies and injustices of nineteenth-century English life. An important minor playwright, one of the most admired and feared wits of his time, and a redoubtable fighter for democratic and liberal causes, Jerrold found the ideal outlet for his comic and imaginative gifts in the world of the emerging Victorian popular press.

Notes
1. Quoted by W. Blanchard Jerrold, *The Life and Remains of Douglas Jerrold* (London: W. Kent, 1859), p. 87. Most theaters still allowed patrons in for half-price if they arrived only for the second part of the show.
2. See on this subject Martin Meisel, *Realizations: Narrative, Pictorial, and Theatrical Arts in Nineteenth-Century England* (Princeton: Princeton University Press, 1983).
3. Quoted by W. Blanchard Jerrold, *The Life and Remains of Douglas Jerrold* (London: W. Kent, 1859), p. 169.
4. *The Best of Mr. Punch: The Humorous Writings of Douglas Jerrold*, ed. Richard M. Kelly (Knoxville: University of Tennessee Press, 1970), p. 5.
5. *The Works of Douglas Jerrold* (London: Bradbury and Evans [1863–1864]), Vol. IV, p. 80.
6. *The Works of Douglas Jerrold*, I, 472. Richard Kelly has pointed out how much Jerrold draws in this and other works on the themes and forms of previous fiction and satire, giving them his own particular ironic and grotesque flavor; see Kelly's *Douglas Jerrold* (New York: Twayne, 1972), pp. 93–97.
7. *The Wit and Opinions of Douglas Jerrold* (London: W. Kent, 1859), p. 2.
8. *Ibid.*, pp. 3, 69.
9. *The Life and Remains of Douglas Jerrold*, p. 96.
10. *The Wit and Opinions of Douglas Jerrold*, pp. 23, 28; *Bon-Mots of Charles Lamb and Douglas Jerrold*, ed. Walter Jerrold (London: J.M. Dent, 1893), p. 177.

Selected Bibliography
Primary Sources

Collections
The Writings of Douglas Jerrold. 8 vols. London: Bradbury and Evans, 1851–1854.
The Wit and Opinions of Douglas Jerrold. Collected and arranged by W. Blanchard Jerrold. London: W. Kent, 1859.
The Works of Douglas Jerrold, with an introductory memoir by his son, W. Blanchard Jerrold. 4 vols. London: Bradbury and Evans, and Philadelphia: Lippincott [1863–1864].
Bon-mots of Charles Lamb and Douglas Jerrold. Ed. Walter Jerrold. Grotesques by Aubrey Beardsley. London: J.M. Dent, 1893.

J

The Essays of Douglas Jerrold. Ed. Walter Jerrold, with illustrations by H.M. Brock. London: J.M. Dent, and New York: E.P. Dutton, 1903.

Douglas Jerrold and "Punch." Ed. Walter Jerrold. London: Macmillan, 1910. Contains an account of Jerrold and *Punch* as well as some of his contributions.

The Best of Mr. Punch: The Humorous Writings of Douglas Jerrold. Ed. with an introduction by Richard M. Kelly. Knoxville: University of Tennessee Press, 1970.

Fiction and Essays

Men of Character. Illustrations by Thackeray. 3 vols. London: Henry Colburn, and New York: Bunce, 1838.

The Handbook of Swindling, by Barabbas Whitefeather. Illustrations by "Phiz." London: Chapman & Hall, 1839. New edition, with an introduction by Walter Jerrold. London: Walter Scott, and New York: A. Lovell [1891].

Punch's Letters to His Son. London: W.S. Orr, 1843.

The Story of a Feather. London: Punch Office, 1844; Philadelphia: Carey and Hunt, 1845.

The History of St. Giles and St. James. New York: Burgess, Stringer, 1845.

Punch's Complete Letter Writer. Illustrations by John Leech and others. London: Punch Office, 1845.

The Chronicles of Clovernook; with Some Account of the Hermit of Ballyfule. London: Punch Office, and New York: Harper, 1846.

Mrs. Caudle's Curtain Lectures. New York: W. Taylor and E. Winchester, and Philadelphia: Carey and Hart, 1845. London: Punch Office, 1846. Many other editions and several translations of this, Jerrold's most popular work, appeared during the nineteenth century.

A Man Made of Money. London: Punch Office [1848–1849]. New York: Lockwood, 1845. Published in 6 parts.

The Brownrigg Papers. Ed. W. Blanchard Jerrold. London: J.C. Hotten, 1860. In addition to the selection of works above (all of which first appeared in periodicals), Jerrold published numerous articles and stories which have not been collected or reprinted. His extensive con-

tributions to *Punch* are partly listed in Walter Jerrold, *Douglas Jerrold: Dramatist and Wit*. His many contributions to the *New Monthly Magazine* are identified in the *Wellesley Index*.

Plays

Mr. Paul Pry. Coburg, November 27, 1827. Farce. Pub. in *English Plays of the Nineteenth Century*. Ed. Michael Booth. London: Oxford University Press, 1969–1973. Vol. 4.

Ambrose Gwinnett. Coburg, October 6, 1828. Melodrama.

Fifteen Years of a Drunkard's Life. Coburg, November 24, 1828. Melodrama.

Black Ey'd Susan: or All in the Downs. Surrey, June 8, 1829. Nautical melodrama. Pub. in *Nineteenth-Century Melodrama*, ed. George Rowell, 2nd ed. (London: Oxford University Press, 1972), and in *English Plays of the Nineteenth Century*, ed. Michael Booth (London: Oxford University Press, 1969–1973), Vol. 1.

Thomas à Becket. Surrey, November 30, 1829. Historical drama.

Sally in Our Alley. Surrey, January 11, 1830. Melodrama.

The Mutiny on the Nore: or British Sailors in 1797. Royal Pavilion, June 7, 1830. Nautical melodrama.

The Bride of Ludgate. Drury Lane, December 8, 1831. Comedy.

The Rent Day. Drury Lane, January 25, 1832. London: C. Chapple, and New York: Clayton, 1832; rpt. with an introduction and notes by C.G. Worth (Department of English, Monash University, 1990). Domestic melodrama.

The Factory Girl. Drury Lane, October 6, 1832. Melodrama.

Nell Gwynne: or, The Prologue. Covent Garden, January 9, 1833. Comedy.

The Housekeeper, or The White Rose. Haymarket, July 17, 1833. Comedy.

Beau Nash, the King of Bath. Haymarket, July 16, 1834. London: J. Miller, 1834. Comedy.

The Painter of Ghent. Strand, April 25, 1836. One-act tragic drama.

Bubbles of the Day. Covent Garden, February 8, 1842. London: How and Parsons, 1842. Comedy.

Time Works Wonders. Haymarket, April 26, 1845. London: Bradbury and Evans,

1845. Comedy.

This is a small selection from Jerrold's dramatic output. Most titles were published in one or another, or several, of the collections of acting editions of plays such as Lacy's or Dick's. Only separate publication is recorded above. See Allardyce Nicoll, *A History of English Drama 1660–1900*, volume 4, *Early Nineteenth Century Drama, 1800–1850*, 2nd ed. (Cambridge: Cambridge University Press, 1960), for further details of Jerrold's theatrical work.

Secondary Sources

Books

Jerrold, W. Blanchard. *The Life and Remains of Douglas Jerrold*. London: W. Kent, 1859. Useful biographical source, though rather hagiographic.

Jerrold, Walter. *Douglas Jerrold, Dramatist and Wit*. 2 vols. London: Hodder and Stoughton [1914]. Key biographical source, and particularly well-informed on Jerrold's early dramatic career.

Kelly, Richard M. *Douglas Jerrold*. New York: Twayne, 1972. Twayne's English Authors Series, number 146. Excellent modern introduction to Jerrold, informative on the *Punch* years, and with some interesting comments on the fiction, including the results of Kelly's detailed work on the sources and analogues of Jerrold's writing. Has detailed bibliography.

The first scholarly and critical biography of Jerrold by Michael Slater of Birkbeck College, University of London, is forthcoming.

Articles and Chapters in Books

Emeljanow, Victor. "Douglas Jerrold." In his *Victorian Popular Dramatists*. Boston: Twayne, 1987, pp. 21–55. Twayne's English Authors Series, number 440. Some lively comments on Jerrold's drama.

Ray, Gordon N. *Thackeray: The Uses of Adversity, 1811–1846*. New York: McGraw-Hill, 1955. On the relations between Thackeray and Jerrold.

Spielmann, M.H. *The History of "Punch."* New York: Cassell, 1895. Standard work on the early years of *Punch*.

Christopher G. Worth

Johnson, Samuel

Born: Lichfield, England; September 7 (September 18, New Style calendar), 1709
Education: Lichfield Grammar School, 1717–1725; Stourbridge Grammar School, 1726; Pembroke College, Oxford University, 1728–1729
Marriage: Elizabeth Jervis Porter, July 9, 1735
Died: London, December 13, 1784

Biography

On September 7, 1709 (Old Style calendar), Samuel Johnson was born in Lichfield, England, to fifty-two-year-old Michael Johnson, a bookseller, and his forty-year-old wife, Sarah Ford. Sent to a nurse, as was the custom, the infant contracted tuberculosis, which left him blind in his left eye, deaf in his left ear, and badly scarred. After attending the local grammar school where he was a brilliant student (1717–1725), Johnson left Lichfield in late 1725 to spend nearly a year with his cousin, Cornelius Ford, at Pedmore. This visit affected Johnson greatly, for it introduced him to a world of elegance and learning previously closed to him. Upon his return to Lichfield he could not continue at the grammar school, so he went to Stourbridge (1726), where his intelligence, according to Bishop Thomas Percy, earned him admission "into the best company of the place, and [he] had no common attention paid to his conversation; of which remarkable instances were long remembered there."

Shortly after his seventeenth birthday, Johnson came back to his native town to work—and more often to read—in his father's bookshop. His voracious intellectual appetite (matched by his physical appetite) prompted Dr. William Adams to remark, when through a legacy of £40 Johnson was able to go up to Pembroke College, Oxford, that the young man "was the best qualified for the University that he [Adams] had ever known come there."

Forced to leave college for lack of money after thirteen months, Johnson taught briefly at Market Bosworth (1732). In 1733, he moved to Birmingham, where he wrote for the local newspaper and earned £5 by translating Father Jerome Lobo's *Voyage to Abyssinia*. In Birmingham he met Harry Porter; Porter died in 1734 and Johnson married the man's widow, Elizabeth, on July 9, 1735, although she was twenty-one years his senior. With her savings he opened a school at Edial, near Lichfield, but the effort failed. Accompanied by his former pupil David Garrick and with a half-finished tragedy in his pocket, in 1737 Johnson went to London, each hoping to succeed in his own way on the stage. Garrick made his fortune, but Johnson could find no producer for *Irene* until his one-time student, who had risen to become manager of Drury Lane Theatre, agreed to perform the work in 1749. Meanwhile, to eke out a precarious living, between 1737 and 1755 Johnson wrote over 200 articles on subjects ranging from agriculture to Chinese architecture. While most of this was hack work, he also produced two fine poems, *London* (1738) and *The Vanity of Human Wishes* (1749), a moving biography of his friend Richard Savage (1744), and *The Rambler* (1750–1752), a collection of moral essays.

In 1755, his *Dictionary* appeared, the first modern lexicon. Although he received more than £1,500 for the project, the money was spent before the two folio volumes were published. Not until 1762, when he was awarded a government pension of £300 a year, would his financial problems end. To defray the costs of his mother's illness in 1759 he wrote *Rasselas* in the course of a week.

The last twenty years of the author's life were passed in relative contentment. In 1763, he met James Boswell, and two years later he became friendly with the Thrales, whose houses at Southwark and Streatham became second homes to him. His own establishment served as a refuge for a variety of destitute, querulous people: Dr. Robert Levett, the blind Anna Williams, Elizabeth Desmoulins, Francis Barber, and Poll Carmichael. Johnson would spend the week with the Thrales and return to his own residence on weekends to ensure that these dependents had at least one good meal. He also helped establish the Literary Club, which included Sir Joshua Reynolds, Edmund Burke, Edward Gibbon, Oliver Goldsmith, Garrick, and James Boswell—in short, the leading cultural figures of late eighteenth-century Britain. This group provided Johnson with the company that he desperately needed, for he was a most clubbable man and feared being alone.

No longer forced to write to earn his living, Johnson nonetheless produced a number of important works during his last two decades. His edition of William Shakespeare's works appeared in 1765, his *Journey to the Western Isles of Scotland*, based on a jaunt with Boswell to the Scottish Highlands, in 1775, and his *Prefaces, Biographical and Critical to the Works of the English Poets* between 1779 and 1781. Together with his earlier publications these established him as the foremost writer of his age. Following his death in London on December 13, 1784, he was buried in Westminster Abbey, one great monument placed inside another, and it would be difficult to determine which did the other more honor.

Literary Analysis

Johnson's greatness as a man, a writer, and a humorist derives from his insistence upon reality; he had no patience with idle speculation that was contrary to sense and observation. To Bishop Berkeley's philosophy he replied by kicking a stone: the stone is real, whatever metaphysicians may ingeniously and pointlessly argue. Hester Thrale, in her *Anecdotes of the Late Samuel Johnson, LL.D.* (1786) reveals this same attitude when she recounts, "He never (as he expressed it) desired to hear of the *Punic* war while he lived: such conversation was lost time (he said), and carried one away from common life, leaving no ideas behind which could serve *living wight* as warning or direction." "Clear your mind of cant," he repeatedly advised Boswell, and he was not one who failed to reck his own rede. Indicative of his frame of mind was his admiration of Reynolds when they first met at the house of Frances and Charlotte Cotterell. The two women were lamenting the death of a person who had helped them greatly. Reynolds remarked, "You have, however, the comfort of being relieved from a burthen of gratitude." The women were shocked, Johnson impressed by Reynolds' insight into the reality of human nature. This rejection of sentimental platitudes could suggest what Boswell described as a lack of "affection, tenderness, or even common civility" in an exchange with Mrs. Thrale. Boswell, relying on Guiseppe Marc' Antonio Baretti's account of this incident, mitigates Johnson's asperity, but Thrale's version in her *Anecdotes* rings true: "When I one day lamented the loss of a first cousin killed in America, —'Prithee, my dear, (said he,) have done with canting; how would the world be the worse for it, I may ask, if all your relations were at once spitted like larks, and roasted for Presto's supper?'—Presto was the dog that lay under the table while we talked."

Johnson sympathized deeply with the human condition. As Goldsmith observed of him, "No man alive has a more tender heart. *He has nothing of the bear but his skin.*" He placed pennies in the hands of poor sleeping children so they could buy breakfast, and he objected when others complained of paupers' seeking comfort. Precisely because he recognized life as "a state in which much is to be endured, and little to be enjoyed," he resented those who willfully added to the burden of sorrow, as he believed Mrs. Thrale was doing in summoning up the memory of a distant relative about whom, he felt, she cared little. When her mother died, Johnson's reaction was far different. His response to an over-scrupulous clerk demonstrates the same distinction between real and imagined trouble. The man was lamenting to Johnson that he suffered pangs of conscience over taking home supplies from work, even though he had his master's permission. "Study algebra," Johnson told the fellow, "and you will leave off tormenting your neighbours about paper and packthread, while we all live in a world that is bursting with sin and sorrow."

His touchstone for merit was fidelity to reality. Thus, he praised Francis Bacon for presenting "the observations of a strong mind operating on life." Despite his own wide reading, he told Mrs. Thrale that "the knowledge of Books . . . will never do without looking on life likewise with an observant Eye," and he maintained that "the only end of writing is to enable the readers better to enjoy life, or better to endure it." He held himself to the same high standard of facing the truth that he demanded of others. Told that a man named Pot had called *Irene* the finest modern tragedy, Johnson replied, "If Pot says so, Pot lies." Similarly, asked by a lady why he had defined "pastern" as the knee of a horse, he confessed, "Ignorance, Madam, pure ignorance." Johnson's humor thus rests on a bedrock of common sense. He delights by puncturing pretension and by demonstrating how people often follow the dictates of Erasmus's Folly rather than those of reason.

London, among Johnson's earliest literary efforts, is in some ways an artificial piece. Exploiting the vogue for classical imitation that Alexander Pope had created with his adaptations of Horace, Johnson turned to Juvenal's Third Satire, already Englished by John Oldham and John Dryden. Johnson echoes the anti-ministerial stance of the age's leading writers. Lycurgus had invited Thales to Sparta to civilize the inhabitants. In *London*, Robert Walpole is the anti-Lycurgus, the bad lawgiver who drives Thales away. Johnson later changed his mind about Walpole and came to regard him as a great prime minister. Indeed, many of the attitudes expressed in the poem hardly seem Johnsonian—the anti-urban stance, the call for war, the attack on luxury. This is the work of a young man who still had much to learn. Yet, the poem's major premise, expressed in a line capitalized for emphasis, is pure Johnson: "Slow rises worth, by poverty depress'd." This much life had already taught him.

By the time he wrote his other, and greater, Juvenalian imitation a decade later, he had found his voice. Significantly, *The Vanity of Human Wishes* is the first work to bear Johnson's name, and it embodies the tragic sense that informs all of his best work. Much of the poet's message is summarized in the line, "Fate wings with ev'ry wish th' afflictive dart." Riches, political power, learning, military success, long life, and beauty fail to produce happiness, not only because they are in themselves hollow gifts that pass away but also because humanity never can rest content. "Wav'ring man" repeatedly is "betray'd by vent'rous pride / . . . Shuns fancied ills, or chases airy good." For proof, Johnson, like Juvenal, turns to history, that embodiment of experience. Whereas the Roman satirist mocks those who pursue vain wishes, though, Johnson sympathizes. Juvenal, for example, paints a ludicrous portrait of the old man who would not die; Johnson's ancient arouses pity.

Johnson also differs from his source in his response to a tragic world. For Juvenal, Stoicism is the last grim hope; man is helpless against "the torrent of his fate." Ever the Christian, howbeit less orthodox than is often imagined, Johnson finds in religion salvation not only in the next world but in this. Temperance, courage, wisdom, faith, hope, and charity—the classical and Christian virtues—can calm "the mind / And [make] the happiness she does not find."

In *The Vanity of Human Wishes*, Johnson's stately couplets play a powerful organ in a minor key. In lines that drove the author himself to tears, he warns the fledgling scholar:

> Yet hope not life from grief and danger free,
> Nor think the doom of man revers'd for thee:
> Deign on the passing world to turn thine eyes,

J

And pause awhile from letters, to be
    wise;
There mark what ills the scholar's life
    assail,
Toil, envy, want, the garret (later, patron)
    and the jail.

King Charles XII of Sweden provided another powerful illustration of the sorrows that flesh is heir to, of great gifts that fail to bring happiness, of shattered dreams. He had hoped to rule "all . . . beneath the polar sky." His legacy proved different: "He left the name, at which the world grew pale, / To point a moral, or adorn a tale." Tragic fate, not unlimited power, induced the pallor.

Yet, even in his two great satires Johnson can raise a laugh. In *London*, he writes, "Here falling buildings thunder on your head, / And here a female atheist talks you dead." In *The Vanity of Human Wishes*, he speaks of Roger Bacon's gatehouse on Folly Bridge. The structure supposedly would fall if a scholar greater than Bacon passed beneath; the young student imagines that it already trembles above him. In his lighter verse this strain of humor shines forth even more brightly. As Johnson's imitations surpass their originals in grandeur, so his parodies reduce their models to the ludicrous. Pseudo-medieval ballads by Thomas Warton and his ilk particularly appealed to his sense of the ridiculous and prompted verses like the following:

Hermit hoar, in solemn cell,
Wearing out life's evening gray,
Smite thy bosom, sage, and tell,
Where is bliss? and which the way?
Thus I spoke; and speaking sigh'd;
—Scarce repress'd the starting tear;—
When the smiling sage reply'd,—
—Come, my lad, and drink some beer.

Though Johnson is a better poet than is sometimes recognized, his reputation rests largely on his prose. Because of Boswell one is inclined to preface the name Johnson with "Dr.," but in his own day the antecedent was more often "Dictionary." The French, Spanish, and Italians had national dictionaries, and England, too, desired one. In 1746, a group of booksellers asked Johnson to prepare such a work; after some hesitation he undertook the project. The forty members of the Académie Française had required over forty years to pro-

duce their lexicon; Johnson, working alone, proposed to complete his in three. Asked about the French experience Johnson replied, "Let me see; forty times forty is sixteen hundred. As three to sixteen hundred, so is the proportion of an Englishman to a Frenchman." Johnson actually required nine years and had the assistance of six amanuenses, but his accomplishment remains astonishing, particularly since during this period he contributed at least eighty pieces to the *Gentleman's Magazine* and wrote all but five of the 208 *Rambler* papers that appeared twice weekly between March 20, 1750 and March 14, 1752.

Johnson's definitions do not always clarify. His explanation of "cough" as "a convulsion of the lungs, vellicated by some sharp serosity" may not be enlightening. Nor is his entry for "network" instantly illuminating: "any thing reticulated or decussated, at equal distances, with interstices between the intersections." Still, to paraphrase his comment on Thomas Gray's *Elegy*, had he written often thus, it had been vain to praise, and useless to blame him. His definitions and 114,000 illustrative quotations reflect deep reading and thought, and those explanations that provoke laughter do so not because they are eccentric but because they penetrate to the core of the matter. Johnson's experience with Lord Chesterfield had taught him what a patron was: "commonly a wretch who supports with insolence, and is paid with flattery." Struggling to earn a living, he understood how one commonly received a pension, that "allowance made to any one without an equivalent. In England it is generally understood to mean pay given to a state hireling for treason to his country." However one might describe an excise, Johnson knew what it was—"a hateful tax levied upon commodities, and adjudged not by the common judges of property, but wretches hired by those to whom excise is paid." He harbored no illusions about his own accomplishment in the dictionary, recognizing that a lexicographer is "a harmless drudge." Perhaps his most famous definition is one that he did not include in the two folio volumes. *London* had echoed the sentiments of the anti-Walpole patriots, but by the 1770s Johnson had learned that patriotism all too often is "the last refuge of the scoundrel."

The "Preface" to the *Dictionary* once more demonstrates Johnson's fund of common sense. Many had hoped, including Johnson himself, that the lexicon would fix the English language in amber, but he had learned from the twin guides of reason and experience that language is a living essence. Though he regarded linguistic change as "degeneration," he acknowledged it as inevitable and confessed the lexicographer's inability "to change sublunary nature, and clear the world at once from folly, vanity, and affectation."

No matter how perdurable these aspects of human nature, in *Rasselas* Johnson cautioned against them. This novel may be viewed as a prose rendition of *The Vanity of Human Wishes*, as Rasselas, his sister, and Pekuah repeatedly imagine schemes of happiness and repeatedly find that reality does not conform to their expectations. In Cairo they encounter a philosopher whose doctrines so impress the prince that he resolves to become a disciple. Imlac warns the youth that "teachers of morality . . . discourse like angels, but they live like men." A few days later Rasselas learns the truth of Imlac's warning; all of the Stoic's preachings have been overturned by his daughter's death. The company hears of a hermit famed for the sanctity of his life; they reach his retreat just as he is about to return to Cairo, having resolved that society is preferable to solitude. Late in the book Rasselas decides to devote himself to study; Imlac introduces him to one who has pursued this course, an astronomer who has come to believe himself in control of the world's weather. Recalled to reason, he recognizes the folly of passing his time away from the world, and he declares that he has paid too high a price for his knowledge. At length the group resolves to return to Abyssinia, though not to the Happy Valley. Still dreaming, the princess intends to master all of the sciences and then establish a college whose graduates will be "models of prudence, and patterns of piety." Her brother would rule a small kingdom that grows ever larger in his imagination, and Pekuah longs for stasis in a world of flux. This ending may be read as a rejection of the need to hope. In the Happy Valley, where the inhabitants have nothing to desire, there are no pleasures; though in the world there are many pains, dreams—however unattainable—give meaning to life.

The characters in the novel, like the figures that illustrate *The Vanity of Human Wishes*, delude themselves with speculation that blinds them to reality and renders them the objects of satire or subjects of tragedy. Nowhere is the author's impatience with such self-imposed shortsightedness more evident than in his review of Soame Jenyns's *A Free Inquiry into the Nature and Origin of Evil* (1757) which blithely echoes Pope's proclamation in *An Essay on Man, Epistle I* (1734): "All Nature is but Art, unknown to thee; / All Chance, Direction which thou canst not see; / All Discord, Harmony not understood; / All partial Evil, universal Good." Johnson despised this philosophy, writing in his *Life of Pope*, "Never were penury of knowledge and vulgarity of sentiment so happily disguised." Jenyns fared even less well by Johnson's pen. *A Free Inquiry* had suggested that human suffering might amuse higher beings. The callous proposition provoked Johnson to Swiftian irony: "As we shoot a bird flying, they take a man in the midst of his business or pleasure, and knock him down with an apoplexy. Some of them, perhaps, are virtuosi, and delight in the operations of an asthma, as a human philosopher in the effects of the air pump . . . Many a merry bout have these frolic beings at the vicissitudes of an ague, and good sport it is to see a man tumble with an epilepsy, and revive and tumble again, and all this he knows not why." But, one particular jest surpasses all others. These superior beings "now and then catch a mortal proud of his parts, and flattered either by the submission of those who court his kindness, or the notice of those who suffer him to court theirs. A head thus prepared for the reception of false opinions, and the projection of vain designs, they easily fill with idle notions, till in time they make their plaything an author" who regales them most with an absurd "treatise of philosophy," like *A Free Inquiry*.

Johnson concluded his review by declaring that "[t]he only end of writing is to enable the readers better to enjoy life, or better to endure it." Measured by this yardstick, Shakespeare is the greatest author because he is truest to nature and humankind, and Johnson defended the playwright against neoclassical strictures that ignored reality. Thus, he accepted the mingling of comedy and tragedy because in life "the reveller is hastening to his wine, and the mourner burying his friend." The unities held no charm for him, either, since there was no reason that the audience could not as easily imagine itself in two places as in one. Did Shakespeare violate decorum by portraying a Roman senator as a fool? Again Johnson defended the choice by pointing to life. Shakespeare "knew that *Rome*, like every other city, had men of all dispositions; and wanting a buffoon, he went into the senate-house for that which the senate-house would certainly have afforded him." In 1765, Johnson objected to the lack of poetic justice in the plays, but in the *Life of Addison* he conceded that in mirroring reality the stage "ought to show us sometime what we are to expect."

Familiarity with and relevance to life were for Johnson the hallmarks of great literature. Imlac tells Rasselas, "I could never describe what I had not seen: I could not hope to move those with delight or terrour, whose interest and opinion I did not understand." The bad critic Dick Minim, whom Johnson satirizes in *Idler* 61 and 62, mouths platitudes but lacks judgment, learning, and experience. Since the purpose of literature is to instruct in the art of living, Johnson observes in *Rambler* 60 that "no Species of Writing seems more worthy of Cultivation than Biography." Such works should not concentrate on the unusual or the public but rather on "the minute Details of daily Life," as these are the elements that provide instruction. Johnson also warned against the panegyric, which detracted from the didactic function of literature and might persuade readers that they could never emulate the subject.

This insistence on truth to experience explains those of Johnson's literary assessments which strike some as anomalous. He disliked pastorals because they do not "imitate real life, require no experience, and exhibiting only the simple operation of unmingled passion, admit no subtle reasoning or deep inquiry" (*Life of Pope*). He preferred Dryden's *Ode for St. Cecilia's Day* to Pope's because Dryden draws on history rather than imagination: "The passions excited by Dryden are the pleasures and pains of real life, the scene of Pope is laid in imaginary existence" (*ibid.*). Though he highly praised John Milton's *Paradise Lost*, he also had reservations about it. His comment about its length is well known, but his greatest objection was its remoteness from common experience: "The man and woman who act and suffer, are in a state which no other man or woman can ever know. The reader finds no transaction in which he can be engaged; beholds no condition in which he can by any effort of imagination place himself; he has, therefore, little natural curiosity or sympathy . . . The want of human interest is always felt" (*Life of Milton*). This remoteness from common experience troubled Johnson about the poetry of William Collins and Gray as well. Johnson anticipates William Wordsworth's strictures on Gray's lan-

guage because it is "remote from common use." On the other hand, Johnson praised Gray's *Elegy Written in a Country Churchyard* because it "abounds with images which find a mirrour in every soul, and with sentiments to which every bosom returns an echo" (*Life of Gray*).

The same practical viewpoint that underlies his literary criticism informs his politics. To Goldsmith's *The Traveler* (1764) Johnson contributed the lines, "How small of all that human hearts endure, / The part which laws or kings can cause or cure." This couplet reflects the same view that he expressed to Boswell in response to a question about political improvement: "Why, Sir, most schemes of political improvement are very laughable things." He had no patience with those who claimed that British liberties were endangered when Parliament expelled John Wilkes (*The False Alarm*, 1770). Nor did he sympathize with the American Revolution, wondering, "How is it that we hear the loudest yelps of liberty from the drivers of Negroes?" (*Taxation No Tyranny*, 1775). But, he was no blind follower of authority. At Oxford he drank a toast to the next slave rebellion in the West Indies. He supported neither the French nor the English during the Seven Years' War, which he regarded as "only the quarrel of two robbers for the spoils of a passenger," the Indians to whom the lands really belonged. When Boswell supported feudal subordination, Johnson reminded him that while the Highland chiefs found the arrangement pleasant enough, their subjects clearly did not, since they fled from it as soon as they could and never returned.

Such trenchant remarks have done as much as his writing to earn Johnson his respected place in English literature. Only Shakespeare is quoted more, and many of Johnson's most familiar lines come from his speech. As Thomas Percy observed, even as a youth his comments were memorable; in later life he moved an auditor to observe that everything that Johnson said was as correct as a second edition. He was very fond of talk. Thrale regarded her biography of Johnson as little more than a collection of the man's sayings, "as his life, at least since my acquaintance with him, consisted in little else than talking, when he was not absolutely employed in some serious piece of work."

Famous for talking for victory at any cost, Johnson nonetheless regarded himself as good-humored, and all who knew him concurred. Dr. William Adams remembered him as "a gay and frolicksome fellow." Recording his first meeting with Johnson, Boswell wrote, "He has great humour and is a worthy man," though in this instance the humor was directed against the Scots. Sir John Hawkins called Johnson "the most humorous man I ever knew," and Garrick observed, "Rabelais and all other wits are nothing compared with him. You may be diverted by them; but Johnson gives you a forcible hug, and shakes laughter out of you, whether you will or no." Thrale rated her acquaintances' humor on a scale of twenty. She gave Johnson a sixteen—only Garrick scored higher (nineteen).

His jests have endured and his name continues to bring a smile to audiences because he does not pretend. He says what is, not what politeness dictates. When Boswell sought to impress him with the amenities of Scotland by pointing out a water closet in an old castle, Johnson told him, "You take very good care of one end of a man, but not of the other." On that tour Johnson brought with him a large oak stick from London. When it vanished, Johnson was certain that it had been stolen: "Consider, sir, the value of such a piece of timber here!" he told Boswell on the treeless landscape of the Highlands. The *Dictionary* had taken far longer than the publishers had anticipated. After Johnson sent the last sheets to Andrew Millar, he asked the messenger what Millar, not noted for his piety, had said. "Sir, he said, thank GOD I have done with him." Johnson smilingly responded, "I am glad that he thanks GOD for any thing."

He harbored no illusions about children, shocking Mrs. Thrale by observing, "I myself should not have had much fondness for a child of my own . . . At least I never wished to have a child." When a fond parent asked him to listen to each of his offspring recite Gray's *Elegy* in turn so that Johnson could judge which performed better, Johnson replied, "No, pray, let the dears both speak it at once; more noise will by that means be made, and the noise will be sooner over." As already noted, he did not share the current enthusiasm for the poetry of Gray and Collins, nor did he admire the then popular Ossian. Asked whether any living man could have written those Gaelic poems, Johnson observed, "Yes, Sir; many men, many women, and many children."

He epitomized in a sentence the sentiment of authors beleaguered by poetasters: "I never did the man an injury; but he would persist in reading his tragedy to me." Likewise, he expressed the general sentiment toward lawyers.

When someone left a gathering, the man sitting next to Johnson asked who that person was. "I cannot exactly tell you Sir," Johnson said, "and I would be loth to speak ill of any person who I do not know deserves it, but I am afraid he is an *attorney*." He had no tolerance for pretension. To a young man complaining of the loss of his Greek, Johnson retorted, "I believe it happened at the same time, Sir, that I lost all my large estate in Yorkshire." Nor did he tolerate fools. When Mrs. Thrale's nephew asked whether or not to marry, Johnson told him, "I would advise no man to marry . . . who is not likely to propogate understanding." Though he respected Lord Monboddo's intelligence, he found ludicrous the man's insistence on being descended from monkeys. "Monboddo is as jealous of his tail as squirrel."

Summary

Samuel Johnson has provided an ocean of *bons mots*. Hester Thrale recorded, "He used to say 'that the size of a man's understanding might always be justly measured by his mirth'; and his own was never contemptible." Among the best known of his remarks is the one concerning a man who wed a second time despite an unhappy first marriage. Johnson described this behavior as "the triumph of hope over experience." His own stance always favored the latter. As he warned in the august opening of *Rasselas*, "Ye who listen with credulity to the whispers of fancy, and pursue with eagerness the phantoms of hope; who expect that age will perform the promises of youth, and that the deficiencies of the present day will be supplied by the morrow; attend to the history of Rasselas, prince of Abissinia." His was the clear vision of the satirist, tempered by compassion that would not long allow him to assume the distance from human suffering that satire requires. Characteristically, after delivering his caustic comment to Thrale's nephew he addressed the question of marriage in such a way that, according to Thrale, "no one ever recollected the offence, except to rejoice in its consequences."

Shunning the Scylla of cynicism and the Charybdis of sentimentality, Johnson navigated by the polestar of common sense. Whatever the subject he addressed, he brought to it not only extensive reading but also keen insight into human nature. What he wrote of Shakespeare applies equally to himself and explains his enduring popularity:

He who has mazed his imagination, in following the phantoms which other writers raise up before him, may here be cured of his delirious extasies, by reading human sentiments in human language; by scenes from which a hermit may estimate the transactions of the world, and a confessor predict the progress of the passions.

Selected Bibliography
Primary Sources

Poetry
London: A Poem, In Imitation of the Third Satire of Juvenal. London: R. Dodsley, 1738.
The Vanity of Human Wishes. London: R. Dodsley, 1749.
The Poetical Works of Samuel Johnson. London: Printed for the Editor, 1785.

Fiction
The Prince of Abissinia. A Tale. London: R. and J. Dodsley, 1759.

Drama
Irene: A Tragedy. London: R. Dodsley, 1749.

Essays
The Rambler. London: J. Payne, 1753.
The Idler. London: John Newbery, 1761.

Political Writings
The False Alarm. London: T. Cadell, 1770.
Thoughts on the Late Transactions Respecting Falkland's Islands. London: T. Cadell, 1771.
The Patriot. London: T. Cadell, 1774.
Taxation No Tyranny. London: T. Cadell, 1775.

Travelogues
A Journey to the Western Isles of Scotland. London: W. Strahan, and T. Cadell, 1775.
A Diary of a Journey into North Wales, in the Year 1774. London: Robert Jennings, 1816.

Biographies
An Account of the Life of Mr. Richard Savage, Son of the Earl Rivers. London: J. Roberts, 1744.
Prefaces, Biographical and Critical to the Works of the English Poets. London: J. Nichols, et al., 1779–1781.

Letters
Letters to and from the Late Samuel Johnson. London: W. Strahan, and T. Cadell, 1788.
Letters of Samuel Johnson. Ed. R.W. Chapman. Oxford: Clarendon, 1952.

Edited Works
A Dictionary of the English Language. London: W. Strahan, for J. and P. Knapton et al., 1755.
The Plays of William Shakespeare. London: J. and R. Tonson, 1765.

Secondary Sources

Bibliographies
Chapman, R.W. "Johnsonian Bibliography: A Supplement to the Courtney." *Proceedings of the Oxford Bibliographical Society*, 5 (1939): 119–66.
Clifford, James L., and Donald Greene. *Samuel Johnson: A Survey and Bibliography of Critical Studies*. Minneapolis: University of Minnesota Press, 1970. Presents 200 years of Johnsonian criticism.
Courtney, William Prideaux and David Nichol Smith. *A Bibliography of Samuel Johnson*. Oxford: Clarendon, 1915. Though dated, this remains the most complete primary bibliography of Johnson's works. Should be supplemented with Chapman's work (cited above).
Greene, Donald, and John A. Vance. *A Bibliography of Johnsonian Studies, 1970–1985*. Victoria, BC: University of Victoria English Literary Studies, 1987. Updates the Clifford-Greene bibliography of secondary material on Johnson.

Biographies
Bate, Walter Jackson. *Samuel Johnson*. New York: Harcourt Brace Jovanovich, 1977. A detailed psychoanalytical approach with much information about the writing as well as the life.
Boswell, James. *The Life of Samuel Johnson, LL.D., with A Journal of a Tour to the Hebrides with Samuel Johnson*. Ed. G.B. Hill and L.F. Powell. 6 vols. Oxford: Clarendon, 1934–1964. The standard edition of the greatest biography in the English language. Though Boswell sometimes errs, the editors have corrected

him. This work is indispensable to any student of Johnson, the place at which study must begin and end.

Clifford, James L. *Young Sam Johnson*. New York: McGraw-Hill, 1955. A fine scholarly biography covering the first forty years of Johnson's life.

———. *Dictionary Johnson*. New York: McGraw-Hill, 1979. Continues the previous volume to 1763.

Krutch, Joseph Wood. *Samuel Johnson*. New York: Holt, 1944. Long regarded as the best biography of Johnson, this remains a readable, informed study that serves as an ideal introduction to the man and his works.

Wain, John. *Samuel Johnson: A Biography*. London: Macmillan, 1975. A personal view of Johnson aimed at the general reader.

Books

Alkon, Paul K. *Samuel Johnson and Moral Discipline*. Evanston, IL: Northwestern University Press, 1967. Alkon examines the sources of Johnson's views (Locke looms large) and the expression of his moral outlook throughout his writings.

Bate, Walter Jackson. *The Achievement of Samuel Johnson*. New York: Oxford University Press, 1955. An excellent discussion of Johnson as writer.

Folkenflick, Robert. *Samuel Johnson, Biographer*. Ithaca, NY: Cornell University Press, 1978. A comprehensive study of this facet of Johnson's achievement.

Greene, Donald J. *The Politics of Samuel Johnson*. New Haven: Yale University Press, 1960; 2nd ed. Athens, GA: University of Georgia Press, 1989. An important study that shatters the stereotype of Johnson as ardent Tory, noting his independent thinking.

———. *Samuel Johnson*. Boston: Twayne, 1970; updated ed. Boston: Twayne, 1989. A good though superficial survey of all facets of Johnson's work. Includes a useful annotated bibliography of criticism.

———, ed. *Samuel Johnson: A Collection of Critical Essays*. Englewood Cliffs, NJ: Prentice-Hall, 1965. A valuable anthology covering many aspects of Johnson's oeuvre.

Hagstrum, Jean H. *Samuel Johnson's Literary Criticism*. Minneapolis: University of Minnesota Press, 1952; 2nd ed. Chicago: University of Chicago Press, 1967. Despite its efforts at Aristotelean classification, an important examination of Johnson's approach to literature.

Hilles, F.W., ed. *New Light on Dr. Johnson*. New Haven: Yale University Press, 1959. Valuable anthology on a wide range of Johnsonian topics.

Korshin, Paul J., ed. *Johnson after Two Hundred Years*. Philadelphia: University of Pennsylvania Press, 1986. A fine collection of fourteen essays dealing with Johnson's life, intellectual development, and writing.

Reddick, Allen. *The Making of Johnson's Dictionary, 1746–1773*. Cambridge: Cambridge University Press, 1990. Not only an excellent account of the creation of the *Dictionary* but also an examination of the various editions to determine Johnson's attitude toward language.

Sledd, James H., and Gwin J. Kalb. *Dr. Johnson's Dictionary: Essays in the Biography of a Book*. Chicago: University of Chicago Press, 1955. Sledd places Johnson within the "lexicographical tradition," noting both his debt to earlier dictionaries and his innovation in the use of quotations.

Wimsatt, W.K., Jr. *Philosophical Words: A Study of Style and Meaning in the Rambler and Dictionary of Samuel Johnson*. New Haven: Yale University Press, 1948. A classic study in Johnson's use of language.

———. *The Prose Style of Samuel Johnson*. New Haven: Yale University Press, 1941. Wimsatt looks at parallelism, antithesis, diction, and other qualities of Johnson's prose, Johnson's ideas about composition, his predecessors, critics, imitators, and parodists.

Articles and Parts of Books

Bronson, Bertrand H. "The Double Tradition of Dr. Johnson." *English Literary History*, 18 (1951): 90–106. Bronson compares the popular view of Johnson with the scholarly attitude.

———. "Johnson Agonistes." In his *Johnson and Boswell: Three Essays*. Berkeley: University of California Press, 1944, pp. 363–98. Johnson seen as torn between intellectual skepticism and emotional enthusiasm.

DeMaria, Robert, Jr. "The Politics of Johnson's *Dictionary*." *Publications of the Modern Language Association of America*, 104 (January 1989): 64–74. DeMaria looks at the political implications of the definitions, quotations, and the creation of the work itself. Finds Johnson a champion of democracy and "economic independence."

Eliot, T.S. "Johnson's 'London' and 'The Vanity of Human Wishes.'" In Samuel Johnson, *London: A Poem* and *The Vanity of Human Wishes*. London: Etchells and Macdonald, 1930. Eliot's introduction to the poems reestablished Johnson's reputation as a poet.

Krutch, Joseph Wood. "Samuel Johnson as Critic." *Nation*, 158 (February 14, 1944): 218–22. Krutch praises Johnson's criticism as "the play of a vigorous and entertaining mind over a wide range of subjects." Johnson is interesting even when he is wrong.

Leavis, F.R. "Johnson as Critic." *Scrutiny*, 12 (Summer 1944): 187–204. Leavis praises Johnson's criticism as "alive and life-giving."

Meier, Thomas K. "Johnson on Scotland." *Essays in Criticism*, 18 (1968): 349–52. Meier responds to earlier critics of Johnson's *Journey*. Sees Johnson as sympathetic to the plight of the Scots, but the book paints a bleak picture of the country.

Noyes, Alfred. "Johnson." In *Pageant of Letters*. New York: Sheed & Ward, 1940, pp. 75–99. A general assessment particularly good on the emotional aspects of Johnson's poetry.

Rawlinson, David H. "Presenting Its Evils to Our Minds: Imagination in Johnson's Pamphlets." *English Studies: A Journal of English Language and Literature*, 70 (1989): 315–27. Rawlinson discusses Johnson's view of imagination and its role in sympathy.

Joseph Rosenblum

Jonson, Ben

Born: Probably in or near London, June 11, 1572 (?)
Education: May have attended a private school in St. Martin's Church; Westminster School, from which he was withdrawn, probably in 1588
Marriage: Probably married Anne Lewis on November 14, 1594; may have married Hester Hopkins in 1623; at least four children
Died: Probably in Westminster, London, August 16, 1637

Biography

Ben Jonson had the good fortune to become one of the best writers and most talented humorists in the history of English literature, but he also had the misfortune to be born a contemporary of William Shakespeare. Shakespeare's shadow looms large in Jonson criticism, and many writers—including Jonson himself—have felt compelled to contrast the two. More recent commentary suggests that the differences between them may have been exaggerated, and in any case Jonson has increasingly been appreciated in his own right and on his own terms. His is the story of an ambitious and dedicated young man who willfully transformed himself into one of the most influential writers of his own and subsequent times. Still, Jonson's beginnings were hardly auspicious.

Ben was born, probably in London, sometime in 1572 (or possibly in 1573), perhaps on June 11, 1572. His father, a dissenting minister who had been imprisoned under the Catholic Queen Mary, died a month before Jonson was born, during the reign of Mary's Protestant sister, Elizabeth I. Within a few years Jonson's mother had married a master-bricklayer. Although young Ben may have attended a private school in St. Martin's Church and studied at Westminster School under William Camden (whom he always revered), his education was cut short when he was withdrawn from the school, probably in 1588, and as an adolescent he was apprenticed as a bricklayer. Although his devotion to learning never abated, he does not seem to have received a formal university education. His achievements and intellectual dedication seem all the more impressive in light of his early disadvantages.

During the first year or so of the 1590s, Jonson appears to have been in the Netherlands as a volunteer soldier in England's conflict with Spain. The natural combativeness that seems to have been part of his personality was expressed in his duel with an enemy soldier, whom Jonson later claimed to have killed and stripped of his weapons. While the details are not definite, it is thought that he returned to London, married Anne Lewis on November 14, 1594, fathered a son and daughter, and became involved in the burgeoning English theater, apparently first as a touring actor and then as a playwright in the employ of Philip Henslowe, the famous entrepreneur. In the fall of 1597, he was imprisoned for his part in producing *The Isle of Dogs*, a play written with Thomas Dekker that the authorities called slanderous and seditious. By the following autumn, though, Jonson had scored his first notable success with the comedy *Every Man in His Humour*, one of his best and most characteristic plays and in which Shakespeare acted a leading role. This work, with its focus on the odd "humours" or obsessive traits of various characters, allowed him to display the heavily satiric bent that typified most of his comic writing. The drama seems to have been the first of his plays that he considered worth preserving, and indeed his regard for it is indicated by the fact that he went to the trouble of revising it carefully, if mainly cosmetically, for publication in his 1616 folio *Workes*.

However, just when Jonson seemed to have distinguished himself as a playwright, he again found himself in legal trouble. Another duel, on September 22, 1598, with the actor Gabriel Spencer, led to Spencer's death and Jonson's imprisonment. Tried for murder, he took advantage of an opportunity to plead "benefit of clergy," that is, to show that he could read a biblical verse in Latin (a tradition inherited from the Middle Ages to prevent civil authorities from improperly punishing priests). A man could use this option only once (a brand on the thumb provided a permanent record), and fortunately Jonson would never need to use it again. While in prison, the young writer became a convert to Catholicism. By the time he left jail he had broken with the Protestant creed of his father (now the official creed of the state), thus exposing himself once again to danger. Later his rivals would mock his religion, and local authorities would investigate his beliefs.

Nonetheless, Jonson's career was progressing. Another comedy, *The Case Is Altered*, seems to have been performed sometime in 1597, although he later chose not to reprint the play in the 1616 *Workes*. This drama is not one of his most memorable efforts, and it has received relatively little attention. It contains satiric thrusts that are recognizably his, but a romantic emphasis seems less obviously charac-

teristic, and the possibility has even been raised that Jonson may have had a collaborator. Certainly he co-wrote on two other plays from this period, the lost tragedies *Page of Plymouth* and *Robert II King of Scots*, which he may have written with Dekker in 1599. The turn of the century witnessed the production of one of his most significant comedies, *Every Man Out of His Humour*, staged at the newly built Globe Theatre. With its complex structure, choric commentators, biting satire, and artistic self-consciousness, the play is an illustration of the kind of innovation (not always wholly successful) of which Jonson was capable. An epilogue addressed to Queen Elizabeth exemplifies his effort at this time to attract the attention of aristocratic patrons—an effort also obvious, for instance, in such poems as the "Epistle to Elizabeth, Countess of Rutland" (*The Forrest*, XII), which displays much of the same concern with social satire and the ridicule of moral failings that characterizes so much of the author's humor. Jonson is often witty, but his wit, whether in his poems, plays, masques, or prose, usually has both an edge and a serious point. Wit simply for its own sake is a luxury in which he rarely indulges.

The early years of the new century involved one of the most important events of his life, the so-called "poetomachia" or "War of the Theatres," a pitched verbal battle fought against Dekker and another playwright, John Marston, in a series of plays. Jonson took offense at Marston's depiction of him in *Histriomastix* (1599), and he responded in *Every Man Out*. Marston responded in turn, and by 1601 Jonson had written a comedy, *Cynthia's Revels*, mocking both Marston and Dekker, followed shortly by another comedy, *Poetaster*, which not only responded to Marston's response (in *What You Will*) but attempted to head off Dekker's *Satiromastix* (1601), in which Jonson is obviously and repeatedly attacked. Once again Jonson's combative instincts seem evident, and this was not the last time that the seriousness with which he took himself and his art (including his comedy) would open him to ridicule. The immediate fallout of his tiff with Marston and Dekker seems to have been a sense of disillusionment with comedy; by the summer of 1602 he was at work on another "lost" tragedy (*Richard Crookback*, about King Richard III), and by 1603 one of his two surviving tragedies, *Sejanus*, had been performed. With its sardonic wit and irony, this play in which Jonson deals with the fall of a corrupt Roman favorite is a demonstration that humor of a sort was never far from the writer's mind. The play's opening exchange—in which one character exclaims to another, "You're rarely met in court!" and the other responds, "Therefore, well met" (1.1.2)—immediately sets a wry, cynical tone that continues throughout. Jonson's basic impulse to satirize vice meant not only that sarcasm was an essential aspect of his sense of humor but also that such humor would turn up at some point in most of his works. The authorities, however, did not always find his satire funny, and the Earl of Northampton thought that he spotted popery and treason in *Sejanus*. Jonson was summoned by the Privy Council, but little else is known of this incident.

The dramatist's latest brush with the authorities did not prevent him from being selected to play an increasingly prominent part in the official literary life of his country. In June 1603, his first royal entertainment was presented before Queen Anne and Prince Henry, who were following King James, the new British monarch, south from Scotland. James's accession marked a turning point in Jonson's career; increasingly he received the kind of patronage, from the new sovereign and from other aristocrats, that he had long desired. The gentle humor and charming compliments found in his first entertainment, presented at Sir Robert Spencer's estate of Althorp, are common to many of Jonson's works in this genre and to his masques. Typical is the passing reference to Mab, the fairy queen, as "She, that pinches country wenches / If they rub not clean their benches" (2.58–59). Typical, too, is the address to the assembled "Queen, Prince, Duke, Earls, / Countesses; you courtly Pearls" (2.244–45). Yet, the work's muted satire on past corruption at court illustrates again the ethical seriousness that underlay practically everything that Jonson wrote. The fact that he was chosen, during 1604, to write three more works celebrating and counseling the new ruler indicates that his talents were being increasingly recognized and legitimized. He had already found a voice of mingled gravity and wit, and now that voice was being heard and apparently appreciated by powerful people. Jonson's desire to use humor (and other devices) to attack vice and endorse virtue had won him both attention and sanction. In plays, entertainments, and nondramatic poems, he used comedy, sarcasm, and satire to promote goodness and the good.

Not everyone, of course, shared Jonson's sense of humor. In 1605, a Scotsman complained to King James about anti-Scottish satire in *Eastward Ho*, a comedy on which Jonson had collaborated with his friend George Chapman and with his old antagonist Marston. Jonson's precise responsibility for the offending passages remains unclear, but he and Chapman soon found themselves in jail, threatened with physical punishment. Jonson protested his innocence in a number of surviving letters to powerful aristocrats, and eventually he was released. That he was not fundamentally anti-Scottish is evidenced by the five years (beginning about 1603) that he spent living in the household of a Scottish nobleman, Lord D'Aubigny. That he was not fundamentally antagonistic to James's government is suggested by his role in the immediate aftermath of the infamous Gunpowder Plot, a conspiracy by dissident Catholics to assassinate the English government by blowing up the houses of parliament in November 1605. Although Jonson had known some of the conspirators, he was also employed by the government to contact a particular priest after the plot was foiled. In the meantime, despite his troubles, his employment as a court poet continued. The performance of his *Masque of Blackness*, his first effort in a type of royal entertainment he would master and transform, occurred in January 1605. A year later (in January 1606) another masque, *Hymenaei*, was staged, this time to help celebrate the union through marriage of two powerful families, but in April of that year Jonson was again accused of promoting popery, of failing to attend Anglican church services, and of refusing to take communion. He denied the first two charges and suggested that he would be willing to take communion if certain scruples were satisfied. Like much else in his life, the outcome of this incident is uncertain, but his run-in with the church does not seem to have damaged his standing at court. In July, his royal entertainment, written to celebrate the visit of King Christian IV of Denmark, was performed at Theobalds, home of Robert Cecil, James's most important minister and one of Jonson's most important patrons. Jonson would write a number of other dramatic and nondramatic works for Cecil within the next few years. His status as the most important poet of the Jacobean court was becoming increasingly clear, and that status depended greatly on his ability to combine good teachings with good humor. His comic muse was rarely trivial or frivolous. His masques, entertainments, and poems are often delightful and amusing, but never insubstantial. Jonson could be quite funny, yet his joking usually had a point and was also often pointed.

Certainly this is true of *Volpone*, one of his finest plays and one of the best comedies in English. First produced in 1606, this work has usually been seen as the first of a series of truly great dramas that have established Jonson's significance. As in *Sejanus*, the tragedy that preceded it, in *Volpone* the playwright presents a world of intrigue centered on a master manipulator and a clever parasite whose power eventually threatens his patron. Also as in *Sejanus*, *Volpone* is illustrative of the relative impotence of simple goodness; Jonson's depictions of scheming, foolish, or malignant egotists are often full of a powerful verbal energy that gives his unsavory characters a vitality and interest that the obviously virtuous sometimes lack. In *Volpone*, for instance, the scheming parasite Mosca exults that "Success hath made me wanton. I could skip / Out of my skin now, like a subtle snake, / I am so limber" (3.1.5–7). In fact, critics have frequently complained that the heavenly Celia and the good Bonario pale beside Volpone and Mosca, not to mention the other rogues and fools who populate the play. Jonson's best writing is often lavished on his worst characters, but that fact indicates part of the advance which he had made. *Volpone* teaches every bit as much as *Cynthia's Revels*, but in the great comedies of Jonson's middle period his teaching is less blatant, more implied.

During the decade beginning in 1606, the dramatist entered a creative period unlike any in his life before or after. He produced a steady stream of masques and entertainments (averaging more than one a year), and he also wrote more of his greatest comedies, including *Epicoene, or the Silent Woman* (first performed in 1609), *The Alchemist* (1610), and *Bartholomew Fair* (1614). He produced as well a somewhat frigid tragedy, *Catiline* (1611), which was badly received when it was first performed. In addition, he found time to escort Sir Walter Ralegh's son on a tour of the continent (1612–1613), and he decided to become an Anglican convert (perhaps in 1610) after all. Moreover, he brought together two collections of his poems, including *The Forrest* (which contains one of his most vital and pleasing works, "To Penshurst") and a volume of *Epigrammes* (which he called his "ripest" studies, and in which poems praising virtuous figures are paired with wickedly funny satires of fools, fops, and frauds). In addition, by this point Jonson had fundamentally altered the masque genre, deemphasizing its dependence on mere spectacle, enhancing its literary value, and injecting it with new life and comic vitality by expanding the role of the often antic *antimasques* that preceded the masques per se.

Thus, by 1616, when he published his *Workes*, Jonson had transformed himself from the stepson of a bricklayer into one of the most significant writers of his day and one of the greatest comic authors in the English language. Furthermore, his unprecedented rise had changed what it could mean to be an English poet, a fact formally acknowledged that year when King James granted him a generous annuity, making him an unofficial Poet Laureate. Ironically, however, many critics have also detected the first indication of his dramatic decline in the comedy that he wrote as 1616 was ending, *The Devil Is an Ass*. The play has been decried for lacking energy and coherence, although its significance as a reflection of contemporary economic problems has frequently been noted.

While *The Devil* has often been seen as the first of Jonson's "dotages," its weakness is only relative. It would probably seem a better play if its author had not so recently written *Volpone*, *Epicoene*, *The Alchemist*, and *Bartholomew Fair*. As with *Epicoene*, Jonson was accused of using *The Devil* to mock powerful figures; King James asked him to conceal such satire in this case, but Jonson's barbs were apparently often aimed at real people. Evidence survives that by 1619 he had completed a pastoral comedy (whether a poem or a drama is unclear) entitled *The May Lord*. This work alluded to contemporary figures, too, but all that survives of it are Jonson's brief and cryptic comments recorded during his famous "Conversations" with William Drummond of Hawthornden, a minor aristocrat whom he visited during a walking tour of Scotland in 1618–1619. Interestingly, Jonson also told Drummond (among much else) that half of the comedies which he had written were not then in print—suggesting that he had been even more prolific in this genre than the number of his published works indicates.

If Jonson wrote any other comedies for the stage during this period, they have not survived. Between 1616 and 1626, he seems to have concentrated chiefly on composing masques and entertainments (again averaging more than one a year), including such notable works as *Pleasure Reconciled to Virtue* (1618) and *The Gypsies Metamorphos'd* (1621). All of these writings are comic to some degree or in some sense, if only because they tend to be celebratory displays of wit ending in affirmations of social concord. Masque-writing paid well, and the now-pensioned Jonson apparently felt no great need to support himself by turning to the stage. Meanwhile, his recognition and prestige continued to grow. In 1619, he was granted an honorary M.A. by Oxford University, and in 1621 he received the reversion to the office of Master of the Revels. Although this position never did revert to him, if it had, he would have been responsible for monitoring—and censoring—all new plays produced for the public stage. It seems significant that powerful figures were willing to trust him with this important assignment.

In addition to writing masques and entertainments, Jonson also continued to write poems, many of them comic. One of the most memorable, his "Execration" on Vulcan, humorously attacks the Roman god of fire for causing the blaze that destroyed Jonson's house (and many of his manuscripts) in the fall of 1623:

> And why to me this, thou lame lord of
> fire,
> What had I done, that might call on
> thine ire?
> I ne're attempted, Vulcan, 'gainst thy life,
> Nor made least line of love to thy loose
> wife . . . (2.1–2; 5–6)

In the poem he details the numerous works that the fire destroyed, and many of his deepest ideals as a writer are strikingly expressed. The mixture of stoic affability and stinging satire exemplifies two of his most characteristic tones, which are also present in another important poem written that same year, the "Tribe of Ben" epistle. The latter work indicates that Jonson had become the center of a circle of young admirers even as it expresses some apprehension about the security of his social position as well. Like a number of other works, this poem is a reflection of Jonson's long-running feud with Inigo Jones, the architect and designer with whom he nonetheless collaborated so fruitfully on so many of his masques. (It was probably Jones to whom Jonson alluded when he once described a creature who would sooner "see its sister naked, ere a sword"; *Epigrammes* 115, 1.22.) There is some evidence that Jonson married Hester Hopkins in 1623.

King James's death in March 1625, brought to the throne King Charles I, who was in some ways quite different from his jocular if hot-tempered father. Charles seemed more distant and reserved than James, and initially, at least, Jonson's influence at court may have diminished somewhat. Partly because of financial constraints on court spending, masque commissions stopped for a while, and in 1626 the aging playwright oversaw the staging of his first new comedy in a decade, *The Staple of News*. As in his previous play, Jonson used this one to satirize contemporary economic practices, commenting on the growth of the English appetite for "news," especially from foreign sources. *The Staple*, like Jonson's other final comedies, seems not to have been particularly well received. These are the works that John Dryden referred to as "dotages," although some recent critics have tried to emphasize their attractions. Still, Jonson's contemporaries seem to have felt that such works as *The New Inn* (1629), *The Magnetic Lady* (1632), and *A Tale of a Tub* (1633) represented a falling-off from their author's greatest accomplishments, and it is difficult to disagree with this assessment.

The final decade of Jonson's life involved mixed frustrations and satisfactions. Sometime in 1628 he suffered a paralytic stroke, but in September he was appointed Chronologer of the city of London only to be questioned a month later about the authorship of verses commending the assassin of the duke of Buckingham, the royal favorite. Jonson denied having written the verses, and within a year and a half King Charles had in fact increased the poet's pension. In the interim, though, *The New Inn* had been acted and disastrously received. Jonson's defensive instincts found expression in a bitter "Ode to Himselfe," in which he lambasted his critics, expressed frustration with the king's disinterest, but promised to turn from the stage and to use his gifts to celebrate the monarch. He did abandon playwriting for a while, turning increasingly to occasional poems and writing two royal masques, both performed in early 1631. Plays, however, followed in 1632 and 1633, and two more entertainments (commissioned by the Earl of Newcastle, an important patron) were written to celebrate royal visits. At the time of his death in London on August 16, 1637, Jonson seems to have been at work on at least one more comedy, *The Sad Shepherd*, a pastoral that survives only as a fragment. The charm and vigor of the work have led some to suppose that it was written much earlier, while others prefer to see it as evidence of a talent that never completely lost its strength and vitality.

Literary Analysis

Although Jonson was occasionally mocked during his lifetime for composing slowly, the sheer length and tenacity of his career meant that he produced quite a few plays, many of them comedies but not all of them extant. He was regarded by contemporaries, and has been regarded since, as one of the greatest dramatists of his time. Although critics generally agree that the quality of Jonson's plays is uneven, there is also general agreement that his best works rank among the finest comedies in English. The great masterpieces of his middle period—*Volpone*, *The Alchemist*, *Epicoene*, and *Bartholomew Fair*—are flanked on either side by works of more questionable value, but none of his comedies lack interest or are unworthy of attention. In addition, his achievements as a comic writer in other genres, particularly in poetry and masques, were as important in their own ways as his accomplishments on the stage. As the author comes to be appreciated more and more on his own terms (rather than simply being regarded as a foil to Shakespeare), the distinctiveness of his comic genius is likely to become increasingly apparent. He was one of the greatest innovators in the history of English comedy, and while not all of his experiments succeeded, many did, and all reveal a man who took quite seriously the business of being funny.

Many of Jonson's comedies share important traits, especially the fundamental purpose of teaching by pleasing, of encouraging virtue by ridiculing or exposing folly and vice. Over the course of his career, he varied the methods and explicitness of this didactic impulse, but teaching ethics seems to have been a constant motive behind nearly everything he wrote. Therefore, his comedies are often satirical in tone and purpose; his plays' endings are rarely "happy" in a romantic or complacent sense, and his focus on selfish misbehavior inevitably disappoints readers who look to comedy for simple affirmation or amusement. Jonson's concern with satirizing vice sometimes leaves his comedies with an apparently hard and bitingly "realistic" edge. The plays are often full of topical allusions; their locale is often the London of the writer's day; their characters are often recognizable contemporary "types"; the language they speak is often vigorous and colloquial, reflecting the jargons or idioms of the era. As a result, Jonson sometimes seems more parochial than Shakespeare, who, as Jonson himself would claim, "was not of an age, but for all time." Yet, Jonson also felt—and rightly so—that the specific traits which he mocked, celebrated, or explored in his plays were rooted in a basic human nature that linked his own time not only with the past but with the future. For all of their emphasis on the English of his day, Jonson's plays are no less relevant and no more "difficult" than the works of his best contemporaries.

Jonson is sometimes accused of creating caricatures rather than fully rounded and complex characters. His tone is sometimes considered cold and harsh, and his frequent stress on punishment and poetic justice has led some critics to view his works as unforgiving, even as occasionally misanthropic. However, such critics miss the point of the writer's intent and judge him by standards that he did not embrace. His characters, for instance, for all of their surface realism, are often meant to represent particular social classes, types, or vices, and, indeed, several critics have traced Jonson's debt to the great tradition of "morality" plays which were typically rooted in the conflict between personified abstractions. The very names of his characters (Manly, Lovewit, Truewit, Subtle, Justice Overdo) often suggest their emblematic functions. At the same time, his tendency toward abstraction is balanced by his astonishing ability to particularize, to draw on his vast knowledge of contemporary life and lore to create characters who speak and act in ways that his audience would have recognized as "real." For Jonson, comedy was a mirror held up to the times, and his works reflect both the individual foibles and the representative traits of the characters depicted in them.

Jonson's debt to the native English tradition of morality plays is enriched by his wide reading in a range of other sources, including the classics of Greek and Roman antiquity, the literature of continental Europe, and the works of his own contemporaries and rivals. Despite the realistic effects often achieved in his plays, his works are also firmly rooted in his familiarity with literary precedents and generic conventions, and it is his ability to adopt, adapt, echo, modify, and parody his sources that gives many of his own works much of their interest. Jonson always hoped for (but rarely encountered) an audience as learned as he, and at times his relations with the people who did attend his plays were marked by tension and ambivalence. His dramas are usually highly self-conscious and ambivalent—a fact indicated not only by his tendency to employ prologues, epilogues, and other devices of authorial commentary, explanation, and self-defense, but also by the emphasis in the plays on the theme and fact of acting. The playwright frequently presents characters who are consciously or unconsciously playing roles and who are either deceived, deceptive, or self-deceiving. As Jonas Barish has emphasized, Jonson's drama normally reflects a suspicion of the dramatic impulse, and much of the comedy in his plays results from the tensions and disparities between illusion and reality, between how people act and who they really are, between what characters believe and what is truly so.

The trickery that is frequently at the heart of Jonson's comedy gives his works a witty, farcical tone, a tone that once again complicates his surface realism. His comedies are populated by dupes and dupers, by gulls and knaves, by characters who are either amazingly stupid or too clever for their own good. In his dramas he frequently deals with the ways that people make fools of themselves or are victimized by others, and the central sin satirized in the plays is pride, which leads to vanity, egotism, self-righteousness, immoderation, willfulness, inflexibility, meanness, greed, hypocrisy, and similarly foolish, vicious, or unattractive traits. Ironically, much of the energy of Jonsonian drama comes from the impulsive drive and verbal wit of the characters who are most morally repugnant, whereas the characters who are most obviously virtuous can sometimes seem the least interesting and most thin. Rich and riotous language is the soul of Jonson's best comedies; he had a fine ear for jargon and hyperbole, for the sounds and rhythms of words. And, since he firmly believed that language showed the man, that the way a character spoke revealed much about his mind, his plays present a veritable babble of speakers and speech. In one of the most memorable speeches that the playwright ever composed, the greedy Sir Epicure Mammon, anticipating how he will dine when he becomes rich, exclaims that he intends to eat "Oiled mush-

rooms; and the swelling unctuous paps / Of a fat pregnant sow, newly cut off, / Dressed with an exquisite and poignant sauce; / For which, I'll say unto my cook, there's gold, / Go forth, and be a knight" (2.2.83–87). Such words say more than enough about their speaker's character; any added satire would have been superfluous.

Although Jonson's early plays can seem a bit too openly preachy, the great comedies of his middle period gain in moral complexity because he makes their lessons less obvious and more ambiguous. Explicitly or implicitly, he invites his audience to recognize their own shortcomings in the follies that he presents, and his great comedies in particular discourage ethical complacency and promote moral alertness and self-vigilance. By encouraging us to evaluate his characters, he invites us to evaluate ourselves as well. His plays were ideally designed to help his audiences grow in ethical maturity, although his own characters seldom show such development. Rather, they exhibit their perversities or foolishness and then are defeated and judged either harshly, as in *Volpone*, or more tolerantly, as in *Bartholomew Fair*. Judgment, in fact, is crucial to the theory and practice of Jonson's comedy, and his plays often involve trials of one sort or another. His characters constantly, if unwittingly, reveal traits that allow us to judge them, and our reactions in turn become tests of our own good judgment. Irony was an abiding trait of Jonson's art, and he could employ it just as easily in dealing with his audience as in presenting his characters. Thus, in the "Induction" to *Bartholomew Fair,* he teases the kind of auditor who prefers old-fashioned dramas: "He that will swear, *Jeronimo,* or *Andronicus* are the best plays, . . . shall pass unexcepted at, here, as a man whose judgment shows it is constant, and hath stood still, these five and twenty, or thirty years."

Besides those already mentioned, there are other traits also included in the definition of "Jonsonian" comedy. The frequent concern with the classical "unities," for instance, usually limits the action to a compressed time and a central location. Jonson shows less interest in romantic love than do many of his contemporaries, and certainly attractive, complex heroines are less prominently emphasized in his comedies than in those by Shakespeare. When women do appear, they are often treated symbolically, either as exemplars of virtue or as examples of vice. However, this tendency to present characters symbolically is hardly confined to Jonson's women, and in general he is not concerned with developing characters of great psychological depth or introspective complexity. The dramatist's least moral characters are often the most intriguing (in several senses), yet for the most part the writer seems to have been less interested in exploring individual personalities than in scrutinizing his characters' ethics, the ways that they interacted socially. Further, the relative lack of rhyme in his comedies helps give them surface realism, as do their contemporary settings and their focus on current fads, manners, and mannerisms, but all of this is balanced by an almost allegorical focus on recurrent behaviors and character types that transcend any particular time or place. Jonson mocks all manner of pretension, obsession, fantasy, and deceit, and it is this emphasis on the enduringly ridiculous that gives his best works their continuing life. With his strong emphasis on examining the ways that characters behave socially, he provided an obvious influence on the so-called comedy of manners that became prominent in the later seventeenth century. This is especially true of *Epicoene*, in which one character is described as the kind of man, who, "between his mistress abroad, and his ingle [page boy] at home, high fare, soft lodging, fine clothes, and his fiddle, . . . thinks the hours ha' no wings" (1.1). Later, a group of assertive women is described as "an order between courtiers and country-madams, that live from their husbands; and give entertainment to all the Wits and Braveries o' the time, . . . [and behave] with most masculine, or rather hermaphroditical authority" (1.1).

Two of Jonson's early works illustrate some of the traits that made his writing so influential and distinctive. *Every Man In His Humour* and *Every Man Out of His Humour*, despite their similar titles, are quite different in structure and effect, yet both plays exemplify Jonson's interest in characters whose excessive or obsessive traits render them ridiculous. Thus, Sogliardo, in the latter work, announces his personal obsession by declaring, "I have land and money, . . . and I will be a gentleman, whatsoever it cost me" (1.2). Such a mania could be congenital, habitual, or deliberately assumed, but in any case it exemplifies an imbalance, an irrationality, an insubstantiality, and a lack of true self-knowledge that Jonson found absurd and socially destructive. Both plays are typical, too, in their critical self-consciousness, in their

explicit concern with the status and purpose of the poet and the functions of poetry. Jonson rarely took his own role for granted, and in his early works (including also *Poetaster* and *Cynthia's Revels*) the problem of what it might mean to be a writer in Elizabethan London is never far from his mind. His comedy is always essentially serious in its sources and intended effects.

Certainly this is true of *Volpone*, his first masterwork and a play of relentless inventiveness and energy. *Volpone* exemplifies many traits typical of Jonsonian comedy, such as the focus on deception and self-deceit, on clever manipulators and self-serving but self-defeated dupes, and on characters who illustrate a wide range of social types and individual obsessions. The comedy's subplot centers on Sir Politic Would-Be and his excruciatingly talkative Lady, whose visit to the title character is thus described:

> All my house,
> But now, steamed like a bath, with her
>   thick breath.
> A lawyer could not have been heard; nor
>   scarce
> Another woman, such a hail of words
> She has let fall. (3.5.7–10)

The Would-Be story line neatly balances the main plot's emphasis on the attempts by various conniving legacy-hunters to convince the equally conniving Volpone, who is only pretending to be mortally ill, to leave them his fortune. Nowhere is the play's basic action more deftly summarized than in the acrostic that Jonson appended to the first edition:

> V olpone, childless, rich, feigns sick, de-
>   spairs,
> O ffers his state to hopes of several heirs,
> L ies languishing; his Parasite receives
> P resents of all, assures, deludes; then
>   weaves
> O ther cross plots, which ope themselves,
>   are told.
> N ew tricks for safety are sought; they
>   thrive; when, bold,
> E ach tempts th' other again, and all are
>   sold.

Many of Jonson's characteristic ironies and themes are suggested here. In retrospect, the acrostic implies Volpone's essential isolation

J

and egotism, his spiritual poverty, his moral sickness, his genuine hopelessness if he continues along his present path, and the senses in which he languishes ethically through his lying and deceit. His ironic dependence on his own "Parasite," the enormously quick-witted and active Mosca, makes him vulnerable to the same kinds of assurance and delusion that he practices on his presumptive "heirs," while the "new tricks" by which the now-competing Volpone and Mosca seek to protect and promote themselves collapse into an ending that even Jonson seems to have felt verged on the tragic.

Significantly, the two transparently virtuous characters, Celia and Bonario, are nowhere mentioned in the acrostic, and their impact within the play is comparably unemphatic. Celia serves mainly as a symbol of all that is good and simple and thus as a foil who makes the malice and manipulations of others all the more apparent.

Jonson's general rejection of romantic or sentimental comedy in favor of a kind that is probing and satirical is typefied by *Volpone*. The symbolic names of the various characters suggest the play's debt to beast fables and allegories. The avarice and role-playing so prominently stressed in many of the author's plays are also strongly emphasized here, while the somewhat harsh and somewhat tainted justice with which the play concludes stresses the playwright's greater interest in moral judgment than in happy endings. A judge tells Volpone that since most of his money "was gotten by imposture, / By feigning lame, gout, palsy, and such diseases, / Thou art to lie in prison, cramped with irons, / Till thou be'st sick and lame indeed" (5.12.121–24). Audiences have often reacted ambivalently to this dark conclusion, but the work's exuberant language, incisive characterization, and hilarious plotting have long made it one of Jonson's best-regarded plays.

Epicoene, perhaps, is less immediately appealing, but it still ranks as one of its author's best efforts. This comedy revolves around the tensions between a small group of generally attractive young gallants, a generally unattractive group of pretentious women (the "Collegiate Ladies"), a number of fools and gulls, and a misanthropic egotist named Morose who is obsessed with a need for quiet. At one point he announces, "all discourses but mine own afflict me; they seem harsh, impertinent, and irksome" (2.1), and he commands his aptly named ser-

vant, Mute, to respond only through hand gestures and bowing. One of the themes is exposure, as various characters reveal their own foolishness or have it exposed and punished by others. An example of this is Epicoene, the young and at first extraordinarily quiet girl whom Morose marries only to discover that she is at least as talkative, annoying, and assertive as the Collegiate Ladies. However, the crowning example of exposure occurs when Dauphine, Morose's nephew, promises to free his uncle from the bondage of marriage in exchange for being made his heir. Morose desperately agrees, only to have Dauphine reveal to his uncle, the other characters, and us that Epicoene has really been a young boy all along. Part of the joke, of course, is that in Jonson's day the role of a young woman would have been played by a young boy, so Dauphine's trick on his uncle is merely part of a larger and more sophisticated trick that Jonson has played on his audience. Such cleverness suggests a great deal about his self-conscious theatricality; he is one of the first great English writers to seem so fully aware of the artifice of his art.

Modern readers are perhaps more likely than Jonson was to sympathize with Morose and feel uneasy at the ways that he is baited and tormented, but *Epicoene* in general seems more ethically complex than some of Jonson's early plays, and it is partly this element that makes the work so fascinating. Even the young gallants are not entirely or uniformly admirable, and although they spend much time mocking others' foolishness, their own flaws are also on display. Judgment is still an important theme in this play, as it is in nearly all of Jonson's works, but here as in all of his best comedies he seems acutely aware of the ambiguities and ambivalence that judgment can entail. The play's emphasis on farce and on the comedy of manners is still quite funny, but the work's overall effect seems deliberately unsettling. Whether this is a strength or a weakness depends on what one wants from comedy. In any case, Jonson once again frustrates any desire for a simple or sentimental "happy ending."

The same is true of his next great comedy, *The Alchemist*, although this play is so full of shenanigans and sheer inventiveness that its immediate appeal is almost irresistible. Jonson's delight and fascination with the clever trickery that he satirizes is nowhere more obvious than in this work in which selfish designs cross and double-cross one another with astonishing rapidity until the entire, elaborate structure of deceit implodes. Alchemy (the vain attempt to use a "philosopher's stone" to transform base metals into gold) is the perfect symbol of the theme of bogus transmutation central to the play, yet the work's gritty comic realism and linguistic exuberance give it a vitality that takes it beyond moral abstractions. Although the drama has been criticized for Jonson's presentation of caricatures rather than fully rounded characters and for being too topically based, few of Jonson's people are more memorable than the aggressive Subtle, the wily Face, or the enormously self-indulgent Sir Epicure Mammon, and few plays deal more effectively with such enduring themes as egotism, deception, gullibility, greed, and self-deceit. The cross-section of London society typifies the range of human variety, and the satire of hypocritical Puritanism seems too topical only until we realize that Jonson's larger target is hypocrisy in general. Thus, at one point a Puritan proclaims that Subtle, the alchemist, "bears / The visible mark of the Beast in his forehead. / And for his stone, it is a work of darkness, / And with philosophy blinds the eyes of man." Nevertheless, his colleague, Tribulation Wholesome, defends the potentially profitable scheme by saying, "Good Brother, we must bend unto all means, / That may give furtherance to the holy cause" (3.1.7–12). In this play as in *Volpone*, Jonson suggests that human beings often worship themselves and idolize material things, and here as in that play and in *Epicoene* he gives us an ending that is not entirely consoling or reassuring and which implicates its audience in the very foibles that it mocks.

Bartholomew Fair was not Jonson's last theatrical comedy, but it is the last whose greatness is almost universally acknowledged. In some ways a summing up of many themes and techniques present in his earlier work, this play has also been seen as a new departure. Many critics have commented on the more forgiving, more generous tone of its conclusion; Jonson's judgment of human folly, while still incisive and probing, is less harsh than that in much of his earlier writing. Some have argued that in this work Jonson shows a greater sympathy and tolerance for his characters' weaknesses and foibles, a greater appreciation of the universality of human limitation. Whether or not this is so, the play is certainly one of his most interesting and innovative compositions. By setting the work in Bartholomew Fair, a yearly gathering

of tradesmen and their customers in the Smithfield section of London, Jonson gave himself an opportunity to present a diverse range of characters and character types. Although the dramatis personae can be divided basically into two large groups (those who inhabit the fair and those who visit it), Jonson has lost none of his ability to create strikingly individual characters and memorable situations. The mere opportunity to meet Ursula, the grotesque "pig woman," or the childishly stupid Cokes, or the irascible Humphrey Waspe, or Zeal-of-the-Land Busy, the hypocritical Puritan fanatic, is worth the price of admission, but Jonson also contrives a number of ridiculous interactions among characters who are themselves patently ludicrous. (Thus, Ursula, the profusely sweating pig-roaster, says of herself, "I am all fire and fat, . . . I shall e'en melt away to the first woman, a rib again, I am afraid. I do water the ground in knots, as I go, like a great garden-pot, you may follow me by the S's I make"; 2.2.) All of the standard vices are mocked, all of the typically Jonsonian themes and concerns are touched on, and the play builds toward a conclusion of exquisite and theatrically self-conscious absurdity, yet the work ends not by stressing the separation and division of the characters but by emphasizing reconciliation and self-understanding.

After writing *Bartholomew Fair*, Jonson completed *The Devil Is an Ass*. Although he seems to have been at work on at least one lost comic drama during the ensuing decade, no new play of his was staged until 1626, and the comedies that he wrote in his final decade were greeted then, and have been greeted since, with mixed reactions. Nonetheless, the comedies composed during his great middle period would be more than enough to ensure his reputation; *Volpone* alone reveals his special genius. However, Jonson's comic talents were not only apparent in his stage plays but also in his seminal contributions to the masque and lyric poetry.

Jonson revolutionized the masque, and although his works in this genre were by their nature tightly tied to particular occasions, he did his best to give them a lasting appeal and significance. Much valuable scholarly work has been done on the ways that he transformed these royal entertainments which combined speeches, music, and dance. Critics such as Stephen Orgel and Richard S. Peterson have demonstrated the intellectual and moral seriousness of these works, while Leah S. Marcus has done more than anyone else to show how Jonson's masques were active responses to social and political stimuli, often functioning themselves as highly political texts. In these works as in everything that he wrote, his fundamental purposes were ethically serious; his masques are hardly fluff or trivially entertaining. Still, entertaining they must have been and still can be; the same vigorous language and vital wit that inform the plays enliven the masques, and despite their frequent emphasis on pageantry and ritual, these works are also full of clever satire and good fun. In fact, Jonson greatly expanded the role of the antimasque, in which the forces of often comic chaos are given full rein before the assertion (or reassertion) of stability and order personified by the king. The later masques bear an increasing similarity in their tones, themes, and techniques to his theatrical comedies.

Jonson's masques are in one sense comic by their very nature: unlike his plays, they almost inevitably have happy endings. Their humor can be variously gentle, teasing, rollicking, biting, boisterous, whimsical, parodic, farcical, and so on. Much depends on the specific purposes and occasion for which a work was written. *The Irish Masque* (1613–1614), for instance, derives much of its humor from a playful use of dialects, as does *For the Honour of Wales* (1618). *Pleasure Reconciled to Virtue*, one of the author's most famous and most accomplished masques, opens with swaggering and energetic bluster ("Room, room! make room for the bouncing belly, / First father of sauce, and deviser of jelly"), while another famous work, *The Gypsies Metamorphos'd*, combines the comic liveliness of a band of wandering gypsies with a scene of teasingly personal fortune telling. On the other hand, *News from the New World Discovered in the Moon* (1621) and *Time Vindicated to Himselfe and to His Honours* (1623) both contain stinging contemporary satire. Within a single basic pattern—the shift from antimasque to masque, from disorder to concord—Jonson displayed an astonishing variety of tones and subjects. Although the humor of his masques is inevitably a bit dated, and although much of the fun of these works must have depended on the specific manner of their performance, the surviving texts still have the power to amuse and instruct. When reading them it is easy to see why Jonson was, and remains, the foremost writer of English masques.

The same range of comic tones that typifies his plays and masques is also present in his nondramatic poems. He seems to have written lyric poetry from the beginning of his career until its very end, and his works in this genre survive in the *Epigrammes* (*Ep.*), *The Forrest* (*For.*), *The Underwood* (*Und.*), and in the posthumously collected group of *Ungathered Verse* (*U.V.*). Humor of various kinds appears in many of Jonson's poems, although satire is often their predominant tone. This is especially true in the *Epigrammes*, in which Jonson, strongly influenced by the Roman poet Martial, skewers all manner of foolishness and pretension. Once again, his fundamental impulse is the same: to promote virtue by attacking vice. In the *Epigrammes*, his satire is often dismissive and contemptuous; the very brevity of some of the poems suggests the ultimate insignificance of their targets. Typical of such concision is the poem "To Pertinax Cob" (*Ep.*, 69), with its implied sexual mockery: "Cob, thou nor soldier, thief, nor fencer art, / Yet by thy weapon liv'st! Thou hast one good part." This poem depends on an exaggeration that is simultaneously a kind of reduction. Like many of the epigrams, it is almost a riddle, with a final twist that drives the joke home without simply spelling it out. The same pattern of set-up and delivery is visible, for instance, in *Ep.* 118, "On Gut":

> Gut eats all day, and lechers all the night,
> So all his meat he tasteth over, twice;
> And striving so to double his delight,
> He makes himself a thoroughfare of vice.
> Thus in his belly he can change a sin:
> Lust it comes out, that gluttony went in.

With its emphasis on such themes as self-indulgence, avarice, egotism, debased pleasure, and bodily corruption as an index of spiritual degradation, this poem exemplifies the scathing and often brutal frankness of Jonson's nondramatic satire. The behaviors that he attacks in such poems are often repulsively funny; readers are meant to glimpse the ugliness as well as the humor. This effect is emphasized, especially in the *Epigrammes*, by the placement of adjacent poems celebrating good persons and their attractive virtues. Thus, an epitaph celebrating a virtuous maiden is followed shortly by one describing the domestic bliss of a couple named Giles and Joan:

> Who says that Giles and Joan at discord
> be?

The observing neighbours no such mood
    can see.
Indeed, poor Giles repents he married
    ever:
But this his Joan doth too. And Giles
    would never,
By his free will, be in Joan's company;
No more would Joan he should. Giles
    riseth early,
And having got him out of doors is
    glad—
The like is Joan—but turning home, is
    sad;
And so is Joan. Oft times, when Giles
    doth find
Harsh sights at home, Giles wisheth he
    were blind:
All this doth Joan. Or that his long-
    yarned life
Were quite out-spun; the like wish hath
    his wife.
The children that he keeps, Giles swears
    are none
Of his begetting; and so swears his Joan:
In all affections she concurreth still.
If now, with man and wife, to will and
    nill
The self-same things a note of concord
    be,
I know no couple better can agree!

Behind even the most whimsical of Jonson's satire is a strong sense of how humans should ideally behave and of how often and how far they fall short of such behavior.

The Forrest contains the beautiful poem "To Penshurst," which praises the country estate of the Sidney family as a kind of latter-day Eden, offering a powerful vision of harmony and concord. Here Jonson's humor can be touchingly gentle, as when he describes the peasants who visit the Sidneys' home:

Some bring a capon, some a rural cake,
Some nuts, some apples; some that think
    they make
The better cheeses, bring 'em; or else
    send
By their ripe daughters, whom they
    would commend
This way to husbands; and whose bas-
    kets bear
An emblem of themselves, in plum or
    pear.

The delicacy of "think," in which Jonson winks at the good-natured pride of the peasants, the playful use of "ripe" to describe the marriageable young women, the sly acknowledgment of the peasants' innocent scheming, the teasing comparison of the shapely girls to succulent fruit—all of this suggests how lovely and loving Jonson's humor could be when he found a subject worth his admiration. This aspect of his writing is easy to forget or overlook when reading his more frequent and more openly satirical poems, but it is worth remembering that it was precisely his love of the good that provoked his derision of the bad.

In "To Penshurst" Jonson demonstrates a nice ability to poke fun at himself as well as others, an ability apparent in additional works such as the lyric sequence "A Celebration of Charis" (*Und.*, 2), the epigram "My Picture Left in Scotland" (*Und.*, 9), a poem to the painter William Burlase (*Und.*, 52), and the "Epistle" to Lady Covell (*Und.*, 56). If Jonson is thought of as the ferocious satirist in such memorable poems as the epistle to Sir Edward Sackville (*Und.*, 13), "An Epistle to a Friend" (*Und.*, 15), the "Speech According to Horace" (*Und.*, 44), the "Tribe of Ben" epistle (*Und.*, 47), or the "Epigram on the Court Pucell" (*Und.*, 49), it should be remembered that the same man was capable of the sheer whimsy of "A Fit of Rhyme Against Rhyme" (*Und.*, 29), of the stoic cheerfulness of the "Execration Upon Vulcan" (*Und.*, 43), and of the simple foolery of his several poems on Thomas Coryate (*U.V.*, 10–12). Jonson's humor was every bit as complicated and various as Jonson the man.

Summary

Ben Jonson was one of the most innovative and influential writers in British comedy. He mastered a number of different genres and left his special stamp on them all—drama, masque, and poetry. Jonsonian humor is complex and various, but nearly all of it is ethically serious. Jonson's strong sense of human absurdity is balanced by a recognition of our potential for dignity and virtue. This double vision gives his satire both its bite and its deeper meaning.

Selected Bibliography
Primary Sources
    Jonson penned several hundred separate
    works in a wide variety of genres, many
    of them comic or tinged with humor.
    Among the more helpful recent editions

are *The Yale Ben Jonson* (general editors, Alvin B. Kernan and Richard B. Young), modernized texts of the masques and of the more important plays, with helpful introductions and notes. Many of Jonson's dramas have been (or will be) published as separate volumes in the series *The Revels Plays*; these editions, issued over several decades by various editors and publishers, are extremely useful. Some of the dramas have also been published as separate volumes of the *Regents Renaissance Drama* series, published by the University of Nebraska Press (Cyrus Hoy, general editor), and separate modernized editions of the plays have recently been issued by the university presses of Oxford (G.A. Wilkes, editor) and Cambridge (edited by Johanna Proctor and Martin Butler).

Ben Jonson. Ed. C.H. Herford and Percy and Evelyn Simpson. 11 vols. Oxford: Clarendon, 1925–1952. Carefully edited texts, thorough introductions and commentary, and many documents dealing with Jonson's life, works, and times. Collection remains the indispensable standard edition of the complete works.

Ben Jonson. Ed. Ian Donaldson. New York: Oxford University Press, 1985. An exceptionally helpful annotated edition of the nondramatic poems that also includes *Volpone* and *The Alchemist*.

Secondary Sources

A *Ben Jonson Journal*, edited by Richard Harp and Stanley Stewart, is due to begin publication in 1993–1994.

Biographies and Reference Works

Brock, D. Heyward. *A Ben Jonson Companion*. Bloomington: Indiana University Press, 1983. Extremely useful and comprehensive encyclopedia.

Judkins, David C. *The Non-Dramatic Works of Ben Jonson: A Reference Guide*. Boston: G.K. Hall, 1982. Brief annotated entries; helpful index.

Lehrman, Walter D., et al. *The Plays of Ben Jonson: A Reference Guide*. Boston: G.K. Hall, 1980. Short summaries of criticism; indexed.

Riggs, David. *Ben Jonson: A Life*. Cambridge, MA: Harvard University Press, 1989. Riggs treats both the works and

life; psychological emphasis.

Books

Arnold, Judd. *A Grace Peculiar: Ben Jonson's Cavalier Heroes*. University Park: Pennsylvania State University Press, 1972. Arnold argues that Jonson identifies with cavalier wits who battle with fools and fops.

Bamborough, J.B. *Ben Jonson*. London: Hutchinson, 1970. A solid survey.

Barish, Jonas A. *The Anti-Theatrical Prejudice*. Berkeley: University of California Press, 1981. A chapter included on Jonson's ambivalence as a dramatist.

———, ed. *Ben Jonson: A Collection of Critical Essays*. Englewood Cliffs, NJ: Prentice Hall, 1963.

———. *Ben Jonson and the Language of Prose Comedy*. Cambridge, MA: Harvard University Press, 1960. Focus is on stylistic traits such as rhythm and syntax; places Jonson's style in larger theoretical contexts.

Barton, Anne. *Ben Jonson: Dramatist*. Cambridge: Cambridge University Press, 1984. A play-by-play survey; offers both synthesis and new insights.

Beaurline, L.A. *Jonson and Elizabethan Comedy: Essays in Dramatic Rhetoric*. San Marino, CA: Huntington Library, 1978. Beaurline focuses on the various stances Jonson took toward his audience.

Blisset, William, ed. *A Celebration of Ben Jonson*. Toronto: University of Toronto Press, 1973. Essays on comedic "incredibility"; distrust of drama; "human nature"; the late plays; poetic "wit"; and social contexts.

Bryant, J.A., Jr. *The Compassionate Satirist: Ben Jonson and His Imperfect World*. Athens, GA: University of Georgia Press, 1972. Bryant studies the poet as "moralist, literary critic, and satirist."

Champion, Larry S. *Ben Jonson's "Dotages": A Reconsideration of the Late Plays*. Lexington, KY: University Press of Kentucky, 1967. The post-1615 plays are championed, with stress on their continuities with earlier masterpieces.

Dessen, Alan C. *Jonson's Moral Comedy*. Evanston: Northwestern University Press, 1971. Jonson's works placed in the morality-play tradition.

Dick, Aliki L. *Paedeia Through Laughter*:

Jonson's Aristophanic Appeal to Human Intelligence. The Hague: Mouton, 1974. Topics include the restorative power of laughter, attitudes toward audiences, alchemy, sophistry, satire, distortion, exaggeration, and obscenity.

Duncan, Douglas J.M. *Ben Jonson and the Lucianic Tradition*. Cambridge: Cambridge University Press, 1979. The "serio-comic balance and teasing rhetoric" of the middle comedies were influenced by Lucian, Erasmus, and More.

Dutton, Richard. *Ben Jonson: To the First Folio*. Cambridge: Cambridge University Press, 1983. Covers the tragedies; the major comedies; the pre-1616 poems; certain masques; and "covert allusions."

Enck, John Jacob. *Jonson and the Comic Truth*. Madison: University of Wisconsin Press, 1957. A chronological survey.

Evans, Robert C. *Ben Jonson and the Poetics of Patronage*. Lewisburg, PA: Bucknell University Press, 1989. Evans stresses the importance of patrons, rivals, and friends; stresses the poems; two chapters on plays and masques.

———. *Jonson in the Contexts of His Time*. Lewisburg, PA: Bucknell University Press, 1994. Essays on Jonson and historical criticism and on personal and political contexts of plays, masques, and poems.

———. *Jonson, Lipsius, and the Politics of Renaissance Stoicism*. Wakefield, NH: Longwood Academic, 1992. Exploration of the parallels between Jonson's reading and his own political ideals.

Gardiner, Judith Kegan. *Craftsmanship in Context: The Development of Jonson's Poetry*. The Hague: Mouton, 1975. Excellent discussion of major themes and specific techniques.

Haynes, Jonathan. *The Social Relations of Jonson's Theater*. Cambridge: Cambridge University Press, 1992. Haynes discusses Jonson's "realism" and "festivity," emphasizing *The Alchemist* and *Bartholomew Fair*.

Helgerson, Richard. *Self-Crowned Laureates: Spenser, Jonson, Milton and the Literary System*. Berkeley: University of California Press, 1983. Helgerson examines Jonson's role in creating a new dignity for the poet in England.

Hibbard, G.R., ed. *The Elizabethan Theatre IV*. Toronto: Macmillan, 1974. Essays on humor, Shakespeare, *Bartholomew Fair*, realism and idealism, "A Celebration of Charis," and on Jonson's view of life.

Jackson, Gabrielle Bernhard. *Vision and Judgment in Ben Jonson's Drama*. New Haven: Yale University Press, 1968. Jonson's "didacticism," "realism," and "classicism" stressed.

Jensen, Ejner J. *Ben Jonson's Comedies on the Modern Stage*. Ann Arbor: UMI Research Press, 1985. Emphasizes performance.

Kernan, Alvin. *The Cankered Muse: Satire of the English Renaissance*. New Haven: Yale University Press, 1959. A pathbreaking study.

Knights, L.C. *Drama and Society in the Age of Jonson*. New York: George W. Steward, 1937. One of the first and most influential historical studies.

Knoll, Robert E. *Ben Jonson's Plays: An Introduction*. Lincoln: University of Nebraska Press, 1964. A survey in which Jonson's Christian humanism is stressed.

Leggatt, Alexander. *Ben Jonson: His Vision and His Art*. London: Methuen, 1981. Leggatt examines works in all genres, stressing ideas they share.

Loewenstein, Joseph. *Responsive Readings: Versions of Echo in Pastoral, Epic, and the Jonsonian Masque*. New Haven: Yale University Press, 1984. Loewenstein sees the myth of Echo as a source of coherence in Jonson's works.

McCanles, Michael. *Jonsonian Discriminations: The Humanist Poet and the Praise of True Nobility*. Toronto: University of Toronto Press, 1992. McCanles argues that Jonson used contrastive techniques to promote a meritocracy.

Marcus, Leah S. *The Politics of Mirth: Jonson, Herrick, Milton, Marvell, and the Defense of Old Holiday Pastimes*. Chicago: University of Chicago Press, 1986. Richly detailed essays on the masques' historical contexts.

Maus, Katharine Eisaman. *Ben Jonson and the Roman Frame of Mind*. Princeton: Princeton University Press, 1984. Maus examines the impact of such Roman moralists as Seneca, Horace, Tacitus, Cicero, Juvenal, and Quintilian.

McDonald, Russ. *Shakespeare and Jonson/ Jonson and Shakespeare*. Lincoln: Uni-

J

versity of Nebraska Press, 1988. A study of parallels and contrasts.

Meagher, John C. *Method and Meaning in Jonson's Masques*. Notre Dame: University of Notre Dame Press, 1966. A thorough introduction.

Miner, Earl. *The Cavalier Mode from Jonson to Cotton*. Princeton: Princeton University Press, 1971. Miner emphasizes the "social" focus of the poems.

Orgel, Stephen. *The Jonsonian Masque*. Cambridge, MA: Harvard University Press, 1965. One of the first efforts to treat the masques fully.

Parfitt, George. *Ben Jonson: Public Poet and Private Man*. London: J.M. Dent, 1976. Parfitt emphasizes various genres, periods, tensions, and attitudes.

Partridge, Edward B. *The Broken Compass: A Study of the Major Comedies of Ben Jonson*. New York: Columbia University Press, 1958. Imagery and metaphor contribute to comic effect.

Peterson, Richard S. *Imitation and Praise in the Poems of Ben Jonson*. New Haven: Yale University Press, 1980. Stress is on how thoroughly Jonson absorbed his reading and used it to stimulate his own creativity.

Randall, Dale B.J. *Jonson's Gypsies Unmasked: Background and Theme of The Gypsies Metamorphos'd*. Durham, NC: Duke University Press, 1975. Richly detailed study; sees the masque as implicit satire on Duke of Buckingham.

Rowe, George E. *Distinguishing Jonson: Imitation, Rivalry, and the Direction of a Dramatic Career*. Lincoln: University of Nebraska Press, 1988. Rowe stresses Jonson's need to establish his own identity by distinguishing himself from others.

Summers, Claude J., and Ted-Larry Pebworth. *Ben Jonson*. Boston: Twayne, 1979. An exceptionally valuable introduction; a model of its kind.

———. *Classic and Cavalier: Essays on Jonson and the Sons of Ben*. Boston: Twayne, 1979. Essays on classical influences; on the book as artifact; on style; on epitaphs and love poems; on rivalry; and on links with Herbert, Carew, Vaughan, Suckling, Marvell, and Milton.

Sweeney, John Gordon III. *Jonson and the Psychology of Public Theater: To Coin the Spirit, Spend the Soul*. Princeton: Princeton University Press, 1985. Conflict between Jonson and his audiences.

Teague, Frances. *The Curious History of Bartholomew Fair*. Lewisburg, PA: Bucknell University Press, 1985. On the play's reception until 1978.

Trimpi, Wesley. *Ben Jonson's Poems: A Study of the Plain Style*. Palo Alto: Stanford University Press, 1963. Trimpi explains Jonson's preference for a curt, "middle" style in the poems.

van den Berg, Sara J. *The Action of Ben Jonson's Poetry*. Newark: University of Delaware Press, 1987. Poems seen as acts of relationship; stresses links between poetic traditions; occasion and history; fact and idea.

Watson, Robert N. *Ben Jonson's Parodic Strategy: Literary Imperialism in the Comedies*. Cambridge, MA: Harvard University Press, 1987. Watson shows how thoroughly Jonson responded to the writings of his contemporaries.

Wayne, Don E. *Penshurst: The Semiotics of Place in the Poetics of History*. Madison: University of Wisconsin Press, 1984. Jonson's famous country-house poem placed in detailed historical context.

Wiltenburg, Robert. *Ben Jonson and Self-Love: The Subtlest Maze of All*. Columbia: University of Missouri Press, 1990. Focus on self-love in *Cynthia's Revels*, *Volpone*, the *Epigrammes*, and *The Forrest*.

Womack, Peter. *Ben Jonson*. Oxford: Basil Blackwell, 1986. Womack emphasizes conflicts and tensions; focuses on character, language, theater, and the struggle between popular entertainment and authoritarian classicism.

Robert C. Evans

Joyce, James

Born: Rathgar, County Dublin, Ireland, February 2, 1882

Education: Clongowes Wood College, 1888–1891; Christian Brothers school, 1893; Belvedere College, 1893–1898; Royal University (later renamed University College), Dublin, 1898, B.A., 1902

Marriage: Nora Barnacle, July 4, 1931; two children

Died: Zurich, Switzerland, January 13, 1941

Biography

James Augustine Joyce was the first surviving child born to John and Mary "May" (Murray) Joyce, on February 2, 1882 in a tidy suburb south of Dublin called Rathgar. The quickly expanding family situation (thirteen pregnancies, nine more surviving children in a twelve-year span), along with the father's declining financial handlings, led to a constant series of moves, each time, it seems, to a less reputable neighborhood. However, beginning in 1888 young James was still able to attend the prestigious Jesuit school, Clongowes Wood College, in County Kildare, for a period of nearly three years. Then, after more than a year of self-study under his mother's direction, Joyce attended the Christian Brothers school near his home on North Richmond Street during the first few months of 1893. Finally, in April 1893 he was placed in Belvedere College, another Jesuit-run institution in Dublin proper. Having completed studies at Belvedere, Joyce entered University College in 1898, where he concentrated on modern language studies. His first publication was a piece in the *Fortnightly Review* called "Ibsen's New Drama" in April of 1900. Another essay, "The Day of the Rabblement," criticizing the policies and politics of the Irish theater movement, was rejected by the college literary journal in 1901 (both essays are reprinted in *The Critical Writings*). A year later, Joyce graduated with a baccalaureate degree and departed for Paris to pursue a medical career near year's end.

His first sojourn in Paris was almost as short-lived as his interest in becoming a doctor; in April 1903, Joyce was summoned back to Dublin due to his mother's fatal illness. May Joyce died in August of that year, but by then her son had decided not to return to Paris. He opted instead to become a writer and to support himself through newspaper book reviews and by teaching (for a short period) at the Clifton School in Dalkey, near his rented Martello tower in Sandycove.

In early January 1904, Joyce tried unsuccessfully to publish an autobiographical essay entitled "A Portrait of the Artist." He quickly proceeded to rewrite it as an equally autobiographical novel, *Stephen Hero*, but later abandoned that, too, for the highly "scrupulous" method found in *A Portrait of the Artist as a Young Man* (1916). Joyce first met Nora Barnacle, formerly of Galway, but then working as a chambermaid at Finn's Hotel in Dublin, in

mid-June 1904. By October, with a promise of a teaching job in Zurich, Joyce, with Nora accompanying him, left Ireland for good (excepting several brief visits in 1909 and 1912). Before leaving, however, Joyce managed to complete his first collection of poems, *Chamber Music* (1907), and to publish three short stories in a local agricultural weekly; those stories were to blossom into the collection entitled *Dubliners* (1914) over the next few years.

By 1905, the Joyces had settled more or less permanently in Trieste (now in northern Italy, but then part of the Austro-Hungarian empire). Their two children, George and Lucia, were born there in 1905 and 1907 respectively. Joyce supported his growing family mostly by giving private English lessons to well-off patrons; he "imported" his brother, Stanislaus, and later, his sisters, Eva and Eileen, to live in Trieste with them. By 1906, Joyce had finished twelve stories for *Dubliners* and they were accepted for publication in Ireland. He soon added two more stories and then began an eight-year battle to get the collection in print. After a hastily decided upon move to Rome, where Joyce had secured employment in a bank, the author relocated his family in Trieste in 1907. There he quickly composed "The Dead," which was included as the fifteenth and final entry in *Dubliners*.

The next few years were ones of extreme hardship for Joyce; they included frustration with publishers, extreme poverty, bouts of drunkenness, entrepreneurial disasters, and frequent changes of address. Nonetheless, Joyce continued to grow as a writer, and his work finally came to the attention of Ezra Pound in 1913, a propitious event largely due to the efforts of W.B. Yeats. Joyce's star slowly began to rise: in 1914, the originally contracted publisher of *Dubliners* finally fulfilled his obligation in London, and the recently revised and still in progress *A Portrait of the Artist as a Young Man* began serialization in Pound's *Egoist* in London. That year also found Joyce beginning to write his only play, *Exiles*, and to plan his next novel, *Ulysses*.

The onslaught of war drove the Joyces to their first extended stay in Zurich, from 1915 to 1919, and it was there that Joyce composed a large portion of *Ulysses*, oversaw the publication of *A Portrait* in 1916, completed and published *Exiles* in 1918, and underwent the first of a long series of painful eye operations in 1917. Following the war, the Joyce family returned briefly to Trieste, but by 1920 Pound had coaxed Joyce to reside in Paris, where he lived for twenty years or, essentially, the rest of his productive life. Also due to Pound's influence, sections of *Ulysses* were serialized for almost two years in the American journal, *Little Review*, before being banned as obscene literature. During the Zurich stay, Joyce also found lifelong patronage in the person of Harriet Shaw Weaver, who often kept the prodigal Joyce and his family from the edges of impoverishment.

On Joyce's fortieth birthday in 1922, the first 1,000 copies of *Ulysses* were published by Sylvia Beach's Shakespeare and Co., a bookstore in Paris. A year later Joyce began composing the first drafts of his next and final novel, the title of which was kept a secret until its publication in 1939. *Finnegans Wake*, fragments of which were serialized in various journals over the next sixteen years, was known simply as *Work in Progress* to a growing circle of critics, friends, and general readers. Herbert Gorman published the first biography of Joyce in 1924; subtitled *His First Forty Years*, the book was actually commissioned by Joyce, who constantly strove for his own self-promotion.

As with both of his earlier works of fiction, Joyce encountered problem after problem with the publishing of *Ulysses*. He was frustrated even before its initial full publication in 1922 by customs seizings, claims of pornography, arrests, and court proceedings. After that date, the book was involved in more seizures, court orders, and even a badly copied, serialized version by an American named Samuel Roth, with whom Joyce fought with the aid of a petition signed by more than a hundred prominent scientists and writers to ban the pirated edition. Roth finally stopped his illegal serialization in 1928.

Joyce had no such trouble publishing his second book of verse, *Pomes Penyeach*, in 1927, or with various sections of *Work in Progress*, which had already been seen in print in Ford Madox Ford's *Transatlantic Review*, T.S. Eliot's *Criterion*, and Eugene and Maria Jolas's *transition*. He did have troubles with his health, though, due mostly to his long years of drinking and bad nutrition. Not only did he suffer through numerous eye operations, he also had badly decayed teeth which were finally removed entirely in 1923, and he developed duodenal ulcers which eventually killed him. Added to Joyce's physical ailments was the increasingly bizarre mental behavior of his daughter Lucia, beginning around 1929 and culminating, after a number of short stays at various sanataria, in her being permanently committed in 1936. In the face of such adversities, Joyce continued to write what was to be his final comic masterpiece.

Despite growing world-wide recognition and praise for *Ulysses* (the first book-length study of the novel, by Stuart Gilbert, came out in 1930), the cryptic style of *Work in Progress* was not without its detractors, including Pound and Joyce's usually agreeable brother Stanislaus, who said that it was "unreadable." To offset claims of the book's inaccessibility, in 1929, Joyce oversaw the publication of *Our Exagmination Round His Factification for Incamination of Work in Progress*, a collection of twelve essays by Joyce's closest associates including Samuel Beckett, William Carlos Williams, and Frank Budgen.

On a more domestic note, Joyce and Nora, his mate of twenty-six years, were married in London on July 4, 1931, ultimately to ensure George's and Lucia's inheritance rights. At the very end of that year, Joyce's father died in Dublin, but the following February saw the birth of Joyce's grandson Stephen. The proximity of these two diametrical events inspired his best poem, "Ecce Puer."

In 1933, an American judge decreed that *Ulysses* was not pornographic, making possible its first legal U.S. publication by Random House a year later. Also in 1934, Budgen, a Zurich-based artist and friend of the Joyces, published *James Joyce and the Making of "Ulysses."* If popular magazine coverage can be a measure of the height of one's fame, then Joyce reached his pinnacle in 1934 with a cover story in *Time* magazine. *Collected Poems* was published in New York in 1936, and the last installment of *Work in Progress* appeared in *transition* in 1938. In 1939, on his fifty-seventh birthday Joyce received the first advance copy of *Finnegans Wake*, but the book actually went on sale in May of that year. Much criticism was favorable, but sales and eventually the novel's fame were slowed somewhat by the advent of war in September 1939.

By Christmas of that year, Paris had become too dangerous and unfriendly a place for the "neutral" Joyce family, so they moved to a village near Vichy, staying with close friends for almost a year. Joyce tried unsuccessfully to secure the release of Lucia, who was housed in a nearby sanitarium, but finally he did manage to obtain visas for the rest of his family, including son George and grandson Stephen, to enter neutral Switzerland. The physical and mental toll proved too much for the writer, who was hospitalized in Zurich for a perforated ulcer on January 11. He died following an unsuccessful operation two days later on January 13, 1941.

Literary Analysis

Joyce began his literary career as a fine imitator of late Victorians such as Oscar Wilde, Algernon Swinburne, and Walter Pater, but ended it as an unparalleled comic innovator in the High Modernist tradition. In literature, High Modernism, though never a true movement encompassing a marked set of beliefs among its major proponents, is said in retrospect to include the time between the two world wars, or approximately 1918 to 1939. Joyce published his two great novels, *Ulysses* and *Finnegans Wake*, within that time frame. Both books helped change the way that novels are written, and perhaps more importantly altered our understanding of what constitutes a funny novel. Other high modernists writing in English, including Virginia Woolf, Ford, Eliot, Pound, D.H. Lawrence, William Faulkner, Gertrude Stein, Djuna Barnes, and Ernest Hemingway, all altered the way that narrative texts are read, but none of them did it with Joyce's comic flair.

Joyce's understanding of the comic is perhaps best described in the Bakhtinian sense of lower body humor. Mikhail Bakhtin places this lower body humor within "the culture of folk humor" and alternately calls it "the concept of grotesque realism": "The essential principle of grotesque realism is degradation, that is, lowering of all that is high, spiritual, ideal, abstract; it is a transfer to the material level, to the sphere of the earth and body in their indissoluble unity." It is descended directly from writers like Geoffrey Chaucer, Miguel de Cervantes, François Rabelais, Jean Baptiste Moliere, Giovanni Boccaccio, Jonathan Swift, Henry Fielding, Laurence Sterne, and Nikolai Gogol. This "school" of comedy takes sex, sexuality, digestion, elimination, and other physiological functions, shunned or taboo subjects in the high comic order, to be not only acceptable but downright fitting topics for humorous treatment. For instance, Joyce's otherwise straightforward attempt at neoclassical poetry, *Chamber Music*, apparently has a cloacal *double entendre* in its title: in *Ulysses*, Joyce likened his first verses to the musical sound of a woman micturating in a chamber pot. Joyce's great comic creation, Leopold Bloom, the Odyssean protagonist of *Ulysses*, is humorously linked to all lower bodily functions, from the quotidian (his morning session in the jakes) to the sexually perverse (his sadomasochism exposed and parodied in Bella Cohen's whorehouse). And, of course, Joyce the artist, through his autobiographical characters (from the Stephen of *Stephen Hero* to his transmogrified self, Shem, in *Finnegans Wake*), equates artistic creation with the act of elimination.

Mimicry and mockery are also elemental to Joyce's comedy. The young Joyce's extremely diverse reading in everything from religious and secular classics to then "unknown" writers such as Henrik Ibsen, Gerhard Hauptmann, Gabriele D'Annunzio, and Giordano Bruno made him a bit of a legend during his university days. This omnivorous literary appetite would later provide him with the very ingredients of his satire and parody, perhaps this Irish author's best comic utensils. However, the high priests of letters and the denizens of popular literature were not the only objects of Joyce's ridicule. After Charles Dickens, Joyce is perhaps the first modern British prose writer to have chronicled the foibles and follies of the common people, particularly the Dublin middle-income and poorer economic classes. Joyce's nine-year struggle to publish *Dubliners* in part was due to ongoing arguments with the publishers and printers who felt that he cut too close to the bone by his insistence on using actual places of business and the names of shop and pub owners in order to portray realistically the middle- and lower-class populace of the city.

Joyce's early works, including *Chamber Music*, *Dubliners*, the unfinished *Stephen Hero*, and *A Portrait of the Artist as a Young Man*, perhaps too often are seen as the stuff of apprenticeship, mere preparation for the masterful comedy of *Ulysses* and *Finnegans Wake*. Nevertheless, beginning with *Dubliners*, but especially in the later compositions of that collection, Joyce was already displaying a seasoned talent for comic creation, taking satirical pokes at contemporary views of courtship, love, sex, religion, art, and politics in and around Dublin. Of course, emotions like pathos and despair *are* intentionally evoked in Joyce's depiction of Dublin's paralysis (a word introduced in the first story and often pointed out by critics as a metaphor for the static nature of many of the collection's characters). Still, the element of levity introduced into each situation usually undercuts its seriousness.

For example, Tom Kernan in "Grace" is a serious alcoholic in need of assistance. His friends devise a plan to aid him by coaxing the former Protestant to attend a Catholic retreat for businessmen; to do so they visit the ailing Tom at home. Ironically, what ensues is a typical Irishmen's drinking bout, made hilarious by all of the participants' spouting of faulty knowledge of the history of their religion. All the men in Kernan's bedroom struggle to understand some complex beliefs of Catholicism; they are especially verbal about papal infallibility (a then recent [1870] dogma of the Church). Mr. Fogarty declares, "Yes, because when the Pope speaks *ex cathedra* . . . he is infallible" (168). Then Mr. Cunningham tries to explain the internal struggle of the Vatican Council to adopt this concept: "There they were at it, all the cardinals and bishops and archbishops from all the ends of the earth . . . until at last the Pope himself stood up and declared infallibility a dogma of the Church *ex cathedra*" (169). The delicious circular logic and fine irony of this statement is not lost on most readers, but Joyce hilariously captures these pretentiously pious men who take it at face value.

Moreover, on a structural level, Joyce heightens the comedy of "Grace" by mimicking the tripartite layout of Dante Alighieri's *Divine Comedy*: hell-purgatory-heaven. By alluding to such highbrow literature, Joyce manages paradoxically to devastate the strained earnestness of these lowbrow do-gooders and to create an affinity with the very high-level art that he is parodying. Of course, the Dantean parallel in *Dubliners* goes beyond the story "Grace." Mary T. Reynolds argues that each of the stories alludes to some episode in the *Inferno*, thus indicating Dublin's "moral death" (159). This also points up Joyce's level of parodic sophistication. Perhaps Joyce's best comic targets, though, were not the literary predecessors to *Dubliners* but the Irish people, specifically those with whom Joyce was most familiar: young students, priests, merchants, artists, minor politicos, hangers-on, ne'er-do-wells, welshers, salesmen, newspapermen, and office workers. Lenehan and Corley, the protagonists of "Two Gallants," though their tale is ultimately one of shameless deceit and pretense, are not without humorous characteristics, as witnessed in the narrator's fitting description of Corley as a walking, tumescent phallus: "He walked with his hands at his sides, holding himself erect and swaying his head from side to side. His head was large, globular, and oily; it sweated in all weathers; and his large round hat, set upon it sideways, looked like a bulb which had grown out of another" (51). In this particular story, the epiphany (Joyce's coinage for moments of "sudden spiritual manifestation" [*Stephen Hero*, 188]) belongs to the reader. It is we who have been duped by Corley's apparent ulterior motive with the slavey, and we who now suddenly realize the true nature of the peripatetic Lenehan's concerns throughout the narrative.

However, in "The Dead," Joyce's best and most anthologized story, the final realization is all Gabriel Conroy's. Because "The Dead" ends with Gabriel's serious questioning of the meaning of his life, it is not often defined as a humorous account or even a satirical story unmasking the hypocritical temperament of turn-of-the-century Dublin, as are many of the preceding stories. Nevertheless, "The Dead" can tickle the funnybone of its readers, even as it touches the heartstrings with fond memories. We smile at Aunt Julia's inability to grasp the connection between guttapercha galoshes and prophylactics, since that was once the main ingredient for condoms: "'Goloshes, Julia!' exclaimed her sister. 'Goodness me, don't you know what goloshes are? You wear them over your . . . over your boots, Gretta, isn't it?'" (181). We also laugh at the drunken antics of Freddy Malins. It is authorial mocking of the mildly pompous Gabriel, though, that best marks the comedy of this story. He is deservedly derided for putting on airs of superiority and aloofness when in fact he often falls dismally short of grasping the truth of a given situation. Until Gabriel's realization of his own frailty and finality, Joyce gently goads this ostentatious would-be writer who is in fact a counterfeit projection of what Joyce might have become had he remained in Ireland.

By contrast, the autobiographical elements in Joyce's first novel, *A Portrait*, are to a large extent a true projection of what the young writer had been and was becoming. Even so, this *Kunstlerroman*, or novel of the adolescent development of an artist-hero, does not always present an authorial empathy toward Stephen Dedalus's lifestyle, or especially, his way of reacting to the world. By the use of third person narration, Joyce in effect distances himself from his fictional hero. This narrative technique historically has been represented, according to Stephen's aesthetic theory which is espoused in chapter 5, by the dramatic form of literature: "The personality of the artist, at first a cry or a cadence or a mood and then a fluid and lambent narrative, finally refines itself out of existence, impersonalizes itself, so to speak . . . The artist, like the God of creation, remains within or behind or beyond or above his handiwork, invisible, refined out of existence, indifferent, paring his fingernails" (215). Thus, the mature Joyce is emancipated from the words and actions of his young artist-hero creation—and yet, ironically, he is a bit too removed. That is to say, the third person narration, though seemingly impartial, has an undercurrent, a distinct appearance of being Stephen's personal account. We as readers seem to be situated in Stephen's consciousness throughout the narrative. And although there are a large number of supporting players in this "drama," we get only Stephen's reactions to the events of the novel, never any other character's.

As a result of this limited viewpoint, and since Stephen is often introspective, somber, and even sullen, the reaction to the novel by most readers is usually less than jocular. In fact, one critic argues "[t]hat there is none of the vigorous wit and philosophical irony of the genial *Dubliners* and of *Ulysses*, while Joyce's own waggish satire is only hinted at."[1] While the humor of *A Portrait* is more subdued than that in his other major works, it does shine through at times. One good example is the Christmas dinner scene in chapter 1. Almost Sternean in its depiction of a familial repast where high rhetoric and blasphemous speech vie for dominance, the dinner is also a brutally realistic history play. A major motif in *A Portrait* is betrayal, and the then-recent fall of Charles Stewart Parnell, Ireland's great parliamentarian and advocate of Home Rule for the Irish State, was defined by many, including Mr. Dedalus and John Casey, as a perfidious action on the part of both the Catholic Church and Parnell's own chosen disciples. The stylistic irony of a heated political argument dealing with this theme on the birthday of one who was also betrayed and defiled and crucified is not lost on most readers, but the more humorous moments are often overshadowed by such a contrast. Lighter scenes include Mr. Casey's teasing Stephen about his "purse of silver in his throat" (28), Simon's take-off of the hotelkeeper with both Stephen and Mr. Casey joining in the merriment (29), the father's perfectly timed wry comment about the "pope's nose" (32), and Casey's spiteful spitting story (the closest approximation to eliminative comedy in the novel).

The subtlety of the humor may also have been affected by Joyce's style in the design and writing of *A Portrait*. In abandoning the sixty-three chapter format of *Stephen Hero* for the streamlined five chapter revision, the novelist forced on his narrative a "scrupulous meanness," greatly reducing the story line while allowing for a certain resultant fragmenting of characterization. Hence, the Stephen of *Stephen Hero* is found in lighter moments laughing aloud with McCann and being laughed at by Lynch when Stephen confesses his spur-of-the-moment decision the day before to ask Emma to sleep with him for one night:

No girl with an ounce of brains would listen to you. That's no way to go about it, man. You run out suddenly after her, come up sweating and puffing and say "Let us lie together." Did you mean it as a joke?

—No, I was quite serious. (179)

Both the original encounter and the two young men's subsequent conversation, in which the narrator allows Lynch to mock Stephen's naivety, are eliminated in the revised *A Portrait* so that there the reader knows only that some strain on their friendship now exists between Stephen and Emma, but the humor behind that breach has been lost.

With *Ulysses*, Joyce loses no such opportunities for comedy. Stephen Dedalus, having flown through the nets that ensnared his artistic soul at the end of *A Portrait*, is back in Dublin, now an even more saturnine young man who is chided by his usurping nemesis, Buck Mulligan, for still mourning his mother's passing nine months after her death. To counterbalance this morose picture, Joyce introduces the Blooms, Leopold and Molly, whose life-affirming actions will parallel and finally intersect with Stephen's pathway on an otherwise nondescript day (eighteen hours or so to be more exact), the sixteenth of June, 1904.

Underlying the entire day's events is Joyce's palimpsestic use of Homer's *Odyssey*. However, the author's parodic intent is not to write a modern sequel to that Greek epic, but merely to pepper his narrative with Homer's ghostly presence, not unlike the case of Stephen's theory about William Shakespeare's dramatic histories and tragedies which is also dependent upon an authorial spiriting within and behind those plays. The final effect is purely comic, since Stephen-Telemachus is less than enthusiastic to find another father to replace his already drunken one; Molly-Penelope is less than patiently faithful in her affair with Blazes Boylan; and Bloom-Odysseus, although a wanderer on this and every day (he is an advertising canvasser for a daily Dublin newspaper), is less than heroic in demeanor as he fights his minor battles and encounters his own psychological demons, sirens, and harpies.

Joyce achieved several technical tours de force in the composition of *Ulysses*. One is his mastery of stream-of-consciousness, or the interior monologue, in order to allow the reader direct access to the mental processes of his major characters, seemingly without a narrator's interpretation. Richard Ellmann points to the diary entries at the end of *A Portrait*, with their sentence fragments and associative connections, as one probable precursor to the style in *Ulysses*.[2] Nevertheless, in the latter work, Joyce perfects it as a comic technique so that, for example, in the "Nausicaa" episode, which is told in the first half by an omniscient narrator whose language approximates that which is found in the glamour and beauty magazines perused by Gerty MacDowell, the reader is suddenly hit in the second portion with Bloom's longest interiority of thought with very little narrative interruption and/or explication. As a consequence, the reader is treated to a hilariously contrasting view of the events which have just transpired. Gerty's perception is of her being in close proximity to "a sterling man, a man of inflexible honour to his fingertips" whose "hands and face were working" inexplicably while she leans back to observe the fireworks, consequently exposing her "graceful beautifully shaped legs" (13:695–98;1961: 365). Less than two pages later, Bloom assumes the narration by revealing a number of things that the first-round reader only suspects. He is, naturally, the dark gentleman about whom Gerty has over-romanticized; she is in fact lame ("Glad I didn't know it when she was on show. Hot little devil all the same"); and Bloom's gestures have been onanistic rather than chivalrous—"Begins to feel cold and clammy . . . Still you have to get rid of it someway. They don't

care. Complimented perhaps" (13:851–53;1961:370).

Another technique initiated by Joyce in *Ulysses* is the mutability of the narration. After the initial "straightforward" style of the first six episodes, the remainder of the novel has what appears to be a constant change of narrators and/or narrative approaches. Something happens to alter the reader's perception of the storytelling modes in the final twelve chapters. Beginning with the interspersed headlines of "Aeolus" and ending with the apparent disappearance of any outside narrator in "Penelope," Joyce intentionally places these narrative stumbling blocks to obfuscate the reader's facility for comprehension. It is a comic as well as a playful narrational ploy; all of these changes actually beg the puzzle-lover in each of us to solve the mystery with the clues given: some easy (the headlines appear in a chapter dealing with newspapermen), and some brain-teasing but solvable (the parodied progressive styles of writing in "Oxen of the Sun," in which the gestation of written English corresponds to the birth of Mrs. Purefoy's child). Still other clues may provide no answer.

In fact, such lacunae are part of the game that Joyce is playing: certain "evidence" was never planted in the text, or else false indicators may exist. A good example is the ongoing critical argument over the discrepancy concerning the number of lovers Molly has had. In the catechetical penultimate episode "Ithaca," which is a series of 309 questions and answers, the scientifically objective questioner asks for a list of Molly's previous bed-sharers to be compiled, and then a complete listing of twenty-five men is supplied. For some years, most critics took this list at face value, and not at all as a jealous projection of Bloom's unconscious desires, as others more recently would have it.[3]

The only other documentation that the reader has to determine the list's accuracy is Molly's saucy but also very funny soliloquy, the "Penelope" episode, which is not only devoid of punctuation and normal paragraph construction but also has no narrator to navigate the reader through the rushing flood of words. Nonetheless, the reading is fairly smooth sailing, due to Molly's way of thinking whole thoughts spliced together with numerous conjunctions and connective phrases. Molly's thoughts understandably center on sex, and in the course of recent and long-ago memories, she seems to negate the extent of her past promiscuity, indicating that Boylan may be her only coitional partner besides her husband, Leopold Bloom, who deflowered her on Howth Hill sixteen years earlier. And yet, the author leaves the reader-detective guessing regarding the recent Boer War casualty Lt. Gardner, whom Molly mentions as a recent suitor but who is not on the list in "Ithaca."

However, in most readers' minds, Leopold is not only still at the center of Molly's consciousness (and vice versa), he is at the heart of Joyce's comedy in *Ulysses*. When Bloom tries himself mentally in "Circe," the only episode in dramatic form, THE VEILED SIBYL testifies that Bloom is "the funniest man on earth" (15:1737;1961:491). Most readers would at least agree that Bloom is imbued with a true comic spirit, as Zack Bowen argues in *"Ulysses" as a Comic Novel*. Bowen sees Bloom as a sort of common man's Ulysses, not Noman but Everyman, a regular *schlemiel* figure (Bloom is of Jewish descent), one with whom the average reader can associate or even feel superior to. Moreover, "as spiritual misfit, Bloom embodies the traditional comic salvation of the powerless against the powerful, the individual against the social order."[4] Bloom also acts as a comic foil to the melodramatic Stephen, who, if he continues to play out his Hamlet fantasy, is in sore need of a Shakespearian father-figure like Bloom to give him a parallactic view of the world, one that can see life's varied problems with a sense of action and resolve (no matter that Bloom's solutions are often half-cocked and unworkable) rather than with reserve and hesitancy. In that sense, the characterizations of Bloom and Stephen anticipate those of Humphrey Chimpden Earwicker and Shem in *Finnegans Wake*.

It took Joyce sixteen years to compose his last novel, *Finnegans Wake*, and throughout much of that time the author was adding constantly to the original drafts of his *Work in Progress*, obscuring literal meanings of words and enveloping the language with multiple possibilities for linguistic, historical, cultural, and mythic interpretations. At the same time, Joyce never lost sight of the fact that he was writing a comic novel, so the humor has been enhanced, not destroyed, by the layers of meaning heaped upon each word, phrase, and sentence in the *Wake*. Like Lewis Carroll before him, Joyce packs full his *portmanteau* words to tease his reader into making aural/oral/verbal associations that should lead to a height-ened understanding of a nonsensical-looking term; but those associations can also be downright funny. A simple case in point is the word "psocoldlogical": the very human science of psychology, the term seems to imply, defines itself as being coldly clinical like the pure sciences, but this "so-called logical" definition does not really fit. Joyce's neologism is not only funny, it is also economical! Indeed, constant poetic explication like the above is an intrinsic part of the process of reading *Finnegans Wake*.

So much for reading a single word, but what about the full scope of understanding in the *Wake*? What is the book about? Beckett explains that the book "is not *about* something; *it is that something itself* . . . When the sense is sleep, the words go to sleep . . . When the sense is dancing, the words dance" (14). Though Beckett's definition of Joyce's language usage is aptly descriptive, most readers still would like to know in whose bed the words are slumbering and who are their dancing partners. In other words, do any of the normative elements of a novel—plot, setting, cast of characters, themes, and so forth—operate in *Finnegans Wake*? Basically, the answer is yes, although critics have argued for and against any and all of the above elements for fifty years.

One major theme is evident from the title, which is taken from an obscure late nineteenth-century Irish-American song called "Finnegan's Wake" about a drunken Irish stonemason who dies from a fall and subsequently revives at his own wake when alcoholic spirits are spilled into his coffin accidentally. This resurrection motif, which Joyce proceeds to cull from every religious, mythological, and legendary source, plays up the cyclical nature of life as well as that of the book itself, perhaps made most obvious by the famous opening sentence, a suspended epic statement which is truly spoken *in medias res*: "rivverrun, past Eve and Adam's, from swerve of shore to bend of bay, brings us by a commodius vicus of recirculation back to Howth Castle and Environs" (*Finnegans Wake*, 3.1–3). Although it continues to be a controversial crux of *Wake* criticism, the very last sentence of the novel *seems* to invite a Viconian return on the reader's part to the above first line: "A way a lone a loved a long the" (628.15–16).

This line also concludes the soliloquy of Anna Livia Plurabelle, the novel's mature woman/mother figure whose fluid nature is representative of the River Liffey, which flows down from the Wicklow hills through Dublin and eventually joins the sea. Anna's journey through life parallels the course of the river (as well as the book), one that mystically implies birth, death, and rebirth, just as seaborne clouds always bring rain to refresh the nascent waters of hillside streams destined to flow into the Liffey. Anna is also the subject of chapter 8 (book 1.8), which is a gossipy but comic tale told by two old women doing their washing near the headwaters of the Liffey. In part, their gossip entails the "situation" around which the loosely framed storyline is built; that is, the alleged wrongdoing in Phoenix Park by Anna's husband, Humphrey Chimpden Earwicker. One of the duties performed by Anna appears to be an attempt to exonerate Humphrey in his fall from grace and to reestablish his good name, at least among his three children, most often called Shem, Shaun, and Issy in the narrative.

The lapsarian motif is exemplified best in Humphrey's "crime," which may have involved his furtively observing two girls relieving themselves in the park, but unbeknownst to him he is spied on in the act by three British soldiers. His fall is echoed in any number of sacred and secular figures, from Adam to Humpty Dumpty to Tim Finnegan to Finn MacCool, the Irish giant of mythical times whose fallen corpse makes up the surrounding topography of Dublin and who is expected to rise again some day. This theme of falling and rising looms large not only in mythology and religion, but also in the historical theories of Giambattista Vico, whose writings, especially *Scienza Nuova*, Joyce emulates at least in part throughout *Finnegans Wake*. Even the structure of the book roughly follows Vico's regal "ages": book 1 (the first eight chapters) relates to the Viconian time when the Gods ruled; book 2 (the next three chapters) encompasses the age when Heroes ruled; book 3 (the three penultimate chapters) signifies the democratic period of Human rule; and book 4 (the final chapter) is the *ricorso*, or the transitional time before the return to the first age.

Although several highly involved concepts like the above are important for an ultimate understanding of this "traumscript" or throwaway dream-script, the novice reader need not be totally immersed in complex theories of Wakean exegesis to appreciate the comedy which is basic to the *Wake*. Perhaps as in real life, those who best embody the comic spirit in Joyce's last novel are the children of Humphrey and Anna. In book 2.1 (chapter 9), the twins,

Shem and Shaun, and their sister Issy (who is paired with her own image, "her grateful sister reflection in a mirror") share a chapter in which they appear to stage a twilight play called "The Mime of Mick, Nick and the Maggies." For Robert M. Polhemus, "Shem and Shaun are the quintessential comic opposites, reverberating as significantly as Yin and Yang or cerebral bipolarity. They create each other, play off each other . . . and out of the implied tension between these mythic figures and their world views comes Joyce's comic vision." The chapter aptly begins with a parody of a playbill, including a cast of characters and an acknowledgement of all those who helped in the production. Listed there is the following: "Jests, jokes, jigs and jorums for the Wake lent from the properties of the late cemented Mr T.M. Finnegan R.I.C." (*Finnegans Wake*, 221.26–7). And, indeed, much humor abounds in this chapter of puns, riddles, nursery rhymes, and children's fun and games. Patrick A. McCarthy sees the children's production on two levels: it is a comic reenactment of their father's fall in Phoenix Park, and it is also a "parody of a morality play."[5] In sum, this central episode of the *Wake* is exemplary of the rich layers of humor extant in every chapter of this "scherzarade [charade; *scherzo*, Italian for joke] of one's thousand one nightinesses" (*Finnegan's Wake*, 51.4–5).

Summary

James Joyce was an Irish self-exile who wrote fiction about his homeland from a critical distance, and despite his youthful rejection of the ideals of the Irish Literary Revival, ironically his writings helped establish Irish literature as the mainstream movement it remains to this day. Joyce's greatest contributions to comic fiction are his two novels of maturity, *Ulysses* and *Finnegans Wake*. *Ulysses*, though difficult at times, is the more accessible of the two. The author's sense of the humorous is rooted in the corporal as well as the cerebral modes of comedy. His best comic creations play off that diametric opposition: Bloom and Molly, Stephen and Buck Mulligan, Humphrey and Anna, Shem and Shaun. His inventive fiction turned the world of literature on its head, in much the same way that Pablo Picasso and the Cubists altered our way of viewing art. Joyce's innovations were directly responsible for further ground-breaking novelistic techniques and more innovative fiction in the latter half of the twentieth century, most notably from writers like Beckett, Vladimir Nabokov, Thomas Pynchon, John Barth, Italo Calvino, and Martin Amis.

Notes

1. John Blades, *James Joyce: A Portrait of the Artist as a Young Man* (New York: Viking Penguin, 1991), p. 187.
2. Richard Ellmann, *James Joyce* (New York: Oxford University Press, 1982), pp. 358–59. Of course, Ellmann and many other critics acknowledge several literary forebears to the stream-of-consciousness technique, including Edouard DuJardin, Leo Tolstoy, Dorothy Richardson, and George Moore.
3. See Phillip Herring's article "The Bedsteadfastness of Molly Bloom," *Modern Fiction Studies*, 15, 1 (Spring 1969): 49–61, for arguments on both sides of this issue. In *James Joyce and the Politics of Desire*, Suzette Henke gives a more recent perceptive defense of Molly's fidelity.
4. Zack Bowen, *"Ulysses" as a Comic Novel* (Syracuse, NY: Syracuse University Press, 1989), pp. 4–11.
5. See Patrick A. McCarthy, *The Riddles of "Finnegans Wake."* (Rutherford, NJ: Fairleigh-Dickinson University Press, 1980), pp. 139–40. McCarthy further argues that the comic inversion comes from satanic Shem (Nick) being cast as the tempted rather than the tempter as in Milton's *Paradise Lost.*

Selected Bibliography

Primary Sources

Each work's original publication is listed first, with current edition(s) immediately following.

Chamber Music. London: Elkin Matthews, 1907. Included in *Collected Poems*. New York: Viking Press, 1957.

Dubliners. London: Grant Richards, 1914; New York: B.W. Huebsch, 1916; *Dubliners: Text, Criticism, and Notes*, ed. Robert Scholes and A. Walton Litz. New York: Viking Press, 1968. Viking Critical Edition.

A Portrait of the Artist as a Young Man. New York: B.W. Huebsch, 1916; London: The Egoist Press, 1917. *A Portrait of the Artist as a Young Man: Text, Criticism, and Notes*, ed. Chester G. Anderson. New York: Viking Press, 1968. Viking Critical Edition.

Exiles: A Play in Three Acts. New York: B.W. Huebsch, and London: Grant Richards, 1918. Rpt., including "Notes by the Author," New York: Viking Press, 1961.

Ulysses. Paris: Shakespeare and Company, 1922; *Ulysses*, "corrected and reset" edition, New York: Random House, 1961; *Ulysses: The Corrected Text*, ed. Hans Walter Gabler, New York: Random House, 1986.

Pomes Penyeach. Paris: Shakespeare and Company, 1927. Included in *Collected Poems*. New York: Viking Press, 1957.

Finnegans Wake. New York: Viking Press, and London: Faber & Faber, 1939. Paperback reprint, New York: Viking Penguin, 1988.

Stephen Hero. Ed. Theodore Spencer. Norfolk, CT: New Directions, 1944. Augmented edition by John J. Slocum and Herbert Cahoon, New York: New Directions, 1963.

Letters of James Joyce. 3 vols. Vol. 1 (1957), ed. Stuart Gilbert; Vols. 2 and 3, ed. Richard Ellmann. New York: Viking Press, 1966.

The Critical Writings of James Joyce. Ed. Ellsworth Mason and Richard Ellmann. New York: Viking Press, 1959. New edition with "forward by Guy Davenport." Ithaca, NY: Cornell University Press, 1989.

Secondary Sources

The following includes full-length studies and collections of essays only. Innumerable articles on Joyce can be found in any of several bibliographical compilations, some of which are listed below. (See also Current Journals below.)

Bibliographies

Deming, Robert H. *A Bibliography of James Joyce Studies*. Boston: G.K. Hall, 1977. 2nd ed. Exhaustive reference source for both articles and full-length studies.

Rice, Thomas Jackson. *James Joyce: A Guide to Research*. New York: Garland, 1982. Annotated bibliography complete to 1981.

Biographies

Ellmann, Richard. *James Joyce*. New York:

Oxford University Press, 1959; rev. 1982. The best and most extensive biography to date.

Gorman, Herbert. *James Joyce: His First Forty Years.* New York: B.W. Huebsch, 1924. First biography, notable historically but not for its accuracy.

Books and Articles

Attridge, Derek, ed. *The Cambridge Companion to James Joyce.* Cambridge: Cambridge University Press, 1990. Most recent multifaceted study of Joyce's life and works. Includes much current critical theory.

———, and Daniel Ferrer, eds. *Poststructuralist Joyce: Essays from the French.* Cambridge: Cambridge University Press, 1984. Small but important collection; contributions by very prominent French scholars on all of Joyce's major works.

Beckett, Samuel, et al. *Our Exagmination round his Factification for Incamination of Work in Progress.* Paris: Shakespeare and Co., 1929; Rpt. New York: New Directions, 1972. Twelve early disciples expound on various aspects of the unfinished *Finnegans Wake*; a historically important document.

Bell, Robert H. *Jocoserious Joyce: The Fate of Folly in "Ulysses."* Ithaca and London: Cornell University Press, 1991. Bell reassesses the nature of comedy extant in *Ulysses*; draws on comic theories from Erasmus to Henri Bergson, and finds *Ulysses* a mix of farce, satire, and the mock-heroic.

Benstock, Bernard. *James Joyce.* New York: Frederick Ungar, 1985. Concise biographical study with critical chapters coinciding with chronological ordering of Joyce's works.

———, ed. *The Augmented Ninth: Papers from the Ninth James Joyce Symposium.* Syracuse: Syracuse University Press, 1988. Important for current critical thought by major Joyceans; also includes essays by Jacques Derrida and Julia Kristeva.

———, and Shari Benstock. *Who's He When He's At Home: A James Joyce Directory.* Urbana: University of Illinois Press, 1980. Exhaustive listing of names and identities of all characters, real and imag-

ined, in every prose work except *Finnegans Wake*.

Blades, John. *James Joyce: A Portrait of the Artist as a Young Man.* Penguin Critical Studies. New York: Viking Penguin, 1991. An investigation of themes, styles, innovations, historical and cultural contexts for the novel; looks closely at its influence on and by Modernism.

Bowen, Zack. *Musical Allusions in the Works of James Joyce: Early Poetry through "Ulysses."* Albany: State University of New York Press, 1974. A thorough study of Joyce's musical references with accompanying critical commentary.

———. *"Ulysses" as a Comic Novel.* Syracuse, NY: Syracuse University Press, 1989. Bowen places *Ulysses* in historic comic novel context dating from Miguel de Cervantes. Also investigates theories of comedy and relates them to *Ulysses*.

———, and James F. Carens, eds. *A Companion to Joyce Studies.* Westport, CT: Greenwood Press, 1984. First and best all-inclusive collection of critical essays on every published work of Joyce. Includes a biography and a textual study.

Budgen, Frank. *James Joyce and the Making of "Ulysses."* London: Grayson and Grayson, 1934; new edition, Bloomington: University of Indiana Press, 1960. Mostly accurate account of how Joyce worked through the completion of the novel by closest friend in Zurich, 1918–1921.

Chace, William M., ed. *Joyce: A Collection of Critical Essays.* Englewood Cliffs, NJ: Prentice-Hall, 1974. Twentieth-Century Views. Excellent collection of important essays on all works of Joyce by eminent scholars.

Deming, Robert H., ed. *James Joyce: The Critical Heritage.* 2 vols. New York: Barnes & Noble, 1970. Reprints of then-current reviews and criticism of Joyce's works.

Epstein, Edmund L. "James Augustine Aloysius Joyce." In *A Companion to Joyce Studies.* Ed. Zack Bowen and James Carens. Westport, CT: Greenwood Press, 1984, pp. 3–37.

Gifford, Don. *Joyce Annotated: Notes for Dubliners and Portrait.* Berkeley: University of California Press, 1982. Large number of entries glossing passages, expressions, terms, names, etc. in both early works.

———, with Robert J. Seidman. *"Ulysses" Annotated: Notes for James Joyce's "Ulysses."* Revised and Expanded Edition. Berkeley: University of California Press, 1988. Though flawed, still an important tool for deciphering the novel; now glossed to both currently used editions of *Ulysses*.

Glasheen, Adaline. *Third Census of "Finnegans Wake": An Index of Characters and Their Roles.* Berkeley: University of California Press, 1977. Last and most complete in an entertaining series of directories of people in the *Wake*.

Hart, Clive, ed. *James Joyce's "Dubliners": Critical Essays.* New York: Viking Press, 1969. Still unsurpassed as critical guide to all of the short stories by eminent scholars.

———, and David Hayman, eds. *James Joyce's "Ulysses": Critical Essays.* Berkeley: University of California Press, 1974. Classic collection of eighteen essays on each episode by important scholars.

Henke, Suzette A. *James Joyce and the Politics of Desire.* New York and London: Routledge, 1990. A radical feminist/psychoanalytic perspective on language and desire in all of Joyce's major works.

Herr, Cheryl. *Joyce's Anatomy of Culture.* Urbana: University of Illinois Press, 1986. Important study of influences of Dublin's popular culture on Joyce's writing; Herr concentrates on his use of the stage, the press, and religious sermons in *Ulysses* and *Finnegans Wake*.

Herring, Phillip. "The Bedsteadfastness of Molly Bloom," *Modern Fiction Studies*, 15, 1 (Spring 1969): 49–61.

Hodgart, Matthew J.C., and Mabel P. Worthington. *Songs in the Works of James Joyce.* New York: Columbia University Press, 1959. Classic reference work that deals mainly with *Finnegans Wake*.

Kenner, Hugh. *Joyce's Voices.* Berkeley and Los Angeles: University of California Press, 1978. Still vital short tome on style and narrative voice, especially in *Ulysses*.

Kershner, R.B. *Joyce, Bakhtin, and Popular Literature: Chronicles of Disorder.* Chapel Hill: University of North Caro-

lina Press, 1989. Excellent study incorporating current literary theory with detailed explications of Joyce's "pop-lit" influences in all early works up to *Exiles*.

Litz, A. Walton. *The Art of James Joyce: Method and Design in "Ulysses" and "Finnegans Wake".* Corrected edition. London: Oxford University Press, 1964. Litz examines Joyce's extraordinary composition process; this is the first critical use of Joyce's early drafts and notes for these two novels.

McCarthy, Patrick A. *The Riddles of "Finnegans Wake".* Rutherford, NJ: Fairleigh-Dickinson University Press, 1980. McCarthy aptly demonstrates how the riddle is Joyce's convention, established as early as *A Portrait*, for the elusiveness of knowledge.

———. *"Ulysses": Portals of Discovery.* Boston: Twayne, 1990. Twayne Masterwork Studies. A very accessible thematic study for neophytes as well as "veteran" readers of the novel.

McCormick, Kathleen, and Erwin R. Steinberg, eds. *Joyce's Ulysses.* New York: Modern Language Association, 1993. Approaches to Teaching World Literature series.

McHugh, Roland. *Annotations to "Finnegans Wake."* Baltimore: The John Hopkins University Press, 1980. Useful, though sometimes baffling, page-by-page glossing of this difficult novel.

Norris, Margot. *The Decentered Universe of "Finnegans Wake": A Structuralist Analysis.* Baltimore: The John Hopkins University Press, 1976. Though theory is less current, still a valuable critical tool to understanding methods of this difficult novel.

Polhemus, Robert M. *Comic Faith: The Great Tradition from Austen to Joyce.* Chicago: University of Chicago Press, 1980. Marries the secular and religious impulses of comedy; excellent long chapter on the *Wake*, especially the Shem chapter.

Reynolds, Mary T. *Joyce and Dante: The Shaping Imagination.* Princeton: Princeton University Press, 1981. Excellent in-depth analysis demonstrating a Dantean influence on all of Joyce's works.

Riquelme, John Paul. *Teller and Tale in*

J

Joyce's Fiction: Oscillating Perspectives. Baltimore: The John Hopkins University Press, 1983. Riquelme makes stylistic, structural, and narrational connections between Joyce's mature fiction and his earlier works.

Scholes, Robert, and Richard M. Kain, eds. *The Workshop of Daedalus.* Evanston, IL: Northwestern University Press, 1965. Pioneering effort in textual study of Joyce: includes important manuscript materials heretofore unpublished—all related to *A Portrait.*

Scott, Bonnie Kime. *Joyce and Feminism.* Bloomington: Indiana University Press, 1984. Especially important for how it treats issue of Joyce's relationship to women in his private and professional life.

Staley, Thomas F., and Bernard Benstock, eds. *Approaches to Joyce's "Portrait": Ten Essays.* Pittsburgh: University of Pittsburgh Press, 1976. An excellent collection of essays by distinguished critics on various aspects of Joyce's first novel.

Thornton, Weldon. *Allusions in "Ulysses": An Annotated List.* Chapel Hill: University of North Carolina Press, 1968. Still the best reference book dealing with *Ulysses.*

Tucker, Lindsey. *Stephen and Bloom at Life's Feast: Alimentary Symbolism and the Creative Process in James Joyce's "Ulysses."* Columbus: The Ohio State University Press, 1984. Detailed analysis of Joyce's use of the digestive process and its relation to ritual and myth.

van Caspel, Paul. *Bloomers on the Liffey: Eisegetical Readings of Joyce's "Ulysses."* Baltimore: The John Hopkins University Press, 1986. Close reexamination of some of the leading (and sometimes misleading) interpretations of the text.

Current Journals

James Joyce Broadsheet. Commentary and reviews. Published three times yearly. c/o The School of English, University of Leeds, Leeds LS2 9JT, England.

James Joyce Literary Supplement. Reviews and special features. Published twice yearly. c/o Bernard Benstock, Department of English, P.O. Box 248145, University of Miami, Coral Gables, FL 33124.

James Joyce Quarterly. Scholarly articles on all aspects of Joyceana. Includes "Current JJ Checklist" for recent publications. c/o Robert Spoo, University of Tulsa, Tulsa, OK 74104.

Joyce Studies. Once a year (first issue 1990); a collection of essays on Joyce. c/o Thomas Staley, P.O. Box 7219, University Station, The University of Texas at Austin, Austin TX 78713.

A "Finnegans Wake" Circular. "Hard facts" scholarship, manuscript studies, and explications of the *Wake*; fills the void left by the demise of *A Wake Newsletter* (1962–1984). Published quarterly, but currently three years behind schedule. c/o Vincent Deane, 38 Anna Villa, Ranelagh, Dublin 6, Ireland.

John S. Slack

K

Kempe, Kemp, or Kempt, William

Born: ca. 1565
Education: Unknown, although grammar
school and an acting apprenticeship are
assumed
Died: London (?), ca. 1603

Biography

Not much is known about William Kempe's early life. He was probably born around 1565; it is uncertain where his birth took place or into what kind of family circumstances he was born. He probably went to grammar school and served an apprenticeship—most likely he would have been apprenticed to a master actor or "merryman." It is also likely that he picked up French, German, and Italian as well as the Latin that he would have learned in school. There is no record of his being married, and even the date and location of his death is uncertain; he may have died in 1603 in London. He is referred to as dead by 1608, although he may not have survived a European tour by more than a couple of years. "William Kempe, a man," was buried in Southwarke Church on November 2, 1603; the last name is too common to permit certain identification, but Southwarke was where many actors and entertainers lived. Still, some scholars believe that Kempe may not have died unti 1608.

Literary Analysis

Kempe was William Shakespeare's first clown, originating the roles of Costard in *Love's Labour's Lost*, Launce (Lance) in *The Two Gentlemen of Verona*, Peter in *Romeo and Juliet*, Launcelot Gobbo in *Merchant of Venice*, Dogberry in *Much Ado about Nothing*, Bottom in *A Midsummer Night's Dream*, and quite pos-

sibly the role of Falstaff. He was also famous as a comic writer, dancer, and composer of "jigs" and "merriments," two kinds of short musical comic entertainments that were extremely popular in Elizabethan England.

Kempe was referred to as "a jesting player" in the early 1580s. By 1586, he was traveling through the Netherlands with the Lord Leicester's Men, a troupe of actors and entertainers who followed their lord on his expedition through northern Europe in 1585 and 1586. Like most Elizabethan comic actors, Kempe was an accomplished musician, singer, dancer, and tumbler. He is mentioned as "Wilhelm Kempe instrumentist" in records of a performance of Leicester's Men in Denmark in 1586. At that time, the "jig," a comic song-and-dance interlude that could range from silly to satirical to bawdy, had become popular in England thanks to clowns such as the great Dick Tarlton. Kempe brought the jig over to the Continent from England and he may have helped start the vogue for *Singspiele*, musical pieces much like the jig that swept through the German-speaking countries.

In 1588, Leicester died, and his troupe became the Lord Strange's Men. Through this group of actors, Kempe met Richard Burbage and a young writer named Shakespeare. Thus began a fruitful decade, for in 1594 the Lord Strange's Men would become the Lord Chamberlain's Men, the most prominent acting troupe of the day. Throughout the 1590s, Kempe was an eminent member of the troupe, holding down the major comic roles as well as performing jigs and merriments at the end of the plays.

Tarlton, the most famous clown in Elizabethan England, had died in 1588. Other clowns—notably Robert Armin—claimed to be heir-apparent to Tarlton, but it is worth noting that contemporaries most often mentioned Kempe in that light. As the semiofficial court fool for Queen Elizabeth, Tarlton had gained notoriety and perhaps political influence. Though Kempe never belonged to the Queen's Men, the special troupe reserved for Elizabeth's pleasure, he was said to have succeeded "as wel in the favour of her majesty as in the opinions and good thoughts of the generall audience." In the pamphlet *An Almond for a Parret* (1590), the author, Thomas Nashe, dedicates the piece to Kempe, "Jest-monger and Vice-gerent generall to the Ghost of Dicke Tarleton." Kempe's clowning is, indeed, clearly directly descended from Tarlton's: hearty, physical, reminiscent of the great medieval minstrel tradition that print and social upheaval were transforming into the early modern entertainment industry.

Like Tarlton, Kempe was an excellent folkdancer and specialist in physical humor. If Tarlton was the king of the jig in the 1580s, Kempe was the same for the 1590s. His jig depicting the welcoming of the King to the city of Goteham ("merriments of the men of Goteham, in receiving the King into Goteham") appears in the otherwise anonymous comedy *A Knack to Know a Knave* (1592), and Kempe may have had a hand in the play proper as well. Other jigs became something like pop hits. The late 1590s saw several jigs licensed in Kempe's name, which argues either great industry on Kempe's part or (most likely) a rush by others to capitalize on his name. People hummed his tunes all over London. In 1598, Edward Guilpin wrote that "Whores, bedles, bawdes, and sergeants filthily / Chaunt Kemps Jigge" all over town. The music to some of these jigs still survives. Kempe was famous for his extemporaneous wit, evidently being able to improvise words for a jig as he was dancing it. It also appears that Kempe could use his jigs as social satire. During the "war" between Puritans and players in the mid-1590s, Kempe danced extemporaneous "mad jigges and merry jestes" aimed at the Puritans.

Kempe became a major force in the company of Burbage and Shakespeare. A 1594 record mentions the three in a payment for two comedies acted on the 26th and 28th of December. (The two comedies were probably *Taming of the Shrew* and *The Comedy of Errors*.) He is mentioned in the list of actors for Ben Jonson's *Every Man in His Humor* (1598) and

as "William Kempt" in "The Names of the Principall Actors" in the First Folio of Shakespeare's works (1623).

The year 1599 was a pivotal year for Kempe, as it was for the history of English comedy. By now, the academic satire *3 Return from Parnassus* (1599–1600) could call him a "very famous" actor. In that year, Burbage created the original company for the Globe. Kempe was one of the original shareholders in that company, but for unknown reasons, he left before the year was out, apparently selling back his share. He was replaced as head funny man by Armin, another heir of the Tarlton tradition. This change in comic actors accompanied a change in Shakespeare's clown roles.

Kempe next appears in his most famous accomplishment. In February of 1600, he accepted a three-for-one wager that he could not dance a morris (an old traditional English folkdance) from London to Norwich. Accompanied only by a drummer and two servants, but eventually attracting a crowd of fans and camp-followers, Kempe completed the dance in what he later claimed was nine days, although he actually took twenty-three. (Because of bad weather and fatigue, Kempe only spent nine days on the road, all of which, he swears, he spent dancing and leaping.) His adventures through the muddy roads with such a crew are recorded both in his own writings and in local records. The dance was well publicized: it was timed to coincide with the accession of the new mayor of Norwich, Roger Weld. When Kempe entered the city, he was received with a triumphal procession, and he hung up his dancing shoes in the Norwich town Guildhall. Mayor Weld awarded him five pounds and a 40-shilling stipend for life.

Kempe's "nine days' wonder" was celebrated throughout England: references to it appeared in private letters and public pamphlets. In fact, the pamphleteers were so quick to capitalize that Kempe felt himself obliged to publish his own brief on it: *Kemps Nine Daies Wonder* (1600). The pamphlet is fronted with a famous woodcut of Kempe morrising down the highway.

With this success behind him, Kempe decided to take his show to Europe. He barnstormed though France, Italy, and Germany, supposedly dancing a morris over the Alps. This was to bring him more triumphant notice at home, but the reality of the trip may have been much harsher. A diary entry on the day of his return refers to his many "wanderings and misfortunes"; he apparently returned home ill and in financial trouble. He may have rejoined the Lord Chamberlain's Men briefly before joining Worcester's Men in 1601 or 1602.

The precise nature of Kempe's contribution to Shakespeare's early comic writing has long been a subject of debate. Kempe was an established comic by the time that Shakespeare came to London, and it seems likely that the two men would at least have consulted closely on the nature and content of the clown roles. For example, in reading Kempe's "merriments of the men of Goteham, in receiving the King into Goteham," one encounters comic rhythms, structures, and voices that will be familiar from Shakespeare's plays. This scene is a comic debate among some tradesmen over which is best suited to deliver a petition to the King. The wit is studded with malapropisms ("Now let us constult among our selves, how to misbehave our selves to the Kings worship"), absurd turns (the Cobbler is chosen because he is the *least* qualified to approach the King), and a genial gaiety that is very reminiscent of early Shakespeare, especially of the comic debates in *A Midsummer Night's Dream*. Most important of all, it is designed with a great deal of room for ad-libbing, horseplay, and dance, which there almost undoubtedly was. (The same was probably the case with most of Shakespeare's comic scenes throughout the 1590s.)

Kempe's trade was, like Tarlton's, a gallimaufry of dancing, satirical songs, extemporaneous rhymes on any theme, imitations and mimicry, musicianship, and much else. We do not have the words to Kempe's jigs, but if they are like Tarlton's, they must have required ingenuity in both creation and performance.

Geniality of an especially spacious and invigorating sort is the informing spirit of *Kemp's Nine Daies Wonder*. This pamphlet is a straightforward account of his famous exploit. Kempe makes sure that we know that he was mobbed all along the way. At one point he is so beset by crowds that he has to lock himself in his inn and wave out his window rather than perform. Very much like the minstrel whose job is to get the audience involved, Kempe is very interested in the people who join him. Many cannot resist dancing along, and Kempe takes on several of them in good-natured competition (which Kempe always wins).

No passage gives us a better idea of Kempe as personality, performer, and narrator than the following. On his way to the town of Braintree, Kempe is traveling a mucky road when he encounters two fellows who want to morris along:

> At length, coming to a broad plash of water and mud, which could not be avoyded, I fecht a rise, yet fell in over the anckles at the further end. My youth that follow'd me took his jump, and stuck fast in the midst, crying out to his companion, Come, George, call yee this dauncing? Ile goe no further, for indeede he could goe no further, till his fellow was faine to wade and help him out. I could not chuse but lough to see how like two frogges they laboured: a hartye farewell I gave them, and they faintly bad God speed me, saying if I daunst that durtie way this seaven yeares againe, they would never daunce after me.

The tales are interspersed with what appears to be improvised snatches of verse. Kempe claims that several of them are written by a friend. Whoever wrote them, they are good examples of the instantaneous poetry a traveling minstrel had to come up with as part of his trade. For example, in one the subject is a large young woman who has a dancing contest with Kempe:

> A Countrye Lasse, browne as a berry,
> Blith of blee [countenance], in heart as
>   merry,
> Cheekes well fed, and sides well larded,
> Every bone with fat flesh guarded,
> Meeting merry Kemp by chaunce,
> Was Marrian in his Morrice daunce.

We may well believe that Kempe and his friend are one and the same.

Summary

William Kempe was a clown for the leading playwright in England for nearly a decade. We must note that he represented a style of clowning that would go out of fashion around 1600, and this may have led to his abandonment of the stage and his tour of homeland and continent. Still, while at the Globe, Kempe and Shakespeare would have been constant collaborators. Little in Kempe's extant work suggests that he was capable of actually *writing* the sorts of roles Shakespeare wrote—but the heritage of Tarlton, the minstrel merriment that enlivens these roles, is what Kempe contributed and what his acting made famous. Thanks to the survival of his *Nine Daies Wonder*, Kempe also survives as a friendly, inviting, ambitious performer, willing to dance across England and over the Alps if it will get him notice and a coin in his cap.

Selected Bibliography

Primary Sources

"Kemps applauded merriments of the men of Goteham, in receiving the King into Goteham." In *A Knack to Know a Knave*. London, 1592. This is the only piece of extant comic writing that is almost certainly by Kempe, though many of the anonymous jigs from the period may be his.

Kemps Nine Daies Wonder. London: N. Ling, 1600. This pamphlet appears to be an autobiographical account of Kempe's pageant from London to Norwich, and several of the details can be corroborated from other sources. It is a gay, madcap work.

Secondary Sources

Biographies

Chambers, E.K. "William Kemp." In *The Elizabethan Stage*. Oxford: Clarendon, 1923. Vol. 2, pp. 325–27.

Lee, Sidney. "William Kemp." In *Dictionary of National Biography*. 21 vols. Ed. Leslie Stephen and Sidney Lee. Oxford: Oxford University Press, 1960. Vol. 10, pp. 1278–79.

Books

Baldwin, T.W. *Organization and Personnel of the Shakespearian Company*. Princeton: Princeton University Press, 1927. An influential study of how Shakespeare's work was shaped by his fellow players, including the clowns.

Baskervill, C.J. *The Elizabethan Jig*. Chicago: University of Chicago Press, 1929. Baskervill discusses the "jig," a popular entertainment form in Elizabethan England, and connects it with the careers of Armin, Kempe, and Tarlton.

Welsford, Enid. *The Fool: His Social and Literary History*. New York: Farrar & Rinehart, 1936. This is the best introduction to the profession of fool in Elizabethan times.

Articles

Ingram, William. "Minstrels in Elizabethan London: Who Were They, What Did They Do?" *English Literary Renaissance*, 14 (1): 29–54. Ingram discusses how the occupation of "minstrel" overlapped with those of the fool and musician.

Palmer, Daryl W. "William Kemp's *Nine Daies Wonder* and the Transmission of Performance Culture." *Journal of Dramatic Theory and Criticism*, 5, 2 (Spring 1991): 33–47. Palmer argues that in writing down his habits of performance, Kempe did not simply transcribe them; he changed them into something new and valuable: a written record. Kempe is not just a performer but a narrator who is at a certain remove from the crowds that mob him and the people who attempt to join in his morris dance.

Somerset, J.A.B. "Shakespeare's Great State of Fools, 1599–1607." In Gray, J.C., *Mirror up to Shakespeare*. Toronto: University of Toronto Press, 1984, pp. 68–81. Somerset discusses Shakespeare's changing "fool" roles, and he argues against the old idea that the shift from Kempe to Armin caused the change in Shakespeare's style.

John Timpane

Kipling, [Joseph] Rudyard

Born: Bombay, India, December 30, 1865
Education: United Services College, Westward Ho!, North Devon, 1878–1882
Marriage: Caroline Balestier, January 18, 1892; three children
Died: London, January 18, 1936

Biography

The son of John Lockwood Kipling and Alice MacDonald, Joseph Rudyard Kipling was born in Bombay, India, on December 30, 1865. His father was at the time Professor of Architectural Sculpture at Bombay and later became the Curator of the Lahore Museum. His mother was one of the five beautiful MacDonald girls, one of whom, Georgina, married Sir Edward Burne-Jones; a second, Agnes, married Sir Edward Poynter; a third married Alfred Baldwin and became the mother of Stanley Baldwin, the first earl. Kipling was thus connected with two eminent Pre-Raphaelite painters and a future prime minister. His lineage also included two grandfathers and one uncle who were Wesleyan ministers.

When Rudyard was five and sister Alice (always called Trix) was three, they were taken to England and, in Anglo-Indian tradition, left with foster-parents, the Holloways of Lorne Lodge Southsea. The Holloways were a retired sea captain, his religiously strict wife, and their twelve-year-old son. Unfortunately, the captain, who liked Rudyard, soon died; Mrs. Holloway was ill-equipped to deal with the precocious, "spoiled" Rudyard. Furthermore, the children's parents gave them no explanation or farewell reassurances, so both Rudyard and Trix felt abandoned. Their unhappiness is fictionalized as "The House of Desolation" in Rudyard's short story "Baa Baa Black Sheep." Rudyard attended school in Southsea and spent holidays with his relatives. In March of 1877, Georgina Burne-Jones wrote Alice Kipling that Rudyard was losing his sight. Mrs. Kipling arrived in England and took both children for a quiet country holiday. However, in January 1878, when Rudyard was enrolled at the United Services College at Westward Ho!, Trix was returned to board with Mrs. Holloway for three more years. Visiting her in 1880, Rudyard met and fell in love with another boarder at Lorne Lodge, Florence Garrard, to whom he was unofficially engaged when he left for India, in September 1882.

The headmaster of United Services College was Cormell Price, a friend of the Kiplings, so although Rudyard was not preparing for military service as were most of the boys and could not participate in sports because of his poor eyesight, he profited from new friendships and the headmaster's guidance that led to his journalistic career. He left Westward Ho! at the end of the summer term 1882 and sailed in September for India to become a sub-editor on the staff of the *Civil & Military Gazette* in Lahore. He lived with his parents and learned his craft under the strict supervision of the editor, Stephen Wheeler; in the summer of 1886, Wheeler was replaced by the younger and more progressive E. Kay Robinson.

Early in his time at Westward Ho! Kipling had written both original and parody poetry. Unknown to him, his mother had had his *Schoolboy Lyrics* privately printed in 1881. In March 1882, his poem "Ave Imperatrix!" (honoring Queen Victoria's escape from the assassination attempt) was printed in the *Chronicle*. In November, his sonnet "Two Lives" was published anonymously in the British periodical *The World*. In the summer of 1883, he spent his first of several vacations in Simla, the Anglo-Indian retreat from Southern India's deadly summers and a considerable source of literary material for the young author. In July 1884, Florence wrote to break their engagement, but Rudyard's feelings were assuaged by the arrival of Trix to join the family, and the publication in September of his first short story, "The Gate of the Hundred Sorrows," in the *Gazette*. In November, *Echoes*, a collection of thirty-nine parodies, thirty-two by Rudyard and seven by Trix, was published.

Life continued to furnish Kipling with a wealth of experiences to be used in his writing. In March 1885, he was sent to Peshawar to cover the ceremonial reception of the Amir Abdurrahman by the new Viceroy, Lord Duffering. He briefly visited the Khyber Pass. At the end of the year, *Quartette*, a collection of prose and verse by the entire family, was published. Only two stories, "The Strange Ride of Morrowbie Jukes" and "The Phantom Rickshaw," were later reprinted. In 1886, the original series of "Departmental Ditties" began appearing in the *Gazette*; later they appeared as a collection, anonymously, in Lahore, then with the author's name, in Calcutta. In October, the "Ditties" were reviewed in England by Andrew Lang in *Longman's Magazine*, and Kipling's rise to fame had begun. In November, his second reputation builder, "Plain Tales from the Hills," began appearing in the *Gazette*. This year also saw his admission to the Masonic Lodge, whose ritual would figure in several of his stories.

In the fall of 1887, he was transferred to the Allahabad *Pioneer*. For eighteen strenuous months he edited "The Week's News," wrote a story for each issue, contributed pieces to the *Gazette*, and traveled widely in quest of material for travel sketches. His stories, poems, and sketches appeared at the average rate of three a week. The year 1888 saw the publication of the story collections *Plain Tales from the Hills*, *Soldiers Three*, *The Story of the Gadsbys*, *In Black and White*, *Under the Deodars*, *The Phantom Rickshaw*, and *Wee Willie Winkie*. In February 1889, he visited his family in Lahore to say goodbye, then sailed for England via Rangoon, Singapore, Hong Kong, Yokohama, San Francisco, and New York, reaching Liverpool on October 5. Throughout the trip he sent back enthusiastic but often irreverent travel reports to the *Pioneer*.

Kipling traveled much of the way with "Alek" and "Ted" (Professor S.A. and Edmonia) Hill. It was the Hills' photographs and descriptions of the Seonee district that became the setting for *The Jungle Book*. He spent nearly two months at Mrs. Hill's parents' home in Pennsylvania where he formed a romantic attachment to "Ted's" younger sister, Caroline Taylor. Professor R.T. Taylor was the president of a small college and a clergyman of fairly strict views. After some months of correspondence, the courtship came to an end, probably in part because of the writer's unorthodox religious views. At Caroline's questioning, he affirmed his belief in "God the Father Almighty, maker of Heaven and Earth and in One filled with His spirit Who did voluntarily die in the belief that the human race would be spiritually bettered thereby."[1] However, he doubted eternal punishment and rewards. This reluctant statement of his theology, when he was twenty-four, cannot be considered a definitive description of his spiritual perceptions throughout his career.

In 1890, he accidentally met Florence again and suffered a renewal of interest and a final rejection. A fictionalized account of this relationship appears in *The Light That Failed*, published in March 1891. More important was the friendship that he developed with Wolcott Balestier, a charismatic young American who was in London to promote the interests of J.W. Lovel Publishing Firm. The friendship took several months to develop, but Kipling acquiesced to Wolcott's request that they collaborate on a novel and became engaged to Wolcott's sister Caroline (Carrie).

In September 1890, Kipling suffered a breakdown in health, so he spent October in Italy. The next August he determined to take a longer vacation and set out on a trip round the world, visiting South Africa, Australia, and New Zealand, and paying his last visit to India. While at Lahore he received news of the death of Wolcott from typhoid. He immediately set out for England, arriving January 10, 1892. On January 18, he married Carrie Balestier; Henry James gave away the bride. Carrie was a small, intense woman who took over the management of affairs for her mother and sister at Wolcott's death and who would be accused through the years of "managing Rudyard." Still, there are many indications that he was happy in her care, although she seems not to have shared his creative world. Years later their daughter Elsie would admit that her mother's possessiveness

and uncertain moods were often difficult for the family, but her father's "kindly nature, patience, and utter loyalty to her"[2] never wavered. The husband and wife were rarely apart during their forty-four years of marriage.

On February 3, 1892, the newlyweds set out on a revised world tour. From New York they visited Carrie's family in Brattleboro, Vermont, then crossed the continent to Vancouver and sailed to Yokohama. Unfortunately, the Oriental Banking Company where they had placed their funds failed; they lost their savings and were compelled to return to Brattleboro. There they lived in a cottage on the Balestier family estate and there their first child, Josephine, was born one day before Rudyard's twenty-seventh birthday. Carrie was thirty.

The novel begun with Wolcott, *Naulahka*, was finished and appeared as a serial, and *Barrack-Room Ballads* and *Many Inventions* were published the same year. By the spring of 1893 the Kiplings could afford to build a home, also on the family estate; they named it Naulakha (the correct spelling). The years spent here were productive and happy, despite some conflict with Carrie's brother Beatty and Rudyard's occasional impatience with American manners. *The Jungle Book* appeared in 1894; *The Second Jungle Book* in 1895. In 1896, *The Seven Seas*, which includes such outstanding poems as "A Song of the English," "M'Andrews' Hymn," and "When Earth's Last Picture Is Painted," was published, and their second child, Elsie, was born. In August, Kipling made the mistake of taking his quarrelsome brother-in-law to court. The resulting publicity drove the Kiplings to England, where they settled first in Torquay.

In 1897, they moved to Rottingdean, Sussex; "Recessional" was published in the *Times*, *Captains Courageous*, Kipling's tribute to New England, was published, and their son John was born. The year ended on a sad note, when Trix, home with her husband from India after many years in which she had been prominent in Simla society, suffered a complete mental breakdown and was placed under her mother's care. Kipling's later writing about "psychic" phenomena was born out of this painful experience. For some time Carrie had wished to see her mother, and Rudyard felt that he must attend to several matters in America, among them the disposition of their home in Brattleboro. They sailed for New York in January 1899. Shortly after their arrival, Carrie suffered a bout of fever but forced herself to resume her family responsibilities when the two younger children came down with whooping cough. Then, on February 20, Rudyard developed a fever, and on February 22, Josephine ran a high temperature. Despite her convalescent condition, Carrie traveled daily between the DeForests' home on Long Island, where the children had been placed, to the hotel where Rudyard was very ill. Her brother had chosen their return to sue them for libel, and news that Kipling was fighting for his life kept crowds of journalists and admirers about the hotel. On March 4, Rudyard was out of danger, but on March 6 Josephine died. Her father was not told for several days, but the loss was a lasting sorrow, only occasionally revealed, as in the short story "They."

Finally, in June the family was able to return to England, knowing that they would never return to live in America, though they did not find the "home" that they sought until they purchased Bateman's in Burwash, Sussex, in 1902. While the Kiplings fought for privacy in their grief and other matters, they continued to react to public events. Eighteen ninety-nine had been disastrous not only for them but also for South Africa, for the Dutch ultimatum on October 9 was answered by the British declaration of war and the dispatch of 47,000 men to the Cape. Kipling's response was to form a volunteer company in the village of Rottingdean and to raise money for the Soldiers' Families' Fund. For the latter effort he wrote "The Absent Minded Beggar," which, set to music by Sir Arthur Sullivan, raised a quarter of a million pounds sterling for this charity. Lord Salisbury sent his private secretary to ask if Kipling would accept a knighthood. The author declined, as he was later to decline all such honors that he felt might limit his freedom to express himself, but he accepted those honors and requests for speeches that permitted him to woo some to his philosophy of hard work, ideals, and creativity.

It was shared ideals that deepened his friendship with Cecil Rhodes. Carrie especially appreciated the cottage, the "Woolshack," that Rhodes built on his property and that they visited every winter from 1901 to 1908. Rhodes rarely enjoyed the company of women, but Carrie was an exception. It was she who encouraged him to increase the Rhodes Scholarships from 250 to 300 pounds a year. She encouraged his schemes for the improvement of the building, native arts, and architecture, and

caring for landscapes, trees, and animals. He was especially pleased when she undertook to raise an orphaned lion cub. Both Rudyard and Carrie sorrowed deeply when this man of great accomplishments and many unfulfilled dreams died. Part of Kipling's obituary verses are inscribed on the Rhodes Monument.

During their 1900 stay in South Africa, Kipling visited the troops and helped to publish a paper for the military. Also, his prose masterpiece, *Kim*, was finished and published. Nineteen hundred two saw the end of the South African war, their move to Bateman's, and the publication of the *Just So Stories*. Other works followed—*The Five Nations* (1903), *Traffics and Discoveries* (1904), and *Puck of Pook's Hill* (1906). In 1907, Kipling received the Nobel Prize for Literature, the first English author to do so, and honorary degrees from Durham and Oxford universities. His *Collected Verse* was published in New York that year and in London in 1912. In 1908, he received an honorary D.Litt. degree from Cambridge. *Actions and Reactions* came out in 1909, *Rewards and Fairies* in 1910. This year closed with the death of Kipling's mother in November; his father's death followed the next January.

Kipling's frequent speeches, poems, and other comments warning England of German aggression offended many, even after World War I began, but he was much admired by soldiers and sailors, and government officials sought his support. In August 1915, he visited the front lines in France; in September he visited the Royal Navy. It is not surprising that their son, John, was eager to enter the fight and that Rudyard used some of his influence to get John into the Irish Guards. When word came on October 2, 1915 that John was "missing in action" expressions of sympathy came from many, but there were those who wrote viciously that this loss was deserved since Kipling had "promoted" war. This ugly side of the public continues to surface even among critics. Martin Seymour-Smith, whose book *Rudyard Kipling* was published in 1989, writes that Kipling "lacked kindness of heart . . . He was not altogether good to his own son: he used him as an instrument, a thing, and was initially happy to sacrifice him for what he saw as his own politics." This distorted attack continues, describing Carrie as "almost pathological in her hatefulness, meanness, and pettiness." As for Kipling's philosophy, Seymour-Smith considers it "cheap, shoddy, cruel, unworthy and impractical" and the man as a "thinker . . . grotesque, merciless and insensitive" (7–8).

The family kept its sorrow private, though Rudyard was able to work out some of his grief in writing a two-volume history of the Irish Guards and in serving as a member of the War Graves Commission. Among the young officers who shared their experiences for this history was Captain George Bainbridge. His friendship with the family continued after the publication of the work (in 1923), and in the spring of 1924, he and Elsie became engaged. While her father was pleased with the match, he was saddened with the inevitable loss of their only remaining child.

Although Kipling abhorred crowds—of "trippers" or "voters"—and suffered the pompous impatiently, he had a legion of friends, from his school roommate "Stalky" (General Dunsterville) to King George V. He carried on a vast correspondence, continued to seek improved health and new knowledge in travel, and wrote both creative and political material. He received an honorary Ph.D. from Athens University in 1924. In 1926, the Kiplings visited South America and *Debits and Credits* was published. In 1927, rather against Kipling's wishes, the Kipling Society was founded. In 1930, on their visit to the West Indies, Carrie became seriously ill, necessitating a three-month stay in a hospital in Bermuda. *Limits and Renewals* was published in 1932 and Kipling worked on *Something of Myself*, a carefully limited autobiography which was not published until 1937.

Early in 1936, the Kiplings planned to go to Cannes, France. On their way they chose to visit Elsie and George Bainbridge in Hampstead. Rudyard was in good health, but Carrie seemed far from well, as indeed she had been for some time. However, during the night of January 12, Rudyard suffered a sudden and violent hemorrhage, was rushed to Middlesex Hospital, and underwent emergency surgery. On January 18, his and Carrie's forty-fourth wedding anniversary, Kipling died in London. The newspapers, which had so recently celebrated Kipling's seventieth birthday, were crowded with news of King George's final illness. Before preparations could be made for Kipling's funeral, the King's death plunged the nation into mourning. Nevertheless, before Westminster Abbey was put in order for the royal ceremony, Kipling was buried in Poet's Corner during a service attended by thousands.

Literary Analysis

Authorized editions of Kipling's works include five novels, 250 short stories, 1,000 pages of verse, and several volumes of speeches, letters, travel reports, and other prose commentary. Since he generally followed the rule of never doing the same thing twice, the writer's poetry includes an incredible range of verse forms, while his short stories include stories in the manner of the Latin masters, stories rising from the pages of the Bible, stories in the language and tone of Muslim thought and lore, stories from the heart and tongue of his famous Soldiers Three (Irish Mulvaney, Cockney Ortheris, and Scotch Learoyd), satiric tales of "naughty" Simla, romantic tales of heroic and/or charming Indians, Anglo-Indians, Americans, Englishmen, and Frenchmen, tales of animals, machines, prehistory, and science fiction, parables, allegories, and more. His novels include a picaresque novel, three very different romances, and a novel of craft.

The quantity, variety, and inclusion of many topics formerly considered inappropriate for literary art have complicated critical evaluation of Kipling's work, but his writing continues to appeal to segments of the public. This is partly due to his remarkable use of "ordinary" people in both common and uncommon circumstances, and discovering new meaning in both the good and the bad events of life. To his truly democratic interests he added the word-power of a poet and the philosophy of a humorist. His pervasive use of biblical language and allusions identifies the spiritual values of his philosophy. In the poem "The Explorer,"[3] he clearly recognizes God as the source of the Whisper that sent his persona across the mountains and desert to discover the truth that God wished to reveal "when He judged His people ready" (204). The explorer alludes to Saul hunting donkeys and finding a kingdom (I Samuel 1, 2) but he gladly accepts not riches or fame but the awesome knowledge that God's Whisper came to him. In "My New Cut Ashlar,"[4] the poet prays to the "Great Overseer" for forgiveness for those times when he has failed to meet God's Design and asks that he may not lose his Vision, because through God's grace he sees nothing on earth "common or unclean," an allusion to Peter's vision on the housetop in Joppa, a vision that declared that the Christian Gospel was for all people (Acts 10).

Proof of this "prophetic call"[5] is well established by many of his poems and at least one extant letter. In 1897, he wrote to C.E. Norton: "I am daily and nightly perplexed with my own responsibilities before God."[6] His sister, Mrs. Alice Fleming, stated in 1937: "Critics today are apt to forget that Kipling felt from the beginning that the word of the Lord was laid upon him, and that he had to do that for which he was sent."[7] It is this sense of spiritual insight that thunders condemnation of those with spiritual blindness and corrupt purposes, as in "The Islanders,"[8] in which he accuses the insular English of caring more for their dogs and horses than for the "souls they sacrifice" (262) by sending untrained and ill-equipped young men into the Boer War. And in "The City of Brass,"[9] he warns those who "fashion a God" (416) who will aid them in their selfish desires that the true God will grant them "the heart of a beast in place of a man's heart" (418).

However, many of his poems and stories mask their serious themes with wit, ambiguity, over-simplification, mistaken identity, paradox, exaggeration, even slapstick. Since comedy requires the reversal of an unjust situation by the exposure of the cause of the injustice, vengeance of some kind is present in many comedies. Sometimes the person whose ignorance, weakness, arrogance, or jealousy has caused the trouble is "converted" to a wiser person; sometimes he is "removed." "A Second Rate Woman,"[10] one of the Simla stories, is filled with the witty exchanges of the very clever Mrs. Hauksbee and her housemate, the not-so-energetic Mrs. Mallowe. Mrs. Hauksbee is indignant at a newcomer, Mrs. Delville, who dresses so badly that she nicknames her The Dowd. However, when the Bent baby nearly chokes to death with diphtheria, Mrs. Delville saves the child and is appreciated—briefly! The introductory paragraph is typical of Mrs. Hauksbee's humor: "Dressed! Don't tell me that woman ever dressed in her life. She stood in the middle of the room while her ayah—no, her husband—it must have been a man—threw her clothes at her. She then did her hair with her fingers, and rubbed her bonnet in the flue under the bed. I know she did, as well as if I had assisted at the orgie. Who is she?" (71).

In "His Wedded Wife,"[11] a young subaltern earns the nickname "The Worm" because he seems incapable of the social skills expected of an English officer and he writes frequently to his mother and sisters at home. When he is "initiated" by his fellow officers, he bears it all meekly, even the continuing torment of the Senior Subaltern. Finally, he responds to an especially unkind practical joke by challenging his tormentor to a bet that he can return the humiliation. Because he is "a pretty boy, without a hair on his face, and a waist like a girl's" (200), he is able to masquerade as the Senior Subaltern's supposedly neglected wife, come all the way from England. His convincing dramatic performance teaches the Senior Subaltern a needed lesson and wins the respect of his fellows, who make him the head of their drama club.

While many of Kipling's stories mask the narrator's sense of humor behind straight-faced reporting, some acknowledge his appreciation of the humor that produces total surrender to laughter. In "The Miracle of St. Jubanus,"[12] a young shell-shocked Frenchman recovers his reason when he is overcome with laughter, along with everyone else in the church, at the sight of the village's lone atheist forced to participate in the church service by becoming entangled in the ritual equipment carried by the acolytes. Such laughter can heal; it can also hurt. In "The Village that Voted the Earth Was Flat,"[13] the village is subjected to a nationwide media exposure that verges on persecution.

Nevertheless, Kipling believed that the Creator included humor in His Divine Design. In the poem "The Necessitarians,"[14] he argues that the same Power that shaped the planet and the rose emptied upon earth "urns of Mirth," justifying his use of humor, even in dealing with such a serious topic as the terrible death toll of war. Of one such story, "On the Gate, a Tale of '16,'"[15] A.E. Purefoy comments: "Half the time I'm reading it I'm doubled up with laughter, and the other half I'm blinking at the print through those exasperating tears that the best stories always squeeze out."[16] The story is told in the metaphor of military logistics, with St. Peter and Death visiting a receiving station where Civil Death is upset that the war rush has forced him into less comfortable quarters and the neglect of many of his traditional services. A seraph explains that "The Lower Establishment are taking advantage of"[17] the inevitable delays in so large an operation. In the list of extra pickets he has called on are "Arc J., Bradlaugh C., Bunyan J., Calvin J., Iscariot J . . . . Also Shakespeare W."[18] St. Peter deals with an insistent mother whom he excuses as the Importunate Widow of the story found in the Gospel of Luke (18:2–5), a Shropshire Yeoman being coaxed in the wrong direction by representa-

K

tives of the Lower Establishment, and finally a cowardly traitor, whose judgment Peter determines by "Samuel Two, Double Fourteen . . . 'For we must needs die and are as water spilled on the ground which cannot be gathered up again. Neither doth God respect any person, yet— . . . Yet doth He devise means (d'you understand that?) *devise means* that His banished be not expelled from Him!'"[19] On this note of mercy the traitor is led off, and Death (the Archangel Azreal) wonders if even he might hope.

With similar empathy Kipling treats the faith of the uneducated, as in poems such as "Mulholland's Contract."[20] The monologue's narrative begins with Mulholland in fear for his life as he manages the lower deck of a freighter carrying cattle through rough weather. Mulholland promises God that if He would bring him safe to port, he "would exalt His Name, / An' praise His Holy Majesty till further orders came" (61). The seaman reaches port but has to spend seven weeks in a hospital, where he has time to learn God's instructions for fulfilling his "contract." He reluctantly accepts the duty of preaching to his unredeemed shipmates. He often suffers blows, "as warned would be the case, / An' turned my cheek to the smiter exactly as Scripture says; / But, following that, I knocked him down an' led him up to Grace" (62).

Much of Kipling's satire is humorous rather than bitter. The poem "Natural Theology"[21] points out mankind's propensity to blame God for all its misfortunes, traces this complaining from "Primitive" through those of "Pagan," "Mediaeval," "Material," and "Progressive":

I ate my fill of a whale that died
And stranded after a month at sea . . .
There is a pain in my inside.
Why have the Gods afflicted me?

A "Chorus" appropriate to his English audience follows:

We had a kettle: we let it leak;
Our not repairing it made it worse,
We haven't had any tea for a week . . .
The bottom is out of the Universe!

To each he applies the "Conclusion":

This was none of the Good Lord's pleasure,

For the Spirit He breathed in Man is free;
But what comes after is measure for measure,
And not a God that afflicteth thee. (399–401)

It is unlikely that there will ever be a consensus on what is Kipling's best writing, either of the verse or the prose. However, many critics agree with Nirad C. Chaudhuri that *Kim*[22] is not only the finest novel in the English language with an Indian theme, but also one of the greatest of English novels.[23] Both a picaresque novel and a novel of initiation, *Kim* presents convincing detail, memorable characters, and a compelling theme, all choreographed with wit, exaggeration, disguise, mirth, and the exposure of ignorance and pomposity. While the hero becomes a skillful player of the "Great Game" played by the Indian Secret Service, he learns other essentials of living and earns the love of such diverse characters as a Tibetan lama, a Moslem horsetrader, a Bengali scholar, and a Hill Country royal widow.

Kimball O'Hara, the streetwise orphaned son of an Irish soldier, becomes an excellent *chela* (servant-disciple) of the saintly Teshoo Lama, whom he meets in front of the Lahore Museum (of which in real life the author's father was curator). He is already a friend of Mahbub Ali, an Afghan horsetrader and British spy who has much to do with Kim's successful integration of his two cultures. Other instructors in Kim's initiation include Hurree Chunder Mookerjee, the Bengali who insists that he is fearful but proves very brave; Colonel Creighton, head of the British Survey Service which masks the spying network, who disguises his competence by inconspicuous authority; the Subiha whose shrewish tongue hides a noble character; and of course the Lama, who argues against involvement in emotions and activities but for love of Kim pays for his education and renounces his opportunity to escape The Wheel of Life.

In the fourth chapter of *Kim*, Kim and the Lama encounter the Subiha's entourage. Cleverly Kim builds his cooking fire as close as he dares to the curtained cart, knowing the leading servant will protest. When he does, Kim responds:

"Huh! It is only a *pahari* (a hillman)," said Kim over his shoulder. "Since when have the hill-asses owned all Hindustan?"

The retort was a swift and brilliant sketch of Kim's pedigree for three generations.

"Ah!" Kim's voice was sweeter than ever, as he broke the dung-cake into fit pieces. "In *my* country we call that the beginning of love-talk." (248)

The hidden Subiha's laugh brings the result that Kim had sought, after more bombast from the servant, who is stopped short of violence by discovering the Lama whom Kim is serving. A bit later, Colonel Creighton happens to ride by and tease the Subiha for exposing her face:

"O mother, do they do this in the *zenanas*? Suppose an Englishman came by and saw that thou hadst no nose?"

"What?" she shrilled back. "Thy own mother had no nose? Why say so then on the open road?"

It was a fair counter. The Englishman threw up his head with the gesture of a man hit at sword-play. She laughed and nodded. "Is this a face to tempt virtue aside?" She withdrew all her veil and stared at him.

It was by no means lovely, but as the man gathered up his reins he called it a Moon of Paradise, a Disturber of Integrity, and a few other fantastic epithets which doubled her up with mirth. [As he rode away he concluded] "Keep thy beauty under a shade—O Dispenser of Delights."

And the Subiha comments, "These be the sort to oversee justice. They know the land and the customs of the land" (253).

At the end of the story, after Kim has recovered from exhaustion, the result of his rescuing the Lama, and the incriminating evidence of Russian plotting, he realizes that despite his love for the Lama he is glad that he can re-enter the teeming life of India, for "Roads were meant to be walked upon, houses to be lived in, cattle to be driven, fields to be tilled, and men and women to be talked to" (520). In contrast,

the Lama still persuades himself that his beloved chela will follow him in seeking release from life; he even invites Mahbub to join them, an insult to a Muslim, but an offense excused by the holy man's simplicity.

Kipling used humor as he believed God did. In the poem "The Legend of Mirth,"[24] he reports that when the four archangels, Raphael, Gabriel, Michael, and Azreal, found the constant problems of earth too much for their lofty sense of duty, God sent the Seraph of Mirth to meet them and develop their saving sense of humor. The writer's own sense of humor enabled him to delight in the company of children and to write such classics as *The Just So Stories* and *The Jungle Book*s. Here the occasionally questionable farce of some of his adult stories gives way to exaggeration and word play, pranks, and challenges to adults appropriate to the world of imagination. Who, having read "The Elephant's Child,"[25] can forget the "satiable curiosity" that got the young elephant into—and eventually out of—trouble, or the "great grey-green, greasy Limpopo River" that figures in his adventure.

Even in Kipling's factual accounts, as in *France At War*,[26] he smilingly cites a Commandant who commented on his effectively modified old gun that "anybody" could have made such improvements, for they were "only an assembly of variations and arrangements." To which Kipling's aside is, "That, of course, is all that Shakespeare ever got out of the alphabet" (62). And when the gun was fired, "she spoke" with a higher pitch than the men, "with a more shrewish tang to the speeding shell. Her recoil was as swift and as graceful as the shrug of a French-woman's shoulders." And somebody closed the incident by laughingly remarking, "They'll be bothered down below to know the meaning of our single shot. We don't give them one dose at a time as a rule" (64).

Summary

The quantity and quality of his original work and the critical comment on it assure Rudyard Kipling of major literary rank. His range of material and skill with language justify his frequent comparison to such other great authors as Shakespeare, Charles Dickens, and Robert Browning. For some readers his prose, especially his stories set in India, are the most memorable, but his poetry has contributed more to language enrichment and literary innovation. Much of this achievement is due to his belief that his talent was God-given and laid on him a Divinely mandated responsibility to present a comprehensive vision of Universal Law and spiritually based ideals. His humor fitted into this vision as one of the tools that men use to deal with both the exalted and the trivial, the exotic and the mundane. T.R. Henn considers "Judson and the Empire" an "intensely funny story"[27] and some of the *Departmental Ditties* "extremely funny."[28] J.M. Tompkins devotes an entire chapter to "Laughter" (33–54) in her *The Art of Rudyard Kipling*.

Kipling used all of the literary techniques of humor, from sophisticated wit to Rabelaisian farce, and applied those techniques to the portrayal of men and machines, animals and governments, tragedy and romance, science and spiritual issues. He was fascinated with how the universe works, including the healing or redemptive effects of humor. While he understood, through personal as well as vicarious experience, the intensity of suffering and tragedy, he lived and wrote in the conviction that life was interesting and worth living, a basically optimistic philosophy essential to a humorist.

Notes

1. C.E. Carrington, *The Life of Rudyard Kipling* (Garden City, NY: Doubleday, 1955), p. 107.
2. *Ibid.*, p. 400.
3. *The Five Nations*, XXVI, pp. 200–04. (All references to Kipling's works will be cited by the original book title and the volume and pages in *The Burwash Edition of the Complete Works in Prose and Verse*.)
4. *Life's Handicap*, IV, pp. 413–14; also *Songs From Books*, XXVII, pp. 31–32.
5. Esther M.G. Smith, "The Prophetic Qualities of Rudyard Kipling's Work," dissertation at University of Florida, 1972.
6. Carrington, p. 248.
7. Alice Fleming, "The Annual Luncheon," *The Kipling Journal*, No. 42 (June 1937), p. 63 (*The Kipling Journal* began using volume numbers with the March 1939 issue, vol. V).
8. *The Five Nations*, XXVI, pp. 258–62.
9. *The Years Between*, XXVI, pp. 415–18.
10. *Under the Deodars*, III, pp. 71–94.
11. *Plain Tales from the Hills*, I, pp. 193–202.
12. *Limits and Renewals*, X, pp. 277–95.
13. *A Diversity of Creatures*, IX, pp. 141–86.
14. *The Years Between*, XXVI, p. 102.
15. *Debits and Credits*, VIII, pp. 229–49.
16. A.E. Purefoy, "'On the Gate' a Lowbrow Commentary," *The Kipling Journal*, XXI, No. 102 (October 1954), p. 10.
17. "On the Gate," *Debits and Credits*, VIII, p. 231.
18. *Ibid.*, p. 231.
19. *Ibid.*, p. 249.
20. *Seven Seas*, XXVI, pp. 60–62.
21. *The Years Between*, XXVI, pp. 399–401.
22. *Kim*, XVI, pp. 187–525.
23. Nirad C. Chaudhuri, "The Finest Story about India—in English," *Encounter*, 8 (1957): 47–53.
24. *A Diversity of Creatures*, IX, pp. 289–92.
25. *The Just So Stories*, XII, pp. 59–75.
26. *The War: A Fleet In Being*, XX, pp. 54–103.
27. T.R. Henn, *Kipling* (New York: Barnes & Noble, 1967), p. 40.
28. *Ibid.*, p. 65.

Selected Bibliography

Primary Sources

Since many of the short stories, poems, and other individual items in Kipling's work appeared originally in newspapers, magazines, or other short-lived publications not now available to the public, the original publication data given here refer to their publication in books, as listed in the Livingston official bibliography; for the convenience of the reader, each entry is also located by volume in *The Burwash Edition of the Complete Works in Prose and Verse of Rudyard Kipling*, published in New York, by AMS Press in 1970, a reprint from a copy of the collection of the Harvard University Libraries, from the 1941 editions.

Plain Tales From the Hills. Calcutta: Thacker, Spink, 1888. I.

The Story of the Gadsbys. Allahabad: Messrs. A.H. Wheeler, 1888. II.

Soldiers Three. Allahabad: Pioneer Press, 1888. II.

In Black and White. Allahabad: Messrs. A.H. Wheeler, 1888. II.

Departmental Ditties, Barrack Room Ballads and Other Verse. New York: United States Book Company, 1890. XXV.

The Light That Failed. London: J.B. Lippincott, 1891. XV.

Life's Handicap, Being Stories of Mine Own
People. London and New York:
Macmillan, 1891. IV.
Naulahka. London: William Heinemann,
1892. XV.
Many Inventions. London and New York:
Macmillan, 1893. V.
The Jungle Book. London and New York:
Macmillan, 1894. XI.
The Second Jungle Book. London and New
York: Macmillan, 1895. XI.
Captains Courageous. London and New
York: S.S. McClure, 1896–1897. XVI.
The Day's Work. New York: Doubleday &
McClure, 1898. VI.
From Sea to Sea and Other Sketches. New
York: Doubleday & McClure, 1899.
XVII, XVIII.
Stalky & Co. London: Macmillan, and New
York: Doubleday & McClure, 1899. XIV.
Kim. London: Macmillan, 1900. XVI.
Letters of Travel. London: Macmillan, 1900.
XIX.
The Just So Stories. London: Macmillan,
1902. XII.
The Five Nations. Garden City, NY:
Doubleday, Page, 1903. XXVI.
Traffics and Discoveries. London: Macmillan,
and New York: Doubleday, Page, 1904.
VII.
Muse Among the Motors. Garden City, NY:
Doubleday, Page, 1904. Collected with
Early Verse and Miscellaneous in Vol.
28.
Puck of Pook's Hill. London: Macmillan,
1906. XIII.
Actions and Reactions. London: Macmillan,
1909. VIII.
Rewards and Fairies. London: Macmillan,
1910. XIII.

Songs From Books. Garden City, NY:
Doubleday, Page, 1912. XXVII.
A Diversity of Creatures. London:
Macmillan, 1917. IX.
The Years Between. Garden City, NY:
Doubleday, Page, 1919. XXVI.
Land and Sea Tales. Garden City, NY:
Doubleday, Page, 1923. XIV.
The Irish Guards in the Great War. London:
Macmillan, 1923. XXI, XXII.
Debits and Credits. Garden City, NY:
Doubleday, Page, 1926. VIII.
Limits and Renewals. Garden City, NY:
Doubleday, Doran, 1932. X.
Something of Myself. Garden City, NY:
Doubleday, Doran, 1937. XXIV.
A Book of Words. XXIV.

Secondary Sources

Bibliographies
Livingston, Flora V. *Bibliography of the
Works of Rudyard Kipling.* New York:
Burt Franklin, 1927; 1968; Supplement,
1968.

Biographies
Carrington, C.E. *The Life of Rudyard
Kipling.* Garden City, NY: Doubleday,
1955. Excellent official biography, both
factual and interpretive.

Books
Bodelsen, C.A. *Aspects of Kipling's Art.* New
York: Barnes & Noble, 1964. Perceptive
insights into Kipling's special qualities.
Tompkins, J.M. *The Art of Rudyard Kipling.*
Lincoln: University of Nebraska Press,
1965.

Esther M.G. Smith

K